I0355874

George Warren Fuller

Report on the Investigations into the Purification of the Ohio River Water at Louisville, Kentucky

George Warren Fuller

Report on the Investigations into the Purification of the Ohio River Water at Louisville, Kentucky

ISBN/EAN: 9783337139940

Printed in Europe, USA, Canada, Australia, Japan

Cover: Foto ©ninafisch / pixelio.de

More available books at **www.hansebooks.com**

REPORT

ON THE INVESTIGATIONS INTO

THE PURIFICATION OF THE OHIO RIVER WATER AT LOUISVILLE KENTUCKY

MADE TO THE

PRESIDENT AND DIRECTORS

OF THE

LOUISVILLE WATER COMPANY

BY

GEORGE W. FULLER

Chief Chemist and Bacteriologist to the Louisville Water Company; Formerly Biologist in charge of the Lawrence Experiment Station, State Board of Health of Massachusetts; Member of the American Chemical Society, American Public Health Association, American Water Works Association, etc.

PUBLISHED UNDER AGREEMENT WITH THE DIRECTORS

NEW YORK

D. VAN NOSTRAND COMPANY

1898

TABLE OF CONTENTS.

WATER PURIFICATION AT LOUISVILLE.

TO THE PRESIDENT AND DIRECTORS OF THE LOUISVILLE WATER COMPANY.

GENTLEMEN:

Herewith is presented the full report of your representative upon the results accomplished during the recent tests by the several filters or systems in the purification of the Ohio River water, together with such descriptions, comments, and conclusions as are deemed pertinent to the subject.

The following filters or systems of water purification were investigated, named in the order in which they were installed at the pumping station of this Company, where the tests and investigations were conducted:

1. The Jewell Filter, of the O. H. Jewell Filter Company, 73 Jackson St., Chicago, Ill.
2. The Warren Filter, of the Cumberland Manufacturing Company, 220 Devonshire St., Boston, Mass.
3. The Western Gravity Filter, of the Western Filter Company, St. Louis, Mo.
4. The Western Pressure Filter, of the Western Filter Company, St. Louis, Mo.
5. The Harris Magneto-Electric System, of the John T. Harris Company, of New York City.
6. The Palmer and Brownell Water Purifier, of Palmer and Brownell, Louisville, Ky.
7. The MacDougall Polarite System, of John MacDougall, Montreal, Canada.

On Oct. 1, 1895, the writer took charge of the tests and investigations, which had for their purpose the determination of the quality of the river water after purification on a practical scale by each of the filters or systems, and the collection and compilation of such data as would indicate the cost of construction and operation of these filters or systems of purification. The first three weeks were devoted chiefly to the construction and equipment of a suitable laboratory, in which chemical, bacteriological, and microscopical analyses of the water could be made after the most approved methods.

From Oct. 21, 1895, to Aug. 1, 1896, daily tests were made, practically without interruption, of the filters or systems which were then ready. On Oct. 21, 1895, the Jewell and Warren filters were the only ones in readiness for operation. The two Western filters were tested beginning December 23, 1895—the date when their construction was completed. No tests were made of the Harris system until June 24, 1896, when it was first offered for official inspection.

The greater part of the month of August, 1896, was devoted to an investigation by the Water Company into the practicability of the principles employed in certain devices operated by the Harris Company during the preceding month. This was made necessary by the incompleteness of the evidence which had been accumulated upon this point by Aug. 1, the close of the tests as originally provided for.

September, October, and November, 1896, were occupied in the preparation of this report, so far as it relates to work done up to that time.

In December, 1896, special tests and investigations were made relating to the action of purified water in the corrosion of boilers and pipes, and in the incrustation of steam-boilers. An examination was also made of an experimental electrolytical device for water purification, submitted for inspection to the Water Company by Profs. Palmer and Brownell in their laboratory at the Louisville Manual Training High School.

From January 1 to March 10, 1897, attention was given to the construction and examination of electrolytical devices for water purification, designed by Profs. Mark and Brownell of Louisville, and to the investigation of points of practical significance connected therewith. The tests of these electrolytical devices were the outcome of the inspection of the above-mentioned laboratory experiments made by Profs. Palmer and Brownell in December, 1896.

When the tests of these electrolytical devices as designed by Profs. Mark and Brownell were brought to a close on March 10, 1897, it had been decided to investigate the MacDougall Polarite System as soon as a test plant could be constructed. It was also arranged on that date that the intervening time, before the polarite system was completed, should be occupied in constructing and testing devices designed by the officers of the Water Company. This work, which was carried on solely by the Water Company, was intended, as far as possible, to be a practical demonstration of some of the leading conclusions drawn from the foregoing tests, and to extend our knowledge along several important but not thoroughly understood lines, so far as time permitted. Owing to several unavoidable delays, the construction of the devices of the Water Company was not completed until April 10. They were then tested until May 10, when the MacDougall Polarite System was offered for official examination. This system was tested from May 10 to 19, and from May 28 to June 12, inclusive.

The remainder of the time up to August 1, 1897, the date of the final close of these investigations, was devoted to work upon the devices of the Water Company referred to above.

Since August 1, the time has been devoted to the preparation of this report so far as it relates to work done after January 1, 1897.

Nature of the Systems of Purification which were Tested.

Before recording the results accomplished by these several methods of purification it is necessary to show in general terms how they differed from each other and from those which have been employed elsewhere. At present the custom prevails to a large extent of calling all devices for water purification by the name of filters. In a majority of cases filtration of some kind is employed in the process of purification, but none of the devices tested by this company at this time consisted of plain filtration, as the term is properly used. Filtration alone means simply the passage of the water taken from its source through a layer of sand or similar material. This process, which is briefly outlined in the following pages, has been successfully employed for many years in Europe, where the yield of filtered water per acre of filtering surface is about 2,000,000 gallons per 24 hours. When river water, which contains much mud, clay, and other suspended matters, reaches the sand layer, the pores of the sand become clogged so that it is soon necessary to scrape off a layer of the surface sand and accumulations which are deposited on it. This treatment would apparently be required at frequent intervals in the filtration by this method of the Ohio River water when in its muddiest condition, even after the water had been subsided for several days, and a large reserve area would probably be necessary to maintain the city supply. The cost of this reserve area of filters, and of the scraping of the sand surface, would probably be great if this method were adopted here, as I understand was indicated to be the case from experiments made by your Chief Engineer, Mr. Charles Hermany, at the Crescent Hill Reservoir during the summer and fall of 1884 and spring of 1885.

In the systems of purification which were recently tested by this company there were tried a number of different methods that were claimed to make the cost of purification less than by sand filtration, such as has been adopted in many European cities in purifying river waters less muddy than that of the Ohio River. With one exception, in all of these systems of purification filtration through sand or quartz was made a very prominent portion of their respective methods, although the various filters were constructed and operated differently from those used in Europe. But the principal difference between the European method of filtration and all but one of those tested at Louisville lies in the fact that in these test systems the water was coagulated by chemical or electrolytical treatment, so that a portion of the suspended matter could settle out more rapidly in basins before the water reached the sand layer; and, further, so that the water could be filtered through sand about fifty times as fast as when no coagulation was afforded the water. In the method of filtration in which there was no coagulation of the water by chemical (or electrolytical) treatment, use was made of two filters for the water to pass through in turn, and this second filter contained a layer of material called polarite, in addition to the sand. The rate of filtration through the polarite filter was about one-half as fast as through those filters receiving coagulated water.

THE WARREN, JEWELL, WESTERN GRAVITY, AND WESTERN PRESSURE FILTERS.

In the Warren, Jewell, Western Gravity, and Western Pressure Filters the general method of procedure was identical, and substantially as follows:

Sulphate of alumina (or alum) was added to the river water, as it entered the devices in quantities varying with the character of the water. By combining with lime naturally dissolved in the river water the sulphate of alumina formed a white, gelatinous, solid compound, called hydrate of alumina. This latter compound gradually coagulated the suspended matter in the river water, in a manner similar to the well-known action of white of egg when added to turbid coffee. In the settling basins, where the river water first entered, this coagulation progressed so that, as the water left the settling basins and entered the sand layer, the river water had lost some of the mud suspended in it, and the mud and clay which it did contain were formed into flakes of sufficient size to allow a very rapid flow of water through the sand layer, with satisfactory results. The claim that this method of water purification was more economical for the Ohio River water than those practised in Europe was based on the assertion that comparatively small amounts of sulphate of alumina permitted a very great reduction in the necessary area of filtering surface.

While in the general method of procedure these four systems were the same, yet they were different in the manner in which the practical details were carried out. That is to say, there were different devices for the application of sulphate of alumina; the settling basins differed in size and arrangement; and in the filters themselves the sand layers were different in depth and size of grain, and were cleaned in somewhat different ways. Detailed accounts of these filters are given beyond, but these statements show the general status of the matter. It may also be added here that when these tests were begun there were no means of telling which system had the best practical devices; or, indeed, whether any of them was adapted to a satisfactory and reasonably economical purification of the Ohio River water at this point.

THE HARRIS DEVICE.

In the Harris Magneto-Electric System of water purification, which was tested for a short period in June, 1896, no use was made of filtration. It consisted in treating the river water directly with an electric (spark) discharge, and the subsequent passage of the water through iron tanks, in which were carbon electrodes, and on which were placed powerful magnets. The electric current was supposed to destroy the germs and the organic matter, while the mud, clay, and silt were to be separated out from the water by the repellent action of the magnets.

In July, 1896, the Harris Company made some experiments with the application of electricity to the purification of the Ohio River water by a method in which the hydrate of alumina (formed in the case of the other filters by the decomposition of sulphate of alumina by lime, as stated above) was prepared by the electrolytic decomposition of metallic aluminum. It was apparently the intention, so far as appliances permitted, to coagulate the water by the same chemical compound as in the sulphate of alumina treatment, and then proceed with subsidence and filtration in a manner similar to that employed in the case of the other filters, the only difference in the methods being in the manner of application of chemicals: in one case a commercial chemical product was employed, while in the other case the coagulating compound was made by the electrolytic action on the pure metal. Aside from the question of cost the electric treatment has certain advantages, which will be explained subsequently.

THE MARK-BROWNELL DEVICES.

During the months of January, February, and March, 1897, electrolytical devices, designed by Profs. Mark and Brownell, were constructed and tested. These devices were an improvement in several ways over those of the Harris Company. Their only difference in general method was the substitution of iron electrodes for aluminum electrodes. The electric current produced hydrate of iron, a compound similar to hydrate of alumina in its coagulating properties, and it was claimed that this would materially reduce the cost of purification.

THE MACDOUGALL POLARITE SYSTEM.

The results of the tests at this point indicated the desirability of reducing the amount of the coagulating chemicals whether produced electrolytically or from commercial products, and, if possible, doing away with them altogether. It was claimed by Mr. MacDougall that, judging from experience in purifying the water of the river Nile and of some English streams, the Ohio River water could be economically purified, without the use of coagulating chemicals, by his polarite filter. By this method the river water was passed through a settling tank (replaced later by a coke strainer) to remove the coarsest matter, thence the water was passed at a rapid rate through a sand filter in order to remove further the particles of mud, silt, and clay. The partially clarified water was finally passed at a slower rate through a filter containing a polarite layer with sand layers above and below it. This polarite is an iron ore which has been treated by a patent process. By doing away with the use of coagulating chemicals, and their attending cost, and at the same time securing a rate of filtration many times greater than in the case of plain sand filtration, the advantage of polarite as a filtering material was claimed to be great. The polarite filter was tested from May 10 to 19, and May 28 to June 12, 1897.

METHODS AND DEVICES OF THE WATER COMPANY.

During the time which was required for the construction of the polarite filter, advantage was taken of the opportunity for the Water Company to test some of their own plans which had arisen as an outcome of the foregoing tests. These methods and plans are described fully beyond, in Chapter XV, but their objects may be briefly outlined as follows:

1. A reduction in the cost of purification by a removal of the bulk of the mud, silt, and clay from the river water before it reaches the filters, thereby doing away with the necessity of a large reserve portion of a filter plant, to be used only at times of muddy water, with its cost of installation and operation. Experiments upon a small scale with the removal of the bulk of the mud by subsidence alone were made during the early summer of 1896, and gave very promising results.

2. The most economical and efficient method of application of coagulating chemicals, in connection with subsidence, to prepare the water for filtration at a rapid rate, with reference to the best period for the coagulation of the matter suspended in the water.

3. The relative economy, advantages, and disadvantages of different coagulating chemicals prepared in various ways.

The investigations along these lines were carried to a logical end so far as was considered possible under the existing conditions.

The State of Development of Water Purification at the Time of These Tests.

While much careful attention has been given to the art of water purification for more than sixty years, yet the general solution of the problem on a practical basis for large cities is far from satisfactory or complete at its present stage of development. This is due partly to varying effects of the adopted processes with different natural waters, partly to the lack of a widely practical and scientific understanding of the influence of a number of factors of the processes themselves, and partly to the great cost involved in the construction of adequate filtration works. With a river water of such exceedingly great variations in its composition as that of the Ohio River, and with proprietary systems of purification about which so little accurate information was available, these tests at Louisville were bound to be pioneer work in a large measure. Nevertheless, valuable data were obtained. But to understand the significance of these data, and to give them their true value in the line of studies necessary to place this line of work on a satisfactory basis and capable of general application, it is essential to trace the development of this subject up to this time.

Brief Historical Résumé.

The filtration of public water supplies was first adopted at London, England. The date of adoption of filtration at London has been generally regarded in this country as 1839. But it is now known that a sand filter, one acre in area, was put in service in 1829, the year following the appointment of the first Royal Commission on the Quality of the Metropolitan Water Supply. This Commission recommended the filtration of the Thames water, and the filter referred to above was constructed by the Chelsea Water Company in compliance therewith.

Progress in the adoption of filtration was slow until after 1849. During this year there was a severe cholera epidemic, and in August, 1849, Dr. Snow first formally announced the theory that drinking water, polluted from those ill or dead of cholera, was the chief means of propagation of this disease. Following this the filtration of river-water supplies advanced less slowly. After December 31, 1855, filtration of all river water supplied to the Metropolitan District of London was made compulsory by an Act of Parliament passed in July, 1852.

Since this date rapid advance in the adoption of filtration for public water supplies has been made in Europe. The population of the European cities now supplied with filtered water aggregates from fifteen to twenty millions, or more. After the severe epidemic of cholera at Hamburg in 1892, caused largely by the polluted Elbe water, the Imperial Board of Health of Germany ordered that all public water supplies in that country drawn from rivers or lakes should be filtered.

During the last thirty years there has been a marked increase in the efficiency of these systems of purification of European water supplies, owing to improvements in both the construction and the operation of the filters. The first important step in this direction was taken at London in 1871, when Parliament made provision for systematic examinations at frequent intervals of the filters and the filtered water. The greatest progress, however, has been made during the past dozen years. This has been due to the establishment of the germ theory of disease, and the general recognition by sanitarians that such diseases as typhoid fever and cholera are transmitted largely by drinking water. And, further, rapid developments in the new science of bacteriology have made it possible to apply this science in the solution of problems in water purification, so as to yield results of substantial and practical value.

The recognition of the need of reliable information from an engineering, chemical, and bacteriological standpoint to facilitate the adoption, construction, and operation of purification systems has led to several important investigations. These have been made in England, Germany, and America.

One of the objects of filtration, in many instances in Europe, has been to remove mud, silt, and clay from river water. In many cases, however, filtration has also been directed to protect the water consumers from those diseases which are carried by the water. This is a very important matter in Europe, where the population has become very dense around the great cities. In America, with its comparatively sparse population, it is not as a rule so pressing at present. But disastrous experience in Europe with some filters built in the early days of water purification show clearly that all filters should be capable at all times of protecting the health of the consumers from water-borne diseases.

General Description of the Most Important Type of Filters Abroad.

Filters such as were introduced into England, and which have since been employed regularly there and in many places on the Continent, consist substantially of a large, open basin ranging as a rule from about 0.5 to 1.5 acres in area and 10 feet or more in depth. In cold climates, such as in Northern Germany, they are covered, to afford protection from ice and frost. The bottom of the basins are made practically water-tight. On the bottom of these basins, drains and pipes are suitably arranged so as to conduct the water from the filter to a collecting well or reservoir, located at some convenient place near the filter. In some cases, instead of using lateral pipes with perforations or open joints, the water is taken to the main underdrain through an arrangement of dry-laid bricks.

Over the underdrains are placed successively layers of broken stone and gravel, the depth of each of which varies usually according to the construction of the underdrains. The size of the stone and gravel in turn becomes gradually finer toward the top, in order that they may better serve their purpose of supporting the layer of sand which rests upon the gravel. The thickness of this layer of sand placed upon the gravel varies in different filters from about 2 to 5 feet. There is also some variation in the size of the sand grains in the filters of the different cities.

In the operation of the filters water flows or is pumped from the river or sedimentation basin onto the filter, and stands several feet in depth above the surface of the sand. The water passes downward through the sand, gravel, and broken stone, in turn, and thence through the underdrains, collecting well, or reservoir, and pumps (if such are necessary) to the consumer. The rate at which the water flows by gravity through the filter is generally controlled and made fairly uniform by regulating devices on the outlet pipe from the filter.

After a time, when a geater or less quantity of water has passed through the filter, there appears at and near the surface of the sand an accumulation of silt and other matters which were suspended in the water when it reached the filter. Eventually this accumulation becomes so great that the interstices of the sand are clogged so that an adequate quantity of water cannot pass through the filter. When this condition of affairs obtains the inlet water is shut off. The water standing on the filter is allowed to drain to some distance below the surface of the sand, and workmen remove with shovels and wheelbarrows the upper layer of the clogged sand ordinarily to a depth of about 0.5 to 0.75 inch. The main body of the sand is cleaned only by the removal of organic matter through the action of bacteria. The filter is slowly filled with water after the surface has been scraped, either by applying the unfiltered water at the top or by letting filtered water flow in from below. This latter procedure, where the construction of the filter will permit it, is much the better, because it tends to prevent the formation of channels in the sand, due to the escaping air which enters the pores of the sand upon draining. Such channels are very objectionable, because they allow the water to pass through them without satisfactory purification.

Once or twice a year the layer of sand is restored to its original thickness by either replacing the removed sand after thorough washing, or adding new clean sand. In some of the important filters of this type use is made of coagulating chemicals, but the rate of filtration is comparatively slow—about 2,000,000 gallons per acre daily. In Holland chemicals for coagulation have been used to some extent.

Principles of Sand Filtration without the Use of Coagulating Chemicals.

There has never yet been given an accurate and concise definition of the principles by which water is purified by the type of filters just described. The reason of this appears to be that there are several factors which have to be taken into consideration; and the relative practical value of these factors seems to vary under different local conditions. As we now understand the subject, the principles of purification by this type of filtration involve three significant phases, namely:

A. Mechanical or Physical.
B. Biological.
C. Chemical.

A. *Mechanical or Physical.*—There are at least two important actions of a mechanical or physical nature which aid in the purification of water by this type of filtration, namely:

1. A *straining* action, by which there are removed from the water those small suspended particles which may be called large when compared with the size of the interstices in the sand layer.

2. An *adhesive* action, by which there are removed those suspended particles, including the bacteria, which are far smaller than the interstices of the sand layer through which the water passes.

This very important adhesive action is influenced by several varying factors and is not thoroughly understood. Its efficiency in filtration, furthermore, is associated to a considerable degree with chemical and biological conditions, as noted below.

B. *Biological.*—This aspect is of practical significance by virtue of its action in removing organic matter which, in places beneath the upper surface, accumulates as films around the sand grains. The removal of organic matter by oxidation and nitrification appears to be a factor in causing indirectly the death of bacteria, which are mechanically arrested by the adhesive action of the sand grains. By some it has been claimed that the bacteria pass into a gelatinous form, the zooglœa stage; and, being attached to the sand grains, they facilitate thereby the removal of bacteria in the active vegetable stage, and of minute suspended particles by means of adhesion.

C. *Chemical.*—The chemical side of filtration deals with the removal of dissolved organic matters and, together with the bacteria, with the removal of organic matters, accumulated on the sand grains. In many cases it appears that an action, more or less chemical in its nature, between certain ingredients in the water and certain ingredients of the sand causes the formation of films, containing organic matter, around the sand grains. This facilitates the mechanical removal from water of bacteria by the adhesive action mentioned above; and it is also probable that this puts the organic matter in a position where the bacteria may do their work of destroying it to better advantage.

In the early days of filtration the mechanical and chemical aspects of the subject were the only ones which received attention. Since the dawn of bacteriology much attention has been given to the question as to how far the biological side aided in the accomplishment of purification by filtration. Biological theories advanced rapidly. By some it was claimed that the whole process was a biological one. These theories, however, reached a point which was untenable, and for several years the mechanical and chemical phases have been regaining more nearly their true significance.

English Filters.

The type of filters which we have been considering, and which was introduced at London, England, by James Simpson in 1829, is called by various names. The number has become so great that they are very confusing. The principal names given to this type of filters are as follows:

1. Filter beds.
2. Sand beds.
3. Sand filters.
4. Artificial sand filters.
5. Natural sand filters.
6. Slow sand filters.
7. Biological filters.
8. English filters.
9. European filters.

Of these various names all have more or

less significance, although some of them convey an impression which is not altogether correct. Thus, "biological filter" in the light of our present knowledge is an unfortunate name, because it gives undue prominence to one of several phases of the process. Quite recently "natural sand filters" has been used by many to designate this type of filters. This expression has considerable significance in that there is imitated in these filters the process in nature by which spring water and other ground waters are purified by filtration through the upper layers of the earth. The use of this name is not strictly correct in this connection, because these filters are actually of artificial construction, and the processes go on under conditions widely different from those in nature. Natural filtration for public water supplies is correctly applied only to those cases where galleries or wells are located in the earth near a river or lake, where the water is naturally filtered, either from the adjoining body of water or, more frequently, from the ground on the land side, where it is naturally filtered through the earth before it reaches the place of collection. Natural filters as thus described are successfully used in France and in some places in this country where the geological conditions are favorable. The water obtained from driven wells is also similarly purified.

It seems practically impossible to find a name which will specifically characterize the construction and operation of this type of filter, now that so many modifications in filters have been introduced. In view of this fact, it is believed that "English filters" is the best name to apply to them, and we shall use this name throughout this report. This type of filter is distinctly of English origin, and English engineers and English capital introduced it on the Continent of Europe at an early date, at Berlin, St. Petersburg, Altona, and other places. For this reason and the fact that there are several modifications in some of the Continental filters we prefer to call them English rather than European filters.

Modifications in Europe of the Original English Filters.

In England there have been no marked changes in the construction of filters, although some attempts have been made to replace sand with other materials, such as carbide of iron, and polarite. Improvements in the efficiency of filtration for the most part have come, however, from more careful operation, and from extensions in the sedimentation basins. In the latter instance there is a notable reduction in the cost of filtration of turbid and muddy river waters.

On the Continent of Europe, however, a number of modifications in the original filters have been introduced. The more important ones are as follows:

Tours, France.—In 1856 two filters were put in service at this place. They were designed with the view to having the accumulation of mud, etc., on the surface of the sand removed by forcing filtered water up through the sand from the bottom, instead of having it scraped off with shovels as in English filters. This idea never worked well in practice at this place, owing to insufficient pressure to force the water up through the filter. These filters were abandoned after a time, owing apparently to a failure to provide sedimentation basins in which the sediment in the river water could subside by gravity.

Holland.—In several places in Holland, notably at Leeuwarden, Groningen, and Schiedam, and also at Antwerp, in Belgium, alum has been used at times to aid in the purification of colored and polluted water by English filters. The practical effect of the application of alum is entered into in detail in a subsequent portion of this report, and it is the purpose here only to record its use in Holland.

Anderson Process.—This process has been in use more or less regularly for some years at Antwerp, Belgium, and in some small towns in Europe. Quite recently a large plant has been installed at Paris, France, for the purification of water from the river Seine.

Essentially this process consists of passing the water first through a revolving cylinder containing iron filings. The carbonic acid in the water dissolves some of the iron, forming ferrous carbonate. By the air contained in the water this salt of iron is oxidized more or less rapidly to ferric hydrate. The iron when changed into this solid, gelatinous form combines with much of the organic matter, and, like aluminum hydrate formed from alum or sulphate of alumina, coagulates the suspended matter, and makes it easier to filter the water subsequently through English filters.

ENGLISH FILTERS IN AMERICA.

Although there are ten or twelve comparatively small filters in America, more or less resembling English filters, it may be safely stated that this system of water purification has never become well established in this country. Among the principal reasons of this are the following:

1. The question of cost.
2. The general absence of State or Federal Boards constituted with adequate authority to enforce the protection of citizens from polluted water supplies, as is the case in the more thickly populated countries of Europe.
3. The absence of severe cholera epidemics, such as have led a number of European cities to adopt filtration with haste.

For a number of years sufficient information has been available to show that practically any water may be satisfactorily purified by English filters, provided sufficient sedimentation is first employed in the case of very turbid or muddy waters, and that the rate of filtration is sufficiently low. With regard to the question of expense, however, it has been, and is still, difficult to estimate even approximately the cost of construction and operation of filters which will purify a turbid or muddy water satisfactorily. The reason of this is that the various elements of cost differ widely with the local conditions, and especially with the character of the water to be purified.

There are two noteworthy points to be mentioned in connection with English filters in America. In the first place this type of water purification was well described in a report by an American engineer. This gentleman, now deceased, was Mr. James P. Kirkwood, Chief Engineer of the Water Commission of St. Louis, Mo. In December, 1865, he was instructed by the commissioners to proceed to Europe and examine into this question of water filtration, with a view to applying this information in connection with the purification of the water supply of St. Louis. The publication of the report made a very valuable work of reference, which has been used by both American and European engineers. The work was of such a high grade that it was translated into German in 1876. In it there are several important suggestions which have led to improvements in the construction and operation of this type of filters. The most noteworthy of these points are that the removal of mud and silt from the water by subsidence in basins before the water reaches the filters reduces the cost, and increases the efficiency of filtration; and, further, that the efficiency of the operation is enhanced by maintaining by suitable devices a uniform flow of water through the filter.

During the past six years, furthermore, the most extensive experimental investigations upon the purification of water by slow filtration through sand, unaided by treatment with a coagulant, have been made in America at the Lawrence Experiment Station of the State Board of Health of Massachusetts. These investigations have yielded a large fund of information on the purification of such clear but polluted waters as that of the Merrimac River.

Another factor which has recently served to explain in part the slowness with which American cities have adopted purification systems for their water supplies is the fact that there has appeared in America within the last dozen years another type of water filter. This type of filter is described below. It is spoken of as the "mechanical," "alum," and "rapid sand" filter. None of these names is particularly appropriate, and in distinction from the English filters we shall refer to it as the American filter.

Both types of filters unquestionably possess merit. But as to their relative merits for the purification of waters in general, or of any particular water, we have little or no information to guide us. In the absence of facts there have arisen in connection with the subject numerous statements and opinions, many of which are partisan and erroneous. This unfortunate state of affairs has recently done much to retard the adoption of municipal systems of water purification, and will probably continue to do so until reliable comparable data are available.

American Filters.

This type of filters is the outgrowth of schemes to purify water for industrial and manufacturing purposes. Its development up to this time has been tentative to a marked degree, and has been in the hands of several competing business corporations. In 1883 it first attracted the attention of those connected with public water supplies. At that time it consisted essentially of a large circular tank in which there was a layer of sand supported by a perforated bottom. Its chief characteristic, other than small size, in distinction from English filters, was the fact that the sand layer was cleansed of the accumulated materials removed from the river water by forcing water under pressure up through the layer of sand. In this respect it resembled the filters constructed in 1856 at Tours, in France.

Patents were taken out in 1884 to cover a modification which consisted of the application of alum, a salt of iron, or other similar coagulating chemical, to the water, just before it passed through the layer of sand. The custom of applying alum to coagulate water, in order to facilitate the removal of foreign matter, has been practised in various ways for many centuries in different parts of the world, and the description of it in scientific literature began about seventy years ago. The apparent object of the application of chemicals under the stated conditions are understood to be a reduction in the cost of treatment, by doing away with subsidence basins, and by diminution of the area of filtering surface.

This type of filters was first employed in the treatment of a public water supply at Somerville, N. J., in 1885. Since that time many towns and small cities have adopted systems of this general type. At present it is said that over 100 town and municipal plants are in operation, but among this number there are none for large cities.

In the last ten years many modifications have been introduced by the several competing companies. These modifications, more or less protected by patents, relate for the most part to devices for supporting the sand layer at the bottom; the introduction of filtered water under pressure below the sand layer, to enable the filter to be cleaned by a reverse flow of water; and of agitating devices to stir the sand during washing, and thus aid the cleansing process. In the present filters of the several companies the coagulating chemicals are applied at points differently located with reference to the sand layer, and with varying provisions to secure not only more complete coagulation, but also to effect a removal of some suspended matter before the water is filtered. To this general account of the American filters it may be added that a majority of them are gravity filters—where the water flows by gravity through a sand layer placed in an open tank. In some cases, however, pressure filters are used. The pressure filters, in addition to customary devices, consist of a sand layer placed in a closed compartment, so that the water can be forced through the filter under pressure, thereby avoiding, it is claimed, additional pumping under some conditions.

Compared with the English filters, the American filters at present show the following principal differences:

1. The American filters are aided by the application to the water of a coagulating chemical, which makes it possible to filter through sand at a much more rapid rate, and thereby the necessary area of filter is much reduced.

2. The American filters are cleaned by passing a stream of water upward through the sand, with or without accompanying agitation, rather than by scraping off the surface layers, as in the case of the English filters.

There are of course many other features of difference, such, for example, as the strainers at the bottom, to hold back the sand, and at the same time furnish an exit for the filtered water; but the two points stated above are the principal differences.

Efficiency of American Filters, and Cost of their Operation.

At the beginning of the Louisville tests

there were no available data which would show whether or not the American type of filter was capable of purifying the Ohio River water; or which of the several companies had the best filter for sale; or whether any of the American filters were capable of purifying the Ohio River water at a reasonable cost. It is true that some scattering data indicated a satisfactory purification of certain waters by this type of filters, but there was other information pointing to work of an inferior grade. With regard to the question of cost, practically nothing was available which would be of any service in considering the purification of such an exceedingly variable water as that of the Ohio River. On the one hand, it was claimed that somewhat similar muddy waters were purified at a comparatively low cost by this type of filter; while, on the other hand, it was known that a system of purification installed at New Orleans by one of the prominent American filter-makers had for some reason been a failure. What the exact facts and conditions of purification were at the several places where this type of filter had been tried could not be learned. In fact there is reason to believe that they were not accurately known.

Very early in these tests the results of some tests of an American filter made at Providence, R. I., were available. The Providence work was of much value in indicating that it was possible with some waters and some conditions to accomplish a satisfactory purification by this type of filter. But the Pawtuxet River water, so far as can be learned from the limited analytical evidence as to its character, is very much easier to purify than the Ohio River water. And it may be safely stated that a thoroughly satisfactory solution of the problem of purifying the Pawtuxet water could not by any means serve as an adequate guide for the purification of the Ohio water. An attempt was also made to learn the relative advantages of the English and American types of filters in purifying the local water, but the conditions were such that in this respect the work at Providence led to no decisive conclusions of value.

With regard to the Harris Magneto-Electric System it was said that an experimental device at Brooklyn had been successful in purifying the local water, but no accurate idea could be obtained as to the cost of treatment.

The Mark and Brownell electrolytical device, in which the current of electricity was applied to the water through iron electrodes, was on the same principle as the Webster Process for sewage purification. Eight or nine years ago the Webster Process was claimed in England to be very promising, but for the past few years little or nothing had been heard about it. As already stated, this electrolytical device replaces the application of chemicals, but it was used in connection with American filters. This portion of the test, therefore, refers to the coagulation preceding filtration. The MacDougall Polarite System had never been tried in America, but fragmentary accounts of its trial in England and Egypt indicated that it probably had some advantages.

Such were the conditions found by the Louisville Water Company when they made these tests, with a view to finding a practicable method of purifying the Ohio River water as delivered to the citizens of Louisville.

Conditions under which the Tests were Conducted.

The investigations and tests described in the following portion of this report were all conducted at the pumping station of the Water Company, about three miles above the city of Louisville on the Kentucky shore of the Ohio River. A plan of the ground at the pumping station is presented on Plate I.

The Water Company constructed six temporary buildings, four of which were occupied by the companies which offered purification systems for examination. One of them was equipped as the laboratory of the Water Company, and under the direction of the writer was furnished with all apparatus and supplies necessary for analytical work in this line after the best modern methods. The remaining building contained a pump with which filtered water under pressure was supplied for washing the filters. Steam, and Ohio River water taken from the force main at a point about 390 feet from the intake, were supplied by the Water Company to these buildings. All the piping leading to and from the buildings, the meters on the water-pipes, and sewer connections were also furnished by the Water Company.

During the period preceding Aug. 1, 1896, the four buildings above mentioned were occupied by the Warren Filter, the Jewell Filter, the two Western Filters, and the Harris Magneto-Electric System of purification, respectively, named in the order of their location, beginning at the laboratory. This order was used in the current note-books, and as a matter of convenience the several systems of purification will be referred to in this report in the above order. In view of the fact that filtration alone was not the only method employed in the purification processes, the term system of purification will be used in this report in speaking of the entire experimental devices of each company, rather than the term filter alone. By the terms of the contracts between the Water Company and the other companies the latter installed their respective systems, each having a capacity of 250,000 gallons per twenty-four hours, in separate temporary houses at their own expense. The several companies, further, managed and operated their systems without any expense, risk, or responsibility to the Water Company. Authority, however, was reserved by the Water Company to make such rules and regulations as it deemed advisable in conducting these tests on a fair competitive basis, and to allow its representatives unrestricted access to the several systems at all times, in order that such information could be obtained as was deemed necessary in the premises.

Mr. George A. Soper was engineer in charge of the Warren Filter. Messrs. William M. Jewell and Ira H. Jewell, officers of the Jewell Filter Company, were in charge of the Jewell Filter. Mr. Charles T. Whittier was chemist in charge of the Western Systems. The writer wishes to express his obligations to these gentlemen for their courteous cooperation with him in conducting these tests.

The Warren Filter and the two Western Filters were removed promptly at the close of the competitive tests, Aug. 1, 1896. The Jewell Filter and the Harris Systems were not removed at once. During August, 1896, arrangements were made with the Harris Company to utilize some of their appliances in supplementary tests made by the Water Company, and, when the investigations were resumed at the beginning of 1897, arrangements were also made by the Water Company whereby these two experimental plants could be used, in order to guard against delays.

In the tests of electrolytical devices from Jan. 1 to March 10, 1897, the professional services of Profs. Mark and Brownell were retained by the Water Company to devise necessary electrical appliances, and to consult with officers of the Water Company with regard to their operation. These new devices were installed at the expense of the Water Company in the temporary house formerly occupied by the Warren Filter.

The settling tank, clay extractor, and polarite filter used in the MacDougall Polarite System were constructed by Mr. MacDougall at his own expense, and in connection with the Jewell Filter were operated under the supervision of Mr. John MacDougall.

The tests of methods and appliances carried on solely by the Water Company were made under the direction of the Chief Engineer and Superintendent, Mr. Charles Hermany, and of the Chief Chemist and Bacteriologist. A large share of the engineering portions of the work was done under the general supervision of Mr. Hermany, and the writer desires to express his obligation to him for much valuable advice and assistance upon the entire work obtained in frequent conferences throughout the progress of the investigations. A large amount of construction and repair work in the course of the tests was ably done by Mr. John Wiest, the engineer in charge of the pumping station.

There was a considerable difference in the amount of work to be done at various times throughout the tests, and, accordingly, the number of assistants employed by the Water Company varied from time to time during the two years of investigation. The number ranged from two to seven, and averaged a little more than three, exclusive of the stenographer and porter. In addition to the construction and repair work on pipes and meters, the Water Company funished an engineer during the competitive tests to operate the wash-water pump.

The following gentlemen were engaged as assistants during these investigations, and to their faithfulness and industry a large share of the success of the work is due:

Mr. Chas. L. Parmelee, Assistant Engineer.
Mr. Robert S. Weston, Assistant Chemist.
Dr. Hibbert Hill, Assistant Bacteriologist.
Mr. Joseph W. Ellms, Assistant Chemist.
Mr. George A. Johnson, Clerk and Assistant Bacteriologist.
Mr. Reuben E. Bakenhus, Assistant.
Mr. Harold C. Stevens, Assistant.

All analytical work connected with these investigations was done in the laboratory of the Louisville Water Company, with the exception of the necessary mechanical analyses of filtering material, which were made at the Lawrence Experiment Station by Mr. Harry W. Clark.

At the outset of these investigations it was arranged that bi-weekly reports of progress should be made by the Chief Chemist and Bacteriologist to the Directors of the Water Company, and to them alone. Early in the competitive tests the Jewell Filter Company and the Cumberland Manufacturing Company requested the Water Company to keep them informed as to the daily results accomplished by their respective filters. The Water Company, in response to this request, offered to furnish the operators of the filters transcripts of analytical results obtained from their own filters (without any comments, summaries, or conclusions), provided the filter companies would reimburse the Water Company for the additional expense incurred, and that the transcript of the results would not be used within a stated period for any purpose other than as an aid to the intelligent operation of their respective filters. The Jewell Filter Company and the Cumberland Manufacturing Company accepted, but the Western Filter Company declined, this proposition. In compliance therewith the amount of analytical work was increased, beginning Feb. 1, 1896.

In order that the present report may be more readily understood it is divided into sixteen chapters, as shown below, giving the full results of the investigations in their logical order. With the exception of Chapter I, on the composition of the Ohio River water, and upon which additional data were obtained in 1897, the first twelve chapters are presented in substantially the same form as prepared in 1896. It will be seen that the remaining chapters deal with the work of the current year. In the appendix are recorded the methods of analyses employed, and several other matters of purely technical interest.

The chapters into which the report is divided are as follows:

CHAPTER I.

Composition of the Ohio River Water.

The water of the Ohio River at Louisville varies widely from time to time in its composition. This variation is caused by a number of factors, among which are the following:

1. The size and varying geological formation of the watershed.
2. The number of comparatively large tributaries which drain areas of distinctly unlike geological character.
3. The amount of precipitation (rain and snow).
4. The distribution of the precipitation over the watershed.
5. The condition of the soil at the beginning of heavy rain-storms.
6. The amount and rate of precipitation during single storms.
7. The stage of the river.
8. The velocity of flow of the river.
9. Agitation of the water in the river, due to wind-storms, etc.

The watershed of the Ohio River above Louisville is about 85,000 square miles in area. This area includes portions of the States of New York, Pennsylvania, Ohio, Indiana, North Carolina, Virginia, West Virginia and Kentucky. Wide extremes in geological formation exist in the watershed.

At Pittsburgh the Alleghany and Monongahela rivers unite to form the Ohio River. West of the city of Pittsburgh the drainage of this portion of the watershed finds its way into the Ohio River through thirty-three principal tributaries and a great number of smaller affluents. East of Pittsburgh there are numerous affluents to the two main streams, but they are correspondingly small in size.

The total population resident on this watershed above Louisville is estimated at 4,500,000, of which 1,575,000 is contained in 220 towns and cities, according to the census of 1890, increased 15 per cent. for the six years of the present decade. The nearest city discharging sewage into the water which passes this pumping station is Madison, Indiana, situated about 50 miles above Louisville, with a population of about 12,000. The next city is Frankfort, Kentucky, situated on the Kentucky River 67 miles from its mouth. This city has a population of about 10,000. The Kentucky River joins the Ohio about 57 miles above Louisville. The nearest large centre of population discharging sewage into this water supply is at Cincinnati, Ohio. Opposite this city are the cities of Newport and Covington, Kentucky. Their aggregate population (three cities) is about 420,000, and they are distant above Louisville about 150 miles by river.

At the pumping station of this Company where the tests and investigations were conducted the Ohio River is about 1700 feet wide and 20 feet in average depth at low water. At the Ohio Falls, which are about three miles below the pumping station and opposite the city of Louisville, the river is about 4400 feet wide at low water. When very heavy freshets or floods occur in the Ohio River in this locality they cause the river to overflow its banks at the pumping station, and reach to the bluffs which run parallel to the river on the Kentucky side. The width of the river is then about 5500 feet.

The rises and floods in the Ohio River, with their associated factors, produce wide and rapidly changing variations in the composition of the river water. Owing to the fact that the composition of the river water is a prominent factor in the cost of purification, analyses were made practically every day during these tests of the water before its application to the systems of purification. Before giving attention to the results of analyses, however, the question of frequency and depth of freshets or floods is to be considered.

Freshets or Floods in the Ohio River.

Freshets or floods may be considered as stages or depths of water in the river which are above the normal. Their frequency and magnitude depend upon a series of factors connected with the rainfall on the watershed, and are very irregular. By virtue of the influence which they exert indirectly upon the cost of purification, and the method leading to the most efficient and economical results, they are worthy of very careful consideration. This is especially true in connection with this report, because inspection of the data presented in the following table shows that during the period covered by the first portion of these tests the magnitude of freshets or floods was below the normal for the past thirty-six years. Practically speaking, this means that the average amount of mud, silt, and clay suspended in a given volume of the Ohio River water during these investigations and tests was abnormally small.

In the following table is given a summary of the number and magnitude of the freshets or floods which occurred in the Ohio River at Louisville during the past thirty-six years, 1861 to 1896, inclusive. This was obtained from curves prepared annually by the Water Company from data obtained daily at the pumping station during the entire period. These annual curves were made from plottings of a convenient scale, in which the abscissæ correspond to the number of days in a year, and the ordinates to depths of water above the low-water level. By connecting the points plotted in this manner curves have been obtained which show the depth of the river water for each day of each year of this period. The number and extent of the freshets or floods were obtained by noting those portions of the curve corresponding to rising, fairly stationary, and falling stages or depths of water in the river. The end of a given freshet or flood is shown by a return to the normal depth of water, or by the beginning of another freshet or flood quickly following the one in question. To obtain the depth of a given freshet or flood from these curves the difference in elevation is noted between the initial and highest point of the given portion of the curve.

Plan of Analytical Work.

In the determination of the composition of the Ohio River water, as shown by analyses, attention was directed to the physical, chemical, and biological characters of the water.

Physical Character.—Upon this point the examinations included observations on the appearance and character of the matters in suspension, and on the odor, color, taste, and temperature of the water.

Chemical Character.—The chemical analyses included the determinations of the total amount by weight of the mineral and organic matters dissolved and suspended in the water; the amount of organic matter in solution and in suspension; the form in which the nitrogen was present in its passage through the cycle from crude organic matter (albuminoid ammonia) to completely mineralized matter (nitrates); the alkalinity, due chiefly to the carbonates and bicarbonates of calcium and magnesium, which indicated the amount of alum that could be effectually decomposed by the water; and the amounts present of chlorine, dissolved alumina, iron, and fixed residue on evaporation after ignition to burn up the organic matter and effect incidental changes. These determinations compose the regular sanitary and technical chemical analysis of water for work of this class.

In addition to the regular chemical analyses, as stated above, there were made from time to time as occasion presented special sanitary and technical analyses. Among these were included the determination of the amounts of free (atmospheric) oxygen and carbonic acid gases, dissolved in the water; and the amounts of incrusting constituents of the water in connection with its adaptability for use in boilers.

Mineral analyses were also made of several samples of water which were representative of different grades in the wide range of composition of the water met with in these investigations. These analyses consisted of the determination of the principal metallic elements and the acids present in the mineral compounds contained in the river water.

Biological Character.—The biological analyses consisted chiefly of the determination of the numbers of bacteria present in the water,

NUMBER AND DEPTH OF FRESHETS OR FLOODS IN THE OHIO RIVER AT LOUISVILLE FROM 1861 TO 1896, INCLUSIVE.

Year.	Depth of Freshet or Flood in Feet. 1	2	3	4	5	6	7	8	9	10	11	12	13	14	15	16	17	18	19	20	21	22	23	24	25	26	27	28	29	30	31	32	33	34	35	36	37	38	39	40	41	42	43	44	45	46	Total.	Year.
1861		3	3	1	5	3	2	2	3	1		2	1	1			1							1																							29	1861
1862	3	1	3	5	5	1		1					1					1	1		1				1			2				1															27	1862
1863	5	5	3	2	2		2	2			1	1	1	2	1	1		1																													29	1863
1864	1	2	1	5	3	5	4	4	3	1		1	1							1																											32	1864
1865		3	4	6	3	6	4	2				1	1	1		1					2					1	1						1														36	1865
1866			2	4	2	1	7	4	4	3			2	2	1		1																														33	1866
1867	4	7	1	2		1	2	3	2	1		1	1																		1					1											27	1867
1868		1	3	2	4	2	4		1	1					2	2		2	2			1																									27	1868
1869		4			2	3	5	3	6	1	1	2			1																																28	1869
1870		4	2	5	3	3	1		5					1						1					1							1															27	1870
1871	2	5	7	3	3		2	2	4				1		1	1																															31	1871
1872	3	3	3	6	4	6	4	1												1																											31	1872
1873	2			5	2	2	3	3	1	1	3	1		3	1	1	1	1																													30	1873
1874	1	2	3	2	2	2	1	1	1	1	2	1	1			1				1	1	1																									24	1874
1875				3	1	2	5	2	2	1	1	1	3				1	1	1									1																			25	1875
1876			1	3	4	4	5	2	1	2	2		1			1				1												1															28	1876
1877		1	3	3	3		4	2	2	4					1	1													1																		25	1877
1878				2	4	5	2	2	5	6	4	1	1		1																																33	1878
1879	1	3	2	3	1	3	1	5	1	1	1	3	1	1	2		1	1																													31	1879
1880			4	2	7	2	1	3	2	3		1	1				1	1	1	1									1																		31	1880
1881	1	2	3	3	1	1	2	1	3	2	1	1	2			2	1					1																									27	1881
1882					4	5	4	7	4			1	1		1	1	1			1	1	2				1											1										35	1882
1883		1	2	1	2	3	5	3	3		5			1				1				1		1																				1			30	1883
1884		5	3		1	5	1	4	1		2						1								1																					1	25	1884
1885			1		2	11	6	1	2	1	2			1								1																									28	1885
1886		1	1	4	2	6		2	5	3	1		1	1	1																	1															29	1886
1887	2	4	4				4	2	2						1					1					1	1					1	1															24	1887
1888				1		2	5	5	2	3	3	2		1		1																															25	1888
1889				3	3	1	4	5	5	2	5	2		1																																	31	1889
1890				1	2		1	6	3	3	2	5			1	1	1	1	1	1														2													31	1890
1891		5		1	2	2	4	8	1			1			1			1		1	3	1										1															32	1891
1892			8	2	1	2	3	16		3		1	1		1						1																										39	1892
1893	2	3	4	2	5	1	2	15			1										1							1																			37	1893
1894	5	2	3		2	3	1	4	3	1	1		1																																		26	1894
1895	3	2	4	3	2	1	1	1			2	2									1																										22	1895
1896			3	2	8	8	1	5		2	1		2		1							1																									34	1896
Total ...	35	69	81	87	97	102	103	129	77	47	41	31	25	16	18	14	10	11	6	10	11	9	0	2	4	3	0	4	2	0	2	6	1	2	0	1	1	0	0	0	0	0	0	1	0	1	1059	

and of the examination of the species of bacteria with special reference to their connection in the causation of disease.

Microscopical examinations were also made from time to time to learn the numbers and kinds of algæ, diatoms, infusoriæ, etc., present in the river water. These microscopical analyses differ distinctly from the bacterial analyses in that the former relate solely to those relatively large micro-organisms which may be counted and classified with the aid of comparatively low powers of the microscope; while the bacteria are so small (about 0.0001 inch in length) that they require for their enumeration and classification special methods of laboratory procedure.

Preceding the several tables showing the results of analyses there will be found explanatory notes, calling attention to the nature of the principal points of practical significance. At the close of the report is an appendix in which is presented a record of some of the more important features of the analytical methods from a technical standpoint.

The plan of analytical work, which has been briefly outlined in the foregoing paragraphs, may be made plainer by the following synopsis:

Synopsis of Analytical Work.

1. Physical: Appearance, odor, color, taste, and temperature.
2. Chemical: Regular sanitary and technical analyses.
   Special sanitary and technical analyses.
   Mineral analyses.
3. Biological: Microscopical examinations.
   Quantitative bacterial analyses.
   Identification of species of bacteria, with special reference to the causation of disease.

Place of Collection of Samples of River Water for Analysis.

Samples of river water for analysis were collected from a tap on a 6-inch pipe. This tap was kept open during working hours. The 6-inch pipe was about 230 feet in length, and connected with the force main leading to the distributing reservoir at Crescent Hill. From the intake to the point where the 6-inch pipe branched from the force main the distance was about 390 feet. In this distance the water passed through the pump well and the pump which was operated to supply the city.

The intake of the water supply is located 3.5 feet below the low-water stage and about 100 feet from the Kentucky shore at low water.

Manner of Collection of Samples of River Water for Analysis.

After the investigations were well under way it was the general custom to collect on each working day, from the above-described place, one sample of water for regular chemical analysis, and two or more samples for the determination of the numbers of bacteria. When the systems of purification were in operation night and day samples of water for both chemical and bacterial analyses were collected once in six hours. In the case of the chemical samples four portions were mixed together to give a representative sample for the day.

Samples of water for other analytical purposes were collected from time to time as occasion demanded, and as the pressure of regular work allowed of their analysis.

All samples were placed in a large ice-box during the period which intervened between their collection and their analysis.

PHYSICAL CHARACTER OF THE OHIO RIVER WATER.

The most noticeable of the physical characters of the Ohio River water is its appearance with regard to the matters suspended in it. At no time was the river water clear and free from suspended matters. During October and the greater part of November, 1895, the water was comparatively clear; but even at that time it had a distinct turbidity due to the presence of minutely divided particles. The first heavy rains caused the water to become muddy. From that time until the close of the investigations the appearance of the river water possessed a wide range of rapidly changing variability.

As a means of expression of the relative appearance of the Ohio River water the use of adjectives fails utterly. The best idea of the varying appearance of the water is obtained from the results of the daily determination of the weight of the matter suspended in it. These results form a portion of the regular chemical analyses; and reference is made to the following tables in which they are presented, and to an explanation of them in the note which precedes the tables. Here it will suffice to state that the weight of organic and mineral matter suspended in the water ranged from 1 to 5,311 parts per million. The ratio between the weights of the maximum and minimum suspended matter, therefore, was 5,311 to 1.

The appearance of the suspended matter itself was quite different from time to time, ranging from a light gray to a dark red color. A series of factors influenced the appearance in this regard. Prominent among them was the character of the soil on which the rain fell. The extreme conditions of muddy water in connection with the appearance of the suspended matter were noted in March and in May, 1896. During March heavy rains fell throughout the valley. All the tributaries were in flood, and during the last days of the month, when the velocity of the Ohio River was great, the water had a decided red appearance. These particles were comparatively large and came, apparently, from the upper portion of the watershed.

In April and May, 1896, there was a period of extended drought and the surface of the earth was very dry. The rains which came during the last week in May produced muddy water, which contained an immense number of minutely divided particles of a light gray color. This gave the water a yellowish appearance. Some of the particles were smaller than bacteria and measured under the microscope less than 0.00001 inch in diameter. Naturally enough this water was very difficult to clarify.

Between these extreme conditions of appearance there was a wide range of intermediate conditions, depending upon the relative influence of the series of factors outlined on page 15.

During 1897 there was a still greater range than during 1895–96 in the amounts and character of the suspended matter in the river water, although at no time were the clay particles finer than in May, 1896. Further, it appears that the heavy mud is most prevalent during the winter and early spring, while the fine clay prevails in the late spring and summer.

Odor of the River Water.

The Ohio River water, when it was not heated, possessed as a rule a faint odor, the intensity of which was somewhat variable. Occasionally the odor was quite pronounced, but often no odor could be detected. During the fall, winter, and early spring the odor was usually musty, sometimes aromatic and resinous. After the rains in the spring the odor had a vegetable character at times.

Upon heating the river water the odor became stronger, especially in the case of the vegetable odor noticed during warmer weather.

In practically no case, however, was the odor disagreeable, or stronger than would be expected in a surface water of this kind.

Color of the River Water.

It is the suspended particles in the river water which give to it a color. This has already been referred to under the appearance of the water.

When the water is freed from its suspended particles it is practically colorless.

In the following tables containing the results of the regular chemical analyses will be found a record of the amount of dissolved color, expressed in units of the platinum-cobalt standard. These color results were obtained after the suspended particles had been removed by the passage of the water through a fine paper filter or a Pasteur filter.

Taste of the River Water.

Disregarding the suspended matter, the taste of the river water is satisfactory, although the salts dissolved in it, especially the lime, give a slight taste which is noticed by those accustomed to drinking a softer water. There is at times a slight earthy taste to the water.

The suspended matter cannot be regarded as other than objectionable. But after persons become familiar with this kind of water there appear to be comparatively few complaints, except when the water is very muddy.

Temperature of the River Water.

The results of observations on the temperature of the river water, expressed in degrees centigrade, are presented in the tables beyond, containing the results of the regular chemical analyses.

Chemical Character of the Ohio River Water.

In the next set of tables there are presented the results of the regular chemical analyses of the river water from a sanitary and technical standpoint.

The times of collection, the temperature, and the color results will be readily understood from the foregoing pages. They are recorded here as a matter of convenience.

The remaining columns contain the resul s of the several chemical determinations. An outline of the analytical methods used in these chemical determinations will be found in the appendix. In order that the practical significance of these results may be understood more clearly a brief explanation of them will be given.

Explanation of the Results of Chemical Analyses.

The several points will be taken up in the order in which they appear in the tables.

Form of Expression.—All of these results are expressed in parts per million. The exact meaning of this is that one million parts of water by volume contained the several substances in parts by weight to the extent indicated by the figures.

These results may be converted into grains per United States gallon (231 cubic inches) by dividing by 17.1.

Oxygen Consumed.—The results of this determination indicate the amount of organic matter present in the water. By analytical methods there is measured the amount of oxygen which is actually consumed by the organic matter in the water, as it is converted into a comparatively stable form not readily capable of farther decomposition by ordinary means.

As nitrogen cannot be oxidized by this method these results are generally considered to be indicative of the amount of organic matter of a carbonaceous nature.

Nitrogen as Albuminoid Ammonia.—When water containing organic matter of a nitrogenous nature is distilled with a strong alkaline solution of potassium permanganate, the organic nitrogen is changed to ammonia. This ammonia is spoken of as "albuminoid ammonia," and the results of determinations by this method indicate the amount of organic matter of a nitrogenous nature.

A comparison of the results of analyses by the last two methods indicates that the nature of the organic matter in the river water varied considerably, according to the relative results by these methods for its determination.

It will also be noted in the tables that the results by the second method show the amounts of organic matter in suspension and in solution, respectively. Comparatively speaking, the amount of nitrogenous organic matter in solution is fairly constant, although it varied somewhat at different seasons of the year.

Nitrogen as Free Ammonia.—Upon the distillation of the river water without chemicals there is obtained in the distillate a small quantity of ammonia. This is known as the "nitrogen in the form of free ammonia." It measures the amount of nitrogenous organic matter which has undergone the initial step in the decomposition of organic matter by nature.

This decomposition in nature is accomplished in the presence of oxygen by bacteria which eventually convert crude organic matter into harmless mineral matter.

Nitrogen as Nitrites.—These results show the amount of organic matter that is in the

RESULTS OF CHEMICAL ANALYSES OF THE OHIO RIVER WATER.

(Parts per Million.)

Serial Number.	Collected. Date.	Collected. Hour.	Stages of River. Feet.	Temperature. Degrees C.	Color.	Oxygen Consumed.	Nitrogen as Albuminoid Ammonia. Total.	Nitrogen as Albuminoid Ammonia. Suspended.	Nitrogen as Albuminoid Ammonia. Dissolved.	Nitrogen as Free Ammonia.	Nitrogen as Nitrites.	Nitrogen as Nitrates.	Chlorine.	Residue on Evaporation. Total.	Residue on Evaporation. Suspended.	Residue on Evaporation. Dissolved.	Fixed Residue after Ignition. Total.	Fixed Residue after Ignition. Suspended.	Fixed Residue after Ignition. Dissolved.	Alkalinity.	Dissolved Alumina.	Iron.
	1895																					
1	Oct. 16	9.00 A.M.	1.1	......	....	3.4	.368	.156	.212	.028	.005	0.9	40.8	239	1	238	184	1	183	98.0	0	0.4
2	" 17	9.05 "	1.0	......	....	4.0	.492	.316	.176	.028	.005	0.9	40.4	243	1	242	179	1	178	98.0	0	0.4
3	" 18	9.00 "	1.0	......	....	3.2	.356	.108	.248	.031	.005	0.9	42.0	240	1	239	173	0	173	99.5	0	0.4
6	" 19	4.40 P.M.	1.0	......	....	3.2	.322	.122	.200	.030	.005	0.4	46.5	249	10	239	179	5	174	101.0	0	0.3
9	" 21	3.50 "	0.9	......	....	2.9	.236	.098	.138	.012	.005	0.6	55.7	306	24	282	217	8	209	94.7	0	0.4
12	" 22	4.05 "	0.9	......	....	2.7	.288	.154	.134	.018	.007	0.4	58.0	290	15	275	200	11	189	95.8	0	0.3
15	" 23	4.05 "	1.0	15.5	....	2.6	.244	.102	.142	.028	.004	0.6	61.6	308	28	280	211	14	197	97.0	0	0.4
18	" 24	2.00 "	1.0	......	....	2.3	.212	.078	.134	.034	.005	0.4	62.0	290	17	273	230	11	219	98.0	0	0.3
22	" 25	2.00 "	1.1	14.0	....	2.6	.290	.154	.136	.022	.007	0.4	65.0	321	25	297	241	17	224	95.3	0	0.3
25	" 26	12.55 "	1.1	14.2	....	2.4	.316	.174	.142	.018	.005	0.5	65.0	323	31	292	243	12	231	99.5	0	0.3
28	" 28	3.30 "	1.0	......	....	2.1	.216	.082	.134	.078	.035	0.6	73.0	332	10	322	240	5	235	96.0	0	0.6
31	" 30	4.20 "	0.9	......	....	2.2	.222	.076	.146	.080	.035	0.5	77.1	342	15	327	259	11	248	95.0	0	0.5
34	" 31	4.30 "	1.0	12.0	....	1.9	.198	.062	.136	.108	.010	0.3	76.6	332	8	324	247	5	242	97.1	0	0.3
36	Nov 1	3.30 "	1.0	......	....	2.3	.252	.116	.136	.028	.010	0.4	54.0	326	6	320	252	6	246	99.0	0	0.3
39	" 2	3.47 "	1.0	......	....	1.9	.204	.068	.136	.064	.010	0.3	72.1	314	8	306	247	8	239	98.5	0	0.3
42	" 7	2.24 "	0.8	12.5	....	2.1	.206	.064	.142	.066	.010	0.4	57.0	278	4	274	210	4	206	102.2	0	0.3
45	" 9	2.35 "	1.0	......	....	2.0	.202	.048	.154	.092	.010	0.4	55.8	270	10	260	205	5	200	101.9	0	0.3
46	" 12	3.00 "	1.0	......	....	1.8	.154	.020	.134	.070	.010	0.4	52.2	266	13	253	205	5	200	103.4	0	0.4
48	" 14	3.05 "	1.0	9.7	....	2.1	......	......	.142	.020	.010	0.4	51.1	262	9	253	201	4	197	104.0	0	0.3
50	" 20	2.40 "	0.9	8.3	....	2.1	.212	.060	.152	.042	.010	0.4	41.9	245	14	231	181	6	175	101.9	0	0.3
52	" 22	3.40 "	1.0	8.7	....	2.2	.220	.040	.180	.072	.010	0.6	42.0	252	17	235	188	12	176	103.0	0	0.3
54	" 23	3.10 "	1.4	......	....	2.4	.244	.064	.180	.176	.016	0.5	40.8	245	10	235	178	10	168	108.7	0	0.2
55	" 25	4.00 "	1.5	8.2	...	2.8	.234	.054	.180	.058	.010	0.5	38.1	255	21	234	185	10	175	103.6	0	0.2
56	" 26	2.35 "	2.7	7.8	...	2.8	.246	.052	.194	.070	.010	0.6	42.0	256	34	222	200	32	168	90.0	0	0.4
59	" 27	2.01 "	2.2	7.8	....	2.7	.232	.026	.206	.058	.010	0.7	38.2	262	25	237	204	17	187	90.5	0	0.5
62	" 29	2.11 "	3.2	6.8	....	2.5	.200	.072	.128	.118	.010	0.9	38.5	254	31	223	192	27	165	93.5	0	0.4
65	Dec. 2	11.00 A.M.	2.8	6.0	....	2.6	.216	.026	.190	.180	.016	0.8	37.1	258	11	247	205	9	196	92.2	0	0.5
68	" 3	2.57 P.M.	2.0	5.4	....	2.8	.230	.040	.190	.182	.016	0.6	35.6	277	25	252	208	25	183	91.2	0	1.1
71	" 4	2.55 "	2.0	4.5	....	2.6	.216	.036	.150	.185	.015	0.7	38.2	281	21	260	214	20	194	100.0	0	1.5
74	" 6	12.06 "	2.2	4.2	....	2.8	.246	.060	.186	.150	.020	0.4	61.4	344	35	309	260	26	234	96.1	0	2.8
79	" 9	3.27 "	4.4	3.8	....	3.0	.234	.108	.126	.140	....	....	....	....	....	....	....	....	....	85.9	0	1.6
82	" 10	3.15 "	4.3	2.8	....	3.0	.184	.072	.112	.126	....	....	....	....	....	....	....	....	....	79.4	0	2.7
85	" 11	2.48 "	3.9	3.0	....	3.1	.192	.076	.116	.176	....	....	....	....	....	....	....	....	....	74.3	0	2.7
A	Average, Nos. 79, 82, 85		....	......	.09	2.9	.203	.085	.118	.147	.030	0.3	50.6	288	33	255	221	24	197	79.9	0	2.3
88	Dec. 13	4.22 P.M.	4.2	2.6	....	3.2	.158	.038	.120	.132	....	....	....	....	....	....	....	....	....	65.9	0	2.7
91	" 14	3.25 "	3.9	2.5	....	3.5	.174	.062	.112	.100	....	....	....	....	....	....	....	....	....	61.7	0	2.8
D	Average, Nos. 88 and 91		....	......	.21	3.1	.166	.050	.116	.116	.030	0.3	53.5	273	36	237	202	20	182	63.8	0	2.7
94	Dec. 16	2.30 P.M.	3.8	2.6	....	3.9	.188	.032	.156	.110	....	....	....	....	....	....	....	....	....	60.0	0	2.5
97	" 17	3.10 "	3.3	3.0	....	4.0	.210	.046	.164	.120	....	....	....	....	....	....	....	....	....	59.0	0	2.8
100	Dec. 18	3.18 "	3.3	3.8	....	3.9	.198	.026	.172	.112	....	....	....	....	....	....	....	....	....	61.2	0	2.7
G	Average, Nos. 94, 97, 100		....	......	.30	3.8	.172	.050	.126	.102	.030	0.7	28.3	206	15	191	154	6	148	60.0	0	2.6

RESULTS OF CHEMICAL ANALYSES OF THE OHIO RIVER WATER.—*Continued*

(Parts per Million.)

Serial Number.	Collected. Date.	Collected. Hour.	Stages of River. Feet.	Temperature. Degrees C.	Color.	Oxygen Consumed.	Nitrogen as Albuminoid Ammonia. Total.	Nitrogen as Albuminoid Ammonia. Suspended.	Nitrogen as Albuminoid Ammonia. Dissolved.	Nitrogen as Free Ammonia.	Nitrogen as Nitrites.	Nitrogen as Nitrates.	Chlorine.	Residue on Evaporation. Total.	Residue on Evaporation. Suspended.	Residue on Evaporation. Dissolved.	Fixed Residue after Ignition. Total.	Fixed Residue after Ignition. Suspended.	Fixed Residue after Ignition. Dissolved.	Alkalinity.	Dissolved Alumina.	Iron.
	1895																					
103	Dec. 20	10.21 P.M.	3.1	5.1	.34	4.2	.228	.044	.184	.102	.010	1.3	27.3	208	15	193	156	8	148	62.0	0	2.7
114	*	*	....	......	.19	6.0	.388	.236	.152	.108	.010	2.0	22.0	408	220	188	352	213	139	74.5	0	5.0
	1896																					
119	Jan. 2	2.41 P.M.	8.7	3.6	.18	12.3	....	....	....	....	....	....	....	....	....	....	....	....	....	....	....	....
124	" 3	10.20 A.M.	8.9	3.2	....	11.8	....	....	....	....	....	....	....	....	....	....	....	....	....	....	....	....
129	Average, Nos. 119 and 124		....	......	.18	12.5	1.181	.984	.197	.118	.016	2.7	24.0	1066	867	199	983	833	150	60.0	0	49.0
134	Jan. 4	2.27 P.M.	8.8	2.1	....	9.0	....	....	....	....	....	....	....	....	....	....	....	....	....	....	....	....
139	" 6	11.54 A.M.	7.7	1.7	....	7.8	....	....	....	....	....	....	....	....	....	....	....	....	....	....	....	....
143	Average, Nos. 134 and 139		....	......	....	6.5	.653	.494	.159	.076	.010	2.8	10.0	515	362	153	444	341	103	45.0	0	14.5
161	†	†	....	......	....	5.8	.423	.200	.223	.066	.030	3.0	7.6	257	120	137	187	97	90	44.5	0	16.4
166	Jan. 11	11.20 A.M.	6.0	1.8	....	5.3	.261	.118	.143	.066	.010	3.1	8.0	267	118	149	210	113	97	47.5	0	10.7
171	" 14	1.45 P.M.	4.8	1.6	....	4.1	....	....	....	....	....	....	....	....	....	....	....	....	....	....	....	....
176	" 15	2.52 "	4.8	1.3	....	4.1	....	....	....	....	....	....	....	....	....	....	....	....	....	....	....	....
181	Average, Nos. 171 and 176		....	1.45	....	4.1	.209	.026	.183	.050	.005	3.4	14.7	225	43	182	164	33	131	57.4	0	5.0
186	Jan. 20	4.07 P.M.	4.0	2.3	....	3.1	....	....	....	....	....	....	....	....	....	....	....	....	....	....	....	....
191	" 22	2.10 "	3.8	3.1	....	3.1	.135	.010	.125	.072	.010	2.3	13.0	192	17	175	143	14	129	54.0	0	1.9
196	" 27	4.05 "	6.0	4.6	....	5.5	....	....	....	....	....	....	....	....	....	....	....	....	....	....	....	....
201	" 28	12.55 A.M.	5.7	4.0	....	6.6	....	....	....	....	....	....	....	....	....	....	....	....	....	....	....	....
204	Average, Nos. 196 and 201		....	4.3	....	6.3	.369	.260	.109	.096	.010	2.5	10.2	493	273	220	412	253	159	101.1	0	17.0
212	Jan. 29	1.53 P.M.	6.5	4.0	....	7.1	.439	.368	.071	.080	.013	2.0	11.7	526	297	229	449	283	166	88.2	0	17.0
215	Feb. 1	9.55 A.M.	8.6	4.0	....	6.6	.365	.380	.085	.056	.008	1.8	23.2	555	243	212	461	313	148	61.0	0	27.5
219	" 3	10.23 "	8.2	5.2	....	4.7	.245	.164	.081	.054	.006	1.8	19.3	454	244	210	302	172	130	72.1	0	5.2
223	" 4	10.10 "	8.2	3.8	.09	5.7	.279	.196	.083	.070	.008	1.8	18.4	436	246	188	322	202	130	66.8	0	6.3
227	" 5	10.07 "	8.4	4.6	.14	8.4	.439	.356	.083	.066	.008	2.7	8.0	625	458	167	548	429	119	82.0	0	8.2
232	" 6	10.03 "	8.5	5.2	.16	8.2	.417	.338	.079	.066	.007	2.7	7.3	618	464	154	550	444	102	71.2	0	33.0
237	" 7	10.08 "	9.0	5.2	.26	11.4	.593	.518	.075	.054	.008	2.7	6.3	810	636	174	709	595	114	74.2	0	42.8
242	" 8	10.25 "	10.1	5.3	...	13.0	.639	.530	.109	.052	.006	2.2	8.5	864	704	160	769	563	106	55.2	0	27.5
245	" 10	10.10 "	12.0	5.2	.06	12.8	.577	.508	.069	.064	.008	2.2	11.6	1099	967	132	1001	907	94	43.0	0	34.3
250	" 11	10.05 "	12.2	5.1	.14	8.9	.437	.346	.091	.060	.007	1.7	8.2	572	409	163	496	376	120	40.2	0	15.0
254	" 12	10.20 "	11.8	4.2	.18	9.1	.391	.298	.093	.040	.009	1.9	9.1	586	418	168	496	394	102	39.0	0	17.5
259	" 13	9.10 "	11.4	7.2	....	4.6	.215	.128	.087	.042	.008	1.8	7.0	270	126	144	212	108	104	40.7	0	9.0
264	" 14	9.00 "	11.4	4.6	.12	7.6	.311	.244	.067	.040	.006	2.4	5.9	456	339	117	398	318	80	48.1	0	13.6
267	" 15	9.48 "	11.2	4.6	.19	8.7	.353	.278	.075	.040	.009	2.8	7.0	646	486	160	576	462	114	50.1	0	23.0
272	" 17	9.30 "	10.5	4.1	.14	7.5	.292	.218	.074	.040	.009	3.0	4.0	511	391	120	449	361	88	54.0	0	10.0
277	" 18	9.22 "	10.3	4.9	.11	9.1	.366	.334	.032	.022	.010	3.1	3.0	310	180	130	256	166	90	40.1	0	10.0
280	" 19	9.07 "	10.2	3.6	.13	11.2	.484	.426	.058	.030	.009	2.8	4.2	684	565	119	612	507	105	41.0	0	28.0
285	" 20	9.25 "	10.0	2.5	.17	6.3	.232	.166	.066	.022	.010	2.0	5.6	383	266	117	333	254	79	37.7	0	14.5
288	" 21	9.10 "	9.6	2.0	.16	7.2	.256	.208	.048	.018	.006	2.2	5.7	464	338	126	422	328	94	37.0	0	13.0
293	" 22	9.10 "	9.1	1.5	.13	6.0	.288	.220	.068	.032	.010	1.6	5.0	424	310	114	391	305	86	35.0	0	15.7
296	" 24	9.15 "	7.8	2.0	.13	4.3	.162	.112	.050	.032	.007	1.7	6.3	258	134	124	214	130	84	39.5	0	10.0

* Average samples collected Dec. 27, 10.05 A.M.; Dec. 28, 9.56 A.M.; Dec. 30, 10.56 A.M.

† Average samples collected Jan. 8, 2.50 P.M.; Jan. 10 1.42 P.M.

RESULTS OF CHEMICAL ANALYSES OF THE OHIO RIVER WATER.—*Continued.*

(Parts per Million.)

Serial Number.	Collected.		Stages of River. Feet.	Temperature. Degrees C.	Color.	Oxygen Consumed.	Nitrogen as Albuminoid Ammonia.			Nitrogen as Free Ammonia.	Nitrogen as Nitrites.	Nitrogen as Nitrates.	Chlorine.	Residue on Evaporation.			Fixed Residue after Ignition.			Alkalinity.	Dissolved Alumina.	Iron.
	Date.	Hour.					Total.	Suspended.	Dissolved.					Total.	Suspended.	Dissolved.	Total.	Suspended.	Dissolved.			
	1896																					
301	Feb. 25	9.10 A.M.	7.3	2.0	.14	3.8	.152	.098	.054	.024	.007	1.6	4.8	260	144	116	204	120	84	41.0	0	7.3
304	" 26	9.10 "	6.6	2.5	.15	3.3	.146	.104	.042	.022	.010	1.6	4.7	238	129	109	202	115	87	43.9	0	7.2
309	" 27	10.00 "	6.1	3.5	.15	4.5	.200	.140	.060	.024	.006	1.7	5.5	282	161	121	242	153	89	48.0	0	9.8
312	" 28	9.10 "	5.8	3.3	....	3.0	.102	.036	.066	.024	.005	1.4	5.5	198	57	141	154	60	94	49.5	0	6.9
317	" 29	9.30 "	5.7	4.0	....	2.8	.088	.038	.050	.022	.010	1.4	5.6	202	62	140	156	58	98	51.0	0	4.9
320	Mar. 2	9.30 "	5.5	3.8	.18	2.6	.084	.042	.042	.018	.007	1.4	5.6	186	54	132	153	53	100	59.6	0	3.6
326	" 3	9.55 "	5.5	4.0	.17	3.2	.118	.062	.056	.020	.006	1.5	6.4	214	89	125	177	89	88	57.6	0	4.6
329	" 4	9.30 "	5.7	4.1	.14	2.5	.088	.050	.038	.016	.006	1.6	6.0	190	55	135	160	55	105	61.0	0	3.6
334	" 5	9.30 "	5.8	4.0	....	2.1	.100	.048	.052	.030	.011	1.7	6.8	199	50	149	155	50	105	59.8	0	3.0
337	" 6	9.30 "	5.8	4.5	....	1.8	.084	.030	.054	.028	.006	1.7	7.6	174	22	152	139	21	118	60.2	0	2.3
342	" 7	9.30 "	6.0	4.7	.16	2.5	.102	.046	.056	.018	.010	1.7	9.0	224	80	144	184	77	107	59.0	0	4.0
346	" 9	9.30 "	6.6	5.0	.12	2.3	.076	.040	.036	.030	.011	1.6	11.3	220	68	152	181	64	117	64.2	0	9.3
351	" 10	9.30 "	6.5	5.4	.18	2.2	.090	.046	.044	.026	.010	1.5	12.5	214	60	154	179	59	120	55.1	0	5.8
354	" 11	9.30 "	6.7	6.0	.08	1.9	.096	.044	.052	.028	.011	1.4	12.0	232	71	161	178	56	122	59.0	0	3.2
359	" 12	9.30 "	6.6	4.5	.13	2.1	.116	.044	.072	.034	.010	1.3	11.5	221	56	165	173	54	119	68.9	0	2.4
363	" 13	9.30 "	6.5	4.0	....	2.1	.094	.046	.048	.032	.010	1.7	10.4	192	45	147	160	43	117	63.3	0	4.4
366	" 14	9.30 "	6.6	4.2	.11	2.3	.108	.058	.050	.028	.011	1.2	9.4	192	52	140	162	49	113	61.1	0	3.6
370	" 16	9.30 "	7.1	4.2	.18	2.5	.110	.046	.064	.034	.008	1.5	7.3	184	50	134	156	47	109	60.7	0	3.4
375	" 17	9.30 "	7.0	4.0	.07	2.9	.130	.076	.054	.026	.005	1.2	8.2	197	62	135	162	60	102	57.5	0	3.3
378	" 18	9.30 "	7.2	4.9	.11	3.0	.132	.066	.066	.030	.007	1.7	9.5	216	88	128	181	83	98	54.8	0	4.0
382	" 19	9.30 "	8.2	5.6	.17	5.0	.238	.174	.064	.032	.003	1.0	6.5	330	210	120	293	201	92	63.0	0	6.4
386	" 20	9.30 "	10.8	4.2	.14	14.2	.700	.628	.072	.082	.005	1.1	9.0	1120	993	127	1038	944	94	47.0	0	22.8
390	" 21	9.45 "	12.6	4.2	.15	17.8	1.046	.980	.066	.108	.007	1.1	4.0	1397	1276	121	1293	1206	87	44.0	0	45.9
394	" 23	9.35 "	13.8	5.9	.15	13.2	.580	.498	.082	.064	.004	1.6	4.0	776	665	111	720	643	77	41.2	0	36.6
399	" 24–25	*	13.7	5.6	.27	9.3	.476	.408	.068	.034	.003	1.7	5.8	622	521	101	567	491	76	37.0	0	37.1
400	" 25–26	*	13.0	5.5	.30	9.1	.414	.358	.056	.022	.005	2.1	8.1	643	516	127	569	486	83	48.0	0	45.2
404	" 26–27	*	12.3	5.6	.14	8.9	.462	.392	.070	.028	.005	2.0	5.4	578	472	106	514	435	79	49.5	0	20.3
408	" 27–28	*	11.9	6.5	.15	7.5	.344	.270	.074	.022	.007	2.1	4.9	480	355	125	422	330	92	53.0	0	15.1
412	" 28–29	*	11.5	6.3	.13	8.3	.454	.382	.072	.032	.009	2.1	5.6	554	428	126	484	396	88	51.6	0	20.0
416	" 29–30	*	11.1	8.0	.15	7.4	.374	.296	.078	.034	.006	2.0	5.2	469	338	131	404	312	92	58.3	0	19.0
420	" 30	11.30 A.M.	10.8	8.0	.17	12.0	.852	.742	.110	.042	.005	1.9	5.5	881	740	141	784	696	88	59.0	0	29.7
424	" 31	9.30 "	11.8	8.8	.18	13.9	.932	.836	.096	.064	.008	2.1	6.1	1145	1004	141	1044	951	93	57.1	0	40.0
428	April 1	9.30 "	12.7	9.8	.17	15.8	1.032	.944	.088	.040	.009	2.4	6.0	1263	1131	132	1163	1063	100	63.0	0	44.9
432	" 2	9.30 "	15.2	9.0	.15	15.6	.960	.890	.070	.034	.009	2.3	6.4	1052	932	120	973	889	84	46.0	0	36.6
436	" 3	9.30 "	18.3	8.5	.18	18.4	1.080	1.004	.076	.056	.005	1.2	6.0	1157	1062	95	1058	990	68	31.4	0	42.0
440	" 4	9.30 "	20.7	8.1	.25	13.0	.620	.522	.098	.054	.006	1.0	4.1	705	628	77	656	604	52	27.1	0	30.0
445	" 6	9.30 "	22.3	9.1	.23	8.6	.500	.416	.084	.058	.005	1.0	3.5	555	485	70	514	464	50	23.1	0	22.2
449	" 7	9.30 "	20.8	8.4	.18	7.5	.380	.306	.074	.058	.005	1.1	3.1	426	352	74	389	338	51	30.0	0	21.3
453	" 8	9.30 "	17.7	9.5	.18	6.7	.370	.278	.092	.054	.005	1.1	3.5	396	302	94	346	280	66	34.7	0	20.0
456	" 9	9.30 "	14.1	9.2	.20	7.7	.380	.300	.080	.034	.006	1.1	3.6	426	329	97	380	308	72	38.2	0	21.3

* Average samples at 11.30 A.M., 5.30 P.M., 11.30 P.M., 5.30 A.M.

RESULTS OF CHEMICAL ANALYSES OF THE OHIO RIVER WATER.—*Continued.*

(Parts per Million.)

Serial Number.	Collected. Date.	Collected. Hour.	Stages of River, Feet.	Temperature, Degrees C.	Color.	Oxygen Consumed.	Nitrogen as Albuminoid Ammonia. Total.	Nitrogen as Albuminoid Ammonia. Suspended.	Nitrogen as Albuminoid Ammonia. Dissolved.	Nitrogen as Free Ammonia.	Nitrogen as Nitrites.	Nitrogen as Nitrates.	Chlorine.	Residue on Evaporation. Total.	Residue on Evaporation. Suspended.	Residue on Evaporation. Dissolved.	Fixed Residue after Ignition. Total.	Fixed Residue after Ignition. Suspended.	Fixed Residue after Ignition. Dissolved.	Alkalinity.	Dissolved Alumina.	Iron.
	1896																					
459	April 10	9.30 A.M.	11.6	9.5	.25	6.3	.312	.232	.080	.036	.006	1.2	4.0	354	252	102	307	235	72	37.8	0	16.1
462	" 11	9.30 "	10.3	10.0	.20	6.5	.286	.206	.080	.036	.006	1.2	4.7	378	284	94	344	274	70	43.0	0	14.0
465	" 13	9.30 "	8.5	......	.20	5.4	.270	.184	.086	.042	.007	1.1	4.7	269	168	101	233	155	78	43.0	0	8.2
468	" 14	9.35 "	8.0	11.3	.23	3.5	.166	.088	.078	.034	.004	1.1	6.2	178	72	106	144	65	79	45.0	0	7.2
469	" 15	9.30 "	7.6	12.6	.15	4.9	.208	.128	.080	.028	.005	1.0	6.5	264	155	109	222	141	81	46.1	0	8.0
471	" 16	9.30 "	7.5	13.2	.27	3.6	.164	.082	.082	.038	.005	1.0	6.9	176	66	110	146	65	81	46.4	0	5.5
473	" 17	9.30 "	7.3	15.5	.18	4.0	.172	.088	.084	.038	.007	1.0	7.0	196	86	110	162	82	80	45.0	0	5.8
475	" 18	9.30 "	7.4	15.0	.22	3.3	.206	.108	.098	.052	.007	1.0	7.5	210	97	113	177	90	87	48.5	0	6.8
477	" 20	9.30 "	7.8	16.6	.12	3.7	.198	.116	.082	.042	.005	.8	10.9	235	116	119	200	107	93	44.2	0	6.8
480	" 21	9.30 "	7.7	16.9	.18	3.4	.188	.110	.078	.038	.005	1.0	10.7	234	118	116	204	109	95	45.0	0	3.2
483	" 22	9.30 "	7.4	16.8	.15	3.1	.160	.090	.070	.034	.005	.9	12.6	217	101	116	193	96	97	45.1	0	2.8
486	" 23	9.30 "	7.1	17.5	.21	2.3	.138	.070	.068	.030	.007	.9	10.8	176	61	115	152	57	95	47.0	0	3.6
489	" 24	9.30 "	6.8	17.7	.25	2.8	.146	.068	.078	.030	.005	.8	8.1	189	75	114	168	74	94	47.8	0	4.0
492	" 25	9.30 "	6.5	18.2	.23	2.3	.152	.080	.072	.030	.005	.7	7.9	183	68	115	154	64	90	47.3	0	2.9
495	" 27–28	*	6.1	......	.15	3.1	.172	.088	.084	.036	.006	.8	6.7	184	72	112	162	72	90	53.2	0	3.6
498	" 28–29	*	6.3	22.0	.16	3.0	.172	.084	.088	.034	.006	.7	6.1	194	78	116	162	73	89	50.0	0	4.0
501	" 29–30	*	6.3	19.8	.18	2.9	.170	.100	.070	.032	.006	.8	6.9	189	72	117	160	68	92	55.0	0	3.2
504	†	*	...	......	.14	2.4	.160	.088	.072	.022	.004	.8	9.5	181	57	124	152	52	100	56.1	0	4.3
507	May 1–2	*	6.2	......	.14	3.1	.174	.088	.086	.038	.005	.9	9.0	184	62	122	162	59	103	54.0	0	2.8
510	" 2	9.00 A.M.	6.3	21.2	.14	2.9	.168	.080	.088	.042	.005	.9	8.4	184	60	124	160	55	105	58.0	0	3.2
513	" 4–5	‡	6.0	23.0	.27	3.6	.188	.096	.092	.036	.006	1.0	11.9	243	103	140	218	98	120	58.5	0	4.0
516	" 5–6	‡	6.0	22.8	.17	3.6	.196	.100	.096	.038	.006	.9	9.7	230	104	126	204	100	104	54.8	.1	4.0
519	" 6–7	‡	5.7	22.7	.21	3.4	.188	.102	.086	.036	.009	1.1	10.0	224	97	127	197	90	107	56.0	0	5.2
522	" 7–8	‡	5.7	22.1	.25	3.5	.164	.068	.096	.030	.008	.9	11.4	214	74	140	190	73	117	54.8	0	5.4
525	" 8–9	‡	5.9	23.0	.19	4.3	.206	.108	.098	.034	.009	.8	12.4	247	111	136	218	107	111	53.5	0	6.3
529	" 9	9.00 A.M.	6.1	23.4	.18	4.1	.194	.112	.082	.034	.007	.7	10.9	255	111	144	222	110	112	51.0	0	6.7
532	" 11–12	§	6.4	24.0	.18	4.7	.286	.190	.096	.034	.007	.8	10.3	321	185	136	285	184	101	51.2	0	11.8
536	" 12–13		6.1	23.5	.11	3.9	.226	.146	.080	.036	.007	.7	11.5	295	168	127	265	164	101	48.0	0	6.0
540	" 13–14		5.9	23.6	.11	3.5	.202	.120	.082	.032	.008	.8	11.1	260	137	123	234	130	104	53.0	0	5.5
544	" 14–15		5.4	23.0	.11	3.7	.200	.130	.070	.022	.007	.5	10.3	263	144	119	229	141	88	53.8	0	2.4
548	" 15–16		5.1	24.1	.13	3.6	.182	.110	.072	.026	.011	.5	11.0	228	100	128	187	94	93	53.1	0	4.5
552	" 16	9.00 A.M.	4.8	23.7	.17	4.0	.190	.114	.076	.028	.010	.5	12.4	264	129	135	225	120	105	53.0	0	2.6
556	" 18–19	¶	4.4	23.6	.16	3.3	.174	.074	.100	.030	.012	.6	14.7	213	77	136	172	68	104	55.6	0	6.8
560	" 19–20	¶	4.4	23.7	.12	3.1	.158	.068	.090	.028	.012	.6	12.8	200	59	141	158	59	99	56.9	0	6.8
564	" 20–21	¶	3.9	23.6	.12	4.0	.228	.142	.086	.034	.010	.7	11.5	285	152	133	249	151	98	57.0	0	7.2
568	" 21–22	¶	3.8	23.6	.13	3.8	.214	.124	.090	.040	.013	.8	10.7	278	132	146	238	125	113	62.0	0	6.4
572	" 22–23	¶	3.6	24.5	.12	4.9	.228	.138	.090	.048	.016	.6	12.0	232	81	151	183	76	107	61.0	0	13.6

* Average samples at 9.30 A.M., 9.00 P.M., 3.00 A.M., 9.00 A.M.
† April 30 and May 1.
‡ Average samples at 3.00 P.M., 9.00 P.M., 3.00 A.M., 9.00 A.M.
§ Average samples at 9.00 A.M., 3.00 P.M., 9.00 P.M., 3.00 A.M.
Average samples at 9.30 A.M., 6.00 P.M., 12.00 P.M., 6.00 A.M.
¶ Average samples at 12.00 M., 6.00 P.M., 12.00 P.M., 6.00 A.M.

RESULTS OF CHEMICAL ANALYSES OF THE OHIO RIVER WATER.—*Continued.*

(Parts per Million.)

Serial Number.	Collected.		Stage of River. Feet.	Temperature. Degrees C.	Color.	Oxygen Consumed.	Nitrogen as Albuminoid Ammonia.			Nitrogen as Free Ammonia	Nitrogen as Nitrites.	Nitrogen as Nitrates.	Chlorine.	Residue on Evaporation.			Fixed Residue after Ignition.			Alkalinity.	Dissolved Alumina.	Iron.
	Date.	Hour.					Total.	Suspended.	Dissolved.					Total.	Suspended.	Dissolved.	Total.	Suspended.	Dissolved.			
575	1896 May 25–26	*	3.5	25.6	.15	2.7	.166	.084	.082	.028	.006	.7	13.2	187	38	149	150	36	114	68.0	0	2.8
579	" 26–27	*	3.3	25.3	.13	2.9	.158	.082	.076	.024	.006	.7	13.9	181	42	139	147	40	107	63.5	0	2.5
582	" 27–28	*	3.9	24.8	.12	3.3	.186	.108	.078	.042	.008	.6	13.0	234	90	144	202	88	114	65.5	0	5.2
585	" 28–29	*	4.1	24.0	.12	8.4	.566	.450	.116	.086	.018	.8	12.3	834	673	161	710	595	115	74.0	0	28.9
589	" 29–30	*	5.1	23.5	.18	9.4	.602	.470	.132	.080	.014	.9	11.1	815	653	162	736	615	121	86.3	0	30.6
593	" 30	9.30 A.M.	4.8	23.6	.18	7.8	.502	.382	.120	.076	.005	.8	9.0	691	534	157	626	503	123	89.8	0	27.1
596	June 1–2	*	4.7	22.1	.17	7.0	.446	.340	.106	.030	.020	.7	13.4	741	573	168	645	534	111	73.5	0	39.1
599	" 2–3	*	4.3	22.2	.20	8.0	.576	.444	.132	.048	.008	.8	12.4	983	829	154	861	754	107	69.8	0	37.5
603	" 3–4	*	4.2	22.8	.22	5.8	.364	.244	.120	.048	.010	.9	12.3	617	459	158	526	417	109	69.0	0	18.0
607	" 4–5	*	3.9	23.8	.18	5.2	.324	.222	.102	.034	.020	.8	10.2	485	338	147	424	317	107	72.1	0	17.4
611	" 5–6	*	3.9	24.2	.20	4.2	.274	.148	.126	.030	.020	.7	13.9	350	186	164	298	186	112	72.0	0	11.4
616	" 6	9.00 A.M.	4.5	24.4	.20	3.0	.192	.092	.100	.034	.019	.7	14.2	328	160	168	268	148	120	73.2	0	10.2
623	" 9	11.30 "	...	27.0	.18	6.8	.404	.324	.080	.080	.010	1.1	14.8	753	582	171	664	533	131	81.9	0	28.0
626	" 10	9.30 "	4.3	25.0	.23	6.1	.340	.246	.094	.032	.007	.9	25.6	542	366	176	478	346	132	74.0	0	17.4
629	" 11	9.30 "	4.6	24.8	.20	4.2	.282	.190	.092	.044	.012	.9	16.1	412	247	165	355	229	126	75.3	0	9.6
632	" 12	9.30 "	4.7	25.0	.26	4.1	.250	.162	.088	.026	.008	.9	17.6	387	197	190	323	190	133	69.7	0	13.5
636	" 13	9.30 "	4.7	24.2	.13	4.2	.232	.146	.086	.022	.012	.7	18.9	383	221	162	318	197	121	74.1	0	7.2
642	" 15	9.30 "	4.7	24.2	.24	5.6	.364	.270	.094	.036	.014	.8	13.5	563	400	163	497	383	114	71.4	0	20.0
646	" 16	9.30 "	4.8	25.0	.16	4.2	.248	.158	.090	.030	.013	1.2	14.8	384	223	161	328	208	120	74.3	0	10.6
649	" 17	9.30 "	5.0	25.2	.17	4.6	.260	.170	.090	.026	.010	.9	13.5	391	223	168	331	216	115	73.0	0	13.4
651	" 18	9.30 "	4.9	25.4	.18	5.0	.288	.194	.094	.034	.006	.6	14.0	423	270	153	368	264	104	69.1	0	10.4
655	" 19	9.30 "	4.9	25.8	.25	5.9	.392	.282	.110	.034	.004	.7	15.0	577	426	151	506	397	109	64.0	0	16.5
658	" 20	9.30 "	4.7	27.2	.16	4.3	.268	.176	.092	.028	.003	.6	17.0	437	262	175	366	243	123	69.5	0	12.2
662	" 22	9.30 "	4.6	27.0	.19	4.0	.222	.118	.104	.032	.003	.6	21.3	383	216	167	306	197	109	72.0	0	7.7
665	" 23	9.30 "	4.4	27.0	.22	3.7	.224	.124	.100	.024	.004	.7	17.3	357	179	178	290	174	116	72.0	0	5.2
668	" 24	9.30 "	4.9	27.4	.24	5.1	.460	.352	.108	.032	.004	.7	22.6	586	402	184	484	360	124	66.0	0	12.2
678	" 25	9.30 "	5.4	27.0	.17	6.0	.326	.212	.114	.036	.005	.7	28.6	503	301	202	427	275	152	74.5	0	12.5
681	" 26	9.30 "	4.8	......	.25	5.1	.304	.188	.116	.026	.007	.8	24.0	482	283	199	394	256	138	75.2	0	16.2
684	" 27	9.30 "	4.7	26.5	.18	5.5	.374	.250	.124	.034	.012	.8	20.6	548	356	192	472	330	142	71.2	0	18.3
686	" 29	9.30 "	6.8	25.5	.17	7.4	.412	.314	.128	.030	.008	.9	15.8	698	534	164	620	503	117	75.9	0	28.7
689	" 30	9.30 "	8.0	26.0	.22	5.6	.356	.256	.100	.028	.007	1.0	13.0	531	357	174	461	332	129	59.3	0	16.5
692	July 1	9.30 "	8.3	26.1	.18	10.7	.628	.516	.112	.036	.002	.9	17.4	1016	867	149	910	812	98	52.2	0	31.1
695	" 2	9.30 "	8.5	26.2	.22	15.0	.962	.856	.106	.056	.002	.9	10.7	1800	1674	126	1663	1575	88	49.1	0	43.2
700	" 3	9.30 "	8.3	26.5	.22	12.1	.640	.528	.112	.044	.002	.5	7.0	1093	996	97	999	937	62	46.2	0	35.3
704	" 6	9.30 "	6.8	26.3	.25	4.8	.258	.148	.110	.022	.001	.9	15.2	354	223	131	294	202	92	49.6	0	9.0
707	" 7	9.30 "	6.5	27.0	.22	7.0	.398	.294	.104	.026	.004	1.0	11.0	646	529	117	584	499	85	50.0	0	26.4
711	" 8	9.30 "	5.9	27.2	.22	6.8	.432	.324	.108	.026	.014	1.0	7.5	571	461	110	500	432	68	50.0	0	22.0
714	" 9	9.30 "	5.5	26.0	.25	6.6	.378	.272	.106	.030	.002	.6	6.9	589	470	119	523	436	87	56.0	0	30.7
720	" 10	9.30 "	5.3	26.0	.25	5.8	.346	.218	.128	.034	.002	.8	5.6	488	354	134	425	328	97	58.2	0	17.6

* Average samples at 12.00 M., 6.00 P.M., 12.00 P.M., 6.00 A.M.

RESULTS OF CHEMICAL ANALYSES OF THE OHIO RIVER WATER.—*Continued*

(Parts per Million.)

Serial Number.	Collected.		Stage of River, Feet.	Temperature, Degrees C.	Color.	Oxygen Consumed.	Nitrogen as Albuminoid Ammonia.			Nitrogen as Free Ammonia.	Nitrogen as Nitrites.	Nitrogen as Nitrates.	Chlorine.	Residue on Evaporation.			Fixed Residue after Ignition.			Alkalinity.	Dissolved Alumina.	Iron.
	Date.	Hour.					Total.	Suspended.	Dissolved.					Total.	Suspended.	Dissolved.	Total.	Suspended.	Dissolved.			
	1896																					
723	July 11	9.30 A.M.	5.3	25.9	.21	4.4	.224	.116	.108	.030	.001	1.0	6.0	318	185	133	263	165	98	53.2	0	11.1
727	" 13	9.30 "	6.9	26.1	.25	7.0	.382	.274	.108	.026	.009	.9	5.0	611	487	124	544	456	89	55.9	0	22.9
730	" 14	9.30 "	8.5	26.4	.24	6.6	.310	.204	.106	.024	.006	.8	7.0	487	373	114	421	342	78	40.1	0	17.4
734	" 15	9.30 "	8.5	26.3	.28	8.3	.420	.294	.126	.030	.002	.8	6.1	598	486	112	542	454	88	47.7	0	24.4
737	" 16	9.30 "	8.3	25.9	.26	7.0	.378	.286	.092	.030	.000	.8	3.4	560	452	108	504	417	87	52.3	0	16.9
740	" 16	12.50 P.M.	....	......	.27	7.0	.362	.214	.148	.030	.000	.6	2.2	540	404	136	480	404	76	52.7	0	15.4
743	" 17	9.30 A.M.	7.6	25.8	.18	7.0	.394	.310	.084	.022	.001	.7	2.5	583	475	108	527	447	80	56.0	0	19.9
744	" 18	9.30 "	6.9	25.7	.19	8.7	.504	.406	.098	.038	.001	.5	4.0	753	637	116	668	594	74	60.3	0	33.3
753	" 20	9.30 "	6.9	23.8	.18	6.5	.318	.222	.096	.030	.001	.7	5.5	486	363	123	428	342	86	53.8	0	19.0
756	" 21	9.30 "	8.0	23.8	.22	7.7	.494	.386	.108	.030	.001	.8	6.1	686	559	127	604	526	78	59.7	0	20.5
760	" 22	9.30 "	9.9	23.6	.23	14.0	.824	.726	.098	.052	.005	.9	10.0	1294	1171	123	1170	1095	75	57.4	0	52.3
763	" 23	9.30 "	10.7	25.3	.37	24.8	1.360	1.228	.132	.056	.008	.7	8.6	2296	2175	121	2096	201	78	61.9	0	97.9
767	" 24	9.30 "	9.9	25.1	.23	35.6	2.400	2.272	.128	.068	.004	1.0	4.6	3470	3347	123	3230	3140	90	71.8	0	184.0
773	" 25	9.30 "	9.7	25.5	.26	22.6	1.320	1.202	.118	.034	.003	.8	8.5	1811	1677	134	1667	1569	98	69.0	0	65.7
777	" 27	9.30 "	11.0	26.0	.28	21.7	1.220	1.068	.152	.052	.018	.8	5.0	1515	1398	117	1405	1334	71	63.0	0	60.5
780	" 28	1.30 P.M.	11.9	26.7	.32	17.8	1.120	1.000	.120	.066	.012	.7	7.4	1523	1416	107	1382	1318	64	51.0	0	70.8
790	" 29	9.30 A.M.	13.0	26.6	.21	19.7	.880	.752	.128	.062	.010	.6	5.0	1886	1770	116	1741	1667	74	54.0	0	57.5
793	" 30	9.30 "	13.8	26.8	.23	23.4	1.200	1.060	.120	.056	.006	.8	3.1	1833	1733	100	1660	1604	65	55.3	0	57.0
798	" 31	9.30 "	14.1	26.6	.24	13.6	.470	.352	.118	.050	.005	.7	3.7	920	805	115	834	754	80	53.2	0	31.0
807	Aug. 7	....	12.5	....	.32	9.7	.430	.298	.132	.044	.002	0.6	5.0	536	415	121	443	353	90	54.0	0	20.2
809	" 11	....	8.7	....	.30	9.8	.430	.292	.138	.032	.000	0.7	5.3	520	389	131	455	375	80	75.4	0	14.4
813	" 14	....	6.6	....	.18	19.7	1.040	.932	.108	.046	.004	0.7	6.1	1524	1388	136	1418	1324	94	74.0	0	46.0
818	" 18	....	6.2	....	.18	6.6	.260	.156	.104	.026	.000	0.7	5.9	380	241	139	331	241	90	74.0	0	12.0
824	Dec. 10	....	7.5	....	....	4.3	.186	.076	.110	.024	.008	0.6	4.9	289	179	110	231	153	78	72.0	0	15.0
	1897																					
831	Feb. 16	9.30 A.M.	12.8	5.0	....	6.4	.326	.216	.110	.062	.024	1.0	4.4	376	234	142	332	230	102	49.0	0	16.0
833	" 17	9.30 "	12.3	6.0	....	6.8	.380	.260	.120	.048	.028	0.7	4.5	428	288	140	388	280	108	50.5	0	24.0
835	" 22	9.30 "	12.2	7.0	.23	9.1	.542	.402	.140	.028	.015	1.5	4.4	620	474	146	561	447	114	61.5	0	60.0
837	" 23	9.30 "	19.6	8.0	.18	50.3	3.084	3.004	.080	.098	.012	1.2	4.1	4501	4372	129	4223	4128	95	62.5	0	340.0
839	" 24	9.30 "	25.2	8.3	.23	48.9	2.360	2.286	.074	.060	.015	1.4	4.4	3732	3604	128	3537	3445	92	56.0	0	340.0
841	" 25	9.30 "	29.1	8.5	.28	18.5	.950	.880	.070	.042	.015	1.5	4.9	1084	957	127	995	903	92	32.0	0	170.0
842	" 26	1.30 P.M.	32.0	8.7	.32	16.3	.538	.472	.066	.064	.009	1.2	2.7	706	629	77	647	599	48	21.2	0	40.0
843	" 27	10.15 A.M.	33.6	8.9	.31	13.9	.554	.492	.062	.056	.007	1.1	2.0	854	787	67	797	756	41	25.0	0	45.0
844	Mar. 1	3.00 P.M.	34.0	9.0	.34	8.9	.388	.312	.076	.044	.018	1.4	1.6	501	424	77	456	407	49	23.5	0	35.0
845	" 2	3.30 "	31.9	9.2	.23	8.1	.402	.316	.086	.054	.024	1.6	1.9	408	324	84	371	215	56	29.0	0	18.0
846	" 3	4.00 "	28.3	9.5	.25	8.4	.466	.370	.096	.048	.008	1.7	2.5	446	343	103	400	325	75	44.0	0	20.0
847	" 4	10.00 A.M.	25.1	9.8	.22	9.9	.644	.550	.094	.044	.006	1.9	2.6	673	562	111	620	540	80	53.2	0	34.0
848	" 5	9.30 "	19.5	9.8	.23	12.0	.762	.654	.108	.036	.007	1.8	3.1	892	761	131	820	726	94	54.7	0	36.0
850	" 6	11.30 "	21.3	10.0	.24	65.0	4.900	4.754	.146	.090	.007	1.4	3.3	5431	5311	120	5165	5076	89	52.9	0	116.0
852	" 7	12.00 M.	22.4	4.5	.23	33.8	2.410	2.268	.142	.120	.006	1.1	3.3	2702	2604	98	2542	2475	67	54.4	0	162.0
853	" 9	4.00 P.M.	16.0	9.8	.22	16.3	.940	.826	.114	.100	.005	0.9	3.5	1039	914	125	959	875	84	58.9	0	44.0

RESULTS OF CHEMICAL ANALYSES OF THE OHIO RIVER WATER.—*Continued.*

(Parts per Million.)

Serial Number.	Collected.		Stage of River. Feet.	Temperature. Degrees C.	Color.	Oxygen Consumed.	Nitrogen as Albuminoid Ammonia.			Nitrogen as Free Ammonia.	Nitrogen as Nitrites.	Nitrogen as Nitrates.	Chlorine.	Residue on Evaporation.			Fixed Residue after Ignition.			Alkalinity.	Dissolved Alumina.	Iron.
	Date.	Hour.					Total.	Suspended.	Dissolved.					Total.	Suspended.	Dissolved.	Total.	Suspended.	Dissolved.			
854	1897 Mar. 10	9.30 A.M.	18.7	10.1	.20	29.5	1.400	1.294	.106	.120	.005	1.2	4.6	1789	1672	117	1708	1630	78	51.5	0	83.0
855	" 11	9.30 "	23.1	10.6	.22	24.6	1.268	1.140	.128	.042	.002	1.1	5.1	1881	1751	130	1766	1664	102	51.9	0	96.0
858	" 12	10.00 "	25.7	10.5	.23	19.1	1.000	892	.108	.044	.003	1.4	5.1	1280	1182	98	1193	1117	76	51.2	0	53.0
859	" 13	9.30 "	26.7	10.2	.28	10.4	.680	.580	.100	.038	.006	1.3	3.6	820	728	92	767	695	72	43.7	0	22.0
860	" 15	9.30 "	25.0	11.2	.28	7.2	.368	.246	.122	.030	.012	1.3	2.9	486	404	82	450	390	60	39.4	0	15.2
861	" 16	9.30 "	22.7	11.0	.27	6.4	.346	.224	.122	.030	.010	1.2	2.6	415	322	93	384	319	65	45.0	0	14.4
862	" 17	1.00 P.M.	20.1	11.5	.22	7.0	.342	.224	.118	.020	.008	1.0	3.0	451	346	105	418	343	75	43.5	0	16.8
863	" 18	9.30 A.M.	18.3	11.7	.20	6.4	.296	.200	.096	.020	.006	0.9	2.8	386	281	105	354	267	87	42.9	0	17.6
864	" 19	9.30 "	18.0	11.6	.21	7.4	.430	.310	.120	.018	.008	1.2	2.5	515	399	116	479	383	96	54.0	0	22.4
865	" 20	9.30 "	18.6	11.7	.20	8.0	.564	.448	.116	.018	.008	1.0	2.5	557	455	102	517	436	81	51.0	0	22.0
866	" 22	10.30 "	16.4	11.2	.19	7.6	.412	.302	.110	.020	.992	1.2	3.5	430	322	108	390	319	71	55.6	0	22.8
867	" 23	11.00 "	15.0	11.0	.19	6.2	.268	.176	.092	.014	.004	1.3	3.6	378	272	106	344	259	85	51.6	0	21.2
868	" 24	10.00 "	15.3	10.4	.20	13.2	.752	.662	.090	.020	.004	1.5	2.4	1084	987	97	1019	950	69	54.7	0	51.2
869	" 25	1.00 P.M.	15.0	......	.15	6.8	.362	.260	.102	.008	.005	1.2	3.1	466	364	102	436	359	77	49.0	0	12.4
870	" 26	4.00 "	13.8	10.0	.15	5.2	.250	.138	.112	.012	.001	1.3	3.2	344	244	100	316	237	79	47.2	0	13.2
871	" 27	2.30 "	12.6	10.2	.15	4.6	.204	.126	.078	.008	.003	1.1	3.0	295	184	111	262	172	90	48.1	0	20.8
872	" 29	2.30 "	11.5	......	.17	4.3	.224	.112	.112	.008	.003	0.8	6.2	287	187	100	262	182	80	43.0	0	10.0
873	" 30	12.00 M.	11.1	......	.19	4.7	.246	.126	.120	.012	.002	1.0	2.7	340	227	113	305	216	89	37.1	0	8.0
874	April 1	10.00 A.M.	10.2	10.4	.14	4.9	.214	.134	.080	.020	.003	0.9	6.6	341	230	111	310	218	92	48.0	0	9.2
875	" 2, 3	*	9.3	10.5	.16	4.5	.248	.166	.082	.020	.002	1.2	4.5	325	213	112	299	209	90	39.2	0	8.8
878	" 3–4	3.30 P.M., 9.30 P.M. 12.30 A.M., 5.30 A.M.	8.4	11.2	.20	4.8	.208	.138	.070	.014	.001	0.8	2.8	309	200	109	281	193	88	43.8	0	12.8
880	" 5	12.30 P.M., 5.30 P.M. 9.30 P.M.	8.1	12.0	.18	6.7	.344	.268	.076	.028	.002	1.6	3.5	466	336	130	420	332	88	56.7	0	9.0
882	" 6	5.30 A.M., 2.00 P.M. 5.30 P.M.	8.4	12.0	.18	6.8	.382	.292	.090	.022	.002	1.0	3.0	495	351	144	444	351	93	68.0	0	12.0
885	" 6–7	11.30 P.M., 6.00 A.M. 3.00 P.M.	8.6	13.0	.17	9.4	.514	.434	.080	.028	.002	1.0	2.2	740	586	154	668	575	93	67.0	0	19.2
887	" 8	3.00 P.M.	9.6	12.5	....	13.6	.680	.586	.094	.024	.003	1.8	3.0	977	839	138	886	790	96	65.0	0	24.8
889	" 9	11.00 A.M.	10.6	12.0	.18	13.3	.612	.486	.126	.036	.002	1.8	2.4	762	634	128	685	585	100	45.5	0	24.0
891	" 9–10	3.30 P.M., 10.30 A.M.	11.5	11.5	.19	12.9	.650	.576	.074	.018	.002	1.9	2.0	920	820	100	844	783	61	43.2	0	25.0
893	" 11	3.00 P.M., 9.00 P.M.	12.7	11.0	.22	13.1	.800	.694	.106	.024	.004	1.8	3.1	903	784	119	833	756	77	60.4	0	26.0
895	" 12	3.00 A.M., 9.00 A.M.	12.6	11.5	.16	12.4	.550	.440	.110	.020	.003	1.6	2.3	720	598	122	663	581	82	61.4	0	22.0
897	" 12	3.00 P.M., 9.00 P.M.	....	11.5	.15	10.2	.480	.400	.080	.020	.002	1.7	2.4	638	518	120	607	518	89	62.8	0	16.0
899	" 13	3.00 A.M., 9.00 A.M.	12.6	11.5	.13	9.8	.400	.334	.066	.024	.002	1.6	2.5	560	452	108	517	441	76	56.9	0	18.0
901	" 13–14	3.00 P.M., 10.00 P.M. 3.00 A.M.	12.8	11.0	.15	9.2	.454	.394	.060	.014	.002	1.5	3.0	584	459	125	527	448	79	53.9	0	18.4
903	" 14–15	9.00 A.M., 5.00 P.M. 10.30 P.M., 3.00 A.M.	13.4	11.0	.15	7.6	.320	.250	.070	.020	.003	1.6	3.1	454	331	123	407	322	85	56.0	0	14.2

* (1) 5.30 P.M., 8.00 P.M. (2) 12.30 A.M., 9.30 A.M.

RESULTS OF CHEMICAL ANALYSES OF THE OHIO RIVER WATER.—*Continued.*

(Parts per Million.)

Serial Number.	Collected. Date.	Collected. Hour	Stage of River. Feet.	Temperature. Degrees C.	Color.	Oxygen Consumed.	Nitrogen as Albuminoid Ammonia. Total.	Nitrogen as Albuminoid Ammonia. Suspended.	Nitrogen as Albuminoid Ammonia. Dissolved.	Nitrogen as Free Ammonia.	Nitrogen as Nitrites.	Nitrogen as Nitrates.	Chlorine.	Residue on Evaporation. Total.	Residue on Evaporation. Suspended.	Residue on Evaporation. Dissolved.	Fixed Residue after Ignition. Total.	Fixed Residue after Ignition. Suspended.	Fixed Residue after Ignition. Dissolved.	Alkalinity.	Dissolved Alumina.	Iron.
	1897																					
907	April 15–16	9.30 A.M., 5.30 P.M. 10.00 P.M., 3.00 A.M.	13.4	11.5	.20	6.8	.350	.258	.092	.016	.002	1.2	3.0	448	347	101	404	332	72	56.3	0	12.5
909	" 15–16	5.30 P.M., 3.00 A.M. 9.00 A.M.	14.0	11.5	.15	8.4	.392	.316	.076	.026	.002	1.1	3.0	534	407	127	478	398	80	54.3	0	12.5
911	" 20–21	5.00 P.M., 9.30 P.M. 3.00 A.M., 9.00 A.M.	11.4	12.5	.15	4.8	.246	.170	.076	.014	.000	1.2	3.0	301	205	96	275	206	69	50.5	0	8.0
913	" 21–22	3.15 P.M., 9.00 P.M. 3.00 A.M.	10.9	13.0	.18	5.0	.238	.176	.062	.016	.001	1.3	3.5	306	193	113	268	195	73	51.0	0	8.2
915	" 22	9.30 A.M., 3.30 P.M.	10.3	13.5	.13	5.5	.310	.218	.092	.016	.001	1.5	3.5	353	231	122	312	233	79	48.6	0	10.4
917	" 22–23	9.30 P.M., 3.00 A.M. 9.30 A.M.	9.7	13.5	.14	5.4	.302	.204	.098	.022	.002	1.4	3.5	365	242	123	324	236	88	48.3	0	11.0
919	" 23–24	4.00 P.M., 12 30 A.M. 9 00 A.M., 2.30 P.M.	9.1	14.5	.12	5.0	.254	.182	.072	.020	.002	1.5	2.5	314	196	118	270	195	75	49.2	0	7.2
921	" 26	9.30 A.M., 3.30 P.M. 9.30 P.M.	7.8	15.5	.12	4.5	.208	.154	.054	.016	.003	1.2	3.9	297	184	113	254	171	83	58.5	0	9.0
923	" 27–28	9.00 P.M., 3.00 A.M.	7.4	16.0	.12	4.4	.234	.166	.068	.022	.003	1.3	3.9	273	160	113	240	151	89	61.4	0	9 6
925	" 28	9.00 A.M., 4.00 P.M. 9.00 P.M.	7.0	16.5	.10	3.3	.188	.126	.062	.024	.004	1.1	2.9	263	133	130	206	133	73	64.1	0	6.0
927	" 29	4.00 A.M., 10.00 A.M.	6.8	17.0	.12	4.1	.224	.158	.066	.022	.003	1.0	3.1	264	136	128	206	125	81	62.8	0	6.0
929	" 29–30	6.00 P.M., 10.00 P.M. 3 00 A.M.	6.5	17.5	.10	3.3	.162	.104	.058	.008	.004	1.0	2.9	253	131	122	198	121	77	63.5	0	4.4
931	" 29 May 1	9.00 A.M., 3.00 P.M. 9.00 P.M., 3.00 A.M. 9.00 A.M., 3.00 P.M.	6.0	18.0	.08	3.2	.150	.092	.058	.008	.005	1.3	2.7	218	77	141	170	77	93	71.2	0	......
933	" 4	4.10 P.M.	....	17.0	.14	14.8	1.000	.878	.122	.054	.006	1.3	3.5	1143	965	178	1067	937	130	82.3	0	30.5
934	" 5	9.30 A.M.	....	16.0	.14	21.7	1.100	.978	.122	.040	.005	1.3	3 0	1441	1301	140	1348	1253	95	86.6	0	40.5
934	" 6–7	11.00 P.M., 5.00 A.M. 10.30 A.M., 4.30 P.M.	9.6	15.0	.14	8.1	.498	.426	.072	.026	.003	1.5	3.2	565	433	132	503	424	79	60.8	0	18.5
935	" 7–8	9.00 P.M., 3.00 A.M. 9.30 A.M., 4.30 P.M.	10.3	15.5	.18	5.9	.340	.254	.086	.036	.001	1.4	2.9	417	301	116	367	290	77	53.1	0	13.0
939	" 8–9	9.00 P.M., 4.30 A.M.	10.0	16.0	.10	6.3	.350	.244	.106	.032	.001	1.2	3.1	427	301	126	384	301	83	53.0	0	12.5
941	" 10–11	3.04 P.M., 9.05 P.M. 3.00 A.M.	9.5	17.0	.13	4.5	.282	.182	.100	.036	.004	1.0	3.0	293	171	122	259	173	86	58.1	0	8.5
944	" 12	10.30 A.M., 4.45 P.M. 9.00 P.M.	8.4	17.5	.14	5.3	.348	.214	.134	.054	.002	1.5	4.5	376	248	128	330	240	90	64 0	0	10.0
947	" 13	3.00 A.M., 10.00 A.M. 4.00 P.M., 9.00 P.M.	9.0	18.1	.14	6.0	.400	.308	.092	.050	.003	1.4	2.5	396	260	136	339	252	87	66 9	0	12.0
950	" 14	3.00 A.M., 9.00 A.M. 11.00 P.M.	9.5	18.1	.14	17.2	.884	.796	.088	.....	.004	1.5	3.2	1324	1200	124	1217	1131	86	65.2	0	39.7
953	" 15	3.00 A.M., 9.00 A M. 3 60 P.M.	9.3	18.0	.15	16.3	1.042	.942	.100	.044	.002	1.5	2.1	1404	1262	142	1301	1207	94	69.1	0	37.6

RESULTS OF CHEMICAL ANALYSES OF THE OHIO RIVER WATER.—*Continued.*

(Parts per Million.)

Serial Number.	Collected. Date.	Collected. Hour.	Stage of River. Feet.	Temperature. Degrees C.	Color.	Oxygen Consumed.	Nitrogen as Albuminoid Ammonia. Total.	Nitrogen as Albuminoid Ammonia. Suspended.	Nitrogen as Albuminoid Ammonia. Dissolved.	Nitrogen as Free Ammonia.	Nitrogen as Nitrites.	Nitrogen as Nitrates.	Chlorine.	Residue on Evaporation. Total.	Residue on Evaporation. Suspended.	Residue on Evaporation. Dissolved.	Fixed Residue after Ignition. Total.	Fixed Residue after Ignition. Suspended.	Fixed Residue after Ignition. Dissolved.	Alkalinity.	Dissolved Alumina.	Iron.
	1897																					
956	May 17, 18, 19	3.30 P.M., 9.00 P.M. 3.30 A.M., 9.00 A.M. 3.00 P.M., 9.00 P.M. 3.00 A.M.	11.5	19.0	.19	10.4	.448	.356	.092	.020	.001	1.3	2.0	581	486	95	523	464	59	39.8	0	17.0
959	" 19–20	11.00 P.M., 3.00 A.M. 9.00 A.M., 3.00 P.M. 9.00 P.M.	11.1	20.0	.16	6.9	.356	.254	.102	.022	.000	1.3	2.5	373	277	96	322	266	56	35.0	0	8.0
961	" 21	3.00 A.M.	9.3	20.0	.15	6.6	.260	.168	.092	.030	.002	1.3	3.0	324	239	85	281	223	58	42.4	0	8.5
963	" 21, 22, 23	10.30 P.M., 3.00 A.M. 9.00 A.M., 3.00 P.M. 9.00 P.M., 3.00 A.M. 9.00 A.M., 3.00 P.M.	8.3	20.0	.14	6.2	.248	.176	.072	.020	.002	1.3	2.6	335	247	88	288	227	61	43.4	0	7.0
965	" 23–24	9.00 P.M., 3.00 A.M. 9.00 A.M.	7.7	20.0	.14	5.2	.280	.190	.090	.020	.002	1.3	2.1	275	188	87	229	170	59	39.2	0	8.0
967	" 24–25	9.30 P.M., 3.00 A.M. 9.00 A.M., 3.00 P.M.	6.7	19.5	.12	5.4	.208	.128	.080	.024	.003	1.1	2.0	233	141	92	202	129	73	53.6	0	7.0
971	" 25–26	10.00 P.M., 3.00 A.M. 9.00 A.M., 3.30 P.M. 8.30 P.M.	6.0	20.0	.09	4.4	.192	.116	.076	.016	.002	1.2	2.0	229	117	112	199	112	87	53.8	0	6.0
973	" 27	3.00 A.M., 9.00 A.M. 3.00 P.M.	5.3	19.5	.12	4.1	.182	.096	.086	.042	.006	0.8	2.3	210	106	104	181	102	79	64.8	0	3.4
975	" 27–28	9.40 P.M., 3.00 A.M. 9.00 A.M.	5.4	19.5	.10	3.8	.185	.109	.076	.016	.003	0.8	2.3	204	91	113	178	88	90	65.4	0	4.6
977	" 28–29	3.30 P.M., 9.00 P.M. 3.00 A.M., 9.00 A.M. 5.00 P.M.	5.3	20.0	.14	3.5	.146	.062	.084	.014	.003	0.7	2.3	205	89	116	179	88	91	68.1	0	6.0
981	" 31 June 1	11.00 A.M., 5.00 P.M. 11.00 P.M., 5.00 A.M.	4.9	20.0	.14	2.8	.138	.056	.082	.014	.002	0.8	2.4	165	35	130	125	31	94	71.7	0	0.6
985	" 2–3	4.00 P.M., 11.00 P.M. 5.00 A.M., 11.30 A.M. 5.00 P.M., 11.00 P.M. 5.00 A.M., 11.00 A.M. 5.00 P.M., 11.00 P.M.	4.2	20.5	.16	3.1	.166	.088	.078	.014	.003	0.8	3.6	174	39	135	133	37	96	72.5	0	1.6
989	" 4–5	5.00 A.M., 12.00 M. 5.00 P.M., 11.00 P.M. 5.00 A.M., 11.00 A.M. 4.30 P.M.	4.1	21.5	.13	3.1	.180	.084	.096	.022	.002	0.8	3.8	166	31	135	127	31	96	74.6	0	1.2
993	" 7–8	11.00 A.M., 5.00 P.M. 11.00 P.M., 5.00 A.M. 11.00 A.M., 4.30 P.M. 11.00 P.M.	3.5	22.5	.17	2.4	.186	.104	.082	.014	.002	0.7	5.6	181	43	138	141	36	105	80.2	0	0.6

RESULTS OF CHEMICAL ANALYSES OF THE OHIO RIVER WATER.—*Continued.*

(Parts per Million.)

Serial Number.	Collected. Date.	Collected. Hour.	Stage of River. Feet.	Temperature. Degrees C.	Color.	Oxygen Consumed.	Nitrogen as Albuminoid Ammonia. Total.	Nitrogen as Albuminoid Ammonia. Suspended.	Nitrogen as Albuminoid Ammonia. Dissolved.	Nitrogen as Free Ammonia.	Nitrogen as Nitrites.	Nitrogen as Nitrates.	Chlorine.	Residue on Evaporation. Total.	Residue on Evaporation. Suspended.	Residue on Evaporation. Dissolved.	Fixed Residue after Ignition. Total.	Fixed Residue after Ignition. Suspended.	Fixed Residue after Ignition. Dissolved.	Alkalinity.	Dissolved Alumina.	Iron.
	1897																					
997	June 9–10	5.00 A.M., 11.00 A.M. 5.00 P.M., 11.00 P.M. 5.00 A.M., 11.00 A.M. 5.30 P.M., 11.00 P.M.	3.2	22.5	.13	2.2	.164	.072	.092	.048	.001	0.8	4.9	168	17	151	131	13	118	84.0	0	0.5
1001	" 11–12	5.00 A.M., 11.00 A.M. 5.00 P.M., 11.00 P.M. 5.00 A.M., 4.30 P.M.	3.1	23.0	.13	2.2	.176	.098	.078	.044	.003	0.8	6.0	171	23	148	117	8	109	82.7	0	0.5
1005	" 15–16	4.00 P.M., 9.30 A.M.	4.7	24.0	.12	2.4	.190	.102	.088	.034	.006	0.6	8.0	203	54	149	145	34	111	66.2	0	5.0
1006	" 17–18	2.00 P.M., 9.30 A.M.	5.0	26.0	.10	2.6	.195	.117	.078	.032	.006	0.6	7.0	250	100	150	200	84	116	69.8	0	6.7
1007	" 19–20	8.15 A.M., 2.30 P.M. 9.30 P.M., 5.00 A.M.	5.3	26.0	.12	4.8	.315	.239	.076	.026	.008	0.6	7.0	528	399	129	480	376	104	67.0	0	13.9
1009	" 20	10.30 A.M., 4.45 P.M.	5.2	26.5	.13	3.9	.295	.219	.076	.042	.006	1.1	7.8	443	273	170	383	275	108	66.0	0	11.7
1011	" 21	12.30 A.M., 3.30 A.M.	5.5	26.0	.12	4.3	.245	.165	.080	.022	.005	0.8	7.6	317	161	156	264	151	113	62.3	0	12.0
1013	" 22	4.30 A.M., 9.00 A.M. 3.30 P.M.	5.8	26.5	.14	4.4	.305	.223	.082	.022	.009	1.1	8.1	558	403	155	485	375	110	62.3	0	13.5
1015	" 23	4.00 A.M., 3.00 P.M. 8.30 P.M.	5.9	26.0	.15	5.4	.350	.248	.102	.042	.011	0.9	8.9	516	346	170	446	332	114	62.3	0	6.9
1017	" 24	3.00 A.M., 9.00 A.M. 3.00 P.M., 9.00 P.M.	6.8	26.0	.14	7.3	.370	.274	.096	.016	.001	0.9	6.0	810	677	133	720	641	79	58.1	0	17.4
1019	" 25	3.00 A.M., 9.00 A.M. 3.00 P.M., 9.00 P.M.	7.5	26.0	.15	6.8	.485	.385	.100	.018	.002	0.8	5.4	657	528	129	573	493	80	54.7	0	14.5
1021	" 26	3.00 A.M., 9.00 A.M. 3.00 P.M., 9.00 P.M.	7.1	26.0	.14	5.7	.385	.285	.100	.022	.001	0.7	4.0	646	517	129	587	493	94	50.4	0	10.0
1022	" 27	3.00 A.M., 9.00 A.M. 3.00 P.M., 9.00 P.M.	6.5	25.5	.14	6.8	.455	.339	.116	.020	.004	1.0	2.9	574	449	125	512	431	81	43.2	0	10.5
1024	" 28	3.00 A.M., 9.00 A.M.	6.1	26.0	.15	5.7	.350	.244	.106	.028	.002	0.7	3.2	529	418	111	460	389	71	44.0	0	19.5
1026	" 29, 30	9.00 P.M., 3.00 A.M. 9.00 A.M., 3.30 P.M. 9.00 P.M.	5.5	26.5	.15	5.5	.370	.260	.110	.046	.000	1.1	3.2	484	359	125	435	352	83	45.6	0	17.0
1029	July 1	3.00 A.M., 9.00 A.M. 3.30 P.M., 9.00 P.M.	4.8	27.0	.20	3.8	.280	.168	.112	.050	.001	1.0	3.2	335	247	88	299	238	61	48.0	0	9.5
1033	" 2	4.00 A.M., 9.00 A.M. 3.30 P.M., 9.00 P.M.	4.5	27.0	.15	4.1	.210	.114	.096	.010	.002	0.8	3.9	269	147	122	237	148	89	48.0	0	6.0
1035	" 3	3.00 A.M., 9.00 A.M.	4.3	28.0	.14	2.8	.160	.074	.086	.028	.005	0.9	3.4	235	150	85	199	141	48	49.0	0	5.7
1038	" 6	10.00 A.M., 4.00 P.M. 9.00 P.M.	4.9	30.0	.14	3.3	.170	.080	.090	.030	.003	0.8	3.9	258	108	150	218	107	111	60.5	0	6.0
1040	" 7	3.00 A.M., 9.00 A.M. 4.00 P.M., 9.00 P.M.	6.5	30.5	.14	6.7	.370	.280	.090	.032	.003	0.3	4.4	609	509	100	554	489	65	58.0	0	14.5
1042	" 8	4.00 A.M., 9.00 A.M. 3.00 P.M.	6.5	30.5	.14	6.1	.350	.256	.094	.024	.001	0.8	8.6	617	502	115	569	480	89	53.2	0	18.0

RESULTS OF CHEMICAL ANALYSES OF THE OHIO RIVER WATER.—*Concluded.*

(Parts per Million.)

Serial Number.	Collected.		Stage of River. Feet.	Temperature. Degrees C.	Color.	Oxygen Consumed.	Nitrogen						Chlorine.	Residue on Evaporation.			Fixed Residue after Ignition.			Alkalinity.	Dissolved Alumina.	Iron.
							as Albuminoid Ammonia.			as Free Ammonia.	as Nitrites.	as Nitrates.										
	Date.	Hour.					Total.	Suspended.	Dissolved.					Total.	Suspended.	Dissolved.	Total.	Suspended.	Dissolved.			
	1897																					
1044	July 9–10	5.00 A.M., 9.30 A.M. 4.45 P.M., 9.00 P.M. 3.00 A.M., 9.00 A.M. 2.30 P.M.	5.5	30.5	.12	4.9	.280	.186	.094	.028	.000	0.7	3.8	502	404	98	444	376	68	46.8	0	18.0
1048	" 12–13	4.00 P.M., 3.00 P.M.	4.8	29.0	.18	4.9	.280	.178	.102	.026	.001	1.3	2.7	379	272	107	334	270	64	39.8	0	12.8
1049	" 14–15	8.30 P.M., 3.00 A.M. 9.00 A.M., 3.00 P.M. 8.30 P.M.	4.3	29.5	.18	4.2	.205	.103	.102	.030	.002	1.2	2.7	293	182	111	251	180	71	47.0	0	9.6
1051	" 16	3.00 A.M., 9.00 A.M. 9.00 P.M.	4.0	31.0	.15	3.8	.190	.104	.086	.008	.016	1.1	3.6	297	178	119	254	175	79	51.0	0	8.8
1053	" 17–18	3.00 A.M., 9.00 A.M. 3.00 P.M., 9.00 P.M. 3.00 A.M., 9.00 A.M.	4.1	30.5	.17	3.9	.195	.107	.088	.008	.006	1.2	5.5	248	113	135	198	111	87	52.3	0	6.0
1055	" 19–20	3.00 P.M., 9.00 P.M. 3.00 A.M., 9.00 A.M. 3.30 P.M., 9.00 P.M. 3.00 A.M., 9.00 A.M. 3.30 P.M., 9.00 P.M.	4.5	30.0	.14	2.8	.180	.090	.090	.014	.004	1.1	9.1	238	87	151	186	83	103	60.0	0	4.6
1057	" 21–22	3.00 A.M., 9.00 A.M. 3.30 P.M., 9.00 P.M. 3.00 A.M., 9.00 A.M. 3.00 P.M., 10.30 P.M.	4.4	27.5	.12	2.8	.198	.092	.106	.024	.003	1.1	8.5	238	90	148	184	86	98	59.6	0	5.1
1059	" 23–24	2.30 A.M., 9.00 A.M. 3.00 P.M., 9.00 P.M. 3.00 A.M., 9.00 A.M.	4.8	29.0	.12	3.3	.206	.094	.112	.024	.005	1.1	9.1	317	160	157	264	155	109	62.4	0	6.4

second intermediate stage of the process in nature by which organic matter is converted to mineral matter.

Nitrogen as Nitrates.—From these results there is learned the amount of organic matter which has been completely oxidized and changed into the form of mineral matter.

Chlorine.—Chlorine is usually supposed to be present in water as common salt for the most part. Some of it very likely comes from mineral deposits on this watershed. Salt is also present in sewage, and this is one of the reasons why it is accurately determined.

The determination of chlorine is also of value in studying the composition of a water by virtue of the fact that it is not affected by any ordinary conditions which waters meet in nature. It is always soluble, and cannot be oxidized or reduced. For this reason it does not pass through a cycle of changes as does nitrogen. A comparison of the nitrogen and chlorine is therefore instructive.

Residue on Evaporation.—The residue on evaporation shows the total weight of the solid matter which the water contained. In the following tables the total residue is subdivided into suspended and dissolved residues.

Attention is especially called to the suspended residue on evaporation. This shows the weight of the matters suspended in the water, and gives a good general idea of what the relative appearance of the water was on the different days.

Fixed Residue after Ignition.—After weighing the total residue of the water upon evaporation it is the custom to heat the platinum dish containing the residue to a dull red point and again weigh it. By this means the fixed residue is obtained.

Formerly it was supposed that this ignition burnt off the organic matter, and the difference in weight of the contents of the dish would give the amount of organic matter present in the water. This is not true, however, because the ignition volatilizes certain mineral constituents of the water, which would be erroneously figured as organic matter.

Nevertheless, the fixed residue on evaporation appeared to be of some value in studying the comparative composition of the mineral constituents of the water.

Alkalinity.—This determination is one of great importance in connection with the purification of water by the method under investigation. These results show the amount of carbonates and bicarbonates of calcium and magnesium which were present in the water. It is these compounds which decompose alum or sulphate of aluminum, as is explained in Chapter III.

The results are expressed in terms of calcium carbonate (lime). They are somewhat similar to the "temporary hardness" determination by the "soap method."

Dissolved Alumina. — No appreciable amount of dissolved alumina could be found in the river water. The results of the tests are recorded, however, as they are of value in the study of the question as to the passage of alum through the systems into the filtered water.

Iron.—The results of the determination of iron are of value in showing variations in the composition of the suspended matter in the water. Practically all of the iron was contained in the suspended matters.

Special Chemical Analyses.

There were several sanitary and technical problems under consideration, which required special chemical analyses from time to time, as follows:

1. Atmospheric oxygen dissolved in the water.

2. Carbonic acid gas (carbon dioxide) dissolved in the water.

3. Those dissolved chemicals in the water which give to the water its "permanent hardness" and its power to produce incrustations in steam-boilers.

The first set of these data was fairly complete, from a practical point of view, during 1895–96, and the analyses were made less frequently in 1897. With regard to the latter sets of data, however, the evidence early in 1897 showed that these constituents were so variable and of such importance that they were included in the regular analyses. As a matter of convenience, however, the results are recorded here; but reference to the foregoing tables will show their relation to other constituents of the water. The significance of these results is explained and discussed in subsequent chapters.

Dissolved Oxygen in the River Water.—These results are of value in connection with the preservation of the quality of the water after purification, and for a comparison of the water before and after treatment, especially in the electrolytic process with iron electrodes. The amount of atmospheric oxygen which may be contained in the river water is limited by the saturation of oxygen gas in the water; and the saturation depends chiefly on the temperature (and pressure), the amount of oxygen necessary for saturation decreasing as the temperature increases. In the adjoining table the amounts of oxygen gas dissolved in the river water are expressed in parts by weight per million parts of water by volume, and in percentages of the amounts necessary for the saturation of the water at the actual temperature at the time of collection.

Carbonic Acid Gas Dissolved in the River Water.—As an aid in an investigation into the influence of carbonic acid gas (carbon dioxide) upon the corrosive action of the river water before and after purification by different methods, the amount of this gas which was naturally dissolved in the river water with the formation of carbonic acid was determined with results given on page 34. It developed in the course of the tests that the determinations of carbonic acid gas are of more importance than was generally supposed to be the case formerly, and, as stated above, the analyses were made with more frequency in 1897 than during the first part of the work. In passing it may be noted that at times the weight of carbonic acid gas dissolved in the river water equalled and even exceeded the weight of all solid matters dissolved in the water.

Hardness of the River Water.—The hardness of a water depends upon the presence of dissolved salts of calcium (lime) and magnesium. These salts consist of the carbonates, bicarbonates, sulphates, chlorides, and nitrates. The bicarbonates are carbonates which are held in solution by carbonic acid. For many years it has been the custom to subdivide hardness into "temporary hardness" and "permanent hardness." Temporary hardness is caused by bicarbonates of lime and magnesia which are precipitated upon boiling, due to the expulsion of carbonic acid gas. The remaining salts of lime and magnesia, as stated above, have been regarded as permanent hardness.

The practical significance of the above-stated salts of lime and magnesia is twofold in connection with these investigations, namely:

PARTS PER MILLION OF ATMOSPHERIC OXYGEN DISSOLVED IN THE OHIO RIVER WATER, WITH PERCENTAGES SHOWING THE RELATION BETWEEN THE AMOUNTS FOUND AND THOSE NECESSARY FOR SATURATION AT ACTUAL TEMPERATURES.

Date. 1895.	Temperature. Degrees C.	Dissolved Atmospheric Oxygen.		
		Parts per Million.		Percentages which the Amounts Found were of the Amounts Required for Saturation.
		Saturation.	Found.	
Dec. 3	3.4	12.32	10.3	78
" 4	4.5	12.57	9.5	76
" 6	4.2	12.69	10.2	80
" 9	4.1	12.88	11.2	87
1896				
Jan. 11	2.1	13.52	11.6	86
Feb. 10	5.9	12.19	11.3	93
" 15	7.0	11.90	11.6	97
" 26	3.4	13.01	13.0	100
Mar. 4	4.4	12.61	11.6	92
" 11	6.5	12.01	10.8	90
" 19	5.2	12.38	12.4	100
Apr. 9	9.9	11.16	10.2	91
May 6	23.1	8.47	7.2	85
" 14	24.0	8.34	6.6	79
" 23	24.5	8.28	6.2	75
" 29	24.7	8.25	5.9	71
June 5	24.2	8.32	6.3	76
" 10	24.7	8.25	6.6	80
" 18	25.3	8.20	6.4	78
" 24	26.8	8.02	6.4	80
July 9	25.5	8.17	5.9	72
" 18	25.6	8.15	5.8	71
1897				
April 10	11.3	10.81	10.1	93
" 20	11.6	10.75	10.1	94
" 29	16.3	9.61	8.5	88
June 4	20.9	8.81	8.7	99
" 5	21.8	8.65	8.7	100
" 17	26.7	8.04	7.4	92
" 18	29.1	7.73	6.6	85
" 25	26.0	8.11	6.7	82
" 27	25.3	8.20	6.9	84
" 28	25.3	8.20	6.6	81
" 30	26.2	8.09	8.0	99
July 1	26.6	8.05	6.7	83
" 3	27.6	7.95	6.2	78
" 9	30.0	7.76	5.4	69
" 13	26.5	8.05	6.8	84
" 14	27.2	7.98	7.0	88
" 16	26.1	8.10	8.0	99
" 20	26.8	8.02	8.0	100
" 21	27.5	7.96	8.0	100
" 23	27.7	7.94	6.5	82
" 27	26.2	8.09	4.6	57

AMOUNT OF CARBONIC ACID GAS (CARBON DIOXIDE) DISSOLVED IN THE OHIO RIVER WATER.

(Parts per Million.)

Date. 1896.	Carbonic Acid Gas.	Date. 1897.	Carbonic Acid Gas.	Date. 1897.	Carbonic Acid Gas.
June 18	30.8*	April 3	53.5	May 29	101.6
" 22	26.4*	" 7	79.6	June 1	66.6
" 24	27.7*	" 8	46.0	" 2	90.5
" 27	29.7*	" 9	91.0	" 4	82.7
July 3	30.6*	" 10	80.0	" 7	89.0
" 8	21.1*	" 12	65.0	" 10	133.0
Nov. 28	83.0	" 13	44.0	" 11	107.6
Dec. 10	98.0	" 14	75.7	" 15	98.8
1897		" 15	88.3	" 16	103.3
Feb. 16	80.4	" 16	50.2	" 17	107.6
Mar. 2	63.4	" 21	41.2	" 18	82.7
" 3	59.0	" 22	42.7	" 19	106.3
" 4	67.8	" 23	43.0	" 20	100.3
" 5	49.3	" 25	55.0	" 21	100.3
" 6	47.6	" 27	94.9	" 22	100.3
" 7	51.4	" 29	85.9	" 23	107.4
" 11	99.5	May 4	86.8	" 24	100.3
" 12	88.0	" 7	57.4	" 25	105.6
" 13	122.4	" 8	110.6	" 26	113.7
" 15	45.8	" 9	66.7	" 27	120.0
" 16	33.4	" 10	72.1	" 28	92.1
" 19	38.8	" 13	65.2	" 30	105.9
" 20	42.6	" 14	76.6	July 1	93.9
" 22	46.4	" 15	50.8	" 2	75.3
" 23	40.4	" 18	67.3	" 3	73.1
" 24	44.9	" 19	71.8	" 6	100.4
" 25	41.9	" 21	88.7	" 7	106.1
" 26	36.5	" 22	95.9	" 8	99.9
" 27	47.0	" 23	94.3	" 12	71.8
" 29	56.6	" 26	80.2	" 15	47.0
" 30	80.0	" 27	80.0	" 16	28.8
April 1	53.6	" 28	107.3	" 17	49.4
" 2	59.0				

* The results of June and July, 1896, were obtained by the Pettenkoffer method, without the Trillich modification, and are probably much too low.

1. It is the carbonates and bicarbonates of lime and magnesia in the river water which possess the power of decomposing such applied chemical products as alum and sulphate of alumina, and thereby forming the gelatinous hydrate of aluminum that acts as a coagulant.

2. It is the remaining salts (sulphates, chlorides, and nitrates) of lime and magnesia which are connected with the formation of incrustations when the water is used in steam-boilers.

By the old Clark method of getting the bicarbonates, called temporary hardness, the full power of the water to decompose the commercial chemicals stated above is not recorded, because it does not include the carbonates. In practice it is found that the carbonates will decompose 3 grains or more of sulphate of alumina per gallon. To use a method which shows only the bicarbonates is, therefore, inadmissible; and Hehner's method was employed. This method furnished what is required, that is, both the carbonates and bicarbonates. For the sake of explicitness these results are recorded as the alkalinity of the water in the foregoing tables of analyses. As the Ohio River possesses no carbonate or bicarbonate of soda or potash, the full alkalinity of the water is due to the carbonates and bicarbonates of lime and magnesia.

By the old Clark method the carbonates of lime and magnesia are recorded with the "incrusting constituents" or "permanent hardness." The facts show that these two compounds are permanent, but they form a sludge, and not an incrustation, in steam-boilers. By the Hehner method, which was employed in these investigations, the carbonates are not included in the following table of results, which, in the absence of a better name, are termed the "incrusting constituents" of the water. These results, which are discussed in Chapter XV, are expressed according to the conventional method in equivalent parts of calcium carbonate. A further consideration of the methods of analyses will be found in the appendix.

The dissolved salts of lime and magnesia are also of importance in connection with the consumption of soap when the water is used for washing purposes. This point is practically uninfluenced by the purification processes under consideration, but the range of variation in this soap-consuming ingredient may be noted by taking the sum of the alkalinity and incrusting ingredients. See first table on page 35. These results approximate the total hardness results obtained by the Clark method.

Mineral Analyses of the Ohio River Water.

A record of the results of the determination of the mineral constituents of the river water is presented in the next table. Eight samples were analyzed with as much completeness as circumstances allowed; and the results show very clearly the marked variations which the

INCRUSTING CONSTITUENTS OF THE OHIO RIVER WATER.

(Parts per Million.)

Date. 1895.	Incrusting Constituents.	Date. 1897.	Incrusting Constituents.	Date 1897.	Incrusting Constituents.
Dec. 9-11	43.9	Mar. 25	10.0	May 19-20	10.8
1896		" 26	13.9	" 21	11.9
May 6	43.0	" 29	12.8	" 21-23	15.9
" 14	33.8	" 30	33.3	" 23-24	10.2
" 22	40.1	Apr. 1	29.1	" 25	20.2
" 29	41.1	" 2-3	18.2	" 25-26	14.5
June 11	44.0	" 3-4	11.0	" 27	16.7
" 18	30.0	" 5	29.9	" 27-28	19.3
July 30	35.0	" 6	23.4	" 28-29	16.8
1897		" 6-7	30.0	" 31 }	17.0
Feb. 17	18.7	" 8	19.8	June 1 }	
" 22	24.7	" 9	14.2	" 2-3	17.6
" 23	17.2	" 9-10	13.3	" 4-5	23.5
" 24	21.2	" 11	9.0	" 7-8	22.5
" 25	16.1	" 12	12.7	" 9-10	23.8
" 26	10.0	" 13-14	16.0	" 11-12	28.8
" 27	8.0	" 14-15	20.0	" 21	28.8
Mar. 1	15.8	" 15-16	18.1	" 22	31.0
" 2	10.0	" 20-21	15.5	" 23	31.8
" 3	8.0	" 21-22	17.5	" 24	27.8
" 4	12.0	" 22	12.0	" 25	21.9
" 5	25.3	" 22-23	14.6	" 27	19.0
" 6	34.6	" 23-24	14.3	" 28	17.5
" 7	16.0	" 27	12.7	" 29-30	25.5
" 9	23.4	" 28	17.0	July 2	20.0
" 10	17.9	" 29	32.0	" 6	20.9
" 11	30.0	" 29-30	21.7	" 7	47.0
" 12	33.0	" 30 }	20.0	" 9-10	11.0
" 15	14.0	May 1 }		" 12-13	12.8
" 16	20.5	" 4	23.0	" 14-15	14.8
" 17	24.6	" 5	17.0	" 16	14.0
" 18	36.0	" 6-7	15.5	" 17-18	12.3
" 19	16.7	" 8-9	15.8	" 19-20	24.2
" 20	22.0	" 13	16.1	" 21-22	24.2
" 22	12.4	" 14	23.2	" 23-24	43.8
" 23	9.0	" 15	11.3		
" 24	10.8	" 17-19	9.0		

composition of the river water possessed during these investigations.

The sample which was collected on May 29 and 30, 1896, was analyzed both before and after filtration through fine filter-paper. At this time the water contained a large amount of very finely divided particles; and it was probably the most difficult water to purify without subsidence that was encountered during the whole work. The sample was collected just after a heavy rain, following an extended period of drought.

From March 23 to 29, inclusive, the sample for analysis was prepared by mixing equal small portions of the river water collected every six hours. During this time the systems of purification were in operation night and day. By automatic devices samples of filtered water were collected, representing the entire period. The analyses of the filtered water are presented in Chapter VII.

According to the general custom the results of the determination of the various elements in the water, both metallic and acid, are expressed in the following table of analyses in the form of oxides (except the chlorine).

As would naturally be expected in the water of a river, the watershed of which offers such a wide range in the possibilities for different kinds of rock disintegration and surface erosion, the relative amounts of the mineral constituents are seen to vary widely. This is shown very forcibly in the following table, in the case of suspended matters, by a comparison of the ratio existing between the alumina and the oxide of iron.

RESULTS OF MINERAL ANALYSES OF THE OHIO RIVER WATER.

(Parts per Million.)

Periods of Collection.	1895			1896					
	Oct. 28 to Nov. 14.	Nov. 22 to Nov. 29.	Dec. 9 to Dec. 20.	Jan. 2 to Jan. 11.	Feb. 7 to Feb. 27.	Feb. 28 to Mar. 18.	Mar. 23 to Mar. 29.	May 29 and 30. Unfiltered.	May 29 and 30. Filtered.
Silica (SiO_2)	11.2	25.9	28.4	227.2	206.7	42.6	299.5	325.3	9.3
Oxide of iron (Fe_2O_3)	0.2	0.4	3.7	21.6	26.0	6.4	39.4	32.8	0.6
Alumina (Al_2O_3)	3.7	3.9	7.3	15.7	70.0	5.9	76.6	131.4	0
Oxide of manganese (MnO)	....	} 0.3	1.4	0.5 }	....	....	2.2	3.4	0
Oxide of nickel (NiO)	....				....	....	1.1	2.9	Trace.
Lime (CaO)	....	58.2	49.0	39.6	35.5	32.7	31.7	69.2	47.7
Magnesia (MgO)	....	17.1	13.8	....	13.0	11.4	14.0	28.1	3.9
Soda (Na_2O)	....	....	10.5	12.5	....	....	8.5	....	....
Potash (K_2O)	....	....	37.1	3.1	....	....	18.1	....	....
Chlorine (Cl)	65.4	39.9	39.9	10.7	6.4	8.2	5.6	10.4	10.4
Nitric acid (N_2O_5)	3.1	4.8	5.0	22.3	16.9	11.6	14.7	3.3	3.3
Carbonic acid (combined) (CO_2)	44.0	43.0	29.8	20.8	19.7	25.9	21.3	38.7	38.7
Sulphuric acid (SO_3)	....	18.0	24.3	19.4	28.2	37.4	23.3	18.1	18.3
Phosphoric acid (P_2O_5)	....	....	Trace.	Trace.	1.2	Trace.	1.6	3.7	Trace.

Biological Character of the Ohio River Water.

Determinations of the number of bacteria in the river water, and a study of their relation to disease, occupied the gerater part of the attention with regard to this portion of the work. Microscopical examinations of the water, however, were made from time to time to learn the numbers and kinds of the larger micro-organisms which were present.

Microscopical Examinations of the River Water.

In the next table (see p. 37) there are presented the results of the microscopical examination of the river water for the presence of algæ, diatoms, etc. As already stated, these micro-organisms are much larger than the bacteria; and may be classified by the aid of low powers of the microscope.

It will be noted that the algæ (cyanophyeæ and chlorophyceæ) and diatoms, which are usually abundant in surface water during hot weather, were present in only very limited numbers after the last of May, 1896. The reason of this was, undoubtedly, that the large amount of suspended matter in the water prevented the sunlight, which is necessary for their development, from reaching them.

In 1897 no microscopical examinations of the river water were made during its muddy condition. The single analysis on June 11, however, when the water was very clear, comparatively speaking, shows the range in numbers and kinds of organisms which may be expected under such conditions.

Identification of Species of Bacteria in the River Water, with special reference to their Causation of Disease.

With regard to this portion of the biological analyses attention was especially directed to the detection of bacteria which are dangerous or suspicious from a hygienic point of view. It is to be stated that during the low water in the river in November, 1895, and again during the last part of April and early part of May, 1896, when there had been a drought for a month or more, there was found in the river water B. coli communis. This germ is the most prominent one in sewage, and it is also the most abundant species in the fecal discharges of man and certain domestic animals. On May 1, five days after the beginning of the period when this germ was repeatedly found in the river water, an examination of the tap water in the city also showed its presence there.

At high stages of the river and when the water was very muddy the results of numerous examinations for sewage bacteria were negative in a great majority of cases. Nevertheless, B. coli communis was found in the river water on June 30, 1896, and closely allied kinds of bacteria were noted from time to time during the investigations. The evidence indicates that with muddy water and high stages of the river there are conditions which aid in causing the disappearance to a marked degree of those germs which appear to come from the entrance of sewage into the river above the pumping station.

The results of tests for the presence of the germs of typhoid fever and other diseases were negative in all cases. It is not to be understood, however, that these negative results are adequate proof that disease germs were entirely absent from the river water.

The reason of this lies in the natural limitation of the most approved laboratory methods, which at best allow an examination of only a very small portion of the quantity of water flowing in the stream. These comments are especially true in view of the fact, as stated above, that at times of low water there were present intestinal bacteria.

In 1897 twelve tests for B. coli communis were made between January 21 and February 4, with negative results in each case. From April 1 to 9, nine more tests were made in which this germ was found in three instances.

The question of the classification of the numerous but harmless species of bacteria in the water received as much attention as time allowed. Owing to the fact that there were several other lines of work which yielded results of greater importance from a practical standpoint, this question was not made one of constant study. Nevertheless, the investigations on the detection of dangerous or suspicious species, and on the comparison of the species of bacteria in the water before and

RESULTS OF MICROSCOPICAL ANALYSES OF THE OHIO RIVER WATER.

(Number of organisms per cubic centimeter.)

Date of Collection.	1896. February.			1896. March.				1896. April.		1896. May.				1896. June.			1896. July.	1897. June.
	18	19	26	4	11	19	27	10	16	6	15	21	29	11	18	27	8	11
Number of Sample.	277	280	304	329	354	382	404	459	471	516	544	564	585	629	651	684	711	1001
Diatomaceæ	340	120	120	16	14	42	8	114	60	18	38	112	44	6	24	2	2	659
Asterionella								16	2									115
Melosira	120		96			4		72			14	40	28					69
Synedra		60	8	8	9	16	5	40	40	8	14	16	8	6	16	2		165
Tabellaria																	2	37
Meridion						12			4									
Fragillaria					3													80
Navicula	160				1	8	3		8		4	24						1
Cyclotella	20	20	8	2				8	2	10		32	8					173
Pinnularia	40																	
Cymbella		40		2		2		8	2		4				8			
Coconeus			8															1
Pleurosigma				1					2		2							1
Diatoma																		17
Cyanophyceæ																		8
Anabæna																		8
Chlorophyceæ	20	0	8	2	1	8	0	0	2	8	26	352	20	4	16	2	0	289
Closterium						2												
Pediastrum															8			22
Protococcus	20		8			4			2	8	26	352	20	4				88
Raphidium				2												2		
Scenedesmus					1													20
Chlorococcus															8			143
Staurogenia																		2
Conferva																		13
Fungi	0	60	8	2	2	12	10	8	2	0	2	0	0	0	0	0	2	0
Crenothrix		60	8	2	2	12	10	8	2		2						2	
Infusoria	0	20	24	2	3	6	0	16	0	6	2	8	20	14	24	2	2	19
Peridinium										4								1
Trachelomonas		20								2			4	4	8		2	2
Monas			24	2	2	4		8				8	16	10	8	2		13
Vorticella					1													
Cilliata															8			
Cases						2		8			2							3
Vermes	0	0	0	4	2	0	0	0	2	0	0	0	8	0	16	0	0	14
Triarthra				2	2										8			
Anguillula													4					1
Rotifera				2					2				4		8			13
Crustacea																		1
Daphnia																		1
Miscellaneous	40	0	8	2	2	2	3	0	0	12	4	24	8	6	0	0	0	3
Zoospores					1	2						16		6				2
Ova	40		8	2	1		2				2	8	4					1
Sponge spicules							1			2								
Vegetable hairs										10	2							
Total number	400	200	168	28	24	70	21	168	66	44	72	496	96	30	80	6	6	993
Genera	6	5	8	10	11	13	5	8	10	7	10	8	9	5	9	3	3	26
Amorphous matter	Very abundant in all cases.																	

after purification, necessarily involved a considerable effort in this direction. Comparison of the results of diagnostic tests used for the identification of species of bacteria with the available published descriptions of bacteria indicated, so far as the similarity of laboratory methods would allow, the presence of several new species as well as a considerable number which have been found elsewhere.

The following list of bacteria and yeasts, together with the results of the microscopical examinations already presented in this chapter, indicate the nature of the microscopic flora of the Ohio River water:

Bacillus arborescens (Frankland).
" aurantiacus (Frankland).
" coli communis (Escherich).
" flavescens (Pohl).
" fluorescens liquefaciens (Flügge).
" fluorescens non-liquefaciens (Eisenberg).
" fulvus (Zimmerman).
" janthinus (Zopf).
" lactis ærogenes (Escherich).
" mesentericus ruber (Globig).

Bacillus nebulosus (Wright).
" prodigiosus (Ehrenberg).
" proteus vulgaris (Hauser).
" radiatus aquatilis (Zimmerman).
" ramosus (Frankland).
" rubidus (Eisenberg).
" subtilis (Ehrenberg).
" venenosus (Vaughan).
" violaceus (Frankland).
Cladothrix castrana (Cohn).
" dichotoma (Cohn).
Micrococcus aquatilis (Bolton).
" cremoides (Zimmerman).
Proteus fluorescens (Jäger).
Sarcina lutea (Schrœter).
Saccharomyces cerevisæ (Mayen).
Rosa Hefe.

Quantitative Bacterial Analyses of the River Water.

The average results for each day of the determination of the numbers of bacteria in the river water are recorded in the following table:

AVERAGE RESULTS OF DAILY DETERMINATIONS OF THE NUMBER OF BACTERIA PER CUBIC CENTIMETER IN THE OHIO RIVER WATER.

Date.	October.	November.	December.	January.	February.	March.	April.	May.	June.
1	....	110	....	....	21 300	....	39 600	5 400	18 800
2	....	125	6 800	10 700	....	44 600	27 500	7 100	15 500
3	....	....	10 200	14 300	62 200	33 400	31 000	....	13 800
4	....	352	6 800	8 600	5 500	29 800	27 000	7 000	8 500
5	....	126	4 900	....	71 000	18 000	....	6 000	6 400
6	....	228	9 900	5 000	30 800	12 200	18 700	5 000	4 900
7	....	135	9 800	4 200	55 000	10 500	18 500	5 200	....
8	....	187	....	4 100	29 800	....	13 800	4 000	....
9	....	274	8 200	1 900	....	14 000	21 000	5 900	11 300
10	....	....	7 200	1 800	14 400	11 500	7 300	....	10 700
11	....	637	2 900	2 500	19 800	7 700	13 000	7 300	6 600
12	....	888	2 800	....	28 000	11 300	....	5 900	6 100
13	....	292	2 200	1 900	14 800	11 000	9 600	3 600	13 400
14	....	112	2 400	800	11 900	12 100	7 500	6 500	....
15	....	180	....	3 000	10 800	....	3 700	6 400	13 500
16	....	223	1 900	3 200	....	16 600	1 700	7 300	8 400
17	....	....	2 000	6 500	21 800	16 300	3 000	....	11 000
18	....	166	2 200	7 300	14 400	19 700	5 900	6 600	10 600
19	....	184	2 000	....	20 700	34 400	....	4 300	18 000
20	....	190	3 200	6 400	17 400	46 700	4 800	4 800	10 500
21	148	74	2 200	3 000	10 700	57 200	4 000	6 100	....
22	158	99	....	2 600	20 000	....	5 500	5 100	7 700
23	127	192	3 700	4 800	....	30 500	4 400	6 100	8 000
24	118	....	3 400	3 600	15 000	37 300	7 700	....	8 300
25	137	5 600	....	7 200	16 200	46 000	8 300	1 900	7 500
26	142	3 400	5 200	....	25 200	47 900	....	1 800	6 000
27	....	2 300	12 000	10 600	4 100	31 900	6 500	4 100	10 800
28	114	....	35 700	14 700	4 500	34 100	6 100	23 400	....
29	128	5 200	....	18 200	14 800	49 200	7 100	26 100	13 300
30	106	6 500	12 000	13 400	....	25 700	4 100	19 700	10 900
31	183	....	13 000	14 300	....	26 700	....	....	....

Date.	July.	August.	December.	February.	March.	April.	May.	June.	July.
1	....	27 900	....	....	....	9 200	....	2 200	3 300
2	24 200	....	....	....	15 100	3 500	....	1 910	3 240
3	12 000	....	....	....	26 900	4 600	....	1 390	3 600
4	....	....	....	....	17 700	5 400	25 100	970	....
5	....	....	....	....	33 300	5 900	37 300	710	....
6	7 400	....	....	....	39 800	19 400	22 100	....	3 330
7	5 500	....	....	....	....	28 700	34 500	770	10 600
8	6 700	....	....	....	....	32 500	19 800	640	16 900
9	9 200	....	....	....	....	34 100	13 100	490	6 700
10	10 000	....	12 000	....	46 500	46 000	15 300	460	8 700
11	9 600	....	....	....	38 600	50 000	11 800	470	....
12	....	....	....	....	30 500	44 400	31 000	590	14 800
13	7 700	....	....	....	23 400	31 700	36 200	....	8 900
14	10 100	17 600	....	....	....	27 700	52 400	....	5 600
15	8 300	....	....	....	....	31 500	49 400	470	5 600
16	5 500	....	....	37 200	11 800	33 500	....	510	5 800
17	5 700	....	....	23 700	27 300	....	22 600	660	6 500
18	9 900	....	....	....	27 500	....	16 500	7 500	4 300
19	....	....	....	....	45 200	....	12 700	10 300	3 700
20	7 000	....	....	....	41 100	14 400	14 300	12 300	2 900
21	17 100	....	....	....	....	14 900	11 800	9 200	3 700
22	33 800	....	7 800	46 800	26 500	14 100	10 800	7 400	4 600
23	27 100	....	....	59 900	17 600	12 500	16 700	7 300	5 200
24	31 000	....	....	31 400	25 200	11 100	10 300	20 100	6 100
25	17 300	....	....	40 100	....	....	9 100	18 600	....
26	....	....	....	37 000	18 200	8 100	13 000	14 900	....
27	17 800	....	....	19 500	11 100	11 700	7 500	12 000	....
28	24 500	....	....	....	10 000	20 700	7 200	7 600	....
29	9 500	....	....	....	....	17 400	7 700	12 600	....
30	12 000	....	....	....	11 900	10 500	....	8 600	....
31	6 800	....	....	....	....	....	2 560	....	....

CHAPTER II.

Description of the Application of Chemicals to the Ohio River Water by the Several Systems of Purification.

With the systems of purification examined during the first portion of these tests, the application of chemicals is a matter of fundamental importance for two reasons:

1. Chemicals are absolutely necessary under normal conditions for successful filtration of water through sand at the rapid rate employed in American filters.

2. The application of chemicals to facilitate the subsidence of suspended matters, in such muddy water as that of the Ohio River, and to insure efficient filtration, makes their use the principal item in the cost of purification of this water by these systems.

The topics which are considered in this chapter are as follows:

Kinds of chemicals used.
Composition of chemicals.
Effect of the application of alum, or sulphate of alumina, to the Ohio River water.
Devices used by the respective systems for the application of chemicals to the Ohio River water.
Uniformity in the rate of application of chemicals by the respective devices.
Strength of solutions of chemicals applied to the river water by the respective systems.
Average daily amounts, in grains per gallon, of sulphate of alumina applied to the river water by the respective systems.

This chapter deals with the problem as it stood on Aug. 1, 1896.

Kinds of Chemicals Used.

During these tests (1895–96) three kinds of chemicals were used:

1. Sulphate of alumina (trade name, "basic sulphate of alumina").
2. Potash alum.
3. Lime.

Electrolytically formed chlorine and scrap-iron were also used in an experimental way with the Jewell System for a few hours on each of several days.

Sulphate of alumina, of different lots and brands, was used regularly in the Warren and Jewell systems, except for a few hours on Feb. 10 in the case of the Warren System, when potash alum was employed. During the time when the Western Company made use of their first device for the application of chemicals, potash alum was used instead of sulphate of alumina, because the former was less soluble in water, and therefore more adaptable under the circumstances, as will be shown beyond.

Potash alum was used by the Western System up to May 20, and from June 4 to 6, inclusive. Sulphate of alumina was used during the remainder of the test.

During a greater part of the time from Feb. 8 to April 1, inclusive, lime was added to the river water with the sulphate of alumina in the case of the Jewell System. The object of this, apparently, was to improve the effect of the application of the sulphate of alumina, and to guard against the passage of the latter through the system into the filtered water.

Sulphate of alumina, known commercially as basic sulphate of alumina, and potash alum are approximately of equal cost. The former contains no potash, less sulphuric acid and water of crystallization, but more alumina, as is shown in the table of analyses in the next section. It is the available (soluble in water) alumina in these two chemicals which give to them their efficiency in connection with the purification of such water as that of the Ohio

River. For this reason sulphate of alumina is better and more economical to employ for this purpose.

Composition of Chemicals.

The average results of duplicate analyses of potash alum crystals used in the Western System, as stated above, are presented in the following table. For the purpose of comparison the theoretical percentage composition of pure potash alum is also given.

PERCENTAGE COMPOSITION OF POTASH ALUM USED IN THE WESTERN SYSTEM.

Source of Sample.	Alum Used in Western System.	Pure Alum (theoretical).
Matter insoluble in water	0.02	0.00
Available alumina (Al_2O_3)....	10.72	10.77
Sulphuric acid (SO_3).........	34.06	33.76
Water (H_2O)................	45.69	45.54
Potash (K_2O)...............	10.00	9.93
Lime (CaO)..................	0	0
Oxide of iron (Fe_2O_3)........	0	0

These results show that the potash alum used in the Western System was absolutely pure, practically speaking.

In the next table are presented results of analyses of the sulphate of alumina used in the several systems. In the Warren System use was made of one brand obtained in three principal lots. For the most part in the Jewell System use was made of one brand, but a different one from that of the Warren System, and also obtained in three principal lots. The second brand (lot No. 4) was used in the Jewell System alternately with the regular brand from June 20 to 30, inclusive, and from July 6 to 11, inclusive. With the Western System use was made of several lots, for the most part of the same brand as that employed in the Warren System.

In order to compare the composition of these commercial products with that of the theoretical sulphate of alumina, the percentage composition of the latter is given in the following table:

PERCENTAGE COMPOSITION OF THE SEVERAL LOTS OF SULPHATE OF ALUMINA.

System.	Number of Lot.	Matter Insoluble in Water.	Available Alumina (Al_2O_3).	Sulphuric Acid (SO_3).	Water (H_2O).	Lime (CaO).	Oxide of Iron (Fe_2O_3).
Warren.......................	1	0.06	17.88	39.87	41.22	0.00	0.43
"	2	0.10	17.90	38.61	42.75	Trace	0.32
"	3	0.02	17.86	37.72	44.62	0.08	0.00
Jewell......................	1	1.98	16.39	37.96	43.46	0.00	0.20
"	2	0.63	16.19	37.87	45.28	Trace	0.00
"	3	0.40	16.12	37.48	46.08	Trace	0.00
"	4	2.17	18.62	42.20	36.90	Trace	0.34
Western.....................	2	0.30	17.20	37.64	44.92	0.02	0.24
Sulphate of alumina (theoretical)..	....	0.00	15.32	36.04	48.64	0.00	0.00

In connection with the above tables it is to be noted that each lot of commercial sulphate of alumina contained considerably more available alumina than the theoretical sulphate of alumina. It is this portion (available alumina) of these compounds that gives to them their efficiency for this particular purpose; and, on an average, these commercial products contained about 60 per cent. more available alumina than the pure potash-alum crystals, analyses of which are presented in a foregoing table. Some of the sulphate of alumina used in the Jewell System contained more alumina than is indicated by the above results. But as it was insoluble in water it was of no value, and is recorded with other matters as "matter insoluble in water."

These lots of sulphate of alumina differed in part from the theoretical sulphate of alumina, in that they contained less water of crystallization owing to the process of their preparation. This fact alone caused the former to be richer in available alumina than the latter. The increase in the available alumina in the commercial products above that in the theoretical sulphate of alumina was also greater than the corresponding increase in sulphuric acid. This point doubtless explains the origin of the trade name, basic sulphate of alumina. The ratio of the alumina (Al_2O_3) to the acid (SO_3) in each lot is shown in the following table, with the corresponding ratio in the theoretical sulphate of alumina taken as one:

System.	Lot.	Ratio.	System.	Lot.	Ratio.
Warren..	1	1.05	Jewell...	1	1.02
" ..	2	1.09	" ...	2	1.01
" ..	3	1.11	" ...	3	1.01
Western.	2	1.07	" ...	4	1.04

In all comparisons and tabulations throughout this report the chemicals applied to the river water for the purpose of coagulation and sedimentation are expressed in terms of sulphate of alumina. Wherever potash alum was used the results are converted into their respective equivalents of sulphate of alumina, on the basis that 10 parts of the latter are equal, from a practical point of view, to 16 parts of potash alum.

Effect of the Application of Alum or Sulphate of Alumina to the Ohio River Water.

When alum or sulphate of alumina is applied to the Ohio River water, it is decomposed for the most part by the lime (calcium carbonate and bicarbonate) dissolved in the water, and there is formed a white, gelatinous precipitate of aluminum hydrate. The magnesium carbonate and bicarbonate in the water also decompose the alum in the same manner as does the lime. Carbonic acid gas is liberated by the decomposition of the alum, but remains dissolved in the water as free acid. The lime and magnesia which combine with and decompose the alum pass into the form of soluble neutral sulphates. The tiny, sticky particles of aluminum hydrate group themselves together; and around the infinite number of centers of coagulation are gathered together more or less completely the matters suspended in the water, including the bacteria, thereby forming flakes of greater or less size and weight. Neither before or after its decomposition has the alum or sulphate of alumina, in amounts which would be permissible in the purification of municipal water supplies, a germicidal effect on the bacteria, but simply aids in their removal, through subsidence and filtration, by their envelopment in the gelatinous flakes. Several factors exerted a marked influence upon the coagulation, upon the subsequent sedimentation, and finally upon the effect of the remaining coagula in the water as it was filtered at a rapid rate through the sand.

The application of chemicals to the Ohio River water where this system of purification is employed is of fundamental importance, influencing both the efficiency and cost of the system, and the whole subject in its different phases will be discussed in detail beyond. At this time it is the purpose simply to point to the matter in a very general way, in order to make plainer and to bring out the significance of the following account of the devices used in the initial step in the process of purification.

Devices Used in the Respective Systems for the Application of Chemicals to the Ohio River Water.

In this section is given a brief description of the principal features of the several devices for the application of solutions of alum and other chemicals. An account of the efficiency with which this was accomplished will be found in subsequent sections of this chapter. In the following chapters are described the decomposition and subsequent disposition of the applied alum or sulphate of alumina, and also the effect which this application produced in connection with the purification of water.

Warren Device.

Sulphate of alumina was applied to the water in the Warren System just after the river water entered the settling basin. The current of water in the inlet water-pipe revolved a small propeller wheel located in the mouth of the pipe. This wheel turned, by means of two sets of beveled gears, a specially designed pump, working in a pump box on the floor above. This pump box received the sulphate of alumina solution from the mixing tanks, the flow from which was regulated by a float valve. From the pump the solution of sulphate of alumina passed through a lead pipe discharging by gravity into the water in the settling basin, opposite the center and approximately 5 inches from the end of the inlet water-pipe.

Two white-pine mixing tanks were located on the floor over the settling basin and adjacent to the pump box. These tanks were used alternately, solutions being made up in one tank while the other was in service. Filtered water pumped from the filtered-water reservoir was used for dissolving the sulphate of alumina; and stirring was done in all cases by hand. The depth of the tanks was 4.5 feet and the diameter about 4 feet. Owing to unsatisfactory working of the meter on the pipe through which the chemicals entered the water, and its final abandonment, glass gauges were employed for measuring the quantity of solution used. Calibrations of the tanks showed an average capacity for each 0.1 foot in depth of 1.24 and 1.18 cubic feet in tanks A and B, respectively. Owing to the distance which the outlet pipe was above the floor of the tanks, the lower portion of the solution in the tanks could not be used. The quantity of solution left in the tanks each time a new solution was prepared varied considerably, but generally amounted to something less than 3 cubic feet.

Pump Box.—The solution of sulphate of alumina flowed into the pump box from the mixing tanks, the flow being regulated by a 2-inch float valve of vulcanized rubber. The pump box was about 2.9 feet long by 1.2 feet wide. The depth of solution in the pump box was capable of regulation by varying the distance of the float from the center of the valve, the float arm being adjustable in length. This was intended as a means of varying the rate of application of solution by increasing or decreasing the depth of immersion of the pump arms. In practice it was not found successful, as the float valve was too irregular to make such an adjustment feasible. The maximum and minimum depths of solution, at the overflow of the pump box and the lowest level at which the device operated, were 11 and 5 inches, respectively.

Propeller.—The propeller wheel was a small screw wheel of about 0.5 foot outside diameter, set on a horizontal shaft directly in the mouth of the inlet water-pipe. When the Warren System was first installed a 5-blade wheel was tried, but this was taken out and a 7-blade wheel substituted Nov. 25, 1895. This wheel was made of cast brass, 0.5 foot in diameter by 0.2 foot deep. There were seven blades, each pitched so that the circumferential distance between their edges was 2 inches. Connections from this propeller wheel to the shaft of the chemical pump above were made by two sets of small beveled gears and a vertical shaft.

Pump.—The pump was a patented device constructed of vulcanized rubber. It was made up of six hollow curved arms, each of which lay in a plane perpendicular to the horizontal shaft on which the pump revolved, and which were connected respectively to six tubes placed parallel to the same shaft. The shape of the curved arms was approximately that of two straight pipes 5 and 3 inches long, respectively, making an angle of 45° and connected by a circular curve of 3 inches radius. The inside diameter of these arms and of the horizontal tubes was 0.5 inch. In operation the pump was revolved by the propeller wheel just described. The shaft of the pump was located upon the top of the pump box, the solution filling the pump box ordinarily to from 1 to 3 inches below the pump shaft. As the pump revolved, each arm was filled as it entered the solution, and as the end was the first part to leave the solution it trapped some of it, the amount varying with the height of the solution in the box. As the pump turned the liquid was dropped back into the arm and emptied out of the horizontal tube into a funnel at the side of the box. To this funnel was connected a lead pipe through which the solution flowed into the settling basin, discharging opposite the mouth of the inlet water-pipe.

Manner of Control of the Application of Chemicals.—When the flow of river water into the settling chamber was not too low (above 18 cubic feet per minute) the discharge of the solution from the pump was supposed to be proportional to the admission of river water. The amount of solution pumped was changed by the removal or insertion of rubber stoppers into the ends of the hollow arms of the pump. In some instances half-stoppers (halved lengthwise) were inserted. Marked changes in the application of alum called for new solutions of different strength.

Elevations.—The relative elevations in feet of the more important points, referred to the bottom of the sand layer of the filter as the datum plane, were as follows:

Maximum flow line in mixing tanks	14.80
Minimum flow line in mixing tanks	10.66
Center of chemical pump	10.60
Maximum flow line in pump box	10.58
Center of discharge in the settling basin	1.03

Jewell Device.

The solution of sulphate of alumina was pumped into the inlet water-pipe against a pressure of about 60 pounds at a point about 10 feet inside the settling chamber. Before the entrance to the settling chamber of the river water containing the solution it passed through a meter and two valves on the main inlet pipe.

Mixing Tanks.—Sulphate of alumina solutions were prepared alternately in two cypress tanks 5.5 feet deep and 3.5 feet in average diameter. Filtered water, taken from the outlet pipe just as it left the filter, was used for dissolving the commercial product after it had been broken into small pieces. This was facilitated at times by heating the water with steam which was allowed to enter the water-pipe just before it reached the tanks.

Pump.—From the tanks the solution was pumped into the inlet pipe by a 3.5 by 4.5 by 6-inch single pump, the suction pipes of which reached to within about 1 inch of the bottom of the tanks. The ends of the suction pipes were capped with screens. The steam supplied to the pump was kept at practically a constant pressure by means of a regulating valve.

Feed Pipe.—The feed pipe from the pump to the inlet pipe was a heavy lead pipe 0.75 inch in diameter. At first all fittings were of wrought iron, but owing to corrosion by the sulphate of alumina they repeatedly broke, and at the close of the test practically all fittings were of brass.

Manner of Control.—At the outset it was the custom to start the pump at a speed to deliver the desired quantity of solution and keep it under general control by means of a float on the water above the sand layer. This float was connected by a chain and pulley with a valve regulating the flow of steam to the pump. This was not a success, and the float was abandoned during the latter part of March, and the application controlled by frequent regulations of the steam-valve, inspections of quantities from the meters and of the speed of the pump being used as guides. Ordinarily, changes in the speed of the pump would allow the desired arrangement in the application of sulphate of alumina, but in extreme cases the strength of the solution was altered.

Elevations.—The relative elevations in feet of the more important points, with the bottom of the sand layer of the filter as the datum plane, were as follows:

Maximum flow line in mixing tanks	− 6.90
Minimum flow line in mixing tanks	− 12.06
Center of discharge into inlet pipe	− 11.13

Western Systems.

As only one settling chamber was used for both the Western Pressure and Western Gravity systems a single device for the application of alum was sufficient. Two separate and distinct devices, however, were used. The first was used from the beginning of the operation of these systems up to April 7, and the second, following an extended period of modifications and repairs, was in service from May 7 till the close of the tests.

First Western Device.

On the main inlet water-pipe to the settling chamber there was a 6-inch gate valve which caused a difference in pressure above and below it. From above this valve a 0.5-inch brass pipe led to the alum tank, which was a cast-iron vertical cylinder 1 foot in inside diameter and approximately 2 feet deep. The alum tank had a top opening with a cover constructed like a hand-hole fitting. The diameter of the opening was 4.5 inches. The brass pipe above mentioned connected with the alum tank at the top and extended into it about 1 foot. From the top of the alum tank a second 0.5-inch brass pipe led to the inlet pipe below the valve above mentioned. Suitable valves cut off the flow in both brass pipes; allowed access to the alum tank; and aided in controlling the flow of alum solution. A mercury column in a celluloid tube was used to indicate the difference in pressure in the two brass pipes. By this arrangement the alum solution was applied to the river water in the inlet pipe about 10 feet from the settling chamber.

Operation.—In use the alum tank was kept filled to a greater or less depth with crystals of potash alum put in through the hand-hole at the top. Differences in pressure in the inlet water-pipe before and after this by-pass caused the flow of a small quantity of water through the tank whereby the alum was dissolved and carried over into the inlet water-pipe. The only means of regulating the quantity of alum solution applied was by differences in the pressure of the water flowing through this by-pass.

Second Western Device.

The entire device for the application of chemicals was changed during April, the final arrangement being as follows:

The separate pipe for the admission of river water to the system, which was introduced Feb. 29, was broken and a duplex pumping engine inserted on the pipe line. To this duplex pump were attached auxiliary pumps by which the solution of chemicals was forced into the main inlet water-pipe beyond the pumps and about 30 feet from the settling chamber. The duplex water pump forced the river water, containing the alum or sulphate of alumina solution, through the settling chamber, and also through the pressure filter, or into the top of the gravity filter.

Mixing Tanks.—Two pine tanks each 4 feet deep by 3 feet in diameter were used alternately for the purpose of preparing the solutions. The solutions were made with filtered water taken from the outlet pipe near its exit from the pressure filter, or with river water when the pressure filter was not in operation.

Main Water Pumps.—The main pumping engine was a Worthington single-expansion duplex engine. The principal dimensions were as follows:

Diameter of steam cylinder.......	9 inches
Diameter of water cylinder.......	8.5 "
Length of stroke................	10 "

Steam was supplied by a 1.5-inch asbestos-covered pipe. The exhaust, a 2-inch pipe, was open to the atmosphere.

Auxiliary Chemical Pumps. — The device used for pumping the solution of alum or sulphate of alumina consisted of small plunger extensions of the main piston-rods on the water pumps above described. These worked in pockets in which they caused alternate suction and pressure. The valve system was a pair of cup valves in the same casting, one opening to allow flow from, and the other to allow flow into, the plunger pocket. These valves were located just outside of the plunger chamber.

Piping System.—From the mixing tanks a system of 0.5-inch brass pipes led to the auxiliary pumps. The arrangement was such that either tank could be used, and either one or both of the auxiliary pumps operated. From the pump the solution of chemicals was forced through a system of 0.75-inch brass pipes into a glass tube. A 3-inch brass air-chamber in the system equalized the flow.

This glass tube was connected at the bottom with a brass pipe which led into the inlet water-pipe, discharging in the center of the inlet pipe through a tee set with its long arm with the current. The glass tube was also connected at the top with the top of a 6-inch air-chamber in the inlet water-pipe. A body of air was always maintained in this chamber, and there was a corresponding vertical air column in the glass tube, as the level of the chamber and of the tube were the same. By this arrangement the alum or sulphate of alumina solution was discharged through an air column, thus making the flow of the solution plainly visible.

Manner of Control.—As the pumps discharged a constant quantity, regulation of the application of chemicals was obtained by relief pipes and valves through which the excess of solution was returned to the mixing tanks and pumped over again.

Elevations.—The relative elevations in feet, with the bottom of the sand layer of the pressure filter as the datum plane, were as follows:

Maximum flow level in mixing tanks...	0.00
Minimum flow level in mixing tanks.	−3.34
Center of pumps..................	−2.70
Center of discharge into inlet........	+1.80

Jewell Device for Application of Lime.

The device used for adding lime to the river water was modified a number of times during its use. At first it consisted simply of an ordinary barrel and suitable piping as described below. The barrel was located on the upper floor. Unslaked lime was put in the barrel and a stream of water let in at the bottom. The flow of water into the barrel was regulated by a float valve. Near the top of the barrel a pipe led to a connection with the suction pipe from the sulphate of alumina tanks. To the lower end of this pipe was attached a glass cylinder in order to make visible the rate of flow. The mixed milk of lime and sulphate of alumina solutions were forced into the main inlet water-pipe by the same pump. At first the solution was stirred by hand, but later an aspirator was introduced.

When the use of lime was resumed on March 21 the milk of lime solution was pumped through a separate pipe into the inlet water-pipe just outside the settling chamber; and the entire lime system was independent of the sulphate of alumina system.

Elevations.—The relative elevations in feet, with the bottom of the sand layer as the datum plane, were as follows:

Discharge level in the lime barrel................	+ 13.00 (approx.)
Center of modified discharge into inlet pipe..	− 5.95

Jewell Device for the Application of Iron.

The device used for the application of iron consisted of a cast-iron tank, approximately 1 foot in diameter and 3 feet long, filled with scrap-iron. The piping was so arranged that the suction from the sulphate of alumina tanks, the suction from the lime barrel, and the force main from the sulphate of alumina pump could be connected with this tank. The iron could be thus introduced at any desired point in the flow of chemicals. It can hardly be said to have been in actual service, but was tried on Feb. 10 and 12, and again for 2.5 hours on Feb. 22. Its use was discontinued on the latter date on account of the very evident presence in the effluent of dissolved iron.

Jewell Device for the Application of Chlorine.

This device consisted of a set of small U-shaped tubes, in which a common salt solution was decomposed by an electric current. A constant flow of water was maintained through the tubes. The water dissolved the hypochlorites and carried them with it to the water in the top of the filter. The apparatus was never used regularly, but was tried on Jan. 21 and 22, and for very short periods at later dates. On Jan. 22 available chlorine was applied in this way during the morning at the rate of 0.1 part per million by weight of applied water.

Uniformity in the Rate of Application of Chemicals in the Respective Systems.

Owing to the marked and comparatively sudden variations in the quality of the river water, the rate of application of chemical solution was varied by necessity from time to time. But with regard to uniformity when the quality of the river water was practically the same the observations revealed several points of an unsatisfactory nature. The amount of attention which was given to the devices for application of chemicals, furthermore, was found to be a very important factor in most instances.

Speaking in general terms, the application of chemicals by the Warren device was fairly satisfactory. Its chief merit lay in the fact that it was automatic. It had a number of shortcomings, however. The rate of application of chemicals during short periods was variable, due to varying heights of solution in the pump box. When the river water entered the settling chamber at a rate of less than about 18 cubic feet per minute the propeller wheel could not be depended upon to operate the pump regularly. So far as was learned the propeller was reasonably uniform in its action when the flow was greater than that stated above. The manner of regulating the operating area of the open arms of the pump by means of rubber stoppers was crude, and under some circumstances would limit the serviceability of the device in purifying such a water as that of the Ohio River.

The operations of the Jewell device showed clearly that its efficiency was closely dependent upon the attention which it received. During the latter part of the test it received sufficient attention to make its operation satisfactory. At times during the first part of the tests, however, the application of chemicals was very erratic. In some instances the rate of application of sulphate of alumina varied five or six hundred per cent. on the same day when the quality of the water was about the same.

Complications arose when lime and sulphate of alumina were both applied by the same device in the Jewell System. At times it appeared that the two chemicals entered the water alternately.

With the first Western device control of the application of alum was repeatedly lost, even with a laborer spending the greater part of his time watching it. The Western Company abandoned this device in April.

The second Western device gave fairly satisfactory results, although it was necessary to give close attention both to the stuffing boxes between the water pumps and chemical pumps, and to the relief valves on the pipes through which the excess of solution was returned to the mixing tanks.

This feature of the application of chemicals is a very important one, both with regard to the cost and the efficiency of purification, and will be discussed in Chapter IX.

Strength of Solutions of Chemicals Applied to the River Water in the Respective Systems.

Samples of the alum and sulphate of alumina solutions used in the several systems were collected at frequent but irregular intervals for examination. The specific gravity of the samples was determined by the aid of a Sartorius balance, and these readings were converted into percentages of applied chemicals from tables of factors which were checked from time to time. In all 1632 determinations were made of the strength of applied chemical solutions. In the next set of tables there are given the daily averages of the percentage strength of the solutions used in each system. Before considering these results there are several comments to be made.

In the Jewell System the uniformity of strength of the sulphate of alumina solutions was very satisfactory, as a rule, during a greater part of the test. During the first portion, however, the variations in the strength of the solution were quite confusing.

For the most part the uniformity of strength of the sulphate of alumina solutions used in the Warren System was fairly satisfactory. Small variations in the strength of even consecutive solutions, however, were repeatedly noted. This was due, apparently, to the complicated system of preparation of the solutions, which involved the consideration of certain quantities of solution in each tank when its use was stopped to prepare new solutions, and to too much dependence upon hydrometer readings.

With the first device used in the Western System the variations in the strength of the alum solutions were so great that this factor placed the whole system at a great disadvantage at times, in spite of the comparatively close attention which it received.

This device, which consisted of allowing a small stream of river water in the inlet pipe to flow through a by-pass in which was placed an iron cyclinder containing potash alum, showed marked weaknesses, among which were the following:

1. The solubility of potash alum crystals varied with the temperature of the river water in the alum tank.

2. The strength of the solution applied to the river water varied with the period of time that the river water remained in the alum tank; that is, it varied inversely with the rate of application of the alum solution.

3. The strength of the solution varied with the amount of potash alum crystals in the tank.

4. There were no ready means of knowing how much alum was being applied to the water; and in several instances the alum crystals in the cylinder became exhausted, or very nearly so.

On many days the strength of the solution was quite uniform, especially during the latter half of the period when this device was used, and when, at times, a small gas flame was placed beneath the inlet pipe leading to the alum tank to increase the temperature of the water. Similar results to the following were frequently obtained, however, during the first two months that the system was in operation.

Date. 1896.	Hour.	Percentage of Alum in Applied Solution.	Date. 1896.	Hour.	Percentage of Alum in Applied Solution.
Jan. 24.	10.28 A.M.	7.8	Feb. 20.	11.25 A.M.	3.9
"	11.35 "	5.0	"	1.20 P.M.	5.7
"	12.32 P.M.	6.2	"	3.30 "	3.3
"	1.30 "	3.2	"	4.00 "	4.6
"	3.07 "	5.1	"	4.30 "	5.2
			"	5.00 "	5.2
			"	5.30 "	5.1

The following results, obtained on Feb. 26, are more representative of the last portion of the period when more care was taken to prevent the exhaustion of alum from the tank.

Hour.	Percentage of Alum in Applied Solution.	Hour.	Percentage of Alum in Applied Solution.
9.30 A.M.	5.9	2.30 P.M.	6.5
11.00 "	4.9	3.00 "	6.4
12.30 P.M.	5.9	3.30 "	6.5
1.00 "	6.1	4.00 "	5.7
1.30 "	6.2	4.30 "	6.6
2.00 "	5.9	5.00 "	6.5

With the second device for the application of chemicals in the Western Systems, there came an improvement in the uniformity of the strength of solutions, but it was not thoroughly satisfactory. This was due in part to mistakes in weighing out the alum or sulphate of alumina, and in part to accidental dilution of the solutions after their preparation. An important factor in these varying strengths of solution, the effect of which is difficult to estimate accurately, was the flow of river water from the water pumps through the stuffing boxes into the pumps containing the solution of alum or sulphate of alumina.

This was repeatedly observed and guarded against in part by frequent packing of the stuffing boxes. The maximum leak noted was about 1 gallon per hour for one of the two pumps. Under the conditions on that day, May 20, the dilution from this single pump amounted to about 10 per cent. of the full quantity of solution in one tank when full. With more nearly normal rates of flow of water and of alum solution this percentage would be somewhat less, but on the other hand the effect of the dilution from this source became cumulative, owing to the passage through the pumps of an excess of the solution, and its return through relief pipes leading back to the mixing tanks. The last portion of the solution from the tank was thereby more diluted than the first.

DAILY AVERAGES OF THE PERCENTAGE STRENGTH OF THE SOLUTIONS OF SULPHATE OF ALUMINA APPLIED TO THE RIVER WATER IN THE WARREN SYSTEM.

Day.	October.	November.	December.	January.	February.	March.	April.	May.	June.	July.
1	....	2.80	....	....	2.00	....	2.70	1.20	2.30	1.90
2	....	2.20	1.30	1.70	....	2.10	2.40	1.20	2.20	1.90
3	....	....	1.20	2.00	2.00	2.00	2.90	......	2.20	2.00
4	....	2 20	1.40	2.00	2.20	2.10	2.80	1.10	2.20	....
5	....	2.20	2.00	....	2.20	2.10	....	1.20	2.00	....
6	....	2.20	2.00	2.00	2.20	2.20	3.20	1.50	2.00	2.00
7	....	2.10	1.25	2.00	2.30	2.00	2.60	1.00	....	2.00
8	....	2.10	....	2.00	2.20	....	2.60	1.10	....	2.20
9	....	2.00	1.20	2.00	....	2.10	2.60	1.00	2.40	2.20
10	....	....	1.10	1.80	1.30	2.00	2.60	....	2.40	2.20
11	....	2.00	1.30	1.80	....	2.10	2.60	1.00	1.90	2.10
12	....	....	1.30	....	....	2.10	....	1 10	2.20	....
13	....	....	1.50	2.20	1.90	2.20	....	1.10	2.20	2.00
14	....	....	1.60	2.20	2.20	2.10	....	1.00	....	1.90
15	....	....	....	2.20	2.00	....	....	1.00	2.20	2.00
16	....	....	1.50	2.20	....	2.00	....	1.10	2.10	2.00
17	....	....	1.70	2.30	2.00	2.00	....	....	2.00	2.00
18	....	....	1.70	2.10	2.10	2.00	....	1.10	2.00	2.00
19	....	....	2.20	....	2.00	2.00	....	1.00	2.10	....
20	....	....	2.20	2.10	2.10	2.50	1.60	1.00	2.10	2.10
21	1.05	....	2.20	2.00	2.20	2.90	1.60	1.00	....	2.20
22	1.08	....	....	2.90	2.10	....	1.90	1.00	1.90	2.10
23	1.20	....	2.20	....	....	3.10	1.80	1.00	2.00	2.50
24	1.00	....	1.80	....	2.00	2.80	1.75	....	2.00	3.00
25	1.06	1.10	....	1.90	2.00	2.50	1 70	1.00	2.00	2.80
26	1.10	1.10	2.00	....	2.00	2.80	....	1.10	....	....
27	....	1.10	2.00	2.20	2.00	2.40	1.55	1.20	....	2.60
28	1.30	....	2.10	2.20	2.00	2.30	1.60	1.20	....	2.60
29	2.60	1.20	....	2.30	2.00	2.30	1.45	1.30	....	3.00
30	2.60	1.20	2.20	2.40	....	2.40	1.20	1.60	2.20	2.20
31	2.80	....	2.00	2.10	......	2.50	....	....	....	2.20

DAILY AVERAGES OF THE PERCENTAGE STRENGTH OF THE SOLUTIONS OF SULPHATE OF ALUMINA APPLIED TO THE RIVER WATER IN THE JEWELL SYSTEM.

Day.	October.	November.	December.	January.	February.	March.	April.	May.	June.	July.
1	....	0.42	....	....	....	....	1.20	0.60	....	1.20
2	....	0.42	0.33	1.20	....	0.80	1.20	0.60	1.20	1.20
3	....	....	0.33	1.20	....	0.75	1.20	....	1.20	1.20
4	....	....	0.33	1.20	....	0.60	1.20	0.60	1.20	....
5	....	0.40	0.39	....	0.70	0.60	....	0.60	1.20	....
6	....	....	0.42	1.20	0.70	0.60	1.20	0.60	1.20	1.30
7	....	0.60	0.42	....	0.85	0.60	1.20	0.60	....	1.10
8	....	0.30	....	1.20	1.40	....	0.95	0.60	....	1.20
9	....	0.32	0.42	1.20	....	0.60	0.60	0.60	1.20	1.20
10	....	....	0.42	1.20	1.34	0.50	0.60	....	1.20	1.20
11	....	0.29	0.42	1.20	1.40	0.35	0.60	0.60	1.20	1.20
12	....	0.34	0.44	....	1.40	0.30	....	0.60	1.20	....
13	....	0.31	0.44	0.85	1.20	0.30	0.60	0.60	1.20	1.20
14	....	0.28	0.44	0.60	1.20	0.30	0.60	0.60	....	1.20
15	....	0.64	....	0.60	1.35	....	0.60	0.60	1.20	1.20
16	....	0.30	0.40	0.60	....	0.53	0.55	0.60	1.20	1.20
17	....	....	0.44	0.60	1.40	0.60	0.53	....	....	1.20
18	....	0.30	0.44	0.60	1.40	0.60	0.50	0.60	1.20	1.20
19	....	0.30	0.68	....	1.40	0.60	....	0.60	1.20	....
20	....	0.30	0.88	0.60	2.00	0.70	0.55	0.60	1.40	1.20
21	0.24	0.30	0.88	0.60	1.00	0.20	0.65	0.60	....	1.20
22	0.24	0.30	....	0.60	1.20	....	0.60	0.60	1.40	1.20
23	0.24	0.30	0.71	0.60	....	1.20	0.60	0.60	0.70	1.20
24	0.26	....	0.80	0.60	1.30	1.20	0.58	....	0.60	1.40
25	0.44	0.39	....	0.62	1.10	1.15	0.60	0.60	0.60	1.80
26	0.38	0.39	0.80	....	0.80	1.20	....	0.60	0.60	....
27	....	0.39	0.80	0.65	0.45	1.20	0.60	0.60	0.90	1.80
28	0.44	....	0.80	0.67	0.80	0.80	0.60	0.90	....	1.50
29	0.50	0.39	....	0.70	0.80	0.60	0.60	1.20	1.20	1.30
30	0.46	0.39	0.95	0.70	....	0.60	0.60	1.20	1.20	1.30
31	0.37	....	1.60	0.70	....	1.20	....	....	....	....

DAILY AVERAGES OF THE PERCENTAGE STRENGTH OF THE SOLUTION OF ALUM AND OF SULPHATE OF ALUMINA APPLIED TO THE RIVER WATER IN THE WESTERN SYSTEMS.

Day.	January.*	February.	March.	April.	May.	June.	July.
1	....	6.0	....	6.7	....	2.6	1.7
2	....	....	5.5	8.0	....	1.4	2.4
3	....	6.0	7.0	7.4	....	1.5	4.2
4	....	3.8	7.0	5.8	....	1.9	....
5	....	6.2	7.1	....	....	2.9	....
6	....	4.3	6.1	7.9	....	3.0	2.2
7	....	4.3	7.0	7.2	3.8	....	2.2
8	....	5.4	....	....	4.0	....	2.0
9	....	....	6.6	....	3.0	3.2	2.0
10	5.2	5.7	6.7	....	....	3.2	1.5
11	5.7	5.9	6.0	....	2.8	2.6	0.8
12	....	5.9	7.9	....	2.9	2.6	....
13	....	6.2	6.9	....	1.9	2.0	3.2
14	4.3	6.0	6.8	....	2.1	....	3.0
15	6.8	4.2	....	....	2.2	2.2	2.9
16	7.2	....	7.1	....	2.2	2.2	2.7
17	5.8	4.6	6.6	....	....	2.2	2.0
18	5.8	4.5	6.5	....	1.2	0.9	1.8
19	....	5.2	6.8	....	1.0	2.5	....
20	4.9	4.7	5.6	....	0.6	2.8	2.2
21	5.8	5.1	6.3	....	0.5	....	1.9
22	5.2	....	....	....	0.6	2.0	1.7
23	5.6	....	5.9	....	0.6	....	2.4
24	5.5	5.6	5.7	....	....	1.9	2.7
25	4.0	5.4	6.0	....	0.6	2.1	1.9
26	....	6.1	6.9	....	0.8	1.7	....
27	6.0	6.0	7.0	....	0.9	2.5	2.0
28	5.2	5.7	6.9	....	0.9	....	2.3
29	....	6.8	7.9	....	1.4	3.0	1.7
30	....	....	7.5	....	2.6	2.6	....
31	5.8	....	7.1	....	....	....	2.0

* The meter on the alum pipe was not attached till Jan. 10; and from Dec. 23 to that time the amount of alum applied to the water was computed from the weight of alum put into the alum tank.

AVERAGE DAILY AMOUNTS, IN GRAINS PER GALLON, OF SULPHATE OF ALUMINA APPLIED TO THE OHIO RIVER WATER IN THE RESPECTIVE SYSTEMS.

The daily average results of the determination of the amounts of sulphate of alumina used in the respective systems (from October, 1895, to July, 1896, inclusive) are presented in the following tables. In the case of the Western Systems, when both filters were in operation, the average results refer to the filters in common.

As already explained alum was used during a large portion of the time in the Western Systems, and in all cases it is converted into equivalent amounts of sulphate of alumina.

As a matter of convenience these results are expressed in grains per gallon. They may be changed to parts per million by multiplying by 17.1, and to pounds per million gallons by multiplying by 143.

AVERAGE DAILY AMOUNTS, IN GRAINS PER GALLON, OF SULPHATE OF ALUMINA APPLIED TO THE OHIO RIVER WATER IN THE WARREN SYSTEM.

Day.	October.	November.	December.	January.	February.	March.	April.	May.	June.	July.
1	....	0.88	....	....	3.97	....	6.53	1.16	4.05	3.82
2	....	0.78	0.72	3.69	....	2.45	5.85	1.03	5.19	5.03
3	....	....	1.51	5.26	3.58	2.03	5.89	....	5.30	5.10
4	....	0.83	1.66	4.18	3.65	2.38	4.35	1.85	4.40	....
5	....	0.93	1.03	....	4.10	2.53	....	1.77	3.27	....
6	....	0.70	0.68	3.86	4.02	2.62	4.77	1.83	3.12	3.36
7	....	1.25	0.92	3.56	3.52	2.15	1.86	1.28	....	3.10
8	....	1.35	....	4.46	4.05	....	2.06	1.32	....	2.88
9	....	1.08	0.79	3.87	....	2.44	1.89	1.59	4.78	2.73
10	....	....	1.00	4.05	2.85	2.42	1.88	....	4.00	3.29
11	....	1.14	2.00	4.47	....	4.41	1.95	2.32	2.40	3.04
12	....	....	1.27	....	....	4.67	....	1.67	1.57	....
13	....	....	0.93	4.10	3.18	4.83	....	1.81	1.78	3.18
14	....	....	1.02	3.15	5.76	5.00	....	1.66	....	2.43
15	....	....	....	3.28	5.99	....	....	1.69	3.49	2.87
16	....	....	1.15	3.22	....	4.48	....	1.89	2.68	2.83
17	....	....	1.22	3.59	4.15	4.30	....	....	1.50	2.97
18	....	....	0.88	3.45	3.61	4.34	....	1.02	2.32	2.76
19	....	....	1.03	....	3.90	4.53	....	0.96	3.09	....
20	....	....	0.94	2.88	4.09	5.57	1.58	1.15	2.65	2.80
21	0.52	....	0.63	3.19	3.82	6.50	0.83	1.54	....	3.19
22	0.44	....	....	3.91	3.00	....	0.85	1.68	1.94	4.33
23	0.60	....	1.58	....	....	6.37	0.77	3.64	2.15	6.45
24	0.44	....	1.36	....	2.16	5.72	0.84	....	2.35	7.41
25	0.42	1.74	....	3.30	2.52	5.31	0.62	0.66	2.38	7.40
26	0.79	1.40	1.64	....	2.21	4.65	....	1.31	....	....
27	....	1.28	2.96	2.98	2.90	3.77	0.54	1.69	....	7.50
28	0.73	....	3.94	3.19	2.43	3.60	0.63	2.57	....	7.03
29	1.20	0.85	....	3.25	2.41	3.38	1.10	3.58	....	5.25
30	0.87	0.65	5.16	5.23	....	5.43	1.07	4.84	3.95	4.42
31	1.11	....	4.55	4.08	....	5.78	....	....	....	4.17

AVERAGE DAILY AMOUNTS, IN GRAINS PER GALLON, OF SULPHATE OF ALUMINA APPLIED TO THE OHIO RIVER WATER IN THE JEWELL SYSTEM.

Day.	October.	November.	December.	January.	February.	March.	April.	May.	June.	July.
1	....	0.85	....	....	....	....	4.68	1.40	....	7.31
2	....	0.45	0.65	3.00	....	0.80	4.93	1.33	5.87	6.71
3	....	....	0.69	2.82	....	1.13	4.55	....	5.94	6.33
4	....	....	0.64	2.71	....	0.94	4.16	1.62	4.31	....
5	....	0.53	0.84	....	2.64	0.97	....	1.69	5.06	....
6	....	....	0.76	2.63	3.56	0.98	4.05	1.65	4.35	4.67
7	....	3.00	0.88	....	4.46	1.18	2.16	1.64	....	4.06
8	....	1.34	....	2.68	3.45	....	1.96	1.61	....	6.36
9	....	1.30	0.81	1.49	....	1.30	1.94	1.61	5.90	6.17
10	....	....	0.47	1.52	2.08	1.00	2.18	....	5.79	5.25
11	....	0.59	0.48	2.09	2.24	0.77	1.72	1.61	4.79	5.92
12	....	0.57	0.59	....	3.22	0.76	....	1.62	5.55	....
13	....	0.58	0.72	1.24	2.31	0.65	1.38	1.64	3.81	6.36
14	....	0.38	0.69	1.38	1.39	0.85	1.40	1.61	....	5.90
15	....	1.05	....	0.94	2.81	....	1.31	1.60	4.70	5.78
16	....	0.14	0.94	1.00	....	1.28	1.10	1.62	5.64	4.24
17	....	....	0.89	1.02	2.48	1.45	1.04	....	....	4.82
18	....	0.17	0.99	0.92	2,41	1.60	0.94	1.00	3.92	5.81
19	....	0.40	1.22	....	3.51	1.47	....	1.07	4.97	....
20	....	0.53	1.20	0.91	2.54	3.08	1.13	1.52	2.85	5.02
21	1.00	0.15	1.20	0.86	1.96	5.27	1.35	1.52	....	5.37
22	0.23	0.52	....	1.09	1.68	....	1.20	1.83	3.32	6.11
23	0.29	0.42	0.99	0.89	....	4.52	1.25	2.14	1.93	8.32
24	0.45	....	1.15	0.74	1.12	4.00	1.27	....	1.40	12.24
25	0.63	0.52	....	0.95	1.66	3.57	1.32	0.98	1.65	10.83
26	0.84	0.49	1.08	....	1.40	3.83	....	1.03	2.69	....
27	....	0.34	1.65	1.17	1.39	3.75	1.22	1.48	3.53	8.75
28	1.74	....	4.03	1.72	1.15	3.11	1.36	3.38	....	6.95
29	2.06	0.59	....	1.71	1.12	2.51	1.39	4.83	6.24	7.58
30	0.41	0.41	4.38	1.53	....	3.24	1.41	4.85	7.49	8.72
31	1.03	....	4.59	2.21	....	5.02	....	....	....	....

AVERAGE DAILY AMOUNTS, IN GRAINS PER GALLON, OF SULPHATE OF ALUMINA APPLIED TO THE OHIO RIVER WATER IN THE WESTERN SYSTEMS.

Day.	January.	February.	March.	April.	May.	June.	July.
1	....	2.54	....	4.30	....	4.38	4.87
2	....	....	0.63	4.01	....	4.27	7.70
3	....	1.49	0.79	3.49	....	4.54	9.02
4	....	1.59	0.72	2.83	....	3.32	....
5	....	2.64	0.55	....	....	4.26	....
6	....	1.79	0.82	3.16	....	4.28	4.02
7	....	3.09	0.73	2.32	1.13	....	5.62
8	....	3.54	....	....	1.11	....	4.61
9	....	....	0.74	....	0.80	6.32	5.30
10	1.32	3.01	0.66	....	....	7.24	3.16
11	1.01	3.22	0.62	....	1.13	5.77	1.48
12	....	4.00	1.07	....	1.22	5.86	....
13	....	2.76	0.89	....	0.79	4.25	5.91
14	1.06	3.25	0.75	....	0.83	....	4.84
15	1.21	2.47	....	....	0.95	5.19	4.60
16	1.66	....	0.97	....	1.01	4.18	5.21
17	1.39	1.99	0.77	....	....	4.00	3.36
18	1.24	2.19	0.84	....	0.51	1.52	3.66
19	....	2.04	1.44	....	0.51	4.35	....
20	1.24	2.05	2.78	....	0.83	5.39	3.70
21	0.87	2.26	3.54	....	1.11	....	3.93
22	0.71	....	....	....	1.58	3.29	4.46
23	0.94	....	3.83	....	1.44	....	7.08
24	0.81	1.36	4.56	....	....	3.64	8.31
25	0.73	1.15	3.17	....	1.63	4.42	5.20
26	....	1.11	3.78	....	0.95	3.73	....
27	1.58	1.16	2.87	....	1.57	5.38	6.01
28	2.60	0.92	2.62	....	2.20	....	5.36
29	....	0.77	3.12	....	6.18	7.05	4.36
30	....	....	3.69	....	6.98	6.71	....
31	1.92	....	3.13	....	....	....	3.83

Amounts of Lime Used in the Jewell System.

DAILY AVERAGES OF PERCENTAGE STRENGTHS OF LIME SOLUTION USED IN THE JEWELL SYSTEM.

Date. 1896.	Strength.	Date. 1896.	Strength.	Date. 1896.	Strength.	Date. 1896.	Strength.
February 8	0.52	February 18	0.55	February 27	0.49	March 7	0.44
" 10	0.52	" 19	0.55	" 28	0.49	" 21	0.19
" 11	0.52	" 20	0.49	" 29	0.53	" 23	0.30
" 12	0.52	" 21	0.49	March 2	0.44	" 25	0.40
" 13	0.55	" 22	0.49	" 3	0.44	" 26	0.25
" 14	0.55	" 24	0.49	" 4	0.44	" 27	0.21
" 15	0.55	" 25	0.52	" 5	0.44	" 31	0.25
" 17	0.55	" 26	0.52	" 6	0.44	April 1	0.30

The daily average results of the amounts of lime used in the Jewell System are presented in the following table:

AVERAGE DAILY AMOUNTS, IN GRAINS PER GALLON, OF LIME APPLIED TO THE OHIO RIVER WATER IN THE JEWELL SYSTEM.

Date. 1896.	Amount.	Date. 1896.	Amount.	Date. 1896.	Amount.	Date. 1896.	Amount.
February 8	0.85	February 18	1.05	February 27	0.32	March 7	0.23
" 10	1.38	" 19	1.17	" 28	0.03	" 21	0.28
" 11	1.67	" 20	0.88	" 29	0.18	" 23	0.72
" 12	1.56	" 21	0.47	March 2	0.19	" 25	0.49
" 13	0.52	" 22	0.32	" 3	0.17	" 26	1.05
" 14	0.72	" 24	0.46	" 4	0.19	" 27	1.41
" 15	0.92	" 25	0.38	" 5	0.18	" 31	2.17
" 17	0.82	" 26	0.53	" 6	0.13	April 1	0.81

CHAPTER III.

Decomposition and Subsequent Disposal of the Alum or Sulphate of Alumina applied to the Ohio River Water.

In some localities objections have been raised to the use of alum and of sulphate of alumina in the purification of public water supplies. The ground for this has been that some of the dissolved chemicals passed through the filter, appeared in the filtered water, and were liable to injure the health of the water consumers. While this might be true with some waters, it can be positively stated that it should not, and need not, be the case with the Ohio River water at Louisville. The reasons for this are that there is dissolved in the Ohio River water an ample supply of lime and magnesia to combine with, and to decompose, more sulphate of alumina than would be necessary to apply under conditions giving a satisfactory and economical purification of the water by the general method under consideration.

The lime and magnesia which are found in the river water, in a form capable of decomposing sulphate of alumina, are present as carbonates and bicarbonates. In the tables of chemical analyses of the river water in Chapter I the amounts of these constituents are recorded as *alkalinity*. These compounds which give to the water its alkalinity possess the power of decomposing sulphate of alumina and alum, by virtue of the fact that the sulphuric acid of the applied chemicals is much stronger than the carbonic acid of the alkaline compounds. The result is that the sulphuric acid (the strong acid) combines with the lime or magnesia (the strong bases); the alumina is thus disengaged and, in the presence of the water, forms aluminum hydrate, which soon appears in the form of a white gelatinous solid compound; and the carbonic acid (the weak acid) remains in the water as free acid. Taking sulphate of alumina, the more efficient of the two chemicals, as an example, and viewing the results of its application to the Ohio River water in the light of the expressions used in water analysis, we find that the following principal changes occur:

1. The alkalinity is reduced by the displacement of carbonic acid by sulphuric acid, which, combining with the lime and magnesia, forms neutral sulphates.

2. The alumina is freed from sulphuric acid when the latter unites with the alkaline constituents, and appears as the gelatinous, solid aluminum hydrate, which possesses the power of coagulating the suspended matters in the water. In its solid form the aluminum hydrate is removed subsequently by sedimentation and filtration.

3. The incrusting constituents are increased, due to the sulphuric acid uniting with the lime and magnesia.

4. The free carbonic acid is increased on account of the liberation of this acid when the alkalinity is reduced, with a resulting increase in the incrusting constituents. At the instant of liberation it exists as a gas, but it immediately takes up water and forms free carbonic acid.

It is noted above that these are the principal changes. If the river contained no suspended matter or dissolved organic matter, there would be no other action; and these changes, furthermore, would be proportional to the amount and composition of the applied sulphate of alumina. In practice it is found that the particles of suspended matter, by an absorptive or mordanting action, dispose of some of the sulphate of alumina, without the above decomposition taking place. This secondary action will be mentioned beyond.

Considering the primary decomposition (in a water free from suspended matters and dissolved organic matter), the reduction in alkalinity in parts per million, for 1 grain per gallon of each lot of the chemicals used in these tests, would be proportional to the sulphuric acid, as follows:

REDUCTION OF ALKALINITY (LIME AND MAGNESIA) BY ONE GRAIN PER GALLON OF EACH LOT OF COMMERCIAL SULPHATE OF ALUMINA.

System.	Number of Lot.	Percentage of Sulphuric Acid.	Reduction in Alkalinity. Parts per Million.
Warren	1	39.87	8.53
"	2	38.61	8.27
"	3	37.72	8.07
Jewell	1	37.96	8.12
"	2	37.87	8.11
"	3	37.46	8.02
"	4	42.20	9.04
Western	1	37.72	8.07
"	2	37.64	8.06

Under the above-mentioned conditions, the increase in incrusting constituents, expressed in the usual way in parts per million, would be exactly proportional to the reduction in alkalinity; and the increase in carbonic acid, expressed in parts per million by weight of carbon dioxide, would be 44 per cent. of the reduction in alkalinity.

Independent of the absorptive and mordanting action with suspended matters and certain dissolved organic matters, the changes in the river water, upon the addition of 1 grain per gallon of the first lot of sulphate of alumina used with the Warren System, may be illustrated as follows:

COMPARISON IN PARTS PER MILLION OF IMPORTANT CONSTITUENTS OF THE OHIO RIVER WATER BEFORE AND AFTER TREATMENT WITH ONE GRAIN PER GALLON OF SULPHATE OF ALUMINA.

Constituents.	Before Treatment.	After Treatment.
Alkalinity	60	51.47 (decrease)
Incrusting constituents	25	33.53 (increase)
Carbonic acid (carbon dioxide)	60	63.75 (increase)

When suspended matter, especially clay, is present in the water, there is a certain amount of the sulphate of alumina absorbed without its decomposition by the alkaline constituents. This causes the alkalinity to be reduced in amounts less than that indicated above. The degree of reduction, furthermore, varies with the amount and character of the matter in suspension. The Ohio River contains so little dissolved organic matter that this factor probably does not cause the actual reduction in alkalinity to depart from the theoretical more than about 5 per cent. But the varying composition of the Ohio River water, with regard to suspended matter, causes a variable relation to exist between the theoretical reduction in alkalinity, due to complete decomposition of the applied sulphate, and the actual reduction after a portion of it has been absorbed by the suspended matter. The significance of this is shown in the following table, where the average results of several determinations are presented, in which the amount of sulphate of alumina was sufficient to produce complete coagulation.

PERCENTAGES WHICH THE ACTUAL REDUCTION OF ALKALINITY BY SULPHATE OF ALUMINA WERE OF THE THEORETICAL, WITH OHIO RIVER WATER CONTAINING DIFFERENT AMOUNTS OF SUSPENDED MATTER.

Suspended Matter in Parts per Million.	Percentages which the Actual were of the Theoretical Reductions.
200	85
400	80
800	75
1200	65

Further information upon this point was obtained in 1897, and the results are recorded in Chapter XV.

Combining the above information concerning the decomposition of sulphate of alumina with the varying amounts of alkalinity in the river water, as recorded in Chapter I, it will be seen that the greatest amount of sulphate of alumina which can be safely applied to the Ohio River water is about 4 grains per gallon for a minimum; the normal ranges from 6 to 10 grains; and the maximum about 15 grains per gallon.

From the outset of these investigations, the importance of determining accurately the presence or absence of the applied alum or sulphate of alumina in the filtered water was clearly recognized. There are two methods which can be utilized in the solution of this problem. These methods, both of which were carefully applied to samples of the filtered water day by day, are as follows:

1. The determination of the alkalinity of the effluents. This proved, if the effluents

were alkaline, that no undecomposed sulphate of alumina was present. If the effluent was acid, however, the opposite of this was true.

2. The test for alumina in the effluent, according to Richards' logwood and acetic acid test.

In the following table are presented all results in which any trace of alumina (Al_2O_3) was found in the filtered water, together with the corresponding alkalinity or acidity of each sample. The amount of sulphate of alumina equivalent to each amount of alumina is also recorded. It will be noted, in those cases where the effluents were acid, that the amounts of alumina and sulphate of alumina were abnormally low. This may have been due to changes in the sulphate of alumina in passing through the filter, or to inaccuracies of the logwood test in measuring such small quantities of alumina, or both.

SUMMARY OF ALL RESULTS SHOWING ALUMINA BY THE LOGWOOD AND ACETIC ACID TEST, WITH THE CORRESPONDING ALKALINITY IN THE EFFLUENT OF EACH SYSTEM.

Date. 1896.	Alkalinity. Parts per Million.	Alumina. Parts per Million.	Sulphate of Alumina. Grains per Gallon.
	WARREN EFFLUENT.		
February 15	6.5	0.2	0.07
" 20	17.0	0.1	0.04
March 16	12.0	0.1	0.04
" 20	13.1	0.1	0.04
" 21	10.1	0.1	0.04
" 23	4.9	0.1	0.04
" 24	4.0	0.1	0.04
April 2	0.2	0.5	0.18
" 3	Acidity 0.1	0.3	0.11
" 6	Acidity 3.1	0.8	0.27
" 7	3.5	0.5	0.18
July 3	10.2	0.1	0.04
	WESTERN GRAVITY EFFLUENT.		
July 2	6.1	0.2	0.07
" 3	6.0	0.1	0.04
	WESTERN PRESSURE EFFLUENT.		
April 3	3.0	0.2	0.07
" 4	Acidity 1.0	0.4	0.13
" 6	5.0	0.2	0.07
	JEWELL EFFLUENT.		
February 10	43.0	0.2	0.07
" 20	14.9	0.2	0.07
March 24	15.4	0.1	0.04
" 26	51.1	0.1	0.04
March 27	59.2	0.1	0.04
" 28	31.9	0.1	0.04
April 2	5.5	0.3	0.17
" 3	1.3	0.2	0.07
" 4	Acidity 4.7	0.7	0.25
" 6	4.0	0.2	0.07
June 2	28.9	0.1	0.04
" 3	39.7	0.1	0.04
" 10	22.5	0.3	0.11
" 16	24.0	0.1	0.04
July 1	Acidity 1.8	0.3	0.11
" 2	Acidity 3.9	0.4	0.13
" 3	4.6	0.8	0.27
" 8	8.8	0.1	0.04
" 13	4.1	0.3	0.11
" 14	Acidity 1.0	0.3	0.11
" 15	2.5	0.2	0.07
" 17	10.0	0.4	0.13
" 20	15.2	0.2	0.07
" 21	17.1	0.1	0.04
" 22	14.0	0.1	0.04
" 23	8.9	0.1	0.04
" 24	Acidity 2.1	0.3	0.11
" 25	Acidity 6.0	0.3	0.11
" 27	Acidity 3.8	0.3	0.11
" 28	Acidity 1.9	0.2	0.07

The above results show that on 2, 8, 0, and 1 days, respectively, the Warren, Jewell, Western Gravity, and Western Pressure effluents were acid, and contained, therefore, undecomposed sulphate of alumina. The acidity on these several occasions was due, of course, to the application of sulphate of alumina in amounts exceeding that capable of decomposition by the alkaline constituents of the river water. On a practical basis of operation, such applications would be inexcusable.

It will also be noted from the results in the last table that on 10, 22, 2, and 2 days, respectively, the Warren, Jewell, Western Gravity, and Western Pressure effluents contained slight traces of alumina, although the effluents were alkaline. In a majority of these cases the effluents were sufficiently alkaline to decompose several grains of sulphate of alumina, and the passage of the latter through the filter in an undecomposed form, under these conditions, was an impossibility. So far as we could learn, these slight traces of alumina in alkaline effluents were due to the passage through the filter of minute flakes of the insoluble aluminum hydrate, and to their subsequent solution by the reagents used in the logwood and acetic acid test. So far as their direct and inherent influence is concerned, these slight traces of alumina in an alkaline effluent cannot be regarded as objectionable.

In conclusion it may be stated that the experience obtained during these tests shows clearly that the Ohio River water contains a sufficient amount of alkaline compounds to decompose adequate quantities of sulphate of alumina; that the alumina appears as a solid gelatinous body, which coagulates the mud silt and clay, and subsequently is completely removed, practically speaking, by sedimentation and filtration; and that the sulphuric acid combines with lime and magnesia to form neutral sulphates of those bases, while an equivalent amount of carbonic acid is formed, and remains dissolved in the water. In a very few instances very slight amounts of undecomposed sulphate of alumina were found in the effluent of these systems. This was due to faults of construction of the systems, and of their operation, which must be improved as explained in Chapters IX and XV.

Under the conditions of efficient and economical purification of this water, the presence of undecomposed sulphate of alumina in the filtered water would be not only inadmissible, but inexcusable.

CHAPTER IV.

Coagulation and Sedimentation of Ohio River Water by Aluminum Hydrate Formed by the Decomposition of the Applied Alum or Sulphate of Alumina.

It has been already shown in the preceding chapters how the gelatinous precipitate of aluminum hydrate is formed, and reference has also been made to the disposal of the alumina in this solid form by subsidence and filtration through sand. In this chapter it is the purpose to explain the nature of coagulation and sedimentation, to describe the devices in the several systems where the coagulation and sedimentation were accomplished, and to point out the practical results which may be obtained by the aid of aluminum hydrate in the purification of such water as that of the Ohio River. Coagulation is the term generally used to express the action which is produced by the application of alum to water. In general terms this action has already been described, but in detail it is as follows:

When the applied alum solution comes in contact with the dissolved lime and magnesia in the river water, the former is immediately decomposed by the latter, which are present in excess. At the instant of the decomposition of the alum it forms aluminum hydrate. The latter is also dissolved in the water at the time when the decomposition or reaction takes place. The great bulk of aluminum hydrate passes very quickly into the form of solid matter. To chemists a solid compound, separating out by the action on each other of two soluble chemical compounds, is known as a precipitate. At first this precipitate of aluminum hydrate is present as innumerable, minute, white particles of a gelatinous and sticky nature; and it is not until the alum has been decomposed and converted into this form that its application in the purification, by this system, of such water as that of the Ohio River begins to be of practical value, by its accomplishment of the initial step in the purification, viz.:

Coagulation.

The process of coagulation consists of a gradual grouping together of the tiny particles of aluminum hydrate which surround, and at the same time envelope, the mineral matter, organic matter, bacteria, and other organisms suspended in the river water. Aluminum hydrate (or, perhaps, sulphate of alumina) also combines with some of the dissolved organic matters, and adds them to the mass of coagulated material. Coagulation of muddy water by aluminum hydrate may be more easily understood by comparing it to the clarification of turbid coffee to which the white of eggs has been added.

The completeness with which coagulation takes place depends upon the relation of several factors. But it may be stated that, disregarding the question of cost, it is possible with sufficient coagulation followed by sufficient sedimentation to render very muddy water perfectly clear. In actual practice the economical aspects must be considered, and coagulation should be carried to such a degree, and under such conditions, that sedimentation will remove the most mud and other suspended matter for the least money. For efficient and economical filtration through sand at a rapid rate, attention must be given also to the coagulated masses in the water as it reaches the filter.

The degree of coagulation is influenced and controlled by several factors. Primarily it is controlled by the amount of alum which is applied and decomposed into aluminum hydrate. It is also influenced, among other things, to a marked degree by the amount of suspended matter in the river water, the relative character of the suspended particles, and the period during which coagulation and subsequent sedimentation may take place. The last factor is of great economical importance.

Coagulation by itself effects no purification in the sense that it removes from the water any objectionable matters. It is simply an initial and very important step in the purification of waters heavily charged with suspended matters, by which the way is paved for economical and efficient purification by means of sedimentation and filtration through sand.

SEDIMENTATION.

Sedimentation consists solely of the subsidence due to gravity of the suspended matters after coagulation. It is a process of purification in that it removes from the water objectionable matters. It occurs in part simultaneously with coagulation in these systems, but the greater part of the sedimentation follows coagulation.

In the following pages are described the portions of each system where the coagulation and sedimentation took place. Beyond this are given some results showing the purification effected by the coagulation and sedimentation in the respective systems, and an account of the relative value of the above-named factors, together with the results of some special experiments made with the view to demonstrating more clearly the economical significance of these portions of this method of purifying the Ohio River water.

These descriptions will be more clearly understood by reference to the accompanying plates.

WARREN SETTLING BASIN.

The settling basin was rectangular in plan, 12.1 feet by 12.0 feet, and 10.25 feet deep. It was constructed entirely of yellow pine. The bottom was made of planks 2.5 inches thick, and the sides for a distance of 5.1 feet above the bottom were 2.5 inches thick: above this height they were 5 inches thick. The basin was strongly braced inside and out by white-pine posts (6 by 8 inches), and the foundation was made of timbers of the same size. Iron rods 0.375 inch in diameter extended across the basin to stay it. Two partitions or baffle-walls divided the basin into three sections as shown on the plan. These walls did not extend entirely across the basin, but left an opening at one end of 2.67 feet.

These partitions were made of 1-inch sheathing fastened to 1.75 by 6-inch posts. The general arrangement of the basin is shown on the plans, as are also the locations of the inlet and outlet water-pipes.

Inlet Water-pipe.—The river water entered the basin through a 6-inch pipe, connecting just inside the basin wall with a 6-inch balanced valve controlled by a float. There was from 45 to 65 pounds pressure on the inlet water-pipe, which branched from the force main leading to the Crescent Hill Reservoir. A small propeller-wheel located in a 6-inch nipple, which extended 5 inches from the valve, drove the chemical pump as previously described.

Outlet.—The outlet was a box channel, 3.4 by 1.1 feet in section. Its crest was 8.7 feet above the floor of the basin.

From the basin outlet an 8-inch cast-iron pipe led to the filter, where it connected with an 8-inch pipe, which in turn connected with the central well. The passage of water from the basin to the filter was controlled by an 8-inch valve in this pipe.

Elevations.—The relative elevations in feet, with the bottom of the sand layer as the datum plane, were as follows:

Center of inlet water-pipe at basin...	+1.02
Floor of basin....................	−1.98
Top of basin......................	+8.52
Average maximum water level.......	+8.02
Crest of outlet (mudsill)............	+6.72
Center of pipe leading to the filter....	+1.60

Depth.—The depths of the chamber in feet were as follows:

At level of mudsill..................	8.7
Average maximum water level........	10.0
Total depth of chamber.............	10.5

Area.—The areas of the chamber in square feet were as follows:

At floor level	139.7
At level of mudsill	143.6
At average maximum water level	147.9

Capacity.—The capacities of the chamber in cubic feet were as follows:

Below level of mudsill	1229
Below average maximum level of water.	1422
Total capacity	1459

These do not include the outlet channel, the contents of which were 33.9 cubic feet.

Storage Period.—Assuming complete displacement, the length of time required for water to pass through the basin at the contract rate (250,000 gallons per 24 hours) was 61 minutes. The distance from the inlet to the outlet along center lines was 36.6 feet.

Concentrated solutions of common salt and of various aniline colors were added to the water on several occasions as it entered the basin, and careful observations made to learn the time taken for passage through the basin. It was found that the first water so charged passed through to the outlet at the contract rate of flow in about 15 minutes. The water containing the greatest amount of these solutions passed through in 58 minutes, but the dilution was so great that it was just 2 hours before the last traces of the substances disappeared from the water as it left the settling basin. In explanation of the short period which elapsed before the first appearance of the substances at the outlet it is to be stated that in the baffle-wall opposite the mouth of the main inlet water-pipe there was an opening, 1 to 2 square inches in area, through which passed an iron rod 0.5 inch in diameter.

Drainage.—A 4-inch flap valve located in one corner of the settling basin was used as a sludge outlet. No provision was made to drain to this valve, the floor of the chamber being level.

Cleaning.—No special arrangements were made for cleaning.

Jewell Settling Chamber.

The settling chamber together with the filter was included in one large circular wooden tank, 14.0 feet high and 13.5 feet outside diameter.

The sides were made of 3 by 9-inch cypress staves, and the bottom of two layers of 3-inch pine planks. The hoops were eleven in number; the first and sixth were 4.5 by 0.18 inches, the second, third, fourth, and fifth were 4 by 0.12 inches, and the upper five were 3 by 0.12 inches. All of them were made of wrought iron.

At a distance of 6.79 feet above the floor of the tank was a second floor 3 inches thick, which formed the lower floor of the filter tank. It was supported on eight 8 by 8-inch white-pine posts, four 8 by 10-inch timbers forming the floor-beams.

The lower part of the tank was used as the settling chamber; the floor and sides of the tank forming the bottom and sides of the settling chamber, respectively, while the bottom floor of the filter formed the top of the settling chamber. The general dimensions as shown on the plan were: diameter, 13.0 feet, and height, 6.89 feet.

Inlet Water-pipe.—This pipe was of wrought iron and was 5 inches in diameter. It was connected to the side of the chamber by a flange joint. The river water contained in it was under from 45 to 65 pounds pressure, and was taken from the force main leading to the distributing reservoir.

Inside the chamber there was a single-seated valve operated by a float in the filter above, and designed to control the flow into the settling chamber.

Chamber Outlet.—The outlet from the chamber was in the center, through an 8-inch central well passing up through the filter.

Elevations.—The elevations in feet, with the bottom of the sand layer as the datum plane, were as follows:

Center of inlet water-pipe	-6.05
Floor of chamber	-7.61
Roof of chamber	-0.82

Height.—The total height of the chamber was 6.79 feet, and the height under the beams supporting the floor of the filter was 5.96 feet.

Area.—The gross area of the settling chamber was 132.7 square feet. The area deducting the supports for the filter floor was 129.2 square feet.

Capacity.—The total capacity of the chamber was about 879 cubic feet.

Storage Period.—Assuming complete displacement of the water, the length of time required for the water to pass from the inlet to the outlet pipe at the contract rate (250,000 gallons per 24 hours) was 36 minutes.

The flow of water through the chamber was traced by the application of salt and various aniline colors in experiments similar to those described in the case of the Warren System. Under the above-stated contract rate of flow the water charged with these substances appeared at the outlet in about 8 minutes after their application at the inlet; the period of passage of the water containing the greatest amount of these substances when it reached the outlet was 22 minutes; and the last appreciable trace of these substances in the water as it left the outlet disappeared in 48 minutes after application at the inlet.

Inspection.—A manhole was provided at a convenient location to allow of inspection of the settling chamber.

Drainage.—An 8-inch valve was connected to the side of the chamber at the bottom by means of a flange joint. This valve discharged into a barrel connected with the sewer. The settling chamber could be drained completely through this valve provided its contents were quite liquid. The floor of the chamber was level, however, so that mud and slime had to be swept or shoveled out.

Cleaning.—It was intended to flush out the settling chamber by allowing waste wash-water to flow over into the central well from the filter above, and discharge into the settling chamber. A curved half-pipe 4 inches in diameter, which was fastened to and turned with the agitator shaft, was used as a trough to direct the flow to different parts of the chamber. This did not prove effective, however, and the method of cleaning resorted to was by hand, aided by occasional flushings from the inlet water-pipe.

WESTERN SETTLING CHAMBER.

The Western Pressure Filter and the settling chamber used by both filters were contained in a large steel cylinder made of 0.62-inch plates. It was 22.5 feet long and 8.0 feet in inside diameter. The ends were dome-shaped, curving outwards 1.25 feet. This cylinder was divided in the center by two curved partitions. The partition plates touched at the center and were bolted together. The vertical joints were all lapped, and the horizontal ones were all butt-joints with two cover plates. Two lines of staggered rivets 0.75 inch in diameter were used throughout. The total weight of the empty cylinder was said to be 27,000 pounds.

The west half of the cylinder was used for the settling chamber, the east half for the pressure filter. This chamber was 11.15 feet long in the center, 8.71 feet long on the sides, and 8.0 feet in inside diameter.

Supply of River Water.—The supply for the Western Systems was at first furnished by the same pipe which supplied the Warren and Jewell systems with river water under from 45 to 65 pounds pressure from the force main to the Crescent Hill Reservoir. The variations in pressure were due to the variations in draft on the supply-pipe.

Objections were made to this by the Western Filter Company on account of the variations in pressure caused by the operation of the other systems. Therefore, on Feb. 29, 1896, a new 4-inch river-water pipe was laid from the force main, to be used solely by the Western Systems. After the change the pressure was held very closely between 60 and 65 pounds.

Up to April 7 this pipe was connected directly with the settling chamber. Among the changes made during the period from April 7 to May 8 was the introduction of a Worthington pump on this pipe. This was done with the view to obtaining better equalization of the pressure in the water-pipe, and also to operate a pair of auxiliary plunger pumps which were used for applying the chemical solution as already described in Chapter II.

Pumping Engine.—The pumping engine was of the the H. R. Worthington pattern. The main dimensions were 9-inch steam-cylinder, 8.5-inch water cylinder and 10-inch stroke. It was a single-expansion duplex engine. The steam was supplied by a 1.5-inch covered pipe. The exhaust was a 2-inch pipe, open to the atmosphere.

Inlet Water-pipe.—As first used the inlet to the settling chamber was a simple pipe with a flange joint screwed on to the bottom of the cylinder. With the other changes in April this was modified, and a distributing pipe was inserted in the chamber. This distributer was formed by a 6-inch nipple 12 inches long screwed into the upper side of the flange joint above mentioned; a 6-inch tee with its long arm horizontal, and two lengths of 6-inch pipe each 2.5 feet long capped at the outer end. On each side of the nipple and pipes was a line of holes 1.5 inches in diameter. There were two holes in the tee, four in each nipple and one in the center of each cap. The center of the holes was 1.30 feet above the floor of the chamber.

Outlet.—The outlet from the settling-chamber was a simple 6-inch pipe connected to the top of the cylinder by a flange joint.

This pipe led down to the front of the cylinder and joined a tee, to the ends of which were attached the pipes leading to the pressure and gravity filters, respectively.

Elevations.—The principal elevations in feet, with the bottom of the sand layer of the pressure filter as the datum plane, were as follows:

Center of inlet pipe.........	-0.80
Bottom of cylinder (inside)..	-2.15
Top of cylinder (inside).....	+5.85

Capacity.—The capacity of the chamber was 503 cubic feet.

Storage Period.—Assuming complete displacement in the chamber the storage interval at the contract rate (250,000 gallons per 24 hours) was 22 minutes.

Experiments with salt and various aniline colors, similar to those described in connection with the other systems, were made to trace the flow of water through the settling chamber. At the contract rate of flow, as stated above, the water containing these applied substances first appeared at the outlet in about 2 minutes after their application; the water containing the largest proportion of these substances passed through the chamber in 9 minutes; and the last appreciable traces of the salt and dyes disappeared from the water at the outlet in 27 minutes after their application to the water at the inlet.

With both filters in operation at the contract rate, the storage period in this chamber would be only one-half as long as stated above.

Inspection.—The settling chamber could be inspected by removing a manhole placed about in the center of the upper front quadrant. A hand-hole was also provided, occupying a similar position in the lower quadrant.

Drainage.—The construction was such that there was no convenient method of draining the chamber. The inlet pipe at its lowest point was, however, provided with a tee, one arm of which was plugged. By removing this plug the water could be drained out to the level of the distributing pipe. As no arrangements were made to carry off the water from this plug it was used but little. The usual method was by siphonage through the manhole in the upper part of the chamber.

Cleaning.—Handwork was mainly relied upon for cleaning. By a system of valves and piping, connection was formed between the wash-water and chamber outlet pipes so that wash-water could be turned in from above to aid in flushing the chamber.

PURIFICATION OF THE OHIO RIVER WATER BY SEDIMENTATION IN THE SEVERAL SYSTEMS.

As sedimentation is an intermediate step in the complete purification by this system of the Ohio River water, and as it varies widely according to the existing conditions, this phase of the tests was not made the subject of detailed daily study. Attention was given to the matter in a general way, however, with the view to learning its practical significance.

Inspection showed very quickly that the degree of purification of the Ohio River water by sedimentation was a variable factor so far as the removal of mud was concerned. With the same river water sedimentation increased with the amount of aluminum hydrate formed from the decomposed alum or sulphate of alumina.

This would be naturally expected, of course, because the greater the number of minute gelatinous particles, forming centers of coagulation, the greater would be the size and weight of the coagulated masses or flakes; and, in turn, the greater and heavier these flakes the more quickly would they subside by gravity to the bottom of the settling chambers.

At times the Ohio River water had suspended in it large quantities of very fine silt and clay, of which the individual particles sometimes ranged as small as 0.00001 inch in diameter. It was after heavy rains following a long period of drought that water of such a character was found. With the same amounts of aluminum hydrate in two samples of river water, one of the character just described, and the other a more nearly normal water containing the same amount by weight of larger suspended matter, the latter water is far more purified by coagulation and sedimentation in the same period of time than is the former water. With plain sedimentation, without coagulation, similar results would be obtained; and the explanation of the results just described is that the coagulation was quite incomplete. With a water containing an innumerable quantity of very finely divided particles, the period necessary for coagulation is unusually long; and it appears that, in some cases at least, the bulk of the aluminum hydrate together with the larger suspended particles subside before a large portion of the fine particles is coagulated.

Another factor which produces a marked effect upon the degree of sedimentation is the period of time during which the coagulation and subsidence take place. The actual storage periods under normal conditions for the respective systems have already been presented in an earlier portion of this chapter. These storage periods were complicated in a good many cases by washing, repairing, and modifying the filters and by delays occasioned by the filters being out of service during the night (except March 24-30 and April 27 to June 6) and on Sundays.

During the six weeks' continuous run (Sundays excepted), from April 27 to June 6, twenty-nine sets of bacterial analyses were made of the river water before treatment, and of the corresponding water after it has passed through, under normal conditions, the Warren settling basin and the Jewell settling chamber, respectively. At the outset the facilities for taking samples of the water after passage through the Western settling chamber were not wholly satisfactory. During the latter part of the period (May 28 to June 1) eight samples were taken from this system. The average results of these analyses are compared with the corresponding ones from the other two systems just after the next table. In the next table are recorded the results of the individual analyses with the percentages of removal, in the full set of tests of the Warren and Jewell systems upon this point. The average quantities of sulphate of alumina applied by each system on the different days are given in Chapter II.

It will be noted that these results, which are tabulated below, are quite variable with regard to the percentages of removal. This was due in part to the amount of applied sulphate of alumina in relation to the quality of the river water; and also to the fact that there were in the water small flakes of coagulated

NUMBERS OF BACTERIA PER CUBIC CENTIMETRE IN THE OHIO RIVER WATER BEFORE AND AFTER PASSAGE THROUGH THE WARREN SETTLING BASIN AND THE JEWELL SETTLING CHAMBER, RESPECTIVELY, WITH THE PERCENTAGES OF REMOVAL.

Date. 1896.	Bacteria per Cubic Centimeter in Water from			Percentage Removal	
	River.	Warren Settling Basin.	Jewell Settling Chamber.	Warren.	Jewell.
April 28	5 700	5 800	4 300	0	25
" 29	7 100	2 800	2 800	60	60
" 30	3 700	2 300	1 700	38	54
May 2	5 600	1 100	4 100	80	27
" 2	9 000	2 800	7 400	69	18
" 4	7 500	2 900	4 700	61	37
" 5	9 000	6 000	4 900	33	46
" 6	4 900	1 800	4 400	63	10
" 7	5 000	4 200	1 700	16	66
" 11	6 900	2 400	3 500	65	49
" 12	7 100	1 700	4 000	76	44
" 13	4 200	1 000	3 400	76	19
" 14	5 800	1 500	3 100	74	47
" 15	7 500	1 300	1 500	83	80
" 16	10 900	1 800	2 400	83	78
" 18	9 500	1 800	4 600	81	52
" 19	7 800	5 400	3 400	26	53
" 20	4 700	4 400	2 300	06	51
" 21	5 900	2 700	4 300	54	27
" 22	4 600	1 800	2 400	61	48
" 28	14 900	6 800	11 900	54	20
" 29	33 900	6 800	21 200	80	37
" 29	23 600	1 400	15 900	94	33
" 30	28 700	5 100	20 300	82	29
" 30	21 800	5 100	15 200	77	30
June 3	18 900	2 200	4 100	88	78
" 5	9 900	2 800	4 100	72	59
" 5	6 200	2 400	3 500	61	44
" 5	5 000	1 600	3 100	68	38
Averages	10 500	3 100	5 900	61	43

material, containing bacteria enveloped within and around them, and which were of necessity broken up in an incomplete and irregular manner as they were mixed with the culture medium for bacterial analysis. That is to say, it was practically impossible to get all the bacteria in these flakes separated into single cells so that each colony on the culture medium should represent only one bacterium, as the method of analysis called for.

During the period from May 28 to June 1, inclusive, when the river water contained the greatest amount of very finely divided particles, and when it was most difficult to coagulate, the average results of bacterial purification by coagulation and sedimentation in the three systems were as follows:

System.	Number of Bacteria per Cubic Centimeter.	Percentage Removal.
Warren	5 000	80
Jewell	16 900	31
Western	16 600	32
(River)	24 600	......

On June 5 and 6 four samples of river water before and after passage through the Warren settling basin and the Jewell settling chamber, respectively, were collected under normal conditions and mixed together for chemical analysis. The results of the analyses showed that 59 and 18 per cent., respectively, of the suspended matter in the river water were removed in these two systems by coagulation and sedimentation.

These results show very forcibly the great economical importance of long storage periods in order to allow the coagulated material to subside, especially as the removal in the Warren System of more than three times that in the Jewell System was effected with only 65 per cent. of the sulphate of alumina employed in the latter system.

The examinations of the removal of suspended matter of the river water in the Western settling chamber indicated that it was more variable than in the case of the other systems, but on an average about equal to that by the Jewell settling chamber.

During June and July several sets of analyses, both chemical and bacterial, were made of the river water before and after it had remained over night or over Sunday in the several respective settling chambers. The results of the analyses bore out the observations as to the appearance of the water in the settling chambers, showing in practically every case a removal of more than 90 per cent. of both bacteria and suspended mineral and organic matter, while in several instances the removal was more than 99 per cent.

These last data show very conclusively the great economical importance of coagulation and sedimentation in the purification of such muddy water as that of the Ohio River.

They also show the superiority in this respect of the Warren over the other systems, owing to a longer storage period in the settling chamber, during which sedimentation takes place. Furthermore, this evidence is abundant proof that in all these systems the storage period in the settling basin and chambers is too short by far to allow full benefit and economy to be derived from sedimentation.

Owing to the great practical importance of sedimentation, some special experiments were made for the purpose of obtaining more information on this subject, as will be found in the next section of this chapter. During 1897 additional experiments were made, and the results are recorded in Chapter XV.

Special Investigations upon the Degree of Purification of the Ohio River Water by Sedimentation under Varying Conditions, both with and without Coagulation by Aluminum Hydrate, and with Special Reference to the Influence of the Period of Subsidence.

This set of experiments was made with the aid of a settling pipe, 20 inches in diameter and 24 feet deep, placed in the boiler house. Suitable piping arrangements were made to allow flushing, filling, and draining the pipe, and at the sides of the pipe was placed a series of pet cocks through which samples of water could be drawn at stated distances from the bottom.

The results of these experiments are given in the following table. Except in those cases where the regular samples (numbers in parentheses) for daily analyses of the river water were used, special serial numbers were given to samples collected for this purpose.

The distances from the bottom of the pipe to the tap from which the sample was taken are given under the heading, source of sample. Analyses were made for the determination of the total suspended solids (insoluble residue on evaporation), and also of the number of bacteria in the water. As explained above, the latter determination was complicated by the presence of masses of suspended matter in the water which made it difficult to separate the individual bacteria. Another factor affecting the determination of the percentage removal of the bacteria was the high and unequal temperature of the water in the pipe at different heights and at different times during the same experiment. The temperature probably exerted a retarding influence upon subsidence, but, on the other hand, the general conditions of sedimentation in a small tank are more favorable than in a large basin or reservoir. In those cases where no coagulants were applied it is probable that, under the conditions of practice with longer periods of subsidence, the variation in the amount of suspended matter in the water at different depths would be reduced materially.

RESULTS OF SEDIMENTATION EXPERIMENTS.

Experiment.		Applied Sulphate of Alumina. Grains per Gallon.	Sample.		Period of Subsidence, Hours.	Temperature, Degrees C.	Suspended Solids.		Bacteria.	
Number.	Date. 1896.		Number.	Source.			Parts per Million.	Per Cent Removed.	Per Cubic Centimeter.	Per Cent Removed.
1	May 29	0.0	1	River.	0	....	590	....	....	....
			2	2 feet	24	....	320	45.8	....	....
			3	4 "	24	....	....	....	....	....
			4	11.75 "	24	....	286	51.5	....	....
			5	20 "	24	....	262	55.6	....	....
			6	2 "	48	....	170	71.2	....	....
			7	4 "	48	....	....	....	....	....
			8	11.75 "	48	....	160	72.8	....	....
			9	20 "	48	....	90	84.7	....	....
2	June 1	0.0	10	River	0	....	390	....	....	....
			11	2 feet	24	....	254	34.9	....	....
			13	11.75 "	24	....	226	42.1	....	....
			14	20 "	24	....	194	50.2	....	....
3	June 2	0.0	15	River	0	....	936	....	....	....
			16	2 feet	24	....	724	22.6	....	....
			18	11.75 "	24	....	580	38.0	....	....
			19	20 "	24	....	514	45.1	....	....
			20	2 "	48	30.0	504	46.1	....	....
			22	11.75 "	48	33.5	338	63.9	....	....
			23	20 "	48	31.0	228	75.6	....	....
4	June 4	0.0	24	River	0	....	320	....	....	....
			25	2 feet	24	29.2	220	31.3	....	....
			27	11.75 "	24	33.0	218	31.9	....	....
			28	20 "	24	35.8	150	53.1	....	....
			29	2 "	48	32.8	186	41.9	....	....
			31	11.75 "	48	34.8	122	61.9	....	....
			32	20 "	48	36.0	92	71.2	....	....
5	June 6	0.0	33	River	0	....	220	....	6 100	....
			34	2 feet	24	....	146	33.6	....	....
			36	11.75 "	24	....	130	40.9	....	....
			37	20 "	24	....	118	46.4	....	....
			38	2 "	48	29.8	114	48.2	2 900	52.4
			40	11.75 "	48	32.0	88	60.0	2 700	55.7
			41	20 "	48	33.7	80	63.6	500	91.8
6	June 10	4.0	(626)	River	0	....	413	....	12 700	....
			50	2 feet	1	....	17	95.9	1 600	87.4
			51	6 "	1	....	19	95.4	1 000	92.1
			52	11.75 "	1	....	20	95.1	1 300	89.8
			53	20 "	1	....	19	95.4	400	96.9
			54	2 "	3	....	9	97.8	....	....
			57	20 "	3	....	10	97.7	....	....
			58	11.75 "	7	....	15	95.1	900	92.9
7	June 10	0.0	59	River	0	....	298	....	....	....
			60	2 feet	18	....	256	14.1	....	....
			61	11.75 "	18	....	198	33.6	....	....
			62	20 "	18	....	152	45.6	....	....
8	June 11	3.0	63	River	0	....	296	....	8 500	....
			64	2 feet	1	....	19	93.6	700	91.8
			66	20 "	1	....	18	93.9	400	95.3
			67	2 "	3	....	11	96.3	....	....
			69	20 "	3	....	11	96.3	....	....
			70	11.75 "	4.5	....	9	97.0	....	....
9	June 11	2.0	71	River	0	....	252	....	....	....
			72	2 feet	1	....	18	92.8	....	....
			73	11.75 "	1	....	14	94.4	....	....
			74	20 "	1	....	11	95.6	....	....
			75	2 "	3	....	4	98.4	....	....
			77	20 "	3	....	3	98.8	....	....
			78	11.75 "	6	....	3	98.8	....	....
			79	11.75 "	12	....	2	99.2	....	....
			80	11.75 "	16	....	2	99.2	....	....
10	June 12	2.0	(632)	River	0	....	234	....	4 100	....
			81	2 feet	1	....	19	91.9	500	87.8
			83	20 "	1	....	19	91.9	300	92.7
			84	2 "	3	....	6	97.4	....	....
			86	20 "	3	....	6	97.4	....	....
11	June 12	3.0	87	River	0	....	245	....	....	....
			88	2 feet	1	....	10	95.9	....	....

RESULTS OF SEDIMENTATION EXPERIMENTS.—*Continued.*

Experiment.		Applied Sulphate of Alumina. Grains per Gallon.	Sample.		Period of Subsidence. Hours.	Temperature. Degrees C.	Suspended Solids.		Bacteria.	
Number.	Date. 1896.		Number.	Source.			Parts per Million.	Per Cent Removed.	Per Cubic Centimeter.	Per Cent Removed.
11	June 12	3.0	90	20 feet	1	....	8	96.7	....	....
			91	2 "	3	....	10	96.2	....	....
			93	20 "	3	....	2	99.2	....	....
12	June 13	1.0	94	River.	0	....	209	....	10 100	....
			95	2 feet	1	....	50	78.0	1 900	71.2
			96	11.75 "	1	....	45	80.3	2 600	74.3
			97	20 "	1	....	43	81.2	2 400	76.2
			98	2 "	3	....	41	83.0	1 200	88.1
			99	11.75 "	3	....	37	84.6	1 000	90.1
			100	20 "	3	....	25	89.6	1 000	90.1
			101	11.75 "	6	....	25	89.6	800	92.1
			102	11.75 "	27	....	11	95.4	900	91.1
			103	11.75 "	50	....	9	96.3	....	....
13	June 15	1.0	(642)	River.	0	....	46	....	14 100	....
			104	2 feet	3	....	11	97.4	500	96.6
			105	20 "	3	....	6	98.6	100	99.3
			106	11.75 "	19	....	4	99.0	....	....
14	June 16	0.5	(646)	River.	0	....	220	....	8 800	....
			107	2 feet	1	....	57	74.1	3 200	63.6
			108	20 "	1	....	51	76.8	2 700	69.3
			109	2 "	3	....	32	80.3	3 100	64.7
			110	20 "	3	....	32	80.3	1 700	80.7
15	June 17	1.0	111	River.	0	....	248	....	8 300	....
			112	2 feet	1	....	64	74.2	3 800	54.3
			113	20 "	1	....	71	71.4	4 100	50.6
			114	2 "	3	....	35	85.9	1 100	86.7
			115	20 "	3	....	28	88.7	2 300	72.3
16	June 17	0.5	116	River.	0	....	266	....	14 100	....
			117	2 feet	1	....	266	0	11 700	13.0
			118	20 "	1	....	220	17.4	7 100	49.6
			119	2 "	3	....	98	63.2	....	....
			120	20 "	3	....	96	63.9	....	....
			121	11.75 "	18	....	49	81.6	1 900	86.5
17	June 18	1.5	(651)	River.	0	....	278	....	9 600	....
			122	2 feet	1.5	....	23	91.8	800	91.7
			123	20 "	1.5	....	15	93.5	1 000	89.6
			124	2 "	3.5	....	12	95.7	....	....
			125	20 "	3.5	....	3	98.9	....	....
18	June 18	0.25	126	River.	0	....	299	....	11 600	....
			127	2 feet	1	....	299	0	12 200	....
			128	20 "	1	....	296	1.0	9 200	20.8
			129	2 "	3	....	297	0.7	3 000	74.2
			130	20 "	3	....	271	9.4	6 000	40.6
			131	11.75 "	20	....	145	51.4	....	....
19	June 19	0.25	(655)	River.	0	....	420	....	14 900	....
			132	2 feet	1	....	84	80.0	3 800	74.5
			133	20 "	1	....	84	80.0	5 400	63.8
			134	2 "	3	....	27	93.5	1 500	90.0
			135	20 "	3	....	23	94.6	....	....
20	June 19	0.75	136	River.	0	....	427	....	6 300	....
			137	2 feet	1	....	353	19.3	4 600	27.0
			138	20 "	1	....	325	23.9	5 000	20.7
			139	2 "	3	....	199	53.5	....	....
			140	20 "	3	....	182	57.4	4 500	28.6
			141	11.75 "	20	....	80	81.3	....	....
21	June 20	2.0	(658)	River.	0	....	297	....	11 400	....
			142	2 feet	1	....	37	87.5	1 200	89.8
			143	20 "	1	....	24	91.8	1 100	90.0
			144	2 "	3	....	18	94.0	900	92.8
			145	20 "	3	....	17	94.2	300	97.4
22	June 20	1.0	146	River.	0	25.8	270	....	9 700	....
			147	2 feet	1	28.0	46	82.9	3 500	63.9
			148	20 "	1	35.5	48	82.2	2 500	74.2
			149	2 "	3	....	21	92.2	2 200	77.3
			150	20 "	3	....	3	98.8	2 700	72.4
23	June 20	0.0	151	River.	0	26.0	261	....	11 200	....
			152	2 feet	22	29.0	199	23.7	....	....
			153	11.75 "	22	33.1	140	44.1	....	....

RESULTS OF SEDIMENTATION EXPERIMENTS.—*Continued.*

Experiment.		Applied Sulphate of Alumina. Grains per Gallon.	Sample.		Period of Subsidence. Hours.	Temperature. Degrees C.	Suspended Solids.		Bacteria.	
Number.	Date. 1896.		Number.	Source.			Parts per Million.	Per Cent Removed.	Per Cubic Centimeter.	Per Cent Removed.
23	June 20	0.0	154	20 feet	22	37.2	129	52.6	....	....
			155	2 "	48	....	125	52.1	3 900	65.2
			156	11.75 "	48	....	67	74.3	900	92.0
			157	20 "	48	....	48	81.6	900	92.0
24	June 23	3.0	(660)	River	0	26.2	235	....	9 400	....
			158	2 feet	1	26.2	31	86.8	400	95.7
			159	20 "	1	30.0	25	89.3	500	94.7
			160	2 "	3	....	9	96.2	....	....
			161	20 "	3	....	5	97.8	....	....
25	June 23	1.0	162	River	0	27.0	218	....	8 000	....
			163	2 feet	1	27.0	42	80.7	4 600	42.5
			164	20 "	1	32.0	39	82.1	3 900	51.3
			165	2 "	3	....	32	85.3	2 200	72.5
			166	20 "	3	....	32	85.3	....	....
26	June 24	2.0	(668)	River	0	27.4	446	....	5 100	....
			167	2 feet	1	27.0	54	87.7	3 100	39.2
			168	20 "	1	36.5	41	90.6	8 000	....
			169	2 "	3	....	22	94.8	4 400	13.7
			170	20 "	3	....	22	94.8	4 200	17.6
27	June 24	0.75	171	River	0	....	267	....	13 800	....
			172	2 feet	1	....	148	59.6	8 100	41.4
			173	20 "	1	....	147	59.8	11 200	18.8
			174	2 "	3	....	58	84.1	7 800	43.5
			175	20 "	3	....	58	84.1	10 200	26.0
			176	11.75 "	20	....	19	94.8	2 800	69.7
28	June 25	0.75	(678)	River	0	27.3	321	....	5 300	....
			177	2 feet	1	....	121	62.2	....	....
			178	20 "	1	....	109	66.1	2 400	54.7
			179	2 "	3	....	46	85.5	2 000	56.6
			180	20 "	3	....	35	89.1	3 800	28.2
			181	11.75 "	24	....	28	91.2	500	90.6
29	June 26	0.75	(681)	River	0	....	296	....	6 000	....
			182	2 feet	1	....	193	34.8	2 400	60.0
			183	20 "	1	....	114	58.2	2 300	61.6
			184	2 "	3	....	52	82.4	700	88.3
			185	20 "	3	....	48	83.7	1 400	76.6
			186	11.75 "	24	....	24	92.0	400	93.3
30	June 27	0.75	(684)	River	0	26.5	358	....	7 900	....
			187	2 feet	1	27.0	358	0.	6 100	22.8
			188	20 "	1	36.0	232	35.2	7 700	2.6
			189	2 "	3	....	100	72.1	4 300	45.6
			190	20 "	3	....	88	75.3	....	....
			191	11.75 "	30	....	32	91.0	....	....
			192	11.75 "	48	....	18	95.1	400	94.9
31	June 29	0.0	(686)	River	0	25.5	505	....	12 500	....
			193	2 feet	3	26.0	493	2.4	10 900	12.8
			194	20 "	3	34.8	465	7.9	9 200	26.5
			195	2 "	24	....	276	45.3	3 000	76.0
			196	20 "	24	....	193	61.8	4 200	66.4
32	July 1	0.0	(692)	River	0	26.5	856	....	....	....
			202	2 feet	24	29.3	435	49.2	8 400	....
			203	20 "	24	38.2	336	60.7	4 200	....
33	July 2	1.0	204	River	0	23.5	636	....	6 200	....
			205	2 feet	1	25.8	1 552	5.2	....	....
			206	20 "	1	31.3	1 385	15.3	....	....
			207	2 "	3	....	1 248	23.7	....	....
			208	20 "	3	....	796	51.3	....	....
			209	11.75 "	17	....	430	73.8	....	....
34	July 6	2.0	(704)	River	0	26.3	244	....	6 300	....
			210	2 feet	1	26.0	40	83.6	2 200	65.0
			211	20 "	1	34.5	30	87.7	1 300	79.4
			212	2 "	3	....	12	95.1	1 100	82.5
			213	20 "	3	....	8	96.7	600	90.5
35	July 6	0.75	214	River	0	....	395	....	9 500	....
			215	2 feet	1	....	209	47.1	7 100	25.2
			216	20 "	1	....	199	49.5	7 400	22.0
			217	2 "	3	....	115	70.9	3 600	62.1
			218	20 "	3	....	103	73.9	4 100	56.8

RESULTS OF SEDIMENTATION EXPERIMENTS.—*Concluded.*

Experiment.		Applied Sulphate of Alumina. Grains per Gallon.	Sample.		Period of Subsidence, Hours.	Temperature. Degrees C.	Suspended Solids.		Bacteria.	
Number.	Date. 1896.		Number.	Source.			Parts per Million.	Per Cent Removed.	Per Cubic Centimeter.	Per Cent Removed.
35	July 6	0.75	219	11.75 feet	20	....	72	81.6	....	....
36	July 7	0.75	(707)	River	0	33.0	525	....	5 400	....
			222	2 feet	3	26.5	438	16.5	3 700	31.5
			223	20 "	3	25.4	388	26.1	6 400	....
			224	11.75 "	24	34.0	229	56.3	3 500	35.2
			225	11.75 "	48	34.3	177	66.2	1 100	79.6
			226	11.75 "	72	35.7	153	70.8	2 400	55.5
37	July 10	1.5	(720)	River	0	26.2	387	....	8 200	....
			227	11.75 feet	24	34.6	21	45.7	1 300	84.1
38	July 11	0.75	(723)	River	0	26.0	208	....	6 800	....
			230	2 feet	3	27.3	166	20.2	7 500	8.5
			231	20 "	3	37.5	154	26.0	5 500	32.8
			232	11.75 "	28	....	74	64.4	....	....
			233	11.75 "	46	34.6	61	70.7	10 100	....
			234	11.75 "	70	35.8	42	79.8	600	....
39	July 14	1.5	(730)	River.	0	26.2	402	....	12 000	....
			235	11.75 feet	24	35.8	28	93.0	1 000	91.6
40	July 18	0.0	(744)	River	0	25.7	637	....	7 600	....
			248	11.75 feet	72	33.4	202	68.2	2 100	72.4
			249	11.75 "	120	35.5	142	77.7	600	92.1
			250	11.75 "	144	36.7	131	79.4	700	90.8
41	July 24	0.0	(767)	River	0	25.5	3 347	....	34 100	....
			251	11.75 feet	24	32.9	872	74.0	5 100	85.0
			252	11.75 "	144	38.9	195	94.2	10	99.9

NUMBER OF BACTERIA PER CUBIC CENTIMETER IN THE OHIO RIVER WATER AFTER PASSAGE THROUGH THE DISTRIBUTING RESERVOIR AND A PORTION OF THE DISTRIBUTING PIPE OF THE LOUISVILLE WATER COMPANY.

In the next table are recorded the results of bacterial analyses of tap water collected in the city of Louisville. In all cases the water was allowed to run from the faucet for some minutes before the sample was collected. The place of collection was 419 West Chestnut Street up to Feb. 1, 1896, and at 820 South Second Street for the remainder of the time.

On its way to the city the river water is pumped to the Crescent Hill Reservoir, which has a capacity of 100 million gallons, equivalent to about six times the average daily consumption of the city.

The chief value of these results is that they show a removal by subsidence and passage through the distributing pipes of about 80 per cent. of the bacteria originally present in the water as it was pumped from the river. In this connection reference may be made to the results of bacterial analyses of the river water already presented in Chapter I.

NUMBER OF BACTERIA PER CUBIC CENTIMETER IN THE TAP-WATER OF THE CITY OF LOUISVILLE, BY DAYS, IN 1895–96.

Days.	November.	December.	January.	February.	March.	April.	May.	June.	July.
1	128	....	....	5 400	....	6 300	1 000	1 600	....
2	116	284	1 500	....	....	4 600	1 200	1 100	800
3	....	322	2 800	....	6 900	4 500	....	....	1 900
4	132	679	1 700	5 300	6 900	6 700	800	1 500	....
5	108	1 848	....	5 600	6 300	....	2 000	1 100	....
6	119	2 500	2 100	6 700	2 000	6 900	1 500	900	1 800
7	....	....	3 100	....	3 000	12 200	1 300	....	3 200
8	178	....	1 700	1 100	....	4 800	....	1 500	1 500
9	228	1 710	400	....	8 000	....	....	1 700	2 000
10	....	2 000	400	1 200	7 800	3 800	....	1 900	....
11	118	1 400	500	4 100	12 500	2 100	4 700	1 000	....
12	118	1 900	....	5 100	9 900	....	400	....	....
13	104	1 000	400	3 500	6 200	2 000	1 300	2 200	2 300
14	120	1 100	400	12 100	8 000	900	1 000	....	2 200
15	136	....	....	1 800	....	2 200	1 200	2 200	2 100
16	164	780	500	....	14 800	....	1 200	3 700	1 000
17	....	640	800	3 800	10 000	600	....	2 600	1 000
18	368	1 100	800	....	1 400	5 300	900	1 600	700
19	212	700	....	3 300	2 200	....	1 500	1 800	....
20	321	1 300	1 400	4 800	3 300	4 000	9 700	2 700	2 100
21	116	1 200	900	4 500	800	1 200	....	....	1 100
22	588	....	900	8 300	....	5 400	900	1 200	....
23	204	500	900	....	1 300	1 600	500	....	1 000
24	....	370	1 500	3 000	3 400	700	....	1 200	....
25	288	....	400	6 300	7 300	1 100	400	1 700	2 000
26	354	380	....	6 900	14 000	....	700	....	....
27	456	700	1 000	1 300	7 100	1 300	1 800	2 000	3 500
28	....	950	300	1 400	11 700	2 300	600	....	....
29	418	....	800	10 900	8 200	600	600	1 900	3 900
30	520	290	....	....	7 000	2 000	1 600	900	2 200
31	....	1 200	800	....	1 500	....	....	....	1 200

CHAPTER V.

Description of the Filters through which the River Water Passed after Coagulation by Aluminum Hydrate and Partial Purification by Sedimentation.

It has already been explained in the introduction that this method of purification consisted of several parts, each of which, to quite a degree, was distinct in its nature and in its application. The last part of the process is the passage of the water downward through a layer of sand either by gravity or pressure, in order to remove from the water the bacteria, aluminum hydrate, mud, clay, and other suspended matters.

This final operation is properly called filtration. It is erroneous, however, to speak of the entire process as filtration, or mechanical filtration, because, so far as waters like the Ohio River are concerned, filtration is only one of several steps in a process of economical purification.

This (American) type of filtration differs in several respects from the older (English) type of filtration which has been adopted and studied in Europe and several places in this country. There are two chief differences, namely:

1. In American filters the aluminum hydrate remaining in the water as it flows from the settling chamber to the filter, by virtue of its gelatinous nature, enveloping the bacteria and other suspended matters, makes it practicable to allow the water to pass through the sand at a much more rapid rate than in the case of English filters.

2. In American filters the accumulation of matters which are removed from the water by the sand (bacteria, aluminum hydrate, mud, clay, and other suspended matters) is in turn removed from the sand by the passage of a reverse current of water through the sand from the bottom to the top, either with or without accompanying agitation of the sand. The corresponding accumulations in English filters of foreign matter from the water, located for the most part at and near the surface of the sand, are removed, practically speaking, by scraping the surface of the sand layer with a shovel or similar implement to a depth ordinarily of 0.5 inch or thereabouts.

By corresponding accumulations on the sand in the English filters is meant, ordinarily, the various kinds of material noted, with the exception of the aluminum hydrate; although it is not to be forgotten that aluminum hydrate, formed from the decomposition of alum added to river water, was used for some years in Holland in connection with the purification of public water supplies by English filters.

The systems which were investigated during these tests are included in the American type of filtration and are all divided into three main divisions. Each division includes the devices used for carrying out one step of the process, and it is to be noted that it was only in the design and construction of these devices that these systems differed. These divisions may be outlined as follows:

1. An arrangement for the preparation and delivery of the chemicals. This included preparation tanks; pumps or other devices for delivering the solutions to the river water; pipes and fittings; valves and other regulating devices; scales, gauges, hydrometers, etc.

2. A chamber or basin for the reception of the treated water and in which coagulation and sedimentation took place to a greater or less degree. This included all the necessary inlet, outlet, and drain pipes, and the devices used for controlling the flow of water through the basin.

3. A filter and appurtenances. This division included a tank which contained the sand layer and water to be filtered; a system of strainers for removing the water from the sand; a system for distributing the wash-water beneath the sand layer; and, in the case of the Warren and Jewell systems, a set of rakes with operating mechanism for stirring the sand. All piping, valves, and regulating devices which pertained to the filter are included in this division.

In Chapter II the devices included in the first division have been described in considerable detail. The second division has been presented in Chapter IV, and it now remains to present the third division, which is the subject of this chapter.

In the next chapter will be found a summary of the principal parts of which each division of each system was composed, together with a record of the repairs, changes, and delays noted during these tests.

The manner of operation of these systems is given in Chapter VII, where a more complete description of the special regulating devices is also presented.

The filters of the respective systems are described in the order which has been followed heretofore.

All elevations used are in feet and refer to the bottom of the respective sand layers as the datum plane. The accompanying drawings will facilitate an understanding of the several filters and their respective appurtenances.

The Warren Filter and Appurtenances.

The filter was placed in a circular wooden tank. About 1.5 feet from the bottom was the strainer system, which was made of perforated copper plates with suitable wooden supports. The layer of sand which was used as a filtering medium was placed upon the strainer system. Above the sand there was an open compartment which contained the water to be filtered. During filtration the water passed by gravity from the upper compartment through the sand layer and strainer system into a closed compartment situated between the strainer system and the bottom of the tank, from which a pipe connected with the weir box, where the rate of filtration was regulated. For washing, the water was removed from the upper compartment and wash-water admitted under pressure into the lower chamber, from which it forced its way up through the sand. After passage through the sand the wash-water was removed from the upper compartment by drain pipes. During washing the sand was stirred by rakes which were supported at the top of the tank. Plans and sections of the Warren System will be found on Plates II and III, respectively.

Filter Tank.—The filter tank was made of alternate cypress and pine staves, the bottom being entirely of cypress. It was 10.6 feet in diameter on the inside and 9.75 feet deep inside. The staves were 2.62 inches thick and 6 inches wide. They were strongly bound with iron hoops, six in number. The hoops were 0.6 inch thick and 2 inches wide.

About 1.5 feet from the bottom of the tank were wooden pieces which served as a support for a copper strainer floor. In the open compartment above the perforated copper floor was the layer of sand. The closed compartment beneath the copper floor was the filtered-water chamber, through which the filtered water passed as it made its exit from the filter. The filtered water used for washing the filter also passed through this closed compartment as it was pumped upward through the sand.

From the bottom of the tank a central well 4.33 feet in height extended through the filtered-water chamber, strainer floor, and the sand layer. For a distance of 1.17 feet from the bottom the diameter of this well was 2.42 feet, and above this point 1.71 feet.

Across the top of the tank lay two timbers, one 12 by 12 inches and the other 6 by 12 inches, on which rested the bulk of the appliances for the operation of the agitator. The main vertical shaft, to which the rakes were fastened, was supported at the top by these timbers and guided at the bottom by a casting on the upper end of the central well.

The height of water above the sand during filtration was normally about 5.75 feet. As described beyond, the total available acting head was 4.17 feet.

The above description in general terms shows the relation to each other of the various devices located in the filter tank. The details of these devices and their piping connections are as follows:

Inlet Water-pipe.—The main inlet water-pipe was 8 inches in diameter and conducted the water by gravity from the outlet of the settling basin. This pipe led into and across the bottom of the filtered-water chamber, at the bottom of the filter tank, and connected with the central well by a flange joint.

Arrangement for the Exit of the Filtered Water.—After passage through the sand the water passed through the strainer system, composed of perforated copper plates and wooden supports; next through the filtered-water chamber; and thence through an 8-inch pipe to the weir box. From the weir box the water passed through about 65 feet of 5-inch pipe to the filtered-water reservoir.

Strainer System.—The original strainer system consisted of punched copper plates supported by a network of radial and circumferential wooden braces. Details of the arrangement of these braces can best be understood by an examination of the accompanying drawings (Plates II, III, VIII).

The radial supports were 2.25 by 2.75 inches, with the long side set vertically. They were supported at the center on a shoulder made for that purpose in the central well, and at the periphery on a ring made of short wooden sections nailed to the inside of the tank. They fitted tightly together at the central well and were 7 inches apart at the periphery. On top of these supports was laid a second set of ribs, each 1.37 by 0.75 inches, with the long side set vertically. Between this upper set of ribs were laid pieces 1.25 by 0.75 inches, set perpendicular to the radius at their center.

These circumferential spacers were supported at each end by the main radial beams, and were level on top with the upper radial strips. The spacers were not accurately circumferential, but were really a series of short chords.

The perforated copper plates were placed on top of the ribs and spacers, and were fastened to them. They were made in sections of the size of the space subtended by the radial ribs. The joints of the plates were over these ribs and were protected by copper strips 1.12 inches wide.

Exit Area.—The orifice area of the copper-plate system was made up of about 681,900 punched holes. These holes averaged 0.043 inch (1.1 millimeter) in diameter. They averaged 10.5 per linear inch radially, and 7.5 per linear inch at right angles thereto.

The size and spacing varied considerably, but the above figures are averages of numerous determinations at different parts of the strainer area. Using these figures as a basis of computation, the total orifice area of the copper-plate system, including all holes exposed on the upper side, was 1032 square inches. No possible method of determining how much water passed through the holes directly over the supports was found. It seems probable, however, that the weight of the sand would press the plates sufficiently close to the supports to obstruct the passage of water to a considerable extent. Deducting all such holes, the net area was 923 square inches.

On April 12, 1896, a finer sand was put in service, and it was found to be too fine to use with the original perforated copper plates described above. Accordingly an auxiliary strainer device, consisting of a fine brass gauze, was added. This gauze was laid directly over the copper plates, the same copper strips being used to keep it in place. Owing to inability to secure readily a sufficient quantity of gauze of the desired size two sizes were used. The first portion, which was used to cover about 80 per cent. of the area, had 65 meshes to the linear inch. For the remaining 20 per cent. of the area a gauze which had 80 meshes per linear inch was used.

By the introduction of the brass gauze the determination of the available exit area of the strainer system was complicated. There were two extreme areas which may be considered, the true area utilized being somewhere between the two, apparently.

1. The brass gauze may be assumed to have reduced the exit area of the perforated copper plates. In this case the gauze is assumed to have allowed water to pass through only those portions of it which were directly above the holes in the copper plate.

2. It may be assumed that the entire exit

area of the holes in the copper plates was available, and that the water could in all cases pass more or less freely between the gauze and the copper plates.

The second supposition appears to be more nearly correct, because, no matter how closely the gauze was pressed upon the copper plate, unless the wires were flattened, innumerable channels must have existed through which the water could flow more or less freely.

Filtered-water Chamber.—Directly beneath the strainer floor and forming the bottom of the filter tank was a closed compartment which was used as a collecting chamber for the filtered water, and also as a distributing chamber for the wash-water. It was simply the space left in the construction of the tank, no finishing being used.

The total depth of the chamber was 1.5 feet, but the upper part was largely obstructed by the braces of the strainer floor, below which the depth was 1.1 feet.

The area of the base of this chamber was somewhat less than that of the main tank, on account of restrictions by the wooden rim which supported the outer side of the strainer floor and by the central well. The area was 70.6 square feet.

The total capacity of the chamber was 94.7 cubic feet, including the spaces between the supports of the strainer floor.

The chamber could be drained through the waste-water pipe to within 0.6 foot of the bottom. No arrangements were made for complete draining.

A small hand-hole was provided in one side of the tank for the purpose of inspection.

The only method for cleaning was by forcing filtered water into the chamber and allowing it to flow out through the waste-water pipe.

Weir Box.—The weir box was an open, rectangular compartment constructed at the northwest corner of the settling basin, and built in connection therewith of the same material. It was connected with the filtered-water chamber by an 8-inch pipe, 8 feet in length.

It was 5.71 feet long by 2.75 feet wide, inside dimensions. The weir partition ran across the short dimension, dividing the box into an inlet and an outlet side. The inlet side was 2.67 by 2.75 feet, and the outlet 3.04 by 2.75 feet. As first constructed the weir was a fixed one with its crest approximately at an elevation of 6.00 feet. On Nov. 25 it was lowered to approximately 5.5 feet.

With other changes previous to Nov. 25 a movable weir was inserted. This weir was made of an iron plate moving in guides at the sides, its position being controlled by a worm shaft operated by a wheel on the floor over the settling basin. It had an available vertical movement from an elevation of 3.85 to the maximum water level (elev. 8.02), a distance of 4.17 feet. The nominal crest was 2.1 feet wide, but on account of leakage in the guides its actual width was probably about 2.5 feet.

A 3-inch valve connecting the two sides was put in the bottom of the weir box Feb. 12 to allow more complete draining of the filter before washing. The center of this valve was at elevation —1.13. From the weir box the water flowed through about 65 feet of 5-inch pipe to the filtered-water reservoir.

Outlet for Filtered Waste Water.—At such times as in the opinion of the operator the filtered water was not of a satisfactory character, a 3-inch pipe leading from the filtered-water chamber to the sewer was used in place of the main outlet through the weir box.

Sand Layer.

During the test several changes were made in the sand layer, the kind of sand, the thickness of the layer, and the area of the surface, all having been changed.

Kinds of Sand Used.—At the opening of the test the sand layer was composed of sand No. 1. This was removed Jan. 22, and sand No. 2 put in place and used up to April 13. On April 17 sand No. 3 was put in place. This was used up to July 25, when 2 inches of sand containing 23 parts of No. 3 and one part of a very fine sand were added. No. 1 was natural sand; the other two were crushed quartz. Mechanical analyses of these sands gave results which are presented on the next page.

Thickness of Sand Layer.—The thickness of the sand layer varied from three causes:

1. Addition of sand by the operators of the filter.

MECHANICAL ANALYSES OF THE SANDS USED IN THE WARREN FILTER.

	No. 1.	No. 2.	No. 3.
	Per cent. by weight.		
Finer than 2.04 millimeters......	100.	100.	100.
" " 0.93 "	100.	15.0	95.5
" " 0.462 "	4.2	0.2	6.5
" " 0.316 "	0.3	....	0.9
" " 0.182 "	0.1	....	....
Effective size { Ten per cent finer than diameter in millimeters.................. }	0.56	....	0.51

2. Losses of some of the finer portions of the sand during the process of washing.

3. Increased compactness of the sand layer.

At different places on the surface of the sand layer the thickness varied owing to the action of the rake-teeth of the agitator. As the agitator revolved during washing a small portion of the sand was moved from the central part of the layer towards the periphery. The effect of this action was cumulative. Observations made on Jan. 20, Feb. 14, April 13, May 22, and July 17 showed differences in the elevations of the surface of the layer at the central well and at the periphery, ranging from 1 to 4 inches.

On Nov. 25, 1895, the average thickness of the sand layer was about 2.36 feet. This thickness was increased on Jan. 3, 1896, by the addition of 0.6 inch of new sand (No. 1).

The average thickness of the layer of sand No. 2 on Jan. 25 was 1.86 feet. On Feb. 12 this thickness was increased to 2.25 feet.

With the third lot of sand the thickness of the layer when new, April 17, was 2.17 feet; on May 22, 2.12 feet; and on July 17, 2.00 feet.

On July 25, 0.25 foot of mixed sand was added.

The average thickness at the close of the test was 2.25 feet.

Area.—As first arranged the sand layer extended to the wall of the filter tank and the surface area of the sand was equal to the area of the filter tank, excepting the central well. 1.8 feet in diameter. This area was approximately 85.70 square feet. Practically all of the tests were made after the completion on Nov. 25 of a new collecting gutter to carry the wash-water to the sewer-pipe. This made the diameter of the sand layer 10.1 feet including the central well above noted.

Allowing 2 square inches for each of 16 teeth which extended into the sand bed during filtration, the net area of the surface of the sand was 77.36 square feet.

From April 17 to July 25 the rake-teeth barely pierced the sand layer, thus increasing the area to 77.50 square feet.

Device for Cleaning the Sand Layer.

The device for cleaning the sand layer by washing comprised the following principal parts which are described in turn below:

1. Pipes through which filtered water was pumped from the filtered-water reservoir into the filtered-water chamber, and thence through the strainer system into the bottom of the sand layer.

2. Auxiliary slotted pipes, located at the bottom of the sand layer just above the strainer system, through which for a short time part of the wash-water was pumped, with the view to getting more uniform distribution.

3. A collecting gutter and pipes to carry to the sewer the last portion of the water on the sand layer just after draining the filter prior to washing, and the wash-water after it had passed through the sand layer.

4. An agitator with the necessary mechanism for stirring the sand during the process of washing.

5. An engine, with pulleys, belting, and shafts, to operate the agitator.

Wash-water Supply Pipe.—The wash-water taken from the filtered-water reservoir was pumped through an 8-inch pipe. This arrangement was used by all the filters in common. From the pump to a point on this pipe where a separate pipe branched to the Warren System was about 100 feet; a 4-inch pipe 10 feet in length led from this point to the filtered-water chamber beneath the sand. At first a 3-inch valve was located on this pipe just outside the filter tank.

With this 3-inch valve on the 4-inch pipe the distribution of wash-water was not satisfactory. The restriction in the pipe caused by the small valve gave something of a nozzle effect, so that the stream of water entered the filtered-water chamber with sufficient velocity to strike the outer wall of the central well, and be deflected up through a comparatively small area of the strainer system and of the sand layer. To remedy this difficulty, and to increase the loss of pressure in the piping, the 3-inch valve was replaced on Feb. 12 by a 4-inch valve.

Auxiliary Slotted Pipes for the Distribution of Wash-water.—In addition to putting a larger valve on the wash-water pipe on Feb. 12, there were also introduced at the same time supplementary pipes to convey a portion of the wash-water to different points at the bottom of the sand layer.

A 2-inch brass pipe branched from the main wash-water supply just outside the filter tank, the flow being regulated by a 2-inch valve. This pipe entered the tank above the perforated copper floor on which the sand rested. It connected directly with a ring of 2-inch iron pipe made of tees and eighth bends.

The water was distributed by six 1-inch slotted tubes of brass and the inlet pipe noted above, which was also slotted. The seven pipes or tubes were laid radially, spaced equally around the central well, and fitted into the respective tees in the iron ring encircling the central well.

Two rows of longitudinal slots 90° apart extended the entire length of each tube. They averaged 2 inches in length, 0.031 inch in width, and were approximately 3 inches apart. All of the tubes were capped at the ends, and in the center of each cap was a hole 0.031 inch in diameter. The tubes were first set with the slots on the under side, with the center of the tube 2.25 inches above the perforated copper bottom at the inner end and 3 inches above at the outer end.

On Feb. 19 the tubes were reversed, bringing the slots on the upper side. The entire device was removed on Feb. 21.

Collecting Gutter and Central Well.—The circular collecting gutter was constructed of wood and galvanized sheet iron. A lining of pine staves 0.25 foot thick, extending from the strainer floor to 2.35 feet above it, was placed inside the filter tank. On the side of the lining towards the inner well a strip of galvanized iron was tacked, its upper edge extending 0.5 foot above the staves. The space thus formed between the metal strip and the main wall of the tank was used as a gutter. The upper edge of the metal strip, or, in other words, the discharge level, was at elevation 2.85 feet. At three equidistant points conections were made with this gutter to a 3-inch pipe which partially encircled the filter tank on the outside.

This 3-inch pipe connected by means of a special casting with a branch from the inlet pipe from the settling basin to the filter, which in turn connected with the sewer.

By means of a tee and suitable valves on the 6-inch inlet pipe to the filter, this pipe was connected with the sewer, thus allowing the use of the central well (1.8 feet in diameter) for the removal of unfiltered waste and wash water.

During the tests the crest of the central well was changed three times. When the depth of the sand was increased on Feb. 12 the height of the well was also increased about 4 inches. It was lowered again on Feb. 14 to the original height in order to try the effect on the sand of discharging all the water during washing through the well. On Feb. 21 it was raised to the same level as the crest of the collecting gutter.

Agitator.—The agitator consisted essentially of two horizontal rake-arms with eight teeth each, and the necessary mechanism to raise and lower the rakes, and to revolve them as desired. Power was furnished by a small engine, and transmitted by a 6-inch belt to a counter-shaft, from which another belt 6 inches wide led to the driving pulley of the mechanism. For simplicity in presentation a general description of the operating mechanism is given, referring to each of the parts by serial numbers. Following this, the several parts are tabulated, and their leading dimensions given.

The rake-arms were hung on the main vertical shaft, which was supported at the upper end by the frame of the machine, and guided at the lower end by a collar on the top of the inlet well. This shaft was turned around by means of a large bevel gear (1), a lug on which fitted into a vertical slot in the shaft. By this arrangement the shaft could be raised or lowered without interfering with the rotary motion. To drive the gear, a pinion (2) on the shaft which carried the main driving pulley drove a gear (3) on a lower parallel horizontal shaft. At the end of this shaft was a bevel pinion (4) which drove the rotating gear. It will be noticed that this arrangement necessitated rotation of the main vertical shaft with its rakes whenever any part of the mechanism was in operation. For raising or lowering the main vertical shaft, power was transferred by gearing from the horizontal driving shaft to an upper parallel shaft, on the end of which a bevel pinion (5) drove the raising and lowering gears. For transferring the power two duplicate sets of gears connected the main driving shaft with the upper shaft. Either of these sets could be used as desired, or they could both be out of operation, hand levers controlling their position. Each set consisted of the driving gear (6); two idle gears (7) and (8), and the driven gear (9); (6) and (9) were the same for both sets, and (7) and (8) duplicates in each set. In the original machine gear (8) was omitted, the increased length of vertical motion of the modified machine, with its necessitated increase in height of the frame, requiring the introduction of the second gear.

The raising and lowering gear proper consisted of a large bevel gear (10), and a sleeve on the main shaft. This sleeve was made of babbitt metal cast on the main vertical shaft in the following manner: In the upper end of the main shaft (the lower end of which held the rake-arms) were cut nine circular slots, each 1 inch wide and 0.35 inch deep. The first one was 1.5 inches from the top of the shaft. Below this the slots were spaced 2.5 inches apart. On the shaft thus prepared was cast a sleeve of babbitt metal 0.75 inch thick and 25 inches long. In casting, a vertical slot 1.5 inches wide and 0.5 inch deep was left in this sleeve. This slot engaged a lug on the framework of the machine, and prevented rotation of the sleeve, the steel core (main shaft) rotating within the sleeve. On the face of the sleeve a helical thread was cut, with three threads to the inch; this formed the worm, which engaged and was driven by a similar thread on the inside of the lifting gear, that worked freely on a loose bearing plate. As above described, a bevel pinion on an upper horizontal shaft drove this gear.

For the purpose of stopping the vertical motion of the main shaft automatically, lugs were provided on the vertical shaft, which at the limits of motion (top or bottom) operated sets of levers, which disengaged the set of idle gears which were in operation, transferring power from the driving shaft to the upper parallel shaft.

The main dimensions of the gears and pinions numbered in the above description are as follows:

1. Bevel gear, 35 inches in diameter with 72 teeth.
2. Pinion, 5.75 inches in diameter with 14 teeth.
3. Gear, 26 inches in diameter with 50 teeth.
4. Bevel pinion, with 13 teeth.
5. Bevel pinion, with 15 teeth.
6. Gear, 4.25 inches in diameter with 24 teeth.
7. Gear, 6.25 inches in diameter with 36 teeth.
8. Gear, 8.25 inches in diameter with 48 teeth.
9. Gear, 8.25 inches in diameter with 48 teeth.
10. Bevel gear, 16.5 inches in diameter with 66 teeth.

Rakes.—Attached by means of a collar and socket bolts to the main vertical shaft were the rake-arms. These were two in number and were set 180° apart. Two shorter arms on the other diameter carried tie-rods to strengthen the rake-arms. The rake-teeth were of cast iron. The original teeth were 27 inches long, but later a change was made, and 35-inch teeth were inserted. There were eight teeth on each arm. They were wedge-shaped in section, the back being rounded. On the original teeth a wedge-shaped shoulder was cast 13.25 inches from the upper part of the teeth. This was not used in the longer teeth.

As first used, the rakes in the upper position were clear of the sand, and in the lower position they averaged 5 inches from the strainer floor. On Feb. 21 they were lowered so that they came within 2 inches of the floor, longer rakes being introduced at the same time to allow for this greater penetration. The lift of the original machine was found to be too small with this new arrangement to raise the rake-teeth clear of the sand; and on April 13 a new machine was put in service as noted above, giving approximately 8 inches greater lift of the rakes. At the close of the test with the sand layer 27 inches thick, the rake-teeth remained about 1 inch in the sand at the upper position.

Engine and Belting.—The engine was a Carlisle single-cylinder, fly-wheel engine. The size was 5.75 by 6 inches, with 77 per cent. cut-off. The engine drove a 6-inch belt over a 12-inch pulley 8.25 inches wide.

From the engine a 6-inch rubber belt drove a 20-inch pulley on a 2.5-inch counter-shaft. Another 6-inch belt from a 16-inch pulley on the counter-shaft drove an 18-inch pulley on the agitator machinery.

Elevations.

The different elevations in feet, referred to the bottom of the sand layer as the datum plane, were as follows:

Bottom of sand layer (top of strainer floor)	0.00
Floor of filtered-water chamber	−1.48
Sand surface (average, Aug. 1, 1896)	+2.27
Crest of central well and circular gutter	+2.85
Lower end of rake-teeth (agitator up)	+1.94
Top of filter tank	+8.27
Average maximum water level	+8.02
Lower floor (main-house floor)	−1.77
Center of inlet pipe at filter	−0.94
Center of outlet pipe at filter	−0.85
Center of wash- and waste-pipes at filter	−0.98
Lowest position of weir	+3.85
Highest position of weir (available as outlet	+8.02
Crest of outlet channel from settling basin (mudsill)	+6.72

THE JEWELL FILTER AND APPURTENANCES.

The layer of sand forming the filtering medium was held in a wooden tank set in the upper compartment of the main tank. The roof of the settling chamber served as a support for a layer of bricks and cement which covered the strainer manifold, and formed a support for the sand layer. Between the inner and outer tanks was a space which was used as a collecting gutter for draining. A central well connected the compartment above the sand with the settling chamber. During filtration the water passed downward through the sand and the strainer system by gravity. The total available acting head was about 14 feet, of which 5.5 feet were positive (above the bottom of the sand layer), and 8.5 negative. Plans and sections of this system are shown on Plates IV and V, respectively. The rate of filtration was regulated by valves on the pipe from the strainer system. When the filter required washing, the water in the compartment above the sand, about 2.5 feet deep, was removed and wash-water admitted to the strainer system under pressure. Wash-water was then forced up through the sand and discharged into the space between the two tanks, from which it was removed to the sewer. During washing the sand was stirred by a set of rakes supported by beams at the top of the main tank.

Filter Tank.—The filter tank was of cypress, 12.15 feet in inside diameter, 5.0 feet high on the outside, and 3.41 feet deep above the strainer floor. It was made of 3-inch staves and was strongly bound by three hoops, each 3 inches wide and 0.125 inch thick. At its bottom, the space between the filter tank and the main tank (about 0.3 foot wide) was filled by a wooden ring 0.33 foot thick. This ring served to brace the bottom of the staves, and also prevented any lateral movement. There was no floor in this tank, the staves resting upon the roof of the settling chamber. The spaces between the pipes of the strainer system were filled with a layer of brick and cement, supported by the roof of the settling chamber. This brick and cement layer in turn supported the sand.

The strainer system, consisting of a set of pipes to collect the water from the cups, and cups through which the water passed from the sand layer, was laid on the roof of the settling chamber, and covered by the layer of bricks and cement, the face of which was flush with the top of the strainer cups.

The set of parallel pipes were all connected to a special cast-iron pipe which ran across the filter tank. On one side this casting was connected by a suitable joint with the outlet pipe. This pipe conveyed the water to the outside of the main tank, where it connected with a cross, which was also connected to the outlet pipe leading to the filtered-water reservoir; to the waste-water pipe leading to the sewer; and the wash-water supply pipe. A central well extended from the settling chamber through the strainer floor and the sand layer to about 1.4 feet above the sand.

At the top of the main tank were two timbers, on which rested the bulk of the appliances for the operation of the agitator. These timbers were supported at either end by suitable iron brackets fastened on the inside of the wall of the main tank, the upper face of the timbers being flush with the top of the main tank. Ordinarily the water above the sand layer partly submerged these timbers. The main vertical shaft, to which were fastened the rake-arms of the agitator, was supported at the top by these timbers, and guided at the bottom by a ring on the inlet well.

The above description in general terms shows the relation to each other of the various devices located in the filter tank. The details of these devices and the piping connections were as follows:

Inlet Water-pipe.—The inlet water-pipe was a central well 0.67 foot in diameter and 4.5 feet high. It was made of cast iron.

Arrangements for the Exit of the Filtered Water.—After passage through the sand the water passed through the strainer system, consisting of 444 strainer cups and suitable collecting pipes, to a connection with a 5-inch pipe. This pipe connected with a cross outside the filter. From the cross there were about 8 feet of 4-inch pipe leading to the automatic controller, from which about 65 feet of 5-inch pipe led to the filtered-water reservoir.

Strainer System.—The strainer system consisted of brass strainer cups screwed into a set of collecting pipes. The shape and size of these cups, of which there were 444, is shown on the drawings. The face of the cup was covered with a punched aluminum bronze plate, the plate being secured to the cup by a ring which was riveted to the cup flange. The strainer cups were screwed directly into the collecting pipes, the arrangement of which is shown on the drawings.

A central casting was fastened to the filter floor by six 0.75-inch studs. In general form this casting was a hollow annular ring with flange joints on two ends of one diameter. To each of these flanges was attached a length of 5-inch pipe, each length being made in three sections 2 feet, 1 foot, and 2 feet long, respectively. The central section in one side was a nipple, and in the other a tee with the short arm passing down through the filter floor. The outlet pipe connected to this arm. Running from the 5-inch pipes above described, and also from the central casting, was a system of 1.5-inch pipes, 23 on each side of the large pipes. These pipes were of different lengths to fit the inner circumference of the filter tank. The shortest was 1.33 feet and the longest 5.0 feet. They were spaced 0.5 foot from center to center. All of the pipes were capped at the ends. The strainer cups were screwed into the tops of the whole system as above described; six in the central casting, twenty in each of the large pipes, and the remainder in the smaller pipes. These cups were all spaced approximately 6 inches from center to center except in the central casting. The distribution was very uniform; the greatest distance from any cup to the nearest other cup, or from any point on the floor to the nearest cup, was 6 inches. The shortest distance between any two cups (4 inches) was at the central casting.

Exit Area.—The diameter of the opening of the strainer cups was 1.69 inches, and the area 2.24 square inches. The aluminum bronze plate was punched with twenty holes to the linear inch, the holes averaging 0.028 inch (0.70 millimeter) in diameter and 0.0006 square inch in area. The orifice area per single strainer cup was therefore 0.54 square inch, giving a total area for the entire system of 240 square inches.

The passage through the neck of the strainer cup was 0.188 inch in diameter. The total area of the whole system was 12.26 square inches, equivalent to a small fraction less than that of a 4-inch pipe.

The major portion of the strainer system was covered with cement, the space between the pipes being filled with bricks. This formed the filter floor. It was level in the main, and flush with the top of the strainer cups. Where the cups were set into the large pipes and central casting they were 1.8 inches higher than where set into the small pipes. There was no cement over the large pipes or central casting.

Outlet Pipe.—The outlet pipe was a 5-inch cast-iron pipe connected to the short arm of the tee in the main pipe of the strainer system. It was made up of 6.2 feet of straight pipe set vertically, a U trap and a length of 5-inch horizontal pipe connecting with a 5-inch cross outside the main tank. The whole length was about 11.5 feet to the center of the cross.

From the cross about 8 feet of 4-inch pipe connected with the automatic controller. The filtered-water meter was located on this pipe.

Automatic Controller.—The automatic controller consisted of a galvanized-iron tank, set vertically, open at the top, and arranged with a sharp-edge orifice at the bottom; an arrangement of the outlet piping to discharge into the top of this tank; a funnel under the tank, on top of the pipe to the filtered-water reservoir, to collect the discharge from the orifice; a butterfly valve on the outlet pipe above the tank; a balance arm, operating the butterfly valve, one end of the arm supporting a weight, the other a copper can; and a connection from the base of the tank with an adjustable overflow which discharged into the can on the balance arm. The device was dependent on the rate of overflow into the can on the balance arm, an increase in height of water in the main tank increasing the overflow, thus increasing the amount of water in the small can, which caused a movement of the balance arm and a consequent closing of the valve.

A 4-inch pipe connected with the outlet pipe just before the latter reached the controller. It was used when the necessary acting head fell below that available with the controller. This pipe emptied into the sewer.

From the controller the water flowed by gravity through about 65 feet of 5-inch pipe, emptying into the filtered-water reservoir inside the house for the wash-water pump.

Outlet for Filtered Waste Water.—A 4-inch pipe connected with the cross above mentioned and conveyed such water as, in the opinion of the operator, was not of a satisfactory character directly to the sewer.

Sand Layer.

During the test the sand was changed twice. The area and thickness were modified somewhat during the test by changes in the tank itself, due to warping.

Kinds of Sand Used.—At the beginning of the test the sand layer was composed of sand No. 4. On Feb. 1 this was removed and sand No. 5 put in its place. This was used till July 3. Sand No. 13 was put in service July 6 and used for the remainder of the test. Sand No. 13 was a natural sand; the other two were crushed quartz. Mechanical analyses of these sands gave the following results:

MECHANICAL ANALYSES OF THE SANDS USED IN THE JEWELL FILTER.

	No. 4.	No. 5.	No. 13.
	Per cent. by weight.		
Finer than 2.04 millimeters........	100.0	100.0	100.0
" " 0.93 "	74.2	91.0	95.5
" " 0.462 "	19.5	11.0	16.6
" " 0.316 "	1.4	1.4	1.4
Effective size { Ten per cent. finer than diameter in millimeters }	0.42	0.45	0.43

Thickness of Sand Layer.—The thickness of the sand layer varied slightly, due to increased compactness during use and slight wastes during washing. The nominal thickness was 34 inches. On Feb. 28 it averaged 34 inches. On July 6 the new sand layer was reported as 34 inches thick, but a measurement on July 8 gave only 32 inches. The thickness at the close of the test was 30.5 inches.

The sand layer was quite uniformly level, only 0.25 inch difference having been recorded between the center and the periphery. During reverse motion the rake-arms cut furrows in the surface varying in depth from 0.25 to 0.75 inch. The impact of the water over the crest of the inlet well also caused a slight depression at about 1 foot from the well. The rake-arms, during filtration, penetrated the surface of the sand layer from 3 to 5 inches.

Area.—An average of several determinations gave 115.8 square feet as the area of the sand surface.

Device for Cleaning the Sand Layer.

The device for cleaning the sand by washing comprised the following principal parts, which are described in turn below:

1. Pipes through which filtered water was pumped from the filtered-water reservoir into the outlet piping system.

2. The strainer system already described, which was used as a system for the distribution of the wash-water beneath the sand layer.

3. A collecting channel to convey to the sewer the wash-water after it had passed through the sand.

4. An agitator with the necessary mechanism for stirring the sand during washing.

5. An engine to drive the main shaft.

Wash-water Supply Pipe.—The wash-water taken from the filtered-water reservoir was pumped through an 8-inch pipe. From the pump to the point where a separate pipe branched to the Jewell and Western systems was about 60 feet. From this point 10 feet of 5-inch pipe led to a point where a separate pipe, made up of about 4 feet of 5-inch pipe, a meter, and about 3 feet of 4-inch pipe, led to a connection outside the main tank.

Device for Distributing the Wash-water under the Sand Layer.—The device used for distributing the water beneath the sand layer comprised the outlet pipe, main casting, set of parallel pipes, and strainer cups, employed during filtration as the collecting strainer system.

As this device has already been described, it will not be repeated here. For the purpose of breaking the nozzle effect of the neck of the strainer cups, a small casting consisting of a ring and four arms connecting at the center was put in the cup when it was made. (See Plate VIII.) The total area of the necks of the strainer cups was equal to a 4.12-inch pipe, or 68 per cent. of the wash-water supply pipe.

Collecting Channel.—The space between the filter tank and the main tank was used as a collecting channel, the water overflowing the edge of the inner tank. This channel was nominally 0.33 foot wide, but owing to warping and other displacements of the inner tank it varied from 0.2 to 0.4 foot. A suitable valve controlled the flow from this channel to the sewer through an 8-inch pipe about 9 feet long.

Agitator.—The agitating device consisted of a set of four rake-arms hung from a vertical shaft on the upper end of which was a horizontal gear engaging a worm on a horizontal shaft. This shaft was driven by a small engine. These portions of the agitator are next taken up and described in detail.

During the first part of the test (up to June 2) a double-thread worm was used. On this date a single-thread worm was installed. The dimensions of this worm were: Outside length, 4 inches; pitch, 1 inch; smallest diameter, 2.75 inches; and largest diameter, 4 inches. Both worms were of steel.

The dimensions of the gear were: Outside diameter, 16.5 inches; inside, 16.188 inches; and pitch, 1 inch. The ratio of revolutions of the agitator shaft to revolutions of the main driving shaft was 1 : 49. The central portion of this gear was of iron, and the teeth were of bronze metal.

The vertical shaft which carried the rake-arms was 1.81 inches in diameter. The weight of the shaft and rake-arms was supported by the bearing of the gear above mentioned, the whole system being hung from this support. At the lower end a collar working on the inlet pipe leading from the settling chamber served as a guide.

Attached to the vertical shaft above mentioned was a casting, in which there were sockets holding the rake-arms, four in number. The casting was fastened to the shaft by two set-screws, and it was also supported by a collar 1.75 inches wide fastened to the shaft by two set-screws.

The arms were steel rods 1.75 inches in diameter. They were fastened into the sockets by key bolts. There were two long and two short arms, set alternately about 90° apart. One of the long arms was 4.67 feet long, the other 4.33 feet long. The short arms were 2.17 feet and 1.58 feet long, respectively. The longest arm had seven teeth, the next six teeth, and each of the short arms three short teeth and chains. On the long arms the teeth averaged 3.69 feet in length below the center of the arms. Short teeth (2 feet long) were used on the short arms, each having 22 inches of 0.44-inch chain attached.

The teeth were made of iron bars, 0.87 inch square in section, set so that one diagonal was tangent to the arc of movement. They were attached to the arms by wrist-joints allowing them to turn freely in a left-hand direction, but holding them vertically when the movement of the agitator was left-handed, the teeth turning in a right-handed direction on the arms. By this device the teeth were made to penetrate the sand to the full depth at once.

When in their lowest position the distance between the teeth and lowest portion of the sand was about 0.25 foot.

Engine.—The engine was a small, double-cylinder, reversible, marine engine, with both pistons connected directly to a single horizontal shaft by crank arms set at 90°. The main dimensions of the engine were: Cylinders, 3 inches in diameter; stroke, 4.125 inches; and cut-off at 85 per cent. On the outer end of the shaft there was a fly-wheel 2 feet in diameter, having an approximate weight of 90 pounds.

The driving shaft was 1.23 inches in diameter. From the center of the engine to the center of the worm the distance was 5.625 feet.

Elevations.

The different elevations in feet, referred to the bottom of the sand layer as the datum plane, were as follows:

Bottom of sand layer (top of strainer floor)	0.00
Top of filter tank (wash-water overflow)	+3.41
Sand surface (average Aug. 1, 1896)	+2.54
Crest of central well	+3.68
Center of rake-arms	+3.93
Lower end of rake-teeth (during washing)	+0.24
Average maximum water level	+5.27
Lower floor (main-house floor)	−9.13
Center of supply pipe at settling basin	−6.05
Center of outlet, wash and waste pipes at cross	−6.38

The Western Gravity Filter and Appurtenances.

Water from the common settling chamber used for both Western Systems passed through this filter by gravity. The sand layer was contained in a vertical wooden tank, and the open compartment in the tank above the sand contained the water to be filtered.

During filtration the water passed downward through the sand and was collected by a manifold of slotted brass tubes into a single outlet pipe, through which it flowed to the sewer. There were two outlets on this pipe, for use as a filtered-water outlet and a waste-water outlet, respectively, as the operator deemed advisable. When it seemed advisable to wash the sand the supply of water from the settling chamber was shut off, and the filter allowed to drain more or less completely. The water remaining above the sand was drawn off by means of a circumferential gutter at the periphery, an outlet from which connected with the sewer. Wash-water was then introduced into the wash-water distributing system and forced up through the sand. The wash-water after passing up through the sand overflowed into the collecting gutter, from which it passed into the sewer.

The total available acting head was about 14 feet.

Before entering into a more detailed description of this filter, it is necessary to state that under the name of the Western gravity filter two essentially different filters were examined.

The original filter (operated up to March 22) differed from the final filter (put in service July 2) in the following points:

1. Location of the sand layer, the final filter having its sand layer 7.0 feet higher than the original one.

2. Washing device, the final filter having a special arrangement for distributing the wash-water, while in the original filter the strainer manifold for the collection of filtered water alone was used.

On account of the many modifications incidental to the changes above noted, it seems best to consider two filters, Western gravity filter (A) and Western gravity filter (B). What has already been said applies to both filters. All elevations used are in feet and refer to the level of the bottom of the sand layer of the Western pressure filter as the datum plane. The drawings (Plates VI and VII) give a plan and section of Western gravity filter (B), with reference lines to the location of the sand layer and the strainer floor of Western gravity filter (A).

Western Gravity Filter (A).

This filter was placed in a circular wooden tank which was open at the top.

About one foot of the lower portion of the tank was filled with a layer of broken stone, concrete, and cement, by which the sand layer was supported. A manifold of slotted brass tubes which formed the strainer system was half buried in the cement. The inlet pipe entered the tank at the top and discharged into a circumferential trough, the crest of which was 1.69 feet above the sand and 8.24 feet below the top of the tank. The upper portion of the tank held the water to be filtered, a column normally about 8 feet deep.

Filter Tank.—The filter tank was made of pine staves 2.75 inches thick and 4 inches wide. It was smaller at the top than at the bottom, being 10.0 feet in inside diameter at the base and 9.5 feet in inside diameter at the top. The depth was 14.37 feet. It was bound strongly by ten iron bands, each 0.25 inch thick, and ranging from 3.5 inches in width at the bottom to 2.5 inches in width at the top.

Inlet Water-pipe.—The supply pipe to the filter connected with the outlet pipe from the settling chamber, and passed up over the edge of the tank and down on the inside, discharging into the circumferential trough. This pipe, from its junction with the outlet from the settling chamber, was 4 inches in diameter. From the settling chamber to the point where this pipe began there were about 10 feet of 6-inch pipe. The total length of pipe from the settling chamber to the discharge in the filter tank was about 41 feet. Flow through this pipe was regulated by a hand-valve and by a plug operated by a float on the water in the filter tank.

Arrangements for the Exit of the Filtered Water.—After passing through the sand, the water passed through the strainer system, consisting of a manifold of slotted brass tubes; a rectangle of iron pipes into which these tubes were screwed, and which served as collecting pipes; and an outlet pipe connecting the rectangle with a branch where two discharge pipes, the filtered-water and waste-water pipe, respectively, connected with the sewer.

Strainer System.—The strainer system was a manifold of slotted brass tubes screwed into a rectangle 5 by 7 feet of 6-inch wrought-iron pipe. The drawings show the arrangement of these tubes in Western gravity filter (B). They were arranged in almost the same manner in Western gravity filter (A), except that short lengths of tube were screwed into the outside of the rectangle also.

The tubes were 1.5 inches in inside diameter and laid in a bed of concrete, the surface of the concrete being just above the center of the tubes. The slots were circumferential, five rows of slots in each section, two above the cement floor and three below, the lower ones of course being covered up with concrete. They were cut from the inside by a circular saw making them wider and longer on the inside of the tube than on the outside. There was considerable variation in the length of the slots, and the widths differed by nearly 50 per cent. An average of several determinations gave a length of 0.719 inch and a width of 0.024 inch. The slotted sections were spaced 0.125 inch from center to center. (See Plate VIII.)

Exit Area.—The total length of cut tubing was 727 inches. The exit area per linear inch was 0.272 square inch, making the total orifice area 198 square inches.

Outlet Pipe.—The outlet was a 4-inch pipe connecting with the strainer manifold in the middle of one of the short sides of the rectangle. From this point it led out through the side of the tank and to the front of the filter, a distance of about 8 feet, where it branched into a filtered-water and a filtered waste-water pipe, the two latter pipes connecting with the sewer 6 feet beyond.

Sand Layer.

The sand layer was the same throughout the use of this filter. Sand No. 6, a natural sand, was used. Mechanical analysis of this sand gave results which are presented on the next page.

Thickness of Sand Layer.—The nominal thickness of the sand layer was about 3 feet. The thickness as determined January 16 was

MECHANICAL ANALYSIS OF THE SAND USED IN THE WESTERN GRAVITY FILTER (A).

	Number 6, Per cent. by weight.
Finer than 2.04 millimeters	100.00
" " 0.93 "	96.00
" " 0.46 "	19.00
" " 0.316 "	3.60
" " 0.182 "	0.00
Effective size { Ten per cent. finer than diameter in millimeters }	0.39

36 inches above the strainers. On March 20 about 2 inches were scraped off the surface after the close of the day's operations. The sand surface was level.

Area.—The area of the sand surface was that of an unbroken circle 9 feet 10 inches in diameter, which is equal to 75.94 square feet.

Device for Cleaning the Sand Layer.

The device for cleaning the sand comprised the following principal parts, which are described in turn below:

1. Pipes through which the filtered water was pumped from the filtered-water reservoir to the wash-water distributing pipes.
2. A system of piping to distribute the water under the sand and thus cause its distribution through the sand layer during its upward passage.
3. A collecting gutter and pipes to carry to the sewer the water remaining above the sand after draining, and the wash-water after passage through the sand during washing.

Wash-water Supply Pipe.—The wash-water, taken from the filtered-water reservoir, was pumped through 60 feet of 8-inch pipe and 55 feet of 5-inch pipe to a point of connection with the outlet pipe.

Wash-water Distributing Pipes.—The strainer system of slotted brass tubes was used as a wash-water distributing system.

Collecting Gutter.—A circular wooden gutter, 12 inches deep and made of 0.375-inch pine boards, was fastened to the inner wall of the tank 0.6 foot above the sand. This was used to carry off the wash-water after passage through the sand, and a pipe at the front with a suitable valve connected it with the sewer.

Elevations.

The different elevations in feet, referred to the bottom of the sand layer of the Western pressure filter as the datum plane, were as follows:

Bottom of sand layer (top of strainer floor)	− 0.78
Sand level (average March 22, 1896)	+ 2.22
Crest of collecting gutter	+ 3.91
Top of tank	+ 12.15
Average maximum water level	+ 11.90
Lower floor (main-house floor)	− 2.22
Center of outlet pipe at filter	− 0.95

Western Gravity Filter (B).

The second filter operated under the name of the Western gravity filter differed from the first one in the location of the sand layer and the device for distributing the wash-water. The manner of operation was practically the same, except that a special wash-water distributing device was used. Connection was also made from the wash-water pipe to the collecting strainer system, whereby the latter could be used to distribute wash-water if desired, and also in order to loosen the sand around the strainers by forcing water through them. The normal depth of water above the sand during filtration was 3 feet.

Filter Tank.—The tank used was the same as that used by the Western gravity filter (A).

Strainer Floor.—The strainer floor was located 8.37 feet above the house floor, or 7 feet higher than in the first filter. This was accomplished by building a second flooring of 3-inch pine planks supported by eight 4 by 6-inch pine posts. The lower part of the tank was not used with this filter, but was kept filled with water throughout the remainder of the test. On the wooden floor was laid a layer of broken stone and concrete faced with cement. The wash-water system, consisting of distributing pipes and ball nozzles, was buried in this cement layer. The top of the cement was flush with the face of the nozzles. The strainer system, consisting of a manifold of slotted brass tubes, was laid on top of the cement floor.

The relation of the inlet, outlet, and waste-water pipes to the sand layer was the same as in the Western gravity filter (A).

Arrangements for the Exit of the Filtered

Water.—After passage downward through the sand the water flowed into the strainer tubes, a manifold of which covered the bottom of the filter tanks. From this manifold a single pipe led to the filtered-water and waste-water outlets as in Western gravity filter (A), the main change being the insertion of 7 more feet of pipe necessitated by the increased elevation of the sand layer.

Strainer System.—The strainer system was composed of slotted brass tubes set in a rectangle of 6-inch wrought-iron pipes. It was laid on top of the cement floor, however, and not imbedded in it, the entire slotted area of the tubes being utilized. Instead of conforming to the sides of the tank as in Western Gravity Filter (A), the strainer tubes formed a rectangle.

The strainer tubes were nominally spaced 12 inches from center to center, but, as will be seen from the drawing (Plate VI), there were several places on the floor of the filter where the nearest tubes were more than 1 foot apart. On the side of the rectangle at the center, the distance to the nearest strainer slot was approximately 15 inches, while at the corners the distance was about 18 inches. In general the arrangement covered the center of the bed uniformly, but was not well arranged to drain the sand at the periphery.

Exit Area.—The total length of strainer tubes used was 39.3 feet. The orifice area per linear inch was 0.680 square inch, making the total area about 320 square inches. (For details of the strainer system see Plate VIII.)

Sand Layer.

The sand layer was made up of a mixture of sands in the following manner: Approximately 12 inches of a natural sand (No. 9) were put into the filter and washed for six minutes. One inch of fine material was then scraped off the top and discarded. Sample No. 10 was taken after this sand had been washed and scraped. The sand which was used in Western gravity filter (A), (No. 7), was then screened through a No. 24 sieve, and all of that which would pass through it (about one-half) was discarded. About two feet in depth of the screened sand were then put in the filter and the coarse and fine washed together for ten minutes. Finally, on April 30, enough more of the screened sand was added to make the layer three feet thick. It was then thoroughly washed and ready for service. Sample No. 11 w● from the final sand when ready for use. Sample No. 14 was collected at the close of the test, Aug. 1, 1896. Mechanical analyses of these sands gave the following results:

MECHANICAL ANALYSES OF THE SANDS USED IN THE WESTERN GRAVITY FILTER (B).

	No. 7.	No. 9.	No. 10.	No. 11.	No. 14.
	Per cent. by weight.				
Finer than 3.90 mm....	100.0	100.0	100.0	100.0	100.0
" " 2.04 "	100.0	95.5	100.0	98.0	100.0
" " 0.93 "	95.5	66.0	93.0	89.0	93.4
" " 0.46 "	22.0	25.0	35.0	19.0	15.1
" " 0.316 "	1.7	12.0	4.0	3.9	0.6
" " 0.182 "	0.0	1.0	0.1	0.9	0.0
" " 0.105 "	0.0	0.0	0.0	0.0	0.0
Effective size { Ten per cent finer than diameter in millimeters }	0.41	0.30	0.38	0.39	0.43

Thickness of Sand Layer.—The nominal thickness was 36 inches. On July 25, however, the thickness was found to be only 31 inches. The same thickness was found at the close of the test, August 1.

Area.—On acount of the sloping sides of the filter tank the area was less than in Western gravity filter (A), being 72.78 square feet.

Device for Cleaning the Sand Layer.

The device for cleaning the sand consisted of the following principal parts, which are described in turn below.

1. Pipes through which the wash-water was supplied to the wash-water distributing system.
2. A system of piping and ball nozzles used to distribute the wash-water under the sand layer.
3. A secondary system for the distribution of the wash-water under the sand layer (comprising the strainer manifold).
4. A collecting gutter and pipes to carry to the sewer the last portion of the water remaining on the sand after draining preparatory to washing the filter, and also to carry off the wash-water after its passage through the sand.

Wash-water Supply Pipes.—The same piping was used as in the Western gravity filter

(A) to convey the filtered water to the connection with the wash-water pipe at the filter.

During the test of this filter, however, unfiltered wash-water was used, except on the last day, July 30.

For the use of unfiltered water a connection was made from the main inlet pipe to the settling chamber with the wash-water pipe at the meter, the filtered wash-water pipe being disconnected.

Beyond the meter there were two branches taken from the main wash-water supply pipe, one of which was connected with a 6-inch pipe which led to the washing device in the filter tank, a distance of about 27 feet. On this pipe was located a swing check valve with a sand pocket. The other branch from the main wash-water supply pipe was connected to the outlet pipe from the strainer system.

When filtered water was used the main supply pipe was disconnected, and in its place connection was made with the filtered-water pipe used in the Western gravity filter (A).

Main Wash-water Distributing Device.—The main wash-water distributing device consisted of a manifold of pipes, feeding eighty-two ball nozzles distributed over the strainer floor as shown in the drawing. The entire system up to the face of the ball nozzles was covered by the cement floor.

Sections of the nozzles are shown on the drawings. The total orifice area at the neck of the nozzles was made up of eighty-two 0.5-inch pipes equaling a 5.188-inch pipe. All of the balls were of solid rubber, and had a diameter of 1.625 inches. The construction allowed them a rise and fall of about 0.5 inch. With the ball at full height the orifice area was approximately 1.4 square inches for each nozzle. The inner face of the nozzle was ground to allow the ball to make a close fit and so shut off the sand and water during filtration.

Secondary Wash-water Distributing System.—A connection was made so that the strainer tubes could be used as wash-water distributers, but the main washing was given through the ball nozzles, the water being turned through the strainers for the last minute only.

Collecting Gutter.—This was the same as was used in the Western gravity filter (A), but it was located 6.33 feet above its former position.

Elevations.

The different elevations in feet, referred to the bottom of the sand layer of the Western pressure filter as the datum plane, were as follows:

Bottom of sand layer (top of strainer floor)	+ 6.19
Sand surface (average Aug. 1, 1896)	+ 8.78
Crest of collecting gutter	+ 10.24
Top of tank	+ 12.15
Lower floor (main-house floor)	− 2.22
Center of inlet pipe (highest point)	+ 12.35
Center of outlet pipe at filter	+ 6.32
Center of outlet (lowest point)	− 1.62
Center of outlet (discharge)	− 1.62

The Western Pressure Filter.

This was a portion of a continuous series of pipes and compartments through which the water passed in the process of purification. There was no restriction of the pressure from the beginning to the end (outlet) of the entire system, except such as was caused by the resistance of the piping, sand layer, and strainer system.

The filtering medium was placed in one-half of a closed steel cylinder, the other half of which was used as a settling chamber. A supply pipe for this filter connected with the cylinder at the top by a flange joint. In the lower part of the filter chamber was a layer of broken stones, concrete and cement. The strainer system, consisting of a set of slotted brass tubes, was half buried in this concrete layer, the surface of which formed the floor for the sand layer.

During filtration the water was admitted under a pressure of from 45 to 65 pounds into the portion of the chamber above the sand layer. After Feb. 29, 1896, the pressure was kept quite uniformly between 60 and 65 pounds. The outlet from the strainer system was then opened and the difference in pressure caused the water to pass downward through the sand layer, through the slots in the strainer tubes and thence through the collecting pipes and outlet to the sewer. The average total available acting head was about 140 feet, as the full pressure in the supply pipe was available, and the filtered water was discharged into the sewer.

At such times as it seemed necessary or advisable to wash the filter, a valve on the supply pipe from the settling chamber was closed. At the same time a valve on a branch from this pipe which led to the sewer was opened. Wash-water was then let into the outlet system through connections between the two pipes, forced up through the sand and out through the inlet pipe and branch to the sewer.

Filter Chamber.—The filter chamber was cylindrical in section with dome-shaped ends. The principal inside dimensions were: Length in the center, 11.15 feet; length on the sides, 8.71 feet; diameter, 8.00 feet. The inlet pipe entered the top of the chamber at the center of the compartment. In the lower portion of the compartment was placed a layer of broken stones, concrete and cement, about 2.1 feet thick in the center. The strainer system, consisting of a frame of iron pipe and a set of slotted brass tubes, was half buried in this layer. On top of this floor was the sand layer, and the upper portion of the compartment for a space about 1.7 feet high contained the water to be filtered. The inlet pipe and a branch therefrom was used as an outlet for waste water during washing.

Inlet Water-pipe.—The inlet pipe was 6 inches in diameter and conducted the water from the outlet of the settling chamber over to and into the filter chamber at the top. It was about 29 feet from the point where it connected with the settling chamber to the connection with the filter chamber. Connection with the steel shell was made by a flange, riveted to the shell. The pipe screwed into this flange. At first there was no provision for breaking the flow, but it was soon found that the impact of the water caused considerable disturbance in the sand surface, and a 6-inch nipple 4 inches long was screwed into the flange from the inside. A 6-inch tee was screwed on the nipple, the long arm of the tee running parallel with the sides of the chamber.

Arrangements for the Exit of the Filtered Water.—After passage through the sand, the water was collected by a manifold of slotted brass tubes set in a frame of iron pipe made in the form of a letter H, 9.0 feet long and 3.5 feet wide. From the center of the crosspiece of the H a single outlet pipe led down through the shell of the cylinder and out in front, where it rose above the floor, dividing into two outlets, for the effluent and filtered waste water, respectively, both of which connected with the sewer.

Strainer System.—The strainer system was made of a manifold of slotted brass tubes screwed into two lines of 6-inch pipe. The arrangement is shown on the drawings. The tubes were 1.5 inches in diameter. They were partially imbedded in a concrete floor, the floor line being just above the center of the tubes. The slots were circumferential, five slots in each section, two of them above the floor and three below. The lower ones were of course covered up. They were cut from the inside by a circular saw, making the slot wider on the inside than on the outside, or, in other words, wedge-shaped. As the depth of cutting varied considerably, the width and length of the slots varied by quite a percentage. An average of many determinations gave a width of 0.024 and a length of 0.719 inch. The slotted sections were spaced 0.125 inch from center to center.

Exit Area.—The area was made up of 731 linear inches of strainer tube, containing, per linear inch, 16 slots of an area of .017 square inch each, giving a total orifice area of 199 square inches.

Outlet Pipe.—The strainer manifold as above described connected by a tee in the center to a 6-inch downcomer, which went through the bottom of the filter and connected with a pipe which passed out from under the filter, and branched up above the floor. The upward bend was made by a tee, the long arm of which was horizontal. To the outer end of the long arm the wash-water pipe was joined. Just above the floor the outlet pipe entered a cross. The opposite arm of this cross connected to the inlet pipe. The two horizontal arms connected to the outlet and waste pipes, respectively. These two pipes passed directly to the sewer. From the strainer to the cross the distance was about 9.5 feet.

Outlet and Waste Discharges.—From the opposite sides of the cross branched the outlet and waste-water pipes, 4 inches in diameter. They both led directly to the sewer, a distance of about 4.5 feet.

Sand Layer.

Kinds of Sand Used.—The character of the sand was changed twice, a slight amount of coarser material being added the first time and some fine sand the second time. Up to April 8, the layer was composed of sand No. 6, a natural quartz sand. Sand No. 8 was the same sand after use, the sample having been collected from the sand which was removed April 8. The new sand layer put in service May 8 was made up in the following manner:

Approximately 12 inches in depth of sand No. 9, a natural sand, were put into the filter and well washed. All of the old sand was then put back, and on top of this 12 inches of the original sand (No. 6) were added. The sand layer was then washed for 10 minutes under unusually high pressure, enough sand being washed out, it was estimated, to lower the level from 3 to 4 inches. On June 3 about 6 inches of the original sand (No. 6) were added. Sample No. 15 was taken of the sand in use at the close of the test. Mechanical analyses of these sands gave the following results:

MECHANICAL ANALYSES OF THE SANDS USED IN THE WESTERN PRESSURE FILTER.

	No. 6.	No. 8.	No. 9.	No. 15.
	Per cent by weight.			
Finer than 3.90 millimeters..	100.0	100.0	100.0	100.0
" " 2.04 " ..	100.0	100.0	95.5	100.0
" " 0.93 " ..	96.0	93.0	66.0	95.5
" " 0.46 " ..	19.0	14.5	25.0	15.1
" " 0.316 " ..	3.6	1.0	12.0	0.4
" " 0.182 " ..	0.0	0.1	1.0	0.0
" " 0.105 " ..	0.0	0.0	0.0	0.0
Effective size { Ten per cent finer than diameter in millimeters. }	0.39	0.43	0.30	0.44

Thickness of Sand Layer.—The thickness of the sand layer was changed twice intentionally. On Jan. 13 it was 4.00 feet deep. Practically no change took place from that date until April 8, when the sand was removed. The new layer put in service May 8 was estimated to be 4.85 feet thick before it was washed. On June 3 the thickness was found to be 4.27 feet or 7 inches less, of which it was estimated that 4 inches was caused by settling and 3 inches by removal in washing. On this date ten sacks of sand (No. 6) were added. The thickness as determined July 15 was 4.71 feet. After the close of the test, Aug. 1, 1896, it was found to be 4.12 feet.

Sand Surface.—The major portion of the sand surface was level. In the center the impact of the water from the inlet formed a depression, about 3 feet in diameter and 3 inches to 4 inches deep. The introduction of a tee on the inlet pipe remedied this trouble.

Area.—The determination of the available filtration area of the sand layer was complicated by the following facts:

The sides and ends of the layer were curves, and every change in thickness changed the area of the layer.

The sand surface did not form a sharp junction with the side wall, but for a depth, apparently, of from 1 to 2 inches the sand curved away from the wall.

As the sides and ends of the sand layer were curved, the upper surface was less in area than a section at the center of the chamber.

Inasmuch as it is the surface of the sand which removes the major portion of the sediment, and as it is customary in this connection to use the surface of the sand as a basis of computation, it is deemed advisable to use this as the filtration area. Further, as the thickness varied considerably during the test it was thought advisable to take the area as first measured and use it in current work, correcting at the close if necessary. The area used was determined from measurements taken Jan. 13, which were as follows: Length at the side, 9.07 feet; length at the center, 10.35 feet; and width, 6.67 feet. The laps at the ends somewhat reduced the area, the surface as determined being 66.22 square feet. Redetermination after the close of the test gave an area of 65.30 square feet, the change being due to the increased depth caused by adding more sand. This area was determined from the following measurements:

Approximate radius of ends of surface	8.92 feet.
Middle ordinate of curve	0.60 "
Length of rectangular portion of surface	9.03 "
Total length of surface at center ..	10.23 "
Width of surface at center	6.67 "

For the purpose of comparison the following areas are presented:

Area of sand surface (Jan. 13, 1896)	66.2 square feet.
Area of sand surface (Aug. 1, 1896)	65.3 " "
Area of surface of strainer floor	72.8 " "
Area of maximum horizontal section of filter chamber	83.3 " "

The difference between the areas as determined Jan. 13 and Aug. 1, 1896, is only 1.4 per cent., and inasmuch as the related observations were liable to a greater percentage error, it has been thought best to use the original area of 66.22 square feet in all computations. On May 8 the area was probably 10 per cent. less than this, but it increased rapidly for three or four days, owing to loss of sand during washing, and was probably not over 2 or 3 per cent. less than this during the balance of the test.

Device for Cleaning the Sand Layer.

The device used for cleaning the sand layer by washing comprised the following parts:

1. Pipes through which the wash-water was conveyed to a connection with the distributing pipes.

2. Pipes for the distribution of the wash-water under the sand layer during washing.

3. An exit pipe for the wash-water after it had passed through the sand.

Wash-water Supply Pipe.—During the major portion of the test filtered water was used as wash-water. From June 4 to July 27, inclusive, unfiltered water was used.

The supply of filtered water was pumped from the filtered-water reservoir, through the same pipes as supplied the gravity filter, to the wash-water meter, a distance of 115 feet. From this point a separate 6-inch pipe led to a connection with the outlet pipe of the pressure filter, a distance of about 18 feet.

For the use of unfiltered wash-water the connection with the filtered-water supply pipe at the meter was disconnected and replaced by a connection with the main river-water pipe leading to the settling chamber.

Pipes for the Distribution of Wash-water.—The outlet pipe conveyed the wash-water to the strainer tubes, which were used to distribute the water under the sand layer during washing.

Exit Pipe for Wash-water.—The inlet or supply pipe was used as an exit pipe for the wash-water after its upward passage through the sand. About 8 feet from the connection of this pipe with the shell of the cylinder a 6-inch pipe branched over to the sewer, a distance of about 10 feet. Suitable valves were provided on these pipes to allow their use as desired.

Elevations.

The different elevations in feet, referred to the bottom of the sand layer as the datum plane, were as follows:

Bottom of sand layer (surface of strainer floor)	0.00
Surface of sand layer (Aug. 1, 1896)	+4.12
Inner side of cylinder at top	+5.84
Center of discharge tee on inlet pipe	+5.25
Lower floor (main-house floor)	−2.22
Center of outlet discharge at sewer	−1.22

CHAPTER VI.

Summary of the Various Parts of the Respective Systems, and a Record of Repairs, Changes and Delays.

It is stated in the introduction to this report that each of the systems described in the foregoing chapters represents the same method of purification, and that they differed only to a certain degree in the various devices employed to put into practical use the same fundamental principles. In this chapter it is the purpose to present a list of all the parts comprised in each of the divisions of the respective systems employed in carrying out this method of purification, which consists of three steps, viz.:

1. Application of chemicals to the river water.
2. Coagulation and sedimentation.
3. Filtration.

The schedules on the following pages (Tables Nos. 1, 2, and 3) show the various parts comprising a system which in each case was installed to purify 250,000 gallons of river water per 24 hours, according to the contracts with the Water Company. They are of value not only as a matter of record, but also as an indication of the attention necessary for their satisfactory operation and maintenance. It will be understood that these schedules refer only to the systems and their immediate connections.

In accordance with the contracts between the several Filter Companies and the Water Company the latter provided the following portions of the experimental plant, in addition to the laboratory:

1. The houses in which the systems were installed, and the necessary foundations on which they rested.
2. All water and steam used by the systems in their operation.
3. All steam and water pipes leading to and from each system.
4. All meters for the measurement of the water.
5. A reservoir of 142,000 gallons capacity for storage of the filtered water for washing the filters.
6. A pumping engine of 3,000,000 gallons capacity per 24 hours to deliver filtered water under pressure to the large filters for washing.

The general location of the chief portions of the experimental plant, including the storage reservoir and wash-water pump, is shown on Plate I.

In Tables Nos. 1, 2, and 3 are given lists of the principal devices employed in the respective systems for carrying on the three steps of this method of purification.

Table No. 1 includes all the principal devices used in connection with the application of the chemicals to the river water.

Table No. 2 contains a list of the principal appurtenances of the settling chambers.

Table No. 3 is a tabulation of the principal devices and appurtenances of the filters.

In the tabulations under this head, only the leading dimensions of the various devices are given, and reference is made in all cases to Chapters II, IV, and V, where descriptions will be found, and to the drawings on which these devices are shown. All devices which were in design or construction peculiar to the respective system in which they were used are marked with a star (*). All other devices are understood to be such as are in common use.

TABLE No. 1.

DEVICES FOR THE APPLICATION OF THE CHEMICALS TO THE RIVER WATER BY THE RESPECTIVE SYSTEMS.

	Warren.	Jewell.	Western-Device No. 1.	Western-Device No. 2.
Mixing Tanks.	Two circular white-pine tanks, 4 feet in diameter, 4.5 feet deep.	Two circular cypress tanks 3.5 feet in diameter, 5.5 feet deep. One ordinary "half-barrel" of oak, iron-bound.	One vertical iron cylinder, 1 foot in diameter, 2 feet deep.*	Two circular white-pine tanks, 3 feet in diameter, 4 feet deep.
Pump Boxes.	One rectangular wooden box, 2.9 by 1.2 feet, by 1.0 feet deep.	....	....	....
Propeller Wheels.	One seven-bladed screw-wheel made of cast brass, diameter 0.5 foot, depth 0.2 foot.*	....	....	....
Pumps.	One vulcanized-rubber pump.*	Two single-acting steam-pumps. Size, 3.5 by 4.5 by 6.0 inches.	....	One Worthington pumping engine. Size 8.5 by 9 by 10 inches. Two auxiliary pumps; plunger extensions of the piston-rods of the main pump.
Air Chambers.	....	....	....	One cast-brass cylinder, 3 inches in diameter, 6 inches long. One cast-iron cylinder, 6 inches in diameter, 2 feet long.
Air Compressors.	....	....	....	One wrought-iron cylinder, 5 inches in diameter, 4 feet long, with fittings.
Gauges.	Two glass sight gauges, 1.0 inch in diameter, 4 feet long, with brass fittings.	Two wooden depth gauges.	One celluloid mercury sight gauge with fittings; diameter approximately 0.25 inch.	Two wooden depth gauges.
Glass Sight Tubes.	....	One 0.75-inch glass sight tube, 1.0 foot long, with brass fittings.	....	One 0.5-inch glass sight tube, 1.5 feet long with brass fittings.
Platform Scales.	One 240-pound platform scale.	One 240-pound platform scale.	One 240-pound platform scale.	One 240-pound platform scale.
Steel Rods.	6 feet 0.5-inch steel rod.	....	....	....
Gears.	Two 1-inch steel bevel gears.* Two 4 inch steel bevel gears.*	....	....	....
Brass Pipes.	12 feet 1.5-inch brass pipe.	10 feet 0.5-inch brass pipe.	10 feet 0.5 inch brass pipe.	10 feet 0.75-inch brass pipe. 6 feet 0.5-inch brass pipe.
Brass Fittings.	Twelve 1.5-inch brass fittings.	Five 0.5-inch brass fittings.	Eight 0.5-inch brass fittings.	Nine 0.75-inch brass fittings. Twenty-two 0.5-inch brass fittings.
Brass Valves.	Two 1.5-inch brass plugs.	Two 0.75-inch brass valves. Three 0.5-inch brass valves. One 0.5-inch brass check valve.	Two 0.5-inch brass valves.	Two 0.75-inch brass valves. Two cast-brass valve chambers with valves. Six 0.5-inch brass valves. One 0.5-inch brass check valve.
Iron Pipes.	24 feet 1.5-inch iron pipe.	95 feet 0.75-inch iron pipe. 30 feet 0.5-inch iron pipe. 10 feet 1.0-inch iron pipe.	....	20 feet 0.75-inch iron pipe. 12 feet 0.5-inch iron pipe.
Iron Fittings.	Five 1.5-inch iron fittings.	Five 1.0-inch iron fittings. Fifteen 0.75-inch iron fittings. Twenty 0.5-inch iron fittings.	....	Twelve 0.75-inch iron fittings. Eight 0.5-inch iron fittings.
Iron Valves.	Two 1.5-inch iron valves.	Five 0.75-inch iron valves. Two 0.5-inch iron valves. Three 1.0-inch iron valves. One 1.0-inch iron steam regulating valve.	....	Four 0.75-inch iron valves. Two 0.5-inch iron valves. One 0.5-inch iron check valve.
Lead Pipes.	7 feet 1.5-inch lead pipe.	25 feet 0.75-inch lead pipe.	....	....
Rubber Valves.	One 1.5-inch rubber float valve.	....	....	....

TABLE No. 2.

DEVICES FOR THE COAGULATION AND SEDIMENTATION OF THE RIVER WATER BY THE RESPECTIVE SYSTEMS.

	Warren.	Jewell.	Western—Device No. 1.	Western—Device No. 2.
Settling Basins or Chambers.	One open rectangular wooden basin, 12.1 feet by 12.0 feet, by 10.25 feet deep.	The lower portion of a circular wooden tank, 13.5 feet in diameter, 14.0 feet high. Main dimensions of settling chamber: Diameter, 13.0 feet; depth, 6.89 feet.	The settling chamber formed one half of a steel cylinder, with dome-shaped ends, 8.0 feet in diameter, 22.5 long. Inside dimensions of the settling chamber: Length in center, 11.15 feet; length on the side, 8.71 feet; diameter, 8.0 feet.	Same as device No. 1.
Iron Rod.	48 feet 0.375-inch iron rod.	......	......	......
Iron Pipes.	2 feet 6-inch iron pipe.	One quarter bend of halved 4-inch iron pipe. Two feet 8-inch iron pipe. 3 feet 4-inch iron pipe. 0.5 foot 5-inch iron pipe.	30 feet 8-inch iron pipe.	24 feet 6-inch iron pipe. 23 feet 4-inch iron pipe.
Iron Fittings.	Four 6-inch iron fittings. Three 4-inch iron fittings.	Two 8-inch iron fittings. Two 5-inch iron fittings. Six 4-inch iron fittings.	Six 6-inch iron fittings.	Seven 6-inch iron fittings. Six 4-inch iron fittings.
Iron Body Valves	One 5-inch balanced iron valve operated by float. One 4 inch flap valve	One 8-inch iron valve. One 5-inch single-seated valve operated by float. One 5 inch iron valve.	One 6-inch iron valve.	One 6-inch iron valve. One 4-inch iron valve.

TABLE No. 3.

DEVICES FOR THE FILTRATION OF THE COAGULATED AND PARTIALLY SUBSIDED WATER BY THE RESPECTIVE SYSTEMS.

	Warren.	Jewell.	Western Gravity (A).	Western Gravity (B).	Western Pressure.
Filter Tanks.	One open circular wooden tank; 10.6 feet in diameter, 9.75 feet deep.	One open circular wooden tank, 12.15 feet in diameter, 5.0 feet deep.	One open circular wooden tank, 9.5 feet in diameter at the top, 10.0 feet in diameter at the bottom, 14.37 feet deep.	Same as listed under Western gravity (A).	One half of the steel cylinder listed under settling chambers. Size of filter compartment: Length in center, 11.15 feet; length on sides, 8.71 feet; diameter, 8.00 feet.
Sand Layers.	Area, 77.36 square feet; thickness, 2.25 feet; volume, 6.5 cubic yards.	Area, 115.8 square feet; thickness, 2.54 feet; volume, 10.9 cubic yards.	Area, 75.94 square feet; thickness, 3.0 feet; volume, 8.4 cubic yards.	Area, 72.78 square feet; thickness, 2.58 feet; volume, 7.0 cubic yards.	Area, 85.30 square feet; thickness, 4.12 feet; volume, 12.0 cubic yards.
Strainer Systems.	88.25 square feet copper plate, 0.031 inch thick, punched with 0.043 inch holes, 78.6 to the square inch.* 61.9 square feet brass gauze, 65 meshes to the linear inch. 15.5 square feet brass gauze, 80 meshes to the linear inch. 172.5 feet copper strips 1.12 inches wide.	Seven iron castings for strainer manifold.* 444 strainer cups.*	39.5 feet 1.5-inch slotted brass pipe.*	38.0 feet 1.5-inch slotted brass pipe.*	61 feet 1.5-inch slotted brass pipe.*
		......	......	......	......
Belts.	60 feet 6-inch rubber belt.				

TABLE No. 3.—*Continued.*

	Warren.	Jewell.	Western Gravity (A).	Western Gravity (B).	Western Pressure.
Engines.	One vertical single-cylinder engine. Diameter of cylinder, 5.75 inches; stroke, 6.0 inches.	One double-cylinder reversible marine engine. Diameter of cylinder, 3.0 inches; stroke, 4.125 inches.	....	....	....
Gears.	One 35-inch iron gear.* One 26-inch iron gear.* One 16.5-inch iron bevel gear. Two 8.25-inch iron gears.* One 6.25-inch iron gear.* One 6.0-inch iron bevel gear.* One 5.75-inch iron gear.* One 4.25-inch iron gear.* One 3.0-inch iron bevel gear.*	One steel worm, single thread: length, 4 inches; pitch, 1 inch; smallest diameter, 2.75 inches; largest diameter, 4 inches.* One gear made of iron and bronze metal: outside diameter, 16.5 inches; pitch, 1 inch.*	....	....	....
Pipes.	One length 8-inch iron pipe, 4 feet long.* One length 8-inch iron pipe, 3.75 feet long.* One iron central well: height, 4.33 feet; diameter, 2.42 and 1.71 feet.* One length 8-inch iron pipe, 6.75 feet long.* 4 feet 2-inch brass pipe. 2 feet 3-inch iron pipe. 12 feet 3-inch iron pipe.* 4 feet 4-inch iron pipe.	18 feet 4-inch iron pipe. 12 feet 5-inch iron pipe. 4.8 feet 8-inch iron pipe.	27 feet 4-inch iron pipe. 28 feet 6-inch iron pipe. 2 feet 8-inch iron pipe.	48 feet 1.5-inch iron pipe. 25 feet 4-inch iron pipe. 60 feet 6-inch iron pipe. 9 feet 8-inch iron pipe.	3 feet 4-inch iron pipe. 62 feet 6-inch pipe.
Shafts.	8.0 feet 2.5-inch steel shaft. 1.81 feet 1.25-inch steel shaft. 2.21 feet 1.75-inch steel shaft. 3.87 feet 2.25-inch steel shaft.	9 feet 1.81-inch steel shaft. 17.2 feet 1.75-inch steel shaft. 8 feet 1.25-inch steel shaft.	....	....	....
Levers.	Two sets shifting levers.*	....	....	....	....
Rakes.	Two rake-arms.* Two stiffener arms.* Two tie-rods 0.75 inch in diameter, 5.5 feet long. Sixteen rake-teeth, 35 inches long.*	One iron casting for support of rake-shafts.* Thirteen wrought-iron teeth, 3.69 feet long, 0.87 inch square. Six wrought-iron teeth, 2.00 feet long, 0.87 inch square. 11 feet 0.44-inch iron chain.			
Pulleys.	One 20-inch pulley. One 18-inch pulley. One friction clutch for 18-inch pulley. One 16-inch pulley. One 12-inch pulley.	....	....	....	....
Special Castings for Agitator.	One babbitt-metal sleeve on vertical shaft, 25 inches long, 0.75 inch thick; cast with a helical thread, three threads to the inch.* Framework for agitator machinery, with bearing plates.	One bearing plate for main gear and shaft. Two cast-iron shaft supports.	....	....	....
Fittings.	Five 8-inch iron fittings. Seven 4-inch iron fittings. Twelve 3-inch iron fittings. Four 2-inch brass fittings. Sixteen 2-inch iron fittings. One 8 by 6 by 3-inch tee.*	Three 8-inch iron fittings. Four 5-inch iron fittings. Eighteen 4-inch iron fittings.	Six 6-inch iron fittings. Nine 4-inch iron fittings.	Two 8-inch iron fittings. Six 6-inch iron fittings. Five 4-inch iron fittings. Twelve 1.5-inch iron fittings.	Twenty-five 6-inch iron fittings. Four 4-inch iron fittings.

TABLE NO. 3.—*Concluded.*

	Warren.	Jewell.	Western Gravity (A).	Western Gravity (B).	Western Pressure.
Brass and Iron Body Valves.	One 2-inch brass valve. Two 8-inch iron valves. One 6-inch iron valve. One 4-inch iron valve. One 3-inch iron valve.	One 8-inch iron valve. Three 5-inch iron valves. Two 4-inch iron valves.	One 8-inch iron valve. Four 4-inch iron valves.	One 8-inch iron valve. Two 6-inch iron valves. Four 4-inch iron valves. One 4-inch brass plug with float and float arm.	Five 6-inch iron valves. Two 4-inch iron valves.
Special Outlet Regulating Devices.	One open rectangular wooden box, 5.71 feet by 2.75 feet, by 10.25 feet deep. One iron plate, 2.25 feet wide, 4.5 feet long. One worm shaft and wheel with stand.	One controller.	....	....	....
Broken Stone, Brick and Cement.	....	2.2 cubic yards brick and cement.	2.9 cubic yards broken stone and concrete.	2.5 cubic yards broken stone and concrete.	3.0 cubic yards broken stone and concrete.
Special Devices for Distributing Wash-water.	30 feet 1-inch slotted brass pipe.* 4.5 feet 2-inch slotted brass pipe.*	....	....	Eighty-two ball nozzles; brass castings with rubber balls.*	

RECORDS OF THE REPAIRS AND CHANGES OF THE VARIOUS DEVICES OF THE RESPECTIVE SYSTEMS.

The next two topics of this chapter, dealing respectively with the repairs and changes which were made during these investigations, are closely allied to each other. The majority of repairs were coincident with changes of more or less importance. As a matter of convenience for reference the repairs and changes are listed separately, so far as it is practicable to do so, on the basis that repairs related to work done on devices which had temporarily failed to serve their purpose, and that changes refer to the installment of new devices or portions thereof where the old devices did not give results satisfactory to the operators. The repairs and changes, with the total periods occupied, are listed in the next two tables. The periods refer to 10 working hours per day from the time that regular operations ceased until they began again. Whenever possible repairs and changes were made outside of the regular hours of operation or during delays due to other causes. When repairs were made at such times the period occupied is estimated, and marked with a star (*).

In some instances the periods for repairs and changes were caused in part by failure to provide necessary materials promptly.

RECORDS OF THE PERIODS OCCUPIED IN REPAIRS OF THE VARIOUS DEVICES OF THE RESPECTIVE SYSTEMS.

Device Repaired.	Total Period Occupied. Hours.		
	Warren.	Jewell.	Western.
Chemical pump..........	0.	*8.0	1.3
Chemical feed pipe..........	0.2	*10.8	1.0
Strainers..........	0.	*1.0	*20.0
Agitator..........	25.9	*2.7	......
Steam-pipes..........	0.	2.8	0.
Lime pump..........	......	0.2	......
Controller..........	......	*2.0	......
Inlet..........	0.	16.0	*3.0
General..........	*10.0	0*.8	*10.0

RECORDS OF THE PERIODS OCCUPIED IN CHANGES OF THE VARIOUS DEVICES OF THE RESPECTIVE SYSTEMS.

Warren.

1895, Nov. 12 to 25. 93 hours 30 minutes. Mainly to change sand layer and modify filter tank.

1896, Jan. 23 to 25. 20 hours 25 minutes. Mainly to change sand layer and modify central well.

1896, Feb. 11 to 13. 19 hours 0 minutes. Mainly to introduce auxiliary wash-water distributing system, add new sand and raise central well.

Feb. 14. 48 minutes. Mainly to change agitator teeth.

Feb. 15. 50 minutes. Mainly to modify auxiliary wash-water distributing system.

Feb. 21. 3 hours 34 minutes. Mainly to remove auxiliary wash-water distributing system, change rakes and modify central well.

March 17. 10 minutes. Mainly to change position of rake-arms.

April 13 to 20. 59 hours 30 minutes. Mainly to change sand layer and strainer system.

April 23. 1 hour 35 minutes. Mainly to change agitating devices.

April 25. 3 hours 0 minutes. Mainly to change agitating devices.

Jewell.

1896, Jan. 31 to Feb. 4. 26 hours 25 minutes. Mainly to change sand layer.

Feb. 14. 47 minutes. Mainly to change outlet valves.

June 2. 1 hour. Mainly to change worm gear of agitator.

July 3 to 5. 30 hours 0 minutes. Mainly to change sand layer.

Other changes were made outside of the regular hours of operation at various times. These were mainly changes in chemical pump, lime apparatus, other chemical devices, float in main tank, chemical feed-pipe fittings, fastenings for rake-arms; the total time so occupied was about 35 hours.

Western Gravity.

March 22 to July 2. 765 hours. During this period the main changes made were in the strainer floor, sand layer, wash-water distributing systems, and piping systems.

The changes in this filter were complete on May 8, but the filter was not put in official operation till July 2.

Western Pressure.

April 7 to May 8. 221 hours 45 minutes. During this period the main changes were made in the devices for the application of the chemicals, the supply, and the distributing piping systems.

Records of the Delays of Operation during the Tests.

In this section is presented a record of the delays which were met with, and a summary of the time occupied in various ways during these investigations. After the work was well begun it was arranged that the systems should be operated as continuously as practicable from 9.00 A.M. to 5.30 P.M. on each week day, unless the Water Company requested otherwise. From March 24, 9.00 A.M., to March 30, 5.30 P.M., the operations were requested to be continuous, as was the case from 9.00 A.M on Monday to 4.00 P.M. on Saturday for each of six weeks beginning April 27. A number of repairs and changes by the operators of the several systems, and operations and observations by the Water Company, reduced somewhat the available period of operation as outlined above. The chief factors which caused delay were:

1. *Repairs and Changes.*—These have already been referred to above. Some of the principal ones necessarily extended into the regular periods of operation. The minor ones frequently were made outside the hours of regular operations, as will be noted from the differences in total time consumed as shown in the first two tables and in the final summary.

2. *Removal of Sediment which had Subsided to the Bottom of the Settling Chambers.*—The average time required by the respective systems for this operation was as follows: Warren, 3 hours; Jewell, 2 hours; Western, 6 hours. In a majority of cases the settling chambers were cleaned at times of washing or when other causes delayed the regular operation of these devices. The delays at such times were therefore less than the actual time required to clean the chambers. Exclusive of operations under prescribed conditions, the

chambers were cleaned on the following dates:

Warren System: December 19, 1895; January 23, 1896; April 13, April 28, June 9, July 2, July 23, and July 28.

Jewell System: December 11, 1895; February 28, 1896; April 25, July 3, and July 17.

Western System: December 31, 1895; January 13, 1896; April 7, June 3, June 8, June 24, and July 23.

3. *Sterilization of the Sand Layer.*—This occurred three times in the case of the Jewell System, on October 30, 1895; January 8, 1896; and February 28, 1896. About four hours were required for the operation each time, and the sand was allowed to cool over night. Sterilization was not attempted in any of the other systems.

4. *Change of Water in Settling Chambers.*—This was occasioned in some instances by the conditions prescribed by the Water Company during the period from May 18 to June 6. The water was usually changed during the time of washing the filters in order to make the delay as small as possible. The periods required for the operation depended on the rate which was being maintained and the size of the respective settling chambers. The dates when these operations took place were:

Warren System: May 18, 19, 20, 21, 25, 27, 28, and 29; June 1, 2, and 4.

Jewell System: May 18, 19, 22, 26, 28, 29, and 30; June 2, 4, and 5.

Western Pressure System: May 28, 29, and June 4.

5. *Observations and Operations by the Water Company.*—These included inspection of systems, collection of sand samples, special tests, repairs of meters and pipes, and examination of various details. The total periods of delay were: Warren, 33.2 hours; Jewell, 56.2 hours; Western Gravity, 15.6 hours; Western Pressure, 22.6 hours.

The following table gives a summary of the total periods available for operation of each system, the periods during which the respective systems were in actual operation, and the periods during which the above-mentioned causes of delay interfered with the regular operation of the systems.

It is to be noted that in this table the actual total time used in operation is presented, while in the final summary in Chapter IX only the period occupied by operations included in averages is given.

SUMMARY OF THE TIME OCCUPIED IN VARIOUS WAYS DURING THE TESTS IN DAYS OF 24 HOURS.

	Warren.	Jewell.	Western	
			Gravity.	Pressure.
Date of official beginning of tests	Oct. 21, '95	Oct. 21, '95	Dec. 23, '95	Dec. 23, '95
Date of official close of tests	Aug. 1, '96	Aug. 1, '96	Aug. 1, '96	Aug 1, '96
Period available for operation (by arrangement)	103.56	102.54	65.45	79.46
Period used for operation	91.63	94.00	26.50	66.05
Period used for repairs	1.09	0.79	0.	0.10
Period used for changes	8.40	3.89	31.88	9.25
Period used for cleaning settling chambers	0.21	0.16	0.05	0.05
Period used to change water in settling chambers	0.75	0.52	....	0.03
Period of delays by water company	1.38	2.34	0.65	0.94
Period used for sterilizing sand layer	0.	0.50	0.	0.
Periods when by request of Filter Company systems were out of service	0.	0.	5.67	2.12
Unclassified	0.10	0.34	0.70	0.92

CHAPTER VII.

The Manner of Operation of the Respective Systems of Purification and the Amount of Attention Given Thereto.

The method of water purification investigated in these tests, generally called up to this time "mechanical filtration," has been held by some to be so simple that practically no attention is required for its satisfactory operation. To many, however, the name conveys a different impression, that of a mechanism or combination of mechanical devices, for the perfect working of which, like that of any other appliance, careful and systematic supervision must be maintained.

It is the purpose of this chapter to show that the latter supposition is correct so far as it relates to the purification of the unsettled Ohio River water, because for the efficient maintenance of the systems examined during these tests constant care and regulation were necessary; and, further, that without this, irregularities, often highly detrimental both to the character of the effluent and the cost of treatment, were bound to occur.

The following topics will be presented in this connection:

1. The general manner of operation of the different systems.
2. The mechanical devices installed and used to aid in the operation of the systems.
3. The attention given to the systems throughout the tests.

Under section No. 1 will be presented a general outline of the manner of operation of the different parts of the respective systems.

Section No. 2 includes a detailed description of the special valves and other devices used to regulate or control the different operations. These have already been referred to briefly under the different portions of Chapters II, IV, and V.

Section No. 3 will include statements of the number of men employed by each system throughout the test.

The General Manner of Operation of the Respective Systems.

The general manner of operation of all the systems represented at these tests may be described as follows:

1. The treatment of the river water with alum or sulphate of alumina for the purpose of obtaining coagulation and subsequent sedimentation.
2. The filtration of the coagulated water, partially purified by sedimentation, through a layer of sand.
3. The washing of the filter (sand layer).

Nos. 1 and 2 were carried on simultaneously, but were quite separate in their methods of control.

In the following pages these different operations for the respective systems will be described in order.

Operation of the Warren System.

Application of Sulphate of Alumina.—The river water was supplied under pressure to the Warren System through a 5-inch pipe which was enlarged to 6 inches at the settling basin. The passage of the water through this pipe was controlled by a 5-inch gate valve, and a 6-inch balanced valve on the mouth of the inlet pipe, the balanced valve being operated by a float in the settling basin. As has already been described in Chapter II, the arrangement used for the application of the sulphate of alumina solution comprised a propeller wheel in the mouth of the inlet pipe; a pump on the upper floor operated by the propeller wheel; and a pair of tanks in which the solution was made, and from which it flowed by gravity to the pump box.

The operation of the whole device was

automatic, as the current of water upon entering the basin operated the propeller; and it in turn drove the pump, to which the solution flowed from the chemical tanks by gravity.

For the successful operation of this portion of the system, regulation of the rate of inflow of the river water was required. Control of the strength solution was also required. The amount of sulphate of alumina applied to the water was regulated in two ways:

1. By varying the strength of solution.
2. By varying the number of arms on the pump into which stoppers were inserted, to prevent the entrance of the solution into the arms. This is more fully described in Chapter II.

It will be seen that the design of this portion of the system called only for the initial application and the regulation of the river water into the settling basin, by hand; attention to the preparation of the sulphate of alumina solution; and the adjustment of the pump to deliver a suitable quantity of chemicals. The balance of the work was automatic. The special construction of the automatic devices will be described in the next section.

From the settling basin the water passed through a pipe to the central well of the filter, and thence to the top of the sand.

Filtration.—Starting with a clean sand layer just after washing, the settling basin full of chemically treated water, and all valves closed, the first operation was to open a valve on the inlet pipe from the settling basin to the filter, allow the water to fill the central well, overflow on top of the sand and slowly rise in the open compartment above the sand. It was necessary to let the filter fill slowly to avoid disturbance of the sand surface. From 8 to 15 minutes were occupied in filling the filter, the average time being about 10 minutes. As soon as the water reached within about 0.5 foot of the maximum level, a valve on the waste pipe was opened slowly and filtration begun. At the same time the valve on the inlet pipe to the filter was opened wide. During the latter and greater portion of the tests no water was wasted in this system following a wash of the filter, and the filtered water was turned immediately into the main outlet pipe leading to the weir box. When wasting was practiced the rate of flow of water was regulated by hand by means of a 4-inch gate valve on this pipe. When the water became satisfactory in appearance, the valve in the waste pipe was closed, and a valve on the main outlet pipe, leading to the weir box, opened. This valve was opened slowly, allowing the filtered water to enter the weir box and rise on the inlet side thereof. As soon as the water began to flow over the crest of the weir, the valve on the outlet pipe was opened wide, and the rate of filtration regulated by means of the weir. The entire system was then in operation. The water was treated with sulphate of alumina as it entered the settling basin through which it flowed on its way to the sand layer. After it was filtered, it was discharged over the weir.

The rate of flow of water through the entire system was regulated solely by the movable weir, which was used only for this purpose and not as a measuring device. The height of this weir was adjusted at varying intervals, depending largely on the amount of suspended matter in the water flowing into the filter. As a general rule, at intervals of half or three quarters of an hour it was lowered an amount necessary to maintain the desired rate of filtration, the meter on the pipe from the weir chamber to the filtered-water reservoir being used for the determination of the actual rate.

During filtration the water passed freely from the settling basin to the compartment at the top of the filter, and stood at the same level in each.

When it was considered necessary to waste the filtered water during filtration, the valve on the pipe connecting the filtered-water chamber beneath the filter and weir box was closed, and the valve on the waste pipe opened, the rate of flow of water being regulated by hand. When the effluent became clear, the change was made to the main outlet pipe as described above in starting filtration. If the effluent did not become clear in a reasonable length of time the filter was prepared for washing in the manner described below.

Decision to Wash the Filter.—This decision was one which required considerable judgment. During the whole test no case was recorded where the Warren filter was washed on account of the entire available head having been used, and the rate falling below the desired quantity. In fact, less than 60 per cent. of the available head obtained with the weir (4.17 feet) was ordinarily utilized. In general it may be said that the only immediate guide to the decision to wash the filter at any particular time was the appearance of the effluent.

In passing it may be stated, further, that the decision as to washing was influenced in a measure by several other features, the relative importance of which varied from time to time. These features related largely to the quality of the river water as it flowed from the settling basin to the filter, and especially in connection with the relative amount of aluminum hydrate present in the water at that point. The significance of these features will be mentioned beyond.

Preparations for Washing the Filter.—When it was decided to wash the filter the valve on the inlet pipe to the filter from the settling basin was closed. The water above the sand was then allowed to filter off through the sand, the rate being carefully regulated to the normal in order to maintain as good a character of effluent as possible. This was continued until the water was drained down as far as desired. With the use of the weir alone, there was left at least 2 feet of water above the sand. By the introduction of the valve (Feb. 12) in the weir chamber further drainage was made possible, only about 0.5 foot of water being left above the sand when this valve was used. During draining the settling basin was allowed to fill till the float closed the valve on the inlet pipe.

Washing of the Filter.—During the draining of the filter, preparatory to washing, the engine used for operating the agitator machinery was "warmed up." As soon as the filter was drained, the engine was started at full speed and the friction-clutch of the agitator engaged. This started the agitator, which was allowed to turn a partial revolution before the lowering gear was engaged. The agitator then slowly descended, revolving at the same time. After about one revolution the wash-water was admitted into the filtered-water chamber at the bottom of the filter. The pressure of the water forced it up through the perforated bottom into and through the sand layer, thus loosening the sand. The agitator continued to descend until it reached the full depth into the sand, when a system of levers automatically disengaged the lowering gears. At times these gears were thrown so far that the raising gears were engaged, necessitating adjustment by hand.

Washing was continued till the sand was, in the opinion of the operator, cleansed sufficiently. During this time the power given to the agitator machinery was left constant, and the amount of wash-water admitted was regulated so as to maintain a regular rate of revolution of the agitator, usually from six to eight revolutions per minute. The rate of admission of wash-water was regulated by a valve operated by hand. The maximum, minimum, and average vertical velocities of the wash-water used (estimating 45 per cent. of the sand layer occupied by water) were 4.05, 0.86, and 1.79 linear feet per minute, respectively.

As soon as the bed was cleansed to the desired degree, the lifting gears were engaged and the rakes raised out of the sand. It was customary at this time to supply a little more steam to the engine and to admit a little extra wash-water, as the greatest load came on the agitating machinery when lifting the rakes. The construction of the machinery was such that the rakes could not be lifted vertically out of the sand, but must continue to revolve while rising. As the rakes approached their highest position, steam was gradually shut off from the engine. For some time it was customary to shut off the wash-water when the rakes were about three-fourths out of the sand. In the early part of February, however, it was found that by continuing the supply of wash-water till the agitator was fully raised and stopped, the ridges in the sand formed by the rake-teeth were lessened. After this date it was customary to shut off the wash-water gradually as the rakes ascended, to stop the agitator by disengaging the friction-clutch as soon as the rakes were fully raised, and then to shut off the wash-water entirely. The engine was then stopped.

The filter was now ready for filling with water from the settling basin preparatory to filtration, as has been described.

Operation of the Jewell System.

The same method of presentation of the operation of this system will be followed as was used with the Warren System.

Application of Sulphate of Alumina.—The river water was supplied to the Jewell System, under a pressure of about 60 pounds, through a 5-inch pipe. The pipe through which the solution of sulphate of alumina was pumped joined the inlet pipe at a point about 10 feet from the entrance to the settling chamber. The river water and chemical solution had to pass through the inlet meter and two valves before they reached the settling chamber.

Two valves (a hand valve and an automatic valve) were used to control the flow through the inlet pipe. The first was a simple globe valve used to regulate the flow when starting the system or to shut off the river water upon stopping operations. The other valve was situated in the mouth of the inlet pipe within the settling chamber. It was controlled by a float in the compartment above the sand in the filter, and was relied upon to regulate the rate of admission of the water into the system as soon as the water rose high enough to set the float in operation. Regulation of the rate of admission of the water to the settling chamber also controlled its passage through the chamber and entrance to the filter.

The rate of application of the chemicals to the river water was regulated solely by the speed of the pump used for that purpose. For large changes in the amount of chemicals applied to the water, the strength of the solution was varied. The speed of the pump was adjusted by regulation of a steam throttle-valve, the pressure of the steam being held nearly constant by a regulating valve on the main steam-pipe. During the early part of the test, the throttle-valve on the pump for the delivery of sulphate of alumina was controlled by a float at the top of the filter. This was found to be unsatisfactory and hand regulation was relied upon throughout the balance of the test. The rate of feeding the sulphate of alumina solution for short intervals was determined by counting the strokes of the pump, the delivery of which was approximately 2.1 cubic inches per stroke. For longer periods control was obtained by comparison of the readings of the meter used for measuring the amount of solution and the meter on the inlet water-pipe. To start or stop the application of the sulphate of alumina solution the throttle-valve was opened or closed. The chemical pump was started just before the valve on the inlet water-pipe was opened, and stopped immediately after the latter was closed. A check-valve on the chemical feed pipe prevented the flow of water through this pipe from the inlet water-pipe when the pump was stopped.

It will be noted that the regulation of the entrance of river water was automatic, but that the regulation of the application of the sulphate of alumina required adjustment by hand of the throttle-valve of the pump.

The application of the mixed lime and sulphate of alumina was regulated at first in the same manner as the application of sulphate of alumina, one pump being used for the delivery of both solutions.

No adequate means were provided to regulate the relative quantities of the two solutions. This was remedied in the latter part of March by the use of an entirely separate arrangement for delivering the lime, including a separate pump and piping system.

Filtration.—The water after passing through the settling chamber rose up through the central well and overflowed in the compartment of the filter above the sand. Its flow was regulated by the entrance of the river water into the settling chamber, and this in turn was controlled for the most part by the float valve described above.

Starting with a clean sand layer just after washing, the settling chamber filled with chemically treated water, and all valves closed, filtration was proceeded with as follows:

The valve on the inlet water-pipe leading to the settling chamber was first opened and the sulphate of alumina pump started. This caused the water to rise in the central well and overflow on top of the sand in the filter. As soon as the water had reached its normal height above the sand, the outlet was opened, and filtration begun. This process of filling the filter usually occupied about 6 minutes, the time being dependent upon the rate used.

In filling the filter the rate of flow was regulated by hand to the required amount, as the float valve did not operate unless the water was almost at its normal height in the filter.

As the main outlet pipe and the waste-water pipe were simply different branches of the same pipe leading from the manifold in which the filtered water was collected beneath the sand, no special difference in the operation occurred whether the main outlet pipe or waste pipe was used. It was customary in this system to turn the filtered water directly into the main outlet pipe. This operation will therefore be described next.

The flow through the main outlet pipe was controlled by a valve operated by hand, which was supplemented during the latter portion of the test by an automatic controller. In starting filtration this valve was opened and the rate of flow regulated to the desired quantity. This was the only means of regulating the rate of filtration up to April 10, when the automatic controller was introduced. This device, which will be described in the next section, was so arranged that a variation in the flow through it closed a valve automatically, if the flow increased, or opened it if the flow decreased. After the introduction of this device, it was customary to open wide the valve on the main outlet pipe as soon as the controller was in operation. Owing to the pressure required to operate this controller, the head available for filtration was reduced about 4 feet. To obviate this difficulty there was placed on the main outlet pipe a by-pass which cut out the controller. This by-pass was used when the available head fell below that necessary when the controller was in operation. Under such circumstances the valve on the main outlet pipe was used to regulate the rate of filtration by hand.

Whenever it was considered necessary to waste the filtered water, the valve on the main outlet pipe was closed and the valve on the waste pipe opened, the rate of flow being adjusted by hand.

Filtration was continued until one of the two following conditions appeared: either the resistance of the filter, due to accumulations of matters removed from the water, became so great that the desired rate could not be maintained with the available head, or the appearance of the effluent became unsatisfactory in the opinion of the operator.

The determination of the course to be pursued under these circumstances rested with the judgment of the operator of the system. At times it was found that the appearance of the effluent might fail for a short period and then improve. Wasting the effluent for a short time was often tried under these conditions. When the available head fell below that necessary to maintain the desired rate of flow, one of the two following operations was adopted: either the filter was washed or the surface of the sand agitated.

Surface agitation consisted in trailing the agitator (generally by hand) in a reverse direction for about one revolution. By this means the surface of the sand was disturbed by the rake-teeth which rested upon it, and the layer of sediment on the top of the sand was broken up more or less. During this operation the passage of water through the system was stopped, but the water above the sand was never removed. Application and filtration of the water were immediately resumed, the whole operation occupying from 1 to 3 minutes. Several times during the early part of the test continuous agitation of the surface of the sand during filtration was tried. It cannot be said to have been a normal procedure, however.

In deciding whether to agitate the surface of the sand or to wash the filter, many considerations had to be borne in mind.

Decision to Agitate the Surface of the Sand.—With a decreasing rate of flow, owing to increasing resistance of the filter, and a satisfactory appearance of the filtered water, the question as to whether it was better to agitate the surface, or wash the filter, involved a consideration by the operator of the following factors:

1. Length of the last run and amount of water filtered during the same.

2. Cause for last wash.

3. Success of surface agitation on last run, if tried.

4. Length of present run and amount of water filtered.

5. Appearance of the water flowing from the settling chamber to the top of the filter.

It was found that under some conditions two and sometimes three surface agitations between washings were successful; while at other times the disturbance of the surface caused a deterioration in the character of the effluent, which did not improve. The degree of coagulation of the water as it entered the sand layer seemed to be a controlling factor.

Decision to Wash the Filter.—Several factors influenced this decision, which was in general only reached after a careful study of the varying conditions under which the system was being operated. Unsatisfactory appearance of the effluent and a utilization of the total available head were the immediate guides to washing. The quality of the river water before and after filtration, as shown by inspection and analytical results, was an important factor.

Preparations for Washing the Filter.—When it was decided to wash the filter the valve on the inlet water-pipe was closed, the chemical pump stopped, and the water above the sand allowed to filter off. When the water, in the opinion of the operator, was seriously deficient in quality it was drained out through the waste pipe for filtered water or drawn off from above the sand by means of the collecting gutter which connected with a pipe leading to the sewer. As a rule, however, the water while draining the filter was allowed to pass into the main outlet pipe to the filtered-water reservoir. During the draining of the filter the engine used for driving the agitator was "warmed up."

Washing the Filter.—As soon as the water above the sand was drained off, the engine was started at full speed in reverse motion. The wash-water was then turned into the outlet pipe and allowed to force its way up through the sand. As soon as it appeared on the surface of the sand (generally about 1 minute) the engine was reversed, and the rake-teeth turning on the arms penetrated the sand to their full available length. The agitator was continued in operation, stirring the sand throughout the wash. Up to May 1 the rate of delivery of the wash-water was regulated to maintain a certain pressure on the sand. After this date the valve on the wash-water pipe was left wide open during washing. The agitator was operated normally at a speed of eight to nine revolutions per minute.

Washing was continued until the sand layer was cleansed sufficiently, in the opinion of the operator, when the valve on the wash-water pipe was closed. The agitator engine was immediately reversed, and the rake-teeth were thrown to the surface by the resistance of the sand, which very quickly settled into place. The engine was then stopped.

In washing this filter the wash-water was passed upward through the sand layer (estimating 45 per cent. of the layer as occupied by water) at the following vertical velocities in linear feet per minute: Maximum, 2.58; minimum, 0.42; average, 1.37.

Operation of the Western Systems.

The arrangement of the Western Systems, as has already been stated, was such that the supply of river water, the apparatus for the application of alum or sulphate of alumina, and the settling chamber were used by both filters in common. The first portion of the description will therefore apply to both the gravity and pressure systems.

Application of Alum—Original Device.—In the original device the river water was supplied under pressure through a 6-inch pipe leading directly to the settling chamber. The flow of water through this pipe was controlled by a valve operated by hand. From this pipe, on each side of the valve, a small brass pipe led to the alum tank. The inlet pipe to the tank, from the upper side of the valve, passed through the cover of the tank, and projected into it about 1 foot. The outlet pipe simply passed through the cover of the alum tank and entered the inlet water-pipe below the valve. This tank was water-tight, and in it were placed crystals of potash alum. After the addition of the alum the cover was returned, and the water from the main inlet water-pipe was admitted to the alum tank through the small brass inlet pipe. A valve was placed on each of the brass pipes to regulate the flow through them.

To start the supply of river water and alum solution to the settling chamber, the valve on the inlet water-pipe was opened nearly wide, but not completely so, thus leaving a difference in pressure on the two sides of the valve. The valve on the brass pipe leading to the alum tank was normally left open. When the valve on the inlet water-pipe was opened, the valve on the brass pipe leading from the alum tank to the inlet water-pipe was also opened. The difference in pressure caused a current of water to pass from the inlet water-pipe through the alum tank and back to the inlet water-pipe. It was considered that this water in passing through the alum tank formed a saturated alum solution. The rate of flow of this solution was regulated by hand, the valve on the brass outlet pipe from the alum tank being used for this purpose. The actual rate of flow was observed by the aid of a small meter. No regulation of the water entering the settling chamber was attempted, as the rate of entrance of water was controlled solely by the rate of removal of water from the settling chamber, which was kept constantly filled and under nearly the full pressure. The water passed through the settling chamber and out at the top into the chamber outlet pipe, which branched in front of the chamber into a supply pipe for the gravity filter and a supply pipe for the pressure filter.

Unless the whole system was taken out of operation for a time no change was made in the valves on the main inlet pipe at all, except to regulate the rate of application of alum as described above.

Application of Alum or Sulphate of Alumina —Second Device.—As has been described in Chapter II, the second device used in this system for the treatment of the river water with alum or sulphate of alumina consisted mainly of two mixing tanks and a pair of small pumps, together with suitable piping.

The arrangement of the inlet pipes was changed but little so far as general operation is concerned. Unless the system was to be taken out of operation, the river water had free passage into the settling chamber at all times. The only change in this portion of the system was the operation of the main water pump. As soon as the valve on the pipe leading from the settling chamber to either filter was opened, and the water drawn from the settling chamber, the pump was started in operation by opening the steam throttle-valve. This valve was opened to a regular position and allowed to remain there till the draft on the settling chamber was stopped, when the pump slowed down owing to the increased pressure to pump against. The throttle-valve was then closed.

The device for the application of alum or sulphate of alumina was put in operation simultaneously with the main water pump, as the chemical pumps were simple extensions of the piston-rods of the water pumps. When starting, the valves cutting off the supply of chemical solution from the tanks to the pumps were opened, the air in the pumps blown off by means of petcocks, and the device was then in operation.

The method of regulation of the chemical application, as in the Warren and Jewell systems, was either by changes in the strength of solutions, or by varying the rate of application. Setting aside leakages, the discharge from the chemical pumps was practically constant. The method used to control the rate of application was to regulate by hand the rate of return from the pumps to the mixing tanks of a portion of the solution. Suitable piping with simple cocks was provided for this purpose. Observations of the rate of flow of the solution were made by the aid of a meter. A glass tube forming part of the piping system made visible the flow of the chemical solution.

The operation of filtering the partially purified (settled) water by the gravity and pressure filters, and the manner of washing these filters, is next presented. The modification in the former filter in April makes it advisable to consider it as two separate filters, gravity filters (A) and (B).

Operation of the Western Gravity Filter (A).

The water from the settling chamber flowed through a 4-inch pipe into the open circumferential gutter in the compartment above the sand, from which it overflowed on top of the sand layer. The flow through this pipe was controlled by a 4-inch gate valve operated by hand, and a 4-inch plug operated by a float in the open compartment referred to above.

Filtration.—Starting with a clean sand layer just after washing, and all valves closed, the operation of filtration was proceeded with as follows:

The gate valve on the inlet from the settling chamber to the filter was opened and the filter allowed to fill slowly to the desired height. As a usual rule, filtration was begun when the open compartment above the sand was half to three-qarters full, and it was then allowed to fill till the flow was stopped by the plug operated by the float. This plug was intended to regulate the rate of flow of the water applied to the filter.

The valve on the filtered waste-water pipe was next opened and the water allowed to pass downward by gravity through the sand. Filtration was usually begun at about half of the normal rate or less. This rate was held fairly constant, the regulation being by hand adjustment of the valve, until the water began to appear clear. The rate of filtration was then slowly increased to the normal. As soon as the water became clear at the normal rate of flow, the valve on the waste-water pipe was closed and the valve on the main outlet pipe opened.

Filtration was continued, the valve on the main outlet pipe being regulated by hand from time to time to maintain the desired rate, till it became necessary or desirable to wash.

Decision to Wash the Filter.—It may be stated that the cause of washing this filter was in practically all cases the exhaustion of the full available head for filtration. When the accumulations on and in the sand caused a resistance so great that, with the outlet valve wide open, the rate of filtration fell below that which, in the opinion of the operator, it was economical or desirable to maintain, the filter was washed.

Preparation for Washing the Filter.—When it was decided to wash the filter, the valve on the pipe from the settling chamber to the filter was closed, and the water above the sand was allowed to filter out. This was, of course, done at a constantly decreasing rate, owing to the increasing resistance and the decreasing head. The time occupied in this operation was often comparatively long, as high as 1 hour and 40 minutes being recorded, while intervals of from 1 to 1.5 hours were quite common. The variations in the quantity of unfiltered waste water (water remaining upon the sand after draining prior to washing) are interesting in this connection and will be presented in tables in Chapter VIII.

After having drained through the sand layer as long as seemed desirable, the remainder of the water above the sand was drawn through the circumferential gutter and pipe which led from it to the sewer.

Washing the Filter.—The operation of washing this filter consisted in opening the valve on the wash-water pipe to its full extent and letting the water under pressure into the strainer system beneath the sand. From the strainer system it forced its way up through the sand, stirring it more or less by the current of the water. This was continued till the sand was sufficiently cleansed in the judgment of the operator, when the wash-water was shut off. The maximum, minimum, and average vertical velocities of the wash-water used with this filter (estimating 45 per cent. of the sand layer as occupied by water) were 3.42, 1.22, and 2.22 linear feet per minute, respectively. The filter was then ready for filling with water from the settling chamber preparatory to filtration, as has been described.

Operation of the Western Gravity Filter (B).

Filtration.—This operation was similar to that followed in Western gravity filter (A), as the methods of regulating the flow into the filter, starting filtration and the regulation of the rate of filtration were all the same as in the original filter.

In this filter, however, washing was often found advisable before the available head was used up.

Decision to Wash the Filter.—This question was, as with the other systems, a matter of judgment with the operator. Either the unsatisfactory appearance of the effluent or the decrease in rate of filtration on account of resistance of the filter were used as immediate guides for the determination of the time of washing. The general features of operation, character of river water, amount and character of water filtered, and several other allied factors, however, were all considered, as a rule.

Preparation for Washing the Filter.—The manner of preparing to wash the filter was practically the same as in the original filter. Owing to the small column of water (only about 3 feet) maintained above the sand, there was but little to drain out, and the operation was performed quite rapidly, eight minutes being the longest time recorded. As a rule, however, no attempt was made to drain the filter, the water above the sand being drawn off through the gutter and drain-pipe to the sewer, as far down as the top of the collecting gutter. The filter was then ready for washing.

Washing the Filter.—As soon as the filter was drained, the valve controlling the supply of wash-water was opened, and the water admitted freely into the ball-nozzle washing system. The water was allowed to pass up through the sand under full pressure, until the sand was considered to be cleansed to the desired degree. The wash-water was then shut off from the ball-nozzle system, and turned into the strainer system for a period of about one minute. The valve on the wash-water pipe was then closed, and the filter was ready for filling with water from the settling chamber preparatory to filtration, as has been described.

In washing this filter an average vertical velocity of the wash-water (estimating 45 per cent. of the sand layer as occupied by water) of 2.25 linear feet per minute was maintained, and the range was from 1.64 to 2.81 linear feet per minute.

Operation of the Western Pressure Filter.

The supply for this filter was taken from the settling chamber through a 6-inch pipe, and admitted to the filter under full pressure (about 45 pounds to 65 pounds). The flow through this pipe was cut off when desired by a valve operated by hand.

Filtration.—Starting with a clean sand layer just after washing, and with all valves closed, the operation was as follows:

Water from the settling chamber was admitted to the filter through the inlet pipe. The valve on this pipe was opened wide by hand. As the pressure filter in reality was only one of several closed compartments through which the water passed, there was no filling or draining the tank such as took place in the gravity filters.

As soon as the valve on the inlet water-pipe was open, the valve on the waste-water pipe was opened, and filtration begun. The most distinctive point in the operation of this filter was the pressure. As noted above, full pressure was carried in the water above the sand, and the valve on the outlet pipe was opened only enough to cause a difference in pressure sufficient to allow the desired amount of water to pass through the filter. The available head in this filter was approximately 115 feet for the ordinary minimum pressure.

In starting filtration it was always customary to waste the effluent for a short period. As in the operation of the Western gravity filter, the rate of wasting was usually about half of the normal rate until the water began to be clear. The rate was then increased up to the desired quantity; the valve on the waste-water pipe was closed; and the valve on the outlet pipe was opened.

Filtration was continued until it was found necessary or desirable to wash the filter. The rate of filtration was regulated from time to time by hand adjustment of the valve on the outlet pipe.

Decision to Wash the Filter.—In this filter two factors were principally used as guides to determine when to wash it. The one most often relied upon was the appearance of the filtered water. The other, which was used mainly during the early part of the test, was the loss of head due to the resistance of the sand layer. As has been explained, the minimum available head was about 115 feet. This was never used entirely, however, as it was deemed advisable to wash the filter when the loss reached about 50 feet. In some cases when the appearance of the filtered water was unsatisfactory it was found that by reducing the rate of flow for a short time the water would again become clear. Under these conditions it was customary to waste at a low rate until the appearance of the water was again satisfactory, when filtration was resumed.

Preparation for Washing the Filter.—The preparation for washing was to close the valve on the main outlet pipe or waste-water pipe (whichever was in use), close the valve on the pipe leading from the settling chamber to the filter, and then open the valve on the branch which led from the inlet pipe to the sewer.

Washing the Filter. — The operation of washing the filter consisted of turning the wash-water under full pressure into the strainer system beneath the sand. The pressure of the water forced it up through the sand layer, from which it passed out through the inlet pipe and its branch to the sewer. Washing was continued until the operator, judging from the appearance of the water discharging into the sewer, thought the sand was cleansed sufficiently. The valve on the wash-water pipe was then closed, shutting off the supply of wash-water. The valve on the sewer pipe was next closed and the filter was at once ready for use.

On account of the curved sides of the filter chamber the velocity of the wash-water varied at different points in the sand layer. The maximum, minimum, and average vertical velocities in linear feet per minute were as follows: At strainer floor, maximum 4.48, minimum 1.40, average 2.68; at maximum horizontal section of sand layer, maximum 4.52, minimum 1.23, average 2.33; at sand surface, maximum 5.68, minimum 1.54, average 2.93.

It will be seen that no automatic devices were employed in connection with the Western Pressure System.

Filtered water was used for washing the filter during the major portion of the tests, but during the period from June 24 to July 27 unfiltered river water, admitted at the full pressure in the main, was used for this purpose.

The Mechanical Devices Installed and Used to Aid in the Operation of the Respective Systems.

Under this section the special devices used by the several systems will be described in the following order:

Devices to regulate the admission of river water to the systems.

Devices to regulate the flow of water from the settling basins or chambers to the filters.

Devices to regulate the admission of chemical solution.

Devices to regulate the rate of filtration.

Devices Used to Regulate the Admission of River Water.

Warren System.—The flow of river water under pressure into the settling basin was regulated by a 5-inch valve operated by hand, and a common 6-inch balanced valve operated by a float in the settling basin. The float was a cylinder fixed on the end of an arm fastened to the side of the basin. The arm was approximately 3 feet long. About 0.75 foot from the fixed end of the arm a chain connected to the valve stem. The relative motion of the float and valve was therefore about 4 to 1.

Jewell System.—The flow of river water under pressure into the settling chamber was regulated by a 5-inch valve operated by hand and a 5-inch single-seated valve operated by a float in the open compartment of the filter above the sand. The float was a metal cylinder attached to an arm 3.67 feet long, one end of which was fastened to the beam supporting the agitator machinery. From the other end of the cylinder extended an arm to which was attached a chain leading down through a small vertical pipe to the valve mechanism on the inlet water-pipe. The total length from the fixed end of the float to the point where the chain was fastened was 5.17 feet. The chain was fastened on the long arm of a bell-crank lever, the arms of which were 1.84 feet and 0.21 foot long, respectively. The short end was fastened by a wrist-pin to an arm 0.18 foot long, which in turn connected with the valve plate by means of a wrist-pin. The valve plate was connected with a fixed arm hinged on one side of the frame. The distance from the wrist-pin on the valve plate to the hinge about which the valve moved was 0.33 feet. This combination of levers caused a motion of the valve, the relation of the movement to that of the float depending upon the position of the float. When the latter was down, the valve was given its greatest proportional movement. When the float approached its highest position, the short arm of the bell-crank and the arm attached to the valve approached a straight line, and the movement of the valve became very small.

Western Systems.—The supply for these systems was regulated only by controlling the rate of flow to the filters as described beyond. The main water pump aided somewhat in maintaining a uniform pressure of the water, but cannot be said to have been used as a device for regulating the flow of water.

Devices Used to Regulate the Flow of Water from the Settling Chambers to the Respective Filters.

Only one special device can be said to have been used directly for this purpose, viz., the plug operated by a float in the Western gravity filter. In operation, however, the device used by the Jewell System for regulating the admission of water to the settling chamber acted as a controlling device in this connection, as did also the similar mechanism in the Warren System.

Devices Used to Control the Application of Alum or Sulphate of Alumina.

Warren System.—The sulphate of alumina solution admitted to the pump box was regulated by a valve operated by a float in the pump box. The float arm was vertical, the relation between the position of the valve and the level of the solution being adjustable by changing the length of the vertical arm. The rate of discharge of solution by the pump for each revolution was capable of variation by means of the insertion of stoppers in the ends of the pump arms.

This operation was, of course, performed by hand. The pump itself was the main regulating device, because it was operated by the flow of the water in the main inlet water-pipe, and its rate of revolution was designed to be proportional to the flow of water through the pipe.

Jewell System.—During the first five months of the test the movement of a float at the top of the filter, as described above, was relied upon to regulate the rate of application of the solution of sulphate of alumina, by adjusting the throttle-valve on the chemical pump. After this was abandoned, hand regulation alone was used.

Western Systems.—In the original device used by these systems the method used for regulating the application of alum solution was by hand adjustment of the valve on the alum pipe. The arrangement of the device allowed adjustment by regulating the difference in pressure in the two alum pipes, which was done by changing the position of the valve on the main inlet water-pipe. This was only used in starting operation, however.

In the second Western device the method of adjusting the application of chemicals was by hand regulation of the return or relief outlet valves.

Devices Used for Regulating the Rate of Filtration.

Warren System.—The regulating device used in this system was a movable weir. This has already been fully described in Chapter V. As a rule it was adjusted about every half-hour. A valve operated by hand was used for regulating the rate of wasting.

Jewell System.—As described in section 1 of this chapter, the rate of filtration was regulated by means of hand valves up to April 10, 1896. On this date a device called an "automatic controller" was installed. The arrangement of this device was as follows:

The main outlet pipe from the filter was raised up and the end turned down, so that it discharged into a galvanized iron tank through a 4-inch butterfly valve. Through this pipe the flow was regulated by the valve, which in turn was controlled by the position of a balance arm on the valve stem. The iron tank, 1 foot in diameter, was hung from the outlet pipe by four arms. Its upper end was open. The outlet from this tank was a sharp-edged orifice at the bottom, through which the water was discharged into a galvanized iron funnel, which led the water into the pipe connected with the filtered-water reservoir.

The regulation of the flow was obtained by the butterfly valve above mentioned, the position of the valve been controlled by the level in the tank in the following manner:

The balance arm of the valve held an iron weight at one end and a copper cylinder at the other. This copper cylinder had a discharge port and funnel at the bottom. From the bottom of the iron tank a flexible pipe, with an overflow, fed into the small copper cylinder above mentioned, and the water in the cylinder flowed back into the funnel on the pipe to the reservoir.

The small overflow pipe was adjustable to any desired height so that it would cause the desired rate of flow through the orifice in the bottom of the iron tank. The parts were so proportioned that if the water remained constantly at the desired level, the overflow into the small cylinder was just sufficient to keep the water in this cylinder at a height necessary to balance the weight on the other end of the lever arm, thus keeping the valve open the required amount. When the flow increased or decreased, the overflow became greater or smaller, and the level of the water in the small cylinder therefore increased or decreased. The balance arm moved correspondingly, thus closing or opening the valve.

Western System.—Hand valves alone were used for regulating the rate of filtration in the Western Systems.

The Attention Given to the Respective Systems.

The general manner of operation of the respective systems, and the special devices installed to aid the operators, have already been presented. In this section, the number of men which the several companies considered necessary to employ to operate the respective systems will be given. It is not the purpose of this section to present any comparative statements for the purpose of showing the number of men necessary to operate any modification or enlargement of these systems, but to show clearly the amount and character of supervision deemed necessary by the different filter companies for the operation of their respective systems.

From March 24 to 29, inclusive, the systems were operated day and night. For six weeks beginning April 27 the systems were operated continuously from 9 A.M. on Monday to 4 P.M. on Saturdays of each week.

The Number of Men Engaged in the Operation of the Respective Systems.

Warren System.—Throughout the test this system was in charge of a trained engineer who was also a chemist. He was assisted by one regular helper. During the continuous run in March, the system was operated at night by a superintendent of the company. During the six weeks' run the regular assistant took charge at night, and a second helper was employed during the day.

Jewell System.—From the beginning of the test till Nov. 11, 1895, the system was operated by one man who was a chemist. After Nov. 11 an officer of the company was in charge. He was assisted till Nov. 18 by the original man in charge. On that date another chemist was employed in place of the original chemist. This chemist was replaced during the second week in December by a mechanic. A boy was employed after the first week in December. This force of two men and a boy remained up to March 23, when a chemist was employed. No change was made in this force of three men and a boy throughout the balance of the test except during the continuous run in March.

During this continuous run the system was operated during the day by an officer of the company assisted by the chemist, and during the night by another officer assisted by the mechanic and the boy. During the six weeks' continuous run the force of three men was divided into three watches, the boy assisting about the place during the day.

Western Systems.—These systems were in charge of a trained chemist throughout the test. He was assisted in the routine operation by one and sometimes two men. Up to March 24 only one helper was employed. A new man was employed to assist during the day at the beginning of the first continuous run, the original helper being on duty at night. Two men were employed from this time till the first week in July. A boy was also employed to assist at night throughout the six weeks' continuous run.

The influence on the results accomplished by the systems of the attention received will be considered further in Chapter IX.

CHAPTER VIII.

COMPOSITION OF THE OHIO RIVER WATER AFTER TREATMENT BY THE RESPECTIVE SYSTEMS OF PURIFICATION, AS SHOWN BY CHEMICAL, MICROSCOPICAL, AND BACTERIAL ANALYSES; TOGETHER WITH A TABULATION OF THE MOST IMPORTANT DATA ON THE OPERATION OF THE RESPECTIVE SYSTEMS.

IN this chapter is recorded the main bulk of the detailed results of the observations and examinations made during the investigations. These results are presented in a series of tables as follows:

Table No. 1, results of regular chemical analyses, indicating the sanitary and technical characters of the water after purification.

Table No. 2, results of mineral analyses of the water after purification.

Table No. 3, results of microscopical examinations of the water after purification.

Table No. 4, results of bacterial analyses of the water after purification, and a record of conditions under which each sample was collected.

Table No. 5, records of the operation of the respective systems, including a brief summary of the analytical results and also the amount of sulphate of alumina used during each run.

The next chapter, in which these results are summarized and discussed, also contains some analytical and other results which were obtained in connection with special points which are outlined in the discussion. This chapter deals solely with the principal detailed records. In the case of each table there are a number of explanations and points to which attention is called, as stated in the following paragraphs. It may again be stated that *effluent* refers to the water, after its passage through one of the systems, which was passed into the outlet provided for the finished product. It is further to be noted that whenever filtration or any related term is used, it refers to effective filtration, i.e., the filtration of water which was passed into the outlet provided for the finished effluent.

Table No. 1.

Samples.—The samples of the several effluents, for regular chemical analysis, are listed in serial numbers. The same series of numbers was used for both the untreated river water and the effluents. During the process of analysis samples were designated by these numbers only, and the source of the samples was not known to the analysts. The conditions under which the samples were collected are presented as a matter of convenience by reference to Table No. 5, which includes the results of bacterial analyses of corresponding samples. During a portion of the time samples for chemical analysis were collected continuously by an automatic device which is briefly described in the appendix. In such cases the period covered by the sample is recorded.

In cases where several portions of effluent were mixed together for a single average sample, the water was kept in an ice-box during the period which intervened between the times of collection and of analysis.

Methods of Analysis.—Substantially the same methods were employed for the analysis of effluents as were used in the case of the untreated river water. They are presented briefly in Chapter I. The only point to be mentioned is that in the present tabulations there are included results indicating the appearance of the effluents. These results are given under the heading, "Degree of Clearness." They were obtained by careful inspection, aided by a diaphanometer such as is briefly described in the appendix, where an outline of the methods followed will be found.

The significance of the five degrees of clearness is substantially as follows:

Degree No. 1, brilliant.
Degree No. 2, clear.
Degree No. 3, slightly turbid.
Degree No. 4, turbid.
Degree No. 5, very turbid.

These expressions relate to perfectly clear water as a basis of comparison, and have nothing to do with such expressions as might be applied to the muddy river water. No objection could be raised by consumers with regard to the appearance of the effluents when it was represented by any of the first three degrees of clearness; with the fourth, the turbidity would probably be noticed by consumers at times, but not uniformly.

Color.—The color of the effluents, so far as related to dissolved matters in the water, was very slight, as is also true of the Ohio River water before treatment. Some of the color results were unavoidably increased by minute particles suspended in the water.

Carbonaceous Organic Matter—Oxygen Consumed.—The carbonaceous organic matter in the effluents, as indicated by the oxygen consumed, was satisfactory, practically without exception, and was less than that dissolved in the river water.

Nitrogenous Organic Matter—Albuminoid Ammonia.—The nitrogenous organic matter in the effluents, as indicated by the nitrogen in the form of albuminoid ammonia, was also satisfactory as a rule, and less than that dissolved in the river water. Very little or no organic matter was suspended in the effluents ordinarily. In effluents which had either of the first two degrees of clearness it is recorded as zero. In the other three degrees of clearness it was appreciable; but it was too small for measurement in a satisfactory manner, and accordingly blanks are inserted in the tables under these conditions.

Nitrogen as Free Ammonia and Nitrites.—As a rule there was a slight reduction in the effluents, as compared with the river water, in these compounds, which represent intermediate steps in the conversion of organic matter in its crude form into completely oxidized mineral matter.

Nitrogen as Nitrates.—There was substantially no change in the water before and after treatment with regard to the amount of nitrogen in the form of nitrates. This determination indicates the amount of organic matter which is completely oxidized ; and it is not to be expected that the amounts would change after treatment of the water by a process in which the organic matter is removed mechanically—not by oxidation and nitrification.

Chlorine.—The chlorine in the water was not affected by the treatment.

Residue on Evaporation.—The suspended matter in the river water was completely removed in a majority of cases by the treatment, as well as some of the dissolved matters. Whenever the effluents had a degree of clearness of No. 4 or No. 5, there was an appreciable amount of mineral matter suspended in it, but it could not be satisfactorily measured.

Fixed Residue on Evaporation.—These results are given as a matter of record for comparison with corresponding results of the water before treatment.

Alkalinity.—The alkalinity of the effluents, caused chiefly by lime (carbonate and bicarbonate of calcium), was less than that of the river water by a quantity almost directly proportional to the amount of sulphate of alumina used in the treatment of the water. In some instances the alkalinity was exhausted, due to an excess of sulphate of alumina, and the effluents were acid.

Dissolved Alumina.—As a rule the analyses indicated the effluents to be completely free from dissolved alumina, although at times mere traces were noted in the course of analysis.

The question of alkalinity and dissolved alumina have already received careful consideration in Chapter III.

Iron.—With the possible exception of very slight traces of dissolved iron, all of the iron in the river water was removed except when the effluents were quite turbid. In many cases it appeared that iron was contained in the particles which made the effluents turbid.

Table No. 2.

In this table are recorded the results of mineral analyses of the several effluents during the period of continuous operation, from March 23 to 29, inclusive. During this time samples of the effluents were collected continuously by automatic devices. As a matter of convenience for comparison, the mineral analyses of the corresponding river samples are also presented.

These results are of value in showing the constituents which composed the mineral matter in the water before and after treatment.

Table No. 3.

This table contains the results of microscopical analyses of the effluents for algæ, diatoms and such micro-organisms as may be enumerated and classified with the aid of the microscope, and without the aid of special methods such as are necessary in the case of the bacteria.

Practically speaking, the effluents were free from this class of living organisms.

Table No. 4.

The results of the determinations of the numbers of bacteria in the effluents are recorded in this table. The samples were given a number in the series which included also the samples of river water. In addition to the hour of collection of the sample a record is also given of the "run" during which the collection was made. This facilitates a detailed study of the entire records, including those of the following table. A run was regarded during these investigations as comprising all the normal operations of the respective systems, from the first opening of the valve on the filtered-water pipe, following a wash, to the next succeeding similar operation.

The rate of filtration, expressed in cubic feet per minute and million gallons per acre per 24 hours, and the loss of head at the time of collection of the samples are also presented. It will be noted that the loss-of-head observations were not made at the outset of the investigations. This was caused by unavoidable delays in providing proper facilities for obtaining full sets of observations. The period of time occupied in filtration, and the quantity of water filtered, between the resumption of filtration following the preceding washing of the sand layer and the collection of the samples, are each recorded. Under the remarks will be found comments upon special features in the operation of the respective systems in association with the sample analyzed. A series of letters will also be noted under the column of remarks. They serve as a guide in showing the basis upon which the average bacterial efficiencies of the respective systems were computed, as follows:

A. Those abnormal results which were obtained at the extreme end of a run just prior to washing, and which are not included in averages.

B. The results of special samples collected in special places, and of those taken after the system had been out of operation for periods of greater or less duration, both of which were therefore not included in averages.

C. When two sets of bacterial samples were collected, one set taken "all at once" and the other collected by an automatic sampler and covering a long period, only one set of results were used for official averages. Those results designated by the letter C were used only as checks.

D. Those results were excluded which were obtained at times when the operations were under conditions known to be abnormal, and which were in the majority of cases caused by the Water Company.

E. Long series of results on certain runs, when the automatic samplers were in use, were excluded from the daily averages, but were used exclusively in obtaining the averages for those particular runs.

Table No. 5.

This table contains the records of the operation of the respective systems tabulated in the form of runs. As stated above, all normal operations of the respective systems from the first opening of the valve on the filtered-water pipe following a wash to the next succeeding similar operation composed a run, according to the system of records employed in these investigations. The several headings, under which the data upon each individual run are grouped, are defined as follows:

Period of Operation.—This includes all the time devoted to normal operation of the system.

Period of Service.—The time during which water passed through the pipe provided for the finished product, i.e., the period of effective filtration.

Period of Wash.—The time occupied in preparing the filter for filtration, comprising the time occupied in washing the sand layer, filling the filter, and wasting the filtered water when considered necessary.

Period of Delay.—The time which was not used in normal operation of the system from the beginning to the end of the run.

Quantities of Water.—These are all expressed in cubic feet as actually recorded by the meters, except the unfiltered waste water, which was determined from gauge observations.

Applied Water.—The total quantity of river water treated by the system.

Filtered Water.—The total quantity of filtered water turned into the outlet provided for the finished product.

Filtered Waste-water.—The total quantity of filtered water which was wasted.

Unfiltered Waste-water.—The total quantity of unfiltered water which was removed from above the sand layer prior to washing.

The remaining headings are self-explanatory, but attention may be called to the summaries for each run of the following data, dealing with the efficiency and economy of purification:

1. The amount of sulphate of alumina applied to the river water in grains per gallon.

2. The estimated amount of suspended matter, in parts per million, in the river water.

3. The average number of bacteria per cubic centimeter in the river water and in the effluents.

4. The maximum and minimum number of bacteria per cubic centimeter found in the effluents.

5. The average bacterial efficiency, which was computed by taking the percentage which the difference in the average numbers of bacteria in the river water and in the effluent was of the average number of bacteria in the river water.

Special features are noted under "Remarks." Those runs marked with a star (*) were made under abnormal conditions and are excluded from subsequent averages and summaries.

TABLE NO. 1.

RESULTS OF CHEMICAL ANALYSES OF EFFLUENTS OF THE RESPECTIVE SYSTEMS.

Warren System.

(Parts per Million.)

Serial Number.	Collected.		Temperature. Degrees C.	Degree of Clearness.	Color.	Oxygen Consumed.	Nitrogen as Albuminoid Ammonia.			Nitrogen as Free Ammonia	Nitrogen as Nitrites.	Nitrogen as Nitrates.	Chlorine.	Residue on Evaporation.			Fixed Residue after Ignition.			Alkalinity.	Dissolved Alumina.	Iron.
	Date.	Corresponding Bacterial Numbers or Period of Collection by Automatic Sampler.					Total.	Suspended.	Dissolved.					Total.	Suspended.	Dissolved.	Total.	Suspended.	Dissolved.			
	1895																					
5	Oct. 18	3.30 P.M.*	...	1	...	2.0	.120	.000	.120	.012	.005	0.9	45.2	236	0	236	173	0	173	92.9	.0	0.00
7	" 19	3.40 " *	...	1	...	2.2	.152	.000	.152	.025	.007	0.9	47.0	247	0	247	174	0	174	101.0	.0	0.00
10	" 21	6	...	1	...	2.3	.156	.000	.156	.014	.007	0.6	56.8	282	0	282	209	0	209	91.2	.0	0.00
13	" 22	16	...	2	...	2.1	.156	.000	.156	.048	.005	0.4	58.5	285	0	285	187	0	187	95.5	.0	0.00
16	" 23	31	...	2	...	2.3	.178	.000	.178	.046	.007	0.6	62.1	284	0	284	197	0	197	93.4	.0	0.45
20	" 24	41	...	2	...	1.5	.164	.000	.164	.024	.007	0.4	62.5	260	0	260	208	0	208	92.5	.0	0.05
24	" 25	64	12.0	2	...	1.7	.196	.000	.196	.054	.007	0.4	64.0	303	0	303	221	0	221	95.6	.0	0.00
26	" 26	69	...	1	...	1.5	.174	.000	.174	.048	.003	0.5	67.0	305	0	305	234	0	234	93.0	.0	0.00
29	" 28	76	...	1	...	1.5	.132	.000	.132	.062	.010	0.6	72.5	310	0	310	238	0	238	95.1	.0	0.00
32	" 30	97	...	1	...	1.3	.134	.000	.134	.052	.010	0.5	77.1	301	0	301	236	0	236	92.4	.0	0.00
37	Nov. 1	113	...	1	...	1.2	.116	.000	.116	.042	.010	0.4	75.5	316	0	316	243	0	243	92.2	.0	0.00
40	" 2	130	...	1	...	1.4	.116	.000	.116	.046	.010	0.3	73.0	311	0	311	241	0	241	93.5	.0	0.00
43	" 7	189	12.5	1	...	1.2	.118	.000	.118	.028	.010	0.4	57.0	273	0	273	214	0	214	94.0	.0	0.00
57	" 26	326	7.8	2	...	1.4	.130	.000	.130	.072	.010	0.6	46.4	235	0	235	180	0	180	90.7	.0	0.00
60	" 27	340	6.9	4	...	1.6	.128	...	...	.072	.010	0.7	37.9	223	...	...	171	...	...	86.4	.0	0.03
63	" 29	358	6.8	3	...	1.8	.114	...	...	.094	.010	0.9	39.7	212	...	...	174	...	174	89.1	.0	0.00
66	Dec. 2	378	6.1	1	...	1.8	.140	.000	.140	.164	.015	0.8	38.1	211	0	211	165	0	165	87.6	.0	0.55
69	" 3	392	5.0	4	...	2.3	.200	...	...	.174	.015	0.5	35.7	266	...	...	211	...	...	88.0	.0	0.00
72	" 4	409	4.8	4	...	2.0	.126	...	...	.184	.015	0.7	38.2	248	...	...	185	...	...	91.9	.0	0.22
75	" 6	441	3.1	4	...	1.7	.126	...	...	.132	.020	0.4	60.4	293	...	...	218	...	...	92.0	.0	0.00
77	" 6	451	3.4	2	...	1.6	.128	.000	.128	.160	.020	0.4	60.4	290	0	290	221	0	221	91.6	.0	0.00
80	" 9	471	3.2	2	...	1.8	.086	.000	.086	.078	...	...	...	...	...	...	...	...	...	85.2	.0	0.21
83	" 10	393	2.8	1	...	1.9	.080	.000	.080	.132	...	...	...	...	...	...	...	...	...	72.4	.0	0.00
86	" 11	505	2.8	1	...	1.8	.068	.000	.068	.174	...	...	...	...	...	...	...	...	...	71.9	.0	0.15
B	" 11	471, 493, 505	2.9	2	.04	1.8	.090	.000	.090	.132	.005	0.4	50.6	250	0	250	192	0	192	76.5	.0	0.18
89	" 13	521	2.5	3	...	2.0	.080	...	...	.168	...	...	...	...	...	...	...	...	...	59.0	.0	0.15
92	" 14	531	2.3	4	...	2.5	.102	...	...	.122	...	...	...	...	...	...	...	...	...	58.6	.0	0.80
E	" 13–14	521, 531	2.4	4	.16	2.5	.104	...	...	.134	.005	0.3	54.4	237	...	...	181	...	...	58.8	.0	0.47
95	" 16	538	2.5	3	...	1.9	.112	...	...	.116	...	...	...	...	...	...	...	...	...	52.4	.0	0.28
98	" 17	545	3.1	4	...	2.1	.132	...	...	.114	...	...	...	...	...	...	...	...	...	51.2	.0	0.16
101	" 18	565	3.7	4	...	2.7	.180	...	...	.114	...	...	...	...	...	...	...	...	...	55.4	.0	0.28
H	" 16–18	538, 545, 565	3.1	4	.16	2.2	.141	...	...	.115	.005	0.7	29.4	183	...	...	143	...	...	56.0	.0	0.36
104	" 20	587	5.4	2	.13	2.2	.106	.000	.106	.096	...	...	...	...	...	...	...	...	...	52.1	.0	0.14
106	" 20	589	...	1	.04	1.7	.078	.000	.078	.104	...	...	...	...	...	...	...	...	...	52.5	.0	0.01
108	" 20	591	...	2	.11	1.9	.096	...	.096	.112	...	...	...	...	...	...	...	...	...	50.5	.0	0.28
110	" 20	594	...	4	.33	3.3	.156	...	...	.116	...	...	...	...	...	...	...	...	...	57.7	.0	0.80
112	" 20	587, 589, 591, 594	...	3	.22	2.5	.122	...	...	.118	.016	1.3	27.3	186	...	...	144	...	...	52.1	.0	0.39

* No corresponding bacterial sample.

TABLE NO. 1.—*Continued.*

Warren System.

(Parts per Million.)

Serial Number.	Collected. Date.	Collected. Corresponding Bacterial Numbers or Period of Collection by Automatic Sampler.	Temperature, Degrees C.	Degree of Clearness.	Color.	Oxygen Consumed.	Nitrogen as Albuminoid Ammonia. Total.	Nitrogen as Albuminoid Ammonia. Suspended.	Nitrogen as Albuminoid Ammonia. Dissolved.	Nitrogen as Free Ammonia.	Nitrogen as Nitrites.	Nitrogen as Nitrates.	Chlorine.	Residue on Evaporation. Total.	Residue on Evaporation. Suspended.	Residue on Evaporation. Dissolved.	Fixed Residue after Ignition. Total.	Fixed Residue after Ignition. Suspended.	Fixed Residue after Ignition. Dissolved.	Alkalinity.	Dissolved Alumina.	Iron.
115	1895 Dec. 27–30	651, 660, 692	7.5	4	...	1.8	.096	...	...	.094	.010	2.0	23.9	206	...	...	164	...	...	55.0	.0	0.42
120	1896 Jan. 2	740	3.6	5	.06	2.5	...	...	...	...	...	...	...	...	...	...	...	...	...	...	.0	...
125	" 3	749	3.6	5	...	1.4	...	...	...	...	...	...	...	...	...	...	...	...	...	...	.0	...
130	" 2–3	740, 749	3.6	5	.06	2.0	.141	...	...	.082	.010	2.7	26.7	255	...	...	210	...	...	37.5	.0	0.80
135	" 4	772	2.4	3	...	1.2	...	...	...	...	...	...	...	...	...	...	...	...	...	...	.0	...
140	" 6	776	2.2	4	...	1.3	...	...	...	...	...	...	...	...	...	...	...	...	...	...	.0	...
144	" 4–6	772, 776	2.3	3	...	1.2	.065	...	...	.054	.010	2.8	10.0	164	...	...	111	...	...	22.0	.0	0.11
148	" 8	802	1.8	2	.01	1.1	...	...	...	...	...	...	...	...	...	...	...	...	...	...	.0	...
152	" 9	816	1.9	2	.01	1.9	...	...	...	...	...	...	...	...	...	...	...	...	...	...	.0	...
157	" 10	827	1.8	2	.01	1.0	...	...	...	...	...	...	...	...	...	...	...	...	...	...	.0	...
162	" 8–10	802, 816, 827	1.8	2	.00	1.6	.111	.000	.111	.060	.010	3.0	7.3	142	0	142	101	0	101	12.4	.0	0.10
167	" 11	836	2.2	3	.00	1.0	.073	...	...	.052	.010	3.0	9.5	140	...	...	101	...	...	13.1	.0	0.05
172	" 14	859	1.5	2	.02	1.6	...	...	...	...	...	...	...	...	...	...	...	...	...	...	.0	...
877	" 15	861	1.5	2	.04	1.1	...	...	...	...	...	...	...	...	...	...	...	...	...	...	.0	...
182	" 14–15	859, 881	1.5	2	.04	1.3	.029	.000	.029	.034	.005	3.4	12.4	154	0	154	113	0	113	26.6	.0	0.00
187	" 20	973	2.3	2	.04	1.2	...	...	...	...	...	...	...	...	...	...	...	...	...	...	.0	...
192	" 22	997	2.8	2	.02	1.2	.059	.000	.059	.066	.010	2.3	12.5	167	0	167	123	0	123	31.9	.0	0.03
197	" 27	1044	3.8	2	.02	1.2	...	...	...	...	...	...	...	...	...	...	...	...	...	...	.0	...
208	" 28	1057	4.4	2	...	1.5	...	...	...	...	...	...	...	...	...	...	...	...	...	...	.0	...
210	" 27–28	1044, 1057	4.1	2	.02	1.3	.071	.000	.071	.082	.010	2.4	11.0	224	0	224	164	0	164	74.6	.0	0.16
213	" 29	1068	4.1	3	.04	1.3	.075	...	...	.076	.011	2.0	9.0	238	...	...	184	...	...	68.0	.0	0.01
216	Feb. 1	1095, 1096, 1099	5.0	1	.04	1.0	.035	.000	.035	.045	.007	1.8	23.5	224	0	224	155	0	155	55.2	.0	0.10
220	" 3	1107, 1110	5.0	2	.04	0.8	.041	.000	.041	.044	.006	1.7	19.9	202	0	202	140	0	140	39.1	.0	0.18
224	" 4	1121, 1124, 1127	5.0	2	.02	0.9	.043	.000	.043	.068	.008	1.8	19.0	190	0	190	134	0	134	40.2	.0	0.18
228	" 5	1136, 1140, 1149	4.8	2	.04	1.0	.061	.000	.061	.070	.006	2.7	7.6	190	0	190	136	0	136	47.0	.0	0.12
233	" 6	1155, 1161, 1163	5.3	2	.01	1.0	.049	.000	.049	.058	.0 4	2.6	6.1	166	0	166	119	0	119	45.9	.0	0.09
238	" 7	1173, 1177	6.5	1	.03	1.0	.039	.000	.039	.054	.005	2.7	6.9	184	0	184	125	0	125	47.2	.0	0.08
243	" 8	1187, 1191, 1195	5.9	2	.05	1.1	.035	.000	.035	.040	.007	2.2	9.2	156	0	156	111	0	111	32.0	.0	0.00
246	" 10	1203, 1207, 1211	5.4	2	.02	1.1	.037	.000	.037	.062	.006	2.1	11.2	137	0	137	104	0	104	21.2	.0	0.10
263	" 13	1258	4.6	3	.04	1.0	.037	...	...	.038	.005	1.9	6.5	130	...	...	92	...	...	19.5	.0	0.13
265	" 14	1265, 1269, 1273	5.1	4	...	1.1	.035	...	...	.030	.002	2.3	6.1	138	...	...	97	...	...	19.0	.0	0.01
268	" 15	1283, 1287, 1291	5.1	3	.06	1.1	.031	...	...	.040	.005	2.8	6.8	150	...	...	110	...	...	6.5	.2	0.23
273	" 17	1302, 1306, 1310	4.0	2	.01	0.9	.042	.000	.042	.030	.004	3.0	3.5	140	0	140	100	0	100	25.8	.0	0.01
278	" 18	1320, 1324, 1328	4.9	2	.02	0.9	.018	.000	.018	.018	.001	3.1	3.3	134	0	134	88	0	88	22.2	.0	0.04
281	" 19	1343, 1347, 1351	4.7	2	.02	0.9	.024	.000	.024	.014	.002	2.8	4.1	121	0	121	91	0	91	18.2	.0	0.09
286	" 20	1362, 1371, 1377	2.6	2	.04	0.9	.038	.000	.038	.022	.004	2.0	5.5	126	0	126	94	0	94	17.0	.0	0.05
289	" 21	1390, 1394	3.2	2	.02	0.7	.020	.000	.020	.018	.002	2.2	5.0	134	0	134	104	0	104	9.8	.0	0.05
294	" 22	1408, 1411, 1412	2.6	2	.01	0.8	.038	.000	.038	.026	.004	1.4	5.1	122	0	122	91	0	91	16.0	.0	0.11
297	" 24	1422, 1423	2.6	2	.01	0.7	.034	.000	.034	.018	.004	1.6	6.6	120	0	120	89	0	89	20.0	.0	0.07
302	" 25	1437, 1441, 1445	2.0	2	.02	0.7	.044	.000	.044	.030	.005	1.7	4.7	118	0	118	88	0	88	19.9	.0	0.04

TABLE No. 1—*Continued.*

Warren System.

(Parts per Million.)

Serial Number.	Collected.		Temperature. Degrees C.	Degree of Clearness.	Color.	Oxygen Consumed.	Nitrogen as Albuminoid Ammonia.			Nitrogen as Free Ammonia.	Nitrogen as Nitrites.	Nitrogen as Nitrates.	Chlorine.	Residue on Evaporation.			Fixed Residue after Ignition.			Alkalinity.	Dissolved Alumina.	Iron.
	Date.	Corresponding Bacterial Numbers or Period of Collection by Automatic Sampler.					Total.	Suspended.	Dissolved.					Total.	Suspended.	Dissolved.	Total.	Suspended.	Dissolved.			
305	1896. Feb. 26	1456, 1460, 1464	2.6	1	.03	0.7	.026	.000	.026	.022	.004	1.7	4.5	116	0	116	85	0	85	21.6	.0	0.00
310	" 27	1478, 1479, 1483	2.8	2	.04	0.8	.042	.000	.042	.026	.003	1.6	5.5	124	0	124	91	0	91	24.7	.0	0.05
313	" 28	1496, 1502	2.9	1	.02	0.9	.044	.000	.044	.032	.005	1.4	5.5	133	0	133	98	0	98	30.7	.0	0.05
318	" 29	1512, 1516, 1520	3.9	2	.02	1.0	.024	.000	.024	.026	.005	1.4	5.6	141	0	141	103	0	103	33.0	.0	0.05
321	Mar. 2	1536, 1540, 1544	4.2	2	.03	0.7	.030	.000	.030	.014	.007	1.4	5.6	140	0	140	102	0	102	40.6	.0	0.05
327	" 3	1557, 1561, 1565	4.0	2	.02	0.6	.038	.000	.038	.026	.004	1.3	6.5	125	0	125	86	0	86	43.0	.0	0.06
330	" 4	1576, 1580, 1584	4.8	3	.08	0.7	.034	......	......	.018	.007	1.6	6.0	132	......	......	109	......	......	43.6	.0	0.08
335	" 5	1595, 1599, 1608	3.9	2	.05	0.8	.026	.000	.026	.022	.008	1.6	6.6	145	0	145	104	0	104	41.4	.0	0.04
338	" 6	1616, 1621, 1625	4.6	2	.08	0.5	.020	.000	.020	.016	.007	1.8	7.5	150	0	150	117	0	117	40.6	.0	0.04
343	" 7	1637, 1641, 1644	5.0	1	.06	0.6	.022	.000	.022	.018	.006	1.7	8.9	158	0	158	115	0	115	42.0	.0	0.02
347	" 9	1656, 1661, 1670.	5.1	2	.08	0.9	.024	.000	.024	.018	.010	1.6	11.2	158	0	158	121	0	121	43.2	.0	0.05
352	" 10	1678, 1682, 1686	5.5	2	.05	0.6	.034	.000	.034	.026	.009	1.5	12.7	158	0	158	127	0	127	38.8	.0	0.04
355	" 11	1699, 1705	6.2	2	.04	0.4	.026	.000	.026	.024	.010	1.2	12.4	164	0	164	124	0	124	31.0	.0	0.10
360	" 12	1719, 1723, 1727	5.5	2	.02	0.6	.030	.000	.030	.028	.009	1.0	11.6	173	0	173	134	0	134	28.1	.0	0.12
364	" 13	1739, 1743, 1747	4.6	3	.05	0.7	.030	......	......	.026	.009	1.7	10.3	158	......	......	126	......	......	25.0	.0	0.20
367	" 14	1758, 1764, 1770	4.8	2	.06	0.8	.038	.000	.038	.028	.009	1.1	8.9	158	0	158	116	0	116	23.8	.0	0.14
371	" 16	1784, 1790, 1796	4.9	3	.06	0.7	.028	......	......	.028	.007	1.4	7.3	149	......	......	118	......	......	12.0	.1	0.11
376	" 17	1810, 1816, 1822	4.6	1	.04	0.8	.030	.000	.030	.028	.005	1.1	8.0	131	0	131	102	0	102	26.0	.0	0.07
379	" 18	1835, 1840, 1847	5.1	1	.04	0.8	.034	.000	.034	.030	.006	1.6	9.0	136	0	136	107	0	107	24.2	.0	0.07
383	" 19	1867, 1873, 1878	4.9	2	.07	0.9	.050	.000	.050	.032	.003	1.0	6.6	122	0	122	90	0	90	29.0	.0	0.15
387	" 20	1887, 1892, 1900	4.8	2	.04	0.9	.036	.000	.036	.964	.003	1.1	8.0	140	0	140	112	0	112	13.1	.1	0.10
391	" 21	1912, 1918, 1925	4.8	2	.04	1.2	.030	.000	.030	.084	.004	1.1	4.2	132	0	132	102	0	102	10.1	.1	0.14
395	" 23	1935, 1940, 1946	6.2	2	.04	0.8	.034	.000	.034	.062	.003	1.5	3.7	116	0	116	90	0	90	4.9	.1	0.20
396	" 24–25	9.00 A.M. to 8.30 A.M.	5.3	3	.08	0.7	.036	......	......	.036	.004	1.7	5.8	122	......	......	94	......	......	4.0	.1	0.14
401	" 25–26	8.30 " " 8.30 "	5.8	5	.10	1.5	.040	......	......	.034	.005	2.1	8.2	142	......	......	96	......	......	11.0	.0	0.12
405	" 26–27	8.30 " " 8.30 "	5.8	3	.04	0.9	.048	......	......	.030	.004	1.9	4.8	123	......	......	98	......	......	15.1	.0	0.07
409	" 27–28	8.30 " " 8.30 "	6.0	2	.04	0.8	.046	.000	.046	.034	.005	2.1	5.0	137	0	137	102	0	102	26.5	.0	0.05
413	" 28–29	5.30 " " 5.30 "	7.0	2	.09	0.9	.054	.000	.054	.032	.005	2.0	5.7	137	0	137	96	0	96	29.8	.0	0.09
417	" 29–30	8.30 " " 8.30 "	8.1	2	.06	0.9	.054	.000	.054	.034	.005	2.0	5.6	150	0	150	102	0	102	32.0	.0	0.04
421	" 30	8.30 " " 5.30 P.M.	8.1	3	.07	0.9	.064	......	......	.036	.005	1.9	5.5	149	......	......	105	......	......	26.4	.0	0.07
425	" 31	9.35 " " 2.30 "	8.7	3	.06	0.9	.046	......	......	.038	.005	1.9	6.5	174	......	......	119	......	......	22.0	.0	0.08
429	*	2.30 P.M. " 2.30 "	9.4	3	.09	1.2	.044	......	......	.032	.007	2.4	6.0	156	......	......	120	......	......	21.0	.0	0.07
433	April 1–2	2.30 " " 2.30 "	9.4	3	.08	0.7	.032	......	......	.022	.008	2.3	6.0	150	......	......	114	......	......	12.5	.0	0.14
437	" 2–3	2.30 " " 2.30 "	9.0	3	.08	0.7	.040	......	......	.034	.006	1.3	6.0	129	......	......	102	......	......	0.2	.5	0.21
441	" 3–4	2.30 " " 2.30 "	7.9	2	.04	0.6	.040	.000	.040	.044	.004	1.0	3.6	104	0	104	78	0	78	†0.1	.3	0.17
446	" 6	9.15 A.M. " 2.30 "	8.9	2	.07	0.6	.048	.000	.048	.052	.004	0.9	3.2	86	0	86	70	0	70	†3.1	.8	0.05
450	" 6–7	2.30 P.M. " 2.30 "	9.5	2	.05	0.6	.040	.000	.040	.038	.004	1.0	3.4	93	0	93	69	0	69	3.5	.5	0.05
454	" 7–8	2.30 " " 2.30 "	9.2	2	.09	0.8	.054	.000	.054	.040	.004	1.2	3.5	92	0	92	64	0	64	16.3	.0	0.03

* March 31 to April 1. † Acidity.

TABLE No. 1.—*Continued.*

Warren System.

(Parts per Million.)

Serial Number.	Collected. Date.	Collected. Corresponding Bacterial Numbers or Period of Collection by Automatic Sampler.	Temperature. Degrees C.	Degree of Clearness.	Color.	Oxygen Consumed.	Nitrogen as Albuminoid Ammonia. Total.	Nitrogen as Albuminoid Ammonia. Suspended.	Nitrogen as Albuminoid Ammonia. Dissolved.	Nitrogen as Free Ammonia.	Nitrogen as Nitrites.	Nitrogen as Nitrates.	Chlorine.	Residue on Evaporation. Total.	Residue on Evaporation. Suspended.	Residue on Evaporation. Dissolved.	Fixed Residue after Ignition. Total.	Fixed Residue after Ignition. Suspended.	Fixed Residue after Ignition. Dissolved.	Alkalinity.	Dissolved Alumina.	Iron.
	1896.																					
457	April 8–9	2.30 P.M. to 2.30 P.M.	9.6	2	.09	0.8	.046	.000	.046	.026	.004	1.2	3.7	98	0	98	75	0	75	23.0	.0	0.07
460	" 9–10	2.30 " " 2.30 "	9.4	2	.10	0.9	.048	.000	.048	.028	.005	1.1	4.1	106	0	106	80	0	80	25.0	.0	0.10
433	" 10–11	2.30 " " 2.30 "	9.9	1	.08	1.1	.064	.000	.064	.034	.006	1.2	4.7	95	0	95	77	0	77	28.4	.0	0.01
478	" 20	2452, 2455, 2458	16.5	2	.06	0.7	.058	.000	.058	.042	.005	0.9	10.4	120	0	120	97	0	97	29.0	.0	0.04
481	" 21	2465, 2468, 2475	17.1	2	.06	0.7	.064	.000	.064	.040	.005	1.0	10.9	116	0	116	95	0	95	33.8	.0	0.04
484	" 22	2481, 2484, 2489	16.1	3	.08	0.7	.062	.....	.....	.036	.005	0.8	12.4	114	.....	.....	96	.....	.....	38.0	.0	0.03
487	" 23	2497, 2502	17.4	2	.08	0.8	.056	.000	.056	.038	.006	0.9	10.2	112	0	112	91	0	91	40.0	.0	0.03
490	" 24	2510, 2513, 2516	17.5	2	.08	0.8	.054	.000	.054	.036	.005	0.8	8.4	110	0	110	93	0	93	40.2	.0	0.01
493	" 25	2522, 2524, 2526	18.0	2	.10	0.7	.070	.000	.070	.040	.005	0.7	7.8	113	0	113	92	0	92	41.0	.0	0.01
496	" 27–28	9.30 A.M. to 9.00 A.M.	......	3	.11	1.0	.078	.....	.....	.042	.005	0.8	6.3	113	.....	.....	92	.....	.....	49.0	.0	0.01
500	" 28–29	2.00 " " 9.00 "	21.2	2	.12	0.9	.064	.000	.064	.036	.006	0.8	6.2	116	0	116	92	0	92	47.5	.0	0.00
502	" 29–30	9.00 " " 9.00 "	20.4	2	.07	0.8	.062	.000	.062	.036	.006	0.8	6.9	116	0	116	96	0	96	44.2	.0	0.00
505	(*)	9.00 " " 9.00 "	20.2	2	.08	0.8	.058	.000	.058	.022	.005	0.8	9.0	124	0	124	98	0	98	48.2	.0	0.03
508	May 1–2	2643, 2650, 2656, 2659	21.3	2	.01	0.8	.060	.000	.060	.034	.005	0.8	9.0	122	0	122	106	0	106	43.0	.0	0.08
511	" 2	2661, 2663	......	2	.01	0.9	.056	.000	.056	.032	.005	0.9	8.5	122	0	122	105	0	105	51.0	.0	0.07
515	" 4–5	7.00 P.M. to 9.00 A.M.	22.3	2	.09	0.9	.058	.000	.058	.034	.006	1.1	11.0	129	0	129	110	0	110	41.0	.0	0.05
518	" 5–6	2721, 2726, 2728, 2732	21.9	2	.08	1.1	.068	.000	.068	.038	.006	0.9	9.7	134	0	134	110	0	110	45.1	.0	0.06
521	" 6–7	2738, 2748, 2751, 2757	......	2	.04	1.1	.060	.000	.060	.040	.007	1.1	9.9	129	0	129	111	0	111	44.0	.0	0.03
523	" 7–8	9.00 A.M. to 9.00 A.M.	22.8	2	.13	1.6	.074	.000	.074	.034	.008	0.9	11.4	137	0	137	116	0	116	45.8	.0	0.05
526	" 8–9	9.00 " " 9.00 "	22.4	2	.08	1.5	.078	.000	.078	.034	.007	0.6	12.3	132	0	132	109	0	109	41.2	.0	0.08
530	" 9	9.00 " " 3.00 "	23.4	2	.04	1.3	.052	.000	.052	.030	.006	0.7	10.4	138	0	138	107	0	107	42.0	.0	0.02
534	" 11–12	2823, 2829, 2856	23.9	2	.03	0.8	.046	.000	.046	.024	.006	0.7	10.2	128	0	128	98	0	98	37.0	.0	0.02
538	" 12–13	2870, 2878, 2880, 2884	22.8	2	.02	1.1	.064	.000	.064	.030	.006	0.6	11.5	145	0	145	115	0	115	41.1	.0	0.00
543	" 13–14	2889, 2895, 2899, 2904	23.2	2	.02	0.9	.060	.000	.060	.034	.006	0.8	11.0	125	0	125	104	0	104	45.5	.0	0.05
545	" 14–15	2908, 2912, 2918, 2922	22.7	1	.01	1.0	.060	.000	.060	.026	.006	0.5	10.3	123	0	123	96	0	96	38.8	.0	0.05
549	" 15–16	2926, 2930, 2960, 2969	23.5	1	.01	0.9	.044	.000	.044	.032	.007	0.5	11.0	128	0	128	98	0	98	38.0	.0	0.07
555	" 16	2980, 2991	23.5	2	.03	1.3	.060	.000	.060	.018	.003	0.5	12.3	148	0	148	113	0	113	49.0	.0	0.06
558	" 18–19	2997, 3007, 3014, 3023	23.4	1	.06	1.4	.074	.000	.074	.030	.007	0.6	14.7	144	0	144	106	0	106	45.0	.0	0.08
561	" 19–20	3031, 3040, 3048, 3056	23.9	2	.04	1.2	.064	.000	.064	.026	.009	0.6	12.7	145	0	145	106	0	106	54.6	.0	0.04
567	" 20–21	3068, 3080, 3085, 3092	24.0	2	.06	1.3	.062	.000	.062	.042	.006	0.7	11.4	130	0	130	100	0	100	52.0	.0	0.02
571	" 21–22	3104, 3111, 3121, 3126	23.6	2	.03	1.1	.062	.000	.062	.046	.006	0.7	11.1	151	0	151	118	0	118	54.0	.0	0.02
573	" 22–23	3136, 3147, 3154, 3160	24.1	1	.05	1.2	.068	.000	.068	.046	.007	0.6	11.9	155	0	155	109	0	109	51.5	.0	0.09
577	" 25–26	3174, 3181, 3188, 3197	25.8	2	.04	1.3	.078	.000	.078	.036	.003	0.7	12.5	149	0	149	113	0	113	62.0	.0	0.03
580	" 26–27	3212, 3221, 3228, 3236	25.0	2	.08	1.2	.066	.000	.066	.026	.001	0.6	13.5	137	0	137	103	0	103	56.0	.0	0.04
584	" 27–28	3243, 3255, 3264, 3272	25.0	1	.06	1.1	.058	.000	.058	.038	.001	0.6	13.0	144	0	144	116	0	116	57.3	.0	0.03
588	" 28–29	3296, 3305, 3332, 3355	24.3	2	.11	1.4	.078	.000	.078	054	.010	0.7	13.0	159	0	159	126	0	126	59.1	.0	0.10
591	" 29–30	3360, 3367, 3378, 3389	23.4	2	.08	1.6	.078	.000	.078	.058	.016	0.9	11.0	173	0	173	146	0	146	62.2	.0	0.04
594	" 30	3402	23.9	2	.08	1.2	.068	.000	.068	.060	.002	0.8	10.2	177	0	177	143	0	143	50.0	.0	0.10

* April 30 and May 1.

TABLE NO. 1.—*Continued.*

Warren System.

(Parts per Million.)

Serial Number.	Collected. Date.	Collected. Corresponding Bacterial Numbers or Period of Collection by Automatic Sampler.	Temperature, Degrees C.	Degree of Clearness.	Color.	Oxygen Consumed.	Nitrogen as Albuminoid Ammonia. Total.	Nitrogen as Albuminoid Ammonia. Suspended.	Nitrogen as Albuminoid Ammonia. Dissolved.	Nitrogen as Free Ammonia.	Nitrogen as Nitrites.	Nitrogen as Nitrates.	Chlorine.	Residue on Evaporation. Total.	Residue on Evaporation. Suspended.	Residue on Evaporation. Dissolved.	Fixed Residue after Ignition. Total.	Fixed Residue after Ignition. Suspended.	Fixed Residue after Ignition. Dissolved.	Alkalinity.	Dissolved Alumina.	Iron.
	1896.																					
597	June 1–2	3406, 3413, 3420, 3425	22.4	2	.04	1.2	.070	.000	.070	.032	.009	0.7	12.5	174	0	174	114	0	114	43.7	.0	0.02
602	" 2–3	3431, 3435, 3444, 3450	22.4	2	.09	1.0	.066	.000	.066	.022	.002	0.8	12.1	174	0	174	123	0	123	36.2	.0	0.08
604	" 3–4	3457, 3467, 3480, 3486	22.4	2	.07	0.9	.050	.000	.050	.024	.003	0.9	12.1	170	0	170	128	0	128	43.2	.0	0.07
609	" 4–5	3494, 3508, 3534, 3542	23.8	2	.07	0.9	.064	.000	.064	.038	.005	0.8	10.2	162	0	162	121	0	121	40.0	.0	0.07
614	" 5–6	3553, 3558, 3585, 3603	24.5	2	.09	1.0	.072	.000	.072	.036	.005	0.7	13.8	158	0	158	113	0	113	31.1	.0	0.04
617	" 6	3623, 3628	25.1	1	.04	0.9	.052	.000	.052	.026	.004	0.7	14.2	168	0	168	129	0	129	46.4	.0	0.00
624	" 9	3656,	26.8	2	.06	1.3	.068	.000	.068	.048	.003	1.1	14.8	175	0	175	134	0	134	55.1	.0	0.06
627	" 10	3668, 3671, 3675	24.6	1	.04	1.2	.066	.000	.066	.026	.001	1.0	16.8	172	0	172	132	0	132	43.0	.0	0.03
630	" 11	3681, 3684, 3692	25.0	2	.05	1.2	.070	.000	.070	.034	.002	0.7	16.0	172	0	172	132	0	132	53.5	.0	0.07
633	" 12	3697, 3704	25.2	2	.08	1.3	.076	.000	.076	.022	.003	0.9	17.6	190	0	190	136	0	136	54.0	.0	0.04
637	" 13	3711, 3718, 3724	24.0	2	.08	1.4	.066	.000	.066	.024	.000	0.7	18.1	170	0	170	128	0	128	61.0	.0	0.01
643	" 15	3740, 3743, 3747	24.4	2	.05	1.4	.078	.000	.078	.030	.007	0.8	13.6	166	0	166	124	0	124	53.0	.0	0.11
647	" 16	3759, 3766, 3767	25.2	1	.06	1.4	.076	.000	.076	.026	.009	0.9	15.0	167	0	167	128	0	128	51.8	.0	0.07
650	" 17	3776, 3780, 3783	25.4	1	.04	1.6	.080	.000	.080	.026	.006	0.9	13.5	170	0	170	116	0	116	57.5	.0	0.07
652	" 18	3796, 3801, 3809	25.2	2	.06	1.8	.080	.000	.080	.032	.004	0.6	12.5	155	0	155	115	0	115	52.8	.0	0.05
656	" 19	3818, 3829	26.0	1	.03	1.3	.068	.000	.068	.018	.002	0.7	14.2	159	0	159	121	0	121	43.0	.0	0.06
659	" 20	3856, 3861, 3870	27.4	2	.07	1.7	.070	.000	......	.020	.001	0.6	17.0	177	0	177	123	0	123	50.0	.0	0.04
663	" 22	3887, 3893, 3898	27.4	1	.06	1.5	.074	.000	.074	.028	.002	0.6	20.2	184	0	184	138	0	138	56.2	.0	0.04
666	" 23	3915, 3926, 3930	27.2	2	.07	1.1	.078	.000	.078	.026	.002	0.7	16.7	189	0	189	129	0	129	54.6	.0	0.08
669	" 24	3938, 3947, 3954	26.8	2	.08	1.4	.092	.000	.092	.026	.002	0.7	24.0	186	0	186	130	0	130	52.6	.0	0.14
690	" 30	4099, 4104	25.8	2	.08	1.5	.074	.000	.074	.026	.003	1.0	12.4	162	0	162	124	0	124	37.1	.0	0.11
693	July 1	4113, 4122, 4131	25.9	1	.08	1.3	.074	000	.074	.024	.002	0.9	14.5	160	0	160	112	0	112	29.0	.0	0.13
696	" 2	4151, 4156	26.0	3	.10	1.4	.076	......	.076	.024	.002	0.9	9.1	147	.....	.....	109	.....	.....	19.0	.0	0.14
701	" 3	4164, 4186, 4196	26.2	2	.05	1.3	.068	.000	.068	.028	.001	0.6	7.1	118	0	118	87	0	87	10.2	.1	0.14
705	" 6	4227	26.5	2	.04	1.3	.080	.000	.080	.016	.001	0.9	12.5	131	0	131	98	0	98	24.2	.0	0.02
708	" 7	4245, 4252, 4255	27.3	2	.06	1.1	.066	.000	.066	.022	.004	1.0	11.0	126	0	126	92	0	92	25.2	.0	0.04
715	" 8	4266, 4267, 4271	......	2	.14	1.2	.074	.000	.074	.022	.014	0.8	7.1	120	0	120	87	0	87	30.0	.0	0.04
716	" 9	4279, 4282, 4301A	26.4	4	.13	1.1	.074	......	......	.022	.001	0.8	6.5	119	.....	.....	91	.....	.....	38.0	.0	0.00
721	" 10	4314, 4317, 4320	26.3	2	.05	2.2	.072	.000	.072	.022	.001	0.9	5.5	124	0	124	88	0	88	35.7	.0	0.04
724	" 11	4328, 4333, 4346	26.1	2	.08	1.0	.060	.000	.060	.022	.001	0.9	5.9	125	0	125	88	0	88	33.0	.0	0.03
729	" 13	4367, 4370, 4375	26.3	2	.04	1.2	.076	.000	.076	.022	.007	0.9	3.8	125	0	125	86	0	86	28.0	.0	0.01
731	" 14	4396, 4422	26.2	2	.06	1.2	.070	.000	.070	.022	.004	0.8	7.5	114	0	114	81	0	81	26.0	.0	0.05
735	" 15	4442, 4443, 4448	26.1	2	.06	1.3	.078	.000	.078	.026	.001	0.8	5.3	103	0	103	74	0	74	26.3	.0	0.05
738	" 16	4459, 4469, 4484	26.2	2	.07	1.0	.062	.000	.062	.020	.000	0.8	2.8	106	0	106	84	0	84	29.0	.0	0.08
749	" 17–18	4503, 4525, 4546	25.7	2	.07	1.2	.060	.000	.060	.020	.000	0.3	4.0	122	0	122	80	0	80	32.9	.0	0.04
755	" 20	4570, 4575, 4576	24.2	2	.06	1.2	.060	.000	.060	.024	.001	0.7	5.5	132	0	132	90	0	90	34.8	.0	0.07
759	" 21	4603, 4608, 4613	23.7	2	.07	1.2	.074	.000	.074	.026	.000	0.8	6.1	141	0	141	86	0	86	37.0	.0	0.03
761	" 22	4618, 4627	23.8	2	.10	1.5	.080	.000	.080	.034	.006	0.9	9.5	146	0	146	96	0	96	31.2	.0	0.07
766	" 23	4637, 4643, 4645	......	5	.05	1.8	.120	......	......	.048	.006	0.7	7.0	178	.....	.....	130	.....	.....	26.0	.0	0.55

TABLE No. 1.—*Continued*.

Warren System.

(Parts per Million.)

Serial Number.	Collected. Date.	Collected. Corresponding Bacterial Numbers or Period of Collection by Automatic Sampler.	Temperature, Degrees C.	Degree of Clearness.	Color.	Oxygen Consumed.	Nitrogen as Albuminoid Ammonia. Total.	Nitrogen as Albuminoid Ammonia. Suspended.	Nitrogen as Albuminoid Ammonia. Dissolved.	Nitrogen as Free Ammonia.	Nitrogen as Nitrites.	Nitrogen as Nitrates.	Chlorine.	Residue on Evaporation. Total.	Residue on Evaporation. Suspended.	Residue on Evaporation. Dissolved.	Fixed Residue after Ignition. Total.	Fixed Residue after Ignition. Suspended.	Fixed Residue after Ignition. Dissolved.	Alkalinity.	Dissolved Alumina.	Iron.
	1896																					
771	July 24	4682	25.9	5	....	1.6	.092	......	......	.026	.001	1.0	3.6	189	....	....	143	....	....	28.6	.0	0.50
776	" 25	4705, 4710, 4712	25.2	4	.13	1.8	.094	......	......	.026	.000	0.7	8.5	189	....	....	138	....	....	26.0	.0	0.18
778	" 27	4727, 4732, 4733	26.3	3	.15	1.5	.090	......	......	.038	.011	0.9	5.0	159	....	....	116	....	....	17.8	.0	0.07
784	" 28	4766, 4780, 4792	26.4	2	.10	1.5	.070	.000	.070	.046	.009	0.7	7.2	136	0	136	99	0	99	6.0	.0	0.07
791	" 29	4830, 4844, 4852	26.3	2	.06	1.7	.074	.000	.074	.042	.005	0.7	5.0	131	0	131	105	0	105	25.4	.0	0.12
802	" 30–31	4869, 4870, 4882, 4887	26.6	2	.07	1.3	.074	.000	.074	.034	.001	0.7	3.1	121	0	121	90	0	90	21.3	.0	0.13
	Jewell System.																					
	1895																					
4	Oct. 18	3.10 P.M.*	......	1	....	2.3	.148	.000	.148	.016	.004	0.9	45.2	231	0	231	171	0	171	93.5	.0	0.00
8	" 19	3.40 " *	......	1	....	2.2	.144	.000	.144	.016	.004	0.4	46.9	239	0	239	167	0	167	96.3	.0	0.00
11	" 21	4	......	1	....	2.0	.136	.000	.136	.016	.004	0.5	56.0	272	0	272	186	0	166	88.1	.0	0.00
14	" 22	17	......	1	....	2.4	.170	.000	.170	.036	.004	0.5	58.2	275	0	275	189	0	189	95.0	.0	0.00
17	" 23	33	......	2	....	2.3	.158	.000	.158	.024	.003	0.6	61.6	275	0	275	220	0	220	93.2	.0	0.00
19	" 24	40	......	3	....	2.8	.206	......	......	.012	.003	0.4	62.0	286	....	....	225	....	....	97.0	.0	0.07
21	" 25	56	......	2	....	1.6	.198	.000	.198	.020	.004	0.5	62.6	295	0	295	225	0	225	95.5	.0	0.00
23	" 25	63	12.0	1	....	1.4	.138	.000	.138	.016	.004	0.4	64.5	294	0	294	226	0	226	94.5	.0	0.00
27	" 26	68	......	1	....	1.6	.162	.000	.162	.022	.004	0.5	65.5	314	0	314	238	0	238	93.0	.0	0.00
30	" 28	72	......	2	....	1.6	.140	.000	.140	.050	.004	0.6	72.2	316	0	316	238	0	238	96.0	.0	0.00
33	" 30	98	......	2	....	1.3	.142	.000	.142	.072	.010	0.5	78.5	282	0	282	208	0	208	89.5	.0	0.00
35	" 31	110	11.0	2	....	1.4	.136	.000	.136	.050	.010	0.3	77.2	245	0	245	150	0	150	92.6	.0	0.00
38	Nov. 1	119	......	2	....	1.3	.096	.000	.096	.042	.010	0.4	75.3	317	0	317	247	0	247	94.5	.0	0.00
41	" 2	129	......	2	....	1.5	.128	.000	.128	.060	.010	0.3	72.3	306	0	306	238	0	238	98.4	.0	0.00
44	" 7	190	......	1	....	1.1	.130	.000	.130	.034	.010	0.4	57.0	282	0	282	215	0	215	91.0	.0	0.00
47	" 12	240	......	1	....	1.6	.120	.000	.120	.024	.010	0.4	52.2	255	0	255	197	0	197	99.3	.0	0.00
49	" 14	253	......	1	....	1.8	.158	.000	.158	.034	.010	0.4	50.7	250	0	250	194	0	194	102.0	.0	0.00
51	" 20	281	8.0	1	....	1.7	.174	.000	.174	.010	.010	0.4	42.1	231	0	231	174	0	174	98.3	.0	0.00
53	" 22	291	7.5	1	....	1.6	.144	.000	.144	.072	.010	0.6	42.0	235	0	235	170	0	170	99.5	.0	0.00
58	" 26	325	7.5	1	....	1.6	.148	.000	.148	.078	.010	0.6	35.0	243	0	243	174	0	174	89.5	.0	0.00
61	" 27	339	7.0	3	....	2.3	.172	......	......	.066	.010	0.7	37.9	220	....	....	167	....	....	87.6	.0	0.00
64	" 29	357	6.7	1	....	1.9	.114	.000	.114	.112	.010	0.9	39.3	207	0	207	161	0	161	91.8	.0	0.00
67	Dec. 2	377	6.1	3	....	2.2	.138	......	......	.156	.015	0.8	37.3	218	....	....	173	....	....	96.0	.0	0.15
70	" 3	393	5.1	1	....	2.1	.130	.000	.130	.180	.015	0.6	36.0	227	0	227	173	0	173	89.2	.0	0.00
73	" 4	411	5.6	1	....	1.8	.120	.000	.120	.182	.015	0.7	37.5	235	0	235	180	0	180	92.2	.0	0.00
76	" 6	442	3.0	1	....	1.5	.102	.000	.102	.140	.020	0.4	61.1	295	0	295	224	0	224	88.4	.0	0.25
78	" 6	452	3.2	1	....	1.3	.100	.000	.100	.154	.020	0.3	60.9	290	0	290	217	0	217	82.8	.0	......
81	" 9	472	3.2	1	....	1.8	.076	.000	.076	.090	.....	.....	.....	.....	0	....	....	0	....	83.1	.0	0.00

* No corresponding bacterial sample.

TABLE No. 1.—*Continued.*

Jewell System.

(Parts per Million.)

Serial Number.	Collected.		Temperature, Degrees C.	Degree of Clearness.	Color.	Oxygen Consumed.	Nitrogen as Albuminoid Ammonia.			Nitrogen as Free Ammonia.	Nitrogen as Nitrites.	Nitrogen as Nitrates.	Chlorine.	Residue on Evaporation.			Fixed Residue after Ignition.			Alkalinity.	Dissolved Alumina.	Iron.
	Date.	Corresponding Bacterial Numbers or Period of Collection by Automatic Sampler.					Total.	Suspended.	Dissolved.					Total.	Suspended.	Dissolved.	Total.	Suspended.	Dissolved.			
	1895																					
84	Dec. 10	494	3.0	2	....	2.4	.106	.000	.106	.124	....	....	....	....	....	....	....	....	....	77.7	.0	0.14
87	" 11	506	2.8	2	....	1.8	.112	.000	.112	.172	....	....	....	....	....	....	....	....	....	71.2	.0	0.15
C	" 11	472, 494, 506	3.0	2	.08	2.0	.088	.000	.088	.134	.005	0.3	50.3	247	0	247	196	0	196	77.3	.0	0.09
90	" 13	522	2.6	1	....	1.9	.082	.000	.082	.182	....	....	....	....	....	....	....	....	....	57.4	.0	0.15
93	" 14	529	2.2	2	....	2.3	.110	.000	.110	.150	....	....	....	....	....	....	....	....	....	58.6	.0	0.11
F	" 13–14	522, 529	2.4	2	.09	2.1	.094	.000	.094	.148	.005	0.3	53.6	232	0	232	183	0	183	58.0	.0	0.13
96	" 16	539	2.6	2	....	2.3	.142	.000	.142	.116	....	....	....	....	....	....	....	....	....	55.1	.0	0.27
99	" 17	549	3.0	2	....	2.6	.132	.000	.132	.114	....	....	....	....	....	....	....	....	....	53.0	.0	0.14
102	" 18	566	3.7	2	....	2.3	.196	.000	.196	.114	....	....	....	....	....	....	....	....	....	54.5	.0	0.14
I	" 16–18	539, 549, 566	3.1	2	.16	2.4	.156	.000	.156	.115	.005	0.7	30.1	180	0	180	139	0	139	55.0	.0	0.18
105	" 20	586	5.4	1	.05	2.1	.092	.000	.092	.096	....	....	....	....	....	....	....	....	....	51.8	.0	0.09
107	" 20	590	....	1	.06	1.8	.088	.000	.088	.108	....	....	....	....	....	....	....	....	....	50.0	.0	0.08
109	" 20	592	....	2	.13	2.3	.102	.000	.102	.114	....	....	....	....	....	....	....	....	....	52.1	.0	0.20
111	" 20	595	....	1	.07	2.0	.080	.000	.080	.110	....	....	....	....	....	....	....	....	....	52.3	.0	0.16
113	" 20	586, 590, 592, 595	....	2	.08	1.8	.088	.000	.088	.110	.005	1.4	27.3	180	0	180	138	0	128	51.5	.0	0.13
116	" 27–30	652, 664, 693	7.1	2	....	1.4	.082	.000	.082	.090	.010	2.0	23.9	181	0	181	142	0	142	57.0	.0	0.03
	1896																					
121	Jan. 2	739	3.9	4	....	1.9	....	....	....	....	....	....	....	....	....	....	....	....	....	....	....	....
126	" 3	750	3.8	5	....	1.9	....	....	....	....	....	....	....	....	....	....	....	....	....	....	....	....
131	" 2–3	739, 750	3.8	5	....	1.9	.127	....	....	.094	.010	2.7	24.8	230	....	....	185	....	....	34.3	.0	0.55
136	" 4	771	2.4	4	....	1.9	.115	....	....	.066	.010	2.7	10.4	180	....	....	133	....	....	23.5	.0	0.49
153	" 9	817	1.9	2	....	1.8	....	....	....	....	....	....	....	....	....	....	....	....	....	....	....	....
158	" 10	829	1.9	2	.10	1.6	....	....	....	....	....	....	....	....	....	....	....	....	....	....	....	....
163	" 8–10	817, 829	1.9	2	.08	1.6	.136	.000	.136	.066	.010	3.1	7.4	130	0	130	89	0	89	32.4	.0	0.11
168	" 11	839	1.7	3	.09	1.5	.097	....	....	.060	.005	3.0	10.0	140	....	....	92	....	....	34.5	.0	0.40
173	" 14	860	1.5	3	....	1.0	....	....	....	....	....	....	....	....	....	....	....	....	....	....	....	....
178	" 15	882	1.2	3	.06	1.5	....	....	....	....	....	....	....	....	....	....	....	....	....	....	....	....
183	" 14–15	860, 882	1.3	3	....	1.3	.079	....	....	.036	.010	3.3	13.0	153	....	....	108	....	....	42.0	.0	0.47
188	" 20	974	2.2	2	.09	1.5	....	....	....	....	....	....	....	....	....	....	....	....	....	....	....	....
193	" 22	998	2.8	2	.03	1.4	.067	.000	.067	.064	.010	2.3	13.4	163	0	163	122	0	122	47.5	.0	0.00
198	" 27	1045	3.8	2	.08	1.7	....	....	....	....	....	....	....	....	....	....	....	....	....	....	....	....
202	" 28	1054	4.1	4	....	2.4	....	....	....	....	....	....	....	....	....	....	....	....	....	....	....	....
205	" 27–28	1045, 1054	4.0	4	....	2.0	.111	....	....	.086	.010	2.5	9.4	....	....	....	....	....	....	86.1	.0	0.28
214	" 29	1069	4.1	5	....	2.1	.117	....	....	.074	.014	2.0	9.2	237	....	....	183	....	....	85.3	.0	0.43
229	Feb. 5	1137, 1141, 1145	4.5	3	.13	1.2	.069	....	....	.060	.007	2.7	7.1	176	....	....	130	....	....	67.1	.0	0.15
234	" 6	1156, 1160, 1164	5.2	4	.17	1.3	.059	....	....	.056	.004	2.5	6.9	167	....	....	124	....	....	66.3	.0	0.33
239	" 7	1174, 1178	5.7	2	.03	1.1	.041	.000	.041	.048	.007	2.7	6.6	177	0	177	131	0	131	50.0	.0	0.05
244	" 8	1190, 1192, 1196	5.8	4	....	1.9	.071	....	....	.046	.003	2.4	9.1	172	....	....	123	....	....	55.1	.0	0.49
247	" 10	1204, 1208, 1212	5.8	3	.11	1.5	.045	....	....	.050	.006	2.2	11.0	150	....	....	120	....	....	43.0	.2	0.12

TABLE No. 1.—*Continued.*

Jewell System.

(Parts per Million.)

Serial Number.	Collected.		Temperature. Degrees C.	Degree of Clearness.	Color.	Oxygen Consumed.	Nitrogen as Albuminoid Ammonia.			Nitrogen as Free Ammonia.	Nitrogen as Nitrites.	Nitrogen as Nitrates.	Chlorine.	Residue on Evaporation.			Fixed Residue after Ignition.			Alkalinity.	Dissolved Alumina.	Iron.
	Date.	Corresponding Bacterial Numbers or Period of Collection by Automatic Sampler.					Total.	Suspended.	Dissolved.					Total.	Suspended.	Dissolved.	Total.	Suspended.	Dissolved.			
	1896																					
251	Feb. 11	1222, 1225, 1228	5.2	2	.04	1.4	.045	.000	.045	0.44	.004	1.7	8.5	142	0	142	107	0	107	37.0	.0	0.06
255	" 12	1241	4.8	5	....	2.4	.081	.016	.065	0.38	.003	1.9	8.7	186	14	172	132	17	115	42.7	.0	2.00
260	" 13	1249, 1252, 1255	4.8	2	.02	1.4	.043	.000	.043	0.40	.005	1.8	6.9	139	0	139	98	0	98	34.0	.0	0.11
266	" 14	1266, 1270, 1274	4.8	2	.11	1.6	.051	.000	.051	0.30	.002	2.4	6.6	149	0	149	103	0	103	56.4	.0	0.03
269	" 15	1284, 1288, 1292	4.6	3	.07	1.4	.055	......	......	0.32	.004	2.8	7.0	154	......	......	116	......	......	48.0	.0	0.03
274	" 17	1303, 1307, 1311	4.5	4	.14	1.3	.054	......	......	0.30	.003	2.8	3.5	138	......	......	108	......	......	52.5	.0	0.09
279	" 18	1321, 1325, 1329	5.1	4	.17	1.4	.038	......	......	0.20	.001	3.1	3.1	136	......	......	90	......	......	59.0	.0	0.30
282	" 19	1344, 1348, 1352	4.6	2	.08	1.0	.028	.000	.028	0.18	.002	3.0	4.0	139	0	139	111	0	111	27.3	.0	0.10
287	" 20	1363, 1372, 1378	2.6	2	.02	0.7	.032	.000	.032	.022	.004	2.0	5.1	137	0	137	109	0	109	14.9	.2	0.04
290	" 21	1393, 1395, 1398	2.5	2	.06	0.7	.036	.000	.036	.020	.003	2.2	5.0	136	0	136	112	0	112	27.1	.0	0.11
295	" 22	1409, 1410, 1413	1.8	5	.11	1.2	.052	......	......	.038	.004	1.6	5.6	127	......	......	99	......	......	26.0	.0	2.24
298	" 24	1421, 1424, 1427	2.7	2	.09	1.1	.042	.000	.042	.024	.004	1.6	5.8	122	0	122	93	0	93	38.7	.0	0.07
303	" 25	1438, 1442, 1446	1.8	3	.17	1.4	.050	......	......	.020	.004	1.7	4.9	117	......	......	87	......	......	45.0	.0	0.14
306	" 26	1457, 1461, 1467	2.7	3	.13	1.2	.040	......	......	.022	.004	1.7	4.7	124	......	......	93	......	......	44.3	.0	0.02
311	" 27	1473, 1480, 1484	3.0	2	....	0.8	.044	.000	.044	.022	.003	1.8	5.4	129	0	129	99	0	99	43.8	.0	0.06
314	" 28	9.20 A.M. to 12.15 P.M.	3.6	3	.12	1.3	.050	......	......	.024	.004	1.4	5.6	141	......	......	105	......	......	45.0	.0	0.08
319	" 29	9.58 " " 3.18 "	4.7	2	.13	1.3	.040	.000	.040	0.26	.005	1.3	5.6	155	0	155	110	0	110	53.2	.0	0.14
322	March 2	9.35 " " 3.15 "	4.2	2	.06	1.5	.042	.000	.042	0.18	.006	1.3	5.5	146	0	146	109	0	109	58.8	.0	0.10
325	" 2–3	3.15 P.M. to 3.20 P.M.	3.8	3	.06	1.2	.038	......	......	0.26	.003	1.3	6.4	136	......	......	102	......	......	56.1	.0	0.09
328	" 3–4	3.20 " " 3.20 "	3.6	3	.07	1.4	.044	......	......	0.24	.006	1.6	6.2	145	......	......	117	......	......	59.0	.0	0.08
333	" 4–5	3.20 " " 3.20 "	4.1	2	.07	1.0	.040	.000	.040	0.26	.010	1.6	6.6	155	0	155	119	0	119	57.0	.0	0.02
336	" 5–6	3.20 " " 3.20 "	4.5	2	.06	0.8	.046	.000	.046	0.26	.007	1.4	7.5	150	0	150	118	0	118	58.1	.0	0.04
341	" 6–7	3.20 " " 3.20 "	4.6	2	.08	0.8	.030	.000	.030	0.20	.007	1.3	8.9	152	0	152	114	0	114	56.4	.0	0.03
344	" 7–9	3.20 " " 3.20 "	4.9	1	.04	0.7	.024	.000	.024	0.22	.010	1.4	11.1	150	0	150	114	0	114	50.0	.0	0.03
349	" 9–10	3.30 " " 3.10 "	5.5	1	.03	0.7	.028	.000	.028	0.24	.009	1.5	12.4	152	0	152	120	0	120	50.9	.0	0.02
353	" 10–11	3.10 " " 3.20 "	5.7	1	.02	0.7	.034	.000	.034	0.22	.010	1.4	12.3	158	0	158	122	0	122	52.1	.0	0.05
357	" 11–12	3.20 " " 3.26 "	4.8	1	.01	0.8	.036	.000	.036	0.26	.009	1.4	11.6	160	0	160	127	0	127	59.7	.0	0.04
361	" 12–13	3.26 " " 3.15 "	4.4	2	.02	1.0	.034	.000	.034	0.26	.010	1.6	10.4	150	0	150	118	0	118	56.0	.0	0.02
365	" 14	1776	4.7	1	.04	0.8	.036	.000	.036	0.26	.008	1.1	8.8	135	0	135	105	0	108	50.1	.0	0.05
368	" 14–16	3.15 P.M. to 3.15 P.M.	4.9	2	.04	1.0	.044	.000	.044	0.30	.007	1.2	7.8	131	0	131	108	0	105	50.3	.0	0.05
373	" 16–17	3.15 " " 3.18 "	4.1	1	.04	1.1	.044	.000	.044	0.26	.005	1.2	8.0	126	0	126	97	0	97	47.1	.0	0.02
377	" 17–18	3.18 " " 3.24 "	5.0	1	.03	0.8	.034	.000	.034	0.28	.006	1.4	9.0	130	0	130	101	0	101	40.0	.0	0.02
381	" 18–19	3.24 " " 3.02 "	4.8	2	.06	1.0	.054	.000	.054	0.32	.002	1.1	7.9	132	0	132	102	0	102	49.1	.0	0.07
384	" 19–20	3.02 " " 3.33 "	4.2	2	.10	1.5	.048	.000	.048	0.64	.003	1.1	7.7	129	0	129	97	0	97	34.1	.0	0.05
389	" 20–21	3.33 " " 3.20 "	4.2	3	.09	1.3	.050	......	......	0.88	.004	1.0	5.3	133	......	......	105	......	......	21.5	.0	0.14
392	" 21–23	3.20 " " 3.00 "	6.3	4	.10	1.0	.044	......	......	0.74	.003	1.4	3.9	129	......	......	104	......	......	25.1	.0	0.18
397	" 24–25	9.00 A.M. to 8.30 A.M.	5.3	3	.06	0.9	.038	......	......	0.44	.003	1.3	5.9	114	......	......	90	......	......	15.4	.1	0.09
402	" 25–26	8.30 " " 8.30 "	5.8	2	.05	0.9	.028	.000	.028	0.26	.004	2.1	8.1	139	0	139	91	0	91	20.1	.0	0.08
406	" 26–27	8.30 " " 8.30 "	5.8	3	.09	1.0	.050	......	......	0.32	.004	2.0	2.4	152	......	......	119	......	......	51.1	.1	0.06

TABLE NO. 1.—*Continued.*

Jewell System.

(Parts per Million.)

Serial Number.	Collected.		Temperature. Degrees C.	Degree of Clearness.	Color.	Oxygen Consumed.	Nitrogen as Albuminoid Ammonia.			Nitrogen as Free Ammonia.	Nitrogen as Nitrites.	Nitrogen as Nitrates.	Chlorine.	Residue on Evaporation.			Fixed Residue after Ignition.			Alkalinity.	Dissolved Alumina.	Iron.
	Date.	Corresponding Bacterial Numbers or Period of Collection by Automatic Sampler.					Total.	Suspended.	Dissolved.					Total.	Suspended.	Dissolved.	Total.	Suspended.	Dissolved.			
	1896																					
410	Mar. 27–28	8.30 A.M. to 8.30 A.M.	5.8	2	.08	1.2	.058	.000	.058	.032	.005	2.1	4.9	172	0	172	138	0	138	59.2	.1	0.06
414	" 28–29	8.30 " " 8.30 "	6.0	2	.04	0.8	.046	.000	.046	.032	.005	2.1	5.9	141	0	141	101	0	101	31.9	.1	0.04
418	" 29–30	8.30 " " 8.30 "	8.1	2	.04	0.9	.068	.000	.068	.034	.004	2.0	5.5	148	0	148	98	0	98	35.3	.0	0.04
422	" 30	8.30 " " 5.30 P.M.	7.8	3	.08	1.0	.056	......	......	.032	.005	1.9	5.4	151	......	151	110	......	......	33.0	.0	0.06
426	" 31	9.15 " " 2.30 "	8.8	3	06	1.0	.064	......	......	.032	.005	2.1	6.6	170	......	170	120	......	......	37.4	.0	0.06
430	*	2.30 P.M. " 2.30 "	9.8	3	.10	1.1	.042	......	......	.032	.007	2.4	6.0	178	......	178	146	......	......	58.2	.0	0.08
434	April 1–2	2.30 " " 2.30 "	9.0	3	.08	0.8	.038	......	......	.024	.008	2.3	6.6	139	......	139	103	......	......	18.8	.0	0.07
438	" 2–3	2.30 " " 11.30 A.M.	8.7	3	.12	0.7	.040	......	......	.034	.005	1.4	6.5	132	......	132	102	......	......	5.5	.3	0.08
412	" 3–4	2.30 " " 2.30 P.M.	8.0	2	.06	0.6	0.36	.000	.036	.042	.004	0.8	3.6	102	0	102	78	0	76	1.3	.2	0.10
447	" 4–5	2.30 " " 2.30 "	9.0	2	.06	0.6	.048	.000	.048	.052	.004	0.8	3.2	88	0	88	71	0	71	†4.7	.7	0.04
451	" 6–7	2.30 " " 2.30 "	9.5	2	.05	0.5	.038	.000	.038	.038	.004	1.0	3.3	92	0	92	65	0	65	4.0	.2	0.07
455	" 7–8	2.30 " " 2.30 "	9.5	2	.02	0.8	.054	.000	.054	.042	.004	1.2	3.4	95	0	95	65	0	65	18.2	.0	0.01
458	" 8–9	2.30 " " 2.30 "	9.5	2	.13	0.8	.046	.000	.046	.028	.004	1.1	2.6	94	0	94	70	0	70	22.3	.0	0.06
461	" 9–10	2.30 " " 2.30 "	9.5	2	.11	1.0	.056	.000	.056	.034	.005	1.2	4.0	107	0	107	83	0	83	25.4	.0	0.00
464	" 10–11	2.30 " " 2.30 "	9.9	1	.08	0.9	.052	.000	.052	.036	.006	1.2	4.6	97	0	97	78	0	78	27.4	.0	0.01
466	" 11–13	2.30 " " 2.30 "	10 0	1	.07	1.1	.070	.000	.070	.040	.005	1.2	4.8	102	0	102	80	0	80	33.0	.0	0.03
467	" 13–14	2419, 2422, 2424	13.2	1	.13	1.1	.056	.000	.056	.032	.003	1.1	6.0	106	0	106	78	0	78	35.1	.0	0.00
470	" 14–15	2425, 2428, 2429	13.0	1	.06	1.1	.064	.000	.064	.032	.005	1.0	6.5	113	0	113	81	0	81	40.5	.0	0.08
472	" 15–16	2431, 2434, 2435	13.4	2	.07	1.1	.056	.000	.056	.038	.004	1.0	6.3	104	0	104	84	0	84	37.1	.0	0.01
474	" 16–17	2437, 2440, 2441	16.4	1	.04	1.1	.064	.000	.064	.052	.006	1.0	6.6	114	0	114	86	0	86	39.1	.0	0.02
476	" 17–18	2443, 2446, 2447	15.5	1	.04	0.9	.074	.000	.074	.046	.006	1.0	7.5	110	0	110	88	0	88	38.8	.0	0.04
479	" 18–20	2449, 2453, 2459	16.6	1	.05	0.6	.056	.000	.056	.042	.005	0.7	10.0	113	0	113	87	0	87	36.5	.0	0.03
482	" 21	2466, 2469, 2476	17.2	2	.05	0.6	.064	.000	.064	.042	.005	1.0	10.9	113	0	113	95	0	95	33.5	.0	0.02
485	" 22	2482, 2485, 2190	16.8	1	.05	0.6	.042	.000	.042	.038	.005	0.9	12.4	117	0	117	96	0	96	36.0	.0	0.01
488	" 23	2494, 2498, 2503	17.2	1	.05	0.6	.048	.000	.048	.034	.006	0.9	10.3	114	0	114	93	0	93	37.0	.0	0.02
491	" 24	2511, 2514, 2517	17.6	1	.05	0.7	.040	.000	.040	.032	.005	0.8	8.4	108	0	108	93	0	93	35.3	.0	0.00
494	" 25	2525, 2527	18.1	2	.05	0.6	.064	.000	.064	.042	.005	0.8	7.8	114	0	114	90	0	90	37.3	.0	0.00
497	" 27–28	3.20 P.M. to 9.00 A.M.	......	2	.08	0.8	.058	.000	.058	.040	.005	0.8	6.6	111	0	111	93	0	93	42.0	.0	0.00
499	" 28–29	9.00 A.M. " 9.00 "	21.2	2	.07	0.8	.056	.000	.056	.036	.005	0.8	6.0	116	0	116	94	0	94	40.0	.0	0.00
503	" 29–30	9.00 " " 9.00 "	20.4	2	.07	0.8	.054	.000	.054	.038	.006	0.8	6.6	118	0	118	98	0	98	45.3	.0	0.00
506	‡April 30 to May 1	9.00 " " 9.00 "	20.4	1	.10	0.8	.068	.000	.068	.030	.004	0.8	9.1	130	0	130	102	0	102	42.6	.0	0.01
509	May 1–2	9.00 " " 9.00 "	21.0	2	.02	0.9	.070	.000	.070	.036	.004	0.8	9.1	121	0	121	103	0	103	45.6	.0	0.03
512	" 2	9.00 " " 3.45 P.M.	......	1	.00	0.8	.054	.000	.054	.034	.005	0.9	8.5	126	0	126	107	0	107	48.3	.0	0.02
514	" 4–5	9.15 " " 9.00 A.M.	22.3	2	.08	1.0	.062	.000	.062	.042	.006	1.2	11.0	142	0	142	116	0	116	48.1	.0	0.05
517	" 5–6	9.00 " " 9.00 "	21.9	1	.05	1.0	.056	.000	.056	.040	.005	1.0	9.6	136	0	136	106	0	106	42.0	.0	0.04
520	" 6–7	9.00 " " 9.00 "	21.9	2	.08	1.1	.058	.000	.058	.040	.006	1.1	9.9	135	0	135	113	0	113	43.8	.0	0.06
524	" 7–8	9.00 " " 9.00 "	21.9	2	.12	1.3	.064	.000	.064	.040	.006	0.9	11.4	137	0	137	117	0	117	43.7	.0	0.03
527	" 8–9	9.00 " " 9.00 "	22.5	2	.04	1.7	.094	.000	.094	.052	.005	0.6	12.3	136	0	136	117	0	117	37.0	.0	0.05

* March 31 to April 1. † Acidity.

TABLE NO. 1—*Continued.*

Jewell System.

(Parts per Million.)

Serial Number.	Collected. Date.	Collected. Corresponding Bacterial Numbers or Period of Collection by Automatic Sampler.	Temperature, Degrees C.	Degree of Clearness.	Color.	Oxygen Consumed.	Nitrogen as Albuminoid Ammonia. Total.	Nitrogen as Albuminoid Ammonia. Suspended.	Nitrogen as Albuminoid Ammonia. Dissolved.	Nitrogen as Free Ammonia.	Nitrogen as Nitrites.	Nitrogen as Nitrates.	Chlorine.	Residue on Evaporation. Total.	Residue on Evaporation. Suspended.	Residue on Evaporation. Dissolved.	Fixed Residue after Ignition. Total.	Fixed Residue after Ignition. Suspended.	Fixed Residue after Ignition. Dissolved.	Alkalinity.	Dissolved Alumina.	Iron.
	1896																					
531	May 9	9.00 A.M. to 3.00 P.M.	23.2	2	.09	1.2	.050	.000	.050	.036	.005	0.7	10.4	141	0	141	110	0	110	40.0	.0	0.03
533	" 11–12	2825, 2830, 2857, 2867	23.8	1	.02	1.0	.054	.000	.054	.024	.003	0.8	10.1	134	0	134	102	0	102	37.0	.0	0.05
539	" 12–13	2873, 2877, 2881, 2685	23.2	1	.02	1.1	.066	.000	.066	.028	.004	0.5	11.5	129	0	129	104	0	104	38.2	.0	0.02
541	" 13–14	2891, 2896, 2900, 2905	23.4	1	.01	0.9	.058	.000	.058	.034	.004	0.8	11.0	121	0	121	104	0	104	38.3	.0	0.08
546	" 14–15	2909, 2914, 2919, 2923	22.9	1	.01	0.8	.048	.000	.048	.028	.002	0.5	10.3	132	0	132	100	0	100	37.1	.0	0.05
550	" 15–16	2927, 2932, 2961, 2970	23.9	1	.02	0.9	.046	.000	.046	.024	.003	0.5	10.9	128	0	128	98	0	98	40.2	.0	0.07
554	" 16	2981, 2992	23.8	2	.14	1.4	.056	.000	.056	.022	.003	0.5	12.3	141	0	141	107	0	107	44.6	.0	0.01
557	" 18–19	3000, 3008, 3015, 3024	23.7	1	.....	.....	.078	.000	.078	.036	.005	0.7	14.7	142	0	142	106	0	106	47.2	.0	.....
563	" 19–20	3032, 3041, 3051, 3057	24.0	2	.06	1.2	.070	.000	.070	.026	.001	0.6	12.7	146	0	146	107	0	107	52.0	.0	0.04
566	" 20–21	3069, 3077, 3086, 3093	23.9	1	.04	1.3	.062	.000	.062	.034	.001	0.7	11.4	131	0	131	104	0	104	49.0	.0	0.01
570	" 21–22	3101, 3112, 3118, 3127	23.8	1	.04	1.3	.068	.000	.068	.038	.000	0.8	10.6	147	0	147	118	0	118	51.0	.0	0.02
574	" 22	3137, 3148, 3155	24.2	2	.12	1.4	.078	.000	.078	.046	.000	0.7	12.0	152	0	152	110	0	110	51.0	.0	0.09
576	" 25–26	3175, 3182, 3189, 3198	26.0	1	.06	1.2	.070	.000	.070	.030	.000	0.7	12.5	150	0	150	113	0	113	63.0	.0	0.03
581	" 26–27	3213, 3222, 3229	25.5	2	.08	1.2	.066	.000	.066	.030	.000	0.8	13.5	139	0	139	105	0	105	56.4	.0	0.02
583	" 27–28	3241, 3256, 3265, 3273	24.0	1	.05	1.1	.064	.000	.064	.040	.000	0.6	12.5	145	0	145	116	0	116	56.2	.0	0.03
587	" 28–29	*	24.2	2	.08	1.4	.084	.000	.084	.056	.004	0.7	12.9	167	0	167	129	0	129	52.2	.0	0.09
592	" 29–30	†	23.6	4	.11	1.6	.080	.....	.....	.060	.007	0.9	10.4	180	....	....	146	....	....	51.8	.0	0.20
595	" 30	340	24.0	1	.05	1.0	.060	.000	.060	.062	.003	0.9	9.2	178	0	178	144	0	144	43 4	.0	0.05
601	June 2–3	3436, 3442, 3451	22.6	3	.08	1.1	.076	.....	.....	.026	.000	0.9	12.1	188	....	....	135	....	....	28.9	.1	0.08
605	" 3–4	3458, 3468, 3478, 3487	22.9	2	.04	0.9	.056	.000	.056	.028	.001	0.9	12.1	174	0	174	132	0	132	30.7	.1	0.05
608	" 4–5	3496, 3509, 3531, 3543	23.9	2	.09	0.9	.062	.000	.062	.028	.001	0.8	10.2	159	0	159	121	0	121	37.8	.0	0.06
615	" 5–6	3556, 3559, 3586, 3596	24.4	2	.11	0.8	.068	.000	.068	.036	.001	0.7	13.7	174	0	174	122	0	122	30.0	.0	0.09
618	" 6	3624, 3629	25.2	1	.06	1.0	.052	.000	.052	.024	.001	0.7	14.1	169	0	169	127	0	127	43.8	.0	0.02
625	" 9	3657	26.6	2	.09	1.1	.060	.000	.060	.038	.000	1.1	14.8	174	0	174	138	0	138	41.8	.0	0.05
628	" 10	3669, 3672, 3676	24.6	1	.04	1.0	.062	.000	.062	.024	.000	0.7	16.8	185	0	185	143	0	143	22.5	.3	0.00
631	" 11	3682, 3685, 3693	25.2	2	.06	1.0	.066	.000	.066	.030	.000	0.6	16.0	178	0	178	138	0	138	31.2	.0	0.05
634	" 12	3699, 3703, 3706	24.8	1	.06	1.0	.062	.000	.062	.018	.000	0.9	17.6	203	0	203	149	0	149	38.3	.0	0.06
638	" 13	3713, 3719, 3725	24.4	1	.04	1.1	.060	.000	.060	.022	.000	0.8	18.0	179	0	179	133	0	133	42.0	.0	0.00
644	" 15	3741, 3744, 3748	24.0	2	.04	1.3	.072	.000	.072	.028	.000	0.8	14.0	172	0	172	131	0	131	36.1	.0	0.08
648	" 16	3760, 3764	25.4	1	.06	1.1	.062	.000	.062	.026	.005	0.9	14.9	179	0	179	136	0	136	24.0	.1	0.07
653	" 18	3797, 3802, 3810	25.4	1	.05	1.1	.070	.000	.070	.028	.000	0.6	12.5	164	0	164	118	0	118	34.6	.0	0.06
657	" 19	3819, 3830	25.9	1	.04	1.5	.074	.000	.074	.030	.000	0.7	14.1	160	0	160	114	0	114	41.9	.0	0.06
660	" 20	3860, 3863, 3872	27.3	1	.04	1.5	.068	.000	.068	.018	.000	0.6	17.0	180	0	180	125	0	125	41.3	.0	0.07
664	" 22	3889, 3895, 3900	27.1	2	.03	1.3	.074	.000	.074	.022	.000	0.6	20.2	189	0	189	135	0	135	47.0	.0	0.00
667	" 23	3921, 3925, 3927	26.8	1	.05	1.3	.084	.000	.084	.030	.001	0.7	16.5	187	0	187	135	0	135	56.0	.0	0.06
670	" 24	3939, 3951, 3955	27.0	2	.12	1.5	.096	.000	.096	.026	.000	0.7	24.1	195	0	195	128	0	128	55.6	.0	0.12
680	" 25	3994, 4002, 4006	26.8	2	.08	1.8	.092	.000	.092	.026	.004	0.7	27.4	208	0	208	147	0	147	60.2	.0	0.07
682	" 26	4024, 4031, 4035	......	1	.10	1.5	.068	.000	.068	.026	.005	0.8	23.9	199	0	199	143	0	143	49.0	.0	0.05

* 3295, 3306, 3333, 3340, 3356.

† 3361, 3368, 3380, 3388, 3394.

TABLE NO. 1.—*Continued.*

Jewell System.

(Parts per Million.)

Serial Number.	Collected. Date.	Collected. Corresponding Bacterial Numbers or Period of Collection by Automatic Sampler.	Temperature, Degrees C.	Degree of Clearness.	Color.	Oxygen Consumed.	Nitrogen as Albuminoid Ammonia. Total.	Nitrogen as Albuminoid Ammonia. Suspended.	Nitrogen as Albuminoid Ammonia. Dissolved.	Nitrogen as Free Ammonia.	Nitrogen as Nitrites.	Nitrogen as Nitrates.	Chlorine.	Residue on Evaporation. Total.	Residue on Evaporation. Suspended.	Residue on Evaporation. Dissolved.	Fixed Residue after Ignition. Total.	Fixed Residue after Ignition. Suspended.	Fixed Residue after Ignition. Dissolved.	Alkalinity.	Dissolved Alumina.	Iron.
	1896																					
685	June 27	4044, 4052, 4055	26.7	1	.08	1.2	.076	.000	.076	.022	.007	0.7	21.1	189	0	189	139	0	139	42.1	.0	0.11
687	" 29	4062, 4068, 4070	25.2	1	.04	1.0	.072	.000	.072	.022	.003	0.9	15.2	190	0	190	146	0	146	14.8	.0	0.11
691	" 30	4082, 4100, 4105	26.2	2	.04	1.1	.064	.000	.064	.026	.001	1.0	12.4	180	0	180	137	0	137	5.8	.0	0.12
694	July 1	4112, 4123	26.3	2	.05	1.0	.054	.000	.054	.022	.000	0.9	10.5	196	0	196	138	0	138	†1.8	.3	0.03
697	" 2	4144, 4153, 4157	26.0	3	.07	1.3	.066	......	......	.020	.001	0.9	8.3	176	......	......	128	......	......	†3.9	.4	0.13
702	" 3	4165, 4182, 4192	26.6	1	.05	1.2	.066	.000	.066	.020	.001	0.6	7.0	130	0	130	99	0	99	4.6	.8	0.12
706	" 6	4229	26.5	1	.04	0.9	.066	.000	.066	.016	.001	0.9	14.2	143	0	143	109	0	109	14.2	.0	0.03
709	" 7	4246, 4253, 4257	27.4	1	.05	1.1	.068	.000	.068	.024	.006	1.0	11.0	130	0	130	94	0	94	16.0	.0	0.03
717	" 8–9	4275, 4280, 4283, 4302	26.5	1	.12	0.9	.062	.000	.062	.024	.005	0.8	7.0	135	0	135	102	0	102	8.8	.1	0.07
722	" 10	4315, 4318, 4321	26.4	1	.05	0.7	.066	.000	.066	.022	.003	0.8	5.2	134	0	134	97	0	97	17.0	.0	0.03
725	" 11	4329, 4334, 4347	26.2	2	.05	0.8	.060	.000	.060	.020	.002	0.9	8.3	136	0	136	100	0	100	8.3	.0	0.07
728	" 13	4369, 4371, 4373	26.1	2	.07	0.9	.060	.000	.060	.024	.009	0.9	3.8	144	0	144	103	0	103	4.1	.3	0.07
733	" 14	4397, 4410, 4423	26.2	2	.02	0.9	.056	.000	.056	.026	.006	0.8	7.0	138	0	138	96	0	96	†1.0	.3	0.14
736	" 15	4440, 4444, 4449	26.2	2	.06	0.9	.066	.000	.066	.024	.001	0.9	4.5	127	0	127	91	0	91	2.5	.2	0.12
739	" 16	4460, 4470, 4474	26.2	2	.05	0.9	.062	.000	.062	.020	.000	0.6	2.3	112	0	112	91	0	91	17.0	.0	0.05
750	" 17–18	4504, 4526, 4545, 4556	26.0	2	.07	0.8	.058	.000	.058	.020	.001	0.5	4.0	136	0	136	95	0	95	10.0	.4	0.02
754	" 20	4571, 4573, 4578	24.0	2	.05	0.9	.052	.000	.052	.018	.001	0.7	5.5	144	0	144	101	0	101	15.2	.2	0.07
758	" 21	4601, 4609, 4612	23.8	1	.04	1.0	.060	.000	.060	.022	.001	0.8	6.2	144	0	144	100	0	100	17.1	.1	0.01
762	" 22	4623, 4625	23.8	2	.06	1.2	.064	.000	.064	.038	.008	0.9	8.6	158	0	158	103	0	103	14.0	.1	0.06
765	" 23	4636, 4644, 4646	......	2	.06	1.3	.084	.000	.084	.048	.010	0.7	7.0	166	0	166	126	0	126	8.9	.1	0.04
772	" 24	4679, 4687, 4688	25.9	3	.06	1.2	.062	......	......	.030	.006	1.0	3.5	222	......	......	184	......	......	†2.1	.3	0.14
774	" 25	4706, 4709, 4713	25.7	2	.05	1.1	.058	.000	.058	.028	.004	0.8	7.4	231	0	231	169	0	169	†6.0	.3	0.12
779	" 27	4728, 4731, 4735	26.2	2	.05	1.1	.066	.000	.066	.042	.020	0.9	4.9	172	0	172	135	0	135	†3.8	.3	0.10
785	" 28	4770, 4782	26.5	2	.05	1.3	.066	.000	.066	.044	.010	0.7	7.5	160	0	160	116	0	116	†1.9	.2	0.12
792	" 29	4828, 4842, 4853	26.5	2	.07	1.8	.068	.000	.068	.042	.006	0.7	5.0	153	0	153	114	0	114	4.2	.0	0.35

Western Gravity System.

Serial Number.	Date.	Corresponding Bacterial Numbers or Period of Collection by Automatic Sampler.	Temperature, Degrees C.	Degree of Clearness.	Color.	Oxygen Consumed.	Alb. Ammonia Total.	Alb. Ammonia Suspended.	Alb. Ammonia Dissolved.	Free Ammonia.	Nitrites.	Nitrates.	Chlorine.	Residue Total.	Residue Suspended.	Residue Dissolved.	Fixed Residue Total.	Fixed Residue Suspended.	Fixed Residue Dissolved.	Alkalinity.	Dissolved Alumina.	Iron.
	1895																					
117	Dec. 27–30	653, 662, 694	7.2	2	.04	1.4	.082	.000	.082	.090	.010	2.0	23.8	199	0	199	158	0	158	59.7	.0	0.01
	1896																					
122	Jan. 2	737	4.1	1	....	1.3	......	......	......	......	......	......	......	......	......	......	......	......	......	......	...	......
127	" 3	751	4.6	1	....	1.5	......	......	......	......	......	......	......	......	......	......	......	......	......	......	...	......
132	" 2–3	737, 751	4.3	1	....	1.3	.088	.000	.088	.088	.010	2.7	25.1	214	0	214	174	0	174	43.2	.0	0.17
137	" 4	770	2.7	3	....	1.0	......	......	......	......	......	......	......	......	......	......	......	......	......	......	...	......
141	" 6	777	2.2	1	....	1.8	......	......	......	......	......	......	......	......	......	......	......	......	......	......	...	......
145	" 4–6	770, 777	2.3	3	....	1.4	.077	......	......	.054	.010	2.8	10.0	171	......	......	113	......	......	28.7	.0	0.05
149	" 8	804	1.8	2	....	1.7	......	......	......	......	......	......	......	......	......	......	......	......	......	......	...	......
154	" 9	818	2.0	2	....	1.9	......	......	......	......	......	......	......	......	......	......	......	......	......	......	...	......

† Acidity.

TABLE No. 1.—*Continued.*

Western Gravity System.

(Parts per Million.)

Serial Number.	Collected. Date.	Collected. Corresponding Bacterial Numbers or Period of Collection by Automatic Sampler.	Temperature, Degrees C.	Degree of Clearness.	Color.	Oxygen Consumed.	Nitrogen as Albuminoid Ammonia. Total.	Nitrogen as Albuminoid Ammonia. Suspended.	Nitrogen as Albuminoid Ammonia. Dissolved.	Nitrogen as Free Ammonia.	Nitrogen as Nitrites.	Nitrogen as Nitrates.	Chlorine.	Residue on Evaporation. Total.	Residue on Evaporation. Suspended.	Residue on Evaporation. Dissolved.	Fixed Residue after Ignition. Total.	Fixed Residue after Ignition. Suspended.	Fixed Residue after Ignition. Dissolved.	Alkalinity.	Dissolved Alumina.	Iron.
	1896																					
159	Jan. 10	830	2.0	2	.07	1.8	...	...	...	...	...	...	...	...	...	...	...	...	...	...	...	...
164	" 8–10	804, 818, 830	1.9	2	.12	1.6	.113	.000	.113	.060	.010	3.2	8.3	139	0	139	99	0	99	36.2	.0	0.13
169	" 11	837	1.9	1	.02	1.3	.091	.000	.091	.056	.005	3.0	9.7	142	0	142	99	0	99	35.2	.0	0.01
174	" 14	861	1.4	1	.04	1.0	...	...	...	...	...	...	...	...	...	...	...	...	...	...	...	...
179	" 15	883	1.5	2	.12	1.6	...	...	...	...	...	...	...	...	...	...	...	...	...	...	...	...
184	" 14–15	861, 883	1.4	2	.08	1.3	.079	.000	.079	.032	.010	3.4	11.7	156	0	156	111	0	111	44.9	.0	0.14
189	" 20	975	2.0	1	.04	1.5	...	...	...	...	...	...	...	...	...	...	...	...	...	...	...	...
194	" 22	999	2.8	2	.06	1.7	.071	.000	.071	.060	.010	2.3	12.8	165	0	165	122	0	122	52.5	.0	0.01
199	" 27	1046	4.6	1	.01	1.2	...	...	...	...	...	...	...	...	...	...	...	...	...	...	...	...
203	" 28	1055	4.0	1	...	2.1	...	...	...	...	...	...	...	...	...	...	...	...	...	...	...	...
206	" 27–28	1046, 1055	4.0	4	...	1.7	.095	...	...	.082	.010	2.5	9.2	243	...	...	185	...	...	84.0	.0	0.18
217	Feb. 1	1097, 1100	4.2	2	.04	1.2	.055	.000	.055	.042	.006	1.7	22.3	224	0	224	154	0	154	47.0	.0	0.15
221	" 3	1108, 1111, 1113	4.8	1	.02	0.8	.049	.000	.049	.058	.005	1.9	18.3	200	0	200	149	0	149	57.0	.0	0.11
225	" 4	1122, 1125, 1128	4.4	2	.01	1.1	.049	.000	.049	.060	.008	1.8	17.5	186	0	186	138	0	138	54.0	.0	0.15
230	" 5	1138, 1142, 1146	4.9	2	.06	1.4	.065	.000	.065	.060	.006	2.7	7.2	186	0	186	130	0	130	70.8	.0	0.02
235	" 6	1157, 1162, 1165	5.0	2	.04	1.3	.071	.000	.071	.062	.004	2.7	7.2	175	0	175	125	0	125	60.2	.0	0.07
240	" 7	1175, 1179	5.5	3	.12	1.5	.061	...	...	.048	.007	2.9	6.3	192	...	...	127	...	...	57.7	.0	0.25
248	" 10	1206, 1209, 1213	5.0	1	.00	1.2	.037	.000	.037	.050	.005	2.5	11.1	136	0	136	108	0	108	24.1	.0	0.04
252	" 11	1223, 1226, 1229	5.0	1	.01	1.1	.035	.000	.035	.046	.004	1.4	8.1	129	0	129	99	0	99	23.3	.0	0.04
256	" 12	1238	4.8	1	.00	0.8	.031	.000	.031	.046	.006	1.9	8.7	165	0	165	118	0	118	12.9	.0	0.10
261	" 13	1250, 1253, 1256	4.9	2	.03	1.2	.051	.000	.051	.040	.005	1.8	7.0	138	0	138	100	0	100	28.3	.0	0.07
270	" 15	1285, 1289, 1293	4.9	3	.07	1.1	.045	...	...	.032	.004	2.4	7.0	145	...	...	113	...	...	35.9	.0	0.10
275	" 17	1304, 1308, 1313	4.4	1	.02	0.9	.046	.000	.046	.030	.003	3.0	3.5	137	0	137	105	0	105	42.4	.0	0.00
283	" 19	1345, 1349, 1353	4.5	2	.09	0.9	.038	.000	.038	.020	.001	2.6	4.0	120	0	120	96	0	96	31.7	.0	0.06
291	" 21	1391, 1396	2.5	2	.02	0.9	.038	.000	.038	.034	.003	2.0	5.6	139	0	139	114	0	114	17.3	.0	0.00
299	" 24	1419, 1425, 1428	2.5	1	.04	0.9	.036	.000	.036	.018	.004	1.7	5.8	126	0	126	98	0	98	28.7	.0	0.07
307	" 26	1458, 1463, 1466	2.7	1	.04	0.8	.032	.000	.032	.022	.004	1.7	4.7	119	0	119	95	0	95	35.9	.0	0.00
315	" 28–29	1498, 1503, 1518	3.9	1	.02	0.9	.036	.000	.036	.020	.005	1.3	5.5	155	0	155	107	0	107	44.0	.0	0.06
323	Mar. 2	1538, 1542, 1546	4.3	2	.07	0.9	.040	.000	.040	.014	.007	1.2	5.5	138	0	138	105	0	105	56.2	.0	0.03
331	" 4	1578, 1582, 1586	3.6	2	.08	1.0	.032	.000	.032	.018	.007	1.6	6.1	136	0	136	106	0	106	58.0	.0	0.06
339	" 6–7	1618, 1628, 1639, 1645	5.4	1	.06	0.8	.032	.000	.032	.024	.009	1.6	8.6	150	0	150	110	0	110	54.5	.0	0.00
345	" 9	1658, 1663, 1667	4.8	1	.03	0.8	.028	.000	.028	.018	.009	1.4	11.2	159	0	159	116	0	116	58.0	.0	0.00
356	" 11	1702, 1704, 1708	5.9	2	.02	0.7	.034	.000	.034	.026	.010	1.3	12.4	157	0	157	121	0	121	54.3	.0	0.02
362	" 13–14	1741, 1749, 1761, 1773	5.0	1	.06	0.9	.036	.000	.036	.026	.109	1.3	9.4	148	0	148	114	0	114	57.7	.0	0.03
372	" 16	1787, 1793, 1799	4.1	1	.05	1.0	.052	.000	.052	.038	.007	1.5	7.3	133	0	133	105	0	105	53.9	.0	0.02
380	" 18–19	1837, 1843, 1850	4.3	2	.08	1.0	.052	.000	.052	.030	.002	1.1	7.5	140	0	140	106	0	106	50.2	.0	0.04
388	" 20	1864, 1872, 1876	4.7	4	.13	1.3	.038	...	...	.058	.003	1.0	8.0	158	...	...	126	...	...	34.0	.0	0.23
698	July 2	4145, 4158	26.4	3	.07	1.5	.080	...	...	.024	.001	0.9	9.5	181	...	...	140	...	...	6.1	.2	0.13
703	" 3	4166, 4183, 4195	26.6	2	.04	1.2	.068	.000	.068	.028	.002	0.6	7.2	136	0	136	97	0	97	6.0	.1	0.16

TABLE No. 1.—*Continued.*

Western Gravity System.

(Parts per Million.)

Serial Number.	Collected. Date.	Collected. Corresponding Bacterial Numbers or Period of Collection by Automatic Sampler.	Temperature, Degrees C.	Degree of Clearness.	Color.	Oxygen Consumed.	Nitrogen as Albuminoid Ammonia. Total.	Nitrogen as Albuminoid Ammonia. Suspended.	Nitrogen as Albuminoid Ammonia. Dissolved.	Nitrogen as Free Ammonia.	Nitrogen as Nitrites.	Nitrogen as Nitrates.	Chlorine.	Residue on Evaporation. Total.	Residue on Evaporation. Suspended.	Residue on Evaporation. Dissolved.	Fixed Residue after Ignition. Total.	Fixed Residue after Ignition. Suspended.	Fixed Residue after Ignition. Dissolved.	Alkalinity.	Dissolved Alumina.	Iron.
	1896																					
726	July 10–11	*	26.5	2	.07	1.2	.068	.000	.068	.024	.001	0.9	6.0	125	0	125	85	0	85	38.0	.0	0.05
751	" 17–18	4505, 4524, 4547, 4555	25.8	2	.07	1.2	.062	.000	.062	.024	.000	0.4	3.8	124	0	124	80	0	80	33.1	.0	0.05
775	" 24–25	4677, 4703, 4707, 4708	26.2	4	.12	1.9	.088	.....	.....	.022	.003	0.7	7.9	171	.....	.....	130	.....	.....	31.0	.0	0.18
803	" 31	4883, 4888, 4892	26.6	2	.08	1.3	.074	.000	.074	.032	.002	0.8	3.4	116	0	116	83	0	83	25.9	.0	0.11
	Western Pressure System.																					
	1895																					
118	Dec. 27–30	654, 663, 695	7.4	2	.04	1.6	.080	.000	.080	.090	.010	2.0	22.8	197	0	197	152	0	152	59.0	.0	0.00
	1896																					
123	Jan. 2	738	4.1	1	....	1.7	.....	.....	.....	.....	.....	.....	.....	.....	.....	.....	.....	.....	.....	.....	.....	.....
128	" 3	752	3.9	1	....	1.2	.....	.....	.....	.....	.....	.....	.....	.....	.....	.....	.....	.....	.....	.....	.....	.....
133	" 2–3	738, 752	4.0	2	.08	1.5	.089	.000	.089	.086	.010	2.7	25.1	200	0	200	160	0	160	42.5	.0	0.00
138	" 4	769	2.8	1	....	1.3	.....	.....	.....	.....	.....	.....	.....	.....	.....	.....	.....	.....	.....	.....	.....	.....
142	" 6	778	2.2	1	....	1.4	.....	.....	.....	.....	.....	.....	.....	.....	.....	.....	.....	.....	.....	.....	.....	.....
146	" 4–6	769, 778	2.4	1	.04	1.2	.077	.000	.077	.058	.010	2.8	9.9	162	0	162	109	0	109	28.3	.0	0.00
150	" 8	805	1.8	1	....	1.7	.....	.....	.....	.....	.....	.....	.....	.....	.....	.....	.....	.....	.....	.....	.....	.....
155	" 9	819	1.9	2	....	1.8	.....	.....	.....	.....	.....	.....	.....	.....	.....	.....	.....	.....	.....	.....	.....	.....
160	" 10	831	1.9	2	.08	1.6	.....	.....	.....	.....	.....	.....	.....	.....	.....	.....	.....	.....	.....	.....	.....	.....
165	" 8–10	805, 819, 831	1.9	2	.13	1.7	.119	.000	.119	.062	.010	3.0	8.2	136	0	136	95	0	95	35.3	.0	0.00
170	" 11	838	1.9	1	.02	1.4	.101	.000	.101	.066	.005	3.0	9.8	143	0	143	98	0	98	36.2	.0	0.00
175	" 14	862	1.4	1	.02	1.4	.....	.....	.....	.....	.....	.....	.....	.....	.....	.....	.....	.....	.....	.....	.....	.....
180	" 15	884	1.5	1	.03	1.7	.....	.....	.....	.....	.....	.....	.....	.....	.....	.....	.....	.....	.....	.....	.....	.....
185	" 14–15	862, 884	1.4	1	.03	1.6	.097	.000	.097	.044	.010	3.4	11.6	158	0	158	113	0	113	43.3	.0	0.00
190	" 20	976	2.2	1	.04	1.4	.....	.....	.....	.....	.....	.....	.....	.....	.....	.....	.....	.....	.....	.....	.....	.....
195	" 22	1000	2.8	2	.04	1.5	.071	.000	.071	.064	.006	2.3	12.7	162	0	162	120	0	120	52.0	.0	0.00
200	" 27	1047	4.0	1	.01	1.4	.080	.000	.080	.....	.....	.....	.....	.....	.....	.....	.....	.....	.....	.....	.....	.....
207	" 28	1056	4.2	3	....	1.7	.101	.....	.....	.088	.....	.....	.....	.....	.....	.....	.....	.....	.....	.....	.....	.....
209	" 28	1062	.....	5	....	9.0	.581	.....	.....	.098	.010	.....	7.5	672	.....	.....	603	.....	.....	79.5	.0	0.00
211	" 27–28	1047, 1056	4.1	2	.04	1.4	.089	.000	.089	.084	.010	2.4	10.2	235	0	235	175	0	175	79.0	.0	0.00
218	Feb. 1	1098, 1101	4.4	1	.04	1.3	.039	.000	.039	.044	.005	1.6	22.4	234	0	234	153	0	153	49.0	.0	0.00
222	" 3	1109, 1112, 1114	4.6	1	.02	0.8	.051	.000	.051	.046	.003	1.8	21.0	211	0	211	153	0	153	55.7	.0	0.00
226	" 4	1123, 1126, 1129	4.4	1	.01	1.1	.051	.000	.051	.058	.008	2.0	17.0	184	0	184	130	0	130	56.7	.0	0.00
231	" 5	1139, 1143, 1147	4.9	3	.09	1.4	.071	.....	.....	.064	.007	3.1	7.2	196	.....	.....	136	.....	.....	67.5	.0	0.00
236	" 6	1158, 1159, 1166	5.2	3	.12	1.6	.073	.....	.....	.060	.011	3.2	6.3	170	.....	.....	126	.....	.....	59.9	.0	0.28
241	" 7	1176, 1180	5.6	3	.14	1.5	.061	.....	.....	.048	.006	3.5	6.8	193	.....	.....	135	.....	.....	57.8	.0	0.22
249	" 10	1205, 1210, 1214	5.0	1	.01	1.1	.041	.000	.041	.050	.005	2.6	11.8	132	0	132	104	0	104	23.0	.0	0.11
253	" 11	1224, 1227, 1230	5.0	2	.03	1.2	.043	.000	.043	.046	.004	1.7	8.0	129	0	129	101	0	101	21.4	.0	0.07

* 4316, 4319, 4322, 4330, 4335, 4348.

TABLE No. 1.—*Continued.*

Western Pressure System.

(Parts per Million.)

Serial Number.	Collected.		Temperature, Degrees C.	Degree of Clearness.	Color.	Oxygen Consumed.	Nitrogen as Albuminoid Ammonia.			Nitrogen as Free Ammonia.	Nitrogen as Nitrites.	Nitrogen as Nitrates.	Chlorine.	Residue on Evaporation.			Fixed Residue after Ignition.			Alkalinity.	Dissolved Alumina.*	Iron.
	Date.	Corresponding Bacterial Numbers or Period of Collection by Automatic Sampler.					Total.	Suspended.	Dissolved.					Total.	Suspended.	Dissolved.	Total.	Suspended.	Dissolved.			
	1896																					
257	Jan. 12	1237, 1239, 1240	4.8	1	.03	1.1	.047	.000	.047	.033	.004	1.9	8.0	156	0	156	103	0	103	16.1	.0	0.10
262	" 13	1251, 1254, 1257	4.8	2	.04	1.0	.047	.000	.047	.034	.005	1.4	7.1	140	0	140	101	0	101	26.0	.0	0.12
271	" 15	1286, 1290, 1294	4.8	2	.08	1.3	.053	.000	.053	.034	.003	3.2	7.2	140	0	140	104	0	104	40.0	.0	0.09
276	" 17	1305, 1309, 1314	4.4	2	.06	1.0	.048	.000	.048	.038	.003	3.0	3.5	135	0	135	102	0	102	42.7	.0	0.08
284	" 19	1346, 1350, 1354	4.5	5	.04	2.3	.076	.046	.030	.022	.003	3.0	4.7	180	.....	.....	145	....	....	30.9	.0	1.00
292	" 21	1392, 1397	2.6	2	.03	1.0	.034	.000	.034	.024	.003	1.6	5.3	139	0	139	111	0	111	17.0	.0	0.07
300	" 24	1420, 1426, 1429	2.5	2	.04	1.2	.036	.000	.036	.024	.005	1.5	5.5	126	0	126	96	0	96	28.2	.0	0.04
308	" 26	1459, 1463, 1465	2.6	1	.04	0.8	.036	.000	.036	.030	.004	1.7	4.5	120	0	120	92	0	92	35.6	.0	0.00
316	Feb. 28–29	1499, 1504, 1519, 1523	4.0	3	.13	1.1	.030	.....	.....	.020	.005	1.7	5.5	139	.....	.....	105	....	....	44.1	.0	0.07
324	Mar. 2	1539, 1543, 1547	3.8	2	.09	1.0	.040	.000	.040	.018	.006	1.2	5.7	136	0	136	98	0	98	57.2	.0	0.02
332	" 4	1579, 1583, 1587	4.0	2	.08	0.9	.030	.000	.030	.022	.006	1.6	6.0	133	0	133	106	0	106	57.6	.0	0.04
340	" 6–7	1619, 1629, 1640, 1646	5.0	2	.08	0.9	.030	.000	.030	.018	.007	1.7	8.8	150	0	150	112	0	112	57.2	.0	0.00
345	" 9	9.00 A.M. to 3.25 P.M.	4.8	1	.03	0.7	.026	.000	.026	.022	.010	1.6	6.3	160	0	160	116	0	116	55.1	.0	0.01
350	" 9–11	3.25 P.M. " 3.27 "	5.3	2	.06	0.9	.048	.000	.048	.026	.010	0.9	12.2	165	0	165	131	0	131	50.5	.0	0.10
358	" 11–14	3.27 " " 3.18 "	4.6	1	.05	1.1	.040	.000	.040	.026	.009	1.1	9.5	153	0	153	119	0	119	57.3	.0	0.03
369	" 14–16	3.18 " " 3.22 "	4.1	1	.03	0.9	.036	.000	.036	.026	.007	1.2	7.8	130	0	130	103	0	103	53.2	.0	0.03
374	" 16–19	3.22 " " 3.11 "	4.7	2	.11	1.2	.070	.000	.070	.034	.003	1.2	8.6	150	0	150	102	0	102	49.1	.0	0.05
385	" 19–20	3.11 " " 3.37 "	4.3	3	.04	1.2	.034	.....	.....	.054	.004	....	8.1	142	.....	.....	112	....	....	35.8	.0	0.20
393	" 23	9.00 A.M. " 4.00 "	6.0	4	.11	1.4	.070	.....	.....	.064	.003	1.5	4.0	140	.....	.....	110	....	....	17.1	.0	0.24
398	" 24–25	9.00 " " 8.30 A.M.	5.3	4	.12	0.9	.040	.....	.....	.052	.002	1.7	5.6	140	.....	.....	112	....	....	11.0	.0	0.12
403	" 25–26	8.30 " " 8.30 "	5.6	4	.08	1.1	.036	.....	.....	.034	.004	2.1	8.3	156	.....	.....	107	....	...	20.9	.0	0.04
407	" 26–27	8.30 " " 8.30 "	5.6	2	.04	0.7	.042	.000	.042	.042	.004	2.0	4.8	148	0	148	113	0	113	26.0	.0	0.06
411	" 27–28	8.30 " " 8.30 "	5.9	2	.05	0.9	.048	.000	.048	.032	.005	2.1	4.3	160	0	160	125	0	125	31.2	.0	0.06
415	" 28–29	8.30 " " 8.30 "	6.0	2	.08	0.9	.052	.000	.052	.034	.006	2.0	5.6	159	0	159	116	0	116	28.1	.0	0.10
419	" 29–30	8.30 " " 8.30 "	7.8	2	.08	0.9	.052	.000	.052	.034	.004	2.1	5.4	166	0	166	109	0	109	31.2	.0	0.05
423	" 30	8.30 " " 5.30 P.M.	.....	4	.09	1.0	.068	.....	.....	.046	.005	1.9	5.5	174	.....	.....	126	....	....	34.5	.0	0.09
427	" 31	9.30 " " 2.30 "	9.0	3	.09	1.1	.076	.....	.....	.038	.005	2.0	6.6	171	.....	.....	122	....	....	38.6	.0	0.08
431	*	2.30 P.M. " 2.30 "	10.2	5	.14	1.2	.048	.....	.....	.036	.007	2.4	6.0	186	.....	.....	148	....	...	28.9	.0	0.46
435	April 1–2	2.30 " " 2.30 "	9.0	4	.13	1.2	.048	.....	.....	.024	.008	2.3	6.1	160	.....	.....	120	....	....	22.1	.0	0.17
439	" 2–3	2.30 " " 2.30 "	8.8	5	.13	1.0	.056	.....	.....	.032	.005	1.4	6.1	142	.....	.....	115	....	....	12.6	.0	0.14
443	" 3–4	2.30 " " 2.30 "	8.0	2	.10	0.6	.038	.000	.038	.044	.004	1.0	3.6	119	0	119	97	0	97	3.0	.2	0.07
448	" 4–6	2.30 " " 2.30 "	9.0	2	.05	0.6	.048	.000	.048	.050	.003	0.9	3.2	103	0	103	86	0	86	†1.0	.4	0.03
452	" 6–7	2.30 " " 2.30 "	9.5	2	.06	0.6	.040	.000	.040	.036	.004	1.0	3.4	104	0	104	80	0	80	5.0	.2	0.06
528	May 8–9	9.00 A.M. " 9.00 A.M.	22.7	2	.10	1.6	.080	.000	.080	.036	.005	0.6	12.4	129	0	129	108	0	108	43.2	.0	0.05
535	" 11–12	10.00 " " 9.00 "	23.2	4	.10	1.5	.062	.....	.....	.022	.003	0.9	10.3	139	.....	.....	104	....	....	46.2	.0	0.04
537	" 12–13	9.00 " " 8.00 "	23.0	2	.05	1.1	.060	.000	.060	.030	.004	0.5	11.6	139	0	139	112	0	112	44.1	.0	0.02
542	" 13–14	8.00 " " 9.00 "	23.4	3	.05	1.2	.074	.....	.....	.034	.004	0.8	11.0	148	.....	.....	127	....	....	47.9	.0	0.09
547	" 14–15	2906, 2910, 2920, 2924	23.2	2	.05	1.4	.068	.000	.068	.028	.002	0.5	10.2	128	0	128	98	0	98	45.5	.0	0.03

* March 31 to April 1. † Acidity.

TABLE No. 1.—*Concluded.*

Western Pressure System.

(Parts per Million.)

Serial Number.	Collected. Date.	Collected. Corresponding Bacterial Numbers or Period of Collection by Automatic Sampler.	Temperature, Degrees C.	Degree of Clearness.	Color.	Oxygen Consumed.	Nitrogen as Albuminoid Ammonia. Total.	Nitrogen as Albuminoid Ammonia. Suspended.	Nitrogen as Albuminoid Ammonia. Dissolved.	Nitrogen as Free Ammonia.	Nitrogen as Nitrites.	Nitrogen as Nitrates.	Chlorine.	Residue on Evaporation. Total.	Residue on Evaporation. Suspended.	Residue on Evaporation. Dissolved.	Fixed Residue after Ignition. Total.	Fixed Residue after Ignition. Suspended.	Fixed Residue after Ignition. Dissolved.	Alkalinity.	Dissolved Alumina.	Iron.
	1896																					
551	May 15–16	2928, 2951, 2962, 2971	23.6	2	.04	1.2	.056	.000	.056	.018	.003	0.5	11.3	137	0	137	101	0	101	45.3	.0	0.05
553	" 16	2982, 2993	23.6	1	.02	1.0	.052	.000	.052	.028	.008	0.5	12.3	145	0	145	109	0	109	43.8	.0	0.00
559	" 18–19	*	23.7	2	.13	1.6	.084	.000	.084	.028	.002	0.6	14.9	145	0	145	105	0	105	53.0	.0	0.08
562	" 19–20	6.00 A.M. to 6.00 A.M.	24.1	3	.13	2.0	.082	......	......	.018	.000	0.6	12.4	145	......	......	107	......	......	52.1	.0	0.10
565	" 20–21	6.00 " " 9.00 "	23.8	2	.07	1.5	.072	.000	.072	.018	.001	0.7	11.4	139	0	139	105	0	105	55.0	.0	0.07
569	" 21–22	9.00 " " 9.00 "	23.8	2	.04	1.7	.076	.000	.076	.022	.001	0.8	10.7	146	0	146	115	0	115	54.8	.0	0.02
578	" 22–26	9.00 " " 9.00 "	25.7	1	.09	1.2	.068	.000	.068	.018	.000	0.7	11.9	147	0	147	111	0	111	53.2	.0	0.04
586	" 26–29	9.00 " " 9.00 "	24.4	2	.09	1.3	.076	.000	.076	.022	.000	0.7	12.9	159	0	159	117	0	117	59.1	.0	0.08
590	" 29–30	9.00 " " 9.00 "	23.5	5	.12	1.8	.100	......	......	.026	.002	0.9	10.1	202	......	......	150	......	......	55.0	.0	0.40
598	†	9.00 " " 12.25 "	22.3	2	.08	1.0	.066	.000	.066	.028	......	0.7	12.4	174	0	174	130	0	130	38.0	.0	0.14
600	June 2–3	12.25 " " 9.00 "	22.6	5	.16	1.3	.084	......	......	.020	......	0.8	12.4	190	......	......	145	......	......	38.1	.0	0.20
606	" 3–4	3469, 3479, 3490	22.6	2	.06	0.9	.060	.000	.060	.012	......	0.9	12.2	187	0	187	134	0	134	33.0	.0	0.03
610	" 4–5	‡	23.5	2	.05	0.9	.062	.000	.062	.018	......	0.8	9.7	193	0	193	137	0	137	37.1	.0	0.04
619	" 5–6	9.00 A.M. to 1 55 P.M.	25.4	3	.10	1.2	.060	......	......	.020	......	0.7	14.1	194	......	......	148	......	......	41.2	.0	0.12
635	" 9–11	1.00 P.M. " 5.30 "	24.8	2	.07	1.0	.062	.000	.062	.016	......	0.9	16.5	209	0	209	137	0	137	33.0	.0	0.07
645	" 12–15	12.00 M. " 3.05 "	24.1	2	.04	1.1	.068	.000	.068	.016	......	0.8	14.5	180	0	180	133	0	133	37.2	.0	0.05
654	" 15–18	3.05 P.M. " 12.37 "	25.4	2	.05	1.3	.076	.000	.076	.024	......	0.6	13.0	168	0	168	113	0	113	46.0	.0	0.04
661	" 18–20	12.37 " " 3.25 "	27.3	2	.08	1.4	.064	.000	.064	.016	......	0.6	13.2	173	0	173	121	0	121	34.1	.0	0.05
683	" 24–26	2.10 " " 3.30 "	......	2	.06	1.5	.062	.000	.062	.012	......	0.6	23.9	200	0	200	150	0	150	43.0	.0	0.07
688	" 26–29	3 30 " " 3.40 "	25.5	2	.08	1.3	.084	.000	.084	.014	......	0.9	18.8	184	0	184	146	0	146	38.0	.0	0.18
699	§	3.40 " " 5.40 "	26.5	3	.10	1.4	.068	......	......	.020	......	0.9	15.0	177	......	......	134	......	......	26.0	.0	0.33
710	July 6–7	9.15 A.M. " 3.00 "	......	3	.09	1.4	.072	......	......	.030	......	1.0	10.3	144	......	......	103	......	......	16.2	.0	0.14
718	" 7–9	3.00 P.M. " 3.27 "	......	2	.13	0.9	.080	.000	.080	.018	......	0.8	7.0	134	0	134	95	0	95	12.1	.0	0.01
732	" 13–15	9.15 A.M. " 2.50 "	26.2	2	.07	1.0	.064	.000	.064	.020	......	0.9	5.4	121	0	121	88	0	88	11.0	.0	0.06
742	" 15–16	2.50 P.M. " 3.30 "	26.4	2	.04	1.1	.064	.000	.064	.040	......	0.7	2.5	114	0	114	89	0	89	14.0	.0	0.05
757	" 20–21	9.15 A.M. " 3.00 "	23.8	2	.08	1.1	.062	.000	.062	.022	......	0.8	6.1	132	0	132	90	0	90	31.0	.0	0.03
764	" 21–23	3.00 P.M. " 12.45 "	25.8	3	.11	1.4	.072	......	......	.032	......	0.7	9.2	160	......	......	111	......	......	25.4	.0	0.09
786	" 27–29	‖	26.7	2	.11	1.6	.078	.000	.078	.030	......	0.8	6.5	141	0	141	99	0	99	13.3	.0	0.09

* May 18, 12 M., and May 18, 6.00 P.M., to May 19, 6.00 A.M. † May 30 to June 2. ‡ June 4, 11.40 A.M., and June 4, 8.45 P.M., to June 5, 9.00 A.M.

§ June 29 to July 1. ‖ July 27, 11.30 A.M., to July 29, 3.00 P.M., and July 29, 3.07 P.M.

TABLE No. 2.
RESULTS OF MINERAL ANALYSES OF THE OHIO RIVER WATER BEFORE AND AFTER PURIFICATION BY THE RESPECTIVE SYSTEMS.
(Parts per Million.)

Source of Sample.	River Water.	Warren Effluent.	Jewell Effluent.	Western Pres. Eff.
Silica (SiO_2)	299.50	4.25	4.00	8.00
Oxide of iron (Fe_2O_3)	39.45	0.15	0.11	0.13
Alumina (Al_2O_3)	76.55	2.05	0.24	0.62
Oxide of manganese (MnO)	2.20	none	trace	trace
Oxide of nickel (NiO)	1.09	less than 1.0	less than 1.0	less than 1.0
Lime (CaO)	31.70	30.60	33.22	34.65
Magnesia (MgO)	13.98	7.03	6.64	6.74
Soda (Na_2O)	8.48	5.02	3.56	8.42
Potash (K_2O)	18.15	8.19	7.85	12.40
Chlorine (Cl)	5.57	5.54	5.78	5.42
Nitric acid (N_2O_5)	14.67	14.67	13.89	14.67
Carbonic acid, combined (CO_2)	21.28	7.75	13.12	10.40
Sulphuric acid (SO_3)	23.28	35.71	33.37	41.33
Phosphoric acid (P_2O_5)	0.79	0.98	0.81	0.47

TABLE No. 3.
RESULTS OF MICROSCOPICAL ANALYSES OF THE EFFLUENTS OF THE RESPECTIVE SYSTEMS
(Number of Organisms per Cubic Centimeter.)*

Date of Collection.	Number of Sample.	Organisms.	Total Number.	Genera.
		Effluent of the Warren System.		
1896 Feb. 18	278	Diatomaceæ: Synedra, 8; Chlorophyceæ: Protococcus, 2; Infusoria: Parts of cases, 6	16	3
" 19	281	Diatomaceæ: Navicula and Cymbella pr.	pr.	2
" 26	305	No organisms present	0	0
March 4	330	Diatomaceæ: Synedra, pr; Fungi: Crenothrix, pr.	pr.	2
" 11	355	Diatomaceæ: Synedra, 3	3	1
" 19	383	Diatomaceæ: Meridion, pr; Miscellaneous: Anguillula, 1	1	2
" 26	405	Miscellaneous: Anguillula, pr.	pr.	1
April 10	460	No organisms present	0	0
May 6	518	Chlorophyceæ: Protococcus, 1; Miscellaneous: Vegetable Hairs, 23	24	2
" 15	545	Diatomaceæ: Synedra, 1; Cymbella, 1; Chlorophyceæ: Protococcus, 1	3	3
" 21	567	Chlorophyceæ: Protococcus, pr; Infusoria: Trachelomonas, pr.	pr.	2
" 29	588	Diatomaceæ: Synedra and Cyclotella, pr.	pr.	2
June 11	630	Chlorophyceæ: Conferva, pr.	pr.	1
" 18	652	Vermes: Ploima, 26; Miscellaneous: Zoospores, 16	42	2
		Effluent of Jewell System.		
Feb. 19	282	Diatomaceæ: Synedra, Navicula, pr.	pr.	2
" 26	306	Diatomaceæ: Pleurosigma, Cymbella, pr; Chlorophyceæ: Protococcus, Scenedesmus, pr.	pr.	4
March 4	328	No organisms present	0	0
" 11	353	No organisms present	0	0
" 19	381	No organisms present	0	0
" 26	406	Fungi: Mould hyphæ, pr.	pr.	1
April 10	461	No organisms present	0	0
" 16	472	Chlorophyceæ: Protococcus, pr.	pr.	1
May 6	517	Chlorophyceæ: Protococcus, 16; Miscellaneous: Anguillula, 1	17	2
" 15	546	Miscellaneous: Zoospores, pr	pr.	1
" 21	566	Diatomaceæ: Synedra, pr; Chlorophyceæ: Protococcus, 1; Scenedesmus, 2; Miscellaneous: Zoospores, pr.	3	4
" 29	587	Diatomaceæ: Synedra, pr; Cyclotella, 1; Chlorophyceæ: Protococcus, 2; Pandorina, pr; Endorina, pr; Vermes: Plorlma, pr.	3	6
June 11	631	Chlorophyceæ: Protococcus, pr.	pr.	1
" 18	653	No organisms present	0	0
" 27	685	Infusoria: Monas, 12; Miscellaneous: Zoospores, pr.	12	2
July 8	709	No organisms present	0	0
		Effluent of Western Gravity System.		
Feb. 26	307	No organisms present	0	0
March 4	331	No organisms present	0	0
" 11	350	Chlorophyceæ: Spyrogyra, 1	1	1
" 19	380	Chlorophyceæ: Protococcus, pr.	pr.	1
		Effluent of Western Pressure System.		
Feb. 16	308	No organisms present	0	0
March 4	332	No organisms present	0	0
" 11	350	No organisms present	0	0
" 19	374	Chlorophyceæ: Protococcus, 1	1	1
" 26	407	No organisms present	0	0
May 21	565	Chlorophyceæ: Protococcus, 5	5	1
" 29	586	Diatomaceæ: Cyclotella, pr	pr.	1
June 18	654	No organisms present	0	0
July 8	718	Chlorophyceæ: Protococcus, pr.	pr.	1

* pr = present.

TABLE NO. 4.

RESULTS OF BACTERIAL ANALYSES OF THE EFFLUENTS OF THE RESPECTIVE SYSTEMS.

Warren System.

Serial Number.	Collected.		Number of Run.	Rate of Filtration.		Loss of Head. Feet.	Period of Service Since Last Washing. Hours and Minutes.	Filtered Water Since Last Washing. Cubic Feet.	Bacteria per Cubic Centimeter.	Remarks.
	Date.	Hour.		Cubic Feet per Minute.	Million Gallons per Acre per 24 Hours.					
	1895									
5	Oct. 21	12.35 P.M.	1	....	.....	....	2h. 35m.	......	47	
6	" 21	3.40 "	1	....	.....	....	5h. 40m.	......	34	
10	" 22	11.51 A.M.	2	24.0	132	....	15m.	......	88	
11	" 22	12.07 P.M.	2	24.0	132	....	31m.	......	32	
12	" 22	1.10 "	2	23.5	129	....	1h. 34m.	......	54	
16	" 22	3.50 "	2	....	.....	....	4h. 14m.	......	64	
21	" 23	10.00 A.M.	2	21.0	115	....	4h. 24m.	......	36	
23	" 23	11.13 "	2	22.0	121	....	5h. 37m.	......	48	
25	" 23	12.05 P.M.	2	21.0	115	....	6h. 29m.	......	44	
27	" 23	1.25 "	2	22.0	121	....	7h. 49m.	......	34	
29	" 23	2.33 "	2	22.0	121	....	8h. 57m.	......	72	
31	" 23	4.30 "	2	22.0	121	....	10h. 54m.	.....	72	
35	" 24	9.56 A.M.	3	21.0	115	....	16m.	239	34	
36	" 24	10.11 "	3	23.0	126	....	31m.	518	99	
37	" 24	10.51 "	3	23.0	126	....	1h. 11m.	1 504	37	
39	" 24	12.22 P.M.	3	22.0	121	....	2h. 42m.	3 472	49	
41	" 24	1.50 "	3	23.5	129	....	4h. 10m.	5 515	196	
43	" 24	3.05 "	3	24.0	132	....	5h. 25m.	7 326	53	
44	" 24	4.01 "	3	25.0	137	....	6h. 21m.	8 535	53	
46	" 24	5.06 "	3	....	.....	....	7h. 26m.	10 197	23	
50	" 25	9.58 A.M.	3	25.0	137	....	7h. 53m.	19 787	36	
52	" 25	11.12 "	3	25.0	137	....	9h. 07m.	12 600	48	
54	" 25	12.12 "	3	25.0	137	....	10h. 07m.	14 117	38	
55	" 25	1.28 P.M.	3	25.0	137	....	11h. 23m.	16 016	34	
57	" 25	2.38 "	4	27.0	148	....	28m.	427	93	
60	" 25	3.35 "	4	24.0	132	....	1h. 25m.	1 825	46	
64	" 25	4.34 "	4	25.0	137	....	2h. 24m.	3 274	33	
66	" 26	10.56 A.M.	4	25.0	137	....	4h. 26m.	7 205	65	
69	" 26	1.12 P.M.	4	24.0	132	....	6h. 42m.	9 493	31	
71	" 26	4.40 "	4	20.0	110	....	10h. 10m.	13 527	32	
73	" 28	12.10 "	5	26.0	143	....	45m.	1 127	61	
74	" 28	1.10 "	5	26.0	143	....	1h. 45m.	2 671	28	
75	" 28	2.30 "	5	23.0	126	....	3h. 05m.	4 554	28	
76	" 28	3.23 "	5	25.0	138	....	3h. 58m.	5 802	30	
79	" 29	12.33 "	6	27.0	148	...	1h. 33m.	2 357	42	
81	" 29	2.00 "	6	28.0	154	....	3h. 00m.	4 676	20	
82	" 29	3.25 "	6	26.0	143	....	4h. 25m.	7 023	18	
85	" 30	9.55 A.M.	7	24.0	132	....	55m.	1 290	46	
86	" 30	10.18 "	7	27.0	148	....	1h. 18m.	1 866	58	
87	" 30	10.37 "	7	26.0	143	...	1h. 37m.	2 330	18	
88	" 30	11.17 "	7	28.0	154	....	2h. 17m.	3 385	15	
89	" 30	12.25 P.M.	7	27.0	148	...	3h. 25m.	5 118	10	
90	" 30	1.40 "	7	24.0	132	....	4h. 40m.	7 052	11	
93	" 30	3.22 "	7	28.0	154	....	6h. 22m.	8 629	16	
97	" 30	4.30 "	7	....	.....	....	7h. 30m.	10 689	14	
108	" 31	2.31 "	8	23.0	126	....	5h. 26m.	6 262	9	
113	Nov. 1	12.07 "	8	25.0	137	....	7h. 12m.	8 014	13	
115	" 1	3.15 "	8	....	.....	....	10h. 20m.	12 238	14	Shut outlet 3.15 P.M.
118	" 1	4.03 "	9	22.0	121	....	38m.	1 062	16	
120	" 1	4.33 "	9	22.0	121	....	1h. 08m.	1 732	11	
124	" 2	11.07 A.M.	9	24.0	132	....	2h. 52m.	4 099	15	
126	" 2	12.31 P.M.	9	26.0	143	....	4h. 16m.	6 232	14	
128	" 2	1.26 "	9	24.0	132	....	5h. 11m.	7 599	43	
130	" 2	3.48 "	9	24.0	132	....	7h. 33m.	9 344	19	
134	" 4	2.32 "	10	26.0	143	....	1h. 25m.	1 802	42	
135	" 4	3.37 "	10	27.0	148	....	2h. 30m.	3 474	38	
137	" 5	9.23 A.M.	10	24.0	132	....	3h. 01m.	4 160	20	
139	" 5	9.46 "	10	26.0	143	....	3h. 24m.	4 736	11	
142	" 5	10.07 "	10	....	.....	....	3h. 45m.	5 254	10	
143	" 5	10.32 "	10	25.0	137	...	4h. 10m.	5 820	12	
150	" 5	11.30 "	10	24.0	132	....	5h. 08m.	7 210	14	

TABLE No. 4.—*Continued.*

Warren System.

Serial Number.	Collected.		Number of Run.	Rate of Filtration.		Loss of Head. Feet.	Period of Service Since Last Washing. Hours and Minutes.	Filtered Water Since Last Washing. Cubic Feet.	Bacteria per Cubic Centimeter.	Remarks.
	Date.	Hour.		Cubic Feet per Minute.	Million Gallons per Acre per 24 Hours.					
	1895									
151	Nov. 5	12.50 P.M.	10	24.0	132	....	6h. 28m.	9 079	13	
153	" 5	3.50 "	10	16.0	88	....	9h. 28m.	11 744	10	
158	" 6	10.30 A.M.	11	....	.....	....	1h. 15m.	......	18	
159	" 6	11.13 "	11	24.0	132	....	1h. 58m.	2 552	15	
160	" 6	1.19 P.M.	11	24.0	132	....	4h. 04m.	5 661	17	
161	" 6	2.55 "	11	24.0	132	....	5h. 40m.	7 952	24	
165	" 7	9.10 A.M.	11	24.0	132	....	6h. 03m.	8 489	138	
166	" 7	9.27 "	11	25.0	137	....	6h. 20m.	8 940	82	
167	" 7	9.49 "	11	24.0	132	....	6h. 42m.	9 452	54	
168	" 7	10.27 "	11	24.0	132	....	7h. 20m.	10 385	21	
173	" 7	11.25 A.M.	11	23.0	126	....	8h. 18m.	11 725	30	
175	" 7	12.24 P.M.	12	30.0	165	....	02m.	26	196	
176	" 7	12.30 "	12	27.0	148	....	08m.	191	54	
177	" 7	12.50 "	12	28.0	154	....	28m.	751	48	
178	" 7	1.09 "	12	24.0	132	....	47m.	1 245	61	
180	" 7	1.35 "	12	26.0	143	....	1h. 13m.	1 938	46	
189	" 7	2.27 "	12	25.0	137	....	2h. 05m.	3 342	31	
193	" 7	3.00 "	12	24.0	132	....	2h. 38m.	4 180	35	
197	" 8	9.50 A.M.	12	24.0	132	....	3h. 43m.	5 113	49	
199	" 8	11.05 "	12	23.0	126	...	4h. 58m.	6 813	42	
202	" 8	12.37 P.M.	12	24.0	.....	....	6h. 30m.	8 822	19	
206	" 8	2.13 "	13	24.0	132	....	07m.	152	180	
208	" 8	2.27 "	13	23.0	126	....	21m.	542	70	
210	" 8	2.50 "	13	6.0	33	....	44m.	1 050	26	
214	" 9	11.33 A.M.	13	24.0	132	....	1h. 22m.	2 015	46	
218	" 9	1.27 P.M.	13	25.0	137	....	3h. 16m.	4 802	50	
221	" 9	2.30 "	13	24.0	132	....	4h. 19m.	6 328	58	
227	" 11	10.47 A.M.	13	25.0	137	....	7h. 01m.	10 215	224	
230	" 11	11.10 "	13	23.0	126	....	7h. 24m.	10 745	136	
231	" 11	2.32 "	14	24.0	132	....	....	1 637	41	
303	" 25	10.20 "	15	....	.....	....	35m.	......	1 584	
306	" 25	11.00 "	15	24.0	146	....	1h. 15m.	1 096	468	
311	" 25	12.20 P.M.	15	20.0	121	....	2h. 35m.	2 044	390	
313	" 25	1.40 "	15	21.0	127	....	3h. 55m.	3 673	414	
315	" 25	3.30 "	15	25.0	152	....	5h. 45m.	5 732	294	
318	" 26	9.28 A.M.	15	23.0	140	....	6h. 18m.	6 745	496	
322	" 26	10.20 "	15	21.0	127	....	7h. 19m.	7 901	372	
324	" 26	11.34 "	15	20.0	121	....	8h. 24m.	9 437	328	
326	" 26	2.00 P.M.	15	20.0	121	....	10h. 50m.	12 445	344	
332	" 27	9.27 A.M.	15	11.0	67	....	11h. 52m.	13 667	680	
335	" 27	10.24 "	15	18.0	109	....	12h. 49m.	14 546	452	
338	" 27	11.53 "	15	25.0	152	....	13h. 42m.	15 890	446	
340	" 27	1.44 P.M.	15	23.5	143	....	15h. 33m.	18 488	564	
343	" 27	3.17 "	15	20.0	121	....	17h. 06m.	20 310	512	
347	" 29	9.52 A.M.	16	11.0	67	....	02m.	31	1 302	
348	" 29	10.03 "	16	10.0	61	....	13m.	132	1 169	
349	" 29	10.14 "	16	10.0	61	....	24m.	248	908	
350	" 29	10.23 "	16	10.0	61	....	33m.	355	1 092	
351	" 29	10.32 "	16	10.0	61	....	42m.	507	876	
352	" 29	10.43 "	16	21.0	127	....	53m.	762	760	
354	" 29	10.54 "	16	20.0	121	....	1h. 04m.	1 006	344	
356	" 29	12.06 P.M.	16	23.5	143	....	2h. 16m.	2 458	624	
358	" 29	1.58 "	16	23.0	140	....	4h. 08m.	4 968	448	
368	" 30	10.41 A.M.	16	24.0	146	....	7h. 17m.	9 416	632	
370	" 30	11.51 "	16	26.0	158	....	8h. 27m.	11 043	840	
372	" 30	1.39 P.M.	16	25.0	152	....	10h. 15m.	13 691	984	
376	Dec. 2	9.47 A.M.	16	20.0	121	....	12h. 15m.	16 533	770	
378	" 2	10.48 "	16	24.0	146	....	13h. 16m.	17 949	945	
381	" 2	12.35 P.M.	16	23.5	143	....	15h. 03m.	20 462	875	
383	" 2	2.38 "	16	23.0	140	....	17h. 06m.	23 122	1 078	
385	" 3	9.35 A.M.	16	25.0	152	....	18h. 06m.	24 401	826	

TABLE NO. 4.—*Continued.*

Warren System.

Serial Number.	Collected. Date.	Collected. Hour.	Number of Run.	Rate of Filtration. Cubic Feet per Minute.	Rate of Filtration. Million Gallons per Acre per 24 Hours.	Loss of Head. Feet.	Period of Service Since Last Washing. Hours and Minutes.	Filtered Water Since Last Washing. Cubic Feet.	Bacteria per Cubic Centimeter.	Remarks.
	1895									
387	Dec. 3	10.35 A.M.	16	25.0	152	....	19h. 06m.	25 866	532	
389	" 3	11.41 "	16	24.5	149	....	20h. 12m.	27 334	665	
391	" 3	1.02 P.M.	16	22.0	133	....	21h. 33m.	29 349	1 036	
392	" 3	2.09 "	16	24.0	146	....	22h. 40m.	30 929	1 169	Shut inlet 2.01 P.M., outlet 2.21 P.M.
395	" 3	3.00 "	17	21.0	127	....	12m.	213	462	
396	" 3	3.10 "	17	22.0	133	....	22m.	401	490	
397	" 3	3.20 "	17	22.0	133	....	32m.	598	392	
398	" 3	3.31 "	17	25.0	152	....	43m.	836	406	
399	" 3	3.40 "	17	24.0	146	....	52m.	1 036	399	
400	" 3	3.50 "	17	21.0	127	....	1h. 02m.	1 259	399	
401	" 3	4.49 "	17	23.0	140	....	2h. 01m.	2 498	334	
403	" 4	10.40 A.M.	17	21.0	127	....	3h. 49m.	4 898	315	
405	" 4	11.06 "	17	20.0	121	....	4h. 15m.	5 481	378	
406	" 4	11.26 "	17	21.0	127	....	4h. 35m.	5 908	357	
407	" 4	11.45 "	17	22.0	133	....	4h. 54m.	6 315	322	
408	" 4	1.12 P.M.	17	25.0	152	....	6h. 21m.	8 281	518	
409	" 4	2.52 "	17	21.0	127	....	8h. 01m.	10 591	594	
412	" 4	4.19 "	18	24.0	146	....	11m.	321	548	
413	" 4	4.29 "	18	22.0	133	....	21m.	533	470	
415	" 4	4.42 "	18	24.0	146	....	34m.	886	320	
416	" 4	4.50 "	18	23.0	140	....	42m.	956	396	
417	" 4	5.00 "	18	20.0	121	....	52m.	1 136	254	
418	" 4	5.11 "	18	23.0	140	....	1h. 03m.	1 239	280	
421	" 5	9.58 A.M.	18	....	....	....	2h. 00m.	2 333	260	
423	" 5	10.42 "	18	24.0	146	....	2h. 54m.	3 468	180	
426	" 5	11.52 "	18	24.0	146	....	3h. 54m.	5 124	236	
428	" 5	2.44 P.M.	18	24.0	146	....	6h. 46m.	9 161	336	
435	" 5	3.40 "	18	24.0	146	....	7h. 42m.	10 464	472	
439	" 6	11.07 A.M.	18	22.0	133	....	10h. 38m.	13 123	386	
441	" 6	11.17 "	18	24.0	146	....	10h. 48m.	14 727	690	
444	" 6	12.50 P.M.	19	18.0	109	....	12m.	131	524	
445	" 6	1.00 "	19	18.0	109	....	22m.	295	476	
446	" 6	1.10 "	19	20.0	121	....	32m.	522	476	
447	" 6	1.20 "	19	22.5	126	....	42m.	738	476	
448	" 6	1.30 "	19	23.0	140	....	52m.	970	440	
450	" 6	1.40 "	19	24.0	146	....	1h. 02m.	1 175	412	
451	" 6	3.38 "	19	22.0	133	....	3h. 00m.	3 984	660	
454	" 7	10.17 A.M.	19	23.0	140	....	5h. 51m.	7 932	450	
456	" 7	12.27 P.M.	19	25.0	152	....	8h. 01m.	11 981	412	
459	" 7	3.50 "	20	23.0	140	....	11m.	182	254	
462	" 9	10.10 A.M.	20	20.0	121	....	2h. 19m.	3 082	324	
464	" 9	11.14 "	20	21.0	127	....	3h 23m.	4 445	250	
466	" 9	12.17 P.M.	20	24.0	146	....	4h. 26m.	5 705	270	
469	" 9	1.57 "	20	24.0	146	....	6h. 06m.	8 060	272	
471	" 9	3.30 "	20	24.0	146	....	7h. 39m.	10 371	324	
475	" 10	9.17 A.M.	20	23.0	140	....	9h. 13m.	12 819	312	
477	" 10	10.20 "	20	23.0	140	....	10h. 16m.	14 018	406	
484	" 10	12.23 P.M.	21	22.0	133	....	20m.	325	288	
485	" 10	12.33 "	21	21.0	127	....	30m.	539	344	
486	" 10	12.43 "	21	20.0	121	....	40m.	779	330	
487	" 10	12.53 "	21	22.0	133	....	50m.	1 032	324	
488	" 10	1.03 "	21	24.0	146	....	1h. 00m.	1 247	246	
489	" 10	1.13 "	21.	24.0	146	....	1h. 10m.	1 494	188	
491	" 10	2.10 "	21	24.0	146	....	2h. 07m.	2 845	266	
493	" 10	3.24 "	21.	24.0	146	....	3h. 21m.	4 564	244	
496	" 11	9.24 A.M.	21.	24.0	146	....	5h. 31m.	7 489	196	
498	" 11	11.11 "	21.	24.0	146	....	7h. 18m.	9 994	210	
500	" 11	12.18 P.M.	21	23.0	140	....	6h. 25m.	11 561	196	
502	" 11	1.18 "	21	20.0	121	....	9h. 25m.	12 923	202	Shut inlet 1.18 P.M., outlet 1.21 P.M.
505	" 11	2.58 "	22	21.0	127	....	54m.	1 137	146	
509	" 12	9.40 A.M.	22	24.0	146	....	4h. 07m.	5 452	128	

TABLE No. 4.—*Continued.*

Warren System.

Serial Number.	Collected.		Number of Run.	Rate of Filtration.		Loss of Head, Feet.	Period of Service Since Last Washing, Hours and Minutes.	Filtered Water Since Last Washing, Cubic Feet.	Bacteria per Cubic Centimeter.	Remarks.
	Date.	Hour.		Cubic Feet per Minute.	Million Gallons per Acre per 24 Hours.					
	1895									
511	Dec. 12	12.04 P.M.	22	24.0	146	....	6h. 31m.	8 851	228	
513	" 12	3.05 "	23	22.0	133	....	1h. 01m.	1 273	190	
518	" 13	10.16 A.M.	23	22.0	133	....	4h. 40m.	6 180	108	
521	" 13	4.38 P.M.	24	22.0	133	....	52m.	1 073	136	
525	" 14	10.09 A.M.	24	23.0	140	....	2h. 52m.	3 811	108	
527	" 14	12.59 P.M.	24	23.0	140	....	5h. 42m.	7 672	135	
531	" 14	3.33 "	25	20.0	121	....	14m.	281	274	
534	" 16	9.30 A.M.	25	21.0	127	....	2h. 25m.	3 109	160	
536	" 16	11.37 "	25	23.0	140	....	4h. 32m.	6 094	126	
538	" 16	2.31 P.M.	25	21.0	127	....	7h. 26m.	9 961	172	
541	" 16	5.17 "	26	23.0	140	....	1h. 08m.	1 492	120	
543	" 17	9.30 A.M.	26	23.0	140	....	1h. 50m.	2 430	111	
546	" 17	12.58 P.M.	26	23.0	140	....	5h. 18m.	7 156	170	
548	" 17	3.21 "	27	23.0	140	....	1h. 06m.	1 260	110	
551	" 17	4.37 "	27	22.0	133	....	2h. 22m.	3 001	148	
554	" 18	9.20 A.M.	27	22.0	133	....	3h. 40m.	4 731	197	
556	" 18	10.41 "	27	23.0	140	....	5h. 01m.	6 509	196	
558	" 18	1.16 "	27	22.0	133	....	7h. 36m.	9 382	185	
559	" 18	2.32 "	28	22.0	133	....	13m.	234	236	
560	" 18	2.42 "	28	22.0	133	....	23m.	444	294	
561	" 18	2.52 "	28	22.0	133	....	33m.	658	274	
562	" 18	3.02 "	28	22.0	133	....	43m.	874	220	
563	" 18	3.12 "	28	22.0	133	....	53m.	1 098	178	
565	" 18	3.22 "	28	22.0	133	....	1h. 03m.	1 306	278	
568	" 18	4.39 "	28	23.0	140	....	2h. 20m.	2 964	158	
570	" 19	9.25 "	28	23.0	140	....	3h. 31m.	4 474	169	
580	" 19	3.23 P.M.	28	24.0	146	....	7h. 39m.	10 212	142	
582	" 19	4.40 "	28	24.0	146	....	8h. 56m.	11 987	165	
587	" 20	10.14 A.M.	29	21.0	127	....	12m.	234	426	
589	" 20	11.59 "	29	24.0	146	....	1h. 57m.	2 590	103	
591	" 20	2.02 P.M.	29	23.0	140	....	4h. 00m.	5 397	188	
594	" 20	3.53 "	29	24.0	146	....	5h. 51m.	7 902	720	
597	" 21	9.19 A.M.	29	21.0	127	....	7h. 47m.	10 460	344	
600	" 21	4.01 "	30	22.0	133	....	3h. 31m.	4 627	164	
603	" 23	9.18 "	30	12.0	73	....	5h. 14m.	6 551	260	
606	" 23	10.39 "	30	19.0	115	....	6h. 35m.	7 754	150	
612	" 23	12.34 P.M.	30	20.0	121	....	8h. 30m.	9 932	132	
616	" 23	3.33 "	30	8.0	49	....	11h. 29m.	13 316	150	Shut inlet 3.20 P.M., outlet 3.40 P.M.
619	" 24	9.29 A.M.	31	23.0	140	....	1h. 49m.	2 466	63	
627	" 24	12.48 P.M.	31	24.0	146	....	5h. 08m.	6 433	78	
628	" 24	3.07 "	31	21.0	127	....	7h. 27m.	9 772	86	
637	" 26	10.09 A.M.	31	22.0	133	....	10h. 48m.	13 578	95	
638	" 26	11.49 "	32	22.0	133	....	32m.	688	59	
639	" 26	12.04 P.M.	32	23.0	140	....	47m.	994	60	
644	" 26	3.49 "	32	22.0	133	....	4h. 32m.	6 134	244	
651	" 27	10.07 A.M.	32	21.0	127	....	7h. 15m.	9 392	1 701	
655	" 27	12.34 P.M.	32	21.0	127	....	9h. 42m.	12 757	1 530	
660	" 27	2.57 "	32	....	....	....	12h. 05m.	15 815	924	Shut outlet 2.57 P.M.
665	" 27	3.42 "	33	24.0	146	....	30m.	641	230	
666	" 27	3.57 "	33	22.0	133	....	45m.	978	128	
671	" 27	4.55 "	33	22.0	133	....	1h. 43m.	2 223	160	
674	" 28	9.56 A.M.	33	22.0	133	....	3h. 11m.	4 131	428	
682	" 28	11.56 "	33	21.0	127	....	5h. 11m.	6 776	1 728	
683	" 28	3.06 P.M.	33	....	....	....	8h. 21m.	11 011	1 350	Shut inlet 3.04 P.M., outlet 3.24 P.M.
692	" 30	10.56 A.M.	34	22.0	133	....	2h. 31m.	2 884	402	
696	" 30	12.15 P.M.	35	21.0	127	....	14m.	179	474	
697	" 30	12.44 "	35	22.0	133	....	43m.	804	210	
701	" 30	1.59 "	35	24.0	146	....	1h. 58m.	2 561	502	
705	" 30	4.53 "	36	23.0	140	....	18m.	378	210	
707	" 30	5.16 "	36	22.0	133	....	41m.	959	170	
711	" 31	10.45 A.M.	36	23.0	140	....	2h. 34m.	4 708	406	

TABLE No. 4.—*Continued.*

Warren System.

Serial Number.	Collected. Date.	Collected. Hour.	Number of Run.	Rate of Filtration. Cubic Feet per Minute.	Rate of Filtration. Million Gallons per Acre per 24 Hours.	Loss of Head. Feet.	Period of Service Since Last Washing. Hours and Minutes.	Filtered Water Since Last Washing. Cubic Feet.	Bacteria per Cubic Centimeter.	Remarks.
	1895									
717	Dec. 31	1.39 P.M.	37	17.0	103	....	15m.	215	440	
718	" 31	2.09 "	37	23.0	140	....	45m.	835	278	
	1896									
730	Jan. 2	10.56 A.M.	38	22.5	136	....	10m.	130	784	
731	" 2	11.26 "	38	25.0	152	....	40m.	690	600	
740	" 2	2.40 P.M.	38	18.0	109	....	3h. 54m.	5 260	1 400	
743	" 2	4.06 "	39	20.0	121	....	15m.	222	405	
749	" 3	10.21 A.M.	39	21.0	127	....	3h. 07m.	3 722	180	
753	" 3	1.22 P.M.	40	20.0	121	....	15m.	186	220	
754	" 3	1.58 "	40	20.5	124	...	51m.	956	97	
765	" 4	11.55 A.M.	41	18.0	109	...	14m.	118	170	
772	" 4	2.26 P.M.	41	21.5	130	....	2h. 45m.	2 558	133	
776	" 6	11.55 A.M.	42	17.0	103	....	30m.	415	102	
780	" 6	3.27 P.M.	42	17.0	103	...	4h. 02m.	3 891	112	
785	" 7	12.24 "	43	14.0	85	....	4h. 19m.	4 159	43	
789	" 7	3.52 "	44	12.0	73	....	2h. 17m.	2 218	66	
794	" 8	11.58 A.M.	45	16.0	97	....	55m.	858	25	
799	" 8	2.28 P.M.	45	16.0	97	....	3h. 25m.	3 235	68	
802	" 8	2.49 "	45	16.0	97	....	3h. 46m.	3 529	84	
809	" 9	10.21 A.M.	46	18.0	109	....	2h. 25m.	2 316	10	
814	" 9	1.26 P.M.	47	16.5	100	...	15m.	210	53	
816	" 9	1.47 "	47	15.0	91	...	36m.	500	21	
826	" 10	1.05 "	48	14.0	85	....	09m.	119	152	
827	" 10	1.42 "	48	15.0	91	....	46m.	699	36	
836	" 11	11.21 A.M.	49	17.5	106	....	2h. 53m.	2 630	36	
843	" 13	12.30 P.M.	51	16.0	97	....	15m.	198	35	
844	" 13	1.00 "	51	15.0	91	....	45m.	633	31	
846	" 13	2.01 "	51	16.0	97	....	1h. 46m.	1 608	10	
850	" 13	4.57 "	52	16.0	97	....	15m.	207	78	
856	" 14	11.56 A.M.	52	17.0	103	....	3h. 44m.	3 516	14	
859	" 14	1.57 P.M.	53	16.0	97	....	15m.	186	31	
863	" 14	2.27 "	53	17.0	103	....	45m.	714	32	
867	" 14	3.25 "	53	17.0	103	....	1h. 43m.	1 606	25	
871	" 15	10.40 A.M.	54	16.0	97	..	15m.	181	62	
875	" 15	11.10 "	54	16.0	97	....	45m.	657	12	
879	" 15	12.59 P.M.	54	16.0	97	....	2h. 34m.	2 327	49	
881	" 15	2.54 "	54	14.0	85	....	4h. 29m.	4 124	77	
886	" 16	10.43 A.M.	55	16.5	100	....	2h. 34m.	2 356	78	
891	" 16	12.58 P.M.	55	14.0	85	....	4h. 49m.	4 486	94	
896	" 16	2.17 "	56	16.0	97	....	15m.	203	73	
897	" 16	2.47 "	56	16.5	100	...	45m.	663	60	
898	" 16	2.59 "	56	16.0	97	....	57m.	853	58	
915	" 17	11.37 A.M.	57	17.0	103	...	15m.	176	126	
920	" 17	12.07 P.M.	57	17.0	103	...	45m.	675	.....	
924	" 17	1.02 "	57	16.0	97	....	1h. 40m.	1 515	65	
931	" 17	2.11 "	57	15.0	91	....	2h. 49m.	2 615	171	
935	" 17	3.53 "	58	17.5	106	....	17m.	240	82	
939	" 17	4.23 "	58	15.0	91	...	47m.	660	76	
941	" 17	4.58 "	58	16.0	97	....	1h. 22m.	1 205	68	
948	" 18	10.08 A.M.	58	16.0	97	....	2h. 54m.	2 620	38	
952	" 18	1.00 P.M.	59	16.0	97	....	15m.	217	67	
956	" 18	1.30 "	59	14.0	85	....	45m.	677	70	
961	" 18	2.50 "	59	15.5	94	....	2h. 05m.	1 887	64	
968	" 20	10.38 A.M.	60	15.0	91	....	2h. 18m.	2 040	102	
971	" 20	2.05 P.M.	61	16.0	97	....	15m.	176	108	
973	" 20	4.09 "	61	15.0	91	....	2h. 19m.	2 086	146	
982	" 21	12.10 "	62	16.0	97	....	15m.	181	86	
983	" 21	12.40 "	62	16.0	97	...	45m.	691	32	
985	" 21	4.12 "	63	16.0	97	....	34m.	453	36	
991	" 22	9.21 A.M.	63	16.0	97	....	2h. 17m.	2 073	33	
997	" 22	2.12 P.M.	64	17.0	103	...	1h. 35m.	1 464	36	
1028	" 25	2.27 "	65	19.0	115	....	2h. 03m.	2 418	60	

TABLE NO 4.—*Continued.*

Warren System.

Serial Number.	Collected. Date.	Collected. Hour.	Number of Run.	Rate of Filtration. Cubic Feet per Minute.	Rate of Filtration. Million Gallons per Acre per 24 Hours.	Loss of Head. Feet.	Period of Service Since Last Washing. Hours and Minutes.	Filtered Water Since Last Washing. Cubic Feet.	Bacteria per Cubic Centimeter.	Remarks.
	1895									
1032	Jan. 27	10.03 A.M.	65	16.0	97	....	5h. 52m.	6 108	113	
1037	" 27	11.22 "	66	16.0	97	....	15m.	216	39	
1038	" 27	11.52 "	66	16.0	97	....	45m.	666	177	
1039	" 27	1.05 P.M.	66	16.0	97	....	1h. 58m.	1 836	41	
1044	" 27	4.06 "	66	15.0	91	....	4h. 59m.	4 636	412	
1050	" 28	9.45 A.M.	67	16.5	100	....	1h. 29m.	1 226	225	
1057	" 28	3.33 P.M.	68	15.0	91	....	1h. 10m.	954	536	
1058	" 28	4.29 "	68	16.0	97	....	2h. 06m.	1 924	650	
1065	" 29	10.09 A.M.	68	16.0	97	....	3h. 58m.	3 504	327	
1068	" 29	1.55 P.M.	69	15.0	91	....	1h. 55m.	1 828	570	
1071	" 29	5.15 "	70	14.0	85	....	17m.	219	679	
1074	" 30	10.56 A.M.	70	14.0	85	....	2h. 28m.	2 279	79	
1076	" 30	12.56 P.M.	70	14.0	85	....	4h. 28m.	4 259	76	
1079	" 30	2.54 "	71	15.5	94	....	56m.	648	58	
1083	" 31	10.42 A.M.	71	10.0	61	....	5h. 14m.	4 788	169	A. Shut inlet 10.42 A.M., outlet 10.56 A.M.
1090	" 31	2.42 P.M.	72	20.0	121	....	2h. 05m.	1 998	59	
1092	" 31	3.43 "	72	16.0	97	....	3h. 06m.	2 948	55	
1095	Feb. 1	9.57 A.M.	72	16.0	97	....	5h. 46m.	5 298	85	
1096	" 1	12.11 P.M.	73	16.0	97	....	47m.	699	39	
1099	" 1	2.40 "	73	16.0	97	....	3h. 16m.	2 959	69	
1103	" 1	4.55 "	74	14.0	85	....	30m.	415	30	
1107	" 3	10.12 A.M.	74	16.0	97	....	2h. 30m.	2 295	174	
1110	" 3	1.10 P.M.	74	16.0	97	....	5h. 15m.	4 875	196	
1116	" 3	4.55 "	75	17.0	103	....	1h. 18m.	1 140	225	
1121	" 4	10.12 A.M.	75	15.5	94	....	3h. 05m.	2 850	240	
1124	" 4	11.45 "	75	16.0	97	....	4h. 38m.	4 290	606	
1127	" 4	2.25 P.M.	75	16.0	97	....	7h. 18m.	6 730	555	
1131	" 4	5.13 "	76	16.0	97	....	1h. 24m.	1 273	4 740	
1136	" 5	10.09 A.M.	76	18.0	109	....	2h. 51m.	2 873	256	
1140	" 5	11.45 "	76	18.0	109	....	4h. 27m.	4 513	752	
1144	" 5	3.02 P.M.	77	16.0	97	....	2h. 30m.	2 570	510	
1149	" 5	5.04 "	78	14.0	85	....	05m.	29	816	
1155	" 6	10.05 A.M.	78	17.0	103	....	1h. 36m.	1 339	232	
1161	" 6	12.19 P.M.	78	17.0	103	....	3h. 50m.	3 519	173	
1163	" 6	3.10 "	79	17.0	103	....	34m.	431	207	
1168	" 6	4.12 "	79	16.5	100	....	1h. 36m.	1 421	270	
1173	" 7	10.10 A.M.	79	16.0	97	....	4h. 09m.	3 701	237	
1177	" 7	1.25 P.M.	80	16.0	97	....	1h. 33m.	1 646	338	
1183	" 7	5.22 "	81	16.0	97	....	1h. 00m.	886	512	
1187	" 8	10.27 A.M.	81	16.0	97	....	2h. 17m.	2 049	556	
1191	" 8	2.10 P.M.	82	16.0	97	....	43m.	677	194	
1195	" 8	3.00 "	82	18.0	109	....	1h. 27m.	1 417	180	
1198	" 8	4.46 "	82	14.0	85	....	3h. 13m.	3 047	530	
1203	" 10	10.12 A.M.	82	16.0	97	....	4h. 57m.	4 797	275	
1207	" 10	12.56 P.M.	83	16.0	97	....	54m.	800	110	
1211	" 10	3.10 "	83	14.0	85	....	3h. 08m.	2 980	384	Shut inlet 3.03 P.M., outlet 3.23 P.M.
1215	" 10	4.57 "	84	17.0	103	....	57m.	862	348	
1258	" 13	2.34 "	85	20.0	121	....	23m.	468	182	
1263	" 13	5.19 "	85	19.0	115	....	3h. 08m.	3 588	678	D. Application of chemicals unsatisfactory; chemical meter out of order.
1265	" 14	10.19 A.M.	85	19.0	115	....	4h. 23m.	4 928	1 670	
1269	" 14	1.12 P.M.	86	21.0	127	....	1h. 44m.	2 047	57	
1273	" 14	3.14 "	86	19.5	118	....	2h. 58m.	3 457	40	
1283	" 15	10.07 A.M.	86	21.0	127	....	4h. 23m.	5 007	84	
1287	" 15	1.25 P.M.	87	22.5	136	....	1h. 10m.	1 487	90	
1291	" 15	2.57 "	87	20.0	121	....	2h. 42m.	3 397	243	
1295	" 15	5.24 "	88	19.0	115	....	1h. 32m.	1 673	.....	
1302	" 17	10.06 A.M.	88	20.0	121	....	2h. 54m.	4 173	109	
1306	" 17	1.35 P.M.	89	19.0	115	....	33m.	521	125	
1310	" 17	3.07 "	89	20.0	121	....	2h. 05m.	2 311	87	
1320	" 18	10.20 A.M.	90	18.0	109	....	30m.	550	20	
1324	" 18	11.55 "	90	19.0	115	....	2h. 05m.	2 260	56	

TABLE NO. 4.—*Continued.*

Warren System.

Serial Number.	Collected. Date.	Collected. Hour.	Number of Run.	Rate of Filtration. Cubic Feet per Minute.	Rate of Filtration. Million Gallons per Acre per 24 Hours.	Loss of Head. Feet.	Period of Service Since Last Washing. Hours and Minutes.	Filtered Water Since Last Washing. Cubic Feet.	Bacteria per Cubic Centimeter.	Remarks.
	1895									
1328	Feb. 18	2.20 P.M.	90	17.0	103	....	4h. 30m.	4 790	198	
1333	" 18	4.55 "	91	18.0	109	....	1h. 39m.	1 804	67	
1337	" 18	5.05 "	91	18.0	109	....	1h. 49m.	1 954	61	
1343	" 19	10.12 A.M.	91	19.0	115	....	3h. 15m	3 434	39	
1347	" 19	11.31 "	91	18.0	109	....	4h. 34m.	4 894	104	
1351	" 19	3.04 P.M.	92	18.5	112	....	1h. 42m.	1 829	55	
1358	" 19	5.10 "	92	18.0	109	....	3h. 48m.	4 069	382	
1362	" 20	11.00 A.M.	92	18.0	109	....	5h. 43m.	6 029	156	
1366	" 20	12.03 P.M.	93	18.0	109	....	15m.	209	116	
1368	" 20	12.18 "	93	18.0	109	...	30m.	459	104	
1369	" 20	12.33 "	93	18.0	109	....	45m.	739	287	
1370	" 20	12.40 "	93	18.0	109	....	52m.	1 009	560	
1371	" 20	1.04 "	93	18.0	109	....	1h. 16m.	1 309	79	
1375	" 20	2.06 "	93	18.0	109	....	2h. 18m.	2 389	135	
1377	" 20	3.08 "	93	17.0	103	....	3h. 20m.	3 469	141	
1382	" 20	4.08 "	93	17.0	103	...	4h. 20m.	4 489	325	
1387	" 20	5.15 "	94	17.5	106	....	08m.	90	200	
1390	" 21	9.56 A.M.	94	16.5	100	....	1h. 20m.	1 330	48	
1394	" 21	12.42 P.M.	94	17.0	103	....	4h. 06m.	4 160	34	
1404	" 21	5.09 "	95	18.5	112	....	14m.	227	147	
1408	" 22	10.20 A.M.	95	18.0	109	....	1h. 55m.	2 077	88	
1411	" 22	1.18 P.M.	95	18.0	109	....	4h. 53m.	5 337	115	
1412	" 22	3.01 "	95	19.0	115	....	6h. 36m.	7 177	528	
1414	" 22	4.53 "	96	17.5	106	....	1h. 14m.	1 315	94	
1422	" 24	10.27 A.M.	96	17.5	106	....	3h. 17m.	3 480	79	
1423	" 24	1.10 P.M.	96	18.5	112	....	6h. 00m.	6 440	77	
1431	" 24	5.16 "	97	18.5	112	....	1h. 35m.	1 611	62	
1437	" 25	10.26 A.M.	97	20.0	121	....	3h. 16m.	3 631	40	
1441	" 25	1.14 P.M.	98	19.0	115	....	48m.	734	52	
1445	" 25	3.07 "	98	17.5	106	....	2h. 41m.	2 824	64	
1452	" 25	5.08 "	98	18.5	112	....	4h. 42m.	4 994	127	
1456	" 26	10.26 A.M.	98	17.5	106	....	6h. 30m.	6 904	122	
1460	" 26	11.43 "	98	15.0	91	....	7h. 47m.	8 214	294	
1464	" 26	3.04 P.M.	99	18.0	109	....	1h. 47m.	1 823	68	
1471	" 26	5.23 "	99	18.0	109	....	4h. 06m.	4 363	326	
1478	" 27	10.36 A.M.	99	18.0	109	....	5h. 49m.	6 193	34	
1479	" 27	1.43 P.M.	100	24.5	149	....	44m.	923	30	
1483	" 27	2.58 "	100	24.0	146	....	1h. 59m.	2 773	53	
1488	" 27	5.07 "	101	23.0	140	....	17m.	341	142	
1496	" 28	10.36 A.M.	101	25.0	152	....	2h. 16m.	3 311	21	
1502	" 28	3.23 P.M.	102	25.0	152	....	1h. 56m.	1 241	33	
1507	" 28	5.00 "	102	23.5	143	....	3h. 33m.	4 961	413	
1512	" 29	10.30 A.M.	103	25.0	152	....	1h. 29m.	2 326	138	
1516	" 29	1.34 P.M.	104	24.0	146	....	24m.	494	176	
1520	" 29	3.14 "	104	25.0	152	....	2h. 04m.	3 024	187	
1528	" 29	5.15 "	105	24.0	146	....	17m.	396	211	
1531	Mar. 2	9.33 A.M.	105	22.5	136	....	1h. 03m.	1 606	130	
1536	" 2	10.21 "	105	25.0	152	....	1h. 51m.	2 766	331	
1540	" 2	1.33 P.M.	106	24.5	149	....	1h. 07m.	1 549	.....	
1544	" 2	3.12 "	106	23.0	140	....	2h. 46m.	3 859	676	
1549	" 2	5.06 "	107	25.0	152	....	22m.	457	333	
1557	" 3	10.37 A.M.	107	24.0	146	....	2h. 23m.	3 547	155	
1561	" 3	12.15 P.M.	107	24.0	146	....	4h. 01m.	5 897	405	
1565	" 3	3.10 "	108	25.0	152	....	1h. 27m.	2 025	95	
1570	" 3	5.10 "	108	24.0	146	....	3h. 27m.	4 845	553	
1576	" 4	10.44 A.M.	108	21.5	130	....	4h. 54m.	6 999	605	
1580	" 4	12.58 P.M.	109	23.0	140	....	1h. 14m.	1 747	80	
1584	" 4	3.19 "	109	24.0	146	....	3h. 35m.	5 093	1 390	
1589	" 4	5.03 "	110	24.0	146	....	1h. 05m.	1 452	116	
1595	" 5	10.30 A.M.	110	25.0	152	....	3h. 02m.	4 442	187	
1599	" 5	12.49 P.M.	111	23.0	140	....	43m.	930	93	
1608	" 5	3.29 "	111	23.0	140	....	3h. 23m.	4 650	590	

TABLE NO. 4.—*Continued.*

Warren System.

Serial Number.	Collected. Date.	Collected. Hour.	Number of Run.	Rate of Filtration. Cubic Feet per Minute.	Rate of Filtration. Million Gallons per Acre per 24 Hours.	Loss of Head. Feet.	Period of Service Since Last Washing. Hours and Minutes.	Filtered Water Since Last Washing. Cubic Feet.	Bacteria per Cubic Centimeter.	Remarks.
	1895									
1612	Mar. 5	5.18 P.M.	112	26.0	158	....	10m.	169	615	
1616	" 6	10.32 A.M.	112	23.0	140	....	1h. 54m.	2 819	48	
1621	" 6	12.38 P.M.	112	23.0	140	....	4h. 00m.	5 699	615	
1625	" 6	3.16 "	113	26.0	158	....	1h. 51m.	2 737	106	
1633	" 6	5.25 "	114	24.5	149	....	37m.	808	59	
1637	" 7	10.40 A.M.	114	24.0	146	....	2h. 20m.	3 468	39	
1641	" 7	12.53 P.M.	114	23.0	140	....	4h. 33m.	6 508	485	
1644	" 7	3.10 "	115	24.0	146	....	1h. 16m.	1 750	40	
1649	" 7	5.15 "	115	24.0	146	....	3h. 21m.	4 710	154	
1656	" 9	10.58 A.M.	115	23.5	143	....	5h. 33m.	7 890	620	
1661	" 9	12.50 P.M.	116	24.5	149	....	1h. 16m.	1 738	40	
1670	" 9	3.40 "	117	24.0	146	....	36m.	837	35	
1671	" 9	5.04 "	117	24.0	146	....	2h. 00m.	2 757	64	
1678	" 10	10.19 A.M.	117	24.0	146	....	3h. 45m.	5 357	139	
1682	" 10	1.33 P.M.	118	25.0	152	....	1h. 43m.	2 344	68	
1686	" 10	3.07 "	118	24.5	149	....	3h. 17m.	4 605	935	
1693	" 10	5.15 "	119	25.0	152	....	1h. 29m.	2 085	61	
1699	" 11	10.18 A.M.	119	25.0	152	....	3h. 02m.	4 375	300	
1706	" 11	3.17 P.M.	121	20.0	121	....	1h. 34m.	1 872	310	
1713	" 11	5.05 "	122	21.5	130	....	29m.	562	60	
1719	" 12	10.15 A.M.	122	19.5	118	....	2h. 09m.	2 622	89	
1723	" 12	12.54 P.M.	123	19.0	115	....	1h. 19m.	1 439	26	
1727	" 12	3.22 "	123	17.5	106	....	3h. 47m.	4 069	485	
1732	" 12	5.08 "	124	20.0	121	....	1h. 07m.	1 311	24	
1739	" 13	10.23 A.M.	124	18.5	112	....	2h. 55m.	3 551	137	
1743	" 13	1.09 P.M.	125	19.5	118	....	1h. 17m.	1 389	26	
1747	" 13	3.10 "	125	18.5	112	....	3h. 18m.	3 639	1 000	
1752	" 13	5.01 P.M.	126	19.5	118	....	1h. 13m.	1 377	11	
1758	" 14	10.27 A.M.	126	18.5	112	....	3h. 09m.	3 827	137	
1764	" 14	1.06 P.M.	127	19.0	115	....	1h. 21m.	1 480	37	
1770	" 14	3.10 "	127	19.5	118	...	3h. 25m.	3 870	451	
1778	" 14	4.50 "	128	20.0	121	....	1h. 06m.	1 182	19	
1784	" 16	10.22 A.M.	128	19.0	115	....	3h. 08m.	3 642	40	
1790	" 16	1.09 P.M.	129	18.0	109	....	1h. 49m.	2 019	34	
1796	" 16	3.12 "	129	17.0	103	....	3h. 52m.	4 169	172	
1803	" 16	5.02 "	130	20.0	121	....	26m.	443	60	
1809	" 17	9.31 A.M.	130	20.0	121	....	1h. 19m.	1 533	8	
1810	" 17	10.24 "	130	20.0	121	....	2h. 12m.	2 583	32	
1816	" 17	1.11 P.M.	131	18.5	112	....	18m.	264	50	
1822	" 17	3.15 "	131	20.0	121	....	2h. 22m.	2 734	34	
1834	" 18	9.31 A.M.	132	19.0	109	....	31m.	551	23	
1835	" 18	10.26 "	132	18.0	109	....	1h. 26m.	1 611	31	
1840	" 18	1.06 "	132	20.0	121	....	4h. 06m.	4 801	51	
1846	" 18	2.06 "	133	19.0	115	....	10m.	203	90	
1847	" 18	3.20 "	133	20.5	124	....	1h. 24m.	1 623	56	
1852	" 18	4.21 "	133	19.5	118	....	2h. 25m.	2 793	43	
1853	" 18	4.59 "	133	20.0	121	....	3h. 03m.	3 523	50	
1859	" 19	9.31 A.M.	133	20.0	121	....	3h. 55m.	4 613	65	
1860	" 19	9.45 "	133	19.5	118	....	4h. 09m.	4 863	78	
1861	" 19	9.55 "	133	20.0	121	....	4h. 19m.	5 063	143	
1862	" 19	10.44 "	134	20.0	121	....	10m.	185	150	
1866	" 19	10.56 "	134	20.0	121	....	22m.	415	105	
1867	" 19	11.05 "	134	19.5	118	....	31m.	585	91	
1873	" 19	2.08 P.M.	135	20.5	124	....	13m.	217	265	
1878	" 19	3.14 "	135	19.5	118	....	1h. 19m.	1 547	76	
1886	" 20	9.30 A.M.	136	20.0	121	....	30m.	610	43	
1887	" 20	10.21 "	136	20.0	121	....	1h. 21m.	1 580	144	
1892	" 20	1.03 P.M.	137	18.0	109	....	58m.	978	137	
1899	" 20	2.18 "	137	18.0	109	....	2h. 13m.	2 318	111	
1900	" 20	3.27 "	138	16.5	100	....	30m.	497	298	
1904	" 20	4.10 "	138	18.5	112	....	1h. 13m.	1 277	116	

Table No. 4.—*Continued.*

Warren System.

Serial Number.	Collected.		Number of Run.	Rate of Filtration.		Loss of Head. Feet.	Period of Service Since Last Washing. Hours and Minutes.	Filtered Water Since, Last Washing. Cubic Feet.	Bacteria per Cubic Centimeter.	Remarks.
	Date.	Hour.		Cubic Feet per Minute.	Million Gallons per Acre per 24 Hours.					
	1896									
1906	Mar. 20	4.46 P.M.	138	18.5	112	....	1h. 49m.	1 877	111	
1912	" 21	10.40 A.M.	139	18.5	112	....	1h. 10m.	1 227	138	
1916	" 21	11.58 "	139	18.0	109	....	2h. 28m.	2 647	148	
1918	" 21	12.51 P.M.	140	19.0	115	....	18m.	266	220	
1925	" 21	3.37 "	141	18.0	109	....	06m.	97	820	
1926	" 21	4.03 "	141	19.0	115	....	32m.	507	229	
1927	" 21	4.33 "	141	18.0	109	....	1h. 02m.	1 087	116	
1929	" 21	5.03 "	141	18.0	109	....	1h. 32m.	1 597	150	
1934	" 23	9.37 A.M.	142	15.5	94	....	07m.	138	147	
1935	" 23	10.20 "	142	18.0	109	....	50m.	828	51	
1939	" 23	11.10 "	142	18.0	109	....	1h. 40m.	1 708	60	
1940	" 23	11.58 "	142	18.0	109	....	2h. 28m.	2 558	60	
1945	" 23	1.01 P.M.	143	18.0	109	....	14m.	183	440	
1946	" 23	2.53 "	143	18.0	109	....	2h. 06m.	2 153	50	
1951	" 23	4.27 "	144	19.5	118	....	13m.	215	435	
1952	" 23	5.00 "	144	18.5	112	....	46m.	845	73	
1958	" 24	9 A.M. to 11.30 A.M.	144	17.7	107	....	....	......	25	
1961	" 24	11.30 " " 2.30 P.M.	144–145	16.4	99	....	....	......	21	
1965	" 24	2.30 P.M. " 5.30 "	145–146	16.3	99	....	....	......	127	
1968	" 24	5.30 " " 8.30 "	146	19.3	117	....	....	......	66	
1972	" 24	8.30 " " 11.30 "	146–147	18.4	111	....	....	......	61	
1975	" 25	12.21 A.M.	147	17.0	103	....	3h. 05m.	3 373	286	C.
1976	" 25	1.04 "	148	17.5	106	....	10m.	131	153	E.
1977	" 25	1.14 "	148	18.0	109	....	20m.	311	170	E.
1978	" 25	1.24 "	148	20.0	121	....	30m.	481	97	E.
1979	" 25	1.39 "	148	18.5	112	....	45m.	751	116	E.
1980	" 25	1.54 "	148	18.0	109	....	1h. 00m.	1 071	75	E.
1981	" 25	2.24 "	148	18.0	109	....	1h. 30m.	1 581	64	E.
1984	" 24–25	11.30 P.M. to 2.30 A.M.	147–148	16.4	99	....	....	......	52	
1985	" 25	2.54 A.M.	148	18.0	109	....	2h. 00m.	2 101	90	E.
1986	" 25	3.54 "	148	18.0	109	....	3h. 00m.	3 241	196	E.
1987	" 25	4.12 "	148	15.0	91	....	3h. 18m.	3 491	252	E.
1988	" 25	2.30 A.M. to 5.30 A.M.	148–149	15.8	96	....	....	......	103	
1992	" 25	5.30 " " 8.30 "	149	19.9	120	....	....	......	62	
1997	" 25	8.30 " " 11.30 "	150	18.2	110	....	....	.....	71	
2000	" 25	11.30 " " 2.30 P.M.	150–151	17.6	103	....	....	......	85	
2004	" 25	2.30 P.M. " 5.30 "	151–152	15.5	94	....	....	......	201	
2007	" 25	5.30 " " 8.30 "	152–153	18.9	114	....	....	....	81	
2011	" 25	8.30 " " 11.30 "	153–154	15.6	95	....	....	......	865	D. Application of chemicals unsatisfactory on Run No. 154; chemical meter out of order.
2020	" 25–26	11.30 " " 2.30 A.M.	154–155	17.3	105	....	....	......	74	
2030	" 26	2.30 A.M. " 5.30 "	155–156	17.5	106	....	....	......	87	
2034	" 26	5.30 " " 8.30 "	156–157	18.1	109	....	....	......	121	
2039	" 26	8.30 " " 11.30 "	157–158	18.3	111	....	....	......	205	
2042	" 26	11.30 " " 2.30 P.M.	158	17.8	108	....	....	......	142	
2046	" 26	2.30 P.M. " 5.30 "	159	17.7	107	....	....	......	228	
2049	" 26	5.30 " " 8.30 "	160	18.4	111	....	....	......	89	
2053	" 26	8.30 " " 11.30 "	160–161	18.4	111	....	....	......	69	
2056	" 26–27	11.30 " " 2.30 A.M.	161–162	15.1	91	....	....	......	59	
2064	" 27	2.30 A.M. " 5.30 "	162–163	17.6	107	...	....	......	209	
2075	" 27	5.30 " " 8.30 "	163	18.3	111	....	....	......	91	
2082	" 27	8.30 " " 11.30 "	163–164	17.8	108	....	....	......	62	
2098	" 27	11.30 " " 2.30 P.M.	164–165	17.8	108	....	....	......	189	
2102	" 27	2.30 P.M. " 5.30 "	165–166	18.7	113	....	....	......	309	
2105	" 27	5.30 " " 8.30 "	166–167	19.4	117	....	....	......	110	
2109	" 27	8.30 " " 11.30 "	167	17.6	107	....	....	......	169	
2112	" 28	12.03 A.M.	167	21.0	127	....	3h. 49m.	4 050	207	C. Shut inlet 12.03 A.M.,
2113	" 28	12.37 "	168	18.0	109	....	10m.	124	535	E. [outlet 12.11 A.M.
2114	" 28	12.47 "	168	18.0	109	....	20m.	324	110	E.
2115	" 28	12.57 "	168	18.0	109	....	30m.	504	97	E.
2116	" 28	1.12 "	168	18.0	109	....	45m.	784	59	E.
2117	" 28	1.27 "	168	18.0	109	....	1h. 00m.	1 004	115	E.

TABLE NO. 4.—*Continued.*

Warren System.

Serial Number.	Collected. Date.	Collected. Hour.	Number of Run.	Rate of Filtration. Cubic Feet per Minute.	Rate of Filtration. Million Gallons per Acre per 24 Hours.	Loss of Head, Feet.	Period of Service Since Last Washing, Hours and Minutes.	Filtered Water Since Last Washing, Cubic Feet.	Bacteria per Cubic Centimeter.	Remarks.
	1896									
2118	Mar. 28	1.57 A.M.	168	18.0	109	....	1h. 30m.	1 494	107	E.
2119	" 28	2.27 "	168	18.0	109	....	2h. 00m.	2 104	134	E.
2120	" 27–28	11.30 P.M. to 2.30 A.M.	167–168	16.8	102	....	....	......	126	
2123	" 28	3.27 A.M.	168	18.0	109	....	3h. 00m.	3 184	160	E.
2124	" 28	4.27 "	168	17.5	106	....	4h. 00m.	4 244	221	E.
2125	" 28	4.33 "	168	16.0	97	....	4h. 06m.	4 354	206	E.
2126	" 28	2.30 A.M. to 5.30 A.M.	168–169	17.1	104	....	....	......	83	
2130	" 28	5.30 " " 8.30 "	169	18.1	110	....	....	......	77	
2135	" 28	8.30 " " 11.30 "	169–170	18.4	111	....	....	......	114	
2138	" 28	11.30 " " 2.30 P.M.	170–171	19.1	116	....	....	......	155	
2142	" 28	2.30 P.M. " 5.30 "	171	18.5	112	....	....	......	169	
2145	" 28	5.30 " " 8.30 "	171–172	18.3	111	....	....	......	187	
2154	" 28	8.30 " " 11.30 "	172–173	18.0	109	....	....	......	135	
2157	" 28–29	11.30 " " 2.30 A.M.	173	17.3	105	....	....	......	21	
2160	" 29	2.30 A.M. " 5.30 "	173–174	17.3	105	....	....	......	40	
2164	" 29	5.30 " " 8.30 "	174–175	17.9	109	....	....	......	67	
2168	" 29	8.30 " " 11.30 "	175	17.8	108	....	....	......	46	
2172	" 29	11.30 " " 2.30 P.M.	175–176	16.2	98	....	....	......	125	
2181	" 29	2.30 P.M. " 5.30 "	176	18.9	115	....	....	......	300	
2184	" 29	5.30 " " 8.30 "	177	17.5	106	....	....	......	69	
2188	" 29	8.30 " " 11.30 "	177–178	17.2	104	....	....	......	180	
2191	" 29–30	11.30 " " 2.30 A.M.	178	17.9	108	....	....	......	52	
2195	" 30	2.30 A.M. " 5.30 "	178–179	19.0	115	....	....	......	92	
2198	" 30	5.30 " " 8.30 "	179	17.3	104	....	....	......	.....	
2202	" 30	8.30 " " 11.30 "	179–180	17.1	103	....	....	......	145	
2207	" 30	11.30 " " 2.30 P.M.	180–181	17.4	105	....	....	......	113	
2209	" 30	2.30 P.M. " 5.30 "	181	17.9	108	....	....	......	117	
2215	" 31	9.35 A.M. " 11.30 A.M.	182	17.8	108	....	....	......	147	
2219	" 31	11.30 " " 2.30 P.M.	182–183	17.2	104	....	....	......	325	
2223	" 31	2.30 P.M. " 5.30 "	184–185	17.5	106	....	....	......	635	
2228	April 1	9.15 A.M. " 11.30 A.M.	185	17.8	108	....	....	......	300	
2233	" 1	11.30 " " 2.30 P.M.	186	17.4	105	....	....	......	220	
2236	" 1	2.30 P.M. " 5.30 "	187–188	16.6	101	....	....	......	270	
2241	" 2	9.15 A.M. " 11.30 A.M.	188	17.8	108	....	....	......	102	
2246	" 2	11.30 " " 2.30 P.M.	188–189	17.6	106	....	....	......	157	
2249	" 2	2.30 P.M. " 5.30 "	189–190	17.4	105	....	....	......	205	
2254	" 3	9.15 A.M. " 11.30 A.M.	190–191	18.4	111	....	....	......	93	
2258	" 3	11.30 " " 2.30 P.M.	191	17.2	104	....	....	......	77	
2261	" 3	2.30 P.M. " 5.30 "	192	18.0	109	....	....	......	76	
2266	" 4	9.15 A.M. " 11.30 A.M.	193	17.0	103	....	....	......	180	
2270	" 4	11.30 " " 2.30 P.M.	193	18.0	109	....	....	......	87	
2275	" 4	2.30 P.M. " 5.30 "	194	18.2	110	....	....	......	81	
2280	" 6	9.15 A.M. " 11.30 A.M.	194	18.2	110	....	....	......	25	
2285	" 6	11.30 " " 2.30 P.M.	194–195	16.6	101	....	....	......	37	
2288	" 6	2.30 P.M. " 5.30 "	195	18.0	109	....	....	......	39	
2293	" 7	9.15 A.M. " 11.30 A.M.	195	17.0	103	....	....	......	37	
2298	" 7	11.30 " " 2.30 P.M.	195–196	17.0	103	....	....	......	25	
2301	" 7	2.30 P.M. " 5.30 "	196	18.5	112	....	....	......	59	
2309	" 8	9.30 A.M. " 11.30 A.M.	196	17.2	104	....	....	......	51	E.
2312	" 8	12.10 P.M.	196	14.0	85	....	8h. 04m.	8 673	.....	Shut inlet 12.08 P.M., toulet 12.24 P.M.
2313	" 8	12.46 "	197	18.0	109	....	03m.	38	.....	
2314	" 8	12.49 "	197	19.0	115	....	06m.	88	124	
2315	" 8	12.52 "	197	18.5	112	....	09m.	148	91	
2316	" 8	12.55 "	197	18.0	109	....	12m.	198	127	
2317	" 8	12.58 "	197	18.0	109	....	15m.	248	117	
2318	" 8	1.13 "	197	18.0	109	....	30m.	518	93	
2319	" 8	1.28 "	197	18.0	109	....	45m.	778	81	
2321	" 8	11.30 A.M. to 2.30 P.M.	196–197	17.4	105	....	....	......	33	C.
2330	" 8	2.30 P.M. " 5.30 "	197	17.5	106	....	....	......	53	C.
2333	" 9	9.15 A.M. " 11.30 A.M.	197	17.3	104	....	....	......	37	C.
2336	" 9	11.32 A.M.	197	18.0	109	....	7h. 19m.	7738	70	

TABLE NO. 4.—*Continued.*

Warren System.

Serial Number.	Collected. Date.	Collected. Hour.	Number of Run.	Rate of Filtration. Cubic Feet per Minute.	Rate of Filtration. Million Gallons per Acre per 24 Hours.	Loss of Head, Feet.	Period of Service Since Last Washing. Hours and Minutes.	Filtered Water Since Last Washing. Cubic Feet.	Bacteria per Cubic Centimeter.	Remarks.
	1896									
2337	April 9	11.47 A.M.	197	17.0	103	....	7h. 34m.	8 008	126	
2339	" 9	12.02 P.M.	197	15.0	91	....	7h. 49m.	8 198	158	Shut inlet 11.52 A.M.,
2342	" 9	11.30 A.M. to 2.30 P.M.	197–198	18.4	111	....	....	......	74	C. [outlet 12.08 P.M.
2345	" 9	2.30 P.M. " 5.30 "	198	18.0	109	....	....	......	126	C.
2350	" 10	10.19 A.M.	198	18.0	109	....	6h. 24m.	6 798	44	
2352	" 10	10.49 "	198	18.0	109	....	6h. 54m.	7 298	51	
2354	" 10	11.19 "	198	18.0	109	....	7h. 24m.	7 838	87	
2355	" 10	9.20 A.M. to 11.30 A.M.	198	17.1	103	....	....	......	42	C.
2357	" 10	11.49 A.M.	198	18.0	109	....	7h. 54m.	8 338	86	
2359	" 10	12.31 P.M.	199	18.0	109	....	03m.	19	32	
2360	" 10	12.34 "	199	18.5	112	....	06m.	79	55	
2361	" 10	12.37 "	199	18.5	112	....	09m.	139	47	
2362	" 10	12.40 "	199	18.5	112	....	12m.	199	29	
2363	" 10	12.43 "	199	18.5	112	....	15m.	259	39	
2364	" 10	12.58 "	199	18.0	109	....	30m.	519	16	
2365	" 10	1.13 "	199	18.0	109	....	45m.	789	15	
2366	" 10	2.20 "	199	18.0	109	....	1h. 52m.	2 009	23	
2367	" 10	11.30 A.M. to 2.30 P.M.	198–199	17.9	109	....	....	......	38	C.
2370	" 10	3.20 P.M.	199	18.0	109	....	2h. 52m.	3 099	29	
2371	" 10	4.20 "	199	17.5	106	....	3h. 52m.	4 149	30	
2372	" 10	5.20 "	199	17.0	103	....	4h. 52m.	5 229	44	
2373	" 10	2.30 P.M. to 5.30 P.M.	199	17.7	107	....	....	......	45	C.
2377	" 11	11.30 A.M.	199	18.0	109	....	7h. 32m.	8 099	17	
2379	" 11	9.15 A.M. to 11.30 A.M.	199	17.8	108	....	....	......	16	C.
2381	" 11	12.00 M.	199	18.0	109	....	8h. 02m.	8 629	16	
2383	" 11	12.30 P.M.	199	18.0	109	....	8h. 32m.	9 119	13	
2385	" 11	1.00 "	199	18.0	109	....	9h. 02m.	9 709	25	
2387	" 11	1.30 "	199	18.0	109	....	9h. 32m.	10 159	12	
2396	" 11	11.30 A.M. to 2.30 P.M.	199	17.2	104	....	....	......	32	C.
2400	" 11	3.45 P.M.	200	16.0	97	....	03m.	10	65	
2401	" 11	3.48 "	200	18.0	109	....	06m.	60	41	
2402	" 11	3.51 "	200	18.0	109	....	09m.	120	62	
2403	" 11	3.54 "	200	18.0	109	....	12m.	170	53	
2404	" 11	3.57 "	200	18.0	109	....	15m.	230	37	
2406	" 11	4.12 "	200	18.0	109	....	30m.	500	19	
2407	" 11	4.27 "	200	18.0	109	....	45m.	770	20	
2409	" 11	4.57 "	200	18.0	109	....	1h. 15m.	1 310	19	
2411	" 11	2.30 P.M. to 5.30 P.M.	200	17.1	104	....	....	......	28	C.
2452	" 20	10.25 A.M.	201	26.0	158	....	1h. 23m.	2 020	30	
2455	" 20	11.58 "	201	26.0	158	....	2h. 56m.	4 400	24	
2458	" 20	2.54 P.M.	201	27.0	164	....	5h. 52m.	8 900	48	
2463	" 21	9.30 A.M.	202	22.5	136	....	30m.	622	46	
2465	" 21	10.22 "	202	23.0	140	....	1h. 22m.	1 782	59	
2468	" 21	12.35 P.M.	202	24.0	146	....	3h. 35m.	4 832	64	
2472	" 21	1.48 "	202	25.0	152	....	4h. 48m.	6 472	96	
2475	" 21	2.55 "	202	24.0	146	....	5h. 55m.	8 002	147	
2479	" 22	9.51 A.M.	203	23.0	140	....	51m.	1 136	104	
2481	" 22	10.45 "	203	23.0	140	....	1h. 45m.	2 356	191	
2484	" 22	12.32 P.M.	203	23.0	140	....	3h. 32m.	4 796	174	
2486	" 22	1.22 "	203	23.5	143	....	4h. 22m.	5 916	162	
2489	" 22	2.56 "	203	22.0	133	....	5h. 56m.	8 076	198	
2495	" 23	11.18 A.M.	204	23.0	140	....	33m.	680	53	
2497	" 23	12.47 P.M.	204	24.0	146	....	2h. 02m.	2 760	73	
2499	" 23	2.00 "	204	24.0	146	....	3h. 15m.	4 410	107	
2502	" 23	3.02 "	204	24.0	146	....	4h. 17m.	5 830	167	
2504	" 23	4.47 "	204	24.0	146	....	6h. 02m.	8 240	151	
2508	" 24	9.31 A.M.	204	24.0	146	....	7h. 16m.	9 920	356	
2510	" 24	11.43 "	204	23.0	140	....	9h. 28m.	12 960	375	
2513	" 24	1.09 P.M.	204	21.5	130	....	10h. 54m.	14 830	460	
2516	" 24	2.44 "	205	23.0	140	....	41m.	882	220	
2518	" 24	4.41 "	205	23.5	143	...	2h. 38m.	3 572	330	

TABLE NO. 4.—*Continued.*

Warren System.

Serial Number.	Collected. Date.	Collected. Hour.	Number of Run.	Rate of Filtration. Cubic Feet per Minute.	Rate of Filtration. Million Gallons per Acre per 24 Hours.	Loss of Head. Feet.	Period of Service Since Last Washing. Hours and Minutes.	Filtered Water Since Last Washing. Cubic Feet.	Bacteria per Cubic Centimeter.	Remarks.
	1896									
2522	April 25	10.15 A.M.	205	20.0	121	....	4h. 42m.	6 292	231	
2524	" 25	12.40 P.M.	205	20.0	121	....	7h. 07m.	9 172	371	
2526	" 25	1.44 "	205	20.0	121	....	8h. 11m.	10 462	324	
2531	" 27	9.30 A.M. to 3.30 P.M.	206	21.3	129	....	....	......	143	
2534	" 27	3.30 P.M. " 9.00 "	206–207	21.2	128	....	....	......	500	
2537	" 27–28	9.30 " " 3.00 A.M.	207	20.6	125	....	....	......	559	
2539	" 28	3.00 A.M. " 9.00 "	207–208	22.3	134	....	....	......	....	Application of chemicals unsatisfactory on run No. 208; alum meter out of order.
2543	" 28	9.00 " " 3.00 P.M.	209	21.9	133	....	....	......	547	
2547	" 28	3.00 P.M. " 9.00 "	209	21.8	132	....	....	......	410	
2550	" 28–29	9.00 " " 3.00 A.M.	210	20.5	124	....	....	......	390	
2556	" 29	3.00 A.M. " 9.00 "	210–211	20.5	124	....	....	......	1 057	
2560	" 29	9.00 " " 3.00 P.M.	211–212	21.3	129	....	....	......	....	
2563	" 29	3.00 P.M. " 9.00 "	212	23.0	140	....	....	......	172	
2588	" 29–30	9.00 " " 3.00 A.M.	212–213	20.3	123	....	....	......	146	
2598	" 30	3.00 A.M. " 9.00 "	213	20.6	125	....	....	......	95	
2602	" 30	9.00 " " 3.00 P.M.	213–214	20.8	126	....	....	......	120	
2607	" 30	3.00 P.M. " 9.00 "	214	20.9	126	....	....	......	76	
2609	May 1	12.46 A.M.	214	21.0	127	....	10h. 34m.	13 136	90	C.
2610	" 1	1.58 "	215	19.0	115	....	02m.	12	193	This series of results on run No. 215 used in obtaining the average bacteria for this run, but not for the day.
2611	" 1	2.00 "	215	24.0	146	....	04m.	52	187	
2612	" 1	2.02 "	215	20.0	125	....	06m.	92	243	
2613	" 1	2.04 "	215	20.0	125	....	08m.	132	170	
2614	" 1	2.06 "	215	20.0	121	....	10m.	182	199	
2615	" 1	2.08 "	215	20.0	121	....	12m.	222	123	
2616	" 1	2.10 "	215	20.0	121	....	14m.	262	144	
2617	" 1	2.12 "	215	20.0	121	....	16m.	302	144	
2618	" 1	2.14 "	215	21.0	127	....	18m.	352	71	
2619	" 1	2.16 "	215	21.0	127	....	20m.	392	64	
2620	" 1	2.18 "	215	21.0	127	....	22m.	432	57	
2621	" 1	2.20 "	215	21.0	127	....	24m.	472	86	
2622	" 1	2.22 "	215	21.0	127	....	26m.	512	145	
2623	" 1	2.24 "	215	21.0	127	....	28m.	552	85	
2624	" 1	2.26 "	215	21.0	127	....	30m.	602	94	
2625	" 1	2.31 "	215	21.0	127	....	35m.	802	101	
2626	" 1	2.41 "	215	21.0	127	....	45m.	1 012	53	
2627	" 1	2.56 "	215	21.0	127	....	1h. 00m.	1 322	107	
2629	Apr. 30–May 1	9.00 P.M. to 3.00 A.M.	214–215	21.4	129	....	....	......	96	
2631	May 1	3.56 A.M.	215	21.0	127	....	2h. 00m.	2 432	98	
2632	" 1	4.56 "	215	21.0	127	....	3h. 00m.	3 692	104	
2633	" 1	5.56 "	215	21.0	127	....	4h. 00m.	4 952	45	
2634	" 1	6.56 "	215	21.0	127	....	5h. 00m.	6 182	53	
2635	" 1	7.56 "	215	21.0	127	....	6h. 00m.	7 442	87	
2637	" 1	8.56 "	215	21.0	127	....	7h. 00m.	8 662	108	
2639	" 1	3.00 A.M. to 9.00 A.M.	215	20.6	125	....	....	......	83	
2641	" 1	9.56 A.M.	215	20.5	124	....	8h. 00m.	9 902	111	
2642	" 1	10.56 "	215	20.5	124	....	9h. 00m.	11 162	132	
2643	" 1	11.56 "	215	20.0	121	....	10h. 00m.	12 352	140	
2644	" 1	12.56 P.M.	215	21.0	127	....	11h. 00m.	13 652	166	
2645	" 1	1.56 "	215	21.0	127	....	12h. 00m.	14 862	158	
2646	" 1	2.43 "	215	14.0	85	....	12h. 47m.	15 712	191	Shut inlet 2.25 P.M., outlet 2.48 P.M.
2650	" 1	9.00 "	216	21.5	130	....	5h. 44m.	7 188	77	
2656	" 2	3.45 A.M.	217	21.0	127	....	18m.	364	95	From May 2–9, inclusive, the results of both single samples and those collected by the sampler were used to obtain the average bacteria for days and for runs.
2659	" 2	9.00 "	217	....	.....	....	5h. 33m.	6 744	140	
2661	" 2	12.40 P.M.	217	21.0	127	....	9h. 13m.	12 374	149	
2663	" 2	3.00 "	217	21.0	127	....	11h. 33m.	14 244	183	
2670	" 4	9.15 A.M. to 3.00 P.M.	217–218	21.7	131	....	....	......	72	
2693	" 4	3.00 P.M. " 9.00 "	218–219	20.5	124	....	....	......	56	
2702	" 4–5	9.00 " " 3.00 A.M.	219	20.3	122	....	....	......	43	
2712	" 5	3.00 A.M. " 9.00 "	219–220	20.6	124	....	....	......	51	
2718	" 5	12.31 P.M.	220	21.0	127	....	7h. 50m.	9 769	66	
2721	" 5	9.00 A.M. to 3.00 P.M.	220	20.5	124	....	....	......	....	

TABLE No. 4.—*Continued.*

Warren System.

Serial Number.	Collected. Date.	Collected. Hour.	Number of Run.	Rate of Filtration. Cubic Feet per Minute.	Rate of Filtration. Million Gallons per Acre per 24 Hours.	Loss of Head. Feet.	Period of Service Since Last Washing. Hours and Minutes.	Filtered Water Since Last Washing. Cubic Feet.	Bacteria per Cubic Centimeter.	Remarks.
	1896									
2726	May 5	3.00 P.M. to 9.00 P.M.	220–221	21.0	127	....	....	......	.....	
2728	" 6	12.15 A.M.	221	21.0	127	....	6h. 55m.	8 876	69	
2730	" 6	9.00 P.M. to 3.00 A.M.	221	21.0	127	....	....	......	.....	
2732	" 6	6.00 A.M.	222	21.0	127	....	52m.	1 076	35	
2738	" 6	12.20 P.M.	222	21.0	127	....	7h. 12m.	8 846	100	
2740	" 6	3.00 "	222	20.5	124	....	9h. 52m.	12 186	52	
2748	" 6	3.00 P.M. to 9.00 P.M.	222–223	20.7	125	....	....	......	.....	
2751	" 6–7	9.00 " " 3.00 A.M.	223	21.0	127	....	....	......	96	
2754	" 7	3.25 A.M.	224	22.0	133	....	11m.	216	100	
2757	" 7	3.00 A.M. to 9.00 A.M.	224	20.9	126	....	....	......	.....	
2758	" 7	9.00 A.M.	224	21.0	127	....	5h. 46m.	7 226	.....	
2762	" 7	3.00 P.M.	224	21.0	127	....	11h. 46m.	14 790	30	
2763	" 7	9.00 A.M. to 3.00 P.M.	224	21.0	127	...	....	......	.....	
2770	" 7	3.00 P.M. " 9.00 "	224–225	21.2	128	....	....	......	.....	
2771	" 7	9.00 P.M.	225	21.0	127	....	4h. 30m.	5 836	51	
2777	" 7–8	9.00 P.M. to 3.00 A.M.	225	20.8	126	....	....	......	.....	
2778	" 8	3.00 A.M.	225	21.0	127	....	10h. 30m.	13 326	167	
2783	" 8	3.00 A.M. to 9.00 A.M.	225–226	20.6	125	....	....	......	113	
2784	" 8	9.00 A.M.	226	21.0	127	....	4h. 39m.	5 674	17	
2789	" 8	9.00 A.M. to 3.00 P.M.	226	20.0	121	....	....	......	.....	
2790	" 8	3.00 P.M.	227	24.0	146	....	05m.	100	.....	Application of chemicals
2797	" 8	3.00 P.M. to 9.00 P.M.	227–228	21.0	127	....	....	......	.....	unsatisfactory on run
2801	" 8–9	9.00 " " 3.00 A.M.	228	20.9	127	....	....	......	.....	No. 227; alum meter
2802	" 9	3.00 A.M.	228	20.5	124	....	7h. 41m.	9 545	58	out of order.
2807	" 9	3.00 A.M. to 9.00 A.M.	228–229	21.0	127	....	....	......	.....	
2812	" 9	9.00 A.M.	229	20.5	124	....	5h. 09m.	6 482	43	
2817	" 9	3.00 P.M.	229	20.0	121	....	11h. 09m.	14 322	49	Shut inlet 2.53 P.M., out-
2823	" 11	3.00 P.M.	230	21.0	127	....	6h. 12m.	7 958	44	let 3.13 P.M.
2829	" 11	9.00 "	230	21.0	127	....	12h. 12m.	15 578	41	
2832	" 11	9.51 "	231	....	....	....	02m.	13	54	
2833	" 11	9.53 "	231	21.5	130	....	04m.	43	100	
2834	" 11	9.55 "	231	22.0	133	....	06m.	93	88	
2835	" 11	9.57 "	231	22.0	133	....	08m.	133	71	
2836	" 11	9.59 "	231	20.5	124	....	10m.	173	49	
2837	" 11	10.01 "	231	21.0	127	....	12m.	213	49	
2838	" 11	10.03 "	231	21.0	127	....	14m.	253	48	
2839	" 11	10.04 "	231	21.5	130	....	15m.	273	30	
2840	" 11	10.05 "	231	22.0	133	....	16m.	303	33	
2841	" 11	10.07 "	231	22.0	133	....	18m.	343	55	
2842	" 11	10.09 "	231	21.5	130	....	20m.	383	23	
2843	" 11	10.11 "	231	21.5	130	....	22m.	423	32	
2844	" 11	10.13 "	231	21.0	127	....	24m.	473	47	
2845	" 11	10.15 "	231	21.0	127	....	26m.	513	25	
2846	" 11	10.17 "	231	21.0	127	....	28m.	553	33	
2847	" 11	10.19 "	231	21.0	127	....	30m.	603	27	
2848	" 11	10.24 "	231	21.0	127	....	35m.	713	33	
2849	" 11	10.34 "	231	21.0	127	....	45m.	963	36	
2850	" 11	10.49 "	231	21.0	127	....	1h. 00m.	1 243	27	
2851	" 11	11.49 "	231	21.0	127	....	2h. 00m.	2 483	76	
2853	" 12	12.49 A.M.	231	21.0	127	....	3h. 00m.	3 733	48	
2854	" 12	1.49 "	231	21.0	127	....	4h. 00m.	4 973	29	
2855	" 12	2.49 "	231	21.0	127	....	5h. 00m.	6 283	32	
2856	" 12	3.00 "	231	21.0	127	....	5h. 11m.	6 443	31	
2859	" 12	3.49 "	231	21.0	127	....	6h. 00m.	7 503	32	
2860	" 12	4.49 "	231	21.0	127	....	7h. 00m.	8 713	36	
2861	" 12	5.49 "	231	20.5	124	....	8h. 00m.	9 913	41	
2863	" 12	6.49 "	231	20.5	124	....	9h. 00m.	11 183	43	
2864	" 12	7.49 "	231	21.0	127	....	10h. 00m.	12 433	42	
2865	" 12	8.45 "	231	21.0	127	....	10h. 56m.	13 683	73	
2870	" 12	12.00 M.	232	21.0	127	....	2h. 11m.	2 790	123	
2878	" 12	8.44 P.M.	233	23.0	140	....	10m.	164	47	

TABLE NO. 4.—*Continued.*

Warren System.

Serial Number.	Collected.		Number of Run.	Rate of Filtration.		Loss of Head. Feet.	Period of Service Since Last Washing. Hours and Minutes.	Filtered Water Since Last Washing. Cubic Feet.	Bacteria per Cubic Centimeter.	Remarks.
	Date.	Hour.		Cubic Feet per Minute.	Million Gallons per Acre per 24 Hours.					
	1896									
2880	May 13	2.00 A.M.	233	21.0	127	....	5h. 26m.	6 534	44	
2884	" 13	8.00 "	234	21.0	127	....	3h. 59m.	4 961	31	
2889	" 13	1.00 P.M.	234	21.0	127	....	8h. 59m.	11 231	13	
2895	" 13	7.00 "	235	21.5	130	....	4h. 03m.	5 136	11	
2899	" 14	3.00 A.M.	236	21.0	127	....	3h. 13m.	3 899	10	
2904	" 14	9.00 "	236	21.0	127	....	9h. 13m.	11 389	15	
2908	" 14	2.00 P.M.	237	22.0	133	....	1h. 47m.	2 330	18	
2912	" 14	8.00 "	237	21.5	130	....	7h. 47m.	9 940	24	
2918	" 15	1.00 A.M.	238	21.0	127	....	56m.	1 139	52	
2922	" 15	8.00 "	238	21.5	130	....	7h. 56m.	9 759	59	
2926	" 15	11.00 "	238	21.5	130	....	10h. 56m.	13 609	47	
2930	" 15	5.09 P.M.	239	21.0	127	....	4h. 56m.	6 250	14	
2960	" 15	11.00 "	239	20.0	121	....	10h. 47m.	13 580	16	
2969	" 16	5.00 A.M.	240	21.0	127	....	3h. 13m.	3 162	25	
2980	" 16	10.00 "	240	22.5	136	....	8h. 13m.	9 362	17	
2991	" 16	3.00 P.M.	240	21.0	127	....	13h. 13m.	15 652	4	
2997	" 18	12.00 M.	241	16.5	100	0.6	16m.	212	103	
3004	" 18	3.05 P.M.	241	18.0	109	1.0	3h. 21m.	3 372	53	
3007	" 18	6.00 "	241	16.5	100	1.2	6h. 16m.	6 212	192	D.
3012	" 18	9.11 "	242	16.0	97	0.6	15m.	210	181	D. Application of chem-
3014	" 18	12.00 "	242	16.5	100	0.9	3h. 04m.	3 040	152	D. icals unsatisfactory
3017	" 19	3.00 A.M.	242	16.0	97	1.3	6h. 04m.	6 110	79	D. on runs Nos. 242
3020	" 19	4.57 "	243	16.5	100	0.6	05m.	33	117	D. and 243; chemical
3021	" 19	5.07 "	243	16.5	100	0.6	15m.	223	127	D. meter out of order.
3023	" 19	6.00 "	243	16.5	100	0.7	1h. 08m.	1 183	118	D.
3026	" 19	8.30 "	243	17.5	106	1.0	3h. 38m.	3 593	74	D.
3031	" 19	12.00 M.	243	16.5	100	1.5	7h. 08m.	7 033	81	D.
3034	" 19	3.00 P.M.	243	16.5	100	2.0	10h. 08m.	9 913	98	D.
3040	" 19	6.00 "	243	17.5	106	2.2	11h. 04m.	10 763	58	D.
3045	" 19	9.03 "	244	16.0	97	0.3	05m.	88	109	
3046	" 19	9.13 "	244	16.0	97	0.6	15m.	238	185	
3048	" 19	12.00 "	244	16.5	100	0.8	3h. 02m.	3 018	41	
3052	" 20	3.00 A.M.	244	17.5	106	1.5	6h. 02m.	6 038	40	
3056	" 20	6.00 "	244	18.0	109	1.9	8h. 42m.	8 688	45	
3059	" 20	8.30 "	244	17.5	106	2.2	11h. 12m.	11 148	75	
3068	" 20	12.00 M.	244	15.5	94	2.6	14h. 42m.	14 508	116	
3071	" 20	3.00 P.M.	244	16.5	100	3.6	17h. 42m.	17 348	13	
3079	" 20	7.35 "	245	15.0	91	0.7	05m.	93	107	
3080	" 20	7.45 "	245	17.0	103	0.6	15m.	243	78	
3081	" 20	9.00 "	245	16.5	100	0.8	1h. 30m.	1 533	47	
3085	" 20	12.00 "	245	17.5	106	1.2	4h. 30m.	4 563	66	
3088	" 21	3.00 A.M.	245	18.0	109	1.4	7h. 30m.	7 393	57	
3092	" 21	6.00 "	245	17.0	103	1.7	10h. 30m.	10 263	49	
3097	" 21	8.30 "	245	17.5	106	2.7	13h. 00m.	12 513	62	
3103	" 21	12.32 P.M.	246	16.0	97	0.5	05m.	11	111	
3104	" 21	12.41 "	246	16.0	97	0.5	15m.	161	201	
3105	" 21	3.00 "	246	16.5	100	....	2h. 33m.	2 491	52	
3111	" 21	6.00 "	246	16.5	100	1.1	5h. 33m.	5 431	42	
3114	" 21	9.00 "	246	17.0	103	1.5	8h. 33m.	10 541	102	
3120	" 22	1.48 A.M.	247	15.7	91	0.5	05m.	97	52	
3121	" 22	1.58 "	247	18.0	109	0.5	15m.	227	67	
3122	" 22	3.00 "	247	17.5	106	0.7	1h. 17m.	1 227	17	
3126	" 22	6.00 "	247	17.5	106	1.0	4h. 17m.	4 127	27	
3129	" 22	8.30 "	247	17.0	103	1.3	6h. 47m.	6 577	33	
3136	" 22	12.00 M.	247	16.5	100	1.6	10h. 17m.	10 018	41	
3139	" 22	2.50 P.M.	247	22.0	133	2.0	13h. 07m.	12 838	22	
3144	" 22	3.47 "	248	16.0	97	0.5	08m.	97	135	
3145	" 22	3.52 "	248	16.0	97	0.5	13m.	177	67	
3147	" 22	6.00 "	248	16.0	97	0.6	2h. 21m.	2 237	36	
3150	" 22	9.00 "	248	17.0	103	0.8	5h. 21m.	5 267	48	
3154	" 22	12.00 "	248	16.5	100	1.2	8h. 21m.	8 127	52	

TABLE NO. 4.—*Continued.*

Warren System.

Serial Number.	Collected.		Number of Run.	Rate of Filtration.		Loss of Head. Feet.	Period of Service Since Last Washing, Hours and Minutes.	Filtered Water Since Last Washing. Cubic Feet.	Bacteria per Cubic Centimeter.	Remarks.
	Date.	Hour.		Cubic Feet per Minute.	Million Gallons per Acre per 24 Hours.					
	1895									
3157	May 23	3.00 A.M.	248	16.0	97	1.3	11h. 21m.	11 017	44	
3160	" 23	6.00 "	248	16.5	100	1.7	14h. 21m.	13 937	30	
3162	" 23	8.30 "	248	16.0	97	1.9	16h. 51m.	16 257	24	
3174	" 25	12.00 M.	249	19.5	118	....	1h. 02m.	1 443	49	
3177	" 25	2.00 P.M.	249	19.5	118	1.1	3h. 02m.	3 613	21	
3181	" 25	6.00 "	249	20.0	121	2.0	7h. 02m.	8 463	39	
3184	" 25	8.00 "	249	20.0	121	2.5	9h. 02m.	9 743	35	
3188	" 25	12.00 "	249	20.0	121	3.5	13h. 02m.	15 513	46	
3191	" 26	2.00 A.M.	249	19.5	118	3.9	15h. 02m.	17 833	35	
3194	" 26	4.36 "	250	20.0	121	0.6	05m.	107	46	
3195	" 26	4.46 "	250	20.0	121	0.7	15m.	357	50	
3197	" 26	6.00 "	250	20.0	121	0.9	1h. 29m.	1 777	30	
3202	" 26	8.30 "	250	20.0	121	1.5	3h. 59m.	4 707	56	
3208	" 26	10.00 "	250	20.0	121	2.2	5h. 29m.	6 557	31	
3212	" 26	2 00 P.M.	250	19.5	118	3.0	9h. 29m.	11 347	29	
3215	" 26	4.00 "	250	20.0	121	3.7	11h. 29m.	13 727	33	
3219	" 26	6.05 "	251	18.5	112	0.7	05m.	68	94	
3220	" 26	6.15 "	251	19.0	115	0.7	15m.	228	37	
3221	" 26	8 00 "	251	19.0	115	1.1	2h. 00m.	2 288	41	
3224	" 26	10.00 "	251	19.5	118	1.5	4h. 00m.	4 638	39	
3228	" 27	2.00 A.M.	251	19.0	115	2.4	8h. 00m.	9 188	26	
3231	" 27	4.00 "	251	19.0	115	3.2	10h. 00m.	11 488	28	
3236	" 27	7.30 "	251	19.5	118	2.0	13h. 30m.	15 718	36	
3240	" 27	11.51 "	252	19.5	118	0.7	05m.	37	912	
3243	" 27	12.01 P.M.	252	20.0	121	0.7	15m.	347	23	
3245	" 27	3.00 "	252	19.5	118	1.5	3h. 14m.	3 727	19	
3255	" 27	6.00 "	252	19.5	118	2.1	6h. 14m.	7 297	36	
3258	" 27	9.00 "	252	20.0	121	3.0	9h. 14m.	10 847	24	
3264	" 27	12.00 P.M.	252	20.0	121	3.8	12h. 14m.	14 337	60	
3269	" 28	3.09 A.M.	253	19.0	115	0.6	05m.	54	63	
3270	" 28	3.19 "	253	19.5	118	0.7	15m.	234	31	
3272	" 28	6.00 "	253	19.5	118	1.1	2h. 56m.	3 374	45	
3275	" 28	7.30 "	253	19.5	118	1.3	4h. 26m.	5 094	90	
3279	" 28	10.00 "	253	19.5	118	1.6	6h. 56m.	8 174	62	
3294	" 28	2.32 P.M.	254	20.0	121	0.7	15m.	67	247	D.*
3295	" 28	2.32 "	254	20.0	121	0.7	15m.	77	207	B.* Collected from weir
8296	" 28	2.42 "	254	20.0	121	0.7	25m.	267	328	D.* box.
3297	" 28	4.00 "	254	20.0	121	0.8	1h. 43m.	1 827	340	D.*
3305	" 28	8.00 "	254	20.0	121	1.3	5h. 43m.	6 577	185	D.*
3314	" 28	10.20 "	255	20.0	121	0.7	28m.	384	312	D.*
3315	" 28	12.33 A.M.	256	19.0	115	0.6	05m.	45	570	D.*
3324	" 29	10.50 P.M.	255	20.0	121	0.8	58m.	974	680	D.* Shut inlet 10.48 P.M.,
3325	" 29	12.43 A.M.	256	19.5	118	0.7	15m.	235	325	D.* outlet 10.53 P.M.
3332	" 29	2.00 "	256	19.0	115	0.8	1h. 32m.	1 735	220	D.*
3343	" 29	4.44 "	257	19.5	118	0.7	15m.	200	157	
3355	" 29	7.30 "	257	19.5	118	1.0	3h. 01m.	3 520	88	
3360	" 29	12.00 M.	258	20.0	121	0.9	2h. 31m.	2 950	89	
3363	" 29	2.00 P.M.	258	20.0	121	1.2	4h. 31m.	5 310	139	
3367	" 29	6.00 "	259	19.5	118	1.0	2h. 32m.	3 070	181	
3373	" 29	8.00 "	259	19.5	118	1.2	4h. 32m.	5 490	80	
3378	" 29	12.00 "	260	19.5	118	0.8	1h. 19m.	1 505	293	
3386	" 30	2.50 A.M.	261	19.5	118	0.7	11m.	294	227	
3389	" 30	6.55 "	262	20.0	121	0.8	16m.	329	246	
3399	" 30	10.10 "	262	19.5	118	1.2	3h. 31m.	4 219	92	
3402	" 30	12.10 P.M.	263	20.0	121	0.9	07m.	112	93	
3406	June 1	12.00 M.	263	21.0	127	1.9	6h. 57m.	9 322	35	
3408	" 1	3.00 P.M.	263	20.0	121	2.5	9h. 57m.	11 952	64	
3413	" 1	6.00 "	264	23.0	140	0.9	30m.	666	31	
3415	" 1	9.00 "	264	23.0	140	1.5	3h. 30m.	4 806	50	
3420	" 1	12.00 "	265	23.0	140	1.0	59m.	1 349	73	
3422	" 2	4.00 A.M.	266	22.5	136	1.0	35m.	790	111	

* Prescribed amount of chemicals insufficient.

TABLE NO. 4.—*Continued.*

Warren System.

Serial Number.	Collected.		Number of Run.	Rate of Filtration.		Loss of Head. Feet.	Period of Service Since Last Washing. Hours and Minutes.	Filtered Water Since Last Washing. Cubic Feet.	Bacteria per Cubic Centimeter.	Remarks.
	Date.	Hour.		Cubic Feet per Minute.	Million Gallons per Acre per 24 Hours.					
	1895									
3425	June 2	6.45 A.M.	267	23.0	140	0.9	09m.	260	64	
3428	" 2	10.20 "	268	23.0	140	4.0	1h. 12m.	1 656	67	
3431	" 2	11.51 "	269	24.0	146	9.7	10m.	180	181	
3435	" 2	4.30 P.M.	271	23.5	143	1.0	22m.	568	121	
3440	" 2	6.50 "	272	18.0	109	0.7	22m.	325	177	
3444	" 2	10.47 "	273	18.0	109	0.7	27m.	414	49	
3446	" 3	3.30 A.M.	274	17.0	103	0.7	37m.	529	81	
3450	" 3	6.00 "	274	16.5	100	0.9	3h. 07m.	2 849	57	
3453	" 3	9.00 "	275	16.5	100	....	1h. 42m.	1 797	77	
3457	" 3	12.00 M.	275	17.5	106	1.0	4h. 42m.	4 837	69	
3459	" 3	2.00 P.M.	275	16.0	97	1.2	6h. 42m.	6 797	71	
3461	" 3	2.58 "	275	17.0	103	....	7h. 40m.	7 897	61	Shut inlet 2.42 P.M., outlet 3.00 P.M.
3462	" 3	4.30 "	276	15.5	94	0.7	1h. 00m.	944	36	
3467	" 3	6.00 "	276	17.0	103	1.0	2h. 30m.	2 424	.....	
3471	" 3	9.00 "	276	17.0	103	1.2	5h. 30m.	5 444	38	
3475	" 3	10.50 "	276	18.5	112	1.2	7h. 20m.	7 304	66	
3477	" 3	12.00 "	277	16.5	100	0.5	05m.	41	28	
3480	" 4	12.10 A.M.	277	17.0	103	0.7	15m.	201	33	
3481	" 4	3.00 "	277	16.5	100	1.0	3h. 05m.	3 101	25	
3486	" 4	6.00 "	277	16.5	100	1.2	6h. 05m.	5 921	26	
3489	" 4	7.00 "	277	....	.....	....	7h. 05m.	6 941	57	
3491	" 4	9.00 "	278	....	.....	....	1h. 09m.	1 119	24	
3494	" 4	10.35 "	278	18.0	109	1.0	2h. 44m.	2 679	34	
3503	" 4	3.52 P.M.	278	17.0	103	0.7	8h. 01m.	8 289	36	
3504	" 4	5.52 "	278	15.5	94	2.9	10h. 01m.	10 189	39	
3508	" 4	8.35 "	279	20.0	121	0.9	46m.	884	28	
3534	" 4	12.00 "	279	20.0	121	1.5	4h. 11m.	4 924	16	
3538	" 5	3.20 A.M.	280	19.5	118	0.6	11m.	201	43	
3542	" 5	6.00 "	280	19.5	118	1.1	2h. 51m.	3 251	33	
3546	" 5	9.00 "	280	20.0	121	1.5	5h. 51m.	6 801	63	
3553	" 5	4.00 P.M.	281	23.0	140	1.8	5h. 33m.	7 521	87	
3558	" 5	10.00 "	282	23.0	140	1.8	5h. 55m.	6 608	40	
3585	" 6	2.27 A.M.	283	22.5	136	1.5	3h. 27m.	4 522	21	
3591	" 6	7.03 "	283	23.0	140	2.1	8h. 03m.	10 642	46	
3598	" 6	7.57 "	284	7.5	45	1.1	02m.	15	31	
3599	" 6	7.57 "	284	....	.....	...	02m.	15	84	
3600	" 6	7.59 "	284	20.0	121	0.8	04m.	55	50	
3601	" 6	8.01 "	284	20.0	121	0.8	06m.	95	34	
3602	" 6	8.01 "	284	20.0	121	0.8	06m.	95	.....	
3603	" 6	8.03 "	284	20.0	121	0.8	08m.	135	25	
3604	" 6	8.05 "	284	20.0	121	0.9	10m.	175	27	
3606	" 6	8.07 "	284	25.0	152	0.9	12m.	225	19	
3607	" 6	8.09 "	284	25.0	152	0.9	14m.	275	14	
3608	" 6	8.11 "	284	23.0	140	0.9	16m.	320	16	
3609	" 6	8.13 "	284	23.0	140	0.9	18m.	365	12	
3610	" 6	8.15 "	284	25.0	152	0.9	20m.	415	9	
3611	" 6	8.17 "	284	23.0	140	0.9	22m.	460	23	
3612	" 6	8.19 "	284	23.0	140	0.9	24m.	505	11	
3613	" 6	8.21 "	284	22.5	136	0.9	26m.	550	8	
3614	" 6	8.23 "	284	22.5	136	0.9	28m.	595	11	
3615	" 6	8.25 "	284	23.0	140	0.9	30m.	640	21	
3616	" 6	8.27 "	284	23.0	140	0.9	32m.	685	14	
3617	" 6	8.32 "	284	22.5	136	0.9	37m.	795	16	
3618	" 6	8.42 "	284	23.0	140	0.9	47m.	1 025	16	
3619	" 6	8.57 "	284	22.0	133	1.0	1h. 02m.	1 345	73	
3622	" 6	9.55 "	284	23.0	140	1.3	2h. 00m.	2 645	14	
3623	" 6	10.55 "	284	23.0	140	1.5	3h. 00m.	3 995	27	
3626	" 6	11.55 "	284	23.0	140	1.8	4h. 00m.	5 415	25	
3627	" 6	12.55 P.M.	284	23.0	140	2.0	5h. 00m.	6 795	21	
3628	" 6	1.55 "	284	23.5	143	2.2	6h. 00m.	8 205	36	
3631	" 6	2.55 "	284	23.5	143	2.4	7h. 00m.	9 595	12	

TABLE NO. 4.—*Continued.*

Warren System.

Serial Number.	Collected.		Number of Run.	Rate of Filtration.		Loss of Head. Feet.	Period of Service Since Last Washing. Hours and Minutes.	Filtered Water Since Last Washing. Cubic Feet.	Bacteria per Cubic Centimeter.	Remarks.
	Date.	Hour.		Cubic Feet per Minute.	Million Gallons per Acre per 24 Hours.					
	1895									
3634	June 6	3.17 P.M.	284	20.0	121	....	7h. 22m.	10 085	42	Shut inlet 3.10 P.M., out-
3656	" 9	12.45 "	285	23.0	140	1.3	3h. 11m.	3 871	171	outlet 3.27 P.M.
3659	" 9	5.00 "	286	22.5	136	0.8	10m.	186	159	
3668	" 10	11.07 A.M.	286	22.0	133	1.2	2h. 43m.	3 656	50	
3671	" 10	1.00 P.M.	286	21.5	130	1.6	4h. 36m.	6 316	57	
3675	" 10	3.30 "	287	22.5	136	0.9	44m.	1 015	40	
3681	" 11	10.28 A.M.	287	21.5	130	1.3	4h. 12m.	5 705	25	
3684	" 11	1.00 P.M.	287	22.5	136	1.8	6h. 44m.	9 245	112	
3687	" 11	2.15 "	288	22.0	133	0.8	26m.	499	16	
3692	" 11	3.40 "	288	22.5	136	1.0	1h. 51m.	2 439	16	
3697	" 12	10.18 A.M.	288	22.5	136	1.4	4h. 59m.	6 729	27	
3704	" 12	2.40 P.M.	289	22.5	136	0.8	33m.	689	53	
3711	" 13	10.11 A.M.	289	23.0	140	1.1	4h. 34m.	6 219	241	
3718	" 13	12.58 P.M.	290	22.5	136	1.0	1h. 48m.	2 417	109	
3724	" 13	2.53 "	290	23.0	140	1.4	3h. 43m.	5 087	48	
3730	" 13	5.28 "	291	23.0	140	0.8	28m.	563	355	
3734	" 15	9.00 A.M.		....	....	....	....	......	67	B. From usual place.*
3735	" 15	9.00 "		....	....	....	....	......	216	B. From weir box.*
3736	" 15	9.00 "		....	....	....	....	......	73	B. From filtered-water
3740	" 15	10.12 "	291	22.5	136	0.9	1h. 42m.	2 223	91	chamber.*
3743	" 15	12.20 P.M.	291	23.0	140	1.4	3h. 50m.	5 203	356	
3747	" 15	2.58 "	292	23.0	140	0.9	50m.	1 130	41	
3753	" 15	4.30 "	292	22.0	133	1.3	2h. 22m.	3 240	42	
3759	" 16	10.22 A.M.	292	24.0	146	1.4	4h. 44m.	6 560	35	
3766	" 16	12.55 P.M.	293	22.5	136	0.8	24m.	439	31	
3767	" 16	3.25 "	293	23.0	140	1.3	2h. 54m.	3 969	28	
3772	" 16	4.30 "	293	23.0	140	1.8	3h. 59m.	5 479	49	
3776	" 17	10.05 A.M.	293	23.5	143	1.8	6h. 04m.	8 449	57	
3780	" 17	12.55 P.M.	294	22.5	136	0.8	32m.	674	81	
3783	" 17	2.51 "	294	22.5	136	1.2	2h. 28m.	3 454	89	
3791	" 17	4.20 "	294	23.0	140	1.6	3h. 57m.	5 414	71	
3796	" 18	10.08 A.M.	295	23.5	143	0.9	1h. 08m.	1 439	177	
3801	" 18	12.32 P.M.	295	23.5	143	1.2	3h. 32m.	4 399	43	
3809	" 18	2.44 "	295	23.0	140	1.7	5h. 44m.	7 789	22	
3818	" 19	9.58 "	296	22.5	136	0.9	1h. 23m.	1 737	61	
3824	" 19	12.40 "	296	....	....	....	4h. 05m.	4 662	111	Shut inlet 12.24 P.M., out-
3829	" 19	2.57 "	297	23.0	140	1.1	1h. 50m.	2 315	61	let 12.41 P.M.
3845	" 19	4.26 "	297	23.0	140	1.3	3h. 19m.	4 495	61	
3853	" 20	9.26 A.M.	297	....	....	....	4h. 49m.	6 999	171	
3856	" 20	11.10 "	298	23.0	140	0.9	36m.	756	77	
3861	" 20	12.38 P.M.	298	24.0	146	1.1	2h. 04m.	2 746	39	
3862	" 20	12.38 "	268	....	....	....	....	......	....	From filtered-water
3870	" 20	3.22 "	298	23.5	143	1.5	4h. 48m.	6 536	77	chamber.
3874	" 20	4.36 "	298	24.0	146	1.6	6h. 02m.	8 256	65	[chamber.†
3881	" 22	9.00 A.M.		....	....	....	....	......	690	B. From filtered-water
3882	" 22	9.00 "		....	....	....	....	......	78	B. From weir box.†
3883	" 22	9.00 "		....	....	....	....	......	145	B. From usual place.†
3887	" 22	10.08 A.M.	299	20.5	124	....	1h. 08m.	1 508	90	
3888	" 22	10.08 "	299	....	....	....	....	......	70	
3893	" 22	1.12 P.M.	299	23.0	140	1.4	4h. 12m.	5 738	61	
3894	" 22	1.12 "	299	....	....	....	....	......	90	B. From filtered-water
3898	" 22	3.00 "	299	23.5	143	1.8	6h. 00m.	8 268	102	chamber.
3899	" 22	3.00 "	299	....	....	....	....	......	525	B. From filtered-water
3902	" 22	4.56 "	299	23.5	143	2.0	7h. 56m.	10 888	75	chamber.[chamber.
3903	" 22	4.56 "	299	....	....	....	....	......	95	B. From filtered-water
3912	" 23	10.03 A.M.	299	....	....	....	9h. 33m.	13 138	49	Shut inlet 10.03 A.M.
3913	" 23	10.05 "	299	15.0	91	....	9h. 35m.	13 168	56	
3914	" 23	10.07 "	299	25.0	152	....	9h. 37m.	13 218	61	
3915	" 23	10.09 "	299	20.0	121	....	9h. 39m.	13 258	49	

* Collected before the filter was in operation, and after period of rest of 39 hours 30 minutes.

† " " " " " " " " " " " " " " 39 " 51 "

TABLE NO. 4.—*Continued.*

Warren System.

Serial Number.	Collected. Date.	Collected. Hour.	Number of Run.	Rate of Filtration. Cubic Feet per Minute.	Rate of Filtration. Million Gallons per Acre per 24 Hours.	Loss of Head. Feet.	Period of Service Since Last Washing. Hours and Minutes.	Filtered Water Since Last Washing. Cubic Feet.	Bacteria per Cubic Centimeter.	Remarks.
	1896									
3916	June 23	10.11 A.M.	299	20.0	121	....	9h. 41m.	13 298	83	
3917	" 23	10.13 "	299	20.0	121	....	9h. 43m.	13 338	106	
3918	" 23	10.15 "	299	20.0	121	....	9h. 45m.	13 373	92	
3919	" 23	10.17 "	299	20.0	121	....	9h. 47m.	13 408	150	
3920	" 23	10.19 "	299	20.0	121	....	9h. 49m.	13 438	72	
3921	" 23	10.21 "	299	20.0	121	....	9h. 51m.	13 473	92	Shut outlet 10.22 A.M.
3924	" 23	11.09 "	300	22.5	136	0.8	20m.	495	560	
3926	" 23	1.25 P.M.	300	23.5	143	1.2	2h. 36m.	3 655	410	
3930	" 23	3.15 "	300	23.0	140	1.7	4h. 26m.	6 225	....	
3935	" 23	5.00 "	300	23.0	140	1.9	6h. 11m.	8 738	58	
3938	" 24	10.14 A.M.	300	23.5	143	1.9	7h. 55m.	10 895	132	
3942	" 24	11.15 "	300	....	....	....	8h. 56m.	12 382	330	Shut outlet 11.15 A.M.
3943	" 24	11.20 "	300	....	....	....	....	......	345	B. From filtered-water chamber.
3947	" 24	12.36 "	301	23.0	140	0.8	38m.	713	275	
3954	" 24	3.20 "	301	23.0	140	1.3	3h. 22m.	4 593	240	
3964	" 24	4.45 "	301	23.0	140	1.5	4h. 47m.	6 493	195	
3977	" 25	9.40 "	301	....	....	....	6h. 12m.	8 393	....	Shut inlet 9.37 A.M., outlet 9.54 A.M.
3978	" 25	9.40 "	301	....	....	....	....	......	52	B. From filtered-water chamber.
4079	" 30	9.30 "	301	....	....	....	....	......	82	
4081	" 30	9.30 "		....	....	....	....	......	41	
4086	" 30	11.27 "	302	25.5	155	0.8	05m.	57	37	
4087	" 30	11.29 "		....	....	....	....	......	57	B. From filtered-water chamber.
4088	" 30	11.32 "	302	26.0	158	0.8	10m.	217	51	
4089	" 30	11.37 "	302	26.0	158	0.8	15m.	347	33	
4090	" 30	11.42 "	302	23.0	140	0.9	20m.	497	21	
4091	" 30	11.47 "	302	23.0	140	0.9	25m.	617	28	
4092	" 30	11.52 "	302	23.0	140	0.9	30m.	727	28	
4093	" 30	11.57 "	302	23.0	140	0.9	35m.	837	42	
4094	" 30	12.02 P.M.	302	24.0	146	0.9	40m.	897	26	
4095	" 30	12.07 "	302	22.0	133	0.9	45m.	967	25	
4096	" 30	12.12 "	302	23.0	140	0.9	50m.	1 047	50	
4097	" 30	12.17 "	302	23.0	140	0.9	55m.	1 167	42	
4098	" 30	12.22 "	302	23.0	140	0.9	1h. 00m.	1 307	29	
4099	" 30	12.38 "	302	23.0	140	0.9	1h. 16m.	1 667	51	
4104	" 30	2.47 "	302	23.0	140	1.1	3h. 25m.	4 657	62	
4109	" 30	4.25 "	303	23.0	140	0.8	37m.	788	40	
4113	July 1	10.22 A.M.	303	23.0	140	1.1	3h. 06m.	4 228	....	
4122	" 1	1.15 P.M.	304	23.0	140	0.6	43m.	934	....	
4131	" 1	3.17 "	304	23.5	143	1.1	2h. 45m.	3 774	....	
4147	" 2	11.28 A.M.	306	23.5	143	....	11m.	159	49	
4151	" 2	12.33 P.M.	306	24.0	146	0.9	1h. 16m.	1 699	130	
4156	" 2	3.03 "	307	23.0	140	1.0	1h. 28m.	1 950	105	
4164	" 3	10.10 A.M.	308	23.0	140	1.1	2h. 32m.	3 493	81	
4167	" 3	11.08 "	308	23.0	140	1.1	3h. 30m.	4 823	57	
4186	" 3	1.45 P.M.	309	23.5	143	1.0	1h. 42m.	3 443	76	
4196	" 3	3.45 "	310	22.5	136	0.7	07m.	117	18	
4197	" 3	4.52 "	310	23.0	140	0.8	1h. 14m.	1 607	167	
4202	" 6	9.00 A.M.		....	....	....	....	......	178	B. From filtered-water chamber.*
4203	" 6	9.00 "		....	....	....	....	......	18	B. From usual place.*
4204	" 6	9.00 "		....	....	....	....	......	122	B. From weir box.*
4216	" 6	2.26 P.M.	311	21.0	127	0.8	05m.	55	186	
4217	" 6	2.31 "	311	22.0	133	0.8	10m.	135	145	
4218	" 6	2.36 "	311	22.5	136	0.8	15m.	255	112	
4219	" 6	2.41 "	311	22.5	136	0.8	20m.	355	77	
4220	" 6	2.46 "	311	22.5	136	0.8	25m.	465	42	
4221	" 6	2.51 "	311	22.5	136	0.8	30m.	565	42	
4222	" 6	2.56 "	311	22.5	136	0.8	35m.	705	40	
4223	" 6	3.01 "	311	22.5	136	0.9	40m.	815	38	
4224	" 6	3.06 "	311	23.0	140	0.9	45m.	945	52	

* Collected before the filter was in operation, and after the period of rest of 63 hours and 30 minutes.

TABLE No. 4.—*Continued.*

Warren System.

Serial Number.	Collected. Date.	Collected. Hour.	Number of Run.	Rate of Filtration. Cubic Feet per Minute.	Rate of Filtration. Million Gallons per Acre per 24 Hours.	Loss of Head. Feet.	Period of Service Since Last Washing. Hours and Minutes.	Filtered Water Since Last Washing. Cubic Feet.	Bacteria per Cubic Centimeter.	Remarks.
	1896									
4225	July 6	3.11 P.M.	311	23.0	140	0.9	50m.	1 065	63	
4226	" 6	3.16 "	311	23.0	140	1.0	55m.	1 185	46	
4227	" 6	3.21 "	311	22.5	136	1.0	1h. 00m.	1 295	36	
4228	" 6	3.26 "	311	22.5	136	1.0	1h. 05m.	1 405	31	
4230	" 6	3.51 "	311	23.0	140	1.1	1h. 30m.	2 005	39	
4233	" 6	4.21 "	311	23.0	140	1.1	2h. 00m.	2 705	26	
4240	" 6	5.25 "	311	22.0	133	1.2	3h. 04m.	4 175	54	
4245	" 7	10.00 A.M.	311	23.0	140	1.4	4h. 09m.	5 685	55	
4252	" 7	1.00 P.M.	312	22.5	136	0.8	18m.	303	112	
4255	" 7	3.00 "	312	23.0	140	1.1	2h. 18m.	3 253	46	
4259	" 7	5.13 "	313	23.0	140	0.8	10m.	160	114	
4266	" 8	10.55 A.M.	313	23.0	140	1.1	2h. 22m.	3 350	51	
4267	" 8	12.35 P.M.	314	22.0	133	0.8	06m.	88	118	
4271	" 8	3.50 "	314	22.0	133	1.1	3h. 21m.	4 438	47	
4274	" 8	5.00 "	315	22.0	133	0.8	14m.	232	62	
4279	" 9	10.20 A.M.	315	22.5	136	1.0	2h. 04m.	2 622	39	
4282	" 9	12.11 P.M.	315	22.0	133	1.3	3h. 55m.	5 232	52	
4285	" 9	1.09 "	316	19.5	118	0.7	05m.	53	9	
4286	" 9	1.14 "	316	21.5	130	0.7	10m.	143	20	
4287	" 9	1.19 "	316	22.0	133	0.8	15m.	263	55	
4288	" 9	1.24 "	316	22.5	136	0.8	20m.	373	51	
4289	" 9	1.29 "	316	23.5	143	0.8	25m.	483	74	
4290	" 9	1.34 "	316	22.5	136	0.8	30m.	603	46	
4291	" 9	1.39 "	316	22.5	136	0.8	35m.	713	82	
4292	" 9	1.44 "	316	23.0	140	0.9	40m.	823	58	
4293	" 9	1.49 "	316	22.5	136	0.9	45m.	943	39	
4294	" 9	1.54 "	316	23.0	140	0.9	50m.	1 053	58	
4295	" 9	1.59 "	316	23.0	140	0.9	55m.	1 173	52	
4296	" 9	2.04 "	316	23.0	140	1.0	1h. 00m.	1 283	24	
4297	" 9	2.09 "	316	23.0	140	1.0	1h. 05m.	1 513	64	
4298	" 9	2.24 "	316	23.5	143	1.1	1h. 20m.	1 773	42	
4299	" 9	2.39 "	316	23.0	140	1.1	1h. 35m.	2 113	33	
4300	" 9	2.54 "	316	23.0	140	1.1	1h. 50m.	2 553	37	
4301	" 9	3.09 "	316	23.0	140	1.1	2h. 05m.	2 913	79	
4301a	" 9	3.24 "	316	23.0	140	1.2	2h. 20m.	3 163	45	
4305	" 9	3.39 "	316	22.0	133	1.2	2h. 35m.	3 513	40	
4306	" 9	3.54 "	316	23.0	140	1.2	2h. 50m.	3 943	75	
4308	" 9	4.09 "	316	19.0	115	....	3h. 05m.	4 183	143	Shut inlet 4.07 P.M., outlet 4.24 P.M.
4314	" 10	11.07 A.M.	317	22.5	136	1.2	2h. 49m.	3 693	54	
4317	" 10	1.01 P.M.	317	22.0	133	1.6	4h. 43m.	6 283	137	
4320	" 10	3.10 "	318	23.0	140	1.1	1h. 19m.	1 708	25	
4323	" 10	5.05 "	318	24.5	149	1.5	3h. 14m.	4 378	69	
4328	" 11	10.31 A.M.	318	22.5	136	1.8	5h. 10m.	6 988	41	
4333	" 11	12.59 P.M.	319	22.5	136	1.1	1h. 01m.	1 469	36	
4346	" 11	3.12 "	319	23.0	140	1.5	3h. 14m.	4 639	43	
4367	" 13	10.10 A.M.	320	22.5	136	0.1	1h. 10m.	1 508	53	
4370	" 13	11.44 "	320	23.0	140	1.2	2h. 44m.	3 658	20	
4375	" 13	3.33 P.M.	321	23.0	140	0.8	30m.	639	42	
4376	" 13	5.08 "	321	22.5	136	1.1	2h. 05m.	2 819	140	
4396	" 14	10.18 A.M.	321	23.0	140	1.2	3h. 45m.	5 139	31	Shut outlet 1.05 P.M.
4409	" 14	1.05 P.M.	....	....	.....	....	6h. 32m.	8 919	51	
4422	" 14	3.21 "	322	22.0	133	1.1	1h. 54m.	2 538	17	
4424	" 14	4.55 "	322	23.0	140	1.4	3h. 28m.	4 728	.....	
4442	" 15	1.11 "	323	23.0	140	0.9	35m.	732	16	
4443	" 15	2.04 "	323	23.5	143	1.0	1h. 28m.	1 972	37	
4448	" 15	3.12 "	323	23.0	140	1.2	2h. 36m.	3 562	37	
4456	" 16	9.35 A.M.	324	22.5	136	0.9	35m.	686	34	
4459	" 16	11.04 "	324	23.0	140	1.1	2h. 04m.	2 756	15	
4469	" 16	1.11 P.M.	324	23.0	140	1.5	4h. 11m.	5 726	.....	
4477	" 16	2.54 "	325	22.5	136	0.8	10m.	184	17	
4478	" 16	2.59 "	325	22.0	133	0.8	15m.	273	32	

TABLE NO. 4.—*Continued.*

Warren System.

Serial Number.	Collected. Date.	Collected. Hour.	Number of Run.	Rate of Filtration. Cubic Feet per Minute.	Rate of Filtration. Million Gallons per Acre per 24 Hours.	Loss of Head. Feet.	Period of Service Since Last Washing. Hours and Minutes.	Filtered Water Since Last Washing. Cubic Feet.	Bacteria per Cubic Centimeter.	Remarks.
	1896									
4479	July 16	3.04 P.M.	325	22.0	133	0.8	20m.	374	69	
4480	" 16	3.09 "	325	22.0	133	0.9	25m.	504	47	
4481	" 16	3.14 "	325	23.0	140	0.9	30m.	614	33	
4482	" 16	3.19 "	325	23.0	140	0.9	35m.	724	38	
4483	" 16	3.24 "	325	22.5	136	0.9	40m.	844	30	
4484	" 16	3.29 "	325	22.5	136	0.9	45m.	954	59	
4485	" 16	3.34 "	325	23.5	143	1.0	50m.	1 074	40	
4486	" 16	3.39 "	325	23.0	140	1.0	55m.	1 184	18	
4487	" 16	3.44 "	325	23.0	140	1.0	1h. 00m.	1 304	27	
4488	" 16	3.59 "	325	23.0	140	1.0	1h. 15m.	1 654	23	
4489	" 16	4.14 "	325	23.0	140	1.1	1h. 30m.	1 994	11	
4490	" 16	4.29 "	325	23.0	140	1.1	1h. 45m.	2 344	33	
4493	" 16	4.44 "	325	23.0	140	1.2	2h. 00m.	2 694	17	
4494	" 16	4.59 "	325	23.0	140	1.2	2h. 15m.	3 054	15	
4497	" 16	5.14 "	325	23.0	140	1.3	2h. 30m.	3 394	29	
4498	" 16	5.29 "	325	23.0	140	1.3	2h. 45m.	3 744	35	
4503	" 17	2.37 "	325	23.5	143	1.3	3h. 46m.	5 124	11	
4525	" 18	11.37 A.M.	326	22.5	136	0.9	31m.	708	23	
4546	" 18	1.52 P.M.	326	23.0	140	1.2	2h. 46m.	3 728	23	
4563	" 18	5.12 "	327	23.5	143	1.1	1h. 17m.	1 683	.....	
4570	" 20	11.07 A.M.	327	22.5	136	1.4	3h. 42m.	4 983	22	
4575	" 20	1.48 P.M.	328	23.0	143	0.8	16m.	305	5	
4576	" 20	3.24 "	328	23.0	143	1.1	1h. 52m.	2 515	21	
4581	" 20	5.12 "	328	21.5	130	3.6	3h. 40m.	4 955	48	
4603	" 21	11.07 A.M.	328	23.5	143	1.8	6h. 05m.	8 195	93	
4608	" 21	1.14 P.M.	329	23.5	143	1.0	1h. 11m.	1 562	57	
4613	" 21	3.19 "	329	23.0	140	1.4	3h. 16m.	4 512	86	
4616	" 21	5.10 "	330	22.5	136	0.9	29m.	616	217	
4619	" 22	11.02 A.M.	330	23.0	140	1.1	2h. 38m.	3 626	383	
4627	" 22	3.47 P.M.	332	23.0	140	0.9	55m.	1 236	818	
4633	" 22	4.52 "	332	23.0	140	1.1	2h. 00m.	2 756	1055	
4637	" 23	11.16 A.M.	333	21.0	127	0.9	50m.	939	367	
4643	" 23	12.54 P.M.	333	23.0	140	1.1	2h. 28m.	3 109	420	
4645	" 23	3.09 "	334	23.0	140	1.0	44m.	875	* 916	
4649	" 23	4.59 "	335	17.0	103	0.8	15m.	143	685	
4682	" 24	1.32 "	336	15.5	94	0.6	20m.	225	288	
4689	" 24	4.20 "	337	15.5	94	0.7	10m.	101	900	
4690	" 24	4.30 "	337	16.0	97	0.7	20m.	361	1300	
4691	" 24	4.40 "	337	16.0	97	0.8	30m.	421	2000	
4691a	" 24	4.50 "	337	16.0	97	0.8	40m.	571	2500	
4692	" 24	5.00 "	337	16.5	100	0.9	50m.	731	2200	
4695	" 24	5.10 "	337	16.0	97	0.9	1h. 00m.	891	392	
4696	" 24	5.25 "	337	15.5	94	1.0	1h. 15m.	1 131	1034	Shut inlet 5.20 P.M., outlet 5.30 P.M..
4705	" 25	11.05 A.M.	338	17.0	103	....	1h. 18m.	1 086	.....	
4710	" 25	1.17 P.M.	338	15.0	91	2.2	3h. 30m.	2 906	416	
4712	" 25	3.15 "	339	13.0	79	2.0	43m.	508	378	
4715	" 25	4.43 "	339	14.0	85	4.0	2h. 11m.	1 698	504	
4722	" 27	9.00 A.M.	....	....	.....	....	....	......	1	B. From filtered-water [chamber.*
4723	" 27	9.00 "	....	....	.....	....	....	......	8	B. From usual place.*
4725	" 27	9.25 "	....	....	.....	....	....	......	22	B. From filtered-water chamber.
4727	" 27	11.49 "	341	14.5	88	0.8	39m.	533	26	
4732	" 27	2.11 P.M.	341	16.0	97	0.7	3h. 01m.	2 763	268	
4733	" 27	3.02 "	341	19.0	115	0.9	3h. 52m.	3 623	624	
4753	" 28	9.45 A.M.	343	22.0	133	0.9	15m.	226	61	
4754	" 28	9.50 "	343	23.5	143	1.0	20m.	336	394	
4755	" 28	9.55 "	343	23.5	143	1.0	25m.	446	113	
4756	" 28	10.00 "	343	23.5	143	1.0	30m.	566	36	
4758	" 28	10.05 "	343	23.5	143	1.0	35m.	696	44	
4759	" 28	10.10 "	343	23.5	143	1.0	40m.	816	53	
4760	" 28	10.15 "	343	23.0	140	1.0	45m.	916	60	

* Collected before the filter was in operation, and after a period of rest of 40 hours and 7 minutes.

TABLE No. 4.—*Continued.*

Warren System.

Serial Number.	Collected. Date.	Collected. Hour.	Number of Run.	Rate of Filtration. Cubic Feet per Minute.	Rate of Filtration. Million Gallons per Acre per 24 Hours.	Loss of Head. Feet.	Period of Service Since Last Washing, Hours and Minutes.	Filtered Water Since Last Washing. Cubic Feet.	Bacteria per Cubic Centimeter.	Remarks.
	1896									
4761	July 28	10.20 A.M.	343	23.0	140	1.0	50m.	1 046	66	
4762	" 28	10.25 "	343	23.0	140	1.0	55m.	1 156	78	
4763	" 28	10.30 "	343	23.0	140	1.0	1h. 00m.	1 266	77	
4765	" 28	10.45 "	343	23.0	140	1.0	1h. 15m.	1 606	31	
4766	" 28	11.00 "	343	22.5	136	1.1	1h. 30m.	1 956	40	
4769	" 28	11.15 "	343	22.5	136	1.0	1h. 45m.	2 396	21	
4771	" 28	11.30 "	343	22.5	136	1.1	2h. 00m.	2 636	59	
4773	" 28	11.45 "	343	23.5	143	1.2	2h. 15m.	2 986	29	
4774	" 28	12.00 M.	343	23.5	143	1.3	2h. 30m.	3 336	27	
4776	" 28	12.15 P.M.	343	23.0	140	1.3	2h. 45m.	3 686	53	
4777	" 28	12.30 "	343	23.0	140	1.3	3h. 00m.	4 046	52	
4779	" 28	12.45 "	343	23.0	140	1.4	3h. 15m.	4 376	61	
4780	" 28	1.00 "	343	23.0	140	1.4	3h. 30m.	4 746	25	
4784	" 28	1.15 "	343	23.0	140	1.4	3h. 45m.	5 096	31	
4785	" 28	1.30 "	343	22.5	136	1.5	4h. 00m.	5 416	46	
4787	" 28	2.00 "	343	23.0	140	1.6	4h. 30m.	6 146	14	
4789	" 28	2.30 "	343	21.0	127	1.7	5h. 00m.	6 826	18	
4792	" 28	3.00 "	343	21.0	127	1.7	5h. 30m.	7 476	33	
4795	" 28	5.02 "	344	21.5	130	0.9	17m.	254	18	
4830	" 29	11.10 P.M.	344	22.5	136	1.3	2h. 55m.	4 024	51	
4844	" 29	1.25 "	345	22.0	133	1.1	1h. 15m.	1 601	90	
4852	" 29	2.56 "	345	22.0	133	1.3	2h. 46m.	3 661	10	
4862	" 29	5.05 "	345	23.0	140	1.6	4h. 55m.	6 581	56	
4869	" 30	1.19 "	346	23.5	143	1.0	37m.	774	12	
4870	" 30	3.43 "	346	23.5	143	1.3	3h. 01m.	4 134	15	
4882	" 31	11.09 A.M.	347	22.5	136	1.2	2h. 09m.	2 874	25	
4887	" 31	1.58 P.M.	347	22.5	136	1.7	4h. 58m.	6 764	7	
4893	" 31	3.44 "	347	23.5	143	2.0	6h. 44m.	9 274	66	

Jewell System.

Serial Number.	Collected. Date.	Collected. Hour.	Number of Run.	Rate of Filtration. Cubic Feet per Minute.	Rate of Filtration. Million Gallons per Acre per 24 Hours.	Loss of Head. Feet.	Period of Service Since Last Washing, Hours and Minutes.	Filtered Water Since Last Washing. Cubic Feet.	Bacteria per Cubic Centimeter.	Remarks.
	1895									
2	Oct. 21	10.47 A.M.	1	25.0	101	....	....	......	76	
3	" 21	12.30 P.M.	2	.....	.....	....	27m.	......	52	
4	" 21	3.46 "	2	.....	.....	....	3h. 43m.	......	38	
6	" 22	9.45 A.M.	2	26.0	105	....	4h. 28m.	6 405	14	
9	" 22	11.25 "	2	28.0	114	....	6h. 08m.	8 465	42	
13	" 22	1.34 P.M.	2	22.0	89	....	8h. 17m.	11 425	66	
14	" 22	1.47 "	2	23.5	95	....	8h. 30m.	11 697	62	Agitated surface of sand layer at 1.39 P.M.
15	" 22	3.05 "	3	28.0	114	....	18m.	504	84	
17	" 22	4.00 "	3	28.0	114	....	1h. 13m.	1 110	49	
20	" 23	9.28 A.M.	3	30.0	122	....	2h. 02m.	2 782	110	
22	" 23	10.57 "	3	30.0	122	....	3h. 31m.	5 319	55	
24	" 23	11.53 "	3	29.0	118	....	4h. 27m.	7 088	53	
26	" 23	1.20 P.M.	3	29.0	118	....	5h. 54m.	9 496	56	
28	" 23	2.30 "	3	28.5	116	....	7h. 04m.	11 475	42	
30	" 23	4.17 "	3	29.0	118	....	8h. 51m.	15 104	38	
33	" 23	5.20 "	3	.....	.....	....	9h. 54m.	16 853	39	
38	" 24	12.12 "	3	29.0	118	....	10h. 52m.	18 423	77	
40	" 24	1.30 "	3	29.0	118	....	12h. 10m.	20 710	67	
45	" 24	4.06 "	3	29.0	118	....	14h. 46m.	25 097	52	
47	" 24	5.12 "	3	.....	.....	....	15h. 52m.	27 022	40	
49	" 25	9.53 A.M.	3	30.0	122	....	16h. 32m.	28 105	34	
51	" 25	11.07 "	3	29.0	118	....	17h. 46m.	30 324	24	
53	" 25	12.05 P.M.	3	26.0	105	....	18h. 44m.	31 908	28	
56	" 25	1.32 "	3	23.0	93	....	20h. 11m.	33 948	27	
58	" 25	2.52 "	4	30.0	122	....	25m.	786	28	
59	" 25	3.30 "	4	30.0	122	....	1h. 03m.	1 971	36	
63	" 25	4.27 "	4	28.0	114	....	2h. 00m.	3 638	29	
65	" 26	10.52 A.M.	4	20.0	81	....	4h. 14m.	7 115	10	
68	" 26	1.03 P.M.	5	26.0	105	....	1h. 13m.	1 951	32	
70	" 26	4.35 "	5	25.0	101	....	4h. 45m.	5 785	12	

TABLE NO. 4.—*Continued.*

Jewell System.

Serial Number.	Collected.		Number of Run.	Rate of Filtration.		Loss of Head. Feet.	Period of Service Since Last Washing. Hours and Minutes.	Filtered Water Since Last Washing. Cubic Feet.	Bacteria per Cubic Centimeter.	Remarks.
	Date.	Hour.		Cubic Feet per Minute.	Million Gallons per Acre per 24 Hours.					
	1895									
72	Oct. 28	10.54 A.M.	5	....	....	....	6h. 19m.	8 916	40	
78	" 29	12.05 P.M.	5	26.0	105	....	8h. 39m	10 507	54	
80	" 29	1.55 "	5	21.0	85	....	10h. 29m.	12 776	20	
92	" 30	3.17 "	6	24.0	97	....	....	772	2	Sterilized filter on this day.
94	" 30	3.50 "	6	24.0	97	....	....	1 585	4	
95	" 30	4.18 "	6	24.0	97	....	....	1 998	2	
98	" 30	5.25 "	6	27.0	109	....	....	2 926	3	
107	" 31	1.43 "	6	22.0	89	...	....	6 527	13	
109	" 31	2.38 "	6	16.0	65	..	....	7 600	16	Agitated surface of sand
110	" 31	4.16 "	6	14.0	57	....	....	9 061	16	layer at 2.38 P.M.
114	Nov. 1	1.52 "	6	21.0	85	....	....	11 790	11	
117	" 1	4.00 "	7	28.0	114	....	....	600	27	
119	" 1	4.30 "	7	28.0	114	....	....	1 351	14	
123	" 2	11.02 A.M.	7	32.0	130	....	....	4 906	17	
125	" 2	12.27 P.M	7	30.0	122	....	....	7 309	28	Agitated surface of sand
127	" 2	1.23 "	7	26.0	105	....	....	8 846	23	layer at 11.22 A.M.
129	" 2	3.27 "	7	27.0	109	....	....	10 547	38	
147	" 5	11.04 A.M.	7	27.0	109	....	....	14 362	520	
148	" 5	11.24 "	7	27.0	109	....	....	14 874	138	
152	" 5	12.54 P.M.	7	27.0	109	....	....	17 241	68	
156	" 5	3.57 "	7	28.0	114	.	....	20 531	102	
170	" 7	10.50 A.M.	7	26.0	105	....	....	22 002	540	
171	" 7	11.20 "	7	24.0	97	....	....	22 761	268	
179	" 7	1.13 P.M.	7	22.0	89	....	....	25 432	186	
184	" 7	1.59 "	8	26.0	105	....	02m.	59	182	
186	" 7	2.09 "	8	25.0	101	....	12m.	334	124	
187	" 7	2.18 "	8	....	....	....	21m.	549	134	
190	" 7	2.36 "	8	24.0	97	....	39m.	1 012	156	
192	" 7	2.50 "	8	24.0	97	....	53m.	1 355	132	
194	" 7	3.09 "	8	24.0	97	...	1h. 12m.	1 852	133	
195	" 7	3.32 "	8	25.0	101	....	1h. 35m.	2 439	178	
198	" 8	11.00 A.M.	8	27.0	109	....	2h. 21m.	4 878	192	Agitated surface of sand
201	" 8	12.35 P.M.	8	20.0	81	...	3h. 56m.	7 077	222	layer from 10.42 A.M. to
203	" 8	1.12 "	8	21.0	85	....	4h. 33m.	7 845	193	1.56 P.M.
207	" 8	2.23 "	9	25.0	101	....	11m.	303	107	
209	" 8	2.46 "	9	25.0	101	....	34m.	842	226	
213	" 9	11.30 A.M.	9	26.0	105	...	1h. 41m.	2 534	128	
217	" 9	1.18 P.M.	9	29.0	118	....	3h. 29m.	5 244	128	
220	" 9	2.27 "	9	24.0	97	...	4h. 38m.	6 863	157	
225	" 11	9.17 A.M.	9	25.0	101	....	5h. 56m.	8 469	1100	Agitated surface of sand
226	" 11	9.50 "	9	24.0	97	....	6h. 29m.	9 267	864	layer all day, Nov. 11.
229	" 11	11.06 "	9	24.0	97	....	7h. 45m.	10 772	396	
232	" 11	2.50 P.M.	9	21.0	85	....	11h. 29m.	15 681	198	
235	" 12	10.44 A.M	10	25.0	101	....	02m.	43	1356	
236	" 12	11.05 "	10	25.0	101	....	23m.	640	178	
237	" 12	11.35 "	10	25.0	101	....	53m.	1 411	308	
238	" 12	12.00 M.	10	25.0	101	....	1h. 18m.	2 040	283	
239	" 12	1.15 P.M.	10	25.0	101	...	2h. 33m.	4 212	260	
240	" 12	3.10 "	10	25.0	101	....	4h. 28m.	6 527	244	
243	" 13	9.20 A.M.	10	24.0	97	....	6h. 54m.	10 308	106	
244	" 13	9.50 "	10	24.0	97	....	7h. 24m.	10 857	136	
245	" 13	10.27 "	10	25.0	101	....	8h. 01m.	11 764	106	
246	" 13	11.27 "	10	23.0	93	....	9h. 01m.	13 290	104	
247	" 13	1.18 P.M.	10	20.0	81	....	10h. 52m.	15 783	74	
248	" 13	2.52 "	10	24.5	99	...	12h. 26m.	18 105	140	
251a	" 14	9.02 A.M.	10	....	.....	....	13h. 15m.	19 505	.....	
251b	" 14	9.50 "	10	25.0	101	..	14h. 03m.	20 482	172	
252	" 14	12.00 M.	10	24.0	97	....	16h. 13m.	23 763	116	
253	" 14	3.00 P.M.	11	25.0	101	....	1h. 43m.	2 390	82	
256	" 15	10.50 A.M.	11	24.0	97	....	5h. 39m.	8 167	68	
257	" 15	12.55 P.M.	11	23.0	93	....	7h. 44m.	11 417	92	

Table No. 4.—*Continued.*

Jewell System.

Serial Number.	Collected. Date.	Collected. Hour.	Number of Run.	Rate of Filtration. Cubic Feet per Minute.	Rate of Filtration. Million Gallons per Acre per 24 Hours.	Loss of Head. Feet.	Period of Service Since Last Washing. Hours and Minutes.	Filtered Water Since Last Washing. Cubic Feet.	Bacteria per Cubic Centimeter.	Remarks.
	1895									
258	Nov. 15	3.29 P.M.	11	22.0	89	....	10h. 18m.	14 961	86	
261	" 16	10.35 A.M.	11	25.0	101	....	....	18 267	116	
263	" 16	12.00 M.	11	25.0	101	....	....	20 584	112	
264	" 16	3.23 P.M.	11	....	101	....	....	......	146	
267	" 18	9.41 A.M.	11	25.0	101	....	....	28 137	276	
268	" 18	11.00 "	11	24.0	97	....	....	30 124	168	
269	" 18	12.35 P.M.	11	24.0	97	....	....	32 329	116	
270	" 18	3.05 "	11	25.0	101	....	....	36 138	98	
273	" 19	9.30 A.M.	11	24.5	99	....	....	37 271	318	
274	" 19	10.20 "	11	24.0	97	....	....	38 403	168	
277	" 20	12.31 P.M.	12	25.0	101	....	21m.	412	304	
278	" 20	12.51 "	12	25.0	101	....	41m.	984	294	
279	" 20	1.05 "	12	25.0	101	....	55m.	1 276	54	
280	" 20	1.20 "	12	25.0	101	....	1h. 10m.	1 714	68	
281	" 20	2.30 "	12	25.0	101	....	2h. 20m.	1 909	49	
284	" 21	9.22 A.M.	12	24.5	99	....	4h. 01m.	6 117	142	
285	" 21	10.10 "	12	24.0	97	....	4h. 49m.	7 237	72	
286	" 21	12.03 P.M.	12	25.0	101	....	6h. 42m.	10 061	76	
287	" 21	2.00 "	12	25.0	101	....	8h. 39m.	13 072	50	
290	" 22	2.22 "	12	24.0	97	....	11h. 06m.	16 687	90	
291	" 22	3.32 "	12	25.0	101	....	12h. 16m.	18 487	36	
294	" 23	9.21 A.M.	12	26.0	105	....	12h. 32m.	19 331	394	
295	" 23	10.24 "	12	26.0	105	....	13h. 35m.	21 046	44	
296	" 23	1.15 P.M.	12	24.0	97	....	16h. 18m.	24 837	58	
299	" 23	3.40 "	12	20.0	81	....	18h. 26m.	27 402	77	
301	" 25	9.45 A.M.	12	19.5	79	....	18h. 43m.	28 002	378	
305	" 25	10.40 "	12	20.0	81	....	19h. 38m.	28 927	420	
307	" 25	11.45 A.M.	13	25.0	101	....	07m.	175	440	
308	" 25	11.55 "	13	25.0	101	....	17m.	413	368	
309	" 25	12.05 P.M.	13	24.5	99	....	27m.	622	364	
310	" 25	12.15 "	13	24.0	97	....	37m.	848	390	
312	" 25	1.35 "	13	24.0	97	....	1h. 57m.	2 605	366	
314	" 25	3.20 "	13	26.0	105	....	3h. 42m.	5 356	484	
320	" 26	9.22 A.M.	13	27.0	109	....	4h. 08m.	6 460	748	
321	" 26	10.15 "	13	25.0	101	....	5h. 01m.	7 474	512	
323	" 26	11.27 "	13	24.0	97	....	6h. 13m.	9 204	664	
325	" 26	1.48 P.M.	13	24.0	97	...	8h 34m.	12 664	394	
328	" 26	3.15 "	13	23.0	93	....	10h. 01m.	14 633	386	
331	" 27	9.20 A.M.	13	25.0	101	....	10h. 36m.	15 617	754	
333	" 27	10.16 "	13	26.0	105	....	11h. 32m.	17 078	875	
337	" 27	11.45 "	13	25.5	103	....	13h. 01m.	19 333	1358	
339	" 27	1.33 P.M.	13	23.5	95	....	14h. 49m.	22 034	972	
342	" 27	3.12 "	13	....	.....	....	16h. 28m.	24 259	704	
345	" 29	9.14 A.M.	13	25.0	101	....	16h. 48m.	24 652	2280	
346	" 29	9.45 "	13	24.0	97	....	17h. 19m.	25 407	665	Agitated surface of sand
353	" 29	10.51 "	13	21.0	85	....	18h. 25m.	26 945	343	layer from 9.28 A.M. to
355	" 29	12.01 P.M.	13	22.0	89	....	19h. 35m.	28 567	444	9.43 A.M.
357	" 29	1.47 "	13	24.0	97	....	21h. 21m.	30 880	328	
362	" 30	9.48 A.M.	14	24.0	97	....	12m.	217	700	
363	" 30	9.58 "	14	24.0	97	....	22m.	511	558	
364	" 30	10.08 "	14	24.0	97	....	32m.	712	540	
365	" 30	10.18 "	14	24.0	97	....	42m.	990	528	
366	" 30	10.28 "	14	24.0	97	....	52m.	1 233	560	
367	" 30	10.38 "	14	24.5	99	....	1h. 02m.	1 368	546	
369	" 30	11.43 "	14	26.0	105	....	2h. 07m.	3 112	658	
371	" 30	1.32 P.M.	14	24.0	97	....	3h. 56m.	5 808	634	
375	Dec. 2	9.42 A.M.	14	25.0	101	....	8h. 35m.	12 213	448	
377	" 2	10.43 "	14	25.0	101	....	9h. 26m.	13 684	322	
380	" 2	12.29 P.M.	14	24.0	97	....	11h. 12m.	16 273	376	
382	" 2	2.32 "	14	24.0	97	....	13h. 15m.	19 148	294	
386	" 3	10.31 A.M.	14	25.0	101	....	15h. 05m.	21 901	392	

TABLE No. 4.—*Continued.*

Jewell System.

Serial Number.	Collected. Date.	Collected. Hour.	Number of Run.	Rate of Filtration. Cubic Feet per Minute.	Rate of Filtration. Million Gallons per Acre per 24 Hours.	Loss of Head. Feet.	Period of Service Since Last Washing. Hours and Minutes.	Filtered Water Since Last Washing. Cubic Feet.	Bacteria per Cubic Centimeter.	Remarks.
	1895									
388	Dec. 3	11.37 A.M.	14	24.0	97	....	16h. 11m.	23 537	350	
390	" 3	12.55 P.M.	14	22.0	89	....	17h. 29m.	25 437	322	
393	" 3	2.15 "	14	22.0	89	....	18h. 49m.	27 206	385	Agitated surface of sand layer at 1.32 P.M.
411	" 4	3.07 "	14	25.0	101	....	20h. 02m.	29 122	372	
414	" 4	4.37 "	14	23.0	93	....	21h. 32m.	31 350	290	
420	" 5	9.47 A.M.	14	23.0	93	....	23h. 09m.	33 716	264	
422	" 5	10.38 "	14	23.0	93	....	24h. 00m.	34 829	150	
425	" 5	11.47 "	14	21.0	85	....	25h. 09m.	36 313	232	Agitated surface of sand layer at 12.23 P.M.
427	" 5	2.40 P.M.	15	24.0	97	....	10m.	271	270	
429	" 5	2.50 "	15	24.0	97	....	20m.	502	244	
430	" 5	3.00 "	15	25.0	101	....	30m.	761	192	
431	" 5	3.10 "	15	26.0	105	....	40m.	1 023	298	
432	" 5	3.20 "	15	24.0	97	....	50m.	1 248	280	
433	" 5	3 30 "	15	24.0	97	....	1h. 00m.	1 482	368	
436	" 5	3.46 "	15	25.0	101	....	1h. 16m.	1 856	156	
438	" 6	10 04 A.M.	15	26.0	105	...	1h. 43m.	2 692	240	
442	" 6	11.27 "	15	24.0	101	....	3h 06m.	4 827	194	
449	" 6	1.36 P.M.	15	24.0	97	....	5h. 15m.	8 029	296	
452	" 6	3.45 "	15	22.0	89	....	7h. 24m.	11 206	236	
453	" 7	9.25 A.M.	15	25.0	101	....	9h. 29m.	14 124	274	
455	" 7	12.24 P.M.	15	23.0	93	....	12h. 28m.	18 442	124	
458	" 7	12.55 "	15	24.0	97	....	14h. 49m.	21 438	864	Agitated surface of sand layer at 2.47 P.M.
461	" 9	10.05 A.M.	15	22.0	89	....	18h. 11m.	26 096	160	
465	" 9	11.18 "	15	22.0	89	....	19h. 22m.	27 655	144	
467	" 9	12.20 P.M.	15	23.0	93	....	20h. 15m.	28 825	192	Agitated surface of sand layer at 11.47 A.M.
468	" 9	1.48 "	15	21.0	85	....	21h. 43m.	30 683	164	
472	" 9	3.38 "	15	21.0	85	....	23h. 26m.	32 836	172	Agitated surface of sand layer at 3.14 P.M.
478	" 10	10.40 A.M.	16	24.0	97	...	14m.	592	224	
479	" 10	10.50 "	16	24.0	97	....	24m.	796	176	
480	" 10	11.00 "	16	24.0	97	....	34m.	1 092	214	
481	" 10	11.10 "	16	24.0	97	....	44m.	1 313	168	
482	" 10	11.20 "	16	24.0	97	....	54m.	1 543	304	
483	" 10	11.30 "	16	24.0	97	....	1h. 04m.	1 755	194	
490	" 10	2.07 P.M.	16	25.0	101	...	3h. 41m.	4 498	268	
494	" 10	3.30 "	16	24.0	97	....	5h. 04m.	6 605	238	
497	" 11	11.08 A.M.	16	28.0	114	....	7h. 35m.	10 370	196	
499	" 11	12.14 P.M.	16	25.0	101	....	8h. 41m.	12 157	224	
503	" 11	1.24 "	16	25.0	101	....	9h. 51m.	13 442	196	
506	" 11	3.11 "	16	24.0	97	....	11h. 38m.	16 532	190	
508	" 12	9.36 A.M.	16	24.0	97	....	14h. 16m.	20 339	142	
510	" 12	12.00 M.	16	23.0	93	....	16h. 40m.	23 717	130	
512	" 12	3.00 P.M.	16	22.0	89	....	19h. 40m.	27 717	176	Agitated surface of sand layer at 4.28 P.M.
517	" 13	10.52 A.M.	16	24.0	97	....	22h. 40m.	31 749	135	
519	" 13	1.50 P.M.	16	20.0	81	....	26h. 18m.	36 428	116	
522	" 13	4.44 P.M.	17	24.0	97	....	30m.	530	127	
524	" 14	10.05 A.M.	17	25.0	101	....	1h. 42m.	3 001	103	
526	" 14	12.55 P.M.	17	21.0	85	....	4h. 32m.	7 195	136	
529	" 14	3.08 "	17	24.0	97	....	6h. 45m.	10 413	164	
533	" 16	9.25 A.M.	17	25.0	101	....	9h. 14m.	14 128	148	
535	" 16	11.32 "	17	25.0	101	....	11h. 21m.	17 561	150	
539	" 16	2.40 P.M.	17	23.0	93	....	14h. 29m.	22 125	186	
540	" 16	5.15 "	17	21.0	85	....	17h. 04m.	25 508	90	
544	" 17	9.48 A.M.	17	20.0	81	....	17h. 29m.	26 059	93	
545	" 17	12.52 P.M.	18	20.0	81	....	24m.	724	88	
549	" 17	3.30 "	18	24.0	97	....	3h. 02m.	4 501	148	
550	" 17	4.31 "	18	24.0	97	....	4h. 03m.	6 061	164	
553	" 18	9.16 A.M.	18	25.0	101	....	5h. 07m.	7 684	168	
555	" 18	10.35 "	18	24.0	97	....	6h. 26m.	9 650	168	
557	" 18	1.05 P.M.	18	22.0	89	....	8h. 56m.	13 038	97	
566	" 18	3.31 "	18	16.0	65	....	11h. 22m.	15 928	130	
567	" 18	4.34 "	18	18.0	73	....	12h. 25m.	16 933	90	

TABLE No. 4.—*Continued.*

Jewell System.

Serial Number.	Collected. Date.	Collected. Hour.	Number of Run.	Rate of Filtration. Cubic Feet per Minute.	Rate of Filtration. Million Gallons per Acre per 24 Hours.	Loss of Head. Feet.	Period of Service Since Last Washing. Hours and Minutes.	Filtered Water Since Last Washing. Cubic Feet.	Bacteria per Cubic Centimeter.	Remarks.
	1895									
571	Dec. 19	9.45 A.M.	18	18.0	73	....	13h. 30m.	18 114	116	Agitated surface of sand
572	" 19	11.48 "	18	18.0	73	....	15h. 33m.	20 187	53	layer at 9.15 A.M.
573	" 19	12.50 P.M.	19	25.0	101	....	10m.	257	46	
574	" 19	1.00 "	19	25.0	101	....	20m.	508	35	
575	" 19	1.10 "	19	25.0	101	...	30m.	646	45	
576	" 19	1.20 "	19	25.0	101	....	40m.	991	56	
577	" 19	1.30 "	19	25.0	101	....	50m.	1 331	71	
578	" 19	1.40 "	19	25.0	101	....	1h. 00m.	1 499	93	
579	" 19	3.19 "	19	24.0	97	....	2h. 39m.	3 841	98	
581	" 19	4.32 "	19	24.0	97	....	3h. 52m	5 444	85	
585	" 20	9.36 A.M.	19	25.0	101	....	5h. 03m.	7 286	94	
586	" 20	10.01 "	19	24.0	97	....	5h. 28m.	7 887	85	
590	" 20	12.02 P.M.	19	24.0	97	....	7h. 29m.	10 798	84	
592	" 20	2.07 "	19	24.0	97	...	9h. 34m.	13 628	144	
595	" 20	3.59 "	19	20.0	81	....	11h. 26m.	16 083	91	
598	" 21	9.26 A.M.	19	24.0	97	....	13h. 15m.	18 234	124	Agitated surface of sand
599	" 21	3.57 P.M.	20	22.0	89	....	2h. 58m.	4 358	102	layer at 8.49 A.M.
604	" 21	9.24 A.M.	20	25.0	101	....	4h. 40m.	7 010	81	
605	" 21	10.26 "	20	24.0	97	....	5h. 42m.	8 486	24	
611	" 21	12.30 P.M.	20	24.0	97	....	7h. 46m.	11 366	62	
615	" 21	3.28 "	20	22.0	89	....	10h. 44m.	15 400	108	
620	" 24	9.36 A.M.	20	23.0	93	....	13h. 08m.	18 366	70	Agitated surface of sand
626	" 24	12.37 P.M.	20	20.0	81	....	16h. 09m.	21 980	92	layer at 9.03 A.M.
630	" 24	3.18 "	21	24.0	97	....	1h. 42m.	2 319	70	
636	" 26	10.02 A.M.	21	25.0	101	....	4h. 45m.	6 766	98	
641	" 26	12.10 P.M.	21	23.0	93	....	6h. 41m.	9 486	97	
646	" 26	3.59 "	21	23.0	93	....	10h. 30m.	14 799	468	
652	" 27	10.29 A.M.	21	20.0	81	....	13h. 25m.	18 641	664	Agitated surface of sand
658	" 27	1.57 P.M.	22	24.0	97	....	18m.	422	235	layer at 12.02 P.M.
659	" 27	2 26 "	22	25.0	101	....	47m.	1 112	336	
664	" 27	3.31 "	22	25.0	101	....	1h. 52m.	2 737	346	
670	" 27	4.52 "	22	25.0	101	....	3h. 13m.	4 745	468	
675	" 28	10.02 A.M.	22	25.0	101	....	4h. 59m.	7 312	855	
681	" 28	11.51 "	22	24.0	97	....	6h. 48m.	9 906	882	
685	" 28	3.15 P.M.	22	21.0	85	....	9h. 53m.	13 914	702	Agitated surface of sand
689	" 30	9.54 A.M.	23	25.0	101	....	17m.	414	126	layer at 1.14 P.M.
690	" 30	10.24 "	23	23.0	93	....	47m.	1 145	302	
693	" 30	11.09 "	23	24.0	97	. ..	1h. 32m.	2 191	880	
698	" 30	1.48 P.M.	23	25.0	101	....	4h. 11m.	6 020	144	
704	" 30	4.48 "	23	23.0	93	....	7h. 02m.	9 601	102	Agitated surface of sand
712	" 31	10.54 A.M.	24	25.0	101	....	15m.	380	83	layer at 4.04 P.M. and
715	" 31	11.24 "	24	25.5	101	....	45m.	2 035	55	Dec. 31, 9.49 A.M.
719	" 31	2.10 P.M.	24	24.0	97	....	3h. 31m.	4 934	560	Agitated surface of sand
	1896					....				layer at 2.38 P.M. and
724	Jan. 2	9.04 A.M.	25	24.0	97	....	22m.	280	140	Jan. 1, 3.26 to 3.34 P.M.
725	" 2	9.27 "	25	25.0	101	....	45m.	825	152	
733	" 2	11 33 "	25	25.0	101	....	2h. 47m.	3 500	290	Agitated surface of sand
739	" 2	2.35 P.M.	25	14.0	57	....	5h. 49m.	7 280	560	layer at 11.16 A.M.
742	" 2	3.59 "	26	25.0	101	....	15m.	273	184	
744	" 2	4.14 "	26	23.0	93	....	30m.	713	240	
750	" 3	10.30 A.M.	26	21.0	85	....	3h. 25m.	4 623	254	
756	" 3	2 05 P.M.	26	22.0	89	....	6h. 48m	8 803	432	Agitated surface of sand
761	" 4	10.57 A.M.	27	24.0	97	....	18m.	425	364	layer at 12.02 P.M.
764	" 4	11.48 "	27	23.5	95	....	1h. 09m.	1 547	368	
771	" 4	2 22 P.M.	27	20.0	81	....	3h. 43m.	4 997	438	
811	" 9	10.30 A.M.	28	25.0	101	....	1h. 20m.	2 014	210	Sterilized filter Jan. 8.
817	" 9	1.56 P.M.	28	23.5	95	....	4h. 46m.	6 914	248	[outlet 11.44 A.M.
822	" 10	11.35 A.M.	28	16.5	67	....	10h. 37m.	14 050	152	Shut inlet 11.32 A.M.,
825	" 10	12.56 P.M.	29	25.0	101	....	46m.	1 000	166	[P.M.
829	" 10	1.52 "	29	25.0	101	....	1h. 42m.	2 420	288	[from 8.52 A.M. to 12.20
839	" 11	11.35 A.M.	29	22.0	89	....	7h. 01m.	1 705	152	Agitated surface of S.L.

TABLE NO. 4.—*Continued.*

Jewell System.

Serial Number.	Collected.		Number of Run.	Rate of Filtration.		Loss of Head. Feet.	Period of Service Since Last Washing. Hours and Minutes.	Filtered Water Since Last Washing. Cubic Feet.	Bacteria per Cubic Centimeter.	Remarks.
	Date.	Hour.		Cubic Feet per Minute.	Million Gallons per Acre per 24 Hours.					
	1896									
841	Jan. 13	9.59 A.M.	30	24.0	97	....	15m.	344	104	Agitated surface of sand
842	" 13	10.38 "	30	25.0	101	....	54m.	1 318	176	layer from 9.44 A.M. to
845	" 13	1.58 P.M.	30	25.0	101	....	4h. 14m.	6 236	290	5.40 P.M.
849	" 13	4.10 "	30	25.0	101	....	6h. 26m.	9 411	204	
855	" 14	11.52 A.M.	30	23.0	93	....	10h. 57m.	15 722	160	Agitated surface of sand
860	" 14	2.05 P.M.	30	23.0	93	....	13h. 10m.	18 819	168	layer from 8.54 A.M. to
866	" 14	3.16 "	30	19.0	77	....	14h. 21m.	20 364	140	9.57 A.M.
868	" 15	9.49 A.M.	31	24.0	97	....	15m.	346	148	
869	" 15	10.19 "	31	24.0	97	....	45m.	987	116	
872	" 15	10.44 "	31	24.0	97	....	1h. 10m.	1 574	168	
878	" 15	12.56 P.M.	31	24.0	97	....	3h. 22m.	4 671	226	
882	" 15	3.07 "	31	24.0	97	....	5h. 33m.	7 658	124	
888	" 16	10.52 A.M.	31	24.0	97	....	9h. 43m.	13 626	120	
893	" 16	1.05 P.M.	31	24.0	97	....	11h. 56m.	16 746	194	
900	" 16	3.05 "	31	23.0	93	....	13h. 56m.	19 626	230	Agitated surface of sand
912	" 17	11.23 A.M.	32	21.0	85	....	05m.	102	430	layer Jan. 17, 10.03
913	" 17	11.28 "	32	24.0	97	....	10m.	222	218	A.M.
916	" 17	11.38 "	32	25.0	101	....	20m.	462	174	
917	" 17	11.48 "	32	23.5	95	....	30m.	672	240	
918	" 17	11.58 "	32	24.0	97	....	40m.	902	292	
921	" 17	12.08 P.M.	32	23.5	95	....	50m.	1 172	194	
922	" 17	12.18 "	32	23.5	95	....	1h. 00m.	1 372	272	
925	" 17	1.06 "	32	23.0	93	....	1h. 48m.	2 532	290	
930	" 17	2.07 "	32	24.0	97	....	2h. 49m.	3 952	332	
932	" 17	3.00 "	32	23.0	93	....	3h. 42m.	5 192	186	
936	" 17	4.00 "	32	24.0	97	....	4h. 42m.	6 602	232	
942	" 17	5.03 "	32	24.0	97	....	5h. 45m.	8 142	298	
949	" 18	10.12 A.M.	32	23.0	93	....	7h. 39m.	10 922	188	
953	" 18	1.19 P.M.	32	23.5	95	....	10h. 46m.	15 342	180	
960	" 18	2.44 "	32	24.5	99	....	12h. 11m.	17 342	198	
963	" 20	9.45 A.M.	33	22.5	91	....	07m.	160	306	
964	" 20	10.00 "	33	25.0	101	....	22m.	470	286	
965	" 20	10.23 "	33	24.0	97	....	45m.	1 010	282	
974	" 20	4.18 P.M.	33	24.0	97	....	6h. 40m.	9 480	44	[layer at 1.39 P.M.
979	" 21	11.32 A.M.	33	23.0	93	....	10h. 24m.	14 830	168	Agitated surface of sand
986	" 21	4.20 P.M.	33	23.5	95	....	15h. 12m.	21 580	173	Agitated surface of sand
992	" 22	9.26 A.M.	33	23.5	95	....	16h. 58m.	24 052	103	layer at 4.30 P.M.
998	" 22	2.21 P.M.	33	23.5	95	....	21h. 53m.	30 700	106	
1002	" 23	10.11 A.M.	34	23.5	95	....	36m.	824	88	
1008	" 23	3.45 P.M.	34	24.0	97	....	6h. 10m.	8 724	318	
1013	" 24	10.15 A.M.	34	23.5	95	....	9h. 14m.	12 994	160	
1015	" 24	1.47 P.M.	34	23.5	95	....	12h. 46m.	18 027	124	
1022	" 25	9.58 A.M.	34	23.0	93	....	17h. 10m.	24 097	128	Agitated surface of sand
1025	" 25	2.15 P.M.	35	25.0	101	....	25m.	266	106	layer at 9.00 A.M., and
1034	" 27	10.10 A.M.	35	25.0	101	....	4h. 51m.	7 186	688	from 9.07 A.M. to 11.32
1040	" 27	1.09 P.M.	35	25.0	101	....	7h. 50m.	11 266	1 196	A.M.
1045	" 27	4.15 "	35	23.0	93	....	10h. 52m.	15 426	952	Agitated surface of sand
1051	" 28	9.15 A.M.	35	23.0	93	....	13h. 10m.	18 906	500	layer at 3.10 P.M.
1054	" 28	1.00 P.M.	36	23.0	93	....	1h. 12m.	1 713	2 500	[layer at 3.42 P.M.
1060	" 28	4.35 "	36	24.0	97	....	4h. 34m.	6 463	1 600	Agitated surface of sand
1066	" 29	10.14 A.M.	36	23.5	95	....	6h. 01m.	8 583	3 016	Agitated surface of sand
1069	" 29	2.04 P.M.	37	23.0	93	....	1h. 24m.	2 024	1 620	layer at 11.43 A.M.
1070	" 29	5.04 "	37	23.5	95	....	4h. 24m.	6 174	675	
1075	" 30	11.03 A.M.	37	24.0	97	....	7h. 13m.	10 194	876	Agitated surface of sand
1077	" 30	1.05 P.M.	37	23.5	95	....	9h. 15m.	13 094	780	layer at 10.09 A.M.
1080	" 30	2.56 "	37	21.0	85	....	11h. 06m.	15 534	804	
1084	" 31	10.55 A.M.	38	24.0	97	....	3h. 30m.	5 001	811	Agitated surface of sand
1089	" 31	2.36 P.M.	38	20.0	81	....	7h. 11m.	10 031	910	layer at 11.29 A.M.
1137	Feb. 5	10.22 A.M.	39	25.0	101	....	27m.	834	612	
1141	" 5	11.50 "	39	24.0	97	....	1h. 55m.	2 924	468	
1145	" 5	3.08 P.M.	39	22.0	89	....	5h. 13m.	7 534	600	

TABLE No. 4.—*Continued.*

Jewell System.

Serial Number.	Collected. Date.	Collected. Hour.	Number of Run.	Rate of Filtration. Cubic Feet per Minute.	Rate of Filtration. Million Gallons per Acre per 24 Hours.	Loss of Head. Feet.	Period of Service Since Last Washing. Hours and Minutes.	Filtered Water Since Last Washing. Cubic Feet.	Bacteria per Cubic Centimeter.	Remarks.
	1896									
1150	Feb. 5	5.08 P.M.	39	22.0	89	....	7h. 13m.	10 144	892	
1156	" 6	10.13 A.M.	39	25.0	101	....	8h. 04m.	11 324	1 620	
1160	" 6	12.14 P.M.	39	23.5	95	....	10h. 05m.	14 174	2 155	Agitated surface of sand
1164	" 6	3.13 "	40	24.5	99	....	40m.	1 014	1 282	layer at 1.54 P.M.
1169	" 6	4.15 "	40	25.0	101	....	1h. 42m.	2 394	1 196	
1174	" 7	10.18 A.M.	40	24.0	97	....	4h. 08m.	5 814	238	[layer at 11.17 A.M.
1178	" 7	1.32 P.M.	40	23.0	93	....	7h. 18m.	10 314	480	Agitated surface of sand
1184	" 7	5.28 "	41	23.5	95	....	1h. 20m.	1 814	1 200	Agitated surface of sand
1190	" 8	10 49 A.M.	41	25.0	101	....	1h. 43m.	2 337	1 785	layer from 4.08 P.M. to
1192	" 8	2.20 P.M.	41	19.0	77	....	5h. 14m.	6 727	500	5.18 P.M.
1196	" 8	3.11 "	41	22.0	89	....	6h. 05m.	7 827	1 900	
1204	" 10	10.22 A.M.	42	25.0	101	....	39m.	908	675	
1208	" 10	1.01 P.M.	42	22.0	89	....	3h. 14m.	4 278	616	Agitated surface of sand
1212	" 10	3.16 "	42	19.0	77	....	5h. 29m.	7 138	516	layer at 11.47 A.M.
1217	" 10	5.02 "	42	22.0	89	....	7h. 11m.	9 328	1 155	Agitated surface of sand
1222	" 11	10.09 A.M.	43	24.5	99	....	24m.	578	415	layer at 3.20 P.M.
1225	" 11	12.50 P.M.	43	24.0	97	....	3h. 01m.	3 978	735	Agitated surface of sand
1228	" 11	3.13 "	43	23.0	93	....	5h. 24m.	7 108	567	layer at 12.40 P.M.
1232	" 11	5.12 "	43	24.0	97	....	7h. 10m.	9 578	2 365	Agitated surface of sand
1241	" 12	3.18 "	45	18.0	73	....	1h. 41m.	2 205	2 420	layer at 4.00 P.M.
1242	" 12	3.40 "	45	26.0	105	....	2h. 03m.	2 695	2 360	
1243	" 12	4.45 "	45	18.5	75	....	3h. 08m.	4 215	324	
1249	" 13	9.48 A.M.	45	23.0	93	....	4h. 36m.	6 115	209	
1252	" 13	12.24 P.M.	45	22.5	91	....	7h. 12m.	9 675	317	
1255	" 13	2.18 "	45	25.0	101	....	9h. 02m.	12 195	740	Agitated surface of sand
1261	" 13	4.50 "	45	23.0	93	....	11h. 34m.	15 615	930	layer at 1.01 P.M.
1266	" 14	10.24 A.M.	46	23.0	93	....	50m.	1 178	234	
1270	" 14	1.17 P.M.	46	23.0	93	....	3h. 38m.	5 013	1 110	Agitated surface of sand
1274	" 14	3.19 "	46	23.5	95	....	4h. 53m.	6 738	1 110	layer at 12.59 P.M.
1278	" 14	4.46 "	46	24.0	97	....	6h. 20m.	8 818	940	
1284	" 15	10.15 A.M.	46	23.0	93	....	8h. 19m.	11 468	790	
1288	" 15	1.29 P.M.	46	23.0	93	....	11h. 28m.	15 688	1 097	Shut inlet 2.56 P.M., out-
1292	" 15	3.02 "	46	18.0	73	....	13h. 01m.	17 788	845	let 3.09 P.M.
1297	" 15	5.20 "	47	24.0	97	....	1h. 46m.	2 353	319	
1303	" 17	10.12 A.M.	47	24.0	97	....	3h. 08m.	4 163	1 100	
1307	" 17	1.40 P.M.	47	24.0	97	....	6h. 31m.	8 783	1 285	Agitated surface of sand
1311	" 17	3.10 "	47	23.0	93	....	8h. 01m.	10 833	1 362	layer at 11.42 A.M.
1317	" 17	5.18 "	48	25.0	101	....	18m.	394	569	
1321	" 18	10.27 A.M.	48	22.5	91	....	1h. 57m.	2 714	1 885	
1325	" 18	11.58 "	48	23.0	93	....	3h. 26m.	4 794	1 250	
1329	" 18	2.23 P.M.	48	22.0	89	....	5h. 51m.	7 994	1 645	Agitated surface of sand
1332	" 18	4.52 "	48	13.0	52	....	8h. 20m.	11 314	1 270	layer at 1.56 P.M.
1340	" 18	5.14 "	48	23.0	93	....	8h. 42m.	11 804	1 855	
1344	" 19	10.18 A.M.	48	16.0	65	....	10h. 01m.	13 414	760	
1348	" 19	11.35 "	48	22.0	89	....	11h. 16m.	15 974	50	Agitated surface of sand
1352	" 19	3.08 P.M.	49	22.5	91	....	20m.	421	695	layer at 11.43 A.M.
1357	" 19	5.03 "	49	26.0	105	....	2h. 15m.	3 011	2 170	
1363	" 20	11.04 A.M.	49	24.0	97	....	3h. 05m.	4 151	28	
1367	" 20	12.05 P.M.	49	23.0	93	....	4h. 06m.	5 591	88	
1372	" 20	1.09 "	49	23.0	93	....	5h. 07m.	6 851	43	Agitated surface of sand
1376	" 20	2.10 "	49	23.0	93	....	6h. 08m.	8 321	59	layer at 12.46 P.M.
1378	" 20	3 12 "	49	24.0	97	....	7h. 10m.	9 771	206	
1381	" 20	4.05 "	49	25.0	101	....	8h. 03m.	10 031	575	
1385	" 20	5.10 "	49	24.0	97	....	9h. 08m.	12 641	1 390	
1393	" 21	11.04 A.M.	49	25.0	101	....	10h. 24m.	14 381	101	
1395	" 21	12.45 P.M.	49	21.0	85	....	12h. 05m.	16 491	120	[layer at 1.22 P.M.
1398	" 21	3.09 "	49	23.0	93	....	14h. 26m.	19 621	490	Agitated surface of sand
1401	" 21	4.55 "	49	22.5	91	....	16h. 12m.	22 011	560	Agitated surface of sand
1409	" 22	10.24 A.M.	50	25.0	101	....	58m.	1 331	65	layer at 5.10 P.M.
1410	" 22	1.08 P.M.	50	21.0	85	....	3h. 42m.	5 071	715	[layer at 1.28 P.M.
1413	" 22	3.05 "	50	24.0	97	....	5h. 46m.	7 781	1 110	Agitated surface of sand

TABLE NO. 4.—*Continued.*

Jewell System.

Serial Number.	Collected. Date.	Collected. Hour.	Number of Run.	Rate of Filtration. Cubic Feet per Minute.	Rate of Filtration. Million Gallons per Acre per 24 Hours.	Loss of Head. Feet.	Period of Service Since Last Washing, Hours and Minutes.	Filtered Water Since Last Washing, Cubic Feet.	Bacteria per Cubic Centimeter.	Remarks.
	1896									
1416	Feb. 22	4.58 P.M.	50	23.0	93	....	7h. 49m.	10 441	700	
1421	" 24	10.24 A.M.	50	23.0	93	....	9h. 25m.	13 225	1 605	
1424	" 24	1.20 P.M.	50	22.5	91	....	12h. 21m.	17 235	404	
1427	" 24	3.26 "	50	24.5	99	....	14h. 24m.	20 115	665	Agitated surface of sand
1432	" 24	5.19 "	50	23.0	93	....	16h. 17m.	22 844	609	layer at 2.15 P.M.
1438	" 25	10.30 A.M.	50	23.0	93	....	17h. 58m.	25 195	960	
1442	" 25	1.18 P.M.	51	23.5	95	....	16m.	335	1 785	
1446	" 25	3.12 "	51	22.5	91	....	2h. 10m.	2 965	1 610	
1451	" 25	5.02 "	51	23.5	95	....	4h. 00m.	5 515	1 450	
1457	" 26	10.29 A.M.	51	25.0	101	....	5h. 47m.	7 755	1 420	
1461	" 26	12.08 P.M.	51	23.0	93	....	7h. 26m.	10 115	1 295	
1467	" 26	3.15 "	51	24.5	99	....	10h. 33m.	14 625	1 770	
1470	" 26	5.18 "	51	20.5	83	....	12h. 36m.	17 495	3 280	
1477	" 27	10.32 A.M.	51	24.0	97	....	13h. 16m.	18 415	191	Agitated surface of sand
1480	" 27	1.45 P.M.	52	26.0	105	....	27m.	670	695	layer at 9.32 A.M. and
1484	" 27	3.02 "	52	30.0	112	....	1h. 44m.	2 810	970	12.18 P.M.
1489	" 27	5.12 "	52	25.5	103	....	3h. 54m.	6 430	1 215	
1495	" 28	9.20 A.M. to 12.15 P.M.	52	30.5	124	..	....	....	.....	C. Sterilized filter, Feb.
1497	" 28	10.42 A.M.	52	29.5	120	....	5h. 54m.	9 950	1 330	28.
1500	" 28	11.50 "	52	33.5	136	....	7h. 02m.	12 050	1 820	
1511	" 29	9.58 A.M. to 3.18 P.M.	53	25.9	122	....	....	......	1 070	C.
1513	" 29	10.39 A.M.	53	27.0	109	....	41m.	1 195	197	
1517	" 29	1.38 P.M.	53	21.5	87	....	3h. 02m.	4 885	2 555	
1521	" 29	3.18 "	53	27.0	109	....	4h. 42m.	7 495	1 910	
1524	" 29	3.38 "	53	27.0	109	....	5h. 02m.	8 035	2 170	
1527	" 29	5.11 "	53	27.0	109	....	6h. 35m.	10 465	1 175	
1532	Mar. 2	9.35 A.M. to 3.15 P.M.	53	25.9	105	....	....	......	1 965	C.
1533	" 2	9.42 A.M.	53	26.0	105	....	7h. 36m.	12 085	3 455	
1537	" 2	10.25 "	53	26.0	105	....	8h. 19m.	13 185	.....	
1541	" 2	1.36 P.M.	53	25.5	103	...	11h. 30m.	18 165	.....	
1545	" 2	3.19 "	53	25.0	101	....	13h. 13m.	20 785	1 545	
1550	" 2	5.10 "	53	25.0	101	....	15h. 03m.	23 575	1 445	
1553	" 2–3	3.18 P.M. to 3.20 P.M.	53	23.2	93	....	....	......	1 570	C.
1558	" 3	10.42 A.M.	53	23.0	93	..	17h. 16m.	26 485	900	
1564	" 3	12.58 P.M.	53	21.0	85	....	19h. 22m.	29 515	1 210	[layer at 2.09 P.M.
1566	" 3	3.13 "	53	22.5	91	....	21h. 31m.	32 395	1 300	Agitated surface of sand
1568	" 3–4	3.20 P.M. to 3.20 P.M.	53–54	25.8	104	....	....	......	1 465	C.
1571	" 3	5.13 P.M.	53	21.5	85	....	23h. 31m.	34 935	1 885	
1577	" 4	10.48 A.M.	54	27.5	111	....	1h. 30m.	2 393	610	
1581	" 4	1.00 P.M.	54	28.0	114	....	3h. 42m.	6 003	880	
1585	" 4	3.20 "	54	28.5	116	....	6h. 02m.	9 853	1 320	
1590	" 4	5.05 "	54	28.0	114	....	7h. 47m.	12 783	595	
1596	" 5	10.39 A.M.	54	28.0	114	....	9h. 51m.	16 253	885	
1600	" 5	12.53 P.M.	54	27.5	111	....	12h. 05m.	19 893	298	
1603	" 4–5	3.20 P.M. to 3.20 P.M.	54	27.8	112	....	....	......	815	C.
1604	" 5–6	3.20 " " 3.20 "	54–55	30.3	123	....	....	.....	650	C.
1605	" 5	3.20 P.M.	54	28.0	114	....	14h. 32m.	24 013	965	
1611	" 5	5.14 "	54	25.0	101	....	16h. 26m.	27 063	725	
1617	" 6	10.35 A.M.	54	23.0	93	....	18h. 17m.	29 743	206	Shut inlet 10.33 A.M.,
1620	" 6	11.17 "	55	38.0	154	....	18m.	536	81	outlet 10.41 P.M.
1622	" 6	12.41 P.M.	55	38.0	154	....	1h. 42m.	3 656	86	
1626	" 6	3.20 "	55	36.0	146	....	4h. 21m.	9 526	570	
1627	" 6–7	3.20 P.M. to 3.20 P.M.	55	28.7	116	....	....	......	.....	C.
1632	" 6	5.22 P.M.	55	34.5	140	....	6h. 23m.	13 606	550	
1638	" 7	10.44 A.M.	55	25.0	101	....	8h. 15m.	17 206	128	
1642	" 7	12.54 P.M.	55	25.0	101	....	10h. 25m.	20 426	150	
1647	" 7	3.20 "	55	25.0	101	....	12h. 51m.	24 046	197	
1648	" 7–9	3.20 P.M. to 3.20 P.M.	55–56	23.5	95	....	....	......	.....	C.
1651	" 7	5.19 P.M.	55	22.5	91	....	14h. 50m.	26 936	108	
1657	" 9	11.00 A.M.	56	25.0	101	....	1h. 35m	2 427	58	
1662	" 9	12.52 P.M.	56	25.5	103	....	3h. 27m.	5 347	61	

TABLE NO. 4.—*Continued.*

Jewell System.

Serial Number	Collected. Date.	Collected. Hour.	Number of Run.	Rate of Filtration. Cubic Feet per Minute.	Rate of Filtration. Million Gallons per Acre per 24 Hours.	Loss of Head. Feet.	Period of Service Since Last Washing. Hours and Minutes.	Filtered Water Since Last Washing. Cubic Feet.	Bacteria per Cubic Centimeter.	Remarks.
	1896									
1668	Mar. 9	3.30 P.M.	56	25.0	101	....	6h. 05m.	9 367	305	
1669	" 9–10	3.30 P.M. to 3.10 P.M.	57	24.4	99	....	....	......	95	C.
1673	" 9	5.07 P.M.	56	24.5	99	....	7h. 42m.	11 739	110	
1679	" 10	10.23 A.M.	56	23.0	93	....	9h. 28m.	14 307	82	
1683	" 10	1.35 P.M.	57	24.5	99	....	2h. 00m.	2 980	111	
1687	" 10	3.10 "	57	25.0	101	....	3h. 35m.	5 400	58	
1688	" 10–11	3.10 P.M. to 3.20 P.M.	57	25.5	103	....	....	.....	166	C.
1694	" 10	5.17 P.M.	57	25.0	101	....	5h. 42m.	8 670	295	
1700	" 11	10.23 A.M.	57	24.0	97	....	7h. 18m.	11 080	79	
1703	" 11	1.30 P.M.	57	26.0	105	....	10h. 02m.	15 290	134	
1707	" 11	3.20 "	57	24.0	97	....	11h. 52m.	18 060	165	
1711	" 11–12	3.20 P.M. to 3.26 P.M.	57–58	25.4	103	....	....	......	325	C.
1714	" 11	5.11 P.M.	57	23.5	95	....	13h. 43m.	20 690	105	
1720	" 12	10.18 A.M.	58	25.0	101	....	53m.	1 303	155	
1724	" 12	12.57 P.M.	58	25.0	101	....	3h. 32m.	5 213	560	
1728	" 12	3.26 "	58	25.0	101	....	6h. 01m.	8 903	165	
1729	" 12–13	3.26 P.M. to 3.15 P.M.	58–59	24.8	100	....	....	......	370	C.
1734	" 12	5.13 P.M.	58	24.0	97	....	7h. 48m.	11 543	121	
1740	" 13	10.32 A.M.	59	21.5	87	....	04m.	104	700	
1744	" 13	1.12 P.M.	59	25.0	101	....	2h. 44m.	4 274	742	
1748	" 13	3.15 "	59	24.5	99	....	4h. 47m.	7 234	325	
1753	" 13	5.03 "	59	24.0	97	....	6h. 35m.	9 854	420	
1759	" 14	9.30 A.M. to 10.30 A.M.	59	23.6	95	....	....	......	230	C.
1760	" 14	10.30 A.M.	59	23.6	95	....	8h. 32m.	12 664	320	
1765	" 14	10.30 A.M. to 1.08 P.M.	59–60	23.5	95	....	....	......	410	C.
1766	" 14	1.08 P.M.	60	25.0	101	....	58m.	1 428	510	
1771	" 14	1.08 P.M. to 3.15 P.M.	60	24.6	99	....	....	......	131	C.
1772	" 14	3.15 P.M.	60	24.5	99	....	3h. 05m.	4 546	64	
1776	" 14	4.02 "	60	25.0	101	..	3h. 52m.	5 706	49	
1779	" 14	4.52 "	60	25.0	101	....	4h. 42m.	6 916	72	
1785	" 16	9.00 A.M. to 10.28 A.M.	60	24.8	100	....	....	......	390	C.
1786	" 16	10.28 A.M.	60	23.0	93	....	6h. 24m.	9 466	169	
1791	" 16	10.28 A.M. to 1.12 P.M.	60–61	24.0	97	....	....	......	147	C.
1792	" 16	1.12 P.M.	61	25.0	101	....	53m.	1 393	98	
1797	" 16	1.12 P.M. to 3.15 P.M.	61	24.7	100	....	....	......	188	C.
1798	" 16	3.15 P.M.	61	24.0	97	....	2h. 56m.	4 433	261	
1804	" 16	5.05 "	61	24.0	97	....	4h. 46m.	7 023	161	
1811	" 17	9.20 A.M. to 10.27 A.M.	61	23.3	94	....	....	......	156	C.
1812	" 17	10.27 A.M.	61	23.5	95	....	6h. 38m.	9 673	128	
1817	" 17	10.27 A.M. to 1.14 P.M.	61–62	24.4	99	..	....	......	95	C.
1818	" 17	1.14 P.M.	62	24.0	97	..	2h. 04m.	3 054	89	
1823	" 17	1.14 P.M. to 3.18 P.M.	62	24.1	97	....	....	......	53	C.
1824	" 17	3.18 P.M.	62	24.5	99	....	4h. 08m.	6 134	67	
1830	" 17	5.13 "	62	23.0	93	....	6h. 03m.	8 784	60	
1836	" 18	10.28 A.M.	63	24.0	97	....	49m.	1 197	17	
1841	" 18	10.28 A.M. to 1.08 P.M.	63	24.7	99	..	....	......	22	C.
1842	" 18	1.08 P.M.	63	24.5	99	....	3h. 29m.	5 197	41	
1848	" 18	1.08 P.M. to 3.24 P.M.	63	23.9	97	....	....	......	47	C.
1849	" 18	3.24 P.M.	63	24.5	99	...	5h. 45m.	8 447	36	
1855	" 18	5.02 "	63	24.5	99	....	7h. 23m.	10 777	47	
1863	" 19	9.00 A.M. to 10.45 A.M.	63	23.6	95	....	....	.. ..	137	C.
1868	" 19	11.08 A.M.	64	24.0	97	....	09m.	210	260	
1870	" 19	12.27 P.M.	64	24.0	97	...	1h. 28m.	2 120	1 200	
1871	" 19	10.45 A.M. to 12.27 P.M.	64	24.1	97	....	....	... ..	530	C.
1874	" 19	3.02 P.M.	64	24.5	99	...	4h. 04m.	5 840	1 155	
1875	" 19	12.27 P.M. to 3.02 P.M.	64	24.0	97	....	....	......	1 200	C.
1881	" 19	5.02 P.M.	64	19.0	77	....	6h. 03m.	8 510	225	
1882	" 19	3.02 P.M. to 5.02 P.M.	64	22.2	90	....	....	.. ..	1 000	C.
1888	" 20	9.00 A.M. " 10.25 A.M.	64–65	24.7	100	....	....	.....	585	C.
1889	" 20	10.25 A.M.	65	24.0	97	...	48m.	1 220	800	
1894	" 20	10.25 A.M. to 1.08 P.M.	65–66	22.8	92	....	....	......	800	C.

TABLE NO. 4.—*Continued.*

Jewell System.

Serial Number.	Collected.		Number of Run.	Rate of Filtration.		Loss of Head. Feet.	Period of Service Since Last Washing. Hours and Minutes.	Filtered Water Since Last Washing. Cubic Feet.	Bacteria per Cubic Centimeter.	Remarks.
	Date.	Hour.		Cubic Feet per Minute.	Million Gallons per Acre per 24 Hours.					
	1896									
1895	Mar. 20	1.08 P.M.	66	24.0	97	....	24m.	593	600	
1901	" 20	1.08 P.M. to 3.33 P.M.	66–67	23.1	93	....	....	......	1 000	C.
1902	" 20	3 33 P.M.	67	23.0	93	....	05m.	113	1 000	
1907	" 20	4.53 "	67	23.5	95	....	1h. 25m.	2 053	1 000	
1908	" 20	3.33 P.M. to 5.30 P.M.	67	24.3	98	....	....	......	1 200	C.
1913	" 21	9.00 A.M. " 10.45 A.M.	67–68	23.2	94	....	....	......	495	C.
1914	" 21	10.45 A.M.	68	24.0	97	....	45m.	1 085	415	[layer at 11.25 A.M.
1919	" 21	12.58 P.M.	68	21.0	85	....	2h. 55m.	4 095	465	Agitated surface of sand
1920	" 21	10.45 A.M. to 12.58 P.M.	68	22.6	91	....	....	......	860	C.
1922	" 21	12.58 P.M. " 3.20 "	68–69	22.8	92	....	....	......	895	C. Agitated surface of
1923	" 21	3.20 P.M.	69	24.0	97	....	1h. 41m.	2 371	1 905	sand layer at 3.05 P.M.
1931	" 21	3.20 P.M. to 5.00 P.M.	69	22.0	89	....	....	......	785	C.
1936	" 23	9.00 A.M. " 10.25 A.M.	70	23.6	95	....	....	......	440	C.
1937	" 23	10.25 A.M.	70	21.0	85	....	1h. 47m.	2 514	405	
1941	" 23	10.25 A.M. to 12 M.	70	21.2	86	....	....	......	700	C. Agitated surface of
1942	" 23	12.00 M.	70	25.0	101	....	3h. 20m.	5 874	1 250	sand layer at 10.29 A.M.
1947	" 23	12.00 M. to 3.00 P.M.	70–71	23.3	94	....	....	......	800	C.
1948	" 23	3.00 P.M.	71	24.0	97	....	1h. 40m.	2 421	475	Agitated surface of sand
1954	" 23	5.16 "	72	24.5	99	....	46m.	1 071	1 245	layer at 3.30 P.M.
1955	" 23	3.00 P.M. to 5.30 P.M.	71–72	24.9	101	....	....	......	1 230	C. [layer at 10.36 A.M.
1959	" 24	9.00 A.M. " 11.30 A.M.	72	25.5	103	....	....	......	179	Agitated surface of sand
1962	" 24	11.30 " " 2.30 P.M.	72–73	23.7	95	....	....	......	80	[layer at 3.54 P.M.
1964	" 24	2.30 P.M. " 4.42 "	73	21.4	86	....	....	......	270	Agitated surface of sand
1969	" 24	4 42 " " 8.30 "	73–74	25.4	102	....	....	......	132	[layer at 9.30 P.M.
1973	" 24	8.30 " " 11 30 "	74	22.6	91	....	....	......	74	Agitated surface of sand
1983	" 24–25	11.30 " " 2.30 A.M.	74–75	23.4	94	....	....	......	306	[layer at 3.41 A.M.
1989	" 25	2.30 A.M. to 5.30 A.M.	75	23.2	94	....	....	......	1 030	Agitated surface of sand
1993	" 25	5.30 " " 8.30 "	75–76	23.8	96	....	....	......	495	[layer at 11.05 A.M.
1998	" 25	8.30 " " 11.30 "	76	24.9	101	....	....	......	48	Agitated surface of sand
2001	" 25	11.30 " " 2.30 P.M.	76–77	25.8	104	....	....	......	158	[layer at 3.51 P.M.
2005	" 25	2.30 P.M. " 5.30 "	77	24.3	98	....	....	......	405	Agitated surface of sand
2008	" 25	5.30 " " 8.30 "	77–78	25.6	103	....	....	......	178	[layer at 10.36 P.M.
2012	" 25	8.30 " " 11.30 "	78	24.2	98	....	....	......	107	Agitated surface of sand
2014	" 26	1.00 A.M.	79	25.0	101	....	12m.	419	156	This series of results on
2015	" 26	1.08 "	79	25.0	101	....	20m.	579	113	run No. 79 was used
2016	" 26	1.18 "	79	25.0	101	....	30m.	829	171	in obtaining the aver-
2017	" 26	1.33 "	79	25.0	101	....	45m.	1 179	229	age bacteria for this
2018	" 26	1.48 "	79	25.0	101	....	1h. 00m.	1 579	420	run, but not for the
2019	" 26	2.18 "	79	25.0	101	....	1h. 30m.	2 339	345	day.
2021	" 25–26	11.30 P.M. to 2.30 A.M.	78–79	22.8	92	....	....	......	215	
2023	" 26	2.48 A.M.	79	25.0	101	....	2h. 00m.	3 049	600	
2024	" 26	3.48 "	79	24.5	99	....	3h. 00m.	4 529	435	
2025	" 26	4.14 "	79	24.5	99	....	3h. 23m.	5 049	460	Agitated surface of sand
2026	" 26	4.48 "	79	24.5	99	....	3h. 57m.	5 789	415	layer at 4.07 A.M.
2027	" 26	5.15 "	79	25.5	103	....	4h. 25m.	6 429	232	
2028	" 26	5.30 "	79	24.5	99	....	4h. 39m.	6 789	221	
2029	" 26	2.30 A.M. to 5.30 A.M.	79	23.6	95	....	....	......	482	
2033	" 26	5.49 A.M.	79	23.0	93	...	4h. 58m.	7159	124	
2035	" 26	5.30 A.M. to 8.30 A.M.	79–80	23.0	93	....	....	......	171	
2040	" 26	8.30 " " 11.30 "	80–81	26.5	107	....	....	......	355	
2043	" 26	11.30 " " 2.30 P.M.	81–82	23.3	94	....	....	......	700	
2047	" 26	2.30 P.M. " 5.30 "	82–83	24.1	97	....	....	......	520	[layer at 7.47 P.M.
2050	" 26	5.30 " " 8.30 "	83	21.1	89	....	....	......	805	Agitated surface of sand
2054	" 26	8.30 " " 11.30 "	84	24.7	100	....	....	......	330	[at 11.54 P.M. & 2.11 A.M.
2057	" 26–27	11.30 " " 2.30 A.M.	84	20.1	89	....	....	......	477	Agitated surface of S.L.
2065	" 27	2.30 A.M. " 5.30 "	84–85	23.2	94	....	....	.....	485	[layer at 6.15 A.M.
2076	" 27	5.30 " " 8.30 "	85	23.6	96	....	....	......	575	Agitated surface of sand
2083	" 27	8.30 " " 11.30 "	86	24.0	97	....	....	......	415	[layer at 11.33 A.M.
2099	" 27	11.30 " " 2.30 P.M.	86	23.8	96	....	....	......	128	Agitated surface of sand
2103	" 27	2.30 P.M. " 5.30 "	87	21.5	87	....	....	......	1 650	[layer at 5.55 P.M.
2106	" 27	5.30 " " 8.30 "	87–88	24.2	98	....	....	......	150	Agitated surface of sand
2110	" 27	8.30 " " 11.30 "	88	23.5	95	....	....	......	117	Agitated surface of sand
2121	" 27–28	11.30 " " 2.30 A.M.	88–89	23.5	95	....	....	......	540	layer at 10.08 P.M.

TABLE No. 4.—*Continued.*

Jewell System.

Serial Number.	Collected.		Number of Run.	Rate of Filtration.		Loss of Head. Feet.	Period of Service Since Last Washing. Hours and Minutes.	Filtered Water Since Last Washing. Cubic Feet.	Bacteria per Cubic Centimeter.	Remarks.
	Date.	Hour.		Cubic Feet per Minute.	Million Gallons Per Acre per 24 Hours.					
	1896									
2127	Mar. 28	2.30 A.M. to 5.30 A.M.	89	23.8	96	....	....	......	407	Agitated surface of sand
2131	" 28	5.30 " " 8.30 "	89-90	24.8	100	....	....	......	321	layer at 3.41 A.M.
2136	" 28	8.30 A.M. " 11.30 "	90	23.9	97	....	....	......	238	Agitated surface of sand
2139	" 28	11.30 " " 2.30 P.M.	90-91	22.9	93	....	....	......	62	layer at 9.26 A.M.
2143	" 28	2.30 P.M. " 5.30 "	91	24.5	99	....	....	......	119	Agitated surface of sand
2140	" 28	5.30 " " 8.30 "	91-92	24.2	98	....	....	......	174	layer at 4.11 P.M.
2148	" 28	10.25 P.M.	92	25.0	101	....	2h. 42m.	3 826	261	C. Agitated surf. of sand
2149	" 28	10.35 "	92	25.0	101	....	2h. 52m.	4 126	186	C. layer at 10.11 P.M.
2150	" 28	10.45 "	92	24.5	99	....	3h. 02m.	4 376	313	C.
2151	" 28	10.55 "	92	24.5	99	....	3h. 13m.	4 556	221	C.
2152	" 28	11.05 "	92	24.5	99	....	3h. 22m.	4 804	243	C.
2155	" 28	8.30 P.M. to 11.30 P.M.	92	23.4	95	....	....	......	193	
2158	" 28-29	11.30 " " 2.30 A.M.	92	22.5	91	....	....	......	119	
2161	" 29	2.30 A.M. " 5.30 "	93	24.1	98	....	....	......	234	
2165	" 29	5.30 " " 8.30 "	93	24.1	98	....	....	......	177	Agitated surface of sand
2169	" 29	8.30 " " 11.30 "	93-94	23.9	97	....	....	......	294	layer at 6.17 A.M.
2173	" 29	11.30 " " 2.30 P.M.	94	23.9	97	....	....	......	580	Agitated surface of sand
2182	" 29	2.30 P.M. " 5.30 "	94	25.1	101	....	....	......	595	layer at 2.14 P.M.
2185	" 29	5.30 " " 8.30 "	94-95	23.5	95	....	....	......	240	
2189	" 29	8.30 " " 11.30 "	95	27.5	111	....	....	......	465	Agitated surface of sand
2192	" 29-30	11.30 " " 2.30 A.M.	95-96	22.7	92	....	....	......	125	layer at 9.31 P.M.
2196	" 30	2.30 A.M. " 5.30 "	96	24.6	99	....	....	......	256	
2199	" 30	5.30 " " 8.30 "	96	23.8	96	....	....	......	476	Agitated surface of sand
2203	" 30	8.30 " " 11.30 "	96-97	23.7	95	....	....	......	581	layer at 5.58 A.M.
2206	" 30	11.30 " " 2.30 P.M.	97	24.4	99	....	....	......	785	Agitated surface of sand
2210	" 30	2.30 P.M. " 5.30 "	98	25.1	101	....	....	......	672	layer at 2.01 P.M.
2216	" 31	9.15 A.M. " 11.30 A.M.	98	24.2	97	....	....	......	650	Agitated surface of sand
2220	" 31	11.30 " " 2.30 "	99-100	23.3	94	....	....	......	390	layer at 10.01 A.M.
2224	" 31	2.30 P.M. " 5.30 P.M.	100-101	24.0	97	....	....	......	1 495	Agitated surface of sand
2229	April 1	9.15 A.M. " 11.30 A.M.	102-103	23.7	95	....	....	......	845	layer at 3.05 P.M.
2234	" 1	11.30 " " 2.30 P.M.	104	23.2	93	....	....	......	545	[layer at 2.39 P.M.
2237	" 1	2.30 P.M. " 5 30 "	104	23.1	93	....	....	......	525	Agitated surface of sand
2242	" 2	9.30 A.M. " 11.30 A.M.	105	24.0	97	....	....	......	240	[layer at 11.25 P.M.
2247	" 2	11.30 " " 2.30 P.M.	105-106	24.0	97	....	....	......	224	Agitated surface of sand
2250	" 2	2.30 P.M. " 5.30 "	106	24 3	98	....	....	......	205	[layer at 11.54 A.M.
2255	" 3	9.20 A.M. " 11.30 A.M.	106-107	24.7	100	....	....	......	92	Agitated surface of sand
2262	" 3	2.30 P.M. " 5.30 P.M.	108	24.3	98	....	....	......	310	Agitated surface of sand
2267	" 4	9.30 A.M. " 11.30 A.M.	108-109	23.7	96	....	....	......	60	layer at 4.27 P.M.
2271	" 4	11.30 " " 2.30 P.M.	109	25 8	104	....	....	......	62	Agitated surface of sand
2276	" 4	2.30 P.M. " 5.30 "	109-110	23.2	94	....	....	......	90	layer at 1.09 P.M.
2281	" 6	9.20 A.M. " 11.30 A.M.	110	23.9	97	....	....	......	30	Agitated surface of sand
2286	" 6	11.30 " " 2.30 P.M.	110-111	25.2	101	....	....	......	36	layer at 9.00 A.M.
2289	" 6	2.30 P.M. " 5.30 "	111	22.9	93	....	....	......	27	Agitated surface of sand
2294	" 7	9.25 A.M. " 11.30 A.M.	112	24.8	100	....	....	......	30	layer at 2.09 P.M.
2299	" 7	11.30 " " 2.30 P.M.	112	24.4	98	....	....	......	44	Agitated surface of sand
2302	" 7	2.30 " " 5.30 "	112-113	24.3	97	....	....	......	118	layer at 12.07 P.M.
2306	" 8	11.00 A.M.	113	25.5	103	....	3h. 26m.	5 014	53	Agitated surface of sand
2307	" 8	11.10 "	113	24.5	99	....	3h. 36m.	5 244	82	layer at 11.42 A.M.
2308	" 8	11.20 "	113	24.0	97	....	3h. 46m.	5 494	88	
2310	" 8	9.20 A.M. to 11.30 A.M.	113	24.3	98	....	....	......	76	C.
2322	" 8	11.30 " " 2.30 P.M.	113	24.7	100	....	....	......	65	C.
2323	" 8	3.32 P.M.	114	22.0	89	....	03m.	61	201	
2324	" 8	3.35 "	114	24.0	97	....	06m.	131	186	
2325	" 8	3.38 "	114	25.0	101	....	09m.	211	125	
2326	" 8	3.41 "	114	25.0	101	....	12m.	291	104	
2327	" 8	3.44 "	114	25.0	101	....	15m.	361	194	
2328	" 8	3.59 "	114	25.0	101	....	30m.	711	185	
2329	" 8	4.14 "	114	25.0	101	....	45m.	1 101	75	
2331	" 8	2.30 P.M. to 5.30 P.M.	113-114	23.4	95	....	....	......	63	C.
2334	" 9	9 20 A.M. " 11.30 A.M.	114	24.0	97	....	....	......	72	C. Agitated surf. of sand
2338	" 9	11.57 A.M.	114	24.0	97	....	4h. 56m.	7 121	157	layer at 10.17 A.M.
2340	" 9	12.32 P.M.	114	24.0	97	....	5h. 31m.	7 961	182	
2341	" 9	1.02 "	114	24.0	97	....	6h. 01m.	8 621	152	

TABLE NO. 4.—*Continued.*

Jewell System.

Serial Number.	Collected. Date.	Collected. Hour.	Number of Run.	Rate of Filtration. Cubic Feet per Minute.	Rate of Filtration. Million Gallons per Acre per 24 Hours.	Loss of Head. Feet.	Period of Service Since Last Washing. Hours and Minutes.	Filtered Water Since Last Washing. Cubic Feet.	Bacteria per Cubic Centimeter.	Remarks.
	1896									
2344	April 9	11.30 A.M. to 2.30 P.M.	114–115	23.4	95	....	....	......	102	C.
2346	" 9	2.30 P.M. " 5.00 "	115	23.6	95	....	....	......	106	C. Agitated surf. of sand
2349	" 10	10.15 A.M.	115	24.0	97	....	3h. 31m.	4 983	62	layer at 4.32 P.M.
2351	" 10	10.45 "	115	24.0	97	....	4h. 01m.	5 683	33	
2353	" 10	11.15 "	115	24.0	97	....	4h. 31m.	6 313	28	
2356	" 10	11.45 "	115	25.0	101	....	5h. 01m.	6 973	39	
2368	" 10	11.30 A.M. to 2.30 P.M.	115	23.1	93	....	....	......	45	C.
2374	" 10	2.30 P.M. " 5.30 "	116	24.1	97	....	....	......	123	C.
2380	" 11	9.20 A.M. " 11.30 A.M.	116	24.5	99	....	....	......	25	C. Agitated surf. of sand
2382	" 11	12.05 P.M.	116	24.0	97	....	6h. 01m.	8 765	42	layer at 9.00 A.M.
2384	" 11	12.35 "	116	24.0	97	....	6h. 31m.	9 454	23	
2386	" 11	1.05 "	116	23.5	95	....	7h. 01m.	10 118	31	
2388	" 11	1.35 "	116	23.0	95	....	7h. 31m.	10 905	30	Shut inlet 1.34 P.M.,
2389	" 11	2.01 "	117	24.0	97	....	03m.	43	78	outlet 1.45 P.M.
2390	" 11	2.04 "	117	25.0	101	....	06m.	123	80	
2391	" 11	2.07 "	117	25.0	101	....	09m.	193	57	
2392	" 11	2.10 "	117	24.0	97	....	12m.	263	32	
2393	" 11	2.13 "	117	24.0	97	....	15m.	343	38	
2394	" 11	2.28 "	117	24.0	97	....	30m.	703	31	
2395	" 11	2.43 "	117	24.0	97	....	45m.	1 093	37	
2397	" 11	11.30 P.M. to 2.30 P.M.	116–117	24.0	97	....	....	......	47	C.
2399	" 11	3.13 P.M.	117	24.0	97	....	1h. 15m.	2 793	27	
2405	" 11	3.58 "	117	24.0	97	....	2h. 00m.	2 903	24	
2408	" 11	4.28 "	117	24.0	97	....	2h. 30m.	3 633	43	
2410	" 11	4.58 "	117	24.0	97	....	3h. 00m.	4 363	38	
2412	" 11	2.30 P.M. to 5.30 P.M.	117	24.0	97	....	....	......	18	C.
2415	" 13	9.20 A.M. " 11.30 A.M.	118	24.0	97	....	....	......	32	C.
2417	" 13	11.30 " " 2.30 P.M.	118	24.3	98	....	....	......	83	C. Agitated surf. of sand
2419	" 13	4.55 P.M.	118	23.0	93	....	6h. 41m.	9 640	81	layer at 11.53 A.M.
2422	" 14	11.30 A.M.	118	22.0	89	....	8h. 03m.	11 617	13	
2424	" 14	2.56 P.M.	119	22.0	89	....	2h. 24m.	3 401	41	[layer at 4.51 P.M.
2425	" 14	5.00 "	119	22.0	89	....	4h. 26m.	6 173	29	Agitated surface of sand
2428	" 15	10.45 A.M.	119	25.0	101	....	6h. 41m.	7 630	20	[layer at 1.26 P.M.
2429	" 15	2.43 P.M.	119	25.0	101	....	10h. 38m.	13 409	20	Agitated surface of sand
2431	" 15	4.54 "	119	25.0	101	....	12h. 47m.	16 160	20	Ag. surf. S. L. 4.53 P.M.
2434	" 16	10.40 A.M.	119	23.0	93	....	15h. 03m.	19 960	15	Shut inl. 10.39, outl. 10.49 A.M.
2435	" 16	3.05 P.M.	120	25.0	101	....	4h. 00m.	5 884	14	Agitated surface of sand
2437	" 16	5.00 "	120	25.0	101	....	5h. 56m.	8 714	5	layer at 2.36 P.M.
2440	" 17	10.40 A.M.	120	24.5	99	....	8h. 05m.	11 898	11	
2441	" 17	2.41 P.M.	121	24.5	99	....	1h. 06m.	1 621	44	
2443	" 17	4.40 "	121	24.5	99	....	3h. 05m.	4 501	44	
2446	" 18	10.35 A.M.	121	24.5	99	....	5h. 38m.	7 991	152	Agitated surface of sand
2447	" 18	2.40 P.M.	121	25.0	101	....	9h. 33m.	14 071	96	layer at 10.33 A.M.
2449	" 18	5.15 "	121	25.0	101	....	12h. 06m.	17 941	53	Agitated surface of sand
2453	" 20	10.30 A.M.	122	25.0	101	....	1h. 07m.	1 676	4	layer at 3.58 P.M.
2454	" 20	11.55 "	122	25.0	101	....	2h. 32m.	3 736	8	
2459	" 20	2.55 P.M.	122	25.0	101	....	5h. 18m.	7 696	6	Agitated surface of sand
2460	" 20	5.16 "	122	25.0	101	....	7h. 39m.	11 186	6	layer at 2.04 P.M.
2464	" 21	9.34 A.M.	122	25.0	101	....	8h. 27m.	12 396	6	
2466	" 21	10.25 "	122	25.0	101	....	9h. 18m.	13 666	19	
2469	" 21	12.41 P.M.	123	25.0	101	....	11m.	247	24	
2473	" 21	1.50 "	123	25.0	101	....	1h. 20m.	1 967	670	
2476	" 21	2.59 "	123	25.0	101	....	2h. 29m.	3 667	17	
2477	" 21	5.11 "	123	24.0	97	....	4h. 40m.	6 857	21	Agitated surface of sand
2480	" 22	9.54 A.M.	123	25.0	101	....	5h. 53m.	8 657	24	layer at 4.39 P.M.
2482	" 22	10.48 "	123	25.0	101	....	6h. 47m.	9 987	19	
2485	" 22	12.39 P.M.	123	25.0	101	....	8h. 38m.	12 727	11	
2487	" 22	1.24 "	123	25.0	101	....	9h. 23m.	13 807	8	
2490	" 22	3.00 "	123	24.0	97	....	10h. 59m.	16 187	17	Agitated surface of sand
2493	" 23	9.42 A.M.	123	24.0	97	....	13h. 00m.	20 857	21	layer at 3.58 P.M.
2494	" 23	10.23 "	123	24.0	97	....	14h. 50m.	21 887	20	Agitated surface of sand
2498	" 23	12.53 P.M.	124	25.0	101	....	28m.	675	32	layer at 10.46 A.M.
2500	" 23	2.03 "	124	24.0	97	....	1h. 38m.	2 405	14	

TABLE No. 4.—*Continued.*

Jewell System.

Serial Number.	Collected. Date.	Collected. Hour.	Number of Run.	Rate of Filtration. Cubic Feet per Minute.	Rate of Filtration. Million Gallons per Acre per 24 Hours.	Loss of Head. Feet.	Period of Service Since Last Washing. Hours and Minutes.	Filtered Water Since Last Washing. Cubic Feet.	Bacteria per Cubic Centimeter.	Remarks.
	1896									
2503	Apr. 23	3.06 P.M.	124	25.0	101	....	2h. 41m.	3 985	24	
2505	" 23	4.50 "	124	24.0	97	....	4h. 25m.	6 515	28	
2509	" 24	9.37 A.M.	124	25.0	101	....	5h. 42m.	8 865	67	
2511	" 24	11 46 "	124	25.0	101	....	7h. 49m.	11 585	41	Agitated surface of sand
2514	" 24	1.14 P.M.	124	25.0	101	..	9h. 17m.	13 795	32	layer at 10.06 A.M.
2517	" 24	[2.49 "	124	25.0	101	...	10h. 42m.	16 235	37	
2519	" 24	4.44 "	124	25.0	101	....	12h. 47m.	19 155	52	
2525	" 25	12.45 "	125	25.0	101	....	1h. 07m.	1 773	56	
2527	" 25	2.57 "	125	25.0	101	....	3h. 19m.	5 047	41	[layer at 7.46 P.M.
2532	" 27	3.20 P.M. to 9.00 P.M.	126	24.9	101	...	....	......	42	Agitated surface of sand
2536	" 27–28	9.00 " " 3.00 A.M.	126–127	24.7	100	..	....	......	47	[layer at 4.19 A.M.
2540	" 28	3.00 A.M. " 9.00 "	127	25.6	104	..	....	......	97	Agitated surface of sand
2544	" 28	9.00 " " 3.00 P.M.	127	25.4	102	...	....	......	.....	Ag. surf. of s. l. at 12.16 P.M.
2548	" 28	3.00 P.M. " 9.00 "	127–128	25.4	102	...	....	......	160	[layer at 12.21 A.M.
2551	" 28–29	9.00 " " 3.00 A.M.	128	24.9	100	...	....	......	.....	Agitated surface of sand
2557	" 29	3.00 A.M. " 9.00 "	128	25.6	103	...	....	......	.....	Ag. surf. of s. l. at 6.54 A.M.
2561	" 29	9.00 " " 3.00 P.M.	128–129	25.3	102	...	....	......	.....	[at 4.03 P.M. and 8.34 P.M.
2565	" 29	3.00 P.M. " 9.00 "	129	24.6	99	...	....	......	86	Agitated surf. of sand layer
2566	" 29	10.39 P.M.	129	22.0	89	...	12h. 30m.	18 788	102	Shut inl. 10.30, outl. 10.46 P.M.
2567	" 29	11.05 "	130	28.0	114	....	02m.	56	139	The series of results on
2568	" 29	11.07 "	130	26.0	105	....	04m.	106	86	run No. 130 was used
2569	" 29	11.09 "	130	27.0	109	...	06m.	156	86	in obtaining the aver-
2570	" 29	11.11 "	130	26.0	105	..	08m.	216	70	age bacteria for the run
2571	" 29	11.13 "	130	26.0	105	....	10m.	266	49	but not for this day.
2572	" 29	11.15 "	130	26.0	105	....	12m.	316	58	
2573	" 29	11.17 "	130	26.0	105	....	14m.	366	38	
2574	" 29	11.19 "	130	26.0	105	....	16m.	426	36	
2575	" 29	11.21 "	130	26.0	105	...	18m.	476	39	
2576	" 29	11.23 "	130	26.5	107	...	20m.	526	24	
2577	" 29	11.25 "	130	26.5	107	....	22m.	576	44	
2579	" 29	11.27 "	130	26.5	107	....	24m.	636	33	
2580	" 29	11.29 "	130	27.0	109	....	26m.	686	113	
2581	" 29	11.31 "	130	27.0	109	....	28m.	736	26	
2582	" 29	11.33 "	130	27.0	109	....	30m.	796	30	
2583a	" 29	11.38 "	130	27.5	111	....	35m.	926	38	
2583b	" 29	11.48 "	130	27.0	109	....	45m.	1 186	29	
2584	" 30	12.03 A.M.	130	26.5	107	....	1h. 00m.	1 596	26	
2585	" 30	1.03 "	130	26.0	105	...	2h. 00m.	3 116	26	
2586	" 30	2.03 "	130	26.0	105	....	3h. 00m.	4 676	24	
2589	" 29–30	9.00 P.M. to 3.00 A.M.	129–130	25.6	103	....	....	.....	74	
2590	" 30	3.03 A.M.	130	26.0	105	....	4h. 00m.	6 206	52	
2591	" 30	4.03 "	130	26.0	105	...	5h. 00m.	7 786	23	
2592	" 30	5.03 "	130	26.0	105	...	5h. 58m.	9 226	27	Agitated surface of sand
2593	" 30	6.03 "	130	26.0	105	....	6h. 58m.	10 816	53	layer at 4.44 A.M.
2594	" 30	7.03 "	130	26.0	105	....	7h. 58m.	12 346	89	
2595	" 30	8.03 "	130	26.0	105	....	8h. 58m.	13 956	34	
2599	" 30	3.00 A.M. to 9.00 A.M.	130	26.0	105	....	....	.....	34	
2600	" 30	12.57 P.M.	130	22.5	91	....	13h. 52m.	21 406	23	
2604	" 30	9.00 A.M. to 3.00 P.M.	130–131	25.0	101	....	....	......	43	[layer at 8.46 P.M.
2608	" 30	3.00 P.M. " 9.00 "	131	25.6	103	....	....	......	46	Agitated surface of sand
2630	Apr. 30–May 1	9.00 " " 3.00 A.M.	131	26.0	105	...	....	......	34	[at 5.05 and 8.03 A.M.
2640	May 1	3.00 A.M. " 9.00 "	131	24.7	100	....	....	......	65	Agitated surf. of sand layer
2647	" 1	9.00 " " 3.00 P.M.	132	27.0	109	....	....	......	52	[layer at 4.11 P.M.
2651	" 1	3.00 P.M. " 9.00 "	132	26.6	107	....	....	......	67	Agitated surface of sand
2653	" 1–2	9.00 " " 3.00 A.M.	132	25.4	103	....	....	......	78	Ag. surf. of s. l. at 1.14 A.M.
2660	" 2	3.00 A.M. " 9.00 "	132–133	25.4	103	....	....	......	46	[layer at 3 07 P.M.
2666	" 2	9.00 " " 3.45 P.M.	133	26.0	105	....	....	......	78	Agitated surface of sand
2672	" 4	9.15 " " 3.15 "	133	28.1	114	....	....	......	37	Ag. surf. s. l. at 3.10 and 6.07 P.M.
2674	" 4	7.30 P.M.	134	25.0	101	....	02m.	53	116	From May 2–9, inclusive, the
2675	" 4	7.32 "	134	25.0	101	....	04m.	113	149	results of both single sam-
2676	" 4	7.34 "	134	25.0	101	....	06m.	183	132	ples and those collected by
2677	" 4	7.36 "	134	25.0	101	....	08m.	223	61	the sampler were used to obtain the bacterial aver-
2678	" 4	7.38 "	134	25.0	101	...	10m.	263	65	ages for days and for runs.

TABLE No. 4.—*Continued.*

Jewell System.

Serial Number.	Collected. Date.	Collected. Hour.	Number of Run.	Rate of Filtration. Cubic Feet per Minute.	Rate of Filtration. Million Gallons per Acre per 24 Hours.	Loss of Head, Feet.	Period of Service Since Last Washing. Hours and Minutes.	Filtered Water Since Last Washing. Cubic Feet.	Bacteria per Cubic Centimeter.	Remarks.
	1896									
2679	May 4	7.40 P.M.	134	26.0	105	....	12m.	313	33	
2680	" 4	7.42 "	134	26.0	105	....	14m.	363	43	
2681	" 4	7.44 "	134	26.0	105	....	16m.	423	44	
2682	" 4	7.46 "	134	26.0	105	...	18m.	473	32	
2683	" 4	7.48 "	134	26.0	105	....	20m.	523	29	
2684	" 4	7.50 "	134	27.0	109	....	22m.	583	33	
2685	" 4	7.52 "	134	27.0	109	....	24m.	633	28	
2686	" 4	7.54 "	134	27.0	109	....	26m.	683	30	
2687	" 4	7.56 "	134	26.5	107	....	28m.	743	42	
2688	" 4	7.58 "	134	27.0	109	....	30m.	793	42	
2689	" 4	8.03 "	134	27.0	109	....	35m.	923	26	
2690	" 4	8.13 "	134	27.0	109	....	45m.	1 193	39	
2691	" 4	8.28 "	134	27.0	109	....	1h. 00m.	1 593	29	
2694	" 4	3.15 P.M. to 9.00 P.M.	133–134	25.0	101	....	....	......	46	
2695	" 4	9.28 P.M.	134	27.0	109	....	2h. 00m.	3 203	37	
2696	" 4	10.28 "	134	27.0	109	..	3h. 00m.	4 823	33	
2697	" 4	11.28 "	134	27.0	109	....	4h. 00m.	6 453	49	
2698	" 5	12.28 A.M.	134	27.0	109	....	5h. 00m.	8 053	47	
2699	" 5	1.28 "	134	27.0	109	....	6h. 00m.	9 663	38	
2700	" 5	2.28 "	134	27.0	109	....	7h. 00m.	11 233	90	
2703	" 4–5	9.00 P.M. to 3.00 A.M.	134	26.5	107	....	....	......	49	
2704	" 5	3.28 A.M.	134	27.0	109	....	8h. 00m.	12 893	96	
2703	" 5	4.28 "	134	27.0	109	....	9h. 00m.	14 473	86	
2706	" 5	5.28 "	134	26.5	107	....	9h. 58m.	15 923	69	Agitated surface of sand
2707	" 5	6.28 "	134	26.5	107	....	10h. 58m.	17 653	28	layer at 5.12 A.M.
2708	" 5	7.00 "	134	26.5	107	....	11h. 58m.	19 163	29	
2709	" 5	8.00 "	134	27.0	109	....	12h. 58m.	20 773	29	
2713	" 5	3.00 A.M. to 9.00 A.M.	134	26.9	109	....	....	......	37	
2714	" 5	9.28 A.M.	134	26.5	107	....	13h. 58m.	22 483	24	
2715	" 5	10.28 "	134	26.5	107	....	14h. 58m.	24 143	58	
2716	" 5	11.28 "	134	26.0	105	....	15h. 56m.	25 633	37	Agitated surface of sand
2717	" 5	12.28 P.M.	134	26.5	107	....	16h. 56m.	27 153	56	layer at 11.19 A.M.
2719	" 5	1.28 "	134	24.5	99	....	17h. 54m.	28 543	46	Agitated surface of sand
2723	" 5	9.00 A.M. to 3.00 P.M.	134–135	26.1	105	....	....	......	40	layer at 1.07 P.M.
2727	" 5	3.00 P.M. " 9.00 "	135	27.3	110	....	....	......	.....	Agitated surface of sand
2731	" 5–6	9.00 " " 3.00 A.M.	135	23.8	96	....	....	......	56	layer at 4.11 P.M.
2733	" 6	3.00 A.M. " 9.00 "	135–136	25.8	103	....	....	......	.....	Agitated surface of sand
2736	" 6	9.35 A.M.	136	26.5	107	....	1h. 40m.	2 763	25	layer at 6.35 A.M.
2743	" 6	9.00 A.M. to 3.00 P.M.	136	26.4	107	....	....	......	....	Agitated surface of sand
2744	" 6	9.00 " " 3.00 "	136	26.4	107	....	....	......	....	layer at 2.48 P.M.
2746	" 6	3.00 P.M.	136	27.0	109	....	7h. 03m.	11 213	16	
2749	" 6	3.00 P.M. to 9.00 P.M.	136	26.7	107	....	....	......	....	
2752	" 6–7	9.00 " " 3.00 A.M.	136–137	25.5	103	...	....	.. ..	85	Agitated surface of sand
2753	" 7	3.00 A.M.	137	27.0	109	...	19m.	519	80	layer at 10.21 P.M. and
2759	" 7	3.00 A.M. to 9.00 A.M.	137	26.9	109	...	....	......	.....	1.08 A.M.
2760	" 7	9.00 A.M.	137	27.0	109	...	6h. 19m.	10 189	32	[layer at 12.34 P.M.
2765	" 7	9.00 A.M. to 3.00 P.M.	137	26.8	109	...	....	......	38	Agitated surface of sand
2773	" 7	3.00 P.M. " 9.00 "	137	27.0	109	....	....	.. ..	46	Agitated surface of sand
2774	" 7	9.00 P.M.	138	26.5	107	....	08m.	192	57	layer at 6.08 and 8.25
2779	" 7–8	9.00 P.M. to 3.00 A.M.	138	26.9	109	....	....	......	... .	P.M.
2780	" 8	3.00 A.M.	138	27.0	109	....	6h. 08m.	9 852	26	
2785	" 8	3.00 A.M. to 9.00 A.M.	138	26.5	107	....	....	......	32	Agitated surface of sand
2786	" 8	9.00 A.M.	138	27.0	109	...	11h. 41m.	18 732	8	layer at 8.19 A.M.
2792	" 8	9.00 A.M. to 3.00 P.M.	138	27.8	113	....	....	......	18	
2793	" 8	3.00 P.M.	138	25.0	101	....	17h. 41m.	26 732	19	Agitated surface of sand
2798	" 8	3.00 P.M. to 9.00 P.M.	138–139	27.0	109	....	....	......	.....	layer at 3.04 P.M.
2803	" 8–9	9.00 " " 3.00 A.M.	139	26.0	105	....	....	......	.....	Agitated surface of sand
2804	" 9	3.00 A.M.	139	27.0	109	....	9h. 56m.	15 907	12	layer at 1.45 A.M.
2808	" 9	3.00 A.M. to 9.00 A.M.	139	27.0	109	....	....	... ..	....	
2813	" 9	9.00 A.M.	139	26.5	107	....	15h. 56m.	25 697	21	Agitated surface of sand
2818	" 9	3.00 "	140	28.0	114	....	4h. 16m.	7 212	39	layer at 9.31 A.M.
2825	" 11	3.00 "	141	27.0	109	....	5h. 42m.	8 955	28	[layer at 4.30 P.M.
2830	" 11	9.00 "	141	27.0	109	....	11h. 40m.	18 290	22	Agitated surface of sand

TABLE NO. 4.—*Continued.*

Jewell System.

Serial Number.	Collected. Date.	Collected. Hour.	Number of Run.	Rate of Filtration. Cubic Feet per Minute.	Rate of Filtration. Million Gallons per Acre per 24 Hours.	Loss of Head. Feet.	Period of Service Since Last Washing, Hours and Minutes.	Filtered Water Since Last Washing, Cubic Feet.	Bacteria per Cubic Centimeter.	Remarks.
	1896									
2857	May 12	3.00 A.M.	142	27.0	109	....	1h. 33m.	2 566	25	
2867	" 12	9.00 "	142	27.0	109	....	7h. 33m.	12 196	54	
2873	" 12	12.00 M.	142	27.0	109	....	10h. 31m.	16 796	22	Agitated surface of sand
2877	" 12	8.30 P.M.	143	23.0	93	....	4h. 10m.	6 711	19	layer at 10.26 A.M.
2881	" 13	2.00 A.M.	143	27.0	109	....	9h. 38m.	15 301	12	Agitated surface of sand
2885	" 13	8.00 "	143	26.5	107	....	15h. 38m.	25 031	12	layer at 1.38 A.M.
2891	" 13	1.00 P.M.	144	27.0	109	....	3h. 22m.	5 183	11	
2896	" 13	7.00 "	144	27.0	109	....	9h. 21m.	14 913	13	Agitated surface of sand
2900	" 14	3.00 A.M.	145	27.0	109	....	48m.	1 258	10	layer at 5.15 P.M.
2905	" 14	9.00 "	145	27.0	109	....	6h. 48m.	10 818	4	
2909	" 14	2.08 P.M.	145	26.0	105	...	11h. 54m.	19 118	37	Agitated surface of sand
2914	" 14	8.00 "	145	27.0	109	....	17h. 46m.	28 748	80	layer at 2.02 P.M.
2919	" 15	1.00 A.M.	146	27.0	109	....	4h. 02m.	6 430	16	
2923	" 15	8.00 "	146	27.0	109	....	11h. 02m.	17 640	16	
2927	" 15	11.00 "	146	27.0	109	....	14h. 00m.	23 340	52	Agitated surface of sand
2932	" 15	5.15 P.M.	147	26.5	107	....	3h. 14m.	5 120	14	layer at 9.09 A.M.
2961	" 15	11.00 "	147	27.0	109	...	8h. 59m.	14 280	15	
2970	" 16	5.00 A.M.	147	26.5	107	....	14h. 57m.	24 020	28	Agitated surface of sand
2981	" 16	10.00 "	148	25.0	101	....	58m.	1 700	19	layer at 4.35 A.M.
2992	" 16	3.00 P.M.	148	26.0	105	....	5h. 58m.	9 610	15	
2999	" 18	1.17 "	149	25.0	101	1.4	05m.	215	108	
3000	" 18	1.27 "	149	25.0	101	1.5	15m.	435	40	
3002	" 18	3.00 "	149	24.8	100	1.9	1h. 48m.	2 805	91	
3008	" 18	6.05 "	149	24.5	99	3.0	4h. 53m.	7 355	192	
3010	" 18	9.00 "	149	25.0	101	3.3	7h. 48m.	11 695	....	
3015	" 18	12.00 "	149	25.0	101	4.0	10h. 48m.	16 145	34	
3018	" 19	3.00 A.M.	149	25.0	101	5.4	13h. 48m.	20 655	57	
3024	" 19	6.00 "	149	25.0	101	6.0	16h. 48m.	25 155	51	
3027	" 19	8.30 "	149	25.0	101	7.0	19h. 13m.	28 845	26	
3032	" 19	12.00 M.	149	24.5	99	8.8	22h. 48m.	34 085	65	[layer at 2.22 P.M.
3036	" 19	3.00 P.M.	149	25.0	101	6.0	25h. 45m.	38 355	43	Agitated surface of sand
3041	" 19	6.00 "	149	25.0	101	8.2	28h. 45m.	42 885	37	[layer at 10.38 P.M.
3044	" 19	9.00 "	149	25.5	103	9.2	21h. 45m.	47 345	315	Agitated surface of sand
3050	" 20	1.00 A.M.	150	26.0	105	....	05m.	112	192	D. Application of chemi-
3051	" 20	1.10 "	150	25.0	101	1.3	15m.	372	99	D. cals unsatisfactory on
3053	" 20	3.00 "	150	25.0	101	1.9	2h. 05m.	3 082	79	D. run No. 150; chem-
3057	" 20	6.00 "	151	25.0	101	1.7	31m.	770	65	ical feed-pipe broken.
3060	" 20	8.30 "	151	25.0	101	2.1	3h. 01m.	4 480	32	
3069	" 20	12.00 M.	151	25.0	101	3.3	6h. 31m.	9 730	57	
3072	" 20	3.00 P.M.	151	25.0	101	5.4	9h. 31m.	14 150	30	
3077	" 20	6.00 "	151	25.0	101	6.1	12h. 31m.	18 620	56	
3082	" 20	9.00 "	151	25.0	101	8.3	15h. 31m.	23 050	41	[layer at 11.11 P.M.
3086	" 20	12.00 "	151	25.0	101	5.9	18h. 29m.	27 260	48	Agitated surface of sand
3089	" 21	3.00 A.M.	151	24.0	97	9.3	21h. 29m.	31 760	62	Agitated surf. S. L., 4.31 A.M.
3093	" 21	6.00 "	151	23.5	95	9.6	24h. 27m.	35 940	73	Agitated surface of sand
3095	" 21	7.54 "	152	25.5	103	2.3	05m.	109	231	layer at 6.16 A.M.
3096	" 21	8.04 "	152	25.5	103	1.6	15m.	379	118	
3098	" 21	8.30 "	152	25.5	103	1.6	41m.	939	60	
3101	" 21	12.00 M.	152	25.0	101	2.7	4h. 11m.	6 289	65	
3108	" 21	3.00 P.M.	152	24.5	99	...	7h. 11m.	10 889	69	
3112	" 21	6.00 "	152	25.0	101	4.3	10h. 11m.	15 319	69	
3115	" 21	9.00 "	152	25.0	101	6.1	13h. 11m.	19 759	47	
3118	" 21	12.00 "	152	25.0	101	8.1	16h. 11m.	24 229	73	
3123	" 22	3.00 "	152	23.5	95	9.6	19h. 11m.	28 639	72	[layer at 3.21 A.M.
3127	" 22	6.00 "	152	25.0	101	9.0	22h. 09m.	32 989	98	Agitated surface of sand
3130	" 22	8.30 "	152	24.0	97	9.8	24h. 37m.	36 559	88	Agitated surface of sand
3133	" 22	10.24 "	153	25.0	101	1.6	05m.	130	87	layer at 7.21 A.M.
3134	" 22	11.34 "	153	24.0	97	1.7	15m.	370	99	
3137	" 22	12.00 M.	153	25.0	101	2.0	1h. 41m.	2 580	66	
3142	" 22	3.00 P.M.	153	24.5	99	3.0	4h. 41m.	7 030	39	
3148	" 22	6.00 "	153	25.5	103	4.3	7h. 41m.	11 560	61	
3151	" 22	9.00 "	153	25.0	101	6.5	10h. 41m.	15 970	41	[layer at 11.54 P.M.
3155	" 22	12.00 "	153	25.0	101	4.2	13h. 39m.	20 340	98	Agitated surface of sand

TABLE NO. 4.—*Continued.*

Jewell System.

Serial Number.	Collected.		Number of Run.	Rate of Filtration.		Loss of Head, Feet.	Period of Service Since Last Washing. Hours and Minutes.	Filtered Water Since Last Washing. Cubic Feet.	Bacteria per Cubic Centimeter.	Remarks.
	Date.	Hour.		Cubic Feet per Minute.	Million Gallons per Acre per 24 Hours.					
	1896									
3164	May 23	9.18 A.M.	154	55.0	222	6.0	08m.	487	35	D. Run No. 154 was a
3165	" 23	9.28 "	154	55.0	222	6.0	18m.	957	23	D. special run at the
3166	" 23	9.38 "	154	55.0	222	6.0	28m.	1 447	26	D. request of Filter
3167	" 23	10.08 "	154	53.0	214	6.0	58m.	2 977	31	D. Company.
3168	" 23	10.38 "	154	50.0	202	6.1	1h. 28m.	6 617	27	D.
3175	" 25	12.00 M.	155	29.5	120	2.7	1h. 49m.	3 322	74	
3178	" 25	2.00 P.M.	155	29.0	118	4.0	3h. 49m.	6 832	43	
3182	" 25	6.00 "	155	30.0	122	5.1	7h. 49m.	14 132	28	
3185	" 25	8.00 "	155	30.0	122	6.5	9h. 49m.	17 932	21	
3189	" 25	12.00 "	155	30.0	122	5.1	13h. 47m.	24 842	34	Agitated surface of sand
3192	" 26	2.00 A.M.	155	30.0	122	6.5	15h. 47m.	28 362	34	layer at 11.09 P.M.
3198	" 26	6.00 "	155	29.0	118	4.4	19h. 45m.	35 172	35	Agitated surface of sand
3200	" 26	7.39 "	156	29.0	118	1.8	05m.	133	114	layer at 5.06 A.M.
3201	" 26	7.49 "	156	30.0	122	1.9	15m.	413	76	
3203	" 26	8.30 "	156	30.0	122	2.1	56m.	1 643	134	
3209	" 26	10.00 "	156	30.0	122	2.8	2h 26m.	4 313	25	
3213	" 26	2.00 P.M.	156	30.0	122	5.0	6h. 26m.	11 533	34	
3216	" 26	4.00 "	156	30.0	122	6.5	8h. 26m.	15 203	46	
3222	" 26	8.00 "	156	30.0	122	5.5	12h. 24m.	22 543	50	Agitated surface of sand
3225	" 26	10.00 "	156	30.0	122	7.0	14h. 24m.	26 143	52	layer at 6.20 P.M.
3229	" 27	2.00 A.M.	156	30.0	122	7.5	18h. 22m.	32 883	46	Agitated surface of sand
3233	" 27	5.10 "	157	25.0	101	1.8	11m.	130	81	layer at 11.58 P.M.
3234	" 27	5.20 "	157	30.0	122	2.1	21m.	490	73	
3237	" 27	7.30 "	157	30.0	122	3.1	2h. 31m.	4 480	46	
3241	" 27	12.00 M.	157	30.0	122	6.0	7h. 01m.	12 670	135	[layer at 2.14 P.M.
3246	" 27	3.00 P.M.	157	29.0	118	5.1	9h. 59m.	17 710	30	Agitated surface of sand
3256	" 27	6.00 "	157	30.0	122	6.9	12h. 59m.	22 980	34	Agitated surface of sand
3261	" 27	9.20 "	158	30.0	122	2.0	05m.	182	206	layer at 7.13 P.M.
3262	" 27	9.30 "	158	30.0	122	2.0	15m.	422	152	
3265	" 27	12.00 "	158	30.0	122	3.3	2h. 45m.	4 982	57	
3267	" 28	3.00 A.M.	158	30.0	122	7.1	5h. 45m.	10 342	51	Agitated surface of sand
3273	" 28	6.00 "	158	30.0	122	5.9	8h. 43m.	15 702	47	layer at 3.11 A.M.
3276	" 28	7.30 "	158	30.0	122	7.3	10h. 13m.	18 362	43	Agitated surface of sand
3280	" 28	10.00 "	158	29.5	120	7.0	12h. 41m.	22 402	54	layer at 7.51 A.M.
3283	" 28	11.00 "	159	29.5	120	1.9	05m.	157	246	
3284	" 28	11.20 "	159	29.0	120	2.0	15m.	447	158	
3295	" 28	2.00 P.M.	159	30.0	122	2.9	2h. 55m.	5 177	162	
3298	" 28	4.00 "	159	30.0	122	4.2	4h. 55m.	8 737	300	
3306	" 28	8.00 "	160	30.0	122	2.7	2h. 30m.	4 497	423	D.
3310	" 28	9.35 "	161	30.0	122	2.0	05m.	193	668	D.
3311	" 28	9.45 "	161	30.0	122	2.0	15m.	443	560	D.
3312	" 28	9.58 "	161	30.0	122	2.0	28m.	633	650	D. Prescribed amount
3316	" 28	11.05 "	162	30.0	122	1.9	05m.	157	460	D. of chemicals in-
3320	" 28	11.25 "	162	30.0	122	2.0	13m.	337	345	D. sufficient.
3326	" 29	12.56 A.M.	163	30.0	122	2.0	05m.	165	715	D.
3330	" 29	1.06 "	163	30.0	122	2.1	15m.	435	394	D.
3333	" 29	2.00 "	163	30.0	122	2.3	1h. 09m.	2 065	510	D.
3340	" 29	4.00 "	163	30.0	122	4.8	3h. 09m.	5 625	363	
3342	" 29	4.35 "	163	30.0	122	5.7	3h. 44m.	6 635	275	
3346	" 29	5.59 "	164	28.0	114	2.1	05m.	293	151	
3348	" 29	6.09 "	164	24.0	97	2.2	15m.	473	149	
3356	" 29	7.30 "	164	25.0	101	2.2	1h. 36m.	2 523	80	
3361	" 29	12.05 P.M.	165	29.5	120	2.5	45m.	875	212	
3364	" 29	2.00 "	166	29.5	120	3.1	1h. 00m.	1 888	129	
3368	" 29	6.00 "	169	30.0	122	2.0	28m.	954	465	
3375	" 29	8.19 "	171	30.0	122	2.1	15m.	493	118	
3380	" 30	12.27 A.M.	174	20.0	81	1.1	15m.	344	128	
3384	" 30	2.00 "	174	20.0	81	1.5	1h. 48m.	2 164	222	
3388	" 30	6.26 "	175	29.5	120	2.1	26m.	720	415	
3394	" 30	8.00 "	176	29.5	120	2.1	14m.	402	275	
3400	" 30	10.15 "	177	30.0	122	2.2	30m.	903	475	
3401	" 30	12.00 M.	178	30.0	122	2.1	28m.	863	169	Agitated surface of sand
3434	June 2	3.50 P.M.	179	34.0	138	3.3	29m.	1 001	289	layer at 3.27 P.M.

TABLE No. 4.—*Continued.*

Jewell System.

Serial Number.	Collected. Date.	Collected. Hour.	Number of Run.	Rate of Filtration. Cubic Feet per Minute.	Rate of Filtration. Million Gallons per Acre per 24 Hours.	Loss of Head. Feet.	Period of Service Since Last Washing. Hours and Minutes.	Filtered Water Since Last Washing. Cubic Feet.	Bacteria per Cubic Centimeter.	Remarks.
	1896									
3436	June 2	4.37 P.M.	179	34.5	140	4.0	1h. 16m.	2 701	620	
3439	" 2	6.20 "	181	20.5	83	2.1	15m.	410	191	
3442	" 2	10.37 "	182	27.0	109	5.1	2h. 25m.	3 989	22	
3447	" 3	3.30 A.M.	183	25.0	101	3.1	2h. 56m.	4 448	36	
3451	" 3	6 00 "	184	25.0	101	2.7	31m.	745	44	
3454	" 3	9.00 "	184	25.0	101	....	3h. 31m.	5 345	26	
3458	" 3	12.00 M.	184	25.0	101	6.7	6h. 26m.	434	25	
3460	" 3	2.00 P.M.	184	20.0	81	9.5	8h. 13m.	2 145	50	Agitated surface of sand
3464	" 3	4.30 "	185	24.5	99	2.5	2h. 10m.	3 356	70	layer at 1 06 P.M.
3468	" 3	6.00 "	185	25.0	101	3.4	3h. 40m.	5 526	144	
3472	" 3	9 00 "	186	25.0	101	2.0	1h. 21m.	2 061	16	
3478	" 3	12.00 "	186	25.0	101	4.6	4h. 21m.	6 451	36	[layer at 1.41 A.M.
3482	" 4	3.00 A.M.	186	25.0	101	8.5	7h. 14m.	10 741	36	Agitated surface of sand
3484	" 4	3.30 "	186	21.0	85	..	7h. 44m.	11 451	64	Shut inlet 3.27 P.M., out-
3487	" 4	6.00 "	187	25.0	101	2.1	2h. 07m.	3 198	43	let 3.38 P.M.
3492	" 4	9 00 "	187	..	.....	....	5h. 07m.	7 588	43	
3496	" 4	10.37 "	187	25.5	103	7.0	6h. 44m.	9 948	54	
3498	" 4	12.02 P.M.	187	23.0	93	9.7	8h. 09m.	11 978	38	
3501	" 4	3.43 "	189	25.0	101	1.7	21m.	851	24	
3506	" 4	6.05 "	189	25.0	101	2.4	2h. 53m.	4 611	116	
3509	" 4	8.40 "	190	25.0	101	2.1	2h. 12m.	3 422	61	
3511	" 4	9.55 "	190	25.0	101	3.2	3h. 27m.	5 442	71	Shut inlet 9.53 P.M., out-
3512	" 4	10.22 "	191	25.0	101	1.7	02m.	50	78	let 10.01 P.M.
3513	" 4	10.24 "	191	25.0	101	1.7	04m.	100	44	
3514	" 4	10.26 "	191	27.5	111	1.7	06m.	155	35	
3515	" 4	10.28 "	191	27.5	111	1.7	08m.	210	33	
3516	" 4	10.30 "	191	25.0	101	1.7	10m.	260	22	
3517	" 4	10.32 "	191	25.0	101	1.7	12m.	310	29	
3518	" 4	10.34 "	191	27.0	109	1.7	14m.	365	33	
3519	" 4	10.36 "	191	25.0	101	1.7	16m.	415	23	
3520	" 4	10.38 "	191	27.0	109	1.7	18m.	470	27	
3521	" 4	10.40 "	191	25.0	101	1.7	20m.	520	43	
3522	" 4	10.42 "	191	27.0	109	1.7	22m.	575	10	
3523	" 4	10.44 "	191	27.0	109	1.7	24m.	630	15	
3524	" 4	10.46 "	191	25.0	101	1.7	26m.	680	87	
3525	" 4	10.48 "	191	25.0	101	1.7	28m.	730	99	
3526	" 4	10.50 "	191	25.0	101	1.7	30m.	780	11	
3527	" 4	10.52 "	191	25.0	101	1.7	32m.	830	114	
3528	" 4	10.55 "	191	25.0	101	1.7	35m.	910	17	
3529	" 4	11.05 "	191	25.0	101	1.7	45m.	1 160	16	
3530	" 4	11.20 "	191	25.0	101	1.8	1h. 00m.	1 540	25	
3531	" 4	11.50 "	191	25.0	101	2.0	1h. 30m.	2 350	52	
3535	" 5	12.20 A.M.	191	25.0	101	2.1	2h. 00m.	3 100	27	
3536	" 5	12.50 "	191	25.0	101	2.1	2h. 30m.	3 870	46	
3537	" 5	1.20 "	191	25.0	101	2.2	3h. 00m.	4 620	33	
3539	" 5	3.22 "	192	30.0	122	2.3	1h. 02m	1 848	18	
3543	" 5	6.00 "	192	29.5	120	3.9	3h. 40m.	6 528	94	
3556	" 5	4.55 P.M.	197	35.0	142	2.5	35m.	1 134	81	
3559	" 5	10.00 "	200	30.0	132	2.1	50m.	1 519	7	
3586	" 6	2.30 A.M.	201	25.0	101	2.1	2h. 12m.	3 386	9	
3596	" 6	7.48 "	203	25.0	101	1.7	53m.	1 312	14	
3624	" 6	10.55 "	203	25.0	101	2.6	4h. 00m.	5 992	29	
3629	" 6	1.55 P.M.	204	34.5	140	2.9	1h. 03m.	2 016	14	
3632	" 6	3.00 "	204	33.5	136	3.1	2h. 08m.	4 116	12	
3657	" 9	12.50 "	205	25.0	101	2.1	1h. 54m.	2 854	170	
3660	" 9	5.00 "	206	25.0	101	1.9	1h. 22m.	2 074	39	
3669	" 10	11.15 A.M.	207	25.0	101	1.6	56m.	1 415	11	Agitated surface of sand
3672	" 10	1.00 P.M.	207	25.0	101	2.6	2h. 41m.	4 045	9	layer at 10.06 A.M.
3676	" 10	3.30 "	207	25.0	101	5.2	4h. 11m.	6 925	13	
3682	" 11	10.32 A.M.	207	25.0	101	5.7	8h. 41m.	12 945	14	
3685	" 11	1.00 P.M.	208	25.0	101	1.7	25m.	644	7	
3693	" 11	3.42 "	208	25.0	101	2.6	3h. 07m.	4 804	10	
3699	" 12	11.11 A.M.	209	25.0	101	1.7	31m.	704	9	

TABLE No. 4.—*Continued.*

Jewell System.

Serial Number.	Collected. Date.	Collected. Hour.	Number of Run.	Rate of Filtration. Cubic Feet per Minute.	Rate of Filtration. Million Gallons per Acre per 24 Hours.	Loss of Head. Feet.	Period of Service Since Last Washing. Hours and Minutes.	Filtered Water Since Last Washing. Cubic Feet.	Bacteria per Cubic Centimeter.	Remarks.
	1896									
3703	June 12	1.38 P.M.	209	25.0	101	2.3	2h. 58m.	4 474	12	
3706	" 12	2.48 "	209	25.0	101	2.8	4h. 09m.	6 184	12	
3713	" 13	11.02 A.M.	210	25.0	101	1.5	22m.	485	23	
3719	" 13	1.00 P.M.	210	25.0	101	2.1	2h. 20m.	3 585	15	
3725	" 13	2.55 "	210	25.0	101	2.7	4h. 15m.	6 465	51	
3728	" 13	5.02 "	210	25.0	101	4.3	6h. 12m.	9 335	71	
3737	" 15	9.00 "	210	....	.....	....	6h. 40m.	10 128	1 153	B. Collected before the filter was in operation and after period of rest of 39 hours 30 minutes.
3741	" 15	10.15 A.M.	211	25.0	101	1.7	50m.	1 248	10	
3744	" 15	12.23 P.M.	211	25.0	101	2.7	2h. 58m.	4 484	25	
3748	" 15	3.02 "	212	25.0	101	1.7	37m.	1 005	19	
3754	" 15	4.31 "	212	25 0	101	2.1	2h. 06m.	3 355	11	
3760	" 16	10.25 A.M.	213	38.0	154	3.7	38m.	1 429	9	
3764	" 16	12.38 P.M.	214	38.0	154	3.1	32m.	1 276	5	
3797	" 18	10.10 A.M.	216	25.0	101	1.7	1h. 07m.	1 718	28	
3802	" 18	12.34 P.M.	216	25.0	101	3.1	3h. 31m.	5 398	15	
3810	" 18	2.49 "	216	25.0	101	5.0	5h. 46m.	8 678	8	
3815	" 18	4.55 "	216	25.0	101	7.4	7h. 47m.	11 678	28	[layer at 11.23 A M.
3819	" 19	10.00 A.M.	216	25.0	101	7.9	9h. 22m.	14 118	39	Agitated surface of sand
3825	" 19	12.56 P.M.	216	....	.....	....	12h. 13m.	18 346	40	Shut outlet 12.56 P.M.
3830	" 19	2.59 "	217	25.0	101	1.8	45m.	1 072	69	
3846	" 19	4.32 "	217	25.0	101	1.8	2h. 18m.	3 422	64	
3860	" 20	11.33 A.M.	218	25.0	101	1.6	38m.	976	67	
3863	" 20	12.43 P.M.	218	25.5	103	1.7	1h. 48m.	2 716	69	
3872	" 20	3.42 "	219	25.0	101	1.6	25m.	638	88	
3875	" 20	4.38 "	219	25.0	101	1.6	1h. 21m.	2 038	101	
3884	" 22	9.00 A.M.	219	....	.....	....	....	......	69	B. Coll. before filter was in operation and after rest of 39h. 30m.
3889	" 22	10.15 "	219	25.0	101	2.0	3h. 28m.	5 258	74	
3891	" 22	12.25 P.M.	219	....	.....	....	5h. 38m.	8 538	300	A. Shut inlet 12.21 P.M., outlet 12.31 P.M.
3895	" 22	1.18 "	220	25.0	101	1.6	23m.	533	96	
3900	" 22	3.01 "	220	25.0	101	2.1	2h. 06m.	3 213	79	
3904	" 22	5.00 "	220	25.0	101	2.6	4h. 05m.	6 243	97	
3910	" 23	9.52 A.M.	220	....	.....	....	5h. 25m.	8 275	.....	Shut outlet 9.52 A.M.
3925	" 23	11.12 "	221	25.0	101	1.8	58m.	1 438	216	
3927	" 23	1.30 P.M.	221	25.0	101	2.1	3h. 16m.	4 918	.....	
3931	" 23	3.20 "	221	25.0	101	1.7	5h. 06m.	7 688	62	
3934	" 23	4.42 "	221	....	.....	....	6h. 28m.	9 759	77	Shut outlet 4.42 P.M.
3039	" 24	10.17 A.M.	222	25.0	101	1.8	1h. 33m.	2 389	840	
3948	" 24	12.39 P.M.	222	....	.....	....	3h. 55m.	5 946	470	Shut outlet 12.39 P.M.
3951	" 24	1.34 "	223	25.0	101	1.6	38m.	793	385	
3955	" 24	3.24 "	223	25.0	101	1.8	2h. 28m.	3 643	355	
3965	" 24	4.51 "	223	25.9	101	2.1	3h. 55m.	5 753	215	
3979	" 25	9.50 A.M.	224	25.0	101	1.4	03m.	93	45	
3980	" 25	9.55 "	224	25.0	101	1.4	08m.	223	.....	
3981	" 25	10.00 "	224	26.0	105	1.4	13m.	353	.....	
3982	" 25	10.05 "	224	25.0	101	1.4	18m.	483	57	
3983	" 25	10.10 "	224	25 0	101	1.5	23m.	613	215	
3984	" 25	10.15 "	224	25.0	101	1.5	28m.	733	515	
3985	" 25	10.20 "	224	25.0	101	1.6	33m.	863	1 750	
3987	" 25	10.25 "	224	25.0	101	1.6	38m.	983	362	
3988	" 25	10.30 "	224	25.0	101	1.6	43m.	1 103	1 780	
3991	" 25	10.35 "	224	25.0	101	1.6	48m.	1 233	215	
3992	" 25	10.40 "	224	25.0	101	1.6	53m.	1 353	445	
3993	" 25	10.45 "	224	25.0	101	1.6	58m.	1 473	950	
3994	" 25	10.50 "	224	26.0	105	1.7	1h. 03m.	1 613	249	
3995	" 25	11.05 "	224	25.0	101	1.7	1h. 18m.	1 983	420	
3996	" 25	11.20 "	224	25.0	101	1.7	1h. 33m.	2 373	990	
3997	" 25	11.35 "	224	25.0	101	1.7	1h. 48m.	2 753	395	
3998	" 25	11.50 "	224	25.0	101	1.9	2h. 03m.	3 163	900	
3999	" 25	12.05 P.M.	224	25.0	101	1.9	2h. 18m.	3 523	365	
4002	" 25	1.15 "	225	25.0	101	1.7	46m.	1 166	510	
4005	" 25	2.31 "	225	....	.....	....	2h. 02m.	3 060	250	Shut outlet 2.31 P.M.
4006	" 25	3.16 "	226	25.0	101	1.4	13m.	236	600	
4009	" 25	4.25 "	226	....	.....	....	1h. 22m.	2 091	173	Shut outlet 4.25 P.M.

TABLE NO. 4.—*Continued.*

Jewell System.

Serial Number.	Collected. Date.	Collected. Hour.	Number of Run.	Rate of Filtration. Cubic Feet per Minute.	Rate of Filtration. Million Gallons per Acre per 24 Hours.	Loss of Head. Feet.	Period of Service Since Last Washing. Hours and Minutes.	Filtered Water Since Last Washing. Cubic Feet.	Bacteria per Cubic Centimeter.	Remarks.
	1896									
4013	June 25	5.00 P.M.	227	25.0	101	1.5	18m.	465	347	
4024	" 26	10.27 A.M.	227	25.0	101	1.8	2h. 14m.	3 235	23	
4028	" 26	11.40 "	227	....	.....	....	3h. 27m.	5 204	61	Shut inlet 11.37 A.M.,
4031	" 26	1.14 P.M.	228	25.0	101	1.9	1h. 16m.	1 921	19	outlet 11.47 A.M.
4034	" 26	2.35 "	228	....	.....	....	2h. 37m.	4 026	79	Outlet closed for wash.
4035	" 26	3.30 "	229	25.0	101	2.0	40m.	1 005	9	
4037	" 26	4.50 "	229	25.0	101	1.8	2h. 00m.	2 945	29	[wasting at end of run.
4042	" 27	9.20 A.M.	229	....	.....	....	....	......	143	Waste. Collected after
4044	" 27	10.26 "	230	25.0	101	1.7	32m.	839	44	
4048	" 27	12.10 P.M.	230	....	.....	....	2h. 16m.	3 425	94	Shut inlet 12.06 P.M.,
4052	" 27	1.58 "	231	25.0	101	1.9	1h. 29m.	2 194	315	outlet 12.16 P.M.
4055	" 27	3.20 "	232	25.0	101	1.5	15m.	441	39	
4056	" 27	4.46 "	232	25.0	101	1.5	1h. 41m.	2 551	41	
4062	" 29	10.16 A.M.	233	25.0	101	1.7	36m.	937	4	
4064	" 29	11.49 "	233	25.0	101	2.1	2h. 09m.	3 577	6	
4068	" 29	1.28 P.M.	233	25.0	101	2.2	3h. 48m.	5 787	9	
4070	" 29	3.38 "	233	25.0	101	6.6	5h. 58m.	9 067	11	
4073	" 29	5.13 "	233	25.0	101	9.6	7h. 33m.	11 267	9	Agitated surface of sand
4082	" 30	10.14 A.M.	234	25.0	101	1.8	23m.	630	7	layer at 9.00 A.M.
4100	" 30	12.45 P.M.	234	23.5	95	2.6	2h. 54m.	4 270	5	
4105	" 30	2.52 "	234	23.5	95	6.1	5h. 01m.	7 290	3	
4108	" 30	4.31 "	234	23.5	95	4.1	6h. 31m.	9 338	4	[layer at 11.20 A.M.
4114	July 1	10.25 A.M.	234	23.5	95	9.0	8h. 53m.	12 730	*	Agitated surface of sand
4116	" 1	11.25 "	234	21.0	85	1.4	9h. 50m.	13 942	.....	Wasting 1 min., 10 cu.ft.
4117	" 1	11.28 "	234	21.0	85	1.4	9h. 50m.	13 942	.....	" 4 " 100 "
4118	" 1	11.31 "	234	21.0	85	1.4	9h. 50m.	13 942	.....	" 7 " 150 "
4119	" 1	11.34 "	234	21.0	85	1.4	9h. 50m.	13 942	.....	Opening outlet.
4120	" 1	11.37 "	234	22.0	89	1.4	9h. 53m.	14 010	.....	
4121	" 1	11.40 "	234	23.5	95	1.5	9h. 55m.	14 060	.....	
4123	" 1	1.17 P.M.	234	23.0	93	10.7	11h. 32m.	16 080	.....	[layer at 2.11 P.M.
4125	" 1	2.08 "	234	15.0	61	11.2	12h. 23m.	16 890	.....	Agitated surface of sand
4126	" 1	2.14 "	234	15.0	61	8.7	12h. 27m.	16 937	.....	Starting to waste.
4127	" 1	2.16 "	234	16.0	65	9.0	12h. 27m.	16 937	.....	Wasting 2 min., 45 cu.ft.
4128	" 1	2.18 "	234	18.0	73	9.5	12h. 27m.	16 937	.....	" 4 " 95 "
4129	" 1	2.22 "	234	18.0	73	9.5	12h. 27m.	16 937	.....	" 8 " 155 "
4130	" 1	2.27 "	234	17.0	69	9.6	12h. 27m.	16 937	.....	Opening outlet.
4135	" 1	4.34 "	235	23.5	95	1.2	39m.	951	.....	
4144	" 2	10.29 A.M.	235	23.5	95	2.1	3h. 01m.	4 231	49	
4148	" 2	11.30 "	235	23.5	95	....	4h. 02m.	5 701	3	
4149	" 2	12.00 M.	235	....	.....	....	4h. 32m.	6 406	115	Shut outlet 12.00 M.
4152	" 2	12.35 P.M.	236	23.5	95	1.1	11m.	325	144	
4153	" 2	1.04 "	236	23.5	95	1.2	40m.	965	111	
4157	" 2	3.05 "	237	23.5	95	1.6	50m.	1 155	9	
4165	" 3	10.14 A.M.	237	23.5	95	6.2	4h. 29m.	6 295	0	
4170	" 3	12.15 P.M.	237	....	.....	....	30m.	8 965	2	Shut outlet 12.15 P.M.
4173	" 3	12.50 "	238	23.5	95	1.2	05m.	114	6	
4174	" 3	12.55 "	238	23.0	93	1.2	10m.	244	10	
4175	" 3	1.00 "	238	20.0	81	1.3	15m.	344	1	
4176	" 3	1.05 "	238	22.0	89	1.4	20m.	454	8	
4177	" 3	1.10 "	238	24.0	97	1.4	25m.	594	15	
4179	" 3	1.15 "	238	25.0	101	1.4	30m.	724	10	
4180	" 3	1.20 "	238	23.0	93	1.5	35m.	834	13	
4181	" 3	1.25 "	238	24.0	97	1.6	40m.	954	8	
4182	" 3	1.30 "	238	23.5	95	1.6	45m.	1 064	7	
4183	" 3	1.35 "	238	24.0	97	1.7	50m.	1 194	13	
4184	" 3	1.40 "	238	23.5	95	1.8	55m.	1 214	6	
4185	" 3	1.45 "	238	23.5	95	1.8	1h. 00m.	1 344	11	
4188	" 3	2.00 "	238	23.0	93	1.8	1h. 15m.	1 794	11	
4189	" 3	2.15 "	238	23.5	95	1.8	1h. 30m.	2 164	125	
4190	" 3	2.30 "	238	23.5	95	1.8	1h. 45m.	2 504	8	
4191	" 3	2.45 "	238	23.5	95	1.9	2h. 00m.	2 864	6	
4192	" 3	3.00 "	238	23.5	95	2.0	2h. 15m.	3 204	24	
4193	" 3	3.15 "	238	23.5	95	2.1	2h. 30m.	3 574	14	

* The bacterial results of July 1 were lost through melting of the culture medium.

TABLE NO. 4.—*Continued.*

Jewell System.

Serial Number.	Collected.		Number of Run.	Rate of Filtration.		Loss of Head. Feet.	Period of Service Since Last Washing. Hours and Minutes.	Filtered Water Since Last Washing. Cubic Feet.	Bacteria per Cubic Centimeter.	Remarks.
	Date.	Hour.		Cubic Feet per Minute.	Million Gallons per Acre per 24 Hours.					
	1896									
4194	July 3	3.30 P.M.	238	23.5	95	2.2	2h. 45m.	3 924	16	
4229	" 6	3.27 "	239	23.5	95	....	37m.	960	281	
4233a	" 6	4.25 "	239	24.0	97	6.8	1h. 35m.	2 380	223	
4234	" 6	5.00 "	239	25.0	101	2.3	2h. 08m.	3 130	357	Agitated surface of sand
4234a	" 6	5.03 "	239	25.0	101	2.5	2h. 11m.	3 210	362	layer at 4.53 P.M.
4235	" 6	5.06 "	239	25.0	101	2.5	2h. 14m.	3 280	372	
4236	" 6	5.09 "	239	25.0	101	2.7	2h. 17m.	3 340	399	
4237	" 6	5.12 "	239	25.0	101	2.7	2h. 20m.	3 420	393	
4238	" 6	5.15 "	239	25.0	101	2.8	2h. 23m.	3 500	435	
4246	" 7	10.00 A.M.	239	25.0	101	5.0	3h. 38m.	5 680	997	[layer at 12.24 P.M.
4253	" 7	1.00 P.M.	239	24.5	99	7.6	7h. 36m.	10 020	341	Agitated surface of sand
4257	" 7	2.43 "	239	25.0	101	2.0	8h. 17m.	12 870	336	Agitated surface of sand
4258	" 7	4.59 "	240	23.5	95	3.3	1h. 34m.	2 364	247	layer at 2.12 P.M.
4275	" 8	5.10 "	241	23.5	95	2.9	54m.	1 360	99	
4280	" 9	10.25 A.M.	242	24.0	97	2.1	22m.	522	15	
4283	" 9	12.20 P.M.	242	23.0	93	4.7	2h. 17m.	3 192	0	
4302	" 9	3.25 "	242	25.0	101	6.3	5h. 20m.	7 562	14	Agitated surface of sand layer
4315	" 10	11.15 A.M.	243	25.0	101	4.9	2h. 11m	4 292	38	at 2.15 P.M. and 4.35 P.M.
4318	" 10	1.09 P.M.	243	21.5	87	9.6	4h. 05m.	5 982	50	Agitated surface of sand
4321	" 10	3.14 "	244	25.0	101	2.3	50m.	1 281	29	layer at 1.27 P.M.
4325	" 10	5.29 "	245	25.0	101	2.0	22m.	534	44	
4329	" 11	10.37 A.M.	245	24.5	99	4.1	2h. 00m.	2 934	39	
4334	" 11	1.08 P.M.	246	25.0	101	2.1	38m.	920	3	
4347	" 11	3.14 "	247	23.5	95	1.9	17m.	394	3	
4362	" 11	5.08 "	247	19.5	79	....	2h. 11m.	3 044	52	
4369	" 13	10.30 A.M.	248	25.0	101	1.9	13m.	363	22	
4371	" 13	11.51 "	248	24.5	99	3.6	1h. 34m.	2 383	25	
4373	" 13	3.00 P.M.	248	25.0	101	5.1	4h. 43m.	6 973	73	
4378	" 13	5.15 "	249	25.0	101	1.7	04m.	180	58	
4397	" 14	10.21 A.M.	249	25.0	101	4.2	1h. 40m.	2 040	5	[layer at 12.16 P.M.
4410	" 14	1.27 P.M.	249	25.0	101	5.1	4h. 44m.	7 020	7	Agitated surface of sand
4423	" 14	3.29 "	249	25.0	101	5.8	6h. 44m.	9 910	9	Agitated surface of sand
4426	" 14	5.21 "	250	25.0	101	1.9	14m.	423	2	layer at 3.21 P.M.
4430	" 15	10.31 A.M.	250	25.0	101	2.8	1h. 55m.	4 203	6	
4431	" 15	11.32 "	250	25.0	101	2.8	2h. 55m.	4 228	23	Agitated surface of sand
4432	" 15	11.33 "	250	25.0	101	2.8	2h. 56m.	4 253	5	layer at 11.28 A.M.
4433	" 15	11.34 "	250	25.0	101	2.8	2h. 57m.	4 278	2	
4434	" 15	11.35 "	250	25.0	101	2.8	2h. 58m.	4 293	5	
4435	" 15	11.36 "	250	25.5	103	2.8	2h. 59m.	4 318	4	
4436	" 15	11.37 "	250	26.0	105	2.8	3h. 00m.	4 348	9	
4437	" 15	11.38 "	250	25.0	101	2.8	3h. 01m.	4 373	11	
4438	" 15	11.39 "	250	25.0	101	2.8	3h. 02m.	4 398	6	
4439	" 15	11.40 "	250	25.0	101	2.8	3h. 03m.	4 423	15	
4440	" 15	11.57 "	250	25.0	101	3.0	3h. 20m.	5 833	9	
4441	" 15	12.58 P.M.	250	25.5	103	5.0	4h. 21m.	6 393	3	
4444	" 15	2.11 "	250	25.0	101	7.7	5h. 34m.	7 233	3	
4449	" 15	3.26 "	250	26.0	105	6.8	6h. 47m.	9 973	16	Agitated surface of sand
4453	" 15	5.20 "	251	25.0	101	2.2	27m.	706	12	layer at 3.04 P.M.
4457	" 16	9.42 A.M.	251	25.0	101	2.9	1h. 19m.	1 846	9	
4460	" 16	11.06 "	251	25.0	101	5.7	2h. 43m.	3 936	8	
4470	" 16	1.14 P.M.	251	25.0	101	4.0	4h. 44m.	6 906	5	Agitated surface of sand
4474	" 16	2.45 "	251	25.0	101	7.1	6h. 15m.	9 136	31	layer at 12.42 P.M.
4496	" 16	5.03 "	252	25.0	101	2.1	29m.	582	2	
4504	" 17	2.45 "	252	25.0	101	3.5	2h. 06m.	3 052	5	
4511	" 18	10.19 A.M.	253	25.0	101	2.0	05m.	146	32	
4512	" 18	10.24 "	253	24.5	99	2.0	10m.	256	19	
4513	" 18	10.29 "	253	25.0	101	2.1	15m.	386	.....	
4514	" 18	10.34 "	253	25.0	101	2.2	20m.	506	.....	
4515	" 16	10.39 "	253	25.0	101	2.3	25m.	636	12	
4516	" 18	10.44 "	253	25.0	101	2.4	30m.	766	10	
4517	" 18	10.49 "	253	25.0	101	2.4	35m.	906	5	
4518	" 18	10.54 "	253	25.0	101	2.5	40m.	1 006	8	
4519	" 18	10.59 "	253	25.0	101	2.5	45m.	1 136	8	

TABLE NO 4.—*Continued.*

Jewell System.

Serial Number.	Collected. Date.	Collected. Hour.	Number of Run.	Rate of Filtration. Cubic Feet per Minute.	Rate of Filtration. Million Gallons per Acre per 24 Hours.	Loss of Head. Feet.	Period of Service Since Last Washing. Hours and Minutes.	Filtered Water Since Last Washing. Cubic Feet.	Bacteria per Cubic Centimeter.	Remarks.
	1896									
4520	July 18	11.04 A.M.	253	25.0	101	2.7	50m.	1 276	5	
4521	" 18	11.09 "	253	25.0	101	2.8	55m.	1 386	235	
4522	" 18	11.14 "	253	25.0	101	3.0	1h. 00m.	1 526	83	
4523	" 18	11.29 "	253	25.0	101	3.1	1h. 15m.	2 006	.....	
4526	" 18	11.44 "	253	25.0	101	4.1	1h. 30m.	2 286	8	
4531	" 18	11.59 "	253	25.0	101	4.7	1h. 45m.	2 676	5	
4532	" 18	12.14 P.M.	253	25.0	101	5.5	2h. 00m.	3 056	5	
4533	" 18	12.44 "	253	25.0	101	7.4	2h. 30m.	3 886	8	
4534	" 18	1.14 "	253	23.0	93	9.1	3h. 00m.	4 516	4	
4535	" 18	1.21 "	253	24.0	97	3.5	3h. 05m.	4 616	4	Agitated surface of sand
4536	" 18	1.22 "	253	23 5	95	3.5	3h. 06m.	4 659	97	layer at 1.19 P.M.
4537	" 18	1.23 "	253	15.0	61	3.5	3h. 07m.	4 659	182	
4538	" 18	1.24 "	253	18.0	73	3.6	3h. 07m.	4 659	62	Wasting 1 min., 20cu. ft.
4539	" 18	1.25 "	253	18.0	73	3.6	3h. 07m.	4 659	30	" 2 " 40 "
4540	" 18	1.26 "	253	22.5	91	3.7	3h. 07m.	4 659	27	" 3 " 65 "
4541	" 18	1.27 "	253	21.5	87	3.7	3h. 07m.	4 659	17	Opening outlet.
4542	" 18	1.28 "	253	22.5	91	3.8	3h. 08m.	4 691	12	
4543	" 18	1.29 "	253	23.0	93	3.8	3h. 09m.	4 721	14	
4544	" 18	1.30 "	253	23.5	95	3.8	3h. 10m.	4 746	6	
4545	" 18	1.44 "	253	25.5	103	4.6	3h. 24m.	5 196	17	
4553	" 18	2.14 "	253	25.5	103	6.6	3h. 54m.	5 846	5	
4554	" 18	2.44 "	253	25.0	101	8.2	4h. 24m.	6 596	4	[layer at 3.19 P.M.
4556	" 18	3.14 "	253	25.0	101	9.7	4h. 54m.	7 286	9	Agitated surface of sand
4557	" 18	3.24 "	253	....	.....	....	4h. 59m.	7 296	157	Wasting 2 min., 45 cu. ft.
4559	" 18	3.44 "	253	25.0	101	7.7	5h. 15m.	7 776	10	
4560	" 18	4.14 "	253	22.0	89	9.3	5h. 45m.	8 496	42	
4565	" 18	5.21 "	254	25.0	101	2.0	21m.	530	5	
4571	" 20	11.15 A.M.	254	25.0	101	5.0	2h. 44m.	4 160	10	
4573	" 20	1.32 P.M.	254	25.0	101	4.1	4h. 59m.	7 430	12	Agitated surface of sand
4578	" 20	3.52 "	255	26.5	107	2.1	16m.	421	3	layer at 1.20 P.M.
4580	" 20	5.09 "	255	25.0	101	3.6	1h. 33m.	2 361	11	
4606	" 21	12.00 M.	256	25.5	103	3.8	47m.	1 180	18	[layer at 1.08 P.M.
4609	" 21	1.21 P.M.	256	25.0	101	2.7	2h. 05m.	3 070	26	Agitated surface of sand
4612	" 21	3.12 "	256	24.0	97	5.8	3h. 56m.	5 850	44	[layer at 4.36 P.M.
4615	" 21	5.07 "	256	24.0	97	7.2	5h. 49m.	8 620	101	Agitated surface of sand
4620	" 22	11.09 A.M.	257	25.0	101	....	45m.	1 495	143	Shut inlet and outlet 11.10 A.M.
4622	" 22	11.59 "	258	....	.....	....	31m.	930	87	Shut outlet 11.59 A.M.
4623	" 22	12.33 P.M.	259	34.0	138	3.4	12m.	354	32	
4625	" 22	2.18 "	260	22.0	89	4.8	54m.	1 441	248	Agitated surface of sand
4631	" 22	4.45 "	261	25.0	101	2.8	33m.	858	745	layer at 2.45 P.M.
4636	" 23	11.23 A.M.	263	21.0	85	3.0	44m.	979	51	
4644	" 23	1.02 P.M.	263	22.0	89	2.0	2h. 21m.	2 969	124	Agitated surface of sand
4646	" 23	3.45 "	264	20.0	81	2.1	39m.	877	96	layer at 12.16 P.M.
4647	" 23	4.54 "	264	20.0	81	9.9	2h. 18m.	2 877	141	
4679	" 24	1.03 "	266	20.0	81	6.0	1h. 32m.	1 737	60	
4687	" 24	2.46 "	266	20.5	83	4.5	3h. 13m.	3 537	27	Agitated surface of sand
4688	" 24	3.18 "	266	22.0	89	8.0	3h. 45m.	4 197	126	layer at 1.54 P.M.
4693	" 24	5.02 "	267	20.5	83	1.8	33m.	657	.....	[layer at 10.23 A.M.
4706	" 25	11.14 A.M.	267	22.0	89	....	3h. 13m.	3 947	52	Agitated surface of sand
4709	" 25	1.07 P.M.	268	21.5	87	1.6	12m.	264	40	[layer at 1.56 P.M.
4713	" 25	3.21 "	268	20.5	83	5.4	2h. 15m.	2 824	.....	Agitated surface of sand
4718	" 25	5.03 "	268	21.0	85	5.0	3h. 46m.	4 614	70	Agitated surface of sand
4724	" 27	9.00 A.M.	268	....	.....	....	....	......	32	layer at 4.10 P.M.
4728	" 27	11.48 "	269	20.5	83	2.2	2h. 17m.	2 778	7	Agitated surface of sand
4731	" 27	2.02 P.M.	269	20.0	81	7.3	4h. 31m.	3 424	38	layer at 11.05 A.M.
4735	" 27	3.16 "	269	21.0	85	4.1	5h. 43m.	7 038	14	Agitated surface of sand
4737	" 27	5.02 "	269	21.0	85	8.7	7h. 22m.	9 078	12	layer at 2.47 P.M.
4770	" 28	11.26 A.M.	270	25.0	101	2.3	21m.	525	4	
4782	" 28	1.06 P.M.	270	23.5	95	2.8	1h. 58m.	2 765	8	Agitated surface of sand
4810	" 29	9.37 A.M.	271	24.0	97	1.7	04m.	110	9	layer at 12.46 P.M.
4811	" 29	9.42 "	271	24.0	97	1.7	09m.	250	6	
4814	" 29	9.47 "	271	24.0	97	....	14m.	350	3	
4815	" 29	9.52 "	271	24.0	97	1.1	19m.	470	17	

TABLE NO. 4.—*Continued.*

Jewell System.

Serial Number.	Collected. Date.	Collected. Hour.	Number of Run.	Rate of Filtration. Cubic Feet per Minute.	Rate of Filtration. Million Gallons per Acre per 24 Hours.	Loss of Head. Feet.	Period of Service Since Last Washing. Hours and Minutes.	Filtered Water Since Last Washing. Cubic Feet.	Bacteria per Cubic Centimeter.	Remarks.
	1896									
4816	July 29	9.57 A.M.	271	23.5	95	2.0	24m.	590	10	
4817	" 29	10.02 "	271	23.5	95	2.1	29m.	700	4	
4820	" 29	10.07 "	271	23.5	95	2.2	34m.	820	3	
4821	" 29	10.12 "	271	23.5	95	2.3	39m.	930	3	
4822	" 29	10.17 "	271	23.5	95	2.6	44m.	1 060	6	
4823	" 29	10.22 "	271	23.5	95	2.8	49m.	1 160	12	
4824	" 29	10.27 "	271	23.5	95	3.1	54m.	1 290	10	
4825	" 29	10.32 "	271	23.5	95	3.5	59m.	1 400	5	
4827	" 29	10.47 "	271	24.0	97	5.1	1h. 14m.	1 760	10	
4828	" 29	11.02 "	271	22.5	91	7.0	1h. 29m.	2 120	10	
4832	" 29	11.17 "	271	22.5	91	9.2	1h. 44m.	2 440	....	
4833	" 29	11.32 "	271	....	....	....	1h. 57m.	2 700	79	Agitated surface of sand
4835	" 29	11.47 "	271	23.0	93	2.3	2h. 06m.	2 970	....	layer at 11.27 A.M.
4836	" 29	12.02 P.M.	271	23.5	95	2.5	2h. 21m.	2 310	13	
4838	" 29	12.17 "	271	23.0	93	2.7	2h. 36m.	3 680	11	
4839	" 29	12.32 "	271	23.0	93	3.0	2h. 51m.	4 040	8	
4841	" 29	12.47 "	271	24.0	97	3.5	3h. 06m.	4 370	1	
4842	" 29	1.02 "	271	24.5	99	3.8	3h. 21m.	4 730	21	
4845	" 29	1.34 "	271	23.5	95	5.0	3h. 53m.	5 530	25	
4848	" 29	2.02 "	271	23.5	95	5.7	4h. 21m.	6 160	10	
4850	" 29	2.32 "	271	22.5	91	6.8	4h. 51m.	6 840	10	
4853	" 29	3.02 "	271	23.0	93	8.1	5h. 21m.	7 520	12	
4859	" 29	3.34 "	271	22.0	89	9.2	5h. 53m.	8 290	71	Agitated surface of sand
4864	" 29	5.30 "	272	24.0	97	1.7	15m.	343	14	layer at 3.49 P.M.
			Western Gravity System.							
	1895									
608	Dec. 23	11.37 A.M.	1	10.0	61	....	1h. 02m.	547	495	
610	" 23	12.27 P.M.	1	10.0	61	....	1h. 52m.	1 018	544	
614	" 23	3.22 "	1	10.0	61	....	4h. 47m.	2 698	328	
622	" 24	9.55 A.M.	2	10.0	61	....	13m.	166	910	
623	" 24	10.25 "	2	10.0	61	....	43m.	475	510	
625	" 24	12.34 P.M.	2	10.0	61	....	2h. 52m.	1 700	220	
632	" 24	3.25 "	2	10.0	61	....	5h. 43m.	3 506	168	
635	" 26	9.57 A.M.	2	10.0	61	....	8h. 32m.	5 281	580	
643	" 26	12.21 P.M.	2	10.0	61	....	10h. 56m.	6 812	580	
648	" 26	4.12 "	2	10.0	61	....	14h. 47m.	9 193	288	
653	" 27	10.35 A.M.	2	10.0	61	....	17h. 30m.	10 822	570	
657	" 27	12.53 P.M.	2	10.0	61	....	19h. 48m.	11 857	540	
662	" 27	3.18 "	2	5.0	30	...	22h. 13m.	12 582	324	
667	" 27	4.28 "	3	18.0	110	....	15m.	232	592	
668	" 27	4.44 "	3	18.0	110	....	31m.	544	480	
677	" 28	10.11 A.M.	3	17.0	103	....	2h. 12m.	2 309	873	
680	" 28	11.47 "	3	8.0	49	....	3h. 48m.	3 329	708	
687	" 28	3.27 P.M.	3	3.0	18	....	7h. 28m.	4 245	1 260	
694	" 30	11.17 A.M.	4	6.0	36	....	3h. 55m.	2 652	332	
699	" 30	1.52 P.M.	5	14.0	85	....	16m.	203	726	
702	" 30	4.38 "	5	11.0	67	....	3h. 02m.	2 456	528	
709	" 31	9.54 A.M.	6	....	....	....	15m.	172	276	
713	" 31	11.05 "	6	23.0	140	....	1h. 26m.	1 140	224	
720	" 31	2.18 P.M.	6	6.0	36	....	4h. 24m.	3 150	260	
	1896									
726	Jan. 2	10.04 A.M.	7	9.0	55	....	15m.	150	200	
728	" 2	10.34 "	7	8.5	52	....	45m.	425	192	
734	" 2	11.36 "	7	11.0	67	....	1h. 47m.	1 050	136	
736	" 2	1.51 P.M.	8	10.0	61	....	15m.	122	392	
737	" 2	2.21 "	8	12.0	73	....	45m.	472	304	
746	" 3	9.51 A.M.	9	7.5	46	....	15m.	93	250	
751	" 3	10.41 "	9	9.0	55	....	1h. 05m.	550	208	
757	" 3	2.08 P.M.	10	8.0	49	....	13m.	119	410	
759	" 3	2.40 "	10	9.5	58	....	45m.	429	432	
762	" 4	11.29 A.M.	11	9.0	55	....	19m.	165	95	
767	" 4	12.04 P.M.	11	9.0	55	..	54m.	437	25	
770	" 4	2.18 "	11	8.5	52	...	3h. 08m.	1 587	122	

TABLE No. 4.—*Continued.*

Western Gravity System.

Serial Number.	Collected. Date.	Collected. Hour.	Number of Run.	Rate of Filtration. Cubic Feet per Minute.	Rate of Filtration. Million Gallons per Acre per 24 Hours.	Loss of Head. Feet.	Period of Service Since Last Washing. Hours and Minutes.	Filtered Water Since Last Washing. Cubic Feet.	Bacteria per Cubic Centimeter.	Remarks.
	1896									
777	Jan. 6	12.10 P.M.	12	14.0	85	....	1h. 27m.	1 103	416	
781	" 6	3.33 "	12	8.0	49	....	4h. 50m.	2 297	320	
784	" 7	12.18 "	12	9.0	55	....	9h. 25m.	5 193	98	
788	" 7	3.49 "	13	11.0	67	....	15m.	172	92	
792	" 7	4.19 "	13	11.0	67	....	45m.	552	88	
797	" 8	12.09 "	13	10.0	61	....	5h. 15m.	3 512	134	
800	" 8	2.33 "	13	10.0	61	....	7h. 39m.	5 002	128	
804	" 8	3.04 "	13	10.0	61	....	8h. 10m.	5 288	190	
808	" 9	10.09 A.M.	14	10.0	61	....	14m.	123	76	
813	" 9	10.39 "	14	11.5	70	....	44m.	443	52	
818	" 9	2.03 P.M.	14	8.5	52	....	4h. 08m.	2 593	172	
823	" 10	11.45 A.M.	15	12.0	73	....	3h. 17m.	2 275	97	
830	" 10	1.56 P.M.	15	12.0	73	....	5h. 28m.	3 935	120	
833	" 11	10.54 A.M.	16	12.5	76	....	29m.	419	53	
837	" 11	11.28 "	16	13.5	82	....	1h. 03m.	849	135	
852a	" 14	11.07 "	17	11.0	67	....	15m.	154	57	
853	" 14	11.37 "	17	11.0	67	....	45m.	518	33	
861	" 14	2.12 P.M.	17	12.0	73	....	3h. 20m.	2 321	94	
864	" 14	3.09 "	17	11.0	67	....	4h. 17m.	2 954	60	
873	" 15	10.47 A.M.	17	14.0	85	....	7h. 55m.	5 554	130	
877	" 15	12.52 P.M.	17	13.0	79	....	10h. 00m.	7 222	90	
883	" 15	3.14 "	17	8.0	49	....	12h. 22m.	8 793	164	
889	" 16	10.58 A.M.	18	14.0	85	....	10m.	89	48	
894	" 16	1.09 P.M.	18	20.0	122	....	2h. 20m.	2 679	192	
901	" 16	3.08 "	18	18.0	110	....	4h. 20m.	4 979	150	
904	" 17	9.59 A.M.	19	15.0	91	....	06m.	70	176	
905	" 17	10.03 "	19	15.0	91	....	10m.	130	124	
906	" 17	10.13 "	19	24.0	146	....	20m.	320	132	
907	" 17	10.23 "	19	25.0	152	....	30m.	550	141	
908	" 17	10.33 "	19	25.0	152	....	40m.	520	102	
909	" 17	10.43 "	19	25.0	152	....	50m.	1 080	132	
910	" 17	10.53 "	19	25.0	152	....	1h. 00m.	1 376	102	
926	" 17	1.11 P.M.	19	20.0	122	....	3h. 18m.	4 500	240	
929	" 17	2.04 "	19	19.0	116	....	4h. 11m.	5 500	140	
933	" 17	3.04 "	19	18.0	110	....	5h. 11m.	6 630	238	
937	" 17	4.04 "	19	16.0	97	....	6h. 11m.	7 620	168	
943	" 17	5.08 "	19	7.5	46	....	7h. 15m.	8 380	198	
946	" 18	9.56 A.M.	20	25.0	152	....	17m.	460	144	
951	" 18	10.20 "	20	26.0	158	....	41m.	940	258	
954	" 18	1.23 P.M.	20	27.0	164	....	3h. 44m.	5 860	256	
959	" 18	2.41 "	20	24.0	146	....	5h. 02m.	7 869	256	
967	" 20	10.34 A.M.	21	22.0	134	....	16m.	276	192	
975	" 20	4.25 P.M.	21	21.0	128	....	6h. 07m.	8 226	246	
981	" 21	11.42 A.M.	22	25.0	152	....	2h. 05m.	3 007	147	
987	" 21	4.25 P.M.	22	16.0	97	....	6h. 48m.	8 857	202	
994	" 22	9.35 A.M.	23	25.0	152	....	15m.	265	136	
995	" 22	10.05 "	23	27.0	164	....	45m.	1 155	174	
999	" 22	2 28 P.M.	23	25.0	152	....	5h. 08m.	7 955	266	
1003	" 23	10.16 A.M.	24	28.0	170	....	50m.	1 345	73	
1007	" 23	3.43 P.M.	24	21.0	128	....	6h. 17m.	9 655	64	
1012	" 24	10.08 A.M.	25	25.0	152	....	19m.	409	49	
1017	" 24	2.00 P.M.	25	25.0	152	....	4h. 11m.	6 649	145	
1020	" 25	9.41 A.M.	26	28.5	173	....	15m.	397	75	
1023	" 25	10.07 "	26	25.0	152	....	1h. 01m.	2 467	65	
1027	" 25	2.23 P.M.	26	20.0	122	....	4h. 57m.	6 509	165	
1031	" 27	9.44 A.M.	27	23.0	140	....	15m.	322	612	
1035	" 27	10.14 "	27	23.0	140	....	45m.	1 102	554	
1041	" 27	1.13 P.M.	27	13.0	79	....	3h. 44m.	4 112	934	
1046	" 27	4.25 "	28	21.0	128	....	34m.	689	504	
1055	" 28	1.08 "	29	14.0	85	....	50m.	1 015	1 586	
1085	" 31	11.00 A.M.	30	20.0	122	....	50m.	870	278	
1088	" 31	2.33 P.M.	31	13.0	79	....	1h. 06m.	1 101	820	
1097	Feb. 1	12.18 "	32	9.0	55	....	2h. 18m.	1 644	326	

TABLE NO. 4.—*Continued.*

Western Gravity System.

Serial Number.	Collected.		Number of Run.	Rate of Filtration.		Loss of Head. Feet.	Period of Service Since Last Washing. Hours and Minutes.	Filtered Water Since Last Washing. Cubic Feet.	Bacteria per Cubic Centimeter.	Remarks.
	Date.	Hour.		Cubic Feet per Minute.	Million Gallons per Acre per 24 Hours.					
	1896									
1100	Feb. 1	2.45 P.M.	33	18.0	110	....	40m.	621	137	
1104	" 1	5.03 "	33	7.0	43	....	2h. 58m.	2 811	118	
1108	" 3	10.35 A.M.	34	17.0	103	....	31m.	442	240	
1111	" 3	1.16 P.M.	34	12.0	73	....	3h. 12m.	3 132	632	
1113	" 3	3.23 "	34	22.0	134	....	5h. 19m.	5 362	560	
1117	" 3	5.00 "	34	6.0	36	....	6h. 56m.	6 742	1 124	
1122	" 4	10.22 A.M.	35	26.0	158	....	32m.	780	421	
1125	" 4	11.49 "	35	19.0	116	....	1h. 59m.	2 810	720	
1128	" 4	2.31 P.M.	35	3.5	21	...	4h. 41m.	4 430	908	
1132	" 4	5.18 "	36	12.0	73	....	1h. 51m.	1 926	900	
1138	" 5	10.26 A.M.	36	14.0	85	....	3h. 29m.	3 466	600	
1142	" 5	11.53 "	36	4.0	25	....	4h. 56m.	4 168	960	
1146	" 5	3.14 P.M.	37	6.0	36	....	2h. 49m.	2 732	324	
1151	" 5	5.09 "	38	15.5	94	....	41m.	694	308	
1157	" 6	10.22 A.M.	38	16.0	97	....	2h. 24m.	2 544	828	
1162	" 6	12.24 P.M.	39	20.0	122	....	04m.	58	1 276	
1165	" 6	3.18 "	39	12.0	73	....	2h. 58m.	3 146	655	
1170	" 6	4.19 "	39	8.0	49	....	3h. 59m.	3 718	460	
1175	" 7	10.22 A.M.	40	18.0	110	....	59m.	1 252	800	
1179	" 7	1.37 P.M.	41	17.0	103	....	1h. 12m.	1 639	1 600	
1188	" 8	10.37 A.M.	42	7.0	43	....	3h. 16m.	2 061	321	
1193	" 8	2.27 P.M.	44	16.0	97	....	32m.	641	825	
1199	" 8	4.53 "	45	4.0	25	....	1h. 05m.	403	860	
1206	" 10	10.35 A.M.	46	20.0	122	....	05m.	82	252	
1209	" 10	1.58 P.M.	47	6.0	36	....	1h. 33m.	1 266	272	
1213	" 10	3.24 "	48	20.0	122	....	26m.	493	290	
1218	" 10	5.07 "	48	13.0	79	....	2h. 09m.	1 573	672	
1223	" 11	10.18 A.M.	49	9.0	55	....	57m.	926	251	
1226	" 11	12.57 P.M.	50	9.0	55	....	1h. 40m.	1 458	461	
1229	" 11	3.19 "	51	8.0	49	....	56m.	983	298	
1233	" 11	5.15 "	52	6.0	36	....	28m.	378	950	
1238	" 12	10.26 A.M.	52	8.0	49	....	2h. 09m.	1 118	250	Shut outlet 10.26 A.M.
1244	" 12	4.53 P.M.	56	10.5	64	....	1h. 22m.	1 197	605	
1250	" 13	9.54 A.M.	57	19.0	116	...	33m.	632	106	
1253	" 13	12.30 P.M.	58	23.0	140	...	21m.	458	235	
1256	" 13	2.25 "	58	4.0	25	....	2h. 16m.	2 158	1 045	
1259	" 13	4.41 "	59	8.5	52	....	1h. 41m.	1 981	425	
1267	" 14	10.30 A.M.	60	18.0	110	...	1h. 05m.	1 348	209	
1271	" 14	1.22 P.M.	60	7.0	43	...	3h. 57m.	3 148	371	
1275	" 14	3.30 "	61	20.0	122	....	45m.	946	372	
1279	" 14	4.52 "	61	6.0	36	....	2h. 07m	2 246	408	
1285	" 15	10 20 A.M.	62	18.0	110	....	1h. 01m.	1 500	390	
1289	" 15	1.33 P.M.	63	17.0	103	....	06m.	104	517	
1293	" 15	3.13 "	63	16.0	97	....	1h. 46m.	2 134	1 975	
1298	" 15	5.24 "	63	9.0	55	....	3h. 57m	3 424	919	
1304	" 17	10.19 A.M.	64	22.0	134	....	1h. 00m.	1 474	865	
1308	" 17	1.45 P.M.	65	23.0	140	...	30m.	609	650	
1312	" 17	3.13 "	65	16.0	97	....	1h. 58m.	2 409	732	
1313	" 17	3.28 "	65	13.5	82	....	2h. 13m.	2 659	1 097	
1316	" 17	5.14 "	65	6.0	36	..	3h. 59m.	3 389	602	
1322	" 18	10.32 A.M.	66	20.5	135	....	1h. 06m.	1 396	1 220	
1326	" 18	12 05 P.M.	66	7.0	43	....	2h. 39m.	2 766	800	
1330	" 18	2.30 "	67	22.0	134	....	41m.	786	465	
1335	" 18	5.00 "	67	9.0	55	....	3h. 11m.	3 068	133	
1338	" 18	5.08 "	67	7.0	43	....	3h. 19m.	3 128	616	
1345	" 19	10.24 A.M.	68	20.0	122	..	1h. 08m.	1 308	158	
1349	" 19	11.40 "	68	8.5	52	...	2h. 24m.	2 498	221	
1353	" 19	3.11 P.M.	69	18.5	113	....	1h. 42m.	2 310	1 305	
1355	" 19	4.55 "	69	5.0	30	...	3h. 26m.	3 310	184	
1364	" 20	11.09 A.M.	70	27.0	164	....	15m.	385	118	
1373	" 20	1.19 P.M.	70	6.0	36	....	2h. 25m.	2 405	240	
1379	" 20	3.22 "	71	25.0	152	....	36m.	828	435	
1383	" 20	5.05 "	71	8.0	49	....	2h. 19m.	2 328	371	

TABLE NO. 4.—*Continued.*

Western Gravity System.

Serial Number.	Collected. Date.	Collected. Hour.	Number of Run.	Rate of Filtration. Cubic Feet per Minute.	Rate of Filtration. Million Gallons per Acre per 24 Hours.	Loss of Head. Feet.	Period of Service Since Last Washing. Hours and Minutes.	Filtered Water Since Last Washing. Cubic Feet.	Bacteria per Cubic Centimetre.	Remarks.
	1896									
1391	Feb. 21	10.03 A.M.	72	24.0	146	....	30m.	613	89	
1396	" 21	12.49 P.M.	72	4.0	25	....	3h. 16m.	2 513	49	
1399	" 21	3.12 "	73	14.0	85	....	1h. 42m.	2 085	310	
1402	" 21	5.00 "	73	4.0	25	....	3h. 35m.	2 805	308	
1419	" 24	10.19 A.M.	74	23.0	140	....	1h. 01m.	1 310	212	
1425	" 24	1.25 P.M.	74	4.0	25	....	4h. 07m.	4 170	262	
1428	" 24	3.30 "	75	15.0	91	....	1h. 49m.	2 282	209	
1433	" 24	5.21 "	75	4.0	25	....	3h. 40m.	3 250	260	
1439	" 25	10.35 A.M.	76	22.0	134	....	1h. 16m.	1 749	1 495	
1443	" 25	1.21 P.M.	76	9.0	55	....	4h. 02m.	5 119	680	
1447	" 25	3.15 "	77	25.0	152	....	42m.	949	605	
1450	" 25	4.55 "	77	5.0	30	....	2h. 22m.	2 543	1 270	
1458	" 26	10.32 A.M.	78	20.0	122	....	06m.	91	475	
1462	" 26	12.15 P.M.	78	21.5	131	....	1h. 49m.	2 471	480	
1466	" 26	3.12 "	78	15.0	91	....	4h. 46m.	5 971	700	
1468	" 26	5.11 "	78	2.0	12	....	6h. 45m.	6 801	962	
1476	" 27	10.30 A.M.	79	25.0	152	....	1h. 20m.	1 829	455	
1481	" 27	1.48 P.M.	79	6.0	36	....	4h. 38m.	5 519	630	
1485	" 27	3.06 "	80	27.5	167	....	48m.	1 177	337	
1490	" 27	5.15 "	80	8.0	49	....	2h. 57m.	4 037	480	
1498	" 28	10.46 A.M.	80	12.0	73	....	4h. 58m.	5 937	129	
1503	" 28	3.26 P.M.	81	24.0	146	....	3h. 14m.	4 864	445	
1505	" 28	4.57 "	81	14.0	85	....	4h. 45m.	6 774	485	
1515	" 29	10.40 A.M.	81	4.0	25	....	6h. 16m.	7 524	235	
1518	" 29	1.40 P.M.	82	25.0	152	....	2h. 48m.	3 880	350	
1522	" 29	3.23 "	82	23.0	140	....	4h. 31m.	6 330	905	
1525	" 29	5.05 "	82	12.0	73	....	6h. 13m.	8 550	1 115	
1534	Mar. 2	9.46 A.M.	82	24.0	146	....	7h. 24m.	9 500	357	
1538	" 2	10.27 "	82	22.0	134	....	8h. 05m.	10 400	.....	
1542	" 2	1.39 P.M.	83	27.0	164	....	26m.	620	1 655	
1546	" 2	3.21 "	83	22.0	134	....	2h. 08m.	2 850	4 000	
1551	" 2	5.13 "	83	15.0	91	....	4h. 00m.	5 380	1 735	
1559	" 3	10.45 A.M.	83	25.0	152	....	6h. 02m.	7 720	1 280	
1563	" 3	12.55 P.M.	83	20.0	122	....	8h. 12m.	10 659	1 005	
1572	" 3	5.16 "	84	16.0	97	....	1h. 57m.	2 512	900	
1578	" 4	10.51 A.M.	84	23.0	140	....	4h. 02m.	5 202	1 175	
1582	" 4	1.02 P.M.	84	23.0	140	....	6h. 13m.	8 212	610	
1586	" 4	3.23 "	84	20.0	122	....	8h. 34m.	11 122	328	
1591	" 4	5.07 "	84	7.0	43	....	10h. 18m.	12 892	660	
1597	" 5	10.42 A.M.	85	19.0	116	....	37m.	759	795	
1601	" 5	12.57 P.M.	85	23.5	143	....	2h. 52m.	3 769	1 085	
1606	" 5	3.24 "	85	23.0	140	....	5h. 19m.	7 129	745	
1610	" 5	5.11 "	85	17.0	103	....	7h. 06m.	9 459	565	
1618	" 6	10.38 A.M.	85	19.0	116	....	9h. 03m.	11 499	390	
1623	" 6	12.44 P.M.	85	7.0	43	....	11h. 09m.	13 449	237	
1628	" 6	3.24 "	86	25.0	152	....	2h. 14m.	2 909	500	
1631	" 6	5.19 "	86	23.0	140	....	4h. 09m.	5 619	245	
1639	" 7	10.50 A.M.	86	20.0	122	....	6h. 10m.	8 159	174	
1645	" 7	3.14 P.M.	87	25.0	152	....	1h. 41m.	2 256	477	
1652	" 7	5.22 "	87	12.0	73	....	3h. 49m.	5 196	345	
1658	" 7	11.06 A.M.	87	12.0	73	....	6h. 03m.	7 456	194	
1663	" 9	12.55 P.M.	88	21.0	128	....	56m.	1 204	401	
1667	" 9	3.27 "	88	24.0	146	....	3h. 28m.	4 634	525	
1674	" 9	5.10 "	88	8.0	49	....	5h. 11m.	6 414	515	
1680	" 10	10.26 A.M.	89	22.5	137	....	1h. 07m.	1 509	265	
1684	" 10	1.38 P.M.	89	23.0	140	....	4h. 19m.	5 649	168	
1689	" 10	3.12 "	89	19.0	116	....	5h. 53m.	7 689	157	
1695	" 10	5.19 "	89	4.0	25	....	8h. 00m.	9 179	210	
1702	" 11	11.25 A.M.	90	25.0	152	....	1h. 14m.	1 629	186	
1704	" 11	1.33 P.M.	90	23.0	140	....	3h. 22m.	4 399	141	
1708	" 11	3.25 "	90	20.0	122	....	5h. 14m.	6 829	234	
1715	" 11	5.16 "	90	8.0	49	....	7h. 05m.	8 789	161	
1721	" 12	10.22 A.M.	91	23.0	140	....	1h. 07m.	1 584	250	

TABLE No. 4.—*Continued.*

Western Gravity System.

Serial Number.	Collected. Date.	Collected. Hour.	Number of Run.	Rate of Filtration. Cubic Feet per Minute.	Rate of Filtration. Million Gallons per Acre per 24 Hours.	Loss of Head. Feet.	Period of Service Since Last Washing, Hours and Minutes.	Filtered Water Since Last Washing. Cubic Feet.	Bacteria per Cubic Centimeter.	Remarks.
	1896									
1725	Mar. 12	1.00 P.M.	91	24.0	146	....	3h. 45m.	5 114	140	
1730	" 12	3.31 "	91	20.0	122	....	6h. 16m.	8 404	146	
1735	" 12	5.17 "	91	5.0	30	....	8h. 02m.	10 014	112	
1741	" 13	10.29 A.M.	92	23.5	143	....	1h. 07m.	1 479	440	
1745	" 13	1.15 P.M.	92	22.5	137	...	3h. 53m.	5 317	213	
1749	" 13	3.19 "	92	19.0	116	....	5h. 57m.	7 927	129	
1754	" 13	5.04 "	92	8.0	49	....	7h. 42m.	9 507	152	
1761	" 14	10.36 A.M.	93	23.0	140	....	1h. 24m.	1 926	127	
1767	" 14	1.11 P.M.	93	22.0	134	....	3h. 59m.	5 426	128	
1773	" 14	3.16 "	93	16.0	97	....	6h. 04m.	7 856	149	
1780	" 14	4.54 "	93	6.0	36	....	7h. 42m.	9 056	158	
1787	" 16	10.33 A.M.	94	22.0	134	....	1h. 14m.	1 736	131	
1793	" 16	1.07 P.M.	94	20.0	122	....	3h. 58m.	5 326	490	
1799	" 16	3.20 "	94	4.0	25	....	6h. 01m.	7 096	200	
1805	" 16	5.07 "	95	22.0	134	....	1h. 20m.	1 824	187	
1813	" 17	10.32 A.M.	95	20.0	122	....	3h. 15m.	4 354	228	
1819	" 17	1.17 P.M.	96	24.0	146	....	40m.	953	157	
1825	" 17	3.23 "	96	22.5	137	....	2h. 46m.	3 803	445	
1829	" 17	5.09 "	96	8.0	49	....	4h. 32m.	5 673	380	
1837	" 18	10.32 A.M.	97	22.0	134	....	1h. 19m.	1 879	730	
1843	" 18	1.16 P.M.	97	11.0	67	....	4h. 03m.	5 269	230	
1850	" 18	3.27 "	98	23.0	140	....	1h. 03m.	1 414	585	
1856	" 18	5.05 "	98	22.0	134	....	2h. 41m.	3 544	535	
1864	" 19	10.50 A.M.	99	19.0	116	....	12m.	179	440	
1872	" 19	1.22 P.M.	100	21.0	128	....	15m.	265	800	
1876	" 19	3.05 "	100	6.0	36	....	1h. 58m.	1 985	580	
1890	" 20	10.30 A.M.	101	24.0	146	....	21m.	468	1 000	
1896	" 20	1.12 P.M.	103	1.0	6	....	51m.	659	700	
1898	" 20	1.46 "	104	20.0	122	..	06m.	137	500	
4145	July 2	10.32 A.M.	107	14.5	88	....	55m.	756	130	
4146	" 2	11.14 "	107	....	.....	....	1h. 37m.	1 239	68	Shut outlet 11.14 A.M.
4154	" 2	2.24 P.M.	109	....	.....	....	1h. 16m.	1 029	1 500	A. Shut outlet 2.24 P.M.
4158	" 2	3.07 "	110	14.0	85	....	18m.	225	52	
4166	" 3	10.18 A.M.	112	14.0	85	3 8	1h. 02m.	899	9	
4178	" 3	1.12 P.M.	112	....	.....	....	3h. 56m.	3 253	10	Shut outlet 1.14 P.M.
4187	" 3	1.56 "	113	15.0	91	....	11m.	166	50	
4195	" 3	3.42 "	114	15.0	91	3.0	10m.	142	77	
4199	" 3	5.00 "	114	14.0	85	7.8	1h. 28m.	1 142	62	
4316	" 10	11.22 A.M.	115	15.0	91	....	1h. 50m.	1 682	46	
4319	" 10	1.22 P.M.	115	20.0	122	3.5	3h. 50m.	3 632	131	
4322	" 10	3.18 "	115	15.0	91	6.8	5h. 46m.	5 242	152	
4330	" 11	10.47 A.M.	116	13.5	82	3.3	1h. 32m.	1 437	118	
4335	" 11	1.15 P.M.	116	16.0	97	4.4	4h. 00m.	3 739	199	*
4338	" 11	2.35 "	116	12.0	73	2.1	0	0	5 000	Wast. 3 min., 52 cu. ft.
4339	" 11	2.40 "	116	14.5	88	2.1	0	0	3 000	" 7 " 112 "
4340	" 11	2.45 "	116	14.5	88	2.2	0	0	1 300	" 12 " 182 "
4341	" 11	2.50 "	116	14.5	88	2.2	0	0	364	" 17 " 252 "
4342	" 11	2.55 "	116	14.5	82	2.2	0	0	392	" 22 " 312 "
4343	" 11	3.00 "	117	18.0	110	1.1	00m.	0	387	Opened outlet 3.00 P.M.
4344	" 11	3.05 "	117	15.5	94	1.5	05m.	56	234	
4345	" 11	3.10 "	117	15.5	94	1.5	10m.	146	213	
4348	" 11	3.15 "	117	16.0	97	2.5	15m.	236	204	
4349	" 11	3.20 "	117	15.5	94	2.5	20m.	326	157	
4350	" 11	3.25 "	117	15.5	94	2.5	25m.	396	142	
4351	" 11	3.30 "	117	16.0	97	2.6	30m.	476	169	
4352	" 11	3.35 "	117	16.0	97	2.6	35m.	546	235	
4353	" 11	3.40 "	117	16.0	97	2.6	40m.	616	216	
4354	" 11	3.45 "	117	16.0	97	2.7	45m.	696	199	
4355	" 11	3.50 "	117	16.0	97	2.7	50m.	776	229	
4356	" 11	3.55 "	117	16.0	97	2.7	55m.	856	207	
4357	" 11	4.00 "	117	16.0	97	2.7	1h. 00m.	936	.....	
4358	" 11	4.15 "	117	16.0	97	3.2	1h. 15m.	1 176	186	
4358a	" 11	4.30 "	117	16.0	97	3.6	1h. 30m.	1 416	271	

* Wasting.

TABLE NO. 4—*Continued.*

Western Gravity System.

Number.	Collected.		Number of Run.	Rate of Filtration.		Loss of Head. Feet.	Period of Service Since Last Washing. Hours and Minutes.	Filtered Water Since Last Washing. Cubic Feet.	Bacteria per Cubic Centimeter.	Remarks.
	Date.	Hour.		Cubic Feet per Minute.	Million Gallons per Acre per 24 Hours.					
	1896									
4359	July 11	4.45 P.M.	117	15.5	94	3.9	1h. 45m.	1 646	.....	
4360	" 11	5.00 "	117	15.0	91	4.0	2h. 00m.	1 876	....	
4361	" 11	5.05 "	117	....	.....	....	2h. 05m.	1 953	176	
4505	" 17	2.52 "	118	15.0	91	4.1	54m.	861	33	
4524	" 18	11.34 A.M.	118	16.0	97	....	6h. 06m.	5 723	46	
4547	" 18	1.57 P.M.	119	16.0	97	2.5	22m.	340	36	
4555	" 18	3.12 "	119	16.0	97	....	1h. 37m.	1 540	61	
4660	" 24	10.50 A.M.	120	10.0	61	2.1	0	0	320	Wasting 33 min., 334 cu. ft.
4661	" 24	11.00 "	121	16.0	97	2.5	05m.	61	158	
4662	" 24	11.05 "	121	15.0	91	2.6	10m.	141	168	
4663	" 24	11.10 "	121	15.0	91	2.6	15m.	211	.....	
4664	" 24	11.15 "	121	15.0	91	2.6	20m.	281	315	
4665	" 24	11.20 "	121	13.0	79	2.1	25m.	351	63	
4666	" 24	11.25 "	121	13.0	79	2.2	30m.	421	268	
4667	" 24	11.30 "	121	13.0	79	2.1	35m.	491	.....	
4668	" 24	11.35 "	121	13.0	79	2.2	40m.	561	161	
4669	" 24	11.40 "	121	14.0	85	2.5	45m.	611	352	
4670	" 24	11.45 "	121	14.0	85	2.4	50m.	691	202	
4671	" 24	11.50 "	121	14.0	85	2.4	55m.	751	446	
4673	" 24	11.55 "	121	14.0	85	2.5	1h. 00m.	821	157	
4674	" 24	12.10 P.M.	121	14.0	85	2.6	1h. 15m.	1 051	214	
4675	" 24	12.25 "	121	14.0	85	2.6	1h. 30m.	1 261	165	
4676	" 24	12.40 "	121	14.0	85	2.6	1h. 45m.	1 481	178	
4677	" 24	12.55 "	121	14.0	85	2.9	2h. 00m.	1 711	112	
4680	" 24	1.10 "	121	14.5	88	2.9	2h. 15m.	1 911	275	
4681	" 24	1.25 "	121	15.0	91	2.9	2h. 30m.	2 111	177	
4683	" 24	1.40 "	121	15.0	91	3.0	2h. 45m.	2 321	237	
4684	" 24	1.55 "	121	15.0	91	3.0	3h. 00m.	2 541	299	
4686	" 24	2.10 "	121	15.0	91	3.1	3h. 15m.	2 761	498	
4702	" 25	10.10 A.M.	122	12.0	73	....	0	0	.....	Wasting 70 min., 763 cu. ft.
4703	" 25	10.38 "	122	13.5	82	....	23m.	300	80	
4707	" 25	11.29 "	122	13.0	79	6.7	1h. 14m.	980	304	
4708	" 25	1.01 "	122	13.0	79	7.2	2h. 46m.	2 130	240	
4714	" 25	4.38 "	123	12.5	76	2.8	48m.	514	511	
4883	" 31	11.20 "	124	14.0	85	3.5	2h. 15m.	1 889	450	
4888	" 31	2.04 P.M.	124	14.0	85	5.1	4h. 59m.	4 319	104	
4889	" 31	2.07 "	124	14.0	85	6.0	5h. 02m.	5 189	166	
4892	" 31	3.38 "	124	13.5	82	5.7	6h. 33m.	5 639	136	

Western Pressure System.

Number.	Date.	Hour.	Number of Run.	Cubic Feet per Minute.	Million Gallons per Acre per 24 Hours.	Loss of Head. Feet.	Period of Service Since Last Washing. Hours and Minutes.	Filtered Water Since Last Washing. Cubic Feet.	Bacteria per Cubic Centimeter.	Remarks.
	1895									
607	Dec. 23	11.33 A.M.	1	18.0	128	...	58m.	1 070	171	
609	" 23	12.24 P.M.	1	20.0	142	....	1h. 49m.	1 934	260	
623	" 23	3.19 "	1	24.0	170	....	4h. 44m.	5 580	172	
621	" 24	9.50 A.M.	1	22.0	156	....	7h. 13m.	9 318	295	
624	" 24	12.31 P.M.	1	21.0	149	....	9h. 54m.	12 960	80	
631	" 24	3.22 "	1	21.0	149	....	12h. 45m.	16 568	90	
634	" 26	9.51 A.M.	1	20.0	142	....	15h. 26m.	19 839	860	
642	" 26	12.17 P.M.	1	17.0	120	....	17h. 52m.	22 596	130	
647	" 26	4.09 "	1	28.0	199	....	21h. 44m.	28 571	242	
654	" 27	10.42 A.M.	1	28.0	199	....	24h. 37m.	33 239	360	
656	" 27	12.50 P.M.	1	28.0	199	...	26h. 45m.	36 582	480	
663	" 27	3.25 "	1	22.0	156	....	29h. 20m.	40 150	268	
669	" 27	4.47 "	1	20.0	142	....	30h. 42m.	41 631	324	
676	" 28	10.09 A.M.	1	19.5	138	....	31h. 56m.	43 336	494	
678	" 28	11.15 "	2	25.0	177	....	19m.	588	810	
679	" 28	11.45 "	2	28.0	199	....	49m.	1 400	1 170	
686	" 28	3.25 P.M.	2	22.0	156	....	4h. 29m.	6 384	1 116	
695	" 30	11.22 A.M.	3	20.0	142	....	55m.	984	246	
700	" 30	1.55 P.M.	3	21.0	149	...	3h. 28m.	4 280	460	
703	" 30	4.43 "	3	23.0	163	....	6h. 16m.	8 067	520	
710	" 31	10.05 A.M.	4	21.0	149	....	15m.	303	380	
714	" 31	11.10 "	4	23.5	166	....	1h. 20m.	2 705	143	
721	" 31	2.20 P.M.	4	22.5	160	....	4h. 30m.	5 228	280	

TABLE NO. 4.—*Continued.*

Western Pressure System.

Serial Number.	Collected. Date.	Collected. Hour.	Number of Run.	Rate of Filtration. Cubic Feet per Minute.	Rate of Filtration. Million Gallons per Acre per 24 Hours.	Loss of Head. Feet.	Period of Service Since Last Washing. Hours and Minutes.	Filtered Water Since Last Washing. Cubic Feet.	Bacteria per Cubic Centimeter.	Remarks.
	1896									
727	Jan. 2	10.18 A.M.	5	15.5	110	....	15m.	192	236	
729	" 2	10.48 "	5	15.5	110	....	45m.	672	121	
735	" 2	11.39 "	5	19.5	138	....	1h. 36m.	1 632	130	
738	" 2	2.28 P.M.	5	16.0	113	....	4h. 25m.	4 752	546	
747	" 3	10.04 A.M.	6	21.0	149	....	15m.	216	160	
752	" 3	10.46 "	6	20.0	142	....	57m.	1 046	140	
758	" 3	2.13 P.M.	6	18.0	128	....	4h. 24m.	4 876	208	
763	" 4	11.30 A.M.	7	12.0	85	....	15m.	194	65	
768	" 4	12.07 P.M.	7	16.0	113	....	52m.	721	116	
769	" 4	2.15 "	7	14.5	102	....	3h. 00m.	2 671	120	
778	" 6	12.14 "	7	14.0	99	....	9h. 51m.	8 671	186	
782	" 6	3.36 "	7	16.0	113	....	13h. 13m.	11 812	228	
787	" 7	3.35 "	8	20.0	142	....	15m.	349	82	
791	" 7	4.05 "	8	20.0	142	....	45m.	936	76	
796	" 8	12.05 "	8	20.0	142	....	5h. 25m.	6 860	210	
801	" 8	2.36 "	8	18.0	128	....	7h. 56m.	8 584	188	
805	" 8	3.10 "	8	18.0	128	....	8h. 30m.	9 176	314	
807	" 9	10.05 A.M.	9	17.0	120	....	21m.	312	73	
812	" 9	10.35 "	9	21.0	149	....	51m.	902	22	
819	" 9	2.06 P.M.	9	20.0	142	....	4h. 22m.	5 152	140	
824	" 10	11.48 A.M.	9	....	....	....	10h. 09m.	11 692	118	
831	" 10	2.00 P.M.	9	18.5	132	....	12h. 11m.	14 152	184	
834	" 11	10.56 A.M.	10	19.5	138	....	28m.	457	130	
838	" 11	11.32 "	10	20.0	142	....	1h. 04m.	1 137	177	
852b	" 14	11.18 "	11	22.5	160	....	15m.	283	42	
854	" 14	11.48 "	11	21.0	149	....	45m.	883	148	
862	" 14	2.18 P.M.	11	20.0	142	....	3h. 15m.	3 578	62	
865	" 14	3.12 "	11	19.0	135	....	4h. 09m.	4 582	100	
874	" 15	10.49 A.M.	11	22.0	156	....	7h. 56m.	9 013	136	
876	" 15	12.50 P.M.	11	22.0	156	....	9h. 57m.	11 732	140	
884	" 15	3.20 "	11	24.0	170	....	12h. 27m.	14 973	166	
890	" 16	11.02 A.M.	11	21.0	149	....	16h. 08m.	19 993	14	
895	" 16	1.14 P.M.	11	29.0	206	....	18h. 20m.	23 543	104	
902	" 16	3.11 A.M.	11	27.0	191	....	20h. 17m.	26 923	248	
911	" 17	11.02 "	12	23.0	163	....	15m.	375	170	
914	" 17	11.32 "	12	28.0	199	....	45m.	1 107	.....	
927	" 17	1.16 P.M.	12	27.0	191	....	2h. 29m.	3 827	156	
928	" 17	2.02 "	12	26.0	184	....	3h. 15m.	5 067	198	
934	" 17	3.17 "	12	28.0	199	....	4h. 30m.	7 177	236	
938	" 17	4.06 "	12	27.0	191	....	5h. 19m.	8 597	214	
944	" 17	5.13 "	12	25.0	177	....	6h. 26m.	10 197	340	
950	" 18	10.16 A.M.	12	30.0	213	....	7h. 29m.	11 897	190	
955	" 18	1.28 P.M.	12	33.5	224	....	10h. 41m.	17 997	268	
958	" 18	2.39 "	12	30.0	213	....	11h. 52m.	20 347	274	
966	" 20	10.32 A.M.	12	23.0	163	....	15h. 42m.	27 057	180	
970	" 20	1.53 P.M.	13	27.0	191	....	30m.	630	212	
976	" 20	4.28 "	13	29.0	206	....	3h. 05m.	4 960	260	
980	" 21	11.37 A.M.	13	28.0	199	....	6h. 24m.	10 340	177	
988	" 21	4.30 P.M.	13	28.0	199	....	11h. 17m.	18 700	211	
993	" 22	9.29 A.M.	13	24.0	170	....	12h. 18m.	20 600	100	
1000	" 22	2.33 P.M.	13	30.0	213	....	17h. 22m.	29 780	140	
1004	" 23	10.19 A.M.	13	29.0	206	....	21h. 14m.	36 250	222	
1006	" 23	3.40 P.M.	13	20.0	142	....	26h. 35m.	45 100	130	
1011	" 24	10.05 A.M.	14	25.0	177	....	17m.	351	59	
1016	" 24	1.55 P.M.	14	30.0	213	....	4h. 07m.	7 091	128	
1021	" 25	9.52 A.M.	14	25.0	177	....	8h. 03m.	14 041	103	
1026	" 25	2.20 P.M.	14	24.0	170	....	12h. 31m.	20 411	170	
1036	" 27	10.17 A.M.	14	26.0	184	....	15h. 09m.	24 151	635	
1042	" 27	1.16 P.M.	14	23.0	163	....	18h. 08m.	28 531	836	
1047	" 27	4.30 "	15	25.0	177	....	39m.	957	770	
1052	" 28	9.58 A.M.	15	26.0	184	....	2h. 04m.	3 017	1 448	
1056	" 28	3.20 P.M.	15	16.0	113	....	6h. 40m.	8 277	736	
1061a	" 28	4.40 "	15	14.0	99	....	8h. 00m.	9 497	444	

TABLE No. 4.—*Continued.*

Western Pressure System.

Serial Number.	Collected. Date.	Collected. Hour.	Number of Run.	Rate of Filtration. Cubic Feet per Minute.	Rate of Filtration. Million Gallons per Acre per 24 Hours.	Loss of Head. Feet.	Period of Service Since Last Washing. Hours and Minutes.	Filtered Water Since Last Washing. Cubic Feet.	Bacteria per Cubic Centimeter.	Remarks.
	1896									
1061b	Jan. 28	4.41 P.M.	15	....	.....	....	....	......	4 080	A.
1062	" 28	4.45 "	15	14.0	99	....	8h. 05m.	9 604	5 000	A.
1086	" 31	11.06 A.M.	16	20.5	146	....	58m.	1 219	336	
1087	" 31	2.29 P.M.	16	14.0	99	....	4h. 21m.	4 829	613	
1098	Feb. 1	12.24 "	17	20.0	142	....	2h. 08m.	2 848	326	
1101	" 1	2.48 "	17	13.0	92	....	4h. 32m.	5 508	102	
1105	" 1	5.07 "	17	16.0	113	....	6h. 51m.	7 528	135	
1109	" 3	10.38 A.M.	18	25.0	177	....	38m.	874	477	
1112	" 3	1.20 P.M.	18	24.5	174	....	3h. 20m.	4 774	607	
1114	" 3	3.26 "	18	25.0	177	....	5h. 26m.	7 824	492	
1118	" 3	5.02 "	18	21.5	152	....	7h. 02m.	10 024	600	
1123	" 4	10.25 A.M.	19	24.0	170	....	39m.	880	.....	
1126	" 4	11.52 "	19	25.0	177	....	2h. 06m.	2 920	1 200	
1129	" 4	2.36 P.M.	19	14.0	99	....	4h. 50m.	6 640	990	
1133	" 4	5 22 "	19	14.0	99	....	7h. 36m.	9 640	255	
1139	" 5	10.34 A.M.	20	22.0	156	....	02m.	33	404	
1143	" 5	11.58 "	20	26.0	184	....	1h. 26m.	2 143	522	
1147	" 5	3.17 P.M.	20	18.5	132	....	4h. 45m.	6 553	1 376	
1152	" 5	5.12 "	20	11.5	82	....	6h. 40m.	8 393	442	
1158	" 6	10.29 A.M.	21	29.0	206	....	57m.	1 619	980	
1159	" 6	12.06 P.M.	21	20.0	142	....	2h. 34m.	3 969	1 024	
1166	" 6	3.21 "	21	23.5	166	....	5h. 49m.	8 619	2 040	
1171	" 6	4.20 "	21	22.0	156	....	6h. 48m.	9 959	1 800	
1176	" 7	10.25 A.M.	22	26.0	184	....	53m.	1 340	600	
1180	" 7	1.40 P.M.	22	23.0	163	....	4h. 08m.	5 360	1 600	
1181	" 7	3.37 "	22	23.0	163	....	6h. 05m.	7 650	700	
1189	" 8	10.45 A.M.	23	22.0	156	....	1h. 27m.	2 054	.....	
1194	" 8	2.31 P.M.	24	25.0	177	....	29m.	744	768	
1197	" 8	4.56 "	24	20.0	142	....	2h. 54m.	3 524	660	
1205	" 10	10.27 A.M.	25	18.0	128	....	1h. 03m.	1 336	166	
1210	" 10	2.02 P.M.	26	20.0	142	....	1h. 32m.	2 005	200	
1214	" 10	3.26 "	26	12.0	85	....	2h. 56m.	3 575	491	
1219	" 10	5.11 "	27	19.0	135	....	1h. 14m.	1 510	1 250	
1224	" 11	10.24 A.M.	27	20.0	142	....	3h. 01m.	2 540	376	
1227	" 11	1.03 P.M.	28	20.0	142	....	1h. 51m.	2 653	151	
1230	" 11	3.22 "	29	22.0	156	....	56m.	1 365	605	
1234	" 11	5.18 "	29	6.0	42	....	2h. 52m.	3 595	390	
1237	" 12	10.23 A.M.	30	23.0	163	...	1h. 05m.	1 426	62	
1239	" 12	1.20 P.M.	30	14.0	99	....	4h. 02m.	4 976	635	
1240	" 12	3.13 "	31	24.5	174	....	1h. 09m.	1 522	252	
1245	" 12	4.57 "	31	21.0	149	....	2h. 53m.	3 802	498	
1251	" 13	9.58 A.M.	32	21.0	149	....	23m.	532	56	
1254	" 13	12.35 P.M.	32	23.0	163	....	3h. 00m.	4 212	117	
1257	" 13	2.29 "	32	22.0	156	....	4h. 54m.	6 782	505	
1260	" 13	4.45 "	32	18.0	128	....	7h. 10m.	9 652	957	
1268	" 14	10.35 A.M.	33	22.0	156	....	1h. 15m.	1 668	227	
1272	" 14	1.26 P.M.	33	21.0	149	....	4h. 06m.	5 288	132	
1276	" 14	3.33 "	33	19.0	135	..	6h. 13m.	6 898	209	
1278	" 14	4.56 "	33	18.5	132	....	7h. 36m.	8 488	296	
1286	" 15	10.24 A.M.	34	27.0	191	....	55m.	1 402	580	
1290	" 15	1.38 P.M.	35	24.0	170	....	06m.	93	1 085	
1294	" 15	3.16 "	35	14.0	99	....	1h. 44m.	2 273	1 290	
1299	" 15	5.27 "	35	19.0	135	....	3h. 55m.	4 683	446	
1305	" 17	10.24 A.M.	36	25.0	177	....	50m.	1 130	925	
1309	" 17	1.48 P.M.	36	23.0	163	....	4h. 14m.	5 910	1 025	
1314	" 17	3.35 "	37	24.0	170	....	06m.	155	441	
1315	" 17	5.11 "	37	22.5	160	....	1h. 42m.	2 355	161	
1323	" 18	10.38 A.M.	37	21.0	149	....	3h. 39m.	4 965	1 160	
1327	" 18	12.07 P.M.	37	20.5	146	....	5h. 08m.	6 925	695	
1331	" 18	2.34 "	38	24.0	170	....	31m.	734	730	
1334	" 18	4.59 "	38	21.0	149	....	2h. 56m.	4 084	848	
1339	" 18	5.11 "	38	21.0	149	....	3h. 08m.	4 314	119	
1346	" 19	10.27 A.M.	38	22.0	151	....	4h. 54m.	6 444	604	

TABLE NO. 4.—*Continued.*

Western Pressure System.

Serial Number.	Collected. Date.	Collected. Hour.	Number of Run.	Rate of Filtration. Cubic Feet per Minute.	Rate of Filtration. Million Gallons per Acre per 24 Hours.	Loss of Head, Feet.	Period of Service Since Last Washing. Hours and Minutes.	Filtered Water Since Last Washing. Cubic Feet.	Bacteria per Cubic Centimeter.	Remarks.
	1896									
1350	Feb. 19	11.43 A.M.	38	20.0	142	....	6h. 10m.	8 804	51 300	A.
1354	" 19	3.13 P.M.	39	23.5	166	....	2h. 49m.	3 980	595	
1356	" 19	4.59 "	39	24.0	170	....	4h. 35m.	6 540	442	
1365	" 20	11.15 A.M.	40	25.0	177	....	13m.	258	197	
1374	" 20	1.23 P.M.	40	24.0	170	....	2h. 21m.	3 498	305	
1380	" 20	3.25 "	40	22.5	160	....	4h. 23m.	6 278	745	
1384	" 20	5.08 "	40	19.0	135	....	6h. 06m.	8 298	881	
1392	" 21	10.07 A.M.	41	20.5	146	....	38m.	1 658	77	
1397	" 21	12.52 P.M.	41	23.0	163	....	3h. 23m.	4 388	145	
1400	" 21	3.13 "	41	18.5	132	....	5h. 44m.	7 208	401	
1403	" 21	5.01 "	42	25.5	180	....	1h. 24m.	2 103	53	
1420	" 24	10.22 A.M.	42	23.0	163	....	3h. 15m.	4 490	187	
1426	" 24	1.30 P.M.	42	22.0	156	....	6h. 23m.	9 030	848	
1429	" 24	3.31 "	43	24.5	174	....	56m.	1 316	338	
1434	" 24	5.24 "	43	23.0	163	....	2h. 49m.	3 956	615	
1440	" 25	10.38 A.M.	43	25.0	177	....	4h. 33m.	6 266	1 205	
1444	" 25	1.23 P.M.	43	22.0	156	....	7h. 18m.	10 066	1 510	
1448	" 25	3.18 "	43	21.5	152	....	9h. 13m.	12 556	720	
1449	" 25	4.53 "	43	16.0	113	....	10h. 48m.	14 456	369	
1459	" 26	10.34 A.M.	44	21.0	149	....	1h. 12m.	1 602	205	
1463	" 26	12.20 P.M.	44	25.0	177	....	2h. 58m.	4 272	595	
1465	" 26	3.11 "	44	25.0	177	....	5h. 49m.	8 512	650	
1469	" 26	5.15 "	44	25.0	180	....	7h. 53m.	11 602	645	
1475	" 27	10.28 A.M.	44	24.5	174	....	9h. 25m.	13 702	887	
1482	" 27	1.50 P.M.	44	16.0	113	....	12h. 47m.	17 812	618	
1486	" 27	3.09 "	45	32.0	227	....	59m.	1 493	990	
1491	" 27	5.25 "	45	26.0	184	....	3h. 15m.	5 213	212	
1499	" 28	10.48 A.M.	45	30.0	213	....	5h. 08m.	8 033	305	
1504	" 28	3.29 P.M.	45	24.0	170	....	9h. 49m.	15 123	710	
1506	" 28	5.00 "	45	20.0	142	....	11h. 20m.	17 243	583	
1514	" 29	10.40 A.M.	45	25.5	180	....	12h. 48m.	19 433	443	
1519	" 29	1.42 P.M.	45	23.0	163	....	15h. 50m.	23 713	1 700	
1523	" 29	3.25 "	45	21.5	152	....	17h. 33m.	25 953	1 140	
1526	" 29	5.08 "	45	21.0	149	....	19h. 16m.	28 043	330	
1535	Mar. 2	9.50 A.M.	46	25.0	177	....	22m.	492	810	
1539	" 2	10.30 "	46	25.5	180	....	1h. 02m.	1 502	.....	
1543	" 2	1.42 P.M.	46	27.0	191	....	4h. 14m.	6 162	1 475	
1547	" 2	3.22 "	46	24.5	174	....	5h. 54m.	8 722	6 000	
1552	" 2	5.16 "	46	25.0	177	....	7h. 48m.	11 462	720	
1560	" 3	10.48 A.M.	46	25.5	180	....	9h. 50m.	14 342	1 600	
1562	" 3	12.52 P.M.	46	25.5	180	....	11h. 54m.	17 452	740	
1567	" 3	3.16 "	46	20.0	142	....	14h. 18m.	20 982	410	
1573	" 3	5.19 "	46	22.5	160	....	16h. 21m.	23 922	442	
1579	" 4	10.53 A.M.	46	20.0	142	....	18h. 25m.	26 772	940	
1583	" 4	1.04 P.M.	46	22.5	160	....	20h. 36m.	29 722	683	
1587	" 4	3.24 "	47	24.5	174	....	39m.	970	222	
1592	" 4	5.08 "	47	24.5	174	....	2h. 23m.	4 260	605	
1598	" 5	10.44 A.M.	47	27.0	191	....	4h. 29m.	6 180	1 040	
1602	" 5	12.59 P.M.	47	25.0	177	....	6h. 44m.	9 520	705	
1607	" 5	3.26 "	47	23.0	163	....	9h. 11m.	12 980	345	
1609	" 5	5.07 "	47	25.0	177	....	10h. 52m.	15 420	370	
1619	" 6	10.40 A.M.	47	23.0	163	....	12h. 55m.	18 140	231	
1624	" 6	12.45 P.M.	47	23.5	166	....	15h. 00m.	20 960	105	
1629	" 6	3.26 "	47	26.0	184	....	17h. 41m.	24 620	585	
1630	" 6	5.19 "	47	26.0	184	....	19h. 34m.	27 460	385	
1640	" 7	10.52 A.M.	48	28.0	199	....	52m.	1 230	845	
1643	" 7	12.59 P.M.	48	25.0	177	....	2h. 59m.	4 530	280	
1646	" 7	3.16 "	48	25.5	180	....	5h. 16m.	7 600	435	
1653	" 7	5.25 "	48	24.0	170	....	7h. 25m.	10 760	320	
1659	" 9	11.09 A.M.	48	22.5	160	....	9h. 39m.	13 930	212	
1660	" 9	9.00 A.M. to 3.25 P.M.	48	23.0	163	....	....	......	.....	
1664	" 9	12.58 P.M.	48	25.5	180	....	11h. 28m.	16 310	235	
1665	" 9	3.25 "	48	24.0	170	....	13h. 55m.	19 710	335	

TABLE NO. 4.—*Continued.*

Western Pressure System.

Serial Number.	Collected.		Number of Run.	Rate of Filtration.		Loss of Head, Feet.	Period of Service Since Last Washing, Hours and Minutes.	Filtered Water Since Last Washing, Cubic Feet.	Bacteria per Cubic Centimeter.	Remarks.
	Date.	Hour.		Cubic Feet per Minute.	Million Gallons per Acre per 24 Hours.					
	1896									
1675	Mar. 9	5.12 P.M.	48	24.0	170	....	15h. 42m.	22 090	175	
1681	" 10	10.28 A.M.	49	22.5	160	....	1h. 12m.	1 618	330	
1685	" 10	1.40 P.M.	49	24.0	170	....	4h. 24m.	6 398	125	
1690	" 10	3.16 "	49	25.0	177	....	6h. 00m.	8 788	204	
1696	" 10	5.20 "	49	24.0	170	....	8h. 04m.	11 778	225	
1701	" 11	10.25 A.M.	49	25.5	180	....	9h. 39m.	13 868	199	
1705	" 11	1.36 P.M.	49	23.5	166	....	12h. 12m.	17 438	165	
1709	" 11	3.27 "	49	23.0	163	....	14h. 03m.	19 938	182	
1666	" 9–11	3.25 P.M. to 3.27 P.M.	49	22.9	162	....	....	......	.....	
1716	" 11	5.19 P.M.	49	24.0	170	....	15h. 55m.	22 518	129	
1722	" 12	10.25 A.M.	49	25.0	177	....	17h. 35m.	24 738	430	
1726	" 12	1.02 P.M.	49	24.0	170	....	20h. 08m.	28 418	298	
1731	" 12	3.33 "	49	22.0	156	....	22h. 39m.	32 058	565	
1736	" 12	5.20 "	49	22.0	156	....	24h. 26m.	34 588	195	
1742	" 13	10.31 A.M.	50	24.0	170	....	1h. 11m.	1 693	181	
1746	" 13	1.17 P.M.	50	23.0	163	....	3h. 57m.	5 603	194	
1750	" 13	3.21 "	50	24.0	170	....	6h. 01m.	8 423	163	
1755	" 13	5.06 "	50	22.0	156	....	7h. 46m.	10 863	110	
1762	" 14	10.40 A.M.	50	23.5	166	....	9h. 50m.	13 633	177	
1763	" 14	9.30 A.M. to 10.40 A.M.	50	22.5	160	....	....	......	225	C.
1768	" 14	1.13 P.M.	50	23.0	163	....	12h. 23m.	17 173	139	
1769	" 14	10.40 A.M. to 1.13 P.M.	50	23.0	164	....	....	......	205	C.
1774	" 14	1.43 P.M. " 3.18 "	50	23.2	164	....	....	......	98	C.
1775	" 14	3.18 P.M.	50	24.0	170	....	14h. 28m.	20 083	187	
1781	" 14	4.55 "	50	24.0	170	....	16h. 05m.	22 333	132	
1788	" 16	9.00 A.M.	50	21.6	131	....	....	......	274	
1789	" 16	10.37 "	50	23.0	163	....	18h. 17m.	25 243	365	
1794	" 16	10.37 A.M. to 1.20 P.M.	50	23.3	165	....	....	......	380	C.
1795	" 16	1.20 P.M.	50	23.0	163	....	21h. 00m.	29 043	322	
1800	" 16	1.20 P.M. to 3.22 P.M.	50	23.7	168	....	....	......	395	C.
1801	" 16	3.22 P.M.	50	24.0	170	....	23h. 02m.	31 933	305	
1806	" 16	5.09 "	50	23.0	163	....	24h. 49m.	34 223	480	
1814	" 17	9 22 P.M. to 10 35 A.M.	51	23.4	166	....	....	......	505	C.
1815	" 17	10.35 A.M.	51	23.5	166	....	1h. 19m.	1 843	685	
1820	" 17	10.35 A.M. to 1.20 P.M.	51	23.2	164	....	....	......	500	C.
1821	" 17	1.20 P.M.	51	23.0	163	....	4h. 04m.	5 663	190	
1826	" 17	1.20 P.M. to 3.25 P.M.	51	23.2	164	....	....	......	118	C.
1827	" 17	3.25 P.M.	51	22.5	160	....	6h. 09m.	8 563	185	
1828	" 17	5.07 "	51	22.5	160	....	7h. 51m.	10 853	420	
1838	" 18	10.34 A.M.	51	22.0	156	....	9h. 48m.	13 543	765	
1839	" 18	9.25 A.M. to 10.34 A.M.	51	22.6	160	....	....	......	425	
1844	" 18	1.19 P.M.	51	23.0	163	....	12h. 33m.	17 263	280	C.
1845	" 18	10.34 A.M. to 1.19 P.M.	51	22.6	156	....	....	......	250	
1851	" 18	1.19 P.M. " 3.30 "	51	21.0	149	....	....	......	325	
1865	" 19	9.30 A.M. " 10.53 A.M.	52	25.0	177	....	....	......	450	
1869	" 19	10.53 " " 12.20 P.M.	52	21.2	149	....	....	......	970	
1877	" 19	12.20 P.M. " 3.11 "	52	21.8	155	....	....	......	780	
1883	" 19	3.11 " " 5.30 "	52	18.8	134	....	....	......	1 000	
1891	" 20	9.00 A.M. " 10.35 A.M.	52–53	19.3	137	....	....	......	500	
1897	" 20	10.35 " " 1.15 P.M.	53–54	16.5	116	....	....	......	400	
1903	" 20	1.15 P.M. " 3.37 "	54	16.3	115	....	....	......	500	
1909	" 20	3.37 " " 5.30 "	55	19.5	138	....	....	......	800	
1915	" 21	10.48 A.M.	56	18.0	128	....	1h. 28m.	1 580	890	
1921	" 21	1.28 P.M.	57	18.5	132	....	18m.	335	980	
1924	" 21	3.27 "	57	13.5	96	....	2h. 17m.	2 085	1 050	
1930	" 21	5.07 "	57	11.0	78	....	3h. 57m.	3 275	1 430	
1938	" 23	9.00 A.M. to 10.30 A.M.	58	18.4	131	....	....	......	1 115	
1943	" 23	10.30 " " 12.05 P.M.	58	17.0	120	....	....	......	1 105	
1949	" 23	12.05 P.M. " 3.05 "	58–59	16.8	119	....	....	......	780	
1950	" 23	3.05 " " 4.00 "	59	19.3	137	....	....	......	740	
1960	" 24	9.00 A.M. " 11.30 A.M.	60	21.4	152	....	....	......	297	
1963	" 24	11.30 " " 2.30 P.M.	60–61	19.7	140	....	....	......	500	
1966	" 24	2.30 P.M. " 5.30 "	61	13.8	98	....	....	......	580	

TABLE No. 4.—*Continued.*

Western Pressure System.

Serial Number.	Collected. Date.	Collected. Hour.	Number of Run.	Rate of Filtration. Cubic Feet per Minute.	Rate of Filtration. Million Gallons per Acre per 24 Hours.	Loss of Head. Feet.	Period of Service Since Last Washing. Hours and Minutes.	Filtered Water Since Last Washing. Cubic Feet.	Bacteria per Cubic Centimeter.	Remarks.
	1896									
1970	Mar. 24	5.30 P.M. to 8.30 P.M.	61–62	15.4	109	....	....	......	208	
1974	" 24	8.30 " " 11.30 "	62	12.6	89	....	....	......	283	
1982	" 24–25	11.30 " " 2.30 A.M.	63	16.0	113	....	....	......	395	
1990	" 25	2.30 A.M. " 5.30 "	63–64	16.0	113	....	....	......	355	
1994	" 25	5.30 " " 8.30 "	64	17.4	123	....	....	......	325	
1999	" 25	8.30 " " 11.30 "	64–65	17.5	124	....	....	......	177	
2002	" 25	11.30 " " 2.30 P.M.	65–66	15.0	106	....	....	......	214	
2006	" 25	2.30 P.M. " 5.30 "	66	14.8	105	....	....	......	825	
2009	" 25	5.30 " " 8.30 "	66	15.1	107	....	....	......	310	
2013	" 25	8.30 " " 11.30 "	67	17.5	124	....	....	......	675	
2022	" 25–26	11.30 " " 2.30 A.M.	67	14.7	104	....	....	......	330	
2031	" 26	2.30 A.M. " 5.30 "	67–68	17.4	124	....	....	......	340	
2036	" 26	5.30 " " 8.30 "	68	16.5	116	....	....	......	360	
2041	" 26	8.30 " " 11.30 "	68–69	17.9	127	....	....	......	270	
2044	" 26	11.30 " " 2.30 P.M.	69	14.8	105	....	....	......	195	
2048	" 26	2.30 P.M. " 5.30 "	69–70	15.4	109	....	....	......	190	
2051	" 26	5.30 " " 8.30 "	70	16.3	115	....	....	......	220	
2055	" 26	8.30 " " 11.30 "	70–71	14.3	101	....	....	......	254	
2058	" 26–27	11.30 " " 2.30 A.M.	71	16.0	113	....	....	......	158	
2059	" 27	2.30 A.M.	71	17.0	120	....	5h. 10m.	5 202	290	E.
2060	" 27	2.45 "	71	17.0	120	....	5h. 25m.	5 452	300	E.
2061	" 27	2.59 "	71	16.5	116	....	5h. 39m.	5 662	400	E.
2062	" 27	3.20 "	72	17.0	120	....	02m.	37	425	The series of results on run No. 72 was used in obtaining the average bacteria for this run, but not for the day.
2063	" 27	3.30 "	72	17.0	120	....	12m.	217	189	
2066	" 27	2.30 A.M. to 5.30 A.M.	71–72	16.3	115	....	....	......	395	
2068	" 27	5.40 A.M.	72	....	.....	....	23m.	447	249	
2069	" 27	5.50 "	72	19.5	138	....	33m.	687	189	
2070	" 27	6.00 "	72	19.0	135	....	43m.	807	295	
2071	" 27	6.10 "	72	18.5	132	....	53m.	987	470	
2072	" 27	6.50 "	72	17.5	124	....	1h. 33m.	1 667	190	
2073	" 27	7.20 "	72	17.5	124	....	2h. 03m.	2 217	185	
2074	" 27	8.20 "	72	16.5	116	....	3h. 03m.	3 187	260	
2077	" 27	5.30 A.M. to 8.30 A.M.	72	17.7	126	....	....	......	225	
2079	" 27	9.20 A.M.	72	17.0	120	....	4h. 03m.	4 237	305	
2080	" 27	10.20 "	72	16.0	113	....	5h. 03m.	5 151	405	
2084	" 27	8.30 A.M. to 11.30 A.M.	72	16.6	117	...	....	......	292	
2085	" 27	11.30 A.M.	72	16.0	113	....	6h. 13m.	6 417	342	
2086	" 27	12.10 P.M.	72	16.0	113	....	6h. 53m.	6 897	302	
2087	" 27	12.20 "	72	15.5	110	....	7h. 03m.	7 057	257	
2088	" 27	12.30 "	72	15.5	110	....	7h. 13m.	7 217	317	
2089	" 27	12.40 "	72	15.5	110	....	7h. 23m.	7 367	266	
2090	" 27	12.50 "	72	15.5	110	....	7h. 33m.	7 517	305	
2091	" 27	1.00 "	72	15.5	110	....	7h. 43m.	7 681	370	
2092	" 27	1.10 "	72	15.5	110	....	7h. 53m.	7 837	408	
2093	" 27	1.20 "	72	15.5	110	....	8h. 03m.	7 987	360	
2094	" 27	1.30 "	72	15.0	106	....	8h. 13m.	8 147	270	
2095	" 27	1.40 "	72	15.0	106	....	8h. 23m.	8 297	309	
2096	" 27	1.50 "	72	15.0	106	....	8h. 33m.	8 447	285	
2097	" 27	2.00 "	72	15.0	106	....	8h. 43m.	8 607	345	
2100	" 27	11.30 A.M. to 2.30 P.M.	72–73	15.8	112	....	....	......	365	
2104	" 27	2.30 P.M. " 5.30 "	73	17.0	121	....	....	......	685	
2107	" 27	5.30 " " 8.30 "	73	17.7	126	....	....	......	148	
2111	" 27	8.30 " " 11.30 "	73–74	16.6	117	....	....	......	166	
2122	" 27–28	11.30 " " 2.30 A.M.	74	17.8	127	....	....	......	98	
2128	" 28	2.30 A.M. " 5.30 "	74	17.0	120	....	....	......	291	
2132	" 28	5.30 " " 8.30 "	74–75	17.1	121	....	....	......	304	
2137	" 28	8.30 " " 11.30 "	75	18.1	129	....	....	......	170	
2140	" 28	11.30 " " 2.30 P.M.	75	17.2	121	....	....	......	215	
2144	" 28	2.30 P.M. " 5.30 "	75–76	16.9	119	....	....	......	199	
2147	" 28	5.30 " " 8.30 "	76	16.2	114	...	....	......	1 955	
2156	" 28	8.30 " " 11.30 "	76–77	15.4	109	....	....	......	[illegible]	
2159	" 28–29	11.30 " " 2.30 A.M.	77	14.9	105	....	....	......	26	
2162	" 29	2.30 A.M. " 5.30 "	77–78	15.9	112	....	....	......	732	

TABLE No. 4.—*Continued.*

Western Pressure System.

Serial Number.	Collected.		Number of Run.	Rate of Filtration.		Loss of Head. Feet.	Period of Service Since Last Washing. Hours and Minutes.	Filtered Water Since Last Washing. Cubic Feet.	Bacteria per Cubic Centimeter.	Remarks.
	Date.	Hour.		Cubic Feet per Minute.	Million Gallons per Acre per 24 Hours.					
	1896									
2166	Mar. 29	5.30 A.M. to 8.30 A.M.	78	15.3	109	....	....	......	323	
2170	" 29	8.30 " " 11.30 "	78–79	16.4	116	....	....	......	1 686	
2174	" 29	11.30 " " 2.30 P.M.	79	16.4	116	....	....	......	1 315	
2175	" 29	3.26 P.M.	80	21.0	149	...	14m.	304	635	C.
2176	" 29	3.32 "	80	20.0	142	....	20m.	404	1 055	C.
2177	" 29	3.42 "	80	17.0	120	....	30m.	564	355	C.
2178	" 29	3.57 "	80	16.5	116	....	45m.	804	95	C.
2179	" 29	4.12 "	80	16.0	113	....	1h. 00m.	1 054	109	C.
2183	" 29	2.30 P.M. to 5.30 P.M.	80	16.9	119	....	....	......	2 475	
2186	" 29	5.30 " " 8.30 "	80	15.7	111	....	....	......	715	
2190	" 29	8.30 " " 11.30 "	80–81	16.9	119	....	....	......	1 056	
2193	" 29–30	11.30 " " 2.30 A.M.	81	17.1	121	....	....	......	2 985	
2197	" 30	2.30 A.M. " 5.30 "	81–82	17.3	122	....	....	......	5 950	
2200	" 30	5.30 " " 8.30 "	82	15.6	111	....	....	......	1 585	
2204	" 30	8.30 " " 11.30 "	82–83	14.1	99	....	....	......	2 725	
2208	" 30	11.30 " " 2.30 P.M.	83	14.7	103	....	....	......	1 265	
2211	" 30	2.30 P.M. " 5.30 "	83	14.3	100	....	....	......	1 145	
2217	" 31	9.30 A.M. " 11.30 A.M.	84	15.9	113	....	....	......	885	
2221	" 31	11.30 " " 2.30 P.M.	84	13.0	92	....	....	......	1 455	
2225	" 31	2.30 P.M. " 5.30 "	85	11.7	83	....	....	......	2 545	
2230	April 1	9.30 A.M. " 11.30 A.M.	86	17.0	120	....	....	......	1 110	
2235	" 1	11.30 " " 2.30 P.M.	86–87	16.1	113	....	....	......	965	
2238	" 1	2.30 P.M. " 5.30 "	87	15.5	110	....	....	......	1 025	
2243	" 2	9.40 " " 11.30 A.M.	88	15.3	108	....	....	......	630	
2248	" 2	11.30 A.M. " 2.30 P.M.	88–89	15.1	107	....	....	......	1 110	
2251	" 2	2.30 P.M. " 5.30 "	89	14.7	104	....	....	......	525	
2256	" 3	9.30 " " 11.30 A.M.	90	17.0	120	....	....	......	1 185	
2259	" 3	11.30 A.M. " 2.30 P.M.	90	13.0	92	....	....	......	1 160	
2263	" 3	2.30 P.M. " 5.30 "	91	15.8	112	....	....	......	475	
2268	" 4	9.30 " " 11.30 A.M.	91	16.0	113	....	....	......	175	
2272	" 4	11.30 A.M. " 2.30 P.M.	91–92	16.0	113	....	....	......	198	
2278	" 4	2.30 P.M. " 5.30 "	92	14.6	103	....	....	......	182	
2282	" 6	9.30 " " 11.30 A.M.	93	19.2	136	....	....	......	57	
2287	" 6	11.30 A.M. " 2.30 P.M.	93	18.4	131	....	....	......	85	
2290	" 6	2.30 P.M. " 5.30 "	93	16.6	117	....	....	......	130	
2295	" 7	9.30 " " 11.30 A.M.	94	18.9	134	....	....	......	64	
2300	" 7	11.30 A.M. " 2.30 P.M.	94	18.8	137	....	....	......	71	
2303	" 7	2.30 P.M. " 5.30 "	94	17.7	125	....	....	......	94	
2768	May 7	3.20 P.M.	95	23.5	166	....	6h. 20m.	8 870	.....	From May 7–9 inclusive, the results of both single samples and those collected by the sampler were used to obtain the average bacteria for days and for runs.
2775	" 7	9.20 "	96	23.5	166	....	07m.	128	289	
2781	" 8	3.05 A.M.	96	24.0	170	....	5h. 52m.	7 988	126	
2787	" 8	9.00 "	96	22.0	156	....	11h. 47m.	16 378	20	
2795	" 8	9.00 A.M. to 3.30 P.M.	96–97	22.6	161	....	....	......	113	
2799	" 8	3.00 P.M. " 9.00 "	97	22.2	156	....	....	......	91	
2805	" 8–9	9.00 " " 3.00 "	97	22.2	156	....	....	......	.....	
2806	" 9	3.00 A.M.	97	23.0	163	....	15h. 05m.	20 023	253	
2809	" 9	3.00 A.M. to 8.30 A.M.	97–98	23.3	164	....	....	......	171	C.
2814	" 9	9.00 A.M.	98	22.5	160	....	4h. 56m.	6 973	346	
2815	" 9	1.20 P.M.	98	23.5	166	....	9h. 16m.	13 033	225	
2819	" 9	3.27 "	98	23.0	163	....	11h. 23m.	15 943	230	
2822	" 11	10.00 A.M. to 1.55 P.M.	99	23.4	165	....	....	......	363	C.
2827	" 11	3.00 P.M.	99	23.5	166	....	5h. 21m.	7 497	287	
2831	" 11	9.00 "	99	22.0	156	....	11h. 21m.	5 637	180	
2858	" 12	3.00 A.M.	100	24.0	170	....	5h. 03m.	7 010	219	
2868	" 12	9.00 "	100	24.0	170	....	11h. 03m.	15 280	242	
2874	" 12	12.00 M.	101	23.0	163	....	1h. 59m.	2 683	278	
2876	" 12	8.30 P.M.	101	22.0	156	....	10h. 29m.	14 154	219	
2882	" 13	2.00 A.M.	102	24.0	170	....	3h. 36m.	5 001	93	
2886	" 13	8.00 "	102	23.5	166	....	9h. 36m.	13 121	115	
2893	" 13	1.00 P.M.	102	23.0	163	....	14h. 36m.	19 731	171	
2897	" 13	7.00 P.M.	103	24.0	170	....	3h. 57m.	5 501	152	
2901	" 14	3.00 A.M.	103	23.5	166	....	11h. 57m.	16 425	156	
2906	" 14	9.00 "	104	23.5	166	....	4h. 30m.	6 443	132	

TABLE NO. 4.—*Continued.*

Western Pressure System.

Serial Number.	Collected.		Number of Run.	Rate of Filtration.		Loss of Head. Feet.	Period of Service Since Last Washing. Hours and Minutes.	Filtered Water Since Last Washing. Cubic Feet.	Bacteria per Cubic Centimeter.	Remarks.
	Date.	Hour.		Cubic Feet per Minute.	Million Gallons per Acre per 24 Hours.					
	1896									
2910	May 14	2.00 P.M.	104	23.0	163	....	9h. 30m.	13 813	131	
2916	" 14	8.00 "	105	24.0	170	....	3h. 34m.	5 190	136	
2920	" 15	1.00 A.M.	105	23.5	166	....	8h. 34m.	12 380	181	
2924	" 15	8.00 "	106	23.0	163	....	3h. 40m.	4 978	222	
2928	" 15	11.00 "	106	26.0	184	....	6h. 40m.	9 268	237	
2934	" 15	5.21 P.M.	106	18.0	128	....	12h. 18m.	17 705	700	Wasting 2 min., 66 cu. ft.
2935	" 15	5.24 "	106	19.0	135	....	12h. 18m.	17 705	705	" 5 " 106 "
2936	" 15	5.27 "	106	22.0	156	....	12h. 18m.	17 705	216	" 8 " 166 "
2937	" 15	5.31 "	107	19.5	138	....	02m.	53	115	
2938	" 15	5.33 "	107	24.0	179	....	04m.	113	151	
2939	" 15	5.35 "	107	24.0	170	....	06m.	153	170	
2940	" 15	5.37 "	107	24.0	170	....	08m.	203	134	
2941	" 15	5.39 "	107	24.0	170	....	10m.	253	122	
2942	" 15	5.41 "	107	24.0	170	....	12m.	293	102	
2943	" 15	5.43 "	107	24.0	170	....	14m.	333	71	
2944	" 15	5.45 "	107	24.0	170	....	16m.	383	54	
2945	" 15	5.47 "	107	24.0	170	....	18m.	443	105	
2946	" 15	5.49 "	107	24.5	174	....	20m.	493	70	
2947	" 15	5.51 "	107	24.5	174	....	22m.	523	68	
2948	" 15	5.53 "	107	24.5	174	....	24m.	573	82	
2949	" 15	5.55 "	107	24.5	174	....	26m.	623	70	
2950	" 15	5.57 "	107	24.5	174	....	28m.	673	82	
2951	" 15	5.59 "	107	24.5	174	....	30m.	703	56	
2952	" 15	6.04 "	107	24.5	174	....	35m.	843	66	
2954	" 15	6.14 "	107	24.5	174	....	45m.	1 093	74	
2955	" 15	6.29 "	107	24.5	174	....	1h. 00m.	1 433	81	
2956	" 15	7.29 "	107	24.5	174	....	2h. 00m.	2 863	65	
2957	" 15	8.29 "	107	24.5	174	....	3h. 00m.	4 303	85	
2958	" 15	9.29 "	107	24.0	174	....	4h. 00m.	5 733	99	
2959	" 15	10.29 "	107	24.5	174	....	5h. 00m.	7 113	90	
2962	" 15	11.00 "	107	25.0	177	....	5h. 31m.	7 873	142	
2964	" 16	12.29 A.M.	107	24.0	170	....	7h. 00m.	10 033	65	
2965	" 16	1.29 "	107	24.5	174	....	8h. 00m.	11 623	400	
2966	" 16	2.29 "	107	23.5	166	....	9h. 00m.	12 913	129	
2967	" 16	3.29 "	107	24.0	170	....	10h. 00m.	14 293	71	
2968	" 16	4.29 "	107	....	.....	....	11h. 00m.	15 813	209	
2971	" 16	5.00 "	107	24.0	170	....	11h. 31m.	16 703	122	
2972	" 16	5.29 "	107	24.0	170	....	12h. 00m.	17 263	109	
2974	" 16	6.29 "	107	23.5	166	....	13h. 00m.	18 753	108	
2975	" 16	7.29 "	107	24.0	170	....	14h. 00m.	20 133	90	
2976	" 16	8.29 "	107	24.0	170	....	15h. 00m.	21 523	90	
2979	" 16	9.29 "	107	22.5	160	....	16h. 00m.	22 983	81	
2982	" 16	10.00 "	107	23.0	163	....	16h. 31m.	23 693	91	
2983	" 16	10.29 "	107	23.0	163	....	17h. 00m.	24 363	63	
2984	" 16	11.29 "	107	23.5	166	....	18h. 00m.	25 753	98	
2985	" 16	12.29 P.M.	107	23.0	163	....	19h. 00m.	27 173	161	
2986	" 16	1.29 "	107	23.0	163	....	20h. 00m.	28 573	136	
2987	" 16	2.29 "	107	23.0	163	....	21h. 00m.	29 933	127	
2993	" 16	3.00 "	107	22.5	160	....	21h. 31m.	30 673	151	
2994	" 16	3.29 "	107	23.0	163	....	22h. 00m.	31 403	142	
2998	" 18	12.00 M.	108	14.5	102	2.3	2h. 45m.	2 406	1 120	
3001	" 18	2.48 P.M.	108	14.0	99	4.6	5h. 33m.	4 826	429	
3009	" 18	6.07 "	108	15.0	106	7.0	6h. 57m.	6 086	265	
3011	" 18	9.00 "	108	15.0	106	4.7	9h. 50m.	8 706	3 000	
3016	" 18	12.00 "	108	15.5	110	7.0	12h. 50m.	11 466	198	
3019	" 19	3.00 A.M.	108	14.5	102	14.7	15h. 50m.	14 096	185	
3025	" 19	6.00 "	108	15.5	110	12.3	18h. 50m.	16 786	215	
3028	" 19	8.30 "	108	16.0	113	10.0	21h. 20m.	18 916	195	
3033	" 19	12.08 P.M.	108	14.5	102	20.8	24h. 58m.	22 046	208	
3038	" 19	3.05 "	108	15.0	106	20.8	27h. 55m.	24 606	300	
3042	" 19	6.00 "	108	14.0	99	18.5	30h. 50m.	27 086	539	
3043	" 19	9.00 "	108	14.0	99	18.5	33h. 50m.	29 586	420	
3049	" 19	12.00 "	108	14.0	99	30.0	36h. 50m.	32 073	582	

TABLE NO. 4.—*Continued.*

Western Pressure System.

Serial Number.	Collected. Date.	Collected. Hour.	Number of Run.	Rate of Filtration. Cubic Feet per Minute.	Rate of Filtration. Million Gallons per Acre per 24 Hours.	Loss of Head. Feet.	Period of Service Since Last Washing. Hours and Minutes.	Filtered Water Since Last Washing. Cubic Feet.	Bacteria per Cubic Centimeter.	Remarks.
	1896									
3054	May 20	3.00 A.M.	108	15.0	106	27.7	39h. 50m.	34 726	68	
3058	" 20	6.00 "	108	14.0	99	27.7	42h. 50m.	37 246	235	
3061	" 20	8.30 "	108	14.0	99	30.0	45h. 20m.	39 266	242	
3063	" 20	9.43 "	109	15.0	106	2.3	06m.	73	340	
3065	" 20	9.53 "	109	14.5	102	2.3	16m.	233	165	
3070	" 20	12.00 M.	109	14.0	99	10.3	2h. 23m.	2 103	310	
3073	" 20	3.00 P.M.	109	14.5	102	4.7	5h. 23m.	4 813	190	
3078	" 20	6.00 "	109	14.5	102	7.0	8h. 23m.	7 353	159	
3083	" 20	9.00 "	109	14.5	102	7.0	11h. 23m.	9 883	146	
3087	" 20	12.00 "	109	14.0	99	11.6	14h. 23m.	12 193	144	
3090	" 21	3.00 A.M.	109	14.0	99	16.3	17h. 23m.	14 693	113	
3094	" 21	6.00 "	109	14.0	99	18.5	20h. 23m.	17 093	139	
3099	" 21	8.30 "	109	13.5	88	19.6	22h. 53m.	19 133	135	
3102	" 21	12.00 M.	109	14.0	99	23.1	26h. 23m.	22 083	162	
3109	" 21	3.06 P.M.	109	14.5	102	27.8	29h. 29m.	24 733	183	
3113	" 21	6.00 "	109	14.5	102	32.4	32h. 23m.	27 223	99	
3116	" 21	9.00 "	109	14.0	99	37.0	35h. 23m.	29 763	89	
3119	" 21	12.00 "	109	14.0	99	41.6	38h. 15m.	32 253	141	
3124	" 22	3.00 A.M.	109	14.0	99	55.4	41h. 15m.	34 793	105	
3128	" 22	6.00 "	109	14.0	99	53.0	44h. 15m.	37 243	146	
3131	" 22	8.30 "	109	14.0	99	55.4	46h. 45m.	39 293	67	
3138	" 22	12.00 M.	110	14.5	102	4.7	2h. 40m.	2 270	71	
3143	" 22	3.00 P.M.	110	14.5	102	7.0	5h. 40m.	4 840	101	
3149	" 22	6.00 "	110	14.0	99	7.0	8h. 40m.	7 390	92	
3152	" 22	9.00 "	110	14.0	99	9.3	11h. 40m.	9 860	69	
3156	" 22	12.00 "	110	14.0	99	7.0	14h. 40m.	12 390	45	
3158	" 23	3.00 A.M.	110	13.5	96	9.3	17h. 40m.	14 940	39	
3161	" 23	6.00 "	110	14.0	99	13.9	20h. 40m.	17 430	33	
3163	" 23	8.30 "	110	13.5	96	16.2	23h. 10m.	19 420	34	
3170	" 23	12.00 M.	110	14.5	102	16.2	26h. 40m.	22 330	72	
3171	" 23	3.00 P.M.	110	14.0	99	18.5	29h. 40m.	24 900	45	
3176	" 25	12.05 "	110	14.5	102	18.5	33h. 45m.	28 260	91	
3179	" 25	2.00 "	110	14.5	102	20.8	35h. 40m.	29 940	64	
3183	" 25	6.00 "	110	14.0	99	30.1	39h. 40m.	32 242	63	
3186	" 25	8.00 "	110	14.0	99	25.5	41h. 40m.	33 990	55	
3190	" 25	12.00 "	110	14.0	99	32.4	45h. 40m.	38 410	45	
3193	" 26	2.00 A.M.	110	14.0	99	32.4	47h. 40m.	40 090	33	
3199	" 26	6.00 "	110	14.0	99	39.3	51h. 40m.	43 340	32	
3204	" 26	8.30 "	110	14.0	99	41.6	54h. 10m.	45 360	369	
3206	" 26	9.28 "	111	18.0	128	2.3	11m.	198	153	
3207	" 26	9.32 "	111	18.0	128	2.3	15m.	278	138	
3210	" 26	10.00 "	111	17.0	120	2.3	43m.	758	138	
3214	" 26	2.00 P.M.	111	17.0	120	11.6	4h. 43m.	4 988	57	
3217	" 26	4.00 "	111	17.5	124	11.6	6h. 43m.	7 088	59	
3223	" 26	8.00 "	111	17.5	124	20.8	10h. 43m.	11 208	48	
3226	" 26	10.00 "	111	17.5	124	20.8	12h. 43m.	13 308	68	
3230	" 27	2.00 A.M.	111	17.0	120	27.8	16h. 43m.	17 488	62	
3232	" 27	4.00 "	111	17.5	124	30.1	18h. 43m.	19 608	27	
3238	" 27	7.30 "	111	17.5	124	32.4	22h. 13m.	23 268	66	
3244	" 27	12.05 P.M.	111	17.5	124	39.3	26h. 48m.	27 878	165	
3247	" 27	3.00 "	111	17.0	120	43.9	29h. 43m.	30 818	36	
3248	" 27	3.12 "	111	20.0	142	4.7	0	0	900	Wasting 2 min., 33 cu.ft.
3249	" 27	3.14 "	111	25.0	177	4.7	0	0	265	" 4 " 63 "
3250	" 27	3.16 "	111	20.0	142	4.7	0	0	210	" 6 " 103 "
3251	" 27	3.18 "	112	15.0	106	4.7	01m.	17	190	
3252	" 27	3.22 "	112	17.0	120	4.7	05m.	87	140	
3253	" 27	3.32 "	112	18.0	128	7.0	15m.	267	119	
3257	" 27	6.00 "	112	17.5	124	7.0	2h. 43m.	2 917	37	
3259	" 27	9.00 "	112	17.5	124	9.3	5h. 43m.	6 027	32	
3266	" 27	12.00 "	112	17.5	124	18.5	8h. 43m.	9 147	25	
3268	" 28	3.00 A.M.	112	17.5	124	23.4	11h. 43m.	12 227	30	
3274	" 28	6.00 "	112	17.0	120	30.1	14h. 43m.	15 537	39	
3277	" 28	7.30 "	112	17.5	124	37.0	16h. 13m.	17 077	500	

TABLE NO. 4.—*Continued.*

Western Pressure System.

Serial Number.	Collected. Date.	Collected. Hour.	Number of Run.	Rate of Filtration. Cubic Feet per Minute.	Rate of Filtration. Million Gallons per Acre per 24 Hours.	Loss of Head, Feet.	Period of Service Since Last Washing. Hours and Minutes.	Filtered Water Since Last Washing. Cubic Feet.	Bacteria per Cubic Centimeter.	Remarks.
	1896									
3281	May 28	10.05 A.M.	112	17.0	120	41.6	18h. 48m.	19 897	74	
3286	" 28	12.14 P.M.	112	24.0	170	4.7	0	0	430	Wasting 2 min., 48 cu.ft.
3287	" 28	12.16 "	112	20.0	142	4.7	0	0	300	" 4 " 88 "
3288	" 28	12.18 "	112	20.0	142	4.7	0	0	282	" 6 " 108 "
3289	" 28	12.20 "	113	15.0	106	4.7	02m.	41	330	
3290	" 28	12.22 "	113	15.0	106	4.7	04m.	71	235	
3291	" 28	12.30 "	113	17.5	124	4.7	12m.	211	267	
3293	" 28	2.00 "	113	19.0	135	4.7	1h. 42m.	1 871	256	
3299	" 28	4.00 "	113	18.0	128	9.3	3h. 42m.	4 021	153	
3307	" 28	8.00 "	113	17.5	124	7.0	7h. 42m.	8 091	165	
3313	" 28	10.00 "	113	18.0	128	9.3	9h. 42m.	10 311	156	
3335	" 29	2.35 A.M.	114	16.0	113	....	10m.	122	152	
3336	" 29	2.45 "	114	17.5	124	9.3	20m.	302	127	
3341	" 29	4.00 "	114	17.0	120	9.3	1h. 35m.	1 652	705	
3344	" 29	5.47 "	115	17.5	124	4.7	05m.	77	325	
3345	" 29	5.57 "	115	17.5	124	4.7	15m.	247	410	
3357	" 29	7.30 "	115	17.5	124	4.7	1h. 48m.	1 847	297	
3362	" 29	12.07 P.M.	116	17.0	120	7.0	59m.	915	78	
3365	" 29	2.03 "	116	15.0	106	7.0	2h. 55m.	2 765	69	
3369	" 29	6.00 "	118	15.5	110	4.7	19m.	439	168	
3374	" 29	8.00 "	118	15.0	106	4.7	2h. 19m.	2 269	34	
3376	" 29	11.23 "	119	....	....	....	2h. 57m.	2 917	86	
3379	" 30	12.24 A.M.	120	17.0	120	4.7	28m.	468	280	
3385	" 30	2.29 "	121	17.5	124	4.7	18m.	298	369	
3392	" 30	7.20 "	123	17.0	120	2.3	40m.	658	118	
3403	" 30	12.24 P.M.	127	17.0	120	7.0	09m.	87	57	
3407	June 1	12.00 M.	129	17.0	120	7.0	2h. 54m.	2 933	67	
3410	" 1	3.00 P.M.	129	17.0	120	4.7	5h. 54m.	5 893	81	
3414	" 1	6.00 "	129	17.0	120	13.9	8h. 54m.	9 213	171	
3416	" 1	9.00 "	132	20.0	142	4.7	04m.	207	27	
3421	" 1	12.00 "	134	20.0	142	4.7	29m.	746	201	
3423	" 2	4.00 A.M.	136	19.5	138	2.3	23m.	700	420	
3426	" 2	6.45 "	138	20.0	142	4.7	16m.	361	187	
3429	" 2	10.25 "	140	11.0	78	13.9	30m.	492	3 900	A.
3430	" 2	11.04 "	141	16.0	113	2.3	01m.	61	68	
3433	" 2	12.00 M.	141	12.0	85	4.7	57m.	831	310	
3437	" 2	4.39 P.M.	143	12.0	85	2.3	1h. 16m.	1 034	5 100	A.
3441	" 2	6.55 "	145	14.0	99	4.7	18m.	225	42	
3443	" 2	10.40 "	148	14.0	99	4.7	35m.	561	41	
3448	" 3	3.30 A.M.	153	14.0	99	4.7	04m.	263	41	
3452	" 3	6.20 "	156	14.0	99	11.6	15m.	237	54	
3469	" 3	6.00 P.M.	158	14.0	99	4.7	41m.	620	79	
3473	" 3	9.00 "	159	14.0	99	4.7	1h. 48m.	1 518	73	
3474	" 3	9.37 "	159	14.0	99	4.7	2h. 25m.	2 038	1 000	A.
3479	" 3	12.00 "	161	14.0	99	4.7	09m.	144	20	
3483	" 4	3.00 A.M.	162	14.0	99	....	1h. 06m.	890	29	
3488	" 4	6.00 "	162	14.0	99	2.3	4h. 06m.	3 260	184	
3490	" 4	7.05 "	163	14.0	99	2.3	36m.	456	29	
3493	" 4	9.00 "	164	....	....	....	47m.	679	8	
3497	" 4	10.40 "	164	14.0	99	2.3	2h. 27m.	2 059	15	
3500	" 4	1.10 P.M.	164	13.5	96	4.7	4h. 57m.	4 079	87	
3502	" 4	3.46 "	165	17.5	124	2.3	1h. 46m.	1 875	23	
3507	" 4	6.28 "	165	17.0	120	2.3	4h. 28m.	4 685	97	
3510	" 4	8.45 "	166	17.0	120	4.7	1h. 49m.	1 809	19	
3533	" 4	12.00 "	167	17.0	120	2.3	2h. 07m.	2 197	174	
3540	" 5	3.25 A.M.	168	17.0	120	2.3	2h. 57m.	2 965	72	
3544	" 5	6.00 "	169	16.5	116	2.3	2h. 16m.	2 294	325	
3545	" 5	6.32 "	169	16.5	116	2.3	2h. 48m.	2 714	1 700	A.
3547	" 5	9.00 "	171	17.0	120	2.3	46m.	647	21	
3554	" 5	4.05 P.M.	175	21.0	149	4.7	1h. 00m.	1 248	89	
3555	" 5	4.42 "	176	20.0	142	2.3	19m.	340	25	
3560	" 5	10.00 "	177	20.0	142	4.7	3h. 18m.	3 857	49	
3564	" 6	12.30 A.M.	177	20.0	142	4.9	0	0	300	Wasting 3 min., 70 cu. ft.

TABLE No. 4.—*Continued.*

Western Pressure System.

Serial Number.	Collected. Date.	Collected. Hour.	Number of Run.	Rate of Filtration. Cubic Feet per Minute.	Rate of Filtration. Million Gallons per Acre per 24 Hours.	Loss of Head, Feet.	Period of Service Since Last Washing, Hours and Minutes.	Filtered Water Since Last Washing, Cubic Feet.	Bacteria per Cubic Centimeter.	Remarks.
	1896									
3665	June 6	12.23 A.M.	177	22.0	156	4.7	0	0	400	Wasting 6 min., 135 cu. ft.
3566	" 6	12.35 "	178	20.0	142	4.7	02m.	31	37	
3567	" 6	12.37 "	178	20.0	142	4.7	04m.	81	43	
3568	" 6	12.39 "	178	18.0	128	4.7	06m.	116	33	
3569	" 6	12.41 "	178	20.0	142	4.7	08m.	156	51	
3570	" 6	12.43 "	178	20.0	142	4.7	10m.	196	22	
3571	" 6	12.45 "	178	20.0	142	4.7	12m.	236	18	
3572	" 6	12.47 "	178	20.0	142	4.7	14m.	276	51	
3573	" 6	12.49 "	178	18.0	128	4.7	16m.	311	37	
3574	" 6	12.51 "	178	20.0	142	4.7	18m.	351	19	
3575	" 6	12.53 "	178	20.0	142	4.7	20m.	391	28	
3576	" 6	12.55 "	178	20.0	142	4.7	22m.	431	25	
3577	" 6	12.57 "	178	20.0	142	4.7	24m.	471	21	
3578	" 6	12.59 "	178	21.0	149	4.7	26m.	516	14	
3579	" 6	1.01 "	178	21.0	149	4.7	28m.	561	67	
3580	" 6	1.03 "	178	21.0	149	4.7	30m.	601	27	
3581	" 6	1.08 "	178	20.0	142	4.7	35m.	701	25	
3582	" 6	1.18 "	178	20.0	142	4.7	45m.	911	39	
3583	" 6	1.33 "	178	20.0	142	4.7	1h. 00m.	1 211	47	
3584	" 6	1.43 "	178	....	....	....	1h. 10m.	1 426	800	A.
3587	" 6	2.33 "	179	20.0	142	2.3	35m.	665	26	
3597	" 6	7.51 "	179	20.0	142	4.7	5h. 53m.	6 815	....	
3625	" 6	10.58 "	179	20.0	142	4.7	5h. 40m.	850	31	
3630	" 6	1.55 P.M.	183	20.0	142	2.3	06m.	273	69	
3633	" 6	3.04 "	183	19.5	138	4.7	1h. 15m.	1 503	31	
3658	" 9	1.30 "	186	20.0	142	2.3	19m.	375	121	
3670	" 10	11.20 A.M.	189	17.5	124	4.7	2h. 14m.	1 374	29	
3673	" 10	1.00 P.M.	189	18.0	128	4.7	3h. 54m.	4 184	104	
3677	" 10	3.30 "	191	17.5	124	2.3	38m.	806	29	
3683	" 11	10.40 A.M.	193	18.0	128	2.3	1h. 15m.	1 463	9	
3686	" 11	1.20 P.M.	194	17.5	124	4.7	12m.	198	19	
3694	" 11	3.45 "	195	17.0	120	2.3	19m.	366	4	
3698	" 12	10.20 A.M.	195	18.0	125	2.3	3h. 24m.	3 596	12	
3705	" 12	2.42 P.M.	196	17.5	124	4.7	35m.	631	17	
3712	" 13	10.14 A.M.	197	20.0	142	4.7	1h. 11m.	1 470	16	
3720	" 13	1.25 P.M.	198	20.0	142	2.3	24m.	501	17	
3726	" 13	2.57 "	198	20.0	142	7.0	1h. 56m.	2 311	320	
3729	" 13	5.03 "	199	18.0	128	2.3	1h. 43m.	1 858	18	
3738	" 15	9.00 A.M.	199	....	.....	..	....	......	118	B.
3742	" 15	10.18 "	199	18.0	128	2.3	3h. 28m.	3 778	23	
3745	" 15	12.25 P.M.	199	17.5	124	7.0	5h. 35m.	6 108	16	
3749	" 15	3.05 "	200	18.0	128	4.7	50m.	933	41	
3755	" 15	4.33 "	201	17.0	120	2.3	43m.	790	27	
3761	" 16	10.29 A.M.	201	18.0	128	4.7	3h. 09m.	3 330	16	
3765	" 16	12.40 P.M.	201	18.0	128	4.7	5h. 20m.	5 600	52	
3768	" 16	3.29 "	202	18.0	128	2.3	2h. 09m.	2 387	46	
3773	" 16	4.32 "	203	18.5	132	2.3	27m.	482	17	
3777	" 17	10.08 A.M.	203	18.5	132	4.7	2h. 33m.	2 882	24	
3779	" 17	12.52 "	203	18.0	128	4.7	5h. 17m.	5 792	21	
3784	" 17	2.55 P.M.	204	17.5	124	2.3	56m.	1 111	37	
3792	" 17	4.22 "	204	18.0	128	2.3	2h. 23m.	2 701	37	
3798	" 18	10.12 A.M.	205	18.0	128	4.7	1h. 05m.	1 273	212	
3803	" 18	12.37 P.M.	205	18.0	128	4.7	3h. 30m.	3 923	103	
3811	" 18	2.52 "	205	18.0	128	4.7	5h. 45m.	6 303	169	
3820	" 19	10.04 A.M.	206	18.0	128	4.7	58m.	1 129	26	
3831	" 19	3.07 P.M.	208	18.0	128	4.7	42m.	702	53	
3847	" 19	4.25 "	208	....	.....	....	2h. 00m.	2 161	11	
3857	" 20	11.18 A.M.	209	18.0	128	2.3	2h. 12m.	2 341	103	
3864	" 20	12.46 P.M.	209	18.0	128	4.7	3h. 40m.	3 941	43	
3871	" 20	3.25 "	210	18.0	128	2.3	1h. 36m.	1 683	54	
3876	" 20	4.40 "	211	18.0	128	2.3	06m.	103	93	
3885	" 22	10.22 A.M.	211	18.5	132	....	2h. 14m.	2 503	41	
3890	" 22	1.23 P.M.	211	18.5	132	...	5h. 19m.	5 923	91	

TABLE No. 4.—*Continued.*

Western Pressure System.

Serial Number.	Collected. Date.	Collected. Hour.	Number of Run.	Rate of Filtration. Cubic Feet per Minute.	Rate of Filtration. Million Gallons per Acre per 24 Hours.	Loss of Head, Feet.	Period of Service Since Last Washing, Hours and Minutes.	Filtered Water Since Last Washing, Cubic Feet.	Bacteria per Cubic Centimeter.	Remarks.
	1896									
3896	June 23	2.22 P.M.	211	....	.....	....	6h. 18m.	7 044	31	
3956	" 24	3.26 "	212	20.5	125	2.3	1h. 36m.	1 919	185	
3966	" 24	4.54 "	212	20.0	142	....	3h. 04m.	3 699	250	
3985	" 25	10.16 A.M.	212	18.0	128	4.7	4h. 56m.	5 949	360	
4003	" 25	1.18 P.M.	212	20.0	142	7.0	7h. 58m.	9 469	35	
4004	" 25	1.54 "	212	....	.....	....	8h. 34m.	10 175	69	
4007	" 25	3.18 "	213	....	.....	....	1h. 04m.	1 300	1 000	
4014	" 25	5.00 "	214	18.0	128	4.7	1h. 19m.	1 354	63	
4025	" 26	10.29 A.M.	214	18.0	128	4.7	3h. 18m.	3 444	12	
4032	" 26	1.17 P.M.	214	18.0	128	7.0	6h. 06m.	6 384	42	
4033	" 26	1.22 "	214	....	.....	....	6h. 11m.	6 481	59	
4036	" 26	3.30 "	215	18.0	128	4.7	1h. 31m.	1 643	81	
4038	" 26	4.54 "	216	18.0	128	4.7	12m.	174	59	
4045	" 27	10.30 A.M.	216	18.0	128	2.3	2h. 16m.	2 434	127	
4051	" 27	1.00 P.M.	216	18.0	128	....	4h. 46m.	5 058	.....	
4053	" 27	2.03 "	217	18.0	128	2.3	42m.	746	.....	
4054	" 27	3.15 "	218	18.0	128	....	09m.	157	370	
4057	" 27	4.51 "	218	18.0	128	2.3	1h. 45m.	1 857	.....	
4063	" 29	10.18 A.M.	219	18.0	128	2.3	1h. 11m.	1 327	12	
4065	" 29	12.30 P.M.	220	18.0	128	7.0	09m.	156	29	
4069	" 29	1.32 "	220	18.0	128	2.3	1h. 11m.	1 306	63	
4071	" 29	3.40 "	221	18.0	128	2.3	30m.	529	69	
4083	" 30	10.16 A.M.	222	18.0	128	4.7	1h. 07m.	1 220	32	
4101	" 30	12.47 P.M.	223	18.0	128	4.7	22m.	356	34	
4106	" 30	2.55 "	224	18.0	128	4.7	24m.	395	32	
4115	July 1	10.27 A.M.	225	18.0	128	4.7	1h. 27m.	1 464	.....	
4124	" 1	1.19 P.M.	226	18.5	132	2.3	35m.	630	.....	
4132	" 1	3.19 "	227	17.5	124	2.3	48m.	830	.....	
4136	" 1	4.37 "	228	18.0	128	2.3	38m.	655	.....	
4206	" 6	10.30 A.M.	229	17.0	120	7.0	1h. 18m.	1 284	13	
4211	" 6	12.43 P.M.	229	17.0	120	7.0	3h. 31m.	3 574	24	
4239	" 6	5.19 "	229	17.5	124	4.7	8h. 07m.	8 334	108	
4247	" 7	10.00 A.M.	230	21.5	152	7.0	49m.	1 265	22	
4254	" 7	1.00 P.M.	231	19.0	135	7.0	25m.	868	49	
4256	" 7	3.00 "	232	18.0	128	....	23m.	567	19	
4265	" 8	10.55 A.M.	233	18.0	128	4.7	1h. 48m.	2 184	11	
4268	" 8	12.45 P.M.	233	18.0	128	....	3h. 38m.	3 984	33	
4272	" 8	3.54 "	234	....	.....	....	2h. 00m.	1 868	20	
4281	" 9	10.30 A.M.	235	17.0	120	4.7	1h. 25m.	1 375	6	
4284	" 9	12.28 P.M.	235	17.0	120	9.3	3h. 23m.	3 345	10	
4303	" 9	3.27 "	236	....	.....	....	1h. 51m.	1 885	112	
4310	" 9	5.13 "	237	16.5	116	7.0	1h. 13m.	1 205	112	
4368	" 13	10.19 "	238	17.0	120	7.0	1h. 08m.	1 074	25	
4372	" 13	12.00 "	238	17.0	120	4.7	2h. 49m.	2 784	98	
4374	" 13	3.05 "	239	17.0	120	4.7	09m.	120	110	
4380	" 14	9.04 A.M.	239	11.0	78	....	0	0	249	Wasting 4 min., 55 cu. ft.
4381	" 14	9.07 "	239	16.0	113	....	0	0	446	Wasting 7 min., 78 cu. ft.
4382	" 14	9.12 "	240	16.5	116	2.3	05m.	82	186	
4383	" 14	9.17 "	240	16.5	116	2.3	10m.	172	71	
4384	" 14	9.22 "	240	16.5	116	2.3	15m.	262	59	
4385	" 14	9.27 "	240	16.5	116	2.3	20m.	342	32	
4387	" 14	9.32 "	240	17.0	120	2.3	25m.	442	45	
4389	" 14	9.37 "	240	17.5	124	2.3	30m.	532	37	
4390	" 14	9.42 "	240	17.5	124	2.3	35m.	622	33	
4391	" 14	9.47 "	240	17.5	124	2.3	40m.	702	14	
4392	" 14	9.52 "	240	17.0	120	2.3	45m.	782	13	
4393	" 14	9.57 "	240	17.5	124	2.3	50m.	872	15	
4394	" 14	10.02 "	240	17.5	124	2.3	55m.	952	7	
4395	" 14	10.07 "	240	17.0	120	2.3	1h. 00m.	1 032	13	
4398	" 14	10.22 "	240	17.0	120	2.3	1h. 15m	1 282	5	
4399	" 14	10.37 "	240	17.0	120	2.3	1h. 30m.	1 532	2	
4400	" 14	10.52 "	240	17.0	120	2.3	1h. 45m.	1 782	7	
4401	" 14	11.07 "	240	17.0	120	2.3	2h. 00m.	2 032	108	

TABLE NO. 4.—*Concluded.*

Western Pressure System.

Serial Number.	Collected. Date.	Collected. Hour.	Number of Run.	Rate of Filtration. Cubic Feet per Minute.	Rate of Filtration. Million Gallons per Acre per 24 Hours.	Loss of Head. Feet.	Period of Service Since Last Washing. Hours and Minutes.	Filtered Water Since Last Washing. Cubic Feet.	Bacteria per Cubic Centimeter.	Remarks.
	1896									
4402	July 14	11.22 A.M.	240	17.0	120	2.3	2h. 15m.	2 292	4	
4403	" 14	11.37 "	240	17.0	120	4.7	2h. 30m.	2 562	8	
4404	" 14	11.52 "	240	17.0	120	4.7	2h. 45m.	2 802	2	
4405	" 14	12.07 P.M.	240	17.0	120	4.7	3h. 00m.	3 042	7	
4406	" 14	12.22 "	240	17.0	120	7.0	3h. 15m.	3 292	9	
4407	" 14	12.37 "	240	17.0	120	9.3	3h. 30m.	3 542	2	
4408	" 14	12.52 "	240	16.5	116	9.3	3h. 45m.	3 792	3	
4413	" 14	1.07 "	240	16.5	116	9.3	4h. 00m.	4 042	1	
4414	" 14	1.22 "	240	17.0	120	7.0	4h. 15m.	4 302	11	
4415	" 14	1.37 "	240	17.0	120	7.0	4h. 30m.	4 562	4	
4416	" 14	1.52 "	240	17.0	120	9.3	4h. 45m.	4 812	6	
4417	" 14	2.07 "	240	17.0	120	9.3	5h. 00m.	5 072	1	
4418	" 14	2.22 "	240	17.0	120	9.3	5h. 15m.	5 322	6	
4419	" 14	2.37 "	240	17.0	120	11.6	5h. 30m.	5 572	10	
4420	" 14	2.52 "	240	17.0	120	9.3	5h. 45m.	5 822	11	
4421	" 14	3.07 "	240	17.0	120	....	6h. 00m.	6 082	54	
4445	" 15	2.19 "	241	16.0	113	7.0	1h. 08m.	1 076	7	
4450	" 15	3.19 "	241	16.5	116	7.0	2h. 08m.	2 096	11	
4451	" 15	4.49 "	241	17.0	120	7.0	3h. 38m.	3 606	15	
4458	" 16	9.47 A.M.	242	17.0	120	4.7	39m.	680	18	
4461	" 16	11.08 "	242	17.5	124	7.0	2h. 00m.	2 080	6	
4471	" 16	1.16 P.M.	243	17.0	120	4.6	22m.	380	31	
4572	" 20	11.21 A.M.	245	17.0	120	7.0	2h. 17m.	2 307	16	
4574	" 20	1.37 P.M.	245	17.0	120	5.9	4h. 33m.	4 607	31	
4577	" 20	3.31 "	245	17.0	120	9.3	6h. 27m.	6 517	20	
4579	" 20	5.06 "	245	17.0	120	9.3	8h. 02m.	8 117	23	
4585	" 21	9.05 A.M.	245	14.0	99	9.3	0	0	820	Wasting 5 min., 78 cu. ft.
4586	" 21	9.10 "	246	17.0	120	9.3	05m.	65	192	
4587	" 21	9.15 "	246	17.0	120	13.9	10m.	145	82	
4588	" 21	9.20 "	246	17.0	120	7.0	15m.	235	72	
4589	" 21	9.25 "	246	17.0	120	7.0	20m.	315	41	
4590	" 21	9.30 "	246	17.0	120	7.0	25m.	405	32	
4592	" 21	9.35 "	246	17.0	120	7.0	30m.	485	190	
4593	" 21	9.40 "	246	16.5	116	7.0	35m.	575	207	
4594	" 21	9.45 "	246	16.5	116	7.0	40m.	645	193	
4595	" 21	9.50 "	246	16.5	116	7.0	45m.	735	171	
4596	" 21	9.55 "	246	16.5	116	7.0	50m.	815	225	
4597	" 21	10.00 "	246	16.5	116	4.7	55m.	895	169	
4598	" 21	10.15 "	246	18.0	128	7.0	1h. 10m.	1 155	195	
4599	" 21	10.30 "	246	18.0	128	7.0	1h. 25m.	1 425	203	
4600	" 21	10.45 "	246	18.0	128	9.3	1h. 40m.	1 685	133	
4601	" 21	11.00 "	246	18.0	128	7.0	1h. 55m.	1 965	154	
4602	" 21	11.02 "	246	18.0	128	7.0	1h. 57m.	1 995	137	
4604	" 21	11.30 "	246	18.0	128	4.7	2h. 25m.	2 485	509	
4605	" 21	12.00 "	246	18.0	128	4.7	2h. 55m.	3 035	498	
4607	" 21	12.30 P.M.	246	18.0	128	7.0	3h. 25m.	3 555	299	
4610	" 21	1.26 "	247	17.0	120	4.7	23m.	370	357	
4611	" 21	3.05 "	248	16.0	113	7.0	15m.	227	292	
4614	" 21	5.05 "	248	16.0	113	7.0	2h. 15m.	2 077	158	
4621	" 22	11.14 A.M.	249	15.5	110	7.0	2h. 09m.	2 001	646	
4626	" 22	2.44 P.M.	251	14.5	102	7.0	46m.	672	37	
4630	" 22	4.03 "	251	14.0	99	16.2	2h. 05m.	1 792	1 186	
4729	" 27	11.58 A.M.	254	14.5	102	7.0	44m.	644	145	
4730	" 27	1.56 P.M.	254	14.0	99	11.6	2h. 32m.	2 364	170	
4734	" 27	3.10 "	254	14.0	99	18.5	3h. 46m.	3 424	138	
4768	" 28	11.06 A.M.	255	15.0	106	....	50m.	723	207	
4783	" 28	1.10 P.M.	255	14.5	102	....	2h. 54m.	2 543	105	
4793	" 28	3.07 "	256	14.5	102	....	15m.	189	.....	
4831	" 29	11.17 A.M.	257	15.0	106	....	2h. 14m.	1 973	.....	
4847	" 29	1.41 P.M.	259	14.0	99	....	29m.	399	101	
4855	" 29	3.16 "	260	14.0	99	....	37m.	517	173	

TABLE No. 5.

RECORDS OF OPERATION OF THE RESPECTIVE SYSTEMS, WITH SUMMARIES OF LEADING ANALYTICAL RESULTS.

Warren System.

Number of Run.	Began.		Ended.		Periods of Time. Hours and Minutes.				Quantities of Water. Cubic Feet.					Percentage which the Sum of the Wash and Waste Water is of Applied Water.	Average Actual Rate of Filtration.		Average Amount of Applied Sulphate of Alumina. Grains per Gallon.	Estimated Average Amount of Suspended Solids in River Water. Parts per Million.	Bacteria per Cubic Centimeter.				Average Bacterial Efficiency.	Number of Run.
	Date.	Hour.	Date.	Hour.	Operation.	Service.	Wash.	Delay.	Applied.	Filtered.	Wash.	Waste. Filtered.	Waste. Unfiltered.		Cubic Feet per Minute.	Million Gallons per Acre per 24 Hours.			River Water.	Effluent. Maximum.	Effluent. Minimum.	Effluent. Average.		
	1895		1895																					
1	Oct. 21	10.00 A.M.	Oct. 22	11.36 A.M.	6h. 05m.	5h. 45m.	20m.	19h. 31m.	7 599	7 325	358	0	400	9	21.2	116	0.52	22	152	47	34	40	73.7	1
2	" 22	11.36 "	" 24	9.40 "	11h. 22m.	11h. 04m.	18m.	34h. 42m.	14 762	14 475	359	0	300	4	21.8	120	0.51	22	138	88	32	54	60.9	2
3	" 24	9.40 "	" 25	2.10 P.M.	12h. 05m.	11h. 50m.	15m.	16h. 05m.	16 970	16 640	328	0	400	4	23.4	125	0.48	21	115	196	23	58	49.6	3
4	" 25	2.10 P.M.	" 28	11.25 A.M.	11h. 30m.	11h. 10m.	20m.	57h. 45m.	13 262	13 701	741	0	400	9	20.5	112	0.75	22	149	93	31	50	66.4	4
5	" 28	11.25 A.M.	" 29	11.00 "	5h. 45m.	5h. 30m.	15m.	17h. 50m.	8 549	8 027	350	0	400	9	24.0	132	1.34	10	114	61	28	37	67.5	5
6	" 29	11.00 "	" 30	9.00 "	4h. 50m.	4h. 35m.	15m.	17h. 10m.	7 724	7 359	355	0	400	10	26.8	147	1.20	12	128	42	18	27	78.9	6
7	" 30	9.00 "	" 31	8.55 "	7h. 55m.	7h. 35m.	20m.	16h. 00m.	9 911	9 791	295	0	250	6	21.5	118	0.91	15	106	58	10	23	78.3	7
8	" 31	8.55 "	Nov. 1	3.25 P.M.	10h. 30m.	10h. 20m.	10m.	20h. 00m.	13 187	12 238	283	0	250	4	19.8	109	0.99	7	144	14	9	12	91.7	8
9	Nov. 1	3.25 P.M.	" 4	1.07 "	9h. 35m.	9h. 15m.	20m.	60h. 07m.	13 848	13 516	326	0	250	4	24.4	134	0.79	7	174	43	11	20	88.5	9
10	" 4	1.07 "	" 6	9.15 A.M.	9h. 48m.	9h. 33m.	15m.	34h. 20m.	12 675	11 798	286	0	250	4	20.6	113	0.92	6	239	42	10	20	91.6	10
11	" 6	9.15 A.M.	" 7	12.22 P.M.	9h. 15m.	8h. 50m.	25m.	17h. 52m.	12 334	12 384	321	0	250	5	23.4	128	0.81	4	228	138	15	44	80.7	11
12	" 7	12.22 P.M.	" 8	2.06 "	7h. 59m.	7h. 43m.	16m.	17h. 45m.	10 408	9 816	307	0	250	5	21.2	116	1.31	7	154	196	19	58	62.3	12
13	" 8	2.06 "	" 11	12.05 "	8h. 37m.	8h. 19m.	18m.	11h. 22m.	12 376	11 874	374	0	250	5	23.8	131	1.08	10	307	224	26	99	67.8	13
14[1]	" 11	12.05 "	" 25	9.45 A.M.	....	....	......	....	4 702	4 375	....	0	250	.....	.....	....	1.29	12	637	41	41	41	93.7	14[1]
15	" 25	9.45 A.M.	" 29	9.50 "	18h. 06m.	17h. 44m.	22m.	53h. 59m.	23 069	21 045	474	0	450	4	19.8	120	1.48	27	3 800	1584	294	524	86.2	15
16	" 29	9.50 "	Dec. 3	2.48 P.M.	23h. 19m.	22h. 52m.	27m.	77h. 39m.	32 102	31 048	540	0	200	2	22.6	137	0.86	22	6 800	1302	344	851	87.5	16
17	Dec. 3	2.48 P.M.	" 4	4.08 "	9h. 17m.	9h. 08m.	09m.	16h. 03m.	12 191	11 709	368	0	180	4	21.4	129	1.66	23	8 000	594	315	413	94.8	17
18	" 4	4.08 "	" 6	12.38 "	11h. 49m.	11h. 15m.	34m.	32h. 41m.	15 967	15 313	436	265	300	6	22.7	137	1.13	28	7 100	690	180	371	94.8	18
19	" 6	12.38 "	" 7	3.39 "	11h. 13m.	10h. 43m.	30m.	15h. 48m.	15 176	14 478	439	254	180	6	22.5	136	1.03	35	9 200	660	412	481	94.8	19
20	" 7	3.39 "	" 10	12.03 "	11h. 28m.	10h. 50m.	38m.	56h. 56m.	15 505	14 626	336	340	180	6	22.5	136	0.75	33	8 400	406	250	301	96.4	20
21	" 10	12.03 "	" 11	2.04 "	10h. 11m.	9h. 35m.	36m.	15h. 50m.	13 851	13 072	376	384	200	7	22.7	137	1.38	33	4 800	344	188	253	94.7	21
22	" 11	2.04 "	" 12	2.04 "	8h. 31m.	7h. 52m.	39m.	15h. 29m.	11 207	10 510	394	469	180	9	22.3	135	1.77	34	3 100	228	128	167	94.6	22
23	" 12	2.04 "	" 13	3.46 "	10h. 10m.	9h. 37m.	33m.	15h. 32m.	13 417	12 554	350	348	180	7	21.8	132	1.03	35	2 500	190	108	149	94.0	23
24	" 13	3.46 "	" 14	3.19 "	7h. 02m.	6h. 23m.	39m.	16h. 31m.	10 460	9 781	297	294	180	7	25.5	155	0.98	36	2 600	136	108	126	95.2	24
25	" 14	3.19 "	" 16	4.09 "	9h. 04m.	8h. 37m.	27m.	39h. 46m.	12 132	11 412	315	331	180	7	22.1	134	1.17	30	2 400	274	126	183	92.4	25
26	" 16	4.09 "	" 17	2.15 "	6h. 35m.	6h. 02m.	33m.	15h. 31m.	8 791	8 126	320	393	200	10	22.4	135	1.17	15	2 000	170	111	137	93.1	26
27	" 17	2.15 "	" 18	2.19 "	8h. 39m.	7h. 58m.	41m.	15h. 25m.	10 418	9 690	315	312	180	8	20.3	123	1.00	15	2 100	197	110	167	92.0	27
28	" 18	2.19 "	" 20	10.02 A.M.	10h. 38m.	9h. 51m.	47m.	33h. 05m	15 268	13 084	380	373	180	6	22.1	134	1.01	15	2 100	294	142	211	90.0	28
29	" 20	10.02 A.M.	" 21	12.30 P.M.	10h. 58m.	10h. 39m.	19m.	15h. 30m.	15 205	13 955	335	0	180	3	21.9	132	0.95	15	2 700	720	103	356	86.8	29
30	" 21	12.30 P.M.	" 23	3.57 "	11h. 53m.	11h. 36m.	17m.	39h. 34m.	14 186	13 357	323	0	180	4	19.2	116	1.51	20	2 900	260	132	171	94.1	30
31	" 23	3.57 "	" 26	11.17 A.M.	11h. 56m.	11h. 36m.	20m.	43h. 24m.	15 106	14 354	391	0	180	4	20.7	125	1.39	50	4 500	95	63	80	98.2	31
32	" 26	11.17 A.M.	" 27	3.12 P.M.	12h. 20m.	12h. 05m.	15m.	15h. 35m.	16 480	15 853	464	0	200	4	21.9	132	1.91	150	9 700	1701	59	753	92.2	32
33	" 27	3.12 P.M.	" 28	4.08 "	2h. 12m.	8h. 39m.	33m.	15h. 44m.	11 497	12 213	723	0	180	8	23.6	144	4.00	220	27 700	1728	128	671	97.9	33
34	" 28	4.08 "	" 30	12.01 "	3h. 36m.	3h. 17m.	19m.	40h. 17m.	4 104	3 804	395	0	200	15	19.3	117	4.71	220	12 100	....	....	402	96.7	34
35	" 30	12.01 "	" 30	4.35 "	4h. 34m.	4h. 15m.	19m.	00m.	5 965	5 736	345	0	200	9	22.5	136	5.25	400	12 000	502	210	395	96.7	35

[1] Available data incomplete.

TABLE NO. 5.—*Continued.*
Warren System.

Number of Run.	Began. Date.	Began. Hour.	Ended. Date.	Ended. Hour.	Periods of Time. Hours and Minutes. Operation.	Service.	Wash.	Delay.	Quantities of Water. Cubic Feet. Applied.	Filtered.	Wash.	Waste. Filtered.	Waste. Unfiltered.	Percentage which the Sum of the Wash and Waste Water is of Applied Water.	Average Actual Rate of Filtration. Cubic Feet per Minute.	Million Gallons per Acre per 24 Hours.	Average Amount of Applied Sulphate of Alumina. Grains per Gallon.	Estimated Average Amount of Suspended Solids in River Water. Parts per Million.	Bacteria per Cubic Centimeter. River Water.	Effluent. Maximum.	Effluent. Minimum.	Effluent. Average.	Average Bacterial Efficiency.	Number of Run.
36	1895 Dec. 30	4.35 P.M.	1895 Dec. 31	1.24 P.M.	5h. 13m.	4h. 58m.	15m.	15h. 36m.	6 695	6 443	317	0	250	8	21.6	131	4.60	400	11 800	406	170	262	97.8	36
37	" 31	1.24 "	1896 Jan. 2	10.46 A.M.	5h. 50m.	5h. 35m.	15m.	39h. 32m.	7 601	7 355	380	0	200	8	22.0	133	2.15	600	14 300	440	278	359	97.6	37
38	1896 Jan. 2	10.46 A.M.	" 2	3.51 P.M.	5h. 05m.	4h. 49m.	16m.	00m.	6 555	6 368	413	0	180	9	22.0	133	2.64	800	10 700	1 400	600	928	91.3	38
39	" 2	3.51 P.M.	" 3	1.07 "	5h. 53m.	5h. 32m.	21m.	15h. 23m.	6 994	6 786	350	0	180	8	20.4	123	4.95	870	13 300	405	180	292	97.8	39
40	" 3	1.07 "	" 4	11.41 A.M.	6h. 15m.	5h. 38m.	37m.	16h. 19m.	6 826	6 378	398	419	180	15	18.9	114	4.54	800	10 700	220	97	158	98.5	40
41	" 4	11.41 A.M.	" 6	11.25 "	5h. 59m.	5h. 18m.	41m.	41h. 45m.	6 416	5 688	334	314	180	13	17.9	108	4.02	400	8 600	170	133	151	98.2	41
42	" 6	11.25 "	" 6	4.28 P.M.	5h. 03m.	4h. 33m.	30m.	00m.	4 566	4 211	271	156	200	14	15.4	93	4.07	300	5 000	112	102	107	97.9	42
43	" 6	4.28 P.M.	" 7	1.35 "	5h. 30m.	5h. 03m.	27m.	15h. 37m.	5 080	4 689	320	160	180	13	15.5	94	2.72	250	4 600	....	....	43	99.1	43
44	" 7	1.35 "	" 8	11.03 A.M.	5h. 55m.	5h. 17m.	38m.	15h. 33m.	5 610	5 052	413	219	300	17	16.0	97	3.54	200	4 200	....	...	66	98.4	44
45	" 8	11.03 A.M.	" 8	4.24 P.M.	4h. 50m.	4h. 22m.	28m.	31m.	4 480	4 102	329	158	200	15	15.7	95	4.25	200	4 100	84	25	59	98.6	45
46	" 8	4.24 P.M.	" 9	1.11 "	5h. 17m.	4h. 47m.	30m.	15h. 30m.	5 276	4 796	285	152	200	12	16.7	101	4.33	170	2 100	....	....	10	99.9	46
47	" 9	1.11 "	" 10	12.56 "	5h. 58m.	5h. 56m.	1h. 02m.	17h. 47m.	6 258	5 541	336	453	180	15	15.6	95	3.92	120	2 500	53	21	37	98.5	47
48	" 10	12.56 "	" 10	4.56 "	4h. 00m.	3h. 22m.	38m.	00m.	3 597	3 139	389	221	200	22	15.5	94	4.02	120	1 800	152	36	94	94.8	48
49	" 10	4.56 "	" 11	3.05 "	6h. 25m.	5h. 52m.	33m.	15h. 44m.	6 025	5 463	316	251	180	12	15.5	94	2.61	120	2 500	....	....	36	98.6	49
50	" 11	3.05 "	" 13	12.15 "	5h. 41m.	5h. 05m.	36m.	15h. 29m.	4 986	4 470	322	224	180	16	14.6	89	5.02	100	1 900	....	....	25	98.7	50
51	" 13	12.15 "	" 13	4.42 "	4h. 27m.	3h. 54m.	33m.	00m.	4 220	3 773	338	263	180	19	16.1	98	3.91	60	1 900	35	10	25	98.7	51
52	" 13	4.42 "	" 14	1.42 "	5h. 30m.	4h. 56m.	34m.	15h. 30m.	5 282	4 701	281	260	200	14	15.9	96	6.08	50	800	78	14	46	94.2	52
53	" 14	1.42 "	" 15	10.25 A.M.	3h. 37m.	3h. 04m.	33m.	17h. 06m.	3 655	2 949	303	244	400	26	16.0	97	3.30	43	900	32	25	44	95.1	53
54	" 15	10.25 A.M.	" 15	4.39 P.M.	6h. 04m.	5h. 29m.	35m.	10m.	5 399	4 938	297	234	180	13	15.0	91	3.14	40	3 000	77	12	50	98.3	54
55	" 15	4.39 P.M.	" 16	2.02 "	5h. 53m.	5h. 20m.	33m.	15h 30m.	5 497	4 983	310	218	200	13	15.6	95	3.27	40	3 200	94	78	86	97.3	55
56	" 16	2.02 "	" 17	11.22 A.M.	5h. 50m.	5h. 15m.	35m.	15h. 30m.	5 274	4 808	312	215	180	13	15.3	93	3.16	35	3 100	73	58	64	97.1	56
57	" 17	11.22 A.M.	" 17	3.36 P.M.	4h. 14m.	3h. 42m.	32m.	00m.	3 707	3 265	244	242	200	19	14.7	89	3.62	30	5 500	171	65	121	97.8	57
58	" 17	3.36 P.M.	" 18	12.45 "	5h. 22m.	4h. 50m.	32m.	15h. 47m.	4 763	4 263	298	228	180	15	14.7	89	3.45	25	7 700	76	38	66	99.1	58
59	" 18	12.45 "	" 18	4.50 "	4h. 05m.	3h. 32m.	33m.	00m.	3 695	3 167	254	229	200	18	15.0	91	3.25	20	7 300	70	64	67	99.1	59
60	" 18	4.50 "	" 20	1.50 "	4h. 15m.	3h. 36m.	39m.	40h. 45m.	3 818	3 244	283	236	250	20	15.0	91	3.05	20	6 400	....	....	102	98.4	60
61	" 20	1.50 "	" 21	11.55 A.M.	6h. 05m.	5h. 21m.	44m.	16h. 00m.	5 491	4 725	283	387	200	19	14.7	89	3.06	20	4 300	146	108	127	97.0	61
62	" 21	11.55 A.M.	" 21	3.38 P.M.	3h. 43m.	3h. 09m.	34m.	00m.	3 285	2 798	235	224	200	20	14.8	90	3.27	20	3 000	86	32	59	98.0	62
63	" 21	3.38 P.M.	" 22	12.37 "	5h. 09m.	4h. 36m.	33m.	15h. 50m.	4 701	4 219	255	198	180	13	15.3	93	4.12	20	2 900	36	33	34	98.8	63
64[1]	" 22	12.37 "	" 25	12.24 "	....	3h. 40m.	....	....	4 146	3 531	....	....	....	....	16.0	97	....	25	2 500	....	....	36	98.6	64
65	" 25	12.24 "	" 27	11.07 A.M.	7h. 11m.	6h. 20m.	51m.	39h. 32m.	7 704	6 472	479	440	300	16	17.1	104	3.64	100	10 300	113	60	86	99.2	65
66	" 27	11.07 A.M.	" 27	4.52 P.M.	5h. 45m.	5h. 07m.	38m.	00m.	5 525	4 770	482	229	250	17	15.6	95	2.99	200	10 600	412	39	167	98.4	66
67	" 27	4.52 P.M.	" 28	2.23 "	3h. 11m.	2h. 37m.	34m.	18h. 20m.	2 771	2 092	432	243	180	31	13.3	81	2.80	270	14 700	....	....	225	98.5	67
68	" 28	2.23 "	" 29	12.00 M.	5h. 59m.	5h. 04m.	55m.	15h. 38m.	5 171	4 396	580	466	180	24	14.5	88	3.31	290	21 800	650	327	504	97.7	68
69	" 29	12.00 M.	" 29	4.58 P.M.	4h. 58m.	4h. 17m.	41m.	00m.	4 431	3 899	586	244	200	23	15.2	92	3.12	297	18 200	....	....	570	96.9	69
70	" 29	4.58 P.M.	" 30	1.58 "	5h. 30m.	4h. 51m.	39m.	15h. 30m.	5 013	4 471	502	245	180	19	15.4	93	4.76	300	14 300	676	76	278	98.1	70
71	" 30	1.58 "	" 31	12.37 "	6h. 12m.	5h. 28m.	44m.	16h. 27m.	5 490	4 960	501	251	180	17	15.1	92	4.88	330	14 700	....	....	58	99.6	71

[1] Available data incomplete.

TABLE No. 5.—*Continued.*

Warren System.

Number of Run.	Began. Date.	Began. Hour.	Ended. Date.	Ended. Hour.	Periods of Time. Hours and Minutes. Operation.	Service.	Wash.	Delay.	Quantities of Water. Cubic Feet. Applied.	Filtered.	Wash.	Waste. Filtered.*	Waste. Unfiltered.	Percentage which the Sum of the Wash and Waste Water is of Applied Water.	Average Actual Rate of Filtration. Cubic Feet per Minute.	Million Gallons per Acre per 24 Hours.	Average Amount of Applied Sulphate of Alumina. Grains per Gallon.	Estimated Average Amount of Suspended Solids in River Water. Parts per Million.	Bacteria per Cubic Centimeter. River Water.	Effluent. Maximum.	Effluent. Minimum.	Effluent. Average.	Average Bacterial Efficiency.	Number of Run.
	1896		1896																					
72	Jan. 31	12.37 P.M.	Feb. 1	11.24 A.M.	7h. 13m.	6h. 37m.	36m.	15h. 34m.	6 642	6 079	488	219	200	14	15.3	93	4.20	340	19 100	85	55	66	99.7	72
73	Feb. 1	11.24 A.M.	" 1	4.25 P.M.	4h. 56m.	4h. 15m.	41m.	05m.	4 245	3 804	447	230	180	20	14.9	90	4.28	343	21 300	69	39	54	99.8	73
74	" 1	4.25 P.M.	" 3	3.37 "	7h. 35m.	6h. 52m.	43m.	39h. 37m.	6 774	6 275	471	233	180	13	15.2	92	3.56	260	47 300	196	30	133	99.7	74
75	" 3	3.37 "	" 4	3.49 "	8h. 42m.	8h. 02m.	40m.	15h. 30m.	8 011	7 487	515	229	180	12	15.5	94	3.40	246	62 900	606	225	406	99.4	75
76	" 4	3.49 "	" 5	12.32 "	5h. 14m.	4h. 38m.	36m.	15h. 29m.	5 173	4 673	472	238	250	18	16.8	102	4.13	353	81 000	752	256	504	99.4	76
77	" 5	12.32 "	" 5	4.59 "	4h. 17m.	3h. 39m.	38m.	10m.	4 090	3 631	474	231	200	22	16.6	101	6.83	458	71 000	....	....	510	99.3	77
78	" 5	4.59 "	" 6	2.36 "	6h. 07m.	5h. 31m.	36m.	15h. 30m.	5 651	3 148	510	225	200	17	15.6	95	4.13	461	38 000	816	173	407	98.9	78
79	" 6	2.36 "	" 7	11.52 A.M.	5h. 51m.	5h. 16m.	35m.	15h. 25m.	5 282	4 765	437	234	250	17	15.1	92	3.64	550	41 200	270	207	238	99.4	79
80	" 7	11.52 A.M.	" 7	4.22 P.M.	4h. 25m.	3h. 47m.	38m.	05m.	3 958	3 487	444	242	250	23	15.4	93	4.87	636	55 000	....	....	338	99.4	80
81	" 7	4.22 P.M.	" 8	1.33 "	5h. 18m.	4h. 42m.	36m.	15h. 53m.	4 934	4 452	518	259	220	20	15.8	96	3.84	670	40 900	556	512	534	98.7	81
82	" 8	1.33 "	" 10	12.02 "	6h. 47m.	5h. 48m.	59m.	39h. 42m.	6 082	5 467	572	407	200	19	15.7	95	3.90	840	20 400	530	180	295	98.6	82
83	" 10	12.02 "	" 10	4.00 "	3h. 58m.	3h. 21m.	37m.	00m.	3 683	3 258	456	247	180	24	16.3	99	2.20	967	14 400	384	110	247	98.3	83
84[1]	" 10	4.00 "	" 13	2.11 "	....	1h. 25m.	......	......	3 490	1 374	....		....	....	16.2	98	1.01	967	18 900	....	....	348	98.2	84[1]
85[2]	" 13	2.11 "	" 14	11.28 A.M.	5h. 03m.	4h. 41m.	22m.	16h. 14m.	6 069	5 191	377	260	180	13	18.5	112	1.10	232	13 900	1670	182	843	93.9	85[2]
86	" 14	11.28 A.M.	" 15	12.15 P.M.	5h. 36m.	5h. 16m.	20m.	19h. 11m.	6 382	5 970	442	0	250	11	18.9	114	6.34	412	11 600	84	40	60	99.5	86
87	" 15	12.15 P.M.	" 15	3.42 "	3h. 27m.	2h. 52m.	35m.	00m.	3 842	3 614	408	311	300	26	21.0	127	6.90	486	10 800	243	90	166	98.5	88
88	" 15	3.42 "	" 17	1.02 "	4h. 20m.	3h. 49m.	31m.	41h. 00m.	4 906	4 292	450	193	200	17	18.8	114	4.35	438	19 800	....	....	109	99.4	87
89	" 17	1.02 "	" 18	9.00 A.M.	4h. 34m.	3h. 53m.	41m.	15h. 24m.	4 861	4 461	416	260	200	18	19.1	116	4.05	390	21 800	125	87	106	99.5	89
90	" 18	9.00 A.M.	" 18	3.16 P.M.	5h. 26m.	4h. 50m.	36m.	50m.	5 534	5 056	295	261	300	16	17.4	105	3.66	180	14 400	198	20	91	99.4	90
91	" 18	3.16 P.M.	" 19	1.22 "	5h. 35m.	4h. 57m.	38m.	16h. 31m.	5 903	5 305	407	409	250	18	17.9	108	3.42	372	17 900	104	39	68	99.6	91
92	" 19	1.22 "	" 20	11.48 A.M.	6h. 31m.	5h. 56m.	35m.	15h. 55m.	7 177	6 330	442	493	180	16	17.8	108	4.21	420	18 500	382	55	198	98.9	92
93	" 20	11.48 A.M.	" 20	5.07 P.M.	5h. 19m.	4h. 41m.	38m.	00m.	5 203	4 779	396	250	180	16	17.0	103	4.27	266	17 400	560	79	218	98.8	93
94	" 20	5.07 P.M.	" 21	4.55 "	4h. 45m.	4h. 23m.	22m.	19h. 03m.	4 844	4 413	323	0	180	10	16.8	102	4.06	338	14 100	200	34	94	99.3	94
95	" 21	4.55 "	" 22	3.39 "	7h. 14m.	6h. 55m.	19m.	15h. 30m.	7 718	7 362	497	0	180	9	17.7	107	3.04	310	15 600	528	88	219	98.6	95
96	" 22	3.39 "	" 24	3.41 "	7h. 51m.	7h. 31m.	20m.	16h. 11m.	8 159	8 059	561	0	220	10	17.9	108	2.45	180	15 900	94	77	83	99.5	96
97	" 24	3.41 "	" 25	12.26 "	5h. 11m.	4h. 49m.	22m.	15h. 34m.	5 651	5 427	482	0	230	13	18.8	114	2.78	140	14 800	62	40	51	99.7	97
98	" 25	12.26 "	" 26	1.17 "	8h. 21m.	8h. 04m.	17m.	16h. 30m.	8 719	8 491	506	0	240	9	17.5	106	2.19	136	19 500	294	52	132	99.3	98
99	" 26	1.17 "	" 27	12.59 "	7h. 41m.	7h. 22m.	19m.	16h. 01m.	8 035	7 800	514	0	180	9	17.8	108	2.28	150	17 900	326	34	143	99.2	99
100	" 27	12.59 "	" 27	4.50 "	3h. 51m.	3h. 21m.	30m.	00m.	4 851	4 672	547	0	200	16	23.2	141	3.19	161	4 100	53	30	41	99.0	100
101	" 27	4.50 "	" 28	1.27 "	5h. 03m.	4h. 39m.	24m.	15h. 34m.	6 832	6 620	641	0	180	19	23.7	144	2.52	78	4 700	142	21	81	98.3	101
102	" 28	1.27 "	" 29	9.01 A.M.	4h. 18m.	3h. 48m.	30m.	15h. 16m.	5 442	5 255	613	0	300	17	23.1	141	2.41	57	4 500	413	33	223	95.0	102
103	" 29	9.01 A.M.	" 29	1.10 P.M.	4h. 04m.	3h. 39m.	25m.	05m.	5 553	5 472	644	0	200	18	25.0	152	2.46	62	14 800	....	....	138	99.1	103
104	" 29	1.10 P.M.	" 29	4.58 "	3h. 40m.	3h. 09m.	32m.	08m.	4 748	4 548	1256	0	200	32	24.2	147	2.50	62	14 800	187	176	181	98.8	104
105	" 29	4.58 "	Mar. 2	12.26 "	3h. 51m.	3h. 30m.	21m.	39h. 37m.	5 309	5 097	546	0	180	14	24.3	148	2.40	56	26 500	331	130	224	99.2	105
106	Mar. 2	12.26 "	" 2	4.44 "	4h. 18m.	4h. 01m.	17m.	00m.	5 825	5 632	489	0	200	12	23.4	142	2.41	54	44 600	....	....	676	98.5	106
107	" 2	4.44 "	" 3	1.43 "	5h. 16m.	4h. 53m.	23m.	15h. 43m.	7 290	7 072	531	0	176	10	24.2	147	1.91	80	37 500	405	155	298	99.2	107

[1] Available data incomplete. [2] Application of chemicals unsatisfactory. Chemical meter out of order.

TABLE No. 5.—*Continued.*

Warren System.

Number of Run.	Began. Date.	Began. Hour.	Ended. Date.	Ended. Hour.	Periods of Time. Hours and Minutes. Operation.	Service.	Wash.	Delay.	Quantities of Water. Cubic Feet. Applied.	Filtered.	Wash.	Waste. Filtered.	Waste. Unfiltered.	Percentage which the Sum of the Wash and Waste Water is of Applied Water.	Average Actual Rate of Filtration. Cubic Feet per Minute.	Million Gallons per Acre per 24 Hours.	Average Amount of Applied Sulphate of Alumina. Grains per Gallon.	Estimated Average Amount of Suspended Solids in River Water. Parts per Million.	Bacteria per Cubic Centimeter. River Water.	Effluent. Maximum.	Effluent. Minimum.	Effluent. Average.	Average Bacterial Efficiency.	Number of Run.
	1896		1896																					
108	Mar. 3	1.43 P.M.	Mar. 4	11.44 A.M.	5h. 53m.	5h. 29m.	24m.	16h. 08m.	8 110	7 752	500	133	176	9	23.6	144	2.26	70	31 700	605	95	418	98.7	108
109	" 4	11.44 A.M.	" 4	3.58 P.M.	4h. 14m.	3h. 59m.	15m.	00m.	5 826	5 651	497	0	176	12	23.6	144	2.47	60	29 800	1 390	80	735	97.5	109
110	" 4	3.58 P.M.	" 5	12.06 "	4h. 33m.	4h. 19m.	14m.	15h. 35m.	6 314	6 102	510	0	176	11	23.6	144	2.52	52	26 300	187	116	151	99.4	110
111	" 5	12.06 "	" 5	5.08 "	4h. 51m.	4h. 18m.	33m.	11m.	6 060	5 881	548	0	176	12	22.8	138	2.59	50	18 000	590	93	341	98.1	111
112	" 5	5.08 "	" 6	1.25 "	4h. 34m.	4h. 16m.	18m.	15h. 43m.	6 207	5 992	492	0	167	11	23.4	142	2.49	25	13 300	615	48	426	96.8	112
113	" 6	1.25 "	" 6	4.48 "	3h. 23m.	3h. 02m.	21m.	00m.	4 586	4 419	433	0	167	13	24.2	147	2.80	22	12 200	....	....	106	99.1	113
114	" 6	4.48 "	" 7	1.54 "	5h. 34m.	5h. 14m.	20m.	15h. 32m.	7 597	7 398	441	0	176	8	23.5	143	2.11	70	10 900	485	39	194	98.2	114
115	" 7	1.54 "	" 9	11.34 A.M.	6h. 04m.	5h. 47m.	17m.	39h. 36m.	8 401	8 182	459	0	176	8	23.6	144	2.32	74	10 500	620	40	271	97.4	115
116	" 9	11.34 A.M.	" 9	3.04 P.M.	3h. 25m.	3h. 12m.	13m.	05m.	4 539	4 351	431	0	176	13	22.7	137	2.57	68	14 000	....	....	40	99.7	116
117	" 9	3.04 P.M.	" 10	11.50 A.M.	4h. 55m.	4h. 40m.	15m.	15h. 51m.	6 773	6 573	460	0	176	9	23.5	143	2.03	64	13 100	139	35	79	99.4	117
118	" 10	11.50 A.M.	" 10	3.46 P.M.	3h. 45m.	3h. 28m.	17m.	11m.	5 039	4 859	443	0	176	12	23.5	143	2.61	60	11 500	935	68	501	95.6	118
119	" 10	3.46 P.M.	" 11	11.02 A.M.	3h. 46m.	3h. 28m.	18m.	15h. 30m.	5 133	4 938	452	0	167	12	23.7	144	2.91	70	11 100	300	61	180	98.4	119
120	" 11	11.02 A.M.	" 11	1.43 P.M.	2h. 26m.	2h. 09m.	17m.	15m.	3 063	2 885	454	0	176	21	22.4	135	4.64	71	7 600	....	....	225	97.0	120
121	" 11	1.43 P.M.	" 11	4.36 "	2h. 48m.	2h. 33m.	15m.	05m.	3 263	3 070	439	0	176	19	20.1	122	4.37	71	7 700	....	....	310	96.0	121
122	" 11	4.36 "	" 12	11.35 A.M.	3h. 27m.	3h. 11m.	16m.	15h. 32m.	4 075	3 853	430	0	176	15	20.3	123	5.20	61	10 100	89	60	74	99.3	122
123	" 12	11.35 A.M.	" 12	4.01 P.M.	4h. 16m.	3h. 59m.	17m.	10m.	4 528	4 338	450	0	176	14	18.2	110	4.22	56	11 300	485	26	255	97.7	123
124	" 12	4.01 P.M.	" 13	11.52 A.M.	4h. 24m.	4h. 07m.	17m.	15h. 27m.	5 010	4 822	475	0	176	13	19.5	118	5.02	49	9 600	137	24	80	99.2	124
125	" 13	11.52 A.M.	" 13	3.48 P.M.	3h. 56m.	3h. 34m.	22m.	00m.	4 076	3 892	452	0	167	15	18.2	110	4.88	45	11 090	1000	26	513	95.3	125
126	" 13	3.48 P.M.	" 14	11.45 A.M.	4h. 27m.	4h. 01m.	26m.	15h. 30m.	4 942	4 717	472	0	176	13	19.6	119	5.06	48	12 500	137	11	74	99.4	126
127	" 14	11.45 A.M.	" 14	3.44 P.M.	3h. 59m.	3h. 41m.	18m.	00m.	4 309	4 128	446	0	176	14	18.7	113	4.36	52	12 100	451	37	244	98.0	127
128	" 14	3.44 P.M.	" 16	11.20 A.M.	4h. 06m.	3h. 45m.	21m.	39h. 30m.	4 427	4 243	421	0	176	13	18.9	114	5.40	51	13 900	40	19	29	99.8	128
129	" 16	11.20 A.M.	" 16	4.36 P.M.	5h. 16m.	4h. 59m.	17m.	00m.	5 398	5 246	433	0	176	11	17.6	107	4.27	50	16 600	172	34	103	99.4	129
130	" 16	4.36 P.M.	" 17	12.53 "	4h. 34m.	4h. 12m.	22m.	15h. 43m.	5 184	4 979	437	0	176	12	19.8	120	4.02	60	17 700	60	8	33	99.8	130
131	" 17	12.53 "	" 18	9.00 A.M.	4h. 42m.	4h. 14m.	28m.	15h. 25m.	5 061	4 899	442	0	176	12	19.3	117	4.67	62	16 300	50	34	42	99.7	131
132	" 18	9.00 A.M.	" 18	1.56 P.M.	4h. 56m.	4h. 36m.	20m.	00m.	5 563	5 368	441	0	176	11	19.4	117	4.28	88	19 700	51	23	35	99.8	132
133	" 18	1.56 P.M.	" 19	10.34 A.M.	4h. 58m.	4h. 36m.	22m.	15h. 40m.	5 720	5 328	478	202	176	15	19.3	117	4.43	110	24 300	143	43	75	99.7	133
134	" 19	10.34 A.M.	" 19	1.55 P.M.	3h. 21m.	3h. 00m.	21m.	00m.	3 646	3 468	470	0	176	18	19.3	117	4.45	210	34 300	150	91	115	99.7	134
135	" 19	1.55 P.M.	" 20	9.00 A.M.	3h. 53m.	3h. 21m.	32m.	15h. 12m.	4 126	3 947	440	0	176	15	19.6	119	4.68	210	36 000	265	76	170	99.5	135
136	" 20	9.00 A.M.	" 20	12.05 P.M.	3h. 05m.	2h. 46m.	19m.	00m.	3 426	3 242	445	0	176	18	19.5	118	5.73	993	41 600	144	43	93	99.8	136
137	" 20	12.05 P.M.	" 20	2.57 "	2h. 50m.	2h. 29m.	21m.	02m.	2 757	2 581	440	0	158	22	17.3	105	5.21	993	60 100	137	111	124	99.8	137
138	" 20	2.57 "	" 21	9.30 A.M.	3h. 03m.	2h. 39m.	24m.	15h. 30m.	3 150	2 800	517	0	324	27	17.6	107	5.38	1 000	56 700	298	111	175	99.7	138
139	" 21	9.30 A.M.	" 21	12.33 P.M.	3h. 03m.	2h. 42m.	21m.	00m.	3 074	2 881	429	0	167	19	17.8	108	6.52	1 276	59 800	148	138	143	99.8	139
140	" 21	12.33 P.M.	" 21	3.31 "	2h. 58m.	2h. 40m.	18m.	00m.	2 968	2 789	466	0	176	22	17.4	105	6.37	1 276	57 100	....	....	220	99.6	140
141	" 21	3.31 "	" 23	9.30 A.M.	2h. 29m.	1h. 59m.	30m.	15h. 30m.	2 569	2 129	513	0	431	37	17.9	108	6.60	1 276	52 100	820	116	329	99.4	141
142	" 23	9.30 A.M.	" 23	12.47 P.M.	3h. 17m.	2h. 56m.	21m.	00m.	3 275	3 065	517	0	176	21	17.4	105	6.29	660	34 700	147	51	79	99.8	142
143	" 23	12.47 P.M.	" 23	4.14 "	3h. 27m.	3h. 06m.	21m.	00m.	3 272	3 098	419	0	176	18	16.7	101	5.93	660	30 400	440	50	245	99.2	143
144	" 23	4.14 "	" 24	12.37 "	4h. 53m.	4h. 32m.	21m.	15h. 30m.	4 874	4 672	482	0	176	13	17.2	104	5.64	521	30 700	435	21	178	99.4	144

TABLE NO. 5.—*Continued.*

Warren System.

Number of Run.	Began. Date.	Began. Hour.	Ended. Date.	Ended. Hour.	Periods of Time. Hours and Minutes. Operation.	Service.	Wash.	Delay.	Quantities of Water. Cubic Feet. Applied.	Filtered.	Wash.	Waste. Filtered.	Waste. Unfiltered.	Percentage which the Sum of the Wash and Waste Water is of Applied Water.	Average Actual Rate of Filtration. Cubic Feet per Minute.	Million Gallons per Acre per 24 Hours.	Average Amount of Applied Sulphate of Alumina. Grains per Gallon.	Estimated Average Amount of Suspended Solids in River Water. Parts per Million.	Bacteria per Cubic Centimeter. River Water.	Effluent. Maximum.	Minimum.	Average.	Average Bacterial Efficiency.	Number of Run.
	1896		1896																					
145	Mar. 24	12.37 P.M.	Mar. 24	5.18 P.M.	4h. 41m.	4h. 18m.	23m.	00m.	4 578	4 426	423	0	176	13	17.2	104	5.93	521	38 000	127	21	72	99.8	145
146	" 24	5.18 "	" 24	9.16 "	3h. 58m.	3h. 34m.	24m.	12h. 00m.	4 019	3 804	448	0	176	16	17.8	108	5.62	521	37 800	127	61	69	99.8	146
147	" 24	9.16 "	" 25	12.54 A.M.	3h. 38m.	3h. 19m.	19m.	00m.	3 730	3 552	507	0	176	18	17.8	108	5.82	521	39 000	61	52	57	99.9	147
148	" 25	12.54 A.M.	" 25	4.44 "	3h. 50m.	3h. 31m.	19m.	00m.	3 796	3 622	456	0	176	17	17.2	104	5.54	521	36 700	252	64	179	99.5	148
149	" 25	4.44 "	" 25	8.45 "	4h. 01m.	3h. 28m.	33m.	00m.	3 868	3 657	377	0	176	14	17.6	107	5.64	521	38 700	103	62	70	99.8	149
150	" 25	8.45 "	" 25	12.33 P.M.	3h. 46m.	3h. 21m.	25m.	02m.	3 894	3 692	441	0	167	16	18.4	111	5.05	516	38 700	85	71	73	99.8	150
151	" 25	12.33 P.M.	" 25	4.10 "	3h. 37m.	3h. 17m.	20m.	00m.	3 668	3 483	428	0	176	16	17.7	107	4.42	516	38 300	201	85	115	99.7	151
152	" 25	4.10 "	" 25	8.09 "	3h. 59m.	3h. 41m.	18m.	00m.	3 694	3 795	396	0	176	16	17.2	104	2.78	516	44 900	201	81	125	99.7	152
153	" 25	8.09 "	" 25	10.43 "	2h. 25m.	2h. 05m.	20m.	09m.	2 256	2 028	415	0	228	28	16.2	98	9.08	516	44 900	865	81	81	99.8	153
154[1]	" 25	10.43 "	" 25	11.55 "	1h. 12m.	52m.	20m.	00m.	1 067	883	374	0	176	52	17.0	103	9.73	516	56 300	865	74	865	99.5	154[1]
155	" 25	11.55 "	" 26	3.27 A.M.	3h. 20m.	3h. 04m.	16m.	12m.	3 418	3 259	455	0	176	18	17.7	107	7.97	516	53 600	87	74	74	99.9	155
156	" 26	3.27 A.M.	" 26	7.03 "	3h. 36m.	3h. 18m.	18m.	00m.	3 554	3 489	411	0	176	17	17.6	107	5.45	516	50 900	121	87	104	99.8	156
157	" 26	7.03 "	" 26	11.03 "	3h. 49m.	3h. 24m.	25m.	11m.	4 050	3 786	556	0	176	18	18.6	113	5.41	494	50 300	205	121	101	99.8	157
158	" 26	11.03 "	" 26	2.32 P.M.	3h. 25m.	3h. 04m.	21m.	04m.	3 536	3 372	411	0	176	17	18.3	111	4.32	472	49 800	205	142	151	99.7	158
159	" 26	2.32 "	" 26	5.31 "	2h. 54m.	2h. 35m.	19m.	05m.	3 101	2 929	418	0	176	19	18.9	114	4.54	472	50 100	....	....	228	95.4	159
160	" 26	5.31 P.M.	" 26	9.08 "	3h. 22m.	3h. 06m.	16m.	15m.	3 565	3 397	430	0	176	17	18.3	111	3.83	472	48 500	89	69	89	99.8	160
161	" 26	9.08 "	" 27	1.00 A.M.	3h. 45m.	3h. 30m.	15m.	07m.	3 863	3 691	404	0	176	15	17.6	107	3.40	472	46 700	69	59	65	99.9	161
162	" 27	1.00 A.M.	" 27	5.04 "	4h. 04m.	3h. 47m.	17m.	00m.	4 106	3 946	443	0	176	15	17.4	105	3.87	472	45 700	209	59	145	99.7	162
163	" 27	5.04 "	" 27	8.59 "	3h. 55m.	3h. 36m.	19m.	00m.	4 038	3 880	435	0	176	15	18.0	109	3.98	472	44 700	209	62	105	99.8	163
164	" 27	8.59 "	" 27	1.00 P.M.	4h. 01m.	3h. 36m.	25m.	00m.	4 083	3 916	511	0	176	17	18.1	110	3.80	360	40 000	189	62	103	99.7	164
165	" 27	1.00 P.M.	" 27	4.46 "	3h. 46m.	3h. 24m.	22m.	00m.	3 857	3 692	470	0	176	17	18.1	110	4.00	360	34 200	309	189	258	99.3	165
166	" 27	4.46 "	" 27	8.14 "	3h. 28m.	3h. 11m.	17m.	00m.	3 631	3 464	353	0	176	15	18.2	110	4.63	360	33 100	309	110	154	99.5	166
167	" 27	8.14 "	" 28	12.27 A.M.	4h. 13m.	3h. 57m.	16m.	00m.	4 335	4 176	400	0	176	13	17.6	107	3.92	360	25 700	169	110	147	99.4	167
168	" 28	12.27 A.M.	" 28	4.58 "	4h. 31m.	4h. 16m.	15m.	00m.	4 615	4 461	419	0	176	13	17.4	105	4.04	360	29 500	555	59	176	99.3	168
169	" 28	4.58 "	" 28	9.12 "	4h. 14m.	3h. 54m.	20m.	00m.	4 387	4 231	420	0	176	14	18.1	110	3.22	360	35 200	114	77	81	99.8	169
170	" 28	9.12 "	" 28	1.31 P.M.	4h. 08m.	3h. 52m.	16m.	11m.	4 465	4 305	448	0	176	14	18.6	113	3.66	428	35 200	155	114	132	99.6	170
171	" 28	1.31 P.M.	" 28	5.52 "	4h. 21m.	4h. 04m.	17m.	00m.	4 761	4 598	444	0	176	13	18.8	114	3.65	428	35 800	187	155	160	99.6	171
172	" 28	5.52 "	" 28	10.27 "	4h. 35m.	4h. 20m.	15m.	00m.	4 830	4 669	423	0	176	12	18.0	109	3.10	428	38 400	187	135	161	99.6	172
173	" 28	10.27 "	" 29	3.12 A.M.	4h. 36m.	4h. 18m.	18m.	09m.	4 597	4 463	440	0	176	13	17.3	105	3.60	428	32 300	135	21	49	99.9	173
174	" 29	3.12 A.M.	" 29	7.44 "	4h. 32m.	4h. 14m.	18m.	00m.	4 730	4 566	425	0	176	13	18.0	109	3.26	428	29 700	67	40	53	99.8	174
175	" 29	7.44 "	" 29	11.53 "	4h. 09m.	3h. 52m.	17m.	00m.	4 157	4 096	430	0	176	15	17.7	107	5.63	383	54 000	125	46	50	99.9	175
176	" 29	11.53 "	" 29	5.29 P.M.	5h. 36m.	5h. 17m.	19m.	00m.	5 889	5 651	456	0	176	11	17.8	108	3.06	338	55 400	300	125	220	99.6	176
177	" 29	5.29 P.M.	" 29	10.55 "	5h. 26m.	5h. 09m.	17m.	00m.	5 650	5 509	449	0	176	11	17.8	108	2.91	338	36 600	180	69	113	99.7	177
178	" 29	10.55 "	" 30	4.23 A.M.	5h. 28m.	5h. 10m.	18m.	00m.	5 883	5 740	494	0	176	11	18.5	112	3.33	338	42 900	180	52	77	99.8	178
179	" 30	4.23 A.M.	" 30	10.17 "	5h. 54m.	5h. 35m.	19m.	00m.	5 995	5 853	490	0	176	11	17.5	106	3.25	650	38 000	145	92	127	99.7	179
180	" 30	10.17 "	" 30	2.26 P.M.	4h. 09m.	3h. 50m.	19m.	00m.	4 185	4 041	434	0	176	15	17.6	107	5.08	740	25 900	145	113	124	99.5	180

[1] Application of chemicals unsatisfactory. Chemical meter out of order.

TABLE No. 5.—*Continued.*

Warren System.

Number of Run.	Began. Date.	Began. Hour.	Ended. Date.	Ended. Hour.	Periods of Time. Hours and Minutes. Operation.	Service.	Wash.	Delay.	Quantities of Water. Cubic Feet. Applied.	Filtered.	Wash.	Waste. Filtered.	Waste. Unfiltered.	Percentage which the Sum of the Wash and Waste Water is of Applied Water.	Average Actual Rate of Filtration. Cubic Feet per Minute.	Million Gallons per Acre per 24 Hours.	Average Amount of Applied Sulphate of Alumina. Grains per Gallon.	Estimated Average Amount of Suspended Solids in River Water. Parts per Million.	Bacteria per Cubic Centimeter. River Water.	Effluent. Maximum.	Effluent. Minimum.	Effluent. Average.	Average Bacterial Efficiency.	Number of Run.
	1896		1896																					
181	Mar. 30	2.26 P.M.	Mar. 31	9.38 A.M.	3h. 22m.	3h. 04m.	18m.	15h. 40m.	3 677	3 271	441	0	430	24	17.8	108	6.47	740	20 900	117	113	117	99.5	181
182	" 31	9.38 A.M.	" 31	12.15 P.M.	2h. 47m.	2h. 31m.	16m.	00m.	2 850	2 670	407	0	158	20	17.7	107	5.28	1 004	22 800	525	147	183	99.2	182
183	" 31	12.15 P.M.	" 31	2.40 "	2h. 18m.	2h. 02m.	16m.	07m.	2 266	2 117	400	0	176	25	17.3	105	6.28	1 004	25 000	....	....	325	98.7	183
184	" 31	2.40 "	" 31	5.03 "	2h. 23m.	2h. 04m.	19m.	00m.	2 313	2 159	463	0	167	27	17.4	105	5.56	1 004	29 600	....	....	635	97.9	184
185	" 31	5.03 "	April 1	11.55 A.M.	3h. 18m.	2h. 59m.	19m.	15h. 34m.	3 254	3 157	439	0	176	19	17.6	107	6.72	1 100	36 500	635	300	300	99.2	185
186	April 1	11.55 A.M.	" 1	2.29 P.M.	2h. 34m.	2h. 15m.	19m.	00m.	2 547	2 400	433	0	176	24	17.8	108	6.68	1 131	39 600	....	....	220	99.4	186
187	" 1	2.29 P.M.	" 1	5.13 "	2h. 44m.	2h. 26m.	18m.	00m.	2 692	2 540	414	0	176	22	17.4	105	6.45	1 131	42 700	....	....	270	99.4	187
188	" 1	5.13 "	" 2	12.49 "	3h. 43m.	3h. 26m.	17m.	15h. 53m.	3 837	3 676	445	0	176	16	17.8	108	6.18	960	31 200	270	102	102	99.7	188
189	" 2	12.49 "	" 2	3.45 "	2h. 56m.	2h. 40m.	16m.	00m.	2 900	2 761	420	0	176	21	17.3	105	5.77	932	19 200	205	157	161	99.2	189
190	" 2	3.45 "	" 3	11.03 A.M.	3h. 48m.	3h. 27m.	21m.	15h. 30m.	3 849	3 675	453	0	176	16	17.7	107	6.07	997	26 800	205	93	149	99.4	190
191	" 3	11.03 A.M.	" 3	2.45 P.M.	3h. 42m.	3h. 22m.	20m.	00m.	3 692	3 578	469	0	176	17	17.7	107	6.30	1 062	31 000	93	77	77	99.8	191
192	" 3	2.45 P.M.	" 4	9.00 A.M.	3h. 04m.	2h. 47m.	17m.	15h. 11m.	3 111	2 975	417	0	176	19	17.8	108	4.82	1 052	29 800	....	....	76	99.7	192
193	" 4	9.00 A.M.	" 4	2.54 P.M.	5h. 54m.	5h. 36m.	18m.	00m.	6 009	5 890	491	0	176	11	17.5	106	4.33	628	29 400	180	67	123	99.6	193
194	" 4	2.54 P.M.	" 6	12.48 "	6h. 24m.	6h. 05m.	19m.	39h. 30m.	6 577	6 723	505	0	176	10	18.4	111	3.90	556	20 100	81	25	55	99.7	194
195	" 6	12.48 "	" 7	12.37 "	8h. 19m.	8h. 00m.	19m.	15h. 30m.	8 515	8 086	521	0	176	8	16.8	102	3.40	400	19 900	39	25	35	99.8	195
196	" 7	12.37 "	" 8	12.43 "	8h. 37m.	8h. 18m.	19m.	15h. 29m.	8 906	8 765	563	0	176	8	17.6	107	1.91	320	16 200	59	25	41	99.7	196
197	" 8	12.43 "	" 9	12.25 "	8h. 12m.	7h. 55m.	17m.	15h. 30m.	8 417	8 278	460	0	176	8	17.4	105	1.92	370	17 800	158	70	110	99.4	197
198	" 9	12.25 "	" 10	12.28 "	8h. 33m.	8h. 14m.	19m.	15h. 30m.	8 737	8 651	495	0	176	8	17.5	106	1.91	300	13 900	87	44	67	99.5	198
199	" 10	12.28 "	" 11	3.42 "	11h. 44m.	11h. 24m.	20m.	15h. 30m.	11 956	11 948	528	0	176	6	17.5	106	1.89	270	13 900	55	12	23	99.8	199
200	" 11	3.42 "	" 20	9.02 A.M.	2h. 08m.	1h. 50m.	18m.	209h. 20m.	2 118	1 959	421	0	176	28	17.8	108	1.88	284	13 200	65	19	39	99.7	200
201	" 20	9.02 A.M.	" 21	9.00 "	8h. 28m.	8h. 04m.	24m.	15h. 30m.	11 672	12 068	438	0	52	4	25.0	152	1.59	116	48 000	48	24	34	99.3	201
202	" 21	9.00 "	" 22	9.00 "	8h. 34m.	8h. 10m.	24m.	15h. 26m.	10 886	11 026	507	0	44	5	22.5	136	0.84	118	4 000	147	46	82	98.0	202
203	" 22	9.00 "	" 23	10.45 "	8h. 37m.	8h. 12m.	25m.	17h. 08m.	11 134	11 136	550	0	70	6	22.7	137	0.85	90	5 500	198	104	166	97.0	203
204	" 23	10.45 "	" 24	2.03 P.M.	11h. 48m.	11h. 20m.	28m.	15h. 30m.	15 366	15 378	570	0	52	4	22.6	137	0.79	70	5 900	460	53	218	96.3	204
205	" 24	2.03 P.M.	" 27	9.00 A.M.	9h. 01m.	8h. 35m.	26m.	57h. 56m.	10 960	10 950	650	0	87	7	21.3	129	0.73	70	8 200	371	220	295	96.4	205
206	" 27	9.00 A.M.	" 27	8.31 P.M.	11h. 31m.	11h. 08m.	23m.	00m.	13 858	14 287	504	0	87	4	21.4	129	0.76	72	6 700	500	143	321	95.2	206
207	" 27	8.31 P.M.	" 28	6.07 A.M.	9h. 36m.	9h. 15m.	21m.	00m.	11 540	11 569	506	0	87	6	20.9	126	0.54	72	5 500	559	500	559	89.9	207
208[1]	" 28	6.07 A.M.	" 28	10.55 "	....	2h. 39m.	....	....	3 911	3 597	426	0	....	....	22.6	137	....	78	5 700	....	....	....	....	208[1]
209	" 28	10.55 "	" 28	9.05 P.M.	10h. 10m.	9h. 48m.	22m.	00m.	14 231	12 831	563	0	44	4	21.8	132	0.73	78	6 200	547	410	478	92.3	209
210	" 28	9.05 P.M.	" 29	6.45 A.M.	9h. 40m.	9h. 19m.	21m.	00m.	11 467	11 465	546	0	44	5	20.5	124	0.49	78	6 800	1075	390	733	89.2	210
211	" 29	6.45 A.M.	" 29	2.40 P.M.	7h. 55m.	7h. 26m.	29m.	00m.	9 256	9 233	546	0	61	7	20.7	125	0.68	72	7 400	....	....	1 075	85.5	211
212	" 29	2.40 P.M.	" 30	1.10 A.M.	10h. 30m.	10h. 05m.	25m.	00m.	12 583	12 646	463	0	44	4	20.9	126	1.32	72	6 900	172	246	159	97.7	212
213	" 30	1.10 A.M.	" 30	2.12 P.M.	13h. 02m.	12h. 37m.	25m.	00m.	15 588	15 675	642	0	52	4	20.7	125	0.97	60	4 200	146	95	120	97.1	213
214	" 30	2.12 P.M.	May 1	1.56 A.M.	11h. 44m.	11h. 18m.	26m.	00m.	13 906	14 005	672	0	50	6	20.7	125	1.14	57	3 800	120	76	95	97.5	214
215	May 1	1.56 A.M.	" 1	3.16 P.M.	13h. 20m.	12h. 52m.	28m.	00m.	15 686	15 795	632	0	51	4	20.5	124	0.99	60	4 600	243	45	119	97.4	215
216	" 1	3.16 P.M.	" 2	3.27 A.M.	12h. 11m.	11h. 47m.	24m.	00m.	14 426	14 653	570	0	44	4	20.7	125	1.29	62	5 700	....	....	77	98.6	216

[1] Application of chemicals unsatisfactory. Chemical meter out of order.

TABLE NO. 5.—*Continued.*

Warren System.

Number of Run.	Began. Date.	Began. Hour.	Ended. Date.	Ended. Hour.	Periods of Time. Hours and Minutes. Operation.	Service.	Wash.[*]	Delay.	Quantities of Water. Cubic Feet. Applied.	Filtered.	Wash.	Waste. Filtered.	Waste. Unfiltered.	Percentage which the Sum of the Wash and Waste Water is of Applied Water.	Average Actual Rate of Filtration. Cubic Feet per Minute.	Million Gallons per Acre per 24 Hours.	Average Amount of Applied Sulphate of Alumina. Grains per Gallon.	Estimated Average Amount of Suspended Solids in River Water. Parts per Million.	Bacteria per Cubic Centimeter. River Water.	Effluent. Maximum.	Effluent. Minimum.	Effluent. Average.	Average Bacterial Efficiency.	Number of Run.
	1896		1896																					
217	May 2	3.27 A.M.	May 4	11.59 A.M.	15h. 23m.	14h. 55m.	28m.	41h. 09m.	18 164	18 283	674	0	44	4	20.4	123	1.07	70	6 900	183	72	128	98.1	217
218	" 4	11.59 "	" 4	8.34 P.M.	8h. 35m.	8h. 11m.	24m.	00m.	10 286	10 340	538	0	44	6	21.1	128	1.15	103	7 200	72	56	64	99.1	218
219	" 4	8.34 P.M.	" 5	4.41 A.M.	8h. 07m.	7h. 42m.	25m.	00m.	9 262	9 352	596	0	44	7	20.2	122	2.32	103	6 300	56	43	47	99.3	219
220	" 5	4.41 A.M.	" 5	5.20 P.M.	12h. 39m.	12h. 07m.	32m.	00m.	14 712	14 893	897	0	60	6	20.5	124	1.80	104	6 800	66	51	58	99.1	220
221	" 5	5.20 P.M.	" 6	5.08 A.M.	11h. 48m.	11h. 22m.	26m.	00m.	14 087	14 240	552	0	44	4	20.9	126	1.80	104	6 300	....	....	69	98.9	221
222	" 6	5.08 A.M.	" 6	4.23 P.M.	11h. 15m.	10h. 45m.	30m.	00m.	13 039	13 169	855	0	44	7	20.4	123	1.43	97	4 600	100	35	62	98.7	222
223	" 6	4.23 P.M.	" 7	3.14 A.M.	10h. 51m.	10h. 25m.	26m.	00m.	13 086	13 211	633	0	44	5	21.1	128	1.46	97	5 400	....	....	96	98.2	223
224	" 7	3.14 A.M.	" 7	4.30 P.M.	13h. 16m.	12h. 47m.	29m.	00m.	15 894	15 970	855	0	44	6	20.9	126	1.92	80	4 700	100	30	65	98.6	224
225	" 7	4.30 P.M.	" 8	4.21 A.M.	11h. 51m.	11h. 25m.	26m.	00m.	14 278	14 522	572	0	44	4	21.2	128	1.01	70	5 300	167	51	109	97.9	225
226	" 8	4.21 A.M	" 8	2.55 P.M.	10h. 34m.	10h. 06m.	28m.	00m.	12 090	12 224	794	0	70	7	20.2	122	1.07	90	4 500	113	17	65	98.6	226
227[*]	" 8	2.55 P.M.	" 8	7.19 "	4h. 24m.	4h. 00m.	24m.	00m.	5 125	5 115	550	0	44	12	21.3	129	1.63	111	3 200	....	...	....	....	227[*]
228	" 8	7.19 "	" 9	3.51 A.M.	8h. 32m.	8h. 06m.	26m.	00m.	9 976	10 063	690	0	44	7	20.7	125	0.93	111	4 300	....	....	58	98.7	228
229	" 9	3.51 A.M.	" 9	3.49 P.M.	11h. 58m.	11h. 22m.	36m.	00m.	14 359	14 534	928	0	44	7	21.3	129	1.33	111	5 800	49	43	46	99.2	229
230	" 9	3.49 P.M.	" 11	9.49 "	13h. 01m.	12h. 36m.	25m.	40h. 59m.	15 781	15 985	689	0	44	5	21.1	128	2.15	180	7 400	44	41	42	99.4	230
231	" 11	9.49 "	" 12	9.49 A.M.	12h. 00m.	11h. 19m.	41m.	00m.	13 738	13 973	841	0	44	6	20.6	125	2.53	180	6 800	100	23	45	99.3	231
232	" 12	9.49 A.M.	" 12	8.34 P.M.	10h. 45m.	10h. 16m.	29m.	00m.	12 922	13 116	705	0	44	6	21.3	129	1.55	168	6 500	....	....	123	98.1	232
233	" 12	8.34 P.M.	" 13	4.01 A.M.	7h. 27m.	6h. 53m.	34m.	00m.	8 240	8 343	848	0	44	11	20.2	122	2.23	168	5 600	47	44	45	99.2	233
234	" 13	4.01 A.M.	" 13	2.57 P.M.	10h. 56m.	10h. 24m.	32m.	00m.	12 805	12 996	970	0	44	8	20.8	126	2.68	150	4 400	31	13	22	99.5	234
235	" 13	2.57 P.M.	" 13	11.47 "	8h. 50m.	8h. 21m.	29m.	00m.	10 256	10 396	811	0	35	8	20.8	126	1.70	137	3 700	....	....	11	99.7	235
236	" 13	11.47 "	" 14	12.13 "	12h. 20m.	11h. 50m.	30m.	06m.	14 435	14 639	1073	0	50	8	20.6	125	1.67	140	4 200	15	10	12	99.7	236
237	" 14	12.13 "	" 15	12.04 A.M.	11h. 51m.	11h. 24m.	27m.	00m.	14 164	14 381	840	0	44	6	21.0	127	1.85	144	6 400	24	18	21	99.7	237
238	" 15	12.04 A.M.	" 15	12.13 P.M.	12h. 09m.	11h. 35m.	34m.	00m.	14 159	14 319	952	0	44	7	20.6	125	1.37	130	7 100	59	47	53	99.3	238
239	" 15	12.13 P.M.	" 16	1.47 A.M.	13h. 34m.	13h. 07m.	27m.	00m.	16 014	17 058	778	0	70	5	21.7	131	1.81	100	7 100	16	14	15	99.8	239
240	" 16	1.47 A.M.	" 18	11.44 "	14h. 42m.	14h. 13m.	29m.	43h. 15m.	17 721	16 840	851	0	104	7	19.7	119	0.91	120	7 400	25	4	15	99.8	240
241[1]	" 18	11.44 "	" 18	8.56 P.M.	9h. 12m.	8h. 47m.	25m.	00m.	10 060	8 622	611	0	61	7	16.4	99	1.01	77	6 600	192	53	116	98.2	241[1]
242[*,1]	" 18	8.56 P.M.	" 19	4.52 A.M.	7h. 56m.	7h. 34m.	22m.	00m.	7 400	7 337	622	0	176	11	16.2	98	0.31	77	3 700	181	79	137	96.3	242[*,1]
243[*,1]	" 19	4.52 A.M.	" 19	8.58 P.M.	14h. 02m.	13h. 35m.	27m.	2h. 04m.	21 991	13 175	932	0	70	5	16.2	98	0.50	59	5 500	127	58	96	98.3	243[*,1]
244[1]	" 19	8.58 P.M.	" 20	7.30 "	21h. 24m.	20h. 54m.	30m.	1h. 08m.	20 334	20 485	872	0	105	5	16.3	99	0.95	100	4 100	185	13	78	98.1	244[1]
245[3]	" 20	7.30 "	" 21	12.27 "	16h. 57m.	16h. 21m.	36m.	00m.	17 302	15 912	1 228	0	100	8	16.2	98	1.35	142	5 400	107	47	67	98.8	245[3]
246[3]	" 21	12.27 "	" 22	1.43 A.M.	12h. 16m.	11h. 47m.	29m.	1h. 00m.	11 291	11 413	943	0	70	9	16.1	98	1.32	132	5 600	201	42	102	98.2	246[3]
247[3]	" 22	1.43 A.M.	" 22	3.39 P.M.	13h. 56m.	13h. 28m.	28m.	00m.	14 490	13 101	1 313	0	44	9	16.2	98	1.70	110	5 500	67	17	37	99.3	247[3]
248[3]	" 22	3.39 P.M.	" 25	10.58 A.M.	18h. 49m.	18h. 19m.	30m.	48h. 30m.	17 350	17 724	1 389	0	150	9	16.1	98	1.76	81	5 300	135	24	54	99.0	248[3]
249[4]	" 25	10.58 A.M.	" 26	4.31 "	17h. 33m.	17h. 02m.	31m.	00m.	21 296	19 906	980	0	61	5	19.5	118	0.83	38	1 900	49	21	37	98.1	249[4]
250[4]	" 26	4.31 "	" 26	6.00 P.M.	13h. 26m.	13h. 05m.	21m.	03m.	15 321	15 469	636	0	44	4	19.7	119	1.32	40	1 500	56	29	39	97.4	250[4]
251[4]	" 26	6.00 P.M.	" 27	11.46 A.M.	16h. 35m.	16h. 08m.	27m.	1h. 11m.	19 271	18 571	1 150	0	44	6	19.2	116	1.09	42	2 800	94	26	43	98.5	251[4]

[1] Prescribed chemicals 1.0 gr., rate 100 mil. gals. [2] Prescribed chemicals 1.5 gr., rate 100 mil. gals. [3] Prescribed chemicals 2.0 gr., rate 100 mil. gals. [4] Prescribed chemicals 1.0 gr., rate 120 mil. gals.

[*] Application of chemicals unsatisfactory. Chemical meter out of order.

TABLE NO. 5.—*Continued.*

Warren' System.

Number of Run.	Began. Date.	Began. Hour.	Ended. Date.	Ended. Hour.	Periods of Time. Hours and Minutes. Operation.	Service.	Wash.	Delay.	Quantities of Water. Cubic Feet. Applied.	Filtered.	Wash.	Waste. Filtered.	Waste. Unfiltered.	Percentage which the Sum of the Wash and Waste Water is of Applied Water.	Average Actual Rate of Filtration. Cubic Feet per Minute.	Million Gallons per Acre per 24 Hours.	Average Amount of Applied Sulphate of Alumina, Grains per Gallon.	Estimated Average Amount of Suspended Solids in River Water. Parts per Million.	Bacteria per Cubic Centimeter. River Water.	Effluent. Maximum.	Effluent. Minimum.	Effluent. Average.	Average Bacterial Efficiency.	Number of Run.
	1896		1896																					
252[1]	May 27	11.46 A.M.	May 28	3.04 A.M.	15h. 18m.	14h. 45m.	33m.	00m.	17 131	16 963	876	0	44	5	19.2	116	1.80	90	4 100	60	19	32	99.2	252[1]
253[1]	" 28	3.04 "	" 28	2.17 P.M.	11h. 13m.	10h. 48m.	25m.	00m.	12 636	12 777	840	0	44	7	19.7	119	1.64	200	10 500	90	31	58	99.4	253[1]
254[*1]	" 28	2.17 P.M.	" 28	9.52 "	6h. 34m.	6h. 08m.	26m.	05m.	6 908	6 993	820	0	44	13	19.0	115	1.48	300	14 200	340	185	275	98.1	254[*1]
255[*2]	" 28	9.52 "	" 29	12.28 A.M.	1h. 24m.	1h. 01m.	23m.	1h. 12m.	2 919	1 089	533	0	369	31	17.9	108	2.09	700	24 400	680	312	496	98.0	255[*2]
256[*3]	" 29	12.28 A.M.	" 29	4.29 "	2h. 42m.	2h. 11m.	31m.	1h. 19m.	4 313	2 525	617	0	369	23	19.3	117	2.96	800	32 400	570	220	372	98.9	256[*3]
257[4]	" 29	4.29 "	" 29	9.29 "	5h. 00m.	4h. 26m.	34m.	00m.	6 876	5 280	884	0	44	13	19.8	120	4.06	673	27 200	157	88	122	99.5	257[4]
258[4]	" 29	9.29 "	" 29	3.28 P.M.	5h. 55m.	5h. 19m.	36m.	04m.	6 183	6 270	780	0	44	13	19.7	119	3.69	653	25 800	139	89	114	99.6	258[4]
259[4]	" 29	3.28 P.M.	" 29	10.41 "	6h. 03m.	5h. 33m.	30m.	1h. 10m.	6 457	6 555	771	0	44	13	19.7	119	3.17	653	27 500	181	80	130	99.5	259[4]
260[4]	" 29	10.41 "	" 30	2.39 A.M.	3h. 50m.	3h. 18m.	32m.	08m.	5 232	3 721	760	0	44	15	18.8	114	4.10	653	28 700	....	....	293	99.0	260[4]
261[4]	" 30	2.39 A.M.	" 30	6.39 "	4h. 00m.	3h. 26m.	34m.	00m.	4 014	4 065	687	0	44	18	19.7	119	3.88	653	25 200	....	....	227	99.1	261[4]
262[4]	" 30	6.39 "	" 30	12.03 P.M.	5h. 24m.	4h. 53m.	31m.	00m.	5 787	5 817	688	0	44	13	19.9	120	4.63	540	20 700	246	92	169	99.2	262[4]
263[5]	" 30	12.03 P.M.	June 1	5.30 "	11h. 14m.	10h. 40m.	34m.	42h. 16m.	12 607	12 786	714	0	44	6	20.0	121	5.70	550	19 100	93	35	64	99.7	263[5]
264[6]	June 1	5.30 "	" 1	11.01 "	5h. 31m.	4h. 59m.	32m.	00m.	8 291	6 727	743	0	44	9	22.5	136	3.78	573	18 800	50	31	40	99.8	264[6]
265[6]	" 1	11.01 "	" 2	3.25 A.M.	4h. 16m.	3h. 49m.	27m.	08m.	5 176	4 839	717	0	298	20	21.1	128	3.45	573	18 600	....	....	73	99.6	265[6]
266[6]	" 2	3.25 A.M.	" 2	6.36 "	2h. 18m.	1h. 54m.	24m.	53m.	2 559	2 500	557	0	44	23	21.9	132	3.16	573	18 600	....	....	111	99.4	266[6]
267[7]	" 2	6.36 "	" 2	9.08 "	2h. 24m.	2h. 03m.	21m.	08m.	4 065	2 814	882	0	44	23	22.9	139	4.34	573	22 300	....	....	64	99.7	267[7]
268[7]	" 2	9.08 "	" 2	11.41 "	2h. 23m	1h. 57m.	36m.	00m.	2 601	2 606	736	0	44	30	22.3	135	4.84	829	22 300	....	...	67	99.7	268[7]
269[7]	" 2	11.41 "	" 2	1.58 P.M.	2h. 17m.	1h. 48m.	29m.	00m.	2 416	2 415	701	0	44	31	22.4	135	5.22	829	26 000	....	....	181	99.3	269[7]
270[7]	" 2	1.58 P.M.	" 2	4.08 "	2h. 10m	1h. 40m.	30m.	00m.	2 319	2 317	640	0	44	30	23.2	141	4.55	829	20 800	....	....	145	99.3	270[7]
271[7]	" 2	4.08 "	" 2	6.28 "	2h. 05m.	1h. 40m.	25m.	15m.	2 254	2 263	588	0	44	28	22.6	137	4.17	829	15 700	....	....	121	99.2	271[7]
272[8]	" 2	6.28 "	" 2	10.20 "	2h. 35m.	2h. 07m.	28m.	1h. 17m.	2 085	2 131	654	0	35	33	16.8	102	4.94	829	14 000	....	....	177	98.7	272[8]
273[9]	" 2	10.20 "	" 3	2.53 A.M.	4h. 33m.	4h. 08m.	25m.	00m.	5 408	3 865	666	0	263	17	15.6	95	5.90	829	12 400	....	....	49	99.6	273[9]
274[9]	" 3	2.53 A.M.	" 3	7.18 "	4h. 25m.	3h. 55m.	30m.	00m.	3 824	3 872	654	0	44	18	16.5	100	5.32	829	10 200	81	57	69	99.3	274[9]
275[9]	" 3	7.18 "	" 3	3.30 P.M.	8h. 12m.	7h. 42m.	30m.	00m.	7 769	7 933	619	0	44	9	17.2	104	5.58	550	8 200	77	61	49	99.2	275[9]
276[9]	" 3	3.30 P.M.	" 3	11.55 "	8h. 25m.	7h. 50m.	35m.	00m.	7 574	7 743	719	0	44	10	16.5	100	5.33	459	14 000	66	36	47	99.6	276[9]
277[9]	" 3	11.55 "	" 4	7.51 A.M.	7h. 56m.	7h. 25m.	31m.	00m.	7 154	7 292	656	0	44	10	16.4	99	4.73	459	13 800	57	25	34	99.8	277[9]
278[9]	" 4	7.51 A.M.	" 4	7.49 P.M.	10h. 53m.	10h. 24m.	29m.	1h. 05m.	10 280	10 545	666	0	44	7	16.9	102	5.20	360	9 600	39	24	33	99.7	278[9]
279[10]	" 4	7.49 P.M.	" 5	3.09 A.M.	7h. 20m.	6h. 49m.	31m.	00m.	9 394	8 013	728	0	44	8	19.6	119	4.18	338	7 600	28	16	22	99.7	279[10]
280[10]	" 5	3.09 A.M.	" 5	10.23 "	7h. 14m.	6h. 48m.	26m.	00m.	7 788	7 920	651	0	44	9	19.4	117	3.96	310	10 700	63	33	46	99.6	280[10]
281[11]	" 5	10.23 "	" 5	5.05 P.M.	6h. 42m.	6h. 14m.	28m.	00m.	8 199	8 323	683	0	44	9	22.3	135	2.32	186	7 200	....	....	87	98.8	281[11]
282[11]	" 5	5.05 P.M.	" 5	11.00 "	5h. 55m.	5h. 31m.	24m.	00m.	7 301	7 506	642	0	44	9	22.7	137	3.31	186	5 400	....	....	40	99.3	282[11]
283[11]	" 5	11.00 "	" 6	7.55 A.M.	8h. 47m.	8h. 20m.	27m.	08m.	10 865	10 927	617	0	44	6	21.9	133	3.99	186	5 600	46	21	33	99.4	283[11]
284[11]	" 6	7.55 A.M.	" 9	9.34 "	8h. 06m.	7h. 32m.	34m.	65h. 33m.	10 080	10 265	684	0	44	7	22.7	137	3.22	160	4 900	84	8	26	99.5	284[11]

[1] Prescribed chemicals 1.5 gr., rate 120 mil. gals.
[2] Prescribed chemicals 2.0 gr., rate 120 mil. gals.
[3] Prescribed chemicals 3.0 gr., rate 120 mil. gals.
[4] Prescribed chemicals 5.0 gr., rate 120 mil. gals.
[5] Prescribed chemicals 4.0 gr., rate 120 mil. gals.†
[6] Prescribed chemicals 3.0 gr., rate 140 mil. gals.†
[7] Prescribed chemicals 4.0 gr., rate 140 mil. gals.†
[8] Prescribed chemicals 4.0 gr., rate 100 mil. gals.
[9] Prescribed chemicals 6.0 gr., rate 100 mil. gals.
[10] Prescribed chemicals 4.0 gr., rate 120 mil. gals.
[11] Prescribed chemicals 4.0 gr., rate 140 mil. gals.

* Application of chemical unsatisfactory. Chemical meter out of order.

† Prescribed amount of chemical insufficient.

TABLE No. 4.—*Continued.*

Warren System.

Number of Run.	Began. Date.	Began. Hour.	Ended. Date.	Ended. Hour.	Periods of Time. Hours and Minutes. Operation.	Service.	Wash.	Delay.	Quantities of Water. Cubic Feet. Applied.	Filtered.	Wash.	Waste. Filtered.	Waste. Unfiltered.	Percentage which the Sum of the Wash and Waste Water is of Applied Water.	Average Actual Rate of Filtration. Cubic Feet per Minute.	Million Gallons per Acre per 24 Hours.	Average Amount of Applied Sulphate of Alumina. Grains per Gallon.	Estimated Average Amount of Suspended Solids in River Water. Parts per Million.	Bacteria per Cubic Centimeter. River Water.	Effluent. Maximum.	Effluent. Minimum.	Effluent. Average.	Average Bacterial Efficiency.	Number of Run.
	1896		1896																					
285	June 9	9.34 A.M.	June 9	4.50 P.M.	7h. 08m.	5h. 10m.	28m.	08m.	6 952	6 496	616	0	44	9	21.0	127	3.86	582	11 300	....	....	171	95.5	285
286	" 9	4.50 P.M.	" 10	2.46 "	6h. 22m.	5h. 54m.	28m.	15h. 34m.	9 779	8 051	585	0	44	8	22.7	137	4.67	400	10 200	159	50	89	99.1	286
287	" 10	2.46 "	" 11	1.49 "	7h. 33m.	7h. 06m.	27m.	15h. 30m.	9 539	9 666	633	0	44	7	22.7	137	3.15	300	7 300	112	25	59	99.2	287
288	" 11	1.49 "	" 12	2.07 "	8h. 33m.	7h. 56m.	37m.	15h. 45m.	10 609	10 760	683	0	44	7	22.6	137	2.26	220	6 900	27	16	20	99.7	288
289	" 12	2.07 "	" 13	11.10 A.M.	5h. 33m.	5h. 06m.	27m.	15h. 30m.	6 824	6 892	570	0	44	9	22.5	136	1.10	210	10 100	241	53	147	98.5	289
290	" 13	11.10 A.M.	" 13	5.10 P.M.	5h. 50m.	5h. 27m.	23m.	00m.	7 385	7 494	559	0	44	8	22.9	139	1.96	221	13 400	109	48	76	99.4	290
291	" 13	5.00 P.M.	" 15	2.08 "	5h. 38m.	5h. 14m.	24m.	15h. 30m.	6 996	7 073	533	0	44	8	22.5	136	3.51	380	13 900	356	91	267	98.1	291
292	" 15	2.08 "	" 16	12.31 "	6h. 44m.	6h. 18m.	26m.	15h. 39m.	8 504	8 621	595	0	44	8	22.8	139	3.01	310	10 900	42	35	39	99.6	292
293	" 16	12.31 "	" 17	12.23 "	8h. 22m.	7h. 58m.	24m.	15h. 30m.	10 812	10 975	579	0	44	6	23.0	140	2.38	223	8 500	57	28	41	99.5	293
294	" 17	12.23 "	" 18	9.00 A.M.	5h. 18m.	4h. 58m.	20m.	15h. 19m.	6 682	6 745	505	0	61	8	22.6	137	1.22	223	11 000	89	71	80	99.3	294
295	" 18	9.00 A.M.	" 18	5.05 P.M.	8h. 05m.	7h. 39m.	26m.	00m.	10 259	10 402	524	0	44	6	22.7	137	2.22	270	10 600	177	22	81	99.2	295
296	" 18	5.05 P.M.	" 19	1.07 "	4h. 32m.	4h. 06m.	26m.	15h. 30m.	5 518	5 562	580	0	44	11	22.6	137	2.69	400	13 200	111	61	86	99.4	296
297	" 19	1.07 "	" 20	10.34 A.M.	5h. 38m.	5h. 11m.	27m.	15h. 49m.	6 869	6 999	513	0	44	8	22.5	136	3.41	410	16 300	171	61	98	99.4	297
298	" 20	10.34 A.M.	" 22	9.00 "	6h. 59m.	6h. 35m.	24m.	39h. 27m.	8 892	8 968	553	0	44	7	22.7	137	2.45	262	10 500	77	39	64	99.4	298
299	" 22	9.00 "	" 23	10.49 "	10h. 19m.	9h. 52m.	27m.	15h. 30m.	13 326	13 473	521	0	44	4	22.8	138	2.08	210	7 800	150	49	81	99.0	299
300	" 23	10.49 "	" 24	11.58 "	9h. 21m.	8h. 56m.	25m.	15h. 48m.	12 015	12 222	538	0	35	5	22.8	138	2.15	250	6 500	560	58	298	95.3	300
301	" 24	11.58 "	" 30	11.02 "	6h. 51m.	6h. 26m.	25m.	136h. 33m.	8 577	8 676	556	0	44	7	22.5	136	2.34	390	8 300	275	41	188	97.7	301
302	" 30	11.02 "	" 30	3.48 P.M.	4h. 26m.	4h. 04m.	22m.	20m.	5 571	5 549	524	0	44	10	22.7	137	3.72	357	10 900	62	21	37	99.7	302
303	" 30	3.48 P.M.	July 1	12.32 "	5h. 14m.	4h. 48m.	26m.	15h. 30m.	6 496	6 594	576	0	44	10	22.9	138	4.22	720	13 500	....	....	40	99.7	303
304	July 1	12.32 "	" 1	5.00 "	4h. 28m.	4h. 06m.	22m.	00m.	5 513	5 609	605	0	44	12	22.8	138	3.64	867	......	....	....	....	....	304
305	" 1	5.00 "	" 2	11.17 A.M.	1h. 53m.	1h. 29m.	24m.	15h. 27m.	2 337	2 030	473	0	369	36	22.9	138	3.37	1 370	14 200	....	....	....	99.7	305
306	" 2	11.17 A.M.	" 2	1.35 P.M.	2h. 18m.	1h. 53m.	25m.	00m.	4 056	2 519	598	0	44	16	23.3	142	6.07	1 674	24 200	130	49	89	99.6	306
307	" 2	1.35 P.M.	" 2	4.08 "	2h. 33m.	2h. 08m.	25m.	00m.	2 811	2 837	507	0	44	20	22.2	134	5.80	1 674	24 200	....	....	105	99.6	307
308	" 2	4.08 "	" 3	12.03 "	4h. 22m.	3h. 48m.	34m.	15h. 33m.	5 133	5 200	528	0	44	11	22.8	138	5.18	1 300	10 400	81	57	69	99.3	308
309	" 3	12.03 "	" 3	3.38 "	3h. 35m.	3h. 12m.	23m.	00m.	4 321	4 386	546	0	44	14	22.8	138	4.85	996	12 000	....	....	76	99.4	309
310	" 3	3.38 "	" 6	2.24 "	2h. 18m.	1h. 52m.	26m.	68h. 25m.	2 836	2 552	670	0	386	41	22.8	138	5.02	996	9 500	167	18	92	99.0	310
311	" 6	2.21 "	" 7	12.42 "	6h. 51m.	6h. 24m.	27m.	15h. 30m.	8 624	8 672	597	0	44	7	22.6	137	3.27	380	7 300	186	26	64	99.1	311
312	" 7	12.42 "	" 7	5.03 "	4h. 11m.	3h. 50m.	21m.	10m.	5 121	5 193	544	0	44	11	22.6	137	2.99	529	5 500	112	46	79	98.6	312
313	" 7	5.03 "	" 8	12.29 "	3h. 56m.	3h. 32m.	24m.	15h. 30m.	4 800	4 832	549	0	44	12	22.8	138	5.75	470	6 400	114	51	82	98.7	313
314	" 8	12.29 "	" 8	4.46 "	4h. 17m.	3h. 53m.	24m.	00m.	5 119	5 186	610	0	44	13	22.3	135	2.91	461	6 700	118	47	82	98.8	314
315	" 8	4.46 "	" 9	1.04 "	4h. 48m.	4h. 28m.	20m.	15h. 30m.	5 849	5 909	533	0	44	10	22.1	134	2.90	470	8 000	62	39	51	99.4	315
316	" 9	1.04 "	" 9	4.48 "	3h. 44m.	3h. 20m.	24m.	00m.	4 451	4 500	593	0	44	14	22.5	136	2.62	470	9 200	143	9	54	99.4	316
317	" 9	4.48 "	" 10	1.51 "	5h. 30m.	5h. 09m.	21m.	15h. 30m.	6 696	6 805	551	0	44	9	22.3	135	2.91	370	10 000	137	54	95	99.1	317
318	" 10	1.51 "	" 11	11.58 A.M.	6h. 31m.	6h 03m.	28m.	15h. 36m.	8 019	8 159	580	0	44	8	22.5	136	3.50	290	10 400	69	25	45	99.6	318
319	" 11	11.58 A.M.	" 13	9.00 "	5h. 32m.	5h. 11m.	21m.	39h. 30m.	7 096	7 222	548	0	44	8	23.2	141	2.94	193	9 300	43	36	39	99.6	319
320	" 13	9.00 "	" 13	3.03 P.M.	6h. 03m.	5h. 40m.	23m.	00m.	7 556	7 699	597	0	44	8	22.7	137	3.25	487	7 700	53	20	36	99.5	320
321	" 13	3.03 P.M.	" 14	1.27 "	6h. 54m.	6h. 32m.	22m.	15h. 30m.	8 739	8 921	585	0	44	7	22.8	138	2.76	420	9 600	140	31	66	99.3	321

TABLE No. 5.—*Continued.*

Warren System.

Number of Run.	Began. Date.	Began. Hour.	Ended. Date.	Ended. Hour.	Periods of Time. Hours and Minutes. Operation.	Service.	Wash.	Delay	Quantities of Water. Cubic Feet. Applied.	Filtered.	Wash.	Waste. Filtered.	Waste. Unfiltered.	Percentage which the Sum of the Wash and Waste Water is of Applied Water.	Average Actual Rate of Filtration. Cubic Feet per Minute.	Million Gallons per Acre per 24 Hours.	Average Amount of Applied Sulphate of Alumina. Grains per Gallon.	Estimated Average Amount of Suspended Solids in River Water. Parts per Million.	Bacteria per Cubic Centimeter. River Water.	Effluent. Maximum.	Effluent. Minimum.	Effluent. Average.	Average Bacterial Efficiency.	Number of Run.
	1896		1896																					
322	July 14	1.27 P.M.	July 15	12.36 P.M.	7h. 38m.	7h. 13m.	25m.	15h. 31m.	10 629	9 826	594	0	44	6	22.7	137	2.29	430	8 300	....	....	17	99.8	322
323	" 15	12.36 "	" 16	9.00 A.M.	4h. 54m.	4h. 30m.	24m.	15h. 30m.	6 056	6 156	515	0	44	9	22.8	138	2.87	496	8 300	37	16	30	99.6	323
324	" 16	9.00 A.M.	" 16	2.44 P.M.	5h. 44m.	5h. 21m.	23m.	00m.	7 194	7 322	581	0	44	9	22.8	138	2.79	452	6 200	34	15	25	99.6	324
325	" 16	2.44 P.M.	" 18	11.06 P.M.	5h. 04m.	4h. 39m.	25m.	39h. 16m.	6 667	6 406	646	0	44	15	23.0	140	2.95	440	5 600	69	11	31	99.4	325
326	" 18	11.06 A.M.	" 18	3.55 P.M.	4h. 49m.	4h. 24m.	25m.	00m.	5 965	5 965	604	0	44	11	23.3	142	2.74	637	9 900	23	23	23	99.8	326
327	" 18	3.55 P.M.	" 20	1.32 "	6h. 00m.	5h. 38m.	22m.	39h. 37m.	7 489	7 638	568	0	44	8	22.6	137	2.66	450	8 800	....	....	22	99.8	327
328	" 20	1.32 "	" 21	12.03 "	6h. 55m.	6h. 32m.	23m.	15h. 36m.	8 822	8 723	542	0	44	7	22.3	135	2.70	480	13 600	93	5	42	99.7	328
329	" 21	12.03 "	" 21	4.41 "	4h. 38m.	4h. 17m.	21m.	00m.	5 748	5 856	530	0	26	10	22.8	138	3.41	559	17 100	86	57	71	99.6	329
330	" 21	4.41 "	" 22	12.20 "	3h. 56m.	3h. 32m.	24m.	15h. 43m.	4 781	4 867	543	0	44	12	23.1	141	3.36	1 050	30 700	383	217	300	99.0	330
331	" 22	12.20 "	" 22	2.52 "	2h. 29m.	2h. 07m.	22m.	03m.	2 814	2 843	520	0	44	20	22.4	135	3.79	1 171	33 300	....	....	665	98.0	331
332	" 22	2.52 "	" 23	10.26 A.M.	4h. 04m.	3h. 36m.	28m.	15h. 30m.	4 808	4 897	640	0	44	14	22.7	137	5.48	1 400	33 300	1055	818	936	97.2	332
333	" 23	10.26 A.M.	" 23	2.25 P.M.	3h. 59m.	3h. 34m.	25m.	00m.	4 557	4 654	610	0	44	14	21.8	132	7.50	2 175	23 800	420	367	393	98.3	333
334	" 23	2.25 P.M.	" 23	4.44 "	1h. 27m.	1h. 03m.	24m.	12m.	1 683	1 362	627	0	395	61	21.7	131	5.43	2 175	27 700	....	....	916	96.7	334
335	" 23	4.44 "	" 24	1.12 "	4h. 59m.	4h. 32m.	27m.	15h. 29m.	4 062	4 168	656	0	44	17	15.3	93	9.62	3 100	34 100	....	....	685	98.0	335
336	" 24	1.12 "	" 24	4.10 "	2h. 01m.	1h. 37m.	24m.	57m.	1 548	1 494	631	0	44	44	15.4	93	8.02	3 347	31 000	....	....	288	99.1	336
337	" 24	4.10 "	" 25	9.47 A.M.	1h. 53m.	1h. 20m.	33m.	15h. 44m.	1 471	1 245	853	0	300	79	15.6	95	7.65	3 347	28 000	2 500	392	1 475	94.7	337
338	" 25	9.47 A.M.	" 25	2.32 P.M.	4h. 45m.	4h. 17m.	28m.	00m.	3 666	3 628	706	0	44	20	14.2	86	6.48	1 677	17 300	....	....	416	97.6	338
339	" 25	2.32 P.M.	" 27	9.00 A.M.	2h. 52m.	2h. 21m.	31m.	15h. 36m.	2 073	1 541	878	0	306	57	13.1	80	7.92	1 677	17 300	504	378	441	97.5	339
340	" 27	9.00 A.M.	" 27	11.10 "	2h. 03m.	1h. 40m.	23m.	07m.	1 906	1 574	574	0	377	50	15.7	95	9.07	1 398	16 000	....	....	320	98.0	340
341	" 27	11.10 "	" 27	3.56 P.M.	4h. 46m.	4h. 22m.	24m.	00m.	4 026	4 150	481	0	44	13	15.9	96	6.40	1 398	17 800	624	26	306	98.3	341
342	" 27	3.56 P.M.	" 28	9.30 A.M.	1h. 07m.	39m.	28m.	16h. 21m.	2 420	617	753	0	412	48	15.8	95	8.15	1 398	19 600	....	....	195	99.0	342
343	" 28	9.30 A.M.	" 28	4.45 P.M.	7h. 15m.	6h. 54m.	21m.	00m.	9 273	9 382	523	0	275	9	22.7	137	7.83	1 416	24 500	394	14	61	99.8	343
344	" 28	4.45 P.M.	" 29	12.10 "	3h. 51m.	3h. 29m.	22m.	15h. 34m.	4 608	4 723	529	0	44	12	22.6	137	4.90	1 680	17 000	51	18	34	99.8	344
345	" 29	12.10 "	" 30	12.42 "	6h. 47m.	6h. 17m.	30m.	17h. 45m.	8 134	8 387	619	0	44	8	22.3	135	5.73	1 750	9 500	90	10	53	99.4	345
346	" 30	12.42 "	" 31	9.00 A.M.	4h. 51m.	4h. 22m.	29m.	15h. 27m.	5 845	5 980	424	0	176	10	22.8	138	4.05	1 733	12 000	15	12	13	99.9	346
347	" 31	9.00 A.M.	" 31	5.30 P.M.	....	8h. 30m.	....	00m.	11 734	11 757	....	....	....	....	23.1	141	....	605	6 800	66	7	33	99.5	347

Jewell System.

Number of Run.	Began. Date.	Began. Hour.	Ended. Date.	Ended. Hour.	Operation.	Service.	Wash.	Delay	Applied.	Filtered.	Wash.	Waste. Filtered.	Waste. Unfiltered.	Percentage.	Cubic Feet per Minute.	Million Gallons per Acre per 24 Hours.	Sulphate of Alumina. Grains per Gallon.	Suspended Solids. Parts per Million.	River Water.	Maximum.	Minimum.	Average.	Average Bacterial Efficiency.	Number of Run.
	1895		1895																					
1[1]	Oct. 21	9.27 A.M.	Oct. 21	12.03 P.M.	....	....	29m.	....	......	......	......	....	....	....	....	....	....	....	148	....	....	76	48.6	1[1]
2	" 21	12.03 P.M.	" 22	2.47 "	9h. 30m.	9h. 00m.	30m.	17h. 14m.	13 797	13 583	581	0	214	6	25.2	102	0.60	20	156	66	14	46	70.5	2
3	" 22	2.47 "	" 25	2.27 "	21h. 06m.	20h. 47m.	19m.	50h. 34m.	36 355	34 677	731	0	150	2	27.8	112	0.40	22	126	110	24	51	59.5	3
4	" 25	2.27 "	" 26	11.50 A.M.	5h. 12m.	4h. 51m.	21m.	16h. 11m.	7 896	7 781	576	0	32	8	26.8	108	0.75	25	154	36	10	26	83.1	4
5[1]	" 26	12.50 A.M.	" 29	3.13 P.M.	....	....	....	....	......	13 944	1 737	0	....	....	....	....	....	20	128	54	12	32	75.0	5[1]
6[1]	" 29	3.13 P.M.	Nov. 1	3.30 "	....	....	....	....	......	13 520	534	0	....	....	....	....	....	10	131	16	2	8	93.9	6[1]
7[1]	Nov. 1	3.30 "	" 7	1.57 "	....	....	20m.	....	28 214	25 889	662	0	....	....	....	....	....	6	131	540	14	151	*	7[1]
8	" 7	1.57 "	" 8	2.12 "	5h. 33m.	5h. 17m.	16m.	18h. 42m.	9 407	8 176	259	0	32	3	25.8	104	2.41	7	152	222	124	165	**	8
9	" 8	2.12 "	" 12	10.42 A.M.	12h. 40m.	12h. 13m.	27m.	79h. 50m.	17 070	16 735	502	0	235	4	22.9	93	1.01	10	401	1 100	107	367	8.5	9

[1] Available data incomplete. * —11.5. ** —10.9.

TABLE NO. 5.—*Continued.*

Jewell System.

Number of Run.	Began. Date.	Began. Hour.	Ended. Date.	Ended. Hour.	Periods of Time. Hours and Minutes. Operation.	Service.	Wash.	Delay.	Quantities of Water. Cubic Feet. Applied.	Filtered.	Wash.	Waste. Filtered.	Waste. Unfiltered.	Percentage which the Sum of the Wash and Waste Water is of Applied Water.	Average Actual Rate of Filtration. Cubic Feet per Minute.	Million Gallons per Acre per 24 Hours.	Average Amount of Applied Sulphate of Alumina. Grains per Gallon.	Estimated Average Amount of Suspended Solids in River Water. Parts per Million.	Bacteria per Cubic Centimeter. River Water.	Effluent. Maximum.	Effluent. Minimum.	Effluent. Average.	Average Bacterial Efficiency.	Number of Run.
	1895		1895																					
10	Nov. 12	10.42 A.M.	Nov. 14	1.17 P.M.	17h. 30m.	17h. 14m.	16m.	33h. 05m.	25 200	25 127	367	0	32	2	24.3	98	0.56	10	590	1 356	74	256	56.6	10
11[1]	" 14	1.17 P.M.	" 20	12.10 "	....	....	26m.	....	......	39 818	702	0	...	.....	.....	.....	.....	12	181	318	68	142	21.5	11[1]
12	" 20	12.10 "	" 25	11.38 A.M.	20h. 36m.	20h. 15m.	21m.	98h. 52m.	29 495	29 463	614	0	32	2	25.0	101	0.40	16	675	420	36	153	77.3	12
13	" 25	11.38 A.M.	" 30	9.36 "	23h. 41m.	23h. 21m.	20m.	94h. 17m.	33 683	33 651	713	0	32	2	24.0	97	0.48	25	4 000	2 280	328	659	83.5	13
14	" 30	9.36 "	Dec. 5	2.30 P.M.	26h. 26m.	26h. 06m.	20m.	98h. 28m.	38 868	37 499	834	0	214	3	24.0	97	0.59	26	6 800	834	150	434	93.6	14
15	Dec. 5	2.30 P.M.	" 10	10.26 A.M.	26h. 13m.	25h. 16m.	57m.	69h. 43m.	35 207	34 987	856	0	214	3	23.0	93	0.82	35	6 700	864	124	256	97.1	15
16	" 10	10.26 A.M.	" 13	4.14 P.M.	28h. 50m.	28h. 11m.	39m.	48h. 58m.	40 391	38 352	624	0	214	2	22.7	92	0.55	34	3 600	304	116	194	94.6	16
17	" 13	4.14 P.M.	" 17	12.28 "	19h. 45m.	19h. 17m.	26m.	72h. 29m.	29 926	28 391	689	0	32	2	24.5	99	0.82	28	2 200	166	90	133	94.0	17
18	" 17	12.28 "	" 19	12.40 "	16h. 36m.	15h. 56m.	40m.	31h. 36m.	21 730	20 488	617	0	32	3	21.5	87	1.26	15	2 100	168	53	122	94.2	18
19	" 19	12.40 "	" 21	12.59 "	16h. 53m.	16h. 14m.	39m.	31h. 26m.	21 883	21 576	534	0	32	3	22.2	90	1.17	15	2 800	144	35	82	97.1	19
20	" 21	12.59 "	" 24	1.36 P.M.	17h. 21m.	16h. 48m.	33m.	55h. 16m.	22 506	22 666	540	0	32	3	22.5	91	1.13	20	2 900	109	24	77	97.3	20
21	" 24	1.36 "	" 27	1.39 "	16h. 18m.	15h. 39m.	39m.	55h. 45m.	21 089	21 335	517	0	32	3	22.8	92	1.25	80	6 600	664	70	279	95.6	21
22	" 27	1.39 "	" 30	9.37 A.M.	12h. 09m.	11h. 16m.	53m.	55h. 49m.	15 327	15 505	733	109	32	6	23.0	93	3.09	220	27 600	882	235	546	98.0	22
23	" 30	9.37 A.M.	" 31	10.39 "	9h. 27m.	8h. 25m.	1h. 02m.	15h. 35m.	11 927	11 669	672	443	32	10	23.1	93	2.86	400	7 000	680	102	311	95.6	23
24	" 31	10.39 "	Jan. 2, '96	8.42 A.M.	7h. 37m.	6h. 56m.	41m.	38h. 26m.	9 282	9 135	661	300	32	11	22.0	89	4.42	600	13 000	560	55	233	98.2	24
	1896		1896																					
25	Jan. 2	8.42 A.M.	Jan. 2	3.44 P.M.	6h. 58m.	6h. 34m.	24m.	04m.	7 932	7 947	685	0	32	9	20.1	81	3.35	800	10 700	560	140	285	97.3	25
26	" 2	3.44 P.M.	" 4	10.39 A.M.	11h. 58m.	11h. 16m.	42m.	30h. 57m.	13 784	13 866	756	250	32	8	20.5	83	2.42	840	13 300	432	184	277	97.9	26
27	" 4	10.39 A.M.	" 9	9.10 "	8h. 56m.	8h. 26m.	30m.	109h 35m.	10 501	10 392	1025	0	32	10	20.6	83	2.84	450	8 600	438	364	390	95.5	27
28	" 9	9.10 "	" 10	12.07 P.M.	11h. 10m.	10h. 46m.	24m.	15h. 47m.	14 792	14 187	467	0	32	3	22.0	89	1.61	120	2 200	248	152	203	90.8	28
29	" 10	12.07 P.M.	" 13	9.44 A.M.	14h. 28m.	14h. 06m.	22m.	54h. 09m.	18 420	18 754	467	0	32	3	22.2	90	1.81	120	1 800	288	152	202	88.8	29
30	" 13	9.44 A.M.	" 15	9.34 "	16h. 58m.	16h. 37m.	21m.	30h. 52m.	23 153	23 320	439	0	32	2	23.4	95	1.12	60	1 300	290	104	177	86.4	30
31	" 15	9.34 "	" 17	11.18 "	18h. 18m.	17h. 51m.	27m.	31h. 26m.	25 190	25 364	433	0	32	2	23.7	96	1.00	40	3 100	230	116	166	94.7	31
32	" 17	11.18 "	" 20	9.38 "	16h. 05m.	15h. 34m.	31m.	54h. 15m.	22 289	22 351	458	301	32	4	24.0	97	0.92	25	6 800	430	174	248	96.3	32
33	" 20	9.38 "	" 23	9.35 "	23h. 33m.	23h. 07m.	26m.	48h. 24m.	35 410	34 946	454	0	32	1	25.2	102	0.94	20	3 400	306	44	183	94.6	33
34	" 23	9.35 "	" 23	2.00 P.M.	19h. 03m.	18h. 44m.	19m.	33h. 22m.	26 278	26 228	432	0	32	2	23.4	95	0.83	30	4 400	318	88	164	96.3	34
35	" 25	2.00 P.M.	" 28	11.48 A.M.	14h. 35m.	14h. 14m.	21m.	55h. 13m.	20 607	20 433	403	0	32	2	24.0	97	1.21	250	10 900	1 196	106	688	93.7	35
36	" 28	11.48 A.M.	" 29	12.40 P.M.	9h. 17m.	8h. 27m.	50m.	15h. 35m.	11 074	10 715	383	310	32	9	21.2	86	1.64	290	17 000	2 016	1 600	2 372	86.0	36
37	" 29	12.40 P.M.	" 30	3.49 "	12h. 04m.	11h. 37m.	27m.	15h. 05m.	16 538	16 253	439	0	32	3	23.4	95	1.59	300	15 300	1 620	675	951	93.8	37
38	" 30	3.49 "	Feb. 5	9.55 A.M.	8h. 33m.	8h. 13m.	20m.	129h. 33m.	11 342	11 337	391	150	32	5	23.0	93	2.06	320	14 300	910	811	860	94.0	38
39	Feb. 5	9.55 A.M.	" 6	2.33 P.M.	12h. 16m.	11h. 50m.	26m.	16h. 22m.	16 934	16 570	617	222	32	5	23.6	95	2.32	460	54 100	2 155	468	1 058	98.0	39
40	" 6	2.33 P.M.	" 7	4.08 "	9h. 38m.	9h. 21m.	17m.	15h. 57m.	13 280	13 127	490	0	32	4	23.4	95	2.39	580	41 200	1 282	238	799	98.1	40
41	" 7	4.08 "	" 10	9.43 A.M.	9h. 05m.	8h. 13m.	52m.	56h. 30m.	11 022	10 609	538	403	32	9	21.5	87	2.17	690	40 900	1 900	500	1 346	96.7	41
42	" 10	9.43 A.M.	" 11	9.45 "	8h. 20m.	7h. 48m.	32m.	15h. 42m.	10 225	10 220	524	0	32	6	21.9	88	2.16	970	14 400	1 155	516	740	94.9	42
43	" 11	9.45 "	" 12	9.33 "	8h. 03m.	7h. 36m.	27m.	15h. 54m.	10 224	10 237	547	0	32	6	22.5	91	2.27	410	19 800	2 365	415	1 020	94.9	43
44[1]	" 12	9.33 "	" 12	1.10 P.M.	3h. 29m.	57m.	2h. 32m.	08m.	4 114	1 296	539	2 643	32	78	22.8	92	1.35	420	28 000	.....	.....	.....	.....	44[2]

[1] Available data incomplete. [2] Application of chemicals un isfactory. Chemical feed pipe choked.

TABLE No. 5.—*Continued.*

Jewell System.

Number of Run.	Began. Date.	Began. Hour.	Ended. Date.	Ended. Hour.	Periods of Time. Hours and Minutes. Operation.	Service.	Wash.	Delay.	Quantities of Water. Cubic Feet. Applied.	Filtered.	Wash.	Waste. Filtered.	Waste. Unfiltered.	Percentage which the Sum of the Wash and Waste Water is of Applied Water.	Average Actual Rate of Filtration. Cubic Feet per Minute.	Million Gallons per Acre per 24 Hours.	Average Amount of Applied Sulphate of Alumina. Grains per Gallon.	Estimated Average Amount of Suspended Solids in River Water. Parts per Million.	Bacteria per Cubic Centimeter. River Water.	Effluent. Maximum.	Effluent. Minimum.	Effluent. Average.	Average Bacterial Efficiency.	Number of Run.
45	1896 Feb. 12	1.10 P.M.	1896 Feb. 14	9.34 A.M.	13h. 12m.	12h. 24m.	48m.	31h. 12m.	16 760	16 827	519	308	32	5	22.7	92	2.96	230	19 200	2420	209	1043	94.6	45
46	" 14	9.34 A.M.	" 15	3.34 P.M.	13h. 42m.	13h. 08m.	34m.	16h. 18m.	17 627	17 925	545	0	32	3	22.8	92	2.75	430	11 500	1110	234	875	92.9	46
47	" 15	3.34 P.M.	" 17	5.00 "	9h. 45m.	9h. 23m.	22m.	39h. 41m.	12 783	12 799	543	0	32	4	22.7	91	4.82	410	21 800	1362	319	1016	95.4	47
48	" 17	5.00 "	" 19	2.48 "	14h. 37m.	13h. 57m.	40m.	31h. 11m.	18 818	18 673	518	164	32	4	22.3	90	2.49	330	16 200	1885	50	1160	92.8	48
49	" 19	2.48 "	" 22	9.26 A.M.	17h. 19m.	16h. 53m.	26m.	49h. 19m.	22 575	22 950	505	0	32	2	22.6	91	3.35	350	15 400	2170	28	504	96.7	49
50	" 22	9.26 A.M.	" 25	1.02 P.M.	20h. 33m.	20h. 04m.	29m.	55h. 03m.	16 328	16 905	638	0	32	4	14.0	57	2.01	200	17 600	1605	65	759	95.7	50
51	" 25	1.02 P.M.	" 27	1.18 "	16h. 30m.	15h. 40m.	50m.	31h. 46m.	21 234	21 698	583	119	32	3	23.1	93	2.26	140	17 000	3280	191	1600	90.6	51
52	" 27	1.18 "	" 29	9.58 A.M.	7h. 57m.	7h. 27m.	30m.	36h. 43m.	12 362	12 915	810	0	32	7	29.0	118	1.36	120	4 700	1820	695	1206	97.4	52
53	" 29	9.58 A.M.	Mar. 4	9.18 "	24h. 10m.	23h. 48m.	22m.	71h. 10m.	35 421	35 292	575	97	214	2	24.7	100	1.03	70	30 900	3455	197	1645	94.7	53
54	Mar. 4	9.18 "	" 6	10.59 "	18h. 41m.	18h. 23m.	18m.	31h. 00m.	29 115	29 947	556	0	32	2	27.2	110	1.00	50	23 400	1320	206	720	96.9	54
55	" 6	10.59 "	" 9	9.25 "	15h. 26m.	15h. 10m.	16m.	55h. 26m.	26 636	27 409	613	0	32	2	30.1	122	0.96	50	10 800	570	81	234	97.9	55
56	" 9	9.25 "	" 10	11.35 "	10h. 40m.	10h. 25m.	15m.	15h. 30m.	15 148	15 487	442	0	32	3	24.8	100	1.32	70	12 700	305	58	123	99.0	56
57	" 10	11.35 "	" 12	9.25 "	14h. 27m.	14h. 10m.	17m.	31h. 23m.	20 996	21 327	559	0	32	3	25.1	101	0.83	70	9 400	295	58	135	98.6	57
58	" 12	9.25 "	" 13	10.28 "	9h. 33m.	9h. 13m.	20m.	15h. 30m.	13 432	13 569	395	0	32	3	24.5	99	0.74	60	11 300	560	121	250	97.8	58
59	" 13	10.28 "	" 14	12.10 P.M.	10h. 12m.	9h. 54m.	18m.	15h. 30m.	14 420	14 526	569	0	0	4	24.5	99	0.65	50	11 300	742	320	501	95.6	59
60	" 14	12.10 P.M.	" 16	12.19 "	8h. 15m.	7h. 58m.	17m.	39h. 54m.	11 551	11 605	572	0	0	5	24.3	98	0.96	50	13 900	510	49	173	98.8	60
61	" 16	12.19 "	" 17	11.10 A.M.	7h. 21m.	7h. 05m.	16m.	15h. 30m.	10 209	10 309	522	0	0	5	24.3	98	1.20	50	17 700	261	98	162	99.1	61
62	" 17	11.10 A.M.	" 18	9.28 "	6h. 48m.	6h. 30m.	8m.	15h. 30m.	9 376	9 447	500	0	0	5	24.2	98	1.52	60	16 300	89	60	72	99.6	62
63	" 18	9.28 "	" 19	10.59 "	9h. 50m.	9h. 31m.	19m.	15h. 41m.	13 752	13 847	560	0	0	4	24.3	98	1.53	100	21 500	47	17	35	98.4	63
64	" 19	10.59 "	" 20	9.37 "	6h. 44m.	6h. 18m.	26m.	15h. 54m.	8 790	8 840	844	0	0	10	23.4	95	1.55	210	34 400	1200	225	710	97.9	64
65	" 20	9.37 "	" 20	12.44 P.M.	3h. 07m.	2h. 47m.	20m.	00m.	3 855	3 887	625	0	0	16	23.2	94	2.88	990	41 600	....	....	800	98.1	65
66	" 20	12.44 P.M.	" 20	3.28 "	2h. 44m.	2h. 23m.	21m.	00m.	3 288	3 350	608	0	0	18	23.4	95	3.09	1 090	60 100	....	....	600	99.0	66
67	" 20	3.28 "	" 21	10.00 A.M.	3h. 02m.	2h. 46m.	16m.	15h. 30m.	3 885	3 948	515	0	0	13	23.8	96	3.84	990	56 700	....	....	1000	98.2	67
68	" 21	10.00 A.M.	" 21	1.35 P.M.	3h. 35m.	3h. 09m.	26m.	00m.	4 437	4 434	558	0	114	15	23.4	95	5.40	1 280	59 800	465	415	440	99.3	68
69	" 21	1.35 P.M.	" 21	5.08 "	3h. 33m.	3h. 11m.	22m.	00m.	4 273	4 327	469	12	0	11	22.6	91	5.16	1 280	57 100	....	....	1905	96.6	69
70	" 21	5.08 "	" 23	1.20 "	4h. 42m.	4h. 21m.	21m.	39h. 30m.	6 021	6 203	611	0	0	10	23.8	96	4.33	730	41 400	1250	405	827	98.0	70
71	" 23	1.20 "	" 23	4.30 "	3h. 10m.	2h. 38m.	32m.	00m.	3 903	3 770	605	245	0	22	23.9	97	5.15	660	30 400	475	475	475	98.4	71
72	" 23	4.30 "	" 24	1.45 "	5h. 45m.	5h. 30m.	15m.	15h. 30m.	7 534	7 769	531	0	0	7	23.5	95	4.22	550	30 700	1245	80	712	97.7	72
73	" 24	1.45 "	" 24	7.20 "	5h. 35m.	5h. 18m.	17m.	00m.	7 396	7 618	519	0	0	8	24.0	97	3.71	520	38 000	270	80	161	99.6	73
74	" 24	7.20 "	" 25	1.10 A.M.	5h. 50m.	5h. 29m.	21m.	00m.	7 548	7 770	575	0	0	8	23.6	95	3.94	520	37 800	306	74	110	99.7	74
75	" 25	1.10 A.M.	" 25	7.41 "	6h. 27m.	6h. 01m.	26m.	04m.	8 352	8 614	430	0	0	5	23.9	97	3.60	520	36 700	1030	1030	731	98.0	75
76	" 25	7.41 "	" 25	1.45 P.M.	5h. 28m.	5h. 12m.	16m.	36m.	7 481	7 727	532	0	0	7	24.8	100	4.46	520	37 800	495	48	103	99.7	76
77	" 25	1.45 P.M.	" 25	7.00 "	5h. 15m.	5h. 00m.	15m.	00m.	7 284	7 534	595	0	0	8	25.1	101	3.40	520	38 300	405	158	247	99.4	77
78	" 25	7.00 "	" 26	12.48 A.M.	5h. 23m.	5h. 08m.	15m.	25m.	7 292	7 260	479	0	0	7	23.6	95	3.32	520	45 000	215	107	167	99.6	78
79	" 26	12.48 A.M.	" 26	6.20 "	5h. 32m.	5h. 11m.	21m.	00m.	7 061	7 420	535	0	0	8	23.9	97	4.09	520	53 600	600	113	299	99.4	79
80	" 26	6.20 "	" 26	9.47 "	3h. 27m.	3h. 14m.	13m.	00m.	4 484	4 618	537	0	0	12	23.8	96	3.72	500	50 900	355	171	224	99.6	80
81	" 26	9.47 "	" 26	1.15 P.M.	3h. 28m.	3h. 16m.	12m.	00m.	4 741	4 944	418	0	0	9	25.2	102	3.10	470	49 800	700	355	528	89.9	81

TABLE NO. 5.—*Continued.*

Jewell System.

Number of Run.	Began. Date.	Began. Hour.	Ended. Date.	Ended. Hour.	Periods of Time. Hours and Minutes. Operation.	Service.	Wash.	Delay.	Quantities of Water. Cubic Feet. Applied.	Filtered.	Wash.	Waste. Filtered.	Waste. Unfiltered.	Percentage which the Sum of the Wash and Waste Water is of Applied Water.	Average Actual Rate of Filtration. Cubic Feet per Minute.	Million Gallons per Acre per 24 Hours.	Average Amount of Applied Sulphate of Alumina. Grains per Gallon.	Estimated Average Amount of Suspended Solids in River Water. Parts per Million.	Bacteria per Cubic Centimeter. River Water.	Effluent. Maximum.	Effluent. Minimum.	Effluent. Average.	Average Bacterial Efficiency.	Number of Run.
	1896		1896																					
82	Mar. 26	1.15 P.M.	Mar. 26	4.39 P.M.	3h. 24m.	3h. 12m.	12m.	00m.	4 484	4 653	440	0	0	10	24.2	98	2.49	470	50 100	700	520	588	98.8	82
83	" 26	4.39 "	" 26	8.54 "	4h. 08m.	3h. 49m.	19m.	07m.	5 067	5 217	501	0	0	10	22.8	92	2.59	470	50 400	805	520	805	98.4	83
84	" 26	8.54 "	" 27	3.23 A.M.	6h. 24m.	6h. 07m.	17m.	05m.	6 139	8 517	483	0	0	6	22.2	94	4.38	470	48 500	485	330	403	99.2	84
85	" 27	3.23 A.M.	" 27	8.38 "	5h. 04m.	4h. 50m.	14m.	11m.	6 491	6 818	514	0	0	8	23.5	95	5.23	470	45 700	575	485	530	98.8	85
86	" 27	8.38 "	" 27	2.23 P.M.	5h. 36m.	5h. 23m.	13m.	09m.	7 309	7 652	419	0	0	6	23.7	96	3.71	360	40 000	415	128	271	99.3	86
87	" 27	2.23 P.M.	" 27	6.42 "	4h. 19m.	4h. 02m.	17m.	00m.	5 274	5 493	404	0	0	8	22.7	92	3.54	360	34 200	1650	150	1 250	99.6	87
88	" 27	6.42 "	" 28	1.04 A.M.	6h. 22m.	5h. 40m.	42m.	00m.	7 886	8 027	395	212	0	8	23.6	95	3.19	360	25 900	540	117	201	99.2	88
89	" 28	1.04 A.M.	" 28	7.00 "	5h. 56m.	5h. 35m.	21m.	00m.	7 733	7 922	529	0	0	7	23.6	95	4.14	360	29 800	540	321	419	98.6	89
90	" 28	7.00 "	" 28	1.14 P.M.	5h. 14m.	6h. 03m.	11m.	00m.	8 025	8 338	502	0	0	6	23.0	93	3.87	380	35 200	321	62	222	99.4	90
91	" 28	1.14 P.M.	" 28	7.40 "	6h. 26m.	6h. 09m.	17m.	00m.	8 540	8 814	508	0	0	6	23.9	97	2.99	430	35 800	174	62	124	99.7	91
92	" 28	7.40 "	" 29	2.55 A.M.	7h. 15m.	6h. 57m.	18m.	00m.	9 391	9 691	522	0	0	6	23.2	94	2.95	430	38 400	193	119	156	99.6	92
93	" 29	2.55 A.M.	" 29	10.34 "	7h. 39m.	7h. 21m.	18m.	00m.	10 271	10 595	581	0	0	6	24.0	97	2.88	410	32 300	294	177	223	99.3	93
94	" 29	10.34 "	" 29	6.20 P.M.	7h. 46m.	7h. 32m.	14m.	00m.	10 697	11 037	515	0	0	5	24.4	99	2.39	340	55 400	595	240	525	99.1	94
95	" 29	6.20 P.M.	" 30	1.40 A.M.	7h. 20m.	7h. 01m.	19m.	00m.	9 945	10 261	532	0	0	5	24.4	99	2.61	340	36 600	465	125	307	99.1	95
96	" 30	1.40 A.M.	" 30	10.30 "	8h. 50m.	8h. 32m.	18m.	00m.	12 181	12 513	617	0	0	5	24.5	99	2.57	400	42 900	581	125	383	99.1	96
97	" 30	10.30 "	" 30	2.34 P.M.	4h. 02m.	3h. 33m.	29m.	02m.	5 269	5 181	577	281	0	16	24.3	98	3.10	740	30 900	785	581	734	97.6	97
98	" 30	2.34 P.M.	" 31	10.33 A.M.	4h. 29m.	4h. 01m.	28m.	15h. 30m.	6 198	6 001	590	142	0	12	24.9	101	4.04	800	20 600	672	650	661	96.8	98
99	" 31	10.33 A.M.	" 31	1.40 P.M.	3h. 07m.	2h. 51m.	16m.	00m.	4 077	4 050	574	0	0	14	23.7	96	4.83	1 000	22 800	....	....	390	98.3	99
100	" 31	1.40 P.M.	" 31	3.28 "	1h. 44m.	1h. 25m.	19m.	04m.	2 216	2 051	464	104	0	26	24.2	98	6.00	1 000	29 600	1495	390	942	96.8	100
101	" 31	3.28 "	" 31	5.04 "	1h. 36m.	1h. 19m.	17m.	00m.	1 910	1 872	496	0	0	26	23.2	94	3.77	1 000	29 600	....	....	1495	95.0	101
102	" 31	5.04 "	April 1	10.36 A.M.	2h. 02m.	1h. 47m.	15m.	15h. 30m.	2 522	2 605	668	0	0	26	24.3	98	5.60	1 090	35 400	....	....	845	97.6	102
103	April 1	10.36 A.M.	" 1	11.41 "	1h. 05m.	09m.	56m.	00m.	776	183	511	592	0	142	20.3	82	6.32	1 130	39 600	....	....	845	97.9	103
104	" 1	11.41 "	" 2	9.16 "	6h. 01m.	5h. 46m.	15m.	15h. 34m.	7 814	8 016	584	0	0	7	23.2	94	4.39	1 130	42 700	545	525	535	98.7	104
105	" 2	9.16 "	" 2	2.09 P.M.	4h. 53m.	4h. 36m.	17m.	00m.	6 462	6 656	632	0	0	10	24.1	97	4.93	930	31 200	240	224	234	99.3	105
106	" 2	2.09 P.M.	" 3	10.08 A.M.	4h. 29m.	4h. 15m.	14m.	15h. 30m.	5 928	6 097	628	0	0	11	23.9	97	4.94	950	26 800	224	92	182	99.3	106
107	" 3	10.08 A.M.	" 3	2.48 P.M.	4h. 32m.	4h. 18m.	14m.	08m.	5 944	6 143	571	0	0	10	23.8	96	4.68	1 060	32 000	....	....	92	99.7	107
108	" 3	2.48 P.M.	" 4	11.08 A.M.	4h. 48m.	4h. 32m.	16m.	15h. 32m.	6 327	6 529	619	0	0	10	24.0	97	4.18	900	27 500	310	60	279	99.0	108
109	" 4	11.08 A.M.	" 4	3.44 P.M.	4h. 36m.	4h. 20m.	16m.	00m.	6 164	6 364	647	0	0	10	24.5	99	4.11	630	27 500	90	60	66	99.8	109
110	" 4	3.44 P.M.	" 6	12.05 "	4h. 51m.	4h. 35m.	16m.	39h. 30m.	6 415	6 647	745	0	0	12	24.2	98	4.25	550	19 700	90	30	58	99.7	110
111	" 6	12.05 "	" 7	9.23 A.M.	5h. 48m.	5h. 34m.	14m.	15h. 30m.	7 729	8 014	669	0	0	9	23.9	97	3.94	490	19 400	36	27	32	99.8	111
112	" 7	9.23 A.M.	" 7	4.04 P.M.	6h. 41m.	6h. 27m.	14m.	00m.	9 114	9 447	636	0	0	7	24.4	99	2.23	350	18 500	118	30	52	99.7	112
113	" 7	4.04 P.M.	" 8	3.29 "	7h. 55m.	7h. 39m.	16m.	15h. 30m.	10 786	11 173	596	0	0	6	24.3	98	1.80	310	13 800	118	53	85	99.4	113
114	" 8	3.29 "	" 9	2.03 "	7h. 04m.	6h. 46m.	18m.	15h. 30m.	9 333	9 668	683	0	0	7	23.8	96	2.00	320	19 000	201	75	164	99.1	114
115	" 9	2.03 "	" 10	2.33 "	7h. 27m.	7h. 09m.	18m.	17h. 03m.	9 625	9 958	655	0	0	7	23.2	94	2.00	290	11 500	62	28	40	99.7	115
116	" 10	2.33 "	" 11	1.58 "	7h. 55m.	7h. 41m.	14m.	15h. 30m.	10 787	11 163	462	0	0	4	24.2	98	1.90	290	11 600	42	23	31	99.7	116
117	" 11	1.58 "	" 13	9.22 A.M.	3h. 54m.	3h. 40m.	14m.	39h. 30m.	5 158	5 286	427	0	0	8	24.0	97	1.74	280	13 200	80	24	44	99.7	117
118	" 13	9.22 A.M.	" 14	12.32 P.M.	9h. 02m.	8h. 50m.	12m.	18h. 08m.	11 245	12 598	495	0	0	4	23.8	96	1.47	140	9 000	81	13	47	99.5	118

TABLE No. 5.—*Continued.*

Warren System.

Number of Run.	Began.		Ended.		Periods of Time. Hours and Minutes.				Quantities of Water. Cubic Feet.			Waste.		Percentage which the Sum of the Wash and Waste Water is of Applied Water.	Average Actual Rate of Filtration.		Average Amount of Applied Sulphate of Alumina. Grains per Gallon.	Estimated Average Amount of Suspended Solids in River Water. Parts per Million.	Bacteria per Cubic Centimeter.	Effluent.			Average Bacterial Efficiency.	Number of Run.
	Date.	Hour.	Date.	Hour.	Operation.	Service.	Wash.	Delay.	Applied.	Filtered.	Wash.	Filtered.	Unfiltered.		Cubic Feet per Minute.	Million Gallons per Acre per 24 Hours.			River Water.	Maximum.	Minimum.	Average.		
	1896		1896																					
119	April 14	12.32 P.M.	April 16	11.03 A.M.	15h. 21m.	15h. 12m.	19m.	31h. 10m.	22 605	22 132	676	0	0	3	24.3	98	1.18	110	4 900	41	15	24	99.5	119
120	" 16	11.03 A.M.	" 17	1.35 P.M.	10h. 18m.	10h. 04m.	14m.	16h. 14m.	14 199	14 683	544	0	0	4	24.3	98	1.00	80	3 100	14	5	10	99.7	120
121	" 17	1.35 P.M.	" 20	9.23 A.M.	12h. 48m.	12h. 30m.	18m.	55h. 00m.	17 984	18 545	690	0	0	4	24.8	100	0.96	90	4 300	152	44	78	98.2	121
122	" 20	9.23 A.M.	" 21	12.30 P.M.	11h. 24m.	11h. 09m.	15m.	15h. 43m.	15 941	16 398	655	0	0	4	24.5	99	1.23	120	4 600	19	4	8	99.8	122
123	" 21	12.30 P.M.	" 23	12.25 "	16h. 55m.	16h. 37m.	18m.	31h. 00m.	23 952	24 483	696	0	0	3	24.5	99	1.21	100	4 600	670	8	77	98.3	123
124	" 23	12.25 "	" 25	11.38 A.M.	13h. 58m.	13h. 42m.	16m.	45h. 15m.	20 248	20 475	1 073	0	0	5	24.9	100	1.30	70	6 700	67	14	36	99.5	124
125	" 25	11.38 A.M.	" 27	9.25 "	6h. 09m.	5h. 55m.	14m.	39h. 38m.	10 000	8 961	611	0	214	8	25.3	102	1.33	70	8 800	56	41	48	99.5	125
126	" 27	9.25 A.M.	" 27	10.08 P.M.	12h. 00m.	11h. 43m.	17m.	43m.	17 592	17 928	674	0	0	4	25.5	103	1.32	70	6 700	47	42	43	99.4	126
127	" 27	10.08 P.M.	" 28	4.40 "	18h. 31m.	18h. 14m.	17m.	01m.	26 900	27 711	686	0	0	3	25.3	102	1.13	80	5 600	160	47	109	98.1	127
128	" 28	4.40 "	" 29	10.03 A.M.	17h. 23m.	16h. 57m.	26m.	00m.	25 188	25 873	759	0	0	3	25.4	103	1.44	80	6 600	....	....	160	97.6	128
129	" 29	10.03 A.M.	" 29	11.03 P.M.	13h. 00m.	12h. 37m.	23m.	00m.	18 390	18 962	681	0	0	4	25.1	101	1.36	70	8 300	....	....	86	99.0	129
130	" 29	11.03 P.M.	" 30	1.28 "	14h. 25m.	14h. 09m.	16m.	00m.	21 032	21 759	874	0	0	4	25.6	103	1.37	70	4 600	139	23	49	98.9	130
131	" 30	1.28 "	May 1	9.29 A.M.	20h. 01m.	19h. 41m.	20m.	00m.	29 362	30 123	421	0	0	1	25.5	103	2.41	60	2 800	65	34	47	98.8	131
132	May 1	9.29 A.M.	" 2	6.29 "	21h. 00m.	20h. 42m.	18m.	00m.	31 319	32 264	398	0	0	1	26.0	105	2.82	60	5 300	67	52	57	98.9	132
133	" 2	6.29 "	" 4	7.28 P.M.	19h. 53m.	19h. 39m.	14m.	41h. 06m.	30 146	30 987	586	0	0	2	26.3	106	3.66	80	7 400	78	37	61	99.2	133
134	" 4	7.28 P.M.	" 5	2.05 "	18h. 37m.	18h. 21m.	16m.	00m.	28 471	29 256	513	0	0	2	26.5	107	1.61	100	5 900	149	24	51	99.1	134
135	" 5	2.05 "	" 6	7.55 A.M.	17h. 45m.	17h. 31m.	14m.	05m.	27 169	27 784	468	0	0	2	26.4	107	1.68	100	6 300	56	40	54	99.1	135
136	" 6	7.55 A.M.	" 7	2.41 "	18h. 46m.	18h. 25m.	21m.	00m.	28 169	28 964	561	0	0	2	26.2	106	1.67	100	5 200	85	16	42	99.2	136
137	" 7	2.41 "	" 7	8.52 P.M.	17h. 50m.	17h. 21m.	29m.	21m.	28 110	28 657	565	176	0	3	27.0	109	1.66	80	4 700	85	32	56	98.8	137
138	" 7	8.52 P.M.	" 8	5.02 "	20h. 10m.	19h. 54m.	16m.	00m.	30 779	31 475	582	0	0	2	26.3	106	1.58	90	4 800	57	8	27	99.4	138
139	" 8	5.02 "	" 9	10.44 A.M.	17h. 42m.	17h. 20m.	22m.	00m.	27 273	27 875	618	17	0	2	26.8	108	1.62	110	4 600	21	12	16	99.7	139
140	" 9	10.44 A.M.	" 11	9.18 "	5h. 34m.	5h. 24m.	10m.	41h. 00m.	8 623	8 817	482	0	0	6	27.2	110	1.60	110	5 900	....	....	39	99.3	140
141	" 11	9.18 "	" 12	1.27 "	16h. 09m.	15h. 55m.	14m.	00m.	24 212	24 769	518	0	0	2	26.8	108	1.61	190	7 400	28	22	25	99.7	141
142	" 12	1.27 "	" 12	4.20 "	14h. 47m.	14h. 35m.	12m.	06m.	22 652	23 385	579	0	0	3	26.7	108	1.54	180	7 000	54	22	34	99.5	142
143	" 12	4.20 "	" 13	9.38 "	17h. 15m.	17h. 03m.	12m.	03m.	26 616	27 329	504	0	0	2	26.7	108	1.67	170	5 400	19	12	14	99.7	143
144	" 13	9.38 "	" 14	2.12 "	16h. 19m.	16h. 04m.	15m.	15m.	25 144	25 724	488	0	0	2	26.7	108	1.59	140	3 700	13	11	12	99.7	144
145	" 14	2.12 "	" 14	8.58 P.M.	18h. 46m.	18h. 33m.	13m.	00m.	29 236	29 928	666	0	0	2	26.8	108	1.69	140	5 100	80	4	33	99.4	145
146	" 14	8.58 P.M.	" 15	2.01 "	17h. 03m.	16h. 48m.	15m.	00m.	26 531	27 150	711	0	0	3	26.9	109	1.55	130	7 300	52	16	28	99.6	146
147	" 15	2.01 "	" 16	9.02 A.M.	19h. 01m.	18h. 49m.	12m.	00m.	29 519	30 230	434	0	0	1	26.8	108	1.61	100	6 100	28	14	19	99.7	147
148*	" 16	9.02 A.M.	" 18	1.12 P.M.	7h. 11m.	6h. 58m.	13m.	44h. 59m.	11 230	11 125	1 266	0	0	11	26.6	107	1.62	130	8 000	19	15	17	99.8	148*
149[1]	" 18	1.12 P.M.	" 20	12.55 A.M.	34h. 46m.	34h. 29m.	17m.	57m.	51 286	51 483	622	93	0	1	24.9	101	0.99	70	5 800	315	26	88	98.5	149[1]
150*†	" 20	12.55 A.M.	" 20	4.05 "	3h. 10m.	2h. 58m.	12m.	00m.	5 330	4 432	524	0	0	10	24.8	100	1.84	60	2 700	192	79	123	95.4	150*†
151[2]	" 20	4.05 "	" 21	7.49 "	26h. 20m.	25h. 59m.	21m.	1h. 24m.	37 095	38 121	508	0	0	1	24.4	99	0.56	130	4 400	73	30	52	98.8	151[2]
152[2]	" 21	7.49 "	" 22	10.19 "	25h. 57m.	25h. 41m.	16m.	33m.	36 882	37 879	732	0	0	2	24.7	100	1.52	130	6 000	231	47	90	98.5	152[2]
153[3]	" 22	10.19 "	" 23	9.10 "	14h. 10m.	13h. 58m.	12m.	8h. 41m.	21 012	20 795	539	0	0	3	24.9	101	1.84	80	5 200	99	39	70	98.7	153[3]

[1] Prescribed chemicals 1 gr., rate 100 mil. gals. [2] Prescribed chemicals 1.5 gr., rate 100 mil. gals. [3] Prescribed chemicals 2.0 gr., rate 100 mil. gals.

* Run shortened at request of Water Company. † Application of chemicals unsatisfactory. Chemical feed pipe broken.

TABLE No. 5.—*Continued.*

Jewell System.

Number of Run.	Began. Date.	Began. Hour.	Ended. Date.	Ended. Hour.	Periods of Time. Hours and Minutes. Operation.	Service.	Wash.	Delay.*	Quantities of Water. Cubic Feet. Applied.	Filtered.	Wash.	Waste. Filtered.	Waste. Unfiltered.	Percentage which the Sum of the Wash and Waste Water is of Applied Water.	Average Actual Rate of Filtration. Cubic Feet per Minute.	Million Gallons per Acre per 24 Hours.	Average Amount of Applied Sulphate of Alumina. Grains per Gallon.	Estimated Average Amount of Suspended Solids in River Water. Parts per Million.	Bacteria per Cubic Centimeter. River Water.	Effluent. Maximum.	Effluent. Minimum.	Effluent. Average.	Average Bacterial Efficiency.	Number of Run.
	1896		1896																					
154*	May 23	9.10 A.M.	May 25	10 11 A.M.	2h. 35m.	2h. 20m.	15m.	46h. 26m.	7 414	7 265	833	0	0	11	51.8	209	2.13	80	5 400	35	23	25	99.5	154*
155[1]	" 25	10.11 "	" 26	7 34 "	21h. 23m.	21h 03m.	20m.	00m.	36 290	37 299	554	0	0	2	25.5	120	0.98	40	1 900	74	21	38	98.0	155[1]
156[1]	" 26	7.34 "	" 27	4.59 "	20h. 27m.	20h. 13m.	14m.	58m.	34 958	35 993	557	0	0	2	29.6	120	0.94	40	1 800	134	25	92	94.9	156[3]
157[2]	" 27	4.59 "	" 27	9.15 P.M.	16h. 16m.	15h. 57m.	19m.	00m.	28 155	28 088	688	0	0	2	29.4	120	1.46	80	2 900	135	30	66	97.7	157[3]
158[2]	" 27	9.15 P.M.	" 28	11 05 A.M.	13h. 46m.	13h. 30m.	16m.	04m.	23 155	23 735	652	0	0	3	29.4	120	1.50	100	6 200	206	43	87	98.6	158[3]
159[2]	" 28	11.05 A.M.	" 28	5.30 P.M.	6h. 20m.	6h. 07m	13m.	05m.	10 567	10 820	573	0	0	6	29.6	120	1.46	400	14 200	300	158	217	98.5	159[3]
160[2]	" 28	5.30 P.M.	" 28	9.30 "	3h. 25m.	3h. 10m.	15m.	35m.	5 562	5 684	501	0	0	9	29.9	122	1.67	670	24 400	....	....	423	98.3	160[3]
161†[2]	" 28	9.30 "	" 28	11.00 "	42m.	29m.	13m.	48m.	1 947	836	460	0	0	24	28.8	117	2.43	670	24 400	668	560	626	97.4	161†[2]
162†[4]	" 28	11.00 "	" 29	12.51 A.M.	1h. 16m.	48m.	38m.	35m.	2 726	1 482	527	354	0	32	30.9	126	3.47	800	33 900	460	345	402	98.8	162†[4]
163†[4]	" 29	12.51 A.M.	" 29	5.54 "	4h. 05m.	3h. 54m.	11m.	58m.	7 558	6 692	639	0	0	8	29.4	120	4.65	670	29 500	715	275	451	98.5	163†[3]
164[4]	" 29	5.54 "	" 29	11.20 "	5h. 26m.	5h. 13m	13m.	00m.	8 494	8 218	757	0	0	9	26.3	106	5.52	660	22 400	151	80	127	99.4	164[4]
165[6]	" 29	11.20 "	" 29	1.00 P.M.	1h. 40m.	1h. 28m.	12m.	00m.	2 582	2 157	517	0	0	20	24.5	99	4.72	650	21 300	....	....	212	99.0	165[6]
166[7]	" 29	1.00 P.M.	" 29	2.20 "	1h. 20m.	1h. 10m.	10m.	00m.	2 020	2 088	607	0	0	30	29.8	121	4.44	650	21 300	....	....	129	99.4	166[7]
167[7]	" 29	2.20 "	" 29	3.45 "	1h. 25m.	1h. 12m.	13m.	00m.	2 042	2 120	639	0	0	31	29.5	120	4.32	650	26 900	....	....	270	99.0	167[7]
168[7]	" 29	3.45 "	" 29	5.32 "	1h. 09m.	57m.	12m.	38m.	1 784	1 716	574	0	0	32	30.0	122	4.64	650	26 900	....	....	270	99.0	168[7]
169[8]	" 29	5 22 "	" 29	6.32 "	1h. 00m.	47m.	13m.	00m.	3 259	1 451	471	0	0	14	30.4	124	2.51	650	32 500	....	....	465	98.6	169[8]
170[9]	" 29	6.32 "	" 29	8.04 "	1h. 27m.	1h. 15m.	12m.	05m.	2 381	2 270	469	0	0	20	30.3	123	3.44	650	32 500	....	....	325	99.0	170[9]
171[9]	" 29	8.04 "	" 29	9.24 "	1h. 20m.	1h. 10m.	10m.	00m.	2 026	2 079	502	0	0	25	29.7	121	4.98	650	30 600	....	....	118	99.6	171[9]
172[10]	" 29	9.24 "	" 29	10.53 "	1h. 29m.	1h. 13m.	16m.	00m.	1 655	1 846	567	0	0	34	25.3	102	5.67	650	30 600	....	....	155	99.5	172[10]
173[11]	" 29	10.63 "	" 30	12.12 A.M.	1h. 19m.	1h. 04m.	15m.	00m.	1 920	1 844	779	0	0	41	28.9	118	5.11	650	28 700	....	....	170	99.4	173[11]
174[12]	" 30	12.12 A.M.	" 30	6.00 "	4h. 55m.	4h. 41m.	14m.	53m.	5 600	5 784	507	0	0	9	20.5	83	4.65	650	25 200	222	128	175	99.3	174[12]
175[13]	" 30	6.00 "	" 30	7.46 "	59m.	45m.	14m.	47m.	2 354	1 268	518	0	0	22	28.1	114	4.70	650	21 800	....	....	415	98.1	175[13]
176[14]	" 30	7.46 "	" 30	9.45 "	1h. 10m.	58m.	12m.	49m.	2 596	1 699	484	0	0	19	29.3	119	5.72	650	20 700	....	....	275	98.7	176[14]
177[15]	" 30	9.45 "	" 30	11.32 "	1h. 39m.	1h. 27m.	12m.	08m.	3 364	2 560	539	0	0	16	29.5	120	6.24	530	19 700	....	....	475	97.6	177[15]
178[16]	" 30	11.32 "	June 2	3.21 P.M.	4h. 08m.	3h. 56m.	12m.	47h. 41m.	6 869	6 742	592	116	0	10	28.6	116	4.16	530	19 700	....	....	169	99.1	178[16]
179[16]	June 2	3.21 P.M.	" 2	5.00 "	1h. 39m.	1h. 26m.	13m.	00m.	3 784	2 967	619	0	0	16	34.5	140	4.47	830	20 800	620	289	454	97.8	179[16]
180[17]	" 2	5.00 "	" 2	6.05 "	1h. 05m.	53m.	12m.	cont.	1 326	1 324	590	0	0	45	25.0	101	4.22	830	15 700	....	....	270	98.3	180[17]
181[17]	" 2	6.05 "	" 2	8.12 "	56m.	38m.	18m.	1h. 11m.	1 032	1 041	487	0	0	47	27.4	111	4.06	830	15 700	....	....	191	98.8	181[17]
182[18]	" 2	8.12 "	" 3	12.34 A.M.	4h. 22m.	4h. 05m.	17m.	00m.	7 636	6 651	799	0	0	10	27.1	111	6.92	830	14 000	....	....	22	99.8	182[18]
183[19]	" 3	12.34 A.M.	" 3	5.29 "	4h. 54m.	4h. 39m.	15m.	00m.	7 027	7 023	619	0	0	9	25.2	102	5.98	830	10 100	....	....	36	99.[illegible]	183[19]
184[19]	" 3	5.29 "	" 3	2.20 P.M.	8h. 33m.	8h. 18m.	15m.	18m.	12 533	12 229	799	206	0	8	24.6	99	5.77	600	8 200	50	25	36	99.6	184[19]
185[19]	" 3	2.20 P.M.	" 3	7.39 "	5h. 19m.	4h. 58m.	21m.	00m.	7 707	7 465	695	70	0	10	25.0	101	5.42	460	13 700	144	70	107	99.2	185[19]
186[19]	" 3	7.30 "	" 4	3.53 A.M.	8h. 12m.	7h. 52m.	20m.	02m.	11 839	11 583	486	100	0	5	24.5	90	6.45	460	16 700	64	161	38	99.8	186[19]

[1] Prescribed chemicals 1.0 gr., rate 120 mil. gals.
[2] Prescribed chemicals 1.5 gr., rate 120 mil. gals.
[3] Prescribed chemicals 2.0 gr., rate 120 mil. gals.
[4] Prescribed chemicals 3.0 gr., rate 120 mil. gals.
[5] Prescribed chemicals 5.0 gr., rate 120 mil. gals.
[6] Prescribed chemicals 5.0 gr., rate 100 mil. gals.
[7] Prescribed chemicals 5.0 gr., rate 120 mil. gals.
[8] Prescribed chemicals 3.5 gr., rate 120 mil. gals.
[9] Prescribed chemicals 5.0 gr., rate 120 mil. gals.
[10] Prescribed chemicals 5.0 gr., rate 100 mil. gals.
[11] Prescribed chemicals 5.0 gr., rate 120 mil. gals.
[12] Prescribed chemicals 5.0 gr., rate 80 mil. gals.
[13] Prescribed chemicals 5.0 gr., rate 120 mil. gals.
[14] Prescribed chemicals 6.0 gr., rate 120 mil. gals.
[15] Prescribed chemicals 7.0 gr., rate 120 mil. gals.
[16] Prescribed chemicals 4.0 gr., rate 140 mil. gals.
[17] Prescribed chemicals 4.0 gr., rate 100 mil. gals.
[18] Prescribed chemicals 7.0 gr., rate 100 mil. gals.
[19] Prescribed chemicals 6.0 gr., rate 100 mil. gals.

* Special run at request of Filter Company. † Prescribed amount of chemicals insufficient.

TABLE No. 5.—*Continued.*

Jewell System.

Number of Run.	Began. Date.	Began. Hour.	Ended. Date.	Ended. Hour.	Periods of Time. Hours and Minutes. Operation.	Service.	Wash.	Delay.	Quantities of Water. Cubic Feet. Applied.	Filtered.	Wash.	Waste. Filtered.	Waste. Unfiltered.	Percentage which the Sum of the Wash and Waste Water is of Applied Water.	Average Actual Rate of Filtration. Cubic Feet per Minute.	Million Gallons per Acre per 24 Hours.	Average Amount of Applied Sulphate of Alumina. Grains per Gallon.	Estimated Average Amount of Suspended Solids in River Water. Parts per Million.	Bacteria per Cubic Centimeter. River Water.	Effluent. Maximum.	Effluent. Minimum.	Effluent. Average.	Average Bacterial Efficiency.	Number of Run.
187[1]	1896 June 4	3.53 A.M.	1896 June 4	1.20 P.M.	8h. 41m.	8h. 27m.	14m.	46m.	12 540	12 463	801	0	0	6	24.6	99	5.80	410	10 100	54	38	44	99.6	187[1]
188[*]	" 4	1 20 P.M.	" 4	3 12 "	1h. 52m.	1h. 33m.	19m.	00m.	3 386	2 494	683	0	0	20	26.8	108	4.34	340	7 900	....	....	45	99.4	188[*]
189[2]	" 4	3.12 "	" 4	6.28 "	3h. 16m.	3h. 04m.	12m.	00m.	4 877	4 879	629	0	0	13	26.5	107	3.61	340	8 600	116	24	70	99.2	189[2]
190[3]	" 4	6.28 "	" 4	10.20 "	3h. 52m.	3h. 33m.	19m.	00m.	5 530	5 532	532	0	0	10	26.0	105	3.98	340	7 600	71	61	66	99.1	190[3]
191[1]	" 4	10.20 "	" 5	1.54 A.M.	3h. 34m.	3h. 18m.	16m.	00m.	5 073	5 072	501	0	0	10	25.6	103	4.07	340	6 700	114	10	40	99.4	191[1]
192[3]	" 5	1.54 A.M.	" 5	6.37 "	4h. 17m.	4h. 04m.	13m.	26m.	7 105	7 120	591	0	0	8	29.2	119	3.84	340	9 100	94	18	56	99.4	192[3]
193[3]	" 5	6.37 "	" 5	9.00 "	2h. 25m.	2h. 11m.	14m.	00m.	3 844	3 877	568	0	0	15	29.6	120	4.97	340	11 600	....	...	55	99.5	193[3]
194[4]	" 5	9.02 "	" 5	11.02 "	2h. 00m.	1h. 48m.	12m.	00m.	3 766	3 803	617	0	0	16	35.2	143	4.44	190	10 700	....	....	65	99.4	194[4]
195[4]	" 5	11.02 "	" 5	1.32 P.M.	2h. 30m.	2h. 17m	13m.	00m.	4 631	4 671	594	0	0	13	34.1	138	4.02	190	9 900	...	...	80	99.2	195[4]
196[4]	" 5	1.32 P.M.	" 5	4 20 "	2h. 01m.	1h. 46m.	15m.	47m.	3 761	3 623	640	62	0	19	34.2	139	3.94	190	7 200	..	....	70	99.0	196[4]
197[5]	" 5	4.20 "	" 5	5.25 "	1h. 05m.	52m.	13m.	00m.	2 637	1 806	515	0	0	20	34.7	141	5.98	190	7 200	....	....	81	98.9	197[5]
198[5]	" 5	5.25 "	" 5	7.17 "	1h. 52m.	1h. 35m.	17m.	00m.	3 417	3 283	530	47	0	17	34.6	140	6.05	190	4 600	....	....	70	99.3	198[5]
199[5]	" 5	7.17 "	" 5	9.10 "	1h. 46m.	1h. 31m.	15m.	07m.	2 970	2 876	550	0	0	18	31.6	128	7.32	190	5 400	...	....	25	99.5	199[5]
200[8]	" 5	9.10 "	" 6	12.18 A.M.	2h. 28m.	2h. 10m.	18m.	40m.	3 977	3 953	596	0	0	15	30.4	124	7.70	190	5 400	....	....	7	99.9	200[8]
201[7]	" 6	12.18 A.M.	" 6	4.50 "	4h. 32m.	4h. 20m.	12m.	00m.	7 457	6 551	573	0	0	8	25.2	102	4.23	190	5 600	....	....	9	99.8	201[7]
202[7]	" 6	4.50 "	" 6	6.55 "	2h. 05m.	1h. 53m.	12m.	00m.	2 822	2 853	486	0	0	17	25.2	102	4.01	190	5 000	..	....	15	99.7	202[7]
203[8]	" 6	6.55 "	" 6	12.52 P.M.	5h. 52m.	5h. 40m.	12m.	05m.	8 648	5 736	559	107	0	8	25.7	104	3.52	170	4 300	29	14	21	99.5	203[8]
204[8]	" 6	12.52 P.M.	" 9	10.56 A.M	3h. 20m.	3h. 08m.	12m.	66h. 44m.	6 551	6 221	436	0	0	9	33 1	134	5.28	160	4 900	14	12	13	99.7	204[8]
205	" 9	10.56 A.M.	" 9	3.38 P.M.	4h. 42m	4h. 28m.	14m.	00m.	6 699	6 740	666	0	0	10	25.1	101	5.73	580	11 300	....	....	170	98.5	205
206	" 9	3.38 P.M.	" 10	10.19 A.M.	3h. 59m.	2h. 47m	12m.	14h. 42m.	4 213	4 219	534	0	0	13	25.2	102	6.55	510	9 300	....	....	39	99.6	206
207	" 10	10.19 A.M.	" 11	12.35 P.M.	10h. 44m.	10h. 28m.	16m.	25h. 32m.	15 488	15 521	739	0	0	5	24.8	100	5.63	330	8 700	14	9	12	99.9	207
208	" 11	12.35 P.M.	" 12	10.40 A.M.	6h. 35m.	6h. 23m.	12m.	15h. 30m.	9 629	9 680	839	0	0	9	25.3	102	4.53	240	6 600	10	7	8	99.9	208
209	" 12	10 40 A.M.	" 13	10.40 "	8h. 27m.	8h. 07m.	20m.	15h. 33m.	11 819	11 709	594	137	0	6	24.1	97	5.58	200	6 100	12	9	11	99.8	209
210	" 13	10.40 "	" 15	9.25 "	7h. 05m.	6h. 49m.	16m.	15h. 40m.	10 315	10 371	817	0	0	8	25.4	103	3.49	220	13 400	71	15	40	99.7	210
211	" 15	9.25 "	" 15	2.25 P.M.	5h. 00m.	4h. 46m.	14m.	00m.	6 997	7 059	549	0	0	8	24.7	100	4.18	400	14 100	25	10	18	99.9	211
212	" 15	2.25 P.M.	" 16	9.47 A.M.	3h. 52m.	3h. 33m.	19m.	15h. 30m	5 638	5 686	608	0	0	11	26.7	108	5.48	400	13 100	19	11	15	99.9	212
213	" 16	9.47 A.M.	" 16	12.06 P.M.	2h. 19m.	2h. 07m.	12m.	00m.	4 384	4 353	530	0	0	12	34.3	139	5.97	220	8 800	..	....	9	99.9	213
214	" 16	12.06 P.M	" 16	2.19 "	2h. 13m.	2h. 00m.	13m.	00m.	4 092	4 077	586	0	0	14	33.9	138	5.04	220	8 400	...	....	5	99.9	214
215	" 16	2.19 "	" 18	9.03 A.M.	1h. 26m.	1h. 11m.	15m.	17h. 18m.	2 801	2 629	656	0	0	23	37.0	150	5.50	220	8 100	...	....	6	99.9	215
216	" 18	9.03 A.M.	" 19	2.14 P.M	12h. 48m.	12h. 13m.	35m.	16h. 23m.	17 833	18 346	1639	71	0	10	25.0	101	3.72	320	12 000	40	3	27	99.8	216
217	" 19	2.14 P.M.	" 20	9.35 A.M.	3h. 35m.	3h. 21m.	14m.	15h. 46m.	5 003	4 856	696	0	0	14	24.3	98	7.20	430	18 000	69	64	66	99.6	217
218	" 20	9.35 "	" 20	3.17 P.M.	4h. 22m.	4h. 02m.	20m.	1h. 20m.	6 234	6 138	951	0	214	19	25.4	103	2.86	260	10 500	69	67	68	99.4	218
219	" 20	3.17 "	" 22	12.55 "	6h. 03m.	5h. 44m.	19m.	39h. 35m.	8 458	8 675	822	26	0	10	25.2	101	2.80	230	8 600	101	74	88	99.0	219
220	" 22	12.55 "	" 23	10.14 A.M.	5h. 47m.	5h. 25m.	22m.	15h. 32m.	8 161	8 275	820	63	0	11	25.5	103	1.60	200	7 700	97	79	91	98.8	220
221	" 23	10.14 A.M.	" 23	5.12 P.M.	6h. 58m.	6h. 28m.	30m.	00m.	9 719	9 759	775	37	0	8	25.1	101	1.66	180	8 000	216	62	118	98.5	221

[1] Prescribed chemicals 6.0 gr., 120 mil. gals.
[5] Prescribed chemicals 6.0 gr., 140 mil. gals.
[2] Prescribed chemicals 4.0 gr., 100 mil. gals.
[6] Prescribed chemicals 6.0 gr., 120 mil. gals.
[3] Prescribed chemicals 4.0 gr., 120 mil. gals.
[7] Prescribed chemicals 4.0 gr., 100 mil. gals.
[4] Prescribed chemicals 4.0 gr., 140 mil. gals.
[8] Prescribed chemicals 6.0 gr., 100 mil. gals.

* Rate at start 120 mil. gals., changed in middle of run to 100 mil. gals.

TABLE No. 5.—*Continued*

Jewell System.

Number of Run.	Began. Date.	Began. Hour.	Ended. Date.	Ended. Hour.	Periods of Time. Hours and Minutes. Operation.	Service.	Wash.	Delay.	Quantities of Water. Cubic Feet. Applied.	Filtered.	Wash.	Waste. Filtered.	Waste. Unfiltered.	Percentage which the Sum of the Wash and Waste Water is of Applied Water.	Average Actual Rate of Filtration. Cubic Feet per Minute.	Million Gallons per Acre per 24 Hours.	Average Amount of Applied Sulphate of Alumina. Grains per Gallon.	Estimated Average Amount of Suspended Solids in River Water. Parts per Million.	Bacteria per Cubic Centimeter. River Water.	Effluent. Maximum.	Effluent. Minimum.	Effluent. Average.	Average Bacterial Efficiency.	Number of Run.
	1896		1896																					
222	June 23	5.12 P.M.	June 24	12.56 P.M.	4h. 10m.	3h. 55m.	15m.	15h. 34m.	5 537	5 946	559	68	0	11	25.3	102	1.46	370	8 300	840	470	655	92.1	222
223	" 24	12.56 "	" 25	9.47 A.M.	5h. 09m.	4h. 35m.	34m.	15h. 42m.	7 106	6 900	683	205	0	12	25.1	101	1.29	400	8 300	385	215	318	96.2	223
224	" 25	9.47 A.M.	" 25	12.29 P.M.	2h. 42m.	2h. 30m.	12m.	00m.	3 709	3 817	647	0	0	17	25.4	103	1.32	300	6 700	1780	45	603	91.0	224
225	" 25	12.29 P.M.	" 25	3.03 "	2h. 32m.	2h. 02m.	30m.	02m.	3 010	3 060	628	312	0	31	25.1	101	1.63	300	8 100	510	250	380	95.3	225
226	" 25	3.03 "	" 25	4.42 "	1h. 36m.	1h. 22m.	14m.	03m.	2 380	2 091	631	0	0	26	25.5	103	2.13	300	8 600	600	173	386	95.5	226
227	" 25	4.42 "	" 26	11.58 A.M.	3h. 46m.	3h. 34m.	12m.	15h. 30m.	5 108	5 204	515	39	0	11	24.3	98	2.73	290	7 600	347	23	144	98.1	227
228	" 26	11.58 A.M.	" 26	2.50 P.M.	2h. 49m.	2h. 37m.	12m.	03m.	3 943	4 026	543	0	0	14	25.6	103	2.26	280	6 000	79	19	49	99.2	228
229	" 26	2.50 P.M.	" 27	9.54 A.M.	2h. 59m.	2h. 40m.	19m.	16h. 05m.	4 439	4 066	599	275	0	20	25.4	103	2.90	280	6 100	29	9	19	99.7	229
230	" 27	9.54 A.M.	" 27	12.29 P.M.	2h. 35m.	2h. 22m.	13m.	00m.	3 476	3 545	614	0	0	18	25.0	101	2.98	360	10 600	94	44	69	99.4	230
231	" 27	12.29 P.M.	" 27	3.05 "	2h. 28m.	2h. 16m.	12m.	08m.	3 366	3 433	544	0	0	16	25.2	102	4.16	360	10 800	....	....	315	97.1	231
232	" 27	3.05 "	" 29	9.40 A.M.	2h. 49m.	2h. 25m.	24m.	15h. 46m.	3 899	3 704	1094	86	0	30	25.5	103	7.54	360	13 700	41	39	40	99.7	232
233	" 29	9.40 A.M.	" 30	9.51 "	8h. 18m.	7h. 50m.	28m.	15h. 53m.	11 973	11 637	918	246	0	10	24.8	100	5.09	530	13 300	11	4	8	99.9	233
234	" 30	9.51 "	July 1	3.55 P.M.	13h. 55m.	13h. 09m.	46m.	16h. 09m.	18 488	17 699	1996	763	0	15	22.4	91	7.61	590	10 900	7	3	5	99.9	234
235	July 1	3.55 P.M.	" 2	12.24 "	4h. 59m.	4h. 32m.	27m.	15h. 30m.	6 773	6 406	958	61	0	16	23.6	95	5.30	1 400	14 200	115	3	56	99.6	235
236	" 2	12.24 "	" 2	2.15 "	1h. 51m.	1h. 26m.	25m.	00m.	2 062	1 860	1004	30	0	51	21.6	87	7.45	1 700	24 200	144	111	127	99.5	236
237	" 2	2.15 "	" 3	12.45 "	7h. 00m.	6h. 30m.	30m.	15h. 30m.	9 046	8 971	1443	81	0	17	23.0	93	6.97	1 300	22 300	9	0	4	99.9	237
238	" 3	12.45 "	" 6	2.50 "	3h. 11m.	2h. 57m.	14m.	70h. 54m.	4 333	4 204	1201	0	0	28	23.8	96	6.22	1 000	12 000	125	1	16	99 9	238
239	" 6	2.50 "	" 7	3.25 "	8h. 58m.	8h. 34m.	24m.	15h. 37m.	12 274	12 396	994	0	0	8	24.1	97	7.15	430	6 900	997	223	409	94.1	239
240	" 7	3.25 "	" 8	4.16 "	2h. 51m.	2h. 30m.	21m.	22h. 00m.	3 647	3 684	1105	128	0	34	24.6	99	5.46	520	5 600	....	....	247	95.6	240
241	" 8	4.16 "	" 9	10.03 A.M.	1h. 59m.	1h. 17m.	42m.	15h. 48m.	2 316	1 888	752	417	0	50	24.5	99	6.25	460	5 600	....	....	99	98.2	241
242	" 9	10.03 A.M.	" 10	9.04 "	6h. 58m.	6h. 31m.	27m.	16h. 03m.	9 989	9 220	977	312	0	13	23.6	95	6.10	470	9 200	15	0	14	99.8	242
243	" 10	9.04 "	" 10	2.24 P.M.	4h. 49m.	4h. 23m.	26m.	31m.	6 732	6 341	849	147	169	17	24.2	98	5.12	350	10 000	50	38	44	99.6	243
244	" 10	2.24 P.M.	" 10	5.07 "	2h. 27m.	2h. 06m.	21m.	16m.	3 311	3 047	745	0	187	28	24.2	98	5.60	350	11 900	....	....	29	99.8	244
245	" 10	5.07 "	" 11	12.30 "	3h. 53m.	3h. 31m.	22m.	15h. 30m.	5 230	5 094	930	0	0	18	24.2	98	5.02	210	9 600	44	39	41	99.6	245
246	" 11	12.30 "	" 11	2.57 "	2h. 27m.	2h. 05m.	22m.	00m.	3 085	2 946	866	0	0	28	23.6	95	5.90	190	9 600	....	....	3	99.9	246
247	" 11	2.57 "	" 13	10.17 A.M.	3h. 43m.	3h. 19m.	24m.	15h. 37m.	4 589	4 591	985	28	0	22	23.1	93	7.17	270	12 500	52	3	27	99.8	247
248	" 13	10.17 A.M.	" 13	5.11 P.M.	6h. 54m.	6h. 32m.	22m.	00m.	9 647	9 543	768	0	0	8	24.4	99	6.27	490	7 700	73	22	40	99.5	248
249	" 13	5.11 P.M.	" 14	5.06 "	8h. 21m.	7h. 49m.	32m.	15h. 34m.	11 789	11 687	1016	0	0	9	24.9	101	5.66	380	10 200	58	5	19	99.8	249
250	" 14	5.06 "	" 15	4.53 "	8h. 17m.	8h. 00m.	17m.	15h. 30m.	11 796	11 717	739	23	0	6	24.4	99	5.83	480	8 400	23	2	8	99.9	250
251	" 15	4.53 "	" 16	4.34 "	8h. 11m.	7h. 51m.	20m.	15h. 30m.	11 568	11 484	861	66	0	8	24.4	99	4.26	450	7 400	31	5	13	99.8	251
252	" 16	4.34 "	" 18	10.14 A.M.	4h. 30m.	4h. 07m.	23m.	36h. 12m.	5 992	6 006	772	0	0	13	24.3	98	4.73	410	5 100	5	2	3	99.9	252
253	" 18	10.14 A.M.	" 18	5.00 P.M.	6h. 46m.	6h. 08m.	38m.	00m.	10 328	8 926	994	176	0	11	24.3	98	5.88	690	9 900	235	4	26	99.7	253
254	" 18	5.00 P.M.	" 20	3.36 "	7h. 06m.	6h. 44m.	22m.	39h. 30m.	10 116	10 029	707	19	0	7	24.9	101	5.07	400	8 800	12	5	9	99.9	254
255	" 20	3.36 "	" 21	11.13 A.M.	4h. 02m.	3h. 46m.	16m.	15h. 35m.	5 617	5 651	582	0	0	10	25.0	101	5.01	470	7 700	11	3	7	99.9	255
256	" 21	11.13 A.M.	" 22	10.24 "	7h. 39m.	7h. 14m.	25m.	15h. 32m.	10 557	10 705	847	0	0	8	24.7	100	5.33	650	17 100	101	18	47	99.7	256
257	" 22	10.24 "	" 22	11.28 "	1h. 00m.	46m.	14m.	04m.	1 653	1 421	508	0	198	43	30.9	126	6.57	1 200	37 300	....	....	143	99.6	257
258	" 22	11.28 "	" 22	12.21 P.M.	43m.	31m.	12m.	10m.	1 161	930	376	0	198	49	30.0	122	6.81	1 200	33 300	....	....	87	99.7	258
259	" 22	12.21 P.M.	" 22	1.24 "	1h. 03m.	48m.	15m.	00m.	1 453	1 363	473	0	0	33	28.4	116	5.78	1 200	29 400	....	....	32	99.9	259

TABLE NO. 5.—*Continued.*

Jewell System.

Number of Run.	Began. Date.	Began. Hour.	Ended. Date.	Ended. Hour.	Periods of Time. Hours and Minutes. Operation.	Service.	Wash.	Delay.	Quantities of Water. Cubic Feet. Applied.	Filtered.	Wash.	Waste. Filtered.	Waste. Unfiltered.	Percentage which the Sum of the Wash and Waste Water is of Applied Water.	Average Actual Rate of Filtration. Cubic Feet per Minute.	Million Gallons per Acre per 24 Hours.	Average Amount of Applied Sulphate of Alumina. Grains per Gallon.	Estimated Average Amount of Suspended Solids in River Water. Parts per Million.	Bacteria per Cubic Centimeter. River Water.	Effluent. Maximum.	Effluent. Minimum.	Effluent. Average.	Average Bacterial Efficiency.	Number of Run.
	1896		1896																					
260	July 22	1.24 P.M.	July 22	4.12 P.M.	2h. 48m.	2h. 27m.	21m.	00m.	3 604	3 773	719	0	0	20	25.7	104	6.16	1 200	32 000	....	....	248	99.2	260
261	" 22	4.12 "	" 23	9.46 A.M.	2h. 04m.	1h. 45m.	19m.	15h. 30m.	2 463	2 504	808	0	0	33	23.8	96	5.76	1 200	34 600	....	....	745	97.8	261
262	" 23	9.46 A.M.	" 23	10.39 "	53m.	37m.	16m.	00m.	858	855	541	0	0	63	23.1	93	5.87	2 200	23 800	....	....	240	99.0	262
263	" 23	10.39 "	" 23	2.36 P.M.	3h. 39m.	3h. 17m.	22m.	18m.	4 219	4 172	797	0	198	23	21.2	86	8.38	2 200	21 800	124	51	87	99.6	263
264	" 23	2.36 P.M.	" 24	10.21 A.M.	4h. 15m.	3h. 56m.	19m.	15h. 30m.	4 643	4 796	804	0	0	17	20.4	83	9.12	2 500	27 500	141	96	118	99.6	264
265	" 24	10.21 A.M.	" 24	11.31 "	1h. 04m.	46m.	18m.	06m.	1 126	914	658	0	0	58	19.9	81	9.00	3 400	34 100	....	....	105	99.7	265
266	" 24	11.31 "	" 24	4.29 P.M.	4h. 51m.	4h. 29m.	22m.	07m.	4 836	4 890	1 019	0	0	21	18.2	74	12.31	3 400	31 000	126	27	71	99.8	266
267	" 24	4.29 P.M.	" 25	12.55 "	4h. 48m.	4h. 23m.	25m.	15h. 38m.	5 239	5 383	1 034	0	0	20	20.5	83	12.62	2 100	22 100	....	....	52	99.8	267
268	" 25	12.55 "	" 27	9.28 A.M.	4h. 36m.	4h. 07m.	29m.	39h. 57m.	5 072	5 016	860	0	0	17	20.3	82	9.68	1 700	17 300	70	32	47	99.7	268
269	" 27	9.28 A.M.	" 28	11.05 "	8h. 31m.	7h. 59m.	32m.	17h. 06m.	9 613	9 903	937	113	0	10	20.7	84	8.72	1 400	17 800	38	7	18	99.9	269
270	" 28	11.05 "	" 29	9.33 "	4h. 27m.	3h. 53m.	34m.	19h. 01m.	5 386	5 405	960	45	0	18	23.2	94	6.45	1 400	24 500	8	4	6	99.9	270
271	" 29	9.33 "	" 29	5.15 P.M.	7h. 42m.	7h. 06m.	36m.	00m.	9 566	9 770	1 078	10	0	11	23.0	93	7.58	1 800	9 500	79	1	15	99.8	271
272	" 29	5.15 P.M.	" 30	11.37 A.M.	3h. 09m.	2h. 39m.	30m.	18h. 22m.	3 439	3 514	776	0	0	22	22.1	89	8.61	1 700	17 300	....	....	14	99.9	272
	Western Gravity System.																							
	1895		1895																					
1	Dec. 23	10.35 A.M.	Dec. 24	9.42 A.M.	7h. 17m.	7h. 00m.	17m.	15h. 00m.	3 867	3 813	615	54	0	18	9.1	57	.....	20	3 700	544	328	456	98.8	1
2	" 24	9.42 "	" 27	4.13 P.M.	23h. 08m.	22h. 45m.	23m.	55h. 23m.	13 036	12 679	505	57	300	5	9.3	58	.....	80	6 900	910	168	469	93.2	2
3	" 27	4.13 P.M.	" 28	3.57 "	7h. 58m.	7h. 41m.	17m.	15h. 46m.	4 413	4 273	451	70	70	13	9.3	58	.....	220	32 400	1 260	480	783	97.6	3
4	" 28	3.57 "	" 30	1.36 "	6h. 14m.	5h. 56m.	18m.	39h. 25m.	3 255	3 072	472	83	100	20	8.6	53	.....	220	12 100	....	....	332	97.3	4
5	" 30	1.36 "	" 31	9.39 A.M.	4h. 29m.	4h. 14m.	15m.	15h. 34m.	3 105	2 980	579	55	70	22	11.6	72	.....	400	11 900	726	528	627	94.7	5
6	" 31	9.39 A.M.	Jan. 2, '96	9.49 "	7h. 39m.	7h. 21m.	18m.	40h. 31m.	4 038	3 750	616	88	200	22	8.5	53	.....	600	13 000	276	224	253	98.1	6
7	Jan. 2, '96	9.49 "	" 2	1.36 P.M.	3h. 47m.	3h. 37m.	10m.	00m.	2 365	1 928	162	37	400	25	8.9	55	.....	800	12 400	200	136	176	98.6	7
8	" 2	1.36 P.M.	" 3	9.36 A.M.	4h. 14m.	3h. 56m.	18m.	15h. 46m.	2 287	2 094	312	143	50	22	8.9	55	.....	870	9 400	392	304	348	96.3	8
9	" 3	9.36 A.M.	" 3	1.55 P.M.	4h. 19m.	4h. 04m.	15m.	00m.	2 607	2 149	285	58	400	28	8.8	55	.....	870	14 300	250	208	229	98.4	9
10	" 3	1.55 P.M.	" 4	11.10 A.M.	2h. 23m.	1h. 53m.	29m.	18h. 52m.	1 564	982	186	182	400	45	8.7	54	.....	800	10 700	432	410	421	96.1	10
11	" 4	11.10 A.M.	" 6	10.43 "	8h. 24m.	8h. 09m.	15m.	39h. 09m.	4 176	4 017	490	59	100	15	8.2	50	.....	360	6 600	122	25	81	98.8	11
12	" 6	10.43 "	" 7	3.34 P.M.	12h. 41m.	12h. 29m.	12m.	16h. 10m.	6 154	5 905	400	49	200	10	7.9	48	.....	250	4 300	416	98	278	93.5	12
13	" 7	3.34 P.M.	" 9	9.55 A.M.	10h. 54m.	10h. 37m.	17m.	31h. 27m.	6 306	6 192	549	64	50	10	9.7	60	.....	200	4 000	190	88	126	96.9	13
14	" 9	9.55 A.M.	" 9	4.22 P.M.	6h. 27m.	5h. 57m.	30m.	00m.	3 646	3 318	367	178	50	17	9.3	58	.....	120	1 900	172	52	100	94.7	14
15	" 9	4.22 P.M.	" 11	10.25 A.M.	10h. 06m.	9h. 41m.	25m.	7h. 57m.	6 328	6 036	424	242	50	11	10.4	64	.....	120	1 800	120	97	108	94.0	15
16	" 11	10.25 A.M.	" 14	10.52 "	7h. 37m.	7h. 15m.	22m.	64h. 50m.	4 880	4 625	494	155	100	15	10.6	66	1.09	100	2 500	135	53	94	96.2	16
17	" 14	10.52 "	" 16	10.48 "	13h. 56m.	13h. 24m.	32m.	34h. 00m.	9 420	9 205	864	215	0	12	11.4	70	1.16	45	1 900	164	33	90	95.3	17
18	" 16	10.48 "	" 17	9.53 "	7h. 02m.	6h. 45m.	17m.	16h. 03m.	7 311	6 989	446	122	200	11	17.3	107	1.65	40	3 200	192	48	130	95.9	18
19	" 17	9.53 "	" 18	9.39 "	8h. 12m.	7h. 53m.	19m.	15h. 34m.	8 986	8 630	431	106	250	9	18.2	112	1.39	30	6 500	240	102	159	97.6	19
20	" 18	9.39 "	" 20	10.18 "	8h. 39m.	8h. 19m.	20m.	40h. 00m.	11 766	11 534	551	132	100	7	21.1	143	1.25	20	7 300	258	144	228	96.9	20
21	" 20	10.18 "	" 21	9.37 "	7h. 04m.	6h. 52m.	12m.	16h. 15m.	9 351	8 979	350	74	300	8	21.8	135	1.24	20	6 400	246	192	219	96.6	21
22	" 21	9.37 "	" 22	9.20 "	8h. 04m.	7h. 48m.	16m.	15h. 39m.	9 720	9 402	501	118	200	8	20.1	125	0.87	20	3 000	202	147	174	94.2	22
23	" 22	9.20 "	" 23	9.26 "	8h. 01m.	7h. 44m.	17m.	16h. 05m.	11 766	11 470	517	146	150	7	24.7	152	0.71	17	2 600	266	136	192	92.6	23

TABLE NO. 5.—*Continued.*

Western Gravity System.

Number of Run.	Began. Date.	Began. Hour.	Ended. Date.	Ended. Hour.	Periods of Time, Hours and Minutes. Operation.	Service.	Wash.	Delay.	Quantities of Water. Cubic Feet. Applied.	Filtered.	Wash.	Waste. Filtered.	Waste. Unfiltered.	Percentage which the Sum of the Wash and Waste Water is of Applied Water.	Average Actual Rate of Filtration. Cubic Feet per Minute.	Million Gallons per Acre per 24 Hours.	Average Amount of Applied Sulphate of Alumina. Grains per Gallon.	Estimated Average Amount of Suspended Solids in River Water. Parts per Million.	Bacteria per Cubic Centimeter. River Water.	Effluent. Maximum.	Effluent. Minimum.	Effluent. Average.	Average Bacterial Efficiency.	Number of Run.
	1896		1896																					
24	Jan. 23	9.26 A.M.	Jan. 24	9.49 A.M.	7h. 57m.	7h. 44m.	13m.	16h. 26m.	11 325	11 026	441	99	200	7	23.8	147	0.94	20	4 800	73	64	68	98.6	24
25	" 24	9.49 "	" 25	9.26 "	8h. 04m.	7h. 47m.	17m.	15h. 33m.	11 518	11 042	359	146	330	7	23.7	146	0.82	20	3 600	145	49	96	97.3	25
26	" 25	9.26 "	" 27	9.29 "	6h. 43m.	6h. 25m.	18m.	41h. 20m.	8 525	8 045	425	133	347	11	20.9	129	0.72	50	7 200	165	65	102	98.6	26
27	" 27	9.29 "	" 27	3.51 P.M.	6h. 22m.	6h. 05m.	17m.	00m.	5 544	5 173	399	141	230	14	14.2	87	1.23	200	13 400	934	554	700	94.8	27
28	" 27	3.51 P.M.	" 28	12.18 "	4h. 16m.	3h. 58m.	18m.	16h. 11m.	3 558	3 114	343	144	300	21	13.1	81	2.07	270	12 400	....	....	504	95.9	28
29	" 28	12.18 "	" 30	10.10 A.M.	5h. 22m.	5h. 04m.	18m.	64h. 30m.	3 784	3 235	839	87	462	37	10.7	66	1.50	270	14 700	....	....	1 586	98.9	29
30	" 30	10.10 A.M.	" 30	1.27 P.M.	3h. 17m.	2h. 59m.	18m.	00m.	2 715	2 009	635	106	600	50	11.2	69	2.23	320	15 600	....	....	278	98.2	30
31	" 30	1.27 P.M.	Feb. 1	10.20 A.M.	4h. 35m.	4h. 18m.	17m.	16h. 18m.	3 410	3 017	568	93	300	28	11.6	72	1.61	320	12 000	....	....	820	93.2	31
32	Feb. 1	10.20 A.M.	" 1	2.05 P.M.	3h. 45m.	3h. 26m.	19m.	00m.	2 305	2 133	606	80	92	34	10.3	64	2.29	340	21 300	....	....	326	98.5	32
33	" 1	2.05 P.M.	" 3	10.04 A.M.	3h. 48m.	3h. 30m.	18m.	40h. 11m.	3 219	3 019	646	100	100	26	14.4	89	2.79	340	17 400	137	118	127	92.7	33
34	" 3	10.04 A.M.	" 4	9.50 "	7h. 54m.	7h. 42m.	12m.	15h. 52m.	7 098	5 982	416	66	50	7	15.1	94	1.51	240	62 200	1 124	240	639	99.0	34
35	" 4	9.50 "	" 4	3.27 P.M.	5h. 37m.	5h. 22m.	15m.	00m.	4 764	4 574	325	40	150	11	14.2	87	1.60	250	55 000	908	421	683	98.7	35
36	" 4	3.27 P.M.	" 5	12.25 "	5h. 28m.	5h. 11m.	17m.	15h. 30m.	4 534	4 223	343	111	200	15	13.6	84	2.55	380	81 000	960	600	820	99.0	36
37	" 5	12.25 "	" 5	4.28 "	4h. 03m.	3h. 47m.	16m.	00m.	3 439	3 089	337	90	260	20	13.6	84	2.22	460	71 000	....	....	324	95.4	37
38	" 5	4.28 "	" 6	12.20 "	4h. 22m.	4h. 05m.	17m.	15h. 30m.	3 945	3 536	336	109	300	19	14.4	89	1.88	460	36 200	828	308	568	98.4	38
39	" 6	12.20 "	" 7	9.23 A.M.	5h. 29m.	5h. 10m.	19m.	15h. 34m.	4 440	4 066	269	174	200	15	13.1	81	1.86	460	30 800	1 276	460	797	97.4	39
40	" 7	9.23 A.M.	" 7	12.25 P.M.	3h. 02m.	2h. 45m.	17m.	00m.	2 935	2 423	409	112	400	32	14.7	91	2.52	640	41 100	....	....	800	98.1	40
41	" 7	12.25 P.M.	" 7	3.49 "	3h. 24m.	3h. 07m.	17m.	00m.	3 375	2 748	433	227	400	31	14.7	91	2.63	640	55 000	....	....	1 600	97.0	41
42.	" 7	3.49 "	" 8	11.11 A.M.	3h. 50m.	3h. 34m.	16m.	15h. 32m.	2 350	2 141	424	109	100	23	10.0	62	3.15	670	45 600	....	....	321	99.3	42
43	" 8	11.11 A.M.	" 8	1.55 P.M.	2h. 44m.	2h. 24m.	20m.	00m.	2 397	1 849	413	148	400	40	12.8	79	3.32	700	27 200	....	....	270	99.0	43
44	" 8	1.55 P.M.	" 8	3.48 "	1h. 53m.	1h. 37m.	16m.	00m.	1 960	1 538	391	122	300	40	15.9	98	.....	700	32 400	....	....	825	97.5	44
45	" 8	3.48 "	" 10	10.30 A.M.	3h. 08m.	2h. 44m.	24m.	15h. 34m.	1 240	951	503	179	110	66	5.8	36	.....	800	21 100	....	....	860	95.9	45
46	" 10	10.30 A.M.	" 10	12.25 P.M.	1h. 55m.	1h. 37m.	18m.	00m.	1 745	1 266	256	179	300	41	13.1	81	.....	970	14 400	....	...	252	98.2	46
47	" 10	12.25 P.M.	" 10	2.58 "	2h. 33m.	2h. 15m.	18m.	00m.	1 951	1 513	353	138	300	42	11.2	69	.....	970	14 400	....	....	272	98.1	47
48	" 10	2.58 "	" 11	9.21 A.M.	2h. 50m.	2h. 32m.	18m.	3h. 33m.	2 358	1 817	450	141	400	41	12.0	74	.....	970	18 900	672	290	481	97.5	48
49	" 11	9.21 A.M.	" 11	11.17 "	1h. 56m.	1h. 44m.	12m.	00m.	1 477	1 308	329	69	100	33	12.6	78	.....	410	20 200	....	....	251	98.8	49
50	" 11	11.17 "	" 11	2.23 P.M.	3h. 06m.	2h. 48m.	18m.	00m.	2 212	1 975	538	137	100	35	11.8	73	.....	410	19 800	....	....	461	97.7	50
51	" 11	2.23 P.M.	" 11	4.47 "	2h. 24m.	2h. 10m.	14m.	00m.	2 005	1 695	335	110	200	32	13.0	80	.....	410	19 400	....	....	298	98.5	51
52	" 11	4.47 "	" 12	10.46 A.M.	2h. 29m.	2h. 09m.	20m.	15h. 30m.	1 642	1 118	351	124	400	53	8.6	53	.....	420	23 700	950	250	600	97.5	52
53	" 12	10.46 A.M.	" 12	12.58 P.M.	2h. 04m.	1h. 46m.	18m.	08m.	2 148	1 809	362	139	200	33	17.0	105	3.22	420	28 000	....	....	840	97.0	53
54	" 12	12.58 P.M.	" 12	1.52 "	30m.	15m.	15m.	24m.	258	79	197	179	100	146	5.3	33	9.33	420	28 000	....	....	280	99.0	54
55	" 12	1.52 "	" 12	3.31 "	1h. 39m.	1h. 16m.	23m.	00m.	917	665	509	152	100	83	8.7	54	3.53	420	28 000	....	....	840	97.0	55
56	" 12	3.31 "	" 13	9.21 A.M.	2h. 14m.	1h. 59m.	15m.	15h. 36m.	1 981	1 475	493	106	400	50	12.4	76	4.13	420	19 400	....	....	605	96.9	56
57	" 13	9.21 A.M.	" 13	12.09 P.M.	2h. 48m.	2h. 36m.	12m.	00m.	2 133	1 784	440	49	300	56	11.4	70	2.80	130	14 800	....	....	106	99.2	57
58	" 13	12.09 P.M.	" 13	3.00 "	2h. 51m.	2h. 39m.	12m.	00m.	3 102	2 267	325	105	730	37	14.3	88	0.78	130	14 800	1 045	235	640	95.7	58
59	" 13	3.00 "	" 14	9.25 A.M.	2h. 44m.	2h. 30m.	14m.	15h. 41m.	2 475	2 293	419	105	80	24	15.3	95	3.51	130	18 800	....	....	425	97.7	59
60	" 14	9.25 A.M.	" 14	2.45 P.M.	4h. 43m.	4h. 25m.	18m.	37m.	3 554	3 322	430	122	110	19	12.5	77	2.77	340	11 900	371	209	290	97.6	60
61	" 14	2.45 P.M.	" 15	9.10 A.M.	3h. 03m.	2h. 45m.	18m.	15h. 31m.	2 691	2 476	415	105	110	23	15.0	93	3.70	340	11 700	408	372	390	96.7	61

TABLE NO. 5.—*Continued.*

Western Gravity System.

Number of Run.	Began. Date.	Began. Hour.	Ended. Date.	Ended. Hour.	Periods of Time. Hours and Minutes. Operation.	Service.	Wash.	Delay.	Quantities of Water. Cubic Feet. Applied.	Filtered.	Wash.	Waste. Filtered.	Waste. Unfiltered.	Percentage which the Sum of the Wash and Waste Water is of Applied Water.	Average Actual Rate of Filtration. Cubic Feet per Minute.	Million Gallons per Acre per 24 Hours.	Average Amount of Applied Sulphate of Alumina. Grains per Gallon.	Estimated Average Amount of Suspended Solids in River Water. Parts per Million.	Bacteria per Cubic Centimeter. River Water.	Effluent. Maximum.	Effluent. Minimum.	Effluent. Average.	Average Bacterial Efficiency.	Number of Run.
	1896		1896																					
62	Feb. 15	9.19 A.M.	Feb. 15	1.27 P.M.	4h. 08m	3h. 53m.	15m.	00m.	3 300	2 996	381	104	200	21	12.9	79	3.48	490	10 800	....	....	390	96.4	62
63	" 15	1.27 P.M.	" 17	9.19 A.M.	4h. 21m.	4h. 03m.	18m.	39h. 31m.	3 647	3 471	451	176	0	17	14.3	88	2.06	490	10 800	1975	517	1137	89.5	63
64	" 17	9.19 A.M.	" 17	1.15 P.M.	3h. 56m.	3h. 41m.	15m.	00m.	3 634	3 414	391	120	100	17	15.4	95	1.91	390	21 800	....	....	865	96.0	64
65	" 17	1.15 P.M.	" 18	9.26 A.M.	4h. 32m.	4h. 15m.	17m.	15h. 39m.	3 608	3 463	490	145	0	18	13.6	84	1.49	390	21 800	1097	602	770	96.5	65
66	" 18	9.26 A.M.	" 18	1.49 P.M.	4h. 20m.	4h. 07m.	13m.	03m.	3 495	3 248	301	116	130	16	13.1	81	2.30	180	14 400	1 220	800	1010	93.0	66
67	" 18	1.49 P.M.	" 19	9.16 A.M.	3h. 57m.	3h. 41m.	16m.	15h. 30m.	3 427	3 270	451	111	50	18	14.8	92	2.58	180	14 400	616	133	405	97.2	67
68	" 19	9.16 A.M.	" 19	1.29 P.M.	4h. 13m.	4h. 02m.	11m.	00m.	3 228	3 008	333	43	180	17	12.4	76	2.41	560	21 000	221	158	189	99.1	68
69	" 19	1.29 P.M.	" 20	10.54 A.M.	4h. 18m.	4h. 01m.	17m.	17h. 07m.	3 748	3 495	482	114	140	20	14.5	90	1.82	560	20 400	1 305	184	744	96.4	69
70	" 20	10.54 A.M.	" 20	2.46 P.M.	3h. 48m.	3h. 36m.	12m.	04m.	2 902	2 727	404	44	130	20	12.6	78	1.81	270	17 400	240	118	179	99.0	70
71	" 20	2.46 P.M.	" 21	9.33 A.M.	2h. 54m.	2h. 44m.	10m.	15h. 53m.	2 517	2 445	343	65	0	16	14.9	92	2.17	270	20 900	435	371	403	98.1	71
72	" 21	9.33 A.M.	" 21	1.25 P.M.	3h. 52m.	3h. 42m.	10m.	00m.	2 801	2 608	351	31	160	19	11.7	72	2.33	340	14 600	89	49	69	99.5	72
73	" 21	1.25 P.M.	" 24	9.18 A.M.	4h. 20m.	4h. 05m.	15m.	63h. 33m.	3 166	2 911	620	101	150	23	11.9	73	2.28	340	10 700	310	308	309	97.1	73
74	" 24	9.18 A.M.	" 24	1.41 P.M.	4h. 23m.	4h. 09m.	14m.	00m.	4 309	4 178	449	54	80	13	16.8	104	1.33	130	18 300	262	212	237	98.7	74
75	" 24	1.41 P.M.	" 25	9.19 A.M.	4h. 03m.	3h. 59m.	14m.	15h. 35m.	3 632	3 283	496	102	250	23	14.4	89	1.31	130	15 000	260	209	234	98.4	75
76	" 25	9.19 A.M.	" 25	2.33 P.M.	5h. 14m.	4h. 57m.	17m.	00m.	5 706	5 460	501	122	120	13	18.4	115	1.04	140	18 000	1 495	680	1087	94.0	76
77	" 25	2.33 P.M.	" 26	10.26 A.M.	4h. 20m.	4h. 07m.	13m.	15h. 33m.	3 544	3 408	488	74	60	18	13.8	85	1.43	140	19 500	1 270	605	937	95.2	77
78	" 26	10.26 A.M.	" 27	9.10 "	7h. 04m.	6h. 48m.	16m.	15h. 40m.	6 967	6 812	480	78	80	9	16.7	103	1.06	130	25 200	962	475	654	97.4	78
79	" 27	9.10 "	" 27	2.18 P.M.	5h. 08m.	4h. 52m.	16m.	00m.	5 778	5 592	527	86	100	12	19.2	118	1.00	160	4 100	630	455	542	98.7	79
80	" 27	2.18 P.M.	" 28	12.12 "	6h. 24m.	6h. 05m.	19m.	15h. 30m.	6 591	6 373	617	138	80	13	17.5	108	1.19	110	4 700	480	129	315	93.3	80
81	" 28	12.12 "	" 29	10.52 A.M.	6h. 28m.	6h. 16m.	12m.	16h. 12m.	7 678	7 525	478	53	100	8	20.0	124	0.99	60	12 100	485	235	388	96.8	81
82	" 29	10.52 A.M.	Mar. 2	1.13 P.M.	10h. 51m.	10h. 32m.	19m.	39h. 30m.	13 035	12 849	523	136	150	8	20.3	126	0.68	60	26 500	1 115	350	682	97.4	82
83	Mar. 2	1.13 P.M.	" 3	3.19 "	10h. 36m.	10h. 18m.	18m.	15h. 30m.	12 700	12 478	455	122	100	5	20.2	125	0.61	80	39 700	4000	1005	1911	95.1	83
84	" 3	3.19 "	" 5	10.05 A.M.	11h. 46m.	11h. 28m.	18m.	31h. 00m.	13 694	13 463	594	131	100	6	19.6	121	0.79	60	29 800	1 175	328	735	97.5	84
85	" 5	10.05 A.M.	" 6	1.10 P.M.	11h. 35m.	11h. 17m.	18m.	15h. 30m.	13 798	13 500	568	218	80	6	20.0	124	0.59	40	15 600	1085	237	636	95.9	85
86	" 6	1.10 P.M.	" 7	1.33 "	8h. 53m.	8h. 37m.	16m.	15h. 30m.	10 199	9 953	587	106	140	8	19.3	119	0.89	50	10 400	500	174	306	97.1	86
87	" 7	1.33 "	" 9	11.59 A.M.	6h. 56m.	6h. 41m.	15m.	39h. 30m.	8 063	7 772	516	75	220	10	19.4	120	0.68	80	11 000	477	194	339	96.9	87
88	" 9	11.59 A.M.	" 10	9.19 "	5h. 42m.	5h. 31m.	11m.	15h. 38m.	6 716	6 575	517	41	100	10	19.9	123	0.68	70	14 000	525	401	480	96.6	88
89	" 10	9.19 "	" 11	9.13 "	8h. 23m.	8h. 11m.	12m.	15h. 31m.	9 360	9 230	513	61	70	7	18.8	116	0.66	60	11 500	265	157	200	98.3	89
90	" 11	9.13 "	" 12	9.15 "	7h. 38m.	7h. 25m.	13m.	16h. 24m.	9 169	8 895	526	81	190	9	20.0	124	0.63	70	7 700	234	141	180	97.7	90
91	" 12	9.15 "	" 13	9.22 "	8h. 27m.	8h. 15m.	12m.	15h. 40m.	10 308	10 087	448	67	150	6	20.2	125	1.07	60	11 300	250	112	162	98.6	91
92	" 13	9.22 "	" 14	9.12 "	8h. 19m.	8h. 08m.	11m.	15h. 31m.	9 888	9 641	443	85	160	7	19.7	122	0.89	45	11 000	440	129	233	97.9	92
93	" 14	9.12 "	" 16	9.19 "	8h. 32m.	8h. 18m.	14m.	39h. 35m.	9 488	9 200	477	87	200	8	18.5	114	0.75	50	12 100	158	127	140	98.9	93
94	" 16	9.19 "	" 16	3.47 P.M.	6h. 28m.	6h. 16m.	12m.	00m.	7 407	7 142	402	88	180	9	19.0	117	0.94	50	15 500	490	131	274	98.2	94
95	" 16	3.47 P.M.	" 17	12.37 "	5h. 06m.	4h. 53m.	13m.	15h. 44m.	6 028	5 781	551	167	80	13	19.7	122	0.83	60	17 700	228	187	207	98.8	95
96	" 17	12.37 "	" 18	9.13 A.M.	5h. 05m.	4h. 53m.	12m.	15h. 31m.	6 102	5 804	565	68	230	14	19.8	123	0.86	60	16 300	445	157	327	98.0	96
97	" 18	9.13 A.M.	" 18	2.24 P.M.	5h. 11m.	4h. 57m.	14m.	00m.	5 870	5 575	587	71	220	15	18.8	116	0.86	90	21 800	739	230	480	97.8	97
98	" 18	2.24 "	" 19	10.38 A.M.	4h. 44m.	4h. 29m.	15m.	15h. 30m.	5 401	5 005	609	87	310	19	18.6	115	0.84	140	19 700	585	535	560	97.2	98

TABLE NO. 5.—*Continued.*

Western Gravity System.

Number of Run.	Began. Date.	Began. Hour.	Ended. Date.	Ended. Hour.	Periods of Time. Hours and Minutes. Operation.	Service.	Wash.	Delay.	Quantities of Water. Cubic Feet. Applied.	Filtered.	Wash.	Waste. Filtered.	Waste. Unfiltered.	Percentage which the Sum of the Wash and Waste Water is of Applied Water.	Average Actual Rate of Filtration. Cubic Feet per Minute.	Million Gallons per Acre per 24 Hours.	Average Amount of Applied Sulphate of Alumina. Grains per Gallon.	Estimated Average Amount of Suspended Solids in River Water. Parts per Million.	Bacteria per Cubic Centimeter. River Water.	Effluent. Maximum.	Effluent. Minimum.	Effluent. Average.	Average Bacterial Efficiency.	Number of Run.
	1896		1896																					
99	June 19	10.38 A.M.	June 19	1.07 P.M.	2h. 29m.	2h. 14m.	15m.	00m.	2 688	2 164	613	100	420	42	16.2	100	1.42	210	31 100	....	....	440	95.6	99
100	" 19	1.07 P.M.	" 20	10.09 A.M.	2h. 46m.	2h. 30m.	16m.	18h. 16m.	2 552	2 087	571	110	360	41	13.9	85	.....	210	36 000	800	580	690	98.1	100
101	" 20	10.09 A.M.	" 20	11.28 "	1h. 14m.	56m.	18m.	05m.	1 485	1 081	552	126	250	64	19.3	119	.....	990	41 600	....	....	1 000	97.6	101
102	" 20	11.28 "	" 20	12.21 P.M.	47m.	32m.	15m.	06m.	1 023	280	474	79	660	119	8.8	55	.....	990	41 600	....	....	830	98.0	102
103	" 20	12.21 P.M.	" 20	1.40 "	1h. 07m.	52m.	15m.	12m.	902	660	512	103	140	84	12.7	78	.....	990	63 500	....	....	700	98.9	103
104	" 20	1.40 "	" 20	2.40 "	55m.	45m.	10m.	05m.	616	490	450	88	40	94	10.9	67	.....	990	60 100	....	....	500	99.2	104
105	" 20	2.40 "	" 21	9.36 A.M.	1h. 12m.	1h. 00m.	12m.	17h. 44m.	816	561	638	59	201	104	9.4	58	.....	990	56 700	....	....	565	99.0	105
106	" 21	9.36 A.M.	July 2	9.37 "	1h. 09m.	34m.	35m.	........*	1 133	411	784	322	400	13	12.1	78	.....	1 300	57 500	....	....	575	99.0	106
107	July 2	9.37 "	" 2	11.49 "	2h. 12m.	1h. 37m.	35m.	00m.	1 602	1 249	622	360	0	61	12.9	83	5.18	1 700	14 200	130	68	99	99.3	107
108	" 2	11.49 "	" 2	1.08 P.M.	1h. 19m.	48m.	31m.	00m.	935	613	523	328	0	91	12.8	83	8.57	1 700	24 200	....	....	120	99.5	108
109	" 2	1.08 P.M.	" 2	2.49 "	1h. 41m.	1h. 16m.	25m.	00m.	1 423	1 029	505	206	50	54	13.5	87	9.75	1 700	34 200	....	....	171	99.5	109
110	" 2	2.49 "	" 2	4.10 "	1h. 21m.	52m.	29m.	00m.	962	663	596	244	50	93	12.8	83	10.55	1 700	34 200	....	....	52	99.9	110
111	" 2	4.10 "	" 3	9.16 A.M.	1h. 15m.	51m.	24m.	15h. 51m.	999	693	470	214	90	77	13.6	88	9.28	1 700	34 200	....	....	35	99.9	111
112	" 3	9.16 A.M.	" 3	1.45 P.M.	4h. 29m.	3h. 58m.	31m.	00m.	3 537	3 253	892	217	60	33	13.7	89	8.36	1 000	10 400	10	9	9	99.9	112
113	" 3	1.45 P.M.	" 3	3.32 "	1h. 47m.	1h. 23m.	24m.	00m.	1 371	1 124	613	179	70	63	13.5	87	8.33	1 000	12 000	....	....	50	99.6	113
114	" 3	3.23 "	" 10	9.32 A.M.	2h. 20m.	1h. 44m.	36m.	159h. 40m.	1 687	1 470	589	338	100	61	14.1	85	6.78	1 000	13 600	77	62	69	99.5	114
115	" 10	9.32 A.M.	" 11	9.15 "	7h. 20m.	6h. 54m.	26m.	16h. 23m.	6 700	6 265	891	196	240	20	15.1	98	3.18	350	10 000	152	46	110	98.9	115
116	" 11	9.15 "	" 11	3.00 P.M.	5h. 45m.	5h. 03m.	42m.	00m.	4 946	4 741	727	382	100	24	15.7	101	1.17	190	9 600	199	118	158	98.4	116
117	" 11	3.00 P.M.	" 17	1.58 "	3h. 43m.	2h. 06m.	37m.	139h. 15m.	2 362	1 953	738	249	160	48	15.5	100	2.24	190	12 500	387	142	216	98.3	117
118	" 17	1.58 "	" 18	1.35 "	8h. 07m.	7h. 22m.	45m.	15h. 30m.	7 023	6 753	930	271	0	17	15.3	99	2.96	560	6 900	46	33	39	99.4	118
119	" 18	1.35 "	" 18	4.11 "	2h. 36m.	2h. 00m.	36m.	00m.	2 125	1 844	790	216	60	50	15.4	99	4.12	640	11 100	61	36	48	99.6	119
120	" 18	4.11 "	" 24	10.55 A.M.	1h. 47m.	1h. 08m.	39m.	136h. 57m.	1 248	1 005	759	393	50	10	14.8	96	5.50	640	23 300	....	....	115	99.5	120
121	" 24	10.55 A.M.	" 25	10.15 "	6h. 14m.	3h. 30m.	2h. 44m.	17h. 06m.	4 788	2 981	1 298	1 672	130	65	14.2	91	4.92	3 300	31 000	498	63	234	99.2	121
122	" 25	10.15 "	" 25	3.50 P.M.	3h. 45m.	3h. 05m.	40m.	1h. 50m.	2 957	2 386	774	332	240	46	12.9	83	5.89	1 700	17 300	304	80	205	98.8	122
123	" 25	0.50 P.M.	" 31	9.05 A.M.	1h. 15m.	1h. 01m.	14m.	136h. 00m.	1 014	715	631	61	230	91	11.7	75	5.03	1 700	18 400	....	....	511	97.2	123
124	" 31	9.05 A.M.	" 31	5.17 P.M.	....	8h. 03m.	....	....	6 804	6 776	574	.....	.....	.....	14.0	90	3.98	810	6 800	450	104	214	96.9	124
							Western Pressure System.																	
	1895		1895																					
1	Dec. 23	10.35 A.M.	Dec. 28	10.56 A.M.	32h. 45m.	32h. 23m.	20m.	87h. 38m.	43 978	43 793	731	185	0	2	22.5	160	.....	110	7 300	860	80	302	95.9	1
2	" 28	10.56 "	" 30	10.27 "	7h. 34m.	7h. 11m.	23m.	39h. 57m.	9 769	9 593	735	176	0	9	22.3	158	.....	220	35 700	1 170	810	1 032	97.1	2
3	" 30	10.27 "	" 31	9.50 "	7h. 35m.	7h. 21m.	14m.	15h. 48m.	9 388	9 297	493	91	0	6	21.1	150	.....	400	12 000	520	246	408	96.6	3
4	" 31	9.50 "	Jan. 2, '96	10.03 "	7h. 11m.	6h. 50m.	21m.	41h. 02m.	8 206	8 051	760	155	0	11	19.6	139	.....	600	13 000	380	143	268	97.9	4
	1896		1896																					
5	Jan. 2	10.03 "	Jan. 3	9.49 "	8h. 02m.	7h. 39m.	23m.	15h. 44m.	7 433	7 276	661	157	0	11	15.9	112	.....	870	10 700	546	121	258	97.4	5
6	" 3	9.49 "	" 4	11.15 "	6h. 33m.	6h. 08m.	25m.	18h. 53m.	6 906	6 745	543	161	0	10	18.3	130	.....	800	14 300	208	140	169	98.8	6
7	" 4	11.15 "	" 7	3.20 P.M.	15h. 52m.	15h. 32m.	21m.	60h. 12m.	13 965	13 805	759	160	0	7	14.8	105	.....	350	6 800	228	65	143	97.9	7
8	" 7	3.20 P.M.	" 9	9.44 A.M.	10h. 41m.	10h. 20m.	21m.	31h. 43m.	11 195	11 114	542	81	0	6	17.9	127	.....	200	4 000	314	76	174	95.7	8

* 103 days 0 hours 1 minute.

TABLE No. 5.—*Continued.*

Western Pressure System.

Number of Run.	Began. Date.	Began. Hour.	Ended. Date.	Ended. Hour.	Periods of Time. Hours and Minutes. Operation.	Service.	Wash.	Delay.	Quantities of Water. Cubic Feet. Applied.	Filtered.	Wash.	Waste. Filtered.	Waste. Unfiltered.	Percentage which the Sum of the Wash and Waste Water is of Applied Water.	Average Actual Rate of Filtration. Cubic Feet per Minute.	Million Gallons per Acre per 24 Hours.	Average Amount of Applied Sulphate of Alumina. Grains per Gallon.	Estimated Average Amount of Suspended Solids in River Water. Parts per Million.	Bacteria per Cubic Centimeter. River Water.	Effluent. Maximum.	Effluent. Minimum.	Effluent. Average.	Average Bacterial Efficiency.	Number of Run.
9	1896 Jan. 9	9.44 A.M.	1896 Jan. 11	10.28 A.M.	17h. 02m.	16h. 43m.	19m.	31h. 42m.	18 607	18 545	581	102	0	4	18.5	132	.....	120	1 800	184	22	107	94.0	9
10	" 11	10.28 "	" 14	11.03 "	7h. 01m.	6h. 37m.	24m.	65h. 34m.	7 449	7 284	723	165	0	12	18.3	130	0.86	100	2 500	177	130	153	93.9	10
11	" 14	11.03 "	" 17	10.47 "	23h. 58m.	23h. 39m.	19m.	47h. 46m.	31 820	31 636	653	184	0	3	22.3	158	1.37	40	2 300	248	14	116	95.0	11
12	" 17	10.47 "	" 20	1.23 P.M.	18h. 33m.	18h. 15m.	18m.	56h. 03m.	31 323	31 147	638	176	0	3	28.4	202	1.24	25	7 000	340	156	223	96.8	12
13	" 20	1.23 P.M.	" 24	9.48 A.M.	28h. 28m.	28h. 05m.	23m.	63h. 57m.	47 172	46 939	683	233	0	2	27.9	198	0.87	20	4 000	260	100	181	95.5	13
14	" 24	9.48 A.M.	" 27	3.51 P.M.	20h. 43m.	20h. 10m.	33m.	33h. 20m.	31 213	30 904	677	309	0	3	25.5	180	0.88	100	6 600	836	59	322	95.1	14
15	" 27	3.51 P.M.	" 31	10.08 A.M.	8h. 44m.	8h. 16m.	28m.	57h. 33m.	9 854	9 638	790	216	0	10	19.4	137	2.50	273	12 400	1 443	444	849	93.2	15
16	" 31	10.08 A.M.	Feb. 1	10.16 "	7h. 57m.	7h. 32m.	25m.	16h. 11m.	7 656	7 431	692	225	0	12	16.4	115	1.93	320	14 300	613	336	474	96.7	16
17	Feb. 1	10.16 "	" 3	10.00 "	7h. 49m.	7h. 24m.	25m.	39h. 55m.	8 170	8 004	656	166	0	10	18.0	128	2.54	340	21 300	326	102	188	99.1	17
18	" 3	10.00 "	" 4	9.46 "	7h. 54m.	7h. 35m.	19m.	15h. 52m.	10 972	10 754	569	218	0	7	23.7	168	1.39	244	62 200	607	477	544	99.1	18
19	" 4	9.46 "	" 5	10.32 "	8h. 03m.	7h. 44m.	19m.	16h. 43m.	10 117	9 837	471	280	0	7	21.2	150	1.84	250	55 000	1 200	255	815	98.5	19
20	" 5	10.32 "	" 6	9.32 "	7h. 15m.	6h. 58m.	17m.	15h. 45m.	8 835	8 624	548	211	0	9	20.6	146	2.64	458	71 000	1 376	404	686	99.0	20
21	" 6	9.32 "	" 7	9.32 "	8h. 21m.	7h. 58m.	23m.	15h. 39m.	11 660	11 479	657	181	0	7	24.0	170	1.79	464	30 800	2 040	980	1 461	95.3	21
22	" 7	9.32 "	" 8	9.18 "	8h. 16m.	7h. 58m.	18m.	15h. 30m.	9 722	9 536	662	186	0	9	19.9	141	3.08	636	55 000	1 600	600	967	98.2	22
23	" 8	9.18 "	" 8	2.02 P.M.	4h. 44m.	4h. 27m.	17m.	00m.	5 442	5 250	579	192	0	14	19.7	140	2.20	704	27 200	....	....	550	98.0	23
24	" 8	2.02 P.M.	" 10	9.24 A.M.	3h. 46m.	3h. 28m.	18m.	15h. 36m.	4 347	4 078	456	269	0	17	19.6	139	0.71	704	32 400	768	660	714	97.8	24
25	" 10	9.24 A.M.	" 10	12.30 P.M.	3h. 06m.	2h. 47m.	19m.	00m.	3 263	3 081	500	182	0	21	18.4	131	.....	967	14 400	....	....	166	98.9	25
26	" 10	12.30 P.M.	" 10	3.57 "	3h. 27m.	3h. 10m.	17m.	00m.	3 794	3 625	431	169	0	16	19.1	136	.....	967	14 400	491	200	345	97.6	26
27	" 10	3.57 "	" 11	11.12 A.M.	2h. 49m.	2h. 33m.	16m.	16h. 26m.	4 198	4 057	492	141	0	15	26.5	188	.....	740	19 500	1 250	376	813	95.8	27
28	" 11	11.12 A.M.	" 11	2.26 P.M.	3h. 14m.	3h. 01m.	13m.	00m.	3 896	3 828	550	68	0	16	21.1	150	.....	409	19 800	....	....	151	99.2	28
29	" 11	2.26 P.M.	" 12	9.18 A.M.	3h. 21m.	3h. 04m.	17m.	15h. 31m.	3 910	3 739	478	171	0	17	20.3	144	.....	409	19 400	605	390	497	97.4	29
30	" 12	9.18 A.M.	" 12	2.04 P.M.	4h. 38m.	4h. 16m.	22m.	08m.	5 386	5 164	492	222	0	13	20.2	143	4.23	418	28 000	635	62	348	98.8	30
31	" 12	2.04 P.M.	" 13	9.35 A.M.	4h. 01m.	3h. 41m.	20m.	15h. 30m.	4 820	4 690	563	130	0	14	21.2	150	3.60	418	28 000	498	252	375	98.7	31
32	" 13	9.35 A.M.	" 14	9.20 "	8h. 14m.	7h. 55m.	19m.	15h. 31m.	10 617	10 474	652	143	0	8	22.1	157	2.78	126	14 800	957	56	409	97.2	32
33	" 14	9.20 "	" 15	9.29 "	7h. 41m.	7h. 20m.	21m.	16h. 28m.	9 271	9 106	639	165	0	9	20.7	147	3.23	339	11 900	296	132	216	98.2	33
34	" 15	9.29 "	" 15	1.32 P.M.	4h. 03m.	3h. 48m.	15m.	00m.	5 472	5 359	375	113	0	9	23.5	166	2.88	486	10 800	....	....	580	94.6	34
35	" 15	1.32 P.M.	" 17	9.34 A.M.	4h. 26m.	4h. 06m.	20m.	39h. 36m.	5 054	4 883	451	171	0	12	19.9	141	2.35	486	10 800	1 290	446	940	91.3	35
36	" 17	9.34 A.M.	" 17	3.29 P.M.	5h. 55m.	5h. 32m.	23m.	00m.	7 986	7 715	648	271	0	12	23.2	164	1.59	391	21 800	1 025	925	975	95.5	36
37	" 17	3.29 P.M.	" 18	2.03 "	7h. 04m.	6h. 45m.	19m.	15h. 30m.	8 824	8 701	734	123	0	10	21.5	152	2.24	240	15 700	1 160	161	614	96.1	37
38	" 18	2.03 "	" 19	12.24 "	6h. 27m.	6h. 10m.	17m.	15h. 54m.	8 229	8 084	657	145	0	10	21.8	155	2.01	370	16 600	848	119	575	96.5	38
39	" 19	12.24 "	" 20	11.02 A.M.	7h. 08m.	6h. 53m.	15m.	15h. 30m.	9 325	9 252	631	73	0	8	22.4	159	1.92	500	17 200	595	442	518	97.0	39
40	" 20	11.02 A.M.	" 21	9.29 "	6h. 43m.	6h. 28m.	15m.	15h. 44m.	8 823	8 730	632	93	0	8	22.5	160	3.77	266	17 400	861	197	532	96.9	40
41	" 21	9.29 A.M.	" 21	3.37 P.M.	6h. 08m.	5h. 50m.	18m.	00m.	7 505	7 325	674	180	0	11	20.9	148	.....	338	10 700	401	77	208	98.1	41
42	" 21	3.37 P.M.	" 24	2.35 "	7h. 21m.	7h. 07m.	14m.	65h. 37m.	9 863	9 734	487	129	0	6	22.8	162	.....	200	12 600	848	53	363	97.1	42
43	" 24	2.35 "	" 26	9.22 A.M.	11h. 45m.	11h. 25m.	20m.	31h. 02m.	15 270	15 114	832	156	0	6	22.1	157	1.15	140	14 700	1 510	339	793	94.6	43
44	" 26	9.22 A.M.	" 27	2.10 P.M.	13h. 07m.	12h. 47m.	20m.	15h. 41m.	17 997	17 819	747	178	0	5	23.2	164	1.06	130	17 900	887	205	633	96.5	44
45	" 27	2.10 P.M.	Mar. 2	9.28 A.M.	20h. 01m.	19h. 38m.	23m.	47h. 17m.	28 740	28 511	898	229	0	4	24.2	171	0.97	80	8 700	1 700	212	713	91.8	45

TABLE NO. 5.—*Continued.*

Western Pressure System.

Number of Run.	Began. Date.	Began. Hour.	Ended. Date.	Ended. Hour.	Periods of Time. Hours and Minutes. Operation.	Service.	Wash.	Delay.	Quantities of Water. Cubic Feet. Applied.	Filtered.	Wash.	Waste. Filtered.	Waste. Unfiltered.	Percentage which the Sum of the Wash and Waste Water is of Applied Water.	Average Actual Rate of Filtration. Cubic Feet per Minute.	Million Gallons per Acre per 24 Hours.	Average Amount of Applied Sulphate of Alumina. Grains per Gallon.	Estimated Average Amount of Suspended Solids in River Water. Parts per Million.	Bacteria per Cubic Centimeter. River Water.	Effluent. Maximum.	Minimum.	Average.	Average Bacterial Efficiency.	Number of Run.
	1896		1896																					
46	Mar. 2	9.28 A.M.	Mar. 4	2.45 P.M.	22h. 17m.	21h. 55m.	22m.	31h. 00m.	31 708	31 482	799	226	0	3	23.9	169	0.69	70	37 500	6 000	410	1 382	96.3	46
47	" 4	2.45 P.M.	" 7	10.00 A.M.	20h. 45m.	20h. 25m.	20m.	46h. 30m.	29 016	28 800	747	216	0	3	23.5	166	0.72	40	18 100	1 040	105	459	97.5	47
48	" 7	10.00 A.M.	" 10	9.16 "	16h. 16m.	16h. 00m.	16m.	55h. 00m.	22 563	22 462	606	101	0	3	23.4	165	0.74	75	12 200	845	175	355	97.1	48
49	" 10	9.16 "	" 13	9.20 "	24h. 56m.	24h. 36m.	20m.	47h. 08m.	35 056	34 825	678	231	0	3	23.6	167	0.78	62	10 200	565	125	254	97.5	49
50	" 13	9.20 "	" 17	9.16 "	25h. 25m.	25h. 10m.	15m.	70h. 31m.	34 777	34 640	733	137	0	2	22.9	162	0.87	50	13 200	480	110	233	98.2	50
51	" 17	9.16 "	" 19	9.19 "	17h. 03m.	16h. 44m.	19m.	31h. 00m.	22 571	22 412	717	159	0	4	22.3	158	0.91	75	18 000	765	185	406	97.7	51
52	" 19	9.19 "	" 20	9.20 "	8h. 30m.	8h. 00m.	30m.	15h. 31m.	10 445	10 001	816	444	0	12	20.8	148	1.44	210	34 400	1 000	450	740	97.8	52
53	" 20	9.20 "	" 20	12.12 P.M.	2h. 44m.	2h. 29m.	15m.	08m.	2 544	2 416	672	128	0	31	16.2	114	2.21	993	41 600	500	400	450	98.9	53
54	" 20	12.12 P.M.	" 20	3.45 "	3h. 07m.	2h. 43m.	24m.	26m.	3 085	2 791	726	294	0	33	17.1	121	.....	993	60 100	500	400	450	99.3	54
55	" 20	3.45 "	" 21	9.20 A.M.	2h. 05m.	1h. 45m.	20m.	15h. 30m.	2 276	2 043	763	233	0	44	19.4	137	.....	993	56 700	....	....	800	98.6	55
56	" 21	9.20 A.M.	" 21	1.10 P.M.	3h. 50m.	3h. 30m.	20m.	00m.	3 787	3 595	625	192	0	22	17.1	121	.....	1 276	59 800	....	...	890	98.5	56
57	" 21	1.10 P.M.	" 23	9.19 A.M.	4h. 39m.	4h. 20m.	19m.	9h. 30m.	3 654	3 520	693	134	0	23	13.5	96	.....	1 276	57 100	1 430	980	1 153	98.0	57
58	" 23	9.19 A.M.	" 23	1.00 P.M.	3h. 41m.	3h. 21m.	20m.	00m.	3 593	3 400	671	193	0	24	16.9	119	.....	660	34 700	1 115	780	1 110	96.8	58
59	" 23	1.00 P.M.	" 24	9.20 A.M.	3h. 20m.	3h. 00m.	20m.	17h. 00m.	3 230	3 070	824	160	0	31	17.1	121	.....	660	25 400	780	740	765	97.0	59
60	" 24	9.20 A.M.	" 24	2.07 P.M.	4h. 47m.	4h. 30m.	17m.	00m.	5 189	5 173	797	58	0	16	19.2	136	3.12	521	39 400	500	297	398	99.0	60
61	" 24	2.07 P.M.	" 24	6.50 "	4h. 43m.	4h. 23m.	20m.	00m.	3 907	3 964	729	156	0	23	15.1	107	4.50	521	38 000	580	208	489	98.7	61
62	" 24	6.50 "	" 24	11.32 "	4h. 42m.	4h. 25m.	17m.	00m.	3 904	3 871	691	87	0	20	14.6	103	3.67	521	37 800	283	208	254	93.3	62
63	" 24	11.32 "	" 25	4.19 A.M.	4h. 47m.	4h. 28m.	19m.	00m.	4 184	4 221	750	137	0	21	15.8	112	4.88	521	36 700	395	355	389	98.9	63
64	" 25	4.19 A.M.	" 25	9.18 "	4h. 58m.	4h. 41m.	17m.	01m.	4 877	4 872	805	112	0	19	17.4	123	3.98	521	38 800	355	177	315	99.2	64
65	" 25	9.18 "	" 25	2.20 P.M.	5h. 02m.	4h. 43m.	19m.	00m.	4 447	4 457	791	112	0	20	15.8	112	3.19	516	38 400	214	177	196	99.5	65
66	" 25	2.20 P.M.	" 25	8.46 "	6h. 26m.	6h. 10m.	16m.	00m.	5 643	5 688	761	88	0	15	15.4	109	3.79	516	41 900	825	214	567	98.7	66
67	" 25	8.46 "	" 26	3.18 A.M.	6h. 32m.	6h. 14m.	18m.	00m.	5 892	5 956	753	123	0	15	15.9	112	3.05	516	53 600	675	330	501	99.1	67
68	" 26	3.18 A.M.	" 26	9.23 "	6h. 00m.	5h. 42m.	18m.	05m.	5 790	5 813	741	124	0	15	17.0	120	2.29	516	50 400	360	270	345	99.3	68
69	" 26	9.23 "	" 26	3.19 P.M.	5h. 56m.	5h. 37m.	19m.	00m.	5 286	5 296	716	129	0	16	15.7	111	4.96	472	50 100	270	190	212	99.6	69
70	" 26	3.19 P.M.	" 26	9.20 "	6h. 01m.	5h. 43m.	18m.	00m.	5 368	5 372	742	126	0	16	15.7	111	3.15	472	48 500	254	190	205	99.6	70
71	" 26	9.20 "	" 27	3.18 A.M.	5h. 58m.	5h. 40m.	18m.	00m.	5 676	5 685	730	176	0	16	16.7	118	3.68	472	46 700	400	290	330	99.3	71
72	" 27	3.18 A.M.	" 27	2.19 P.M.	9h. 02m.	8h. 44m.	18m.	1h. 59m.	8 596	8 619	962	95	0	12	16.4	115	1.96	400	40 000	470	185	305	99.2	72
73	" 27	2.19 P.M.	" 27	11.12 "	8h. 53m.	8h. 36m.	17m.	00m.	8 797	8 907	717	150	0	10	17.3	122	5.78	355	26 700	685	148	333	98.7	73
74	" 27	11.12 "	" 28	7.17 A.M.	7h. 59m.	7h. 42m.	17m.	06m.	7 978	8 036	713	124	0	10	17.4	123	2.36	355	29 500	304	98	201	99.3	74
75	" 28	7.17 A.M.	" 28	3.17 P.M.	8h. 00m.	7h. 43m.	17m.	00m.	7 986	8 059	683	112	0	10	17.4	123	2.36	400	35 800	304	170	211	99.4	75
76	" 28	3.17 P.M.	" 28	9.20 "	6h. 03m.	5h. 45m.	18m.	00m.	5 618	5 648	692	162	0	15	16.4	115	2.75	430	38 400	1 955	199	1 178	96.9	76
77	" 28	9.20 "	" 29	3.19 A.M.	5h. 59m.	5h. 42m.	17m.	00m.	5 354	5 317	678	125	0	15	15.6	111	2.83	428	35 000	732	265	370	98.9	77
78	" 29	3.19 A.M.	" 29	9.16 "	5h. 55m.	5h. 41m.	14m.	02m.	5 315	5 328	704	129	0	16	15.6	111	3.10	428	32 300	1 666	323	595	98.2	78
79	" 29	9.16 "	" 29	3.12 P.M.	5h. 56m.	5h. 44m.	12m.	00m.	5 640	5 659	625	128	0	13	16.4	115	3.58	338	54 000	1 686	1 315	1 463	97.3	79
80	" 29	3.12 P.M.	" 29	9.14 "	6h. 02m.	5h. 47m.	15m.	00m.	5 581	5 605	708	123	0	15	16.2	114	3.01	338	55 400	2 475	715	1 596	97.1	80
81	" 29	9.14 "	" 30	3.15 A.M.	6h. 01m.	5h. 46m.	15m.	00m.	5 643	5 683	783	93	0	16	16.4	115	3.86	338	40 800	5 950	1 056	2 553	93.7	81
82	" 30	3.15 A.M.	" 30	9.14 "	5h. 59m.	5h. 45m.	14m.	00m.	5 664	5 733	655	169	0	15	16.6	117	2.50	338	42 900	5 950	1 585	3 276	92.4	82

TABLE No. 5.—*Continued.*

Western Pressure System.

Number of Run.	Began. Date.	Began. Hour.	Ended. Date.	Ended. Hour.	Periods of Time. Hours and Minutes. Operation.	Service.	Wash.	Delay.	Quantities of Water. Cubic Feet. Applied.	Filtered.	Wash.	Waste. Filtered.	Waste. Unfiltered.	Percentage which the Sum of the Wash and Waste Water is of Applied Water.	Average Actual Rate of Filtration. Cubic Feet per Minute.	Million Gallons per Acre per 24 Hours.	Average Amount of Applied Sulphate of Alumina. Grains per Gallon.	Estimated Average Amount of Suspended Solids in River Water. Parts per Million.	Bacteria per Cubic Centimeter. River Water.	Effluent. Maximum.	Effluent. Minimum.	Effluent. Average.	Average Bacterial Efficiency.	Number of Run.
	1896		1896																					
83	Mar. 30	9.14 A.M.	Mar. 31	9.15 A.M.	8h. 31m.	8h. 16m.	15m.	15h. 30m.	7 224	7 266	739	184	0	13	14.7	104	3.66	740	25 700	2725	1145	1712	93.3	83
84	" 31	9.15 "	" 31	2.34 P.M.	5h. 19m.	4h. 59m.	20m.	00m.	4 325	4 270	764	210	0	22	14.3	101	2.94	1 004	22 800	1455	885	1170	94.9	84
85	" 31	2.34 P.M.	April 1	9.28 A.M.	3h. 17m.	2h. 56m.	21m.	15h. 37m.	2 307	2 062	672	245	0	40	11.7	83	....	1 004	29 600	....	....	2545	91.4	85
86	April 1	9.28 A.M.	" 1	1.43 P.M.	4h. 06m.	3h. 52m.	16m.	07m.	3 933	3 812	673	158	0	21	16.4	115	5.16	1 131	36 500	1110	965	1038	97.2	86
87	" 1	1.43 P.M.	" 2	9.34 A.M.	4h. 07m.	3h. 47m.	20m.	15h. 44m.	3 636	3 574	706	203	0	25	15.7	111	3.35	1 131	39 600	1025	965	995	97.5	87
88	" 2	9.34 A.M.	" 2	2.00 P.M.	4h. 20m.	4h. 04m.	16m.	06m.	3 868	3 783	656	102	0	20	15.5	110	3.72	932	31 200	1110	630	870	95.2	88
89	" 2	2.00 P.M.	" 3	9.18 A.M.	3h. 47m.	3h. 30m.	17m.	15h. 31m.	3 103	3 098	673	169	0	27	14.7	104	3.78	932	19 200	1110	525	709	96.3	89
90	" 3	9.18 A.M.	" 3	2.34 P.M.	5h. 09m.	4h. 46m.	23m.	07m.	4 550	4 519	744	146	0	20	15.8	112	3.14	1 062	32 000	1185	1160	1172	96.3	90
91	" 3	2.34 P.M.	" 4	12.40 "	6h. 36m.	6h. 22m.	14m.	15h. 30m.	6 012	6 062	722	86	0	13	15.9	112	3.65	840	27 500	475	175	283	99.0	91
92	" 4	12.40 "	" 6	9.16 A.M.	5h. 05m.	4h. 50m.	15m.	39h. 31m.	4 395	4 454	715	133	0	19	15.4	109	2.40	628	27 500	198	182	190	99.3	92
93	" 6	9.16 A.M.	" 7	9.14 "	8h. 28m.	8h. 14m.	14m.	15h. 30m.	8 746	8 875	695	110	0	9	18.0	128	3.16	485	18 700	130	57	91	99.5	93
94	" 7	9.14 "	May 7	9.00 "	7h. 48m.	7h. 31m.	17m.	........*	8 196	8 343	710	129	0	10	18.5	132	.....	352	18 500	94	64	76	99.6	94
95	May 7	9.00 "	" 7	9.13 P.M.	12h. 13m.	11h. 52m.	21m.	00m.	21 111	16 512	673	124	0	4	23.2	164	1.97	70	5 000	....	....	150	97.0	95
96	" 7	9.13 P.M.	" 8	11.55 A.M.	14h. 34m.	14h. 20m.	14m.	08m.	10 935	19 835	659	85	0	4	23.1	164	1.20	80	4 800	289	20	145	97.0	96
97	" 8	11.55 A.M.	" 9	4.04 "	16h. 09m.	15h. 50m.	19m.	00m.	22 217	21 000	627	169	0	4	22.1	157	1.07	111	4 300	253	91	152	96.5	97
98	" 9	4.04 "	" 11	9.39 "	12h. 20m.	11h. 56m.	24m.	41h. 15m.	16 449	16 576	650	270	0	6	23.2	164	0.87	111	5 800	346	225	267	95.4	98
99	" 11	9.39 "	" 11	9.57 P.M.	12h. 18m.	12h. 02m.	16m.	00m.	16 451	16 467	595	155	0	5	22.8	162	1.15	185	7 900	287	180	233	97.1	99
100	" 11	9.57 P.M.	" 12	10.01 A.M.	12h. 04m.	11h. 45m.	19m.	00m.	16 048	16 196	561	159	0	4	23.0	163	1.17	180	7 400	242	219	230	96.9	100
101	" 12	10.01 A.M.	" 12	10.24 P.M.	12h. 23m.	12h. 00m.	23m.	00m.	15 913	16 053	623	221	0	5	22.3	158	1.17	168	6 600	278	219	248	96.2	101
102	" 12	10.24 P.M.	" 13	3.03 "	16h. 39m.	16h. 22m.	17m.	00m.	21 813	22 016	684	158	0	4	22.5	160	1.07	150	5 200	171	93	140	97.3	102
103	" 13	3.03 "	" 14	4.30 A.M.	13h. 27m.	13h. 03m.	24m.	00m.	17 749	17 952	791	215	0	6	22.9	162	0.82	137	3 600	156	152	154	95.7	103
104	" 14	4.30 A.M.	" 14	4.26 P.M.	11h. 56m.	11h. 37m.	19m.	00m.	16 689	16 803	451	187	0	4	24.2	171	0.68	140	5 100	132	131	131	97.4	104
105	" 14	4.26 P.M.	" 15	4.20 A.M.	11h. 54m.	11h. 36m.	18m.	00m.	17 446	16 552	741	191	0	5	23.8	169	0.85	144	6 600	181	136	158	97.6	105
106	" 15	4.20 A.M.	" 15	5.29 P.M.	12h. 36m.	12h. 18m.	18m.	33m.	16 579	17 705	736	182	0	6	24.0	170	0.98	120	6 900	237	222	229	96.7	106
107	" 15	5.29 P.M.	" 18	9.15 A.M.	22h. 35m.	22h. 22m.	13m.	41h. 11m.	31 494	31 807	725	68	0	3	23.7	168	0.92	120	6 300	400	54	109	98.3	107
108[1]	" 18	9.15 A.M.	" 20	9.37 "	46h. 27m.	45h. 55m.	32m.	1h. 55m.	39 253	39 733	637	329	0	2	14.4	102	0.51	70	5 400	3000	68	512	90.5	108[1]
109[2]	" 20	9.37 "	" 22	9.20 "	47h. 35m.	47h. 15m.	20m.	08m.	40 833	39 703	783	128	0	2	14.0	99	1.08	140	5 500	340	67	157	97.1	109[2]
110[3]	" 22	9.20 "	" 26	9.17 "	54h. 57m.	54h. 40m.	17m.	41h. 00m.	45 180	45 752	630	146	0	2	14.0	99	1.57	60	3 900	369	32	75	98.1	110[3]
111[4]	" 26	9.17 "	" 27	3.17 P.M.	30h. 00m.	29h. 46m.	14m.	00m.	30 324	30 841	658	115	0	3	17.3	122	0.96	50	2 500	165	27	85	96.6	111[4]
112[5]	" 27	3.17 P.M.	" 28	12.18 "	20h. 52m.	20h. 38m.	14m.	09m.	21 446	21 786	648	107	0	4	17.6	125	1.87	150	6 800	500	25	119	98.3	112[5]
113[6]	" 28	12.18 "	" 29	2.25 A.M.	14h. 07m.	13h. 00m.	1h. 07m.	00m.	13 454	13 659	635	1167	0	13	17.5	124	1.91	400	23 300	330	153	223	99.0	113[6]
114[7]	" 29	2.25 A.M.	" 29	5.42 "	3h. 06m.	1h. 42m.	1h. 24m.	11m.	2 811	1 705	1058	1255	0	82	16.7	117	3.84	800	27 200	705	127	328	98.6	114[7]
115[8]	" 29	5.42 "	" 29	11.08 "	5h. 20m.	5h. 04m.	16m.	06m.	6 895	5 092	623	88	0	10	16.7	117	4.10	663	22 400	410	297	344	98.5	115[8]
116[8]	" 29	11.08 "	" 29	3.00 P.M.	3h. 48m.	3h. 33m.	15m.	04m.	3 366	3 328	723	79	0	24	15.6	111	5.38	653	26 900	78	69	73	99.7	116[8]
117[8]	" 29	3.00 P.M.	" 29	5.41 "	2h. 41m.	2h. 24m.	17m.	00m.	2 338	2 288	593	68	0	28	15.9	112	4.62	653	26 900	....	....	135	99.5	117[8]

[1] Prescribed chemicals 1.0 gr., rate 100 mil. gals.
[2] Prescribed chemicals 1.5 gr., rate 100 mil. gals.
[3] Prescribed chemicals 2.0 gr., rate 100 mil. gals.
[4] Prescribed chemicals 1.0 gr., rate 120 mil. gals.
[5] Prescribed chemicals 1.5 gr., rate 120 mil. gals.
[6] Prescribed chemicals 2.0 gr., rate 120 mil. gals.
[7] Prescribed chemicals 3.0 gr., rate 120 mil. gals.
[8] Prescribed chemicals 5.0 gr., rate 120 mil. gals.

* 29 days 23 hours 46 minutes.

TABLE NO. 5.—*Continued.*

Western Pressure System.

Number of Run.	Began. Date.	Began. Hour.	Ended. Date.	Ended. Hour.	Periods of Time. Hours and Minutes. Operation.	Service.	Wash.	Delay.	Quantities of Water. Cubic Feet. Applied.	Filtered.	Wash.	Waste. Filtered.	Waste. Unfiltered.	Percentage which the Sum of the Wash and Waste Water is of Applied Water.	Average Actual Rate of Filtration. Cubic Feet per Minute.	Million Gallons per Acre per 24 Hours.	Average Amount of Applied Sulphate of Alumina. Grains per Gallon.	Estimated Average Amount of Suspended Solids in River Water. Parts per Million.	Bacteria per Cubic Centimeter. River Water.	Effluent. Maximum.	Effluent. Minimum.	Effluent. Average.	Average Bacterial Efficiency.	Number of Run.
	1896		1896																					
118[1]	May 29	5.41 P.M.	May 29	8.26 P.M.	2h. 45m.	2h. 30m.	15m.	00m.	2 357	2 344	687	71	0	32	15.6	111	5.35	653	30 600	168	34	101	99.7	118[1]
119[1]	" 29	8.26 "	" 29	11.56 "	3h. 30m.	3h. 16m.	14m.	00m.	2 959	2 917	701	87	0	27	14.9	105	7.27	653	30 600	....	....	86	99.7	119[1]
120[2]	" 29	11.56 "	" 30	2.11 A.M.	2h. 11m.	1h. 56m.	15m.	04m.	1 846	1 790	680	105	0	43	15.4	109	5.80	653	28 700	....	....	280	99.0	120[2]
121[2]	" 30	2.11 A.M.	" 30	3.41 "	1h. 17m.	1h. 04m.	13m.	13m.	1 136	1 058	714	77	0	70	16.6	117	7.07	653	25 200	....	....	369	98.5	121[2]
122[2]	" 30	3.41 "	" 30	6.40 "	2h. 55m.	2h. 40m.	15m.	04m.	3 254	2 682	740	124	0	27	16.8	119	5.95	653	21 800	....	....	220	99.0	122[2]
123[3]	" 30	6.40 "	" 30	8.48 "	2h. 08m.	1h. 50m.	18m.	20m.	1 848	1 747	534	65	0	32	15.9	112	4.43	653	20 700	....	....	118	99.4	123[3]
124[3]	" 30	8.48 "	" 30	10.13 "	1h. 25m.	1h. 16m.	09m.	00m.	1 353	1 291	397	52	0	33	17.0	120	4.09	534	19 700	....	....	120	99.4	124[3]
125[3]	" 30	10.13 "	" 30	11.19 "	58m.	49m.	09m.	08m.	832	780	479	44	0	63	15.9	112	5.00	534	19 700	....	....	120	99.4	125[3]
126[3]	" 30	11.19 "	" 30	12.15 P.M.	55m.	45m.	10m.	01m.	808	783	310	56	0	45	17.4	123	10.70	534	19 700	....	....	55	99.7	126[3]
127[3]	" 30	12.15 P.M.	" 30	2.39 "	2h. 24m.	2h. 10m.	14m.	00m.	2 224	2 194	545	78	0	28	16.9	119	7.50	534	19 700	....	....	57	99.7	127[3]
128[3]	" 30	2.39 "	June 1	9.06 A.M.	1h. 15m.	1h. 01m.	14m.	17h. 12m.	1 125	1 060	669	67	0	65	17.4	123	8.47	534	19 700	....	....	55	99.7	128[3]
129[4]	June 1	9.06 A.M.	" 1	6.31 P.M.	9h. 21m.	9h. 08m.	13m.	04m.	9 308	9 322	637	75	0	8	17.0	120	5.16	573	19 100	171	67	106	99.4	129[4]
130[4]	" 1	6.31 P.M.	" 1	7.25 "	47m.	33m.	14m.	07m.	907	685	728	85	0	90	20.8	148	5.56	573	19 100	....	....	115	99.4	130[4]
131[4]	" 1	7.25 "	" 1	8.56 "	1h. 21m.	1h. 10m.	11m.	10m.	1 458	1 399	534	82	0	42	20.0	142	4.23	573	19 100	....	....	115	99.4	131[4]
132[4]	" 1	8.56 "	" 1	10.04 "	1h. 03m.	54m.	09m.	05m.	1 141	1 079	431	80	0	45	20.0	142	5.82	573	19 100	....	....	27	99.9	132[4]
133[4]	" 1	10.04 "	" 1	11.31 "	52m.	41m.	11m.	35m.	877	812	428	69	0	57	19.8	141	3.46	573	18 800	....	....	95	99.5	133[4]
134[5]	" 1	11.31 "	" 2	12.46 A.M.	1h. 04m.	54m.	10m.	11m.	1 114	1 063	400	103	0	45	19.7	140	2.39	573	18 800	....	....	201	98.9	134[5]
135[5]	" 2	12.46 A.M.	" 2	3.37 "	2h. 01m.	1h. 49m.	12m.	40m.	1 857	1 783	607	105	0	38	16.4	115	3.02	573	18 800	....	....	470	97.5	135[5]
136[5]	" 2	3.37 "	" 2	4.54 "	1h. 12m.	59m.	13m.	05m.	1 028	917	551	99	0	63	15.5	110	3.62	573	18 800	....	....	420	97.8	136[5]
137[5]	" 2	4.54 "	" 2	6.29 "	43m.	33m.	10m.	52m.	721	632	487	115	0	84	19.2	136	2.63	573	18 600	....	....	370	98.0	137[5]
138[5]	" 2	6.29 "	" 2	8.15 "	1h. 41m.	1h. 29m.	12m.	05m.	1 664	1 523	658	108	0	46	17.1	121	3.20	573	18 600	....	..	187	99.0	138[5]
139[5]	" 2	8.15 "	" 2	9.55 "	1h. 35m.	1h. 20m.	15m.	05m.	1 334	1 246	667	88	0	57	15.6	110	4.84	700	22 300	....	....	220	99.0	139[5]
140[5]	" 2	9.55 "	" 2	11.03 "	52m.	31m.	21m.	16m.	620	531	1 257	93	0	218	17.1	121	4.27	829	22 300	....	....	220	99.0	140[5]
141[6]	" 2	11.03 "	" 2	12.55 P.M.	1h. 48m.	1h. 35m.	13m.	04m.	1 436	1 324	772	71	0	59	14.0	99	3.42	829	26 000	310	68	189	99.3	141[6]
142[6]	" 2	12.55 P.M.	" 2	3.23 "	2h. 25m.	2h. 11m.	14m.	03m.	1 706	1 653	652	60	0	42	12.6	89	5.06	829	20 800	....	....	105	99.5	142[6]
143[6]	" 2	3.23 "	" 2	5.10 "	1h. 41m.	1h. 27m.	14m.	06m.	1 206	1 157	698	73	0	64	13.3	94	4.27	829	20 800	....	....	105	99.5	143[6]
144[6]	" 2	5.10 "	" 2	6.37 "	56m.	44m.	12m.	31m.	705	622	447	124	0	81	14.1	100	3.11	829	15 700	....	....	80	99.5	144[6]
145[6]	" 2	6.37 "	" 2	8.08 "	1h. 09m.	56m.	13m.	22m.	858	744	477	175	0	76	13.3	94	2.62	829	15 700	....	....	42	99.7	145[6]
146[6]	" 2	8.08 "	" 2	9.10 "	57m.	45m.	12m.	05m.	749	567	510	87	0	80	12.6	86	4.47	829	14 000	....	....	40	99.7	146[6]
147[6]	" 2	9.10 "	" 2	10.05 "	50m.	37m.	13m.	05m.	638	553	445	104	0	86	14.9	105	5.34	829	14 000	....	....	40	99.7	147[6]
148[6]	" 2	10.05 "	" 2	11.10 "	59m.	48m.	11m.	06m.	763	667	477	64	0	71	13.9	98	5.32	829	14 000	...	....	41	99.7	148[6]
149[7]	" 2	11.10 "	" 2	11.57 "	43m.	32m.	11m.	04m.	539	481	429	105	0	99	15.0	106	4.10	829	12 400	....	....	35	99.7	149[7]
150[6]	" 2	11.57 "	" 3	1.02 A.M.	1h. 01m.	49m.	12m.	04m.	732	634	348	117	0	64	12.9	91	4.26	829	12 400	....	....	35	99.7	150[6]
151[6]	" 3	1.02 A.M.	" 3	2.19 "	1h. 09m.	58m.	11m.	08m.	957	849	479	84	0	59	14.6	103	3.28	829	12 400	....	....	50	99.6	151[6]

[1] Prescribed chemical 5.0 gr., rate 120 mil. gals. [2] Prescribed chemical 7.0 gr., rate 120 mil. gals. [3] Prescribed chemical 4.0 gr., rate 120 mil. gals. [4] Prescribed chemical 3.0 gr., rate 140 mil. gals.
[5] Prescribed chemical 4.0 gr., rate 140 mil. gals. [6] Prescribed chemical 4.0 gr., rate 100 mil. gals. [7] Prescribed chemical 6.0 gr., rate 100 mil. gals.

TABLE No. 5.—*Continued.*

Western Pressure System.

Number of Run.	Began. Date.	Began. Hour.	Ended. Date.	Ended. Hour.	Periods of Time. Hours and Minutes. Operation.	Service.	Wash.	Delay.	Quantities of Water. Cubic Feet. Applied.	Filtered.	Wash.	Waste. Filtered.	Waste. Unfiltered.	Percentage which the Sum of the Wash and Waste Water is of Applied Water.	Average Actual Rate of Filtration. Cubic Feet per Minute.	Million Gallons per Acre per 24 Hours.	Average Amount of Applied Sulphate of Alumina. Grains per Gallon.	Estimated Average Amount of Suspended Solids in River Water. Parts per Million.	Bacteria per Cubic Centimeter. River Water.	Effluent. Maximum.	Effluent. Minimum.	Effluent. Average.	Average Bacterial Efficiency.	Number of Run.
	1896		1896																					
152[1]	June 3	2.19 A.M.	June 3	3.26 A.M.	1h. 03m.	53m.	10m.	04m.	833	757	425	70	0	59	14.3	101	4.34	829	12 400	....	....	50	99.6	152[1]
153[1]	" 3	3.26 "	" 3	4.26 "	1h. 00m.	46m.	14m.	00m.	707	644	506	69	0	81	14.0	99	4.08	829	10 100	....	....	41	99.6	153[1]
154[1]	" 3	4.26 "	" 3	5.12 "	42m.	32m.	10m.	04m.	549	464	454	96	0	100	14.5	102	3.67	829	10 100	....	....	60	99.4	154[1]
155[1]	" 3	5.12 "	" 3	6.05 "	53m.	40m.	13m.	00m.	637	548	397	63	0	72	13.7	97	3.71	829	7 900	....	....	55	99.3	155[1]
156[1]	" 3	6.05 "	" 3	7.19 "	1h. 14m.	1h. 00m.	14m.	00m.	876	825	646	52	0	80	13.7	97	3.97	829	7 900	....	....	54	99.3	156[1]
157[2]	" 3	7.19 "	" 3	5.19 P.M.	1h. 33m.	1h. 22m.	11m.	8h. 27m.	1 230	1 161	777	49	0	67	14.4	102	5.95	829	7 900	....	....	50	99.4	157[2]
158[2]	" 3	5.19 P.M.	" 3	6.52 "	1h. 28m.	1h. 14m.	14m.	05m.	1 189	1 152	492	136	0	53	15.6	111	4.54	459	13 700	....	....	79	99.4	158[2]
159[2]	" 3	6.52 "	" 3	10.00 "	2h 39m.	2h. 27m.	12m.	29m.	2 194	2 065	451	110	0	26	14.0	99	3.81	459	18 900	....	....	73	99.6	159[2]
160[2]	" 3	10.00 "	" 3	11.51 "	1h. 51m.	1h. 37m.	14m.	00m.	1 482	1 389	536	58	0	40	14.3	101	7.48	459	16 700	....	....	50	99.7	160[2]
161[2]	" 3	11.51 "	" 4	1.54 A.M.	1h. 51m.	1h. 39m.	12m.	12m.	1 471	1 404	483	85	0	38	14.2	100	3.61	459	14 600	....	....	20	99.9	161[2]
162[2]	" 4	1.54 A.M.	" 4	6.29 "	4h. 30m.	4h. 18m.	12m.	05m.	3 436	3 344	506	45	0	16	13.0	92	3.86	459	13 800	184	29	106	99.2	162[2]
163[2]	" 4	6.29 "	" 4	8.13 "	1h. 38m.	1h. 26m.	12m.	06m.	1 262	1 197	641	62	0	56	13.9	98	5.87	459	13 100	....	....	29	99.8	163[2]
164[2]	" 4	8.13 "	" 4	2.00 P.M.	5h. 33m.	5h. 01m.	32m.	14m.	4 768	4 114	857	286	0	24	13.7	97	4.63	360	10 100	67	8	37	99.6	164[2]
165[3]	" 4	2.00 P.M.	" 4	6.56 "	4h. 43m.	4h. 30m.	13m.	13m.	4 946	4 706	508	115	0	13	17.4	123	3.43	338	7 900	97	23	60	99.2	165[3]
166[3]	" 4	6.56 "	" 4	9.53 "	2h. 53m.	2h. 40m.	13m.	04m.	2 747	2 672	568	78	0	24	16.7	118	3.26	338	7 600	....	....	19	99.8	166[3]
167[3]	" 4	9.53 "	" 5	12.28 A.M.	2h. 31m.	2h. 17m.	14m.	04m.	2 422	2 362	491	112	0	25	17.2	122	3.55	338	6 700	....	....	174	97.4	167[3]
168[3]	" 5	12.28 A.M.	" 5	3.44 "	3h. 16m.	3h. 01m.	15m.	00m.	3 081	3 001	497	85	0	19	16.6	117	3.17	338	9 100	....	....	72	99.2	168[3]
169[3]	" 5	3.44 "	" 5	6.45 "	3h. 01m.	2h. 49m.	12m.	00m.	2 795	2 731	679	110	0	28	16.2	114	3.48	338	9 100	....	....	325	96.4	169[3]
170[3]	" 5	6.45 "	" 5	8.14 "	1h. 29m.	1h. 13m.	16m.	00m.	1 401	1 296	609	119	0	52	17.8	126	2.89	338	11 600	....	....	448	97.0	170[3]
171[3]	" 5	8.14 "	" 5	11.21 "	3h. 01m.	2h. 49m.	12m.	06m.	2 767	2 692	498	84	0	21	15.9	112	4.08	220	10 800	....	....	21	99.8	171[3]
172[4]	" 5	11.21 "	" 5	12.13 P.M.	48m.	39m.	09m.	04m.	823	750	451	69	0	63	19.2	136	5.85	186	9 900	....	....	50	99.5	172[4]
173[4]	" 5	12.13 P.M.	" 5	1.18 "	1h. 00m.	50m.	10m.	05m.	1 068	998	445	84	0	49	20.0	142	4.63	186	9 900	....	....	80	99.2	173[4]
174[4]	" 5	1.18 "	" 5	3.05 "	1h. 42m.	1h. 32m.	10m.	05m.	1 862	1 779	497	78	0	31	19.4	137	4.90	186	7 200	....	....	70	99.0	174[4]
175[5]	" 5	3.05 "	" 5	4.23 "	1h. 18m.	1h. 04m.	14m.	00m.	1 385	1 318	583	74	0	47	20.6	147	5.74	186	7 200	....	....	39	98.8	175[5]
176[5]	" 5	4.23 "	" 5	6.42 "	2h. 10m.	1h. 57m.	13m.	09m.	2 341	2 263	435	94	0	23	19.4	137	5.55	186	4 600	....	....	25	99.5	176[5]
177[4]	" 5	6.42 "	" 6	12.33 A.M.	5h. 46m.	5h. 32m.	14m.	05m.	6 557	6 376	404	136	0	8	19.2	136	5.13	186	5 400	....	....	49	99.1	177[4]
178[4]	" 6	12.33 A.M.	" 6	1.58 "	1h. 20m.	1h. 10m.	10m.	05m.	1 539	1 426	434	127	0	36	20.4	145	5.35	186	6 200	67	14	34	99.4	178[4]
179[4]	" 6	1.58 "	" 6	9.20 "	7h. 22m.	7h. 05m.	17m.	00m.	8 224	8 215	419	86	0	6	19.3	137	2.43	186	5 600	....	....	26	99.5	179[4]
180[4]	" 6	9.20 "	" 6	10.18 "	58m.	48m.	10m.	00m.	1 049	970	380	65	0	42	20.2	143	4.17	160	4 300	....	....	215	99.5	180[4]
181[4]	" 6	10.18 "	" 6	12.13 P.M.	1h. 55m.	1h. 43m.	12m.	00m.	1 982	1 939	652	82	0	37	18.8	134	4.02	160	4 900	....	....	31	99.4	181[4]
182[4]	" 6	12.13 P.M.	" 6	1.49 "	1h. 30m.	1h. 19m.	11m.	06m.	1 622	1 558	477	103	0	36	19.8	141	4.83	160	4 900	....	....	35	99.3	182[4]
183[4]	" 6	1.49 "	" 9	9.45 A.M.	1h. 56m.	1h. 41m.	15m.	66h. 00m.	2 016	1 935	573	122	0	34	19.2	136	4.25	160	6 100	69	31	50	99.2	183[4]
184	" 9	9.45 A.M.	" 9	11.41 "	1h. 41m.	1h. 30m.	11m.	15m.	1 965	1 862	470	99	0	29	20.7	147	7.73	582	13 400	....	....	135	99.0	184
185	" 9	11.41 "	" 9	1.11 P.M.	1h. 19m.	1h. 09m.	10m.	11m.	1 478	1 361	479	85	0	38	19.8	141	6.62	582	11 300	....	....	115	99.0	185

[1] Prescribed chemical 4.0 gr., rate 100 mil. gals. [2] Prescribed chemical 6.0 gr., rate 100 mil. gals. [3] Prescribed chemical 4.0 gr., rate 120 mil. gals.
[4] Prescribed chemical 4.0 gr., rate 140 mil. gals. [5] Prescribed chemical 6.0 gr., rate 140 mil. gals.

TABLE No. 5.—*Continued.*

Western Pressure System.

Number of Run.	Began. Date.	Began. Hour.	Ended. Date.	Ended. Hour.	Periods of Time. Hours and Minutes. Operation.	Service.	Wash.	Delay.	Quantities of Water. Cubic Feet. Applied.	Filtered.	Wash.	Waste. Filtered.	Waste. Unfiltered.	Percentage which the Sum of the Wash and Waste Water is of Applied Water.	Average Actual Rate of Filtration. Cubic Feet per Minute.	Million Gallons per Acre per 24 Hours.	Average Amount of Applied Sulphate of Alumina. Grains per Gallon.	Estimated Average Amount of Suspended Solids in River Water. Parts per Million.	Bacteria per Cubic Centimeter. River Water.	Effluent. Maximum.	Effluent. Minimum.	Effluent. Average.	Average Bacterial Efficiency.	Number of Run.
	1896		1896																					
186	June 9	1.11 P.M.	June 9	2.43 P.M.	1h. 23m.	1h. 13m.	10m.	09m.	1 455	1 387	448	92	0	37	19.0	135	5.27	582	11 300	....	....	121	98.9	186
187	" 9	2.43 "	" 9	3.48 "	46m.	34m.	12m.	19m.	797	713	575	86	0	83	21.0	149	5.38	582	9 300	....	....	95	99.0	187
188	" 9	3.48 "	" 10	9.06 A.M.	1h. 28m.	1h. 15m.	13m.	15h. 50m.	1 447	1 371	324	109	0	30	18.3	130	7.10	582	9 300	....	....	75	99.2	188
189	" 10	9.06 A.M.	" 10	1.30 P.M.	4h. 18m.	4h. 06m.	12m.	06m.	4 466	4 364	536	92	0	14	17.7	125	7.07	366	10 600	104	29	66	99.4	189
190	" 10	1.30 P.M.	" 10	2.52 "	1h. 22m.	1h. 06m.	16m.	00m.	1 263	1 184	508	72	0	46	18.0	128	7.38	366	10 600	....	....	55	99.5	190
191	" 10	2.52 "	" 10	4.47 "	1h. 50m.	1h. 38m.	12m.	05m.	1 823	1 768	477	111	0	32	18.1	129	7.41	366	6 600	....	....	29	99.7	191
192	" 10	4.47 "	" 11	9.25 A.M.	1h. 02m.	48m.	14m.	15h. 36m.	930	825	491	94	0	63	17.2	122	7.57	366	8 600	....	....	15	99.8	192
193	" 11	9.25 A.M.	" 11	1.08 P.M.	3h. 38m.	3h. 29m.	09m.	05m.	4 043	3 965	385	72	0	11	19.0	135	5.70	247	6 600	....	....	9	99.9	193
194	" 11	1.08 P.M.	" 11	3.26 "	2h. 10m.	2h. 00m.	10m.	08m.	2 317	2 262	401	86	0	21	18.9	134	5.57	247	8 500	....	....	19	99.8	194
195	" 11	3.26 "	" 12	2.07 "	6h. 45m.	6h. 34m.	11m.	15h. 56m.	7 112	7 045	447	68	0	75	17.9	127	5.82	220	6 300	12	4	8	99.9	195
196	" 12	2.07 "	" 13	9.05 A.M.	3h. 13m.	3h. 03m.	10m.	15h. 45m.	3 340	3 271	572	89	0	20	17.9	127	6.04	200	8 100	....	....	17	99.8	196
197	" 13	9.05 A.M.	" 13	1.01 P.M.	3h. 51m.	3h. 39m.	12m.	05m.	4 516	4 459	541	98	0	14	20.4	145	4.07	220	13 400	....	....	16	99.9	197
198	" 13	1.01 P.M.	" 13	3.20 "	2h. 13m.	2h. 01m.	12m.	06m.	2 449	2 383	489	85	0	23	19.7	140	4.48	220	14 700	320	17	168	98.9	198
199	" 13	3.20 "	" 15	2.15 "	7h. 14m.	7h. 00m.	14m.	39h. 41m.	7 637	7 595	528	115	0	84	18.1	129	4.58	350	14 400	23	16	19	99.9	199
200	" 15	2.15 "	" 15	3.50 "	1h. 28m.	1h. 15m.	13m.	07m.	1 467	1 363	495	106	0	41	18.2	129	6.17	400	13 000	....	....	41	99.7	200
201	" 15	3.50 "	" 16	1.20 "	5h. 56m.	5h. 42m.	14m.	15h. 34m.	6 061	6 023	647	106	0	12	17.6	125	4.37	270	10 900	52	16	32	99.7	201
202	" 16	1.20 "	" 16	4.05 "	2h. 38m.	2h. 26m.	12m.	07m.	2 744	2 675	489	93	0	21	18.3	130	3.95	220	8 400	....	....	46	99.5	202
203	" 16	4.05 "	" 17	1.59 "	6h. 10m.	5h. 58m.	12m.	15h. 44m.	6 635	6 621	570	78	0	10	18.5	132	3.98	220	10 100	24	17	21	99.8	203
204	" 17	1.59 "	" 18	9.07 A.M.	3h. 19m.	3h. 03m.	16m.	15h. 49m.	3 429	3 408	565	149	0	21	18.6	133	4.13	220	11 000	....	....	37	99.7	204
205	" 18	9.07 A.M.	" 19	9.06 "	7h. 41m.	7h. 29m.	12m.	16h. 18m.	8 210	8 164	582	105	0	8	18.2	129	1.52	270	11 600	212	103	161	98.6	205
206	" 19	9.06 "	" 19	12.44 P.M.	3h. 32m.	3h. 20m.	12m.	06m.	3 829	3 758	588	82	0	17	18.8	134	4.22	430	14 900	....	....	26	99.8	206
207	" 19	12.44 P.M.	" 19	2.25 "	1h. 20m.	1h. 07m.	13m.	21m.	1 322	1 259	564	96	0	50	18.8	134	4.27	430	18 000	....	....	35	99.8	207
208	" 19	2.25 "	" 20	9.06 A.M.	2h. 13m.	2h. 00m.	13m.	16h. 28m.	2 227	2 161	668	71	0	33	18.0	128	4.62	430	21 200	53	11	32	99.6	208
209	" 20	9.06 A.M.	" 20	1.49 P.M.	4h. 43m.	4h. 25m.	18m.	00m.	4 810	4 768	656	108	0	16	18.0	128	5.47	260	10 500	103	43	73	99.3	209
210	" 20	1.49 P.M.	" 20	4.34 "	2h. 37m.	2h. 24m.	13m.	08m.	2 607	2 540	645	108	0	29	17.6	125	3.68	260	9 700	....	....	54	99.4	210
211	" 20	4.34 "	" 24	1.50 "	6h. 30m.	6h. 18m.	12m.	86h. 46m.	7 056	7 044	675	53	0	12	18.6	133	3.44	220	7 400	93	31	64	99.1	211
212	" 24	1.50 "	" 25	2.14 "	8h. 54m.	8h. 34m.	20m.	15h. 30m.	10 111	10 175	557	144	0	7	19.8	141	4.17	340	8 400	360	35	180	97.9	212
213	" 25	2.14 "	" 25	3.41 "	1h. 27m.	1h. 04m.	23m.	00m.	1 420	1 300	539	185	0	51	20.3	144	3.94	300	6 700	....	....	1000	98.5	213
214	" 25	3.41 "	" 26	1.59 "	6h. 38m.	6h. 11m.	27m.	15h. 40m.	6 615	6 481	646	150	0	12	17.5	124	3.82	290	7 600	63	12	44	99.4	214
215	" 26	1.59 "	" 26	4.42 "	2h. 33m.	2h. 13m.	20m.	10m.	2 518	2 409	552	191	0	30	18.1	129	3.56	280	6 000	....	....	81	98.7	215
216	" 26	4.42 "	" 27	1.21 "	5h. 07m.	4h. 46m.	21m.	15h. 32m.	5 224	5 058	643	157	0	15	17.7	125	7.22	340	7 000	127	59	93	98.7	216
217	" 27	1.21 "	" 27	3.06 "	1h. 45m.	1h. 23m.	22m.	00m.	1 658	1 519	658	180	0	51	18.3	130	7.21	360	10 800	....	....	162	98.5	217
218	" 27	3.06 "	" 29	9.07 A.M.	2h. 31m.	2h. 12m.	19m.	15h. 30m.	2 501	2 350	768	103	0	35	17.8	126	2.38	360	13 700	....	....	370	97.3	218
219	" 29	9.07 A.M.	" 29	12.21 P.M.	3h. 41m.	2h. 53m.	21m.	00m.	3 152	3 061	783	170	0	30	17.7	125	8.48	530	13 600	....	....	12	99.9	219
220	" 29	12.21 P.M.	" 29	3.10 "	2h. 49m.	2h. 24m.	25m.	00m.	2 796	2 657	771	253	0	37	18.4	131	7.08	530	14 700	63	29	46	99.7	220
221	" 29	3.10 "	" 30	9.09 A.M.	1h. 50m.	1h. 31m.	19m.	16h. 09m.	1 858	1 609	709	129	0	45	17.7	125	6.05	530	12 700	....	....	69	94.6	221
222	" 30	9.09 A.M.	" 30	12.25 P.M.	3h. 16m.	2h. 51m.	25m.	00m.	3 221	3 094	771	247	0	32	18.1	129	4.68	360	10 900	....	....	32	99.7	222
223	" 30	12.25 P.M.	" 30	2.31 "	2h. 06m.	1h. 39m.	27m.	00m.	1 864	1 651	645	219	0	46	16.7	118	8.58	360	13 500	....	....	34	99.7	223

TABLE NO. 5.—*Concluded.*

Western Pressure System.

Number of Run.	Began. Date.	Began. Hour.	Ended. Date.	Ended. Hour.	Periods of Time. Hours and Minutes. Operation.	Service.	Wash.	Delay.	Quantities of Water. Cubic Feet. Applied.	Filtered.	Wash.	Waste. Filtered.	Waste. Unfiltered.	Percentage which the Sum of the Wash and Waste Water is of Applied Water.	Average Actual Rate of Filtration. Cubic Feet per Minute.	Million Gallons per Acre per 24 Hours.	Average Amount of Applied Sulphate of Alumina. Grains per Gallon.	Estimated Average Amount of Suspended Solids in River Water. Parts per Million.	Bacteria per Cubic Centimeter. River Water.	Effluent. Maximum.	Effluent. Minimum.	Effluent. Average.	Average Bacterial Efficiency.	Number of Run.
	1896		1896																					
224	June 30	2.31 P.M.	July 1	9.00 A.M.	1h. 32m.	1h. 08m.	24m.	16h. 57m.	1 397	1 161	794	195	0	71	17.1	121	8.55	360	13 500	....	....	32	99.8	224
225	July 1	9.00 A.M.	" 1	12.44 P.M.	3h. 44m.	3h. 12m.	32m.	00m.	3 513	3 304	767	287	0	30	17.2	122	4.53	870	......	....	....	....	....	225
226	" 1	12.44 P.M.	" 1	2.31 "	1h. 47m.	1h. 14m.	33m.	00m.	1 526	1 240	798	296	0	72	16.8	119	5.48	870	......	....	....	....	....	226
227	" 1	2.31 "	" 1	3.59 "	1h. 28m.	55m.	33m.	00m.	1 251	935	735	274	0	81	17.0	120	4.60	870	......	....	....	....	....	227
228	" 1	3.59 "	" 6	9.12 A.M.	1h. 26m.	1h. 03m.	23m.	111h. 47m.	1 347	1 061	764	79	0	63	16.9	119	5.58	870	......	....	....	....	....	228
229	" 6	9.12 A.M.	" 7	9.11 "	8h. 29m.	8h. 07m.	22m.	15h. 30m.	8 553	8 359	729	159	0	10	17.2	122	3.97	220	7 400	108	13	48	99.4	229
230	" 7	9.11 "	" 7	12.35 P.M.	3h. 24m.	2h. 56m.	28m.	00m.	3 765	3 557	725	283	0	27	20.2	143	4.62	530	5 400	....	....	22	99.6	230
231	" 7	12.35 P.M.	" 7	2.37 "	2h. 02m.	1h. 35m.	27m.	00m.	1 967	1 661	631	188	0	42	17.5	124	7.00	530	5 500	....	....	49	99.1	231
232	" 7	2.37 "	" 8	9.07 A.M.	2h. 10m.	1h. 56m.	14m.	16h. 20m.	2 226	1 993	566	78	0	29	17.2	122	5.42	530	5 600	....	....	19	99.[illegible]	232
233	" 8	9.07 A.M.	" 8	1.54 P.M.	4h. 47m.	4h. 15m.	32m.	00m.	4 823	4 651	796	254	0	22	18.3	130	4.36	460	6 700	33	11	22	99.7	233
234	" 8	1.54 P.M.	" 9	9.05 A.M.	2h. 15m.	2h. 00m.	15m.	16h. 56m.	2 270	1 868	776	55	0	37	15.6	110	5.11	460	5 600	....	....	20	99.6	234
235	" 9	9.05 A.M.	" 9	1.36 P.M.	4h. 22m.	3h. 55m.	27m.	09m.	4 046	3 900	936	222	0	29	16.6	117	4.95	470	8 600	10	6	8	99.9	235
236	" 9	1.36 P.M.	" 9	4.00 "	2h. 24m.	1h. 51m.	33m.	00m.	2 152	1 890	777	272	0	49	17.0	120	4.33	470	9 200	....	....	112	98.8	236
237	" 9	4.00 "	" 13	9.11 A.M.	1h. 29m.	1h. 13m.	16m.	87h. 42m.	1 578	1 281	800	54	0	54	17.5	124	6.38	470	9 900	....	....	112	98.9	237
238	" 13	9.11 A.M.	" 13	2.56 P.M.	5h. 45m.	5h. 14m.	31m.	00m.	5 477	5 324	681	283	0	18	17.0	120	4.23	490	6 900	98	25	61	99.1	238
239	" 13	2.56 P.M.	" 14	9.07 A.M.	1h. 44m.	1h. 25m.	19m.	16h. 27m.	1 736	1 408	788	78	0	50	16.6	117	7.55	490	7 700	....	....	110	98.6	239
240	" 14	9.07 A.M.	" 15	1.11 P.M.	6h. 47m.	6h. 11m.	36m.	21h. 17m.	6 307	6 096	766	374	0	18	16.9	119	4.82	370	10 100	186	1	25	97.5	240
241	" 15	1.11 P.M.	" 16	9.08 A.M.	4h. 27m.	4h. 09m.	18m.	15h. 30m.	4 602	4 116	812	96	0	20	16.5	116	4.58	490	8 300	15	7	11	99.9	241
242	" 16	9.08 A.M.	" 16	12.54 P.M.	3h. 46m.	3h. 15m.	31m.	00m.	3 503	3 360	796	270	0	30	17.2	122	4.54	450	6 200	18	6	12	99.8	242
243	" 16	12.54 P.M.	" 16	2.49 "	1h. 55m.	1h. 30m.	25m.	00m.	1 842	1 552	564	207	0	42	17.2	122	5.38	450	5 300	....	....	31	99.4	243
244	" 16	2.49 "	" 20	9.04 A.M.	2h. 34m.	2h. 17m.	17m.	87h. 41m.	2 620	2 381	831	53	0	34	17.4	123	5.95	450	5 000	....	....	25	99.5	244
245	" 20	9.04 A.M.	" 21	9.05 "	8h. 31m.	8h. 16m.	15m.	15h. 30m.	8 468	8 352	765	78	0	10	16.8	119	3.67	360	7 000	31	16	22	99.7	245
246	" 21	9.05 "	" 21	1.03 P.M.	3h. 58m.	3h. 30m.	28m.	00m.	3 736	3 645	765	211	0	26	17.4	123	2.63	560	8 800	509	32	195	97.8	246
247	" 21	1.03 P.M.	" 21	2.50 "	1h. 47m.	1h. 22m.	25m.	00m.	1 578	1 373	570	221	0	50	16.8	119	3.28	560	17 100	....	....	357	97.9	247
248	" 21	2.50 "	" 22	9.05 A.M.	2h. 43m.	2h. 27m.	16m.	15h. 32m.	2 506	2 266	801	70	0	35	15.4	109	6.42	560	25 400	292	158	225	99.1	248
249	" 22	9.05 A.M.	" 22	12.27 P.M.	3h. 22m.	2h. 50m.	32m.	00m.	2 716	2 633	743	272	0	37	15.5	110	3.58	1 170	33 300	....	....	646	98.1	249
250	" 22	12.27 P.M.	" 22	1.58 "	1h. 31m.	55m.	36m.	00m.	1 131	856	831	333	0	103	15.6	111	4.29	1 170	29 400	....	....	558	98.1	250
251	" 22	1.58 "	" 23	9.06 A.M.	3h. 00m.	2h. 42m.	18m.	16h. 08m.	2 658	2 322	744	75	0	31	14.4	101	5.41	1 170	32 100	1 186	37	611	98.1	251
252	" 23	9.06 A.M.	" 23	11.52 "	2h. 46m.	2h. 04m.	42m.	00m.	1 949	1 866	795	358	0	59	15.1	101	7.67	2 170	23 800	....	....	452	98.5	252
253	" 23	11.52 "	" 27	11.14 "	2h. 09m.	51m.	1h. 18m.	93h. 13m.	1 025	680	799	742	0	150	13.3	94	9.69	2 170	27 700	....	....	275	99.0	253
254	" 27	11.14 "	" 28	10.16 "	4h. 18m.	4h. 02m.	16m.	18h. 44m.	4 261	3 511	613	91	0	17	14.6	103	6.02	1 400	17 800	170	138	151	99.1	254
255	" 28	10.16 "	" 28	2.52 P.M.	4h. 24m.	2h. 11m.	13m.	12m.	3 725	3 684	640	64	0	19	14.7	104	5.79	1 420	24 500	207	105	156	99.4	255
256	" 28	2.52 P.M.	" 29	9.03 A.M.	1h. 42m.	1h. 32m.	10m.	16h. 29m.	1 335	1 296	611	37	0	48	14.1	100	3.91	1 420	24 500	....	....	245	99.0	256
257	" 29	9.03 A.M.	" 29	11.50 "	2h. 32m.	2h. 20m.	12m.	15m.	2 077	2 068	555	50	0	29	14.8	105	5.02	1 770	9 500	....	....	76	99.2	257
258	" 29	11.50 "	" 29	1.12 P.M.	1h. 15m.	1h. 01m.	14m.	07m.	877	856	488	36	0	60	14.0	99	3.20	1 770	9 500	....	....	95	99.0	258
259	" 29	1.12 P.M.	" 29	2.39 "	1h. 19m.	1h. 07m.	12m.	08m.	949	932	484	39	0	55	13.9	98	5.22	1 770	9 500	....	....	101	98.9	259
260	" 29	2.39 "	" 29	3.43 "	55m.	44m.	11m.	09m.	647	617	598	27	0	97	14.0	99	3.73	1 770	9 500	....	....	173	98.2	260
261	" 29	3.43 "	" 29	5.12 "	....	1h. 12m.	....	....	1 077	1 061	506	....	0	....	14.7	104	4.14	1 770	9 500	....	....	....	....	261

CHAPTER IX.

SUMMARY OF THE PRINCIPAL DATA UPON THE EFFICIENCY AND ELEMENTS OF COST OF PURIFICATION, BY THE RESPECTIVE SYSTEMS, OF THE OHIO RIVER WATER, DIVIDED INTO TWENTY PERIODS, ACCORDING TO THE CHARACTER OF THE UNPURIFIED WATER; TOGETHER WITH A DISCUSSION OF SOME OF THE MORE IMPORTANT FEATURES.

BEFORE the presentation of a summary of the principal data obtained during 1895–6 upon the efficiency and the elements of cost of the purification of the Ohio River water, in twenty periods, according to the character of the unpurified water, there will be given as a matter of record some tabulations showing the character of the purified water by days. For a detailed account of the composition of the Ohio River water by days, and of the amount of sulphate of alumina applied to the river water, reference is made to Chapters I and II, respectively. The question of the decomposition of the sulphate of alumina and its removal from the water was discussed carefully in Chapter III.

Table No. 1.

The first set of tables in this chapter contains a daily statement of the appearance of the water after purification by the respective systems. As already explained the appearance of the filtered water is designated by five degrees of clearness, which may be described briefly as follows:

Degree No. 1 signifies a brilliant water.

Degree No. 2 signifies a clear water.

Degree No. 3 signifies a slightly turbid water.

Degree No. 4 signifies a turbid water.

Degree No. 5 signifies a very turbid water.

The first three degrees of clearness refer in each case to an appearance of the water which is satisfactory. It is doubtful if the consumers would distinguish between these three degrees of clearness unless their attention were directed to the matter. Degrees Nos. 4 and 5 would be noted by the consumers, but it is to be stated that the adjectives used above have only a comparative value in relation to a brilliant water.

In both cases the turbidity would be very slight when compared with the river water before purification.

Degree No. 4 refers to an appearance which would not be unsatisfactory for short periods if the water were of a proper character in all other particulars. Degree No. 5 was objectionable both in its direct and indirect bearings, and was seldom noted for periods of long duration.

Table No. 2.

In the second set of tables are recorded the percentages of removal from the river water, by the respective systems, of the carbonaceous and nitrogenous organic matter, as indicated by the oxygen consumed and the nitrogen in the form of albuminoid ammonia, respectively. As a matter of convenience the total amount of nitrogen in the form of albuminoid ammonia in the river water, and the percentage of the total amount which was found to be undissolved in the water, are given. It will be obsereved that the total amount of nitrogeneous organic matter in the filtered water was less than the amount dissolved in the river water before purification.

Table No. 3.

The third set of tables contains a record of the daily average number of bacteria per cubic centimeter in the Ohio River water before and after purification by the respective systems, and also the daily average bacterial efficiency of each system. Bacterial efficiency means the percentage which the difference in the numbers of bacteria in the water before and after purification is of the number of bacteria originally present in the river water.

Table No. 4.

In the next set of tables are presented the principal data obtained during the investigations with regard to the efficiency and cost of purification by this method. As stated at the outset of this chapter the results are divided into twenty periods, according to the character of the unpurified river water. This was necessitated by the marked variations in the composition of the river water, affecting both the efficiency and the cost of purification; and also by the varying conditions under which the respective systems were operated.

The official investigations of the several systems of purification by the method in question began on Oct. 21, 1895. For a number of weeks after that time the investigations were less exhaustive than they were during the later portion of the period when the laboratory work had been more fully planned to meet the requirements of the problem. The Warren System began operations during the latter half of September. On October 21 the operators of this system contemplated some modifications in its construction. Owing to the remarkably low stage of the river at that time it was desirable for the Water Company to obtain data with this character of water.

Accordingly they were officially requested to postpone their changes for a short time and operate the system with varied amounts of sulphate of alumina from day to day. This they consented to do, but protested against the merits of their system being judged from operations preceding their contemplated changes.

Operation of the Jewell System began early in July, 1895, and was said to have been continued nearly every day up to October 21, the commencement of the official tests.

The installation of the Western Systems did not begin until early in November, and it was not until December 23 that they were ready for regular official inspection. Explanation has already been given of the lengthy delays in these systems after about April 1. From March 24 to 30 and April 27 to June 6 all systems were requested by the Water Company to be operated twenty-four hours per day, excepting Sundays during the latter period. Otherwise the systems were operated about 8.5 hours per day (from 9 A.M. until 5.30 P.M.).

A brief account is next given of the several periods into which the investigations are divided according to the grade of the river water and other conditions of operation.

Outline of the Periods into which the Investigations are Divided.

Period No. 1.—This period extended from Oct. 21 to Nov. 25, 1895. It represents the last portion of the most severe and extended drought which had been noted for many years. With the low stage of the river there was an absence, comparatively speaking, of suspended organic and mineral matters in the river water; the amounts of dissolved organic and mineral matter were abnormally high; and the bacteria, while comparatively few in number, contained an unusually large proportion of species coming from the sewage of cities situated farther up in the valley.

The Jewell System was the only one that was in service during the full period. The Warren System was in service for a considerable portion of the time, but under the conditions stated above; while the installation of the Western Systems was not completed.

Period No. 2.—This period extended from Nov. 25 to Dec. 24. During this time light rains fell. The water varied somewhat in character. At times the indications of sewage pollution were more marked than during the first period. The water became more muddy, and the chlorine and alkalinity decreased in a marked degree toward the end, although this did not follow in the case of the other soluble constituents. In fact there was an increase in some of them, notably in the nitrogen as free ammonia. With the rains the number of bacteria increased considerably.

The Warren and Jewell systems were in

regular service during this period, but the Western Systems did not begin operation until it was practically ended.

Period No. 3.—This period extended from Dec. 24, 1895, to Jan. 13, 1896. It represents the rising, maximum and falling stage of the river after the first heavy storm of the season. From this time to the close of the tests the chief variation in the river water was the amount of suspended matter which it contained. These amounts will be noted in the tables.

All four systems were in service.

Period No. 4.—This period extended from Jan. 13 to 27, 1896. It represents a fairly uniform grade of the river water from the fall of the preceding rise to the beginning of the next subsequent one.

All four systems were in service during the greater part of the time. The sand layer of the Warren System was changed on Jan. 23.

Period No. 5.—This period extended from Jan. 27 to Feb. 6, and represents a rising stage of the river and increasing amounts of suspended matter in the river water.

For unavoidable reasons the Western Systems were out of service on Jan. 29 and 30.

On Feb. 1 the scope of the investigations was enlarged. The sand layer of the Jewell System was changed on this date.

Period No. 6.—This period extended from Feb. 6 to 13, and represents the height of a rise in the river when of course the suspended matter in the water was unusually high in amount.

From Feb. 8 until about April 1 lime was applied to the river water in the case of the Jewell System.

All four systems were in service, but the Warren System was delayed from time to time by changes in the devices for the introduction of wash-water beneath the sand layer.

Period No. 7.—This period extended from Feb. 13 to 27, and represents a falling stage of the river with decreasing amounts of suspended matter in the river water.

The most noteworthy features in the operation of the several systems, speaking in general terms, were the irregular results along several lines, particularly those of bacterial efficiency and application of chemicals.

Period No. 8.—This period extended from Feb. 27 to March 20, and represents comparatively clear water between successive rises.

All of the systems were quite regularly in service. On March 16 the operators of the respective systems were officially asked to comply with certain requests, leading to more regular and more efficient results of purification. On Feb. 29 a new and separate pipe for the supply of river water was connected with the Western Systems.

Period No. 9.—This period included March 20 and 21, and represents very muddy water at the beginning of an extended freshet.

The Western Gravity System went out of service owing to its failure to purify enough water to serve for washing its own sand layer.

Period No. 10.—This period extended from March 23 to 30, and represents a muddy condition of the water and a high stage of the river. The suspended matter for the most part had a red color, however, and was much coarser than was noted under other conditions.

From March 24, 9.00 A.M., to March 30, 5.30 P.M., the systems were operated continuously, with the exception of the Western Gravity System, which was not operated at all.

Period No. 11.—This period extended from March 30 to April 7, and represents a muddy water and falling stage of the river. Rains caused the water to vary considerably in character.

All systems except the Western Gravity System were in service.

On April 3 the representatives of the respective systems were officially requested to get in readiness to operate, upon 48 hours' notice, their systems night and day for such periods as the Water Company deemed advisable.

Period No. 12.—This period extended from April 7 to 27, and represents a falling stage of the river and comparatively clear water. The end of this period marked the beginning of a six weeks' period of continuous operation during each week from 9.00 A.M. on Monday to 4 P.M. on Saturday.

This period was chiefly characterized by repairs, following the official communications of March 16 and April 3, as noted above.

In the Warren System the sand layer was changed. This caused a delay from April 13 to 20. The Jewell System was in regular service. Neither of the Western Systems was operated at all during this period.

Period No. 13.—This period extended from April 27 to May 18, and represents a period of comparatively clear water in the middle of a protracted drought. It also represents the first half of the six weeks' period of continuous operation.

The Warren and Jewell systems were regularly in service. From May 7 until the close of the period the Western Pressure System was in regular operation. At about the same date the repairs of the Western Gravity System were also completed. It was operated unofficially on several occasions, but it was not put in official operation until after the Water Company requested an official explanation of the reason of its withdrawal from the tests. This request was made during the last week in June. During the intervening period this system was left out of consideration by all parties so far as active operations were concerned.

Period No. 14.—This period extended from May 18 to 28, during the time of continuous operation, and represented the last portion of the comparatively clear water, before the end of the long drought. During this period the conditions of operation, with regard to rate of filtration and amount of applied sulphate of alumina, were prescribed by the Water Company as shown in table No. 4 of the last chapter.

No unusual delays occurred in the case of the Warren, Jewell, and Western Pressure systems, except as occasioned by the prescribed conditions.

Period No. 15.—This period extended from May 28 to June 3, and represents a rapidly rising stage of river when the suspended matter was in part exceedingly fine, as noted in Chapter I.

Great difficulty in securing coagulation, even with large amounts of sulphate of alumina, was experienced. Conditions of continuous operations, as above outlined, were prescribed by the Water Company so far as it was practicable.

Period No. 16.—This period extended from June 3 to 9, and represents the last of the continuous operations for 24 hours per day; and also the last of the prescribed conditions. The water was muddy but rather variable in character.

The Warren, Jewell, and Western Pressure systems were in operation without any serious delays.

Period No. 17.—This period extended from June 9 to July 1, and represents three consecutive minor rises of the river. The period closed with the beginning of a marked rise which caused the water to become very muddy.

The Warren, Jewell, and Western Pressure systems were regularly in operation with the exception of three days in the case of the Warren System. This delay was caused by repairs of a break in the agitator machinery.

Period No. 18.—This period extended from July 1 to 6, and represents very rapidly rising and falling stages of the river. Heavy rains fell on the local watershed and the water became very muddy. The rise quickly subsided, and the period ended at the beginning of a minor rise.

During this period the remodeled Western Gravity System was put in operation according to a proposition offered by the Western Filter Company. It was agreed that for the balance of the investigations the pressure system was to be operated on the first four days of each week, and the gravity on the last two days. This proposition was made in reply to a request from the Water Company for an official explanation of the fact that at that time the Western Gravity System had been withdrawn from the tests for a period of more than three months. The communication received from the Western Filter Company, under date of June 26, 1896, is as follows:

"The difficulties experienced in the earlier part of the filter tests occasioned by running both our filters on the same main with the other filters, which we hoped to remedy by the changes made in April, have been but partially removed. We find now after several unofficial trial runs that, owing to wide variations in the pressure due to changes in velocity in a 4-inch main, brought about by opening and closing either outlet, it is liable to impair seriously the results of our work to run both filters at the same time. We have therefore continued the service of our pressure filter, beliving that we obtained better results, at least mechanically, from that portion of our plant.

"We are prepared, however, if it be desirable for the information of the Water Company, to run our gravity filter at such intervals and for such periods as may be deemed advisable, discontinuing the service of our pressure filter during such periods."

Operations of all systems were suspended on July 4, and on July 4 and 5 the sand layer of the Jewell System was changed.

Period No. 19.—This period extended from July 6 to 22, and represents a fairly uniform stage of the river with comparatively muddy water. Occasional rains on the local watershed caused several minor rises, but none of any large amount or extended duration.

The Jewell System was operated with higher amounts of sulphate of alumina than the condition of the water warranted, and consequently the effluent of this system was frequently acid.

The Warren System was in regular operation, and the Western Systems were operated under the arrangement outlined above.

Period No. 20.—This period extended from July 22 to the close of the investigations on Aug. 1. It represents the most marked rise noted during the investigations, and throughout this period the river water contained suspended solids ranging from 805 to 3347 parts per million.

Great difficulty was experienced by all the systems in handling this water, owing to the frequent washings of the sand layer necessitated by the large amounts of mud in the water after the short subsidence and before filtration. Relatively high amounts of sulphate of alumina were used with the view of securing satisfactory coagulation.

During this period the operation of the systems was delayed in a number of instances in order that the Water Company might make a number of tests and observations of an engineering nature. A very slight excess of sulphate of alumina above the amount capable of decomposition by the river water was applied during the majority of the period in the case of the Jewell System. Complications of a greater or less degree arose in the case of the Warren System, beginning about July 22, from the passage of sludge from the settling basin on to the filter. This was remedied on July 27 by cleaning the settling basin.

Just how far this complication affected the results of this system is difficult to say. But it doubtless caused the sand layer to be washed at abnormally frequent intervals and caused a greater or less increase in the amount of applied sulphate of alumina, and something of a decrease in bacterial efficiency.

Explanation of the Data presented in Table No. 4, and of the Methods of Computation thereof.

This table comprises all the qantitative and the leading qualitative data, arranged and compiled for each of the twenty periods into which, as has already been explained, the results of the investigations are divided. Maximum and minimum results during the periods were obtained by inspection of the records presented in Table No. 5 of Chapter VIII.

The exact significance of all expressions not explained here was presented in Chapter VIII. The data presented in this table, and the methods of averaging employed, are as follows:

Periods of Time.—The average length of time per run included in the periods of "operation," "service," and "wash" are expressed in hours and hundredths of hours.

These results were obtained in each case by dividing the total respective times by the number of runs included in the period.

Quantities of Water.—The average quantities of water per run are given in cubic feet. These were all computed by dividing the respective total quantities for the period by the number of runs included in the period. In all computations for this table the actual quantities registered by the meters were used.

Percentage which the Sum of the Wash and Waste Water was of the Applied Water.—These results were obtained by dividing the total quantity of wash and waste water for the period by the total quantity of applied water.

Actual Rate of Filtration.—The average actual rate of filtration in cubic feet per minute was determined by dividing the total quantity of water registered by the filtered-water meter by the total period of service. These results are also given in million gallons per acre per twenty-four hours by multiplication of the rates in cubic feet per minute by the proper constants.

Average Net Rate of Filtration.—These results were obtained by dividing the difference between the quantity of applied water and the quantity of wash and waste water by the period of operation, using in all cases the totals for the period. The rates in million gallons per acre per twenty-four hours were obtained from these rates by the use of the proper constants.

Net Quantity of Filtered Water per Run in Million Gallons per Acre.—These results were obtained by deducting the quantity of wash and waste water from the quantity of the applied water, and multiplying the results by the proper constant value of 1 cubic foot in million gallons per acre. Averages were obtained by using total quantities for the period.

Estimated Suspended Solids in River Water.—Under this head are given the maximum and the minimum average amounts of suspended solids estimated for the different runs, and the average amount for the entire period. The averages were obtained by multiplying the average solids for each run by the quantity of applied water on that run, and dividing the sum of these products by the total quantity of applied water for the period.

Grains of Applied Sulphate of Alumina per Gallon of Applied Water.—The maximum and minimum amounts averaged for any run during the period are given, and also the weighted averages for the period. The latter were obtained in the same manner as the average suspended solids.

Average Grains of Applied Sulphate of Alumina per Gallon of Net Filtered Water.—These results were obtained by dividing the amounts of sulphate of alumina per gallon of applied water by the percentages which the net filtered water was of the applied water, using in both cases averages for the period.

Degree of Clearness.—The maximum, minimum and average degrees of clearness are given. The average degree given in each case is the sum of degrees recorded as averages for each run divided by the number of runs.

Bacteria per Cubic Centimeter in River Water.—The maximum and minimum average numbers per run, and the average number for the period, of the bacteria in the river water are given. The averages were obtained in the same manner as the average amounts of suspended solids.

Average, Maximum and Minimum Numbers of Bacteria per Cubic Centimeter in the Filtered Water.—These results are actual averages of the observations recorded as maximum and minimum numbers of bacteria for the several runs. Where the number of observations was less than one half of the number of runs for the period no average is given.

Average Numbers of Bacteria per Cubic Centimeter in Filtered Water.—The averages per run which were the maximum and minimum during the period are given, and also the average number for the periods. The averages were obtained by multiplying the average for each run by the quantity of filtered water on that run, and dividing the sum of these products by the total quantity of filtered water for the period.

Average Bacterial Efficiencies.—The average efficiencies per run, which were the maximum and minimum for the period, are given, and also the averages for the periods. The latter were obtained by dividing the difference between the average numbers of bacteria in the river water and in the effluent by the average numbrr in the river water, these averages having been determined as described above.

Table No. 5.

In this table are presented the total periods of time devoted to operation, service and preparing the filters for filtration; the total quantities of water recorded by the meters; and averages of each of these periods and quantities per run, obtained by dividing the respective total amounts by the number of runs. The records of the runs not included in averages are omitted from this as well as all other tables. There are presented also in this table the following averages:

Average Actual Rate of Filtration.—These results were obtained by dividing the total quantities of filtered water by the total periods of operation, rates in cubic feet per minute being transferred into million gallons per acre per twenty-four hours by the use of the proper constants.

Average Grains of Sulphate of Alumina.—The average amounts of sulphate of alumina per gallon of filtered water were obtained in each case by multiplying the average amount for each run by the total quantity of applied water on that run, and dividing the sum of these products by the total quantity of applied water. The average amounts per gallon of net filtered water were obtained by dividing the respective amounts per gallon of applied water by the percentages which the net filtered water were of the applied water.

Average Bacterial Efficiencies.—These results were obtained in the same manner as were the average amounts of sulphate of alumina used per gallon of applied water.

Table No. 6.

In this table are given summaries of the leading results obtained from the entire investigation and from certain portions thereof.

Summary No. 1 includes the data obtained during the entire investigation (excluding those runs not included in averages).

Summary No. 2 includes all the data given in Summary No. 1, except those obtained during the periods when the operations were under conditions prescribed by the Water Company in regard to rates of filtration and amounts of sulphate of alumina applied (Periods 14, 15 and 16).

Summary No. 3 includes all the data used in Summary No. 2 except those obtained during Period No. 1, when the operations of the Warren System were under protest of the Cumberland Manufacturing Company, but were continued at the request of the Water Company.

Summary No. 4 includes the data from all the periods when the Warren, Jewell and Western Pressure systems were in service, except those when the conditions of operation were prescribed as noted above.

Summary No. 5 includes those periods when all of the systems were in operation, except Periods 14, 15 and 16.

In this table the same expressions which have been used throughout are employed, and reference is made to the explanation of Table No. 5 of Chapter VIII, where the exact significance of the several expressions is explained.

The data presented and the methods of computation employed are as follows:

The periods of service and of wash are expressed in percentages of the period of operation.

The quantities of water used for washing, the quantities of filtered water wasted, the quantities of unfiltered water wasted, and the quantities of effluent are, respectively, expressed in percentages which they were of the corresponding quantities of water applied to the respective systems. It is to be noted that in all cases in this table the quantity of filtered water (effluent) is the difference between the applied water and the waste water, and not the quantity measured by the meter.

Average actual rates are given, the rates in cubic feet per minute being obtained by dividing the total quantity of effluent by the total period of service. The rates in million gallons per acre per twenty-four hours were obtained by the usual method of transference from comparative tables.

The average net rates were obtained in the same manner as the actual rates, except that the net filtered water and net period of operation were used.

The average amounts of sulphate of alumina per gallon of applied water were obtained in each case by multiplying the average amounts per run by the quantity of applied water on that run, and dividing the sum of the products by the total quantity of applied water. The amounts per gallon of net filtered water were obtained by dividing the amounts per gallon of applied water by the percentages which the net filtered water was of the applied water.

The average bacterial efficiencies were calculated in the usual manner of obtaining efficiencies, using for average numbers of bacteria results obtained in the same manner as the average amounts of sulphate of alumina.

Table No. 1.

SUMMARY BY DAYS OF THE APPEARANCE OF THE EFFLUENTS OF THE RESPECTIVE SYSTEMS,

Expressed in Degrees of Clearness.

Day of Month.		1	2	3	4	5	6	7	8	9	10	11	12	13	14	15	16	17	18	19	20	21	22	23	24	25	26	27	28	29	30	31
1895 October	Warren																		1	1		1	2	2	2	2	1		1		1	
	Jewell																		1	1		1	1	2	3	2	1		2		2	2
	Western Gravity																															
	Western Pressure																															
November	Warren	1	1					1																			2	4		3		
	Jewell	2	2					1					1		1						1		1				1	3		1		
	Western Gravity																															
	Western Pressure																															
December	Warren		1	4	4		3			2		1		3	4		3	4	4		3							4			4	
	Jewell		3	1	1		1			1	7	2		1	2		2	2	2		1							2			2	
	Western Gravity																											2			2	
	Western Pressure																											2			2	
1896 January	Warren		5	5	3		4		2	2	2	3			2	2					2		2					2	2	3		
	Jewell		4	5	4					2	2	3			3	3					2		2					2	4	5		
	Western Gravity		1	1	3		1		2	2	2	1			1	2					1		2					1	4			
	Western Pressure		1	1	1		1		1	2	2	1			1	1					1		2					1	3			
February	Warren	1		2	2	2	2	1	2		2			3	4	3		2	2	2	2	2	2		2	2	1	2	1	2		
	Jewell					3	4	2	4		3	2	5	2	2	3		4	4	2	2	2	5		2	3	3	2	3	2		
	Western Gravity	2		1	2	2	2	3			1	1	1	2		3		1		2		2			1		1		1	1		
	Western Pressure	1		1	1	3	3	3			1	2	1	2		2		2		5		2			2		1		3	3		
March	Warren		2	2	3	2	2	1		2	2	2	2	3	2		3	1	1	2	2	2		2	3	5	3	2	2	2	3	3
	Jewell		2	3	3	2	2	2		1	1	1	1	2	1		2	1	1	2	2	3		4	3	2	3	2	2	2	3	3
	Western Gravity		2		2		1	1		1		2		1	1		1		2	2	4											
	Western Pressure		2		2		2	2		1	2	2		1	1		1	2	2	2	3			4	4	4	2	2	2	2	4	3
April	Warren	3	3	3	2		2	2	2	2	2	1									2	2	3	2	2	2		3	2	2	2	
	Jewell	3	3	3	2		2	2	2	2	2	1		1	1	1	2	1	1		1	2	1	1	1	2		2	2	2	1	
	Western Gravity																															
	Western Pressure	5	4	5	2		2	2																								
May	Warren	2	2		2	2	2	2	2	2		2	2	2	1	1	2		1	2	2	2	1	1		2	2	1	2	2	2	
	Jewell	2	1		2	1	2	2	2	2		1	1	1	1	1	2		1	2	1	1	2			1	2	1	2	4	1	
	Western Gravity																															
	Western Pressure								2	2		4	2	3	2	2	1		2	3	2	2	1	1		1	2	2	2	5	2	
June	Warren	2	2	2	2	2	1			2	1	2	2	2		2	1	1	2	1	2		1	2	2						2	
	Jewell		4	2	2	2	1			2	1	2	1	1		2	1		1	1	1		2	1	2	2	1	1		1	2	
	Western Gravity																															
	Western Pressure	2	3	2	2	3	3			2	2	2	2	2		2	2	2	2	2	2				2	2	2	2		2	3	
July	Warren	1	3	2			2	2	2	4	2	2		2	2	2	2	2	2		2	2	2	5	5	4		3	2	2	2	2
	Jewell	2	3	1			1	1	1	1	1	2		2	2	2	2	2	2		2	1	2	2	3	2		2	2	2		
	Western Gravity		3	2							2	2							2	2					4	4						2
	Western Pressure	3					3	3	2	2				2	2	2	2				2	2	3	3				2	2	2		

TABLE No. 2.

DAILY RESULTS OF THE DETERMINATION OF ORGANIC MATTER IN THE OHIO RIVER WATER, EXPRESSED IN PARTS PER MILLION OF NITROGEN AS ALBUMINOID AMMONIA, AND OF OXYGEN CONSUMED, RESPECTIVELY, TOGETHER WITH THE PERCENTAGES OF REMOVAL OF ORGANIC MATTER BY THE RESPECTIVE SYSTEMS OF PURIFICATION.

Date.	Nitrogen as Albuminoid Ammonia in River Water		Percentage Removal by the Respective Systems of Organic Matter Expressed as Nitrogen in the Form of Albuminoid Ammonia.				Total Oxygen Consumed in River Water.	Percentage Removal by the Respective Systems of Organic Matter Expressed as Oxygen Consumed.			
	Total.	Percentage which was in Suspension	Warren.	Jewell.	Western Gravity.	Western Pressure.		Warren.	Jewell.	Western Gravity.	Western Pressure.
1895										......	......
Oct. 18	.356	30	66	59	......	......	3.2	37	28	......	......
" 19	.322	38	53	55	......	......	3.2	31	31	......	......
" 20	......	......	......	......	......	......	......	......	......	......	......
" 21	.236	41	34	42	......	......	2.9	21	31	......	......
" 22	.288	53	46	41	......	......	2.7	22	11	......	......
" 23	.244	42	27	35	......	......	2.6	11	11	......	......
" 24	.212	37	23	7	......	......	2.3	35	30	......	......
" 25	.290	53	32	52	......	......	2.6	35	46	......	......
" 26	.316	55	45	49	......	......	2.4	37	33	......	......
" 27	......	......	......	......	......	......	......	......	......	......	......
" 28	.216	38	39	35	......	......	2.1	29	24	......	......
" 29	......	......	......	......	......	......	......	......	......	......	......
" 30	.222	34	40	36	......	......	2.2	41	41	......	......
" 31	.198	31	......	31	......	......	1.9	......	26	......	......
Nov. 1	.252	46	54	62	......	......	2.3	48	43	......	......
" 2	.204	33	43	37	......	......	1.9	26	21	......	......
" 3	......	......	......	......	......	......	......	......	......	......	......
" 4	......	......	......	......	......	......	......	......	......	......	......
" 5	......	......	......	......	......	......	......	......	......	......	......
" 6	......	......	......	......	......	......	......	......	......	......	......
" 7	.206	31	43	37	......	......	2.1	43	47	......	......
" 8	......	......	......	......	......	......	......	......	......	......	......
" 9	.202	24	......	......	......	......	2.0	......	......	......	......
" 10	......	......	......	......	......	......	......	......	......	......	......
" 11	......	......	......	......	......	......	......	......	......	......	......
" 12	.154	12	......	22	......	......	1.8	......	11	......	......
" 13	......	......	......	......	......	......	......	......	......	......	......
" 14	......	......	......	......	......	......	2.1	......	14	......	......
" 15	......	......	......	......	......	......	......	......	......	......	......
" 16	......	......	......	......	......	......	......	......	......	......	......
" 17	......	......	......	......	......	......	......	......	......	......	......
" 18	......	......	......	......	......	......	......	......	......	......	......
" 19	......	......	......	......	......	......	......	......	......	......	......
" 20	.212	28	......	18	......	......	2.1	......	19	......	......
" 21	......	......	......	......	......	......	......	......	......	......	......
" 22	.220	18	......	35	......	......	2.2	......	27	......	......
" 23	.244	26	......	......	......	......	2.4	......	......	......	......
" 24	......	......	......	......	......	......	......	......	......	......	......
" 25	.234	23	......	......	......	......	2.8	......	......	......	......
" 26	.246	21	47	40	......	......	2.8	50	43	......	......
" 27	.232	11	45	26	......	......	2.7	41	15	......	......
" 28	......	......	......	......	......	......	......	......	......	......	......
" 29	.200	36	43	43	......	......	2.5	28	24	......	......
" 30	......	......	......	......	......	......	......	......	......	......	......
Dec. 1	......	......	......	......	......	......	......	......	......	......	......
" 2	.216	12	35	36	......	......	2.6	31	15	......	......
" 3	.230	17	13	43	......	......	2.8	18	25	......	......
" 4	.216	17	42	44	......	......	2.6	23	31	......	......
" 5	......	......	......	......	......	......	......	......	......	......	......
" 6	.246	24	48	59	......	......	2.8	43	50	......	......
" 7	......	......	......	......	......	......	......	......	......	......	......
" 8	......	......	......	......	......	......	......	......	......	......	......
" 9	.234	46	63	67	......	......	3.0	40	40	......	......
" 10	.184	39	56	42	......	......	3.0	37	20	......	......
" 11	.192	40	65	42	......	......	3.1	42	42	......	......
" 12	......	......	......	......	......	......	......	......	......	......	......
" 13	.158	24	50	48	......	......	3.2	37	41	......	......

TABLE NO. 2.—*Continued.*

Date.	Nitrogen as Albuminoid Ammonia in River Water.		Percentage Removal by the Respective Systems of Organic Matter Expressed as Nitrogen in the Form of Albuminoid Ammonia.				Total Oxygen Consumed in River Water.	Percentage Removal by the Respective Systems of Organic Matter Expressed as Oxygen Consumed.			
	Total.	Percentage which was in Suspension	Warren.	Jewell.	Western Gravity.	Western Pressure.		Warren.	Jewell.	Western Gravity.	Western Pressure.
1895											
Dec. 14	.174	36	41	37	....	....	3.5	28	34	....	....
" 15	....	....	....	....	....	....	....	....	....	....	....
" 16	.188	17	40	24	....	....	3.9	51	44	....	....
" 17	.210	22	37	37	....	....	4.0	48	35	....	....
" 18	.192	10	....	....	....	....	3.9	31	41	....	....
" 19	....	....	....	....	....	....	....	....	....	....	....
" 20	.228	19	53	60	....	....	4.2	48	50	....	....
" 21	....	....	....	....	....	....	....	....	....	....	....
" 22	....	....	....	....	....	....	....	....	....	....	....
" 23	....	....	....	....	....	....	....	....	....	....	....
" 24	....	....	....	....	....	....	....	....	....	....	....
" 25	....	....	....	....	....	....	....	....	....	....	....
" 26	....	....	....	....	....	....	....	....	....	....	....
" 28	....	....	....	....	....	....	....	....	....	....	....
" 29	....	....	....	....	....	....	....	....	....	....	....
Av. 27–30	.388	61	75	79	79	79	6.0	70	77	77	73
Dec. 31	....	....	....	....	....	....	....	....	....	....	....
1896											
Jan. 1	....	....	....	....	....	....	....	....	....	....	....
" 2	1.187	83	89	89	93	92	12.3	80	84	89	86
" 3	1.187	83	89	89	93	92	11.8	88	84	87	90
" 4	....	....	....	....	....	....	9.0	87	79	89	86
" 5	....	....	....	....	....	....	....	....	....	....	....
Av. 4 & 6	.653	76	90	82	88	88	7.8	83	....	77	82
Jan. 7	....	....	....	....	....	....	....	....	....	....	....
							6.5	83	....	74	74
Av. 8, 9, 10	.423	48	74	63	73	72	5.4	65	67	65	67
							5.8	83	72	69	72
Jan. 11	.261	45	72	63	65	61	5.3	81	72	75	74
" 12	....	....	....	....	....	....	....	....	....	....	....
" 13	....	....	....	....	....	....	....	....	....	....	....
Av. 14, 15	.209	12	86	62	62	54	4.1	61	76	76	66
							4.1	73	63	61	58
Jan. 16	....	....	....	....	....	....	....	....	....	....	....
" 17	....	....	....	....	....	....	....	....	....	....	....
" 18	....	....	....	....	....	....	....	....	....	....	....
" 19	....	....	....	....	....	....	....	....	....	....	....
" 20	....	....	....	....	....	....	3.1	61	52	52	55
" 21	....	....	....	....	....	....	....	....	....	....	....
" 22	.135	7	56	50	47	47	3.1	61	55	45	52
" 23	....	....	....	....	....	....	....	....	....	....	....
" 24	....	....	....	....	....	....	....	....	....	....	....
" 25	....	....	....	....	....	....	....	....	....	....	....
" 26	....	....	....	....	....	....	....	....	....	....	....
Av. 27, 28	.369	70	81	70	74	76	5.5	78	69	78	75
							6.6	77	64	68	74
Jan. 29	.439	84	83	73	....	....	7.1	82	70	....	....
" 30	....	....	....	....	....	....	....	....	....	....	....
" 31	....	....	....	....	....	....	....	....	....	....	....
Feb. 1	.365	77	90	....	85	89	6.6	85	....	82	80
" 2	....	....	....	....	....	....	....	....	....	....	....
" 3	.245	67	83	....	80	79	4.7	83	....	83	83
" 4	.279	70	85	....	82	82	5.7	84	....	81	81
" 5	.439	81	86	84	85	84	8.4	82	86	83	83
" 6	.417	81	88	86	83	82	8.2	88	84	84	80
" 7	.593	87	93	93	90	90	11.4	91	90	87	87
" 8	.639	83	95	89	....	....	13.0	92	85	....	....
" 9	....	....	....	....	....	....	....	....	....	....	....
" 10	.577	88	94	92	94	93	12.8	91	88	91	91
" 11	.437	79	....	90	92	90	8.9	....	84	88	87
" 12	.391	76	....	79	92	88	9.1	....	74	91	88
" 13	.215	60	83	80	76	78	4.6	78	70	74	78
" 14	.311	78	89	84	....	....	7.6	85	79	....	....
" 15	.353	78	91	84	87	85	8.7	87	84	87	85

TABLE NO. 2.—*Continued.*

Date.	Nitrogen as Albuminoid Ammonia in River Water.		Percentage Removal by the Respective Systems of Organic Matter Expressed as Nitrogen in the Form of Albuminoid Ammonia.				Total Oxygen Consumed in River Water.	Percentage Removal by the Respective Systems of Organic Matter Expressed as Oxygen Consumed.			
	Total.	Percentage which was in Suspension	Warren.	Jewell.	Western Gravity.	Western Pressure.		Warren.	Jewell.	Western Gravity.	Western Pressure.
1896											
Feb. 16	…	…	…	…	…	…	…	…	…	…	…
" 17	.292	75	86	82	84	84	7.5	88	83	88	87
" 18	.366	91	95	90	…	…	9.1	90	85	…	…
" 19	.484	88	95	94	92	84	11.2	92	91	92	79
" 20	.232	72	84	86	…	…	6.3	86	89	…	…
" 21	.256	81	92	86	85	87	7.2	90	90	87	86
" 22	.288	76	87	82	…	…	6.0	87	80	…	…
" 23	…	…	…	…	…	…	…	…	…	…	…
" 24	.162	69	79	74	78	78	4.3	84	74	79	72
" 25	.152	64	71	67	…	…	3.8	82	63	…	…
" 26	.146	71	82	73	78	75	3.3	79	64	76	76
" 27	.200	70	79	78	…	…	4.5	82	82	…	…
" 28	.102	35	57	51	{ 62	{ 68	3.0	70	57	{ 69	{ 62 .
" 29	.088	43	73	55			2.8	64	54		
Mar. 1	…	…	…	…	…	…	…	…	…	…	…
" 2	.084	50	64	50	52	52	2.6	73	42	65	62
" 3	.118	53	68	68	…	…	3.2	81	63	…	…
" 4	.088	57	61	50	64	66	2.5	72	44	60	64
" 5	.100	48	74	60	…	…	2.1	62	52	…	…
" 6	.184	36	76	45	{ 66	{ 68	1.8	72	56	{ 63	{ 58
" 7	.102	46	78	71			2.5	76	68		
" 8	…	…	…	…	…	…	…	…	…	…	…
" 9	.076	53	68	68	63	66	2.3	61	70	65	70
" 10	.090	51	62	69	…	{ 48	2.2	73	68	…	{ 56
" 11	.096	46	73	65	65		1.9	79	63	63	
" 12	.116	38	74	69	…		2.1	71	62	…	
" 13	.094	49	68	64	{ 64	{ 62	2.1	67	52	{ 59	{ 50
" 14	.108	54	65	67			2.3	65	65		
" 15	…	…	…	…	…	…	…	…	…	…	…
" 16	.110	42	75	60	53	67	2.5	72	60	60	64
" 17	.130	58	77	68	…		2.9	72	62	…	
" 18	.132	50	74	74	{ 72	{ 58	3.0	73	73	{ 75	{ 67
" 19	.238	73	79	77			5.0	82	80		
" 20	.700	90	95	93	95	{ 96	14.2	94	89	91	{ 93'
" 21	1.046	94	97	95	…		17.8	93	93	…	
" 22	…	…	…	…	…	…	…	…	…	…	…
" 23	.580	86	94	92	…	88	13.2	94	92	…	89
" 24	.476	86	92	92	…	92	9.3	92	90	…	90
" 25	.414	86	90	93	…	91	9.1	84	90	…	88
" 26	.462	85	90	89	…	91	8.9	90	89	…	92
" 27	.344	78	87	83	…	86	7.5	89	84	…	88
" 28	.454	84	88	90	…	89	8.3	89	90	…	89
" 29	.374	79	85	82	…	86	7.4	88	88	…	88
" 30	.852	87	95	93	…	92	12.0	93	92	…	92
" 31	.932	90	95	93	…	92	13.9	94	93	…	92
April 1	1.032	91	96	96	…	95	15.8	92	93	…	92
" 2	.960	93	97	96	…	95	15.6	96	95	…	92
" 3	1.080	93	96	96	…	95	18.4	96	96	…	95
" 4	.620	84	94	94	…	94	13.0	95	95	…	95
" 5	…	…	…	…	…	…	…	…	…	…	…
" 6	.500	83	90	90	…	90	8.6	93	93	…	93
" 7	.380	81	90	90	…	90	7.5	92	93	…	92
" 8	.370	75	85	85	…	…	6.7	88	88	…	…
" 9	.380	79	88	88	…	…	7.7	90	90	…	…
" 10	.312	74	85	82	…	…	6.3	86	84	…	…
" 11	.286	72	78	82	…	…	6.5	83	86	…	…
" 12	…	…	…	…	…	…	…	…	…	…	…
" 13	.270	68	…	74	…	…	5.4	…	80	…	…
" 14	.166	53	…	66	…	…	3.5	…	69	…	…
" 15	.208	62	…	69	…	…	4.9	…	78	…	…
" 16	.164	50	…	66	…	…	3.6	…	69	…	…
" 17	.172	51	…	63	…	…	4.0	…	72	…	…
" 18	.206	52	…	64	…	…	3.3	…	73	…	…
" 19	…	…	…	…	…	…	…	…	…	…	…

TABLE No. 2.—*Continued.*

Date.	Nitrogen as Albuminoid Ammonia in River Water.		Percentage Removal by the Respective Systems of Organic Matter Expressed as Nitrogen in the Form of Albuminoid Ammonia.				Total Oxygen Consumed in River Water.	Percentage Removal by the Respective Systems of Organic Matter Expressed as Oxygen Consumed.			
	Total.	Percentage which was in Suspension	Warren.	Jewell.	Western Gravity.	Western Pressure.		Warren.	Jewell.	Western Gravity.	Western Pressure
1896											
April 20	.198	59	71	72	....	....	3.7	81	84	....	......
" 21	.188	59	66	66	....	....	3.4	79	82	....	......
" 22	.160	56	61	74	....	....	3.1	77	81	....	......
" 23	.138	51	59	65	....	....	2.3	65	74	....	......
" 24	.146	47	63	73	....	....	2.8	71	75	....	......
" 25	.152	53	54	58	....	....	2.3	70	74	....	......
" 26	....	....	....	....	....	....	....	....	....	....	......
" 27	.172	51	55	68	....	....	3.1	68	74	....	......
" 28	.172	49	63	67	....	....	3.0	70	73	....	......
" 29	.170	59	64	68	....	....	2.9	72	72	....	......
" 30	.160	55	64	58	....	....	2.4	67	67	....	......
May 1	.174	50	65	60	....	....	3.1	74	71	....	......
" 2	.168	48	67	68	....	....	2.9	69	72	....	......
" 3	....	....	....	....	....	....	....	....	....	....	......
" 4	.188	51	69	67	....	....	3.6	75	72	....	......
" 5	.196	51	65	71	....	....	3.6	69	72	....	......
" 6	.188	54	68	69	....	....	3.4	68	68	....	......
" 7	.164	41	55	61	....	....	3.5	54	63	....	......
" 8	.206	52	62	54	....	61	4.3	65	60	....	63
" 9	.194	58	73	74	....	....	4.1	68	71	....	......
" 10	....	....	....	....	....	....	....	....	....	....	......
" 11	.286	66	84	81	....	78	4.7	83	79	....	68
" 12	.226	65	72	71	....	73	3.9	72	72	....	72
" 13	.202	59	70	71	....	63	3.5	74	74	....	66
" 14	.200	65	70	76	....	66	3.7	73	78	....	62
" 15	.182	60	76	75	....	69	3.6	75	75	....	67
" 16	.190	60	69	71	....	73	4.0	68	73	....	75
" 17	....	....	....	....	....	....	....	....	....	....	......
" 18	.174	43	57	55	....	52	3.3	58	....	....	52
" 19	.158	43	59	56	....	48	3.1	61	61	....	35
" 20	.228	62	73	73	....	68	4.0	68	68	....	63
" 21	.214	58	71	68	....	65	3.8	71	66	....	55
" 22	.228	61	70	66	....	....	4.9	75	71	....	......
" 23	....	....	....	....	....	65*	....	....	....	....	68*
" 24	....	....	....	....	....	....	....	....	....	....	......
" 25	.166	51	53	58	....	....	2.7	52	56	....	......
" 26	.158	52	58	58	....	}	2.9	59	59	....	}
" 27	.186	58	69	66	....	} 75	3.3	67	67	....	} 73
" 28	.566	79	86	85	....	}	8.4	83	83	....	}
" 29	.602	78	87	87	....	83	9.4	83	83	....	81
" 30	.502	76	86	88	....	....	7.8	85	87	....	......
" 31	....	....	....	....	....	....	....	....	....	....	......
June 1	.446	76	84	....	....	86†	7.0	83	....	....	86†
" 2	.576	77	89	87	....	85	8.0	88	86	....	84
" 3	.364	67	86	85	....	83	5.8	84	84	....	84
" 4	.324	69	80	81	....	81	5.2	83	83	....	83
" 5	.274	54	74	75	....	} 74	4.2	76	81	....	} 67
" 6	.192	48	73	73	....	}	3.0	70	67	....	}
" 7	....	....	....	....	....	....	....	....	....	....	......
" 8	....	....	....	....	....	....	....	....	....	....	......
" 9	.404	80	83	85	....	}	6.8	81	84	....	}
" 10	.340	72	81	82	....	} 82	6.1	80	84	....	} 82
" 11	.282	68	75	77	....	}	4.2	71	76	....	}
" 12	.250	65	70	75	....	....	4.1	68	76	....	......
" 13	.232	63	72	74	....	76‡	4.2	67	74	....	76‡
" 14	....	....	....	....	....	....	....	....	....	....	......
" 15	.364	74	79	80	....	....	5.6	75	77	....	......
" 16	.248	64	69	75	....		4.2	67	74	....	
" 17	.260	65	69	....	....	71§	4.6	65	....	....	73§
" 18	.288	67	72	76	....		5.0	64	78	....	
" 19	.392	72	83	81	....	} 81	5.9	78	75	....	} 73
" 20	.268	66	74	75	....	}	4.3	60	65	....	}

* Average for 22, 23, and 25. † Average May 30 and June 1. ‡ Average 12, 13, and 15.
§ Average 16, 17, and 18.

TABLE No. 2.—*Concluded.*

Date.	Nitrogen as Albuminoid Ammonia in River Water. Total.	Nitrogen as Albuminoid Ammonia in River Water. Percentage which was in Suspension	Percentage Removal by the Respective Systems of Organic Matter Expressed as Nitrogen in the Form of Albuminoid Ammonia. Warren.	Jewell.	Western Gravity.	Western Pressure.	Total Oxygen Consumed in River Water.	Percentage Removal by the Respective Systems of Organic Matter Expressed as Oxygen Consumed. Warren.	Jewell.	Western Gravity.	Western Pressure
1896											
June 21	....	....	....	....	....	....	....	....	....	....	....
" 22	.222	53	67	67	....	....	4.0	63	67	....	....
" 23	.224	55	65	62	....	....	3.7	70	65	....	....
" 24	.460	77	80	79	....	....	5.1	73	71	....	....
" 25	.326	65	....	72	....	{80	6.0	....	70	....	{73
" 26	.304	62	....	78	....		5.1	....	71	....	
" 27	.374	67	....	80	....	{79	5.5	....	78	....	{80
" 28	....	....	....	....	....		....	....	....	....	
" 29	.442	71	....	84	....		7.4	....	86	....	
" 30	.356	72	79	82	....	....	5.6	73	80	....	....
July 1	.628	82	88	91	....	86*	10.7	88	91	....	83*
" 2	.964	89	92	93	92	....	15.0	91	91	90	....
" 3	.640	83	89	90	89	....	12.1	89	90	90	....
" 4	....	....	....	....	....	....	....	....	....	....	....
" 5	....	....	....	....	....	....	....	....	....	....	....
" 6	.258	57	69	74	....	{78	4.8	73	81	....	{76
" 7	.398	74	83	83	....		7.0	84	84	....	
" 8	.432	75	83	{85	....	{80	6.8	82	{87	....	{87
" 9	.378	72	80		....		6.6	83		....	
" 10	.346	63	79	81	{76	....	5.8	79	88	{76	....
" 11	.224	52	73	73		....	4.4	77	82		....
" 12	....	....	....	....	....	....	....	....	....	....	....
" 13	.382	72	80	84	....	{81	7.0	83	87	....	{85
" 14	.310	66	77	82	....		6.6	82	86	....	
" 15	.420	70	81	84	....	{84	8.3	84	89	....	{86
" 16	.378	76	84	84	....		7.0	86	87	....	
" 17	.394	79	{87	{87	{86	....	7.0	{85	{90	{85	....
" 18	.504	81				....	8.7				....
" 19	....	....	....	....	....	....	....	....	....	....	....
" 20	.318	70	81	84	....	{85	6.5	82	86	....	{85
" 21	.494	78	85	87	....		7.7	84	87	....	
" 22	.824	89	90	92	....	{93	14.9	90	92	....	{93
" 23	1.360	90	91	94	....		24.8	93	95	....	
" 24	2.400	95	96	97	{95	....	35.8	96	97	{93	....
" 25	1.320	91	93	96		....	22.6	92	95		....
" 26	....	....	....	....	....	....	....	....	....	....	....
" 27	1.200	89	93	95	....	{93	21.7	93	95	....	{92
" 28	1.120	89	94	94	....		17.8	92	93	....	
" 29	.880	85	92	92	....		19.7	91	91	....	
" 30	1.200	90	{91	....	....	....	23.4	{93	....	....	....
" 31	.470	75		....	84	....	13.6		....	90	....

* Average June 30, July 1.

Table No. 3.

AVERAGE DAILY NUMBER OF BACTERIA PER CUBIC CENTIMETER, IN THE OHIO RIVER WATER AND IN THE SEVERAL EFFLUENTS, TOGETHER WITH THE AVERAGE BACTERIAL EFFICIENCY OF THE RESPECTIVE SYSTEMS OF PURIFICATION.

Date.	Bacteria per Cubic Centimeter.					Bacterial Efficiency of the Respective Systems.			
	River Water.	Effluents of the Respective Systems.							
		Warren.	Jewell.	Western Gravity.	Western Pressure.	Warren.	Jewell.	Western Gravity.	Western Pressure.
1895									
Oct. 21	148	40	55	....	....	73.0	62.8	....	....
" 22	158	59	53	....	....	62.7	66.5	....	....
" 23	127	51	56	....	....	60.0	55.9	....	....
" 24	118	50	59	....	....	57.6	50.0	....	....
" 25	137	47	29	....	....	65.7	78.8	....	....
" 26	142	43	18	....	....	69.7	87.3	....	....
" 27	....	....	....	....	....	....	....	....	....
" 28	114	37	40	....	....	67.5	64.8	....	....
" 29	128	27	37	....	....	78.9	71.1	....	....
" 30	106	23	3	....	....	78.3	97.2	....	....
" 31	183	9	15	....	....	95.1	91.8	....	....
Nov. 1	110	13	17	....	....	88.2	84.5	....	....
" 2	125	23	26	....	....	81.6	79.2	....	....
" 3	....	....	....	....	....	....	....	....	....
" 4	352	40	....	....	....	88.6	....	....	....
" 5	126	13	....	....	....	89.7	....	....	....
" 6	228	18	....	....	....	92.1	....	....	....
" 7	135	66	203	....	....	51.1	− 33.5	....	....
" 8	187	83	188	....	....	55.6	− 0.5	....	....
" 9	274	52	138	....	....	81.0	49.6	....	....
" 10	....	....	....	....	....	....	....	....	....
" 11	637	134	639	....	....	79.0	0	....	....
" 12	888	....	438	....	....	....	51.0	....	....
" 13	292	....	114	....	....	....	61.0	....	....
" 14	112	....	123	....	....	....	− 8.9	....	....
" 15	180	....	82	....	....	....	54.4	....	....
" 16	223	....	125	....	....	....	43.9	....	....
" 17	....	....	....	....	....	....	....	....	....
" 18	166	....	165	....	....	....	0	....	....
" 19	184	....	243	....	....	....	− 24.3	....	....
" 20	190	....	154	....	....	....	18.9	....	....
" 21	74	....	85	....	....	....	− 12.9	....	....
" 22	99	....	63	....	....	....	36.4	....	....
" 23	192	....	143	....	....	....	25.5	....	....
" 24	....	....	....	....	....	....	....	....	....
" 25	5 600	630	400	....	....	88.7	92.9	....	....
" 26	3 400	385	540	....	....	88.7	84.1	....	....
" 27	2 300	531	934	....	....	76.9	59.4	....	....
" 28	....	....	....	....	....	....	....	....	....
" 29	5 200	836	812	....	....	83.9	84.4	....	....
" 30	6 500	819	615	....	....	87.4	90.5	....	....
Dec 1	....	....	....	....	....	....	....	....	....
" 2	6 800	917	360	....	....	86.5	94.7	....	....
" 3	10 200	592	362	....	....	94.2	96.5	....	....
" 4	6 800	396	331	....	....	94.2	95.1	....	....
" 5	4 900	297	245	....	....	93.9	95.0	....	....
" 6	9 900	504	241	....	....	94.9	97.6	....	....
" 7	9 900	372	421	....	....	96.2	95.7	....	....
" 8	....	....	....	....	....	....	....	....	....
" 9	8 200	288	166	....	....	96.5	98.0	....	....
" 10	7 200	295	223	....	....	95.9	96.9	....	....
" 11	2 900	190	201	....	....	93.4	93.1	....	....
" 12	2 800	182	149	....	....	93.5	94.7	....	....
" 13	2 200	122	126	....	....	94.5	94.3	....	....
" 14	2 400	172	134	....	....	92.8	94.4	....	....
" 15	....	....	....	....	....	....	....	....	....
" 16	1 900	147	143	....	....	92.3	92.5	....	....
" 17	2 000	135	123	....	....	92.2	93.8	....	....
" 18	2 200	221	131	....	....	90.0	94.0	....	....
" 19	2 000	159	70	....	....	92.1	96.5	....	....
" 20	3 200	359	100	....	....	88.8	96.9	....	....
" 21	2 200	254	113	....	....	88.5	94.9	....	....
" 22	....	....	....	....	....	....	....	....	....
" 23	3 700	173	69	456	201	95.3	98.1	87.7	94.6
" 24	3 400	76	77	452	155	97.8	97.7	86.7	95.4
" 25	....	....	....	....	....	....	....	....	....
" 26	5 200	114	221	483	411	97.9	95.8	90.9	92.2

TABLE NO. 3.—*Continued.*

Date.	Bacteria per Cubic Centimeter. River Water.	Effluents of the Respective Systems. Warren.	Jewell.	Western Gravity.	Western Pressure.	Bacterial Efficiency of the Respective Systems. Warren.	Jewell.	Western Gravity.	Western Pressure.
1895									
Dec. 27	12 000	779	410	501	358	93.5	96.6	95.8	97.0
" 28	35 700	1 169	813	947	897	76.7	97.7	97.3	97.5
" 29	....	....	....	....	....	....	....	....	....
" 30	12 000	328	311	529	409	97.3	97.4	95.6	96.6
" 31	13 000	375	233	253	268	97.1	98.2	98.1	97.9
1896									
Jan. 1	....	....	....	....	....	....	....	....	....
" 2	10 700	797	261	245	258	92.6	97.6	97.7	97.6
" 3	14 300	166	343	325	169	98.8	97.6	97.7	98.8
" 4	8 600	151	390	81	100	98.2	95.5	99.1	98.8
" 5	....	....	....	....	....	....	....	....	....
" 6	5 000	107	....	368	207	97.9	....	92.6	95.9
" 7	4 200	54	....	93	79	98.7	....	97.8	98.1
" 8	4 100	59	....	151	237	98.6	....	96.3	94.2
" 9	1 900	28	229	100	78	98.5	87.9	94.7	95.9
" 10	1 800	44	202	108	151	94.8	88.8	94.0	91.6
" 11	2 500	36	152	94	153	98.6	93.9	96.2	93.9
" 12	....	....	....	....	....	....	....	....	....
" 13	1 900	38	193	....	....	98.0	89.8	....	....
" 14	800	25	156	61	88	96.9	80.5	92.4	89.0
" 15	3 000	50	156	128	147	98.3	94.8	95.7	95.1
" 16	3 200	73	181	130	122	97.7	94.3	95.9	96.2
" 17	6 500	98	262	159	219	98.5	96.0	97.6	96.6
" 18	7 300	60	189	228	244	99.2	97.4	96.9	96.6
" 19	....	....	....	....	....	....	....	....	....
" 20	6 400	119	229	219	218	98.1	96.4	96.6	96.6
" 21	3 000	51	170	174	194	98.3	94.3	94.2	93.5
" 22	2 600	34	104	192	120	98.7	96.0	92.6	95.4
" 23	4 800	....	203	68	176	....	95.8	98.6	96.3
" 24	3 600	....	142	96	93	....	96.1	97.3	97.4
" 25	7 200	60	117	102	136	99.2	98.4	98.6	98.1
" 26	....	....	....	....	....	....	....	....	....
" 27	10 600	156	945	651	747	98.5	91.1	93.9	93.0
" 28	14 700	470	1 533	1 586	876	96.8	89.6	89.2	94.0
" 29	18 200	525	1 770	....	....	97.1	90.3	....	....
" 30	23 400	72	820	....	....	99.5	93.9	....	....
" 31	14 300	57	860	549	475	99.6	94.0	96.2	96.7
Feb. 1	21 300	56	....	194	188	99.7	....	99.1	99.1
" 2	....	....	....	....	....	....	....	....	....
" 3	62 200	197	....	639	544	99.7	....	99.0	99.1
" 4	55 000	1 535	....	737	815	97.2	....	98.7	98.5
" 5	71 000	583	643	548	686	99.2	99.1	99.2	99.0
" 6	30 800	220	1 563	805	1 461	99.3	94.9	97.4	95.3
" 7	55 000	362	639	1 200	967	99.3	98.8	97.8	98.2
" 8	29 800	365	1 395	669	714	98.8	95.3	97.8	97.6
" 9	....	....	....	....	....	....	....	....	....
" 10	14 400	279	740	371	527	98.1	94.9	97.4	96.3
" 11	19 800	....	1 020	490	380	....	94.9	97.5	98.1
" 12	28 000	....	1 701	427	362	....	93.9	98.5	98.7
" 13	14 800	430	549	453	409	97.1	96.9	96.9	97.2
" 14	11 900	589	848	340	216	95.1	92.9	97.1	98.2
" 15	10 800	139	763	950	850	98.7	92.9	91.2	92.1
" 16	....	....	....	....	....	....	....	....	....
" 17	21 800	107	1 079	789	638	99.5	95.1	96.4	97.1
" 18	14 400	80	1 581	647	710	99.4	89.1	95.5	95.1
" 19	20 700	145	919	467	547	99.3	95.6	97.7	97.4
" 20	17 400	210	341	291	532	98.8	98.0	98.3	96.9
" 21	10 700	76	318	189	169	99.3	97.0	98.2	98.4
" 22	20 000	206	647	....	....	99.0	97.8	....	....
" 23	....	....	....	....	....	....	....	....	....
" 24	15 000	73	821	236	497	99.5	94.5	98.4	96.7
" 25	16 200	71	1 451	1 012	951	99.6	91.0	93.8	94.1
" 26	25 200	202	1 941	654	574	99.2	92.3	97.4	97.7
" 27	4 100	65	768	476	676	98.4	81.3	88.4	83.5
" 28	4 500	156	1 575	353	533	96.5	65.0	92.2	88.2
" 29	14 800	178	1 601	651	903	98.8	89.2	95.6	93.9
Mar. 1	....	....	....	....	....	....	....	....	....
" 2	44 600	367	2 148	1 944	2 251	99.2	95.2	95.6	95.0
" 3	33 400	302	1 324	1 062	798	99.1	96.0	96.8	97.6
" 4	29 800	548	851	693	612	98.2	97.2	97.7	97.9
" 5	18 000	371	718	797	615	97.9	96.0	95.6	96.6
" 6	12 200	207	299	343	326	98.3	97.6	97.2	97.3
" 7	10 500	180	146	332	470	98.3	98.6	96.8	95.5

TABLE No. 3.—*Continued.*

Date.	Bacteria per Cubic Centimeter. River Water.	Effluents of the Respective Systems. Warren.	Jewell.	Western Gravity.	Western Pressure.	Bacterial Efficiency of the Respective Systems. Warren.	Jewell.	Western Gravity.	Western Pressure.
1896 Mar. 8	....	....	....	....	....	....	....	....	....
" 9	14 000	190	133	409	239	98.6	99.0	97.1	98.3
" 10	11 500	301	137	200	221	97.4	98.8	98.3	98.1
" 11	7 700	223	121	180	169	97.1	98.4	97.7	97.8
" 12	11 300	156	251	162	372	98.6	97.8	98.6	96.7
" 13	11 000	293	547	233	162	97.3	95.0	97.9	98.5
" 14	12 100	161	203	140	159	98.7	98.3	98.8	98.7
" 15	....	....	....	....	....	....	....	....	....
" 16	16 600	76	172	252	349	99.5	99.0	98.5	97.9
" 17	16 300	31	86	302	370	99.8	99.5	98.1	97.7
" 18	19 700	49	35	520	441	99.8	99.8	97.4	97.8
" 19	34 400	122	710	606	800	99.6	97.9	98.2	97.7
" 20	46 700	137	850	733	550	99.7	98.2	98.4	98.8
" 21	57 200	260	928	....	1 087	99.5	98.4	....	98.1
" 22	....	....	....	....	....	....	....	....	....
" 23	30 500	164	844	....	935	99.5	97.2	....	96.9
" 24	37 300	64	321	....	368	99.8	99.1	....	99.0
" 25	46 000	103	182	....	404	99.8	99.6	....	99.1
" 26	47 900	136	531	....	256	99.7	98.9	....	99.5
" 27	31 900	141	466	....	294	99.6	98.5	....	99.1
" 28	34 100	111	164	....	537	99.7	99.5	....	98.4
" 29	49 200	123	379	....	2 221	99.8	99.2	....	95.5
" 30	25 700	125	679	....	1 712	99.5	97.4	....	93.3
" 31	26 700	369	845	....	1 628	98.6	96.8	....	93.9
April 1	39 600	263	638	....	1 023	99.3	98.4	....	97.4
" 2	27 500	155	223	....	755	99.4	99.2	....	97.3
" 3	31 000	82	201	....	940	99.7	99.3	....	97.0
" 4	27 000	116	71	....	185	99.6	99.7	....	99.3
" 5	....	....	....	....	....	....	....	....	....
" 6	18 700	34	31	....	91	99.8	99.8	....	99.5
" 7	18 500	40	64	....	76	99.8	99.7	....	99.6
" 8	13 800	105	129	....	....	99.2	99.1	....	....
" 9	21 000	118	164	....	....	99.4	99.2	....	....
" 10	7 300	42	40	....	....	99.4	96.5	....	....
" 11	13 000	25	41	....	....	99.8	99.7	....	....
" 12	....	....	....	....	....	....	....	....	....
" 13	9 600	....	81	....	....	....	99.2	....	....
" 14	7 500	....	28	....	....	....	99.6	....	....
" 15	3 700	....	20	....	....	....	99.5	....	....
" 16	1 700	....	11	....	....	....	99.7	....	....
" 17	3 000	....	33	....	....	....	98.9	....	....
" 18	5 900	....	100	....	....	....	98.3	....	....
" 19	....	....	....	....	....	....	....	....	....
" 20	4 800	34	6	....	....	99.3	99.9	....	....
" 21	4 000	82	126	....	....	98.0	99.7	....	....
" 22	5 500	166	16	....	....	97.0	99.7	....	....
" 23	4 400	110	23	....	....	97.5	99.5	....	....
" 24	7 700	348	46	....	....	95.5	99.4	....	....
" 25	8 300	309	48	....	....	96.3	99.4	....	....
" 26	....	....	....	....	....	....	....	....	....
" 27	6 500	401	62	....	....	93.8	99.0	....	....
" 28	6 100	605	160	....	....	90.1	97.4	....	....
" 29	7 100	138	64	....	....	98.1	99.1	....	....
" 30	4 100	94	42	....	....	97.7	99.0	....	....
May 1	5 400	104	61	....	....	98.1	98.9	....	....
" 2	7 100	157	78	....	....	97.8	98.9	....	....
" 3	....	....	....	....	....	....	....	....	....
" 4	7 000	55	52	....	....	99.2	99.3	....	....
" 5	6 000	57	45	....	....	99.1	99.2	....	....
" 6	5 000	87	48	....	....	98.3	99.0	....	....
" 7	5 200	76	34	....	145	98.5	99.3	....	97.2
" 8	4 000	50	17	....	201	98.8	99.6	....	95.0
" 9	5 900	49	39	....	227	99.2	99.3	....	96.2
" 10	....	....	....	....	....	....	....	....	....
" 11	7 300	44	32	....	232	99.4	99.6	....	96.8
" 12	5 900	61	16	....	176	99.0	99.7	....	97.0
" 13	3 600	12	10	....	153	99.7	99.7	....	95.8
" 14	6 500	37	37	....	167	99.4	99.4	....	97.4
" 15	6 400	25	27	....	111	99.6	99.6	....	98.3
" 16	7 300	10	17	....	117	99.9	99.8	....	98.4
" 17	....	....	....	....	....	....	....	....	....
" 18	6 600	120	75	....	701	98.2	98.9	....	89.4
" 19	4 300	81	93	....	324	98.1	97.8	....	92.5

TABLE No. 3.—*Concluded.*

Date.	River Water.	Bacteria per Cubic Centimeter. Effluents of the Respective Systems				Bacterial Efficiency of the Respective Systems.			
		Warren.	Jewell.	Western Gravity.	Western Pressure.	Warren.	Jewell.	Western Gravity.	Western Pressure.
1896									
May 20	4 800	66	78	...	184	98.6	98.4	...	96.2
" 21	6 100	70	73	...	124	98.9	98.8	...	98.0
" 22	5 100	50	70	...	60	99.0	98.6	...	98.8
" 23	6 100	...	28	...	59	...	99.5	...	99.0
" 24	...	...	...	...	...	...	...	...	...
" 25	1 900	41	59	...	94	97.8	96.9	...	95.1
" 26	1 800	39	50	...	82	97.8	97.2	...	95.4
" 27	4 100	130	84	...	119	96.8	98.0	...	97.1
" 28	23 400	102	194	...	261	99.6	99.2	...	98.9
" 29	26 100	179	245	...	150	99.3	99.1	...	99.4
" 30	19 700	92	322	...	57	99.5	98.4	...	99.7
" 31	...	...	...	...	...	...	...	...	...
June 1	18 800	61	...	...	165	99.7	...	...	99.1
" 2	15 500	101	208	...	93	99.3	98.7	...	99.4
" 3	13 800	45	53	...	60	99.7	99.6	...	99.6
" 4	8 500	36	45	...	93	99.6	99.5	...	98.9
" 5	6 400	28	28	...	36	99.6	99.6	...	99.4
" 6	4 900	25	18	...	44	99.5	99.6	...	99.1
" 7	...	...	...	...	...	...	...	...	...
" 8	...	...	...	...	...	...	...	...	...
" 9	11 300	165	104	...	121	98.5	99.2	...	98.9
" 10	10 700	49	11	...	54	99.5	99.9	...	99.5
" 11	6 600	42	10	...	11	99.4	99.8	...	99.8
" 12	6 100	40	11	...	14	99.3	99.8	...	99.8
" 13	13 400	188	40	...	93	98.6	99.7	...	99.3
" 14	...	...	...	...	...	...	...	...	...
" 15	13 500	132	16	...	27	99.0	99.9	...	99.8
" 16	8 400	36	7	...	33	99.6	99.9	...	99.6
" 17	11 000	74	...	...	30	99.3	...	...	99.7
" 18	10 600	81	20	...	161	99.2	99.8	...	98.5
" 19	18 000	73	53	...	30	99.6	99.7	...	99.8
" 20	10 500	86	61	...	73	99.2	99.2	...	99.3
" 21	...	...	...	...	...	...	...	...	...
" 22	7 700	80	86	...	56	98.9	98.9	...	99.3
" 23	8 000	141	118	...	...	98.2	98.5	...	...
" 24	8 300	234	453	...	218	97.2	94.5	...	97.4
" 25	7 500	52	550	...	305	99.3	92.7	...	95.9
" 26	6 000	...	37	...	51	...	99.4	...	99.2
" 27	10 800	...	107	...	248	...	99.0	...	97.7
" 28	...	...	...	...	...	...	...	...	...
" 29	13 300	...	8	...	43	...	99.9	...	99.7
" 30	10 900	37	5	...	33	99.7	99.9	...	99.7
July 1	...	...	...	...	...	...	...	...	...
" 2	24 200	95	72	83	...	99.6	99.7	99.7	...
" 3	12 000	80	16	42	...	99.3	99.9	99.6	...
" 4	...	...	...	...	...	...	...	...	...
" 5	...	...	...	...	...	...	...	...	...
" 6	7 400	64	353	...	48	99.1	95.1	...	99.3
" 7	5 500	82	480	...	30	98.5	91.3	...	99.4
" 8	6 700	69	99	...	21	99.0	98.5	...	99.7
" 9	9 200	53	10	...	60	99.4	99.9	...	99.4
" 10	10 000	71	40	110	...	99.3	99.6	98.9	...
" 11	9 600	40	24	208	...	99.6	99.7	97.8	...
" 12	...	...	...	...	...	...	...	...	...
" 13	7 700	64	44	...	78	99.2	99.4	...	99.0
" 14	10 100	33	6	...	25	99.7	99.9	...	98.2
" 15	8 300	30	8	...	11	99.6	99.9	...	99.9
" 16	5 500	31	11	...	18	99.4	99.8	...	99.7
" 17	5 700	11	5	33	...	99.8	99.9	99.4	...
" 18	9 900	23	34	48	...	99.8	99.7	99.5	...
" 19	...	...	...	...	...	...	...	...	...
" 20	7 000	24	9	...	22	99.7	99.9	...	99.7
" 21	17 100	113	47	...	204	99.3	99.7	...	98.8
" 22	33 800	752	251	...	623	97.8	99.3	...	98.2
" 23	27 100	597	103	...	...	97.8	99.6	...	...
" 24	31 000	1 327	71	234	...	95.7	99.8	99.2	...
" 25	17 300	433	54	284	...	97.5	99.7	98.4	...
" 26	...	...	...	...	...	...	...	...	...
" 27	17 800	306	19	...	151	98.3	99.9	...	99.2
" 28	24 500	60	6	...	156	99.8	99.9	...	99.4
" 29	9 500	52	15	...	137	99.5	99.8	...	98.6
" 30	12 000	12	...	...	...	99.9	99.9	...	...
" 31	6 800	33	...	214	...	99.5	...	96.9	...

TABLE

SUMMARIES OF

Warren

Number of period		1	2	3	4	5	6	7	8
Began	Date	Oct. 21, '95	Nov. 25	Dec. 26	Jan. 13, '96	Jan. 27	Feb. 6	Feb. 13	Feb. 27
	Hour	10.00 A.M.	9.45 A.M.	11.17 A.M.	12.15 P.M.	11.07 A.M.	2.36 P.M.	2.11 P.M.	4.50 P.M.
Ended	Date	Nov. 25, '95	Dec. 26	Jan. 13, '96	Jan. 27	Feb. 6	Feb. 13	Feb. 27	Mar. 20
	Hour	9.45 A.M.	11.17 A.M.	12.15 P.M.	11.07 A.M.	2.36 P.M.	2.11 P.M.	4.50 P.M.	9.00 A.M.
Runs included in period		1–14	15–31	32–50	51–65	66–78	79–84	85–100	101–135
Period of operation. (Hours.)	Maximum	12.08	23.32	12.33	7.18	8.70	6.78	8.35	6.07
	Minimum	4.83	6.58	3.60	3.62	3.18	3.97	3.45	2.43
	Average	8.87	11.22	5.98	5.10	5.82	5.27	5.72	4.32
Period of service. (Hours.)	Maximum	11.83	22.87	12.08	6.33	8.03	5.80	8.07	5.78
	Minimum	4.58	6.03	3.28	3.07	2.62	3.35	2.87	2.15
	Average	8.58	10.72	5.50	4.50	5.15	4.59	5.25	3.97
Period of wash. (Hours.)	Maximum	0.42	0.78	1.03	0.73	0.92	0.98	0.68	0.55
	Minimum	0.17	0.15	0.25	0.53	0.57	0.58	0.28	0.22
	Average	0.28	0.50	0.48	0.60	0.67	0.68	0.47	0.35
Quantity of applied water. (Cubic feet.)	Maximum	16 970	32 102	16 480	7 704	8 011	6 082	8 719	8 401
	Minimum	7 599	8 791	3 597	3 285	2 771	3 683	3 842	3 063
	Average	11 816	14 944	6 685	4 749	5 307	4 788	6 119	5 379
Quantity of filtered water. (Cubic feet.)	Maximum	16 640	31 048	15 853	6 472	7 487	5 467	8 491	8 182
	Minimum	7 359	8 126	3 139	2 798	2 092	3 258	3 614	2 885
	Average	11 457	14 007	6 215	4 165	4 745	4 286	5 735	5 171
Quantity of wash water. (Cubic feet.)	Maximum	741	540	723	479	586	572	561	1 286
	Minimum	283	297	271	244	432	437	295	421
	Average	360	376	374	298	497	485	446	509
Quantity of filtered waste water. (Cubic feet.)	Maximum	0	469	453	440	466	407	493	202
	Minimum	0	0	0	198	219	234	0	0
	Average	0	221	144	258	253	278	145	10
Quantity of unfiltered waste water. (Cubic feet.)	Maximum	400	450	300	400	250	250	300	300
	Minimum	250	180	180	180	180	180	180	167
	Average	312	206	198	218	197	220	219	181
Percentage which wash and waste water was of applied water.	Maximum	10	10	22	26	31	24	26	32
	Minimum	4	2	4	13	12	17	9	8
	Average	6	6	11	16	18	21	13	15
Actual rate of filtration — Cubic feet per min.	Maximum	26.8	25.5	23.6	17.1	16.8	16.3	23.2	25.0
	Minimum	19.8	19.2	14.6	14.7	13.3	15.1	16.8	17.6
	Average	22.3	21.8	18.9	15.4	15.4	15.6	18.2	21.7
Actual rate of filtration — Mil. gals. per acre per 24 hours.	Maximum	147	155	144	104	102	99	141	152
	Minimum	109	116	89	89	81	92	102	107
	Average	122	132	114	93	93	95	110	131
Ave. net rate of filtration.	Cubic feet per minute	20.9	20.0	16.6	13.0	12.5	12.0	15.5	18.1
	Mil. gals. per acre per 24 hr.	115	121	101	79	76	73	94	110
Net quantity of filtered water per run, in mil. gals. per acre	Maximum	68	131	66	27	29	21	31	32
	Minimum	30	33	12	11	8	12	12	10
	Average	46	59	26	17	18	16	22	20
Average estimated suspended solids in river water. (Parts per million.)	Maximum	22	50	870	100	461	967	486	210
	Minimum	4	15	100	20	200	550	136	22
	Average	13	27	230	410	320	730	290	40
Grains of applied sulphate of alumina per gallon of applied water.	Maximum	1.34	1.77	5.25	6.08	6.83	4.87	6.90	5.40
	Minimum	0.48	0.75	1.91	3.05	2.80	2.20	2.19	1.91
	Average	0.84	1.17	3.79	3.61	3.99	3.70	3.66	3.36
Average grains of applied sulphate of alumina per gallon of net filtered water		0.89	1.25	4.26	4.31	4.87	4.69	4.21	3.87
Degree of clearness of filtered water	Maximum	2	4	5	2	3	3	4	3
	Minimum	1	1	2	2	1	1	1	1
	Average	1.4	2.5	3.3	2.0	2.0	2.0	2.2	1.9
Bacteria per cubic centimeter in river water	Maximum	307	9 200	27 700	10 300	81 000	55 000	21 800	44 000
	Minimum	106	2 000	1 800	800	10 600	14 400	4 100	4 500
	Average	168	4 700	10 100	4 600	34 400	33 800	16 000	17 900
Average maximum number of bacteria per cubic centimeter in filtered water		96	479	559	84	474	432	238	365
Average minimum number of bacteria per cubic centimeter in filtered water		20	183	157	46	136	252	55	59
Bacteria per cubic centimeter in filtered water	Maximum	99	851	928	127	570	534	219	735
	Minimum	12	80	10	25	54	238	41	29
	Average	42	349	328	72	290	350	121	224
Average bacterial efficiency	Maximum	91.7	98.2	99.9	99.2	99.8	99.4	99.7	99.8
	Minimum	60.9	86.2	91.3	94.2	96.9	98.3	98.5	95.0
	Average	75.0	92.6	96.8	98.4	99.1	99.0	99.2	98.8

No. 4.

RESULTS BY PERIODS.

System.

9	10	11	12	13	14	15	16	17	18	19	20
Mar. 20	Mar. 23	Mar. 30	Apr. 7	Apr. 27	May 18	May 28	June 3	June 9	June 30	July 6	July 21
9.00 A.M.	9.30 A.M.	4.23 P.M.	12.37 P.M.	9.00 A.M.	11.14 A.M.	2.17 P.M.	3.30 P.M.	9.34 A.M.	3.48 P.M.	2.21 P.M.	4.41 P.M.
Mar. 23	Mar. 30	Apr. 7	Apr. 27	May 18	May 28	June 3	June 9	June 30	July 6	July 21	July 31
9.30 A.M.	4.23 P.M.	12.37 P.M.	9.00 A.M.	11.14 A.M.	2.17 P.M.	3.30 P.M.	9.34 A.M.	3.48 P.M.	2.21 P.M.	4.41 P.M.	9.00 A.M.
136–141	142–178	179–195	196–205	206–240	241–253	254–275	276–284	285–302	303–310	311–329	330–346
3.08	5.60	8.32	11.80	15.38	21.40	11.23	10.88	10.32	5.23	7.63	7.25
2.48	2.42	2.30	2.13	7.45	9.20	2.08	5.92	4.43	2.30	3.73	1.22
2.92	4.02	3.95	8.57	11.27	15.15	4.47	7.91	6.77	3.33	5.46	3.71
2.77	5.28	8.00	11.40	14.92	20.90	10.67	10.40	9.87	4.80	7.22	6.90
1.98	2.08	2.03	1.83	6.88	8.78	1.67	5.52	4.07	1.48	3.33	0.65
2.53	3.70	3.65	8.20	10.80	14.67	3.97	7.43	6.34	2.90	5.08	3.28
0.50	0.55	0.35	0.47	0.68	0.60	0.60	0.58	0.62	0.57	0.47	0.55
0.30	0.25	0.27	0.28	0.35	0.35	0.35	0.40	0.33	0.37	0.33	0.35
0.37	0.32	0.30	0.37	0.47	0.48	0.50	0.48	0.43	0.43	0.38	0.43
3 426	5 889	8 515	15 366	18 164	21 296	12 607	10 865	13 326	6 496	10 629	9 273
2 569	2 256	2 266	2 118	8 240	10 060	2 085	7 154	5 518	2 337	4 451	1 471
2 991	4 112	4 016	10 015	13 394	16 044	5 049	8 737	8 617	4 188	6 876	3 981
3 248	5 740	8 086	15 378	18 283	20 485	12 786	10 927	13 473	6 594	9 826	9 382
2 129	2 028	2 117	1 959	8 343	8 622	2 131	7 292	5 549	2 030	4 500	617
2 737	3 952	3 857	10 016	13 485	15 540	4 672	8 726	8 590	3 966	6 890	3 871
517	556	521	650	1 073	1 389	884	725	683	670	646	878
429	353	400	421	463	611	557	617	506	473	515	424
468	440	450	518	684	985	707	672	569	563	572	622
0	0	0	0	0	0	0	0	0	0	0	0
0	0	0	0	0	0	0	0	0	0	0	0
0	0	0	0	0	0	0	0	0	0	0	0
431	228	430	176	404	150	298	44	61	386	44	412
158	167	158	44	35	44	35	44	35	44	26	44
239	177	189	118	61	70	68	44	44	127	43	158
37	28	27	28	11	9	33	10	11	41	15	79
18	11	8	4	4	4	6	6	4	10	6	8
24	15	16	6	6	7	16	8	7	17	9	19
19.5	18.9	18.4	25.0	21.8	19.7	23.2	22.7	23.0	23.3	23.3	23.1
17.3	16.2	16.8	17.4	19.7	16.1	15.6	16.4	21.0	22.2	22.1	13.1
17.9	17.8	17.6	20.6	20.8	17.7	19.7	19.6	22.6	22.7	22.6	19.7
118	114	111	152	132	119	141	137	140	142	142	141
105	98	102	105	119	98	95	99	127	134	134	80
108	108	107	125	126	107	119	119	137	137	137	119
13.0	12.7	14.2	18.3	18.5	17.1	15.9	16.9	19.7	17.4	19.1	14.3
79	77	86	111	112	104	96	102	119	105	116	87
12	22	33	61	73	84	49	43	53	24	34	35
6	7	7	6	31	35	6	27	20	7	16	5
10	15	14	39	52	52	18	31	33	15	26	13
1 276	660	1 131	370	180	200	829	459	582	1 674	637	3 347
993	338	400	70	57	38	540	160	210	720	190	1 050
1 130	450	800	180	100	90	680	290	295	1 090	440	1 740
6.60	9.08	6.72	1.92	2.68	1.80	5.90	5.33	4.67	6.07	5.75	9.62
5.21	2.78	3.25	0.73	0.49	0.83	3.16	2.32	1.10	3.37	2.29	3.36
5.97	4.43	5.07	1.33	1.41	1.33	4.52	4.03	2.64	4.61	3.02	6.27
7.85	5.22	6.03	1.42	1.50	1.43	5.50	4.38	2.84	5.55	3.32	7.75
2	5	3	3	3	2	2	2	2	3	4	5
2	2	2	1	1	1	2	1	1	1	2	2
2.0	2.8	2.6	2.0	2.1	1.6	2.0	1.7	1.7	2.0	2.2	3.1
60 100	55 400	42 700	17 800	7 400	10 500	28 700	14 000	13 900	24 200	17 100	34 100
41 600	25 700	19 200	4 000	3 700	1 500	8 200	4 900	6 500	9 500	5 500	9 500
54 600	40 300	27 700	9 500	5 600	4 500	20 100	8 600	9 500	15 000	8 900	22 100
309	211	203	165	140	112	....	55	163	....	89	604
104	78	111	62	73	29	....	23	45	....	30	225
329	245	635	295	1 075	116	293	87	298	105	95	1 475
93	50	35	23	11	32	40	22	20	40	17	13
181	120	145	113	137	57	106	40	106	70	47	354
99.8	99.9	99.8	99.8	99.8	99.4	99.8	99.8	99.7	99.7	99.8	99.9
99.4	95.4	99.7	96.3	85.5	97.4	98.7	99.8	95.3	99.0	98.6	94.7
99.7	99.7	99.5	98.8	97.5	98.7	99.5	99.5	98.9	99.5	99.5	98.4

TABLE NO

SUMMARIES OF RESULTS

Jewel

Number of period		1	2	3	4	5	6	7	8
Began	Date	Oct. 21, '95	Nov. 21	Dec. 24	Jan. 13, '96	Jan. 25	Feb. 6	Feb. 11	Feb. 29
	Hour	12.03 P.M.	11.38 A.M.	1.36 P.M.	9.44 A.M.	2.00 P.M.	2.33 P.M.	9.45 A.M.	9.58 A.M.
Ended	Date	Nov 21, '95	Dec. 24	Jan. 13, '96	Jan. 25	Feb. 6	Feb. 11	Feb. 29	Mar. 20
	Hour	11.38 A.M.	1.36 P.M.	9.44 A.M.	2.00 P.M.	2.33 P.M.	9.45 A.M.	9.58 A.M.	9.37 A.M.
Runs included in period		1–12	13–20	21–29	30–34	35–39	40–42	43–52	53–64
Period of operation. (Hours.)	Maximum	21.10	28.83	16.30	23.55	14.58	9.63	20.55	24.17
	Minimum	5.20	16.60	6.97	16.08	8.55	8.33	7.95	6.73
	Average	13.17	21.97	11.00	18.80	11.35	9.02	13.52	11.84
Period of service. (Hours.)	Maximum	20.78	26.10	15.65	23.12	14.23	9.35	20.07	23.80
	Minimum	4.85	15.93	6.57	15.57	8.22	7.80	7.45	6.30
	Average	12.82	21.40	10.38	18.38	10.87	8.45	12.95	11.54
Period of wash. (Hours.)	Maximum	0.50	0.95	1.03	0.52	0.83	0.87	0.83	0.43
	Minimum	0.27	0.33	0.37	0.32	0.33	0.28	0.37	0.25
	Average	0.35	0.57	0.62	0.42	0.48	0.57	0.57	0.30
Quantity of applied water. (Cubic feet.)	Maximum	36 355	40 391	21 089	35 410	20 607	13 280	22 575	35 421
	Minimum	7 896	21 730	7 932	22 289	11 074	10 225	10 224	8 790
	Average	19 889	30 524	13 673	26 464	15 299	11 509	16 523	17 404
Quantity of filtered water. (Cubic feet.)	Maximum	34 677	38 352	21 335	34 946	20 433	13 127	22 950	35 292
	Minimum	7 781	20 488	7 947	22 351	10 715	10 220	10 237	8 840
	Average	19 363	29 701	13 643	26 442	15 062	11 319	16 770	17 634
Quantity of wash water. (Cubic feet.)	Maximum	731	856	1 025	458	617	538	810	844
	Minimum	259	534	467	432	383	490	505	442
	Average	519	676	665	443	447	517	579	559
Quantity of filtered waste water. (Cubic feet.)	Maximum	0	0	443	301	310	403	308	97
	Minimum	0	0	0	0	0	0	0	0
	Average	0	0	122	60	136	134	66	8
Quantity of unfiltered waste water. (Cubic feet.)	Maximum	235	214	32	32	32	32	32	214
	Minimum	32	32	32	32	32	32	32	0
	Average	104	100	32	32	32	32	32	31
Percentage which wash and waste water was of applied water	Maximum	8	3	11	4	9	9	7	10
	Minimum	2	2	3	1	2	4	2	2
	Average	3	3	6	2	4	6	4	3
Actual rate of filtration — Cubic feet per min.	Maximum	27.8	24.5	23.1	25.2	24.0	23.4	29.0	30.1
	Minimum	22.9	21.5	20.1	23.4	21.2	21.5	14.0	23.4
	Average	25.3	23.1	21.9	24.0	23.1	23.3	21.6	25.5
Actual rate of filtration — Mil. gals. per acre per 24 hours	Maximum	112	99	93	102	97	95	118	122
	Minimum	93	87	81	95	86	87	57	95
	Average	102	93	89	97	93	94	87	103
Ave. net rate of filtration	Cubic feet per minute	24.4	22.5	19.5	24.1	21.6	22.5	19.6	24.5
	Mil. gals. per acre per 24 hr.	99	91	79	97	87	91	79	99
Net quantity of filtered waste per run, mil. gals. per acre	Maximum	99	105	57	97	56	35	62	96
	Minimum	20	59	20	60	28	27	27	22
	Average	54	82	36	73	41	30	44	47
Average estimated suspended solids in river water. (Parts per million)	Maximum	25	35	850	60	460	970	430	210
	Minimum	7	15	80	20	250	580	120	50
	Average	16	26	345	35	320	730	290	70
Grains of applied sulphate of alumina per gallon of applied water	Maximum	2.41	1.26	4.42	1.12	2.32	2.39	4.82	1.55
	Minimum	0.40	0.48	1.25	0.83	1.21	2.16	1.36	0.65
	Average	0.68	0.87	2.35	0.96	1.72	2.25	2.78	1.06
Average grains of applied sulphate of alumina per gallon of net filtered water		0.70	0.90	2.50	0.98	1.80	2.40	2.90	1.11
Degree of clearness of filtered water	Maximum	3	3	5	3	5	4	5	5
	Minimum	1	1	2	2	2	2	2	2
	Average	1.6	1.6	3.2	2.6	3.7	3.0	2.9	1.7
Bacteria per cubic centimeter in river water	Maximum	675	8 700	27 600	6 800	54 100	41 200	21 800	34 400
	Minimum	126	2 100	1 800	1 300	10 900	14 400	4 700	9 400
	Average	371	4 400	9 700	3 800	22 900	33 100	15 600	18 500
Average maximum number of bacteria per cubic centimeter in filtered water		473	611	550	315	1 779	1 446	2 002	779
Average minimum number of bacteria per cubic centimeter in filtered water		56	115	162	105	912	418	245	124
Bacteria per cubic centimeter in filtered water	Maximum	367	659	546	248	2 372	1 346	1 600	1 645
	Minimum	26	77	202	164	688	740	504	35
	Average	154	271	297	186	1 088	960	1 015	533
Average bacterial efficiency	Maximum	83.1	97.3	98.2	96.3	98.0	98.1	97.4	99.6
	Minimum	0.0	83.5	88.8	86.4	86.0	94.9	90.6	94.7
	Average	59.0	93.8	96.9	95.1	95.3	97.1	93.5	97.1

4.—*Continued.*

BY PERIODS.

System.

9	10	11	12	13	14	16	16	17	18	19	20
Mar. 20	Mar. 21	Mar. 30	Apr. 7	Apr. 27	May 18	May 28	June 3	June 9	July 1	July 6	July 22
9.37 A.M.	5.08 P.M.	10.30 A.M.	9.23 A.M.	9.25 A.M.	1.12 P.M.	11.05 A.M.	2.20 P.M.	10.56 A.M.	3.55 P.M.	2.20 P.M.	10.24 A.M.
Mar. 21	Mar. 30	Apr. 7	Apr. 27	May 18	May 28	June 3	June 9	July 1	July 6	July 22	July 30
5.08 P.M.	10.30 A.M.	9.23 A.M.	9.25 A.M.	1.12 P.M.	11.05 A.M.	2.20 P.M.	10.56 A.M.	3.55 P.M.	2.20 P.M.	10.24 A.M.	11.37 A.M.
65–69	70–96	97–111	112–125	126–148	149–158	159–184	185–204	205–234	235–238	239–256	257–272
3.58	8.83	6.02	16.92	21.00	34.77	8.55	8.68	13.68	7.00	8.97	8.52
2.73	3.17	1.08	3.90	5.57	13.77	0.93	1.08	1.43	1.85	1.98	0.72
3.20	5.65	3.86	9.79	16.90	21.63	2.65	3.55	5.02	4.25	5.55	3.48
3.18	8.53	5.77	16.62	20.70	34.48	8.30	8.45	13.15	6.50	8.57	7.98
2.38	2.63	0.15	3.67	5.40	13.50	0.63	0.82	1.18	1.43	1.28	0.52
2.85	5.35	3.53	9.52	16.62	21.35	2.43	3.30	4.70	3.85	5.13	3.10
0.43	0.70	0.93	0.32	0.48	0.35	0.30	0.35	0.77	0.50	0.38	0.60
0.27	0.18	0.23	0.20	0.17	0.20	0.17	0.20	0.20	0.23	0.27	0.20
0.35	0.30	0.33	0.27	0.28	0.28	0.22	0.25	0.32	0.40	0.42	0.38
4 437	12 181	7 814	23 952	31 319	51 286	12 533	12 540	18 448	9 046	12 274	12 274
3 288	3 903	776	5 158	8 623	21 012	1 032	2 637	2 380	2 062	2 316	858
3 948	7 427	5 050	13 641	25 565	33 604	4 220	5 627	7 129	5 553	7 699	4 024
4 434	12 513	8 015	24 483	32 264	51 483	12 229	12 463	17 699	8 971	12 396	9 903
3 350	3 770	183	5 286	8 817	20 795	1 041	1 806	2 091	1 860	1 888	855
3 989	7 659	5 094	13 927	26 225	34 174	3 904	5 443	7 105	5 360	7 497	4 038
625	617	745	1 073	874	732	799	801	1 996	1 443	1 105	1 078
469	395	464	427	398	508	469	486	515	958	582	376
555	510	598	636	580	606	591	587	756	1 151	860	772
12	245	592	0	176	93	206	107	763	81	417	113
0	0	0	0	0	0	0	0	0	0	0	0
2	17	75	0	9	12	15	19	78	43	73	10
114	0	0	274	0	0	0	0	214	0	187	198
0	0	0	0	0	0	0	0	0	0	0	0
23	0	0	15	0	0	0	0	7	0	20	37
18	22	142	8	6	3	47	20	31	51	50	63
11	5	7	3	1	1	6	5	5	16	6	10
15	7	13	5	2	2	15	11	12	21	12	20
23.8	25.2	24.9	25.3	27.2	29.6	34.5	35.2	37.0	23.8	25.0	30.9
22.6	22.7	20.3	23.2	25.1	24.4	20.5	24.5	22.4	21.6	23.1	18.2
23.3	23.8	24.0	24.4	26.3	26.7	26.8	27.5	25.2	23.2	24.2	21.8
96	102	101	102	110	120	140	143	150	96	101	126
91	92	82	94	101	99	83	99	91	87	93	74
94	96	97	99	106	108	108	111	102	94	98	88
17.5	20.2	19.0	22.2	24.6	25.4	22.6	23.5	20.7	17.1	20.1	15.5
71	82	77	90	100	103	91	95	84	69	81	63
105	32	20	65	86	141	32	33	45	21	31	24
7	8	0	13	22	57	2	5	5	3	3	1
9	19	12	36	70	91	10	14	17	12	19	9
1 280	730	1 130	350	190	130	830	460	590	1 700	690	3 400
990	340	490	70	60	40	400	160	180	1 000	190	1 200
1 130	450	850	160	100	80	640	300	340	1 310	450	1 860
5.40	5.23	6.32	2.23	3.66	1.84	6.92	7.70	7.61	7.45	7.17	12.62
2.88	2.39	3.10	0.96	1.13	0.56	1.46	3.52	1.29	5.30	4.26	5.76
4.17	3.44	4.36	1.34	1.76	1.26	4.76	4.96	4.29	6.35	5.65	8.58
4.91	3.70	5.02	1.41	1.80	1.29	5.60	5.58	5.00	8.14	6.58	10.72
3	4	3	2	2	2	4	2	2	3	2	3
3	2	2	1	1	1	1	1	1	1	1	2
3.0	2.6	2.6	1.4	1.2	1.4	2.7	1.8	1.3	1.7	1.6	1.2
60 100	53 000	42 700	19 000	8 300	6 200	32 500	16 700	18 000	24 200	17 100	37 300
41 600	25 900	19 400	3 100	3 700	1 800	8 200	4 300	6 000	12 200	5 100	9 500
55 300	40 100	28 100	8 000	5 700	4 300	19 300	8 800	9 300	18 000	9 300	22 100
....	581	449	123	684	158	....	....	219	98	122	....
....	244	264	27	25	33	....	....	68	29	26	....
1 905	1 250	1 495	164	160	92	475	107	655	127	409	745
440	103	32	8	12	38	22	7	5	4	3	6
968	416	522	50	48	73	190	47	91	43	62	86
99.3	99.7	99.8	99.8	99.7	98.8	99.8	99.9	99.9	99.9	99.9	99.9
96.6	97.7	95.0	98.2	97.6	94.9	97.6	98.9	91.0	99.5	94.1	97.8
98.3	99.0	98.1	99.4	99.2	98.3	99.0	99.5	99.0	99.8	99.3	99.6

TABLE

SUMMARIES OF

Western Gravity

Number of period		1	2	3	4	5	6	7	8
Began	Date	....	....	Dec. 24, '95	Jan. 14, '96	Jan. 27	Feb. 7	Feb. 11	Feb. 28
	Hour	....	....	9.42 A.M.	10.52 A.M.	9.29 A.M.	9.23 A.M.	9.21 A.M.	12.12 P.M.
Ended	Date	....	....	Jan. 14, '96	Jan. 27	Feb. 7	Feb. 11	Feb. 28	Mar. 20
	Hour	....	....	10.52 A.M.	9.29 A.M.	9.23 A.M.	9.21 A.M.	12.12 P.M.	10.09 A.M.
Runs included in period		....	....	2–16	17–26	27–39	40–48	49–80	81–100
Period of operation. (Hours.)	Maximum	....	....	23.13	13.93	7.90	3.83	7.07	11.77
	Minimum	....	....	2.38	6.72	3.28	1.88	0.50	2.48
	Average	....	....	8.02	8.37	4.95	2.82	3.68	7.30
Period of service. (Hours.)	Maximum	....	....	22.75	13.40	7.70	3.57	6.80	11.47
	Minimum	....	....	1.88	6.42	2.98	1.62	0.25	2.23
	Average	....	....	7.70	8.07	4.67	2.52	3.43	7.07
Period of wash. (Hours.)	Maximum	....	....	0.50	0.53	0.32	0.40	0.38	0.32
	Minimum	....	....	0.17	0.20	0.20	0.27	0.17	0.18
	Average	....	....	0.32	0.30	0.28	0.30	0.25	0.23
Quantity of applied water. (Cubic feet.)	Maximum	....	....	13 036	11 766	7 098	3 375	6 967	13 798
	Minimum	....	....	1 564	7 311	2 305	1 240	258	2 552
	Average	....	....	4 544	9 969	4 058	2 257	3 206	8 502
Quantity of filtered water. (Cubic feet.)	Maximum	....	....	12 679	11 534	6 982	2 748	6 812	13 500
	Minimum	....	....	982	6 989	2 009	951	79	2 087
	Average	....	....	4 267	9 632	3 705	1 805	2 951	8 236
Quantity of wash water. (Cubic feet.)	Maximum	....	....	616	864	839	503	620	613
	Minimum	....	....	162	350	269	256	97	402
	Average	....	....	419	448	466	404	425	527
Quantity of filtered waste water. (Cubic feet.)	Maximum	....	....	242	215	174	227	179	218
	Minimum	....	....	37	74	40	109	31	41
	Average	....	....	101	129	103	151	104	98
Quantity of unfiltered waste water. (Cubic feet.)	Maximum	....	....	400	347	600	400	730	420
	Minimum	....	....	50	0	50	100	0	70
	Average	....	....	169	208	250	301	154	178
Percentage which wash and waste water was of applied water	Maximum	....	....	48	12	50	66	146	42
	Minimum	....	....	5	7	7	23	9	5
	Average	....	....	15	8	20	38	21	9
Actual rate of filtration. Cubic feet per min.	Maximum	....	....	11.6	24.7	15.1	15.9	19.2	20.3
	Minimum	....	....	7.9	11.4	10.7	5.8	5.3	13.9
	Average	....	....	9.2	19.9	13.2	11.7	14.4	19.5
Actual rate of filtration. Mil. gals. per acre per 24 hours	Maximum	....	....	72	152	94	98	118	126
	Minimum	....	....	48	70	64	36	33	85
	Average	....	....	57	123	81	72	89	121
Ave. net rate of filtration.	Cubic feet per minute	....	....	8.0	18.3	11.0	8.3	11.5	17.7
	Mil. gals. per acre per 24 hr.	....	....	49	113	68	51	71	109
Net quantity of filtered waste per run, in mil. gals. per acre	Maximum	....	....	51	45	28	10	27	56
	Minimum	....	....	4	28	6	2	0	6
	Average	....	....	17	39	14	6	11	33
Average estimated suspended solids in river water. (Parts per million.)	Maximum	....	....	870	50	460	970	560	210
	Minimum	....	....	80	17	200	640	110	40
	Average	....	....	290	27	320	780	280	67
Grains of applied sulphate of alumina per gallon of applied water	Maximum	....	....	....	1.65	2.79	....	9.33	1.42
	Minimum	....	....	....	0.71	1.23	....	0.78	0.59
	Average	....	....	2.67	1.07	1.86	3.22	1.94	0.78
Average grains of applied sulphate of alumina per gallon of net filtered water		....	....	3.14	1.16	3.32	5.20	2.46	0.86
Degree of clearness of filtered water	Maximum	....	....	3	2	4	3	3	2
	Minimum	....	....	1	1	1	1	1	1
	Average	....	....	1.7	1.6	2.2	2.0	1.5	1.5
Bacteria per cubic centimeter in river water	Maximum	....	....	32 400	7 300	81 000	55 000	28 000	39 700
	Minimum	....	....	1 800	1 900	12 000	14 400	4 100	7 700
	Average	....	....	8 200	4 800	37 600	34 500	16 200	22 000
Average maximum number of bacteria per cubic centimeter in filtered water		....	....	396	195	880	....	652	735
Average minimum number of bacteria per cubic centimeter in filtered water		....	....	214	98	386	....	311	285
Bacteria per cubic centimeter in filtered water	Maximum	....	....	783	228	1 586	1 600	1 137	1 941
	Minimum	....	....	81	68	127	252	69	140
	Average	....	....	302	148	679	679	541	520
Average bacterial efficiency	Maximum	....	....	98.8	98.6	99.0	99.3	99.5	98.9
	Minimum	....	....	93.2	92.6	92.7	95.9	93.0	95.1
	Average	....	....	96.3	96.9	98.2	98.0	96.7	97.6

No. 4.—*Continued.*

RESULTS BY PERIODS.

System.

9	10	11	12	13	14	15	16	17	18	19	20
Mar. 20	......	......	......	......	......	......	......	......	July 2	July 10	July 24
10.09 P.M.	......	......	......	......	......	......	......	......	9.37 A.M.	9.32 A.M.	10.55 A.M.
July 2	......	......	......	......	......	......	......	......	July 10	July 24	July 31
9.37 A.M.	......	......	......	......	......	......	......	......	9.32 A.M.	10.55 A.M.	5.17 P.M.
101–106	......	......	......	......	......	......	......	......	107–114	115–120	121–123
1.23	......	......	......	......	......	......	......	......	4.48	8.12	6.23
0.78	......	......	......	......	......	......	......	......	1.25	1.78	1.25
1.07	......	......	......	......	......	......	......	......	2.05	4.70	3.75
1.00	......	......	......	......	......	......	......	......	3.97	7.37	3.30
0.53	......	......	......	......	......	......	......	......	0.80	1.13	1.01
0.79	......	......	......	......	......	......	......	......	1.57	4.08	2.53
0.58	......	......	......	......	......	......	......	......	0.60	0.75	2.73
0.17	......	......	......	......	......	......	......	......	0.40	0.43	0.23
0.28	......	......	......	......	......	......	......	......	0.48	0.62	1.22
1 133	......	......	......	......	......	......	......	......	3 537	7 023	4 788
616	......	......	......	......	......	......	......	......	935	1 248	1 014
996	......	......	......	......	......	......	......	......	1 564	4 067	2 920
1 081	......	......	......	......	......	......	......	......	3 253	6 753	2 981
280	......	......	......	......	......	......	......	......	613	1 005	715
580	......	......	......	......	......	......	......	......	1 262	3 760	2 027
784	......	......	......	......	......	......	......	......	892	930	1 298
450	......	......	......	......	......	......	......	......	470	727	631
568	......	......	......	......	......	......	......	......	601	806	901
322	......	......	......	......	......	......	......	......	360	393	1 672
59	......	......	......	......	......	......	......	......	179	196	61
129	......	......	......	......	......	......	......	......	261	284	688
660	......	......	......	......	......	......	......	......	100	240	240
40	......	......	......	......	......	......	......	......	0	0	130
287	......	......	......	......	......	......	......	......	52	102	200
119	......	......	......	......	......	......	......	......	93	50	91
13	......	......	......	......	......	......	......	......	33	10	46
99	......	......	......	......	......	......	......	......	58	29	61
19.3	......	......	......	......	......	......	......	......	14.1	15.7	14.2
8.8	......	......	......	......	......	......	......	......	12.8	14.8	11.7
12.5	......	......	......	......	......	......	......	......	13.5	15.3	13.3
119	......	......	......	......	......	......	......	......	89	101	91
55	......	......	......	......	......	......	......	......	83	96	75
77	......	......	......	......	......	......	......	......	87	99	86
1.6	......	......	......	......	......	......	......	......	5.3	10.2	5.1
10	......	......	......	......	......	......	......	......	34	65	33
2	......	......	......	......	......	......	......	......	11	26	8
0	......	......	......	......	......	......	......	......	0	6	0
0	......	......	......	......	......	......	......	......	3	13	6
1 300	......	......	......	......	......	......	......	......	1 700	640	3 300
990	......	......	......	......	......	......	......	......	1 000	190	1 700
1 110	......	......	......	......	......	......	......	......	1 420	400	2.590
......	......	......	......	......	......	......	......	......	10.55	5.50	5.89
......	......	......	......	......	......	......	......	......	5.18	1.17	4.92
4.36	......	......	......	......	......	......	......	......	8.58	2.71	5.24
436.0	......	......	......	......	......	......	......	......	20.4	3.94	13.4
4	......	......	......	......	......	......	......	......	3	2	4
4	......	......	......	......	......	......	......	......	2	2	2
4.0	......	......	......	......	......	......	......	......	2.5	2.0	3.0
63 500	......	......	......	......	......	......	......	......	34 200	23 300	31 000
41 600	......	......	......	......	......	......	......	......	10 400	6 900	17 300
51 800	......	......	......	......	......	......	......	......	18 900	9 900	24 900
......	......	......	......	......	......	......	......	......	......	169	406
......	......	......	......	......	......	......	......	......	......	75	71
1 000	......	......	......	......	......	......	......	......	171	216	511
500	......	......	......	......	......	......	......	......	9	39	208
736	......	......	......	......	......	......	......	......	65	107	257
99.2	......	......	......	......	......	......	......	......	99.9	99.6	99.2
97.6	......	......	......	......	......	......	......	......	99.3	98.3	97.2
98.6	......	......	......	......	......	......	......	......	99.7	98.9	99.0

TABLE NO.

SUMMARIES OF

Western Pressure

Number of period		1	2	3	4	5	6	7	8
Began	Date	...	...	Dec. 23, '95	Jan. 14, '96	Jan. 27	Feb. 7	Feb. 11	Feb. 27
	Hour	...	...	10.35 A.M.	11.03 A.M.	3.51 P.M.	9.32 A.M.	11.32 A.M.	2.10 P.M.
Ended	Date	...	...	Jan. 14, '96	Jan. 27	Feb. 7.	Feb. 11	Feb. 27	Mar. 20
	Hour	...	...	11.03 A.M.	3.51 P.M.	9.32 A.M.	11.32 A.M.	2.10 P.M.	9.20 A.M.
Runs included in period		...	...	1–10	11–14	15–21	22–27	28–44	45–52
Period of operation. (Hours.)	Maximum	...	...	32.72	28.47	8.73	8.27	13.12	25.42
	Minimum	...	...	6.55	18.55	7.25	2.72	3.23	8.50
	Average	...	...	12.02	22.92	8.00	4.35	6.55	19.40
Period of service. (Hours.)	Maximum	...	...	32.38	28.08	8.27	7.97	12.78	25.17
	Minimum	...	...	6.13	18.25	6.97	2.55	3.02	8.00
	Average	...	...	11.67	22.54	7.63	4.07	6.25	19.05
Period of wash. (Hours.)	Maximum	...	...	0.42	0.55	0.47	0.32	0.38	0.50
	Minimum	...	...	0.22	0.30	0.28	0.27	0.22	0.25
	Average	...	...	0.35	0.38	0.37	0.28	0.30	0.35
Quantity of applied water. (Cubic feet.)	Maximum	...	...	43 978	47 172	11 660	9 722	17 997	35 056
	Minimum	...	...	6 906	31 213	7 656	3 263	3 896	10 445
	Average	...	...	13 690	35 382	9 609	5 128	8 368	26 859
Quantity of filtered water. (Cubic feet.)	Maximum	...	...	43 793	46 939	11 479	9 536	17 819	34 825
	Minimum	...	...	6 745	31 147	7 431	3 081	3 739	10 001
	Average	...	...	13 550	35 156	9 395	4 938	8 219	26 642
Quantity of wash water. (Cubic feet.)	Maximum	...	...	760	683	790	662	832	898
	Minimum	...	...	493	638	471	431	375	606
	Average	...	...	653	663	626	520	602	749
Quantity of filtered waste water. (Cubic feet.)	Maximum	...	...	185	309	280	269	271	444
	Minimum	...	...	81	176	166	141	68	101
	Average	...	...	143	225	214	190	149	218
Quantity of unfiltered waste water. (Cubic feet.)	Maximum	...	...	0	0	0	0	0	0
	Minimum	...	...	0	0	0	0	0	0
	Average	...	...	0	0	0	0	0	0
Percentage which wash and waste water was of applied water	Maximum	...	...	12	3	12	21	17	12
	Minimum	...	...	2	2	7	9	5	2
	Average	...	...	6	2	9	14	9	4
Actual rate of filtration: Cubic feet per min.	Maximum	...	...	22.5	28.4	24.0	26.5	23.5	24.2
	Minimum	...	...	14.8	22.3	16.4	18.4	19.9	20.8
	Average	...	...	19.4	27.8	20.5	20.2	21.9	23.3
Actual rate of filtration: Mil. gals. per acre per 24 hours	Maximum	...	...	160	202	170	188	166	171
	Minimum	...	...	105	158	115	131	141	148
	Average	...	...	138	197	146	143	155	165
Ave. net rate of filtration	Cubic feet per minute	...	...	17.9	25.2	18.3	16.9	19.4	22.2
	Mil. gals per acre per 24 hr.	...	...	127	178	130	119	138	157
Net quantity of filtered waste per run, in mil. gals. per acre	Maximum	...	...	209	225	53	43	83	166
	Minimum	...	...	32	142	33	13	16	44
	Average	...	...	62	168	42	21	39	125
Average estimated suspended solids in river water. (Parts per million.)	Maximum	...	...	870	100	464	967	500	210
	Minimum	...	...	100	20	244	636	126	40
	Average	...	...	320	42	340	750	290	70
Grains of applied sulphate of alumina per gallon of applied water	Maximum	...	...	...	1.37	2.64	3.08	4.23	1.44
	Minimum	...	...	...	0.87	1.39	0.71	1.06	0.69
	Average	...	...	2.67	1.06	2.04	3.22	2.25	0.84
Average grains of applied sulphate of alumina per gallon of net filtered water		...	...	2.84	1.08	2.24	3.75	2.48	0.86
Degree of clearness of filtered water	Maximum	...	...	2	2	5	3	5	3
	Minimum	...	...	1	1	1	1	1	1
	Average	...	...	1.6	1.1	2.4	2.0	2.4	1.8
Bacteria per cubic centimeter in river water	Maximum	...	...	35 700	7 000	71 000	55 000	28 000	37 500
	Minimum	...	...	1 800	2 300	12 400	14 400	10 700	8 700
	Average	...	...	9 200	4 800	39 000	32 500	16 600	17 800
Average maximum number of bacteria per cubic centimeter in filtered water		...	...	459	421	1 087	1 027	829	1 549
Average minimum number of bacteria per cubic centimeter in filtered water		...	...	183	82	428	459	257	221
Bacteria per cubic centimeter in river water	Maximum	...	...	1 032	322	1 461	967	975	1 382
	Minimum	...	...	107	116	188	166	151	233
	Average	...	...	287	206	760	681	544	556
Average bacterial efficiency	Maximum	...	...	98.8	96.8	99.1	98.9	99.2	98.2
	Minimum	...	...	93.9	95.0	93.2	95.8	91.3	91.8
	Average	...	...	96.9	95.7	98.1	97.9	96.7	96.9

4.—*Concluded.*

RESULTS BY PERIODS.

System.

9	10	11	12	13	14	15	16	17	18	19	20
Mar. 20	Mar. 23	Mar. 30	....	May 7	May 18	May 28	June 3	June 9	July 1	July 6	July 22
9.20 A.M.	9.19 A.M.	9.14 A.M.	....	9.00 A.M.	9.15 A.M.	12.18 P.M.	5.19 P.M.	9.45 A.M.	9.00 A.M.	9.12 A.M.	9.05 A.M.
Mar. 23	Mar. 30	May 7	....	May 18	May 28	June 3	June 9	July 1	July 6	July 22	July 29
9.19 A.M.	9.14 A.M.	9.00 A.M.	....	9.15 A.M.	12.18 P.M.	5.19 P.M.	9.45 A.M.	9.00 A.M.	9.12 A.M.	9.05 A.M.	3.43 P.M.
53–57	58–82	83–94	....	95–107	108–112	113–157	158–183	184–224	225–228	229–248	249–260
4.65	9.03	8.52	....	22.58	54.62	14.12	7.37	8.90	3.73	8.52	4.40
2.08	3.33	3.28	....	11.90	20.87	0.70	0.80	0.77	1.43	1.48	0.92
3.28	5.95	5.55	....	13.94	39.97	2.09	2.62	3.32	2.10	3.77	2.43
4.33	8.73	8.27	....	22.37	54.67	13.00	7.08	8.57	3.12	8.27	4.18
1.75	3.00	2.93	....	11.60	20.63	0.52	0.65	0.57	0.92	1.22	0.73
2.95	5.67	5.27	....	13.62	39.65	1.82	2.40	3.05	1.60	3.37	2.03
0.40	0.33	0.38	....	0.40	0.53	1.40	0.53	0.45	0.55	0.60	1.30
0.25	0.20	0.23	....	0.22	0.23	0.15	0.15	0.15	0.38	0.23	0.17
0.33	0.28	0.28	....	0.32	0.32	0.27	0.22	0.27	0.50	0.40	0.40
3 787	8 797	8 746	....	31 494	45 180	13 454	8 224	10 111	3 513	8 553	4 261
2 276	3 230	2 307	....	16 048	21 446	539	823	797	1 251	1 578	647
3 069	5 566	5 025	....	19 223	35 407	1 906	2 555	3 458	1 909	3 688	1 946
3 595	8 907	8 875	....	31 807	45 752	13 659	8 215	10 175	3 304	8 359	3 684
2 043	3 070	2 062	....	16 053	21 786	464	750	713	935	1 281	617
2 873	5 577	5 010	....	18 883	35 563	1 764	2 448	3 369	1 635	3 451	1 777
763	962	764	....	791	783	1 257	857	794	798	936	831
625	625	656	....	481	630	310	350	324	735	564	484
696	737	706	....	657	671	587	522	577	766	744	658
294	193	245	....	270	329	1 255	286	253	296	374	742
128	58	86	....	68	107	44	45	53	79	53	27
196	124	156	....	168	165	134	100	121	234	175	177
0	0	0	....	0	0	0	0	0	0	0	0
0	0	0	....	0	0	0	0	0	0	0	0
0	0	0	....	0	0	0	0	0	0	0	0
44	31	40	....	6	4	218	63	84	81	54	150
22	10	9	....	3	2	8	6	7	30	10	17
29	15	17	....	4	2	38	24	20	32	25	43
19.4	19.2	18.5	....	24.2	17.6	20.8	20.6	21.0	17.2	20.2	15.6
13.5	14.6	11.7	....	22.1	14.0	12.6	13.0	16.7	16.8	15.4	13.3
16.2	16.4	15.9	....	23.1	14.9	16.2	17.3	18.4	17.0	17.1	14.6
137	136	132	....	171	125	148	147	149	122	143	111
96	103	83	....	157	99	89	92	118	119	109	94
114	115	112	....	164	106	114	122	131	120	121	103
11.1	13.3	12.5	....	22.1	14.5	9.5	12.4	13.9	7.3	12.2	7.6
79	94	88	....	157	102	67	88	98	51	86	53
14	38	38	....	148	215	57	37	45	12	13	17
6	11	7	....	73	104	0	1	1	1	2	0
11	23	20	....	89	168	6	10	13	4	13	5
1 276	660	1 131	....	185	150	829	459	582	870	560	2 170
993	338	352	....	70	50	400	160	200	870	220	1 170
1 140	450	780	....	130	90	600	280	320	870	440	1 530
....	4.96	5.16	....	1.97	1.87	10.70	7.48	8.58	5.58	7.55	9.69
....	1.96	2.40	....	0.68	0.51	1.91	2.43	1.52	4.53	2.63	3.20
3.16	3.23	3.46	....	1.06	1.16	4.41	4.06	4.84	4.91	4.62	5.50
4.45	3.80	4.17	....	1.10	1.19	7.11	5.35	5.12	10.20	6.18	10.00
3	4	5	....	4	3	5	3	3	3	2	3
3	2	2	....	1	1	2	2	2	3	2	2
3.0	3.0	3.2	....	2.2	2.0	4.0	2.3	2.1	3.0	2.0	2.5
60 100	55 400	39 600	....	7 900	6 800	30 600	18 900	21 200	....	25 400	33 300
41 600	25 400	18 500	....	3 600	2 500	7 900	4 300	6 000	....	5 000	9 500
56 300	40 600	26 000	....	5 800	3 900	23 900	8 300	10 400	....	8 100	22 600
810	1 168	967	....	248	875	....	....	....	....	130	....
593	419	614	....	145	44	....	....	....	....	27	....
1 153	3 276	2 545	....	267	512	470	448	1 000	....	357	646
450	196	76	....	109	75	27	19	8	....	8	76
778	726	776	....	180	195	191	72	76	....	58	314
99.3	99.6	99.6	....	98.3	98.3	99.9	99.9	99.9	....	99.9	99.4
98.0	92.4	91.4	....	95.4	90.5	97.5	96.4	94.6	....	97.5	98.1
98.6	98.2	97.0	....	96.9	95.0	99.2	99.1	99.3	....	99.3	98.6

TABLE No. 5.

GRAND TOTALS AND AVERAGES FOR THE ENTIRE INVESTIGATIONS.

			Warren System.	Jewell System.	Western Gravity System.	Western Pressure System.
Total periods in days of 24 hours		Operation	89.76	90.40	25.81	65.99
		Service	83.76	86.68	24.15	62.72
		Wash	6.00	3.72	1.66	3.27
Total number of runs			347	272	124	261
Total number of runs included in averages			334	260	122	260
Total quantities of water by meter, in cubic feet		Applied	2 473 518	3 061 073	565 207	1 773 994
		Filtered	2 404 357	3 077 341	526 112	1 739 628
		Wash	176 285	162 997	60 771	164 658
		Filtered waste	17 292	9 739	17 442	38 371
		Unfiltered waste	49 611	4 387	22 422	0
Average per run	Periods of time	Operation	6h. 27m.	8h. 21m.	5h. 05m.	6h. 05m.
		Service	6h. 01m.	8h. 00m.	4h 45m.	5h. 47m.
		Wash	26m.	21m.	20m.	18m.
	Quantities of water	Applied	7 405	11 808	4 633	6 823
		Filtered	7 124	11 831	4 312	6 691
		Wash	528	627	498	633
		Filtered waste	51	37	143	148
		Unfiltered waste	149	18	188	0
Average actual rate		Cubic feet per minute	19.9	24.7	15.1	21.7
		Million gallons per acre per 24 hours	114	100	92	154
Average grains of sulphate of alumina		Per gallon of applied water	2.70	2.49	2.90	2.41
		Per gallon of net filtered water	3.00	2.65	3.53	2.72
Average bacterial efficiency			96.7	96.0	97.4	97.3

TABLE NO. 6.

SUMMARIES OF LEADING RESULTS.

		Percentages which the Periods of Service and Wash were of the Period of Operation.		Percentages which the Filtered, Wash, Filtered and Unfiltered Waste Water, respectively, were of the Applied Water.				Average Actual Rates of Filtration.		Average Net Rates of Filtration.			Average Grains of Applied Sulphate of Alumina.		Average Bacterial Efficiencies.
		Period.		Filtered.	Wash.	Waste.		Cubic Feet per Minute.	Million Gallons per Acre per 24 Hours.	Cubic Feet per Minute.	Million Gallons per Acre per 24 Hours.	Gallons per 24 Hours.	Per Gal. of Applied Water.	Per Gal. of Net Filtered Water.	
		Service.	Wash.			Filtered.	Unfiltered								
Summary No. 1, entire investigation.	Warren	93.31	6.69	97.30	7.10	0.70	2.00	19.9	120	17.3	105	186 000	2.70	3.00	96.7
	Jewell	95.88	4.12	99.54	5.33	0.32	0.14	24.7	100	22.2	90	239 000	2.49	2.65	96.0
	Western Gravity	93.57	6.43	92.95	10.75	3.08	3.97	15.1	96	12.5	76	135 000	2.90	3.53	97.4
	Western Pressure	95.05	4.95	97.84	9.28	2.16	0.00	21.7	154	16.5	116	178 000	2.41	2.72	97.3
Summary No. 2, excluding periods 14, 15, 16.	Warren	93.16	6.84	97.02	6.85	0.81	2.17	16.7	101	17.6	106	190 000	2.68	2.98	96.2
	Jewell	95.76	4.24	99.49	5.13	0.34	0.17	24.1	97	21.8	88	235 000	2.43	2 58	95.6
	Western Gravity	93.57	6.43	92.95	10.75	3.08	3.97	15.1	96	12.5	76	135 000	2.90	3.53	97.4
	Western Pressure	95.05	4.95	98.00	8.40	2.00	0.00	24.9	176	17.6	124	191 000	2.37	2.65	97.4
Summary No. 3, excluding periods 1, 14, 15, 16.	Warren	92.85	7.15	96.95	7.14	0.87	2.18	20.0	121	17.2	104	186 000	2.82	3.14	97.8
	Jewell	95.81	4.19	99.49	5.29	0.36	0.15	23.9	97	21.7	88	234 000	2.53	2.69	97.6
	Western Gravity	93.57	6.43	92.95	10.75	3.08	3.97	15.1	96	12.5	76	135 000	2.90	3.53	97.4
	Western Pressure	95.05	4.95	98.00	8.40	2.00	0.00	20.2	143	17.6	124	191 000	2.37	2.65	97.4
Summary No. 4, excluding 1, 2, 12, 14, 15, 16.	Warren	92.43	7.57	96.82	7.92	0.83	2.35	19.8	120	16.9	102	182 000	3.17	3.57	98.5
	Jewell	95.45	4.55	99.43	5.72	0.44	0.13	23.9	97	21.6	87	232 000	2.84	3.04	97.9
	Western Gravity	93.57	6.43	92.95	10.75	3.08	3.97	15.1	96	12.5	76	135 000	2.90	3.53	97.4
	Western Pressure	95.05	4.95	98.00	8.40	2.00	0.00	20.2	143	17.6	124	191 000	2.37	2.65	97.4
Summary No. 5, excluding periods 1, 2, 10.	Warren	90.61	9.39	95.20	8.89	1.64	3.16	19.4	117	16.2	98	174 000	3.84	4.45	98.6
	Jewell	94.86	5.14	99.25	5.92	0.50	0.25	23.1	93	20.6	83	222 000	2.90	3.11	96.7
	Western Gravity	93.57	6.43	92.95	10.75	3.08	3.97	15.1	96	12.5	76	135 000	2.90	3.53	97.3
	Western Pressure	95.10	4.90	98.03	7.29	1.97	0.00	21.3	151	18.7	153	201 000	2.14	2.36	97.1

Outline of the Methods followed in the Discussion of the Results of the Investigations.

At the outset of this discussion the fact is to be recorded that the amount of strictly comparable data forms only a small proportion of those presented in the foregoing tables. This was due to conditions which unavoidably caused results to be influenced by more than one varying factor at the same time. To keep conditions parallel with regard to certain important factors was impracticable, owing to the arrangements under which the tests were conducted. Nevertheless, considerable light was obtained upon those laws which appear to control, practically speaking, the efficiency and elements of cost of purification by this method. This is especially true of the laws when taken as a whole. When single laws or principles are considered, it will be found that in many cases they are intimately associated with others, and the data lead to valuable and practical suggestions, rather than to well-defined and specific conclusions. This was not true in all cases, however, as much definite information of practical significance was obtained.

The discussion is presented under five main sections, as follows:

1. The quality of the Ohio River water after purification, with reference to the respective systems.
2. Prominent factors, which influenced the qualitative efficiency of purification in the case of the respective systems.
3. Prominent factors which influenced the elements of cost of purification in the case of the respective systems.
4. Comparison of the elements of cost of purification, by the respective systems, of twenty-five million gallons of Ohio River water daily, based on the foregoing results.
5. General conclusions.

The discussions and conclusions in this chapter relate solely to the information obtained up to August 1, 1896. In 1897 additional light was obtained on a number of important points connected with this general method of purification, as is stated in Chapter XV. For a complete understanding of the practical significance of these tests it is necessary to study, together, both Chapters IX and XV, but it must be borne in mind that they refer to distinctly separate data, which were obtained under different conditions.

Section No. 1.

The Quality of the Ohio River Water after Purification, with Reference to the Efficiency of the Respective Systems.

For the sake of explicitness the quality of the water after purification is discussed with the following points in view:

A. Physical character.
B. Chemical character.
C. Biological character.

It will be remembered that this method was followed in Chapter I, where the composition of the Ohio River water before purification was described; and reference is made here to that chapter for detailed data for comparison with those presented in this chapter and the preceding one.

Physical Character of the Effluents.

Appearance.—As a rule the appearance of the effluents of the respective systems was satisfactory with regard to freedom from turbidity. Each of the effluents was turbid at times, but the operation of the systems was usually modified promptly, so as to correct a failure in appearance.

In the case of the Western Systems, but not in the Warren or Jewell systems, the effluents were usually turbid immediately after washing the filters, and it was the custom to waste the effluent until it became clear. In the Warren and Western Pressure systems, the effluent usually became turbid after the loss of head had reached a certain but varying amount, and in these systems it was the turbidity of the effluent which determined the time of washing the filter. This was true in a great many instances of the Jewell System, but by no means uniformly so. The composition of the river water with its minute particles of clay, and the degree of coagulation of the river water with reference to the actual conditions of filtration, were important factors associated with the appearance of the effluent, as will be evident from the following portions of this chapter.

The foregoing summary of the data on the appearance of the several effluents, in Table No. 1, shows that the effluent of the Jewell System was the most satisfactory in this respect.

Color.—As the river water itself, independent of its suspended matters, is practically colorless all of the effluents were naturally satisfactory with regard to color. Whenever they showed a noticeable color it was not due to dissolved coloring matter in the filtered water, but to a turbidity which has been referred to under "Appearance."

Taste.—The taste of the several effluents was satisfactory, although it differed somewhat from that of the river water, owing to the varying amounts and kinds of suspended matters in the latter.

Odor.—The slight musty, aromatic or vegetable odor of the river water was substantially unchanged by the purification of the water by this method. In practically no case was the odor objectionable, or more intense than would be expected from a surface water.

Chemical Character of the Effluents.

Organic Matter.—With the possible exception of those abnormal conditions when the appearance of the effluent failed to be satisfactory, the organic matter in the river water was reduced to a satisfactory degree by each of the systems of purification. The summary of the data upon this point, presented in Table No. 2 of this chapter, shows the percentages of removal. It will be noted that practically all of the suspended organic matter, and a certain amount of dissolved organic matter which was dependent upon the quantity of applied sulphate of alumina, were removed from the water in the case of each of the respective systems of purification.

Dissolved Oxygen.—The amount of free atmospheric oxygen dissolved in the water was substantially unchanged by treatment by the Jewell and Western Gravity systems. There was a slight increase as a rule in the case of the Warren System, due to passage of the effluent over the weir by which the rate of filtration was regulated. In the Western Pressure System there was apparently no change until the warm weather of June and July, when there was a reduction in the amount of oxygen dissolved in the water. The results of determinations of the amounts of oxygen dissolved in the river water and in the effluents of the respective systems of purification are given in the following table:

PERCENTAGES WHICH THE FREE OXYGEN DISSOLVED IN THE OHIO RIVER WATER, AND IN THE EFFLUENTS OF THE RESPECTIVE SYSTEMS OF PURIFICATION, WAS OF THAT NECESSARY FOR SATURATION AT THE ACTUAL TEMPERATURE.

Date.	Temperature. Deg. C.	River Water.	Effluents.			
			Warren.	Jewell.	Western Gravity.	Western Pressure.
1895						
Dec. 3	5.4	78	81	78	....	....
" 4	4.5	76	80	79	....	....
" 6	4.2	80	82	78	....	....
" 9	4.1	87	86	82	....	....
1896						
Jan. 11	2.1	86	93	88	84	....
" 17	2.4	98	100	97	97	....
Feb. 10	5.9	93	97	91	92	....
" 15	7.0	97	100	....	95	....
" 26	3.4	100	100	92	99	....
Mar. 4	4.4	92	92	92	92	....
" 11	6.5	90	90	88	90	....
" 19	5.2	100	100	100	98	....
April 9	9.9	91	93	91	....	....
May 6	23.1	85	96	85	....	....
" 14	24.0	79	83	74	....	....
" 23	24.5	75	....	....	....	75
" 29	24.7	71	87	71	....	71
June 5	24.2	76	85	87	....	73
" 10	24.7	80	88	80	....	70
" 18	25.3	78	87	78	....	68
" 24	26.8	80	91	85	....	67
July 9	25.5	72	78	76	....	60
" 18	25.6	71	83	77	76	....

Undecomposed Sulphate of Alumina.—The question of the passage of undecomposed sulphate of alumina was presented and discussed with care in Chapter III. It may be again stated that with the skill and care requisite for the efficient and economical operation of a system of purification by this method there is no occasion for the passage into the effluent of undecomposed chemical, applied for the purpose of coagulation, so far as can be judged from the quality of the Ohio River water met with during these investigations. The only instance where the effluent was acid, due to an excess of sulphate of a'umina, for several days in succession was in the case of the Jewell System during July.

This was due solely to carelessness on the part of the operators of the system. In all of the systems the lack of adequate provisions for subsidence made the possibilities of this occurrence much greater than should be permitted in practice.

Carbon Dioxide.—From a practical point of view the amount of carbon dioxide, more familiarly known as carbonic acid gas and dissolved in water in the form of free carbonic acid, is of considerable significance by virtue of the part which it plays in the corrosion of iron pipe, tanks and boilers. Corrosion of uncoated iron receptacles for water by the joint action of carbonic acid and free atmospheric oxygen gas dissolved in the water is substantially as follows:

Carbonic acid attacks the iron, when incompletely protected by paint or other preparations, and forms what appears to be the ferrous carbonate of iron.

The oxygen in the water changes this compound, formed by the action of the carbonic acid, into the insoluble ferric hydrate of iron, and at the same time liberates carbonic acid gas. This carbonic acid attacks more iron and the action goes on by a repetition of this process, aided by such additional amounts of carbonic acid and oxygen as the water brings to the attacked surface. The rate at which the iron surface is corroded depends upon a series of factors, the relative importance of which is not accurately known. There is no conclusive proof, however, so far as is known, that the action is a self-limited one in the case of pipes and tanks. In boilers the high temperature drives off these gases, and corrosion appears to be more irregular and less marked, and would be located at the water line.

By means of this process there is formed in the iron a depression of greater or less size, according to the period of exposure and other conditions. In this depression, and reaching out from it, is a formation which is called a tubercle. These tubercles have been found to consist principally of iron hydrate or oxide, together with a little silica, lime, magnesia and carbonic acid, and such compounds from the water as are coagulated by the iron hydrate. It will be noted that this action is an illustration of the principles employed in the preliminary treatment of water by the Anderson process of purification, with which you are familiar in a general way.

This corroding action is possessed by the Ohio River water before purification, by virtue of the carbonic acid and oxygen dissolved in it. Whether or not the other substances in the river water influence to an appreciable degree (practically speaking) the corrosion of iron is not now accurately known. But concerning such ingredients, if any are present they are in solution and there are strong reasons for the belief that they would be substantially unaffected by the treatment in question. The corrosion of iron by the river water was shown by an inspection of the water-pipes at the laboratory and pumping station. In the Ohio River water after purification by this method, this corroding action is apparently increased, practically speaking, by an amount proportional to the composition and quantity of alum or sulphate of alumina added to the water to effect coagulation. This increased corroding action is indicated by the following experiment:

On July 8, 1896, two glass flasks containing a considerable quantity of cast-iron borings were filled with river water and Jewell effluent, respectively. The amount of oxygen dissolved in the water of the two flasks was practically the same—about 75 per cent. of that necessary for saturation. The effluent of course contained more carbonic acid, due to the decomposition of the applied sulphate of alumina, which on that day averaged 4.67 grains per gallon. The flasks and their contents were allowed to stand forty-eight hours with occasional stirring. Analyses were then made with the following results:

PARTS PER MILLION.

Sample.	Carbonic Acid Before Treatment.	Dissolved Iron After Treatment.
River water	21.1	8.70
Jewell effluent	40.9	21.30

The above experiment was repeated with like results, and serves to show the increased corroding action of the water after purification. These results, however, must not be taken as a basis for computation of the rate of corrosion in actual practice, because the various conditions affecting this action were not sufficiently parallel to yield data for any other purpose than that for which the experiment was made.

To what extent steam boilers, and cast iron, wrought iron or other metal used for distributing and service pipes or fittings, in the case of this water, are, or may be, effectually protected from corrosion by a suitable surface coating, is a matter which the writer has not investigated, and upon which he has no opinion to express at this time.

In Chapter I it was shown that during June and July, 1896, the Ohio River water contained from 21.1 to 30.8 parts per million of carbonic acid gas by weight. At some seasons of the year the water doubtless contains much more than the above quantity of carbonic acid. The evidence indicates that in Nov., 1895, it was at least 75 parts. A considerable portion of the carbonic acid, and at times perhaps all of it, is engaged in holding the carbonates of calcium and magnesium in solution in the form of bicarbonates. The bicarbonates are not stable compounds, relatively speaking, and there is substantial proof that they give up their carbonic acid to facilitate the corroding action in question. With regard to the relative rates of corroding action by free carbonic acid gas and partially engaged carbonic acid in the form of bicarbonates, there are no available data to lead to a satisfactory expression of opinion.

The amount of carbonic acid gas liberated by the decomposition of alum or sulphate of alumina, is capable of both approximate determination and estimation. The latter requires, however, an exact knowledge of the amount and composition of the applied alum or sulphate of alumina. From the data presented in Chapters I and II the amount of carbonic acid liberated in the water by the decomposition of the applied chemical during these tests may be estimated with sufficient closeness for practical purposes.

The amount of liberated carbonic acid gas per unit quantity of applied chemical varied somewhat in the several lots which were used, owing to the different percentages of sulphuric acid. But taking a chemical of average composition, and assuming that the chemical united wholly with the alkaline compounds, and not with organic or suspended matters, the amount of liberated carbonic acid gas may be adequately shown as follows:

In the case of the potash alum used by the Western Company each grain per gallon would liberate about 2.5 parts per million of carbonic acid gas by weight.

With the several different lots of sulphate of alumina, the parts per million by weight of liberated carbonic acid gas would range from 3.6 to 4.0, and average about 3.7, for each grain per gallon of applied chemicals. These figures refer solely to the liberation of chemically combined carbonic acid gas. In addition thereto, in the case of bicarbonates an equal amount of carbonic acid, partly engaged by holding calcium carbonate in solution, would also be set free. It is very questionable, however, whether this last action would affect corrosion appreciably, if at all.

From the above statements, together with the foregoing tabulations in detail of the amounts of chemical applied by the respective systems, correct information may be obtained as to the average quantity of carbonic acid gas liberated in each case, for runs, days or periods.

Some observations worthy of mention were made upon the wrought-iron reservoir used for the storage of filtered water for use in washing the filters. Throughout the investigations, this iron reservoir, which was not protected on its inner surface by a coating of paint, tar or other material, was practically filled with filtered water. In fact its use for this purpose began early in July, 1895. From the close of the tests on Aug. 1, 1896, the reservoir remained full of filtered water, in an undisturbed condition, until Oct. 17, when one of the systems was operated for a few hours. It then remained undisturbed for another month, when it was drained. Several days after draining, the inner surface of the iron was examined and found to be corroded to a considerable degree. Tubercles were found ranging in size from that of a pin-head to about 0.4 inch in height, and 1 inch in diameter as a maximum. Their size was very variable. It is of course certain that the corroding action was increased somewhat by the acid effluent of the Jewell System during a number of successive days in July. This inexcusable acidity was perhaps not the chief factor, however, as the effluents regularly had considerable corroding action, as was shown by the iron in the effluents which stood over Sunday in the iron outlet pipes.

A more exhaustive study of this subject was made in 1897, and in passing it may be noted, the corroding action of the undecomposed chemical in the effluent even at rare intervals was of great significance, as it accelerated the action of the carbonic acid. The suspended matter in the river water forms a partial protective coating to the metal, and this explains for the most part the results of the experiment on July 8, 1896. Furthermore, the more extended data of 1897 showed that the evidence obtained in 1896 indicated an abnormally high percentage increase of carbonic acid after purification. Additional information upon this subject is given in Chapter XV.

Analysis of one of the tubercles mentioned above showed it to be composed very largely of iron in the ferric oxide state, with a small amount of calcium carbonate (lime).

The percentage composition was found to be as follows:

Water	11.42
Silica (SiO_2)	0.19
Oxide of iron (Fe_2O_3), by difference	85.11
Alumina (Al_2O_3)	Trace
Lime (CaO)	1.77
Magnesia (MgO)	0.03
Sulphuric acid (SO_3)	0.08
Carbonic acid (CO_2), by estimation	1.40
Organic matter	Trace

In concluding this account of the increased corroding action of the water after purification, due to increased amounts of carbonic acid gas proportional to the quantity of alum or sulphate of alumina added to the water, it may be stated that the adoption of this method of purification would call for especial care in coating the inner surface of pipes, and for all feasible means of keeping the amount of applied sulphate of alumina at a minimum.

So far as experience teaches us, the corroding action of this water before and after purification, on lead, would not give trouble, because it quickly forms a coating by itself which protects the lead from further action.

It may also be added, that the carbonic acid gas may be removed from water by lime water or caustic soda, with subsequent subsidence or filtration. It is not probable, however, that such steps would ever be necessary.

Passage of Lime from the Form of Carbonates to that of Sulphate.—It has been explained in Chapter III that the alkalinity of this water was produced, for the most part, if not wholly, by the carbonates and bicarbonates of lime and magnesia, respectively, and that it was reduced by an amount approximately proportional to the quantity of alum or sulphate of alumina added to it. With sulphate of alumina of average composition the alkalinity has been found by actual tests to be reduced about 8.1 parts per million for 1 grain of this chemical added to 1 gallon of ordinary river water. This means practically, since the evidence indicates that the lime is more abundant than magnesia, that this amount of lime and magnesia, but principally lime, is converted from the form of carbonate or bicarbonate to that of sulphate. That is to say, the permanent hardness or incrusting constituents is increased by about 8.1 parts per million, according to the conventional method of expressing permanent hardness in terms of calcium carbonate. The actual weight of the compounds increasing the incrusting constituents would be more than this, because calcium sulphate weighs 1.37 times as much as an equivalent amount of calcium carbonate.

With potash alum, such as was used by the Western Company, the application of 1 grain per gallon was found to reduce the alkalinity, and increase the incrusting constituents about 4.5 parts per million.

The data presented in Chapter I show that the incrusting constituents of the Ohio River water ranged from 30 to 51 parts per million, when tested during this period. With the above data on the increase of incrusting constituents due to the application of alum or sulphate of alumina, and the foregoing records of the amounts of these chemicals employed by the respective systems, a correct idea may be obtained as to the increased incrusting constituents of the several effluents.

It is the amount of incrusting constituents of a water, due to the chlorides, nitrates and sulphates of lime and magnesia, which chiefly determines its fitness for boiler use. When proper care is taken of boilers, it appears that the Ohio River water does not give serious trouble except during low water in the fall, by the formation of boiler scale; although the suspended matter in the water forms a sludge, which requires frequent flushing of the boilers, and occasional removal by manual labor. With the probable exception of magnesium chloride, due to its tendency to decomposition and formation of hydrochloric acid, there is no more objectionable ingredient of water for boilers than sulphate of lime. This compound, which is formed by the addition of alum or sulphate alumina to water, as explained above, and which is soluble at ordinary temperature, produces at boiler temperatures a fine hard scale, in which practically all of the suspended matters of the water become embodied, when those matters consist of fine clay. In the case of heavy mud, these incrustations are attached to the sludge. Unless removed, the scale formed in this manner eventually causes a marked waste in the consumption of fuel by retarding the transmission of heat to the water; and it is completely removed with great difficulty.

Such a scale was found in Boiler No. 3 at the pumping station of this Company, as you have been advised.

This boiler was said to have been filled with the effluent of the Warren and Jewell systems on July 7. During the next run of five weeks, muddy river water was introduced to replace the steam which was not condensed and returned from the engine to the boiler. The boiler was carefully examined after one subsequent run to this one was made, without cleaning during the interval of rest. On examination the tubes and plates were found to be covered with a hard rough incrustation such as above described. This was especially noticeable on the iron plates around the firebox. In places there were evidences of corrosion. A portion of this incrustation was removed and analyzed, with results which show the following percentage composition:

Water, with organic and volatile matters	16.52
Silica (SiO_2)	19.65
Oxide of iron (Fe_2O_3)	4.30
Alumina (Al_2O_3)	9.66
Lime (CaO)	37.97
Magnesia (MgO)	0.60
Soda (Na_2O)	Undetermined
Potash (K_2O)	Undetermined
Chlorine (Cl)	Trace
Nitric acid (N_2O_5)	Trace
Carbonic acid (CO_2)	Trace
Sulphuric acid (SO_3)	11.87

The alumina which was found in the incrustation came from the silicates (clay) of the river water subsequently added to the boiler, and not from the chemical applied in the course of purification.

At the time when the boiler was said to have been filled with the effluent, there were about four grains per gallon of sulphate of alumina being added to the river water on an average. This practically doubled the incrusting constituents of the water, and added to the effluent about 44 parts per million of calcium sulphate by weight. This sulphate was soluble as it entered the boiler, but the high temperature caused it to be insoluble, with the result that a very hard scale was formed, which included a large portion of the suspended matter of the water subsequently added to the boiler.

In fact the analyses show that less than 20 per cent. of the incrustation was composed of sulphate of lime.

The above experience shows that all reasonable steps should be taken to keep the amount of applied sulphate of alumina to a minimum. In this connection, however, it is to be stated that the amount of sulphate of alumina added to the river water on the date when the boiler was said to have been filled, was about 50 per cent. greater than the average amount employed during these tests.

Furthermore, the mud, silt and clay in the water subsequently put into the boiler, added very materially to the incrustation, as shown by the results of the chemical analyses.

By the use of soda, it is possible to remove the sulphates of lime and magnesia from the water; and trisodium phosphate will also serve this purpose, should manufacturing establishments choose to remove these ingredients before the water enters the boilers.

Further discussions of the incrusting power of the Ohio River water, before and after purification, with additional data, will be found in Chapter XV. At this point, it may be briefly noted that when the river water is muddy and requires the largest quantities of coagulant, the incrusting constituents naturally present in the water are so low in amount that the total incrusting power of the effluent would be much less than that of the natural river water during the fall months.

Biological Character of the Effluents.

Microscopical Organisms.—The tables in Chapter VIII show that practically no diatoms, algæ or other microorganisms, which may be readily recognized by the aid of the microscope, were present in the effluents. This would be naturally expected under the circumstances, owing to their greater size when compared with the bacteria. It is to be noted, however, that very few organisms of this nature were found in the river water, owing to unfavorable natural conditions existing there.

In this connection there arises a question of much practical significance, as was pointed out in a communication addressed to you on July 11, 1896; that is, the conditions under which the growth of microorganisms, notably algæ, in the effluents could be prevented during the period when the water is stored prior to distribution. In the case of all the effluents the conditions for growth of algæ would be favorable in the presence of sunlight; and should these forms once become established in the distributing reservoir the probability of the production of objectionable tastes and odors in the effluent, no matter how satisfactory was its character as it left the filters, would be a very serious state of affairs.

There are no specific data to offer upon this subject.

Bacteria.—The removal of bacteria from a water which at times shows such marked proof of sewage pollution as is the case with the Ohio River, is a very important matter. This is particularly so in view of the rapidly increasing population in the Ohio River valley, and the set of data upon this point was made as complete as practicable. Comprehensive summaries of these data have already been presented in this chapter. The bacterial efficiency of the respective systems, as shown by the total averages, was as follows:

System.	Bacterial Efficiency.
Warren	96.7
Jewell	96.0
Western Gravity	97.4
Western Pressure	97.3

The above results are not directly comparable, because the length of service and the condition of the river water during service were quite unlike, as shown by the data of each of the twenty periods of different grades of river water.

Excluding the Western Gravity System on the grounds of failure to purify enough water, when the river water was in a muddy condition, to wash its own sand layer, and taking the averages of all those periods in which the remaining systems were in operation without any prescriptions from this Company, the following bacterial efficiencies are obtained:

System.	Bacterial Efficiency.
Warren	98.5
Jewell	97.9
Western Pressure	97.4

The above figures show the relative efficiency which the systems possessed in the removal of bacteria from the river water. During the early part of the tests the bacterial efficiency was irregular and unsatisfactory at times in the case of all the systems, but least so in the case of the Warren. This was due in part to limitations of the devices employed in the respective systems, and in part to a lack of care and skill in adapting the operation of the system to meet the requirements of the rapidly varying character of the river water. In February and March the bacterial efficiencies of the systems, speaking in general terms, were so unsatisfactory that an official communication was addressed on March 16 to the operators of the systems. The request was made among others that they should keep the bacterial efficiency of their systems above 97 at all times when the number of bacteria per cubic centimeter in the river water exceeded 7000, and when the bacteria in the river water were less than this number there should not be more than 200 per cubic centimeter in the effluents.

Following this official request for greater uniformity in bacterial efficiency, the application of chemicals and the rate of filtration, a number of changes and improvements were made in the systems.

As a rule the removal of bacteria from that time to the close of the test was satisfactory, provided we disregard the amount of chemicals employed to effect the purification.

There was one prominent point of much practical value learned in connection with the bacterial efficiency of the systems. The opinion has generally prevailed that the quality of the effluent of a filter of the type employed in these tests would not be satisfactory immediately after washing the sand layer, and for some minutes it would be necessary to waste the filtered water. The satisfactory bacterial results obtained from the Warren and Jewell systems, in which the sand layer was quite thoroughly washed as a rule, show clearly that the unsatisfactory quality of the filtered water just after washing is not an inherent feature of this type of filters under the existing conditions, but a consequential one, arising from incomplete washing of the sand layer, and other factors.

Inspection of the results showing the average bacterial efficiency of the systems indicates them to be fairly satisfactory when compared with available data upon the efficiency of filters of the English type. Such comparisons of data, however, require the careful consideration of several facts. In the first place, the growths of harmless bacteria generally recognized to prevail to a greater or less degree in the underdrains and lower portions of filters of the English type, did not become established to any marked degree in the corresponding portions of these filters of the American type, owing evidently to the washing of the sand layer at frequent intervals. This was especially true of the filters of the Warren and Jewell systems, in which the thoroughness of washing was enhanced by the accompanying agitation of the sand. Another fact bearing directly upon this point is, that if any slight growth of bacteria within the lower portions of a filter of the American type should take place, the rate of filtration would cause the bacteria to be diluted in the effluent to about fifty times the extent that would be the case in English filters. These facts, together with the results of numerous comparative observations of the species of bacteria in the water before and after purification, show that, in order to insure to the consumers of the same water the same protection from disease germs, the bacterial efficiency by this method of purification must be somewhat higher than in the case of English filters.

Several years ago it was demonstrated by a series of separate investigations in different parts of the world, that English filters were not "germ-proof," but with skill and care in their construction and operation, they could be made very nearly so. It follows from the experience gained in these tests, as stated above, that skill and care are apparently more necessary in the case of the method of purification as practiced and investigated in these tests, than in the case of the English filters. With more adequate provision for subsidence, the necessary skill and attention in operation would be materially reduced. This fact of not being "germ-proof" was confirmed by the marked similarity from time to time of the bacteria in the water before and after purification. Evidence upon this point was also obtained from the artificial application of bacteria, which in their life-history in water resemble the bacillus generally recognized as the specific germ of typhoid fever.

Bacillus Prodigiosus.—This germ was applied to the filters of each of the systems on a number of different occasions during the month of July, 1896. It was not considered prudent to apply these germs to the filters at an earlier period. The reason of this was to guard against the possibility of having any bacterial growth within the filter, if such should occur, attributed to any actions of the Water Company. In passing, it may be added that the introduction of *Bacillus prodigiosus* requires the addition to the water of a certain, but very small, amount of organic matter in which the germs were grown. When these germs were applied to the filters it was done very cautiously, and with scarcely an appreciable addition to the amount of organic matter naturally present in the water. The method consisted of applying to the water above the sand layer a measured quantity of a solution which contained millions of this germ to each cubic centimeter. These applications were made every five minutes for several hours, and the applied germs distributed in the water as uniformly as practicable. During these applications, samples of the effluent were collected at frequent intervals for analysis.

The results of these applications of *Bacillus prodigiosus* to the several filters are summarized in the next table. They show clearly that under the existing conditions an appreciable number of these germs was able to pass through the filters. Owing to the limited amount of data, all of which were obtained under a narrow range of conditions, they are of little value in the consideration of the absence of bacterial growths within the filters.

SUMMARY OF THE RESULTS OF THE APPLICATION OF BACILLUS PRODIGIOSUS TO THE FILTERS OF THE RESPECTIVE SYSTEMS.

Date. 1896.	Number of Applied B prodigiosus per Cubic Centimeter of Filtered Water.	Number of Samples of Effluent Analyzed.	Number of B. prodigiosus per Cubic Centimeter of Filtered Water.			Average Percentage of Removal
			Max.	Min.	Average.	
			WARREN FILTER.			
July 9	465	20	18	0	3	99.4
" 16	3 470	18	16	0	7	99.8
" 24	800	7	2	0	0.7	99.9
" 28	150	28	4	0	0.2	99.9
			JEWELL FILTER.			
July 3	170	23	3	0	0.4	99.8
" 18	1 170	35	4	0	1	99.9
" 29	350	29	8	0	1	99.7
			WESTERN GRAVITY FILTER.			
July 11	975	21	6	0	2	99.8
" 24	940	23	29	0	10	98.9
			WESTERN PRESSURE FILTER.			
July 14	450	33	19	0	3	99.3
" 21	480	22	27	0	7	98.6

SECTION No. 2.

PROMINENT FACTORS WHICH INFLUENCED THE QUALITY OF THE OHIO RIVER WATER AFTER PURIFICATION IN THE CASE OF THE RESPECTIVE SYSTEMS.

The following pages contain a brief discussion of the influence of the factors which from a practical point of view appeared to be of the most importance in the purification of this water. As a rule these factors affected both the quality of the effluents and the cost of treatment. Their influence upon the quality of the effluents is considered in this section, and their relation to the cost of treatment is presented in the next section of this chapter. In some cases the factors were common to all the systems, but in others they differed to a marked degree in the respective systems. An outline and comparison of the factors affecting the systems differently are given.

Composition of the River Water.

The quality of the effluents in all cases was affected by the composition of the river water, on account of the widely varying amounts of chemical which were added to the water in its various stages, as shown in the foregoing summary of results by periods. Owing to the large quantity of suspended matter frequently present in the river water, it was necessary at such times in the case of all the systems, to add to the water comparatively large amounts of alum or sulphate of alumina. As already explained, such additions caused an increase in the corroding action of the effluents, due to the increased amounts of carbonic acid gas set free; and also made the water less desirable for boiler use, owing to the comparatively large amount of lime changed from carbonate into the form of sulphate. Large amounts of alum or sulphate of alumina did not necessarily affect the quality of the effluents in other respects, provided the quantity was kept below that which could be decomposed by the carbonates and bicarbonates (alkalinity) of the river water.

One observation of much practical significance, which was repeatedly noted, may be recorded here.

This observation refers to the relation of the amounts of sulphate of alumina necessary to produce a perfectly clear effluent, and that necessary to give a satisfactory efficiency to the system in the removal of bacteria. Early in the investigations it was noted that as the composition of the river water varied from time to time, the amounts of sulphate of alumina necessary to produce the two above-named results, respectively, were far from parallel.

The most marked examples of this were observed in March and May, 1896. During the latter days of March, the suspended matter in the river water was comparatively large in size, and of a red color; and the effluents in many cases were clear, even brilliant, without a satisfactory removal of bacteria. During the latter part of May, however, the rains which fell after a long period of drought produced such a character of the water in the river, that the suspended matters were very light and minute. In some cases, the suspended particles were finer than bacteria and not more than 0.00001 inch in diameter as measured under the microscope.

Under these circumstances the appearance of the effluent became unsatisfactory in less than one-half hour after the filters were put in service after a thorough washing, and when the number of bacteria in the effluent remained normal. But the most interesting observation made upon these conditions was that the effluent became unsatisfactory in appearance before there was a perceptible increase in the acting head necessary to produce filtration at the given rate. These effects were evidently due to an inadequate degree of coagulation of the water as it entered the sand layer to be filtered at the given rate.

Application of Alum or Sulphate of Alumina.

Preparation of Solutions.—This question was referred to in general terms in Chapter II. In the case of the solutions of sulphate of alumina, with a very few exceptions, it is not probable that the quality of the effluents was affected by irregularities in their preparation. In all cases, however, it would be desirable in the operation of a large system to employ more careful and systematic methods than were noted at times.

The point to which attention is especially invited at this time is in connection with the first device used by the Western Company for the preparation of solutions of potash alum. In winter weather, when the temperature of the water was low, the strength of the solutions, obtained by the passage of a current of water through an alum tank placed on a by-pass on the main water-pipe, was so irregular that the method may be pronounced a failure, so far as its application for the coagulation of the rapidly changing Ohio River water is concerned. The use of this device was discontinued by the Western Company on April 9.

Uniformity of Application of Solutions.—With regard to the regular application of solutions of chemicals in suitable amounts to effect proper coagulation of the varying river water, all devices gave the appearance of being crude, so far as their part in the production of a satisfactory effluent was concerned. With a water of a certain grade the application of chemicals by the Warren device was fairly satisfactory on the whole. With the Jewell and second Western devices satisfactory results could be obtained by giving them close attention. Such attention, however, was not regularly given to them, especially during the earlier part of the investigation.

In its use during these tests the first Western device was a failure, even when an attendant stood over it practically all the time. Not only did the operators lose control of the rate of application of the solution, but, as noted above, their inability to control the rate of application was increased by the widely varying strength of the chemical solutions. In warmer weather when the water would dissolve greater quantities of alum the operation of the device would be still more unsatisfactory.

Application of Lime.

Lime was applied to the river water only by the Jewell System. Under the existing circumstances its application was unnecessary. The object of its application was apparently to guard against the passage of undecomposed sulphate of alumina into the effluent, and perhaps to facilitate the coagulation of the water by the regular chemicals. The trial of the application of lime by the Jewell System was followed by disastrous results so far as the quality of the effluent was concerned. This was due chiefly to the manner of application of the lime. At times the lime and sulphate of alumina must have reached the river water alternately, and produced of course an effluent of unsatisfactory character. At other times the sulphate of alumina was decomposed in the feed pipe leading from the pump to the main inlet water-pipe. After the adoption of the separate feed pipes, shortly before the abandonment of the use of lime, the above difficulties were removed to a greater or less degree. In this connection reference is made to some comparative experiments upon the coagulation of the Ohio River water by aluminum hydrate under different conditions made by the Water Company, and recorded in Chapter XII.

It is not to be inferred from these comments that the use of lime would not be advantageous for some conditions and for some waters. The above criticism refers only to the fact that its application during these tests was unnecessary, and that its manner of application in the Jewell System was not well advised.

Quantity of Applied Alum or Sulphate of Alumina.

For all the varying conditions of the river water there was doubtless a certain amount of sulphate of alumina, which, by virtue of its coagulating power, was best adapted for the purification of the water by each of the systems. To define this optimum amount for any given conditions is impossible with the available data. Inspection of the records and summaries shows that all of the systems were operated far from this mark at times. This was more noticeable during the early than during the later part of the investigations, when the operators had some experience to guide them. It will readily be seen that the liberal use of chemical by the Warren and Jewell systems was reversed at times during the tests. Comparing the effect of the actual quantities used upon the quality of the effluent with that of the optimum, it may be stated that in numerous cases the actual quantity appeared to be below the optimum, and showed its effect by high bacteria in the effluent, or unsatisfactory appearance, or both. At times the actual quantity was in excess of the optimum, and affected the effluent by an unnecessary increase in its corroding action and capacity to form scale in boilers, as already discussed in this chapter. Comments along this line will be found in the next section, under the cost of applied chemicals. For further information in this connection reference is made to the detailed data in foregoing tables.

Provision for the Removal of Suspended Matter from the River Water by Sedimentation.

At times of flood the Ohio River water contains large quantities of heavy mud, and experience indicates that in the neighborhood of 75 per cent. of this mud on an average may be removed economically by plain subsidence without the use of coagulating chemicals. At other times, especially during the spring and early summer, the river water contains large quantities of very finely divided suspended matter, which would require days and perhaps weeks for the removal of the bulk of it by plain subsidence. The evidence presented in Chapter IV, however, indicates that it could be removed after relatively short subsidence, following the application of comparatively small amounts of a coagulating chemical.

In all cases not only were provisions for plain subsidence entirely lacking, but the period for coagulation and subsidence was far too short. Turning to the summaries of results it will be noted in the case of all the systems that the increase in applied chemical, due to muddy water, reached at times as high as 8 grains per gallon. The effect of the application of large quantities of chemical, with reference to corrosion and incrustation, has been referred to above. With plain subsidence followed by longer periods of coagulation and subsidence these high amounts of coagulant could be reduced materially. There are also indications that at times it would be advisable to make more than one application of coagulant. The Warren System was superior to the others with regard to provisions for the removal of suspended matter from the river water by subsidence, but even in this case the provisions were wholly inadequate to prevent the use of excessive amounts of an expensive chemical, and their attending effects. In fact this was the weakest feature of all these systems.

Provisions for Cleaning.—All of the systems were very weak in provisions for ready and economical cleaning of the compartments in which sedimentation took place. How far this affected the character of the effluent it is difficult to estimate, as apparently these compartments were cleaned in the case of each of the respective systems at as frequent intervals as was thought necessary. It is probable, however, that the difficulties of cleaning, due to lack of provision for the ready and economical performance of this operation, often led to delay in cleaning, and to the consequent passage of sludge from the basin or chamber upon the filter.

Provisions for Inspection.—The need for regular and systematic inspection of the interior of the compartments in which sedimentation took place, and of the contents of these compartments, seemed to have been almost wholly ignored in these systems. This was especially true in the case of the Western Systems, where the arrangements were such as to necessitate the draining of the settling chamber, to examine its contents. The failure to inspect the condition of the contents of these compartments, with regard to the amount or sludge, undoubtedly led also to delays in cleaning the compartments, with the resultant effect of the passage of sludge from the basin or chamber upon the filter. The most notable example of this was found in the Warren System on July 22–27.

Degree of Coagulation of the Partially Subsided Water as it entered the Sand Layer.

The degree of coagulation of the water as it entered the sand layer was found to be the most important feature of satisfactory and efficient purification by this type of filter. To an experienced observer the proper degree could be told with considerable accuracy by the size of the flakes or masses of coagulated material and the rapidity with which they subsided. The coagulation had to be thorough; that is, the volume of hydrate had to be practically sufficient to envelop all suspended matters or furnish enough gelatinous surface to which the particles could adhere. It is believed that just after washing this is absolutely true, but after a filter had been operated for a time and flakes of coagula had accumulated in the sand there might be permissible a slight departure from thorough coagulation. Thorough coagulation of the water above the sand, or very nearly thorough, was absolutely essential in order to remove the fine clay particles; and during the greater part of the year the removal of bacteria was satisfactory when the effluent was free from turbidity.

At times during the winter, however, when the suspended matter was very coarse the bacterial efficiency required especial attention.

Taking everything into consideration it may be safely concluded that the volume of available hydrate in the water as it entered the sand layer was the most important feature of successful filtration; and that when the amount of hydrate present departed materially from that necessary for complete coagulation a uniformly satisfactory quality of the effluent could not be expected.

Sand Layers of the Several Filters.

Very little information upon the relative value of each of the more important features of the sand layers is available, as was stated to you July 11, 1896. This is explained by the fact that a series of factors unavoidably worked together to disguise the influence of any particular factor. The two principal factors which affected the efficacy of the sand layers in purifying the water were the degree of coagulation of the water and the rate of filtration. Both of these factors are referred to in their proper order.

All things considered the sand layers of the Jewell System were the most efficient in producing an effluent of satisfactory character.

A brief outline of the more important points as the systems stood at the close of the tests is as follows:

Thickness.—The thickness of the sand layers in the respective systems was as follows:

System.	Thickness in Inches.
Warren	27.0
Jewell	30.5
Western Gravity	31.0
Western Pressure	49.5

Although the Jewell sand layer gave the best results it is still an open question what the thickness of the sand layer should be to give the best results under favorable circumstances with regard to other conditions. The Western sand layers did not appear to advantage, owing, it seems, to failure to wash them satisfactorily and at times to the degree of coagulation with reference to the rate of filtration.

Size of Grain.—A comparison of the sizes of the grains in the several sand layers, as shown by their effective sizes (10 per cent. of the material finer than the diameter given in millimeters), is as follows:

System.	Effective Size.
Warren	0.51
Jewell	0.43
Western Gravity	0.43
Western Pressure	0.44

The Warren material was apparently too coarse to give uniformly the most efficient results under the existing conditions. The fine material of the two Western systems was mixed in both cases with very coarse sand, giving the resultant layer a rather higher effective size. These mixed sands were, however, as fine in effective size as that of the Jewell, but their use was handicapped by factors mentioned under Thickness of Sand Layer.

Composition.—The available evidence, so far as it goes, points to as satisfactory results under suitable conditions from natural sands, of uniform and proper size, as from the more expensive crushed quartz.

Rate of Filtration.

Unless some abnormal and disturbing features appeared, the rates of filtration were maintained so as to give as nearly as possible the contract capacity of 250,000 gallons per 24 hours for each system. At times of very muddy water none of the systems reached the prescribed amount, owing to the incomplete preliminary subsidence. The rates differed somewhat in the different systems, due for the most part to the different areas of the sand layers in relation to the contract rate. As a rule the rates were held fairly uniform under the same conditions of river water, the range of variation under parallel conditions being usually less than 10 per cent. The widely varying factors which influenced the results at different times in addition to changes in rate prevent the drawing of any specific conclusions.

In the following table are given the rates in million gallons per acre daily, the amounts of suspended solids in the river water in parts per million, the amounts of sulphate of alumina used, in grains per gallon, and the bacterial efficiencies of the several systems, for those runs on which the unit rates were the maximum and the minimum, and also the average of these quantities for the entire investigation.

TABLE OF LEADING RESULTS WITH MAXIMUM AND MINIMUM UNIT RATES, AND AVERAGE RESULTS FOR THE ENTIRE INVESTIGATION.

	Warren.			Jewell.		
	Min.	Max.	Aver.	Min.	Max.	Aver.
Rate	80	155	120	57	150	100
Solids	1677	36	......	200	220	......
Sulph. of alumina	7.92	0.98	2.70	2.01	5.50	2.49
Bacterial efficiency	97.5	95.2	96.7	95.7	99.9	96.0

	Western Gravity.			Western Pressure.		
	Min.	Max.	Aver.	Min.	Max.	Aver.
Rate	33	152	96	83	202	154
Solids	420	17	......	1 004	25	......
Sulph. of alumina	9.33	0.71	2.90	......	1.24	2.41
Bacterial efficiency	99.0	92.6	97.4	91.4	96.8	97.3

As stated above, the wide variations in the controlling factors make it practically impossible to draw any definite conclusions from the results in regard to the relative efficiencies of different unit rates. That within the ranges employed, the lower rates did not give uniformly any better results than the higher ones, and that the maximum limits of safe rates were not reached in this work is indicated by the results of the last table and clearly shown by the next table. In this table are given averages of the leading results of the Warren and Jewell systems, omitting Periods Nos. 1 and 2. These averages have been arranged with regard to the unit rates in order to allow comparison of the results from this standpoint. In the case of the Western Systems the degree of coagulation and other factors were too irregular for these systems to be given a place in this table. The headings and results have all been used and explained before.

LEADING AVERAGE RESULTS OF THE WARREN AND JEWELL SYSTEMS, ARRANGED ACCORDING TO UNIT RATES OF FILTRATION.

Warren System.

Rates included in averages	80–89	90–99	100–109	110–119	120–129	130–139	140–149
Number of runs averaged	7	46	69	45	41	58	25
Rates in million gallons per acre per 24 hours	86.5	97.4	105.0	114.9	125.4	136.4	143.3
Amounts of suspended solids in river water in parts per million	511	534	976	317	157	526	258
Amounts of applied sulphate of alumina in grains per gallon	4.46	4.18	4.04	3.87	1.97	3.25	2.80
Amounts of water filtered per run in cubic feet	2 868	5 630	4 120	6 430	12 050	7 360	5 660
Percentages which the water used for washing and wasted was of the applied water on each run	25	19	14	13	7	11	14
Bacterial Efficiencies	98.0	98.4	98.2	99.1	97.9	98.9	98.5

Jewell System.

Rates included in averages	80–89	90–99	100–109	110–118	119–130	138–143
Number of runs averaged	17	100	76	10	18	8
Rates in million gallons per acre per 24 hours	85.0	96.4	104.5	114.6	122.0	139.7
Amounts of suspended solids in river water in parts per million	1310	591	220	476	458	278
Amounts of applied sulphate of alumina in grains per gallon	5.80	3.90	2.88	3.85	3.95	5.06
Amounts of water filtered per run in cubic feet	7 660	10 837	15 080	7 804	10 580	3 573
Percentages which the water used for washing and wasted was of the applied water on each run	19	12	10	20	18	16
Bacterial efficiencies	97.3	98.0	97.6	98.7	98.6	99.2

These data show conclusively that within these limits in rate of filtration and under the given conditions there were other factors of more practical significance than the rates of flow through the sand. Unquestionably, the most prominent of these factors was the degree of coagulation of the water as it entered the sand layer.

How high it would be possible or practicable to carry the rate of filtration in efficient and economical purification by this method cannot be stated at present; and it would require for its proper solution conditions where the bulk of the suspended matters was removed by subsidence. Some data showing the inadvisability of employing rates of less than 100 million gallons per acre daily were obtained in 1897, and are recorded in Chapter XV.

Regulation and Control of Operation of the Filters.

While considerable care was necessary in the operation of the filters in order to secure a satisfactory effluent it was very seldom that moderate irregularities in the rate of filtration made their influence apparent. The presence of certain irregularities in the pressure or acting head upon the Western pressure filter was found to be a very disturbing and disastrous element, and as a rule caused filtration to be stopped and the filter washed.

Loss of Head.

As the frictional resistance to the passage of water of the sand layers and their accumulation increased, the necessary acting head, or loss of head, increased and approached towards the maximum available head. The several filters behaved quite differently in this respect. The Warren filter contained a coarse sand layer and almost without exception the appearance and quality of the effluent became unsatisfactory when the loss of head was much less than the total available head. As a rule the filter of the Warren System was washed when the loss of head was less than 3 feet.

During a large part of the time the Jewell System employed the full available head (12–14 feet) on their filter before the sand layer was washed, although it is to be noted that the last two feet of head (from 10 to 12 feet) were not of great value as the resistance increased very rapidly above 10 feet. This was not always possible, however, especially when the coagulation of the water as it entered the filter from the settling chamber was incomplete. This factor was also a very important one in connection with the employment of surface agitation during the runs. From the detailed data in Chapter VIII, it will be noted that in many instances this operation was successfully used in the Jewell System.

In the Western Gravity System the filter was washed because the loss of head reached the maximum in the case of the Western gravity filter (A), and in very few cases did the quality or appearance of the effluent deteriorate as the loss of head increased. The opposite of this was uniformly true in the case of the Western gravity filter (B).

Frequent "breaks" were noted in the Western pressure filter when the loss of head was a small fraction of the available head, which was equal approximately to the pressure in the force main to the reservoir. These breaks, evidently due for the most part to irregularities in pressure, causing the water to pass through some channel or place of lessened resistance at an abnormal rate, caused, in turn, the effluent to become turbid, and necessitated washing the filter. Previous to June 1, this filter was operated with widely varying maximum acting heads, the apparent custom being to wash at from 30 to 50 feet loss of head, unless the effluent showed deterioration. After this date the practice was changed, 20 feet being apparently adopted as a maximum. It was seldom, however, that more than 15 feet of acting head were employed, and as a rule it was found advisable to wash the filter when the loss of head was less than 10 feet.

With a water which contained such a large amount of very finely divided suspended matter, as was the case during the last days of May, all the filters gave a poor effluent before there was any marked increase in the loss of head, as already noted.

There were no well-marked indications that there was any difference in the action of the negative head of the Jewell filter, as compared with the positive head of the other filters.

Washing the Sand Layer.

By some the belief has been held that just after washing filters of this type, the effluent is of an unsatisfactory character, and that it is necessary to waste the first portion of the filtered water. One of the most important points learned in these tests was that such was not necessarily the case, provided the sand layer was thoroughly washed and the applied water sufficiently coagulated. As a rule the sand layers in the Warren and Jewell systems were washed quite thoroughly, but more especially and uniformly so in the case of the Warren; and it was very rare during the later part of the tests that the first portion of these effluents after washing was inferior in appearance or character to the remaining portions. In connection with this important and practical point it is to be noted that both of the above systems employed constant agitation of the sand layer during washing. The sand layers of both of these systems were usually washed until the filtered water, which was pumped into them from below the sand layer, was comparatively clear as it overflowed from the filter above the sand.

All of the systems regularly employed filtered water for washing the sand layer during these tests, except in the case of the Western Systems from June 24 to July 27, inclusive, when river water was used by these two systems. From the fact that the operators of the Western Systems abandoned the use of unfiltered water for washing it may be inferred that its use was not wholly satisfactory.

One reason why the Western Systems tried the use of unfiltered water for washing, apparently, was that it was their uniform custom to waste the first portion of effluent after washing the sand layer. It seems very clear that this was required partly by incomplete washing and partly by incomplete coagulation of the applied water. Several factors affected the thoroughness of washing the sand layers of these filters. The most important one was the absence of accompanying agitation. Another important one was the unsatisfactory device used for the distribution of the wash-water beneath the sand layer. As already described in Chapter V, this was accomplished by means of slotted brass tubes, which also served for the collection of the effluent when the filters were in service. These slots were wedge shaped, with the smallest width on the outside forming the opening. It was expected that by this arrangement the openings would not clog up, but that any matters small enough to lodge in them would pass through. This was in a measure found to be true at first, but as comparatively large numbers of sand grains passed through the slots the thin edges soon became worn, resulting in the passage through of more grains or in their lodgment in the opening.

When the flow of water was reversed during washing, some of the sand grains in the tubes were doubtless forced into the beveled openings and obstructed the flow. When these strainer tubes were removed about the first of April many of them were found to be one-third full of sand. This state of affairs naturally caused the sand layer to be incompletely washed, especially in the absence of agitation.

The ball nozzles which were used for the distribution of wash-water in the Western gravity filter (B), after the above experience with the slotted brass tubes, did not at the outset possess the action for which they were designed. This filter in its modified form was not operated long enough to demonstrate the practicability of these devices.

Sand samples from the various filters were collected from time to time and analyzed chemically and bacterially with the following results:

RESULTS OF CHEMICAL AND BACTERIAL ANALYSES OF SANDS OF THE RESPECTIVE SYSTEMS.

Nitrogen in the form of Albuminoid Ammonia expressed in Parts per Million by weight of dry Sand.
Bacteria expressed in Numbers per Gram of dry Sand.

Depth below Surface.		0-0.25 Inch.		1 Inch.		3 Inches.		6 Inches.		12 Inches.		24 Inches.		Bot. of Layer.	
Date.	System.	Nitrogen.	Bacteria.	Nitrogen.	Bacteria.	Nitrogen.	Bacteria.	Nitrogen.	Bacteria.	Nitrogen.	Bacteria.	Nitrogen.	Bacteria.	Nitrogen.	Bacteria.
							Before Washing.								
1896															
Jan. 20	Warren	26.0		20.0		12.0		9.0		7.6				1.9	
May 22		80.0	65 100					11.8	31 500	8.0	35 500	3.4	12 600		
July 17		38.8	44 800					6.0	45 700			2.9	3 300		
Jan. 8	Jewell	365.0		56.8				21.6		17.6		9.6		6.0	
Feb. 28		45.0						11.0						7.0	
July 8		73.3	126 000					6.3	21 000			2.4	14 700	2.7	452 000
Jan. 16	Western Gravity	171.5		41.2		13.0		10.0		10.3		11.1		12.7	
July 25		100.8	870 000							6.1	9 600	8.5	111 900	13.4	21 100
Jan. 12	Western Pressure	114.2		80.5				23.6		14.4		9.6		11.2	
June 13								10.9				11.6			
July 14		110.0	43 700					16.3	26 100			14.7	27 300	15.2	46 700
							After Washing.								
Jan. 2[illegible]	Warren							7.1				8.5			
Feb. 1[illegible]		2.7	2 200									1.9	14 800	1.9	7 200
April 1[illegible]		1.9						2.1				2.2			
May 22		2.2	1 500					2.2	3 700			2.1	13 300		
July 17		2.9	300					3.1	1 300			2.9			
1895															
Oct. 30	Jewell							14.4							
" 30								13.4*	*						
1896															
Jan. 8								34.0							
" 8								28.9*	*						
Feb. 28								2.4				3.2			
" 28								2.4*	*			2.4*	*		
May 22		4.3						4.2				4.0			
July 3		3.9	500					4.0	900			3.9	1 800		
Mar. 21	Western Gravity							9.5				9.0			
July 25		25.8	65 100					5.5				5.8	7 900		
" 14	Western Pressure	11.5	10 500					8.8	5 800			9.0			

* After steaming the sand. Sand was practically sterile.

Relation of Proper Attention to the Efficiency of Purification of the Ohio River Water by this Method.

This subject was touched upon in Chapter VII, where the manner of operation of the several systems was outlined. In connection with the factors which exerted an appreciable influence on the quality of the filtered water, this one must be clearly borne in mind. The impression which some people have that large systems of water purification by this method will at all times yield an effluent of satisfactory character with merely nominal attendance is wholly incorrect so far as the Ohio River water is concerned. In the first place both efficiency and economy require that very close attention be given to the application of chemicals. Setting aside the question of cost, any excess of the chemical above the optimum is attended with increased amounts of corroding and incrusting constituents in the filtered water, and, under unskilled supervision, chemical in excess of the amount which the water will decompose might be added at times, resulting of course in the inadmissible presence of undecomposed chemical in the effluent. On the other hand a reduction of the amount of chemical by a small percentage below the optimum would cause immediate deterioration in the character of the effluent, a deterioration which at times could not be determined for several days, as in the case of the Ohio River water a clear effluent is not necessarily a pure effluent, especially during the winter months.

It will be seen, therefore, that the efficiency of filtration requires very close adherence to the optimum amount of chemical treatment, a problem which is very difficult of solution in the present state of the art, and the solution of which by unskilled hands is absolutely out of the question. Among the many other different factors which affect the quality of the effluent and which are to a greater or less degree dependent on the character of the attendants for their efficiency may be mentioned the following: The decision to wash the sand layer, the process of washing, the operation of the many mechanical devices, and finally the general supervision and systematic methods of procedure without which no system of this kind can be successful.

With adequate facilities for the removal of the coarse matter by plain subsidence the amount of attention for successful operation would be largely reduced, because it would make the water just prior to its filtration much more uniform in character.

SECTION No. 3.

PROMINENT FACTORS WHICH INFLUENCED THE ELEMENTS OF COST OF PURIFICATION OF THE OHIO RIVER WATER IN THE CASE OF THE RESPECTIVE SYSTEMS.

The factors which will be considered in relation to the elements of cost are substantially the same as those noted in the last section with regard to the quality of the effluents. In many respects the two sections should be considered side by side.

In the following pages of this chapter comparisons are made of the different factors as they were found at times of fairly clear and muddiest water and, so far as possible, under normal conditions, respectively.

For this purpose averages are used as follows: For fairly clear water, averages during Period No. 13; for muddiest water, averages during Period No. 20, excluding those runs which were affected by the period of subsidence over night or Sunday; for normal water in most cases, averages for the entire investigation. When the Western Gravity System is referred to, Periods Nos. 8 and 9 are used in place of Periods Nos. 13 and 20.

It must be borne in mind that the averages as obtained above do not represent the conditions as they would exist under the actual times of muddiest water in the Ohio River, but they are taken as the best figures obtained during the investigation, and as sufficiently marked to illustrate the points under discussion.

Composition of the River Water.

Inspection of the records for the several periods shows clearly that the amount of suspended matter in the water exerted a marked influence upon the cost for the chemical. The extreme quantities of sulphate of alumina applied to the river water were 12.60 and 0.40

grains per gallon of applied water. At 1.5 cents per pound this would make on this basis the daily cost for the chemical in the operation of a plant of 25,000,000 gallons daily capacity range from $678 to $21 by these systems.

The above figures, however, do not show the full influence exerted by the composition of the river water upon the cost of chemical in purification by this system. When the river water was comparatively clear the average percentages of applied water which was wasted and used for washing the sand layers in the Warren, Jewell, Western Gravity and Western Pressure systems were 6, 2, 9, and 4, respectively. When the water was in its muddiest condition these average percentages became 34, 25, 99, and 58, respectively.

In view of the fact that the evidence indicates that the Western Gravity System (A) was unable at times of muddiest river water to purify enough water to wash its own sand layer properly, and that the data in regard to the Western Gravity System (B) are not sufficiently extended to permit the drawing of any comparisons, these systems will be omitted from further comparisons at this time. As will be seen by inspection of Table No. 4, and of the tables in Chapter VIII, where the full records are presented, the amounts of wash and waste water in the case of the Jewell and Western Pressure systems, exceeded at times 100 per cent. of the filtered water. The contiguous records indicate, however, that these results were abnormal and not likely to occur under regular conditions of practice.

Figuring the amount of applied chemical upon the average quantity of net purified water, the following range of daily cost for the chemical for the purification of 25,000,000 gallons of Ohio River water is obtained:

System.	Daily Cost.	
	Minimum.	Maximum.
Warren	$80	$547
Jewell	96	584
Western Pressure	59	676

From the above-stated increased percentages of water wasted and used for washing at times of muddy river water, it follows that the appliances and their operation, for supplying this increased amount of water, would be factors in the cost of purification. It is to be noted, however, that under suitable arrangements, water which was wasted either before or after purification, might be purified subsequently. Water which was used for washing the sand layers, however, would probably have to be discharged into the sewer.

The composition of the river water, with regard to its suspended matter, influenced the cost of purification by reducing the net capacity of the respective systems. This is shown by the following table, in which the actual average net capacities of each system as operated, is recorded in gallons per 24 hours at times of clear and muddiest water.

System.	Daily Net Capacity in Gallons.		
	By Contract.	With Clear Water.	With Muddiest Water.
Warren	250 000	200 000	120 000
Jewell	250 000	266 000	160 000
Western Pressure	250 000	238 000	64 000

The above data indicate the size of the reserve portion of the respective systems which would be necessary in order to obtain the full quantity of purified water when the river was in the muddiest condition, as shown by these tests. They do not indicate an adequate reserve portion for all conditions, because the Ohio River water contains at times more mud than was the case in any instance during the tests of these filters.

Application of Alum or Sulphate of Alumina.

Kind of Chemical.—Since sulphate of alumina on an average contains about 60 per cent. more available alumina than potash alum, and the two chemicals are of approximately equal cost, the former is cheaper than the latter in the ratio of about 16 to 10.

Preparation of Solutions.—On the grounds of cost alone the preparation of chemical solutions, in the process of application, should receive fully as much attention as was the case in these tests. In some instances economy demands more care in this particular than was regularly given to it in each of the systems. The chief point in this connection, however, is to record the failure of the first Western device to yield solutions of even approximately uniform strength, such as economy demands in the treatment of the Ohio River water in its rapidly changing conditions.

Method and Uniformity of Application.—Irregularities in the application of the chemical were frequently so marked that they would affect the cost of operations on a large scale. They were more noticeable during the early part of the tests, before the operators of the respective systems were cautioned on this point in an official communication dated March 16, 1896, in which among other points their attention was called to such irregularities.

The Warren device was more satisfactory than the others, all things considered, because it was most nearly automatic. It had several crude features, however, and it is by no means clear that its use would be thoroughly satisfactory in a large system.

The Jewell and second Western devices were satisfactory provided they received sufficient attention. At different times during the same day and with the same water the rate of application varied several fold. This means that if the minimum rate of application was sufficient for its purpose the higher rates caused a waste of chemical equal to their excess over the minimum. It may be noted that the use of sufficient chemical to insure proper coagulation, and a sufficient amount of aluminum hydrate in the water as it passes onto the sand layer, are absolutely essential for the success of this method of purification, and that the use of an insufficient amount of chemical is out of the question. To do this on a large scale with the devices submitted for investigation would be less easy than would be thought at first to be the case.

The first device of the Western Company for the application of chemical was a failure as operated at the beginning of these tests; and it was abandoned shortly after the official communication of the Water Company on March 16, as mentioned above.

The cost of power for the application of the chemical depends of course on the method of application used and the strength of solutions, but with any of these devices it would be comparatively insignificant. With the Warren device the power would be practically only that required to lift the chemicals and water to the mixing tanks. The first Western device required substantially no increase in power over that required for handling the river water. The Jewell and the second Western devices both involved the pumping of the solution against the full pressure in the mains. Assuming an average percentage strength of one per cent. and an average amount of chemical of 2.50 grains per gallon, and that the necessary water and the chemical were delivered on the level of the main house floor, the approximate amount of power required on a basis of 25,000,000 gallons per 24 hours would be in each case as follows:

Warren System........	0.4 H.P.
Jewell System.........	4.0 H.P.
Western Press. System.	4.0 H.P. (2d device)

In the case of the Warren device a very small amount of power was used in turning the propeller wheel which operated the chemical pump. The power thus used was probably only a very small fraction of the total power used in the application of the solutions, and was furnished by the velocity pressure in the water supply pipe.

Quantity of Applied Sulphate of Alumina.

The principal element of cost of purification of the Ohio River water by this method would be the sulphate of alumina used for coagulation. That is to say, this element would exceed any other one, including the interest on the cost of construction of the system. The cost for sulphate of alumina would of course be proportional to the amount, and the amount used would depend upon a series of factors, of which the following are the most important:

1. Composition of river water, with regard to the quantity and character of suspended matter.

2. The optimum quantity of coagulant under the given conditions. The chief variable factor affecting this was the composition of the river water, and the chief fixed factor was the period of coagulation and sedimenta-

tion. In practice plain sedimentation should precede coagulation, and reduce the required amount of coagulant.

3. Relation of the actual to the optimum quantity of applied chemical necessary to secure the proper degree of coagulation in the water during and after subsidence.

A brief discussion of the several factors will be found in this chapter in their logical order.

Application of Lime.

The application of lime as tried in an experimental way by the Jewell System increased, apparently, the cost of proper treatment, disregarding the cost of the lime itself, because it seemed to diminish the coagulating power of the resulting aluminum hydrate.

Under other and better conditions of application this might not be the case. In this connection, see the results of comparative experiments recorded in Chapter XII, on the coagulating power of aluminum hydrate prepared in several different ways.

Provisions for Coagulation and Sedimentation.

In relation to the quality of the effluent it was indicated that in this respect all of the systems were very weak, although the Warren was least so. When it comes to a question of cost this weakness of all the systems in their present form would make their adoption expensive to an unnecessary degree, and therefore of questionable admissibility. The merely nominal period of subsidence with coagulation in the Jewell and Western systems, and for one hour or less in the Warren System, and with no plain subsidence in any case to remove coarse matter, materially increases the cost of purification as follows:

1. It increases the cost for chemical.
2. It necessitates a reserve portion of the system with all appurtenances to handle the water when in its muddiest condition.
3. It necessitates the waste of an unusually large amount of filtered water for the purpose of washing the sand layers.
4. The increase of water wasted as indicated above increases the amount of water to be pumped, and therefore the aggregate cost of pumping.
5. The use from time to time of a comparatively large reserve portion of the system would require the constant employment of a full set of trained attendants, capable of operating the entire system. This would be necessary because the freshets in the Ohio River frequently appear in a most irregular and unexpected manner.

Inspection of the records of the freshets in the Ohio River during the past thirty-five years, presented in Chapter I, shows that during many years the river was in a state of flood for longer and more frequent periods than was the case during these investigations. This means that in many cases the river water contained more suspended matter than was encountered during these tests, and therefore the five factors of cost stated above would be correspondingly increased.

In this connection it is not to be forgotten that the Western Gravity System as first designed was voluntarily taken out of service by the Western Filter Company on March 21, because it was unable to yield enough filtered water to serve for wash-water.

The investigations demonstrate conclusively that economy demands plain subsidence suplemented by a considerable period of coagulation and subsidence, followed at times by further application of chemicals to effect coagulation for filtration, in the case that high rates of filtration should be employed. With regard to the best manner of carrying into practice such an improvement there are very few specific data to serve as a guide, as was first pointed out to you in a general way in a preliminary report dated July 11, 1896.

The closing pages of Chapter IV contain the only evidence to offer upon the subject which was obtained in 1896. Much additional evidence along this line was obtained in 1897, and is recorded in Chapter XV.

Provisions for Cleaning the Settling Basin or Chamber.—This matter was not economically handled in the case of any of the systems. Except in the case of the Jewell it was almost ignored, practically speaking, and in this system the provisions were inadequate for economical use.

Provisions for Inspection of the Condition of the Settling Basin or Chamber.—This factor was apparently lost sight of in all of the systems, and the failure to determine the condition of the contents of these compartments and if necessary remove the accumulation of sludge, undoubtedly led at times to the passage upon the filters of mud which should have been held in the settling basins. The effect of this passage of mud on to the filters on the cost of operation was to decrease the length of runs and therefore to increase the percentage of water wasted and used for washing. The most notable occurrence of this kind took place in the Warren System on July 22 to 27.

Degree of Coagulation of the Water as it Entered the Sand Layer.

One of the most clearly established points in connection with these tests was the absolute necessity of thorough coagulation of the water as it entered the sand layer. With different characters of water the required degree of coagulation varied somewhat, but it was made perfectly clear that with the high rates of filtration employed in these filters of the American type a high degree of coagulation is very essential.

Structure of the Systems.

In the adoption of a system of 25,000,000 gallons capacity, to last for many years, it is very questionable whether wooden structures as employed in the Warren, Jewell, and Western Gravity systems would be advisable in preference to metal. In all of the systems it would be very desirable and probably practicable to make the more important parts of the filters, such as strainer systems, more readily accessible. The unsatisfactory results from the use of wood was illustrated by the foul and slimy deposits upon the walls of the filtered-water compartment beneath the sand layer of the Warren filter when that system was removed after the close of the tests. This particular construction could and should be improved.

In the filters of both the Jewell and the Western systems, but especially in the case of the latter filters, there was a considerable sticking together of the sand grains at the bottom of the sand layers. This segregation of the sand grains was evidently associated with the use of cement, and it is possible that this might lead to serious difficulty in time.

Sand Layers of the Several Filters.

The more important data upon the several sand layers, as they appeared at the close of the tests, are reported in the foregoing section in relation to the quality of the effluent. As stated there, the various data were so complicated by a series of factors that it is impossible to draw conclusions with regard to several points of great practical significance. The more important points are noted in turn as follows:

Thickness.—While the Jewell filter was able to yield the most economical results there is no proof that it was the best one which could be adopted with regard to thickness.

Size of Sand Grain.—In the case of the Jewell sand layer the most economical results were obtained. But in the case of size of grain as well as thickness of layer there are no data to show what would be the most economical conditions to adopt in practice. Taking everything into consideration, especially the frequency of tiny flakes of aluminum hydrate in the Jewell effluent, it is probable that a finer size of grain would be more advantageous.

Composition of Sand.—It appears from the available evidence that as satisfactory results may be obtained under suitable conditions from natural sand layers as from those made from the more expensive crushed quartz.

Location of Sand Layers in Gravity Filters.

The location of the sand layer in the upper part of the filter, with a depth of three feet or less of water above the sand, such as was the case in the Jewell and Western gravity (B) filters, is a marked step in advance. By the use of a trap, and a suitable location of the point of discharge of the effluent, the total available head may be undiminished and at the same time the following economical advantages may be insured:

1. The difficult and in a measure impossible task of satisfactorily filtering all of the

water remaining above the sand just prior to washing is readily removed under normal conditions.

2. The quantity of chemically treated water, which it is necessary to remove before washing and to either waste or pump again, is materially reduced.

The second weakness was most noticeable in the Western gravity filter (A).

There is no evidence, however, to indicate that the use of a negative head (suction) has any advantage other than those stated above.

Loss of Head.

Initial.—The initial loss of head is an influential factor in the cost of operation of a system of purification, in that the available head is reduced during filtration by the amount of the initial loss of head. It is also indirectly connected with the successful practice of surface agitation. The initial loss of head was determined mainly in the case of these systems by the resistance of the several sand layers. In all cases the strainer systems when clean offered apparently no measurable resistance to the flow at the contract rate. In the case of the two Western systems, the presence of sand in the strainer tubes as above noted probably increased the initial loss of head to a greater or less degree.

Maximum.—The maximum loss of head (maximum acting head) which can be utilized is an important factor in the cost of operation, in that it influences the length of runs (period between washes) and thus affects the relation between the actual and net rates of filtration.

In this respect the respective filters behaved very differently. The Warren and the Western pressure filters were practically always washed because of the failure in character of the effluent and not because the resistance of the sand layers required greater available head than the construction allowed. The reverse was true, except in cases of peculiar conditions of the river water, with the Jewell filter. This matter was discussed in the preceding section of this chapter, in regard to its effect on the quality of the effluent. A very noticeable point in this connection was mentioned there, that is, that during the last of May the composition of the river water was such that, with the amounts of chemicals used, none of the systems was able to obtain a degree of coagulation of the water as it entered the sand layer, sufficient to clog appreciably the layer before the character of the effluent failed.

Almost without exception during this period the filters were washed without any appreciable increase in loss of head over the initial.

A comparative idea of the relative significance of these factors under the contract rate of 250,000 gallons per twenty-four hours is indicated in the following table:

System.	Loss of Head in Feet.		
	Initial.	Maximum.	
		Normal.	Extreme.
Warren	1.0	1.7	4.5
Jewell	1.6	12.0	13.6
Western Pressure	3.3	20.0	65.4

Pressure System.

One of the economical advantages claimed for pressure systems as compared with gravity systems is that they would lessen the cost of purification by removing the necessity of a secondary pumping of the water if such should be the case with gravity systems. This would depend upon local conditions, and under some circumstances it might be true. But the experience obtained during these tests indicates clearly that, with the muddy Ohio River water at Louisville, a single pumping of the river water to and through a pressure system is out of the question on the grounds of unnecessary cost. The excessive cost attending the use of a pressure system would be caused by the large closed compartments which it would be necessary to insert between the main (primary) pumps and the pressure filters, in order to secure, under the existing conditions, the removal of mud, etc., which the economical treatment of this water before its filtration demands.

It may occur to some that a combined pressure and gravity system might be desirable for the purification of this water supply. That is to say, pump the water from the river to an elevated open subsidence basin of adequate size, and then allow the properly treated water to flow through pressure filters on its way from the subsidence basin to the consumers. From the experience obtained with the Western pressure filter the adoption of this scheme would lead to serious difficulties, owing to irregularities in operation arising from variation in the rate of consumption at different hours (and minutes) of the day, such as the ordinary necessities of the consumers demand.

Unusual rates of consumption such as might occur in putting out large fires, etc., would increase these difficulties. That irregularities such as would occur in this way were a very serious matter in the operation of the Western System was shown conclusively, and is so indicated by the official communication received from the Western Filter Company on June 26, in explanation of the withdrawal from these tests of their gravity system for a period of three months. This letter was given in an earlier part of this chapter, in the description of Period No. 18. In passing it may be mentioned that all experiences in water filtration, with which the writer is familiar, point clearly to the advisability, if not to the necessity, of placing a reservoir, not necessarily large, between the filters and the distributing system in order to maintain as uniform pressure as possible in the pipes and to guard against irregularities in the operation of the filters, with their attending difficulties.

Rate of Filtration.

The rate of filtration is a very prominent factor in the cost of construction of a large system. It also affects the cost of operation. The available data can only be regarded as suggestive upon this point. The fact that the Western pressure filter, however, yielded for comparatively long periods at a time an effluent which compared favorably with the others in character, at a much higher rate per unit of sand surface, is a matter which cannot be ignored or considered lightly. This is especially true when it is remembered that the Western pressure filter was operated in the face of many complications, including irregular coagulation, a faulty strainer system, and absence of agitation of sand layer to secure complete washing, etc.

The actual average rates of filtration employed in the case of the several filters with fairly clear and muddiest water, respectively, are as follows:

Filter.	Rate of Filtration.			
	Normal Clear Water.		Muddiest Water.	
	Cubic Feet per Minute.	Million Gallons per Acre per 24 Hours.	Cubic Feet per Minute.	Million Gallons per Acre per 24 Hours.
Warren..........	20.8	126	20.1	122
Jewell........ ..	26.3	106	22.2	90
Western Pressure..	23.1	164	13.7	97

The contract rate of 250,000 gallons per twenty-four hours is equivalent to 23.21 cubic feet per minute. Owing to different areas of filtering surface this rate per unit of area differed for the several filters, as follows:

Filter.	Area in Square Feet.	Contract Rate in Million Gallons per Acre per 24 Hours.
Warren..........	77.36	141
Jewell....	115.80	94
Western Pressure..	66.20	157

That comparatively wide ranges in unit rates did not affect the cost for chemicals by a corresponding amount will be seen by an inspection of the tables given in connection with the discussion of the effect of rate of filtration on the quality of the effluent in the preceding section. Some further investigations along this line were made by the Water Company during 1897, and are recorded in Chapter XV.

Washing the Sand Layer.

The washing of the sand layer was a considerable item in the cost of operation of the respective systems, for two reasons:

1. The net rate of purification was reduced as the frequency of washing increased, because of the increased percentage of water wasted and used for washing.

2. The cost of the operation of washing was a considerable item, and this was also increased in total expense as the number of washes increased.

The chief factors affecting the frequency

of washing have been discussed in the preceding pages. It was mainly determined by the relation between the degree of coagulation of the water as it entered the sand layer, type of sand layer, rate of filtration, character of filtered water, and available acting head. The relation of the agitation of the surface of the sand layer to the frequency of washing is discussed beyond.

The cost of the operation of washing was dependent upon the amount of water used, the pressure at which it was delivered, and the cost of agitation of the sand, if employed.

Amount of Water Used.—The comparative amounts were determined entirely by the method of washing employed. In the case of the Warren, Jewell, and Western Pressure systems, the average quantities for each wash during the entire investigation were 528, 627, and 633 cubic feet, respectively.

Method of Washing.—All indications point to the conclusion that the most economical method of washing is to carry the process to a point where all detachable materials are removed from the sand, but no further. This means that it seems best to wash the sand until the wash-water after passage through it is practically clear.

The amount required depends principally upon the amount and character of the matter accumulated on the sand grains, and upon the relative efficiency of equal quantities of water. The latter factor is dependent upon the distribution of the water throughout the sand layer and upon the agitation of the sand layer, notably the rubbing together of the sand grains by the agitator teeth.

During the latter part of these tests the Warren filter was uniformly washed to a satisfactory degree. This was the case as a rule in the Jewell filter, but not uniformly so. The Western pressure filter was almost never washed as thoroughly as it should have been. This was probably the chief reason why it was necessary in this system to waste the first portion of the effluent after washing, owing to its unsatisfactory character. The amount wasted was usually only a small percentage of the total water filtered on the run, but during muddy conditions of the river water the amount of filtered water wasted became proportionately large and at times exceeded in amount the quantity of satisfactory effluent obtained.

Distribution of Water throughout the Sand Layer.—The distribution of the water during washing was affected by the agitation of the sand layer and in turn reduced the cost of agitation. The main factor affecting the distribution was the system used for this purpose.

The Warren distributing system was handicapped for a time during the early part of the tests by having an undue portion of the wash water deflected from the central well through a small area of the strainer system and sand layer. This was apparently remedied to a large extent by the changes made on February 12, 1896.

The distributing system of the Jewell filter was apparently quite satisfactory. The most notable points about this device were the restriction of the neck of the strainer cups, and the small deflector in the cups just above the neck. By the first arrangement the greatest resistance to the passage of the water was met at this point, thus causing a distribution of the water throughout the entire system. The small casting which was placed in the cups just above the neck served to break and deflect the stream of water just before it entered the sand layer.

The distributing systems of the Western pressure and Western gravity (A) filters were handicapped by the presence of sand in the tubes, as was noted in the last section. It is difficult to determine how far these distributing systems affected the quantity of water used, as these filters were never washed thoroughly.

In connection with the distributing systems of the Western filters, it is to be noted that when they were clean there was less restriction to the passage of the water through the distributing system than in the supply pipe. Such an arrangement naturally involved the passage of the water most rapidly through those portions of the system nearest the connection with the supply pipe. The accumulations of sand in the strainer tubes reduced the total outlet area and therefore increased the resistance of the tubes. These accumulations, furthermore, increased the tendency of the water to pass into comparatively small portions of the sand layer.

The ball-nozzle system of the Western gravity filter (B) was not in use for a sufficient length of time to determine its relative efficiency. Observations during and after construction, however, indicated unequal distribution of the water at different parts of the sand layer.

The mechanical agitation of the sand layer during washing greatly aided in distributing the wash-water and increased the relative efficiency of equal quantities of water. The Jewell and Warren systems used mechanical devices for agitating the sand throughout the tests. The current of water was relied upon for agitation in both the Western filters. In this connection it is to be noted that a modification in the mechanical agitators whereby the sand would be floated to a less degree and the grains rubbed together more than was the practice in these tests suggests an economical advance, as equally satisfactory results might be obtained with the use of less wash-water.

Pressure of Wash-water.—The pressure under which the water was delivered at the inlet of the distributing systems is the second factor in the cost of the operation of washing. This was widely different in the case of the several filters at times during the tests, on account of changes in other factors. The efficiency of the various pressures used depended largely upon the amount and distribution of the resistances of the distributing systems. The increased resistance of the distributing systems of the Western filters, due to the presence of sand in the tubes, was clearly shown by the increases made from time to time in the pressure employed. The use of mechanical agitators greatly decreased the pressure required, as was shown by the increase in pressure used by the Jewell filter, as the efficiency of the agitator decreased. Owing to these and other factors it is difficult to estimate the pressure necessary under normal conditions of operation. The following table gives the pressures which were used at the close of the tests, in pounds, of the water at the inlet to the several distributing systems:

System.	Pressure of Water. Pounds.
Warren	2.0
Jewell	7.5
Western Pressure	5.9

Agitation of the Sand Layer.—In the Western pressure filter the sand layer was never agitated except by the current of wash-water —unless the removal of sand to repair the strainer system be so regarded. Agitation was regularly employed in the Warren and Jewell sand layers. All indications point to a decided advantage in the constant agitation during washing.

The Warren agitator was changed and repaired several times, and during the later part of the tests appeared to fulfill its purpose. Considerable difficulty was experienced with the Jewell agitator on acount of its stopping and refusing to work at frequent intervals. At first this was thought to be due to the use of too small an engine (nominally 5 H.P.) or, perhaps, to some obstructions of the strainer system. Careful inspection, however, led to the conclusion that it was caused by a binding of the gears, due to a warping of the timbers upon which the agitator rested. This could be readily remedied by a more careful construction. The devices for agitation could and should be improved in simplicity of construction, and in both the Warren and Jewell systems the devices were too weak for their purpose. As noted above, an improvement in these devices whereby the sand grains would be rubbed together more energetically would probably result in a saving of wash-water.

Power Used for Agitation.—At the close of the tests, with the pressure and quantities of wash-water then in use, the power required to operate the agitators of the Warren and Jewell systems was as follows:

System.	Horse-power Required.	
	Maximum.	Normal.
Warren	9	6
Jewell	10	7

The maximum power required occurred in the Warren at the time of lifting the rakes and in the Jewell at the time of forcing the rakes into the sand and starting them in motion.

Surface Agitation.

In the case of the Jewell System it was found that with certain conditions of river water, and of its coagulation, the resisting layer of mud on the surface of the sand could be broken up and filtration then continued without washing the filter or injuring the character of the effluent. This operation, when successful, reduced the resistance of the sand layer and so lengthened the run. It was therefore an element of more or less magnitude in the consideration of cost, in that it decreased the frequency of washing. The success of surface agitation was very closely dependent on the degree of coagulation of the water as it entered the sand layer, and on the character of the sand. In these tests the use of surface agitation at times of very muddy water, or when the river water contained large amounts of fine clay, was not as a rule attempted, and when tried was not successful. The cause of the failure seems clearly to have been the incomplete coagulation of the water at these times.

Relation of Proper Attention and Supervision to the Economy of Purification of the Ohio River Water by this Method.

This subject has been referred to in Chapter VII, and again in this chapter in relation to the efficiency of filtration. The most marked effect of proper supervision of the operation of these systems was on the cost of treatment. As has already been presented, there is at all times a certain optimum amount of chemical, below which satisfactory results cannot be obtained, and above which all chemical used is practically wasted. In the light of our present knowledge the determination of this optimum amount, for such a rapidly and widely varying character of water as that of the Ohio River, is a very difficult problem. At times the optimum amount could be very clearly determined by one thoroughly familiar with the methods of procedure, while at other times, especially with water which would give a clear effluent containing large numbers of bacteria, the decision required judgment based on extended experience.

A system of purification of the Ohio River water is clearly one of combinations of methods and devices, which experience has demonstrated cannot be handled economically by unskilled labor. It would be easy for untrained attendants to waste many thousands of dollars annually by the needless use of the chemical. A comparison of the average daily cost of the chemical used during each of the periods by the Warren, Jewell, and Western pressure systems, on a net basis of 25 million gallons daily, is represented in the following table and shows this point.

DAILY COST FOR CHEMICAL.

Period.	Warren System.	Jewell System.	Western Pressure System.
1	$47.00	$37.00	....
2	67.00	49.00	....
3	229.00	134.00	$152.00
4	231.00	52.00	57.00
5	261.00	225.00	120.00
6	252.00	129.00	201.00
7	226.00	155.00	134.00
8	208.00	60.00	46.00
9	423 00	264.00	239.00
10	280.00	199.00	204.00
11	324.00	269.00	224.00
12	76.00	76.00	....
13	80.00	96.00	59.00
14	76.00	69.00	64.00
15	295.00	300.00	395.00
16	235.00	300.00	288.00
17	152.00	267.00	275.00
18	297.00	437.00	548.00
19	179.00	354.00	335.00
20	416.00	575.00	536.00

In less skilled hands these variations would probably have been more marked. With an adequate employment to its economical limits of subsidence both with and without coagulation, the necessity for variation in the amount of applied chemical would be much less, and the opportunity for departure from the optimum amount would be reduced materially. Nevertheless, there would be no condition where this river water could be economically purified except by skilled labor and supervision.

It is true that the above data are complicated by other factors, some of which vary from time to time, but they serve to illustrate the point in question to a very considerable degree.

SECTION No. 4.

COMPARISON OF THE ELEMENTS OF COST OF PURIFICATION OF TWENTY-FIVE MILLION GALLONS OF OHIO RIVER WATER DAILY BY THE RESPECTIVE SYSTEMS, BASED ON THE RESULTS OF THESE INVESTIGATIONS.

In the following pages are given the elements of probable cost, so far as it is feasible, of the purification of 25 million gallons of Ohio River water daily by each of the systems representing the method in which coagulation and partial sedimentation by aluminum hydrate formed from sulphate of alumina, and subsequent rapid filtration, were employed. As a matter of convenience the elements of cost are subdivided into those of construction and those of operation. All of these estimates are based on the results obtained from these investigations, upon the operation of small test systems contracted to purify 250,000 gallons per twenty-four hours. From the nature of the existing conditions at this time, and in the absence of definite knowledge as to the cost of the various devices, these estimates of necessity deal for the most part with elements of cost. They are so arranged that when the exact cost of the several devices is known, the aggregate cost may be readily computed. Wherever the existing conditions permit of it, actual estimates of cost are given.

The following data are summaries of the principal elements of cost of the respective systems as demonstrated in the previously described investigations. In so far as possible the several amounts have been determined and estimated on the basis of a normal or slightly muddy river water containing about 100 parts per million of suspended matter, and also for a fairly muddy river water containing about 1800 parts. The majority of the comparisons call for normal and maximum figures, but in some cases representative averages for these tests are required. In the latter instance the data presented in Table No. 5 are used. Under the conditions of proper preliminary treatment before filtration by subsidence with and without the aid of coagulants, it might be expected that the water which reached the filters would compare with the normal river water as used in these summaries. On the other hand, the figures given for the muddiest water do not represent the extremes which would be obtained under conditions of actual muddiest water in the Ohio River. Such conditions are, however, unusual and of comparatively short duration, and for these data reference is made to the tables of individual runs which were presented in Chapter VIII. As a rule the figures given as maximum in the following summaries are averages for Period No. 20, excluding those runs which were affected by the period of subsidence over night, or were otherwise abnormal. It will be seen by reference to Chapter VIII that on July 24, 1896, the amount of suspended matter in the river water was 3347 parts per million, or nearly double the amount which is considered as the average muddiest water. (The maximum amount of suspended solids found during the entire investigations was 5311 parts per million on March 6, 1897.)

These excessively high amounts would probably never reach the filter in practice, where proper provision for preliminary plain subsidence was made; and, with the use of coagulation and subsidence as mentioned above, the water reaching the filters would probably not be excessively muddy.

The Western gravity filter (A) does not appear in these comparisons because it was found to be unable to purify at all times enough water to wash its own sand layer, and its operation was discontinued by the Western Filter Company.

The Western gravity filter (B) was not operated long enough to yield adequate data, but there are no indications of its being comparable to the Warren or Jewell filters. As will be seen on examinations of the tables in Chapter VIII, the percentage which the wash and waste water was of the applied, exceeded 100, three times in the case of the Western pressure filter and once in the case of the Jewell filter. As the contiguous results indicate that these percentages were abnormal, they have not been considered as liable to occur in regular practice.

Summaries of Elements of Cost.

NORMAL PERIOD OF SERVICE OF THE FILTERS OF THE RESPECTIVE SYSTEMS BETWEEN WASHES. HOURS AND MINUTES.

System.	Ordinary Water.	Muddiest Water.
Warren	10h. 48m.	2h. 08m.
Jewell	16h. 38m.	2h. 17m.
Western Pressure	13h. 38m.	1h. 38m.

NORMAL PERIOD REQUIRED FOR WASHING THE SAND LAYERS OF THE RESPECTIVE SYSTEMS. MINUTES.

System.	Average.
Warren	26m.
Jewell	21m.
Western Pressure	18m.

NORMAL PERIOD USED FOR WASTING UNSATISFACTORY FILTERED WATER AFTER WASHING THE SAND LAYERS OF THE RESPECTIVE SYSTEMS. MINUTES.

System.	Ordinary Water.	Muddiest Water.
Warren	0	0
Jewell	0	0
Western Pressure	8	14

NORMAL QUANTITY OF RIVER WATER APPLIED TO THE RESPECTIVE SYSTEMS, IN GALLONS PER 24 HOURS.

System.	Ordinary Water.	Muddiest Water.
Warren	206 000	782 000
Jewell	271 000	213 000
Western Pressure	248 500	152 000

NORMAL QUANTITY OF COAGULATED AND PARTIALLY CLARIFIED WATER WASTED BY THE RESPECTIVE SYSTEMS PRIOR TO WASHING THE SAND LAYERS, IN GALLONS PER 24 HOURS.

System.	Ordinary Water.	Muddiest Water.
Warren	960	14 000
Jewell	0	4 000
Western Pressure	0	0

NORMAL QUANTITY OF FILTERED WATER USED IN WASHING THE SAND LAYERS OF THE RESPECTIVE SYSTEMS, IN GALLONS PER 24 HOURS.

System.	Ordinary Water.	Muddiest Water.
Warren	10 800	47 200
Jewell	6 200	49 200
Western Pressure	8 500	71 700

NORMAL QUANTITY OF FILTERED WATER WASTED BY THE RESPECTIVE SYSTEMS, OWING TO UNSATISFACTORY APPEARANCE, IN GALLONS PER 24 HOURS.

System.	Ordinary Water.	Muddiest Water.
Warren	0	0
Jewell	0	300
Western Pressure	2 200	16 300

NORMAL NET QUANTITY OF FILTERED WATER (EXCLUSIVE OF WASH WATER AND WASTE WATER) YIELDED BY THE RESPECTIVE SYSTEMS, IN GALLONS PER 24 HOURS.

System.	Ordinary Water.	Muddiest Water.
Warren	200 000	120 000
Jewell	266 000	160 000
Western Pressure	238 000	64 000

NORMAL NET QUANTITY OF FILTERED WATER (EXCLUSIVE OF WASH WATER AND WASTE WATER) YIELDED BY THE RESPECTIVE SYSTEMS, IN MILLION GALLONS PER 24 HOURS PER ACRE OF FILTERING SURFACE.

System.	Ordinary Water.	Muddiest Water.
Warren	112	68
Jewell	100	60
Western Pressure	157	40

NORMAL PERCENTAGE WHICH THE SUM OF THE WASH WATER AND WASTE WATER FORMED OF THE RIVER WATER APPLIED TO THE RESPECTIVE SYSTEMS.

System.	Ordinary Water.	Muddiest Water.
Warren	6	34
Jewell	2	25
Western Pressure	4	58

NORMAL RATE AND PRESSURE AT WHICH THE FILTERED WATER WAS SUPPLIED FOR WASHING THE SAND LAYERS OF THE RESPECTIVE SYSTEMS.

System.	Rate in Gallons per Minute.	Pressure in Pounds per Square Inch at the Bottom of the Sand Layer.
Warren	460	2.0
Jewell	530	7.5
Western Pressure	650	5.9

NORMAL QUANTITY OF APPLIED SULPHATE OF ALUMINA IN GRAINS PER GALLON OF RIVER WATER SUPPLIED TO THE RESPECTIVE SYSTEMS.

System.	Ordinary Water.	Muddiest Water.
Warren	1.41	6.77
Jewell	1.76	8.14
Western Pressure	1.06	5.27

NORMAL QUANTITY OF APPLIED SULPHATE OF ALUMINA IN GRAINS PER GALLON OF NET FILTERED WATER YIELDED BY THE RESPECTIVE SYSTEMS.

System.	Ordinary Water.	Muddiest Water.	Average for Full Period Covered by these Tests.
Warren	1.50	10.20	3.00
Jewell	1.80	10.86	2.65
Western Pressure	1.10	12.60	2.72

Using the foregoing data as a basis of computation, the following principal elements of cost of installation and operation of a system of 25 million gallons daily capacity are presented, with actual estimates of cost wherever it is feasible.

NUMBER OF THE RESPECTIVE UNIT SYSTEMS WHICH WOULD BE NECESSARY TO FURNISH 25 MILLION GALLONS DAILY OF PURIFIED WATER AT TIMES OF ORDINARY RIVER WATER.

Warren System	124
Jewell System	94
Western Pressure System	105

NUMBER OF THE RESPECTIVE UNIT SYSTEMS WHICH IT WOULD BE NECESSARY TO HOLD IN RESERVE IN ORDER TO SUPPLY 25 MILLION GALLONS DAILY OF PURIFIED WATER AT TIMES OF MUDDIEST RIVER WATER.

Warren System	85
Jewell System	62
Western Pressure System	287

TOTAL NUMBER OF THE RESPECTIVE UNIT SYSTEMS WHICH WOULD BE REQUIRED TO SUPPLY UNIFORMLY 25 MILLION GALLONS DAILY OF PURIFIED OHIO RIVER WATER.

Warren System	208
Jewell System	156
Western Pressure System	391

RATE IN CUBIC FEET PER MINUTE AT WHICH THE WASH WATER WOULD HAVE TO BE SUPPLIED TO WASH THE SAND LAYERS OF A 25 MILLION GALLON PLANT.

	Maximum.	Normal.
Warren System	2 650	312
Jewell System	1 775	177
Western Pressure System	8 560	219

The head against which the pump would have to operate in furnishing the wash-water would depend largely upon the relative location of the pump and the different filters with reference to the source of supply, but it would be such that the available pressure on the bottom of the sand layer would be about 5, 10, and 8 pounds for the Warren, Jewell, and Western Pressure systems, respectively.

There would be required, in the case of the Warren and Jewell systems, engines to furnish the power necessary to operate the agitating machinery when the sand layers were being washed. On the basis of the above data, the maximum and average amounts of power required for this purpose would be as follows:

	Maximum.	Average.
Warren System	383 H.P.	45 H.P.
Jewell System	280 "	25 "

In addition to the above elements of cost of installation of a 25 million-gallon plant there would be the cost of suitable preparation of the grounds upon which to locate the system, and also the buildings to house the filters.

The area occupied by the total number of required unit systems on the above basis would be as follows:

Warren System	125 000 sq. ft.	or 2.9 acres.
Jewell System	68 000 "	" 1.5 "
Western Pressure System	211 000 "	" 4.7 "

With regard to the cost of application of the sulphate of alumina, the very small amount of power required depends largely upon the location and arrangement of the system, strength of solution used, etc., in the case of all of the systems.

Another important factor connected with the cost of operation of such a system of purification, and also with the installation, is the extra pumping of the supply of water. To a great extent this factor is dependent upon other details of construction and would probably exceed somewhat the minimum. A very close idea can be obtained of the importance and significance of this factor by considering simply the difference in level of the water above and below the sand layers of the several filters (loss of head). Taking these figures as presented in foregoing tables, 4.5, 13.6, and 65.4 feet for the Warren, Jewell, and Western Pressure systems, respectively, and adding to the total net capacity of 25 million gallons daily the average percentages of water wasted and used for washing the sand layers, 6, 2, and 4 per cent. for ordinary water, and 34, 25, and 58 per cent. for muddiest water for the three systems in the order above given, the following amounts of power required are obtained:

	Maximum.	Average.
Warren System	26 H.P.	20 H.P.
Jewell System	75 "	60 "
Western Pressure System	460 "	300 "

In regard to the Western Pressure System it is only fair to state that with the normal maximum loss of head of 20 feet these figures would be reduced to about 30 per cent. of the figures given. The question of the insertion of pressure filters in the direct line of pipe from the main pumps to the reservoir or from the reservoir to the city has already been shown to be out of the question; and it is only necessary to add that the cost of increased pumping is represented by the above figures no matter where the filters are located.

The principal cost of operation would be that of the sulphate of alumina required for coagulation of the river water. Using the present quotations of 1.5 cents per pound for commercial sulphate of alumina delivered in carload lots free on board cars at Louisville, the estimates of cost based on the above data are as follows:

DAILY COST OF SULPHATE OF ALUMINA IN THE PURIFICATION OF 25 MILLION GALLONS OF OHIO RIVER WATER BY THE RESPECTIVE SYSTEMS.

	Ordinary Water.	Muddiest Water.	Average.
Warren System	$80	$547	$161
Jewell System	96	584	142
Western Pressure System	59	676	146

ANNUAL COST OF SULPHATE OF ALUMINA IN THE PURIFICATION OF 25 MILLION GALLONS OF OHIO RIVER WATER DAILY BY THE RESPECTIVE SYSTEMS, BASED ON THE RESULTS OF THE TESTS FROM OCTOBER, 1895, TO AUGUST 1, 1896.

Warren System	$58 800
Jewell System	51 800
Western Pressure System	53 300

QUANTITY OF WATER IN GALLONS PER DAY, WHICH WOULD BE WASTED AND USED FOR WASHING THE SAND LAYERS OF THE RESPECTIVE SYSTEMS IN THE PURIFICATION OF 25 MILLION GALLONS DAILY OF THE OHIO RIVER WATER.

	Ordinary Water.	Muddiest Water.	Average.
Warren System	1 600 000	12 880 000	2 720 000
Jewell System	512 000	8 375 000	1 660 000
Western Pressure System	1 000 000	34 500 000	3 220 000

Experience during these tests showed clearly enough that to purify 25 million gallons of the Ohio River water daily in all its varying stages and conditions, without wasting sulphate of alumina and at the same time giving a purified water of a satisfactory character, was absolutely out of the question in the absence of constant care and skillful supervision. The attention given to each system of a rated capacity of 250,000 gallons per twenty-four hours was of course several times greater than would be necessary in a portion of corresponding size in a system having a capacity of 25 million gallons daily. The amount and scope of necessary analytical work would also be much modified in actual practice, especially after a large system had been in operation for a sufficient period for the formulation of a practical and systematic method of procedure.

The best idea which can be given you at this time as to the cost of the necessary attention for the operation of a system to purify 25 million gallons of the Ohio River water daily is afforded by the statement that it would certainly not be less than that for the proper operation and maintenance of your present pumping station, which I understand is 14,000 dollars per annum.

Section No. 5.

General Conclusions.

The practical results of these tests, as applied to the problem of purifying the Ohio River water for the supply for the city of Louisville may be summed up in the following manner, in which reference is made to the general applicability of the method investigated and to the relative merits and demerits of the respective systems.

Applicability of the Method to the Clarification and Purification of the Ohio River Water.

These tests and investigations have proved conclusively that the general method embodying subsidence, coagulation and filtration is most suitable for the proper and economical purification of the Ohio River water at this city. With regard to the use of coagulants it may be stated in unqualified terms that their use is imperative for this water, because for at least six to ten weeks in the spring and early summer the Ohio River water contains such large quantities of fine clay particles, many of which are smaller than bacteria, that clarification and purification without coagulation would be impracticable if not impossible.

While this general method, which was fundamentally adopted by each of these systems, is the most suitable one, in the light of our present knowledge concerning the science and art of water purification, yet in no case did the systems tested carry out these principles in a manner demanded by the economical and efficient purification of this water. Expressed in briefest terms, the reason of this was that they failed to remove the suspended matter sufficiently before the water reached the sand layer. With regard to the relative advantages of American and English filters for the purification of the water, after its partial clarification by subsidence, aided at times by coagulation, no data were obtained at this time, although in Chapter XVI the question is referred to briefly in reference to an earlier series of tests with English filters, made by this Company.

The general defects, with their practical significance, will next be pointed out by a full comparative summary of the principal features and devices of the several systems. After this is presented in brief the quality of the filtered water; and, at the end, the final conclusion from this portion of the investigation.

General Defect of all Systems, with its Results in the Application of this Method of Purification to the Ohio River Water.

In this connection it is to be clearly borne in mind that the Ohio River water possesses a marked variability, both as to character and amount of suspended matter contained in it, and at times the amounts are extraordinarily large. This water, it may be fairly said, is a much more difficult one to purify than those waters concerning which data upon purification are available, and which have been treated on a large scale by American filters. In justice to the several filter companies it is to be stated that they entered these tests with systems which represented their best devices based upon their general information and experience when arrangements were made for these tests, and not with devices designed to meet the specific requirements of this case.

Of the defects possessed by the systems in these tests there is one which causes all others to drop into almost complete insignificance. As stated above, this great defect was the failure to remove suspended matter sufficiently from the water as it reached the sand layer of the filter, in each case. This would produce the following effects upon the process:

1. It would increase to an excessive degree the cost of a chemical to serve as a coagulant, which is the principal item of expense in this method of purification of this water.

2. It would necessitate a reserve portion of the system with all the appurtenances to handle the water when in its muddiest condition. In the best systems this reserve portion would have to be from 60 to 80 per cent. of the system regularly in use.

3. It would necessitate at times of muddy water the waste of an unusually large amount of filtered water for the purpose of washing the sand layers. When the river water is in its muddiest condition this percentage in the case of the best system would average from 25 to 35 per cent., and might for short intervals reach nearly double the average.

4. It would necessitate, by virtue of the water thus disposed of, an increase in the normal pumping appliances, and, therefore, the aggregate cost of pumping.

5. Owing to the wide variations in the character of the water as it reached the sand layer, it would make very difficult the task of operating the systems so as to secure efficient purification at the least possible cost.

6. It would necessitate regularly a large set of trained attendants to operate the reserve portion of the system, beside those regularly engaged in operating the portion of the system regularly employed.

7. It would increase certain undesirable features of the filtered water with reference to its corroding and incrusting powers.

This defect was so great in the case of the Western gravity filter (A) that when the river was very muddy it was unable to yield enough filtered water to wash its own sand layer, as already stated. For this reason this filter will not be mentioned further. With regard to the Western gravity filter (B), it was not operated long enough to allow adequate data to be secured, but gave no indications of being comparable to the Warren or Jewell filters. It will not be mentioned again in this connection.

The systems were not perfect in other respects, but none of the remaining weaknesses were of such vital importance as was the one above.

Comparison of the Principal Devices of the Respective Systems.

Herewith is presented a comparison of corresponding devices of the respective systems with regard to their applicability in treating the Ohio River water successfully by the method of purification under consideration.

Plain Subsidence.—All of the systems were totally lacking in this very essential requisite for the most economical and efficient clarification and purification of this water.

Kind of Chemical Used.—Sulphate of alumina was the principal coagulating chemical used in these tests. So far as could be learned at this time its use was satisfactory for the required purpose.

Potash alum was used in the Western Systems only because of its physical characters, and was abandoned after an improvement was made in the device for the application of coagulants. It is too expensive for regular use.

Lime, electrolytically decomposed salt and metallic iron were tried experimentally in the Jewell System, but were abandoned.

Preparation of Chemical Solutions.—The first Western device was a failure. In all other cases the addition of known weight of chemicals to known volumes of water was satisfactory when it received sufficient care and attention.

Application of Coagulant.—The first Western device was a failure. Experience showed that the Warren device was most nearly automatic and on the whole did the best work under these conditions. Satisfactory results were obtained from the Jewell and second Western devices when they received sufficient attention and regulation.

It is quite probable that in practice the most satisfactory results could be obtained by gravity discharge of the solutions.

The use of iron pipes, fittings and pumps

to handle solutions of sulphate of alumina is not admissible. Brass and aluminum bronze were not attacked.

Quantity of Coagulant Used.—The summaries already presented show that the grains of sulphate of alumina used per gallon of net filtered water in the case of the several systems were as follows:

	Warren.	Jewell.	Western Pressure.
With muddiest water (average) ...	10.20	10.86	12.60
With fairly clear (normal) water (average)	1.50	1.80	1.10
Total average	3.00	2.65	2.72

The available information indicates that the river water during these tests was somewhat easier to purify by these systems than would be the average water year by year. Therefore it is concluded that in no case would any of these systems treat the water with less than an annual average of at least 3 grains per gallon of ordinary sulphate of alumina.

The Period of Coagulation.—The effective period of coagulation in minutes at the contract rate, including the settling basins and the compartments in the filters above the sand layers, was in each case as follows:

Warren.	Jewell.	Western Pressure.
65	28	9

In no case were provisions made to allow a division to be made in the application of the coagulant to allow favorable conditions for coagulation and subsidence, and of coagulation and filtration. It appears that at times this will be necessary.

None of the above periods with a single point of application of coagulant would be advisable in practice. At times they ought to be much longer. In this connection it may be noted that the value of secondary application of coagulant was appreciated by the operators of the Warren System, as shown by its trial of July 22, under the conditions which were available.

Coagulation and Sedimentation.—As noted above, coagulation and sedimentation, independent of coagulation and filtration, would be a great benefit at times, but was not provided in any of the systems, although its importance was recognized by the operators of the Warren System.

Inspection and Cleaning of Settling Basins.—No adequate arrangements in this particular were made in any of the systems, although the Jewell was superior to the others.

Coagulation of Water on Sand Layer.—This is a point of great practical importance and depends upon the quantity of coagulant and provisions for coagulation and sedimentation. The latter points are mentioned above.

Structure and Type of Filter.—The use of wood in a permanent plant would not be advisable, although for experimental purposes wood suffices. In this respect the Western pressure filter was superior. The disadvantage of wood was shown by the foul odors in the filtered water compartment at the bottom of the Warren filter.

Compared with pressure systems the gravity filters were found to be more practicable for the purification of this class of water under ordinary circumstances.

The location of the sand layer near the top of the filtered tank, and the use of a negative pressure, as in the case of the Jewell filter, was a distinct advantage in that it reduced the wasting of coagulated but unfiltered water above the sand layer at times of wasting and similar operations. In other respects no advantages of a negative pressure were noted.

In practice all important parts should be made as accessible as possible, and in this respect several modifications in all the filters could be made to advantage.

Size of Filters.—All of the filters were built to purify 250,000 gallons per twenty-four hours, and this size, and, so far as our knowledge goes, this is the prevailing one in practice. On a large scale the cost of construction and of operation with regard to attendants could be materially reduced by increasing the size of the filters. The limit in size, apparently, would be determined by the arrangements for successful agitation.

In this connection it is said that the Jewell Company is now building large filters.

Sand Layer.—The data upon this point are so obscured by other factors that it is difficult to compare them fairly. The indications are that the Warren sand layer was too coarse and that the greater frictional resistance of the Western pressure sand layer made other operations much more nearly satisfactory under the existing conditions than would have been the case had a coarser sand been employed. This observation is based upon the comparative freedom from fine particles of aluminum hydrate in the effluent of this filter in the presence of irregular coagulation of the applied water (see Chapter III). Whether it would be better to use a greater thickness of layer or finer sand, to secure increased frictional resistance, is not plain. The latter would probably be advisable, as it would not increase the cost of construction.

The sand layer of the Jewell filter gave the best results under the existing conditions, but in the opinion of the writer it would be better to use an equal depth of finer sand.

There were no indications that crushed quartz was distinctly superior to the cheaper natural sand.

Filtered-water Exits.—To secure a uniform and regular rate of flow of water through the sand layer, the exit area for the filtered water and the inlet area for the wash-water, at the bottom of the sand layer, should apparently be less than that of the main pipe beneath them. In respect to this condition the Jewell filter alone fulfilled it. It would seem advisable, however, to decrease the distance between the strainer cups to secure more uniform flow in the lower portion of the sand layer.

The Western exit devices were very poor, because in the slotted tubes sand accumulated in a short time.

So far as could be noted, the exits of the Warren filter served their purpose fairly well, but the varying space occupied beneath them by the supporting frame was undesirable.

In no case were these portions accessible without removing the sand.

Loss of Head.—The indications were that about 10 feet of maximum available head, as ordinarily utilized in the Jewell filter, was best. Amounts above this, as in the Western pressure filter, could be used too seldom to be advisable. In the Warren filter not more than 4 feet were used, owing chiefly to the coarseness of the sand layer.

With regard to pressure filters and negative head, see foregoing remarks on types of filters.

Rate of Filtration.—There are no indications that it would be advisable to employ rates of less than 100 million gallons per acre daily, and it is quite possible that this limit could be safely raised. The data, however, are too complicated by other factors to make this a decisive conclusion. But it is probable in view of the results from the Western pressure filter that in practice under favorable conditions the plant could be operated so as to make increased (uniform) rates in a measure meet increased demands for filtered water.

Regulation and Control.—This is an important point both with regard to necessity of uniform rate to give satisfactory results and also in respect to cost of operation. The automatic controller of the Jewell filter was very crude, but a step in the right direction.

Washing the Sand Layer.—Thorough washing of the sand layer is very important. To secure this it is necessary to distribute the wash-water uniformly under the sand layer. In this respect the Jewell filter was the most satisfactory, though as mentioned before a smaller distance between the cups seems desirable.

Agitation of the sand layer during washing was an advantage as shown by the operation of the Warren and Jewell filters. Of the two agitating devices, that of the Jewell filter was less cumbersome and did not move the sand from the center toward the periphery. It worked poorly at times, apparently due to a binding of the gears occasioned by the warping of the partly submerged timbers upon which the agitator rested. Both the Warren and Jewell devices lacked simplicity of detail and were too weak for the purpose. These defects could and should be remedied.

Surface Agitation.—This procedure to relieve clogging was used in the Jewell filter and was a decided step in advance. Its success is associated closely with the degree of coagulation of the water entering the sand layer, the character of the sand layer and the arrangement of the tank containing the sand layer. The successful employment of this method could probably be extended by a modification of the above factors.

Steaming.—This did not seem to be necessary during these tests, although it might be the case in some instances. This disadvantage of it is that it makes the organic matter on the sand serve as a better food for micro-organisms.

Quality of the Filtered Ohio River Water.

With proper attention to the operation of the systems, and an adequate degree of coagulation of the water as it entered the sand layer, these systems could produce a quality of filtered water which would be thoroughly satisfactory under all ordinary conditions with regard to appearance and sanitary character.

From an industrial standpoint, the filtered water would have a greater corroding action upon uncoated iron receptacles but not upon lead pipe; and it would contain more incrusting constituents when used in steam boilers. Concerning this last point the total quantities would not be excessive, compared with average Western waters, and the removal of the suspended matters would largely if not wholly offset the added sulphate of lime.

Owing to inherent qualities of the Ohio River water, the storage of the effluent in open reservoirs in this climate would require very careful consideration, and the period could not be a long one, owing to conditions favoring growths of algæ, etc.

Final Conclusions.

In all these systems the provision for subsidence, both with and without coagulation, was thoroughly inadequate in each case; but with regard to filtration proper the Jewell filter was the most satisfactory.

CHAPTER X.

Description of the Harris Magneto-electric System of Purification, and a Record of the Results Accomplished Therewith.

This system consisted essentially of a series of large, iron-covered tanks, and a set of electrical and magnetic appliances. According to the terms of the contract this experimental system was to have a capacity of 250,000 gallons per twenty-four hours. A brief general description of the system is as follows:

On the inlet water-pipe there was a small iron cylinder with a porcelain lining. As the water passed through this cylinder, called a spark drum, it met the discharge of an electric current of high voltage. From this cylinder the water passed in succession through three large, round iron tanks with conical bottoms. Each of these tanks contained a lining for the purpose of insulation. The water entered each of these tanks, in turn, at the side about two feet from the top. In the upper portion of the tanks were electrodes between which the water flowed as it passed out of the tanks at the top. On the top of each of the tanks was a set of electro-magnets. The outlet pipe connected with an opening in the cover and between the magnets. The three tanks were similar in construction, and the outlet pipes from the first two tanks entered the second and third tanks, respectively.

The fundamental principles upon which this system was based were never accurately explained to me. Electro-chemical action was considered to be an important factor in connection with the destruction of the bacteria and organic matter in the water. It was intended that all suspended matter would be repelled by the action of the magnets situated at the top of the three tanks; and the magnets were to force the suspended matters, including the bacteria, to the bottom of the tanks, where pipes leading to the sewer were provided.

There will next be presented a more detailed description of these devices and the accompanying electrical machines and appliances. Before doing so, however, it is to be recorded that, owing to delays in the preparation of castings, etc., the construction of this system was not begun until March 27, 1896. No official attention from the laboratory was given to the system until June 24. A large portion of the intervening period of three months was occupied in improvements, especially with regard to an insulating lining for the three large iron tanks, as will be explained beyond.

Spark Drum.

The spark drum, at the beginning of the system, was a cast-iron cylinder of a special design. It was 18 inches long and 10 inches in diameter. Near each end on opposite sides, a branch was taken off to connect with the inlet and outlet water-pipes, respectively. The cylinder and branches were one casting and were all lined with porcelain. The ends were closed with caps which were bolted on to the drum. At the center of each end there was a stuffing box, through which there were passed, respectively, the two pole pieces of the high voltage circuit from a Ruhmkorff coil. When the system was in operation these pole pieces were said to be 3 inches apart.

Iron Tanks containing the Electrodes and Electro-magnets.

These tanks, three in number, were made of cast iron, 1 inch in thickness. The upper half of each tank was cylindrical in form, and the lower half was in the form of a cone with the apex at the bottom.

The inside dimensions were as follows: Diameter of cylinder, 35.5 inches; depth of cylinder, 36 inches; depth of cone, 36 inches; and diameter of opening at the apex of the cone (bottom of the tank), 3 inches. This opening at the bottom of the tank connected with a pipe which led to the sewer. Brass covers closed the top of the tanks, and supported the electro-magnets in the manner described below. The tanks were placed on suitable pedestals.

The lining of the tanks was originally of cement. This did not give satisfactory insulation and at the time that the system was examined officially the tanks were lined with soft rubber sheets.

The inlet water pipes, 3 inches in diameter, entered at the side of the tanks, 2 feet from the top. The opening for the inlet pipe was lined with porcelain. A porcelain hood, 0.625 inch thick, 3 inches in diameter and 4 inches long, was provided at the inlet opening to break the currrent of the water. At the apex of the conical bottom of the tanks there was a 3-inch opening which connected with a 3-inch pipe leading to the sewer. Plug valves controlled the flow through these blow-off pipes. The main exits from the tanks were openings in the covers; and into cast-iron chambers on these covers were connected the outlet water pipes, 3 inches in diameter.

Electro-magnets.—On the brass casting, 1 inch in thickness, which formed the cover of each tank, there rested a set of 5 electro-magnets. In the center there was a large one, 15 inches in diameter, with a core of 12 inches. Four small magnets, each 8 inches in diameter with a core of 6 inches, surrounded the central one. The core of the large central magnet passed through an opening in the brass cover and was fastened on the under side to an iron disc 16 inches in diameter and 1 inch thick, which formed the negative pole. The cores of the four outer magnets passed through the brass plate and connected with an iron ring on the under side, which formed the positive pole. This ring was 10 inches wide and 1 inch thick. Between the disc and the ring was a circular opening 0.25 inch wide and 16 inches in diameter. Communication with the outlet recess on the top of the cover was obtained by a number of small holes drilled through the brass cover just above this circular opening.

The magnets were connected at the upper end by a cast-iron cross about 6 inches thick. With a full current from the generator (45 amperes) the lifting force of each set of (5) magnets was said to be about 6 tons.

Electrodes.—The size and arrangement of the electrodes were changed a number of times during the period covered by the preliminary trials of the system. On the date of the official examination the positive electrode consisted of a series of pressed carbon plates. The plates were 0.25-inch in thickness and 12 inches in width. They were placed in a parallel and vertical position, and suitable insulation and support were provided to keep them about 1 inch apart. The lengths of the carbon plates varied with the length of the parallel chords which they formed with the periphery of the tank, respectively. The total area of these plates (one side) was about 96,000 square inches.

The top of the carbon plates was about 6 inches below the brass top of the tanks. From the bottom of the plates to the plane in which the water entered the tanks the distance was 6 inches.

The negative pole was placed near the bottom of the tanks. It was a small sheet of metallic aluminum about 0.06 inch in thickness, and about 150 square inches in area.

Suitable openings in the tanks were provided for the connection of the wires to the electrodes.

Piping.—The inlet and outlet pipes of the spark drum were 4 inches in diameter. With this exception all the piping, including inlet, and blow-off pipes of the respective tanks, was 3 inches in diameter. The outlet pipe from the third and last tank led to a condenser where the exhaust steam from the engine which operated the generator was condensed.

All of the tanks and also the spark drum were closed compartments. The rate of flow of water through the system was controlled by a valve on the main inlet pipe which contained the river water under about 60 pounds pressure. Suitable valves were also provided on the inlet and outlet pipes of each tank.

The blow-off pipes at the bottom of each

tank were 3 inches in diameter and connected directly with the sewer. The flow through these pipes was controlled by 3-inch plug valves.

Engine.—A simple stationary engine was used to drive the generator. Its principal dimensions were as follows: Diameter of steam cylinder, 9.25 inches; length of stroke, 8.75 inches; and cut-off, 70 per cent. The fly-wheel and driving-pulley were combined, and had a diameter of 4 feet and a rim 12.5 inches in width. Its weight was about 1200 pounds.

From the engine the power was conveyed to the generator a distance of about 20 feet, by means of a leather belt 6 inches wide.

Dynamo-generator.—The generator was a compound-wound, bi-polar machine. It was wound to generate a direct current of 220 volts and 45 amperes, at a speed of 1125 revolutions per minute. The driving pulley was 8.75 inches in diameter and 6 inches wide. A rheostat was provided to regulate the intensity of the field by regulating the amount of current passing through the shunt winding. It was, however, seldom used.

Electric Circuits.—At the switch-board the main circuit was divided into three principal sub-circuits. The first of these sub-circuits passed directly to the electro-magnets situated on top of the tanks; the second led to the electrodes within the tanks; and the third passed through an interrupter to a Ruhmkorff coil from which the induced current of high voltage passed to the spark drum. All of these circuits were arranged in parallel on the main circuit. A fourth sub-circuit was also taken off to a small electric motor which turned the interrupter on the third circuit.

Resistance coils were used to control the electric current. They were made of 50 coils of No. 14 galvanized iron wire, about 4000 feet in all being used. Connections were made so that any number of coils could be used as desired.

Results Accomplished by the Harris Magneto-electric System.

This system was in official operation only for one hour, from 4.00 to 5.00 P.M. on June 24, 1896. The record of its operation, with the results of analyses of the river water before and after passage through the system, is as follows:

The rate at which the water passed through the full system was gradually increased until at 4.10 P.M. it had reached 23.5 cubic feet per minute, equivalent to 254,000 gallons per 24 hours. For ten minutes this rate was held approximately constant. At the end of this time, 4.20 P.M., samples of water, the analyses of which appear in the next tables, were collected as follows:

Bacterial sample No. 3959 was taken from the water as it left the spark drum.

Bacterial sample No. 3960 was taken from the water as it left the last tank.

Chemical sample No. 671 was taken from the water which was "blown off" at the bottom of the tanks.

Chemical sample No. 672 was taken from the water as it left the last tank.

For the next ten minutes the average rate of flow of the water through the entire system was 16.5 cubic feet per minute, equivalent to 178,000 gallons per 24 hours.

At the end of this time, 4.30 P.M., the following samples were collected for analysis:

Bacterial sample No. 3961 was taken from the water as it left the spark drum.

Bacterial sample No. 3962 and chemical sample No. 673 were collected from the water which had passed through the entire system.

During the next period of fifteen minutes there was maintained an average rate of flow of 12.5 cubic feet per minute, equivalent to 105,000 gallons per 24 hours. At 4.45 P.M. samples corresponding to those noted above were taken as follows:

Bacterial sample No. 3968 was collected from the water after passage through the spark drum.

Bacterial sample No. 3969 and chemical sample No. 674 were collected from the water after passage through the entire system.

From 4.45 to 5.00 P.M. the average rate of flow of water through the system was 6.2 cubic feet per minute, equivalent to 67,000 gallons per 24 hours. The following samples were collected at 5.00 P.M. which was the end of the test of this system.

Bacterial sample No. 3971 was collected from the water after passage through the spark drum.

Bacterial sample No. 3970 and chemical sample No. 675 were collected from the water after passage through the entire system.

At 4.44 P.M. chemical and bacterial samples of the river water, having the following numbers, respectively, 679 and 3963, were collected for analysis.

The electric current, during the period from 4.00 to 5.00 P.M., June 24, had an average voltage of 206 and an amperage of 20 to 21, as it left the generator on its way to the full system which was in use at this time.

In the next table are presented the results of analyses of the several samples of water described above. They show no appreciable purification of the water after its passage through the system.

This system was never put in official operation after this date. Various portions of it, however, were utilized in the devices which were operated by the Harris Company during the following month.

RESULTS OF BACTERIAL ANALYSES OF SAMPLES DESCRIBED ABOVE.

Number of Sample.	Source of Sample.	Collected June 24. Hour.	Bacteria per Cub. Centimeter.
3959	Spark Drum	4.20 P.M.	10 400
3960	Effluent	4.20 "	11 800
3961	Spark Drum	4 30 "	7 600
3962	Effluent	4.30 "	10 100
3963	River	4.44 "	11 600
3968	Spark Drum	4.45 "	13 100
3969	Effluent	4.45 "	8 800
3970	Effluent	5.00 "	9 800
3971	Spark Drum	5.00 "	9 900

RESULTS OF CHEMICAL ANALYSES OF SAMPLES DESCRIBED ABOVE.

(Parts per Million.)

Serial Number.	Collected.		Temperature. Degrees C.	Color.	Oxygen Consumed.	Nitrogen						Chlorine.	Residue on Evaporation.			Fixed Residue after Ignition.			Alkalinity.	Dissolved Alumina.	Iron.
						as Albuminoid Ammonia.			as Free Ammonia.	as Nitrites.	as Nitrates.										
	Date, 1896.	Hour.				Total.	Suspended.	Dissolved.					Total.	Suspended.	Dissolved.	Total.	Suspended.	Dissolved.			
670*	June 24	4.44 P.M.	...	.23	5.4	.334	.170	.164	.022	.003	.6	28.0	524	326	198	450	304	146	73.0	0.0	12.30
671†	" 24	4.18 "	....	.15	6.4	.414	.312	.102	.036	.003	.6	27.5	596	397	199	498	371	127	70.0	0.0	18.30
672‡	" 24	4 20 "	....	.15	7.0	.404	.308	.096	.034	.003	.7	27.6	586	383	203	487	351	136	69.8	0.0	19.50
673‡	" 24	4.30 "	....	.16	5.7	.346	.248	.098	.032	.003	.6	27.5	527	324	203	443	304	139	70.0	0.0	12.50
674‡	" 24	4.45 "	...	.18	5.9	.348	.250	.098	.034	.004	.5	27.5	521	330	191	447	308	139	70.3	0.0	12.20
675‡	" 24	5.00 "	....	.23	5.8	.370	.272	.098	.038	.004	.7	27.5	514	310	204	427	276	151	70.3	0.0	10.10

* River water † "Blow-off" at bottom of tanks. ‡ Effluent.

CHAPTER XI.

Description of the Devices Operated by the Harris Company in July, and a Record of the Results Accomplished Therewith.

During the month of July, 1896, a number of devices, more or less alike, were operated by the Harris Company with the view to purifying the Ohio River water. Various portions of the original system were utilized in the several devices, as will appear in the descriptions beyond where they are taken up in turn.

The devices of July appeared to be based mainly, as I understand the matter, on the results of some experiments made in a small glass jar during the last week in June. These experiments may be summarized briefly as follows:

Small Glass Jar Experiments.

A glass jar, of about one gallon capacity, was filled about three-fourths full of river water, and in the water were placed two circular strips of aluminum sheet. The thickness of the aluminum sheets was about 0.06 inch. The two strips were separated from each other by suitable blocks of an insulating material, about 0.125 inch thick. The cross section of the electrolyte (equal to the area of one side of one of the strips) was about 30 square inches.

Through these electrodes there was passed a current of electricity from the generator. A considerable quantity of gas, practically all of which was hydrogen, was set free at the negative pole by the action of the current. There was formed a white gelatinous substance which appeared for the most part, if not wholly, at the positive pole. It was found that this substance was aluminum hydrate. This is the same compound that is formed by the decomposition of alum or sulphate of alumina by lime, as has been explained in preceding chapters.

The aluminum hydrate coagulated the suspended matters in the water, in a similar manner as when sulphate of alumina was added to the water. Instead of the coagulated masses subsiding at the bottom, as in the application of sulphate of alumina, the greater part of them were carried to the surface by the rising currents of hydrogen gas.

When the electric current was turned off a portion of the matters suspended throughout the water settled to the bottom of the jar, while some of them joined the thick scum which formed on the surface of the water. At the end of a few minutes, five or less, the main bulk of the water became quite clear, with the exception of a few scattering particles of aluminum hydrate.

With regard to the length of time necessary to coagulate and clarify the water, this depends upon the strength (amperage) of the electric current. The reason of this lies in the fact that it is the strength of the current which determines the rate of conversion of metallic aluminum into the form of aluminum hydrate, disregarding any secondary solvent action of the initial compounds. In the experiments which received official attention the current was applied for 5 and 10 minutes, respectively. It was estimated that the amounts of aluminum which were converted to aluminum hydrate were about 7 and 17 grains per gallon, respectively.

By the aid of a siphon portions of the clarified water were removed from the jar for analysis. The bacterial results showed that the numbers of bacteria in the river water ranged from 8 100 to 11 600, while in the clarified water from the jar the numbers were 6, 68, and 120 per cubic centimeter, respectively. Disregarding the scattering particles of aluminum hydrate, the chemical results showed the removal of all the suspended organic and mineral matters present in the river water; and, further, that there had been an appreciable reduction in the organic matter which was dissolved in the water.

Status of the Situation on July 1, with Regard to the Magneto-electric System and Devices.

The magneto-electric system having been abandoned, practically speaking, by the Harris Company after the official test of one hour on June 24, there were operated during July several devices in which use was made of the principles illustrated by the jar experiments described above. It is to be recorded here that aluminum electrodes were known to have been employed by others for the purification of certain waters at a date earlier than that of these experiments. But it is also to be stated that the Harris Company claimed that their magnets would supplement and increase the action of the electrodes; and, further, that the magnets would facilitate the clarification of the coagulated water, and, perhaps, do away with the necessity of subsequent filtration through sand.

The devices operated in July will be described in turn, together with the results which they accomplished, respectively.

Device No. 1.

The first device was offered by the Harris Company for official examination on July 9. It consisted essentially of a closed iron tank lined with porcelain, which contained a set of aluminum electrodes. At the bottom of the tank was placed a set of magnets. After treatment in this tank the water passed to the top of a small stand pipe, through which it flowed from top to bottom, and thence to the sewer.

The Tank in which the Water was Treated.

The tank in which the water was subjected to electrolytic action was a small cast-iron cylinder surmounted by a brass dome. It was lined with porcelain. The principal inside dimensions were: Diameter of cylinder and base of dome, 1.71 feet; height of cylinder, 2 feet; and height of dome, 1 foot.

The water entered this tank at the top and passed out at the bottom, from which point it was conveyed to the top of the stand pipe.

Electrodes.—Aluminum sheets, arranged in the form of a manifold, composed the electrodes which were placed within the porcelain-lined tank. They were made of sheets of about 0.06 inch thick, which were held together by hard rubber bolts, the desired distance between the plates, 1.75 inches, being maintained by the use of hard rubber separators. Alternate sheets of metallic aluminum in the manifold formed the positive and negative poles, respectively. The total area of active electrode surface (anodes) was about 2550 square inches.

Magnets.—The magnets were similar in their arrangement to those of the three tanks of the original system, described in the last chapter, except that they were placed on the bottom instead of the top of the tank. There were five magnets in the set. The central one, forming the negative pole, was 8 inches in diameter. The other pole was formed by four smaller magnets of a diameter of 4 inches. The latter were placed around, and connected with, a ring which surrounded the central magnet.

Stand Pipe.—The stand pipe, into which the water passed after treatment in the iron tank, consisted of a single 12-foot length of iron pipe. Its diameter was 20 inches, and both ends were closed by caps. At four equidistant points in the stand pipe there were placed tin cones each 12 inches high and 20 inches in diameter. At the apex of each cone was an opening 1 inch in diameter, through which the water flowed downward in its passage through the stand pipe. The cones were all placed with the apex upward. At the side of the tanks were four openings, one above the base of each of the respective cones. These openings connected with blow-off pipes leading to the sewer. The main exit was about 3 feet from the bottom.

Piping.

The inlet and outlet water pipes of the tank and stand pipe were 1 inch in diameter. River water was supplied to the device under a pressure of about 60 pounds. The blow-off pipes leading to the sewer were 0.50 inch in diameter.

Electrical Machines and Appliances.

The engine and generator were the same that were used in the system described in the preceding chapter.

The circuits were similar except that the interrupter and Ruhmkorff coil were not used.

Results Accomplished by Device No. 1.

This device was in operation, officially, from 2.30 P.M. to 5.00 P.M. on July 9. In that time 514 cubic feet of water passed through it. The rate of flow ranged from 3 to 4 cubic feet per minute, and averaged 3.43 cubic feet per minute, which is equivalent to 37,000 gallons per 24 hours.

The amount of metallic aluminum, which was converted electrolytically into aluminum hydrate, was estimated to be equivalent to about 0.10 grain per gallon of water treated.

Observation on the electric current employed in the operation of this device showed that the amperage averaged 18.8 and the voltage 211. The average current was equivalent to .0122 ampere-hour per gallon and the power was 144 electric H.P. per million gallons of water treated per 24 hours.

Samples of water for chemical and bacterial analyses were collected as the water left the stand pipe at 3.30 P.M. and 4.30 P.M., after the device had been in operation 1 and 2 hours, respectively.

CHEMICAL RESULTS—DEVICE No. 1.

Analyses of Samples Described Below.

(Parts per Million.)

Serial Number.	Collected.		Teperature. Degrees C.	Color.	Oxygen Consumed.	Nitrogen as Albuminoid Ammonia.			Nitrogen as Free Ammonia.	Nitrogen as Nitrites.	Nitrogen as Nitrates.	Chlorine.	Residue on Evaporation.			Fixed Residue after Ignition.			Alkalinity.	Dissolved Alumina.	Iron.
	Date.	Hour.				Total.	Suspended.	Dissolved.					Total.	Suspended.	Dissolved.	Total.	Suspended.	Dissolved.			
714	July 9	9.30 A.M.	26.0	.25	6.6	.378	.272	.106	.030	.002	.6	6.9	589	470	119	523	436	87	56.0	0.0	30.70
719	" 9	Av. 2 samples.	....	.15	6.4	.404	.302	.102	.062	.006	.9	7.1	594	475	119	521	435	86	54.0	0.0	22.00

The two corresponding chemical samples of the treated water were mixed together and analyzed as sample No. 719. The results of the analysis of this sample and that of the river water on that day, sample No. 714, collected at 9.30 A.M., are given above.

The results of bacterial analysis of these samples and of the river water on that day are as follows:

BACTERIAL RESULTS—DEVICE No. 1.

Source of Sample.	Collected. Date. 1896.	Collected. Hour.	Bacteria per Cubic Centimeter.
River	July 9	9.30 A.M.	8 600
Treated water	" 9	3.30 P.M.	7 200
River	" 9	3.55 "	9 900
Treated water	" 9	4.30 "	8 700

No substantial purification of the water by this device is shown by the above results. After this test of July 9 modifications and additions to the device were made.

DEVICE No. 2.

On July 16 a second device was offered for official inspection. It was simply an elaboration and extension of the first device. There were added two duplicates, practically speaking, of the porcelain-lined iron tank containing electrodes and magnets as above described. The original one was also used, making three in all. The total area of active electrode surface (anodes) was about 4000 square inches, and the distance between the plates averaged 1.75 inches.

To facilitate clarification of the water after the treatment in these tanks there were used, in addition to the stand pipe, the three large iron tanks employed in the original system. The flow of water through the stand pipe was reversed; that is to say, it entered at the bottom and passed out at the top.

In the passage of the water through each

of these seven closed vessels successively, it was first treated in the three porcelain-lined tanks containing the electrodes and magnets; and thence it passed through the stand pipe and the three large iron tanks for clarification by subsidence. The cubical capacity of all the vessels was about 126 cubic feet, as follows: each of the three porcelain-lined tanks, 5.5 cubic feet; stand pipe, 26 cubic feet; each of the three iron tanks of the original system, 28 cubic feet; and piping (1 and 3 inches in diameter), 5 cubic feet.

Results Accomplished by Device No. 2.

The device was put in operation on the above-mentioned date, but only for 26 minutes after the water appeared at the outlet pipe. At the commencement of the test all the tanks and the stand pipe were drained. Water was applied at 11.52 A.M., and first appeared at the outlet at 12.39 P.M. The operation of the device was stopped at 1.05 P.M.

The period of operation was too short to yield any decisive information, except that there was no improvement in the appearance of the water after treatment at the average rate of 4 cubic feet per minute.

Samples of water, before and after treatment, were collected for analysis, and the results are presented below as a matter of record. It will be noted that the numbers of bacteria in the water increased during the passage through the device. The reason of this appeared to be that there were accumulations on the walls of the three rubber-lined tanks through which the water last passed.

BACTERIAL RESULTS—DEVICE No. 2.

Source of Sample.	Collected.		Bacteria per Cubic Centimeter.
	Date. 1896.	Hour.	
River	July 16	9.30 A.M.	6 800
Treated water	" 16	12.45 P.M.	22 900
Treated water	" 16	12.50 "	....
River	" 16	12.50 "	5 600
Treated water	" 16	12.55 "	13 700
Treated water	" 16	1.00 "	9 600
Treated water	" 16	1.05 "	10 200
River	" 16	5.00 "	5 000

With regard to the following results of chemical analyses, sample No. 740 was collected from the river water at 12.50 P.M.; while sample No. 741 represents a mixture of three equal portions of the treated water, collected at 12.45 P.M., 12.55 P.M., and 1.05 P.M., respectively.

CHEMICAL RESULTS—DEVICE No. 2.

Analyses of Samples Described Above.

(Parts per Million.)

Serial Number.	Collected.		Temperature Degrees C.	Color.	Oxygen Consumed.	Nitrogen as Albuminoid Ammonia.			Nitrogen as Free Ammonia.	Nitrogen as Nitrites.	Nitrogen as Nitrates.	Chlorine.	Residue on Evaporation.			Fixed Residue after Ignition.			Alkalinity.	Dissolved Alumina.	Iron.
	Date. 1896.	Hour.				Total.	Suspended.	Dissolved.					Total.	Suspended.	Dissolved.	Total.	Suspended.	Dissolved.			
740	July 16	12.50 P.M.	....	.27	7.0	.362	.214	.148	.030	.000	.6	2.2	540	404	136	480	404	76	52.7	0.0	15.40
741	" 16	Av. 3 samples	....	.14	6.6	.370	.260	.110	.044	.012	.4	2.5	490	370	120	429	366	63	52.3	0.0	15.30

DEVICE NO. 3.

The third device was offered for official inspection on July 18. It comprised the seven closed vessels described as the second device, and in addition there was a small filter of sand. Concerning the portions of the device common to the second one, it is to be stated that the second and third porcelain-lined tanks were used only as settling chambers. Aluminum electrodes, the anode area of which was about 2300 square inches, were placed only in the first porcelain-lined tank where the river water entered the device. The direct use of the magnets was also abandoned, and they were used only as resistance coils to control the current and prevent the passage of a greater current than the fittings were designed for. The water passed through the seven closed vessels in the same order as in the second device. When the water reached the last tank a portion of it was passed through the filter.

Filter.

The filter was made by filling with sand a galvanized iron tank, which was 2 feet in diameter and 3 feet deep. The outlet of this tank was a common 0.5-inch tap. On the bottom of the tank were placed three pieces of slotted brass pipe, which were to serve as strainers and allow the water to pass to the outlet tap while the sand was kept in place. These tubes were 1.5 inches in diameter on the inside. The length of one was 10 inches and of each of the other two 8 inches. They were all screwed into a cross which connected with the outlet tap. In each tube there were 5 rows of circumferential slots which averaged 0.024 inch in width and 0.72 inch in length. These slots were spaced about 0.125 inch from center to center.

Sand Used.—Coarse sand of an effective size of 0.56 millimeter was placed on the bottom of the tank to a depth of 6 inches, surrounding and covering the slotted tubes. Above this layer of sand were 24 inches of a somewhat finer sand having an effective size of 0.51 millimeter. The surface of the sand was about 6 inches below the top of the tank.

Resistance of Strainers and Sand Layer.—With the sand entirely removed from the tank, the maximum rate at which the strainer tubes and the outlet tap allowed water to flow was 0.37 cubic feet per minute, equivalent to 55 million gallons per 24 hours per acre of tank area. With the sand in place, and the surface free from accumulations of suspended matter, this rate was 0.28 cubic foot per minute, equivalent to 42 million gallons per acre per 24 hours.

Piping.—Suitable piping was provided to carry a portion of the water, as it passed through the outlet of the last tank, to the filter. Connections were made with the outlet pipe so that purified water could be forced up through the sand for the purpose of washing. The sand was stirred by hand during the process of washing.

Results Accomplished by Device No. 3.

This device was operated during four hours on July 18. At 10.05 A.M. operation was begun, with the tanks and filter empty. River water was applied to the device at a rate of about 3.0 cubic feet per minute. The full set of (seven) tanks was filled with water at 10.47 A.M. At that time water from the outlet of the last tank was applied to the filter. The rate of flow of water through the tanks was then increased to about 5 cubic feet per minute. For the greater part of the time the water passed through the filter at about the maximum rate; and observations showed this to be from 0.16 to 0.21 cubic foot per minute, equivalent to 24 and 31 million gallons per acre per 24 hours, respectively. After 12.05 P.M. the water passed through the tanks at an average rate of about 1.3 cubic feet per minute, equivalent to 14,000 gallons per 24 hours. The operation of the device was stopped at 2.05 P.M.

After the tanks were filled the blow-off pipes at the bottom of the tanks were opened for a few seconds every fifteen minutes, to remove suspended matters which had settled to the bottom. Of the 630 cubic feet of river water which were applied to the device from 10.05 A.M. to 2.05 P.M., 20 cubic feet were disposed of in this manner; 484 cubic feet passed through the tanks; and the remaining 126 cubic feet were retained in the tanks and the piping system.

During the operation of the device the voltage and amperage of the main circuit averaged 210 and 29, respectively. The voltage on the electrodes was 52.

An opportunity to obtain adequate observations on the amount of metallic aluminum used was not afforded. However, taking the results of later experiments as a basis, it is estimated that the amount of metallic aluminum converted electrolytically into aluminum hydrate averaged about 0.15 grain per gallon of applied water. The amount of electric current was .0129 ampere-hours per gallon up to 12.05 P.M., and .0497 ampere-hours per gallon after that time. The corresponding amounts of electric power were 152 and 583 electric H.P. per million gallons of water per 24 hours, respectively.

After the operation of this device was stopped at 2.05 P.M., the filter was washed. River water without previous treatment was then allowed to flow through it for thirty-five minutes (2.30–3.05 P.M.) at a maximum rate of about 30 million gallons per acre per 24 hours.

Samples of water before and after treatment by this device were collected and analyzed with the results indicated in table opposite.

It will be noted in connection with the above results that the number of bacteria in the water decreased in passage through the tanks, but increased after filtration. The explanation of this is that the filter was not operated long enough to wash out the bacteria originally contained in the sand.

In the next table are presented the results of analyses of chemical samples on this date.

Sample No. 744 was collected from the river water at 9.30 A.M.

Samples Nos. 745 and 747 were collected at 11.55 A.M. and 2.00 P.M., respectively, from the water as it left the outlet of the last tank.

Samples Nos. 746 and 748 were collected at 11.55 A.M. and 2.00 P.M., respectively, from the water after it passed through all the tanks and through the filter.

BACTERIAL RESULTS—DEVICE No. 3.

Source of Sample.	Hour of Collection.	Bacteria per Cubic Centimeter.
River water	9.30 A.M.	7 600
Treated water from outlet of last tank	12.00 M.	3 900
Treated water after filtration	12.00 "	7 100
Treated water from outlet of last tank	12.05 P.M.	5 900
Treated water after filtration	12.05 "	9 100
Treated water from outlet of last tank	2.00 "	900
Treated water after filtration	2.00 "	13 000
Treated water from outlet of last tank	2.05 "	2 700
Treated water after filtration	2.05 "	8 400
River water	2.00 "	9 600
River water after filtration without preliminary treatment	3.04 "	251
Treated water from outlet of last tank (12.00 M.) after 5 hours' sedimentation	5.00 "	1 200
Treated water from outlet of last tank (2.00 P.M.) after 3 hours' sedimentation	5.00 "	280
River water	5.13 "	12 400

Sample No. 752 was collected at 3.04 P.M. and represents river water after filtration without preliminary treatment in the tanks.

CHEMICAL RESULTS—DEVICE No. 3.

Analyses of Samples Described Above.

(Parts per Million.)

Serial Number.	Collected. Date. 1896.	Collected. Hour.	Temperature, Degrees C.	Color.	Oxygen Consumed.	Nitrogen as Albuminoid Ammonia. Total.	Nitrogen as Albuminoid Ammonia. Suspended.	Nitrogen as Albuminoid Ammonia. Dissolved.	Nitrogen as Free Ammonia.	Nitrogen as Nitrites.	Nitrogen as Nitrates.	Chlorine.	Residue on Evaporation. Total.	Residue on Evaporation. Suspended.	Residue on Evaporation. Dissolved.	Fixed Residue after Ignition. Total.	Fixed Residue after Ignition. Suspended.	Fixed Residue after Ignition. Dissolved.	Alkalinity.	Dissolved Alumina.	Iron.
744	July 18	9.30 A.M.	25.7	.19	8.7	.504	.406	.098	.038	.001	.5	4.0	753	637	116	668	594	74	60.3	0.0	33.30
745	" 18	11.55 "	....	.10	6.3	.352	.264	.088	.062	.004	.5	4.1	496	387	109	434	363	71	57.6	0.0	29.10
746	" 18	11.55 "	....	.13	0.6	.082	.000	.082	.060	.004	.4	4.0	107	0	107	66	0	66	57.9	0.0	.07
747	" 18	2.00 P.M.	....	.07	1.2	.128	.036	.092	.146	.004	.4	4.0	172	69	103	134	69	65	59.0	0.6	4.16
748	" 18	2.00 "	....	.08	0.9	.092	.000	.092	.098	.004	.4	2.5	98	0	98	66	0	66	59.0	0.0	.05
752	" 18	3.04 "	....	.18	1.9	.178	....	....	.030	.007	.4	4.0	127	....	....	101	....	....	60.0	0.0	9.20

DEVICE No. 4.

The fourth device presented for official inspection was operated continuously from 9.50 A.M. to 3.25 P.M. July 23, and from 6.30 P.M. July 23, to 9.00 A.M. July 24. It was intended to operate this device continuously up to August 1, but the Harris Company decided to make a further modification after the operation as above noted. This device comprised all of the seven closed vessels which had been used before, and the small sand filter. The first small porcelain-lined tank alone contained electrodes of metallic aluminum, the active area (anode surface) of which was about 2300 square inches. The set of magnets in this tank was also used. On top of this tank was set the 20-inch stand pipe. The cover of the tank and bottom of the stand pipe were removed, as were also the tin cones in the pipe. Water to be treated entered at the bottom of the small tank, and passed up through the stand pipe, from the top of which it passed to and through the series of two small tanks, and three large ones, for the purpose of sedimentation. The records of the operation of this device are presented in the next tables. For convenience in presentation, two tables are given, the first giving the record of the device exclusive of the sand filter, and the second, the records of operation of the filter. Following these two tables are presented the results of analyses of samples of river water before and after treatment by this device.

Aluminum Used.—Satisfactory observations of the amount of metallic aluminum used in the treatment of the water were not obtained. The river water was very muddy at this time, and examination of the porcelain-lined tank at the close of the runs showed that it was filled with a very thick deposit of mud, which had subsided during the passage of the water through this tank and the stand pipe placed on the top of it. Another observation of importance was that, at the bottom of the porcelain-lined tank, there was found a large number of scales of aluminum oxide, which had been formed on and removed from the metallic electrodes by the action of the electric current.

RECORDS OF OPERATION—DEVICE No. 4.

Number of Run....	1	2
Began...	July 23, 9.50 A.M.	July 23, 6.20 P.M.
Ended...	" 23, 3.25 P.M.	" 24, 9.00 A.M.
Period of service...	5 hrs. 35 min.	14 hrs. 30 min.
Period of filling....	0 " 35 "	0 " 15 "
Cubic feet of water treated*....	2 275	4 464
Cubic feet of water wasted..........	0	0
Average rate of treatment		
Cubic feet per min.	6.77	5.35
Gallons per 24 hrs.	72 900	57 600
Average voltage (entire system)...	206	214
Average amperage (entire system)...	29.6	26.0
Average electric ampere hours per gallon†.........	.0098	.0108
Average electric H.P. per mil. gals. per 24 hours†....	112	129

* After system was filled.
† Determined from switchboard readings of entire current.

RECORDS OF OPERATION OF THE FILTER—DEVICE No. 4.

Number of Run..................................	1	2	3
Began..................................	July 23, 9.50 A.M.	July 23, 2.00 P.M.	July 24, 2.50 A.M.
Ended..................................	" 23, 2.00 P.M.	" 24, 2.50 A.M.	" 24, 9.00 "
Period of operation..................................	5 hours 10 minutes.	9 hours 50 minutes.	....
Period of service..................................	4 " 53 "	9 " 30 "	6 hours 10 minutes.
Period of wash..................................	17 "	20 "	....
Cubic feet of filtered water..................................	45.6	87.8	67.8
Cubic feet of wash-water..................................	7.5	10.2	....
Average rate:			
Cubic feet per minute..................................	0.12	0.15	0.18
Million gallons per acre per 24 hours..................................	18	22	27

RESULTS OF BACTERIAL ANALYSES OF SAMPLES COLLECTED JULY 23, 12.00 M.—DEVICE No. 4.

Source of Sample.	Bacteria per Cubic Centimeter.
River..................................	25 800
Treated water from outlet of stand pipe..	23 200
Treated water from outlet of last tank..	29 500
Treated water after filtration..........	4 300

Results of Analyses—Device No. 4.

Samples of water before and after treatment by this device were collected and analyzed with the results presented beyond. Of the chemical samples, No. 763 was collected from the river water before treatment, No. 768 was collected from the water after it had passed through the first small tank and stand pipe extension thereof, No. 769 was taken from the water after it had passed through the entire system of tanks, just before it was turned into the filter, and No. 779 was taken from the effluent from the sand filter.

After the run ending July 24, 9.00 A.M., the stand pipe was removed from the top of the porcelain-lined tank, and placed on the floor again, owing to the complications in the electrolytic cell arising from the sedimentation which took place when in the first-mentioned position. The remaining operations are described as those of Device No. 5.

CHEMICAL RESULTS—DEVICE No. 4.

Analyses of Samples Described Above.

(Parts per Million.)

Serial Number.	Collected. Date. 1896.	Collected. Hour.	Temperature. Degree C.	Color.	Oxygen Consumed.	Nitrogen as Albuminoid Ammonia. Total.	Sus-pended.	Dis-solved.	Nitrogen as Free Ammonia.	Nitrogen as Nitrites.	Nitrogen as Nitrates.	Chlorine.	Residue on Evaporation. Total.	Suspended.	Dissolved.	Fixed Residue after Ignition. Total.	Suspended.	Dissolved.	Alkalinity.	Dissolved Alumina.	Iron.
763	July 23	9.30 A.M.	25.1	.37	24.8	1.360	1.228	.132	.056	.008	.7	8.6	2 296	2 175	121	2 096	2 018	78	61.9	0.0	97.90
768	" 23	12.00 M.	....	.23	24.5	1.280	1.168	.112	.026	.007	.7	8.1	2 192	2 080	112	2 008	1 927	81	68.6	0.0	131.40
769	" 23	12.00 "	....	.23	24.0	1.360	1.154	.206	.080	.011	.7	8.1	2 182	....	...	2 004	....	....	63.9	0.0	93.90
770	" 23	12.00 "	....	.23	3.7	.206	....	....	.038	.011	.7	8.1	254	....	...	203	....	....	64.0	0.0	12.50

Device No. 5.

The fifth and last device was presented for official inspection on July 27. Five runs were made from July 27 to August 1, the device being operated day and night so far as was feasible. In this device, as in the preceding, all seven of the closed vessels were used as well as the filter. In all of the three small tanks were sets of aluminum electrodes and the magnets on these tanks were also used. The electrode manifold in the first tank was somewhat larger than in the second and third, the current (circuits in parallel) dividing as follows: Electrodes Number 1, 7.6 amperes; electrodes Number 2, 5.8 amperes; electrodes Number 3, 6.0 amperes. The total active area of the electrodes (anode surface) was about 4000 square inches.

The river water entered the first small tank at the bottom, passed through it and thence upward through the stand pipe. This pipe was set on the ground as when first used, the top of the small tank and the bottom of the pipe being closed. The tin cones were used in this pipe as in the third device, and piping was provided to flush out the sediment at the base of the cones and the bottom of the pipe. From the stand pipe the water passed successively through the second and third small tanks, thence through the three large tanks (used as settling chambers) and finally a portion of it passed through the filter. From July 30, 5.50 P.M., to July 31, 4.00 P.M., the water filtered was taken from the third small tank, instead of from the third large tank which was the last one of the series.

The records of operation of this device and the results accomplished therewith are presented in the following tables. As before, the records of operation of the device exclusive of the filter, and of the filter itself, are presented separately. Following these tables are presented observations on the amount of aluminum used and the efficiency of the electric generating plant.

RECORDS OF OPERATION—DEVICE No. 5.

Records of Operation of Device Exclusive of Filter.

Number of run	1	2	3	4	5
Began	July 27, 7.47 P.M.	July 28, 4.20 P.M.	July 29, 12.45 P.M.	July 30, 5.30 P.M.	July 31, 4.10 P.M.
Ended	July 28, 9.00 A.M.	July 29, 6.00 A.M.	July 30, 9.00 A.M.	July 31, 12.07 P.M.	Aug. 1, 9.43 A.M.
Period of service, hours and minutes	13h. 13m.	13h. 40m.	20h. 35m.	18h. 37m.	17h. 33m.
Period of filling, " " "	0h. 47m.	2h. 55m.	0h. 00m.	1h. 00m.	1h. 00m
Cubic feet of water treated*	2 599	959	1 415	1 343	4 932
Cubic feet of water wasted	191	100	27	21	176
Average rate of treatment. Cubic feet per minute	3.28	1.17	1.15	1.20	4.68
Gallons per 24 hours	35 300	12 600	12 400	12 900	50 400
Average voltage (entire system)	208	204	198	199	182
Average amperage (entire system)	23.6	27.9	28.8	29.1	31.1
Average electric ampere-hour per gallon †	.016	.053	.056	.054	.015
Average electric horse-power per million gallons per 24 hours †	186	605	617	601	150

* After system was filled. † Determined from switchboard readings of entire current.

Records of Operation of Filter.

Number of Run.	Began.	Ended.	Periods of Time. Hours and Minutes.			Quantities of Water. Cubic Feet.		Average Rate.	
			Operation.	Service.	Wash.	Filtered.	Wash.	Cubic Ft. per Min.	Million Gallons per Acre per 24 H.
1	July 27, 7.47 P.M.	July 27, 11.18 P.M.	4h. 18m.	4h. 05m.	13m.	21.0	3.3	0.11	16
2	" 27, 11.18 "	" 28, 4.30 A.M.	5h. 12m.	4h. 57m.	15m.	19.6	7.3	0.07	11
3	" 28, 4.30 A.M.	" 28, 5.50 "	1h. 20m.	1h. 00m.	20m.	6.0	17.3	0.18	27
4	" 28, 5.50 "	" 28, 8.00 "	2h. 32m.	2h. 15m.	17m.	20.2	12.1	0.15	22
5	" 28, 8.22 "	" 29, 6.00 "	....	15h. 18m.	....	177.0	......	0.19	28
6	" 29, 12.25 P.M.	" 30, 5.50 P.M.	20h. 58m.	20h. 38m.	20m.	255.8	10.5	0.21	31
7	" 30, 5.50 "	" 30, 8.40 "	2h. 50m.	2h. 40m.	10m.	20.0	10.0	0.12	18
8	" 30, 8.40 "	" 31, 1.25 A.M.	4h. 45m.	4h. 33m.	12m	35.0	12.0	0.13	19
9	" 31, 1.25 A.M.	" 31, 6.20 "	3h. 55m.	3h. 45m.	10m.	25.0	13.5	0.11	16
10	" 31, 5.20 "	" 31, 3.50 P.M.	6h. 54m.	6h. 47m.	07m.	54.5	14.8	0.13	19
11	" 31, 3.50 P.M.	" 31, 4.00 "	0h. 32m.	0h. 20m.	12m.	4.4	13.8	0.22	33
12	" 31, 4.00 "	Aug. 1 9.43 A.M.	....	17h. 13m.	....	202.9	....	0.20	30

During runs numbers 7 to 11, inclusive, the water to be filtered was taken from the third small porcelain-lined tank. During all the other runs it was taken from the last large tank.

Results of Analyses—Device No. 5.

In the following tables are presented results of frequent analyses of the water before and after treatment by this device. Samples were collected from the water before treatment, after it had passed through the first tank, after it left the last tank, and after it had passed through the filter.

The first table shows the results of the bacterial analyses of the river water before treatment, during the periods when this device was in operation.

In the second table are given the results of bacterial analyses of the treated water after it had passed through the first tank.

The third and fourth tables contain the results of bacterial analyses of the treated water from the last tank and of the effluent from the filter, respectively.

Following these are tables containing the results of the corresponding chemical analyses, the time and place of collection being given by reference to the corresponding bacterial samples. When two or more bacterial numbers are given it is to be understood that portions collected at the same time and place as these bacterial samples were mixed and the analysis made of the mixture.

BACTERIAL RESULTS—RIVER WATER.

Number of Sample.	Collected.		Bacteria per Cubic Centimeter.
	Date. 1896.	Hour.	
4726	July 27	9.30 A.M.	16 000
4736	" 27	5.00 P.M.	19 600
4741	" 27	9.00 "	14 400
4745	" 28	3.00 A.M.	18 500
4750	" 28	9.30 "	24 500
4796	" 28	6.00 P.M.	12 400
4800	" 28	12.00 "	8 600
4804	" 29	6.00 A.M.	10 700
4812	" 29	9.30 "	9 500
4861	" 29	5.00 P.M.	....
4866	" 30	9.30 A.M.	17 300
4871	" 30	5.00 P.M.	6 800
4878	" 31	9.30 A.M.	6 800
4881	" 31	10.45 "	7 900
4891	" 31	3.35 P.M.	5 800
4898	" 31	4.30 "	8 600
4899	" 31	4.30 "	9 600

BACTERIAL RESULTS—DEVICE No. 5.

Effluent from first tank.

Number of Sample.	Collected.		Rate.*	Bacteria per Cubic Centimeter.
	Date. 1896.	Hour.		
4738	July 27	9.00 P.M.	2.6	12 700
4742	" 28	3.00 A.M.	2.5	12 900
4747	" 28	9.00 "	4.4	15 000
4797	" 28	6.00 P.M.	1.0	2 900
4801	" 28	12.00 "	1.0	3 900
4805	" 29	6.00 A.M.	1.0	5 700
4856	" 29	3.05 P.M.	1.3	5 800
4866a	" 30	9.00 A.M.	1.2	5 800
4872	" 30	5.30 P.M.	1.0	1 500
4875	" 31	8.00 A.M.	1.1	3 600
4879	" 31	10.20 "	1.2	5 600
4884	" 31	12.05 P.M.	1.2	2 800
4894	" 31	4.10 "	4.2	10 100
4900	" 31	5.00 "	3.8	4 600
4904	Aug. 1	9.00 A.M.	4.0	2 000

* Rate of treatment in cubic feet per minute.

BACTERIAL RESULTS—DEVICE No. 5.

Effluent from last tank.

Number of Sample.	Collected.		Rate.*	Bacteria per Cubic Centimeter.
	Date. 1896.	Hour.		
4730	July 27	9.00 P.M.	2.6	1 800
4743	" 28	3.00 A.M.	2.5	5 300
4748	" 28	9.00 "	4.4	15 000
4798	" 28	6.00 P.M.	1.0	215
4802	" 28	12.00 "	1.0	192
4806	" 29	6.00 A.M.	1.0	252
4857	" 29	3.05 P.M.	1.3	700
4867a	" 30	9.00 A.M.	1.2	900
4876	" 30	9.00 "	1.2	900
4883a	" 31	11.40 "	1.2	310
4885	" 31	12.05 P.M.	1.2	250
4895	" 31	4.10 "	4.2	7 800
4901	" 31	5.00 "	3.8	2 000
4905	Aug. 1	9.00 A.M.	4.0	3 500

* Rate of treatment in cubic feet per minute.

BACTERIAL RESULTS—DEVICE No. 5.

Effluent from Filter.

Number of Sample.	Collected.		Rate.*	Bacteria per Cubic Centimeter.
	Date. 1896.	Hour.		
4740	July 27	9.00 P.M.	0.26	132
4744	" 28	3.00 A.M.	0.09	80
4749	" 28	9.00 "	0.11	1 800
4799	" 28	6.00 P.M.	0.20	262
4803	" 28	12 00 "	0.20	399
4807	" 29	6.00 A.M.	0.20	188
4858	" 29	3.05 P.M.	0.25	171
4863	" 29	5.12 "	0.24	700
4868a	" 30	9.00 A.M.	0.14	435
4873	" 30	5.30 P.M.	0.14	130
4877	" 31	8.00 A.M.	0.15	173
4880	" 31	10.20 "	0.13	300
4886	" 31	12.05 P.M.	0.13	505
4896	" 31	4.10 "	0.21	1 500
4902	" 31	5.00 "	0.24	700
4906	Aug. 1	9.00 A.M.	0.23	700

* Cubic feet per minute.

CHEMICAL RESULTS—DEVICE No. 5.

(Parts per Million.)

Serial Number.	Date of Collection. 1896.	Temperature. Degrees C.	Degree of Clearness.	Color.	Oxygen Consumed.	Nitrogen						Chlorine.	Residue on Evaporation.			Fixed Residue after Ignition.			Alkalinity.	Dissolved Alumina.	Iron.
						as Albuminoid Ammonia.			as Free Ammonia.	as Nitrites.	as Nitrates.										
						Total.	Sus-pended.	Dis-solved.					Total.	Suspended.	Dissolved.	Total.	Suspended.	Dissolved.			
781[1]	July 27	....	....	.27	18.8	1.120	1.002	.118	.124	.019	.7	6.5	1 496	1 387	109	1 356	1 286	70	55.1	0.0	70.80
782[2]	" 27-28	....	....	.31	13.2	.740	.622	.118	.092	.018	.6	6.5	1 061	952	109	950	880	70	55.2	0.0	20.00
783[3]	" 27-28	....	....	.30	3.5	.158	.040	.118	.044	.011	.6	6.5	166	57	109	124	54	70	51.0	0.0	2.00
787[4]	" 28-29	....	....	.10	7.2	.320	.230	.090	.228	.022	.6	6.7	435	346	89	381	318	63	45.0	0.0	11.00
788[5]	" 28-29	....	....	.10	2.4	.102	.012	.090	.216	.033	.6	6.0	115	26	89	94	31	63	46.8	0.0	.70
789[6]	" 28-29	....	....	.12	2.1	.080	.....	.....	.144	.100	.5	4.0	87	.....	...	62	.....	..	49.0	0.0	.12
794[7]	" 29-30	...	....	.11	11.8	.630	.530	.100	.202	.023	.8	3.1	926	826	100	841	774	67	56.0	0.0	34.50
795[8]	" 29-30	....	....	.11	3.0	.150	.050	.100	.194	.032	.9	3.0	194	94	100	163	96	67	52.2	0.0	6.50
796[9]	" 29-30	....	....	.10	1.9	.104	.000	.104	.102	.166	.9	3.1	100	0	100	79	0	79	55.1	0.0	.12
799[10]	" 31	....	....	.13	10.2	.680	.588	.092	.248	.012	.7	3.6	628	536	92	560	493	67	52.6	0.0	28.70
800[11]	" 31	...	....	.07	2.0	.088	.000	.088	.140	.333	.6	3.6	92	0	92	68	0	68	53.1	0.0	.05
801[12]	" 31	....	....	.13	2.3	.110	.018	.092	.208	.020	.6	3.1	130	38	92	101	34	67	51.1	0.0	.70
804[13]	" 31, Aug. 1	...	....	.27	11.3	.540	.418	.122	.042	.006	.8	4.0	699	576	123	634	544	90	62.0	0.0	25.30
805[14]	" 31, " 1	...	....	.27	11.9	.510	.388	.122	.040	.006	.8	3.7	658	535	123	583	493	90	43.0	0.0	24.50
806[15]	" 31, " 1	....	....	.27	4.3	.198	.076	.122	.026	.004	.8	3.8	204	81	123	163	73	90	50.0	0.0	9.00

Corresponding bacterial numbers: [1] 4738, 4742, 4747. [2] 4739, 4743, 4748. [3] 4740, 4744, 4749. [4] 4797, 4801, 4885. [5] 4798, 4802, 4806. [6] 4799, 4803, 4807. [7] 4856, 4866a. [8] 4857, 4867a. [9] 4858, 4868a. [10] 4879. [11] 4880. [12] 4883a. [13] 4900, 4904. [14] 4901, 4905. [15] 4902, 4906.

Summary of Analytical Results—Device No. 5.

The degree of purification accomplished by the fifth device, at different points in the passage of the water through it, is indicated by the following tables. The removal of organic matter as indicated by the nitrogen in the form of albuminoid ammonia and oxygen consumed is first presented. Following this is given a summary of the bacterial analyses of the water at different points on its passage through the device.

PERCENTAGE REMOVAL OF ORGANIC MATTER FROM THE RIVER WATER AT DIFFERENT POINTS ON ITS PASSAGE THROUGH THE DEVICE.

Percentage Removal of Nitrogen as Albuminoid Ammonia.

Date. 1896.	Point of Collection of Sample.		
	First Tank.	Last Tank.	Filter.
July 28	0	34	93
" 29	63	88	91
" 30	48	88	91
" 31	0	77	81
Aug. 1	0	0	58
Percentage Removal of Oxygen Consumed.			
July 28	0	23	90
" 29	64	88	89
" 30	50	87	92
" 31	25	83	85
Aug. 1	17	12	68

SUMMARY OF BACTERIAL RESULTS.

BACTERIA PER CUBIC CENTIMETER IN THE RIVER WATER BEFORE TREATMENT AND AT DIFFERENT POINTS ON ITS PASSAGE THROUGH THE DEVICE.

Date, 1896.	July 27	July 28	July 28	July 28	July 28	July 29	July 29
Hour	9 P.M.	3 A.M.	9 A.M.	6 P.M.	12 P.M.	6 A.M.	3 P.M.
River	14 400	18 500	24 500	12 400	8 600	10 700	9 500
First Tank	12 700	12 900	15 000	2 900	3 900	5 700	5 800
Last Tank	1 800	5 300	15 000	215	192	252	700
Filter	132	80	1 800	262	399	188	171

Date, 1896.	July 30	July 30	July 31	July 31	July 31	July 31	July 31	Aug. 1
Hour	9 A.M.	5 P.M.	8 A.M.	10 A.M.	12 M.	4 P.M.	5 P.M.	9 A.M.
River	17 300	6 800	6 800	6 800	7 900	9 100	9 100	6 800
First tank	5 800	1 500	3 600	5 600	2 800	10 100	4 600	2 000
Last tank	900	.....	1 200	......	250	7 800	2 000	3 500
Filter	435	130	173	310	505	1 500	700	703

AVERAGE BACTERIA IN RIVER WATER AND AT DIFFERENT POINTS IN ITS PASSAGE THROUGH THE DEVICE, AND THE AVERAGE PERCENTAGE REMOVAL AT THESE POINTS.

	River.	First Tank.	Last Tank.	Filter.
Average bacteria per c. c.	11 300	6 320	3 000	500
Average percentage removal	......	49	76	96

Amount of Metallic Aluminum Used.

From July 27, 7.47 P.M., to July 30, 9.00 A.M., 37 440 gallons of water were treated and the weight of the aluminum electrodes decreased 18 620 grains, equal to 0.5 grain per gallon.

From July 30, 9.00 A.M., to July 31, 12.07 P.M., 9465 gallons of water were treated and the weight of the aluminum electrodes decreased 7490 grains, equal to 0.78 grain per gallon.

From July 31, 12.07 P.M., to Aug. 1, 9.43 A.M., 34 500 gallons of water were treated but there was no reduction in weight of electrodes, owing to a failure in the electrical connections.

It is to be stated that, of the amount of aluminum noted above, a considerable portion passed into the oxide state; scaled off the electrodes, fell to the bottom of the tanks and was of no aid in the purification of the water. Further, it was impracticable, under the existing circumstances, to determine how much of the aluminum which was removed from the electrodes by the electric treatment was actually utilized in the purification of the water.

Rate of Sedimentation of Water Treated with Electrolytically Prepared Aluminum Hydrate.

Arrangements were made to study this point, but after some work had been done it was seen that no results of practical value were being obtained, because it was not known how much aluminum in the form of available hydrate had actually been added to any sample of water for analysis.

This work was stopped and taken up under more favorable conditions after Aug. 1 and is described in the next chapter.

Efficiency of the Electric Generating Plant of the Harris Magneto-electric Water Purification System.

Three tests were made of the relation between the steam and electrical power, showing the average combined efficiency of the generating plant to be 21.8 per cent.

STATUS OF THE SITUATION ON AUGUST 1, WITH REGARD TO THE MAGNETO-ELECTRIC SYSTEM AND DEVICE.

The more important features of the situation on Aug. 1, when the investigations upon the other systems of purification were brought to a close, may be briefly summarized as follows:

1. The original system was a complete failure at the time of official examination; and, practically speaking, it was abandoned thereafter by the Harris Company.

2. It is possible to purify the Ohio River water to a greater or less degree by the application of aluminum hydrate prepared electrolytically from metallic aluminum. With other waters purification in this or a similar manner had been previously claimed by other persons.

3. The available data, so far as they went, indicated that the direct effect of the electric action and the magnetic action was of little or no practical value.

4. It is possible to purify the Ohio River

water to a satisfactory degree with electrolytically formed aluminum hydrate by the employment of subsequent sedimentation and filtration. Further, no lime in the river water is required with this process, and there is no increase in the corroding and incrusting constituents of the filtered water.

5. The available data, so far as they went, indicated that the manner of purification last stated would be costly to an excessive and unreasonable degree if applied to the water supply of a large city. It appeared, further, that in continuous service it might allow periods of marked irregularity in efficiency.

6. Viewed from a practical point, the data which it was feasible for the Water Company to obtain, under the existing circumstances, were very limited and unsatisfactory. This was due chiefly to the poor and ill-advised construction of the devices as they were assembled together, and, further, to the fact that the total period, during which the devices were operated for official inspection, was less than 119 hours.

7. The situation may be comprehensively described by the statement that this method of purification had not advanced beyond the experimental stage, where laboratory experiments are best adapted to show the practicability and merits of the method.

From the above statements it is plain that at the close of the regular investigations the situation with regard to the magneto-electric devices was quite unsatisfactory, from the Water Company's point of view, as well as from that of the Harris Company.

The indications were that the method was not a commercial success, so far as the purification of the Ohio River water is concerned. But, owing to the unsatisfactory manner of the construction and operation of the several devices, the very limited evidence was obscured by a variety of complications; and there was really obtained very little information of positive value.

A conference was held at this time by the officers of the Water Company to discuss the situation. The advisability of continuing the investigation with the makeshift devices offered for inspection was out of question. The real problem was to decide whether it would be wiser for the interests of the Water Company to dismiss the subject as it stood, or to have the fundamental principles of the method investigated by the experts who were regularly employed by the Water Company at that time. It was decided to pursue the latter course. The Chief Chemist and Bacteriologist was instructed to retain the services of the assistant analysts for two or three weeks or so. An arrangement was also made with the Harris Company to make use of their dynamo and other electrical appliances; and the services of the man who had operated the devices were also availed of.

The results of these investigations by the Water Company are presented in the next chapter.

CHAPTER XII.

INVESTIGATIONS BY THE WATER COMPANY IN AUGUST INTO THE PRACTICABILITY AND ECONOMY OF THE DEVICES OPERATED BY THE HARRIS COMPANY.

IN this chapter there are recorded the results of the various experiments, which were made by the Water Company under my direction during August, 1896, with the view to learning the practicability and economy of the principles upon which the magneto-electric treatment of water was claimed to be based.

The principal points of importance, to which attention was directed, may be outlined as follows:

1. The direct and indirect effect of the application of electricity upon the bacteria and organic matter in the Ohio River water.

2. The direct and indirect effect of the application of electricity in the purification of the Ohio River water through the formation of aluminum hydrate, from metallic aluminum electrodes.

3. A comparison of the efficiency, in the purification of the Ohio River water by coagulation and sedimentation, of aluminum hydrate formed electrolytically from the metallic aluminum, and of aluminum hydrate formed from the decomposition of sulphate of alumina by lime.

4. The effect of the action of the electromagnets upon the constituents of the Ohio River water, and upon the rate at which aluminum hydrate is formed from aluminum electrodes.

5. Rate at which aluminum hydrate is formed electrolytically from metallic aluminum.

6. Regularity during continuous service of the rate at which aluminum hydrate is formed electrolytically from metallic aluminum.

7. Amount of metallic aluminum which is wasted in the electrolytic production of aluminum hydrate.

8. A comparison of the cost of aluminum hydrate formed by the application of sulphate of alumina, and by the action of electricity on metallic aluminum, respectively.

9. Observations on the amount of power which would be required to produce aluminum hydrate in a large scale by means of electricity.

The experiments which were made on the several problems will be described in order.

THE DIRECT AND INDIRECT EFFECT OF THE APPLICATION OF ELECTRICITY UPON THE BACTERIA AND ORGANIC MATTER IN THE OHIO RIVER WATER.

Experiment No. 1.

This experiment was made to learn the effect of a current of high voltage, such as used in the "spark drum" of the original system (Chapter X).

River water was treated with an electric current of high voltage for one hour in the porcelain-lined "spark drum" with the poles 2.56 inches apart. The voltage of the current as it left the Ruhmkorff coil used could not be accurately measured, but was estimated by the representative of the Harris Company to be about 200,000, with an amperage equivalent to a very small fraction of one unit. This experiment was performed in duplicate. The temperature of the river water increased about 2° C. during this treatment for one hour. At the beginning of the experiments the temperature of the river water was 31° C. The average results of bacterial analyses of a corresponding set of samples in the two experiments are as follows:

REMOVAL OF BACTERIA IN OHIO RIVER WATER BY ELECTRIC TREATMENT IN THE "SPARK DRUM."

Length of Treatment of River Water. Minutes.	Bacteria per Cubic Centimeter.	Percentage Removal.	Length of Treatment of River Water. Minutes.	Bacteria per Cubic Centimeter.	Percentage Removal
0	27 400	....	15	19 400	29
3	23 600	14	30	16 900	38
5	20 500	25	45	17 200	37
10	20 600	25	60	14 100	48

The carbonaceous organic matter in the river water was reduced by this treatment, as indicated by the "oxygen consumed," from 9.8 to 7.9 and 7.3 parts per million in 15 and 60 minutes, respectively. No effect was apparently produced upon the nitrogenous organic matter in the river water.

Experiment No. 2.

This experiment was made to learn the effect of currents of comparatively high density, and to study the effect of amount of current. It was performed in duplicate with small carbon electrodes using as high amperage and low voltage as it was practicable to obtain under the circumstances. River water was treated in a glass jar for 10 minutes, when the temperature of the water became so high that it was necessary to stop the experiment in each case. The average amperage and voltage of the current in these experiments were 10.5 and 40, respectively, and the density of the current was about 90 amperes per square foot of cross-section of electrolyte. The average results of bacterial analyses of a corresponding set of samples in the two experiments were as follows:

REMOVAL OF BACTERIA IN OHIO RIVER WATER BY ELECRIC TREATMENT, AS ABOVE STATED.

Length of Treatment of River Water. Minutes.	Ampere-hours per Gallon.	Bacteria per Cubic Centimeter.	Percentage Removal.
0	0	28 500	....
1	0.23	22 200	22
3	0.70	13 300	53
5	1.17	7 700	73
10	2.33	2 700	91

The average temperature at the close of the tests was 53° C., which was so high that by actual experiment it was found to be the explanation for the removal of 70 per cent. of the bacteria originally present in the river water.

There was a noticeable disintegration or change in the nitrogenous organic matter, but there was practically no purification by the direct application of electricity. The change in carbonaceous organic matter could not be determined owing to the presence of carbon from the electrodes.

No apparent effect directly or indirectly on the rate of sedimentation of the river water was noted after these electric treatments with carbon electrodes.

It may be added here that experiments in 1897 bore out this fact that, directly, the electric current had no practical effect in the purification of the Ohio River water.

THE DIRECT AND INDIRECT EFFECT OF THE APPLICATION OF ELECTRICITY IN THE PURIFICATION OF THE OHIO RIVER WATER THROUGH THE FORMATION OF ALUMINUM HYDRATE FROM METALLIC ALUMINUM ELECTRODES.

In this connection experiments similar to the one last described were made except that metallic aluminum electrodes were used in place of carbon ones. River water was treated in a glass jar for 10 minutes with a current having an average amperage and voltage of 6.3 and 97, respectively. At the conclusion of the experiment the contents of the jar were well mixed, and a portion removed for analysis.

Sedimentation rapidly took place in the remaining portion in the jar. The supernatant liquid was clear and of a satisfactory quality with regard to organic matter and bacteria. About 0.75 gallon was used in this experiment, and the amount of treatment was 1.05 ampere hours. Assuming full rate of decomposition, the amount of aluminum added to the water was therefore about 11.0 grains.

This indirect purification of the river water by means of the production of aluminum hydrate was very marked and will be more clearly presented in the next section.

For the purpose of learning the direct effect of this electrical treatment, independent of the subsiding action, analyses were made of the unsettled portion of the treated water. Here it may be stated that analyses of the gas, which was liberated quite rapidly from the negative pole, showed it to be composed very largely, if not wholly, of hydrogen. The number of bacteria in the river water before and after this treatment were found to be 3800 and 4200 per cubic centimeter, respectively.

The results of chemical analyses of the water before and after treatment without subsidence, represented by samples Nos. 807 and 808, respectively, are presented in the next table. It will be noted that the oxygen consumed (carbonaceous matter) was reduced from 9.7 to 8.3 parts. With regard to the nitrogen as free ammonia and albuminoid ammonia, the results show that a certain change was effected in the nitrogenous organic matter. But as there was no marked increase in nitrogen in the oxidized form of nitrites or nitrates, this condition cannot be regarded as one of purification,—it was simply an initial step in that direction.

This experiment, which was duplicated in its most important parts, leads to the conclusion that the direct action of the electricity applied to the river water by means of aluminum electrodes, without subsidence, effected practically no purification.

RESULTS OF CHEMICAL ANALYSES OF SAMPLES AS DESCRIBED ABOVE.

(Parts per Million.)

Serial Number.	Collected.		Temperature. Degrees C.	Color.	Oxygen Consumed.	Nitrogen						Chlorine.	Residue on Evaporation.			Fixed Residue after Ignition.			Alkalinity.	Dissolved Alumina.	Iron.
						as Albuminoid Ammonia.															
	Date. 1896.	Hour.				Total.	Suspended.	Dissolved.	as Free Ammonia.	as Nitrites.	as Nitrates.		Total.	Suspended.	Dissolved.	Total.	Suspended.	Dissolved.			
807	Aug. 7	....	....	.32	9.7	.430	.298	.132	.044	.002	.6	5.0	536	415	121	443	353	90	54.0	0.0	20.20
808	" 7	....	....	.03	8 3	.520	.440	.080	.224	.007	.6	5.0	839	737	102	686	620	66	48.0	0.2	23.00

A Comparison of the Efficiency, in the Purification of the Ohio River Water by Coagulation and Sedimentation, of Aluminum Hydrate Formed Electrolytically from Metallic Aluminum, and of Aluminum Hydrate Formed from the Decomposition of Sulphate of Alumina by Lime.

Preliminary experiments indicated that aluminum hydrate, formed from the decomposition of sulphate of alumina, was somewhat more effective in the purification of the river water than was the case with the same amount of aluminum hydrate when prepared electrolytically from metallic aluminum. The reason of this appeared to be that the particles of aluminum hydrate in the first instance were smaller and more numerous than in the case where this compound was formed electrolytically. This explanation of the observations seemed plausible by virtue of the fact that electrolytically formed aluminum hydrate, being present in larger particles at the beginning, could produce fewer centers of coagulation; and that, since the purification was brought about by coagulation and sedimentation, the finer particles of the precipitate formed from sulphate of alumina gave a better opportunity for the cumulative, enveloping and coagulating action of the aluminum hydrate.

Three sets of carefully prepared experiments were made to obtain accurate data upon this point, and to learn the correctness of the theory presented above. A description of each set of these experiments is next presented, followed by a summary of the practical results obtained therefrom and a record of the results of analyses.

Experiment No. 1.

On August 11 three separate portions of the same sample of river water were treated, respectively, with 0.88 grain of aluminum hydrate prepared in the following manner:

In the first portion this amount of aluminum hydrate was prepared electrolytically in the water from metallic aluminum.

In the second portion the given amount of aluminum hydrate was obtained by adding a calculated quantity of sulphate of alumina, which was decomposed in the water by the lime and magnesia present there.

In the third portion there was added the stated amount of aluminum hydrate in the form of a gelatinous mass, prepared from suitable chemicals in the laboratory.

This amount of aluminum hydrate (1.08 grains per gallon) corresponds to 0.31 grain of metallic aluminum per gallon of water.

The experiments were made with about 2 gallons of water.

At the conclusion of the treatment the water was well mixed and allowed to remain undisturbed for 24 hours. Samples of the clarified water were removed by means of a siphon and subjected to chemical and bacterial analyses with results which are presented beyond, together with those of the untreated water.

Experiment No. 2.

On August 14 the above experiment was duplicated with the river water of that day, with the exception that the amount of aluminum hydrate added in each case was 0.51 grain per gallon, equivalent to 0.18 grain of metallic aluminum per gallon of water.

Chemical and bacterial analyses were made of the river water after subsidence for 24 hours. Determinations were also made of the number of bacteria and amount of suspended matter in the clarified water after sedimentation for 5 and 20 hours, respectively.

Experiment No. 3.

On August 18 the above experiment was duplicated, for the most part, with the river water of that day. The amount of aluminum hydrate, and its equivalent of metallic aluminum, were 0.14 and 0.05 grain per gallon, respectively.

In this experiment an important modification in the manner of application of aluminum hydrate to the third portion of the water was made, with the view to demonstrating more positively the accuracy of the above stated theory in explanation of the varying results obtained. Instead of adding to the third portion the stated amount of aluminum hydrate in the form of a gelatinous mass, the following procedure was adopted:

The calculated amount of sulphate of alumina (the same as was added to the second portion) was added to 10 per cent of the prescribed volume of water. After standing 15 minutes, during which the sulphate of alumina was decomposed by the lime and magnesia into aluminum hydrate, the remaining quantity of untreated river water was added. In this manner the prescribed amount of aluminum hydrate was added in the form of larger initial particles, as it was mixed with the full quantity of water, than in the case of the second portion.

Samples of water were collected for analysis after the plan stated in the last experiment.

In the following tables are summarized the principal analytical results obtained from each portion of water treated in these three sets of experiments.

The first table contains the percentages of removal from the water, after 24 hours subsidence, of organic matter, as indicated by albuminoid ammonia and oxygen consumed, respectively; of the suspended matter, and of the bacteria.

The second table contains the results of the determination of the respective amounts of suspended matter in the several treated waters of experiments Nos. 2 and 3, after subsidence for different periods.

The third table contains the number of bacteria found in the several portions of treated water in experiments Nos. 2 and 3, after different periods of subsidence.

SUMMARY OF ANALYTICAL RESULTS FROM THE LAST THREE EXPERIMENTS, SHOWING THE PERCENTAGES OF REMOVAL OF ORGANIC MATTER, SUSPENDED MATTER, AND BACTERIA, AFTER 24 HOURS' SUBSIDENCE.

Percentage Removal of Albuminoid Ammonia.

Number of Experiment.	Portion of Water Treated.		
	First.	Second.	Third.
1	64	80	55
2	83	93	80
3	43	69	58

Percentage Removal of Oxygen Consumed.

Number of Experiment.	Portion of Water Treated.		
	First.	Second.	Third.
1	66	87	54
2	80	92	78
3	52	67	65

Percentage Removal of Suspended Matter of the River Water.

1	93	100	78
2	96	100	93
3	78	96	88

Percentage Removal of Bacteria.

1	37	86	37
2	74	94	57
3	39	88	73

SUMMARY OF ANALYTICAL RESULTS FROM EXPERIMENTS NOS. 2 AND 3, SHOWING THE AMOUNTS OF SUSPENDED MATTER IN THE WATER AFTER DIFFERENT PERIODS OF SUBSIDENCE.

Experiment No. 2.

Period of Subsidence. Hours.	Parts per Million of Suspended Solids.		
	First Portion.	Second Portion.	Third Portion.
0	1 397	1 397	1 397
5	136	5	199
20	60	4	99
24	52	0	99

Experiment No. 3.

Period of Subsidence. Hours.	Parts per Million, Suspended Solids.		
	First Portion.	Second Portion.	Third Portion.
0	243	243	243
6	104	33	83
20	56	13	33
24	54	10	33

SUMMARY OF ANALYTICAL RESULTS FROM EXPERIMENTS NOS. 2 AND 3, SHOWING THE NUMBERS OF BACTERIA IN THE WATER AFTER DIFFERENT PERIODS OF SUBSIDENCE.

Experiment No. 2.

Period of Subsidence. Hours.	Bacteria per Cubic Centimeter in River Water after Treatment.		
	First Portion.	Second Portion.	Third Portion.
0	17 600	17 600	17 600
5	20 700	900	17 400
20	5 900	600	7 700
24	4 500	1 200	8 100

Experiment No. 3.

0	25 600	25 600	25 600
6	18 200	10 800	18 900
20	16 700	3 500	7 000
24	15 600	3 200	7 000

On the next page are given the results of chemical analyses of the original river water and of the several portions of treated water in each experiment after subsidence for 24 hours. As already stated, samples of the treated water were removed from the bottles by means of a siphon, without disturbance of the solid matters which had settled to the bottom.

Attention is especially called to the fact that the electrolytically produced aluminum hydrate, as well as that prepared in the laboratory, did not decrease the alkalinity of the water. This means that no carbonic acid gas was set free, and that no lime passed into the form of sulphate, because the formation of this compound in these cases was independent of the lime in the water.

The samples of water for chemical analysis were numbered as follows:

Number of Experiment.	Original River Water.	Treated Water after 24 Hours' Subsidence.		
		First Portion.	Second Portion.	Third Portion.
1	809	810	811	812
2	813	814	815	816
3	818	819	820	821

THE EFFECT OF THE ACTION OF THE ELECTRO-MAGNETS UPON THE CONSTITUENTS OF THE OHIO RIVER WATER AND UPON THE RATE AT WHICH ALUMINUM HYDRATE IS FORMED FROM METALLIC ALUMINUM.

So far as could be learned from a series of experiments directed to this point the electro-magnets produced no appreciable effect in the purification of the Ohio River water, either directly or indirectly, by facilitating subsidence or increasing the rate of formation of aluminum hydrate.

RATE AT WHICH ALUMINUM HYDRATE IS FORMED ELECTROLYTICALLY FROM METALLIC ALUMINUM.

One of the most important points in connection with the treatment of water by electrical devices is information upon the cost of the production of aluminum hydrate. It was definitely known that the rate of forma-

RESULTS OF CHEMICAL ANALYSES OF SAMPLES DESCRIBED ABOVE.

(Parts per Million.)

Serial Number.	Collected.		Temperature. Degrees C.	Color.	Oxygen Consumed.	Nitrogen as Albuminoid Ammonia.			Nitrogen as Free Ammonia.	Nitrogen as Nitrites.	Nitrogen as Nitrates.	Chlorine.	Residue on Evaporation.			Fixed Residue after Ignition.			Alkalinity.	Dissolved Alumina.	Iron.
	Date. 1890.	Hour.				Total.	Sus-pended.	Dis-solved.					Total.	Suspended.	Dissolved.	Total.	Suspended.	Dissolved.			
809	Aug. 11	....	....	.30	9.8	.430	.292	.138	.032	.000	.7	5.3	520	389	131	455	375	80	75.4	0.0	14.40
810	" 11	....	....	.11	3.3	.156	.018	.130	.030	.003	.6	5.4	158	27	131	112	32	80	75.0	0.0	2.60
811	" 11	....	....	.09	1.3	.084	.000	.084	.022	.000	.6	5.3	163	0	163	118	0	118	21.5	0.0	0.07
812	" 11	....	....	.23	4.5	.194	.056	.138	.020	.000	.6	5.3	219	88	131	169	89	80	75.4	0.0	6.50
813	" 14	....	..	.18	19.7	1.040	.932	.108	.046	.004	.7	6.1	1 524	1 358	136	1 418	1 324	94	74.0	0.0	46.00
814	" 14	....	....	...	3.9	.168	.060	.108	.016	.002	.7	5.5	188	52	136	150	56	94	73.0	0.0	6.00
815	" 14	....	....	.08	1.6	.074	.000	.074	.022	.002	.6	6.1	160	0	160	119	0	119	46.2	0.0	0.07
816	" 14	....	....	...	4.4	.200	.092	.108	.020	.000	.6	6.1	235	99	136	193	99	94	74.0	0.0	5.00
818	" 18	....	....	.18	6.6	.260	.156	.104	.026	.000	.7	5.9	380	241	139	331	241	90	74.0	0.0	12.00
819	" 18	....	....	.18	3.2	.142	.038	.104	.010	.002	.6	5.7	193	54	139	154	64	90	72.0	0.0	4.00
820	" 18	....	....	.16	2.2	.080	.000	.080	.010	.002	.6	5.7	141	10	131	106	11	95	66.0	0.0	0.80
821	" 18	....	....	.16	2.3	.110	.024	.086	.010	.001	.6	5.9	161	30	131	116	21	95	66.0	0.0	1.48

tion of this compound would be proportional to the strength (amperage) of the current, provided no irregularities occurred. But adequate data were lacking, both with regard to the rate of formation and to the likelihood of irregularities such as would affect the cost and efficiency of the treatment.

In the course of 54 experiments, which were made during the first three weeks in August, attention was directed to this point so far as was practicable. The experiments were made in glass jars of one gallon capacity and in the porcelain-lined tanks described in the last chapter. Early in the work it was learned that the quality of the water apparently exerted little or no influence upon the rate of formation of aluminum hydrate, or the influence of other factors disguised its effect. In a majority of cases river water, from which the suspended matters had been removed by filtration, was employed. The amount of aluminum hydrate, which was formed under certain recorded conditions, was determined both by weighing the amount of hydrate formed and by noting the decrease in the weight of the metallic aluminum electrodes.

Several important observations were made as to the manner in which the aluminum hydrate was formed. When both electrodes were of metallic aluminum the electric current caused the hydrate to appear at both poles, but for the most part at the positive pole. A considerable quantity of gas was liberated at the negative pole. Gas was also set free at the positive pole, but less uniformly and only about 20 per cent. of the volume of that which came from the negative pole. Analyses of the gas from the negative pole showed it to be practically all hydrogen. If there were any oxygen (in excess of that coming from the atmosphere), ozone, or hydrogen peroxide present in the water or gas, the quantities were so small that they escaped detection. Upon shutting off the electric current and allowing the electrodes to remain in the treated water it was repeatedly noted that aluminum hydrate continued to appear for 20 seconds or more after the current ceased. This observation in connection with other information indicated that the electric current does not form the hydrate directly from the metallic aluminum, but it prepared the water by partial decomposition so that certain constituents of the water were able to produce the aluminum hydrate.

When an electric current had passed through the aluminum electrodes for several hours it was found that the positive poles became coated with aluminum oxide (aluminum rust), and that from time to time this coating fell off in the form of scales of a considerable size and number. At the negative poles there appeared a fine black coating, which was found to be composed of minute particles of aluminum in a (spongy) metallic state. From an economical and practical point of view these observations have considerable significance, as will be shown in following sections.

In the next table are recorded all the results of determinations of the rate of formation of aluminum hydrate, electrolytically. These results are expressed in the number of grains and grams of aluminum decomposed from the metal electrodes in one hour for each ampere of electric current, according to the conventional method. The weights of aluminum hydrate which these amounts of metal would form may be obtained by multiplying the respective figures by 2.85. The results were obtained from small electrodes (of bright metal at the beginning of each experiment) during short periods, as a rule, in order that the maximum results, free from abnormal irregularities, might be obtained. The irregularities have already been referred to and will be mentioned again beyond. To make a comprehensive study of them on a small scale was impossible. It will be noted that a variety of combinations of electrodes were tried. The experiments whose numbers do not appear in this table are referred to the foregoing portion of this chapter. The tabulations are self-explanatory, except that it is to be stated that chemical symbols are used as abbreviations of the substances used as electrodes. Thus, Al means aluminum; C, carbon; and Pt, platinum.

SUMMARY OF RESULTS SHOWING THE RATE OF ELECTROLYTIC DECOMPOSITION OF METALLIC ALUMINUM.

Number of Experiment.	Duration of Experiment. Hours and Minutes.	Area of Aluminum Electrodes, Square Inches.	Connection of Electrodes.		Current on Magnets.		Current on Electrodes.						Total Current in Ampere Hours.	Rate of Decomposition of Metallic Aluminum Per Ampere-Hour.	
							Amperes.			Volts.					
			Positive.	Negative.	Amperes.	Volts.	Maximum.	Minimum.	Average.	Maximum.	Minimum.	Average.		Grains.	Grams.
1	oh. 10m.	300	Al.	Al.	0	0	1.2	0.9	1.00	134	131	133	0.17	12.3	0.80
2	oh. 10m.	300	"	"	0	0	3.4	0.8	1.23	228	223	224	0.20	6.0	0.39
3	oh. 05m.	300	"	"	0	0	9.0	4.1	5.65	95	72	84	0.47	14.2	0.92
6	oh. 05m.	300	"	"	0	0	10.0	2.0	5.20	101	83	91	0.43	9.2	0.60
6a	oh. 05m.	300	"	"	0	0	8.0	6.0	6.79	93	83	88	0.57	8.0	0.52
7	oh. 05m.	300	"	"	0	0	8.1	5.6	6.55	98	81	90	0.55	8.9	0.58
7a	oh. 05m.	300	"	"	0	0	8.3	6.0	6.86	93	80	87	0.57	9.0	0.58
15	oh. 10m.	200	"	"	0	0	7.2	4.1	5.08	113	98	107	0.85	7.2	0.47
16	oh. 19m.	200	"	"	0	0	6.2	3.9	4.76	111	98	105	0.79	9.0	0.59
17	oh. 10m.	200	"	"	0	0	5.6	5.0	5.10	108	105	106	0.85	9.2	0.60
22	oh. 10m.	200	"	"	0	0	5.7	4.1	4.75	112	102	107	0.79	9.2	0.60
37	oh. 05m.	200	"	"	0	0	6.5	5.1	5.73	107	103	105	0.48	8.3	0.54
39	1h. 00m.	200	"	"	0	0	8.3	3.8	5.20	113	95	105	5.20	8.7	0.57
41	1h. 00m.	200	"	"	0	0	8.1	3.8	5.27	111	85	103	5.30	6.2	0.41
42	4h. 30m.	200	"	Pt.	0	0	4.3	1.7	2.33	131	114	125	10.50	7.6	0.49
48	oh. 05m.	100	Pt.*	Al.	0	0	9.8	8.7	9.44	231	230	231	0.79	3.9	0.25
49	oh. 03m.	100	Al.	Pt.	0	0	10.5	8.4	9.42	210	207	209	0.47	5.2	0.34
50	oh. 10m.	100	"	C.	0	0	3.9	3.6	3.83	213	212	212	0.64	6.7	0.44
51	oh. 05m.	100	C.*	Al.	0	0	6.4	5.0	6.02	215	213	214	0.50	4.2	0.37
52	3h. 00m.	200	Al.	"	7.2	222	8.3	3.5	5.30	112	85	92	15.90	8.0	0.52
53	2h. 00m.	200	"	Iron†	7.2	222	2.3	2.1	2.18	215	189	200	4.36	8.6	0.56

* The formation of aluminum hydrate in those cases where metallic aluminum formed the negative pole only (the positive pole being carbon or platinum), is not understood and seems to be at variance with the present views of electrochemistry. Similar results, but with much lower rates, were obtained subsequently; and, so far as our knowledge goes, the above results are correct.

† In the last experiment the negative wire was attached to the iron pipe which served as an outlet from the tank in which the experiment was made. This pipe led to the sewer.

In the consideration of the results in the foregoing table it is to be borne in mind that the amounts of metal decomposed include the oxide as well as the hydrate of aluminum; as the oxide came off irregularly in films or scales, it is probable that the highest results are associated with this factor. Concerning the low results, the utilization of electric current in the formation of oxygen at the positive pole appears to be the explanation of them.

Taking the average of all these experiments, it is found that rate of decomposition of aluminum was equal to 8.16 grains or 0.53 gram per ampere-hour. The entire current used in this set of experiments was 50.42 ampere-hours, and the total amount of metal decomposed was 395.3 grains or 25.67 grams. Computing the rate of decomposition on this basis, the rate of 7.84 grains or 0.509 gram per ampere-hour is obtained. This is practically an exact agreement with the results of

Watt ("Electro-Deposition of Metals," page 548), who states that the rate of decomposition of aluminum is 7.92 grains or 0.514 gram per ampere-hour.

This subject is taken up more at length in Chapter XV, Section No. 4, where an explanation of the difference between the above rate of decomposition and that indicated by the electro-chemical equivalent of aluminum is offered.

Regularity during Continuous Service of the Rate at which Aluminum Hydrate is Formed Electrolytically from Metallic Aluminum.

When the metallic aluminum electrodes were bright and clean the rate of formation of aluminum hydrate per ampere-hour, with other conditions equal, seemed to be fairly uniform. After a time, however, the positive pole became coated with oxide of aluminum, and the rate of formation of the hydrate decreased. In time this coating of oxide became so thick that it fell off, and the rate temporarily increased.

On a large scale of operation this would doubtless be an important matter for consideration. From the available evidence, with runs of not more than five hours, variations of 20 per cent. in the formation of aluminum hydrate per ampere-hour were noticed, when the conditions other than the coating on the electrodes were apparently parallel.

Amount of Metallic Aluminum which is Wasted in the Electrolytic Production of Aluminum Hydrate.

Upon passing electricity through aluminum electrodes this metal passes into three different forms:

1. Aluminum hydrate which appears at both poles, but for the most part at the positive pole. It is this form which serves in the purification of water as has been described and discussed.

2. Some of the metal passes into the solution and is deposited at the negative pole. This is probably deposited in a spongy metallic state somewhat similar to that noted under some conditions with other metals in electroplating. The amount of the metal which passes into this state is very small as far as could be learned.

3. After the positive pole has been in service for some time it becomes coated with a layer of aluminum oxide, which, as stated above, gradually becomes thicker until it scales and falls off. The aluminum oxide serves no purpose in water purification and is a waste product which would be expensive in a large plant.

The results of the experiments show that the amount of metallic aluminum which was wasted by passage into the oxide state ranged from 25 to 40 per cent. of that which was converted into the form of aluminum hydrate. It may also be added that this was borne out by the experiences with the devices operated in July. In two instances during the last week in July where the periods of observed operation were 5 and 20 hours, the percentages of metallic aluminum which were wasted were estimated to be 51 and 53, respectively.

A Comparison of the Cost of Aluminum Hydrate Formed by the Application of Sulphate of Alumina to Water, and by the Action of Electricity on Metallic Alumina, Respectively.

It has already been stated that of the two methods of production of aluminum hydrate the electrolytic one furnished a product which was less efficient in the coagulation and sedimentation of the Ohio River water, and which was associated with a wastage of 25 to 40 per cent. of the metallic aluminum from which it was prepared. Aside from the question of cost of power to produce aluminum hydrate electrolytically, which is referred to in the next section, there is a marked difference in the cost of the commercial product used in the two methods of preparation of aluminum hydrate.

Current quotations (Aug., 1896) give the cost of metallic aluminum and sulphate of alumina as 56 and 1.5 cents per pound, respectively. To produce 100 pounds of aluminum hydrate by the two methods it would require 35 pounds of metallic aluminum and 420 pounds of sulphate of alumina of average composition, respectively. The cost of these two commercial products, on the above basis, would be $19.60 and $6.30, respectively. The facts show conclusively that electrolytically prepared aluminum hydrate is more than three times as expensive as that prepared from sulphate of alumina, independent of the wastage of metallic aluminum and the cost for electric power.

Observations on the Amount of Power which would be Required to Produce Aluminum Hydrate on a Large Scale by Means of Electricity.

In the purification of the Ohio River water by the aid of aluminum hydrate prepared by the two methods under consideration, the first point of practical importance which suggests itself is this one: The electric method would require boilers, engines, and a generating plant large enough to supply the needful amount of aluminum hydrate when the water is muddiest, while in the other method such a condition of the water would require in addition to the normal appliances simply a stronger solution of sulphate of alumina and a more rapid addition of the chemical solution.

To estimate the amount of electric power necessary for the formation of aluminum hydrate from metallic aluminum in the purification of the Ohio River water, the necessary quantity (amperage) and electric-motive force (potential) of the current must be known. The formation of hydrate is proportional to the amount (amperage) of current and data on this point are presented in the foregoing tables.

With regard to the voltage (corresponding to pressure in hydraulics) necessary in a plant on a large scale, this cannot be stated from the evidence available at this time. It would doubtless be much less than 210, however, which was the voltage supplied to the devices operated by the Harris Company.

As a matter of convenience and record, it may be stated that to treat one million gallons of water in 24 hours with electrolytically prepared aluminum hydrate equivalent to one grain per gallon of sulphate of alumina, the number of horse-power of electricity actually used, according to these tests, would be about one-half the potential of the current.

Conclusions.

From these investigations made in August upon the purification of the Ohio River water by electricity the following conclusions may be drawn:

1. The direct application of electricity and electro-magnets, as used in these devices, produced no substantial purification of the Ohio River water.

2. The electrolytic formation of aluminum hydrate in the Ohio River water enabled substantial purification to be effected, provided sedimentation and filtration were subsequently employed, as was similarly done by the other systems investigated in these tests and which used aluminum hydrate obtained from the application of sulphate of alumina.

3. The use of electrolytically prepared aluminum hydrate has the advantage of the application of sulphate of alumina in the following points, as was indicated to be the case by the operation of the devices of the Harris Company in July, as stated at the close of Chapter XI.

A. No lime in the river water is required for the successful application of the process.

B. There is no opportunity of getting dissolved chemicals into the filtered water.

C. There is liberated no carbonic acid gas, which in time might injure boilers and distributing pipes.

D. There is dissolved in the filtered water no additional sulphate of lime, which at times might give annoyance and trouble when the water is used in boilers.

4. For the purification of the Ohio River water on a large scale the electric method, as compared with the method in which sulphate of alumina is used, is not a commercial success because of its excessive cost.

During 1897 some further investigations under different conditions, in connection with the use of metallic aluminum electrolytically decomposed for the coagulation of the Ohio River water, were made by the Water Company. The results of these investigations are recorded in Chapter XV, but it may be noted here that the conclusions given in this chapter were confirmed.

CHAPTER XIII.

Description of the Mark and Brownell Electrolytical Devices,* and a Record of the Results Accomplished Therewith.

After devoting the early part of December, 1896, largely to investigations on the increased corroding and incrusting power of water which had been treated with sulphate of alumina, attention was again directed to methods of preparing coagulants by electrolytic means, whereby the use of commercial sulphates might be avoided.

Several Louisville gentlemen called the attention of the Water Company at this time to some electrolytical experiments upon water purification, which had been in progress for several weeks. At their request, the directors and officers of the Water Company, on Dec. 21, 1896, inspected the operation of two small experimental devices along this line, which were operated by Profs. Palmer and Brownell in their laboratory at the Louisville Manual Training High School. Among the other gentlemen interested in these experiments was Prof. Mark, who, with Prof. Brownell, had been retained in consultation upon electrical matters by the Harris Company in July, 1896; and in this way they were introduced to the electrical and electrolytical treatment of the Ohio River water.

The object of these devices, and of their operation, was to indicate the relative merits of the application of electricity to electrodes composed of metallic iron and metallic aluminum, respectively, in the preliminary treatment of the Ohio River water, in order to secure coagulation in a system of purification, of which filtration through sand is the last step.

A general idea of these two devices, which were intended to be duplicates, with the exception of the metal used for the electrodes, may be obtained from the following outline:

Tap water (which was equivalent to Ohio River water from which a portion of the suspended matter had been removed by passage through the Crescent Hill Reservoir and some of the distributing pipes) was led through a meter to two glass cylinders, each about 4 inches in diameter, and 1.5 to 2.0 feet in height. On the top of each cylinder there was fastened a suitable cover, in which were perforations for the glass inlet and outlet pipes, respectively. The glass cylinders of the two devices contained, respectively, metallic iron and metallic aluminum electrodes, which were fairly similar in shape and size. In each case the electrodes were made of sheets fastened together, about 0.5 inch apart, with suitable insulating materials. The electric current was supplied by a dynamo generator. The water was admitted to the cylinders at the top, and was drawn off at the bottom. A second perforation in each of the covers contained a glass tube, to which a rubber tube was attached. Each rubber tube was controlled by a clamp, so that from time to time the gas, which accumulated at the top of the cylinders, could be removed. From the glass cylinders of the two devices, the water passed to the respective filters. Each filter was made by putting a layer of fine sand in a metal cylinder, about 6 inches in diameter, and 2 to 3 feet high. It was said that each filter contained about 1 foot of fine sand, beneath which were several inches of coarse sand, and a metal strainer, which was placed above the outlet at the bottom of the cylinders. All the water from the electrolytic cells (glass cylinders) passed on to the filters, but in each case a considerable portion of the treated water overflowed, owing to the relatively small size of the filters.

* Including the "Palmer and Brownell Water Purifier," as explained beyond.

The experiments were begun before the arrival of the party from the Water Company. The writer understood that the electrodes had been weighed, and that, in the case of the iron device, 65 cubic feet of water had been treated after weighing, but before our arrival. It was said that the operation of the aluminum device, which was in service when we arrived, began about 1.30 P.M. This device was operated until about 4.10 P.M. Before this time chemical and bacterial samples for analyses were collected of the tap water before treatment, of the electrolytically treated water as it overflowed from the top of the filter, and of the effluent as it passed from the outlet at the bottom of the filter. The time required to collect a gallon of this effluent was 30 minutes. It was said that the quantity of water passed through this electrolytic cell from 1.30 P.M. to 4.10 P.M., was 30 cubic feet. The electric current varied a little while we were present, but the amperage and voltage averaged 3.6 and 32, respectively.

From 4.20 P.M. to 4.50 P.M., about 7 cubic feet of water were passed through the iron device. The amperage and voltage averaged 5.4 and 27, respectively. Samples of water for analysis, corresponding to those taken from the aluminum device, were collected, with the exception of the tap water. The flow of water through the filter of this device was much faster than it was in the case of the other filter. This filter was said to be less satisfactory in its construction than the other one, but it was apparently much less clogged at the surface. It required 7 minutes to fill a gallon bottle with this effluent.

In the case of each electrolytic cell, the formation of gas was only slightly in excess of the amount which was absorbed by the flowing stream of water, and only a very small quantity accumulated at the top of the cell.

The samples were taken to the laboratory of the Water Company and analyzed. The results of the bacterial analyses are given in the following table, in which reference by serial numbers is made to the results of the chemical analyses, as stated in the second table.

RESULTS OF BACTERIAL ANALYSES.

Source of Sample	Number of Chemical Sample.*	Number of Bacterial Sample.	Bacteria per Cubic Centimeter.
Tap water............	826	4968	7 800
Electrolytically (aluminum) treated water, before filtration.....	827	4969	6 500
The same, but after filtration............	828	4970	216
Electrolytically (iron) treated water, before filtration............	829	4971	6 300
The same, but after filtration............	830	4972	2 950

* See the following table.

RESULTS OF CHEMICAL ANALYSES.

(Parts per Million.)

Serial Number.	Collected. Date. 1896.	Collected. Corresponding Bacterial Numbers.	Temperature. Degrees C.	Degree of Clearness.	Color.	Oxygen Consumed.	Nitrogen as Albuminoid Ammonia. Total.	Nitrogen as Albuminoid Ammonia. Suspended.	Nitrogen as Albuminoid Ammonia. Dissolved.	Nitrogen as Free Ammonia.	Nitrogen as Nitrites.	Nitrogen as Nitrates.	Chlorine.	Residue on Evaporation. Total.	Residue on Evaporation. Suspended.	Residue on Evaporation. Dissolved.	Fixed Residue after Ignition. Total.	Fixed Residue after Ignition. Suspended.	Fixed Residue after Ignition. Dissolved.	Alkalinity.	Dissolved Alumina.	Iron.
826	Dec. 21	4968	....	...	...	6.8	.346	.234	.112	.072	.009	0.9	4.9	266	117	149	215	104	111	73.5	0	28 0
827	" 21	4969	....	...	...	4.6	.200	.088	.112	.054	.030	0.8	4.9	241	92	149	204	93	111	71.0	0	17.0
828	" 21	4970	....	1	...	2.5	.104	.000	.104	.080	.014	0.8	4.9	137	0	137	103	0	103	70.3	0	0.1
829	" 21	4971	....	...	...	4.1	.162	.050	.112	.052	.011	0.7	4.9	219	70	149	178	67	111	70.0	0	48.0
830	" 21	4972	....	2	...	2.6	.112	.000	.112	.076	.016	0.8	4.9	145	0	145	110	0	110	69.3	0	0.9

The above data indicate that the amounts of electric power used in the iron cell and the aluminum cell were at the rate of 197 and 75 E.H.P. per million gallons per 24 hours, respectively. From the loss in weight of the iron and aluminum electrodes, it was stated that the consumption of these two metals was at the rate of 86 and 60.7 pounds per million gallons, respectively.

It is estimated from the above data, that the amount of electric current applied to the water in its passage through the aluminum and iron devices, was equal to 0.042 and 0.070 ampere-hour per gallon, respectively.

The analytical results show that with the aluminum device, the water was well purified, but in the case of the iron device, due in part, apparently, to the construction of the filter, the effluent contained some iron, and a high number of bacteria. The greater part, if not all, of this iron apparently came from the silt in the tap water, and not from the electrodes.

Taking the results of these experiments in general terms, it may be stated that they were on too small a scale, and of too short duration, to convey any practical specific information on the purification of the Ohio River water, other than that iron, a comparatively cheap metal, may be electrolytically decomposed in a manner similar to aluminum with the formation of a gelatinous hydrate, capable of coagulating the mud, silt, and clay in water.

Plans for Testing the Treatment of the Ohio River Water Electrolytically with the Use of Iron Electrodes.

Arrangements were completed on Jan. 1, 1897, whereby the Water Company should test the practicability of an experimental system of water purification, the electrical appliances of which were to be designed by, and constructed under the supervision of, Profs. Mark and Brownell. This experimental system included a set of appliances which would enable 250,000 gallons of river water to be treated electrolytically with iron electrodes, in order to secure coagulation, preparatory to filtration. As a matter of convenience, it was arranged with the O. H. Jewell Filter Company to make use of their test filter, which at that time was the only one remaining at the pumping station.

Comparing this process with those systems of purification which were tested during the preceding year, it will be noted that with the exception of the magneto-electric system, the general principles of the methods of procedure were substantially the same, in that they consisted of the following:

1. Treatment of the river water with a coagulating chemical.

2. Partial clarification of, and removal of suspended matter from, the treated water by subsidence in a settling chamber.

3. Rapid filtration of the coagulated and partially subsided water through a sand layer.

The most marked feature of difference in the Mark and Brownell devices, from the original Jewell System, was the kind and method of formation of the coagulating chemical. The electricity by itself does practically nothing in the purification of the river water. Its action is almost wholly, if not completely, an indirect one, in preparing a coagulating chemical. This was clearly demonstrated in the devices operated in July, 1896, by the Harris Company, and investigated further by the Water Company in August, 1896, as stated in the two preceding chapters. The preparation of hydrate of aluminum by the electrolytic decomposition of metallic aluminum, was found to possess an advantage as a coagulant when compared with hydrate of alumina prepared from the decomposition of sulphate of alumina by the lime which is naturally present in the river water, in that there are added to the purified water no chemical properties to corrode iron vessels, or to incrust steam boilers. Hydrate of iron possesses gelatinous and coagulating properties somewhat similar to those of the hydrate of alumina. Metallic iron is much cheaper than metallic aluminum, and the indications were that similar advantages in the coagulation of the Ohio River water might be obtained electrolytically in this manner, at a reduced cost. To ascertain the efficiency of this process, and to obtain data indicating the cost of installation and of operation of such a system for the purification of the water supply of this city, was the object in testing the devices of Profs. Mark and Brownell. Arrangements were made whereby Profs. Mark and Brownell were engaged by the Water Company to design and superintend the construction of the necessary electrical devices. These devices in connection with the Jewell filter, were to be operated and tested by the Water Company under the direction of the Chief Chemist and Bacteriologist, but Profs. Mark and Brownell were to inspect daily the devices designed by them, and make such recommendations as seemed advisable.

The time from Jan. 1 to Feb. 12 was occupied in constructing electrodes, electrolytic cells, and a dynamo generator, especially adapted to this class of work; in making suitable piping and electrical connections; and in installing an engine to operate the generator. During this period, considerable attention was given to the practical significance of several features of the process, so far as the available appliances permitted. These special investigations made by the Water Company during this unavoidable delay in the regular work, are recorded in Chapter XV.

Construction of the Mark and Brownell Devices.

The devices consisted of an engine, dynamo generator, two electrolytic cells and two sets of electrodes, in addition to the necessary piping, cables and wiring, to give them the required water, steam and electrical connections. The electrolytic cells were in duplicate in order to test two forms of electrodes. One set was made of wrought-iron plates, designed by Prof. Brownell, and the other designed by Prof. Mark, was made of cast-iron pipes placed within each other. Each cell with its set of electrodes was tested separately, in connection with the Jewell filter.

It may be added here that these electrolytic cells, and the electrodes which were made according to the plans of Prof. Brownell, were found, after the work had been begun, to represent "The Palmer and Brownell Water Purifier—Patent applied for." So far as is known, an application for a patent for the devices designed by Prof. Mark was not made. The tests of the Water Company at this time, therefore, included, but extended beyond, that of the "Palmer and Brownell Water Purifier," which was mentioned in the introduction to this report. For this reason the more comprehensive expression of "Mark and Brownell Devices". is used as the title of this chapter.

The principal details of the construction of these devices were as follows:

Engine.—The engine was a new, horizontal, fly-wheel machine of the Atlas make. Its principal dimensions were as follows: Diameter of steam cylinder, 11 inches; length of stroke, 14 inches; diameter of fly wheel, 4 feet; and diameter of driving wheel, 4 feet. The speed was regulated by a fly-wheel centrifugal governor. It was connected to the dynamo generator by a 10-inch leather belt.

Dynamo-generator.—The dynamo-generator, driven by the Atlas engine, was made by James Clark, Jr., & Co., of Louisville. It was a direct, four-pole, compound machine, rated at 50 volts and 400 amperes at a speed of 800 revolutions per minute. The current was regulated with the aid of a field rheostat, and could be controlled at practically any desired amperage within the range of the machine.

Electrolytic Cells.—The two duplicate cells were made of wrought-iron plates, 0.25 inch thick. The main body of the cells was cylindrical in form, 2.5 feet in diameter, and 6.0 feet high. At the top, the cells were capped by a dome-shaped cover, and the bottom of each was in the shape of a cone. The shell was riveted together with 0.5-inch rivets. A flange was riveted to the upper edge of the plate, to form a connection with the cover, which was bolted to it. The cover was a dome-shaped iron casting, 1.0 inch thick, 30 inches in diameter, and 12 inches high on the inside. On the bottom of the cover was a suitable flange, to allow the cover to be bolted to the shell. In the center of the cover at the top, there was a shoulder suitably tapped for connection with the inlet water pipe. A 0.5-inch pipe with a valve was tapped into the cover, to enable the operator to blow off the gas which accumulated at that point when the device was in operation. A sight gauge was connected to the cover, also, to allow the quantity of accumulated gas to be noted. The conical bottom of the cell was of wrought iron, 27 inches in diameter and 12 inches deep on the inside. The upper portion of the cone was capped with a short cylindrical shoulder, by which the conical bottom was riveted to the main shell. At the apex of the cone (the bottom of the cell) there was a flange for connection with the 3-inch blow-off pipe. The 4-inch outlet pipe was connected with the shell by means of a flange joint at a point 6 inches above the bottom of the cylindrical portion of the cell, and extended into the cell about 8 inches. The inner surface of the cell containing the Brownell electrodes was covered with a heavy coat of asphaltum paint. The inner surface of the other cell acted as part of the negative electrode, and was not insulated.

Brownell Electrodes.—In one of the electrolytic cells the manifold of wrought-iron plates, designed by Prof. Brownell, was placed. The other cell contained the Mark electrodes, which are described in the following section:

The Brownell electrodes were made of 28 wrought-iron plates, each 0.25 inch thick, and 50.375 inches long. The manifold was arranged in two sections of 9 plates each, and one section of 10 plates. Of these sections, the middle one was made of 10 plates of practically the same width, 24 inches. But the width of the plates in each of the two outer sections ranged from 22 to 10 inches, in order to keep the distance between the inner periphery of the cell and the edge of the plates approximately uniform. The plates of each section were fastened together by six 0.75-inch bolts, which were covered with hard rubber tubes to secure insulation. On these hard rubber tubes were placed hard rubber washers, 0.5 inch thick, to serve as insulating distance pieces in keeping the plates separated from each other. All three sections of the manifold were supported on a frame of oak, made of four 2- by 4-inch pieces. This frame itself rested on an angle iron at the bottom of the cell, and had suitable appliances attached to it to aid in lifting the electrodes out of the cell. The space between the sections of the manifold was 2 inches.

The total area of one side of these plates was 27,400 square inches, and the cross-section of the electrolyte (the water between the plates) was 22,400 square inches.

On Feb. 26, 1897, an annular wooden frame was put into the cell just above the top of the electrodes, to fill the space between the electrodes and the wall of the cell, and the supporting frame at the bottom was also filled in to close the corresponding space there.

Mark Electrodes.—These consisted of ten pieces of cast-iron water-pipes, and of the wall of the electrolytic cell in which they were placed. They were 42 inches long, and 1, 3, 6, 9, 12, 15, 18, 21, 24, and 27 inches in diameter, respectively. At the bottom of the cell was a frame of 2- by 4-inch oak pieces, resting on an angle iron, and the electrodes were placed on this frame. The electrodes were not fastened together, but were separated from each other by insulating distance pieces of vulcanized fiber. The distance between the several pieces of pipe ranged from 0.5 to 1.5 inches, and averaged about 0.93 inch.

With regard to the thickness of the electrodes, there was also considerable variation, but the average thickness was about 0.5 inch.

The total superficial area of one side of these pipes was 20,200 square inches, and the cross-section of the electrolyte was 17,900 square inches.

Electrical Connections.—From the generator, the current was led to a switch-board, where an automatic circuit breaker and a suitable ammeter and voltmeter for measuring the current and potential were provided. The potential of the dynamo was regulated by means of a rheostat on the shunt of the magnet circuit. Cables conveyed the current to the two cells. At no time were both cells used at the same time, so the one set of main connections served for the two. In the case of each cell there were two openings near the top. There were placed in these openings wooden plugs, through which iron bars with binding posts at each end were driven. These bars formed part of the electrical circuit, and the wooden plugs were relied upon for insulating them from the cell. To the outer binding posts the cables connecting with the switch-board were attached, and to the inner binding posts were fastened the cables connecting the anodes (positive plates) and cathodes (negative plates), respectively.

In the case of the Brownell electrodes, the plates were connected with the cable by means of a brass lug bolted to each plate. The corners of the alternate plates on each upper side were cut off, to give ample space, and the two cables were passed through and soldered into the holes in the brass lugs, which were bolted on to the uncut corners of the plates. In this way every other plate was made positive or negative, as the case might be. To arrest electrolytic action on the brass lugs and the copper cable, they were coated with insulating paint.

In the case of the Mark electrodes, the two cables attached to the inner binding posts of the cell, were connected with alternate pipes by means of brass lugs, in a manner quite similar to that used on the Brownell electrodes. The outer wall of the cell was one of the plates forming the cathode (negative pole).

Piping.—Each of these electrolytic cells was provided with 4-inch piping and fittings, so that the river water entered the cells at the top, and left them at the side near the bottom, and passed to the settling basin below the Jewell filter, which was operated as usual, except that the application of sulphate of alumina was omitted. At the conical bottom of these cells, there was a 3-inch blow-off pipe leading to the sewer.

All of these pipes were provided with valves and meters wherever necessary, and the only remaining points worthy of mention are the devices at the inlets of the cells, to facilitate the distribution of the river water between the electrodes. In the cell containing the Brownell electrodes, there was attached to the inlet pipe a cast-iron dome, 24 inches in diameter, and 8 inches high. It was screwed on to a nipple which was connected to a flange on the cover of the cell. The plate which formed the base of the dome was slotted to correspond with the water spaces between the electrodes, and in setting the electrodes in place, care was taken to have the water spaces and the slots in the dome come opposite each other. The base of the dome was 3.5 inches above the top of the electrodes. A similar dome was attached to the inlet pipe in the cover to the other cell, containing the Mark electrodes. In this case, however, the base of the dome, which was 12 inches above the top of the electrodes, was perforated with forty 0.5-inch holes, arranged uniformly over the plate.

Operation of the Mark and Brownell Devices—Brownell Electrodes.

These devices and appurtenances were assembled together ready for operation on Feb. 12, 1897. On the afternoon of Feb. 13, and the whole day of Feb. 15, the devices were in preliminary operation, and the Jewell filter was washed five times with filtered water to put it in normal condition, following a long period of rest. Official operation began on Feb. 16. The rate of electrolytic treatment, and of filtration, was to be 250,000 gallons per 24 hours, or 23.2 cubic feet per minute. A brief general account of the operations will now be given, followed by a summary of the principal data, including the results of analyses of the river water before and after treatment.

The river water was fairly muddy at this time; while the filtered water was not of satisfactory appearance or quality, and showed marked signs of insufficient coagulation to secure satisfactory results under these conditions. The average voltage and amperage on Feb. 16, were 37 and 450, respectively; and on Feb. 17, these figures were 32 and 395. On the evening of Feb. 17, it was necessary to stop operations, in order to make some repairs and modifications on the dynamo generator. The dynamo generator was not ready for operation again until Feb. 22, and the tests were suspended during the intervening time.

Mud, iron hydrate formed from the electrolytic decomposition of the electrodes, and a limited amount of other suspended matter, such as silt, clay, and bacteria, accumulated in the conical bottom of the cell beneath the outlet pipe during operation, and, at Prof. Brownell's request, about 2 cubic feet of this liquid and solid material were blown off into the sewer once an hour. The accumulation of gas at the top of the cell was also blown off hourly, to prevent the electrodes from becoming uncovered and consequently out of active service.

Operations were resumed on Feb. 22, at 12.38 P.M., following the repairs of the dynamo. The filter was washed, and the water and mud removed from the settling chamber of the Jewell System. The rate of treatment and of filtration was 23.2 cubic feet per minute, as provided for in the plans and designs. But the filtered water was very turbid and unsatisfactory in appearance, and at 1.55 P.M., operations were stopped, and the filter washed again. The devices were then started at the rate of 15 cubic feet per minute. As the filtered water did not improve materially in appearance, the rate was reduced to about 12 cubic feet at 4.00 P.M., and at 5.00 P.M. it was further reduced to about 10 cubic feet per minute. During the afternoon, the current was approximately constant, and the voltage and amperage averaged 27 and 402, respectively. At no time was the filtered water free from a distinct muddy appearance, although the removal of coarse suspended particles caused it to look much better than the untreated river water.

On the morning of Feb. 23, the devices were operated for a short period at the rate of 13 cubic feet per minute, but the electrolytic treatment, under the existing conditions, was insufficient to give satisfactory results. The river water, however, was exceedingly muddy at this time, which was the early portion of a period of a very heavy flood in the Ohio River. During the balance of this day, and during the following day, Feb. 24, the devices were operated at the rate of 4.9 and 9.8 cubic feet per minute, respectively. On both days the quantity of electric current was as great as the appliances would allow (400 amperes), but the filtered water was decidedly muddy.

As it was clearly evident that these devices were unable to purify the Ohio River water when it was in the existing condition, and further tests without modifications would be a waste of time and money, the writer reported the condition of affairs to President Long, and requested instructions in the premises, as follows:

(Copy.)

Feb. 25, 1897.

Mr. Chas. R. Long, President Louisville Water Company, Louisville, Kentucky.

Dear Sir: Since Monday noon of this week, we have operated daily the electrical devices designed by Profs. Mark and Brownell, with the view to purifying the present, very muddy, water of the Ohio River, at rates ranging from 23.2 (contract) to 5 cubic feet per minute. At no time have we obtained an effluent after filtration which could be properly called purified, or which could be compared with our earlier results during this series of tests.

So far as my knowledge goes, whatever suggestions that may have been made by Profs. Mark and Brownell, have been followed out in the operation of these devices, but thus far I have received no formal notice as to their wishes in this matter.

In view of the fact that the results obtained from these devices last week were not satisfactory with regard to the quality of the filtered water, and that the results of this week appear to be of no practical value to this Company, either with regard to capacity to handle this water, or with regard to its satisfactory purification, I have stopped the operation of these devices. I hereby notify you officially of the present conditions, and respectfully request instructions in the premises.

Very respectfully,

[Signed] George W. Fuller,
Chief Chemist and Bacteriologist.

On Feb. 25, the makers of the dynamo made some changes in the machine, as recommended by Prof. Brownell. Unofficial tests showed that on this, and several following days, there was a marked reduction in the maximum amount of current which the dynamo could put through the electrolytic cell. On preceding days, 500 amperes could be obtained at a potential of about 40 volts. It was now found that conditions had changed so, that with 55 volts, the maximum potential of the machine, only about 375 amperes of current could be obtained. The devices were carefully examined by Profs. Mark and Brownell. This marked reduction of 45 per cent. in the maximum amount of current which could be passed through the electrolytic cell, when the dynamo was operated at its maximum potential, means practically a similar increase in the cost of electrolytic treatment under the conditions stated, and is a factor which is given consideration beyond in the discussion of these results.

At the request of Prof. Brownell, there was placed on Feb. 26 an annular wooden frame both at the top and the bottom of the electrolytic cell, in order to reduce the space through which the river water could pass without treatment.

Profs. Mark and Brownell examined the devices on Feb. 27, and requested that an unofficial run be made with the maximum electric current, and a rate of flow of water of 10 cubic feet per minute. Their request was complied with. But in spite of the fact that the river water contained only about one-fifth as much mud as was the case earlier in the week, it was not possible, even at this low rate of treatment, to obtain a filtered water which was not muddy in appearance. The Brownell electrodes were not used again, except in some special comparative experiments, as requested by President Long. The results of analyses of the water before and after treatment, with summaries of the principal data and discussions thereon, are presented beyond.

The devices were not operated again until March 5, when the second electrolytic cell, containing the Mark electrodes, was used. The rate of treatment, and of filtration, was 10 cubic feet per minute on March 5, and on March 6 the rate was 5 cubic feet. On both days the dynamo was run at the maximum output which could be safely handled. The filtered water, however, was unsatisfactory in appearance, and the greater water space between these electrodes made it impossible, with the available appliances, to secure as much coagulation of the river water as in the case of the Brownell cell, on account of the decrease in current, due to the increased resistance which the current met in its passage through the Mark cell.

As Profs. Mark and Brownell formally announced at this time that they had no further modifications or suggestions to make, these devices in their present form were not regularly operated again.

Summary and Discussion of the Results Accomplished by the Mark and Brownell Devices.

There were nine official runs made with the devices during the period from Feb. 16 to March 6. Seven of these runs were with the Brownell electrodes, and the last two were with the Mark electrodes. In the case of the latter, very little information was obtained, so the discussion will be confined to the results obtained from operations with the Brownell electrodes. To obtain more light upon the work accomplished by these devices, President Long requested, first, that a comparison be made of the results accomplished by the electrolytical devices with the Brownell electrodes in connection with the Jewell filter and those obtained with the same river water by this filter without any treatment whatever; and, second, that a set of aluminum electrodes be made to duplicate the iron electrodes designed by Prof. Brownell, and then compare the results obtained with the respective electrodes, in connection with the Jewell filter, in purifying the same river water. Owing to unavoidable delays in securing aluminum sheets, these comparative tests were not completed until April 4. The results obtained from them are recorded just beyond this discussion, and are followed by the detailed results of analyses of samples connected with the tests of these devices.

The following set of tables contain a summary of the principal data obtained with reference to the rate of treatment and filtration, the amount of electrolytic treatment employed, the amount of electric power used, and the degree of purification after the treated river water had passed through the Jewell filter, and also the results of bacterial and chemical analyses of the individual samples of the water before and after treatment.

BACTERIA PER CUBIC CENTIMETER IN THE OHIO RIVER WATER TREATED BY THE MARK AND BROWNELL DEVICES AND THE JEWELL FILTER.

Number of Sample.	Date. 1897.	Hour.	Bacteria per Cubic Centimeter.
4973	Feb. 16	9.30 A.M.	22 600
4975	" 16	1.30 P.M.	25 100
4979	" 16	4.30 "	34 000
4979a	" 17	9.30 A.M.	22 100
4982	" 17	12.30 P.M.	24 900
4985	" 17	5.00 "	24 200
4986	" 22	9.30 A.M.	20 500
4989	" 22	2.35 P.M.	60 400
4992	" 22	5.00 "	59 500
4993	" 23	9.30 A.M.	63 400
4996	" 23	12.30 P.M.	59 700
4999	" 23	5.00 "	56 500
5000	" 24	9.30 A.M.	41 000
5003	" 24	12.30 P.M.	16 700
5006	" 24	4.30 "	36 500
5039	Mar. 5	9.30 A.M.	37 900
5041	" 5	4.30 P.M.	28 700
5056a	" 6	11.30 A.M.	31 500
5058	" 6	2.00 P.M.	41 000
5061	" 6	5.00 "	47 000

SUMMARY OF RESULTS ACCOMPLISHED BY THE MARK AND BROWNELL DEVICES.

Number of Run.	Began. Date. 1897.	Began. Hour.	Electric Current. H.P. per Million Gallons per 24 Hours.	Electric Current. Ampere Hours per Gallon.	Quantities of Water. Cubic Feet. Filtered.	Quantities of Water. Cubic Feet. Wash.	Average Rates of Filtration. Cubic Feet per Minute.	Average Rates of Filtration. Million Gallons per Acre per 24 Hours.	Periods of Service.
				Brownell Electrodes.					
1	Feb. 16	11.44 A.M.	93	0.044	5 383	820	22.6	92	3h. 56m.
2	" 16	4.05 P.M.	78	0.041	6 344	595	22.5	91	4h. 42m.
3	" 17	1.22 "	66	0.040	6 273	943	23.0	93	4h. 33m.
4	" 22	2.22 "	97	0.064	2 574	542	14.0	57	3h. 02m.
5	" 23	9.52 A.M.	121	0.070	626	381	13.0	52	0h. 48m.
6	" 23	11.05 "	283	0.181	1 902	455	4.9	20	6h. 25m.
7	" 24	9.52 "	175	0.091	4 735	674	9.8	40	8h. 05m.
				Mark Electrodes.					
1	March 5	4.20 P.M.	194	0.099	711	....	10.1	41	1h. 10m.
2	" 6	1.27 "	384	0.197	1 081	....	5.1	20	3h. 33m.

Number of Run.	Estimated Average Suspended Solids in River Water. Parts per Million.	Degree of Clearness of Effluent.	Nitrogen as Albuminoid Ammonia. Parts per Million. River Water.	Effluent.	Per Cent. Removed.	Oxygen Consumed. Parts per Million. River Water.	Effluent.	Per Cent. Removed.	Average Bacteria per Cubic Centimeter. River Water.	Effluent.	Average Bacterial Efficiency.
					Brownell Electrodes.						
1	254	3	.326	.116	64	6.4	2.0	69	23 800	5 400	77.3
2	254	3	....	....	....	......	......	....	27 000	3 580	86.7
3	308	3	.380	.114	70	6.8	2.0	71	22 300	3 780	83.0
4	474	4	.542	.182	66	9.1	3.9	57	60 000	8 000	86.7
5	4 372	4	3.084	.110	96	50.3	2.3	95	63 400	4 400	93.1
6	4 372	4	3.084	.110	96	50.3	2.4	95	58 100	4 200	92.8
7	3 604	4	2.360	.084	96	48.9	2.5	95	31 400	4 260	86.5
					Mark Electrodes.						
1	205	5	.762	.260	66	12.0	4.2	65	28 700	7 300	74.5
2	5 311	5	4.900	.198	96	65.0	3.0	95	39 800	22 100	44.6

BACTERIA PER CUBIC CENTIMETER IN THE OHIO RIVER WATER AFTER TREATMENT BY THE MARK AND BROWNELL DEVICES AND THE JEWELL FILTER.

Serial Number.	Collected. Date. 1897.	Collected. Hour.	Number of Run.	Rate of Filtration. Cubic Feet per Minute.	Rate of Filtration. Million Gallons per Acre per 24 Hours.	Loss of Head. Feet.	Period of Service Since Last Washing. Hours and Minutes.	Filtered Water Since Last Washing. Cubic Feet.	Bacteria per Cubic Centimeter.	Remarks.
				Brownell Electrodes.						
4974	Feb. 16	12.30 P.M.	1	23.5	95	4.7	0h. 46m.	1 241	7 200	
4976	" 16	1.30 "	1	23.5	95	5.2	1h. 44m.	2 541	5 200	
4977	" 16	2.30 "	1	23.5	95	......	2h. 44m.	3 881	3 800	
4978	" 16	4.30 "	2	23.5	95	3.5	0h. 25m.	588	4 400	
4980	" 17	10 20 A.M.	2	23.5	95	8.2	2h. 25m.	3 244	3 090	
4981	" 17	12.30 "	2	23.5	95	8.4	4h. 35m.	6 068	3 250	
4983	" 17	2.30 P.M.	3	23.5	95	4.4	1h. 08m.	1 584	4 120	
4984	" 17	5.00 "	3	23.0	93	7.2	3h. 36m.	4 964	3 160	
4987	" 22	1.30 "	3	23.0	93	7.7	4h. 08m.	5 738	4 050	
4988	" 22	2.35 "	4	20.0	81	2.8	0h. 13m.	285	8 100	
4990	" 22	3.30 "	4	16.0	65	2.7	1h. 08m.	1 175	10 200	
4991	" 22	5.00 "	4	12.0	48	2.0	2h. 35m.	3 385	5 830	
4994	" 23	10.30 A.M.	5	10.0	41	......	0h. 38m.	380	4 400	
4995	" 23	12.30 P.M.	6	5.0	20	0.4	1h. 25m.	424	4 700	
4997	" 23	2.30 "	6	5.0	20	0.4	3h. 25m.	980	4 030	
4998	" 23	5.00 "	6	5.0	20	0.5	5h. 55m.	1 295	3 890	
5001	" 24	10.30 A.M.	7	10.0	41	0.7	1h. 05m.	645	3 050	
5002	" 24	12.30 P.M.	7	9.5	40	1.3	3h. 05m.	1 815	6 000	
5004	" 24	2.30 "	7	10.0	41	1.9	5h. 05m.	3 005	4 400	
5005	" 24	4.30 "	7	10.0	41	2.8	7h. 05m.	4 155	3 500	
				Mark Electrodes.						
5056	Mar. 5	5.30 P.M.	1	10.0	41	1.6	1h. 10m.	711	7 300	
5057	" 6	2.00 "	2	5.0	20	0.5	0h. 33m.	170	12 700	
5059	" 6	3.30 "	2	5.0	20	0.7	2h. 03m.	630	29 500	
5060	" 6	5.00 "	2	5.0	20	0.9	3h. 33m.	1 093	24 000	

RESULTS OF CHEMICAL ANALYSES OF THE OHIO RIVER WATER BEFORE AND AFTER TREATMENT BY THE MARK AND BROWNELL DEVICES AND THE JEWELL FILTER.

(Parts per Million.)

Serial Number.	Collected, Date, 1897.		Temperature, Degrees C.	Degree of Clearness.	Color.	Oxygen Consumed.	Nitrogen as Albuminoid Ammonia. Total.	Suspended.	Dissolved	Nitrogen as Free Ammonia.	Nitrogen as Nitrites.	Nitrogen as Nitrates.	Chlorine.	Residue on Evaporation. Total.	Suspended.	Dissolved.	Fixed Residue after Ignition. Total.	Suspended.	Dissolved.	Alkalinity.	Dissolved Alumina.	Iron.
*																						
							River Water.															
831[1]	Feb	16	5.0	.	...	6.4	.326	.204	.122	.062	.024	1.0	4.4	376	254	122	332	240	92	49.0	0	16.0
833[2]	"	17	6.0	.	...	6.8	.380	.262	.118	.048	.028	0.7	4.5	428	308	120	388	300	88	50.5	0	26.0
835[3]	"	22	7.0	..	.23	9.1	.542	.402	.140	.028	.015	1.5	4.4	620	474	146	561	447	114	61.5	0	60.0
837[4]	"	23	8.0	..	.18	50.3	3.084	3.004	.080	.098	.012	1.2	4.1	4 501	4 372	129	4 223	4 128	95	62.5	0	340.0
839[5]	"	24	8.5	..	.23	48.9	2.360	2.286	.074	.060	.015	1.4	4.4	3 732	3 604	128	3 537	3 445	92	56.0	0	340.0
848[6]	Mar.	5	10.0	..	.23	12.0	.762	.654	.108	.039	005	1.8	3.1	892	761	131	820	726	94	64.3	0	34.0
850[7]	"	6	10.0	..	.24	65.0	4.900	4.754	.146	.090	.007	1.4	3.3	5 431	5 311	120	5 165	5 076	89	62.2	0	116.0
							Effluent with Brownell Electrodes.															
832[8]	Feb.	16	5.0	3	...	2.0	.116	...	...	.060	.012	0.9	4.6	115	...	...	89	...	...	49.5	0	0.7
834[9]	"	17	6.0	3	...	2.0	.114	...	...	.058	.016	0.7	4.6	114	...	...	91	...	...	51.0	0	0.8
836a[10]	"	22	7.0	5	..	4.5	...	...	...	...	...	...	...	332	186	146	294	180	114	...	0	24.0
836b[11]	"	22	...	5	...	4.5	...	...	...	...	...	...	...	292	146	146	256	140	114	...	0	21.0
836c[12]	"	22	...	4	...	2.7	...	...	...	...	...	...	...	186	40	146	156	42	114	...	0	7.6
836[13]	"	22	...	5	.17	3.9	.182	.042	.140	.034	.018	1.5	4.3	284	138	146	244	130	114	62.0	0	19.0
838a[14]	"	23	8.0	4	...	2.3	...	...	...	...	...	...	...	158	29	129	122	27	95	...	0	56.0
838b[15]	"	23	8.5	4	...	2.7	...	...	...	...	...	...	...	182	53	129	143	48	95	...	0	64.0
838c[16]	"	23	...	3	...	2.3	...	...	...	...	...	...	...	134	5	129	101	6	95	...	0	45.0
838[17]	"	23	...	4	.22	2.4	.110	.030	.080	.070	.014	1.2	4.0	152	23	129	127	32	95	62.0	0	58.0
840a[18]	"	24	9.0	3	...	2.4	...	...	...	...	...	...	...	132	4	128	97	5	92	...	0	2.5
840b[19]	"	24	...	4	...	2.8	...	...	...	...	...	...	...	184	56	128	147	55	92	...	0	5.5
840c[20]	"	24	...	4	...	2.7	...	...	...	...	...	...	...	163	35	128	128	36	92	...	0	5.0
840[21]	"	24	...	4	.22	2.5	.084	.010	.074	.062	.016	1.3	4.6	163	35	128	127	35	92	54.0	0	4.5
							Effluent with Mark Electrodes.															
851a[22]	Mar.	6	10.0	5	...	3.2	...	...	...	...	...	...	...	309	189	120	272	183	89	...	0	13.0
851b[23]	"	6	...	5	...	2.9	...	...	...	...	...	...	...	273	153	120	237	148	89	...	0	9.6
851c[24]	"	6	...	5	...	2.7	...	...	...	...	...	...	...	218	98	130	188	99	89	...	0	4.6
851[25]	"	6	...	5	.23	3.0	.198	.052	.146	.094	.008	1.1	3.0	257	137	120	220	131	89	62.8	0	9.2

* Corresponding bacterial numbers, or period of collection by automatic sampler: [1] 9.30 A.M. [2] 4.30 P.M. [3] 9.30 A.M. [4] 9.30 A.M. [5] 9.30 A.M. [6] 9.30 A.M. [7] 11.30 A.M. [8] 4974, 4976, 4977. [9] 4980, 4981, 4983. [10] 4988. [11] 4990. [12] 4991. [13] 4988, 4990, 4991. [14] 4994. [15] 4995. [16] 4996. [17] 4994, 4995, 4996. [18] 5001. [19] 5002. [20] 5004. [21] 5001, 5002, 5004. [22] 5017. [23] 5019. [24] 5019a. [25] 5017, 5019a.

Decomposition of the Brownell Iron Electrodes—Loss of Metal.

During the period covered by the official tests of the Brownell electrodes the total quantity of water treated was 29 965 cubic feet; the duration of treatment for this total quantity of water was 33.25 hours, and the average number of amperes of current was 401. The difference in the weights of these electrodes, at the beginning and at the end of these tests, showed a loss of 17.5 pounds. This indicates an average decomposition of 0.59 gram (9.02 grains) of metallic iron per ampere hour. Carefully conducted experiments made on a small scale with bright iron, free from all rust, showed that the rate of decomposition was rather variable, but, on an average, it approached the theoretical rate of 1.05 grams (16.17 grains) per ampere hour. These small experiments also showed, however, that the rate of decomposition diminished as the electrodes continued in service. The reason of this appeared to be associated with coatings of rust on the surface of the electrodes, especially on the anode (positive pole). It will be noted that in these official tests the actual average rate of decomposition of iron was only 56 per cent. of the theoretical rate. This question of the rate of the electrolytical decomposition of metallic iron is one of great practical importance in this connection, because it is a controlling factor in determining the size of power plant which would be required in the application of this process. Further investigations were made along this line after the close of the work on the Mark and Brownell devices, and the results are recorded in Chapter XV.

Loss of Electrolytically Formed Hydrate of Iron in the Brownell Cell due to the Arrangement of its Outlet Pipe.

From the foregoing description of the electrolytic cell, it will be recalled that the outlet water-pipe was not placed at the bottom of the cell, but at the side, about 6 inches above the apex of the conical bottom. The portion of the cell beneath the outlet pipe had a capacity of about 2.8 cubic feet, equal to 21 gallons. At Prof. Brownell's recommendation the liquid and solid materials at the bottom of the cell were blown into the sewer about once an hour. The quantity removed each time was about 2 cubic feet on an average.

It was very soon noticed that the liquid, which was removed in this way from time to time, subsided very quickly, and evidently contained a large amount of iron hydrate. On Feb. 23, when the river water was very muddy and contained 4372 parts per million of suspended matter, a test was made to learn the amount of iron hydrate which passed to the sewer through the blow-off pipe.

Samples of the semi-liquid matter, which was blown off into a cask before passing to the sewer, were carefully collected after thorough mixing, and corresponding samples of the untreated river water were also taken. The experiment was continued during the afternoon of this day. The results of the analyses of the several samples of river water and blow-off water, respectively, indicated that the iron coming from the electrodes and leaving the cell in this manner, was equivalent to 0.52 gram (7.94 grains) of metallic iron decomposed per ampere-hour during this test.

It is impossible to state accurately what the rate of decomposition of iron was during the afternoon of Feb. 23, but it is probable that it was not far from the average rate for all the runs, as stated in the last section. This would mean that 84 per cent. of the iron which came from the electrodes and left the cell, passed to the sewer with a portion of the heaviest mud, before there was an opportunity for it to coagulate the finer particles in the water, and prepare it for efficient filtration. Owing to the very muddy condition of the river water on this date, it is probable that the above experiment exaggerates the practical significance of this point, with reference to ordinary river water. Nevertheless, it throws much light on the actual conditions at that time, and illustrates a weakness in the arrangement of the cell.

Passages in the Cell containing the Brownell Electrodes, through which the River Water could pass with little or no direct Electrolytical Treatment.

In the electrolytic cell containing the Brownell electrodes, the regular spaces between the electrodes for the passage of the water to be treated were 0.5 inch. There were also two spaces 2 inches in width, between the sections in which the plates were arranged; and in addition to this, there was an annular space, ranging from 3 to 3.5 inches in width, between the edge of the electrodes and the wall of the cell. The quantity of electric current which can pass through a 2-inch water space is only one-fourth as much as can pass through a half-inch water space, other conditions being equal; and there was practically no current passing through the annular space between the cell and the electrodes. The percentages of the total sectional area of the cell which was occupied by the electrodes and the water spaces, respectively, together with the percentages which the treatment of the water passing through each of the sections was of the maximum, are as follows:

Electrodes	21 per cent.	
0.5-inch water space..	35 " "	(full treatment).
2.0 " " " ..	13 " "	(one-quarter treatment).
Annular space around wall...............	31 " "	(no treatment).

These figures show that, originally, there was an opportunity for fully one-half of the water to pass through the cell without direct electrolytic treatment.

On Feb. 26, an annular wooden frame, 3 inches wide, was placed in the cell at both the top and the bottom of the electrodes, and which reduced the outer annular water space, in which there was no treatment, from 31 to about 6 per cent. of the total sectional area of the cell. This corrected in part the defect of having some of the water pass through the cell without coming at once in intimate contact with the coagulant during its initial formation. All the official runs with this cell, however, were made before the frames were put in place. But on the following day the cell was used in its modified form, on an unofficial run, and the devices failed to purify the water satisfactorily.

With the conditions which would be obtained upon a large scale of operation, it is very probable that this defect in the arrangement of the cell would reduce the efficiency of the treatment, owing to the lack of uniform distribution of the solid hydrate in the water. In this experimental cell, however, it is doubtful whether the point in question exerted any influence, because the piping was so arranged that after leaving the cell, the water passed through several elbows, valves, and meters, all of which aided in mixing well together the treated and untreated portions of the water.

Variations in the Resistance of Ohio River Water to the Passage of an Electric Current.

As already stated in the description on the operation of these devices, it was found that up to, and including, Feb. 24, it was possible to pass, for a short time, 500 amperes of current at a potential of 40 volts through the cell containing the Brownell electrodes. But on several days following this date the maximum potential (55 volts) of the dynamo could give only about 375 amperes. On account of the fact that it is the amperage of the current which controls the amount of electrolytic decomposition, this reduction of about 45 per cent. in the efficiency of the plant, with substantially the same expenditure of power, is a very serious problem from a practical point of view. Considerable study was given to the matter, and it was found that it was caused during this flood by the dilution of the dissolved chemical compounds in the river water. So far as could be learned, the mud and other suspended matters in the river water exerted practically no influence on its conductivity. That is to say, with small electrodes placed in two-gallon jars, it apparently made no difference in the resistance of the same river water, whether the suspended matters were present or whether they were removed by the passage of the water through filter paper or a Pasteur filter. The results of further studies along this line are recorded and discussed in Chapter XV.

In the following table are presented comparative results, showing the specific resistance of the Ohio River water, expressed in the conventional form, during the period of flood from Feb. 22 to March 6. They serve to show the variations which were encountered in the river water; and they also indicate the range in power which would be required to do the same amount of efficient work, other things being equal. As will be seen by the comparison of these results with small electrodes (150 centimeters square) with the results referred to in Chapter XV, and which were obtained from the use of large electrodes, these figures can be safely used in estimating the required amount of electromotive force for different services in which the Ohio River water is used as an electrolyte.

SPECIFIC RESISTANCE OF THE OHIO RIVER WATER, EXPRESSED IN OHMS PER CENTIMETER CUBE.

Number of Corresponding Chemical Sample.*	Date. 1897.	Specific Resistance.
835	February 22	7 300
837	" 23	5 900
839	" 24	8 700
841	" 25	11 600
842	" 26	13 200
843	" 27	16 700
844	March 1	12 300
845	" 2	14 900
846	" 3	11 250
847	" 4	14 000
848	" 5	7 900
850	" 6	7 200

* The chemical composition of these samples may be seen by reference to Chapter I.

Electric Power used by these Electrolytical Devices with the Brownell Electrodes.

In the foregoing summary of results, the electric horse-power used during each run is given. The relation between the electric power and the actual steam power used, both with regard to these conditions and the practical conditions on a large scale, are discussed in Chapter XV. As a more accurate idea of the cost of generating electric power, it may be stated here, that these generating appliances, under the most favorable conditions, yielded about 80 per cent. of the power contained in the steam which was used. On a large scale it may be reasonably expected that this efficiency could be maintained or slightly increased.

General Status of this Process at the Close of these Tests.

A.—Brownell Electrodes.

The summary of analytical results obtained in connection with the Brownell electrodes, already presented, shows that at no time was the filtered water satisfactory, either with regard to appearance or to the number of bacteria contained in it. The amount of organic matter in the filtered water, as indicated by the nitrogen in the form of albuminoid ammonia, and by the oxygen consumed, was several times as great as was normally present in the filtered water during the previous year. Owing to the very muddy condition of the river water, however, and the consequently large amount of organic matter which it contained, the percentages of removal of organic matter were high.

B.—Mark Electrodes.

The Mark electrodes, composed of circular cast-iron pipes, were placed in a duplicate cell, and were used in connection with the same generating appliances as in the case of the Brownell electrodes, for two runs, which were made on March 5 and 6, respectively.

At this period the river water was very muddy, and on March 6 it was in the muddiest condition which existed during the entire investigations. Very little information was obtained from the results of these two tests, other than that the filtered water was muddy, showing that the devices were wholly inadequate to coagulate the water properly, even at one-fifth of the regular rate of treatment and of filtration.

Considering these electrodes in general terms, however, they seemed to possess some advantages over the Brownell electrodes in arrangement for operation on a large scale, in that the water was uniformly treated. But in these experimental cells, the outlet pipe leading to the Jewell settling chamber was so arranged that it is doubtful whether any such advantage existed here. It is also possible that the cost of construction of complete sets of electrodes on a large scale would be less in the case of the Mark electrodes. These latter electrodes possessed a disadvantage when compared with the former, in that the water space between the individual electrodes was twice as great, and, accordingly, the amount of power required would be twice as great, other things being equal.

It seems hardly necessary to state that these poor results were caused by inadequate preparation of the river water before its passage through the Jewell filter; and, further, that in the absence of sufficient coagulation these results cannot be taken as a measure of the merits and practicability of the general method of water purification, in which the electrolytic treatment is a preliminary step preceding filtration. These results refer only to a particular set of devices, possessing a number of weaknesses, which might be remedied in a large measure by practical means.

In this connection, it must not be overlooked that, as already stated, the electrolytic treatment of water adds to it no sulphuric acid to combine with lime and form incrustations in steam boilers; nor does it liberate in the water carbonic acid gas to increase the corroding action of the water on wrought-iron receptacles. This advantage of the electrolytic formation of coagulating chemicals (either aluminum hydrate or iron hydrate), over the decomposition of the commercial sulphates of these metals by the lime dissolved in the water, is a matter of importance. Another advantage of the electrolytic treatment is that it is independent of the amount of lime dissolved in the river water, and the possibility of undecomposed sulphates passing into the filtered water is obviated. A further consideration of this process in its various phases will be found in Chapter XV.

COMPARISON OF THE QUALITY OF THE OHIO RIVER WATER AFTER FILTRATION FOLLOWING ELECTROLYTIC TREATMENT IN THE BROWNELL CELL, AND AFTER FILTRATION WITHOUT ANY PRELIMINARY TREATMENT.

As requested by President Long, two runs were made with the Jewell filter on March 11. The first run was made at the regular rate of

23.5 cubic feet per minute, and the river water before filtration was treated with the maximum electric current (400 amperes) in the Brownell electrolytic cell. The second run was made at the same rate, but the river water received no preliminary coagulating treatment whatever. In each case the settling basin of the Jewell System was drained and cleaned, and the filter thoroughly washed before filtration was begun. Both runs were continued until the filter became clogged so that it would not allow the passage of water at the prescribed rate.

A comparison of the result obtained from these two runs is shown in the following table:

BACTERIA PER CUBIC CENTIMETER IN THE OHIO RIVER WATER TREATED DURING THE COMPARATIVE TESTS DESCRIBED ABOVE.

Number of Sample.	Date.	Hour.	Bacteria per Cubic Centimeter.
	1897		
5081	March 11	9.30 A.M.	38 100
5084	" 11	1.00 P.M.	41 500
5087	" 11	3.25 "	36 200

COMPARATIVE SUMMARY OF RESULTS ACCOMPLISHED BY THE JEWELL FILTER WITH (RUN NO. 1) AND WITHOUT (RUN NO. 2) PRELIMINARY TREATMENT BY THE MARK AND BROWNELL DEVICES. (Brownell Electrodes.)

Number of Run.	Began.		Electric Current.		Quantities of Water. Cubic Feet.		Average Rates of Filtration.		Periods of Service. Hours and Minutes.
	Date. 1897.	Hour.	H.P. per Million Gallons per 24 Hours.	Ampere Hours per Gallon.	Filtered.	Wash.	Cubic Feet per Minute.	Million Gallons per Acre per 24 Hours.	
1	March 11	11.51 A.M.	85	0.045	1 517	....	23.4	95	1h. 05m.
2	" 11	2.13 P.M.	....	....	2 237	....	21.9	89	1h. 42m.

SUMMARY OF RESULTS.—*Concluded.*

Estimated Average Suspended Solids in River Water. Parts per Million.	Degree of Clearness Of Effluent.	Nitrogen as Albuminoid Ammonia. Parts per Million.			Oxygen Consumed. Parts per Million.			Average Bacteria per Cubic Centimeter.		Average Bacterial Efficiency.
		River Water.	Effluent.	Per Cent. Removed.	River Water.	Effluent.	Per Cent. Removed.	River Water.	Effluent.	
1 751	Muddy.	2.400	.374	84	24.6	6.4	74	39 800	13 100	67.0
1 751	"	2.400	.566	76	24.6	9.0	63	36 200	20 200	44.0

NUMBER OF BACTERIA IN THE EFFLUENT OF THE JEWELL FILTER WITH AND WITHOUT ELECTROLYTIC TREATMENT.

Serial Number.	Collected.		Number of Run.	Rate of Filtration.		Loss of Head. Feet.	Period of Service Since Last Washing. Hours and Minutes.	Filtered Water Since Last Washing. Cubic Feet.	Bacteria per Cubic Centimeter.	Remarks.
	Date. 1897.	Hour.		Cubic Feet per Minute.	Million Gallons per Acre per 24 Hours.					
	Effluent with Electrolytic Treatment.									
5082	March 11	12.50 P.M.	1	23.5	95	10.0	0h. 55m.	1 287	12 700	
5083	" 11	1.00 "	1	23.5	95	10.8	1h. 05m.	1 517	13 500	
	Effluent with No Coagulating Treatment.									
5085	March 11	3.15 P.M.	2	23.0	93	5.6	1h. 02m.	1 386	17 700	
5086	" 11	3.25 "	2	23.0	93	7.9	1h. 12m.	1 636	19 700	
5088	" 11	3.55 "	2	23.0	93	11.0	1h. 42m.	2 197	23 200	

RESULTS OF CHEMICAL ANALYSES OF THE OHIO RIVER WATER BEFORE AND AFTER FILTRATION THROUGH THE JEWELL FILTER WITH AND WITHOUT ELECTROLYTIC TREATMENT.

(Parts per Million.)

Serial Number.	Collected.		Temperature, Degrees C.	Degree of Clearness.	Color.	Oxygen Consumed.	Nitrogen						Chlorine.	Residue on Evaporation.			Fixed Residue after Ignition.			Alkalinity.	Dissolved Alumina.	Iron.
	Date, 1897.	Corresponding Bacterial Numbers or Hour of Collection.					as Albuminoid Ammonia. Total.	Suspended.	Dissolved.	as Free Ammonia.	as Nitrites.	as Nitrates.		Total.	Suspended.	Dissolved.	Total.	Suspended.	Dissolved.			
855[1]	Mar. 11	9.30 A.M.	11.0	...	.22	24.6	2.400	2.274	.126	.042	.002	1.1	5.1	1881	1751	130	1766	1664	102	61.0	0	96.0
856[2]	" 11	5082, 5083	11.0	5	...	6.4	.374	.248	.126	.036	.003	1.1	5.0	587	547	130	537	435	102	60.7	0	21.0
857[3]	" 11	5085, 5086	11.0	5	...	9.0	5.66	.440	.126	.034	.005	1.3	5.2	763	633	130	704	602	102	63.1	0	28.0

[1] River water. [2] Effluent with electrolytic treatment. [3] Effluent with no coagulating treatment.

A COMPARISON OF THE EFFICIENCY IN THE ELECTROLYTIC TREATMENT OF WATER BEFORE FILTRATION, OF THE BROWNELL ELECTRODES AND OF ALUMINUM ELECTRODES OF THE SAME SIZE AND ARRANGEMENT.

At President Long's request, a set of aluminum electrodes was made to duplicate as nearly as possible the iron electrodes devised by Prof. Brownell. Owing to delays in securing the aluminum plates, it was not until April 2 that these comparative tests could be made. These aluminum electrodes were placed in the cell which formerly contained the Mark electrodes. From April 2, at 3.41 P.M., to April 4, at 6.30 A.M., nine runs were made in connection with the Jewell System. The first five were made with the iron (Brownell) electrodes, and in the last four runs the aluminum electrodes were used. The rate of treatment and filtration was kept as nearly as possible to the regular rate of 23.5 cubic feet per minute, and the conditions of operation, other than the amount of current used, were as nearly the same as possible. In the case of each cell, no sediment was blown off at the bottom.

It was found that a current of 100 amperes on the aluminum electrodes was sufficient to secure a perfectly clear effluent, while with 450 amperes of current on the iron electrodes the effluent was not clear. The iron electrodes, however, were somewhat covered with rust from their earlier use, while the aluminum electrodes were new and bright. It was found that the iron electrodes, following the long period of disuse, gave more efficient coagulation as they continued in service. While these experiments were continued sufficiently to serve their general purpose, yet they were of too short duration to allow satisfactory determinations of the amount of metal used, owing to complications from mud, rust and water. The principal data of these comparative tests are presented in the following summary and results of analyses:

BACTERIA PER CUBIC CENTIMETER IN THE OHIO RIVER WATER TREATED DURING THE COMPARATIVE TESTS DESCRIBED ABOVE.

Serial Number.	Date, 1897.	Hour.	Bacteria per Cubic Centimeter.
5226	April 2	5.30 P.M.	3 700
5228	" 2	8.00 "	3 420
5230	" 3	12.30 A.M.	2 940
5232	" 3	3.30 "	3 500
5234	" 3	9.30 "	3 150
5243	" 3	3.30 P.M.	4 200
5249	" 3	9.30 "	6 400
5252	" 4	12.30 A.M.	5 100
5259	" 4	5.30 "	5 700

COMPARATIVE SUMMARY OF RESULTS ACCOMPLISHED BY THE JEWELL FILTER AND MARK AND BROWNELL DEVICES WITH IRON ELECTRODES (RUNS NOS. 1 TO 5) AND ALUMINUM ELECTRODES (RUNS NOS. 6 TO 9).

Number of Run.	Began.		Electric Current.		Quantities of Water, Cubic Feet.		Average Rates of Filtration.		Periods of Service. Hours and Minutes.
	Date. 1897.	Hour.	H. P. per Million Gallons per 24 Hours.	Ampere Hours per Gallon.	Filtered.	Wash.	Cubic Feet per Minute.	Million Gallons per Acre per 24 Hours.	
1	April 2	4.28 P.M.	95	0.047	5 214	518	23.5	95	3h. 42m.
2	" 2	8.33 "	78	0.042	7 265	603	23.6	95	5h. 08m.
3	" 3	2.07 A.M.	65	0.041	5 902	602	21.8	88	4h. 31m.
4	" 3	7.07 "	35	0.029	4 970	568	23.2	94	3h. 34m.
5	" 3	11.12 "	80	0.044	4 230	....	23.0	93	3h. 04m.
6	" 3	3.36 P.M.	24	0.024	4 092	514	23.2	94	2h. 55m.
7	" 3	6.57 "	20	0.020	4 552	541	22.5	91	3h. 23m.
8	" 3	10.45 "	10	0.015	4 982	....	22.9	93	3h. 37m.
9	" 4	2.44 A.M.	6	0.008	4 974	....	21.2	86	3h. 54m.

Number of Run.	Estimated Average Suspended Solids in River Water Parts per Million.	Degree of Clearness of Effluent.	Nitrogen as Albuminoid Ammonia. Parts per Million.			Oxygen Consumed. Parts per Million.			Average Bacteria per Cubic Centimeter.		Average Bacterial Efficiency.
			River Water.	Effluent.	Per Cent. Removed.	River Water.	Effluent.	Per Cent. Removed.	River Water.	Effluent.	
1	213	3	.248	.075	71	4.5	1.2	73	3 300	311	90.4
2	213	3	.248	.075	71	4.5	1.1	76	2 900	133	93.3
3	213	3	.248	.075	71	4.5	1.0	78	3 500	154	95.6
4	213	3	.248	.075	71	4.5	1.1	76	3 100	240	92.3
5	200	3	.248	.075	71	4.5	1.0	78	3 700	207	94.4
6	200	1	.208	.050	76	4.8	0.8	83	5 300	94	98.2
7	200	1	.208	.050	76	4.8	0.8	83	5 700	100	98.2
8	200	1	.208	.050	76	4.8	0.8	83	5 700	126	97.8
9	200	1	.208	.050	76	4.8	0.9	81	5 400	138	97.6

RESULTS OF CHEMICAL ANALYSES OF THE OHIO RIVER WATER BEFORE AND AFTER TREATMENT BY THE MARK AND BROWNELL DEVICES AND THE JEWELL FILTER WITH IRON ELECTRODES AND ALUMINUM ELECTRODES, RESPECTIVELY.

(Parts per Million.)

Serial Number.	Collected.		Temperature, Degrees C.	Degree of Clearness.	Color.	Oxygen Consumed.	Nitrogen as Albuminoid Ammonia.			Nitrogen as Free Ammonia.	Nitrogen as Nitrites.	Nitrogen as Nitrates.	Chlorine.	Residue on Evaporation.			Fixed Residue after Ignition.			Alkalinity.	Dissolved Alumina.	Iron.
	Date. 1897.	Corresponding Bacterial Numbers or Hour of Collection.					Total.	Suspended.	Dissolved.					Total.	Suspended.	Dissolved.	Total.	Suspended.	Dissolved.			
	River Water.																					
875	Apr. 2, 3	5.30 P.M., 8.00 P.M., 12.30 A.M., 9.30 A.M.	10.5	...	.16	4.5	.248	.166	.082	.020	.002	1.2	4.5	325	213	112	229	209	90	39.2	0	8.8
878	" 3, 4	3.30 P.M., 9.30 P.M., 12.30 A.M., 5.30 A.M.	11.0	...	.20	4.8	.208	.138	.070	.014	.001	0.8	2.8	309	200	109	281	193	88	43.8	0	12.8
	Effluent with Iron Electrodes.																					
876a	Apr. 2	5227	11.0	3	...	1.3	....	....	....	....	...	...	...	119	...	...	103	...	...	....	0	...
876b	" 2	5229	....	3	...	1.2	....	....	....	...	....	...	...	116	...	...	98	...	...	....	0	....
876c	" 3	5231	....	3	...	1.1	....	....	....	....	....	...	...	113	...	...	93	...	...	....	0	....
876d	" 3	5233	....	3	...	1.0	....	....	....	....	....	...	...	113	...	...	96	...	...	....	0	....
876	" 2, 3	5227, 5229, 5231, 5233	...	3	.32	1.2	.076	....	...	.014	.001	1.0	3.0	112	...	...	93	...	...	42.0	0	1.0
877	" 3	5235, 5241	11.0	3	.20	1.0	.074	....	....	.016	.000	0.9	3.0	108	...	...	92	...	...	42.0	0	0.5
	Effluent with Aluminum Electrodes.																					
879a	Apr. 3	5245	11.4	1	...	0.8	....	....	....	....	....	...	...	106	...	...	90	...	...	....	0	....
879b	" 3	5247	....	1	...	0.8	....	....	....	....	....	...	...	104	...	...	87	...	...	....	0	....
879c	" 4	5253	....	1	. .	0.8	...	....	....	....	....	...	...	100	...	...	85	...	...	...	0	....
879d	" 4	5258	....	1	...	0.9	....	....	...	....	....	...	...	106	...	...	84	...	...	....	0	....
879	" 3, 4	5245, 5247, 5253, 5258	....	1	.10	0.8	.050	.000	.050	.016	.002	1.3	2.9	103	0	103	83	0	83	41.1	..	0.0

NUMBER OF BACTERIA IN THE EFFLUENT OF THE JEWELL FILTER FOLLOWING TREATMENT IN THE MARK AND BROWNELL DEVICES WITH IRON ELECTRODES AND ALUMINUM ELECTRODES, RESPECTIVELY.

Serial Number.	Collected. Date. 1897.	Collected. Hour.	Number of Run.	Rate of Filtration. Cubic Feet per Minute.	Rate of Filtration. Million Gallons per Acre per 24 Hours.	Loss of Head. Feet.	Period of Service Since Last Washing. Hours and Minutes.	Filtered Water Since Last Washing. Cubic Feet.	Bacteria per Cubic Centimeter.	Remarks.
				Effluent with Iron Electrodes.						
5227	April 2	5.30 P.M.	1	24.0	97	3.5	1h. 02m.	1 499	385	
5229	" 2	8.00 "	1	24.0	97	......	3h. 32m.	4 964	250	
5231	" 3	12.30 A.M.	2	24.0	97	7.3	3h. 57m.	5 555	193	
5233	" 3	3.30 "	3	24.0	97	3.9	1h. 23m.	1 710	154	
5235	" 3	9.30 "	4	23.5	95	5.3	2h. 23m.	3 378	267	
5236	" 3	10.00 "	4	23.5	95	7.5	2h. 53m.	4 088	239	
5237	" 3	10.30 "	4	22.0	89	9.7	3h. 23m.	4 768	214	
5238	" 3	12.00 M.	5	23.5	95	3.5	0h. 48m.	1 148	219	
5239	" 3	12.30 P.M.	5	23.5	95	3.9	1h. 18m.	1 868	198	
5240	" 3	1.00 "	5	23.5	95	4.3	1h. 48m.	2 538	181	
5241	" 3	1.30 "	5	23.5	95	5.3	2h. 18m.	3 208	222	
5242	" 3	2.00 "	5	20.0	81	8.6	2h. 48m.	3 928	217	
				Effluent with Aluminum Electrodes.						
5244	April 3	4.00 P.M.	6	24.0	97	3.1	0h. 24m.	588	107	
5245	" 3	4.30 "	6	23.0	93	3.4	0h. 54m.	1 238	85	
5246	" 3	5.30 "	6	23.5	95	5.7	1h. 54m.	2 718	91	
5247	" 3	8.00 "	7	23.5	95	3.8	1h. 03m.	1 594	106	
5248	" 3	9.00 "	7	23.5	95	5.7	2h. 03m.	2 976	95	
5250	" 3	10.00 "	7	23.5	95	10.9	3h. 03m.	4 306	120	
5251	" 3	11.30 "	8	23.5	95	3.0	0h. 45m.	1 074	159	
5253	" 4	12.30 A.M.	8	23.5	95	4.0	1h. 45m.	2 474	110	
5254	" 4	1.30 "	8	23.5	95	7.0	2h. 45m.	3 834	110	
5255	" 4	2.00 "	8	23.0	93	9.8	3h. 15m.	4 544	139	
5256	" 4	3.30 "	9	23.5	95	3.0	0h. 46m.	812	199	
5257	" 4	4.30 "	9	23.5	95	3.9	1h. 46m.	2 342	93	
5258	" 4	5.30 "	9	23.5	95	6.5	2h. 46m.	3 692	121	

CHAPTER XIV.

Description of the MacDougall Polarite System of Purification, and a Record of the Results Accomplished Therewith.

On March 3, 1897, just as the tests of the Mark and Brownell devices were being completed, arrangements were made whereby the efficiency and cost of operation of the MacDougall Polarite System should be investigated, with reference to the purification of the water supply of this Company. In order that the results accomplished by this system might be comparable with those of the foregoing tests, the rate of treatment was arranged to be 250,000 gallons per 24 hours.

In brief, this system, known abroad both as the International System and the Howatson System, was represented to consist of a double filtration of river water, without the use of coagulating chemicals, obtained either electrolytically or from commercial chemical products. The first filtration was to be through a layer of sand, with the view to removing the coarser matters suspended in the river water; and the second filtration was to be through a layer of a special material, called polarite, which is described below. This system of water purification has never been tried in this country, but it is said to be in successful operation in purifying turbid or muddy waters in several places in England, Egypt, and India.

In order to guard against delays, it was mutually agreed that for the first (sand) filter use should be made in an undisturbed condition of the Jewell filter, which was then at the disposal of the Water Company. Owing to the fact that it was necessary to send to England for the polarite, this system, however, was not ready to be tested until May 10.

With the exception of Sundays, and several unavoidable periods of delay, this system was operated night and day from May 10 to June 12, inclusive. During the remaining time, from the close of the tests of the Mark and Brownell devices until the end of the investigations, attention was directed to some plans and devices of the Water Company, as are described in Chapter XV.

When the MacDougall Polarite System was being constructed, it was found that a separate tank with baffle plates was to be substituted for the settling basin under the Jewell filter. On May 28, a "clay extractor," consisting of an iron tank with two compartments, each filled with about 14 feet in depth of coarse coke, was substituted for this tank containing baffle plates. The settling basin and filter of the Jewell System have been fully described in the foregoing chapters, and a plan and section have also been presented. A correct understanding of the other devices used in connection with the polarite system may be obtained from the following description. Meters and gauges were provided wherever necessary, in order to secure measurements of the quantities of water which were treated, and also of the resistance which the water met as it passed through the several layers of filtering material.

Iron Tank with Baffle Plates.

This tank, placed just outside of the Jewell house, was cylindrical in form, 3 feet in diameter, 16 feet high, 113 cubic feet in capacity and made of boiler iron, 0.19 inch in thickness. It was put together with 0.5-inch rivets. The bottom of the tank was conical in form, 2 feet high and tapered at the lowest point to an apex 3 inches in diameter, where a blow-off pipe leading to the sewer was connected. The inlet pipe, leading from the river water main, was 4 inches in diameter, and entered the tank by a flanged joint about 5.5 inches above the point where the conical bottom with a shoulder was riveted to the main cylinder. In this main cylinder were six baffle plates, placed at 0.25, 2.25, 4.25, 6.25, 8.25 and 10.25 feet, respectively, from the center of the inlet pipe. These baffle plates were circular in form, and riveted to the shell of the tank. In order to provide a passage for the water, a small segment of each plate was cut away, leaving a maximum perpendicular distance between the edge of the plates and the adjoining shell, of about 4 inches. The lowest plate was cut away on the side diametrically opposite the point where the inlet pipe entered; and the openings through the remaining baffle plates were arranged alternately with reference to the inlet pipe and the opening in the first plate. Perpendicular to the upper baffle plate, which was 3 feet from the top of the tank, two iron plates were riveted to the baffle plate and to the shell of the tank. Each of these partition plates extended to within 12 inches of the top of the tank, and they were each 22 inches in length. In the center of the tank, and parallel to these two partitions, which were in the same vertical plane as the cut edge of the lower baffle plate, was another partition, 2.83 feet in height, extending from the top of the tank to within 14 inches of the upper baffle plate. Across the bottom of this central partition, and extending to the two outer partitions, was a false bottom, made of a screen with meshes of about 0.25 linear inch. In the inner compartment, formed by the two outer vertical partitions and the shell of the tank, the upper baffle plate and the screen, was placed excelsior, which rested on the baffle plate. The superficial area of the excelsior was 7.85 square feet. It was removed on May 11.

When the water, in its upward flow through the tank, reached the last baffle plate, it passed through the normal opening and the space above it, bounded by the shell of the tank and one of the outer partitions; and thence it flowed over this partition into the central compartment. As described above, this compartment was divided into halves by a central partition, which extended to the excelsior compartment at the bottom. From one side to the other, the water passed by flowing through the excelsior and underneath the central partition. Thence rising in the other half of the central compartment, the water overflowed the outer partition, into a compartment between this partition and the shell of the tank. The outlet pipe, 6 inches in diameter, connected with the tank by a flange joint at the center of this compartment, and 24 inches below the top of the tank. From the tank, the outlet extended directly into the open compartment above the sand of the Jewell filter, ending in an elbow and a 6-inch nipple turned down. No arrangement was provided to break the stream of water as it entered the filter. The lower end of the nipple forming the outlet was on a level with the staves of the outer tank, and 35 inches above the sand. It was 12 inches from the edge of the outer tank to the center of the nipple. At the contract rate of flow, 250,000 gallons per 24 hours, the vertical velocity in the iron tank was 3.28 lineal feet per minute, or 1.2 per cent. of the velocity in a 4-inch pipe. This tank was used from May 10 to May 19, inclusive. On May 11, the excelsior was removed from the inner compartment; but no further changes were made. The system was not in operation from May 19 to 28.

Clay Extractor.

This device consisted of a rectangular iron tank, 6 by 3 feet, and 16 feet high. It was made of 0.19-inch plates of boiler iron, riveted together, and was divided into two equal compartments by a central partition. At points 1.75 and 1.0 feet from the top and bottom, respectively, there were angle irons riveted to the wall of the tank, and upon which rested screens of about 0.625-inch mesh. The space between the screens in each compartment, 14.3 feet in height, was filled with crushed coke. The diameter of the pieces of coke ranged from 0.5 to 2 inches, and averaged more than 1.0 inch. A stay bolt, 0.5 inch in diameter, was passed through the tank from end to end, and through the central partition about 5 feet from the top. Midway in each of the compartments at the bottom of the tank, an iron plate, 1 foot high and 3 feet long, was placed beneath the above-mentioned screens, parallel to the central partition. These plates relieved the angle irons of some of the weight of the layer of coke above them. In the corners of each of the two compartments at the bottom of the tank, where the river water entered and the wash-water left it, curved iron plates were arranged, to guard against accumulations of mud and other deposits. At the center of each side of the two lower compartments, there were openings, to which 4-inch flanges were attached. The two 4-inch pipes entering the tank at the front by means of these flanges were used to admit the river water to the tank; and the two corresponding pipes at the rear conducted the wash-water to the sewer. At the center, on the front side of each of the two open compartments above the coke at the top of the tank, there were openings, to which the two 6-inch outlet pipes were connected by flange joints. The two inlet river-water pipes, the outlet river-water pipes, and the two wash-water outlet pipes, were in each case branches of a single main pipe of the same diameter; and on the first and last pair of pipes gate valves were provided, with the view to using the two compartments either separately or together. In practice, however, both compartments were used together, as the central partition was unable to prevent the water from passing from one to the other.

It was arranged that, when the coke should become clogged and require cleaning, the water could be drained out through the outlet leading to the sewer; and connections were provided so that the effluent of the Jewell filter could be pumped through a 2-inch pipe to the open compartment at the top of the tank, and then flow by gravity to the wash-water outlet pipe at the bottom. A 10- by 18-inch hand-hole, with its center 1.5 feet from the bottom and the side of the tank, was placed at each end of the tank, with the view to taking out some of the clogged coke at the bottom, if it should become too much clogged to be cleaned by the above-stated method of washing.

The main inlet and outlet pipes were the same as were used with the iron tank containing baffle plates. On the inlet there was a meter and a pressure gauge, to show the head required to force the water up through the clay extractor. This new device was completed May 28.

Polarite Filter.

The polarite filter consisted originally of a layer of polarite placed between layers of sand, with all the filtering material resting upon the underdrains in a large open wooden tank. This tank was rectangular in form, 23 feet long, 10.2 feet wide and 7.3 feet deep, as shown by inside measurements. It was made of 2-inch smooth pine planks, fastened to supports as follows: The floor was supported by eight pieces of timber, 10 by 3 inches, which extended about 5 feet beyond each side of the tank. These timbers were connected together at each end by planks. On each side of the tank there were eight upright pieces of timber of the same size as those at the bottom, and in each case a timber 6 by 3 inches extended from the end of the bottom supports to about midway on the upright supports. The floor and sides were laid first, and spiked to the supports mentioned above. The planks at the end were fitted into a shallow vertical groove, which was cut on the inside of the side planks, and the side planks were spiked to those on the end. Midway on each end, there was an upright oak timber, 6 by 6 inches, to which the planks were also spiked. Two stay-rods, 0.75 inch in diameter, passed lengthwise through the tank, and were fastened at the ends to these oak timbers.

On the bottom of the tank, there were placed at right angles to each other, two layers of 3-inch tiles, with the long dimension horizontal, and the ends about 0.5 inch apart at the joints. The space between the tiles was filled with coarse gravel. In addition to the tiles at the bottom of the filter, there were laid on one side, both ends and across the center from end to end, rectangular troughs of wire, with 0.5-inch meshes. These troughs were 4 inches square in section, open at the bottom, and were intended to serve as an aid to the tiles, in conducting the filtered water to the end of the tank, where the outlet pipe was placed. The slope of the bottom of the tank toward the outlet, was about 1 inch in its length of 23 feet. At each of the four corners, on the inside of the tank, there was constructed a stand pipe, made of 3-inch hard tile, with cemented joints. These pipes extended above the level of the water which stood upon the sand when the filter was in operation, and were designed to act as air vents.

On the top of the tile drains (and the wire troughs) the following layers of filtering material were placed, successively: 6 inches of coarse gravel; 3 inches of coarse sand; 6 inches of fine sand; 20 inches of polarite; and 6 inches of fine sand. The original depth of filtering material in the polarite filter, not counting the coarse sand and gravel at the bottom, was 32 inches, and the area of filtering surface was 234.8 square feet, a little more than double that of the Jewell filter (115.8 square feet). The proposed area of the polarite filter was determined by Mr. MacDougall, on the assumption that the polarite filter could be operated with satisfactory results at one-half of the rate of filtration employed in the case of the Jewell filter, or about 50 million gallons per acre per 24 hours. A rectangular wooden trough, 6 inches wide and 6.5 inches deep, extended completely around the inside of the tank, 4.5 feet from the bottom. The 6-inch inlet pipe discharged the effluent of the Jewell filter into this trough at the northwest corner of the tank. At the southwest corner of the tank, a 6-inch pipe led the wash-water from this trough to the sewer. The main outlet pipe was 6 inches in diameter, placed as near as practicable to the bottom of the tank, on the end near the northeast corner. The effluent of the polarite filter discharged into the wrought-iron reservoir, in order to store enough water for wash-water during operation. Arrangements were made whereby this effluent could be pumped under pressure through a 3-inch pipe which entered the polarite filter at the bottom, about midway on the north side. Valves, meters, and gauges were inserted wherever convenience required.

The sand in the polarite filter was taken from several sources. A part of it came from lots which remained at the pumping station from the preceding year, and a part was taken from the bed of the Ohio River. All of these materials were washed carefully in a wheelbarrow with filtered water from a hose. Analyses of the more important filtering materials are given beyond.

Changes in the Polarite Filter.

A number of changes were made in the polarite filter as follows:

1. On May 11, it was found that the joints of the air-vents (stand pipes at the corners) leaked, and allowed some of the water to reach the bottom of the filter without passing through the filtering materials. The two upper sections of each vent were removed, and the lower sections were filled with filtering materials, to correspond with the main filter layers.

At the same time there were added above the filtering materials just mentioned, 5 inches of coarse coke and 5 inches of fine coke. This increased the depth of the filtering materials to 42 inches, and owing to the fact that the coke reached the sides of the distributing trough, which was placed around the tank on the inside, the surface area was reduced to about 200 square feet.

2. On May 14, there were placed on the top of the above-mentioned coke, 2 inches of fine sand. This increased the depth to 44 inches, but the surface area was unchanged.

3. On May 17, air vents were placed in the northwest and southeast corners of the filter, as follows: Three pieces of pipe, 1.5 inches in diameter, were put through the side of the tank at 12, 40, and 48 inches from the bottom, respectively; and by the aid of an elbow, each pipe was extended above the water level. The object of this was to take out accumulations of air at different levels within the filter.

4. During the period from May 19 to 28, inclusive, this system was out of service, and a number of changes were made. The principal one was the substitution of the clay extractor, for the small upright settling tank, as already described. The upper layer of sand and both layers of coke were removed. After the removal of these materials, the lower layers were washed by pumping filtered water into the bottom of the filter for about 3 hours. During this time about 3,600 cubic feet of wash-water were used. The surface of the 6-inch layer of fine sand, resting upon the polarite, was leveled, and upon it were placed 3 inches in depth of fine coke, which had been

carefully washed with filtered water from a hose. Above this coke layer, 3 inches of fine sand, washed in the same manner as the coke, were placed. This left the surface of the filter below the bottom of the distributing trough, and consequently the area was restored to 234.8 square feet. The depth of the filtering material was 38 inches.

Character of Filtering Materials.

The leading features concerning the several filtering materials are as follows:

Polarite.—Polarite is the trade name of a hard, black, porous and magnetic iron substance, which does not rust or dissolve in water. It is understood that it is prepared from a suitable natural ore by a patented process, and by crushing and screening, any desired size of grain may be obtained. By virtue of its numerous and minute pores, in which atmospheric oxygen may be occluded, polarite is claimed to possess a powerful action in the destruction of organic matter by oxidation. The chemical composition of the polarite used in these tests was as follows:

PERCENTAGE COMPOSITION OF POLARITE.

Silica (SiO_2)	22.65
Magnetic oxide of iron (Fe_3O_4)	49.17
Alumina (Al_2O_3) {with a trace of manganese and phosphoric acid.}	12.16
Lime (CaO)	0.85
Baryta (BaO)	0.02
Magnesia (MgO)	7.00
Undetermined, chiefly water and carbon	8.15
	100.00

It was found that the nitrogen in the form of albuminoid ammonia in the polarite was 5.4 parts per million.

The grains of polarite were very coarse for a filtering material, as shown by the following mechanical analysis:

MECHANICAL ANALYSIS OF POLARITE.

	Per cent. by weight.
Finer than 12.00 millimeters	100.0
" " 5.89 "	93.4
" " 3.90 "	50.1
" " 2.04 "	15.1
" " 0.93 "	1.6
" " 0.46 "	0.4
Effective size (ten per cent. finer than the given diameter in millimeters)	1.78

Sand.—There were three lots of sand used in the polarite filter; one lot was coarse, and the other two were fine sand. The coarse sand resting upon the coarse gravel at the bottom of the filter, and the fine sand at the surface, were taken from the river bed; while the fine sand forming the layer just beneath the porlarite was obtained at the pumping station, where it had been left by some of the filter companies from the preceding year. All of this material, as already stated, was washed with filtered water from a hose in iron wheelbarrows. The amount of organic matter remaining on the sand after washing is indicated by the nitrogen in the form of albuminoid ammonia, as follows:

Number of Sand.	Source.	Location in Filter.	Nitrogen as Albuminoid Ammonia. Parts per Million.
16	River bed.	Layer above gravel.	9.2
17	Pumping station.	Layer between gravel and polarite.	6.8
18	River bed.	Layer at surface.	17.4

The efficient size of these filtering materials, as shown by mechanical analyses, was as follows:

MECHANICAL ANALYSES OF SAND USED IN THE POLARITE FILTER.

	Per cent. by weight. No. 16.	No. 17.	No. 18.
Finer than 3.90 millimeters	100.0	100.0	97.8
" " 2.04 "	100.0	100.0	95.5
" " 0.93 "	3.1	95.5	89.2
" " 0.46 "		24.0	67.6
" " 0.316 "		2.8	9.1
" " 0.182 "		0.1	0.3
Effective size (ten per cent. finer than given diameter in millimeters)	1.23	0.39	0.32

Coke.—The coke was of the ordinary commercial variety. The coarse coke was of the grade commonly called nut size, and it contained when new 40.0 parts per million of nitrogen in the form of albuminoid ammonia. In the case of the fine coke when new the nitrogen in this form amounted to 49.8 parts. For this line of work the amount of lime and iron contained in coke is of some significance. The amounts of these constituents in the two grades were as follows:

	Coarse Coke.	Fine Coke.
Ash	5.42 per cent.	17.43 per cent.
Lime (CaO)	0.18 " "	0.95 " "
Iron (Fe)	0.70 " "	1.83 " "

The size of the finer grade is indicated by the results of the following mechanical analyses:

MECHANICAL ANALYSES OF FINE COKE USED IN THE POLARITE FILTER.

	Per cent. by weight.
Finer than 12.0 millimeters.............	100.0
" " 5.89 "	91.3
" " 3.90 "	83.2
" " 2.04 "	67.6
" " 0.93 "	44.7
" " 0.46 "	27.6
" " 0.316 "	18.7
" " 0.182 "	8.1
" " 0.105 "	3.3
Effective size (ten per cent. finer than given diameter in millimeters)	0.21

Operation of the Polarite System.

The operation of the polarite system was divided into two periods, namely: From May 10 to 19, and from May 28 to June 12, 1897, inclusive. During the intervening time between the two periods changes were made in the filter, and the clay extractor was substituted for the small iron settling tank, as has been described.

The general features of the operation were arranged by the Water Company to be as follows:

The operation of this system was under the direction of Mr. MacDougall, or his representative. The required rate of treatment was 250,000 gallons per 24 hours, equivalent to 23.2 cubic feet per minute; the system was under operation as continuously as practicable from 6.00 A.M. on Monday until 6.00 P.M. on Saturday, during each week. It was also understood by the Water Company that no chemical coagulants would be used in connection with this system.

A record of the most important points connected with the operation of this system is as follows:

Period No. 1.

The first period of operation extended from May 10 to May 19, when the system was shut down for alterations and repairs for a considerable length of time. The river water was fairly uniform in character for the first four days, ranging from 171 to 260 parts per million of suspended solids. On May 14 and 15 a slight rise caused the suspended matter to increase to 1,260 parts per million. For the remaining three days the solids averaged 486 parts per million.

The operation of the system began on May 10 at 9.10 A.M. At 3.45 A.M. on May 11 the system was stopped in order to remedy leaks in the air vents of the polarite filter, and to add to the filter 10 inches of coke, as already stated.

Operations were resumed on May 12, at 9.04 A.M., but the rate of filtration was reduced to 12.0 cubic feet per minute, which was about one-half of the normal rate. This reduced rate was held until May 13, at 9.00 A.M., when it was increased to 18.0 cubic feet per minute (about three-quarters of the normal rate), which was held until May 14, at 9.44 A.M. Up to this time the effluent was never clear in appearance as it left the polarite filter; although the water was clearer at this point than it was when it left the Jewell filter.

The system was stopped on May 14, at 9.44 A.M., and 2 inches of fine sand were added to the surface of the polarite filter, after it had been washed for several hours by pumping filtered water through from below, at the rate of 12 to 14 cubic feet per minute. During this time 2,083 cubic feet of wash-water were used.

On May 14, at 7.46 P.M., the operation of the system was resumed; and from that time until May 15, at 9.00 A.M., a solution of sulphate of alumina was applied to the water as it left the Jewell filter on its way to the polarite filter. During this period the rate of application of sulphate varied. It ranged from 11.09 to 1.00 grains per gallon, and averaged 4.39 grains. The rate of filtration was 13 cubic feet per minute from the last resumption of operation until May 15, at 6.00 P.M., when the system was stopped from Saturday night until Monday morning. During the greater portion of the night of May 14, when sulphate of alumina was applied to the water as it entered the polarite filter, the effluent of this filter was clear. At all other times it possessed a decided turbidity.

Whenever the system was out of service it was repeatedly noted that many air bubbles, some of which were quite large, appeared on the surface of the water on the polarite filter, near the edge of the tank. On the morning of May 17, the water in this filter was allowed to drain out, and it was found that there was a scum of aluminum hydrate, clay, etc., about

0.25 inch thick deposited upon the surface of the filter. There was also seen a large number of holes around the edges of the filter, some of which ranged from 3 to 8 inches in width and depth. Air vents, as previously described, were inserted at this time, and about three wheelbarrows of fine sand were added, to fill the holes at the sides. The thick scum cracked in places, and the entire surface of the polarite filter was raked. Filtered water was pumped into this filter from below, until the gauge showed that the water level was 32 inches above the bottom. The Jewell filter was put in operation at 13 cubic feet per minute on May 17, 11.39 A.M.; and, above the point just stated, the polarite filter was filled from the top. This caused a good many bubbles to appear at the surface, especially along the edge of the filter. From the beginning of the operation of the system on this date, until 2.28 P.M., sulphate of alumina was applied to the water as it left the Jewell filter at an average rate of 1.06 grains per gallon. At 2.00 P.M. the rate of filtration was increased to 18 cubic feet per minute; at 4.00 P.M. it was increased to 23.5 cubic feet; and at 4.45 P.M. it was decreased to 18 cubic feet. The system was out of operation from 5.00 to 5.21 P.M. on this date, in order to allow air to escape from the polarite filter. The surface of this filter was also raked, and the water above the sand drained off to a depth of 1 foot at this time. From May 17, at 5.21 P.M., until May 19, at 8.45 A.M. (the close of the first period of operation) this system was operated at a rate of about 18 cubic feet per minute, without any special features of importance. The effluent of the polarite filter was at no time, during this portion of the period, free from a decided turbidity.

Independent of repairs, and of the wash-water pump, this system required the attention of one regular attendant to control the rate at which the river water entered the settling tank; to regulate the outlet valves of the Jewell and polarite filters, so that the depth of water upon them was approximately constant; to apply sulphate of alumina solutions; and to agitate and wash the Jewell filter.

During this period, from May 10 to 19, there were available by arrangement, 7.48 days, of 24 hours, in which to operate the system. Of this time 5.73 days were devoted to regular operations, and the balance of 1.75 days (23 per cent. of the period) to repairs and changes. Of the 5.73 days devoted to regular operations, 3.8 per cent. of the time was occupied in washing and agitating the Jewell filter.

The quantity of water passed through the Jewell filter during this period was 120,865 cubic feet, and the quantity of effluent of the polarite filter was practically the same. This made the actual rates of treatment of water by the two filters, expressed in different forms, as follows:

AVERAGE ACTUAL RATES OF FILTRATION IN THE POLARITE SYSTEM.

	Jewell Filter.	Polarite Filter.
Gallons per 24 hours	164 000	164 000
Cubic feet per minute	15.2	15.2
Million gallons per acre per 24 hours	62	*30.5–†36.0

* Original area. † Modified area.

Of the total quantity of water treated, 120,865 cubic feet, sulphate of alumina was applied to 11,919 cubic feet (9.9 per cent. of total quantity) at an average rate of 3.80 grains per gallon. This amount of sulphate of alumina was equivalent to 0.37 grain per gallon of the total quantity of water treated during the period.

The accumulation of sediment, etc., on the surface of the Jewell filter was removed in a manner somewhat different than was previously the case, in that the filter was washed less frequently, and surface agitation was employed more frequently, with the modification that, at the close of agitation, the water above the top of the staves of the inside tank was allowed to pass to the sewer. The average quantity of unfiltered water thus wasted at the time of each agitation was about 200 cubic feet.

A record of the washes of the filter is as follows:

WASHING OF THE JEWELL FILTER—PERIOD No. 1.

Number of Washing.	Date of Washing.		Period of Washing.	Quantity of Wash Water. Cubic Feet.	Filtered Water since Last Washing. Cubic Feet.	Number of Agitations.
	Day.	Hour.				
1*	May 10	5.20 P.M.	20m.	750	10 953	0
2	" 11	4.30 "	20m.	739	11 815	0
3	" 14	10.47 A.M.	19m.	529	40 720	6
4	" 18	4.25 P.M.	18m.	644	41 938	14
5†	" 19	....	......	......	15 439	4

* Washed by Water Company to prevent stopping at night, in the absence of instructions to the operator from Mr. MacDougall.

† Washed by Water Company, preparatory to use with Water Company's devices.

As the operation of this system progressed, the Jewell filter was washed less frequently, and agitated more often, as seen by the next table, in which the principal data are recorded. It will be noted that the loss of head following an agitation gradually became greater, as the agitations wtihout washing increased.

The polarite filter did not become clogged except by the air which was trapped in its pores at times. The bulk of this air rose to the surface when the outlet was closed.

AGITATIONS OF THE JEWELL FILTER—PERIOD No. 1.

Number of Agitation.	Date of Agitation.		Period of Agitation. Minutes.	Quantity of Filtered Water. Cubic Feet.		Initial Loss of Head in Feet following Agitations—Rate 23.5 Cubic Feet per Minute.
	Day.	Hour.		Since Last Washing.	Since Last. Agitation.	
	1897					
1	May 13	2.06 A.M.	36m.	11 919	....	3.5
2	" 13	9.05 "	26m.	16 674	4 755	4.0
3	" 13	1.14 P.M.	23m.	20 665	3 991	3.9
4	" 13	5.37 "	28m.	24 869	4 204	....
5	" 13	10.09 "	24m.	39 125	4 256	5.2
6	" 14	4.07 A.M.	23m.	45 095	5 970	6.0
7	" 14	11.32 P.M.	30m.	3 054	....	3.1
8	" 15	4.49 A.M.	26m.	6 864	3 810	3.1
9	" 15	11.30 "	32m.	11 800	4 936	....
10	" 15	3.30 P.M.	30m.	14 564	2 764	....
11	" 17	11.33 A.M.	....	16 157	1 593	....
12	" 17	5.00 P.M.	30m.	21 129	2 106	....
13	" 17	8.19 "	21m.	23 899	2 770	5.7
14	" 17	11.40 "	22m.	27 038	3 137	6.5
15	" 18	2.45 A.M.	22m.	30 015	2 979	6.7
16	" 18	6.10 "	22m.	33 309	3 294	....
17	" 18	8.00 "	23m.	34 793	1 484	7.0
18	" 18	9.45 "	22m.	36 216	1 423	....
19	" 18	11.45 "	21m.	37 944	1 728	....
20	" 18	2.00 P.M.	20m.	39 914	970	7.1
21	" 18	8.03 "	23m.	3 427	....	2.6
22	" 18	11.39 "	22m.	6 926	3 299	2.6
23	" 19	3.34 A.M.	23m.	10 691	3 765	2.7
24	" 19	7.10 "	20m.	14 083	3 392	....

Period No. 2.

This period, following repairs and changes which have been enumerated, extended from May 28, 12.35 P.M., until June 12, 6.00 P.M., the close of the tests of this system.

During this time the system was operated continuously, excepting from Saturday nights until the following Monday mornings, at approximately the full rate. The exact rate called for in the contract was 23.2 cubic feet per minute; but it was the general custom throughout all these tests to maintain the rate as nearly to 23.5 cubic feet as practicable. There were no delays, changes or repairs of importance during this period.

The river water contained very little mud at the beginning of this period, but mostly very fine clay particles, averaging in amount about 90 parts per million of suspended matter for the first two days; and the effluent of the polarite filter was decidedly turbid.

On May 31 and June 1, sulphate of alumina was applied to the water as it flowed to the Jewell filter, as follows: May 31, 7.51 to 8.45 A.M., 0.60 grain per gallon; May 31, 9.00 A.M. to 3.00 P.M., 0.24 grain; May 31, 5.00 to 9.00 P.M., 0.21 grain; May 31, 11.30 P.M., to June 1, 3.05 P.M., 0.18 grain per gallon. During those portions of the time between May 31, 7.51 A.M., and June 1, 3.05 P.M., which are included above, there was no application of chemicals. From June 1 3.05 P.M. to 5.20 P.M., sulphate of alumina at the rate of 0.18 grain per gallon was applied to the water as it left the Jewell filter on its way to the polarite filter. After this there was no further application of chemicals.

In the absence of rains in the Ohio Valley, the river water rapidly became clearer, and during the remaining portion of this test the suspended solids averaged only about 30 parts per million. The effect of this is shown very clearly by the fact that from May 31 till June 8 the Jewell filter was neither washed nor agitated during continuous operation at the normal rate. During this time, without any additional application of chemicals (a large portion of the above-stated applications remaining in and upon the filters), the effluent was clear or slightly turbid. At no time, however, was it bright and perfectly free from visible suspended matter.

In addition to the washing at the beginning of this period the Jewell filter was washed on May 31, 7.19 A.M., and on June 11, 8.53 A.M., the quantities of effluent of the polarite filter used for wash-water being 543 and 644 cubic feet, respectively. The quantity of water filtered between the last two washings was 315,199 cubic feet. The Jewell filter was agitated, and about 200 cubic feet of unfiltered water drained from the surface of the sand, eight times during the last three days of the eleven days between washings, as follows:

AGITATION OF JEWELL FILTER—PERIOD No. 2.

Number of Agitation.	Date of Agitation.		Period of Agitation.	Quantity of Filtered Water. Cubic Feet.	
	Date. 1897.	Hour.		Since Last Washing.	Since Last Agitation.
25	June 8	1.25 P.M.	30m.	226 860	....
26	" 9	2.00 "	31m.	260 611	33 751
27	" 10	6.35 A.M.	30m.	282 914	22 303
28	" 10	4.51 P.M.	31m.	296 558	12 644
29	" 10	9.30 "	24m.	302 358	5 801
30	" 10	12.00 "	24m.	395 204	2 845
31	" 11	3.00 A.M.	25m.	308 735	3 531
32	" 11	7.17 "	34m.	313 844	5 109

The data on loss of head before and after each agitation are not complete, but it may be stated that the latter agitations did very little in decreasing the frictional resistance of the sand layer, and that the filter was exceedingly dirty on June 11, when it was absolutely necessary to wash the filter.

During this period the polarite filter was not washed, raked, or scraped, and at the close of June 12, the loss of head was 21 inches, with the normal rate of filtration.

It was also found that the clay extractor did not become clogged during service. Both compartments were regularly used, although neither of them was washed. The acting head necessary to force the water through this device remained 1.9 feet during this period.

From May 28 to June 12, there were available by arrangement 12.22 days of 24 hours, in which to operate this system. Of this time, 12.07 days were devoted to regular operations, and the balance of 0.15 day was devoted to unavoidable delays, largely in making preparations to apply sulphate of alumina. Of the 12.07 days devoted to regular operations, 1.6 per cent. of the time was occupied in washing and agitating the Jewell filter.

The quantity of water passed through the Jewell filter during this period was 397,355 cubic feet; and the quantity of effluent of the polarite filter was substantially the same. About 399,000 cubic feet of water passed through the clay extractor, the increase here (1645 cubic feet, equal to 0.4 per cent. of total) being due to the water which was drained from the surface of the Jewell filter. This made the actual rates of treatment of water by the three devices, expressed in different forms, as follows:

AVERAGE ACTUAL RATES OF FILTRATION IN THE POLARITE SYSTEM.

	Clay Extractor.	Jewell Filter.	Polarite Filter.
Gallons per 24 hours...	246 000	245 000	245 000
Cubic feet per minute..	22.9	22.8	22.8
Million gallons per acre per 24 hours........	593.	92	42

Of the total quantity of water treated, 397,355 cubic feet, sulphate of alumina was applied to 40,328 cubic feet (10 per cent. of total quantity) at an average rate of 0.25 grain per gallon. This amount of sulphate of alumina was equivalent to 0.026 grain per gallon of the total quantity of water treated during this period.

Quality of the Ohio River Water after Treatment by the Polarite System.

In the next two tables are presented summaries of analytical results, showing the bacterial efficiency of the system, and also the percentage of removal of organic matter from the river water by it. Beyond these tables are the results of individual bacterial analyses of the river water, and of the water after it passed through the several devices comprising the system; and also the results of chemical analyses of the water at different stages of treatment. For further information concerning the composition of the river water during this period, in addition to that shown by the summaries of results, reference is made to Chapter I.

The summaries of analytical results are divided into two periods, which are the same as have been used in the foregoing pages concerning the operation of this system. It will be noted at once from the summaries that the river water was quite muddy during the first period; while during the second period it was very clear, comparatively speaking. During the two periods, the suspended solids in the river water averaged 604 and 40 parts per million, respectively.

As was reported to you at the time of occurrence, the collection of samples for analysis, during the first day of operation of this system, was informally protested by Mr. MacDougall, on the ground that this system was not yet ready for normal work. No official notice was received as to the time when this protest was withdrawn, if at all, and no further mention of the subject was made to the writer.

Owing to the fact that so many changes were made during the first period, in an effort to adapt the system to the purification of the Ohio River water, it does not seem fair to give the results obtained during this portion of the operation serious consideration.

Concerning the results obtained during the second period, following several changes, it will be seen that the system accomplished no substantial bacterial purification of the water until sulphate of alumina was applied to the water, as it flowed to the Jewell filter. It further appears that the aluminum hydrate, deposited upon and within the Jewell filter, and which was not removed to a marked degree by the surface agitations of the sand, or by the single short washing which this filter received after the application of sulphate of alumina ceased, was clearly a more important factor in the purification of the river water, than was the polarite.

The coke in the clay extractor contained lime, metallic iron and organic matter. The latter served as a food for the river water bacteria; and while there was no increase after the second day of operation in the albuminoid ammonia in the water as it passed through the extractor, the growths of bacteria continued until nearly the close of operations. It was especially noticeable that the growths were greatest for a short time following a period of rest, such as the first few hours of operation on Monday mornings.

The lime and metallic iron in the coke were steadily removed by the carbonic acid contained in the river water. This explains the usual increase of about 2 parts in the alkalinity of the water during passage through the clay extractor. The still greater increase in alkalinity of the water, during passage through the polarite filter, is similarly explained by the coke layers in this filter.

It was found, from an average of three sets of analyses on June 4, that the river water was practically saturated with atmospheric oxygen at that time, and that the effluent of the polarite filter contained about 90 per cent. of that necessary for saturation at the actual temperature (21° C.).

Contrary to experience sometimes met with effluents of filters containing coke, the oxygen consumed results were apparently not affected, practicaly speaking, by the iron and organic matter contained in the coke. In all cases, the nitrogen in the form of albuminoid ammonia, and the residue on evaporation, were determined in the water as collected, and also after it had been passed through a Pasteur filter. The difference in the corresponding results is recorded in each case as the amount in suspension. During the last few days of the tests, the effluents were so clear that the amount of suspended matter could not be satisfactorily weighed, although it was generally visible in minute quantities. With regard to the nitrogen in the form of albuminoid ammonia, which was suspended in the effluents at this time; the analyses indicate that small amounts were present, although they approached so nearly to the limits of accuracy of the method of analysis that full weight cannot be given to them.

In conclusion, it may be stated that the evidence obtained during these tests, taken as a whole, shows that the MacDougall Polarite

System (which was investigated with the view to dispensing with the use of coagulating chemicals) was not applicable, in the form in which it was tested by this Company, to the efficient and economical purification of the Ohio River water.

SUMMARY OF THE AVERAGE RESULTS BY DAYS OF BACTERIAL ANALYSES OF THE OHIO RIVER WATER BEFORE AND AFTER TREATMENT BY THE POLARITE SYSTEM.

Period No. 1.

Date. 1897.	Bacteria per Cubic Centimeter. River Water.	Jewell Effluent.	Polarite Effluent.	Bacterial Efficiency. Jewell Filter.	Polarite Filter.
May 10	15 300	7 500	14 900	51.0	2.6
" 11	11 800	3 600	9 500	69.5	19.6
" 12	31 000	9 700	30 000	68.7	3.2
" 13	36 200	16 000	34 900	55.7	3.6
" 14	52 400	38 200	72 200	27.0	− 38.7
" 15	49 400	19 500	22 700	60.5	54.0
" 17	22 600	9 000	21 100	60 2	7.1
" 18	16 500	13 900	14 900	15.7	9.7
" 19	12 100	17 000	10 300	− 45.0	14.9

Period No. 2.

Date. 1897.	Bacteria per Cubic Centimeter. River Water.	Extractor Effluent.	Jewell Effluent.	Polarite Effluent.	Bacterial Efficiency. Clay Extractor.	Jewell Filter.	Polarite Filter.
May 28	7 900	8 300	5 360	3 645	− 5	32	54
" 29	7 700	7 600	5 100	3 770	1	34	51
" 31	2 560	10 300	3 280	2 040	− 303	− 28	20
June 1	2 200	2 810	2 470	1 270	− 28	− 12	42
" 2	1 910	1 770	1 157	716	7	37	63
" 3	1 390	1 530	388	250	− 10	72	82
" 4	970	1 490	194	180	− 53	80	81
" 5	710	1 190	158	116	− 67	78	84
" 7	770	1 160	222	192	− 50	71	75
" 8	640	1 260	118	81	− 97	82	87
" 9	490	910	78	44	− 86	84	91
" 10	460	700	55	45	− 52	88	90
" 11	470	547	48	36	− 16	90	92
" 12	590	590	40	36	0	93	94

SUMMARY OF THE RESULTS OF CHEMICAL ANALYSES OF THE OHIO RIVER WATER, BEFORE AND AFTER TREATMENT BY THE POLARITE SYSTEM, SHOWING THE REMOVAL OF ORGANIC MATTER, AS INDICATED BY THE NITROGEN AS ALBUMINOID AMMONIA, AND BY OXYGEN CONSUMED.

(Results in Parts per Million.)

Period No. 1.

Date. 1897.	Nitrogen as Albuminoid Ammonia. River Water.	Jewell Effluent.	Polarite Effluent.	Percentage Removal. Jewell Effluent.	Polarite Effluent.	Oxygen Consumed. River Water.	Jewell Effluent.	Polarite Effluent.	Percentage Removal. Jewell Filter.	Polarite Filter.
May 10, " 11	.282	.112	.108	60	62	4.5	2.0	1.8	56	60
" 12	.348	.176	.140	51	60	5.3	2.7	2.4	49	55
" 13	.406	.232	.160	43	60	6.0	3.5	1.4	42	77
" 14	.884	.334	.110	62	88	17.2	6.8	2.4	60	86
" 15	1.042	.396	.116	62	89	16.3	6.0	2.0	63	88
" 17, " 18, " 19	.448	.260	.130	42	71	10.4	4.9	2.9	53	62

Period No. 2.

Date. 1897.	Nitrogen as Albuminoid Ammonia. River Water.	Extractor Effluent.	Jewell Effluent.	Polarite Effluent.	Percentage Removal. Extractor Effluent.	Jewell Effluent.	Polarite Effluent.	Oxygen Consumed. River Water.	Extractor Effluent.	Jewell Effluent.	Polarite Effluent.	Percentage Removal. Clay Extractor.	Jewell Filter.	Polarite Filter.
May 28, " 29	.146	.152	.108	.096	−4	26	34	3.5	3.2	2.7	2.5	9	23	29
" 31, June 1	.138	.144	.092	.098	−4	35	29	2.8	2.6	2.3	1.8	7	18	36
" 2, " 3	.166	.148	.106	.102	11	36	39	3.1	2.7	2.3	1.9	13	26	39
" 4, " 5	.180	.166	.112	.096	8	38	47	3.1	2.4	1.9	1.9	23	39	39
" 7, " 8	.186	.144	.126	.104	23	32	44	2.4	2.3	1.8	1.4	4	25	42
" 9, " 10	.164	.132	.106	.078	20	35	52	2.2	2.0	1.6	1.5	9	27	32
" 11, " 12	.176	.122	.094	.082	31	47	53	2.2	2.1	1.6	1.3	5	27	41

POLARITE SYSTEM.

Results of Chemical Analyses of the Effluent of the Clay Extractor.

Serial Number.	Collected. Date.	Collected. Corresponding Bacterial Numbers.	Temperature, Degrees C.	Degree of Clearness.	Color.	Oxygen Consumed.	Nitrogen as Albuminoid Ammonia. Total.	Nitrogen as Albuminoid Ammonia. Suspended.	Nitrogen as Albuminoid Ammonia. Dissolved.	Nitrogen as Free Ammonia.	Nitrogen as Nitrites.	Nitrogen as Nitrates.	Chlorine.	Residue on Evaporation. Total.	Residue on Evaporation. Suspended.	Residue on Evaporation. Dissolved.	Fixed Residue after Ignition. Total.	Fixed Residue after Ignition. Suspended.	Fixed Residue after Ignition. Dissolved.	Alkalinity.	Dissolved Alumina.	Iron.
	1897																					
978	May 28–29	6151, 6158, 6166, 6173, 6180	20.0	5	.12	3.2	.152	.064	.088	.018	.001	0.8	2.3	164	46	118	142	49	93	69.7	0	3.40
982	May 31–June 1	6188, 6192, 6199, 6206, 6217, 6224	20.0	5	.11	2.6	.144	.074	.070	.014	.000	0.7	2.7	157	29	128	125	17	108	71.9	0	0.67
986	June 2–3	6231, 6238, 6245, 6252, 6259, 6266, 6273, 6280	20.5	4	.22	2.7	.148	.078	.070	.014	.002	0.8	3.5	156	20	136	123	17	106	74.3	0	1.35
990	" 4–5	6287, 6294, 6301, 6308, 6315, 6322, 6329	21.5	4	.12	2.4	.166	.062	.104	.024	.002	0.8	3.9	151	14	137	116	15	101	77.6	0	1.00
994	" 7–8	6336, 6343, 6350, 6357, 6361, 6365, 6372	22.5	4	.17	2.3	.144	.056	.088	.034	.002	0.7	5.8	159	19	140	123	15	108	82.0	0	0.65
998	" 9–10	6379, 6386, 6393, 6100, 6407, 6414, 6421, 6428	22.5	4	.13	2.0	.132	.056	.076	.056	.005	0.7	4.9	165	7	158	130	3	127	84.3	0	0.40
1002	" 11–12	6435, 6442, 6449, 6456, 6460, 6470	23.0	3	.13	2.1	.122	.044	.078	.042	.004	0.9	6.0	160	....	....	111	....	....	84.1	0	0.40
Results of Chemical Analyses of the Effluent of the Jewell Filter.																						
942	May 10–11	5814, 5821, 5828	17.0	4	.09	2.0	.112	......	......	.028	.002	1.1	3.1	148	39	109	116	31	85	56.8	0	6.20
945	" 12	5834, 5846	17.5	4	.13	2.7	.176	.046	.130	.042	.006	1.5	3.8	189	67	122	152	63	89	63.1	0	6.60
948	" 13	5854, 5865, 5873, 5877	18.2	4	.14	3.5	.232	.126	.106	.032	.003	1.4	2.5	279	155	124	234	148	86	62.0	0	7.80
951	" 14	5884, 5889, 5897	18.1	4	.15	6.8	.334	.250	.084	.042	.004	1.4	2.3	496	378	118	431	350	81	65.2	0	20.00
954	" 15	5902, 5909, 5917	18.0	4	.14	6.0	.396	.286	.110	.030	.003	1.5	2.1	471	339	132	412	324	88	68.7	0	19.00
957	" 17–19	5922, 5926, 5933, 5938, 5945, 5951, 5958	19.0	4	.18	4.9	.260	.178	.082	.018	.002	1.3	3.0	284	202	82	247	193	54	41.2	0	9.00
979	" 28–29	6152, 6159, 6167, 6174, 6181	20.0	4	.14	2.7	.108	.022	.086	.012	.002	0.8	2.3	144	25	119	124	27	97	70.5	0	1.70
983	" 31–June 1	6189, 6193, 6201, 6208, 6219, 6226	20.0	3	.20	2.3	.092	.018	.074	.012	.000	0.8	2.7	130	....	....	99	....	....	70.4	0	.50
987	June 2–3	6232, 6239, 6246, 6253, 6260, 6267, 6274, 6281	20.5	3	.22	2.3	.106	.030	.076	.016	.000	0.9	3.4	140	....	....	111	....	....	75.4	0	.75
991	" 4–5	6288, 6295, 6302, 6309, 6316, 6323, 6330	21.5	3	.15	1.9	.112	.008	.104	.021	.000	0.8	3.9	136	....	....	103	....	....	77.6	0	.30
995	" 7–8	6337, 6344, 6351, 6358, 6362, 6366, 6373	22.5	3	.13	1.8	.126	.038	.088	.034	.000	0.7	5.2	157	....	....	121	....	..	82.6	0	.10
999	" 9–10	6380, 6387, 6394, 6401, 6408, 6415, 6422, 6429	22.5	3	.14	1.6	.106	.030	.076	.034	.000	0.7	4.8	156	....	....	128	....	....	84.9	0	.05
1003	" 11–12	6436, 6443, 6450, 6457, 6461, 6471	23.0	3	.14	1.6	.094	.020	.074	.024	.000	0.8	6.0	156	....	...	110	....	....	84.2	0	.05
Results of Chemical Analyses of the Effluent of the Polarite Filter.																						
943	May 10–11	5813, 5822, 5829	17.0	4	.10	1.8	.108	.022	.086	.016	.004	1.0	3.1	142	35	107	108	23	85	61.2	0	2.40
946	" 12	5835, 5847	17.5	4	.10	2.4	.140	.046	.094	.020	.003	1.3	4.6	163	33	130	132	26	106	65.8	0	1.80
949	" 13	5855, 5866, 5874, 5878	18.2	4	.14	1.4	.160	.074	.086	.028	.003	1.4	2.6	188	55	133	143	54	89	71.2	0	0.68
952	" 14	5885, 5890, 5898	18.1	4	.14	2.4	.110	.026	.084	.038	.004	1.5	2.3	215	82	133	172	71	101	74.0	0	4.44
955	" 15	5903, 5910, 5918	18.0	4	.13	2.0	.116	.022	.094	.026	.003	1.4	2.0	150	21	129	115	20	95	74.2	0	1.20
958	" 17–19	5923, 5927, 5934, 5939, 5946, 5952, 5959	19.0	4	.12	2.9	.130	.048	.082	.012	.003	1.3	3.0	136	40	96	106	40	66	50.0	0	1.52
980	" 28–29	6153, 6160, 6168, 6175, 6182	20.0	4	.14	2.5	.096	.014	.082	.016	.002	0.8	2.3	138	23	115	129	22	107	77.2	0	0.40
984	" 31–June 1	6190, 6194, 6201, 6208, 6219, 6226	20.0	3	.20	1.8	.098	.014	.084	.018	.000	0.7	2.5	137	....	....	110	....	....	78.6	0	0.30
988	June 2–3	6233, 6240, 6247, 6254, 6261, 6268, 6275, 6282	20.5	3	.19	1.9	.102	.026	.076	.012	.000	0.8	3.6	144	....	....	115	....	....	80.4	0	0.55
992	" 4–5	6289, 6296, 6303, 6310, 6317, 6324, 6331	21.5	3	.14	1.9	.096	.000	.096	.020	.000	0.8	3.9	139	....	....	105	....	....	82.3	0	0.23
996	" 7–8	6338, 6345, 6352, 6359, 6363, 6367, 6374	22.5	3	.12	1.4	.104	.016	.088	.032	.001	0.7	5.5	159	....	.	124	....	....	86.9	0	0.08
1000	" 9–10	6381, 6388, 6395, 6402, 6409, 6416, 6423, 6430	22.5	2	.14	1.5	.078	.002	.076	.024	.001	0.8	5.0	160	0	160	131	0	131	88.4	0	0.04
1004	" 11–12	6437, 6444, 6451, 6458, 6462, 6472	23.0	2	.14	1.3	.082	.010	.072	.014	.000	0.7	5.9	155	0	155	110	0	110	87.1	0	0.05

BACTERIA PER CUBIC CENTIMETER IN THE OHIO RIVER WATER[1] BEFORE AND AFTER TREATMENT BY THE POLARITE SYSTEM.

Date.	Hour.	Rate of Filtration. Cubic Feet per Minute.	Bacteria per Cubic Centimeter.				Remarks.
			River Water.	Settling Pipe Effluent.	Jewell Effluent.	Polarite Effluent.	
1897							
May 10	11.00 A.M.	23.5	....	....	5 800	21 100	
" 10	1.15 P.M.	23.5	....	....	6 400	18 200	
" 10	3.04 "	23.5	17 000	....	5 800	15 100	
" 10	5.00 "	23.5	....	....	11 000	15 800	
" 10	8.10 "	23.5	....	....	10 450	13 100	
" 10	9.05 "	23.5	13 700	....	8 300	8 900	
" 10	11.00 "	23.5	....	....	4 500	12 220	
" 11	1.00 A.M.	20.0	....	....	3 490	8 550	
" 11	3.00 "	10.0	11 800	....	3 690	10 500	
" 12	10.30 "	....	45 700	42 900	....	....	
" 12	11.30 "	....	46 500	....	....	....	
" 12	12.30 P.M.	12.0	43 100	....	12 700	34 700	
" 12	2.40 "	12.0	....	....	19 050	38 600	
" 12	4.45 "	....	27 200	....	....	....	
" 12	5.00 "	12.0	....	....	7 300	36 000	
" 12	9.00 "	11.5	21 700	....	5 250	25 000	
" 12	11.00 "	12.0	....	....	4 190	17 500	
" 13	1.00 A.M.	12.0	....	....	3 110	12 050	
" 13	3.00 "	12.0	24 100	....	27 950	18 950	
" 13	5.00 "	12.0	....	....	19 200	39 000	
" 13	8.00 "	12.0	33 000	35 300	19 500	60 000	
" 13	9.00 "	....	38 700	....	....	....	
" 13	10.00 "	18.0	39 700	....	15 900	48 000	
" 13	12.00 M.	18.0	....	....	7 700	37 200	
" 13	2.00 P.M.	18.0	....	....	11 500	21 500	
" 13	4.00 "	18.0	36 500	....	20 800	54 100	
" 13	9.00 "	18.0	45 200	....	19 300	39 000	
" 13	11.00 "	18.0	....	....	15 100	18 900	
" 14	1.00 A.M.	18.0	....	....	20 500	38 500	
" 14	3.00 "	18.0	36 800	....	18 200	45 100	
" 14	5.00 "	18.0	....	....	81 500	255 000	
" 14	9.00 "	18.0	49 100	57 100	64 500	64 200	
" 14	9.00 P.M.	13.0	62 700	....	21 900	*17 000	* Application of sulphate of alumina began at 7.46 P.M.
" 14	11.00 "	13.0	61 000	....	22 600	13 200	
" 15	1.00 A.M.	13.0	....	....	17 400	15 000	
" 15	3.00 "	13.0	63 900	....	19 800	15 000	
" 15	5.30 "	13.0	....	....	24 000	32 400	
" 15	7.00 "	13.0	....	....	37 000	19 500	
" 15	9.00 "	13.0	59 700	64 500	31 700	†13 500	† Application of sulphate of alumina stopped at 9.00 A.M.
" 15	11.00 "	13.0	....	....	13 800	32 500	
" 15	1.00 P.M.	14.0	....	....	13 750	24 500	
" 15	3.00 "	13.0	24 500	....	8 500	33 750	
" 15	5.30 "	13.5	....	....	9 500	18 000	
" 17	3.30 "	18.0	26 400	....	9 400	34 500	
" 17	5.05 "	....	....	....	....	27 200	
" 17	9.00 "	18.0	18 800	....	8 900	12 500	
" 17	11.00 "	18.0	....	....	8 700	10 100	
" 18	1.00 A.M.	18.0	....	....	9 300	12 500	
" 18	3.30 "	18.0	16 100	....	11 500	11 400	
" 18	5.00 "	18.0	....	....	8 600	16 900	
" 18	9.00 "	18.0	21 200	....	21 900	18 500	
" 18	11.00 "	18.0	....	....	18 900	30 500	
" 18	1.00 P.M.	18.0	....	....	14 800	13 900	
" 18	3.00 "	18.0	19 500	10 710	15 000	9 120	
" 18	5.30 "	18.5	....	....	27 300	10 640	
" 18	9.00 "	18.0	9 200	....	8 000	17 200	
" 18	11.00 "	18.0	....	....	3 900	8 900	
" 19	1.00 A.M.	18.0	....	....	4 800	9 700	
" 19	3.00 "	18.0	12 100	....	27 800	8 400	
" 19	5.00 "	18.0	....	....	18 500	12 800	

[1] As a matter of convenience, the numbers of the bacterial samples are omitted. Samples Nos. 5809 to 5962 were collected from May 10 to 19, and samples Nos. 6150 to 6472 from May 28 to June 12.

BACTERIA PER CUBIC CENTIMETER IN THE OHIO RIVER WATER BEFORE AND AFTER TREATMENT BY THE POLARITE SYSTEM.—*Continued.*

Date.	Hour.	Rate of Filtration. Cubic Feet per Minute.	Bacteria per Cubic Centimeter.				Remarks.
			River Water.	Clay Extractor Effluent.	Jewell Effluent.	Polarite Effluent.	
1897							
May 28	3.30 P.M.	23.0	7 300	6 500	5 980	....	
" 28	6.30 "	23.5	....	10 100	6 450	4 400	
" 28	9.00 "	23.5	8 500	8 300	3 660	2 890	
" 29	1.00 A.M.	23.5	10 100	5 600	3 750	3 140	
" 29	3.00 "	23.5	6 100	9 200	3 900	3 120	
" 29	6.00 "	23.5	....	7 900	4 900	3 120	
" 29	9.00 "	23.5	6 700	7 400	5 400	3 220	
" 29	12.00 M.	23.5	....	7 100	6 500	4 950	
" 29	5.00 P.M.	23.0	8 000	8 400	6 950	5 100	
" 31	9.00 A.M.	23.5	2 890	21 000	*5 120	3 750	* Application of sulphate of alumina began at 7.51 A.M.
" 31	11.00 "	23.5	2 420	21 500	3 190	2 150	
" 31	5.00 P.M.	23.5	2 010	2 970	2 400	1 440	
" 31	8.00 "	23.5	....	3 200	2 990	1 580	
" 31	11.00 "	23.5	2 930	4 100	2 720	1 270	
June 1	2.00 A.M.	23.5	....	3 420	2 520	1 430	
" 1	5.00 "	23.5	3 600	3 710	2 420	1 350	
" 1	8.00 "	23.5	....	5 610	4 550	1 935	
" 1	11.00 "	23.5	1 580	1 650	2 720	1 750	
" 1	4.00 P.M.	23.5	1 850	2 520	†1 950	† 640	† Began application of sulphate of alumina at Polarite filter and stopped application at Jewell filter.
" 1	9.00 "	23.5	....	1 430	1 270	‡ 695	
" 1	11.00 "	23.5	1 750	1 350	1 890	1 120	
" 2	2.00 A.M.	23.5	....	1 910	1 980	1 525	
" 2	5.00 "	23.5	1 290	1 690	1 320	870	‡ Application of sulphate of alumina permanently stopped.
" 2	8.00 "	23.5	....	1 690	1 490	850	
" 2	11.30 "	23.5	2 110	2 390	1 040	650	
" 2	2.00 P.M.	23.5	....	1 620	1 540	595	
" 2	5.00 "	23.5	2 290	2 040	640	302	
" 2	8.00 "	23.5	....	1 510	715	489	
" 2	11.00 P.M.	23.5	1 950	1 310	529	451	
" 3	2.00 A.M.	23.5	....	1 840	610	258	
" 3	5.00 "	23.5	1 360	1 250	430	281	
" 3	9.00 "	23.5	....	2 090	660	385	
" 3	11.00 "	23.5	1 510	1 970	339	306	
" 3	1.30 P.M.	23.5	....	1 450	286	222	
" 3	5.00 "	23.5	1 530	1 140	301	178	
" 3	8.00 "	23.5	....	1 510	254	173	
" 3	11.00 "	23.5	1 170	1 020	219	200	
" 4	2.00 A.M.	23.5	....	1 000	241	286	
" 4	5.00 "	23.5	1 060	930	242	149	
" 4	8.30 "	23.5	....	1 580	219	191	
" 4	12.00 M.	23.5	990	950	184	319	
" 4	2.00 P.M.	23.5	....	1 950	179	125	
" 4	5.00 "	23.5	970	1 570	161	129	
" 4	8.00 "	23.5	....	2 170	151	146	
" 4	11.00 "	23.5	880	1 740	172	99	
" 5	2.00 A.M.	23.5	....	1 170	126	109	
" 5	5.00 "	23.5	860	3 180	145	87	
" 5	8.00 "	23.5	....	620	154	111	
" 5	11.00 "	23.5	650	710	157	95	
" 5	2.00 P.M.	23.5	....	620	202	153	
" 5	4.30 "	23.5	610	840	167	143	
" 7	8.30 A.M.	23.5	....	1 580	415	399	
" 7	11.00 "	23.5	790	890	237	223	
" 7	1.30 P.M.	23.5	....	690	194	181	
" 7	5.00 "	23.5	670	870	190	103	
" 7	8.00 "	23.5	....	1 520	152	141	
" 7	11.00 "	23.5	660	1 420	144	108	
" 8	2.00 A.M.	23.5	....	850	117	108	
" 8	5.00 "	23.5	780	910	93	81	
" 8	11.00 "	23.5	550	1 970	163	....	
" 8	4.30 P.M.	23.5	610	1 740	§123	53	§ Agitated and drained water from surface of sand layer at 1.25 P.M.
" 8	8.00 "	23.5	....	990	118	87	
" 8	11.00 "	23.5	610	1 090	96	74	
" 9	2.00 A.M.	23.5	....	1 420	97	53	

BACTERIA PER CUBIC CENTIMETER IN THE OHIO RIVER WATER BEFORE AND AFTER TREATMENT BY THE POLARITE SYSTEM.—*Concluded.*

Date.	Hour.	Rate of Filtration. Cubic Feet per Minute.	Bacteria per Cubic Centimeter.				Remarks.
			River Water.	Clay Extractor Effluent.	Jewell Effluent.	Polarite Effluent.	
1897							
June 9	5.00 A.M.	23.5	570	1 310	104	58	
" 9	8.30 "	23.5	....	1 230	102	43	
" 9	11.00 "	23.5	390	540	88	37	
" 9	2.00 P.M.	23.5	....	930	*84	53	* Agitated and drained water from surface of sand layer at 2.00 P.M.
" 9	5.00 "	23.5	500	640	55	53	
" 9	8.00 "	23.5	....	690	39	32	
" 9	11.00 "	23.5	500	510	54	27	
" 10	2.00 A.M.	23.5	....	540	61	33	
" 10	5.00 "	23.5	510	620	55	53	
" 10	8.00 "	23.5	....	580	†59	75	† Agitated and drained water from surface of sand layer at 6.35 A.M.
" 10	11.00 "	23.5	450	970	49	41	
" 10	2.00 P.M.	23.5	....	340	57	52	‡ Agitated and drained water from surface of sand layer at 4.51 P.M.
" 10	5.30 "	23.5	370	950	‡59	47	
" 10	8.00 "	23.5	....	1 140	37	23	§ Agitated and drained water from surface of sand layer at 9.30 P.M.
" 10	11.00 "	23.5	520	460	§60	39	
" 11	2.00 A.M.	23.5	....	450	‖45	37	‖ Agitated and drained water from surface of sand layer at 12.00 A.M.
" 11	5.00 "	23.5	530	300	¶54	27	
" 11	8.30 "	23.5	....	1 140	*59	27	
" 11	11.00 "	23.5	390	1 090	†51	30	¶ Agitated and drained water from surface of sand layer at 3.00 A.M.
" 11	2.00 P.M.	23.5	....	310	43	41	
" 11	5.00 "	23.5	530	370	47	40	* Agitated and drained water from surface of sand layer at 7.17 A.M.
" 11	8.00 "	23.5	....	300	45	32	
" 11	11.00 "	23.5	410	420	37	52	† Washed Jewell filter from below at 8.53 A.M., using 644 cubic feet of wash water.
" 12	5.00 A.M.	23.5	390	370	41	43	
" 12	7.30 "	23.5	....	450	29	26	
" 12	1.15 P.M.	23.5	....	1 050	38	28	
" 12	4.30 "	23.5	790	490	53	48	

CHAPTER XV.

INVESTIGATIONS OF THE WATER COMPANY FROM APRIL TO JULY, 1897, AND A RECORD AND DISCUSSION OF THE RESULTS ACCOMPLISHED IN CONNECTION THEREWITH.

THE status of the problem of the purification of the Ohio River water, for the water supply of the city of Louisville, on March 10, 1897, when it was decided that the Water Company should conduct further investigations along this line, and independent of the companies previously associated in the tests, may be briefly stated as follows:

1. The Warren, Jewell, Western Gravity, and Western Pressure Systems, in the form in which they were tested, were not capable of purifying the Ohio River water in a practicable manner, for the following principal reasons:

a. The absence of suitable provisions to allow the suspended matters to subside by gravity caused the use of coagulating chemicals in amounts which made their use expensive to an excessive degree, and which were objectionable with regard to the quality of the filtered water.

b. The absence of suitable settling basins to allow subsidence (sedimentation) to be employed to its economical limits caused, at times of muddy water in the river, so much suspended matter to pass on to the filter, that in at least one case the filter was unable to purify enough water to wash it properly; and in the case of the best filters, it would be necessary in practice to provide reserve filters, with an area of 65 to 75 per cent. of those normally in service. The cost of construction and of operation at irregular, but unknown, intervals, of such a large reserve portion of a plant, would increase the cost of purification very materially.

c. The absence of suitable settling basins to allow subsidence to be employed to its economical limits, would cause, at times, in practice with the best available filters, the wasting of from 25 to 35, and occasionally even a greater, per cent. of filtered water, in order to wash the filters properly. This large waste of water would call for the use of more pumping machinery, and would thus increase the cost of pumping the water which actually reached the consumers. Furthermore, the waste of filtered water, which would be used in washing the filters, and thence run into the sewer, would mean practically a corresponding waste of coagulating chemicals.

d. It was demonstrated conclusively that, owing to the very frequent and marked changes in the composition of the water in the Ohio River, it was difficult to give to the systems of purification suitable attention to guard against, on the one hand, an imperfectly purified effluent, and, on the other hand, an unnecessarily large application of coagulating chemicals, with its needless increase in the cost of chemical, and in certain objectionable results in consequence thereof. With a proper employment of subsidence, it would be much easier to operate a large system of purification satisfactorily, independent of the consideration of a large and needless reserve portion of the system.

2. The Harris Magneto-electric System was a complete failure.

3. The use of an electrolytic action upon metallic aluminum plates, such as was tried by the Harris Company in July, 1896, and investigated further by the Water Company, in August, 1896, with a view to its substitution for sulphate of alumina, as a means of securing a coagulating chemical, did not give promise of practicability, owing to its cost. This method possessed certain advantages over

sulphate of alumina, however, as was pointed out in foregoing chapters.

4. The substitution of iron plates for aluminum plates, in the electrolytic method, reduced the cost, but the results obtained in connection with the Mark and Brownell devices were so inadequate that the practicability of this method was an open question at this time.

5. The results of laboratory experiments indicated the advisability of considering other coagulating chemicals than sulphate of alumina, notably the iron compounds.

In connection with the importance of the last mentioned point, it may be added that the results of the experiments in 1884, and of more recent observations, indicated, but did not prove conclusively, that, after the removal of coarse particles by plain subsidence, the Ohio River water would require, at times, coagulation and further subsidence before economical filtration, either by the English or American type of filters, could be adopted. As was stated in the last chapter, it was decided shortly before this time to test the polarite system, in which it was claimed that no use was made of chemicals. It was learned, however, before these investigations were half completed, that this last system was impracticable.

Objects of the Investigations.

The objects of the investigations were to obtain practical information, so far as was possible on an experimental scale, and with appliances which could be made promptly available, on the following principal points:

1. The removal of mud, silt, and clay from the river water by plain subsidence (i.e., unaided by coagulating chemicals).

2. The relative economy, advantages, and disadvantages of all available coagulating chemicals, prepared by various methods (chemical and electrolytical).

3. The most economical and efficient application of coagulating chemicals to aid in the removal of the bulk of various suspended matters by subsidence.

4. The most economical and efficient application of coagulating chemicals, to aid in the rapid filtration of the water, following a partial purification by preliminary subsidence.

5. The consideration of the best method of grouping together the available information upon the foregoing points, with the view to determining the system of purification which would give at a minimum cost, an effluent of the best quality from a practical point of view.

Plan of Presentation of the Results of these Investigations.

There were two principal lines of evidence obtained during these investigations. The major portion came from experiments made with a series of devices, including settling basins, electrical and other appliances, for the preparation and application of different coagulating chemicals, and also the Jewell filter. Additional data of importance were also obtained from laboratory experiments, and from the separate operation of portions of the above-mentioned series of devices, notably those for the electrolytic production of coagulating chemicals.

The plan adopted for the presentation and discussion of the results of these investigations is as follows:

A description is first given of the devices which were employed. The conditions under which these devices were operated are next described. A detailed record of the results of analyses is then presented, followed by a summary of all the principal data obtained from the operation of these devices.

The remaining portion of the chapter, containing a discussion upon various points directly related to the above-stated objects of the investigations, is of most importance. In it use is made of such portions of the summary which precedes it as bear upon the point in question; and the results of the laboratory and other special experiments are recorded in their appropriate place in the discussion.

It will be noted that, at the close of each section of the discussion, conclusions are drawn, so far as the available information upon the point in question will permit. These conclusions, with those from other portions of the report, are grouped together as a matter of convenience in Chapter XVI.

Description of the Devices Arranged and Operated by the Water Company.

For the purpose of carrying on investigations along the several lines referred to above, use was made in so far as possible of apparatus and devices available at the pumping station. Supplementary devices were designed of such style and construction as would be convenient in carrying on this work without prolonged delays for construction, and at the same time conform to the arrangement of devices already at hand.

In order to make the results of operation comparable with those of earlier work, the system was arranged to be operated on a basis of 250,000 gallons per 24 hours (23.2 cubic feet per minute), as was the case with the other systems investigated. Except for the purpose of comparing the effects of different rates of filtration, and in some cases of increasing the amount of electrolytic treatment, this rate was maintained as nearly as possible.

The full system of devices, which were in use wholly or in part during these investigations, included the following:

1. Two circular wooden tanks of about 4000 and 1000 cubic feet capacity, respectively. These were used as settling (subsidence) basins.

2. Four wooden tanks of about 400 gallons capacity each, for the preparation of chemical solutions.

3. One electric generating plant, consisting of a 50-H.P. steam-engine, and a 20-kilowatt dynamo. (See Chapter XIII.)

4. Four electrolytic cells for the preparation of coagulants electrolytically. (See Chapters X and XIII.)

5. Four sets of metal electrodes, two of iron and two of aluminum.

6. The settling chamber and filter of the Jewell System of purification. (See Chapters IV and V.)

7. Necessary pumps, piping, valves, and meters, to allow the desired operations and observations.

This system of devices, or portions thereof, was arranged at various times in a manner to permit several different ways of operation, as indicated below:

1. River water was admitted directly to the inlet of the Jewell settling chamber; and various coagulants were applied at the inlet or the outlet of this chamber, as desired.

2. River water was admitted at the bottom of the large basin (basin No. 1), removed from the top of this basin, and pumped into the bottom of basin No. 2. Thence it was removed from the top of basin No. 2, and pumped into the Jewell settling chamber. Different coagulants were applied at the inlet to basin No. 2, and the inlet to the Jewell settling chamber, or at only one of these places, as desired.

3. In this case the use of basin No. 2 was omitted, and the water passed from basin No. 1 directly to the Jewell settling chamber. Coagulants were applied at the inlet to basin No. 1 (chemicals only), and at the inlet or outlet of the Jewell settling chamber, as desired.

A more detailed description of the various devices is next presented.

Settling Basins.

Basin No. 1.—This was a circular pine tank, placed in the house formerly occupied by the Western Systems, and had the following inside dimensions: Diameter at the bottom, 17.0 feet; diameter at the top, 16.33 feet; and height, 19.0 feet. Its total capacity, and average working capacity were 4110 and 4000 cubic feet, respectively. The staves and the bottom of the tank were 3 inches in thickness. It was held together by 13 iron bands, varying in width from 4 inches to 2 inches, and each 0.125 inch thick. The lowest band was at the bottom of the tank, and above it the successive bands were placed at distances apart increasing from 1 foot at the bottom to 3 feet at the top.

The 4-inch inlet pipe entered at the side, about 2.5 feet above the bottom, and extended into the tank a distance of about 8 feet. The flow of water was regulated by a gate valve placed on the inlet pipe outside the tank, supplemented by a single-seated check valve, operated by a float on the inside of the tank. In front of the mouth of the inlet pipe, which lay horizontally, was a small baffle plate, distant about 3 inches, arranged with the view to breaking the current of water. The 4-inch outlet pipe was connected to the tank about 15 inches from the top, and on the same side as the inlet pipe.

Connections were made for draining into the sewer through an 8-inch opening in the bottom of the tank at one side. During operation this opening to the sewer was closed by a plug. The bottom of the tank was nearly level, and it was necessary to use a stream of water from a hose, and a broom, to remove the accumulation of sediment.

Applications of aniline dyes, and of caustic soda, were made to the water as it entered the basin, and tests were made to note the appearance of the chemicals at the outlet. The results of these tests, to learn the way in which the water passed through this basin, are summarized just beyond, together with corresponding results from the other settling basins.

Basin No. 2.—This basin was made by repairing the tank formerly used as the Western gravity filter. (See Chapter V.) The inside dimensions were as follows: Diameter at the bottom, 10.0 feet; diameter at the top, 9.5 feet; and height, 14.0 feet. Its total capacity, and average working capacity were 1045 and 1000 cubic feet, respectively.

The 4-inch inlet pipe was connected to the side of the tank by a flange joint, 2.0 feet above the bottom. A 4-inch pipe, which was connected to the tank on the opposite side from the inlet, and 2.5 feet below the top, formed the outlet. There were no baffle plates or other devices in this tank to assist in making uniform the displacement of water. A 3-inch pipe was connected to an opening in the bottom, to allow drainage to the sewer. The sediment on the bottom was removed by a stream of water from a hose and by a broom.

The results of the application of chemicals to the water, in order to learn the manner in which the water passed through this basin, are summarized beyond, with corresponding results from the other basins.

Jewell Settling Chamber. — This chamber has already been described in full in Chapter IV. It was a closed compartment cylindrical in form, 6.79 feet high and 13.5 feet in diameter, inside dimensions, having a capacity of 879 cubic feet. It was used without modifications in all operations up to June 19. On this date wooden boxes were inserted to cover the portions of the inlet and outlet pipes lying within the chamber. The end of the inlet pipe was enclosed in a box, so that the water entered the chamber at the bottom instead of 1.55 feet above the bottom as formerly, as the sides and front of the box were 3 inches above the floor of the chamber. By means of wooden framing the outlet pipe (at the top of the chamber) was closed in, leaving an opening 6 inches wide and 24 inches long, about diametrically opposite to the inlet pipe. The water passed through this opening into the portion enclosed by the wooden partitions, and thence to the filter, by means of the regular central pipe which served as an outlet to the settling chamber.

The results of the application of chemicals to the water (after the above stated modification was made), in order to learn the manner in which the water passed through the chamber, are summarized in the next table, together with corresponding results from basins Nos. 1 and 2.

TABLE SHOWING A SUMMARY OF THE RESULTS OF THE TESTS OF THE DISPLACEMENT OF WATER ON ITS PASSAGE THROUGH SETTLING BASINS NOS. 1 AND 2, AND THE JEWELL SETTLING CHAMBER.

	Basin No. 1.	Basin No. 2.	Jewell Settling Basin.
Normal capacity in cubic feet.......	4 000	1 000	879
Time of filling at the regular rate (23.2 cubic feet per minute)......	2h. 52m.	43m.	38m.
Time elapsing between application of chemicals at the inlet and first appearance at the outlet...	39m.	4m.	6m
Time elapsing between application of chemicals at the inlet and maximum appearance at the outlet....	1h. 10m.	10m.	18m.
Percentage which chemical appearing at the end of "time of filling" was of maximum which appeared	24	33	17
Time elapsing between application of chemicals at the inlet and appearance of 50 per cent. at the outlet........................	2h. 49m.	30m.	22m.

Application of Chemical Solutions to Secure Coagulation.

For preparing chemical solutions four wooden tanks, each of about 400 gallons capacity, were used. They were arranged in pairs, one above the other, and the corresponding upper and lower tanks were used for the same kind of chemicals. Solutions were prepared in the upper tanks, and admitted to the corresponding lower tanks as required, the lower tanks serving for pump wells and storage basins.

Pumps.—In addition to the small pump used by the Jewell Company in 1895–96 (described in Chapter II), a small duplex pump, having the following principal dimensions, was placed in operation: Diameter of steam cylinder, 1.125 inches; diameter of water cylinder, 2 inches; length of stroke, 2.75 inches.

Piping.—Each pump was provided with two suction pipes, 0.75 inch in diameter, which reached to within 1 inch of the bottom of the lower tanks. By this arrangement the pumps could be supplied with solution from either tank. For delivery pipes, use was made of such small piping as was available at the pumping station. In the case of the old (simplex) pump, the 0.75-inch heavy lead pipe used in the Jewell System was utilized. It was connected to the inlet pipe of the settling chamber, at a point about 6 feet from the chamber, or lowered about 3 feet into the pipe leading from the top of the settling chamber to the filter, as it was desired to apply the chemicals before or after the water had passed through the settling chamber, respectively. The delivery pipe from the new (duplex) pump was connected to the inlet to basin No. 1, or to the inlet to basin No. 2, as desired. It was mainly made up of 0.5-inch iron pipe, but for connection to the inlet to basin No. 1 about 40 feet of 0.75-inch iron pipe were also used.

Kinds of Chemicals.—In connection with the operation of the devices under consideration five different chemicals, as follows, were used at various times:

1. Sulphate of alumina (two different lots).
2. Persulphate of iron.
3. Potash alum.
4. Protosulphate of iron (copperas).
5. Caustic soda.

A number of other chemicals were used in laboratory experiments, as will appear in a subsequent portion of this chapter.

The composition of the above chemicals is given in the next section. No special features are to be noted here, except in the case of the persulphate of iron. In making solutions (from 0.3 to 0.9 per cent., according to the quantity to be applied) of this chemical in filtered water, it was difficult to dissolve it. It was found, however, that a solution could be made best by adding, successively, small quantities of water to the substance at the outset, and decanting the solution into another tank. Hot water could not be used, because it decomposed the chemical, and with cold water there was also a tendency for the iron to form the sticky hydrate, which retarded the solution of the portion covered by it. This chemical contained considerable material which was completely insoluble (see the analysis below), and it was necessary to remove this by straining through cloth, because it cut the fittings of the pumps and meters. There was also enough free sulphuric acid (2.73 per cent.) in the persulphate of iron to corrode the brass and iron pipes and fittings very rapidly. It is possible, however, to obtain a commercial product of this kind which does not possess these disadvantages, except perhaps a small amount of insoluble matter.

In the case of the potash alum, which contained a small quantity of ammonia, all quantities are calculated, as was the case in 1896, as sulphate of alumina, on the basis that sixteen parts of the former equal ten parts of the latter.

Composition of Chemicals.—The two lots of sulphate of alumina, and the lot of persulphate of iron, were analyzed with the following results:

PERCENTAGE COMPOSITION OF COAGULATING CHEMICALS.

	Sulphate of Alumina.		Persulphate of Iron.
	Lot No. 1	Lot No. 2.	
Matter insoluble in water	0.22	0.06	5.56
Available alumina (Al_2O_3)	15.96	19.64	0.00
Sulphuric acid (SO_3)	34.26	36.85	55.08
Oxide of iron (Fe_2O_3)	0.00	Trace	34.90
Lime (CaO)	0.56	0.06	0.00
Water (H_2O)	49.00	43.39	4.46

The potash alum was of high grade and had about 10.7 and 34.0 per cent. of alumina and sulphuric acid, respectively.

The copperas crystals were also of a good quality, and contained 57.55 and 28.78 per cent. of iron oxide and sulphuric acid, respectively.

Analyses of the caustic soda showed that it contained 73.4 per cent. of sodium oxide.

Devices for the Application of Electrolytic Treatment to Secure Coagulation.

Two electrolytically prepared coagulants (hydrate of aluminum and hydrate of iron) were used at various times. Each was prepared by the electrolytic decomposition of electrodes of the respective metal. For the purpose of preparing these hydrates, electrodes in the form of manifolds of plates were placed in closed iron cells, and the river water and electric current passed through them. The following devices, all of which were placed in the house formerly occupied by the Warren System, were used:

Generating Plant.—The electric generating plant used in connection with the Mark and Brownell devices was employed for generating the necessary electric current.

The dynamo was rated at 400 amperes and 50 volts, but could be operated as high as 450 amperes safely for short periods. For a full description of this engine and dynamo see Chapter XIII. As already described, the electric current was regulated by means of a field rheostat. In order to maintain the resistance necessary to balance the potential of the machine, when operating with low amperage, a large rheostat was inserted on the main circuit. At the close of these investigations, Aug. 1, 1897, tests were made of the engine and dynamo, with the following results:

RESULT OF TESTS OF ELECTRIC GENERATING PLANT.

ENGINE TEST.

Indicated Horse Power.	Efficiency = Brake Horse Power. / Indicated Horse Power.
50	95 per cent.
37.5	93 "
25.0	85 "
12.0	70 "

DYNAMO TEST.

Electric Horse Power.	Efficiency = Brake Horse Power. / Electric Horse Power.
28	*80 per cent.
21	85 "
14	85 "
7	85 "

* This result is abnormally low, due to sparking during the test, caused by a plate in the commutator becoming slightly loosened.

Owing to the fact that the engine (50 I.H.P.) was a much larger machine than the dynamo (28 E.H.P.), and was accordingly at all times operated considerably below the point of maximum efficiency; and, further, owing to the fact that at times the entire plant was too large to give economically the small amount of electric power required for the treatment of fairly clear water, the combined efficiency of the engine and dynamo was very low in some cases. In practice, however, a generating plant would be arranged in several units, and such portions of it used as would furnish the electric current most economically. Under such circumstances the above tests show that 80 per cent. of the indicated horse power at the engine could be obtained as electric power. This agrees fairly well with the results of good modern practice.

Electrolytic Cells.—Four electrolytical cells, with covers, were used in this work. Cells Nos. 1 and 2 were those of the Mark and Brownell devices, and have been fully described in Chapter XIII. Cells Nos. 3 and 4 were two of the large cells of the Harris Company, with whom arrangements for their use were made. These cells have been described in Chapter X. Several changes in all of these cells were made, as follows:

Changes in Cells Nos. 1 and 2.—These duplicate cells were 30 inches in diameter, had a capacity of 35.2 cubic feet, and were not insulated on the inner walls. The special distributing devices, attached to the inner side of the dome at the top, were removed, and, in each case, the 4-inch inlet pipe was connected by a flange joint to the center of the dome-shaped cover. The original outlets on the side were closed by plugs, and the 3-inch opening at the apex of the conical bottom in each cell was used as an outlet.

Changes in Cells Nos. 3 and 4.—These duplicate cells were removed from the Harris house to a position by the side of cells Nos. 1 and 2. They were 35.5 inches in diameter, and had a capacity of 28 cubic feet. The insulating rubber linings, and the covers of a special casting, with magnets resting upon them, were removed. A slightly arched and circular iron plate, to which the 4-inch inlet pipe was attached in the center, served as a cover in each case. A wooden frame was built in the bottom, so that the electrodes when placed upon it reached within 0.25 inch of the flange to which the cover was attached. There was tapped in each cover a hole, to which a 0.25-inch pipe, with a pet-cock, was attached, in order to allow the escape from time to time of accumulated gases. The 3-inch opening in the bottom of the cone was connected with a 4-inch pipe, which served as an outlet and waste pipe.

Electrodes.—New electrodes, numbered the same as the cells in which they were placed, were constructed, and used exclusively in the tests described in this chapter. Electrodes Nos. 1 and 3 were each made of a manifold of wrought-iron plates 0.125-inch thick. Electrodes Nos. 2 and 4 were made of aluminum, to duplicate Nos. 1 and 3.

In the method of construction these four electrodes were identical. The size of the cells used necessitated slightly different forms, however. Each manifold contained fifty-six plates.

Size of Plates.—Electrodes Nos. 1 and 2 were made of plates 50 inches long. In order to fit the cell the widths of the plates varied from 24 to 12 inches, averaging 20.4 inches. The total area of one side of the plates was 56,000 square inches, and the cross section of the electrolyte was 55,400 square inches. When new, these sets of plates weighed 1780 and 674 pounds, respectively. Electrodes Nos. 3 and 4 were made of plates 36 inches long. The widths varied from 30 to 22 inches, and averaged 27.4 inches. The total area of one side of these plates was 56,200 square inches, and the cross section of the electrolyte was 55,500 square inches. When new, these sets of plates weighed 1824 and 682 pounds, respectively.

Formation of Manifolds.—All of the four manifolds were formed alike. The plates were held together by six 1-inch iron bolts, and the desired distance between the plates, 0.25 inch, was maintained by the use of washers, or separators. These bolts were set as far to the edge of the sets as the width of the outer plates would allow. The plates were so thin, however, that they buckled badly, and it was necessary to insert many small pieces of insulating material between them at different places. In order to relieve this difficulty to some extent, 0.5-inch bolts with separators were placed in the corners of the electrodes, at the same time that the other changes were made, and which were completed May 30.

One of the upper corners of each plate was cut off, and the plates arranged in the manifold so that the cut and uncut corners came alternately on each side. To the uncut corners on each upper side brass lugs were riveted. The cables carrying the electric current were soldered to these lugs.

Extensions of six of the plates of each set, with openings which coincided along the center line, were arranged as lifting lugs to aid in handling the electrodes. When placed in the cells the electrodes rested upon a wooden framework arranged in the bottom. The space between the edge of the plates and the uninsulated inner wall of the cell ranged from 0.5 to 3 inches, and averaged about 2 inches. The outer portion of the framework at the bottom was solid, so that there was no opportunity for water to pass downward through a cell, except through the spaces between the plates of the electrodes.

Insulation of Electrodes.—Owing to inability to secure, without long delay, hard rubber fittings for the insulation of the electrodes, it was decided to proceed as follows:

The iron bolts by which the manifold of plates was held together were covered with steam hose, and circular separators of vulcanized fiber 0.25 inch thick were placed on the bolts between each pair of adjoining plates. This method of insulation proved to be a failure, owing to a certain, but not accurately known, portion of the current passing through the cell on the fittings. This portion of the current was consequently wasted, so far as the treatment of the water is concerned, and the greater part of the results obtained with these devices during the month of April, is of very little or no value. The cause of this failure was the presence of small particles of metal in the hose or the fiber, or both. An arc was probably formed between the plates, and the metallic particles and molten metal were deposited in the intervening space. Repeated attempts, with only partial success, were made to remedy these difficulties by the liberal use of insulating tape and paint on the hose, and the removal and repair of fibers showing evidence of metallic particles. Wooden bolts were also substituted for the iron ones. But, as the electrodes continued in service, it was found that the vulcanized fiber separators absorbed water so that they swelled to a degree that caused the electrodes to lose their original form, and stripped off the heads of the wooden bolts. During the first week in May it was decided to abandon the original insulating appliances, and procure an entire set of hard rubber fittings to cover the iron bolts, and to separate the plates. On the large bolts the new separators were 3 inches in diameter, and on the small bolts, 2 inches. These changes, which proved to be thoroughly satisfactory, were completed on May 30. In the modified form the fittings weighed about the same for each set, 84 pounds.

Electrical Connections.—The main electrical circuit was the same, for the most part, as in the case of those devices described in Chapter XIII. Near the switchboard there was placed a rheostat, by which the current passing through the cells could be more satisfactorily regulated. The circuit was arranged so that any, or all, of the cells could be connected at once, and the direction of the current through any of the cells could be promptly reversed.

Connections with the electrodes in cells Nos. 1 and 2 were made through two openings filled with wooden plugs, through which iron binding posts were driven. The main circuit was connected to the outer binding posts, and to the inner binding posts the cables attached to the lugs riveted to alternate plates were connected. Similar arrangements were made for connecting the main circuit with the electrodes in cells Nos. 3 and 4, except that the connection through the openings in the cells were brass binding posts, placed in hard rubber stuffing boxes.

Modification of Electrode No. 1.—In order to give greater treatment to the water than the original form allowed, electrode No. 1 was changed, on July 9, into two electrodes in series. This was accomplished by dividing the set in halves, electrically, and connecting one-half of the plates on one side to half of the plates on the diagonally opposite side. No changes were made other than in the wiring, as described.

Piping.—As the iron electrodes (Nos. 1 and 3) were never used in connection with the filter at the same time as the aluminum electrodes (Nos. 2 and 4), the inlet and outlet pipes of each pair of cells (Nos. 1 and 2 and Nos. 3 and 4) were branches of the same main pipe, respectively. The inlet and outlet pipes were 4 inches in diameter, except that the outlet pipes were reduced to 3 inches at the connections with the cells. Further, the outlet pipe of each cell was itself branched, so that by suitable valves and pipe connections it could also serve as a waste pipe to the sewer.

When basin No. 1 was in service the water as it left that basin could be pumped through either cell No. 3 or cell No. 4, on its way to basin No. 2. Similarly, as the water was pumped from basin No. 2 to the Jewell settling chamber, it could pass through either cell No. 1 or cell No. 2. Cells Nos. 3 and 4 could not be used when basins Nos. 1 and 2 were out of service. At such times river water could be taken from the old Warren inlet pipe (after slight changes) and passed through either cell No. 1 or cell No. 2, on its way to the Jewell settling chamber. During the last of the tests, after July 9, the piping was arranged so that the water could be pumped from basin No. 1 through either cell No. 3 or 4, and then through No. 1 or 2 to the Jewell settling chamber. A further modification at this time, as stated above, allowed the passage of river water from the old Warren inlet directly through cell No. 1 or No. 2, and to the Jewell settling chamber.

When chemical solutions were applied to the water prior to filtration, by-passes and valves made the electrical appliances independent of the other devices. At such times special experiments were usually made with these appliances, and water for that purpose was taken from the main through the old Warren inlet pipe, located by the side of cell No. 1.

The Jewell Filter.

It was arranged with the O. H. Jewell Filter Company to make use of the Jewell filter, which was the only one remaining at the pumping station. No modifications were made in this filter, which has been fully described in Chapter V.

Pipes, Valves, Pumps, and Meters.

From the foregoing account of the ways in which the several devices could be connected, a general idea may be obtained as to the arrangement of the piping. Further details are not of importance. But it may be recalled here that a majority of the piping was 4 inches in diameter. A small portion was 5 inches, and for a short distance from the outlets of the electrolytical cells the diameter was 3 inches. Suitable valves, meters, and gauges were placed where convenience required.

Owing to the fact that the elevation of the Jewell filter was very nearly as high as that of basins Nos. 1 and 2, and that the water passed through some 350 feet of old pipe, with quite a number of turns, valves, meters, and electrodes, it was necessary to set up pumps on the pipe between basins Nos. 1 and 2 and basin No. 2 and the Jewell System. These two pumps had capacities of about 250,000 and 400,000 gallons per 24 hours, under the pressure used, respectively, and were ones which the Water Company had on hand at the time.

Adaptation to Existing Conditions in the Construction and Arrangement of These Devices.

In the consideration of the construction and arrangement of the devices which have been described in the foregoing pages, it must be borne clearly in mind that they were designed to enable as much practical information as possible to be obtained in connection with other appliances at hand, and were not intended to be illustrative of the best forms for adoption in practice. They were arranged to yield data, with a minimum expenditure of time and money, which would show the lines which it would be most practicable to follow on a large scale.

There were many features in the devices which cannot be taken as models of good practice, although they served their purpose in this work. Thus, at the outset of these tests, it was known that the settling basins were all far too small to give the most economical and efficient results; the electrical appliances were not well arranged to meet the requirements of all kinds of river water. The question of closed electrolytical cells as compared with open channels or conduits, the thickness of metal plates, the water space between the plates, and the manner of fastening together and insulating them, were all open questions; and the desirability of testing filters with different depths and sizes of sand was unquestioned. In the discussion following the results of these tests, mention will be made in several instances of methods for securing practicable results from fundamental principles established by these tests.

DESCRIPTION OF THE CONDITIONS AND METHODS OF OPERATION OF THE DEVICES ARRANGED BY THE WATER COMPANY.

The principal features concerning the general operation of these devices during the several periods from April 5 to July 24, inclusive, 1897, are as follows:

Composition of the River Water.—It is during the period of the year covered by these tests that the Ohio River water contains the largest amount of very minute clay particles, which, although less in total weight than the heavy mud of the winter freshets, make the water most difficult to clarify and to purify economically. For further reference to the composition of the river water during the spring and early summer, in addition to comments beyond, see Chapter I.

Interruption of Tests.—These investigations were not continuous, owing to the fact that the polarite system was tested during this period, according to earlier arrangements. This caused the regular operations of the devices of the Water Company to be suspended from May 10 to 19, and from May 28 to June 12. On account of the abnormal clearness of the river water, the operation of all the devices was not resumed after the close of the polarite tests until June 19, except the electrical appliances, which were tested almost constantly from May 30 to June 30. No other abnormal interruptions occurred, except from May 3 to 5, when it was impossible to obtain river water which had not settled for several days in the force mains.

Different Provisions for Subsidence.—Three settling basins, already described, were used in different ways during these tests, according to the amount and character of the suspended matter in the river water and the nature of the point under investigation. The Jewell settling chamber was used without exception. Basins Nos. 1 and 2 were both used on 119 different runs, as follows: April 11 to May 28, 73 runs; June 20 to 22, 5 runs; June 24 to July 8, 41 runs. From July 14 to 15, and 16 to 19, basin No. 1 was used without basin No. 2.

Comparison of Different Coagulants. — A comparison was made of the efficiency and economy of hydrate of iron, obtained electrolytically, and from commercial sulphates; and of hydrate of aluminum prepared electrolytically, and from commercial sulphates. So far as practicable the several coagulants were applied to practically the same water, so as to obtain comparable results.

From earlier statements, it will be recalled that faulty insulation of electrodes during April caused the electrolytic results of that month to be of uncertain value. The remodeled electrodes were tested, independent of the filter, from May 30 to June 20.

Quantity of Coagulants. — For obvious reasons the investigations were conducted with the view to determining the *minimum* quantity of coagulants which would yield an effluent of satisfactory purity. In doing so it was necessary of course, at times, to establish definitely that certain quantities were insufficient. At such times (usually short runs with the filter) the effluent was unsatisfactory; and, in a measure, the results were negative, although they possessed a positive value.

Application of Coagulants.—In studying the optimum method of application of the different coagulating chemicals, they were applied so as to give a range of conditions with regard both to the period of coagulation and subsidence, and to the period of coagulation prior to filtration, in the case of waters of different character. This range was limited by the capacity and facilities of the settling basins, already described.

Filtration.—The Jewell filter was operated, in general terms, in a manner similar to that described in Chapter VII, except that there was no controller on the outlet pipe, and the above-mentioned conditions of operation called for some changes at times in the rate of filtration, and frequency of washing, as noted below.

Rate of Filtration.—As a rule the rate of filtration was kept as nearly as possible at 250,000 gallons per 24 hours, or 94 million gallons per acre daily. This is equivalent to 23.2 cubic feet per minute, but it was the custom to adjust the valves to give 23.5 cubic feet. Owing to the fact that the electrical appliances were too small to furnish sufficient electric current to treat the water properly when in a very turbid condition, it was necessary at times to reduce the rate of flow of water through the electrolytic cells, and, consequently, the rate of filtration. On several occasions the rate of filtration was reduced for this reason to about 16 cubic feet per minute.

Early in these tests it was found that a larger amount of coagulating chemicals was required just after washing the filter than was the case during the major portion of the run, providing the same rate was maintained. With the view to reducing the amount of coagulating chemicals to a point sufficient for the latter portion of a run, the rate of filtration was reduced several times to about one-half the normal, for a short period just after washing the filter.

Length of Runs.—While the regular custom of allowing a run to continue until the available head was exhausted or the quality of the effluent failed prevailed for the most part, there were a number of occasions when a comparison of coagulants required runs of only about 1000 cubic feet of effluent. These short runs served the special purpose for which they were made, and, therefore, are placed in the records, although they were abnormal so far as length of run is concerned.

Washing the Filter.—Surface agitation of the sand layer was employed whenever it was practicable. In all cases of washing, it was carried to a point where the wash-water flowing to the sewer was comparatively clear. The filter was always washed after short special runs, regardless of their length.

Delays in Operation.—In addition to the short delays incidental to such work, there were two sources of extended delays. The first occurred several times in April, when repairs of the electrodes were necessary. A far greater cause for delay was the change of water in all the settling basins in service which held treated water, when there was a change either in the rate or kind of treatment to coagulate the water. It is estimated that this necessary cause of delay covered about 28 per cent. of the time devoted to the actual tests.

Records of Operation, and Samples for Analysis.—In this respect the same general plan which was adopted in the tests of 1895–96 was followed.

As a matter of convenience, and for the sake of clearness, the records of operation, with summaries of analytical results, are presented in the next section by runs listed in serial number, rather than by days.

The general operations are divided into three periods, viz:

Period No. 1, which extended from April 5 to May 10, the beginning of the tests of the polarite system.

Period No. 2, which covered the time occupied by the changes made in the polarite system.

Period No. 3, which extended from the close of the tests of the polarite system until the conclusion of the experimental work.

In order to facilitate a more thorough understanding of the conditions of operation, and the summary of results beyond, the following outline of the important special features of each period is presented.

Period No. 1.

This period extended from the beginning of operations with these devices on April 5 to the time when the polarite system was ready for operations on May 9. From April 5 to 8 operations were continuous, day and night. On April 8, 9 and 10, operations were from 7.00 A.M. to 6.00 P.M. on each day. Continuous day and night operations were begun again on April 11, and continued throughout the period. From April 16, 2.00 P.M., to April 20, 4.00 P.M., and from April 24, 2.44 P.M., to April 26, 6.20 A.M., operations were suspended, to allow work in repairing the insulation of the electrodes. The system was closed down on May 1, and from May 3 to 5, inclusive, attention was given to laboratory experiments, as the main pumping engines were not in service, and it was not possible to obtain river water which had not been affected by a varying period of subsidence in the reservoir and pipes. Operations were begun again on May 6, and were continued till 5.12 A.M. on May 9, when the filter was put in shape for use with the polarite system.

The river water at the beginning of this period was about of a normal character, the suspended solids averaging about 350 parts per million. A slight rise increased the suspended matter on April 9 to about 840 parts per million. From this date to May 1 the water gradually became clearer, the suspended solids on the latter date averaging only 77 parts. From May 6 to 9 the suspended solids ranged from 453 to 301 parts per million.

During this period 66 (Nos. 1 to 66) runs were made. From April 5 to 10, including the first 14 runs, operations were with the original Jewell System, in an unmodified form. Attention was devoted to a comparison of the efficiency of the hydrates of iron and aluminum obtained from persulphate of iron and sulphate of alumina, respectively. The first 6 runs were without agitation of the surface of the filter. After this the use of surface agitation was made a regular feature in all runs continued to their normal length, providing the effluent remained satisfactory.

On April 11 the full system of devices arranged by the Water Company was put in service. This system included the three settling basins and the Jewell filter, together with the various devices for preparing and applying the several coagulants, all of which have been described above.

Coagulants were applied in equal amounts at the inlets to basin No. 2 and the Jewell settling chamber, respectively, except on runs Nos. 53, 54, 65 and 66. On run No. 53 the entire chemical was applied at the inlet to the Jewell settling chamber, and on runs Nos. 54, 65 and 66 at the inlet to basin No. 2.

Four differently prepared coagulants were used: Electrolytically decomposed iron, electrolytically decomposed aluminum, sulphate of alumina and persulphate of iron. Explanation has already been presented of the difficulties met with in the insulation of the electrodes, and it will only be noted here that considerable uncertainty is attached to the electrolytic work during this period.

There were two leading points under consideration throughout this period.

1. Comparison of the efficiency of the four coagulants used.

2. Determination of the minimum coagulant which could be used with safety under normal conditions of operation of the system used.

Practically all of the runs were intended to throw light on the first point, and, in so far as possible, all coagulants were used on the same character of water. Of the 66 runs, 25 were made with sulphate of alumina, 10 with persulphate of iron, 20 with electrolytically decomposed aluminum, and 11 with electrolytically decomposed iron.

In regard to the second point, the rapidly changing character of the river water, and the difficulties experienced with the electrodes, interfered to a large extent with this line of investigation. Much information can be gained, however, by a comparative study of consecutive runs.

Operations were regular throughout this period, the rate of 250,000 gallons per 24 hours (23.2 cubic feet per minute) being maintained as closely as possible, except when the necessity of greater treatment than the capacity of the electrolytic plant would allow required a reduction in the rate.

Period No. 2.

This period extended from May 19 to May 26, inclusive, and included runs Nos. 67 to 87. Operations were continuous during the day and night, except for a short delay from 4.58 A.M. to 9.42 P.M. on May 21, to examine the strainer system of the Jewell filter.

The river water contained about 280 parts per million of fine suspended matter at the beginning of the period. Absence of rains caused the water to become clearer during the latter part of the period, the suspended matter decreasing to 100 parts per million.

Attention was devoted solely to the determination of the safe minimum amount of coagulant for filtration, in connection with subsidence; and for this purpose the full system of three settling basins and the filter was employed. Sulphate of alumina alone was used. It was applied in all cases at the inlet to basin No. 2. By the use of these basins, together with the chemical treatment at basin No. 2, the amount of suspended matter in the water at the top of the filter was usually kept below 100 parts per million.

As it was found that the character and the rate of clearing of the first water filtered after washing was usually the controlling feature in the consideration of the minimum amount of coagulant, several runs were stopped after the effluent had reached a fairly normal or constant character. This procedure caused a number of the runs to be very short, the object of several being accomplished with 1000 cubic feet of effluent, or less.

The principal modification of the operation was the successive use of several rates, 9, 12, 18, and 24 cubic feet per minute, in order to compare the net amounts of coagulants needed for filtration at the several rates.

Period No. 3.

This period extended from June 19 to July 24, when regular operations were finally suspended. In all 98 runs were made, Nos. 88 to 185, inclusive. Operations with the filter were suspended on July 4 and 5, and from July 10, at 5.45 P.M., to July 14, at 8.01 P.M. Attention was directed during the latter period to special laboratory tests. Aside from these delays, and some minor ones incidental to the methods of operation of the system as arranged, operations were continuous during the day and night.

Two minor rises of the river occurred during this period, causing considerable variations in the amounts of suspended matter. The range was from 66 to 711 parts per million, with an average of 320 parts.

Investigations were mainly along the following lines:

1. Comparison of efficiencies of sulphate of alumina and electrolytically decomposed iron, and a determination of their relative efficiency. Other coagulants, including persulphate of iron, in which the free acid had been neutralized with caustic soda, copperas (protosulphate of iron), alone and with caustic soda, and electrolytically decomposed aluminum, were also tried for short periods. The bulk of the work, however, was with the first two coagulants, 62 runs having been made with sulphate of alumina, and 26 with electrolytically decomposed iron.

It is to be noted that the uncertainties attached to the early electrolytic work were removed during the last of May and early part of June by the insertion of new insulating materials. On July 9 electrode No. 1 was remodeled to give double the treatment which was previously available.

2. Comparison of efficiencies of various periods of coagulation preceding filtration, and determination of minimum coagulant allowable with each. For this purpose the place of application of the last dose of chemicals was changed from time to time to the following points: Inlet to basin No. 1; inlet to basin No. 2; inlet to the Jewell settling chamber; and the outlet of the Jewell settling chamber (top of filter). For the effective period of coagulation in the several basins reference is made to the description of these basins in the early part of this chapter.

3. Investigations of the rate of clearing of the effluent following a washing of the filter. This point was studied more or less throughout the period under different rates of filtration, and with different amounts of coagulant. Several runs were made specially for this point, in which the filter was washed after the first 1000 cubic feet or so of water had been filtered.

In order to carry on these studies, use was made of basins Nos. 1 and 2, and the Jewell settling chamber and filter, together with the devices necessary to prepare and apply the various coagulants. As the river water changed in composition several times, it was necessary to modify the arrangement from time to time during the period. River water was admitted directly to the Jewell settling chamber without any preliminary subsidence on runs Nos. 88 to 91, 97 to 105, 147 to 156, 164 to 167, and 174 to 185, inclusive. Basin No. 1 only was used on runs Nos. 157 to 163, and 168 to 173, inclusive. On the other runs, Nos. 92 to 96 and 106 to 146, inclusive, basins Nos. 1 and 2 were used.

The principal points of significance in connection with the various runs are given in serial order in the following list. After the list is the section containing the several tables showing the results of the operation of these devices.

Notes on Special Features of these Runs.

Nos. 1 to 7. Comparison of efficiency of persulphate of iron and sulphate of alumina, using the original Jewell System, without agitation of surface of sand layer.

Nos. 8 to 14. Same as Nos. 1 to 7, but the surface of the sand layer was agitated whenever practicable.

No. 15. First run with new devices, including three settling basins, filter, and devices for preparing and applying coagulants. Iron plates of electrodes were new and bright.

No. 18. The filter was run dry; that is, the sand layer was so heavily loaded with suspended matter that surface agitation neither affected the rate of filtration or the character of effluent.

No. 19. Amount of applied chemicals was reduced during run, resulting shortly in failure in the character of the effluent.

No. 20. First run with aluminum electrodes. Plates were new and bright.

Nos. 20 to 23. Using aluminum electrodes. Effluent failed suddenly after from 2 to 4 hours' filtration, apparently due to accumulations of gas within the sand layer.

No. 24. Electrode No. 3 found touching wall of the cell after a short run. This was remedied, and run continued.

No. 26. Chemical pump broke down, and

lack of coagulant caused an early failure of the effluent.

No. 27. Low voltage on cell No. 3 indicated a leakage of electric current.

April 16. Repaired insulations of bolts and electrodes.

No. 32. Amount of treatment varied three times during the run.

Nos. 32 to 34. Resistance of electrodes Nos. 1 and 3 steadily falling, indicating steadily increasing leakage of electric current.

No. 42. Electrode No. 3 found short circuited after this run.

April 25, 26. Removed iron bolts from electrodes and put in wooden ones. Cleaned separators.

No. 44. First run with repaired electrodes. Plates had been exposed to the air, and were therefore heavily rusted.

No. 54. Period of service was shortened by closing work for the day.

No. 70. This is the only run recorded in which the hydrate came through the sand layer into the filtered water so as to be plainly visible.

May 30. Iron electrodes reassembled with iron bolts and hard rubber insulators, and put in service to study the rate of decomposition of the metal.

June 3. Aluminum electrodes reassembled with iron bolts and hard rubber insulators, and put in service to study the rate of decomposition of the metal.

No. 91. Several changes in the rate of treatment and filtration were made during this run.

No. 112. Failed to drain settling basins after No. 111. This run was therefore affected by previous rate of treatment.

No. 127. Shortened the run to work with copperas.

Nos. 133 to 135. Used old aluminum electrodes, which were very heavily coated with oxide. Direction of electric current was reversed several times.

Nos. 138, 139. Application of caustic soda removed accumulations of organic matter in the sand layer, and carried them into the effluent.

No. 147. Began to use remodeled electrode No. 1.

No. 149. Failure to supply coagulant caused an early failure of the effluent.

No. 156. Period of service was shortened by closing work for the day.

Results Accomplished by the Devices Arranged and Operated by the Water Company.

The results of chemical analyses of the river water after treatment by these methods and devices are presented in a series of tables, in which all of the data obtained with the use of each coagulant is presented separately. With regard to the collection and notation of samples, methods of analysis, and significance of results, reference is made to Chapter VIII, where the corresponding data of 1895–96 were presented. For detailed information concerning the composition of the untreated river water, the tables of analyses in Chapter I may be consulted; and the amounts of suspended matter, and numbers of bacteria which on numerous occasions were determined in samples collected as the water left the several settling basins, are recorded in a subsequent portion of this section.

With regard to features in the chemical composition of the effluents, as shown by special analyses, a full account of these matters will be found in the discussion of results, which is the closing portion of this chapter. At this place it may be briefly stated that in the case of sulphate of alumina, persulphate of iron, and protosulphate of iron, the increase in carbonic acid and sulphate of lime (incrusting constituents) in the effluent, was proportional to the decrease in alkalinity of the river water by the respective treatments. With sulphate of alumina, and persulphate of iron, none of the applied chemicals in an undecomposed form appeared in the filtered water, and there was no diminution in the oxygen dissolved in the water. But when copperas (protosulphate of iron) was used, the carbonic acid in the water retarded the oxidation of the ferrous compounds by the dissolved oxygen, so that when this chemical alone was used, some of the iron passed into the effluent. The use of caustic soda in connection with copperas changed the carbonic acid to carbonate of soda, and, under these conditions, copperas could be satisfactorily applied as a coagulant, provided the amount applied was not in excess of that capable of oxidation by the constituents of the water. It caused a reduction for each grain per gallon of about 0.5 part of dissolved oxygen, which was required in order to convert the iron into a completely insoluble form. In passing, it may be noted, that the application of caustic soda caused a marked removal of the organic matter accumulated on the sand grains of the filter, as shown by the analyses. In those cases where common alum crystals were used as a coagulant the normal free ammonia in the effluents is estimated because the coagulant contained some ammonia.

Concerning the special chemical features of the effluent obtained with electrolytic treatment, there were no additional carbonic acid, incrusting constituents, or dissolved metal in the water as it left the filter under ordinary conditions. With aluminum electrodes this was true under all conditions; but with iron electrodes the decomposed iron had to be oxidized by dissolved oxygen, in order to convert it into a completely insoluble form. As in the case of copperas, therefore, the electrolytic iron treatment could not be safely employed beyond a certain amount, which was limited by the oxygen dissolved in the water. Otherwise, dissolved iron would pass into the filtered water.

Microscopical analyses were not made regularly, but from occasional examinations of the effluents, it may be stated that, as was the case during 1895–96, the effluents were practically free from microscopical organisms.

The results of the bacterial analyses of the effluent with each coagulant are presented in the set of tables following the chemical results, and are given in the same form as was used and explained in Chapter VIII. There are no special features worthy of comment in this connection, except perhaps to point out the fact that, repeatedly, turbid effluents were found to give a fairly satisfactory bacterial efficiency. In no case, however, was an admissible bacterial efficiency obtained when the coagulation of the water passing on to the sand layer was lacking to a marked degree.

These analytical results are summarized by runs, together with a record of the kind, method of application, and quantity of coagulating teatment, and of quantities of water treated, with corresponding periods of time, at the close of this section. A full explanation of this summary precedes it.

RESULTS OF CHEMICAL ANALYSES OF THE EFFLUENT OF THE JEWELL FILTER WITH SULPHATE OF ALUMINA.

(Parts per Million.)

Serial Number.	Collected.		Temperature. Degrees C.	Degree of Clearness.	Color.	Oxygen Consumed.	Nitrogen as Albuminoid Ammonia.			Nitrogen as Free Ammonia.	Nitrogen as Nitrites.	Nitrogen as Nitrates.	Chlorine.	Residue on Evaporation.			Fixed Residue after Ignition.			Alkalinity.	Dissolved Alumina.	Iron.
	Date.	Corresponding Bacterial Numbers.					Total.	Suspended.	Dissolved.					Total.	Suspended.	Dissolved.	Total.	Suspended.	Dissolved.			
	1897																					
881	April 5	5260, 5265, 5268	12.0	2	.11	0.9	.054	.000	.054	.014	.002	1.5	2.8	125	0	125	92	0	92	52.6	.0	0
884	" 6	5285	12.5	1	.05	0.9	.050	.000	.050	.018	.002	1.0	2.5	156	0	156	104	0	104	62.0	.0	0
888	" 8	5316	12.6	1	.08	1.0	.054	.000	.054	.008	.002	1.9	2.5	138	0	138	106	0	106	53.1	.0	.10
890	" 9	5327	12.0	2	.07	0.9	.042	.000	.042	.012	.002	1.8	2.0	103	0	103	76	0	76	29.0	.0	.11
900	" 13	5398, 5405	11.5	3	.14	0.7	.044	.....	.....	.006	.001	1.7	2.2	129	.....	.....	100	.....	.....	33.9	.0	.11
906	" 15	5435, 5437	11.5	3	.18	0.6	.050	.....	.....	.010	.001	1.2	2.7	105	.....	.....	95	.....	.....	36.6	.0	.00
908	" 15–16	5444, 5447	11.5	1	.09	0.9	.050	.000	.050	.006	.002	1.3	2.2	89	0	89	85	0	85	36.0	.0	.05
916	" 22	5499, 5599	13.5	3	.13	1.1	.062	.....	.....	.006	.001	1.4	3.5	114	.....	.....	91	.....	.....	35.9	.0	.30
920	" 24	5523, 5538	14.5	3	.13	0.6	.070	.....	.....	.016	.002	1.4	2.8	110	.....	.....	80	.....	.....	38.5	.0	.15
928	" 29	5591, 5595	17.0	1	.07	0.6	.048	.000	.048	.014	.003	1.1	3.0	124	0	124	78	0	78	53.1	.0	.07
938	May 7–8	5763, 5773, 5780, 5794	15.5	1	.02	1.0	.056	.000	.056	.012	.001	1.4	3.0	112	0	112	84	0	84	32.0	.0	.13
940	" 8–9	5796, 5804	16.0	1	.00	0.8	.058	.000	.058	.016	.001	1.2	3.1	113	0	113	90	0	90	27.8	.0	.06
960	" 19–20	5964, 5972, 5976, 5980, 5986	20.0	3	.14	1.5	.076	.....	.....	.020	.000	1.3	2.4	91	.....	.....	58	.....	.....	25.0	.0	.07
962	" 21	5990 [6027, 6030	20.0	2	.10	1.1	.072	.000	.072	.014	.000	1.3	2.6	86	0	86	58	0	58	25.7	.0	.03
964	" 21–23	5998, 6008, 6011, 6016, 6023,	20.0	2	.10	1.4	.070	.000	.070	.012	.000	1.3	2.6	92	0	92	65	0	65	38.2	.0	.03
966	" 20	6034, 6040	20.0	2	.08	1.3	.068	.000	.068	.026	.000	1.3	2.0	94	0	94	67	0	67	39.1	.0	.03
968	" 24	6047	19.5	3	.17	1.6	.074	.....	.....	.020	.000	1.2	2.5	105	.....	.....	79	.....	.....	36.2	.0	.08
969	" 25	6048	19.5	3	.17	1.7	.074	.....	.....	.014	.000	1.1	2.2	117	.....	.....	90	.....	.....	46.7	.0	.14
970	" 25	6051, 6058, 6062	20.0	2	.10	1.4	.074	.000	.074	.020	.000	1.1	2.0	110	0	110	82	0	82	46.7	.0	.10
972	" 26	6081, 6087, 6090	20.0	2	.08	1.5	.064	.000	.064	.020	.000	0.8	1.9	114	0	114	88	0	88	50.5	.0	.15
974	" 27	6112, 6119, 6122	19.5	2	.11	1.6	.080	.000	.080	.022	.000	0.8	2.3	116	0	116	91	0	91	57.4	.0	.06
976	" 28	6138, 6146	19.5	1	.08	1.3	.058	.000	.058	.006	.001	0.7	2.3	115	0	115	91	0	91	58.2	.0	.20
1010	June 20	6523	26.5	1	.06	0.9	.072	.000	.072	.042	.000	1.1	7.8	171	0	171	121	0	121	51.8	.0	.05
1012	" 21	6532, 6539, 6548	26.0	1	.09	0.8	.076	.000	.076	.022	.001	0.9	7.6	160	0	160	125	0	125	47.0	.0	.00
1014	" 22	6566, 6568, 6579	26.5	2	.13	1.2	.080	.000	.080	.020	.003	1.1	8.9	166	0	166	128	0	128	52.9	.0	.09
1016	" 23	6593, 6605	26.0	1	.12	1.2	.086	.000	.086	.036	.016	0.8	8.9	176	0	176	124	0	124	50.7	.0	.04
1018	" 24	6632	26.0	2	.13	1.3	.080	.000	.080	.014	.005	0.9	6.3	173	0	173	125	0	125	49.3	.0	.04
1025	" 28	6732	26.0	2	.14	1.3	.108	.000	.108	.016	.008	0.7	3.3	128	0	128	81	0	81	26.8	.0	.14
1027	" 29–30	6740, 6742, 6749	26.5	1	.05	1.3	.110	.000	.110	.018	.015	1.1	2.9	123	0	123	91	0	91	24.8	.0	.04
1030	June 30–July 1	6766, 6784	26.5	1	.10	1.3	.108	.000	.108	.032	.012	1.0	3.2	123	0	123	93	0	93	26.0	.0	.10
1032	July 2	6810	27.0	1	.09	1.1	.076	.000	.076	.026	.000	0.9	3.8	104	0	104	79	0	79	46.2	.0	.04
1034	" 3	6827, 6841	27.5	1	.08	1.0	.070	.000	.070	.010	.015	0.8	3.4	122	0	122	89	0	89	33.2	.0	.10
1039	" 6	6863, 6867	30.0	1	.12	1.1	.074	.000	.074	.030	.010	0.8	3.9	160	0	160	109	0	109	51.2	.0	.03
1041	" 7	6876, 6897, 6906	30.5	2	.09	1.1	.076	.000	.076	.032	.006	0.8	4.4	148	0	148	111	0	111	47.2	.0	.03
1043	" 8	6914	30.5	1	.07	1.1	.064	.000	.064	.024	.202	1.5	8.6	141	0	141	105	0	105	34.2	.0	.04
1046	" 9–10	6948, 6970, 6987	29.5	1	.05	0.9	.068	.000	.068	.050	.003	0.8	3.5	109	0	109	73	0	73	22.9	.0	.23
1050	" 15	7012, 7032	29.5	1	.07	1.2	.074	.000	.074	.024	.002	1.2	3.2	108	0	108	66	0	66	31.0	.0	.00
1052	" 16	7044, 7050, 7055, 7065	30.0	2	.06	1.1	.072	.000	.072	.020	.014	1.1	4.0	123	0	123	86	0	86	31.8	.0	.05
1054	" 17–18	7076, 7091, 7099, 7109, 7122,	30.0	1	.08	1.2	.078	.000	.078	.028	.006	1.1	5.5	134	0	134	86	0	86	36.0	.0	.05
1056	" 19–20	7140, 7157, 7165 [7130	30.0	1	.07	1.1	.078	.000	.078	.020	.002	1.1	9.1	144	0	144	96	0	96	47.8	.0	.05
1058	" 21–22	7202, 7223	28.0	1	.05	1.1	.078	.000	.078	.014	.000	1.1	8.5	153	0	153	101	0	101	48.9	.0	.05
1060	" 23–24	7252, 7277, 7290	29.0	1	.11	1.3	.096	.000	.096	.024	.004	1.1	8.7	158	0	158	109	0	109	57.0	.0	.00

RESULTS OF CHEMICAL ANALYSES OF THE EFFLUENT OF THE JEWELL FILTER WITH PERSULPHATE OF IRON.

(Parts per Million.)

Serial Number.	Collected. Date.	Collected. Corresponding Bacterial Numbers.	Temperature, Degrees C.	Degree of Clearness.	Color.	Oxygen Consumed	Nitrogen as Albuminoid Ammonia. Total.	Nitrogen as Albuminoid Ammonia. Suspended.	Nitrogen as Albuminoid Ammonia. Dissolved.	Nitrogen as Free Ammonia.	Nitrogen as Nitrites.	Nitrogen as Nitrates.	Chlorine.	Residue on Evaporation. Total.	Residue on Evaporation. Suspended.	Residue on Evaporation. Dissolved.	Fixed Residue after Ignition. Total.	Fixed Residue after Ignition. Suspended.	Fixed Residue after Ignition. Dissolved.	Alkalinity.	Dissolved Alumina.	Iron.
	1897																					
883	April 6	5273, 5277, 5283	12.0	1	.05	0.8	.044	.000	.044	.018	.002	1.2	3.0	135	0	135	106	0	106	52.0	.0	.00
886	" 7	5302, 5311	13.0	2	.07	0.8	.042	.000	.042	.020	.002	1.0	2.2	141	0	141	106	0	106	56.2	.0	.20
892	" 9–10	5338, 5342	11.5	1	.04	0.6	.030	.000	.030	.012	.002	1.9	2.0	105	0	105	74	0	74	27.5	.0	.04
898	" 12	5381	11.5	2	.05	0.7	.042	.000	.042	.012	.002	1.6	2.2	126	0	126	104	0	104	38.1	.0	.10
905	" 14	5426	11.0	1	.10	0.9	.054	.000	.054	.010	.001	1.6	2.6	124	0	124	90	0	90	46.4	.0	.00
910	" 16	5451	11.5	2	.10	0.8	.048	.000	.048	.006	.000	1.3	3.0	114	0	114	93	0	93	34.7	.0	.23
914	" 21	5489, 5492	13.0	1	.14	0.6	.038	.000	.038	.008	.001	1.2	2.7	118	0	118	78	0	78	30.0	.0	.21
930	" 29–30	5606, 5611	17.5	1	.03	0.5	.050	.000	.050	.018	.003	1.1	2.9	133	0	133	88	0	88	53.8	.0	.03
1047	July 10	6981	29.5	1	.05	0.9	.064	.000	.064	.024	.000	0.7	3.9	102	0	102	69	0	69	24.0	.0	.03

RESULTS OF CHEMICAL ANALYSES OF THE EFFLUENT OF THE JEWELL FILTER WITH COPPERAS.

Serial Number.	Date.	Corresponding Bacterial Numbers.	Temperature, Degrees C.	Degree of Clearness.	Color.	Oxygen Consumed	Alb. Amm. Total.	Alb. Amm. Suspended.	Alb. Amm. Dissolved.	Free Ammonia.	Nitrites.	Nitrates.	Chlorine.	Residue Total.	Residue Suspended.	Residue Dissolved.	Fixed Total.	Fixed Suspended.	Fixed Dissolved.	Alkalinity.	Dissolved Alumina.	Iron.
1028	June 30	6756	26.5	1	.08	1.1	.090	.000	.090	.140	.001	1.4	2.9	156	0	156	121	0	121	0.6	.0	11.08
1036	July 2	6849	28.0	5	.21	4.8	.298	.122	.176	.600	.020	1.6	4.2	244	71	173	208	71	137	51.0	.0	5.80
037	" 3	6855	29.0	2	.15	1.0	.180	.000	.180	.104	.002	0.9	5.0	403	0	403	374	0	374	268.0	.0	.10

RESULTS OF CHEMICAL ANALYSES OF THE EFFLUENT OF THE JEWELL FILTER WITH ELECTROLYTICALLY PREPARED HYDRATE OF ALUMINA.

Serial Number.	Date.	Corresponding Bacterial Numbers.	Temperature, Degrees C.	Degree of Clearness.	Color.	Oxygen Consumed	Alb. Amm. Total.	Alb. Amm. Suspended.	Alb. Amm. Dissolved.	Free Ammonia.	Nitrites.	Nitrates.	Chlorine.	Residue Total.	Residue Suspended.	Residue Dissolved.	Fixed Total.	Fixed Suspended.	Fixed Dissolved.	Alkalinity.	Dissolved Alumina.	Iron.
902	April 14	5411, 5415	11.0	1	.08	0.9	.058	.000	.058	.130	.004	1.4	3.0	94	0	94	67	0	67	54.0	.0	.05
918	" 22–23	5514, 5515, 5517, 5520	13.5	1	.10	1.1	.074	.000	.074	.096	.002	1.4	3.1	101	0	101	77	0	77	50.0	.0	.15
922	" 26	5544, 5547, 5550	15.5	1	.10	0.8	.048	.000	.048	.080	.003	1.2	3.4	105	0	105	84	0	84	52.0	.0	.10
926	" 28	5571, 5583, 5585	16.5	1	.08	0.6	.050	.000	.050	.052	.003	1.1	2.9	118	0	118	75	0	75	61.0	.0	.12
932	April 30–May 1	5622, 5640, 5646, 5653	18.0	1	.04	0.6	.050	.000	.050	.024	.003	1.2	2.6	131	0	131	97	0	97	62.4	.0	.05
936	May 7	5738, 5744, 5751, 5760	15.0	1	.07	0.7	.064	.000	.064	.100	.002	1.4	3.1	124	0	124	90	0	90	59.2	.0	.05
1032	July 2	6810	27.0	1	.04	1.1	.076	.000	.076	.026	.000	0.9	3.8	104	0	104	79	0	79	46.2	.0	.04

RESULTS OF CHEMICAL ANALYSES OF THE EFFLUENT OF THE JEWELL FILTER WITH ELECTROLYTICALLY PREPARED HYDRATE OF IRON.

Serial Number.	Date.	Corresponding Bacterial Numbers.	Temperature, Degrees C.	Degree of Clearness.	Color.	Oxygen Consumed	Alb. Amm. Total.	Alb. Amm. Suspended.	Alb. Amm. Dissolved.	Free Ammonia.	Nitrites.	Nitrates.	Chlorine.	Residue Total.	Residue Suspended.	Residue Dissolved.	Fixed Total.	Fixed Suspended.	Fixed Dissolved.	Alkalinity.	Dissolved Alumina.	Iron.
894	April 11	5346, 5347	11.5	4	....	2.4	.078	....	......	.024	.004	1.7	2.0	128	......	......	99	....	....	58.8	.0	.95
896	" 12	5371, 5373	11.5	2	.14	1.0	.056	.000	.056	.066	.002	1.8	2.1	110	0	110	84	0	84	60.3	.0	.18
904	" 14	5417	11.0	1	.10	0.8	.050	.000	.050	.072	.003	1.6	2.7	97	0	97	72	0	72	53.1	.0	.16
912	" 20–21	5461, 5469, 5474	12.5	2	.13	1.1	.056	.000	.056	.018	.000	1.1	3.0	72	0	72	63	0	63	50.2	.0	.30
924	" 27–28	5560, 5567	16.0	1	.08	0.7	.050	.000	.050	.026	.002	1.3	3.5	107	0	107	88	0	88	61.4	.0	.12
1008	June 19–20	6483, 6491, 6500, 6513	26.0	2	.12	1.2	.082	.000	.082	.040	.000	0.9	7.0	150	0	150	122	0	122	67.0	.0	.06
1020	" 25	6648, 6649, 6663	26.0	2	.09	1.4	.078	.000	.078	.008	.133	0.3	5.5	.....	.....	.....	.....	.....	.....	52.0	.0	.60
1023	" 27	6715	26.0	2	.10	1.2	.088	.000	.088	.018	.160	0.1	3.8	102	0	102	67	0	67	43.2	.0	.40
1031	July 1	6791	27.0	2	.13	1.2	.098	.000	.098	.026	.001	1.0	2.2	102	0	102	75	0	75	45.3	.0	.07
1045	" 9	6940	29.0	2	.08	1.4	.082	.000	.082	.038	.003	0.7	4.1	95	0	95	66	0	66	49.2	.0	.03
1061	" 23	7262	28.5	1	.08	1.4	.098	.000	.098	.020	.001	1.1	7.5	146	0	146	99	0	99	62.0	.0	.00

RESULTS OF BACTERIAL ANALYSES OF THE EFFLUENT OF THE JEWELL FILTER WITH SULPHATE OF ALUMINA.

Serial Number.	Collected.		Number of Run.	Rate of Filtration.		Loss of Head, Feet.	Period of Service Since Last Washing, Hours and Minutes.	Filtered Water Since Last Washing, Cubic Feet.	Bacteria per Cubic Centimeter.	Remarks.
	Date.	Hour.		Cubic Feet per Minute.	Million Gallons per Acre per 24 Hours.					
	1897									
5260	April 5	12.30 P.M.	1	24.0	97	3.0	0h. 57m.	1 442	278	
5262	" 5	4.00 "	2	24.0	97	2.8	0h. 45m.	1 068	219	
5263	" 5	4.30 "	2	24.0	97	3.0	1h. 15m.	1 808	290	
5264	" 5	5.00 "	2	24.0	97	3.3	1h. 45m.	2 478	311	
5265	" 5	5.30 "	2	23.5	95	3.8	2h. 15m.	3 178	292	
5267	" 5	8.00 "	3	23.5	95	3.1	0h. 06m.	154	305	
5268	" 5	9.30 "	3	23.5	95	3.6	1h. 36m.	2 284	620	
5270	" 5	11.30 "	3	23.5	95	6.5	3h. 36m.	5 009	410	
5284	" 6	11.00 P.M.	8	24.0	97	5.0	1h. 16m.	8 853	78	
5285	" 6	11.30 "	8	23.5	95	6.8	1h. 46m.	2 423	42	Agitated surface of sand layer at
5287	" 7	12.30 P.M.	8	23.5	95	3.9	2h. 41m.	3 853	185	11.49 P.M.
5288	" 7	1.30 "	8	23.5	95	4.8	3h. 41m.	5 303	350	
5289	" 7	3.00 "	8	23.5	95	7.1	5h. 11m.	7 303	322	
5290	" 7	5.00 "	9	23.5	95	3.0	0h. 25m.	643	545	
5291	" 7	6.00 "	9	23.5	95	4.0	1h. 25m.	2 053	1 250	Closed outlet at 6.20 A.M.
5314	" 8	12.00 M.	12	23.5	95	5.5	1h. 35m.	2 248	100	
5316	" 8	3.00 P.M.	13	23.5	95	3.8	1h. 45m.	2 619	780	
5318	" 8	4.00 "	13	23.0	93	9.1	2h. 45m.	3 895	355	
5320	" 8	4.21 "	13	23.5	95	....	3h. 04m.	4 379	5 780	Agitated surface of sand layer at
5321	" 8	4.23 "	13	23.5	95	....	3h. 06m.	4 429	2 500	4.15 P.M.
5322	" 8	4.25 "	13	23.5	95	....	3h. 08m.	4 469	950	
5323	" 8	4.27 "	13	23.5	95	....	3h. 10m.	4 519	405	
5324	" 8	4.29 "	13	23.5	95	....	3h. 12m.	4 569	337	
5325	" 9	10.00 A.M.	13	23.5	95	5.3	5h. 16m.	6 246	179	
5327	" 9	11.00 "	13	23.5	95	6.0	6h. 16m.	8 429	870	
5329	" 9	11.50 "	13	23.5	95	....	7h. 06m.	9 749	780	Agitated surface of sand layer at
5330	" 9	11.57 "	13	23.5	95	....	7h. 08m.	9 799	1 800	11.50 A.M.
5331	" 9	11.59 "	13	23.5	95	....	7h. 10m.	9 839	2 510	
5332	" 9	12.01 P.M.	13	23.5	95	....	7h. 12m.	9 889	2 150	
5333	" 9	12.03 "	13	23.5	95	....	7h. 14m.	9 929	1 890	
5334	" 9	12.06 "	13	23.5	95	....	7h. 17m.	9 999	1 680	
5335	" 9	12.09 "	13	23.5	95	....	7h. 20m.	10 066	1 590	
5336	" 9	12.12 "	13	23.5	95	....	7h. 23m.	10 131	1 200	
5337	" 9	12.15 "	13	23.5	95	....	7h. 26m.	10 200	1 170	
5398	" 13	9.00 A.M.	19	23.5	95	3.8	2h. 57m.	3 756	1 275	
5399	" 13	10.00 "	19	24.0	97	4.1	3h. 57m.	5 176	9 910	
5400	" 13	11.00 "	19	23.5	95	4.9	4h. 57m.	6 556	410	
5401	" 13	12.00 M.	19	23.0	93	5.2	5h. 57m.	7 916	1 650	
5402	" 13	1.00 P.M.	19	23.0	93	6.4	6h. 57m.	9 306	2 690	
5403	" 13	2.00 "	19	23.0	93	6.9	7h. 57m.	10 676	1 270	
5405	" 13	3.00 "	19	23.0	93	7.0	8h. 57m.	11 986	1 350	
5435	" 15	9.30 A.M.	26	23.5	95	3.5	2h. 16m.	3 241	59	
5436	" 15	10.30 "	26	23.5	95	4.0	3h. 16m.	4 641	1 020	
5437	" 15	11.30 "	26	23.0	93	4.6	4h. 01m.	5 691	1 080	
5443	" 15	10.30 P.M.	28	23.5	95	2.3	0h. 45m.	955	204	
5444	" 15	11.30 "	28	23.5	95	3.5	1h. 45m.	2 345	142	
5445	" 16	12.30 A.M.	28	23.5	95	4.0	2h. 45m.	3 755	471	
5447	" 16	3.00 "	28	23.5	95	3.1	1h. 38m.	2 329	269	
5448	" 16	5.00 "	30	23.5	95	3.1	0h. 38m.	1 031	68	
5449	" 16	6.00 "	30	23.0	93	3.0	1h. 38m.	2 401	49	
5499	" 22	9.30 "	36	23.5	95	3.0	1h. 33m.	2 099	61	
5500	" 22	10.30 "	36	23.5	95	3.4	2h. 33m.	3 499	1 450	
5501	" 22	11.30 "	36	23.5	95	3.8	3h. 33m.	4 959	37	
5502	" 22	12.30 P.M.	36	23.5	95	4.0	4h. 33m.	6 349	68	
5503	" 22	1.30 "	36	23.5	95	4.3	5h. 33m.	7 659	55	
5504	" 22	2.30 "	36	23.5	95	4.8	6h. 33m.	8 859	165	
5509	" 22	3.30 "	36	23.0	93	5.0	7h. 33m.	10 269	335	
5533	" 24	9.00 A.M.	43	23.5	95	3.7	2h. 40m.	3 521	24	
5534	" 24	10.00 "	43	23.5	95	3.9	3h. 40m.	4 881	26	
5535	" 24	11.00 "	43	23.0	93	4.2	4h. 40m.	6 221	26	
5536	" 24	12.00 M.	43	23.5	95	4.9	5h. 40m.	7 611	21	
5537	" 24	1.00 P.M.	43	23.5	95	5.0	6h. 40m.	9 011	59	

RESULTS OF BACTERIAL ANALYSES—WITH SULPHATE OF ALUMINA.—*Continued.*

Serial Number.	Collected.		Number of Run.	Rate of Filtration.		Loss of Head. Feet.	Period of Service Since Last Washing. Hours and Minutes.	Filtered Water Since Last Washing. Cubic Feet.	Bacteria per Cubic Centimeter.	Remarks.
	Date.	Hour.		Cubic Feet per Minute.	Million Gallons per Acre per 24 Hours.					
	1897									
5538	April 24	2.30 P.M.	43	23.5	95	6.0	8h. 10m.	11 001	242	Closed outlet at 2.44 P.M.
5589	" 29	4.00 A.M.	50	23.0	93	....	0h. 39m.	764	43	
5591	" 29	5.00 "	50	23.0	93	....	1h. 39m.	2 024	44	
5592	" 29	6.00 "	50	23.0	93	3.0	2h. 39m.	3 424	23	
5593	" 29	9.00 "	50	23.5	95	4.5	5h. 39m.	8 664	24	
5595	" 29	10.00 "	50	23.5	95	5.2	6h. 39m.	9 044	22	
5596	" 29	11.00 "	50	23.5	95	6.2	7h. 39m.	10 454	45	
5600	" 29	12.00 M.	50	23.5	95	7.5	8h. 39m.	11 907	107	Agitated surface of sand layer at
5601	" 29	1.00 P.M.	50	23.5	95	6.0	9h. 37m.	13 397	117	12.24 P.M.
5602	" 29	2.00 "	50	23.0	93	6.6	10h. 37m.	14 747	173	
5603	" 29	3.00 "	50	23.5	95	7.7	11h. 35m.	16 120	510	Closed outlet at 3.08 P.M.
5762	May 7	9.00 "	59	23.5	95	2.7	0h. 48m.	1 158	46	
5763	" 7	10.00 "	59	23.5	95	3.0	1h. 48m.	2 588	149	
5767	" 7	11.00 "	59	23.5	95	3.2	2h. 48m.	3 968	71	
5768	" 7	12.00 "	59	23.5	95	3.6	3h. 48m.	5 318	123	
5773	" 8	4.00 A.M.	60	23.5	95	2.6	0h. 57m.	1 369	189	
5774	" 8	5.00 "	60	23.5	95	3.0	1h. 57m.	2 769	58	
5780	" 8	9.30 "	61	23.5	95	3.5	2h. 30m.	3 510	76	
5781	" 8	10.00 "	61	23.5	95	3.8	3h. 00m.	4 220	311	
5782	" 8	11.00 "	61	23.5	95	3.9	4h. 00m.	5 660	116	Closed outlet at 11.04 A.M.
5783	" 8	12.00 M.	62	23.5	95	3.0	0h. 33m.	747	18	
5784	" 8	1.00 P.M.	62	23.5	95	2.6	1h. 33m.	2 197	89	
5785	" 8	2.00 "	62	23.5	95	3.4	2h. 33m.	3 577	110	
5786	" 8	2.30 "	62	23.0	93	3.7	3h. 03m.	4 167	129	Closed outlet at 2.35 P.M.
5787	" 8	3.05 "	63	23.5	95	....	0h. 05m.	119	122	
5788	" 8	3.08 "	63	23.5	95	....	0h. 10m.	239	37	
5789	" 8	3.13 "	63	23.5	95	....	0h. 15m.	359	57	
5794	" 8	4.30 "	63	23.0	93	2.6	1h. 32m.	2 089	22	
5795	" 8	5.30 "	63	23.5	95	3.0	2h. 32m.	3 546	105	
5796	" 8	8.00 "	64	23.5	95	2.8	0h. 28m.	671	191	
5797	" 8	9.00 "	64	23.5	95	3.4	1h. 28m.	2 051	142	
5799	" 8	11.00 "	65	23.5	95	2.5	0h. 27m.	735	189	
5800	" 8	12.00 "	65	23.5	95	2.7	1h. 27m.	2 055	74	
5801	" 9	1.00 A.M.	65	23.5	95	2.9	2h. 27m.	3 445	142	
5802	" 9	1.30 "	65	23.5	95	3.0	2h. 57m.	4 105	92	Closed outlet at 1.43 A.M.
5803	" 9	3.30 "	66	23.5	95	2.5	0h. 01m.	23	41	
5804	" 9	4.30 "	66	23.5	95	2.7	1h. 01m.	1 433	45	
5964	" 19	11.00 P.M.	67	23.5	95	2.1	0h. 56m.	1 246	272	
5968	" 19	12.00 "	67	23.5	95	2.8	1h. 56m.	2 606	196	
5969	" 20	1.00 A.M.	67	23.5	95	2.9	2h. 56m.	3 966	490	
5971	" 20	3.00 "	68	12.0	48	0.8	0h. 33m.	381	274	
5972	" 20	4.00 "	68	12.0	48	0.9	1h. 33m.	1 181	144	
5973	" 20	5.00 "	68	12.0	48	1.0	2h. 33m.	1 821	139	
5974	" 20	6.00 "	68	12.0	48	1.2	3h. 33m.	2 621	1 080	
5976	" 20	9.00 "	68	12.0	48	1.8	6h. 33m.	4 891	3 900	
5977	" 20	11.00 "	68	12.0	48	1.9	8h. 33m.	6 381	244	
5978	" 20	1.00 P.M.	68	12.0	48	2.2	10h. 33m.	7 841	308	
5980	" 20	3.00 "	68	12.0	48	2.8	12h. 33m.	9 381	395	
5981	" 20	5.30 "	68	12.0	48	3.1	14h. 53m.	11 261	165	
5985	" 20	8.00 "	68	12.0	48	4.1	17h. 33m.	13 221	230	
5986	" 20	9.00 "	68	12.0	48	4.4	18h. 33m.	13 951	343	
5988	" 20	11.00 "	69	23.5	95	2.5	0h. 48m.	1 080	401	
5989	" 20	12.00 "	69	23.5	95	2.6	1h. 48m.	2 460	4 500	
5990	" 21	1.00 A.M.	69	23.5	95	2.8	2h. 48m.	3 810	307	
5991	" 21	2.00 "	69	23.5	95	3.0	3h. 48m.	5 180	635	
5993	" 21	3.00 "	69	23.5	95	3.2	4h. 48m.	6 680	1 760	
5994	" 21	4.00 "	69	23.5	95	3.5	5h. 48m.	7 950	215	
5995	" 21	4.30 "	69	23.5	95	3.7	6h. 18m.	8 630	375	Closed outlet at 4.41 A.M.
5997	" 21	10.30 P.M.	70	12.0	48	1.0	0h. 38m.	480	417	
5998	" 21	12.00 "	70	12.0	48	1.0	2h. 08m.	1 480	397	
5999	" 22	1.00 A.M.	70	12.0	48	1.1	3h. 08m.	2 400	259	
6000	" 22	2.00 "	70	12.0	48	1.2	4h. 08m.	3 110	460	
6002	" 22	3.00 "	70	12.0	48	1.5	5h. 08m.	3 860	257	
6006	" 22	5.00 "	70	12.0	48	1.8	7h. 08m.	5 380	423	

RESULTS OF BACTERIAL ANALYSES—WITH SULPHATE OF ALUMINA.—*Continued.*

Serial Number.	Collected.		Number of Run.	Rate of Filtration.		Loss of Head. Feet.	Period of Service Since Last Washing. Hours and Minutes.	Filtered Water Since Last Washing. Cubic Feet.	Bacteria per Cubic Centimeter.	Remarks.
	Date.	Hour.		Cubic Feet per Minute.	Million Gallons per Acre per 24 Hours.					
	1897									
6008	May 22	9.00 A.M.	70	12.0	48	3.2	11h. 08m.	7 943	241	
6009	" 22	12.00 M.	70	12.0	48	5.5	14h. 08m.	1 015	380	
6011	" 22	3.00 P.M.	70	12.0	48	8.2	17h. 08m.	12 303	362	
6012	" 22	5.30 "	70	12.0	48	11.7	19h. 38m.	14 203	546	Agitated surface of sand layer at
6013	" 22	5.45 "	70	12.0	48	3.0	19h. 49m.	14 403	635	5.30 P.M.
6014	" 22	7.00 "	70	12.0	48	3.2	21h. 04m.	15 543	472	
6016	" 22	9.00 "	70	12.0	48	3.9	23h. 04m.	17 013	498	
6020	" 22	11.00 "	70	12.0	48	4.0	25h. 04m.	18 513	578	
6021	" 23	1.00 A.M.	70	12.0	48	4.5	27h. 04m.	20 013	497	
6023	" 23	3.00 "	70	12.0	48	5.1	29h. 04m.	21 543	262	
6024	" 23	6.00 "	70	12.0	48	6.0	32h. 04m.	23 643	810	
6025	" 23	7.00 "	70	12.0	48	6.1	33h. 04m.	24 433	750	
6027	" 23	9.00 "	70	12.0	48	6 5	35h. 04m.	25 643	995	
6028	" 23	12.30 P.M.	70	12.0	48	8.1	39h. 04m.	28 223	1 270	
6030	" 23	3.00 "	70	12.0	48	9.1	41h. 04m.	30 093	610	
6031	" 23	4.30 "	70	12.0	48	10.1	42h 34m.	31 203	1 000	Agitated surface of sand layer at
6032	" 23	6.30 "	71	23.5	95	2.0	0h. 30m.	720	2 290	4.30 P.M. Closed outlet at 4.45 P.M.
6033	" 23	7.00 "	71	23.5	95	2.2	1h. 00m.	1 410	1 890	Closed outlet at 7.11 P.M.
6034	" 23	9.00 "	72	23.5	95	2.1	0h. 43m.	935	1 020	
6036	" 23	10.00 "	72	23.5	95	2.3	1h. 43m.	2 275	261	
6037	" 24	12.30 A.M.	72	23.5	95	2.8	4h. 13m.	5 645	242	
6038	" 24	2.00 "	72	23.5	95	3.4	5h. 43m.	7 635	418	
6040	" 24	3.00 "	72	23.5	95	3.6	6h. 43m.	9 005	725	
6041	" 24	4.00 "	72	23.5	95	3.9	7h. 43m.	10 565	460	
6042	" 24	6.00 "	72	23.5	95	4.8	9h. 43m.	13 075	185	
6044	" 24	9.00 "	72	23.5	95	6.8	12h. 43m.	17 135	235	Closed outlet at 9.10 A.M.
6046	" 24	9.30 P.M.	73	12.0	48	....	....	......	1 260	
6047	" 24	10.00 "	73	12.0	48	1.1	1h. 10m.	480	2 250	" " " 10.24 P.M.
6048	" 25	1.00 A.M.	74	12.0	48	1.0	0h. 32m.	362	4 500	
6049	" 25	2.00 "	74	12.0	48	1.0	1h. 32m.	1 062	2 950	Closed outlet at 2.18 A.M.
6051	" 25	5.00 "	75	12.0	48	1.0	0h. 52m.	479	540	
6056	" 25	6.00 "	75	12.0	48	1.1	1h. 52m.	1 219	235	
6058	" 25	9.00 "	75	12.0	48	1.6	4h. 52m.	3 559	260	
6059	" 25	11.00 "	75	12.0	48	1.8	6h. 52m.	5 159	125	
6060	" 25	1.00 P.M.	75	12.0	48	2.0	8h. 52m.	6 649	263	
6062	" 25	3.00 "	75	12.0	48	2.8	10h. 52m.	8 119	375	
6063	" 25	5.30 "	75	12.0	48	3.3	13h. 22m.	9 949	342	
6064	" 25	7.30 "	75	12.0	48	4.2	15h. 22m.	11 449	495	Closed outlet at 7.30 P.M.
6066	" 25	10.10 "	76	12.0	48	....	0h. 15m.	174	595	
6067	" 25	10.15 "	76	12.0	48	....	0h. 20m.	234	540	
6068	" 25	10.20 "	76	12.0	48	....	0h. 25m.	295	520	
6069	" 25	10.25 "	76	12.0	48	....	0h. 30m.	354	391	
6070	" 25	12.00 "	77	9.0	34	...	0h. 29m.	284	420	
6071	" 26	2.00 A.M.	78	23.5	95	2.1	0h. 45m.	996	223	
6072	" 26	2.36 "	79	23.5	95	2.8	0h. 05m.	88	419	
6073	" 26	2.41 "	79	23.5	95	....	0h. 10m.	208	435	
6074	" 26	2.46 "	79	23.5	95	....	0h. 15m.	308	352	
6075	" 26	2.51 "	79	23.5	95	3.0	0h. 20m.	418	315	
6077	" 26	3.15 "	79	23.5	95	....	0h. 44m.	958	109	Closed outlet at 3.25 A.M.
6078	" 26	5.45 "	80	23.5	95	....	0h. 18m.	393	497	
6079	" 26	6.00 "	80	23.5	95	2.1	0h. 33m.	713	510	
6081	" 26	9.00 "	81	23.5	95	2.2	0h. 30m.	697	301	
6082	" 26	10.00 "	81	23.5	95	2.6	1h. 30m.	2 067	356	
6083	" 26	11.00 "	81	23.5	95	2.8	2h. 30m.	3 477	339	
6084	" 26	12.00 M.	81	23.5	95	3.0	3h. 30m.	4 847	268	
6085	" 26	2.00 P.M.	81	23.0	93	3.5	5h. 30m.	7 597	229	
6087	" 26	3.30 "	81	23.0	93	3.8	7h. 00m.	9 657	235	
6088	" 26	5.30 "	81	23.5	95	4.8	9h. 00m.	12 497	319	
6089	" 26	7.00 "	81	23.5	95	5.4	10h. 30m.	14 397	216	
6090	" 26	8.30 "	81	23.5	95	6.4	12h. 00m.	16 517	304	
6095	" 26	10.52 "	81	23.0	93	....	14h. 22m.	19 597	338	Agitated surface of sand layer at
6096	" 26	11.05 "	81	23.5	95	....	14h. 31m.	19 747	432	10.53 P.M.
6097	" 26	11.10 "	81	23.5	95	5.0	14h. 36m.	19 847	263	
6098	" 27	1.00 A.M.	81	23.5	95	6.0	16h. 26m.	22 327	311	

RESULTS OF BACTERIAL ANALYSES—WITH SULPHATE OF ALUMINA.—*Continued.*

Serial Number.	Collected.		Number of Run.	Rate of Filtration.		Loss of Head. Feet.	Period of Service Since Last Washing. Hours and Minutes.	Filtered Water Since Last Washing. Cubic Feet.	Bacteria per Cubic Centimeter.	Remarks
	Date.	Hour.		Cubic Feet per Minute.	Million Gallons per Acre per 24 Hours.					
	1897									
6100	May 27	3.00 A.M.	81	23.5	95	7.0	18h. 26m.	25 057	382	
6101	" 27	4.05 "	82	23.5	95	....	0h. 07m.	145	522	
6102	" 27	4.10 "	82	23.5	95	....	0h. 12m.	245	575	
6103	" 27	4.22 "	82	23.5	95	...	0h. 24m.	545	499	
6104	" 27	4.43 "	82	23.5	95	....	0h. 45m.	1 045	370	Closed outlet at 4.44 A.M.
6105	" 27	5.23 "	83	12.0	48	....	0h. 10m.	128	411	
6106	" 27	5.34 "	83	12.0	48	....	0h. 21m.	235	298	
6107	" 27	5.54 "	83	12.0	48	....	0h. 41m.	498	453	
6109	" 27	9.05 "	84	12.0	48	....	0h. 10m.	150	590	
6110	" 27	9.18 "	84	12.0	48	....	0h. 23m.	298	382	
6111	" 27	9.35 "	84	12.0	48	....	0h. 40m.	498	272	
6112	" 27	10.16 "	84	12.0	48	....	1h. 21m.	998	197	
1113	" 27	10.24 "	84	23.5	95	....	1h. 29m.	1 168	193	
6114	" 27	11.00 "	84	23.5	95	....	2h. 05m.	2 018	227	
6115	" 27	12.00 M.	84	23.5	95	....	3h. 05m.	3 388	215	
6116	" 27	1.00 P.M.	64	23.5	95	....	4h. 05m.	4 788	161	
6117	" 27	2.00 "	84	23.5	95	....	5h. 05m.	6 188	305	
6119	" 27	3.00 "	84	23.5	95	5.0	6h. 05m.	7 558	167	
6120	" 27	4.00 "	84	12.5	50	3.7	7h. 05m.	8 368	162	
6121	" 27	5.00 "	84	12.0	48	4.3	8h. 05m.	9 098	195	
6122	" 27	6.00 "	84	12.0	48	5.0	9h. 05m.	9 838	164	Closed outlet at 6.00 P.M.
6123	" 27	8.14 "	85	12.0	48	....	0h. 12m.	150	529	
6124	" 27	8.22 "	85	12.0	48	....	0h. 20m.	250	342	
6125	" 27	8.43 "	85	12.0	48	....	0h. 41m.	530	302	
6126	" 27	9.15 "	85	12.0	48	....	1h. 13m.	950	233	
6127	" 27	9.25 "	85	23.5	95	....	1h. 23m.	1 150	269	
6128	" 27	9.30 "	85	23.5	95	....	1h. 28m.	1 250	371	
6129	" 27	9.35 "	85	23.5	95	....	1h. 33m.	1 380	337	Closed outlet at 9.45 P.M.
6131	" 27	10.17 "	86	23.5	95	....	0h. 06m.	138	480	
6132	" 27	10.23 "	86	23.5	95	....	0h. 12m.	258	295	
6133	" 27	10.32 "	86	23.5	95	....	0h. 21m.	498	311	" " " 10.46 P.M.
6134	" 28	12.43 A.M.	87	23.5	95	....	0h. 08m.	145	228	
6135	" 28	12.48 "	87	23.5	95	....	0h. 13m.	245	263	
6136	" 28	12.58 "	87	23.5	95	....	0h. 23m.	495	117	
6138	" 28	3.00 "	87	23.5	95	2.5	2h. 25m.	3 225	89	
6142	" 28	4.30 "	87	23.5	95	2.8	3h. 55m.	5 305	231	
6143	" 28	6.00 "	87	23.5	95	3.5	5h. 25m.	7 335	104	
6144	" 28	8.00 "	87	23.5	95	4.0	7h. 25m.	10 065	510	
6146	" 28	9.00 "	87	23.0	93	4.7	8h. 25m.	11 435	188	
6147	" 28	10.00 "	87	23.0	93	5.4	9h. 25m.	12 805	222	
6148	" 28	11.00 "	87	23.5	95	6.4	10h. 25m.	14 185	197	
6149	" 28	11.30 "	87	23.5	95	6.9	10h. 55m.	14 885	254	Closed outlet at 11.34 A.M.
6520	June 20	4.53 P.M.	92	23.0	93	....	0h. 05m.	114	396	
6521	" 20	4.58 "	92	20.0	81	....	0h. 10m.	211	400	
6522	" 20	5.03 "	92	24.0	97	....	0h. 15m.	309	388	
6523	" 20	5.13 "	92	23.5	95	...	0h. 25m.	564	295	
6524	" 20	6.00 "	92	23.5	95	3.0	1h. 12m.	1 574	357	
6525	" 20	7.00 "	92	23.5	95	3.8	2h. 12m.	2 904	157	
6526	" 20	8.00 "	92	23.5	95	4.7	3h. 12m.	4 254	247	Closed outlet at 8.10 P.M.
6527	" 20	11.45 "	93	23.5	95	....	0h. 05m.	111	198	
6528	" 20	11.53 "	93	23.5	95	....	0h. 13m.	311	153	
6529	" 20	12.00 "	93	23.5	95	2.2	0h. 20m.	501	130	
6530	" 21	12.10 A.M.	93	23.5	95	....	0h. 30m.	701	184	
6532	" 21	12.30 "	93	23.5	95	2.5	0h. 50m.	1 161	117	
6533	" 21	1.30 "	93	23.5	95	3.0	1h. 50m.	1 541	138	
6534	" 21	2.30 "	93	23.5	95	3.7	2h. 50m.	3 861	345	
6536	" 21	3.30 "	93	23.5	95	4.7	3h. 50m.	5 231	945	Closed outlet at 3.45 A.M.
6537	" 21	5.20 "	94	23.5	95	....	0h. 07m.	184	115	
6538	" 21	5.30 "	94	23.5	95	2.3	0h. 17m.	434	138	
6539	" 21	6.00 "	94	23.5	95	2.5	0h. 47m.	1 214	76	
6541	" 21	9.00 "	94	22.0	91	3.0	3h. 47m.	5 304	94	
6542	" 21	10.00 "	94	26.0	105	4.0	4h. 47m.	6 654	155	
6543	" 21	11.00 "	94	23.5	95	4.0	5h. 47m.	8 054	425	
6544	" 21	12.00 "	94	23.5	95	4.5	6h. 47m.	9 444	395	

RESULTS OF BACTERIAL ANALYSES—WITH SULPHATE OF ALUMINA.—*Continued.*

Serial Number.	Collected.		Number of Run.	Rate of Filtration.		Loss of Head. Feet.	Period of Service Since Last Washing. Hours and Minutes.	Filtered Water Since Last Washing. Cubic Feet.	Bacteria per Cubic Centimeter.	Remarks.
	Date.	Hour.		Cubic Feet per Minute.	Million Gallons per Acre per 24 Hours.					
	1897									
6545	June 21	1.00 P.M.	94	23.5	95	4.8	7h. 47m.	10 854	315	
6546	" 21	2.00 "	94	23.5	95	5.1	8h. 47m.	12 254	169	
6548	" 21	3.00 "	94	23.5	95	5.7	9h. 47m.	13 644	287	
6549	" 21	4.30 "	94	23.5	95	6.0	11h. 17m.	15 754	.....	
6550	" 21	5.00 "	94	23.5	95	6.3	11h. 47m.	16 424	328	
6551	" 21	8.03 "	95	23.5	95	2.2	0h. 05m.	126	162	
6552	" 21	8.10 "	95	23.5	95	....	0h. 12m.	266	156	
6554	" 21	8.30 "	95	23.5	95	2.8	0h. 32m.	736	126	
6555	" 21	8.40 "	95	23.5	95	....	0h. 42m.	986	105	Closed outlet at 8.41 P.M.
6556	" 22	12.52 A.M.	96	23.5	95	....	0h. 05m.	103	198	
6557	" 22	1.00 "	96	23.5	95	2.5	0h. 13m.	343	218	
6558	" 22	1.10 "	96	23.5	95	....	0h. 23m.	503	253	
6559	" 22	1.20 "	96	23.5	95	....	0h. 33m.	733	290	
6560	" 22	1.30 "	96	23.5	95	2.6	0h. 43m.	1 023	314	Closed outlet at 1.34 A.M.
6562	" 22	4.45 "	97	23.5	95	...	0h. 05m.	95	390	
6563	" 22	4.53 "	97	23.5	95	....	0h. 13m.	275	495	
6564	" 22	5.00 "	97	23.5	95	2.5	0h. 20m.	475	415	
6565	" 22	5.30 "	97	23.5	95	2.5	0h. 50m.	1 165	157	
6566	" 22	6.00 "	97	23.5	95	2.6	1h. 20m.	1 865	305	Closed outlet at 6.11 A.M.
6568	" 22	9.10 "	98	24.0	97	....	0h. 05m.	140	146	
6569	" 22	9.15 "	98	23.5	95	....	0h. 10m.	260	81	
6570	" 22	10.00 "	98	24.0	97	2.7	0h. 55m.	1 380	79	
6571	" 22	11.00 "	98	24.0	97	3.0	1h. 55m.	2 820	128	
6572	" 22	12.00 "	98	23.5	95	3.2	2h. 55m.	4 240	149	
6573	" 22	1.00 P.M.	98	23.5	95	3.6	3h. 55m.	5 640	194	
6574	" 22	1.10 "	98	23.5	95	....	4h. 05m.	5 870	241	Closed outlet at 1.12 P.M.
6575	" 22	3.13 "	99	......	.....	....	0h. 05m.	148	350	
6576	" 22	3.18 "	99	20.0	81	....	0h. 10m.	253	265	
6577	" 22	3.23 "	99	23.5	95	....	0h. 15m.	378	330	
6579	" 22	3.38 "	99	23.5	95	....	0h. 30m.	738	189	
6580	" 22	4.00 "	99	23.5	95	2.6	0h. 44m.	1 068	233	
6581	" 22	5.30 "	99	23.5	95	4.0	2h. 14m.	3 098	82	
6582	" 23	1.30 A.M.	101	23.5	95	2.5	0h. 06m.	168	269	
6583	" 23	1.35 "	101	23.5	95	....	0h. 11m.	248	265	
6584	" 23	1.40 "	101	24.0	97	....	0h. 16m.	368	255	
6585	" 23	1.50 "	101	23.5	95	....	0h. 26m.	578	180	
6586	" 23	2.00 "	101	23.5	95	2.7	0h. 36m.	888	173	Closed outlet at 2.07 A.M.
6588	" 23	4.17 "	102	23.5	95	....	0h. 05m.	119	297	
6589	" 23	4.23 "	102	20.0	81	....	0h. 11m.	239	415	
6590	" 23	4.30 "	102	23.5	95	2.1	0h. 18m.	419	274	
6591	" 23	5.00 "	102	23.5	95	2.4	0h. 48m.	1 099	295	
6592	" 23	5.30 "	102	23.5	95	2.6	1h. 18m.	1 789	272	
6593	" 23	6.00 "	102	23.5	95	2.7	1h. 45m.	2 469	268	
6594	" 23	8.00 "	102	23.5	95	3.0	3h. 10m.	4 379	261	Closed outlet at 8.10 A.M.
6595	" 23	2.40 P.M.	103	......	.....	....	0h. 05m.	120	157	
6596	" 23	2.45 "	103	24.0	97	....	0h. 10m.	240	136	
6597	" 23	2.50 "	103	23.5	95	....	0h. 15m.	370	142	
6599	" 23	3.00 "	103	23.5	95	2.7	0h. 25m.	630	161	
6600	" 23	3.30 "	103	23.5	95	2.8	0h. 55m.	1 360	187	
6601	" 23	4.35 "	103	23.5	95	....	2h. 00m.	2 860	272	Closed outlet at 4.35 P.M.
6602	" 23	6.00 "	104	23.5	95	2.0	0h. 16m.	374	153	
6603	" 23	8.00 "	104	23.5	95	2.9	2h. 14m.	3 274	45	
6605	" 23	8.30 "	104	23.5	95	2.9	2h. 44m.	4 014	41	
6606	" 23	9.30 "	104	23.5	95	3.1	3h. 44m.	5 434	86	
6607	" 23	10.30 "	104	23.5	95	3.3	4h. 44m.	6 854	181	
6608	" 23	11.30 "	104	23.5	95	3.5	5h. 44m.	8 284	212	Closed outlet at 11.35 P.M.
6628	" 24	2.13 "	107	20.0	81	....	0h. 05m.	133	230	
6629	" 24	2.18 "	107	21.0	85	....	0h. 10m.	273	169	
6630	" 24	2.23 "	107	21.0	85	....	0h. 15m.	378	147	
6632	" 24	3.00 "	107	20.0	81	2.0	0h. 52m.	1 168	151	
6633	" 24	4.00 "	107	20.0	81	2.2	1h. 52m.	2 388	825	Closed outlet at 4.10 P.M.
6637	" 24	9.11 "	109	18.0	73	....	0h. 05m.	76	605	
6638	" 24	9.16 "	109	18.0	73	....	0h. 10m.	166	625	
6639	" 24	9.30 "	109	18.0	73	....	0h. 24m.	406	580	Closed outlet at 9.34 P.M.

RESULTS OF BACTERIAL ANALYSES—WITH SULPHATE OF ALUMINA.—*Continued.*

Serial Number.	Collected. Date.	Collected. Hour.	Number of Run.	Rate of Filtration. Cubic Feet per Minute.	Rate of Filtration. Million Gallons per Acre per 24 Hours.	Loss of Head. Feet.	Period of Service Since Last Washing. Hours and Minutes.	Filtered Water Since Last Washing. Cubic Feet.	Bacteria per Cubic Centimeter.	Remarks.
	1897									
6687	June 26	9.30 P.M.	116	23.5	95	2.2	0h. 06m.	145	127	
6688	" 26	9.35 "	116	23.5	95	....	0h. 11m.	245	73	
6689	" 26	9.45 "	116	23.5	95	....	0h. 16m.	555	81	
6690	" 26	10.00 "	116	23.5	95	2.3	0h. 36m.	865	39	
6691	" 26	10.20 "	116	23.5	95	....	0h. 56m.	1 295	89	Closed outlet at 10.21 P.M.
6692	" 27	12.20 A.M.	117	23.5	95	....	0h. 07m.	207	86	
6693	" 27	12.30 "	117	23.5	95	2.2	0h. 17m.	447	51	
6694	" 27	12.45 "	117	23.5	95	....	0h. 32m.	745	77	
6695	" 27	1.00 "	117	23.5	95	2.0	0h. 47m.	1 147	99	Closed outlet at 1.04 A.M.
6697	" 27	3.00 "	118	23.5	95	2.0	0h. 05m.	156	580	
6698	" 27	3.15 "	118	23.5	95	....	0h. 20m.	456	3 800	Closed outlet at 3.15 A.M.
6726	" 28	3.50 "	124	23.5	95	....	0h. 05m.	122	......	
6727	" 28	3.55 "	124	23.5	95	....	0h. 10m.	242	......	
6728	" 28	4.00 "	124	23.5	95	....	0h. 15m.	342	......	
6729	" 28	4.30 "	124	23.5	95	2.5	0h. 45m.	1 052	880	Closed outlet at 4.30 A.M.
6730	" 28	8.00 "	125	23.5	95	2.5	0h. 54m.	1 263	29	
6732	" 28	9.00 "	125	23.5	95	2.8	1h. 54m.	2 663	26	
6733	" 28	10.30 "	125	23.5	95	3.0	3h. 24m.	4 763	20	
6734	" 28	12.00 M.	125	23.5	95	3.7	4h. 54m.	6 853	32	
6735	" 28	2.00 P.M.	125	23.5	95	3.9	6h. 54m.	9 653	39	
6737	" 29	10.47 "	126	23.5	95	....	0h. 05m.	152	372	
6738	" 29	10.51 "	126	23.5	95	....	0h. 11m.	252	163	
6739	" 29	11.02 "	126	23.5	95	....	0h. 22m.	522	204	
6740	" 29	11.24 "	126	23.5	95	....	0h. 44m.	992	256	
6741	" 30	12.30 A.M.	126	23.5	95	2.6	1h. 50m.	2 532	269	
6742	" 30	1 30 "	126	23.5	95	2.7	2h. 50m.	3 882	1 250	
6743	" 30	2.30 "	126	23.5	95	3.0	3h. 50m.	5 262	91	
6745	" 30	3.30 "	126	23.5	95	3.4	4h. 50m.	6 682	49	
6746	" 30	4.30 "	126	23.5	95	3.5	5h. 50m.	8 112	92	
6747	" 30	5.30 "	126	23.5	95	3.7	6h. 50m.	9 492	94	
6749	" 30	9.00 "	127	23.5	95	2.1	0h. 51m.	1 232	127	
6750	" 30	9.30 "	127	23.5	95	....	1h. 21m.	1 891	26	Closed outlet at 9.35 A.M.
6763	" 30	8.10 P.M.	130	23.5	95	....	0h. 06m.	150	119	
6764	" 30	8.15 "	130	23.5	95	....	0h. 11m.	250	69	
6765	" 30	8.25 "	130	23.5	95	....	0h. 21m.	500	59	
6766	" 30	8.45 "	130	23.5	95	....	0h. 41m.	1 000	84	
6771	" 30	10.00 "	130	23.5	95	2.6	1h. 56m.	2 750	61	
6772	" 30	11.00 "	130	23.5	95	2.8	2h. 56m.	4 130	34	
6773	" 30	12.00 "	130	23.5	95	2.9	3h. 56m.	5 470	100	
6774	July 1	1.00 A.M.	130	23.5	95	3.2	4h. 56m.	6 870	84	
6775	" 1	2.00 "	130	23.5	95	3.4	5h. 56m.	8 270	......	
6776	" 1	3.00 "	130	23.5	95	3.7	6h. 56m.	9 610	......	
6778	" 1	5.41 "	131	23.5	95	....	0h. 06m.	142	81	
6779	" 1	5.47 "	131	23.5	95	....	0h. 12m.	242	39	
6780	" 1	5.57 "	131	23.5	95	....	0h. 22m.	492	8	
6784	" 1	6.19 "	131	23.5	95	....	0h. 44m.	992	68	
6785	" 1	8.00 "	131	23.5	95	2.7	2h. 25m.	3 262	84	
6787	" 1	9.00 "	131	23.5	95	3.0	3h. 25m.	4 662	23	
6788	" 1	10.00 "	131	23.5	95	3.2	4h. 25m.	6 042	25	
6789	" 1	11.00 "	131	23.5	95	3.7	5h. 25m.	7 442	......	
6824	" 2	5.00 P.M.	136	23.5	95	2.0	0h. 04m.	109	67	
6825	" 2	5.30 "	136	23.5	95	....	0h. 34m.	809	......	
6826	" 2	7.30 "	136	23.5	95	2.9	2h. 34m.	3 519	20	
6827	" 2	8.30 "	136	23.5	95	3.7	3h. 34m.	4 869	18	
6832	" 2	9.30 "	136	23.5	95	4.3	4h. 34m.	6 259	57	
6833	" 2	10.30 "	136	23.5	95	4.5	5h. 34m.	7 649	61	
6834	" 2	11.30 "	136	23.5	95	4.6	6h. 34m.	8 999	22	
6835	" 3	1.00 A.M.	136	23.5	95	5.0	8h. 04m.	11 079	21	
6837	" 3	3.02 "	137	23.5	95	....	0h. 07m.	142	99	
6838	" 3	3.05 "	137	23.5	95	....	0h. 10m.	242	87	
6839	" 3	3.22 "	137	23.5	95	....	0h. 27m.	602	66	
6840	" 3	4.00 "	137	23.5	95	....	1h. 05m.	1 502	26	
6841	" 3	5.00 "	137	23.5	95	3.0	2h. 05m.	2 842	31	
6845	" 3	6.00 "	137	23.5	95	3.8	3h. 05m.	4 252	25	

RESULTS OF BACTERIAL ANALYSES—WITH SULPHATE OF ALUMINA.—*Continued.*

Serial Number.	Collected.		Number of Run.	Rate of Filtration.		Loss of Head. Feet.	Period of Service Since Last Washing. Hours and Minutes.	Filtered Water Since Last Washing. Cubic Feet.	Bacteria per Cubic Centimeter.	Remarks.
	Date.	Hour.		Cubic Feet per Minute.	Million Gallons per Acre per 24 Hours.					
	1897									
6846	July 3	8.00 A.M.	137	23.5	95	4.8	5h. 05m.	7 022	39	
6848	" 3	9.00 "	137	23.5	95	5.5	6h. 05m.	8 412	72	
6859	" 6	1.30 P.M.	140	23.5	95	2.2	0h. 10m.	272	291	
6860	" 6	1.45 "	140	23.5	95	2.5	0h. 25m.	652	98	
6861	" 6	2.30 "	140	24.0	97	2.5	1h. 10m.	1 692	47	
6863	" 6	4.00 "	140	23.5	95	2.9	2h. 40m.	3 792	62	
6865	" 6	5.30 "	140	23.5	95	3.5	4h. 10m.	5 912	41	
6866	" 6	8.30 "	140	23.5	95	4.8	7h. 10m.	10 192	49	
6867	" 6	9.00 "	140	23.5	95	5.0	7h. 40m.	10 902	33	
6870	" 6	10.00 "	140	23.5	95	5.6	8h. 40m.	12 282	38	
6871	" 6	11.00 "	140	23.5	95	6.0	9h. 40m.	13 622	37	
6872	" 6	12.00 "	140	23.5	95	6.9	10h. 40m.	14 972	31	
6873	" 7	1.00 A.M.	140	23.5	95	7.5	11h. 40m.	16 322	92	
6874	" 7	2.00 "	140	23.5	95	7.8	12h. 40m.	17 602	126	
6876	" 7	3.00 "	140	23.5	95	8.3	13h. 40m.	18 912	49	Agitated surface of sand layer at
6877	" 7	4.00 "	140	23.5	95	5.2	14h. 32m.	20 022	58	3.37 A.M.
6878	" 7	5.00 "	140	23.5	95	5.7	15h. 32m.	21 352	111	
6879	" 7	6.00 "	140	23.5	95	6.6	16h. 32m.	22 522	143	
6881	" 7	9.00 "	140	23.5	95	7.6	19h. 28m.	26 592	405	Closed outlet at 9.03 A.M.
6882	" 7	10.24 "	141	23.5	95	....	0h. 05m.	146	330	
6883	" 7	10.30 "	141	23.5	95	2.1	0h. 11m.	286	295	
6885	" 7	11.00 "	141	23.5	95	2.3	0h. 41m.	1 008	200	Closed outlet at 11.13 A.M.
6886	" 7	11.46 "	142	23.5	95	2.3	0h. 06m.	148	195	
6887	" 7	11.51 "	142	23.5	95	....	0h. 11m.	258	156	
6888	" 7	12.00 M.	142	23.5	95	2.1	0h. 20m.	478	156	
6889	" 7	1.00 P.M.	142	23.5	95	2.9	1h. 20m.	928	61	
6890	" 7	2.00 "	142	23.5	95	3.7	2h. 20m.	3 318	98	
6892	" 7	2.30 "	142	23.0	93	3.8	2h. 50m.	4 008	144	Closed outlet at 2.39 P.M.
6893	" 7	3.56 "	143	23.5	95	2.1	0h. 06m.	148	320	
6894	" 7	4.00 "	143	23.5	95	2.1	0h. 10m.	238	305	
6897	" 7	4.11 "	143	23.5	95	....	0h. 24m.	498	282	
6898	" 7	4.30 "	143	23.5	95	2.2	0h. 40m.	948	259	
6899	" 7	5.30 "	143	23.5	95	2.3	1h. 40m	1 668	191	
6901	" 7	9.32 "	144	23.5	95	....	0h. 06m.	141	310	
6902	" 7	9.36 "	144	23.5	95	....	0h. 10m.	241	242	
6903	" 7	9.48 "	144	23.5	95	....	0h. 22m.	471	625	
6905	" 7	10.30 "	144	23.5	95	2.7	1h. 04m.	1 481	133	
6906	" 7	11.00 "	144	23.5	95	2.9	1h. 34m.	2 171	192	
6907	" 7	11.30 "	144	23.5	95	....	2h. 04m.	2 871	182	Closed outlet at 11.35 P.M.
6008	" 8	12.54 A.M.	145	23.5	95	....	0h. 07m.	145	261	
6909	" 8	1.00 "	145	23.5	95	2.0	0h. 13m.	275	198	
6910	" 8	1.30 "	145	23.5	95	2.1	0h. 43m.	965	174	
6911	" 8	2.00 "	145	23.5	95	2.1	1h. 13m.	1 535	82	
6914	" 8	4.00 "	145	23.5	95	2.2	3h. 13m.	4 375	61	
6915	" 8	5.00 "	145	23.5	95	2.7	4h. 13m.	5 725	68	
6916	" 8	6.00 "	145	23.5	95	2.9	5h. 13m.	7 055	69	
6917	" 8	9.00 "	145	23.5	95	3.6	8h. 13m.	11 245	147	Closed outlet at 9.15 A.M.
6920	" 8	10.03 "	146	23.5	95	....	0h. 06m.	151	245	
6921	" 8	10.12 "	146	23.5	95	....	0h. 15m.	371	260	
6922	" 8	11.30 "	146	23.5	95	2.2	1h. 33m.	2 191	138	
6923	" 8	1.00 P.M.	146	23.5	95	2.7	3h. 03m.	4 281	152	
6924	" 8	2.30 "	146	23.5	95	2.9	4h. 33m.	6 321	145	
6945	" 9	4.52 "	149	23.5	95	....	0h. 07m.	251	305	
6947	" 9	5.00 "	149	23.5	95	2.2	0h. 15m.	381	127	
6948	" 9	8.00 "	149	23.5	95	2.8	3h. 15m.	4 751	56	
6949	" 9	9.00 "	149	23.5	95	2.9	4h. 15m.	6 171	61	
6966	" 10	4.40 A.M.	153	23.5	95	....	0h. 05m.	146	117	
6967	" 10	4.45 "	153	23.5	95	....	0h. 10m.	246	67	
6969	" 10	5.30 "	153	23.5	95	2.3	0h. 46m.	1 036	64	
6970	" 10	6.00 "	153	23.5	95	2.4	1h. 16m.	1 746	60	
6971	" 10	8.00 "	153	23.5	95	2.6	3h. 16m.	4 616	295	
6972	" 10	9.00 "	153	23.5	95	3.6	4h. 16m.	6 036	70	
6975	" 10	10.00 "	153	23.5	95	3.9	5h. 16m.	7 436	72	Closed outlet at 10.05 A.M.
6985	" 10	5.24 P.M.	156	23.5	95	....	0h. 06m.	150	171	

RESULTS OF BACTERIAL ANALYSES—WITH SULPHATE OF ALUMINA.—*Continued.*

Serial Number.	Collected. Date.	Collected. Hour.	Number of Run.	Rate of Filtration. Cubic Feet per Minute.	Rate of Filtration. Million Gallons Per Acre per 24 Hours.	Loss of Head. Feet.	Period of Service Since Last Washing. Hours and Minutes.	Filtered Water Since Last Washing. Cubic Feet.	Bacteria per Cubic Centimeter.	Remarks.
	1897									
6986	July 10	5.32 P.M.	156	23.5	95	....	0h. 14m.	300	192	
6987	" 10	5.40 "	156	23.5	95	....	0h. 22m.	500	72	
6992	" 14	8.55 "	157	23.5	95	....	0h. 06m.	150	193	
6993	" 14	8.59 "	157	23.5	95	....	0h. 10m.	250	251	
6994	" 14	9.10 "	157	23.5	95	....	0h. 21m.	500	340	
6995	" 14	9.30 "	157	23.5	95	2.2	0h. 41m.	960	182	
6998	" 14	10.00 "	157	23.5	95	....	1h. 11m.	1 655	143	Closed outlet at 10.01 P.M.
6999	" 14	11.23 "	158	23.5	95	....	0h. 06m.	148	244	
7000	" 14	11.27 "	158	23.5	95	....	0h. 10m.	248	225	
7003	" 14	11.38 "	158	23.5	95	....	0h. 21m.	498	217	
7004	" 14	12.00 "	158	23.5	95	2.3	0h. 43m.	998	229	Closed outlet at 12.03 A.M.
7006	" 15	4.49 A.M.	159	23.5	95	...	0h. 10m.	254	260	
7007	" 15	4.53 "	159	23.5	95	....	0h. 14m.	354	274	
7010	" 15	5.04 "	159	23.5	95	....	0h. 25m.	514	177	
7011	" 15	5.30 "	159	23.5	95	2.2	0h. 51m.	1 294	230	
7012	" 15	6.00 "	159	23.5	95	2.4	1h. 21m.	1 884	145	
7013	" 15	8.00 "	159	23.5	95	2.7	3h. 21m.	4 634	96	
7015	" 15	9.00 "	159	23.5	95	3.3	4h. 21m.	5 984	138	Closed outlet at 9.18 A.M.
7018	" 15	10.06 "	160	23.5	95	....	0h. 06m.	150	122	
7019	" 15	10.10 "	160	23.5	95	....	0h. 10m.	250	84	
7022	" 15	10.30 "	160	24.0	97	2.3	0h. 30m.	730	74	
7023	" 15	11.30 "	160	23.5	95	3.0	1h. 30m.	2 110	80	
7024	" 15	12.30 P.M.	160	23.5	95	3.7	2h. 30m.	3 470	88	
7025	" 15	2.52 "	161	23.5	95	....	0h. 06m.	143	96	
7026	" 15	3.00 "	161	23.5	95	2.3	0h. 14m.	303	86	
7030	" 15	3.30 "	161	23.5	95	2.6	0h. 44m.	1 063	177	
7031	" 15	4.30 "	161	23.5	95	3.2	1h. 44m.	2 573	88	
7032	" 15	8.00 "	162	23.5	95	2.2	1h. 30m.	2 059	166	
7036	" 15	9.00 "	162	23.5	95	2.6	2h. 30m.	3 419	31	
7037	" 15	10.00 "	162	23.5	95	3.0	3h. 30m.	4 799	73	Closed outlet at 10.00 P.M.
7038	" 15	11.16 "	163	23.5	95	....	0h. 06m.	149	59	
7039	" 15	11.20 "	163	23.5	95	....	0h. 10m.	249	38	
7040	" 15	11.30 "	163	23.5	95	2.1	0h. 20m.	499	34	
7043	" 15	12.00 "	163	23.5	95	..	0h. 50m.	1 159	48	
7044	" 16	1.00 A.M.	163	23.5	95	2.9	1h. 50m.	2 539	43	
7046	" 16	3.56 "	164	23.5	95	....	0h. 06m.	148	81	
7047	" 16	4.00 "	164	23.5	95	2.1	0h. 10m.	232	92	
7049	" 16	5.00 "	164	23.5	95	2.2	1h. 10m.	1 628	49	
7050	" 16	6.00 "	164	24.0	97	2.5	2h. 10m.	3 078	65	
7052	" 16	9.00 "	165	23.5	95	2.3	0h. 46m.	1 098	128	Closed outlet at 9.04 A.M.
7053	" 16	10.17 "	166	23.5	95	...	0h. 05m.	151	55	
7054	" 16	10.22 "	166	23.5	95	....	0h. 10m.	251	57	
7055	" 16	11.00 "	166	23.5	95	2.4	0h. 48m.	1 161	37	
7057	" 16	12.00 M.	166	23.5	95	2.6	1h. 48m.	2 561	30	
7058	" 16	1.00 P.M.	166	23.5	95	2.9	2h. 48m.	3 991	98	Closed outlet at 1.12 P.M.
7061	" 16	9.58 "	167	23.5	95	....	0h. 06m.	142	63	
7062	" 16	10.02 "	167	23.5	95	....	0h. 10m.	242	51	
7064	" 16	10.12 "	167	23.5	95	....	0h. 20m	492	55	
7065	" 16	11.00 "	167	23.5	95	2.3	1h. 08m.	1 572	37	
7066	" 16	12.00 "	167	23.5	95	2.9	2h. 08m.	3 022	26	
7067	" 17	1.00 A.M.	167	23.5	95	3.0	3h. 08m.	4 352	33	
7068	" 17	2.00 "	167	23.5	95	3.2	4h. 08m.	5 582	25	
7070	" 17	4.14 "	168	23.5	95	....	0h. 07m.	146	23	
7071	" 17	4.18 "	168	23.5	95	....	0h. 11m.	246	17	
7072	" 17	4.30 "	168	23.5	95	2.2	0h. 23m.	536	14	
7075	" 17	5.00 "	168	23.5	95	2.3	0h. 53m.	1 236	11	
7076	" 17	6.00 "	168	23.5	95	2.5	1h. 53m.	2 666	27	
7077	" 17	8.00 "	168	23.5	95	2.9	3h. 53m.	5 456	7	
7079	" 17	9.00 "	168	23.5	95	3.1	4h. 53m	6 876	31	
7080	" 17	10.00 "	168	23.0	93	3.6	5h. 53m.	8 266	22	
7081	" 17	11.00 "	168	23.5	95	3.8	6h. 53m.	9 666	19	
7082	" 17	12.00 M.	168	23.5	95	3.9	7h. 53m.	11 086	37	
7083	" 17	1.00 P.M.	168	23.0	93	4.0	8h. 53m.	12 456	49	
7084	" 17	2.00 "	168	23.5	95	4.4	9h. 53m.	13 856	72	

RESULTS OF BACTERIAL ANALYSES—WITH SULPHATE OF ALUMINA.—*Continued.*

Serial Number.	Collected. Date.	Collected. Hour.	Number of Run.	Rate of Filtration. Cubic Feet per Minute.	Rate of Filtration. Million Gallons per Acre per 24 Hours.	Loss of Head. Feet.	Period of Service Since Last Washing. Hours and Minutes.	Filtered Water Since Last Washing. Cubic Feet.	Bacteria per Cubic Centimeter.	Remarks.
	1897									
7090	July 17	5.13 P.M.	169	23.5	95	....	0h. 07m.	153	12	
7091	" 17	5.30 "	169	23.5	95	2.1	0h. 22m.	563	23	
7094	" 17	7.30 "	169	23.5	95	2.9	2h. 22m.	3 433	35	
7095	" 17	8.30 "	169	23.5	95	3.1	3h. 22m.	4 763	14	
7097	" 17	9.30 "	169	23.5	95	3.7	4h. 22m.	6 113	19	
7098	" 17	11.00 "	169	23.5	95	4.6	5h. 52m.	8 253	7	
7099	" 17	12.00 "	169	23.5	95	4.9	6h. 52m.	9 693	13	
7102	" 18	1.00 A.M.	169	23.5	95	5.3	7h. 52m.	11 403	30	
7103	" 18	2.00 "	169	23.5	95	5.6	8h. 52m.	12 503	32	
7105	" 18	3.00 "	169	23.5	95	5.8	9h. 52m.	13 893	44	Closed outlet at 3.07 A.M.
7106	" 18	4.50 "	170	23.5	95	....	0h. 05m.	134	36	
7107	" 18	5.00 "	170	23.5	95	2.1	0h. 15m.	374	17	
7108	" 18	5.30 "	170	23.5	95	2.1	0h. 45m.	1 054	20	
7109	" 18	6.00 "	170	23.5	95	2.2	1h. 15m.	1 744	13	
7113	" 18	9.00 "	170	23.5	95	2.4	4h. 15m.	5 954	29	
7116	" 18	11.00 "	170	23.5	95	3.7	6h. 15m.	8 754	11	
7117	" 18	1.00 P.M.	170	23.5	95	4.1	8h. 15m.	11 544	14	
7119	" 18	3.00 "	170	23.5	95	4.8	10h. 15m.	14 344	26	
7120	" 18	4.00 "	170	23.5	95	5.0	11h. 15m.	15 754	81	Closed outlet at 4.06 P.M.
7121	" 18	5.22 "	171	23.5	95	....	0h. 06m.	150	15	
7122	" 18	5.30 "	171	23.5	95	2.1	0h. 14m.	340	19	
7125	" 18	8.00 "	171	23.5	95	2.8	2h. 44m.	3 910	18	
7126	" 18	9.00 "	171	23.5	95	....	3h. 44m.	5 270	4	
7128	" 18	10.00 "	171	23.5	95	3.8	4h. 44m.	6 610	5	
7129	" 18	11.00 "	171	23.5	95	4.2	5h. 44m.	8 030	2	
7130	" 18	12.00 "	171	23.5	95	4.8	6h. 44m.	9 450	3	
7133	" 19	1.00 A.M.	171	23.5	95	5.2	7h. 44m.	10 890	21	
7134	" 19	2.00 "	171	23.5	95	5.7	8h. 44m.	12 320	26	
7136	" 19	3.00 "	171	23.5	95	5.9	9h. 44m.	13 730	36	
7137	" 19	4.00 "	171	23.5	95	6.2	10h. 44m.	15 130	124	
7138	" 19	8.56 "	172	23.5	95	....	0h. 06m.	151	14	
7140	" 19	9.00 "	172	23.5	95	2.2	0h. 10m.	286	21	
7141	" 19	10.00 "	172	23.5	95	2.4	1h. 10m.	1 686	2	
7144	" 19	12.00 M.	172	23.5	95	2.9	3h. 10m.	4 526	7	
7145	" 19	2.00 P.M.	172	23.5	95	3.4	5h. 10m.	7 326	8	
7147	" 19	3.30 "	172	23.5	95	3.6	6h. 40m.	9 456	5	
7148	" 19	5.00 "	172	23.5	95	4.0	8h. 10m.	11 536	18	
7149	" 19	7.30 "	172	23.5	95	4.7	10h. 40m.	15 066	111	Closed outlet at 7.49 P.M.
7151	" 19	9.09 "	173	23.5	95	...	0h. 06m.	150	52	
7152	" 19	9.13 "	173	23.5	95	....	0h. 10m.	250	26	
7155	" 19	9.30 "	173	23.5	95	2.1	0h. 27m.	650	43	
7156	" 19	10.00 "	173	23.5	95	2.1	0h. 57m.	1 370	32	
7157	" 19	10.30 "	173	23.5	95	2.2	1h. 27m.	2 070	49	
7158	" 19	12.00 "	173	23.5	95	2.3	2h. 57m.	4 180	36	
7161	" 20	1.00 A.M.	173	23.5	95	2.4	3h. 57m.	5 580	21	
7162	" 20	3.00 "	173	23.5	95	2.7	5h. 57m.	8 390	30	
7164	" 20	5.00 "	173	23.5	95	2.9	7h. 57m.	10 090	27	
7167	" 20	6.00 "	173	23.5	95	3.1	9h. 57m.	12 500	31	
7168	" 20	8.00 "	173	23.5	95	3.5	10h. 57m.	15 300	23	
7170	" 20	10.00 "	173	23.5	95	3.7	12h. 57m.	18 100	31	
7171	" 20	12.00 M.	173	23.5	95	3.9	14h. 57m.	20 950	25	
7172	" 20	2.00 P.M.	173	23.5	95	4.1	16h. 57m.	23 780	28	
7174	" 20	3.30 "	173	23.5	95	4.3	18h. 37m.	25 900	31	
7177	" 20	5.00 "	173	23.5	95	4.8	19h. 57m.	28 990	33	
7178	" 20	8.00 "	173	23.5	95	5.0	22h. 57m.	32 100	30	Closed outlet at 8.04 P.M.
7180	" 20	9.15 "	174	23.5	95	....	0h. 06m.	153	21	
7181	" 20	9.19 "	174	23.5	95	....	0h. 10m.	253	27	
7182	" 20	9.30 "	174	23.5	95	2.2	0h. 21m.	493	21	
7183	" 20	10.00 "	174	23.5	95	2.2	0h. 51m.	1 173	......	
7185	" 20	11.00 "	174	23.5	95	2.5	1h. 51m.	2 573	41	
7186	" 20	12.00 "	174	23.5	95	2.8	2h. 51m.	3 953	39	
7187	" 21	1.00 A.M.	174	23.5	95	3.0	3h. 51m.	5 373	25	
7188	" 21	2.00 "	174	23.5	95	3.2	4h. 51m.	6 612	16	
7190	" 21	3.30 "	174	23.5	95	4.1	6h. 21m.	8 613	12	

RESULTS OF BACTERIAL ANALYSES—WITH SULPHATE OF ALUMINA.—*Concluded.*

Serial Number.	Collected.		Number of Run.	Rate of Filtration.		Loss of Head, Feet.	Period of Service Since Last Washing, Hours and Minutes.	Filtered Water Since Last Washing, Cubic Feet.	Bacteria per Cubic Centimeter.	Remarks.
	Date.	Hour.		Cubic Feet per Minute.	Million Gallons per Acre per 24 Hours.					
	1897									
7191	July 21	5.00 A.M.	174	23.5	95	4.7	7h. 51m.	10 693	21	
7192	" 21	6.00 "	174	23.5	95	5.2	8h. 51m.	12 143	14	
7195	" 21	9.00 "	174	23.5	95	6.8	11h. 51m.	16 293	48	Agitated surface of sand layer
7196	" 21	9.51 "	174	23.5	95	....	12h. 40m.	17 443	38	at 9.39 A.M.
7197	" 21	11.30 "	174	23.5	95	5.8	14h. 19m.	19 763	31	
7198	" 21	1.17 P.M.	175	23.5	95	....	0h. 06m.	155	73	
7199	" 21	2.00 "	175	23.5	95	2.7	0h. 49m.	205	24	
7202	" 21	3.30 "	175	23.5	95	3.0	2h. 19m.	3 335	26	
7215	" 21	5.00 "	175	23.5	95	4.1	3h. 49m.	5 425	27	
7216	" 21	8.00 "	175	23.5	95	4.9	6h. 49m.	9 635	25	
7218	" 21	10.55 "	176	23.5	95	....	0h. 05m.	145	58	
7219	" 21	11.00 "	176	23.5	95	2.1	0h. 10m.	300	48	
7221	" 21	11.30 "	176	23.5	95	2.2	0h. 40m.	965	51	
7222	" 22	12.30 A.M.	176	23.5	95	2.5	1h. 40m.	2 505	57	
7223	" 22	1.30 "	176	23.5	95	2.7	2h. 40m.	3 775	33	
7224	" 22	2.30 "	176	23.5	95	3.1	3h. 40m.	5 175	41	
7226	" 22	3.30 "	176	23.5	95	3.4	4h. 40m.	6 595	45	
7227	" 22	5.00 "	176	23.5	95	4.0	6h. 10m.	8 715	49	
7228	" 22	8.00 "	176	23.5	95	5.3	9h. 10m.	12 825	67	
7230	" 22	9.00 "	176	23.5	95	5.8	10h. 10m.	14 225	86	
7231	" 22	10.00 "	176	23.5	95	6.4	11h. 10m.	15 635	88	
7232	" 22	11.00 "	176	23.5	95	6.7	12h. 10m.	17 035	94	
7233	" 22	12.00 M.	176	23.0	93	7.2	13h. 10m.	18 435	73	Closed outlet at 12.00 M.
7243a	" 22	11.08 P.M.	179	23.5	95	....	0h. 06m.	155	170	
7244	" 22	11.12 "	179	23.5	95	....	0h. 10m.	255	162	
7245	" 22	11.24 "	179	23.5	95	....	0h. 22m.	505	134	
7247	" 22	11.45 "	179	23.5	95	....	0h. 43m.	1 005	107	Closed outlet at 11.45 P.M.
7248	" 23	12.51 A.M.	180	23.5	95	....	0h. 06m.	148	111	
7249	" 23	12.56 "	180	23.5	95	....	0h. 11m.	248	152	
7251	" 23	1.30 "	180	23.5	95	2.2	0h. 45m.	1 048	89	
7252	" 23	2.30 "	180	23.5	95	2.5	1h. 45m.	2 438	61	
7254	" 23	4.00 "	180	23.5	95	2.7	3h. 15m.	4 638	68	
7255	" 23	5.30 "	180	23.5	95	3.5	4h. 45m.	6 808	77	
7265	" 23	8.24 P.M.	182	23.5	95	....	0h. 06m.	150	283	
7266	" 23	8.28 "	182	23.5	95	....	0h. 10m.	250	273	
7267	" 23	8.39 "	182	23.5	95	....	0h. 21m.	500	136	
7271	" 23	9.00 "	182	23.5	95	....	0h. 42m.	1 000	188	Closed outlet at 9.00 P.M.
7272	" 23	10.18 "	183	23.5	95	....	0h. 10m.	144	223	
7273	" 23	10.22 "	183	23.5	95	....	0h. 14m.	244	258	
7274	" 23	10.33 "	183	23.5	95	....	0h. 25m.	494	275	
7275	" 23	11.00 "	183	23.5	95	2.3	0h. 52m.	1 164	231	
7277	" 23	12.00 "	183	23.5	95	2.4	1h. 52m.	2 554	193	
7278	" 24	1.00 A.M.	183	23.5	95	2.7	2h. 52m.	4 054	119	
7279	" 24	2.00 "	193	23.5	95	2.8	3h. 52m.	5 454	82	Closed outlet at 2.00 A.M.
7281	" 24	3.05 "	184	23.5	95	....	0h. 05m.	147	208	
7282	" 24	3.09 "	184	23.5	95	....	0h. 09m.	247	200	
7283	" 24	3.20 "	184	23.5	95	....	0h. 20m.	497	138	
7285	" 24	3.45 "	184	23.5	95	....	0h. 45m.	1 067	92	Closeo outlet at 3.45 A.M.
7286	" 24	4.50 "	185	23.5	95	....	0h. 06m.	146	102	
7287	" 24	4.54 "	185	23.5	95	....	0h. 10m.	246	126	
7289	" 24	5.30 "	185	23.5	95	2.2	0h. 46m.	1 096	91	
7290	" 24	6.00 "	185	23.5	95	2.5	1h. 16m.	1 836	82	
7291	" 24	8.00 "	185	23.5	95	2.8	3h. 16m.	4 696	133	
7293	" 24	9.00 "	185	23.5	95	3.0	4h. 16m.	6 116	167	
7294	" 24	10.00 "	185	23.5	95	3.2	5h. 16m.	7 546	253	Closed outlet at 10.02 A.M

RESULTS OF BACTERIAL ANALYSES—WITH PERSULPHATE OF IRON.

	1897									
5271	Aprll 6	3.30 A.M.	4	23.5	95	3.3	0h. 43m.	1 119	141	
5272	" 6	4.30 "	4	23.5	95	4.0	1h. 43m.	2 469	192	
5273	" 6	5.30 "	4	23.5	95	5.8	2h. 43m.	3 755	89	
5275	" 6	10.30 "	5	23.5	95	4.0	2h. 05m.	2 760	247	

RESULTS OF BACTERIAL ANALYSES—WITH PERSULPHATE OF IRON.—*Continued.*

Serial Number.	Collected.		Number of Run.	Rate of Filtration.		Loss of Head. Feet.	Period of Service Since Last Washing. Hours and Minutes.	Filtered Water Since Last Washing. Cubic Feet.	Bacteria per Cubic Centimeter.	Remarks.
	Date.	Hour.		Cubic Feet per Minute.	Million Gallons per Acre per 24 Hours.					
5276	1897 April 6	12.00 M.	6	23.5	95	....	....	......	840	
5277	" 6	2.00 P.M.	6	23.5	95	3.1	1h. 18m.	1 714	191	
5278	" 6	3.00 "	6	23.5	95	5.6	2h. 18m.	3 154	172	
5280	" 6	3.30 "	6	23.5	95	7.7	2h. 48m.	3 814	172	Closed outlet at 3.42 P.M.
5281	" 6	5.00 "	7	23.5	95	3.1	1h. 00m.	1 382	228	
5283	" 6	5.30 "	7	23.5	95	3.7	1h. 30m.	2 082	319	
5293	" 7	10.00 A.M.	10	23.5	95	5.2	2h. 00m.	2 837	168	
5294	" 7	10.30 "	10	23.5	95	7.5	2h. 30m.	3 517	177	Agitated surface of sand layer at
5295	" 7	10.37 "	10	23.5	95	....	2h. 35m.	3 617	397	10.32 A.M.
5296	" 7	10.40 "	10	23.5	95	....	2h. 38m.	3 688	415	
5297	" 7	10.43 "	10	23.5	95	....	2h. 41m.	3 756	239	
5298	" 7	10.46 "	10	23.5	95	....	2h. 44m.	3 824	198	
5299	" 7	10.49 "	10	23.5	95	....	2h. 47m.	3 892	182	
5300	" 7	10.52 "	10	23.5	95	....	2h. 50m.	3 963	159	
5301	" 7	10.55 "	10	23.5	95	....	2h. 53m.	4 035	177	
5302	" 7	11.30 "	10	23.5	95	5.2	3h. 28m.	4 917	166	
5303	" 7	1.00 P.M.	10	23.5	95	6.6	4h. 58m.	7 027	145	
5304	" 7	2.00 "	10	23.5	95	....	5h. 58m.	8 472	142	
5305	" 7	2.06 "	10	23.5	95	....	6h. 01m.	8 540	260	
5306	" 7	2.09 "	10	23.5	95	....	6h. 04m.	8 612	810	
5307	" 7	2.12 "	10	23.5	95	....	6h. 07m.	8 679	211	
5308	" 7	2.15 "	10	23.5	95	....	6h. 10m.	8 749	169	
5309	" 7	2.18 "	10	23.5	95	....	6h. 13m.	8 817	126	
5310	" 7	2.21 "	10	23.5	95	....	6h. 16m.	8 887	141	[4.48 P.M.
5311	" 7	3.00 "	10	23.5	95	7.0	6h. 55m.	9 747	160	Agitated surface of sand layer at
5313	" 7	4.50 "	10	23.5	95	7.9	8h. 42m.	12 117	181	Closed outlet at 5.00 P.M.
5338	" 9	3.30 "	14	23.5	95	3.5	0h. 35m.	836	137	
5340	" 9	5.00 "	14	23.5	95	6.2	2h. 05m	2 848	289	
5341	" 9	5.25 "	14	23.5	95	6.8	2h. 30m.	3 278	187	
5342	" 9	10.30 A.M.	14	23.5	95	6.0	5h. 49m.	6 862	232	
5344	" 9	12.00 M.	14	23.5	95	6.5	6h. 15m.	8 643	390	
5381	" 12	7.30 P.M.	18	23.0	93	4.5	2h. 05m.	3 093	1 375	
5382	" 12	8.30 "	18	23.5	95	5.1	3h. 05m.	4 413	191	
5384	" 12	9.30 "	18	23.5	95	5.9	4h. 05m.	5 922	88	
5385	" 12	10.30 "	18	23.5	95	6.6	5h. 05m.	6 813	120	
5386	" 12	11.30 "	18	23.5	95	6.9	5h. 41m.	7 983	195	
5387	" 13	12.30 A.M.	18	23.5	95	7.7	6h. 41m.	9 413	183	Agitated surface of sand layer at
5388	" 13	1.30 "	18	23.5	95	6.5	7h. 30m.	10 693	100	12.53 A.M.
5389	" 13	2.30 "	18	23.5	95	6.7	8h. 35m.	12 043	470	
5391	" 13	3.21 "	18	23.5	95	....	9h. 23m.	13 123	425	Agitated surface of sand layer at
5392	" 13	3.24 "	18	23.5	95	....	9h. 26m.	13 193	910	3.18 A.M.
5393	" 13	3.27 "	18	23.5	95	....	9h. 29m.	13 273	256	
5394	" 13	3.30 "	18	23.5	95	7.7	9h. 32m.	13 353	202	[4.12 A.M. and 4.59 A.M.
5395	" 13	4.30 "	18	23.5	95	7.9	10h. 30m.	14 653	147	Agitated surface of sand layer at
5396	" 13	5.30 "	18	23.5	95	....	11h. 27m.	15 853	287	Closed outlet at 5.46 A.M.
5425	" 14	10.30 P.M.	25	23.5	95	2.5	0h. 30m.	665	192	
5426	" 14	11.30 "	25	23.5	95	4.0	1h. 30m.	2 075	310	
5427	" 15	12.30 A.M.	25	23.5	95	4.4	2h. 30m.	3 475	120	
5428	" 15	1.30 "	25	23.5	95	4.8	3h. 30m.	4 865	47	
5429	" 15	2.30 "	25	23.5	95	5.5	4h. 30m.	6 255	78	
5431	" 15	3.30 "	25	23.5	95	6.8	5h. 30m.	7 645	7	
5432	" 15	4.30 "	25	23.5	95	7.0	6h. 30m.	9 035	69	Agitated surface of sand layer at
5433	" 15	5.30 "	25	23.5	95	7.8	7h. 25m.	10 305	264	4.37 A.M.
5451	" 16	9.00 "	31	23.5	95	3.0	1h. 00m.	1 392	58	
5452	" 16	10.00 "	31	23.5	95	3.5	2h. 00m.	2 782	98	
5453	" 16	11.00 "	31	23.5	95	4.0	3h. 00m.	4 182	159	
5454	" 16	12.00 M.	31	23.5	95	4.4	3h. 35m.	4 932	119	
5455	" 16	1.00 P.M.	31	23.5	95	5.0	4h. 35m.	6 322	239	
5459	" 16	2.00 "	31	23.5	95	5.7	5h. 35m.	7 732	310	Closed outlet at 2.13 P.M.
5489	" 21	8.00 "	35	23.5	95	3.9	1h. 28m.	2 135	183	
5491	" 21	10.30 "	35	23.0	93	4.5	3h. 26m.	4 775	71	
5492	" 21	11.30 "	35	23.0	93	5.0	4h. 26m.	5 635	109	
5493	" 22	12.30 A.M.	35	23.5	95	6.4	5h. 26m.	7 425	60	
5494	" 22	1.30 "	35	23.5	95	8.0	6h. 26m.	8 775	114	

RESULTS OF BACTERIAL ANALYSES—WITH PERSULPHATE OF IRON.—*Concluded.*

Serial Number.	Collected.		Number of Run.	Rate of Filtration.		Loss of Head. Feet.	Period of Service Since Last Washing. Hours and Minutes.	Filtered Water Since Last Washing. Cubic Feet.	Bacteria per Cubic Centimeter.	Remarks.
	Date.	Hour.		Cubic Feet per Minute.	Million Gallons per Acre per 24 Hours.					
	1897									
5496	April 22	3.00 A.M.	35	23.0	93	8.8	7h. 56m.	10 805	115	Agitated surface of sand layer at
5497	" 22	4.00 "	35	23.5	95	8.0	8h. 54m.	12 115	495	3.02 A.M.
5605	" 29	7.00 P.M.	51	23.5	95	2.7	0h. 16m.	384	45	
5606	" 29	9.00 "	51	23.5	95	3.9	2h. 16m.	3 174	43	
5607	" 29	10.00 "	51	23.5	95	4.1	3h. 16m.	4 564	29	
5609	" 29	11.00 "	51	23.5	95	5.6	4h. 16m.	5 924	47	
5610	" 29	12.00 "	51	23.5	95	6.4	5h. 16m.	7 304	32	
5611	" 30	1.00 A.M.	51	23.5	95	8.3	6h. 16m.	8 694	44	Agitated surface of sand layer at
5612	" 30	2.00 "	51	23.5	95	5.8	7h. 11m.	9 964	29	1.19 A.M.
5614	" 30	3.00 "	51	23.5	95	8.0	8h. 11m.	11 314	28	
5615	" 30	3.59 "	51	23.0	93	8.8	9h. 06m.	12 544	19	
5616	" 30	4.07 "	51	23.5	95	8.0	9h. 09m.	12 624	47	
5617	" 30	4.10 "	51	23.5	95	8.1	9h. 12m.	12 674	28	
5618	" 30	4.13 "	51	23.5	95	8.2	9h. 15m.	12 734	11	
5619	" 30	4.16 "	51	23.5	95	8.3	9h. 18m.	12 814	16	
5620	" 30	4.30 "	51	21.0	89	9.3	9h. 32m.	13 144	33	Closed outlet at 4.49 A.M.
6976	July 10	12.18 P.M.	154	23.5	95	....	0h. 06m.	150	199	
6977	" 10	12.26 "	154	23.5	95	....	0h. 14m.	342	186	Closed outlet at 12.26 P.M.
6978	" 10	2.15 "	155	23.5	95	....	0h. 07m.	167	97	
6980	" 10	2.30 "	155	23.5	95	2.2	0h. 22m.	497	114	
6982	" 10	2.45 "	155	23.5	95	....	0h. 37m.	807	76	
6983	" 10	3.00 "	155	23.5	95	....	0h. 52m.	1 187	54	
6984	" 10	4.00 "	155	23.5	95	3.5	1h. 52m.	2 537	58	Closed outlet at 4.04 P.M.

RESULTS OF BACTERIAL ANALYSES—WITH COPPERAS.

	1897									
6720	June 28	12.50 A.M.	123	23.5	95	....	0h. 06m.	141	.....	
6721	" 28	12.55 "	123	23.5	95	....	0h. 11m.	251	.....	
6722	" 28	1.00 "	123	23.5	95	2.8	0h. 16m.	371	.....	
6723	" 28	1.10 "	123	23.5	95	....	0h. 26m.	581	.....	
6751	" 30	11.56 "	128	23.5	95	....	0h. 06m.	154	34	
6752	" 30	12.00 M.	128	23.5	95	2.0	0h. 10m.	254	41	
6756	" 30	12.30 P.M.	128	24.0	97	2.6	0h. 40m.	964	121	
6757	" 30	1.00 "	128	23.0	93	2.9	1h. 10m.	1 644	170	
6758	" 30	1.30 "	128	23.0	93	3.2	1h. 40m.	2 324	229	
6759	" 30	2.00 "	128	22.0	89	....	2h. 10m.	2 934	147	Closed outlet at 2.00 P.M.
6761	" 30	4.05 "	129	23.5	95	2.7	0h. 09m.	220	254	
6762	" 30	4.30 "	129	23.5	95	2.7	0h. 34m.	800	188	
6849	July 3	1.40 "	....	23.5	95	....	0h. 07m.	204	1 700	Samples 6849–6857 with cop-
6853	" 3	2.00 "	138	23.5	95	3.4	0h. 27m.	734	219	peras and caustic soda.
6854	" 3	2.15 "	138	23.5	95	....	0h. 42m.	1 074	113	Closed outlet at 2.16 P.M.
6855	" 3	3.30 "	139	23.5	95	2.8	0h. 22m.	577	0	
6856	" 3	4.00 "	139	23.5	95	2.9	0h. 52m.	1 247	12	
6857	" 3	4.30 "	139	23.5	95	2.9	1h. 22m.	1 847	10	

RESULTS OF BACTERIAL ANALYSES—WITH ELECTROLYTICALLY PREPARED HYDRATE OF ALUMINUM.

	1897									
5406	April 13	5.30 P.M.	20	23.0	93	2.5	0h. 04m.	110	325	
5407	" 13	8.00 "	20	23.5	95	4.0	2h. 34m.	4 580	2 111	Closed outlet at 8.08 P.M.
5409	" 14	1.00 A.M.	21	23.5	95	4.2	1h. 11m.	1 599	670	
5410	" 14	2.00 "	21	23.5	95	5.8	2h. 11m.	2 959	1 100	Closed outlet at 2.10 A.M.
5411	" 14	3.00 "	22	23.5	95	2.9	0h. 23m.	521	369	
5413	" 14	4.00 "	22	23.5	95	4.7	1h. 23m.	1 911	236	
5414	" 14	5.00 "	22	23.5	95	5.8	2h. 23m.	3 291	1 290	Closed outlet at 5.10 A.M.
5415	" 14	6.00 "	23	22.0	89	3.1	0h. 27m.	619	387	
5510	" 22	8.30 P.M.	37	23.5	95	4.0	2h, 20m.	3 135	242	Closed outlet at 8.32 P.M.
5511	" 22	9.30 "	38	23.5	95	3.5	0h. 30m.	721	1 125	
5513	" 22	10.30 "	38	23.5	95	3.3	1h. 30m.	2 111	99	
5514	" 22	11.30 "	38	23.5	95	5.0	2h. 30m.	3 511	173	
5515	" 23	1.30 A.M.	39	23.5	95	2.7	0h. 48m.	1 122	117	Closed outlet at 1.35 A.M.

RESULTS OF BACTERIAL ANALYSES—WITH ELECTROLYTICALLY PREPARED HYDRATE OF ALUMINUM.—*Continued.*

Serial Number.	Collected.		Number of Run.	Rate of Filtration.		Loss of Head. Feet.	Period of Service Since Last Washing. Hours and Minutes.	Filtered Water Since Last Washing. Cubic Feet.	Bacteria per Cubic Centimeter.	Remarks.
	Date.	Hour.		Cubic Feet per Minute.	Million Gallons per Acre per 24 Hours.					
	1897									
5517	April 23	4.30 A.M.	40	23.5	95	3.0	0h. 56m.	1 325	217	
5518	" 23	5.30 "	40	23.5	95	4.2	1h. 58m.	2 685	.....	
5520	" 23	10.30 "	41	23.5	95	2.8	0h. 50m.	1 157	142	
5521	" 23	11.30 "	41	23.5	95	3.7	1h. 50m.	2 557	148	
5522	" 23	12.30 P.M.	41	23.5	95	4.8	2h. 50m.	3 917	107	
5523	" 23	1.30 "	41	23.5	95	7.5	3h. 50m.	5 257	179	Closed outlet at 1.45 P.M.
5544	" 26	9.30 A.M.	44	23.5	95	3.3	1h. 14m.	1 722	380	
5545	" 26	10.30 "	44	24.0	97	4.2	2h. 02m.	2 852	254	
5546	" 26	11.30 "	44	23.5	95	6.5	3h. 02m.	4 232	247	
5547	" 26	12.30 P.M.	44	23.5	95	8.7	4h. 02m.	5 602	232	Agitated surface of sand layer at
5548	" 26	1.30 "	44	23.5	95	6.9	5h. 00m.	6 962	485	12.40 P.M.
5550	" 26	5.30 "	45	23.5	95	2.7	2h. 21m.	2 798	145	
5551	" 26	6.30 "	45	23.5	95	3.6	3h. 21m.	4 288	595	
5552	" 26	7.30 "	45	23.5	95	4.9	4h. 21m.	5 608	400	
5553	" 26	8.30 "	45	23.5	95	7.5	5h. 21m.	6 838	233	Agitated surface of sand layer at
5554	" 26	9.30 "	45	23.5	95	5.3	6h 19m.	8 168	67	9.04 P.M.
5559	" 26	10.30 "	45	23.5	93	8.0	7h. 19m.	9 538	141	Closed outlet at 10.35 P.M.
5571	" 28	9.00 A.M.	48	24.0	97	7.2	2h. 56m.	4 093	169	Agitated surface of sand layer at
5572	" 28	10.00 "	48	24.0	97	4.5	3h. 56m.	5 423	201	9.44 A.M.
5573	" 28	11.00 "	48	23.5	95	6.2	4h. 54m.	6 930	435	
5577	" 28	12.00 "	48	23.5	95	7.0	5h. 54m.	8 320	455	
5578	" 28	1.00 P.M.	48	23.0	93	7.6	6h. 54m.	9 680	995	
5583	" 28	4.00 "	49	23.0	93	2.6	0h. 32m.	598	237	
5584	" 28	5.30 "	49	23.5	95	3.0	2h. 02m.	2 678	199	
5585	" 28	8.30 "	49	23.5	95	6.4	5h. 02m.	6 868	319	[9.52 P.M.
5587	" 28	9.30 "	49	23.5	95	8.0	6h. 02m.	8 228	453	Agitated surface of sand layer at
5588	" 28	10.30 "	49	23.5	95	4.8	6h. 59m.	8 848	585	Closed outlet at 10.43 P.M.
5622	" 30	9.30 A.M.	52	23.5	95	2.4	0h. 05m.	147	115	
5623	" 30	10.30 "	52	23.5	95	3.0	1h. 05m.	1 557	110	
5624	" 30	11.30 "	52	23.5	95	4.8	2h. 05m.	2 957	177	
5625	" 30	12.30 P.M.	52	23.5	95	5.3	3h. 05m.	4 357	47	[2.06 P.M.
5626	" 30	1.30 "	52	23.5	95	7.1	4h. 05m.	5 747	195	Agitated surface of sand layer at
5627	" 30	2.30 "	52	23.5	95	5.6	5h. 03m.	7 047	253	[4.10 P.M.
5632	" 30	4.00 "	52	23.5	95	7.7	6h. 33m.	9 087	410	Agitated surface of sand layer at
5633	" 30	5.00 "	52	23.5	95	7.9	7h. 31m.	10 297	333	Agit. surf. of sand layer at 5.04 P.M.
5634	" 30	5.30 "	52	23.0	93	8.0	7h. 59m.	11 067	429	Closed outlet at 5.44 P.M.
5635	" 30	8.00 "	53	23.5	95	2.4	0h. 31m.	698	141	
5640	" 30	9.00 "	53	23.5	95	3.0	1h. 31m.	2 258	158	
5641	" 30	10.00 "	53	23.5	95	4.1	2h. 31m.	3 538	95	
5642	" 30	11.00 "	53	23.5	95	5.7	3h. 31m.	4 908	90	
5643	" 30	12.00 "	53	23.5	95	8.1	4h. 24m.	6 248	83	Agitated surface of sand layer at
5644	May 1	1.00 A.M.	53	23.5	95	6.3	5h. 24m.	7 478	87	12.17 A.M.
5645	" 1	2.00 "	53	23.5	95	7.3	6h. 24m.	8 818	164	
5646	" 1	3.00 "	53	23.5	95	....	7h. 19m.	10 088	321	Agitated surface of sand layer at
5648	" 1	4.00 "	53	23.5	95	7.2	8h. 19m.	11 568	143	12.55 A.M.
5649	" 1	5.00 "	53	23.5	95	....	9h. 14m.	12 678	429	Agitated surface of sand layer at
5650	" 1	5.03 "	53	23.0	93	....	9h. 17m.	12 768	243	4.55 A.M.
5651	" 1	5.06 "	53	23.5	95	....	9h. 20m.	12 838	179	
5653	" 1	9.00 "	54	23.5	95	2.8	0h. 45m.	1 031	121	
5654	" 1	10.00 "	54	23.5	95	3.2	1h. 45m.	2 441	93	
5655	" 1	11.00 "	54	23.5	95	3.5	2h. 45m.	3 881	95	
5656	" 1	12.00 "	54	23.5	95	3.8	3h. 45m.	5 251	92	
5657	" 1	1.00 P.M.	54	23.0	93	5.0	4h. 45m.	6 601	100	
5658	" 1	2.00 "	54	23.5	95	6.0	5h. 45m.	7 981	69	
5663	" 1	3.00 "	54	23.5	95	7.7	6h. 42m.	9 381	121	Agitated surface of sand layer at
5738	" 7	1.00 A.M.	55	23.5	95	4.5	1h. 18m.	1 528	136	3.08 P.M.
5739	" 7	4.30 "	56	23.5	95	2.5	0h. 23m.	611	114	
5744	" 7	5.00 "	56	23.5	95	2.6	0h. 53m.	1 331	129	
5745	" 7	6.00 "	56	23.5	95	4.4	1h. 53m.	2 761	92	
5746	" 7	9.30 "	57	23.5	95	2.7	0h. 28m.	577	252	
5751	" 7	10.30 "	57	23.5	95	3.1	1h. 28m.	1 947	214	

RESULTS OF BACTERIAL ANALYSES—WITH ELECTROLYTICALLY PREPARED HYDRATE OF ALUMINA.—*Concluded.*

Serial Number.	Collected. Date.	Collected. Hour.	Number of Run.	Rate of Filtration. Cubic Feet per Minute.	Rate of Filtration. Million Gallons per Acre per 24 Hours.	Loss of Head, Feet.	Period of Service Since Last Washing. Hours and Minutes.	Filtered Water Since Last Washing. Cubic Feet.	Bacteria per Cubic Centimeter.	Remarks.
	1897									
5752	May 7	11.30 A.M.	57	23.5	95	4.1	2h. 28m.	3 287	319	
5753	" 7	12.30 P.M.	57	23.5	95	5.5	3h. 28m.	4 537	289	Closed outlet at 12.33 P.M.
5754	" 7	2.30 "	58	23.5	95	2.2	0h. 17m.	397	.....	
5755	" 7	3.30 "	58	23.5	95	3.2	1h. 17m.	1 797	139	
5760	" 7	4.30 "	58	23.5	95	4.7	2h. 17m.	3 187	175	
6806	July 2	4.45 A.M.	133	23.5	95	....	0h. 06m.	150	170	
6807	" 2	4.50 "	133	23.5	95	....	0h. 11m.	250	89	
6808	" 2	5.00 "	133	23.5	95	2.1	0h. 21m.	480	136	
6809	" 2	5.30 "	133	23.5	95	2.2	0h. 51m.	1 170	60	
6810	" 2	6.00 "	133	23.5	95	2.3	1h. 21m.	1 830	52	
6815	" 2	9.00 "	133	23.0	93	4.0	4h. 13m.	5 830	127	
6816	" 2	10.30 "	134	23.5	95	2.2	0h. 09m.	214	112	
6817	" 2	11.30 "	134	23.5	95	2.7	1h. 09m.	1 594	73	
6821	" 2	1.00 P.M.	134	23.5	95	3.3	2h. 39m.	3 704	126	
6823	" 2	3.53 "	135	23.5	95	....	0h. 13m.	311	147	Closed outlet at 3.53 P.M.

RESULTS OF BACTERIAL ANALYSES—WITH ELECTROLYTICALLY PREPARED HYDRATE OF IRON.

Serial Number.	Collected. Date.	Collected. Hour.	Number of Run.	Rate of Filtration. Cubic Feet per Minute.	Rate of Filtration. Million Gallons per Acre per 24 Hours.	Loss of Head, Feet.	Period of Service Since Last Washing. Hours and Minutes.	Filtered Water Since Last Washing. Cubic Feet.	Bacteria per Cubic Centimeter.	Remarks.
	1897									
5346	April 11	3.00 A.M.	15	23.0	93	2.8	0h. 50m.	1 153	4 000	
5347	" 11	4.30 P.M.	15	23.0	93	3.9	2h. 20m.	3 123	5 410	
5350	" 11	5.30 "	15	23.0	93	4.2	3h. 20m.	4 403	7 900	
5351	" 11	6.30 "	15	23.0	93	5.0	4h. 20m.	5 723	6 000	
5352	" 11	7.30 "	15	24.0	97	6.0	5h. 20m.	7 123	9 800	
5353	" 11	8.30 "	15	22.0	89	7.3	6h. 20m.	8 353	24 000	
5355	" 11	9.30 "	15	22.0	89	8.0	7h. 19m.	9 663	21 000	Agitated surface of sand layer
5356	" 11	9.43 "	15	23.5	95	6.6	7h. 32m.	10 073	6 650	at 9.37 P.M.
5357	" 11	9.46 "	15	23.5	95	....	7h. 35m.	10 143	44 500	
5359	" 11	9.49 "	15	23.5	95	....	7h. 38m.	10 203	10 000	
5360	" 11	9.52 "	15	23.5	95	7.1	7h. 41m.	10 263	12 000	
5364	" 11	11.30 "	16	18.0	73	2.0	0h. 38m.	662	2 720	
5365	" 12	12.30 A.M.	16	18.0	73	2.7	1h. 38m.	1 712	2 900	
5366	" 12	1.30 "	16	18.0	73	3.2	2h. 38m.	2 772	1 680	
5367	" 12	2.30 "	16	18.0	73	4.0	3h. 38m.	3 802	2 200	
5369	" 12	3.30 "	16	17.0	69	5.0	4h. 38m.	4 842	2 350	
5370	" 12	5.00 "	17	18.0	73	2.1	0h. 50m.	892	1 600	
5371	" 12	6.00 "	17	18.0	73	3.0	1h. 50m.	1 992	2 030	
5373	" 12	9.00 "	17	17.5	71	5.0	4h. 50m.	4 932	15 200	
5374	" 12	10.00 "	17	16.0	65	5.9	5h. 50m.	5 902	12 600	
5375	" 12	11.00 "	17	18.5	75	7.0	6h. 50m.	6 882	13 500	
5376	" 12	12.00 M.	17	14.0	57	6.0	7h. 50m.	7 882	12 700	
5377	" 12	1.00 P.M.	17	18.0	73	7.0	8h. 50m.	8 782	4 640	
5378	" 12	2.00 "	17	16.5	67	8.0	9h. 50m.	9 782	6 400	
5379	" 12	3.00 "	17	17.0	69	8.2	10h. 50m.	10 762	9 450	
5417	" 14	1.30 "	24	.....	.....	....	0h. 15m.	355	371	
5418	" 14	5.00 "	25	23.5	95	3.9	1h. 05m.	1 715	429	
5420	" 14	5.30 "	25	23.0	93	4.0	1h. 35m.	2 375	755	
5461	" 20	8.30 "	32	23.5	95	5.8	3h. 56m.	5 400	1 240	
5462	" 20	9.30 "	32	23.5	95	7.0	4h. 56m.	6 776	1 450	
5468	" 20	12.00 "	33	23.5	95	3.0	1h. 00m.	1 404	449	
5469	" 21	1.00 A.M.	33	23.5	95	4.2	2h. 00m.	2 744	397	
5470	" 21	2.00 "	33	20.0	81	5.9	3h. 00m.	3 994	295	
5471	" 21	3.00 "	33	20.0	81	6.8	4h. 00m.	5 154	267	
5472a	" 21	4.00 "	33	20.0	81	7.5	5h. 00m.	6 324	347	
5474	" 21	9.00 "	34	18.0	73	3.5	3h. 25m.	3 497	167	
5475	" 21	10.00 "	34	18.0	73	4.7	4h. 25m.	4 357	200	
5476	" 21	11.00 "	34	18.0	73	5.0	5h. 25m.	5 647	139	
5477	" 21	12.00 M.	34	18.0	73	6.0	6h. 25m.	6 697	172	
5478	" 21	1.00 P.M.	34	18.0	73	7.0	7h. 25m.	7 747	217	[at 1.35 P.M.
5479	" 21	2.00 "	34	18.0	73	5.6	8h. 25m.	8 777	138	Agitated surface of sand layer
5480	" 21	3.00 "	34	18.0	73	7.8	9h. 25m.	9 823	184	Agitated surface of sand layer
5481	" 21	3.06 "	34	18.0	73	....	9h. 31m.	9 917	420	at 3.02 P.M.

RESULTS OF BACTERIAL ANALYSES—WITH ELECTROLYTICALLY PREPARED HYDRATE OF IRON.—*Continued.*

Serial Number.	Collected. Date.	Collected. Hour.	Number of Run.	Rate of Filtration. Cubic Feet per Minute.	Rate of Filtration. Million Gallons per Acre per 24 Hours.	Loss of Head. Feet.	Period of Service Since Last Washing. Hours and Minutes.	Filtered Water Since Last Washing. Cubic Feet.	Bacteria per Cubic Centimeter.	Remarks.
	1897									
5482	April 21	3.09 P.M.	34	18.0	73	....	9h. 34m.	9 967	212	
5483	" 21	3.12 "	34	18.0	73	....	9h. 37m.	10 017	192	
5488	" 21	4.00 "	34	18.0	73	6.8	10h. 19m.	10 867	232	Agitated surface of sand layer at 3.49 P.M.
5560	" 27	8.30 "	46	23.5	95	3.3	2h. 29m.	3 477	420	
5565	" 27	9.30 "	46	23.5	95	3.9	3h. 29m.	4 807	740	
5566	" 28	1.00 A.M.	47	23.5	95	2.8	1h. 00m.	1 347	248	
5567	" 28	2.00 "	47	23.5	95	3.1	2h. 00m.	2 707	179	
5568	" 28	3.00 "	47	23.5	95	4.1	3h. 00m.	4 037	202	
6478	June 19	10.05 "	88	23.5	95	....	0h. 05m.	131	387	
6479	" 19	10.10 "	88	20.0	81	....	0h. 10m.	231	292	
6480	" 19	10.15 "	88	20.0	81	....	0h. 15m.	331	427	
6481	" 19	10.30 "	88	22.0	89	....	0h. 30m.	661	237	
6482	" 19	10.45 "	88	24.5	99	....	0h. 45m.	1 031	295	
6483	" 19	11.00 "	88	24.5	99	....	1h. 00m.	1 401	302	
6484	" 19	11.40 "	89	10.0	40	....	0h. 05m.	82	251	
6485	" 19	11.45 "	89	10.0	40	....	0h. 10m.	132	299	
6486	" 19	11.50 "	89	12.0	48	....	0h. 15m.	192	249	
6487	" 19	11.55 "	89	12.0	48	...	0h. 20m.	252	261	
6488	" 19	12.00 P.M.	89	18.5	75	....	0h. 30m.	437	301	
6489	" 19	12.15 "	89	18.5	75	....	0h. 40m.	622	235	
6490	" 19	12.32 "	89	23.0	93	....	0h. 57m.	1 012	263	
6491	" 19	1.30 "	89	24.0	97	1.0	1h. 55m.	2 442	197	
6492	" 19	2.30 "	89	23.5	95	1.5	2h. 55m.	3 842	142	
6494	" 19	3.30 "	89	23.5	95	1.8	3h. 55m.	5 272	99	
6495	" 19	4.30 "	89	23.5	95	2.0	4h. 55m.	6 662	260	
6496	" 19	5.30 "	89	23.5	95	2.1	5h. 55m.	8 062	141	
6497	" 19	6.30 "	89	23.5	95	2.1	6h. 55m.	9 352	154	
6498	" 19	8.00 "	89	23.5	95	2.3	8h. 25m.	11 402	145	
6500	" 19	9.30 "	89	23.5	95	2.4	9h. 55m.	13 222	201	
6501	" 19	10.09 "	89	23.5	95	....	10h. 34m.	14 152	250	Agitated surface of sand layer at 10.09 P.M.
6502	" 19	10.21 "	89	23.5	95	6.5	10h. 39m.	14 252	192	
6503	" 19	11.57 "	90	23.5	95	....	0h. 05m.	71	342	
6504	" 20	12.05 A.M.	90	23.5	95	2.2	0h. 13m.	381	278	
6505	" 20	12.29 "	90	23.5	95	....	0h. 37m.	811	292	
6506	" 20	1.30 "	90	23.5	95	2.6	1h. 01m.	1 391	223	
6507	" 20	2.00 "	90	23.5	95	2.6	1h. 31m.	2 277	183	
6508	" 20	4.21 "	91	12.0	48	1.0	0h. 05m.	69	295	
6509	" 20	4.26 "	91	12.0	48	1.0	0h. 10m.	129	377	
6510	" 20	4.30 "	91	12.0	48	0.9	0h. 14m.	189	380	
6511	" 20	4.45 "	91	12.0	48	....	0h. 29m.	359	281	
6513	" 20	5.00 "	91	18.5	75	1.6	0h. 44m.	609	280	
6514	" 20	5.30 "	91	20.0	81	1.7	1h. 14m.	1 229	274	
6555	" 20	6.00 "	91	20.0	81	2.0	1h 44m.	1 739	271	
6516	" 20	6.30 "	91	15.0	61	1.7	2h. 14m.	2 259	205	
6517	" 20	7.00 "	91	15.0	61	1.7	2h. 44m.	2 749	219	Closed outlet at 7.00 A.M.
6609	" 24	12.50 "	105	23.5	95	....	0h. 05m.	107	470	
6610	" 24	12.55 "	105	23.5	95	....	0h. 10m.	227	450	
6611	" 24	1.00 "	105	23.5	95	2.3	0h. 15m.	347	565	
6612	" 24	1.10 "	105	23.5	95	....	0h. 25m.	577	360	
6613	" 24	1.20 "	105	23.5	95	....	0h. 35m.	807	268	
6614	" 24	1.29 "	105	23.5	95	....	0h. 44m.	1 047	385	Closed outlet at 1.29 A.M.
6616	" 24	4.40 "	106	20.0	81	....	0h. 06m.	90	315	
6617	" 24	4.45 "	106	20.0	81	....	0h. 11m.	190	485	
6618	" 24	4.50 "	106	20.0	81	..	0h. 16m.	290	535	
6619	" 24	5.00 "	106	20.0	81	1.9	0h. 26m.	550	390	
6620	" 24	5.30 "	106	20.0	81	....	0h. 56m.	1 090	435	
6621	" 24	6.00 "	106	20.0	81	2.0	1h. 26m.	1 710	465	
6623	" 24	9.00 "	106	20.5	83	3.0	4h. 26m.	5 330	198	
6624	" 24	10.00 "	106	20.0	81	3.7	5h. 26m.	6 480	258	
6625	" 24	11.00 "	106	20.0	81	4.5	6h. 26m.	7 820	229	
6626	" 24	12.00 M.	106	20.0	81	4.7	7h. 26m.	8 908	395	
6627	" 24	12.30 P.M.	106	19.0	77	4.8	7h. 56m.	9 480	475	Closed outlet at 12.30 P.M.

RESULTS OF BACTERIAL ANALYSES—WITH ELECTROLYTICALLY PREPARED HYDRATE OF IRON.—*Continued.*

Serial Number.	Collected.		Number of Run.	Rate of Filtration.		Loss of Head, Feet.	Period of Service Since Last Washing, Hours and Minutes.	Filtered Water Since Last Washing, Cubic Feet.	Bacteria per Cubic Centimeter.	Remarks.
	Date.	Hour.		Cubic Feet per Minute.	Million Gallons per Acre per 24 Hours.					
	1897									
6634	June 24	5.45 P.M.	108	18.0	73	1.7	0h. 05m.	145	590	
6635	" 24	7.30 "	108	18.0	73	2.0	1h. 50m.	2 065	625	Closed outlet at 7.50 P.M.
6640	" 24	11.55 "	110	23.5	95	....	0h. 06m.	151	1 495	
6641	" 24	12.00 "	110	23.5	95	....	0h. 11m.	281	1 680	
6642	" 25	12.15 A.M.	110	23.5	95	....	0h. 26m.	581	2 750	Closed outlet at 12.32 A.M.
6644	" 25	3.12 "	111	18.0	73	....	0h. 05m.	105	695	
6645	" 25	3.20 "	111	18.0	73	....	0h. 13m.	285	710	
6646	" 25	3.30 "	111	18.0	73	1.5	0h. 23m.	485	545	
6647	" 25	4.00 "	111	18.0	73	1.5	0h. 53m.	1 025	575	
6648	" 25	5.00 "	111	18.0	73	1.7	1h. 53m.	2 065	260	
6649	" 25	6.00 "	111	18.0	73	2.0	2h. 53m.	3 035	244	
6650	" 25	8.00 "	111	18.0	73	2.6	4h. 53m.	5 275	166	
6652	" 25	9.00 "	111	18.0	73	3.0	5h. 47m.	6 445	152	
6653	" 25	10.00 "	111	18.0	73	3.5	6h. 47m.	7 435	86	
6654	" 25	11.00 "	111	18.0	73	4.0	7h. 47m.	8 515	111	
6655	" 25	12.00 "	111	18.0	73	4.5	8h. 47m.	9 625	131	
6656	" 25	1.00 P.M.	111	18.0	73	4.8	9h. 47m.	10 745	123	
6657	" 25	2.00 "	111	18.0	73	5.2	10h. 47m.	11 835	107	
6659	" 25	3.00 "	111	18.0	73	5.7	11h. 39m.	12 935	93	
6660	" 25	4.30 "	111	19.0	77	6.0	13h. 09m.	14 455	181	
6661	" 25	7.30 "	111	18.0	73	7.2	16h. 09m.	17 815	151	
6663	" 25	9.00 "	111	18.0	73	7.8	17h. 39m.	19 365	192	
6664	" 25	11.00 "	111	18.0	73	9.0	19h. 39m.	21 455	179	
6665	" 26	12.30 A.M.	111	18.0	73	9.5	21h. 09m.	23 055	127	Agitated surface of sand layer at 12.36 A.M.
6666	" 26	12.45 "	111	18.0	73	6.2	21h. 20m.	23 245	385	
6667	" 26	12.50 "	111	18.0	73	6.3	21h. 25m.	23 355	177	
6668	" 26	1.00 "	111	18.0	73	6.5	21h. 35m.	23 535	194	
6670	" 26	3.00 "	111	18.0	73	7.8	23h. 35m.	25 585	187	
6671	" 26	5.00 "	111	18.0	73	8.8	25h. 35m.	27 695	142	
6672	" 26	6.00 "	111	18.0	73	9.0	26h. 35m.	28 725	106	Closed outlet at 6.00 A.M.
6673	" 26	7.38 "	112	23.5	95	....	0h. 44m.	1 053	212	
6675	" 26	11.22 "	113	23.5	95	....	0h. 06m.	138	295	
6676	" 26	11.27 "	113	23.5	95	....	0h. 11m.	288	258	
6677	" 26	11.37 "	113	23.5	95	....	0h. 21m.	498	281	
6678	" 26	12.00 M.	113	23.5	95	....	0h. 44m.	1 008	275	Closed outlet at 12.13 P.M.
6680	" 26	3.19 P.M.	114	18.0	73	....	0h. 07m.	150	395	
6681	" 26	3.25 "	114	18.0	73	....	0h. 13m.	250	410	
6682	" 26	3.38 "	114	18.0	73	....	0h. 26m.	500	335	Closed outlet at 3.40 P.M.
6683	" 26	5.40 "	115	23.5	95	....	0h. 06m.	150	315	
6684	" 26	5.50 "	115	23.5	95	....	0h. 16m.	370	295	
6685	" 26	7.30 "	115	23.5	95	2.5	1h. 56m.	2 690	340	Closed outlet at 7.33 P.M.
6699	" 27	5.30 A.M.	119	23.5	95	2.0	0h. 05m.	116	1 020	
6700	" 27	5.40 "	119	23.5	95	....	0h. 15m.	326	690	
6701	" 27	6.00 "	119	23.5	95	....	0h. 35m.	796	385	Closed outlet at 6.00 A.M.
6703	" 27	9.00 "	120	23.5	95	3.0	1h. 00m.	1 383	136	Closed outlet at 9.05 A.M.
6704	" 27	11.33 "	121	18.0	73	....	0h. 05m.	148	260	
6705	" 27	11.39 "	121	18.0	73	....	0h. 14m.	248	335	
6706	" 27	12.00 M.	121	18.5	75	1.7	0h. 35m.	578	320	
6707	" 27	12.30 P.M.	121	17.0	69	1.9	1h. 05m.	1 278	146	
6708	" 27	1.00 "	121	18.0	73	2.1	1h. 35m.	1 718	189	
6709	" 27	1.30 "	121	19.0	77	....	2h. 05m.	2 366	181	Closed outlet at 1.30 P.M.
6710	" 27	2.13 "	122	18.0	73	....	0h. 08m.	152	223	
6711	" 27	2.18 "	122	18.0	73	....	0h. 13m.	252	272	
6712	" 27	2.32 "	122	18.0	73	...	0h. 27m.	502	198	
6713	" 27	3.00 "	122	17.5	71	....	0h. 55m.	1 012	187	
6715	" 27	4.00 "	122	18.5	75	2.4	1h. 50m.	2 062	119	
6716	" 27	5.30 "	122	19.0	77	3.3	3h. 20m.	3 722	......	
6717	" 27	8.00 "	122	18.0	73	4.4	5h. 50m.	6 442	......	
6718	" 27	9.00 "	122	18.0	73	....	6h. 50m.	7 494	218	Closed outlet at 9.00 P.M.
6794	July 1	5.00 "	132	23.5	95	2.0	0h. 06m.	158	84	
6795	" 1	5.30 "	132	23.5	95	2.2	0h. 36m.	938	92	

RESULTS OF BACTERIAL ANALYSES—WITH ELECTROLYTICALLY PREPARED HYDRATE OF IRON.—*Concluded.*

Serial Number.	Collected.		Number of Run.	Rate of Filtration.		Loss of Head. Feet.	Period of Service Since Last Washing. Hours and Minutes.	Filtered Water Since Last Washing. Cubic Feet.	Bacteria per Cubic Centimeter.	Remarks.
	Date.	Hour.		Cubic Feet per Minute.	Million Gallons per Acre per 24 Hours.					
	1897									
6796	July 1	8.00 P.M.	132	23.5	95	2.9	3h. 06m.	4 308	39	
6798	" 1	9.00 "	132	23.5	95	3.4	4h. 06m.	5 678	49	
6799	" 1	10.00 "	132	23.5	95	4.3	5h. 06m.	7 058	......	
6800	" 1	11.00 "	132	23.5	95	4.7	6h. 06m.	8 448	94	
6801	" 1	12.00 M.	132	23.5	95	5.0	7h. 06m.	9 858	67	
6927	" 9	4.39 A.M.	147	23.5	95	....	0h. 05m.	140	420	
6928	" 9	4.44 "	147	23.5	95	....	0h. 10m.	240	360	
6929	" 9	4.55 "	147	23.5	95	....	0h. 21m.	490	325	
6932	" 9	5.20 "	147	23.5	95	....	0h. 46m.	1 090	244	
6933	" 9	6.30 "	147	20.0	81	2.2	1h. 56m.	2 510	154	
6934	" 9	8.00 "	147	18.0	73	2.4	3h. 26m.	4 160	259	Closed outlet at 8.14 A.M.
6935	" 9	8.55 "	148	18.5	75	....	0h. 08m.	152	226	
6936	" 9	9.02 "	148	18.0	73	....	0h. 15m.	302	212	
6937	" 9	9.30 "	148	18.0	73	1.7	0h. 43m.	908	176	
6940	" 9	10.00 "	148	18.0	73	1.9	1h. 13m.	1 338	124	
6941	" 9	11.00 "	148	18.0	73	2.1	2h. 13m.	2 418	88	
6942	" 9	12.00 M.	148	18.0	73	3.0	3h. 13m.	3 488	83	
6943	" 9	1.00 P.M.	148	18.0	73	3.5	4h. 13m.	4 558	96	
6952	" 9	11.39 "	150	20.0	81	....	0h. 08m.	153	315	
6953	" 9	11.44 "	150	20.0	81	....	0h. 13m.	253	340	
6954	" 9	12.00 "	150	20.0	81	....	0h. 29m.	443	555	Closed outlet at 12.00 P.M.
6956	" 10	1.19 A.M.	151	18.0	73	....	0h. 08m.	147	330	
6957	" 10	1.24 "	151	18.0	73	....	0h. 13m.	247	430	
6959	" 10	1.38 "	151	18.0	73	....	0h. 27m.	497	340	
6960	" 10	2.00 "	151	18.0	73	....	0h. 49m.	907	173	Closed outlet at 2.00 A.M.
6961	" 10	2.40 "	152	18.0	73	....	0h. 15m.	251	275	
6962	" 10	2.45 "	152	18.0	73	....	0h. 20m.	351	275	
6963	" 10	3.00 "	152	18.0	73	....	0h. 35m.	601	269	Closed outlet at 3.10 A.M.
7234	" 22	1.20 P.M.	177	23.0	93	....	0h. 06m.	154	151	
7235	" 22	1.30 "	177	23.0	93	2.1	0h. 16m.	394	174	
7236	" 22	2.00 "	177	23.0	93	2.1	0h. 46m.	1 084	202	Closed outlet at 2.00 P.M.
7238	" 22	3.09 "	178	23.0	93	....	0h. 06m.	149	139	
7239	" 22	3.24 "	178	23.0	93	....	0h. 21m.	499	138	
7241	" 22	5.00 "	178	23.5	95	2.3	1h. 57m.	3 449	63	
7242	" 22	8.00 "	178	23.5	95	3.7	4h. 57m.	6 899	38	
7257	" 23	9.58 A.M.	181	23.5	95	....	0h. 06m.	146	165	
7258	" 23	10.13 "	181	23.5	95	....	0h. 21m.	496	139	
7259	" 23	11.00 "	181	23.5	95	2.2	1h. 08m.	1 596	128	
7260	" 23	12.00 M.	181	23.5	95	2.7	2h. 08m.	3 006	111	
7261	" 23	1.00 P.M.	181	23.5	95	3.0	3h. 08m.	4 386	116	
7262	" 23	2.00 "	181	23.5	95	3.6	4h. 08m.	5 806	90	
7263	" 23	3.00 "	181	23.0	93	4.0	5h. 08m.	7 206	163	Closed outlet at 3.10 P.M.

Summary of Results, showing the Amount of Suspended Matter and Number of Bacteria in the River Water as it passed through the several Settling Basins.

In this table are given all of the determinations of the amount of suspended matter and number of bacteria in the effluents from the several settling basins, together with corresponding determinations of the river water. It will be seen that in several instances the determinations in the case of the effluents gave larger results than were found with the river or with the effluent from preceding basins. This is mainly accounted for by the fact that it was not found practicable to collect samples from the same water as it passed through the system, but all samples from the settling basins were taken at the same time, and are tabulated with samples of river water collected from one to three hours earlier. The samples do not, therefore, represent the actual condition of the same water as it passed through the system, but the condition of the various effluents at the hour given.

All of the columns given are explained by their headings, except that headed "Treatment." Under this heading and subheading "Kind," two letters are given. The first letter refers to the kind of coagulant used, and the second to the place of application. These letters refer to coagulants and places as follows:

Kind of Coagulant.

A. Hydrate of alumina from sulphate of alumina.

B. Hydrate of iron from persulphate of iron.

C. Hydrate of alumina prepared electrolytically from aluminum.

D. Hydrate of iron prepared electrolytically from iron.

E. Hydrate of iron from protosulphate of iron.

F. E. with caustic soda. The soda was applied at basin No. 2, and the copperas at the Jewell settling chamber.

Place of Application.

A. Basin No. 2 and Jewell settling chamber, in equal amounts.

B. Jewell settling chamber.

C. Top of filter.

D. Basin No. 1 and Jewell settling chamber.

E. Basin No. 1 and top of filter.

F. Basin No. 1.

G. Basin No. 2.

Coagulants were always applied at the inlet pipes.

Under subheading "Amount" the total amounts of chemicals used are given in grains per gallon in the case of commercial chemicals and in ampere hours per gallon in the case of electrolytic treatment; and, in the case of application at D or E, the separate amounts are given as foot-notes in the order in which they were applied, the upper one being first and the lower second.

Where a settling basin was not in use the fact is so recorded in the column for that basin.

AMOUNT OF SUSPENDED MATTER AND NUMBER OF BACTERIA IN THE RIVER WATER AS IT PASSED THROUGH THE SEVERAL SETTLING-BASINS.

Date. 1897.		Number of Run.	Treatment.		River Water.		Effluent of Basin No. 1.		Effluent of Basin No. 2.		Effluent of Jewell Settling Chamber.	
Day.	Hour.		Kind and Place.	Amount.	Suspended Solids. Parts per Million.	Bacteria per Cubic Centimeter.	Suspended Solids. Parts per Million.	Bacteria per Cubic Centimeter.	Suspended Solids. Parts per Million.	Bacteria per Cubic Centimeter.	Suspended Solids. Parts per Million.	Bacteria per Cubic Centimeter.
April 11	4.30 P.M.	15	D-A	.084	784	47 100	413	68 500	476	57 000	....	....
" 14	10.30 "	25	B-A	2.83	322	38 100	185	47 900	225	24 200	87	11 200
" 15	10.00 "	28	A-A	3.01	347	28 700	216	34 500	237	31 700	129	11 500
" 16	1.00 "	31	B-A	3.37	407	37 000	268	29 500	166	14 100	73	3 500
" 20	9.30 "	32	D-A	.080	205	16 800	151	18 700	160	19 400	128	11 800
" 21	4.00 "	34	D-A	.136	183	12 600	192	10 700	120	7 900	97	7 300
" 22	3.30 "	35	B-A	1.81	231	14 600	295	12 100	131	5 600	95	3 900
" 24	2.30 "	43	A-A	1.44	196	9 400	133	4 000	106	4 200	80	2 900
" 26	9.30 "	45	C-A	.030	184	7 400	107	3 900	71	2 400	50	1 800
" 27	9.00 "	46	D-A	.078	160	11 700	115	11 400	119	12 900	81	10 200
" 28	11.00 A.M.	48	C-A	.018	133	22 900	95	....	82	21 100	60	11 700
" 28	4.00 P.M.	49	C-A	.014	133	19 500	107	22 400	92	23 100	76	14 900
" 29	11.00 A.M.	50	A-A	1.17	136	14 800	127	15 800	116	8 200	83	5 800
" 30	3.00 P.M.	52	C-A	.019	77	10 200	76	5 100	47	6 300	34	3 800
" 30	9.00 "	53	C-H	.019	77	9 700	68	8 800	67	9 100	37	4 300
May 1	3.00 "	54	C-G	.019	77	7 900	59	7 800	74	6 100	47	4 600
" 7	5.00 A.M.	56	C-A	.048	453	51 500	181	35 900	38	36 700	8	33 100
" 7	10.30 "	57	C-A	.040	453	31 100	175	19 600	212	12 000	104	7 100
" 7	4.30 P.M.	58	C-A	.028	453	27 000	175	17 300	....	12 100	115	8 800
" 7	10.00 "	59	A-A	2.47	301	28 500	172	27 900	153	15 100	94	12 000
" 8	4.00 A.M.	60	A-A	3.02	301	19 100	168	25 500	147	10 650	84	8 500
" 8	9.30 "	61	A-A	3.60	301	24 200	157	23 200	88	10 100	88	6 100
" 8	4.30 P.M.	63	A-A	3.67	301	21 100	148	20 200	83	9 400	72	6 200
" 9	4.30 A.M.	66	A-G	3.75	301	13 100	110	14 200	115	10 800	84	9 300
" 19	11.00 P.M.	67	G-A	1.96	273	13 400	201	13 600	184	8 900	122	6 200
" 20	5.30 "	68	G-A	1.92	277	10 500	195	9 200	170	8 800	99	5 400
" 22	3.00 A.M.	70	G-A	1.12	260	9 700	144	11 000	139	9 900	122	6 400
" 22	9.00 P.M.	70	G-A	1.12	255	7 400	138	10 000	128	5 800	90	3 900
" 23	9.00 "	72	G-A	1.14	249	....	209	....	123	....	97	....
" 25	5.00 A.M.	75	G-A	0.80	113	9 300	108	8 800	79	6 300	55	5 500
" 26	8.30 P.M.	81	G-A	0.92	100	18 200	86	15 700	77	10 100	75	8 400
" 28	3.00 A.M.	87	G-A	1.26	98	6 700	92	6 900	102	6 100	85	5 200
June 21	3.30 "	93	G-C	1.92	140	....	154	....	174	....	145	....
" 21	12.00 M.	94	G-B	2.11	149	....	145	....	132	....	....	....
" 21	8.30 P.M.	95	G-G	2.71	184	....	166	....	152	....	123	....
" 22	9.30 A.M.	98	G-B	1.46	298	....	Not in use		Not in use		125	....
" 22	1.10 P.M.	98	G-B	1.46	295	....	" " "		" " "		165	....
" 22	4.00 "	99	G-C	1.42	295	....	" " "		" " "		270	....
" 23	8.00 A.M.	102	G-B	1.69	368	....	" " "		" " "		82	....
" 23	3.00 P.M.	103	G-C	1.92	368	....	" " "		" " "		280	....
" 23	8.30 "	104	G-B	1.88	438	....	" " "		" " "		120	....
" 24	1.30 A.M.	105	D-B	0.037	521	....	" " "		" " "		278	....
" 24	5.00 "	106	D-B	0.045	557	....	505	....	....	....	163	....
" 24	12.00 M.	106	D-B	0.045	605	....	581	....	557	....	396	....
" 25	12.15 A.M.	110	D-A	0.078	616	....	609	....	593	....	196	....
" 25	4.00 "	111	D-A	0.099	585	....	532	....	155	....	64	....
" 25	12.00 M.	111	D-A	0.099	514	....	461	....	334	....	71	....
" 25	12.00 P.M.	111	D-A	0.099	444	....	451	....	158	....	45	....
" 26	12.00 M.	113	D-B	0.038	425	....	413	....	426	....	237	....
" 26	5.40 P.M.	115	D-A	0.064	350	....	374	....	383	....	281	....
" 26	9.30 "	116	A-A	2.01	600	....	572	....	542	....	99	....
" 27	12.30 A.M.	117	A-A	2.00	622	....	583	....	620	....	145	....
" 27	3.00 "	118	A-A	1.02	673	....	575	....	627	....	632	....
" 27	6.00 "	119	D-A	0.064	711	....	586	....	567	....	309	....
" 27	12.00 M.	121	D-A	0.094	535	....	539	....	452	....	65	....
" 28	4.00 A.M.	124	A-A	2.35	454	....	426	....	473	....	341	....
" 29	11.15 P.M.	126	A-A	3.47	408	....	389	....	379	....	144	....
" 30	9.00 A.M.	127	A-A	2.90	354	....	....	....	....	....	....	....
" 30	12.00 M.	128	E-A	6.88	354	9 300	352	7 100	....	4 400	....	2 200
" 30	9.00 P.M.	130	A-A	2.98	308	6 100	297	....	250	....	144	....
July 1	6.10 A.M.	131	A-A	2.52	297	4 900	280	4 700	253	4 200	112	2 600
" 1	11.30 "	131	A-A	2.52	279	4 900	256	4 600	248	....	115	1 300

SUSPENDED MATTER AND BACTERIA.—*Concluded.*

Date. 1897.		Number of Run.	Treatment.		River Water.		Effluent of Basin No. 1		Effluent of Basin No. 2.		Effluent of Jewell Settling Chamber.	
Day.	Hour.		Kind and Place.	Amount.	Suspended Solids. Parts per Million.	Bacteria per Cubic Centimeter.	Suspended Solids. Parts per Million.	Bacteria per Cubic Centimeter.	Suspended Solids. Parts per Million.	Bacteria per Cubic Centimeter.	Suspended Solids. Parts per Million.	Bacteria per Cubic Centimeter.
July 1	12.00 P.M.	132	D-A	0.078	218	2 900	214	....	235	2 200	116	....
" 2	6.00 A.M.	133	C-A	0.037	159	2 200	172	1 900	167	....	71	1 000
" 2	12.00 M.	134	C-A	0.028	151	2 210	148	2 100	138	....	99	....
" 2	8.30 P.M.	136	A-B	1.96	147	5 000	140	6 100	128	4 600	62	2 700
" 3	5.30 A.M.	137	A-C	2.06	135	4 800	143	4 300	139	2 500	170	1 400
" 6	4.30 P.M.	140	A-B	1.67	121	3 900	......	....	......	....	71	1 310
" 6	9.00 "	140	A-B	1.67	127	3 800	......	....	......	....	57	1 700
" 7	11.00 A.M.	141	A-C	1.59	552	12 100	......	....	......	....	191	3 700
" 7	2.30 P.M.	142	A-C	2.02	753	12 600	......	....	......	....	324	6 600
" 7	4.00 "	142	A-C	2.02	343	13 100	......	....	......	....	226	3 700
" 7	10.00 "	144	A-C	2.60	455	....	......	....	......	....	400	3 450
" 8	4.00 A.M.	145	A-B	1.92	438	14 100	......	....	......	....	134	1 355
" 8	3.00 P.M.	146	A-B	1.99	633	17 900	......	....	......	....	143	3 300
" 9	5.00 A.M.	147	D-B	.089	488	7 300	Not in use		Basin No. 2 was not used again after Run No. 146.		181	3 400
" 9	10.00 "	148	D-B	.099	419	5 900	" " "				138	2 100
" 9	5.00 P.M.	149	A-B	2.41	455	6 300	" " "				116	1 400
" 9	9.00 "	149	A-B	2.41	478	7 400	" " "				148	1 890
" 9	12.00 "	150	D-B	.091	445	8 500	" " "				157	2 300
" 10	1.30 A.M.	151	D-B	.096	430	9 000	" " "				84	2 150
" 10	3.00 "	152	D-B	.104	312	9 600	" " "				123	1 700
" 10	5.00 "	153	A-B	2.69	320	....	" " "				105	....
" 10	9.00 "	153	A-B	2.69	364	7 100	" " "				124	850
" 10	2.30 P.M.	155	B-B	2.66	379	9 400	" " "				85	2 900
" 10	5.40 "	156	A-B	2.69	305	9 400	" " "				142	3 100
" 14	9.30 "	157	A-D	1.85[1]	191	5 600	186	3 900			92	1 380
" 14	11.30 "	158	A-E	1.81[2]	195	5 600	182	4 600			77	4 400
" 15	5.00 A.M.	159	A-D	2.22[3]	199	5 900	183	4 700			107	2 200
" 15	9.00 "	159	A-D	2.22[3]	171	4 600	100	2 700			71	800
" 15	10.30 "	160	A-B	2.18[4]	171	4 600	127	4 600			65	1 100
" 15	3.00 P.M.	161	A-E	2.19[5]	180	6 100	154	3 900			124	2 400
" 15	8.00 "	162	A-D	2.16[6]	185	6 100	135	1 930			71	1 210
" 15	11.30 "	163	A-E	2.19[6]	189	6 000	142	2 500			139	1 700
" 16	4.00 A.M.	164	A-B	1.81	189	5 800	Not in use				120	980
" 16	11.00 "	166	A-B	2.14	189	5 300	" " "				91	1 500
" 16	10.05 P.M.	167	A-B	2.82	129	5 900	" " "				79	760
" 17	4.30 A.M.	168	A-D	2.32[7]	152	6 400	28	940			0	840
" 17	2.00 P.M.	168	A-D	2.32[7]	131	6 100	71	1 400			30	1 190
" 17	5.30 "	169	A-E	2.30[8]	125	6 100	55	1 250			25	1 180
" 17	12.00 "	169	A-E	2.30[8]	119	5 600	39	1 150			17	680
" 18	6.00 A.M.	170	A-D	2.29[9]	113	4 500	26	....			20	810
" 18	11.00 "	170	A-D	2.29[9]	109	3 900	26	980			22	770
" 18	5.30 P.M.	171	A-E	2.32[10]	108	4 800	42	780			33	770
" 18	12.00 "	172	A-D	2.18[11]	109	3 900	19	810			6	730
" 19	10.00 A.M.	172	A-D	2.18[11]	120	3 800	37	1 080			17	810
" 19	9.30 P.M.	173	A-F	1.51	78	3 400	16	590			20	570
" 19	12.00 M.	173	A-F	1.51	78	3 000	14	860			18	700
" 20	5.00 A.M.	173	A-F	1.51	75	2 700	21	880			16	495
" 20	4.00 P.M.	173	A-F	1.51	66	3 250	51	1 020			31	960
" 20	10.00 "	174	A-B	1.60	70	2 550	Not in use				49	1 120
" 21	9.00 A.M.	174	A-B	1.60	76	3 350	" " "				43	2 180
" 21	3.30 P.M.	175	A-C	1.60	130	4 850	" " "				86	2 780
" 21	11.00 "	176	A-B	1.02	130	4 250	" " "				70	1 670
" 22	5.00 "	178	D-B	.040	128	4 760	" " "				15	3 400
" 22	11.30 "	179	A-C	1.04	127	4 800	" " "				37	1 900
" 23	1.30 A.M.	180	A-D	0.78	140	4 600	" " "				......	1 300
" 23	9.00 P.M.	182	A-G	9.77	171	6 200	84	3 400			82	3 600
" 23	11.00 "	183	A-B	0.77	173	6 200	Not in use				35	3 800
" 24	3.30 A.M.	184	A-C	1.10	174	5 300	" " "				163	....
" 24	5.30 "	185	A-B	1.03	173	5 300	" " "				108	....

[1] 0.63 + 1.22. [2] 0.63 + 1.18. [3] 1.06 + 1.16. [4] 1.06 + 1.12. [5] 1.06 + 1.13. [6] 1.06 + 1.10. [7] 1.49 + 0.83. [8] 1.50 + 0.80. [9] 1.50 + 0.79. [10] 1.52 + 0.80. [11] 1.57 + 0.66.

Final Summary, showing the Leading Results of Operation.

In the following table will be found a summary of all of the leading results of operation of the Water Company's devices. The devices, methods of operation, and general periods of operation, have already been presented, as well as complete tables of analytical results. It is only necessary, therefore, to explain the various headings in the table.

Settling Basins in Service. — Under this heading the basins used for preliminary treatment of the water previous to its entrance to the Jewell settling chamber are given. It is understood that the latter was in use at all times.

Treatment.—For economy of space letters have been used in the two columns under this head. The letters refer to the coagulant used, or place of application, as follows:

Kind (of Coagulant Used).

A. Hydrate of alumina from sulphate of alumina.

B. Hydrate of iron from persulphate of iron.

C. Hydrate of alumina prepared electrolytically from aluminum.

D. Hydrate of iron prepared electrolytically from iron.

E. Hydrate of iron from copperas.

F. E. with caustic soda. The caustic soda was applied to basin No. 2, and the copperas at the inlet to the Jewell settling chamber.

Place (of Application).

A. Equal amounts at basin No. 2 and Jewell settling chamber.

B. Jewell settling chamber.

C. Top of filter. (Outlet of Jewell settling chamber.

D. Basin No. 1 and Jewell settling chamber.

E. Basin No. 1 and top of filter.

F. Basin No. 1.

G. Basin No. 2.

In all cases coagulant was applied at the inlets of the settling basins or chamber, unless otherwise recorded.

Grains of Chemical per Gallon.—The total amount of chemical used per gallon of applied water is given under this heading. Where it was applied at more than one point the separate amounts are given as foot-notes in the order they were applied.

Electric Current.—The electric horse-power per million gallons of treated water per 24 hours is given from calculations based on the amperage and voltage of the electric current. Ampere hours of electric current per gallon of treated water is used to express the amount of electrolytic treatment. For the amounts of metal used see discussion in the last portion of this chapter on the rate of electrolytic decomposition of the metal.

Average Suspended Solids.—In so far as was feasible, the suspended solids in the river water, and in the water above the sand layer in the filter, were determined for each run. The results are given in these two columns.

The headings in the balance of the table have already been described in Chapter VIII, and do not need further explanation.

On runs Nos. 154 and 155 the free acid in the persulphate of iron was neutralized by caustic soda.

Several runs were not continued to their normal length, owing to either the completion of the special study for which the run was made, the necessity of taking up other work at a certain time, or, in two cases, by closing operations for the week. Where the run ended on a good water for these reasons, the period of service is marked with a star (*); and it is to be noted that in most of these cases the bacterial efficiency is probably lower than it would have been had the run been continued to its normal end, as the samples collected at the beginning of the run generally represented the poorest water of the run.

FINAL SUMMARY SHOWING THE LEADING RESULTS OF OPERATION.

Number of Run.	Began. Date. 1897.	Began. Hour.	Settling Basins in Service.	Treatment. Kind.	Treatment. Place.	Grains Chemical per Gallon.	Electric Current. Ampere-hour per Gallon.	Electric Current. H.P. per Million Gallons per 24 Hours.	Average Suspended Solids. Parts per Million. River Water.	Average Suspended Solids. Parts per Million. At Top of Filter.	Period of Service. Hours and Minutes.	Quantities of Water. Cubic Feet. Filtered.	Quantities of Water. Cubic Feet. Wash.	Average Rate of Filtration. Cubic Feet per Minute.	Average Rate of Filtration. Million Gallons per Acre per 24 Hours.	Degree of Clearness of Effluent.	Nitrogen as Albuminoid Ammonia. Parts per Million. River Water.	Nitrogen as Albuminoid Ammonia. Parts per Million. Effluent.	Nitrogen as Albuminoid Ammonia. Parts per Million. Per Cent Removed.	Oxygen Consumed. Parts per Million. River Water.	Oxygen Consumed. Parts per Million. Effluent.	Oxygen Consumed. Parts per Million. Per Cent Removed.	Bacteria per Cubic Centimeter. River Water.	Bacteria per Cubic Centimeter. Effluent.	Bacterial Efficiency.	Number of Run.
1	Apr. 5	11.33 A.M.	None	A	B	1.32	....	.....	336	....	3h. 22m.	5 004	545	24.8	100	2							6 700	275	95.9	1
2	" 5	3.15 P.M.	"	A	B	1.06	....	.....	336	....	4h. 22m.	6 194	560	23.6	95	2	.344	.054	....	6.7	0.9	87	6 500	275	95.7	2
3	" 5	7.54 "	"	A	B	0.58	....	.....	336	....	5h. 10m.	6 765	622	21.8	88	2							5 600	443	92.1	3
4	" 6	2.47 A.M.	"	B	B	1.23	....	.....	351	....	4h. 27m.	5 859	625	22.0	89	2							6 700	141	97.9	4
5	" 6	8.00 "	"	B	B	1.08	....	.....	351	....	2h. 14m.	3 086	511	23.0	93	2	.382	.044	68	6.7	0.8	88	8 600	247	97.1	5
6	" 6	11.44 "	"	B	B	0.96	....	.....	351	....	3h. 00m.	4 052	553	22.5	91	2							13 600	344	97.5	6
7	" 6	4.00 P.M.	"	B	B	0.76	....	.....	351	....	3h. 10m.	4 610	831	24.2	98	2							27 400	319	98.8	7
8	" 6	9.44 "	"	A	B	1.33	....	.....	586	....	6h. 09m.	8 540	524	23.1	93	1	.382	.050	87	6.8	0.9	87	23 000	195	99.2	8
9	" 7	4.35 A.M.	"	A	B	0.93	....	.....	586	....	1h. 45m.	2 596	652	24.7	100	3							28 700	877	96.9	9
10	" 7	8.00 "	"	B	B	1.36	....	.....	586	....	8h. 49m.	12 446	801	23.5	95	2	.514	.042	92	9.4	0.8	91	26 700	192	99.3	10
11	" 8	7.15 "	"	A	B	0.95	....	.....	839	....	2h. 32m.	3 593	595	23.6	95	...	......	....	...	......	....	...	......	......	....	11
12	" 8	10.25 "	"	A	B	1.57	....	.....	839	....	2h. 00m.	2 919	594	24.3	98	1	.680	.054	92	13.6	1.0	93	32 200	100	99.7	12
13	" 8	1.15 P.M.	"	A	B	3.19	....	.....	839	....	8h. 42m.	11 951	1 218	22.9	93	2	.612	.042	93	13.3	0.9	93	32 800	960	97.1	13
14	" 9	2.55 "	"	B	B	4.23	....	.....	634	....	6h. 38m.	9 134	....	23.0	93	2	.650	.030	95	12.9	0.6	95	40 300	247	99.4	14
15	" 11	2.10 "	1 and 2	D	A	.....	.084	32.7	784	....	8h. 11m.	11 071	713	22.5	91	4	.800	.078	90	13.1	2.4	81	54 100	13 700	74.7	15
16	" 11	10.52 "	"	D	A	.....	.114	59.5	784	....	4h. 53m.	5 100	630	17.4	71	3	......	....	...	......	....	...	56 000	2 370	95.8	16
17	" 12	4.10 A.M.	"	D	A	.....	.122	38.0	598	....	11h. 10m.	11 060	1 199	16.5	67	2	.554	.056	90	12.4	1.0	92	39 800	8 190	79.4	17
18	" 12	5.25 P.M.	"	B	A	3.99	....	.....	518	....	11h. 43m.	16 177	847	23.4	95	2	.480	.042	91	10.2	0.7	93	39 100	321	99.2	18
19	" 13	6.03 A.M.	"	A	A	3.98	....	.....	452	...	8h. 57m.	11 986	1 270	22.3	90	2	.400	.044	89	9.8	0.7	93	30 800	1 434	95.3	19
20	" 13	5.26 P.M.	"	C	A	.....	.056	23.8	452	....	2h. 42m.	3 741	515	23.1	93	2							29 400	1 218	95.9	20
21	" 13	11.49 "	"	C	A	.....	.064	28.7	459	....	2h. 21m.	3 288	492	23.3	94	2	.454	.058	87	9.2	0.9	90	28 100	855	96.9	21
22	" 14	2.37 A.M.	"	C	A	.....	.072	36.8	459	....	2h. 33m.	3 502	495	22.9	93	2							28 800	624	97.8	22
23	" 14	5.33 "	"	C	A	.....	.082	46.2	459	....	3h. 37m.	4 984	1 244	22.9	93	2							23 200	387	98.3	23
24	" 14	1.03 P.M.	"	D	A	.....	.080	32.7	331	....	4h. 07m.	5 510	935	33.5	95	2	.320	.050	84	7.6	0.8	89	20 900	518	97.5	24
25	" 14	10.00 "	"	B	A	2.83	....	.....	322	87	8h. 10m.	11 304	1 022	23.1	93	1	.320	.054	83	7.6	0.9	88	37 000	136	99.6	25
26	" 15	7.14 A.M.	"	A	A	3.10	....	.....	347	....	4h. 15m.	6 041	1 083	23.6	95	2	.350	.050	86	6.8	0.6	91	30 400	72	97.6	26
27	" 15	1.47 P.M.	"	D	A	.....	.080	30.4	347	....	4h. 10m.	5 595	1 015	22.4	91	1	......	....	...	......	....	...	......	......	....	27
28	" 15	9.45 "	"	A	A	3.01	....	.....	347	129	3h. 11m.	4 356	508	22.8	92	2	......	....	...	......	....	...	28 700	272	99.1	28
29	" 16	1.22 A.M.	"	A	A	2.88	....	.....	407	....	2h. 37m.	3 628	531	23.1	93	2	.350	.050	86	6.8	0.9	87	29 300	269	99.1	29
30	" 16	4.22 "	"	A	A	1.96	....	.....	407	....	3h. 16m.	4 599	801	23.4	95	2	......	....	...	......	....	...	30 000	68	99.8	30
31	" 16	8.00 "	"	B	A	3.37	....	.....	497	73	5h. 48m.	8 013	919	23.0	93	1	.392	.048	88	8.4	0.8	90	37 000	164	99.6	31
32	" 20	4.34 P.M.	"	D	A	.....	.080	44.8	205	128	6h. 02m.	8 236	598	22.3	90	3							14 400	1 345	90.7	32
33	" 20	11.00 "	"	D	A	.....	.086	39.0	183	97	5h. 52m.	7 347	747	20.9	85	2	.246	.056	77	4.8	1.1	78	15 000	351	97.7	33
34	" 21	5.35 A.M.	"	D	A	.....	.136	40.3	231	97	10h. 59m.	11 522	1 390	17.5	71	1							12 300	192	98.4	34
35	" 21	6.32 P.M.	"	B	A	1.81	....	.....	193	95	10h. 55m.	14 556	1 119	22.3	90	1	.238	.038	84	5.0	0.6	88	17 800	164	99.1	35
36	" 22	7.57 A.M.	"	A	A	1.05	....	.....	231	....	8h. 13m.	11 296	665	22.9	93	2	.310	.062	80	5.5	1.1	80	14 700	120	99.2	36
37	" 22	6.10 P.M.	"	C	A	.....	.028	7.3	231	....	2h. 22m.	3 274	721	23.0	93	3	......	....	...	......	....	...	13 800	242	98.2	37
38	" 22	9.00 "	"	C	A	.....	.030	7.4	242	....	3h. 14m.	4 429	669	22.8	92	3							13 000	132	99.0	38
39	" 23	12.42 A.M.	"	C	A	.....	.028	7.3	242	....	0h. 53m.	1 217	633	23.0	93	3	.302	.074	76	5.4	1.1	80	14 300	117	99.2	39
40	" 23	3.32 "	"	C	A	.....	.038	11.6	242	....	4h. 10m.	5 918	661	23.6	95	2							15 300	217	98.6	40
41	" 23	9.40 "	"	C	A	.....	.020	3.7	242	....	4h. 05m.	5 569	785	22.7	92	1							14 900	144	99.0	41
42	" 23	3.39 P.M.	"	D	A	.....	.076	22.7	196	....	4h. 30m.	6 350	595	23.6	95	3	......	....	...	......	....	...	16 300	376	97.7	42
43	" 24	6.20 A.M	"	A	A	1.44	....	.....	196	30	8h. 24m.	11 209	569	22.3	90	1	.254	.070	72	5.0	0.6	88	8 700	66	99.2	43

FINAL SUMMARY.—*Continued.*

Number of Run.	Began. Date. 1897.	Began. Hour.	Settling Basins in Service.	Treatment. Kind.	Treatment. Place.	Grains Chemical per Gallon.	Electric Current. Ampere-hour per Gallon.	Electric Current. H.P. per Million Gallons per 24 Hours.	Average Suspended Solids. Parts per Million. River Water.	Average Suspended Solids. At Top of Filter.	Period of Service. Hours and Minutes.	Quantities of Water. Cubic Feet. Filtered.	Quantities of Water. Cubic Feet. Wash.	Average Rate of Filtration. Cubic Feet per Minute.	Average Rate of Filtration. Million Gallons per Acre per 24 Hours.	Degree of Clearness of Effluent.	Nitrogen as Albuminoid Ammonia. Parts per Million. River Water.	Nitrogen. Effluent.	Nitrogen. Per Cent Removed.	Oxygen Consumed. Parts per Million. River Water.	Oxygen. Effluent.	Oxygen. Per Cent Removed.	Bacteria per Cubic Centimeter. River Water.	Bacteria. Effluent.	Bacterial Efficiency.	Number of Run.
44	Apr. 26	8.16 A.M.	1 and 2	C	A	.....	.028	7.3	184	....	5h. 47m.	7 984	677	23.0	93	2	.208	.048	77	4.5	0.8	82	8 400	320	96.2	44
45	" 26	2.44 P.M.	"	C	A	.....	.030	7.7	184	50	7h. 24m.	9 671	653	21.8	88	2							6 100	263	95.7	45
46	" 27	6.01 "	"	D	A	.....	.078	35.1	160	81	4h. 17m.	5 900	624	23.0	93	2	.234	.050	79	4.4	0.7	84	11 400	560	94.9	46
47	" 27	12.00 "	"	D	A	.....	.078	34.9	160	....	4h. 11m.	5 724	621	22.8	92	1							12 600	210	98.3	47
48	" 28	6.04 A.M.	"	C	A	.....	.018	3.4	133	60	7h. 37m.	10 752	755	23.6	95	1	.188	.050	73	3.3	0.6	82	22 900	451	98.0	48
49	" 28	3.28 P.M.	"	C	A	.....	.014	2.3	133	76	7h. 12m.	9 784	681	22.6	91	1							23 200	359	98.5	49
50	" 29	12.24 A.M.	"	A	A	1.17	.....	.....	136	83	11h. 47m.	16 282	664	23.1	93	1	.224	.048	79	4.1	0.6	85	17 200	110	99.4	50
51	" 29	6.44 P.M.	"	B	A	1.23	.....	.....	131	...	9h. 51m.	13 597	596	22.9	93	1	.162	.050	69	3.3	0.5	85	15 500	36	99.8	51
52	" 30	9.25 A.M.	"	C	A	.....	.019	3.5	77	34	8h. 13m.	11 339	639	23.1	93	1							10 300	230	97.8	52
53	" 30	7.29 P.M.	"	C	B	.....	.019	6.5	77	37	10h. 28m.	14 324	679	22.9	93	1	.150	.050	67	3.2	0.6	81	12 700	157	98.8	53
54	May 1	8.15 A.M.	"	C	G	.....	.019	6.4	77	47	9h. 31m.*	13 391	496	23.5	95	1							11 800	99	99.2	54
55	" 6	11.42 P.M.	"	C	A	.....	.060	31.8	433	...	2h. 36m.	3 547	641	22.7	92	1							22 100	136	99.4	55
56	" 7	4.03 A.M.	"	C	A	.....	.048	20.6	453	8	3h. 16m.	4 544	654	23.2	94	1	.198	.064	85	8.1	0.7	91	36 800	112	99.7	56
57	" 7	9.02 "	"	C	A	.....	.040	14.8	453	104	3h. 31m.	4 710	584	22.3	90	1							41 300	268	99.4	57
58	" 7	2.13 P.M.	"	C	A	.....	.028	9.1	453	115	2h. 47m.	3 949	564	23.6	95	1							29 000	157	99.5	58
59	" 7	7.59 "	"	A	A	2.47	.....	.....	301	94	4h. 58m.	6 899	608	23.1	93	1							28 500	97	99.7	59
60	" 8	3.03 A.M.	"	A	A	3.02	.....	.....	301	84	3h. 32m.	5 059	616	23.9	97	1							21 600	123	99.4	60
61	" 8	7.00 "	"	A	A	3.60	.....	.....	301	88	4h. 04m.	5 753	612	23.6	95	2	.340	.056	84	5.9	1.0	85	24 200	168	99.3	61
62	" 8	11.27 "	"	A	A	3.84	.....	.....	301	....	3h. 08m.	4 298	611	22.8	92	1							24 200	86	99.6	62
63	" 8	2.58 P.M.	"	A	A	3.67	.....	.....	301	72	3h. 34m.	4 875	520	22.6	92	1							21 100	69	99.7	63
64	" 8	7.32 "	"	A	A	4.29	.....	.....	301	....	2h. 00m.	2 786	575	23.2	94	1							17 900	167	99.1	64
65	" 8	10.33 "	"	A	G	1.89	.....	.....	301	...	3h. 10m.	4 392	573	23.1	93	1	.350	.058	83	6.3	0.8	87	14 000	124	99.1	65
66	" 9	3.29 A.M.	"	A	G	3.75	.....	.....	301	84	1h. 43m.	2 424	....	23.5	95	1							13 100	43	99.7	66
67	" 19	10.04 P.M.	"	A	G	1.96	.....	.....	273	122	3h. 56m.	5 315	652	22.5	91	2	.356	.076	79	6.9	1.5	78	13 400	319	97.6	67
68	" 20	2.27 A.M.	"	A	G	1.92	.....	.....	277	99	19h. 17m.	14 531	619	12.6	51	2							14 500	259	98.2	68
69	" 20	10.12 P.M.	"	A	G	1.85	.....	.....	277	....	6h. 29m.	8 882	630	22.7	92	2	.260	.072	72	6.6*	1.1	83	12 700	327	97.4	69
70	" 21	9.52 "	"	A	G	1.12	.....	.....	258	106	42h. 44m.	31 997	931	12.5	50	2	.248	.070	72	6.2	1.4	77	12 300	551	95.5	70
71	" 23	5.00 "	"	A	G	1.16	.....	.....	249	....	1h. 11m.	1 645	573	23.2	94	4	.....	.....	.....	.....	.....	.....	17 400	2 090	88.0	71
72	" 23	8.17 "	"	A	G	1.14	.....	.....	249	97	12h. 53m.	17 395	750	22.5	91	2	.280	.068	79	5.2	1.3	75	14 300	443	96.9	72
73	" 24	8.50 "	"	A	G	0.59	.....	.....	150	....	1h. 34m.	1 118	460	11.9	48	4	.208	.074	65	5.4	1.6	70	9 900	1 755	82.3	73
74	" 25	12.28 A.M.	"	A	G	0.77	.....	.....	125	....	1h. 50m.	1 263	353	11.5	46	4	.208	.074	65	5.4	1.7	69	9 500	3 725	60.8	74
75	" 25	4.08 "	"	A	G	0.80	.....	.....	113	55	15h. 22m.	11 449	621	12.4	50	2	.....	.....	.....	.....	.....	.....	8 900	330	96.3	75
76	" 25	9.55 P.M.	"	A	G	1.70	.....	.....	110	....	1h. 14m.*	860	449	11.6	46	3	.....	.....	.....	.....	.....	.....	9 100	512	94.4	76
77	" 25	11.31 "	"	A	G	1.32	.....	.....	110		0h. 29m.*	284	346	9.8	39	3	.....	.....	.....	.....	.....	.....	7 500	420	94.6	77
78	" 26	1.15 A.M.	"	A	G	1.56	.....	.....	110	..	0h. 50m.*	1 098	413	22.0	89	3	.....	.....	.....	.....	.....	.....	7 800	223	97.1	78
79	" 26	2.31 "	"	A	G	1.15	.....	.....	110	....	0h. 54m.*	1 195	406	22.2	90	2	.....	.....	.....	.....	.....	.....	7 800	326	95.8	79
80	" 26	5.27 "	"	A	G	0.84	.....	.....	110	....	0h. 57m.*	1 176	347	20.7	84	3	.....	.....	.....	.....	.....	.....	9 900	503	94.9	80
81	" 26	8.30 "	"	A	G	0.92	.....	.....	100	75	18h. 50m.	25 422	699	22.5	91	2	.192	.064	67	4.4	1.8	59	14 200	312	97.8	81
82	" 27	3.58 "	"	A	G	0.89	.....	.....	100	...	0h. 46m.*	1 077	463	23.4	95	3	.....	.....	.....	.....	.....	.....	14 400	491	96.6	82
83	" 27	5.13 "	"	A	G	1.00	.....	.....	100	....	1h. 22m.*	1 000	443	12.2	49	2	.....	.....	.....	.....	.....	.....	10 700	387	96.4	83
84	" 27	8.55 "	"	A	G	0.61	.....	.....	100	....	9h. 05m.	9 838	644	16.0	73	3	.182	.080	56	4.1	1.8	56	6 100	248	95.9	84
85	" 27	8.02 P.M.	"	A	G	0.76	.....	.....	100	...	1h. 43m.*	1 652	522	16.0	65	2	.....	.....	.....	.....	.....	.....	6 500	340	94.8	85
86	" 27	10.11 "	"	A	G	0.77	.....	.....	100	...	0h. 35m.*	813	419	23.2	94	2	.....	.....	.....	.....	.....	.....	7 100	362	94.9	86

FINAL SUMMARY.—*Continued.*

Number of Run.	Began. Date. 1897.	Began. Hour.	Settling Basins in Service.	Treatment. Kind.	Treatment. Place.	Grains Chemical per Gallon.	Electric Current. Ampere-hour per Gallon.	Electric Current. H.P. per Million Gallons per 24 Hours.	Average Suspended Solids. Parts per Million. River Water.	Average Suspended Solids. Parts per Million. At Top of Filter.	Period of Service. Hours and Minutes.	Quantities of Water. Cubic Feet. Filtered.	Quantities of Water. Cubic Feet. Wash.	Average Rate of Filtration. Cubic Feet per Minute.	Average Rate of Filtration. Million Gallons per Acre per 24 Hours.	Degree of Clearness of Effluent.	Nitrogen as Albuminoid Ammonia. Parts per Million. River Water.	Nitrogen as Albuminoid Ammonia. Effluent.	Nitrogen as Albuminoid Ammonia. Per Cent Removed.	Oxygen Consumed. Parts per Million. River Water.	Oxygen Consumed. Effluent.	Oxygen Consumed. Per Cent Removed.	Bacteria per Cubic Centimeter. River Water.	Bacteria per Cubic Centimeter. Effluent.	Bacterial Efficiency.	Number of Run.
87	May 28	12.35 A.M.	1 and 2	A	G	1.26			98	85	10h. 55m.	14 967	699	22.9	93	2	.195	.058	70	3.8	1.6	58	6 700	189	97.2	87
88	June 19	10.00 "	None	D	B		.038	10.7	330		1h. 00m.*	1 399	607	23.3	94	2							5 200	323	93.8	88
89	" 19	11.35 "	"	D	B		.040	10.1	330		11h. 41m.	15 551	755	22.2	90	2	.315	.082	74	4.8	1.2	75	13 300	213	98.4	89
90	" 19	11.52 P.M.	"	D	B		.039	9.9	400		2h. 07m.*	2 877	798	22.7	92	3							18 000	264	98.5	90
91	" 20	4.16 A.M.	"	D	B		.053	13.3	600		2h. 44m.	2 745	571	16.8	68	3							16 800	287	98.3	91
92	" 20	4.48 P.M.	1 and 2	A	C	2.47			210		3h. 22m.	4 463	842	22.1	89	2	.295	.072	74	3.9	0.9	77	10 000	320	96.8	92
93	" 20	11.40 "	"	A	C	1.92			140	145	4h. 05m.	5 567	720	22.7	92	1							8 200	153	98.1	93
94	" 21	5.13 A.M.	"	A	B	2.11			149		12h. 47m.	17 898	639	23.3	94	1	.245	.076	69	4.3	0.8	81	10 800	227	97.9	94
95	" 21	7.58 P.M.	"	A	C	2.71			184	123	0h. 43m.*	1 013	561	23.6	95	1							10 600	137	98.7	95
96	" 22	12.47 A.M.	"	A	C	1.31			300		0h. 47m.	1 048	471	22.3	90	3							7 800	255	96.7	96
97	" 22	4.40 "	None	A	B	1.33			300		1h. 31m.	2 105	569	22.1	89	3							8 000	352	95.6	97
98	" 22	9.05 "	"	A	B	1.46			296	145	4h. 07m.	5 942	1 030	24.1	97	1	.305	.080	74	4.4	1.2	73	7 300	145	98.0	98
99	" 22	3.08 P.M.	"	A	C	1.42			295	270	3h. 53m.	5 518	673	23.7	96	2							6 300	273	95.7	99
100	" 22	7.48 "	"	A	C	1.30			325		3h. 12m.	4 380	609	22.8	92	2										100
101	" 23	1.24 A.M.	"	A	C	1.87			350		0h. 43m.	999	398	23.2	94	3							9 100	228	97.5	101
102	" 23	4.12 "	"	A	B	1.69			368	82	3h. 20m.	4 609	606	23.0	93	1	Av	era	ged	with	No.	104	9 100	297	96.7	102
103	" 23	2.35 P.M.	"	A	C	1.92			368	280	2h. 00m.	2 856	616	23.8	96	2							9 300	176	98.1	103
104	" 23	5.46 "	"	A	B	1.88			438	120	5h. 49m.	8 367	626	24.0	97	1	.350	.086	75	5.4	1.2	78	10 400	120	98.8	104
105	" 24	12.45 A.M.	"	D	B		.037	27.2	521	278	0h. 44m.	1 047	351	23.8	96	3							11 000	416	96.2	105
106	" 24	4.34 "	1 and 2	D	B		.045	35.0	581	163	7h. 56m.	9 480	633	19.9	81	2							14 800	380	97.4	106
107	" 24	2.08 P.M.	"	A	B	2.19			870		2h. 02m.	2 583	529	21.2	86	2	.370	.080	78	7.3	1.3	82	22 600	304	98.7	107
108	" 24	5.40 "	"	D	B		.049	16.3	870		2h. 10m.	2 379	498	18.3	74	4							24 600	607	97.5	108
109	" 24	9.06 "	"	A	B	3.51			650		0h. 28m.	475	552	17.0	69	3							28 700	603	97.9	109
110	" 24	11.49 "	"	D	A		.078	32.9	616	196	0h. 43m.	976	502	22.7	92	4							26 100	1 975	92.4	110
111	" 25	3.07 A.M.	"	D	A		.099	36.0	515	60	26h. 35m.	28 725	631	18.0	73	1	.485	.076	84	6.8	1.4	79	17 500	243	98.6	111
112	" 26	6.54 "	"	D	A		.072	23.0	517		1h. 06m.	1 654	595	25.0	101	1							15 500	212	98.6	112
113	" 26	11.16 P.M.	"	D	B		.038	12.9	425	237	0h. 57m.*	1 313	720	23.1	93	3							18 100	277	98.5	113
114	" 26	3.12 "	"	D	B		.045	15.3	425		0h. 28m.	545	531	19.5	79	3							19 000	380	98.0	114
115	" 26	5.34 "	"	D	A		.064	20.4	350	281	1h. 59m.	2 715	683	22.8	92	3							19 000	317	98.3	115
116	" 26	9.24 "	"	A	A	2.01			600	99	0h. 57m.*	1 298	364	22.6	92	1							14 400	82	99.4	116
117	" 27	12.13 A.M.	"	A	A	2.02			622	145	0h. 51m.*	1 191	383	23.4	95	1							9 800	78	99.2	117
118	" 27	3.55 "	"	A	A	1.01			673	632	0h. 20m.	460	477	23.0	93	5							10 600	2 190	79.3	118
119	" 27	5.25 "	"	D	A		.064	20.5	711	309	0h. 35m.	793	665	22.7	92	5							11 400	698	93.9	119
120	" 27	8.00 "	"	D	A		.078	30.5	711		1h. 05m.	1 485	701	22.9	93	3							11 700	136	98.8	120
121	" 27	11.25 "	"	D	A		.094	39.3	535	65	2h. 05m.	2 366	706	19.0	77	2							12 000	238	98.0	121
122	" 27	2.05 P.M.	"	D	A		.097	40.8	535		6h. 50m.	7 494	501	18.3	74	2	.355	.088	75	6.8	1.2	82	12 700	203	98.4	122
123	" 28	12.34 A.M.	"	E	A	4.81			469		1h. 09m.	1 579	550	22.9	93	4										123
124	" 28	3.45 "	"	A	A	2.35			454	341	0h. 45m.	1 050	525	23.4	95	4							7 600	454	94.0	124
125	" 28	7.06 "	"	A	A	3.59			454		7h. 26m.	10 381	563	23.3	94	1	.350	.108	69	5.7	1.3	77	7 600	29	99.6	125
126	" 29	10.40 P.M.	"	A	A	3.47			408	144	7h. 20m.	10 188	531	23.1	93	2							11 400	171	98.5	126
127	" 30	8.09 A.M.	"	A	A	2.90			354	131	1h. 26m.*	2 037	627	23.7	96	1	.370	.110	70	5.5	1.3	76	9 300	76	99.2	127
128	" 30	11.50 "	"	E	A	6.38			354		2h. 10m.	2 934	632	22.6	91	2	.370	.090	76	5.5	1.1	80	9 300	124	98.7	128
129	" 30	3.56 P.M.	"	E	A	3.39			354		1h. 34m.	2 190	628	23.3	94	4							8 900	221	97.5	129

FINAL SUMMARY.—*Continued.*

Number of Run.	Began. Date. 1897.	Began. Hour.	Settling Basins in Service.	Treatment. Kind.	Treatment. Place.	Grains Chemical per Gallon.	Electric Current. Ampere-hour per Gallon.	Electric Current. H.P. per Million Gallons per 24 Hours.	Average Suspended Solids. Parts per Million. River Water.	Average Suspended Solids. Parts per Million. At Top of Filter.	Period of Service. Hours and Minutes.	Quantities of Water. Cubic Feet. Filtered.	Quantities of Water. Cubic Feet. Wash.	Average Rate of Filtration. Cubic Feet per Minute.	Average Rate of Filtration. Million Gallons per Acre per 24 Hours.	Degree of Clearness of Effluent.	Nitrogen as Albuminoid Ammonia. Parts per Million. River Water.	Nitrogen as Albuminoid Ammonia. Effluent.	Nitrogen as Albuminoid Ammonia. Per Cent. Removed.	Oxygen Consumed. Parts per Million. River Water.	Oxygen Consumed. Effluent.	Oxygen Consumed. Per Cent. Removed.	Bacteria per Cubic Centimeter. River Water.	Bacteria per Cubic Centimeter. Effluent.	Bacterial Efficiency.	Number of Run.
130	June 30	8.04 P.M.	1 and 2	A	A	2.98	......	.....	308	144	7h. 34m.	10 558	588	23.3	94	1	.280	.108	61	3.8	1.1	71	6 100	76	98.8	130
131	July 1	5.35 A.M.	"	A	A	2.52	......	.....	288	114	5h. 55m.	8 034	699	22.6	91	1							4 900	53	98.9	131
132	" 1	4.54 P.M.	"	D	A	.....	.078	32.5	218	116	7h. 41m.	10 598	601	23.0	93	1	.280	.098	65	3.8	1.3	66	3 000	74	97.5	132
133	" 2	4.39 A.M.	"	C	A	.....	.037	81.2	159	71	4h. 45m.	6 556	640	23.0	93	2	.210	.076	64	4.1	1.1	73	2 200	106	95.2	133
134	" 2	10.21 "	"	C	A	.....	.028	68.0	151	99	3h. 09m.	4 394	543	23.2	94	2	......	.....	...	......	...	...	2 400	104	95.7	134
135	" 2	3.40 P.M.	"	C	A	.....	.025	63.3	151	....	0h. 13m.	311	332	23.9	97	4	......	.....	...	......	...	...	2 500	147	94.1	135
136	" 2	4.56 "	"	A	B	1.96	......	.....	147	62	8h. 41m.	11 887	575	22.8	92	1	.210	.070	67	4.1	1.0	76	5 000	38	99.2	136
137	" 3	2.55 A.M.	"	A	C	2.06	......	.....	135	170	6h. 35m.	9 098	669	23.0	93	2							3 600	55	98.5	137
138	" 3	1.31 P.M.	"	F	C	*	......	.....	160	....	0h. 45m.	1 097	620	24.3	98	4	.160	.298	−186	2.8	4.8	−172	2 500	677	73.0	138
139	" 3	3.08 "	"	F	C	†	......	.....	160	....	1h. 52m.	2 530	459	22.6	91	1	.160	.180	−112	2.8	1.0	64	2 500	2	99.9	139
140	" 6	1.20 "	"	A	B	1.67	......	.....	124	64	19h. 31m.	26 640	731	22.8	92	1	.170	.074	66	3.3	1.1	67	5 500	100	98.2	140
141	" 7	10.19 A.M.	"	A	C	1.59	......	.....	552	191	0h. 54m.	1 300	606	24.1	97	3	......	.....	...	......	...	...	12 100	275	97.7	141
142	" 7	11.40 "	"	A	C	2.02	......	.....	548	275	2h. 59m.	4 210	703	23.5	95	2	......	.....	...	......	...	...	12 600	135	98.9	142
143	" 7	3.50 P.M.	"	A	B	1.52	......	.....	548	...	4h. 11m.	6 137	611	24.4	99	2	.370	.076	79	6.7	1.1	84	13 100	271	97.9	143
144	" 7	9.26 "	"	A	C	2.60	......	.....	455	400	2h. 09m.	2 966	659	23.0	93	1							13 500	281	97.9	144
145	" 8	12.47 A.M.	"	A	B	1.92	......	.....	438	134	8h. 18m.	11 584	548	23.2	94	1	.350	.064	82	6.1	1.1	82	16 500	132	99.2	145
146	" 8	9.57 P.M.	"	A	B	1.99	......	.....	633	143	5h. 03m.	7 121	465	23.5	95	2	......	.....	...	......	...	...	18 900	188	99.0	146
147	" 9	4.34 A.M.	None	D	B	.....	.089	114.0	488	181	3h. 40m.	4 392	679	20.0	81	3	......	.....	...	......	...	...	17 600	293	98.3	147
148	" 9	8.47 "	"	D	B	.....	.099	122.0	419	138	4h. 43m.	5 082	733	18.0	73	2	.280	.082	71	4.9	1.4	71	6 600	144	97.8	148
149	" 9	4.45 P.M.	"	A	B	2.41	......	.....	464	132	5h. 19m.	7 618	594	23.9	97	1	Averaged with No. 153.						6 800	137	98.0	149
150	" 9	11.32 "	"	D	B	.....	.091	143.0	445	157	0h. 28m.	546	387	19.5	79	4	......	.....	...	......	...	...	7 400	403	94.6	150
151	" 10	1.11 A.M.	"	D	B	.....	.096	151.0	430	84	0h. 49m.	906	540	18.5	75	3	......	.....	...	......	...	...	8 500	320	96.2	151
152	" 10	2.25 "	"	D	B	.....	.104	162.0	312	123	0h. 45m.	775	461	17.2	70	4	......	.....	...	......	...	...	8 500	273	96.8	152
153	" 10	4.35 "	"	A	B	2.69	......	.....	352	114	5h. 21m.	7 679	560	23.9	97	1	(.280	.068	76	(4.9	0.9	82	8 300	106	98.7	153
154	" 10	12.12 P.M.	"	B[1]	B	1.88	......	.....	352	....	0h. 14m.	342	356	24.4	99	4	......	.....	...	......	...	...	8 200	192	97.7	154
155	" 10	2.08 "	"	B[1]	B	2.66	......	.....	379	85	1h. 56m.	2 617	636	22.6	91	2	......	.....	...	......	...	...	9 400	86	99.1	155
156	" 10	5.18 "	"	A	B	2.69	......	.....	305	142	0h. 27m.*	633	.....	23.5	95	1	Averaged with No. 153.						9 400	145	98.5	156
157	" 14	8.49 "	No. 1	A	D	1.85[2]	......	.....	191	92	1h. 12m.	1 672	551	23.3	94	1	......	.....	...	......	...	...	5 600	222	96.0	157
158	" 14	11.17 "	"	A	E	1.81[3]	......	.....	195	77	0h. 46m.	1 054	434	22.9	93	4	......	.....	...	......	...	...	5 600	229	95.9	158
159	" 15	4.39 A.M.	"	A	D	2.32[4]	......	.....	185	89	4h. 39m.	6 384	632	22.9	93	2	Averaged with No. 162.						5 200	190	96.3	159
160	" 15	10.00 "	"	A	D	2.18[5]	......	.....	171	65	3h. 30m.	4 937	605	23.5	95	1	......	.....	...	......	...	...	5 300	90	98.3	160
161	" 15	2.46 P.M.	"	A	E	2.19[6]	......	.....	180	124	2h. 28m.	3 514	545	23.7	96	2	......	.....	...	......	...	...	5 300	89	98.3	161
162	" 15	6.30 "	"	A	D	2.16[7]	......	.....	185	71	3h. 30m.	4 800	572	22.9	93	1	(.205	.075	64	(4.2	1.2	71	6 000	90	98.5	162
163	" 15	11.10 "	"	A	E	2.19[8]	......	.....	189	139	2h. 58m.	4 071	544	22.9	93	2	Averaged with No. 164.						6 200	44	99.3	163
164	" 16	3.50 A.M.	None	A	B	1.81	......	.....	189	120	3h. 00m.	4 200	579	23.5	95	2	(.190	.072	62	(3.8	1.1	71	6 400	72	98.9	164
165	" 16	8.14 "	"	A	C	2.10	......	.....	189	....	0h. 50m.	1 187	568	23.7	96	4	......	.....	...	......	...	...	5 800	128	97.8	165
166	" 16	10.12 "	"	A	B	2.14	......	.....	189	91	3h. 00m.	4 218	545	23.4	95	1	......	.....	...	......	...	...	5 800	55	99.0	166
167	" 16	9.52 P.M.	"	A	B	2.82	......	.....	129	79	4h. 51m.	6 556	529	22.6	91	2	Averaged with No. 164.						6 100	41	99.3	167
168	" 17	4.07 A.M.	No. 1	A	D	2.32[9]	......	.....	141	15	10h. 55m.	15 296	540	23.4	95	1	.195	.078	60	3.1	0.9	71	7 100	33	99.5	168
169	" 17	5.08 P.M.	"	A	E	2.30[10]	......	.....	122	21	9h. 59m.	14 049	536	23.5	95	1							5 400	23	99.6	169
170	" 18	4.45 A.M.	"	A	D	2.29[11]	......	.....	111	21	11h. 21m.	15 894	597	23.4	95	1							4 400	27	99.4	170
171	" 18	5.16 P.M.	"	A	E	2.32[12]	......	.....	108	33	11h. 49m.	16 634	580	23.5	95	1							4 100	25	99.4	171

[1] Free acid neutralized with caustic soda. [2] 0.63 + 1.22. [3] 0.63 + 1.18. [4] 1.06 + 1.16. [5] 1.06 + 1.12. [6] 1.06 + 1.13. [7] 1.06 + 1.10. [8] 1.06 + 1.13. [9] 1.49 + 0.83. [10] 1.50 + 0.80. [11] 1.50 + 0.79. [12] 1.52 + 0.80.

* 14.60 grains caustic applied at B and 4.89 grains copperas at C. † 7.97 grains caustic applied at B and 3.02 grains copperas at C.

FINAL SUMMARY.—*Concluded.*

Number of Run.	Began. Date. 1897.	Began. Hour.	Settling Basins in Service.	Treatment. Kind.	Treatment. Place.	Grains Chemical per Gallon.	Electric Current. Ampere hour per Gallon.	Electric Current. H.P. per Million Gallons per 24 Hours.	Average Suspended Solids. Parts per Million. River Water.	Average Suspended Solids. At Top of Filter.	Period of Service. Hours and Minutes.	Quantities of Water. Cubic Feet. Filtered.	Quantities of Water. Wash.	Average Rate of Filtration. Cubic Feet per Minute.	Average Rate of Filtration. Million Gallons per Acre per 24 Hours.	Degree of Clearness of Effluent.	Nitrogen as Albuminoid Ammonia. Parts per Million. River Water.	Nitrogen. Effluent.	Nitrogen. Per Cent Removed.	Oxygen Consumed. Parts per Million. River Water.	Oxygen. Effluent.	Oxygen. Per Cent Removed.	Bacteria per Cubic Centimeter. River Water.	Bacteria. Effluent.	Bacterial Efficiency.	Number of Run.
172	June 19	8.50 A.M.	No. 1	A	D	2.18[1]	...	...	114	12	10h. 59m.	15 508	550	23.6	95	1							3 600	23	99.4	172
173	" 19	9.03 P.M.	"	A	F	1.51	...	...	74	21	23h. 01m.	32 227	517	23.2	94	1	.180	.078	57	2.8	1.1	61	3 200	32	99.0	173
174	" 20	9.00 "	None	A	B	1.60	...	...	73	45	14h. 49m.	20 438	622	23.1	93	1							2 800	27	99.0	174
175	" 21	1.11 "	"	A	C	1.60	...	...	130	86	7h. 32m.	10 565	597	23.4	95	1	.198	.078	61	2.8	1.1	61	4 100	35	99.2	175
176	" 21	10.50 "	"	A	B	1.02	...	...	130	70	13h. 10m.	18 431	619	23.4	95	1							4 700	61	98.8	176
177	" 22	1.14 "	"	D	B	...	.028	7.1	128	...	0h. 46m.	1 085	581	23.6	95	3	...	...	...	...	...	...	4 900	176	96.4	177
178	" 22	3.03 "	"	D	B	...	.040	14.1	128	15	5h. 12m.	7 274	552	23.3	94	2	...	...	...	...	...	...	4 600	94	98.0	178
179	" 22	11.02 "	"	A	C	1.04	...	...	127	37	0h. 43m.	1 007	486	23.4	95	3	...	...	...	...	...	...	4 800	143	97.0	179
180	" 23	12.45 A.M.	"	A	B	0.78	...	...	140	...	7h. 17m.	10 322	599	23.6	95	1	Av	era	ged	with	No.	184.	4 500	95	97.9	180
181	" 23	9.52 "	"	D	B	...	.040	12.3	160	...	5h. 18m.	7 426	470	23.3	94	2	.206	.098	52	3.3	1.4	58	5 200	130	97.5	181
182	" 23	8 18 P.M.	No. 1	A	F	0.77	...	...	171	82	0h. 42m.	1 006	432	23.9	97	4	...	...	...	...	...	...	5 600	220	96.1	182
183	" 23	10.08 "	None	A	B	0.77	...	...	173	35	3h. 52m.	5 457	470	23.5	95	2	.206	.096	53	3.3	1.3	61	5 600	197	96.6	183
184	" 24	3.00 A.M.	"	A	C	1.10	...	...	174	163	0h. 45m.	1 671	452	23.8	96	3	...	...	...	...	...	...	5 300	160	97.0	184
185	" 24	4.41 "	"	A	B	1.03	...	...	173	108	5h. 18m.	7 576	530	23.8	96	1	Av	era	ged	with	No.	184.	6 100	136	97.8	185

[1] 1.52 + 0.66.

Outline of the Method followed in the Discussion of the Results of these Investigations.

In the following pages are presented the full discussions of the results of the investigations made during 1897 in connection with the devices arranged by the Water Company, or in connection with laboratory experiments on a small scale. These discussions are presented in fifteen main sections as follows:

Section No. 1. Purification of the Ohio River water by plain sedimentation.

Section No. 2. Account of the commercial chemicals available as coagulants for the Ohio River water, and of the manner of their behavior when applied to this water.

Section No. 3. Status at the beginning of this portion of the investigation, with a general description, of the formation of coagulating chemicals by the electrolytic decomposition of metal plates.

Section No. 4. Detailed account of the electrolytic formation of iron hydrate in the Ohio River water.

Section No. 5. Detailed account of the electrolytic formation of aluminum hydrate in the Ohio River water.

Section No. 6. Relative efficiency of available coagulants based on equal weights of metal used, and also on the amount of electric current in the case of electrolytically formed coagulants.

Section No. 7. Economical application of coagulants, in terms of sulphate of alumina, to aid in the removal of suspended matter by sedimentation.

Section No. 8. Effect of the period of coagulation of the Ohio River water before filtration.

Section No. 9. Degree of coagulation of the water before filtration and the minimum amount of coagulant required for that purpose.

Section No. 10. On the conditions of successful filtration.

Section No. 11. Quality of the effluent, after proper sedimentation, coagulation, and filtration—independent of the nature of the coagulant.

Section No. 12. Manner in which the nature of the coagulant affected the quality of the effluent.

Section No. 13. Amounts of the different available coagulants which would be required with optimum conditions of subsidence and filtration to purify satisfactorily the Ohio River water.

Section No. 14. Degree to which the several coagulants in their respective amounts would affect the quality of the effluent, with its practical significance, and a consideration of the advisability and cost of the removal of the added constituents.

Section No. 15. Relative costs of equivalent amounts of the different available coagulants, together with an estimate of the yearly cost for coagulants for the purification of the Ohio River water.

Section No. 1.

Purification of the Ohio River Water by Plain Sedimentation.

Plain sedimentation means the removal of suspended matters from the water by gravity in the absence of any coagulating treatment. In many cases in this report subsidence is used synonymously with sedimentation; and in some places other expressions, such as settling and settlement, are also used in referring to this same action.

In the early summer of 1896 a series of sedimentation experiments upon a small scale were undertaken to show the relation of coagulation and period of subsidence. The results of these experiments have been recorded in Chapter IV, where it will be seen that a number of them throw light upon the present question. As a matter of convenience, the results of those experiments in which no coagulants were used are repeated, as follows:

Suspended Matter in River Water. Parts per Million.	Percentage Removal.	
	24 Hours.	48 Hours.
590	52	73
936	38	64
320	32	62
220	41	60
261	44	74
Averages 469	41	67

From a practical point of view the conditions under which the above experiments were carried on were abnormal in two respects. In the first place, the diameter of the tank (2 feet) was such that the friction of the water upon the sides caused the vortex motion of the suspended particles to decrease more rapidly than in large basins or reservoirs; or, in other words, it caused the water to reach a state of rest more quickly. Owing to the fact that subsidence is very closely associated with the vortex motion of the particles, the above results, so far as this point is concerned, show higher percentages of removal than would occur in practice. Secondly, the high and varying temperature of the boiler-house in which the tank was placed caused the presence of currents which retarded the subsidence by increasing the vortex motion.

The significance of these points is shown clearly by the results of plain sedimentation experiments made in one-gallon bottles, which were kept at approximately the same temperature. It will be noted that the average amount of suspended matter in these experiments was substantially the same as in the case of those recorded in the last table; and the general character of the water was fairly similar.

Suspended Matter in River Water. Parts per Million.	Percentage Removal.	
	24 Hours.	48 Hours.
521	81	84
516	80	86
472	76	80
428	71	86
338	77	86
Averages 455	77	84

In addition to showing that by 24 hours of *quiescent* subsidence about 75 per cent. of the suspended matter in fairly normal muddy water may be removed, the above results demonstrate that under these conditions economical subsidence cannot be carried beyond this period (24 hours). Comparing the last results with those in the first table, it is clear that the conditions of subsidence, as already noted, were important factors, and that 24 hours' subsidence in gallon bottles was more efficient than 48 hours in the settling tank placed in the boiler house. In this connection it may be stated that some analyses made in June, 1896, of the water leaving the Crescent Hill reservoir, which holds about 6 days' supply, indicated a removal by subsidence of about 60 per cent. of the suspended matters in the general class of water under consideration.

Concerning the efficiency of basin No. 1 in the removal of suspended matters by plain subsidence, the summary of results on pages 371 to 375 show that, during the early spring, when the suspended matter was rather coarse, the removal ranged from 20 to 50 per cent., when the basin held about 3 hours' supply. With the water later in the spring, and in the summer, when the suspended particles were much finer, the removal of suspended matters in this basin ranged from 0 to 15 per cent., but for the most part the water as it left this basin showed no substantial purification.

With regard to the removal of bacteria by plain subsidence, the influence of the temperature is considerable. In general terms it appears that the percentage removal of bacteria follows quite closely that of the suspended lifeless particles. This is to be expected, because the bacteria to a considerable degree appear to be attached to the grosser suspended particles. The removal of bacteria by plain subsidence is not a very important factor, however, because with little or no extra expense to the general process they may be removed subsequently by the necessary coagulation and filtration.

The character of the suspended matter in the river water is a point of great importance in purification by subsidence; and, farther, the amount of suspended matter influences materially the percentage removal. The latter point in a measure follows from the first, because when the particles are large the stage of the river, etc., is such that the total weight of the suspended matter is bound to be great, comparatively speaking. This is shown by the following results, obtained by plain sedimentation in one-gallon bottles.

	No. I.	No. II.	No. III.
Parts per Million of Original Suspended Matter..................	965	393	130
Percentage Removal in 3 hours....	85	24	17
" " " 24 "	96	66	32
" " " 48 "	97	73	41

The above experiments show that, with the first water (No. I), containing coarse and heavy particles, the suspended matters decreased from 965 to 29 parts; while in the third water containing fine clay particles, the corresponding decrease was from 130 to 77 parts. This brings out the important fact that with the water containing clay particles, such as is found here for two or three months in the year, the removal of suspended matter is not only much less rapid than in the water containing the heavier mud and silt, but the amount (weight) of suspended matter at the end of practicable limits of subsidence is greater in the case of the clay-bearing water. In fact, with the third water it would require weeks, if not months, to remove from it substantially all of the clay. With the second water, resembling a mixture of the other two, the removal of suspended matters was intermediate in its nature.

From the above statements it will be perfectly clear that the efficiency of plain subsidence depends very largely, so far as any given period is concerned, upon the conditions under which subsidence takes place. The main thing is to bring the water into a state of comparative rest, in order to reduce the vortex motion of the particles due to eddies and similar movements of the water. Experience shows that the water is brought to a state of rest much more quickly in small receptacles than in large reservoirs such as would be required in practice. The results obtained from small experimental devices, accordingly, can be taken only as indications in general terms of what may be accomplished practically in this manner, and as a guide for the construction of large subsiding basins might be quite misleading. Furthermore, it was not considered feasible during these investigations to secure conditions on a sufficiently large scale to enable the efficiency of plain subsidence on a practical basis to be studied in a thorough manner. The following conclusions upon the purification of the Ohio River water at Louisville, therefore, are in part presented in general rather than in specific terms.

Conclusions.

1. It is possible to remove, economically,

about 75 per cent. of the suspended matter in normal muddy water by plain sedimentation (subsidence). At times of freshets during the winter and early spring the percentage might exceed 90; while in the late spring and summer it might fall to 50 or less.

2. The removal of bacteria by plain sedimentation follows the removal of suspended matter in a general way. But the removal of bacteria by this portion of an efficient system of purification is not important, because they can be effectively disposed of subsequently by filtration without extra cost in the operation of the complete system, and their removal by the filters does not affect the quantitative efficiency of filtration, as is the case with mud and other suspended matters.

3. After treatment to its economical limits by plain sedimentation, the Ohio River water would ordinarily be discolored by suspended matters, which it would contain in sufficient amounts to preclude the probability of growth in the open subsidence basins of algæ and other organisms, giving rise to objectionable tastes and odors.

4. At times of freshets during the spring and summer all the evidence goes to indicate that plain subsidence cannot economically remove a sufficient amount of the fine clay carried in the Ohio River water at Louisville to prepare the water satisfactorily for filtration; and, regardless of whether the English or American type of filter is used, economy demands the use of coagulating treatment to aid subsidence at such times.

5. The period of economical plain subsidence of the Ohio River water does not exceed the equivalent of 24 hours' quiescent subsidence, such as is secured in one-gallon bottles. With the heavy coarse mud of the winter freshets this period is doubtless shorter than 24 hours; and in the case of the clay-bearing waters, for which the use of coagulants is imperative, the period could to advantage be somewhat shorter than this. But with the intermediate class of water, resembling a mixture of these extremes and illustated by No. II water in the last table, we are led to believe that plain quiescent subsidence could be economically carried to 24 hours, or to very nearly that period.

6. With regard to the period of subsidence, under the conditions of practice, equivalent to 24 hours' quiescent subsidence in one-gallon bottles, the available conditions of these investigations were not such as to make the solution of this problem feasible.

7. Concerning the arrangement of the subsidence basins, with reference to size, depth, and location of division walls; and their operation, with regard to the question of constant flow, intermittent flow, or successive fillings and drawings, there are no data available from these investigations, and it will be necessary to rely upon information from other sources.

Section No. 2.

Account of the Commercial Chemicals Available as Coagulants for the Ohio River Water and of the Manner of Their Behavior when Applied to this Water.

In this section it is the purpose to take the entire list of metals and show which of them form commercial compounds capable of coagulating the Ohio River water in a safe manner. The way in which the leading available compounds of the suitable metals are decomposed when applied to this water is described, together with the relative advantages and disadvantages of each. A full description of the formation of coagulating chemicals by the electrolytic decomposition of metal plates is presented in sections Nos. 3, 4, and 5. In Section No. 6 the relative efficiency and economy of the several available coagulants is shown, and in section No. 15 a comparison is made of the costs of the chemicals most adaptable for this use. Chapter III contains a description of the action of sulphate of alumina when applied to the Ohio River water, as far as it was understood in 1896; and this portion of the present chapter is, in a measure, an elaboration of Chapter III, and contains all of our additional information upon this subject at the close of these investigations.

Classification of Metals in their Applicability to the Purification of the Ohio River Water.

The next table contains a list of all metals, excepting the rare and precious ones, subdivided into groups according to their general adaptability for the purpose in question. In the first column are given those metals which are either well-known poisons, or which in small quantities are regarded in the absence of precise data as suspicious from a hygienic point of view. The second column contains those metals the normal compounds of which form soluble salts when added to this water; and in the third column are found those metals capable of forming in the Ohio River water compounds of a solid granular nature, wholly or partially insoluble under the existing conditions. In this connection frequent use will be made of "precipitate," which is the chemical name for a solid compound. Finally, there are presented in the fourth column those metals which form insoluble and gelatinous precipitates when applied in a suitable manner to this water.

CLASSIFICATION OF METALS.

Division No. 1.	Division No. 2.		
	Permissible Metals from a Sanitary Standpoint.		
Metals Inadmissible or Undesirable from a Sanitary Standpoint.	Group No. 1. Forming Soluble Compounds.	Group No. 2. Forming Granular Precipitates Partly or Wholly Insoluble.	Group No. 3. Forming Gelatinous Insoluble Precipitates.
Lead	Sodium	Calcium	Aluminum
Silver	Potassium	Magnesium	Iron
Mercury			Manganese
Tin			
Antimony			
Arsenic			
Copper			
Bismuth			
Cadmium			
Nickel			
Cobalt			
Zinc			
Barium.			
Strontium			

The metals of division No. 1, in the light of our present knowledge, cannot be considered as applicable for this work. Taking up the metals of division No. 2, the use of the several groups may be briefly outlined as follows:

Group No. 1.—These metals may be used in the form of hydrate (caustic soda) to remove carbonic acid from water. This treatment produces sodium carbonate (if caustic soda were added), which will decompose incrusting constituents (permanent hardness). Sodium or potassium may also be added directly to water in the form of carbonates or tribasic phosphates for the purpose of removing incrusting constituents.

Group No. 2.—These metals may be applied to the water in the form of hydrates (e. g. lime water) in order to remove carbonic acid. From such an application there is formed calcium carbonate, which is soluble in water free of carbonic acid, to the extent of 2 to 3 grains per gallon. Quantities in excess of this amount settle out, upon standing, in the form of a fine white powder, which has little or no power as a coagulant.

Group No. 3.—These metals may be added to this water in proper quantities and in a suitable form with the result that ultimately an insoluble gelatinous precipitate is formed, capable of coagulating the suspended matter.

The metals of groups Nos. 1 and 2 refer solely to metals for the reduction of corroding and incrusting constituents, and will be taken up subsequently in connection with these matters; at present we will consider the metals of group No. 3, which are the only ones available for the coagulation of the water, preparatory to subsidence of fine clay and the rapid filtration of the water through sand.

Most Suitable Compounds of the Metals (Group No. 3) capable of producing Coagulating Precipitates, and a General Description of their Behavior upon Application to the Ohio River Water.

A comparative outline of the leading commercial compounds (salts) of these metals is as follows:

Compounds of Aluminum.

In addition to sulphate of alumina and potash alum there are several other commercial compounds which have been investigated in the laboratory. It was explained in Chapters II and IX that the sulphate was the better of the two former; and accordingly this compound will be briefly described and the others referred to it in comparative terms.

Sulphate of Alumina.—The behavior of this

chemical when added to the Ohio River water has been fully described in general terms in Chapter III. As a matter of convenience it may be repeated that, briefly, it is decomposed for the most part by the alkaline compounds (lime and magnesia) in the river water; and that the increase in carbonic acid and incrusting constituents in the water is proportional to the decrease in alkalinity. The rate of decrease in alkalinity (6 to 9 parts per million for 1 grain per gallon of the ordinary chemical) depends upon the amount of sulphuric acid in the chemical and the amount of suspended matters in the water capable of absorbing this compound. The alumina in the commercial product is precipitated and removed by sedimentation and filtration, while the increased carbonic acid and incrusting constituents (principally sulphate of lime) remain in the water. It has already been made plain that the two latter additions to the water are not desirable from an industrial standpoint, although they do not injure the sanitary quality of the water, when the process is carried on under suitable conditions. From an economical point of view the amount of sulphate of alumina wasted by absorption by the surfaces of the suspended particles of mud and silt, and by the organic matter, is a matter of much importance. For the sake of explicitness this topic for all the chemicals is discussed by itself in this section just after this more general account.

Potash Alum.—The crystals of this commercial chemical are a mixture of sulphate of alumina and sulphate of potash. The latter portion is of no practical influence in water purification, while the sulphate of alumina in it behaves in a manner similar to commercial sulphate of alumina as described in the last paragraph. Potash alum contains only about two-thirds as much sulphate of alumina as the commercial form of this last chemical; costs substantially the same; possesses no advantages in current methods of use; and, therefore, is eliminated from the problem on the ground of cost.

Chloride of Alumina.—This compound behaves in a precisely similar manner to sulphate of alumina in forming a precipitate of hydrate of aluminum and reducing in the same ratio the alkalinity, with the formation of carbonic acid and incrusting constituents. The only difference is that the increased amounts of incrusting constituents would be composed of chlorides of lime and magnesia in place of the sulphates of these metals. This change would produce only a very slight and nominal difference in the character of the water, because when heated in a steam-boiler under pressure of 50 pounds the added chloride of lime reacts with the sulphate of magnesia originally in the water, and the effect is similar to the conditions when commercial sulphates are applied. There probably would not be enough magnesium sulphate in the water to complete this change at all times; but even in this event it is to be stated that the magnesium chloride formed from this chemical by the above reaction is the compound which is most injurious to boilers, as it is decomposed by heat in boilers with the formation of free hydrochloric acid.

This chemical is more expensive than sulphate of alumina, because the hydrochloric acid used in its preparation is more costly than sulphuric acid; and as there are no substantial advantages to offset the increased cost its use is not practicable.

Acetate of Alumina.—In trade this chemical is known as "red-liquor" and is used in dyeing. It is decomposed by the alkaline constituents of the river water the same as sulphate of alumina, with the formation of aluminum hydrate and the same rate of reduction in alkalinity and increase in carbonic acid. The other resultant compounds, acetates of lime and magnesia, in place of sulphates, are soluble and would appear in the filtered water. They are not injurious to health, and do not act as incrusting constituents. The absence of increased amounts of the latter compounds would be desirable, but, as the acetate costs about four times as much as the sulphate, the evidence in section No. 14 of this chapter shows that the use of this chemical would not be advisable.

Sodium Aluminate.—This compound of aluminum differs essentially from sulphate of alumina in that in this case the aluminum acts as an acid instead of a base. When carbonic acid is applied to sodium aluminate solutions in certain industrial chemical processes aluminum hydrate is formed and sodium carbonate appears as a by-product. In water coagulation such an action would be very desirable if the conditions allowed it to behave like this, as the same gelatinous hydrate would be obtained, with no increase in corroding or incrusting constituents; in fact the latter would be reduced because the sodium of the applied chemical would unite with carbonic acid to form sodium carbonate, which in turn would decompose an equivalent amount of incrusting constituents without forming any objectionable compounds. In other words, the single compound would give the combined effect of the metals of groups Nos. 1 and 3 of division No. 2 of the table.

Experience, however, showed that its use was impracticable in the case of the Ohio River water because it would not decompose in the manner stated. The reason of this appeared to be that the solution in the river water of this chemical and of carbonic acid was too weak.

Compounds of Iron.

Owing to the fact that iron is a cheap metal, and that its hydrate in the oxidized or ferric state is an excellent coagulant, these compounds are entitled to careful consideration. At the outset it is to be recalled that there are two series of iron compounds, the ferrous (incompletely oxidized) and the ferric (completely oxidized). We shall first consider the ferrous compounds.

Ferrous Sulphate.—This is also known as the protosulphate of iron and as green vitriol, and is the cheapest form in which iron compounds are on the market. When added to the Ohio River water it acts similarly to sulphate of alumina except that ferrous hydrate is formed in place of aluminum hydrate. With equal weights of metal the reduction in alkalinity and increase of carbonic acid and incrusting constituents by ferrous sulphate and sulphate of alumina are in the ratio of 1.0 to 1.3. Ferrous hydrate is not a suitable coagulant because it dissolves in the water to the extent of about 7 parts per million: and to make the iron compounds available it is necessary to have the iron ultimately in the form of the ferric (oxidized) hydrate. In the case of ferrous sulphate there is enough atmospheric oxygen dissolved in the water to accomplish this under favorable conditions. Experience, however, shows that this is impracticable in this water, owing to complications in the oxidation caused by carbonic acid. When ferrous sulphate is added to this water, white ferrous hydrate, mostly insoluble, is formed. Very quickly this precipitate passes into solution, due to the action of carbonic acid and resulting probably in the formation of a soluble basic carbonate. When the iron is in this form the atmospheric oxygen, although present in excess, oxidizes it very slowly and with great difficulty. Furthermore, the iron when it does reach the oxidized state does not form the normal gelatinous ferric hydrate, but a partially granular compound which is some lower hydration of ferric oxide as nearly as could be learned.

In short, the carbonic acid in this water renders the use of ferrous sulphate (and all other ferrous compounds) inadmissible for coagulation, owing to the passage of dissolved iron through the filters. To remove the carbonic acid before applying the ferrous compounds would be too costly to be practicable.

Ferric Sulphate.—Of the commercial forms of iron in the oxidized or ferric condition, ferric sulphate or persulphate of iron is the best one for this line of work when economy is considered, for the same reason that the sulphate is the best compound of aluminum. Ferric sulphate is decomposed by the alkaline constituents of the Ohio River water in a manner precisely similar, so far as could be learned, to sulphate of alumina. The resulting precipitate of ferric hydrate is very gelatinous and is insoluble; therefore it makes an excellent coagulant. With equal weights of iron and aluminum, in the form of sulphates, the ratio of the decrease in alkalinity and increase in carbonic acid and incrusting constituents is 1.0 to 2.1. The waste of ferric sulphate by absorption on the surfaces of silt and mud is similar to that in the case of sulphate of alumina.

Commercial ferric sulphate is a little cheaper than sulphate of alumina, free of water of crystallization, and contains about three times as high a percentage of metal. It was these features of the compound that originally attracted our attention. It is difficult to dissolve, and the sample with which our tests were made contained some free sulphuric acid and insoluble residue. Neutral ferric sulphate can be procured without difficulty, however, and the suspended particles could be removed from the solution by ready means.

Metallic Iron by the Anderson Process.—This process consists in obtaining in the water by contact with metallic iron a carbonate (ferrous) of iron by the solvent action of the carbonic acid in the water, and the oxidation of this compound to insoluble ferric hydrate. It is referred to in Chapter IX, page 244. Bottle experiments indicated that its use with the Ohio River water was not satisfactory, owing to the retarding action of large amounts of carbonic acid such as are present for months at a time in this water. The nature of this retarding action is similar to that in the case of the protosulphate of iron.

Aeration was tried on a small scale to supplement this action, but it did not work well. The oxide was granular in form, showing the absence of normal hydration, and the value of the iron as a coagulant was lost for the most part.

Compounds of Manganese.

Manganese forms manganous, manganic, and permanganate compounds. The manganous compounds cannot be safely used to advantage with this water, owing to complications with carbonic acid in the manner explained in the case of ferrous sulphate. Manganic compounds in a suitable form are not on the market. Permanganates of lime and potash were used in the laboratory; they are manufactured in considerable quantities, but they cost, according to the best quotations, $12.70 and $0.40 per pound, respectively. Their expense renders their use inadmissible for purification of municipal supplies. A study of them, however, has made plainer our understanding of the coagulation of the muddy Ohio River water, and for the sake of completeness they will receive brief consideration.

Permanganate of Potash.—When added to the Ohio River water in proper amounts the organic matter slowly withdraws oxygen from this compound, and the carbon and hydrogen of the organic matter are oxidized to carbonic acid and water, respectively. The result is that after a time the manganese is converted to mangano-manganic hydrate, which is a gelatinous, insoluble precipitate. Experience shows that the action is very slow, at least 3 hours ordinarily being required for its completion; but the time varies with the amount and character of the organic matter. When the reaction is completed the manganese does not pass through the filter, but it will do so until it is converted into the insoluble hydrate. As fast as the carbon dioxide is formed it unites with the potash of the applied chemical to form carbonate of potash, which is an alkaline but not a corroding or incrusting constituent. The nominal increase in alkalinity is the only change in the composition of the filtered water, as the removal of organic matter would be effected by subsidence and filtration independent of this oxidizing action.

In addition to the slowness with which this action takes place this process developed an important fact—that the manganese compounds are not at all or very little absorbed by the surface of the mud or silt.

Permanganate of Lime.—The behavior of this chemical when applied to the Ohio River water is precisely similar to that of permanganate of potash, except that the resulting carbonate in this case is that of lime instead of potash.

Comparative Summary of Coagulants.

Experience shows that the sulphates of alumina and ferric iron are the most suitable commercial chemicals for the coagulation of the Ohio River water. In order to make more explicit the next topic, on absorption of coagulants by silt and clay, the permanganates will be briefly reviewed in comparison with the sulphates, although the former are too expensive and are incapable of being applied in sufficient amounts to be practicable. For convenience we will refer to the sulphates as type A, and to the permanganates as type B.

1. Nature of Reaction.—This has been carefully explained above, but in brief a type A chemical is partly and as a rule mostly decomposed by alkaline constituents, while the remainder is absorbed by the surface of the matters in suspension. The latter action appears to be largely if not wholly a chemical one. With type B the dissolved organic matter decomposes the chemical, and a resultant gelatinous precipitate is formed. So far as we could learn type B appears to be affected not at all, practically speaking, by absorption by silt and clay, and its reaction progresses with suspended organic matter only so fast as the latter becomes disintegrated and passes into solution.

2. Germicidal Action. — The chemicals of each type if applied in sufficiently large quantities will destroy bacteria. But when applied to the water in such amounts as are practicable for the purification of a municipal water supply they do not kill bacteria, practically speaking, although they cause many of them to die either by direct effect or by enveloping them in masses of coagula. In any case under practicable conditions in this connection the destruction of bacteria would not be complete from a hygienic point of view.

3. Speed of Reaction.—With type A the reaction is completed almost instantaneously, although there are indications that at times there is a selective action in respect to the alkaline constituents and the suspended particles which absorb the chemicals. Concerning the time which elapses before the coagula appear in suitable size for efficient subsidence and filtration, this period deals wholly with the period of coagulation following the initial reaction, which occurs immediately.

In the case of type B the initial reaction takes place very slowly; in fact it would probably never be complete in less than 3 hours, and in many instances it would continue for more than 24 hours. This is due to the nature of the reaction as explained above, as the chemical has first to disintegrate and make soluble a large part of the organic matter which is oxidized.

4. Safe Maximum Limit of Application.—The maximum limit of safe application of type A depends upon the absorptive capacity of suspended matters, and the alkalinity of the river water, and the amount of sulphuric acid in the applied chemicals. Expressed in grains per gallon the range of maximum application of sulphate of alumina would be from 4 to 15. For persulphate of iron these figures would range approximately from 3 to 10 grains per gallon.

In the case of permanganate of potash, type B, the safe maximum application would range from 0.1 to 0.2 grain per gallon, with a period of reaction of not less than 3 hours.

5. Applicability in the Purification of the Ohio River Water. — The permanganates, type B, are not applicable to this problem because of their cost, the slowness of their action, and the low limits in the amount of safe application. A study of them, however, was very fruitful in showing inherent weakness of type A chemicals, and indicating how those weaknesses might be remedied in part in practice. They relate to absorption and are discussed as the next topic.

Absorption of Commercial Sulphates of Alumina and of Ferric Iron by the Silt and Clay in the Ohio River Water, with Special Reference to the Waste of Chemicals and the Necessity for the Removal of Coarse Silt by Plain Sedimentation.

In the course of these investigations a number of observations were made which cooperated to bring out the marked significance from a practical point of view, of a phenomenon which we shall call absorption. To illustrate this by an action which is familiar to everyone, we may compare it to the somewhat similar observation of iron stains as they appear upon linen. This action is not the same, but it is believed that its nature is parallel. At this point it may be stated that of all the chemical actions seen in daily life, there is probably none which is more obscure than the action of liquids upon solids, as illustrated by the ones in question. To explain these observations and facts in a comprehensive manner is impossible in the present state of applied chemical science. Accordingly we shall present the evidence in a series of observations characteristic of the nature of this phenomenon, and at the close point out its practical significance.

I.

Loss of Coagulants when Applied in Small Quantities to Ohio River Water, containing Coarse and Fine Particles.

This is shown by the following experiment, in which a series of one-gallon bottles were filled with river water containing 424 parts per million of mixed coarse and fine silt and clay. Beginning with none, the samples were treated with sulphate of alumina, each bottle being given 0.25 grain per gallon more than the preceding one. The bottles were then well shaken, and samples of the supernatant liquid removed by a siphon after 24 hours subsidence. The results were as follows:

Applied Sulphate of Alumina. Grains per Gallon.	After Settling 24 Hours.		Additional Percentage Removal for Successive Portions of 0.25 Grain.
	Suspended Solids. Parts per Million.	Percentage Removal.	
None.	55	70	....
0.25	47	74	4
0.50	44	76	2
0.75	35	81	5
1.00	3	97	16
1.25	1	99	2
1.50	0	100	1

This experiment is not an extreme case, but it serves to illustrate the fact that with successive equal amounts of applied sulphate of alumina the work accomplished is not regularly progressive, and that for some reason in the ordinary river water the specific efficiency of the first portion of chemicals is very low, and less than that of subsequent ones.

II.

Necessity of Applying Different Amounts of Coagulants to secure complete Coagulation of Equal Weights of Suspended Matters of Different Character.

This was repeatedly noted in the operation of the filter, but is illustrated in a very characteristic manner by the following experiment:

Waters A and B each contained 66 parts per million of suspended matter. A represents unusually fine particles, while in B the particles were abnormally coarse. As in the foregoing experiment, successive portions of sulphate of alumina were added to a series of bottles containing the two waters, respectively, and samples of the supernatant liquid were collected for analysis after the coagulant and water had been shaken and then allowed to subside for 18 hours.

Applied Sulphate of Alumina. Grains per Gallon.	After Settling 18 Hours.			
	Water A.		Water B.	
	Percentage Removal of Suspended Solids.	Additional Removal for Successive Portions of 0.25 Grain.	Percentage Removal of Suspended Solids.	Additional Removal for Successive Portions of 0.25 Grain.
None.	10	....	50	....
0.25	10	0	57	7
0.50	10	0	72	15
0.75	15	5	92	20
1.00	30	15	96	4
1.50	82	52*	99	3*
2.00	92	10*	100	1*

* For increases of 0.50 grain.

These results show that 0.75 grain effected as much purification by coagulation and subsidence with the water B, containing the coarse matters, as did 2.00 grains in the case of the water A, with very fine clay. With water A the first point in this evidence is brought out very forcibly, as 0.5 grain was applied with no purification in addition to that accomplished by plain subsidence.

III.

Varying Departures from the Theoretical Rate of Reduction in Alkalinity when Coagulants are applied to Water containing Equal Amounts of Different Kinds of Suspended Matter.

In Chapter III it was shown that theoretically the reduction in alkalinity would be strictly proportional to the amount of chemical added and to the percentage of sulphuric acid contained in the applied sulphate, provided there were no organic or suspended matters present. Data were presented at that time showing that the departure from the theoretical reduction was dependent upon the amount of suspended matter; and here it is the purpose to show that the reduction is also affected by the character of the suspended matter.

The following experiment illustrates this point. The five samples of river water contained approximately equal amounts of suspended matter, while the actual reduction in alkalinity by adequate amounts of the same lot of sulphate of alumina showed wide variations in departure from the theoretical reduction.

Number of Sample.	Suspended Solids. Parts per Million.	Percentage which the Actual Reduction in Alkalinity was of the Theoretical.
1	500	57
2	534	74
3	584	77
4	516	80
5	558	84
Averages	550	74

These data show clearly that different kinds of suspended matter dispose of varying amounts of coagulant by an action which for the want of a better name we call absorption. This is most marked in the case of clay, and appears to be largely, if not wholly, a chemical action. The reason of this belief is based on the fact that there is no diminution in the conductivity of a solution in which absorption takes place, and the assumption that this indicates the absence of a physical change which would withdraw and not interchange ions and thus increase the resistance of the solution containing these particles.

The absorption of chemical solutions by various materials containing alumina has been known for some time to agricultural chemists, and at the Lawrence Experiment Station this action was found to be a factor in connection with the efficiency of filters of the English type. In the case of clay this absorption, it is important to note, produces some coagulation. With regard to the coagulation of clay by other salts, such as common table salt, or by acids, so far as our observations go, there would be nothing practicable in their use.

IV.

Conclusive Indications of the Necessity of having to Saturate some Capacity of the Suspended Particles before complete Coagulation is possible.

The foregoing data bring out very forcibly the fact that with ordinary conditions of the river water the first portions of the coagulant have a very low specific efficiency in purification; and after a certain amount has been applied a very small additional amount causes complete coagulation, provided sufficient time is allowed to elapse after the application of the coagulant. This capacity is the absorption previously referred to, and varies materially with different waters.

V.

Comparison of the Relative Efficiencies as Subsiding Coagulants, of Type A (sulphates) and Type B (permanganates), and with Reference to Discrepancies between the above Relation and the Percentages which the Actual were of the Theoretical Reduction in Alkalinity.

At the outset it may be stated that in general terms experience indicates that to secure equal efficiencies for coagulation, it is necessary to provide substantially equal volumes of gelatinous hydrate. This is demonstrated by the data given in section No. 6, but here it may be noted that ordinary commercial sulphate of alumina and persulphate of iron yield about the same volume of hydrate, and as coagulants their efficiency is substantially the same in all conditions which we have studied.

On the basis of equal volumes of hydrate, sulphate of alumina and permanganate of potash should have relative efficiencies of 1.00 to 1.14. In practice with the unsubsided Ohio River water the relative efficiency of sulphate of alumina was far less than this, as is indicated by the following representative results obtained from a series of experiments, in which in all cases coagulants were added to give a fairly complete and corresponding degree of efficiency, as shown by the removal of suspended matters by subsidence for 24 hours. The comparative efficiencies of types A and B are expressed with reference to the above ratio.

Amount of Coagulant in Grains per Gallon.		Suspended Solids, Parts per Million.	Percentage which the Actual Reduction of Alkalinity was of the Theoretical. Type A.	Percentage which the Efficiency of Type A was of that indicated by the Theoretical Ratio.
Type A.	Type B.			
1.00	0.10	542	58	15
2.00	0.20	542	64	14
1.00	0.14	129	89	13
1.00	0.14	83	91	24
1.00	1.00*	200	95	127*

* In this case an excess of dissolved organic matter was applied to the water so as to increase very largely the speed of reaction.

Bearing in mind the fact that with type A the reaction is practically instantaneous, while in type B it is exceedingly slow, with river water, it will be understood that the coagulating hydrate in type A is formed very quickly and in type B very slowly. It is also to be remembered that type A, but not type B, is absorbed by suspended matter.

If the absorption were the only point of difference in the behavior of the two types then the percentage efficiency which type A gave of that indicated by the theoretical ratio would correspond to the percentage which the actual was of the theoretical rate of reduction of alkalinity in a general way. If the absorption produced no coagulation of clay particles this last statement would be true in absolute terms. But it is shown in the last table that in the case of the first four (normal) waters the percentage efficiency of type A fell far below the percentage which the actual reduction in alkalinity was of the theoretical. In other words, the amount of aluminum hydrate, which was proven to be formed by the actual decomposition of alkaline constituents, failed to accomplish as much work as an equal volume of hydrate of manganese as produced by type B.

The explanation of these results, and of others of a similar nature, was that the hydrate with type A was formed instantaneously, or nearly so, and became attached by some means to the coarse particles, which subsided quickly and carried to the bottom much of the hydrate before it had an opportunity to coagulate those fine particles which needed it most. This explanation was proved conclusively to be correct by adding enough soluble organic matter to the last water in the case of type B to form this hydrate almost immediately, as was normally the case with type A. Under these circumstances the relative efficiency of type A as compared with type B exceeded the theoretical ratio stated above, which was based on the relative volumes of hydrate.

It is now seen that in addition to the absorptive action which with coarse matters means a waste of chemicals, there is also an attachment of hydrate, in the case of sulphate of alumina and persulphate of iron, and the coarse particles, on which this attachment occurs, subside quickly and thus cause a waste of coagulants. Whether or not this attachment is entirely physical or mechanical in its nature is not known.

Conclusions.

1. The suspended matters in the Ohio River water have a certain, but varying, power of absorbing sulphate of alumina and persulphate of iron. With fine clay particles this absorption produces coagulation in a measure, but with the coarsest particles it appears to be a total loss of chemicals. This absorption of the coagulant causes the actual rate of reduction of alkalinity to become variable, and the departure from the theoretical rate measures the absorption of the applied chemicals by the suspended (and soluble organic) matters.

2. In order to secure complete coagulation for any given water containing suspended matter it is necessary to apply a certain definite amount of the coagulant, which varies with different kinds and amounts of suspended matter, in order to saturate their absorptive power before substantial coagulation takes place. When applied in amounts less than this the chemicals are largely wasted.

3. Owing to the fact that with the commercial sulphates the respective hydrates are formed almost instantaneously, the presence of coarse particles which subside quickly cause a waste of chemicals in amounts equal to the quantities of original chemical ab-

sorbed, plus a certain amount of hydrate which becomes attached to their surfaces. The attached hydrate is thus removed before it coagulates to its full power the fine particles in the water.

4. The above facts are decisive proof that it is impracticable to apply coagulants to a water which contains suspended matter which may be economically removed by plain subsidence.

For the sake of completeness it may be stated that in the electrolytical formation of coagulating hydrates the salts of the metals are formed initially, and the general effect is similar to that recorded for the sulphates in this section. So far as our observations extend at present, plain subsidence is the only practical step to take to obviate these actions in part.

Section No. 3.

Status at the Beginning of this Portion of the Investigation, with a General Description, of the Formation of Coagulating Chemicals by the Electrolytical Decomposition of Metal Plates.

At the outset of this portion of the investigation the evidence upon this point may be briefly outlined as follows:

1. Copper, lead, tin, and zinc are inadmissible for electrolytic decomposition for this purpose, because the resultant chemicals are partially soluble in water, and would therefore be liable to injure the health of persons drinking the water after such treatment.

2. Aluminum and iron are the only metals of commerce which can be electrolytically decomposed into chemicals adapted to the coagulation of water. The available information concerning them at that time was as follows:

3. One pound of metallic aluminum, electrolytically decomposed into aluminum hydrate, is substantially equivalent to one pound of aluminum in the form of aluminum sulphate, when the latter is applied to a water containing lime in solution. One pound of metallic aluminum in sheet form costs 27 cents, and one pound of aluminum in the form of sulphate of alumina costs 16 cents. The alumina in the form of the commercial chemical, therefore, costs only 60 per cent. as much as in the form of metal plates, disregarding the expensive items of power, electrolytic cells, and waste of metal in the latter case.

4. One pound of metallic iron electrolytically decomposed into iron hydrate is substantially equivalent to one pound of iron in the form of persulphate of iron, when the latter is applied to water containing lime in solution. One pound of metallic iron, in the form of plates suitably arranged in an electrolytical cell, costs about 2 cents; and one pound of iron in the form of persulphate of iron costs 5 cents. There was a difference, therefore, of 3 cents per pound, to cover the cost of electric power and waste of metal. This was a substantial margin on the right side, and made the electrolytic production of iron hydrate a factor in the problem.

5. Electrolytically produced hydrates (either aluminum or iron) do not, as in the case of commercial chemicals like the sulphates, add to the water a strong acid, to combine with lime and increase the incrusting power of the water when used in steam-boilers; nor is there a practically equivalent amount of carbonic acid gas liberated, to increase the corrosive action of the filtered water on iron vessels.

In short, it will be seen that the electrolytic production of iron hydrate was a promising factor, while the electrolytic production of aluminum hydrate gave no indications of being practicable for regular use, owing to excessive cost. It was decided, however, to investigate the electrolytic production of the hydrates of both of these metals. In the case of aluminum this was done, not only for the purpose of securing comparable data on the same scale as was used in 1895–96, but also with the possibility in mind that the use of aluminum during periods of maximum treatment of the water might reduce the size of power plant, because it appeared that aluminum is decomposed with less power than iron, relatively speaking.

A description of the formation of iron hydrate and of aluminum hydrate, by the electrolytic decomposition of the respective metals, is presented in considerable detail, from a practical point of view, in the next two sections. Before this is done, however, it will be well to consider some of the general features of electrolysis.

General Description of Electrolysis.

Electrolysis is the name of the process by which a liquid is decomposed by means of an electric current. As a rule, such liquids are aqueous solutions of various chemical salts and compounds which are capable of splitting (dissociating) into two component parts. Liquids which can be electrolyzed are called electrolytes. Absolutely pure water cannot be electrolyzed, practically speaking, and liquids possess this capacity by virtue of the chemical compounds dissolved in them. These compounds serve as conductors of the electrical current, and electrolytes are called conductors of the second class, in distinction from the metals, which are known as conductors of the first class.

A receptacle in which electrolysis takes place is called an electrolytic cell. The plates attached to the ends of the wires running from the electric generator to the cell and return are spoken of as the electrodes. To distinguish the two plates, or two sets of plates, the electrode by which the electric current enters is termed the positive pole, or anode, and that by which it leaves, the negative pole, or cathode. The dissolved chemicals in the water are dissociated into two component parts, which are called ions. When an electric current is passed through an electrolytic cell the ions move to the electrodes. The metallic (including hydrogen) constituents or ions of the substances dissolved in the water pass to the cathode or negative pole, while the acid ions move to the anode. The former ions are called cathions, and the latter anions. This movement toward the respective electrodes, of the metallic and acid portions of the compounds dissolved in the liquid, explains the manner in which an electric current is conducted through ordinary water. Having made this point clear, we will now proceed to consider the most important point in question, viz.: the action of the ions when they reach electrodes of different composition.

Electrodes may be divided into two classes, according to their ability or non-ability to be dissolved by the ions which reach the positive pole, with the formation of new chemical compounds. Some electrodes, such as carbon and platinum, are not dissolved by the anions, which find it easier to attack water and decompose it. Such electrodes are called passive or insoluble. Other electrodes, such as aluminum and iron, form new chemical compounds by the solvent action of the anions, which find it easier, wholly or in part, to unite with the metal electrodes than to attack and decompose water. Such electrodes are called active or soluble. Of the two expressions, passivity and solubility of electrodes, the former is preferred, and hereafter we shall use it exclusively. As implied above, all negative poles, regardless of their composition, are considered to be passive.

Passive Electrodes.—When carbon or other passive electrodes are employed in the electrolysis of a liquid there are no new chemical compounds permanently formed, but the water is gradually decomposed into its constituent parts, hydrogen and oxygen gases. To illustrate this we will consider the electrolysis with carbon electrodes of a solution of common salt, sodium chloride, in pure water. The chemical symbol of salt is Na Cl, in which Na refers to sodium and Cl to chlorine.

When an electric current is applied to an electrolytic cell in which the electrolyte is a salt solution the united action is as follows:

Before Application of the Current.

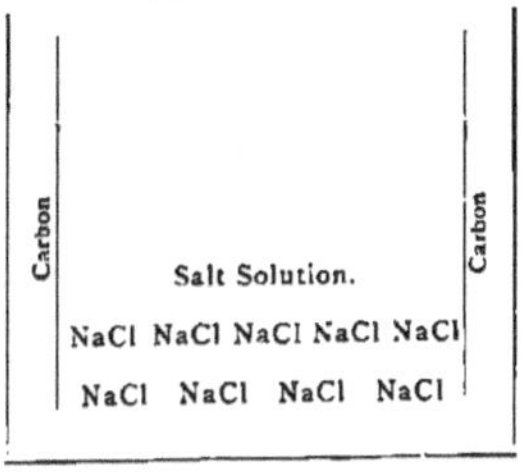

After Application of the Current.

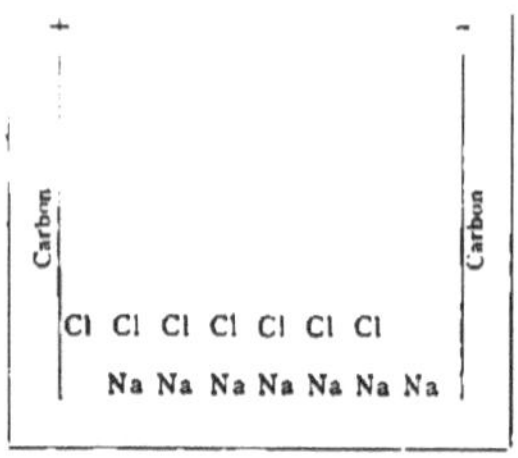

That is, the electric current is conducted through the liquid by the passage of the sodium and chlorine ions to the negative and positive poles, respectively. When the ions reach the electrodes their electric charges are neutralized, and they find in each case that the carbon poles are *passive* and do not offer any opportunity for chemical combination.

Under these circumstances the second step in the process consists of the ions at each electrode attacking water. At the positive pole the chlorine ions unite with water and form hydrochloric acid (HCl), which remains dissolved in the water, and oxygen (O), which escapes as a gas. The sodium ions at the negative pole also unite with water and form sodium hydrate (NaOH), commonly called caustic soda, which remains dissolved in the water, and hydrogen (H), which escapes as a gas. This second step in the process may be illustrated as follows:

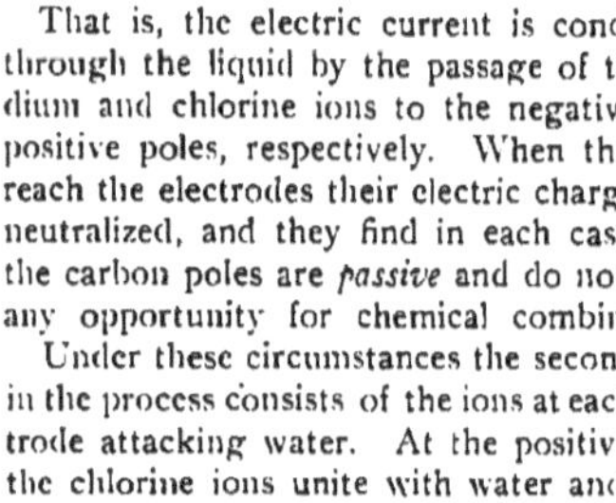

If a porous (parchment) partition were placed in the cell between the electrodes, it would be found that the water in the vicinity of the positive electrode becomes more and more acid as the passage of the electric current continues, and the water in the vicinity of the negative electrode becomes correspondingly alkaline. Hydrochloric acid and sodium hydrate have a strong affinity for each other, and in the absence of a partition unite and form salt, the substance which was started with, and water. This combination of two of the intermediate products to form the original product constitutes the third and last step of the process.

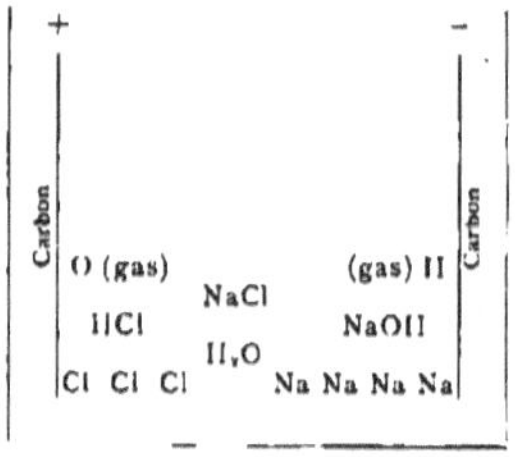

It will thus be seen that with passive electrodes, electrolysis of salt solution effects indirectly the separation of water into its component elements, and that by a recombination of other secondary products the original substance is produced, and the process is therefore continuous.

Active Electrodes.—In order to make this parallel with the preceding account of passive electrodes we will consider the electrolysis of a salt solution when the electrodes are of iron. Here the first step in the process, the conduction of the electric current by the movement of the chlorine and sodium ions to the positive and negative poles, respectively, is precisely the same as in the foregoing description.

With regard to the second step in the process, the action of the sodium ions at the negative pole is also the same (because all negative poles are theoretically passive), attacking water with the formation of sodium hydrate and hydrogen gas. The action of the chlorine ions at the positive pole shows the difference between carbon and iron electrodes. In this latter case it is easier for the chlorine to dissolve the iron electrodes than to attack water. Under the most favorable conditions iron chloride is formed without any oxygen, and under ordinary circumstances the amount of oxygen formed appears to be very small, and perhaps *nil.*

The third step, the combination of iron chloride and sodium hydrate to form sodium chloride (the initial compound) and iron hydrate, is precisely similar to the corresponding step in the case of passive electrodes. The only difference in this particular is that iron hydrate instead of water (which may be regarded as hydrogen hydrate) is formed.

From the above description it will be seen that the activity of iron and aluminum electrodes makes their use possible as a means of producing hydrates of these metals. The degree of passivity, even of the same metal, with different salts dissolved in the water varies widely under the conditions of practice. A consideration of this, and several other important factors, in the electrolytic production of iron hydrate and aluminum hydrate, is taken up in the next two sections, in which the matter is described in detail from a practical point of view.

Fundamental Laws and Principles of Electrolysis, as Applied to the Electrolytic formation of Hydrates of Iron and Aluminum in the Ohio River Water.

The leading laws and principles dealt with in this work are as follows:

1. Faraday's Quantitative Law.—This law may be expressed in a number of different ways, among which is the following: The amount of an ion liberated at an electrode in a given length of time is equal to the strength (amperage) of the electric current, multiplied by the electro-chemical equivalent of the ion. The electro-chemical equivalent of hydrogen for one ampere of current for one hour is equal to 0.375 gram (5.78 grains). On this basis the electro-chemical equivalent of any ion may be obtained by multiplying the above figures by the chemical equivalent weight of the ion. In the case of elementary ions, this chemical equivalent weight is the atomic weight divided by the valency, and in the case of compound ions, it is the molecular weight divided by the valency.

From Faraday's law it follows that, other conditions being equal, the amount of hydrate of iron or aluminum formed is proportional to the amperage of the current; and the amount of coagulating chemicals is therefore controlled by regulating the amperage of the current.

2. Ohm's Law.—Ohm's law, that the number of amperes of current flowing through a circuit is equal to the number of volts of electro-motive force, divided by the number of ohms of resistance in the entire circuit, holds good for electrolytic construction.

3. Resistance of Electrolytic Cell.—In view of the fact that it is the amperage of the current and not its potential which determines the rate of formation of hydrates, it is obvious that the resistance of the cell should be kept as nearly as possible at a certain minimum for economical reasons. The minimum potential is determined by the polarization of the cell, as stated more fully in a following paragraph. The resistance of the cell is due to several factors, among which are: the area of electrodes; the distance between electrodes; the amount of dissolved salts in the river water (electrolyte); and the formation of non-conducting coatings on the electrodes. From Ohm's law it follows that the resistance of an electrolytic cell increases directly with the water space between the electrodes, and inversely with the cross-section of the electrolyte (or area of the electrodes).

4. Resistance to the Passage of an Electric Current of Ohio River Water.—This subject has been referred to in Chapter XIII, where it was seen that during the period of flood in February and March, 1897, the resistance of the river water increased nearly threefold, due to the decrease in amount of dissolved chemical compounds. That, practically speaking, the suspended matters in the water, including those partially dissolved constituents, exerted no influence on the conductivity was also presented at that time.

Estimating the conductivity or resistance (which is the reciprocal of the conductivity) of the river water from the observations on different combinations of various solutions of the salts normally present in it, the resistance in ohms per centimeter cube should be theoretically 6100, 930, and 2080 ohms for maximum, minimum, and average, respectively, corresponding to 72, 260, and 122 parts per million of dissolved chemical compounds, not including carbonic acid gas. As will be shown in connection with the study of passivity of iron electrodes, it is not possible to draw specific mathematical conclusions in regard to the behavior of combinations of ions, based on the results of observations in individual ions. It will be also shown in this connection that dissolved carbonic acid gas is only very slightly ionized, and from a practical point of view need not be considered as a conductor at all.

It is therefore necessary to rely upon observations on the river water itself, though as will be seen, the theoretical and observed resistances follow closely the same curve.

On Feb. 22, 1897, the observed resistance of the electrolyte in the Brownell cell was 7600 ohms per centimeter cube, and on Feb. 27 this figure became 16.750. The amounts of dissolved chemical compounds on these days were 146 and 67 parts per million, respectively. On Feb. 17, with 120 parts per million of dissolved compounds, the resistance was observed to be 9200 ohms.

In connection with the devices of the Water Company the average resistance was observed to be about 7000 ohms per centimeter cube, when the river water contained about 130 parts of dissolved solids.

From these results combined with numerous special observations, including those in Chapter XIII, it is estimated that the maximum, minimum, and average resistance of the Ohio River water as an electrolyte would be 17 000, 2000, and 7000 ohms per centimeter cube, corresponding to 67, 324, and 130 parts per million of dissolved chemical compounds, exclusive of carbonic acid, which, as was shown, is only very slightly ionized. In times of great freshets the dilution of the compounds in the river water might be so great that it would be advisable to add commont salt to the water to increase its conductivity to the normal. Investigations during the heavy freshet of February and March, 1897, showed that this could be accomplished by the addition of common salt in amounts not exceeding 5 grains per gallon. Such additions would not cause the total amount of salt to be greater than was normally present in the river water during the low stages of the river in the fall of 1895.

5. *Polarization of Electrodes.*—When a current of electricity flows through an electrolytic cell, and causes changes in the electrolyte, or on the electrode, the electromotive force of the current is thereby reduced. This action is known as polarization. In explanation of this point, which determines the minimum potential of current that can be safely employed, it is to be stated that all ions possess a certain force or intensity of fixation wherewith they attempt to retain their electric charges when they reach the electrodes. Accordingly, a certain potential, slightly above that corresponding to the intensity of fixation, is necessary in order to overcome this force, and free the ions at the electrodes of their electric charges. The existence of this intensity of fixation, with an opportunity to measure it, is shown by the reverse current which takes place for a short time when the primary current is shut off. With active electrodes, polarization becomes less marked. The potential of polarization varies in the line of work in question. So far as we know, there would be no case where the polarization would require over 2.35 volts to overcome it. Ordinarily it would be much less than this. Records show that in the investigation of electrolysis of iron pipes lying in the ground near electric lines of street-cars (a subject similar in a measure to the present one), decomposition of the iron has taken place at a potential of only 0.001 volt. In all cases a difference in potential of 2.5 volts, or less between adjoining electrodes, would suffice to overcome the intensity of fixation of all ions, while much less than this would probably be adequate for a majority of the ions. Practical investigations along this line are recorded in section No. 4 of this chapter, where it will be seen that potential differences as low as 1.0 volt can be safely employed with iron electrodes.

6. *Passivity of Electrodes.* — As already stated, all negative electrodes, so far as is known, are passive to the ions, and certain positive electrodes such as iron and aluminum, are active. From Ampere's law it follows that the same quantity of electric current always causes in electrolysis the same equivalent amount of acid ions (anions) to go to the positive electrodes, and have their electric charges neutralized. They then pass into the atomic state. With passive electrodes, they attack water, and equal currents produce equal amounts of oxygen gas. Pro-

vided that active electrodes were completely active (not at all passive or insoluble under the action of these liberated acid atoms), the amount of metal decomposed from the positive electrode would also be proportional to the amperage of the current, and to the amount of liberated acid ions, in accordance with Ampere's law.

In the case of iron and aluminum electrodes, however, experience shows that the metal of the positive electrodes is not dissolved in quantities proportional and equivalent to the total quantity of acid ions liberated at the positive electrode. From a practical point of view this fact is a matter of vital importance, because it relates to the amount of hydrate formed, and consequently to the commercial merits of the process. Stating this in another way, we may say that only a portion of the current forms the hydrate of the metal used as the positive electrode; and therefore such metals as iron and aluminum are only partially active, as a portion of the current causes the formation of oxygen, just as in the case of completely passive electrodes, such as carbon or platinum.

It follows from the above statements of facts that, under practical conditions, iron and aluminum electrodes are only partially active, and when employed in this process utilize efficiently only a portion of the current. Hence, in the following sections, in which this process is described in detail, use must be made of degree of activity or degree of passivity of electrode. In view of the fact that the latter expression is in use by chemists, we shall adopt it in future cases where reference is made to this phase of the process.

The degree of passivity of iron and aluminum electrodes is due to the two following factors:

1. The initial passivity of the metal to the various acid ions naturally present in the river water. Thus it is well known that hydrochloric acid has a higher solvent action on these metals than carbonic acid.

2. The acquired passivity of the metal to the various acid ions, due to the formation of thin films of metallic oxide, caused by the oxygen formed by the weaker ions, upon the metal.

In practice the varying composition of the river water caused a wide range in the relative amounts of the different acid ions, and the consequent total dissolving action upon the electrodes. Experience shows that another important factor, especially in the case of aluminum, is the fact that the film of metallic oxide on the positive pole causes a material increase in the resistance which the electric current meets in its passage through the cell. In the case of iron electrodes, however, this is relatively slight, owing to the fact that the film cracks and falls off in scales at frequent but irregular intervals.

7. Secondary Reactions. — Normally there are formed with active electrodes a hydrate of the metal, hydrogen, and, varying with the degree of passivity, a certain amount of oxygen. These reactions have been explained in the foregoing account of electrolysis, and may be called primary reactions, or perhaps the primary group of reactions. Other reactions (independent of coagulation), called secondary reactions, will now be referred to.

When iron electrodes are employed the iron is dissolved from the plates in the form of ferrous or unoxidized salts, which would be converted into the partially soluble ferrous hydrate by the alkaline hydrates coming from the negative electrode. Accordingly, oxygen is necessary, in order to convert the ferrous into the ferric forms. As practically all of the electrolytically formed oxygen attacks the positive iron electrodes, it is necessary that the atmospheric oxygen, naturally dissolved in the water, serves to effect this oxidation. This oxidation is necessary in order to convert the iron into a completely insoluble form, so that it can coagulate the suspended matter in the water without any dissolved iron passing through the filter into the purified water.

The secondary reactions in the case of aluminum electrodes are less clearly understood, but are referred to beyond.

Concerning hydrogen at the negative electrode, small portions of it in the nascent condition combine with atmospheric oxygen dissolved in the water, and reduce iron compounds and nitrates; while the bulk of it, after saturating the pores of the metal, escapes as a gas in a molecular condition.

SECTION NO. 4.

DETAILED ACCOUNT OF THE ELECTROLYTIC FORMATION OF IRON HYDRATE IN THE OHIO RIVER WATER.

A full record and discussion of this process is presented under several leading topics as follows:

Degree of Passivity of Iron Electrodes due to the Different Acid Ions of the Ohio River Water.

The dissolved acids which are present in appreciable amounts in the Ohio River water are hydrochloric, sulphuric, nitric, silicic, and carbonic.

As is well known to chemists, these acids differ in their ability to dissolve iron. This capacity of being dissolved by acids under the conditions of electrolysis measures the passivity of iron in electrolytes containing the acid in question. Several experiments were made in which solutions containing the respective acids alone and in various combinations (in the form of salts of the alkalies) were placed in sets of cells containing electrodes of bright wrought iron and of rusty iron from the same sheet. The cells were arranged in series, and an electric current of from 2 to 47 amperes per square foot was passed through them for periods of from 2 to 30 minutes.

Aliquot portions of the contents of each cell, after rinsing the electrodes, were collected for determinations of the amounts of iron. The average results of these determinations, together with the average specific resistances of the several electrolytes, are presented in the following table.

Percentages which the metal decomposed was of the theoretical rate (1.05 grams per ampere hour) are also given.

The potential difference between the plates varied in these experiments from 12 to 220 volts.

SUMMARY OF RESULTS SHOWING AVERAGE RATES OF ELECTROLYTIC DECOMPOSITION OF NEW AND OLD IRON IN ELECTROLYTES OF VARIOUS ACID IONS.

Acid Ions.	Parts per Million.*	Average Rate of Decompositoin. Grams per Ampere-Hour.†		Per Cent. of the Theoretical Rate.		Average Resistance of Electrolyte. Ohms per Centimeter Cube.
		New Iron.	Old Iron.	New Iron.	Old Iron.	
Hydrochloric acid	10	1.11	0.83	106	79	4 330
Sulphuric acid	15	0.92	0.85	88	81	6 880
Nitric acid	5	0.95	0.72	91	69	10 700
Carbonic acid (carbonate)	60	0.86	0.51	82	49	2 300
Carbonic acid (dissolved gas)	50	0.80	0.65	76	62	20 000
Silicic acid	10	0.79	0.73	75	70	6 960
Hydrochloric acid Sulphuric acid	10 15	1.00	0.63	95	60	3 360
Hydrochloric acid Nitric acid	10 5	1.12	0.90	107	86	4 170
Hydrochloric acid Carbonic acid (carbonate)	10 60	0.97	0.64	93	61	1 690
Hydrochloric acid Carbonic acid (dissolved gas)	10 50	0.90	0.73	86	70	6 540
Hydrochloric acid Sulphuric acid Nitric acid Carbonic acid (carbonate)	10 15 5 60	1.04	0.44	99	42	1 240
Hydrochloric acid Sulphuric acid Nitric acid Carbonic acid (carbonate) Carbonic acid (dissolved gas)	10 15 5 60 50	1.03	0.48	98	46	1 310

* These quantities are equivalent to the estimated average amounts of the several acids contained in the Ohio River water.

† To change grams per ampere-hour into grains per ampere-hour multiply by 15.4.

The above data indicate quite clearly one point which is, that the result of combinations of two or more ions under these conditions is not the mathematical result of their sum except by chance. If the observations of the resistances of the combined electrolytes (chlorine with the other ions) be compared it will be seen that there is a marked difference from the theoretical resistance of the combinations.

The only apparent explanation to account for this is that when two or more ions are combined in these amounts in the same electrolyte their degrees of ionization are different than in the case when any one of them is presented alone.

The relation between the calculated and observed results becomes then a somewhat variable one, dependent upon the relative degrees of ionization of the several acids.

The conclusions which may be drawn from these experiments are that the relative amounts of the different ions present in the river water would affect the rate of decomposition, but the influence of the several factors under practical conditions is so variable that the present data are insufficient to determine the exact laws for the estimation of these amounts.

Cause of Passivity—Initial and Acquired.

In the last section a table of results was presented of some experiments with new bright wrought-iron and old (rusty) iron electrodes. Both sets were cut from the same plate, and one set cleaned to bright metal while the other remained rusty. It will be seen that the results of observation on the behavior of the new iron gave rates of decomposition varying from 79 per cent. of the theoretical with silicic acid to 111 per cent. with dissolved chlorides, averaging 90.5 per cent. That new bright iron behaves differently toward the several ions is clearly shown, and while it is difficult to account for the results over 100 per cent., it seems clear that in the case of all but hydrochloric acid a certain percentage of the electric current is not directly utilized in dissolving the metal. The explanation of this lies in the relative affinities of these ions for the metal and for water. When the electric current is transferred by means of the ions and the ions are discharged or neutralized at the positive pole, they attack the water of the electrolyte and the metal in the proportion of their affinities for the liquid and the metal. The acid ions which attack the water can be said to represent the passivity of the iron, because they would attack the iron were it not passive. The results on new iron may be taken to indicate the relative passivities which bright iron has to the several acid ions. The data are not sufficient, however, to warrant the use of these figures except in a comparative manner.

Those ions to which the metal is passive attack and decompose water, setting free oxygen gas in a nascent condition. Between this gas and the metal there is at all times great affinity, and therefore a considerable amount of the oxygen attacks the metal and forms the oxide. As this continues the plate becomes covered with a coating of oxide scale which grows thicker and thicker until it begins to crack off. Practically speaking, the rate at which the scale is removed from the plate by cracking and peeling becomes eventually as great as the rate of its formation, and equilibrium is established with reference to the respective attacking of the metal and of water.

The presence of this oxide scale changes the relation of the acid ions to the metal, as they must either attack and dissolve the oxide or pass through the scale to attack the pure bright metal beneath. As either of these processes requires more energy than the simple solution of the metal, an increased percentage of the ions does not attack the metal, but decomposes water, and by this action the iron has an *acquired passivity*.

During the process of formation of the scale and before equilibrium has been established between the formation of the oxide and its scaling off, the acquired degree of passivity increases rapidly as the scale forms.

As the formation of the oxide is dependent on the passivity of the metal and this in turn increases with the oxide present on the face of the plate, the process is a reciprocal one, one action increasing the other. For this reason the length of time elapsing between the beginning and end of the action (establishment of equilibrium) is comparatively short and is dependent upon the density of the current used. Furthermore, it is probable that the passivity of the metal may become greater, before the scale begins to come off, than it is after equilibrium has been established.

The results with old iron, presented in the last section, may be taken as fairly representative of the total passivity of iron as it would be used in practice.

As will be presented beyond, there are no indications to warrant the belief that the potential difference between the plates has any effect upon the passivity of the metal.

Within the limits employed in these investigations the difference in initial passivity due to the composition of the metal was not apparent, cast iron, wrought iron of different grades, and mild steel all giving apparently parallel results, or very nearly so.

Form in which Iron leaves the Plates.

The iron leaves the positive electrodes only, and in order to make the full set of plates serviceable it is necessary to reverse the electric current from time to time.

At the positive electrodes the iron leaves the plates in two ways, namely:

1. Those acid ions, which are neutralized electrically at the pole by dissolving some of the metal, form iron salts of the various acids, such as iron chloride, iron sulphate, and iron carbonate. These compounds, furthermore, are in the ferrous (unoxidized) condition, as explained in the next section.

2. Those acid ions which, by virtue of the degree of passivity of the iron anode, find it easier to react with water upon neutralization than to dissolve the equivalent amounts of iron, form oxygen. This oxygen unites with the iron to form iron oxide, which appears as films.

In the first case the solution of iron is regular and proportional to the amperage of the current when the degree of passivity is constant. With those ions to which the iron electrode is passive, the formation of films of iron oxide is regular, but the films crack and peel off from the electrode in an irregular manner.

Influence on the Process of Oxygen.

With the Ohio River water the oxygen in an electrolytic cell comes from two sources, the atmospheric oxygen naturally dissolved in the water, and the oxygen which is formed eleectrolytically at the anode. We shall consider them separately.

Atmospheric Oxygen. — The atmospheric oxygen performs a very important part in this process, by virtue of the fact that it unites with the ferrous compounds as they are dissolved from the electrode, and changes them to ferric or oxidized salts of iron. Apparently this action takes place partly before the iron salts are acted upon by the alkaline hydrates coming from the negative pole, and partly after this reaction.

The result is that after the completion of the secondary group of reactions, the dissolved iron is converted into the form of insoluble ferric hydrate, which is an excellent coagulant. The importance of this oxidation from a practical point of view is great, because without it ferrous hydrate alone would be formed; and, owing to its partial solubility, there would be difficulties arising from its passage through the filter.

A small amount of atmospheric oxygen also unites with hydrogen, which is given off as a gas at the negative electrodes. As this combination cannot take place except when the hydrogen is in the nascent state, the action is confined to the oxygen in the immediate vicinity of the cathode.

Electrolytic Oxygen.—So far as could be learned, practically all of the oxygen which is formed at the anode by the decomposition of water attacks the metal electrodes and forms films of iron oxide. As stated above, these films crack off and leave the cell in an irregular manner.

Of course the scales or films of iron oxide are of no assistance in the purification of water.

Comparing the influence of the oxygen from the two sources we see that the atmospheric oxygen performs a very important part, and without it the process could not be put in practice with satisfactory results. The influence of the electrolytic oxygen and the factors which produce it, on the other hand, is a very serious drawback to the process, because it means a large waste of electric power and of metallic iron. The amount of power and of metal wasted is shown beyond.

Influence on the Process of Free Carbonic Acid.

Viewed in the present connection, as a factor in a series of secondary reactions which occur in this process after the iron is dissolved from the anode, carbonic acid did not give indications of retarding the oxidation of the resulting ferrous salts, as was the case when commercial protosulphate of iron (copperas) was applied to the water. So far as could be learned the practical effect of carbonic acid upon any secondary reaction was *nil*.

With regard to the relation of free carbonic acid to the passivity of iron electrodes and the degree of its ionization, the evidence has already been presented. Briefly, it showed that the degree of ionization of free carbonic acid in the water is very low, and in this connection its practical significance is very slight.

Influence on the Process of Hydrogen.

Under all conditions hydrogen gas is produced at the negative electrode in amounts proportional to the formation of alkaline hydrates. Owing to the fact that iron possesses the capacity to occlude large quantities of hydrogen gas within its pores, a portion of the hydrogen is disposed of in this manner, and there are reasons for believing that the negative electrode after a time is practically composed of hydrogen, from an electrical point of view. A small portion of the hydrogen when in a nascent condition unites with atmospheric oxygen to form water. The bulk of it, however, after the saturation of the pores of the iron cathode and of the water, escapes as a gas.

The only practical influence of hydrogen, other than the slight consumption of the atmospheric oxygen, is in connection with subsequent sedimentation and filtration, as mentioned beyond, together with the relation of other factors of the process upon the following steps in the purification of water.

Influence on the Process of the Solubility of the Initial Iron Compounds.

It has been stated that when the iron is first dissolved from the positive electrode the compounds are in a form of soluble ferrous salts. Experience shows that some of these iron salts, before they are converted into insoluble ferric hydrate, become conductors of the electric current just like lime and other salts dissolved in the water. The result of this is that a portion of the iron is conducted to the negative electrode; and, in a manner similar to that in electroplating, is deposited there in what appears to be a metallic form.

From a practical point of view the influence of this state of affairs is to cause a waste of electric current, as no good is accomplished by transferring the metal from one pole to the other. So far as could be learned this metal is not wasted, but is available for electrolytic decomposition when the direction of the electric current is reversed.

Form in which the Iron leaves the Cell.

A portion of the iron which leaves the cell is in a form available for coagulation, while a portion is not available. We shall consider the two separately in this connection.

Available Iron.—Analyses of the treated water as it leaves the cells show that the greater proportion of the available iron compounds is in the form of ferric hydrate. Some of the iron which may be actually available for coagulation a little farther along in the flow of the water is at times in the form of ferrous compounds as the water leaves the cell. At no time in regular practice was the amount of iron in the form of ferrous compounds found to exceed 3.8 parts per million. Under these conditions it is probable that all the ferrous iron was in the form of hydrate. When the rate of electrolytic treatment is so great that the atmospheric oxygen is all utilized, then additional treatment causes the iron to leave the cell in the form of ferrous hydrate. Under these conditions there would be about seven parts per million of iron which would be soluble.

Non-Available Iron.—As a consequence of the passivity of iron and the formation of films or scales of oxide of the metal, a portion of the iron leaves the cell at irregular intervals in the form of flakes or scales.

The evidence showing the relative amounts of iron in these two forms is presented just below.

Natural Limitations of the Electrolytic Treatment with Iron Electrodes.

From the foregoing account of this process it is clear that this treatment cannot be safely applied beyond the point where atmospheric oxygen in the water is entirely utilized to convert the iron compounds into the form of insoluble ferric hydrate. The limit of safe application of this process depends therefore on two factors, namely, the rate of formation of iron compounds and the amount of oxygen in the water; both of these vary, and their mutual relation is referred to beyond. after the presentation of further evidence.

Rate of Decomposition of Iron at the Positive Electrode.

Owing to faulty insulation of the large electrodes the data prior to May 29, when hard rubber fittings were put in service, are disregarded. In the following tables the weights of iron decomposed electrolytically from the positive electrodes of each of the two sets are recorded for the several periods between weighings, together with the corresponding electric current (expressed in ampere-hours) for each period.

During the first week of June the sets of electrodes were weighed nearly every day, after washing with a stream of water from a hose. It was found, however, that these weighings were of no account, owing to the metal deposited on the negative electrodes and to remaining accumulations of mud and silt. In a number of cases such weighings showed an increase in the weight of the electrodes. Beginning June 9, the electrodes were dismantled from time to time and the positive and negative plates weighed separately, after cleaning each one carefully with a broom and a stream of water. After June 16 the direction of the electric current was rereversed from time to time, and the positive and negative plates were also weighed separately from time to time. The periods of service between weighings were considerably longer than formerly, and an effort was made to choose such times for weighing when the amount of metal deposited on the negative plates formed a comparatively small per cent. of the total loss of metal. After June 29 the plates were not weighed until Sept. 25, when the entire electric plant was finally dismantled. From the close of the regular tests until Sept. 25 the electrodes were used for several special tests and exhibitions, the last of which was on Sept. 23. When not in service the water was drawn out of the cells in which the electrodes were placed.

In studying the following table it is to be recalled that the rate of decomposition of iron at the positive electrode would be 16.2 grains (1.05 grams) per ampere-hour, provided that the iron plates were completely active, or, in other words, soluble in the acid ions discharged at that point. For convenience in comparison this is called the theoretical rate of decomposition.

SUMMARY OF RESULTS.

Period. 1897.	Electric Current in Ampere-Hours.	Loss in Weight of Positive Electrodes. Pounds.	Average Rate of Decomposition.		
			Per Ampere-Hour.		Per Cent. of Theoretical.
			Grains.	Grams.	
Electrodes No. 1.					
May 29 – June 9	46 760	50.0	7.5	0.49	46
" 9 – " 16	34 100	86.5	17.8	1.16	110
" 16 – " 20	23 660	78.75	23.3	1.52	144
" 20 – " 28	31 520	72.75	16.2	1.05	100
" 29 – Sept. 25	109 500	288.25*	18.4	1.19	113
Totals	245 540	576.25	16.42	1.07	102
Electrodes No. 3.					
June 2 – " 11	15 750	30.5	13.6	0.88	84
" 11 – " 18	46 750	104.0	15.6	1.02	96
" 18 – " 29	23 600	46.0	13.6	0.88	84
" 29 – Sept. 25	72 420	200.25	19.4	1.26	120
Totals	158 500	380.75*	16.82	1.09	104
Total for both Electrodes.					
	404 040	957.00	16.57	1.075	102

* Plates scraped with metal scrapers.

The slight excess of the total average rate of decomposition over the theoretical was probably due largely to the fact that at the close of the test the plates were freer from rust than at the beginning of these tests, as at the close the plates were cleaned with metal scrapers. Similarly the irregularities in some of the periods were due largely, if not wholly, to different degrees of thoroughness with which the plates were cleaned with a broom and a stream of water.

Rate of Deposition of Iron on the Negative Electrode.

The rate at which the iron, removed from the positive electrodes in a soluble form, may become a conductor of the electric current and may be deposited in the metallic state, is indicated by the following summary:

SUMMARY OF RESULTS.

Set of Electrodes.	Period. 1897.	Electric Current in Ampere-Hours.	Gain in Weight of Negative Electrodes. Pounds.	Average Rate of Deposition. Per Ampere-Hour. Grains.	Per Ampere-Hour. Grams.	Per Cent. of Theoretical Decomposition.
1	May 29 – June 9	46 760	14.0	2.1	0.14	8.6
3	June 2 – June 7	15 730	6.0	2.7	0.18	11.1

Owing to the fact that it was found advisable to reverse the direction of the electric current at the end of the above period, no further data upon this point were obtained. It is possible that slight amounts of silt from the river water were mixed with the deposited metal, and caused the above results to be a trifle high. This was not a serious factor, however, because the river water at this time was very clear, comparatively speaking.

During the above periods the current density was varied from time to time. On electrodes No. 1, from May 29 to June 7, the current ranged from 100 to 400 amperes and averaged 253 amperes, corresponding to 0.26, 1.03, and 0.65 amperes per square foot of the active surface of the cathodes (corresponding approximately to the cross-section of the electrolyte). With electrodes No. 3 for the above period the maximum, minimum, and average currents were 234, 171, and 196 amperes, respectively, corresponding to 0.60, 0.44, and 0.50 amperes per square foot of cathode surface. From May 29 to June 2, inclusive, it required about 0.8 minute for the water to pass through the portion of cell No. 1 occupied by the electrodes. From June 2 to 9 the rate of flow in both cells Nos. 1 and 3 was such that the water remained in the portion of these cells occupied by the electrodes for about 1 minute. With the same rate of flow of water through a cell, it is probable that the rate of deposition of metal would increase directly with the current density and with the specific resistance of the electrolyte. For the composition of the river water at this time see Chapter I.

Rate and Uniformity of Formation of Available Iron Hydrate.

We have considered the rate of decomposition of iron at the positive electrode, some of which is non-available for coagulation, as it is in the form of scales of iron oxide, and the deposition of some of the soluble iron, capable of forming ferric hydrate, at the negative electrode. It remains to show the rate of formation of iron hydrate which is the only form capable of coagulating the river water. From time to time during the regular operation the amount of iron leaving the cell was determined by tests with ferricyanide and ferrocyanide. By these well-known tests it was learned, in addition to the total amount, how much iron was in the two states of oxidation (ferrous and ferric iron). But these tests do not show the difference between the hydrate and the scales of oxide which are given off at an irregular rate. To note the rate of hydrate formation it is necessary to compare a series of observations, and study the low and uniform rates, which are affected but little, comparatively speaking, by scales of oxide.

In order to make this evidence as complete as practicable, numerous special tests with electrodes Nos. 1 and 3 were begun on July 23 and continued until July 28. The results of these tests, with the percentage which the total iron was of the amount indicated by the theoretically normal rate of formation, are presented in the set of tables on pages 400 and 401. In these tables sufficient notes will be found to make plain the conditions of operation.

It will be seen that the results of these tests, which confirm earlier and more fragmentary data, indicate a normal amount of iron in the water leaving the cells, or something less than 50 per cent. of the quantity corresponding to the theoretical rate of decomposition. In some instances the amount of iron exceeded 100 per cent. of the theoretical rate, showing an abnormal removal of scale of oxide. So far as could be learned the amount of iron corresponding to more than about 50 per cent. of the theoretical rate was ordinarily present for the most part in the form of scales. At times it will be seen that the rate was considerably less than 40 per cent. Among the principal factors which aided in producing the low results are the reversal of the electric current, exposure of the plates to air when not in service, and coatings of mud mixed with the scale and films. These factors are referred to beyond the tables.

At the beginning of these experiments electrodes No. 3 were dry, not having been used since 8.30 P.M., July 16. Electrodes No. 1 had been in use on July 22 and had only partially dried off during the night. Throughout this series a uniform rate of flow of water of 23.5 cubic feet per minute through each cell was maintained while in operation. At the start a current of 210 amperes was used, which gave an effective current of 0.020 ampere-hour per gallon in cell No. 3, and 0.040 ampere-hour per gallon in cell No. 1, which contained the modified electrodes No. 1. The potential difference between the plates at the start (at 210 amperes) was 6 volts on No. 1 and 4 volts on No. 3. When the current was increased on July 23 to 400 amperes the potential differences were increased to 11 and 6 respectively. The current density at 210 amperes was 0.51 ampere per square foot of anode in electrodes No. 3 and 1.00 ampere per square foot of anode in modified electrodes No. 1. The corresponding figures for 400 amperes were 0.97 and 1.91, respectively.

Influence on the Formation of Hydrate of Potential Difference between the Plates.

Potential difference can be defined as the electric pressure necessary to cause the passage of the desired strength of electric current through the electrolyte from plate to plate of the electrodes. This pressure is necessary to cause the ions to carry their respective charges to the poles, and is therefore dependent on the density of the current and length of the electrolyte. There is, furthermore, a certain potential difference necessary to overcome the resistance which the ions have against neutralization. This is the polarization resistance. In the case of passive electrodes the available data indicated that as a maximum this resistance may reach as high as 2.35 volts; and in practice it was assumed early in these tests that 3 volts was the lowest safe minimum difference in potential to secure a utilization of all ions uniformly.

So far as could be learned the practical influence upon the formation of hydrate, of the potential difference above this limit, is *nil.* During the use of the large electrodes potential differences between the plates of from 3 to 12 volts were employed. In laboratory experiments the potential difference was carried at times as high as 220 volts, although the usual range was from 20 to 50 volts.

The most serious factor against the economy of this process of formation of coagulants is the passivity of the iron to the various dissolving ions in the river water. As has been shown in previous portions of this discussion, the passivity of iron is represented by the percentage which the actual amount decomposed and converted into hydrate is of the total theoretical rate of decomposition, and ranged during the observations on this point, including laboratory tests, from about 30 to 50.

As the ions which do not dissolve the metal attack water, it appeared, as the report on these matters neared completion, that by lowering the potential difference to an amount below that which is commonly accepted as necessary to maintain a steady decomposition of water, with passive electrodes, this partial passivity of active electrodes might be overcome in a measure.

For this purpose two electrodes of steel were prepared and operated from 1.20 P.M, Sept. 28, to 9.00 A.M., Sept. 30. The area

TABLE SHOWING THE CONDITION OF OXIDATION AND AMOUNTS OF ELECTROLYTICALLY DECOMPOSED IRON LEAVING THE CELLS, EXPRESSED IN PARTS PER MILLION AND IN PERCENTAGES OF THE THEORETICAL RATE.

Date. 1897.	Hour.	Cell No. 1.				Cell No. 3.				Remarks.
		Parts per Million.			Per Cent. of the Theoretical Rate.	Parts per Million.			Per Cent. of the Theoretical Rate.	
		Ferrous Iron.	Ferric Iron.	Total Iron.		Ferrous Iron.	Ferric Iron.	Total Iron.		
										Conditions at start described in text.
July 23	9.55 A.M.	0.5	8.0	8.5	77	......	......	......	......	
" 23	10.05 "	1.0	9.0	10.0	90	......	......	......	......	
" 23	10.20 "	0.5	11.0	11.5	104	0.0	10.0	10.0	70	
" 23	10.50 "	0.3	13.0	13.3	120	......	......	......	......	
" 23	11.06 "	0.1	10.0	10.1	91	0.4	10.0	10.4	73	
" 23	11.47 "	0.3	8.0	8.3	75	......	......	......	......	
" 23	11.57 "	0.3	8.0	8.3	75	......	......	......	......	
" 23	12.25 P.M.	0.0	5.5	5.5	50	0.0	9.0	9.0	63	
" 23	1.00 "	0.3	10.0	10.3	93	0.3	10.0	10.3	72	
" 23	1.20 "	0.2	9.0	9.2	83	0.0	9.5	9.5	67	
" 23	1.50 "	0.1	9.0	9.1	82	0.1	9.5	9.6	67	
" 23	2.05 "	0.4	9.0	9.4	85	0.3	9.0	9.3	65	
" 23	2.20 "	0.4	7.5	7.9	71	0.4	7.5	7.9	56	
" 23	2.35 "	0.3	7.0	7.3	66	0.3	7.0	7.3	51	
" 23	2.50 "	0.3	7.0	7.3	66	0.2	7.5	7.7	54	
" 23	3.05 "	0.2	7.0	7.2	65	0.3	7.2	7.5	53	
" 23	3.20 "	0.1	5.5	5.6	50	0.1	4.8	4.9	83	
" 23	3.30 "	0.1	5.3	5.4	49	0.2	4.0	4.2	75	
" 23	3.40 "	0.3	7.0	7.3	66	0.1	4.5	4.6	82	
" 23	3.50 "	0.1	10.0	10.1	90	0.2	5.0	5.2	93	
" 23	4.10 "	0.6	4.0	4.6	41	0.0	1.0	1.0	18	Direction of flow of electric current reversed in both cells at 4.00 P.M.
" 23	4.20 "	0.5	4.0	4.5	40	Trace	Trace	0.1	2	
" 23	4.30 "	0.3	4.5	4.8	43	0.1	Trace	0.1	2	
" 23	4.40 "	0.3	4.3	4.6	41	0.1	0.2	2.1	5	
" 23	4.50 "	0.3	5.2	5.5	49	0.0	1.0	1.0	18	
" 23	5.00 "	0.2	5.2	5.4	49	Trace	1.0	1.0	18	Electric current increased to 0.076 and 0.038 ampere-hour per gallon in cells Nos. 1 and 3 respectively.
" 23	5.10 "	0.2	10.0	10.2	48	0.1	3.5	3.6	34	
" 23	5.20 "	0.1	9.8	9.9	47	0.3	4.0	4.3	41	
" 23	5.30 "	0.2	11.0	11.2	53	0.1	3.8	3.9	37	Current shut off and cells drained at 5.45 P.M.
" 24	11.15 A.M.	0.0	4.5	4.5	21	0.3	1.5	1.8	17	Began operations at 11.10 A.M. with conditions unchanged.
" 24	11.25 "	0.0	6.5	6.5	31	0.1	3.5	3.6	34	
" 24	11.35 "	0.0	7.0	7.0	33	0.1	4.0	4.1	39	
" 24	11.45 "	0.0	7.5	7.5	35	0.1	4.1	4.2	40	
" 24	11.55 "	0.3	9.5	9.8	46	0.3	5.2	5.5	52	
" 24	12.12 P.M.	0.0	10.0	10.0	47	0.1	6.0	6.1	57	
" 24	12.25 "	0.2	12.0	12.2	58	0.2	6.0	6.2	58	
" 24	12.40 "	0.3	12.0	12.3	58	0.2	6.0	6.2	58	
" 24	12.55 "	0.0	11.0	11.0	52	0.0	6.0	6.0	57	
" 24	1.10 "	0.0	12.0	12.0	57	0.0	5.0	5.0	47	
" 24	1.25 "	0.1	12.5	12.6	59	0.2	4.8	5.0	47	
" 24	1.45 "	0.2	12.2	12.4	58	0.1	4.8	4.9	46	
" 24	1.55 "	0.0	12.2	12.2	58	0.1	4.8	4.9	46	
" 24	2.10 "	0.2	12.2	12.4	58	0.1	5.0	5.1	48	
" 24	2.25 "	0.2	12.2	12.4	58	0.1	5.5	5.6	53	
" 24	2.40 "	0.2	13.0	13.2	52	0.2	5.0	5.2	49	
" 24	2.55 "	0.2	12.0	12.2	58	0.2	5.0	5.2	49	
" 24	3.10 "	0.1	11.5	11.6	55	0.1	5.2	5.3	50	
" 24	3.25 "	0.1	11.0	11.1	52	0.1	5.0	5.1	48	
" 24	3.40 "	0.1	11.0	11.1	52	0.2	4.8	5.0	47	
" 24	3.55 "	0.1	11.0	11.1	52	0.1	5.0	5.1	48	
" 24	4.10 "	0.1	10.5	10.6	50	0.1	5.0	5.1	48	
" 24	4.25 "	0.1	10.5	10.6	50	0.1	5.0	5.1	48	
" 24	4.40 "	0.1	10.5	10.6	50	0.1	5.0	5.1	48	
" 24	4.55 "	0.1	10.5	10.6	50	0.1	4.8	4.9	46	
" 24	5.10 "	0.1	10.0	10.1	48	0.1	5.0	5.1	48	
" 24	5.25 "	0.0	10.0	10.0	47	0.0	5.0	5.0	47	
" 24	5.40 "	0.1	10.0	10.1	48	0.0	6.0	6.0	56	Current shut off and cells drained at 5.45 P.M.

CONDITIONS OF OXIDATION AND AMOUNTS OF ELECTROLYTICALLY DECOMPOSED IRON LEAVING THE CELLS.—*Concluded.*

Date. 1897.	Hour.	Cell No. 1. Parts per Million. Ferrous Iron.	Ferric Iron.	Total Iron.	Per Cent. of the Theoretical Rate.	Cell No. 3. Parts per Million. Ferrous Iron.	Ferric Iron.	Total Iron.	Per Cent. of the Theoretical Rate.	Remarks.
July 26	9.10 A.M.	0.0	9.0	9.0	42	0.0	4.0	4.0	38	Began operations at 7.00 A.M. with conditions unchanged.
" 26	9.25 "	0.0	8.5	8.5	40	0.0	3.5	3.5	33	
" 26	9.40 "	0.6	9.0	9.6	45	0.7	4.0	4.7	44	
" 26	9.55 "	0.0	9.5	9.5	45	0.0	4.0	4.0	38	
" 26	10.10 "	0.2	9.5	9.7	46	0.2	4.5	4.7	44	
" 26	10.25 "	0.1	10.0	10.1	48	0.1	4.5	4.6	43	
" 26	10.40 "	0.1	10.1	10.1	48	0.1	5.0	5.1	48	
" 26	10.55 "	0.1	10.0	10.1	48	0.0	6.0	6.0	57	
" 26	11.10 "	0.1	10.0	10.1	48	0.0	5.0	5.0	47	
" 26	11.25 "	0.1	9.5	9.6	45	0.0	5.0	5.0	47	
" 26	12.55 P.M.	0.1	10.0	10.1	48	0.1	5.0	5.1	48	
" 26	1.10 "	0.1	10.0	10.1	48	0.0	5.0	5.0	47	
" 26	1.25 "	0.1	9.5	9.5	45	0.0	5.0	5.0	47	
" 26	1.40 "	0.1	10.0	10.1	48	0.1	5.1	5.2	48	
" 26	1.55 "	0.1	10.0	10.1	48	0.1	5.1	5.2	48	
" 26	2.25 "	0.0	10.0	10.0	47	0.1	5.1	5.2	48	
" 26	2.55 "	0.0	10.0	10.0	47	0.1	5.1	5.2	48	
" 26	3.25 "	0.0	10.0	10.0	47	0.0	5.0	5.0	47	
" 26	3.55 "	0.0	10.0	10.0	47	0.0	5.0	5.0	47	
" 26	4.25 "	0.0	10.0	10.0	47	0.0	5.0	5.0	47	
" 26	4.55 "	0.0	9.5	9.5	45	0.0	4.5	4.5	42	
" 26	5.25 "	0.0	10.0	10.0	47	0.0	5.0	5.0	47	
" 27	9.05 A.M.	0.0	10.0	10.0	47	0.0	7.5	7.5	71	Ran continuously over night.
" 27	9.15 "	0.0	10.0	10.0	47	0.0	7.0	7.0	66	
" 27	11.15 "	0.0	10.0	10.0	47	2.0	5.0	7.0	66	
" 27	11.30 "	0.0	9.0	9.0	42	2.0	5.5	7.5	71	
" 27	11.45 "	0.0	10.0	10.0	47	2.0	5.0	7.0	66	
" 27	12.00 M.	0.3	11.0	11.3	53	4.0	6.0	10.0	94	
" 27	12.45 P.M.	0.0	10.0	10.0	47	4.0	5.0	9.0	85	
" 27	1.00 "	0.5	10.0	10.5	50	6.0	8.0	14.0	132	
" 27	1.15 "	0.0	6.0	6.0	28	1.0	7.0	8.0	75	
" 27	1.30 "	0.0	5.0	5.0	24	1.0	6.5	7.5	71	Ran continuously over night.
" 28	9.15 A.M.	0.0	6.0	6.0	28	0.0	5.0	5.0	47	
" 28	9.25 "	0.0	7.0	7.0	33	0.0	5.0	5.0	47	
" 28	9.35 "	0.0	6.0	6.0	28	0.0	5.0	5.0	47	
" 28	9.45 "	0.0	6.0	6.0	28	0.0	4.0	4.0	38	
" 28	9.55 "	0.0	5.0	5.0	24	0.0	4.5	4.5	42	
" 28	3.10 P.M.	0.0	9.0	9.0	42	0.2	7.0	7.2	68	Shut down from 10.00 A.M. to 3.00 P.M. and cleaned scale and mud from electrodes No. 1.
" 28	3.40 "	0.0	9.5	9.5	45	0.0	6.0	6.0	57	
" 28	4.10 "	0.0	9.0	9.0	42	0.0	6.0	6.0	57	
" 28	4.30 "	0.0	9.0	9.0	42	0.1	3.0	3.1	29	Direction of flow of electric current reversed in both cells at 4.15 P.M.
" 28	4.40 "	0.3	9.0	9.3	44	0.1	2.5	2.6	25	
" 28	5.10 "	0.5	9.0	9.5	45	0.2	2.5	2.7	25	

of the positive plates (equal to one side of all plates) of set No. 1 was 1510 square inches, and the area of the electrolyte was 1360 square inches. In set No. 2 the corresponding figures were 3320 and 3170, respectively. A potential difference of 1.5 volts was maintained on set No. 1, and of 1.0 volt on set No. 2. From 10.00 A.M. to 2.00 P.M., Sept. 30, set No. 1 was operated at a potential difference of 3.5 volts. The rate of flow of water was maintained uniformly throughout the first run at 0.5 cubic foot per minute through each cell, and determinations were made every two hours of the amounts of iron in the water as it left the cells. During this run the electric current was held uniformly at 6.0 amperes. On the second run the strength of electric current averaged 15 amperes. The rate of flow of water was 1.0 cubic foot per minute.

The results of the determinations of the amounts of iron in the water as it left the cells, and the percentages which these amounts were of the theoretical, are given in the next table.

During the first run the gas evolved in cell No. 1 appeared to be almost constant in amount. In cell No. 2 almost no gas was observed up to 6.30 A.M., Sept. 29. From this time the formation of gas steadily increased in amount till at the close of the run there was nearly as much gas being formed in No. 2 as in No. 1.

On examination the positive plates of set No. 2 were found to be covered with a heavy coating of what appeared to be an irregularly hydrated form of red oxide, somewhat granular in form. In the bottom of this cell was found a heavy accumulation of red oxide, green hydrate, and scale.

TABLE SHOWING THE AMOUNTS OF IRON LEAVING THE TWO CELLS CONTAINING STEEL ELECTRODES ON WHICH POTENTIAL DIFFERENCES OF 1.5 AND 1.0 VOLTS, RESPECTIVELY, WERE MAINTAINED.

Date, 1897.	Hour.	Cell No. 1—1.5 Volts.		Cell No. 2—1.0 Volt.	
		Iron in Water. Parts per Million.	Per Cent. of the Theoretical.	Iron in Water. Parts per Million.	Per Cent. of the Theoretical.
Sept. 28	2.00 P.M.	8.0	110	6.4	88
" 28	3.00 "	7.5	101	5.2	71
" 28	5.00 "	9.8	134	7.2	98
" 28	7.00 "	8.0	108	5.3	72
" 28	9.00 "	5.8	79	6.5	89
" 28	11.00 "	6.0	82	7.0	95
" 29	1.00 A.M.	6.3	86	7.4	100
" 29	3.00 "	8.0	108	6.5	88
" 29	5.00 "	6.0	81	6.0	81
" 29	7.00 "	5.8	79	7.3	99
" 29	9.00 "	9.0	122	5.8	78
" 29	11.00 "	8.0	108	6.1	83
" 29	1.00 P.M.	6.1	83	5.8	78
" 29	3.00 "	5.9	80	6.3	85
" 29	5.00 "	5.2	70	5.7	77
" 29	7.00 "	5.9	80	6.4	86
" 29	9.00 "	6.2	84	5.8	78
" 29	11.00 "	7.9	107	6.1	83
" 30	1.00 A.M.	7.8	105	5.6	77
" 30	3.00 "	6.7	91	5.7	77
" 30	5.00 "	6.6	89	5.8	78
" 30	7.00 "	6.7	91	8.3	112
" 30	9.00 "	6.7	91	8.0	108
Averages		6.8	92	6.2	84
Increased voltage on No. 1, to 3.5 and stopped No. 2.					
Sept. 30	11.00 A.M.	11.5	125	....	....
" 30	1.00 P.M.	10.8	118	....	....
" 30	1.30 "	11.0	120	....	....
" 30	2.00 "	8.5	93	....	....

It will be seen that the amounts of iron leaving cell No. 1 were somewhat greater than in the case of cell No. 2, the averages being 92 and 84 per cent. of the theoretical rate, respectively.

A slight increase in the amount of iron leaving the cell was noticed after increasing the voltage and current in No. 1, but as this soon returned to the normal it was concluded that the first high results were due to the effect of the increased volume of water and electric current removing the metal previously decomposed, from the plates and portions of the cell upon which they had lodged.

It was evident from these experiments that iron could be decomposed at a potential difference as low as 1.0 volt, and that gas was formed in the process.

There was some indication that the higher potential was slightly more efficient than the lower, but the differences were not great enough to make certain that differences in arrangement of supporting framework under the electrodes, or slight variations in the displacement of the water in the cells, were not the explanation of these results. To make this point clear new electrodes were prepared of the same metal, and river water treated at 10, 5, 2.5, 1.75, and 1.5 volts difference in potentials, respectively. Each experiment was continued to the equivalent of 0.05 ampere-hour per gallon of treated water and the amounts of iron were determined. Within the limits of accuracy no difference could be found in the rate of hydrate formation at the several potential differences.

It was therefore concluded that potential differences between the limits of 1.0 and 220 volts exerted no apparent influence on the rate of formation of hydrate; that scale and gas formed with apparently the same rapidity at all potential differences; and that the practical limits of construction with references to the area of electrode surface and length of electrolyte would be the controlling factors in determination of the potential difference to employ in practice.

Influence on the Formation of Hydrate of Current Density.

The current density ranged from 0.30 to 2.08 amperes per square foot of active electrode surface during these tests. For the most part it was about 1.04 amperes with the large devices. In the case of some laboratory experiments a current density as high as 50.4 amperes per square foot was employed at times, but the usual density was about 15 amperes per square foot.

In connection with the low potential experiment described above, current densities as low as 0.26 ampere per square foot were employed.

Within these limits no marked influence of current density upon the formation of hydrate was noticed, but it is probable, as noted above, that the deposition of iron at the negative pole was somewhat greater with the high than with the low densities, though the increased rapidity of replacement of electrolyte due to increased flow of water through the cells would probably compensate for this in a measure. Theoretically, as has been explained above, the lower the current density the lower the rate of deposition of metal on the negative pole. Current density as low as admissible with economic construction of cells should therefore be employed.

Influence on the Formation of Hydrate of the Composition of the Iron.

The rolled wrought-iron plates used in this work were of the following percentage composition:

Carbon	0.06
Silica	0.28
Sulphur	1.58
Phosphorus	0.14
Manganese	0.00
Iron	97.94

So far as was learned the only way in which the composition of the iron might affect the formation of hydrate was indirectly through its effect upon the passivity of the metal to the acid ions of the water. This subject has been dealt with above in connection with passivity, when it was stated that no difference in hydrate formation was apparent in the various grades of metal used here, which were clearly due to differences in the composition of the several irons and steel.

From a practical point of view the differences in passivity of electrodes due to variations in the composition of the metal would, under the conditions of these tests, have been almost completely disguised by the acquired passivity caused by coatings of iron oxide.

Influence on the Formation of Hydrate of the Composition of the River Water.

Directly, the composition of the river water influences the formation of hydrate principally through the action of the atmospheric oxygen dissolved in the water in converting the iron into the insoluble ferric hydrate. This action is a very important one. It is also probable that the suspended matter affects the character of the surface coatings especially on the negative electrode.

Indirectly, the relative amounts of the different acid ions in the river water influence the formation of hydrate through their different relations to the passivity of the iron. In connection with the current density, also, the composition of the river water is a factor in the consideration of deposition of metallic iron on the cathode. The last two points are referred to in detail at the beginning of this section.

Influence on the Formation of Hydrate of Reversing the Direction of the Electric Current.

When the direction of flow of the electric current passing through the electrodes and electrolyte is reversed, the positive electrode (which was previously the negative) is at the outset saturated with hydrogen gas and the surface is coated with metallic iron, probably mixed somewhat with suspended matters from the water. Comparison in the last set of tables of the amount of iron in the water as it left the cells before and after reversals of current on July 23 at 4.00 P.M., and on July 28 at 4.15 P.M., shows that in three of the four instances the rate of decomposition of iron suffered a marked diminution for more than an hour. The cause of this is not clearly understood, but it appears to be associated with the occluded hydrogen in the pores of the metal and with the surface coatings, which will vary of course with the frequency of reversal and the character of the river water. In practice these marked diminutions in the formation of hydrate would be a serious matter and for a time would require the operation of a reserve portion of the plant, both with regard to the cells and the generating appliances.

Effect on the Subsequent Formation of Hydrate of allowing Electrodes to remain out of Service.

When the electric current was shut off from the electrodes and the cells kept full of water it was repeatedly noted that the decomposition of iron and formation of gas continued for a long time. This was due to a galvanic action, the metal being electro-positive to the surface coating of oxide. During the month of April and early part of May, when the electrical devices were out of service on numerous occasions while tests with chemicals were being made, it is estimated that the total weight of the electrodes decreased 65 pounds, due to this factor alone. On the grounds of economy and of comparable conditions for reliable data, it became necessary to drain the water from the cells as soon as the electric current was stopped. So far as is known the subsequent formation of hydrate, when the electric current was applied following a period of rest in which the electrodes were covered with water, was not seriously influenced by this procedure, which, however, for the reasons stated above, was found to be impracticable.

After the first of June the water was drained out of the cells as soon as the current was turned off. In consequence of the action of the air it was found that the rusting of the electrodes thus produced, increased the acquired passivity of the iron, and, when the electrodes were again put in service, the rate of formation of hydrate was abnormally low for a time. This is shown in the table on page 400 by the results on the morning of July 24, when, following a rest after draining the cells, of about 41 hours, the electrodes did not yield the normal amount of iron for half or three-quarters of an hour. In other cases, where the period of rest was longer the evidence shows a more prolonged diminution in the rate.

Per Cent. of Metal Wasted in this Process.

When the potential difference of the current between adjoining plates was 3 volts or more the evidence showed a rate of decomposition of iron on the positive plate equivalent to about 100 per cent. of the theoretical rate of 1.05 grams, or 16.2 grains per ampere-hour. Of this iron an amount equivalent to about 10 per cent. of the theoretical rate was found deposited on the negative plate. The amount of iron leaving the cell in the form of available hydrate seemed to vary considerably, but averaged about 40 per cent. of the theoretical rate. Taking into consideration the fact that eventually the plates become too thin for use and have to be discarded, it seems fair to conclude that in this process of producing iron hydrate substantially one-half of the metal is wasted by passing into the water in the form of non-hydrated and non-available scales of iron oxide.

The experiments of Sept. 28 to 30 indicate that no substantial advantage in this respect would be obtained with potential differences as low as 1 volt.

Resistance to the Passage of Electric Current of Films of Iron Oxide.

The results of analyses and of observations of scales in the water leaving the cells showed that the films of iron oxide attached to the positive electrodes remained there only temporarily, and came off at an irregular rate from time to time. In consequence thereof it is not probable that the entire surface was covered at any one time, in the course of regular operations, with a film which very materially increased the resistance of the electrodes. Compared with new metal the plates doubtless offered a certain resistance, but within the ranges of service to which these electrodes were subjected the increase in resistance was within the limits of observation, or less than 1 volt at 400 amperes or .0025 ohm.

Percentage of Electric Power Wasted in this Process.

Under the above-described conditions of operation, with potential differences between the electrodes of 3 volts or more, the evidence shows that between 50 and 60 per cent. of the electric current was wasted in removing iron in the form of scales, due to the formation of oxygen at the surface of the plates, and in depositing some of the available metal upon the negative electrodes. This does not include the effect of scales in offering increased resistance to the electric current, as noted in the last paragraph. Combining the three items, the waste of electric power may be safely placed at 60 per cent.

The experiments of Sept. 28 to 30 with potential differences as low as 1 volt indicate that there is no reason under these conditions for modifying the above figures.

Influence of this Process on Subsidence and Filtration.

Comparing the effect of this process upon the efficiency of subsidence and filtration of water with that of chemical treatment such as persulphate of iron or sulphate of alumina, when the degree of coagulation is the same, it is to be pointed out that under the conditions tested the hydrogen gas evolved at the cathode has a slight effect in retarding subsidence, and also at times reduces the length of run between washings of the filter by plugging up some of the pores of the sand layer.

Compared with aluminum the iron electrodes offer much less difficulty with gas formation when equal coagulation is obtained. Some laboratory observations in May showed that the ratio of gas formed by equivalent coagulation with aluminum and iron electrodes was about 2 to 1. In practice as the electrodes become covered with scale this ratio is greatly increased. Thus the ratio of gas formation with aluminum and iron electrodes after long service in connection with the filter, and under the same conditions other than the surface coatings, was found on June 8 to be 150 to 4. It is to be noted that these ratios refer to amounts of evolved gas. As the amount required to saturate the water formed different percentages of the total, the ratios are not absolutely exact.

Influence of the Process on the Composition of Filtered Water.

Like all electrolytic processes of this general type, the iron process does not add to the filtered water any mineral acid to make the water less desirable when used in boilers, and it does not add to the water any free carbonic acid to affect corrosion. In addition to the ordinary removal of suspended mineral and organic matters and a slight removal of dissolved organic matter, however, it removes the atmospheric oxygen in the water in amounts proportional to the iron obtained as hydrate. Up to a certain point this factor is of little practical significance, but when the process is carried to a degree where the oxygen is all or nearly all used for this purpose there is danger of some of the iron passing into the filtered water. A filtered water containing no oxygen would also be undesirable in several ways. Up to a certain point, therefore, this process can be used with satisfaction so far as composition of the filtered water is concerned. Beyond this point (exhaustion of atmospheric oxygen) the application of this process is inadmissible.

Conclusions.

From the evidence presented in this section it may be concluded:

1. Under practical conditions this process can be used to produce ferric hydrate, a good coagulant, up to the point where the atmospheric oxygen dissolved in the water is not completely exhausted.

2. The evolution of gas is fairly small, comparatively speaking, but the indications were that at times the gas might exert a retarding influence upon subsidence and a clogging effect upon filters.

3. The rate of production of ferric hydrate was reasonably uniform at its minimum limit, except for periods in the vicinity of one hour following a reversal of the direction of the current and an exposure of the plates to the atmosphere.

4. Owing to galvanic action when the coated plates were allowed to remain in water when out of service, the loss of metal made it imperative to avoid this procedure except for very short intervals.

5. Under conditions of good practice the amount of metal wasted as oxide scale would be substantially 50 per cent.

6. Under conditions of good practice the amount of power wasted would reach about 60 per cent.

Section No. 5.

Detailed Account of the Electrolytic Formation of Aluminum Hydrate in the Ohio River Water.

During the latter part of 1896 and first part of 1897, several factors operated together to bring forward again the process of the formation of a coagulant by the electrolytic decomposition of metallic aluminum. As was explained at the close of Chapter XII, investigations in July and August, 1896, led to the conclusion that the use of electrolytically prepared aluminum hydrate was out of the question because of its excessive cost, but that the use of an electrolytically prepared coagulant presented certain distinct advantages over the use of sulphate of alumina. Chief among the factors which led to further consideration of this process were the following:

1. The operations with iron electrodes showed clearly that potential differences very much lower than those employed during July and August, 1896, could be used in this general process with equally satisfactory results, thus greatly decreasing the cost of power.

2. The cost of metallic aluminum had decreased to about one-half its cost in August, 1896.

3. It appeared that the electric current gave results nearly twice as effective when new aluminum electrodes were used as when iron plates were employed. This was of much practical significance in consideration of the construction and maintenance of a plant.

4. President Long requested that the proposed investigations of coagulants be made as full and thorough as consistent with the practicability of the results obtained.

For these reasons the use of electrolytically prepared aluminum hydrate was again given attention in connection with other coagulants.

Early in the course of the investigations it was found that aluminum in the form of electrolytically prepared hydrate was no more effective than when in the form of hydrate obtained from the decomposition of the sulphate by the lime in the river water. It was also seen that the efficiency of aluminum plates in practice was very much less, both in amount and in regularity, than was indicated to be the case by the results with new plates.

It seemed inadvisable, therefore, to make the study of the details of this process as exhaustive as those of the formation of iron hydrate electrolytically, although in the main the investigations of both processes were carried on simultaneously. The following account, while it covers the bulk of the ground fully investigated in connection with iron electrodes, is, accordingly, not as complete as the investigation in the case of iron as recorded in section No. 4; and, furthermore, owing to the peculiar and widely varying results, it has been necessary in some instances in order to account for certain observations to introduce explanations and theories, as an exhaustive study of these points was not warranted by the available time and the impracticability of the process.

The same general plan as was employed in the presentation of the investigations of the iron process is followed here.

Passivity of Aluminum Electrodes.

As has been presented in the general discussion of the process of decomposition of metals under the action of an electric current, the percentage of the acid ions which attacks and decomposes water may be stated to represent the degree of passivity of the electrodes, on the assumption that when an electrode is perfectly non-passive (completely active), all of the acid ions attack the plate and no water is decomposed at the anode.

The principal points learned in regard to the action of the acid ions upon aluminum electrodes, so far as it was considered practicable to investigate the subject, were as follows:

1. The fact that in all cases within the limits employed a gas appeared to be liberated at the positive pole when aluminum electrodes of bright metal were used in electrolytes formed of pure solutions of each of the several acid ions normally present in the Ohio

River water, indicates that aluminum is normally passive to all of these ions to a certain but variable degree.

2. Aluminum seems to be most passive to the ions of nitric acid. This would be expected from the fact that aluminum is not readily soluble in nitric acid.

3. The acquired passivity of aluminum electrodes, that is, the passivity due to the formation of a coating of oxide on the face of the plates, continually increases in practice; and while it fluctuates somewhat, due to the scaling of the plates, there is strong evidence to indicate that after considerable service the rate of formation of the hydrate might decrease to almost nothing on this account.

It is to be noted in this connection that the metallic aluminum used during these investigations was the very best grade of commercial rolled plate. How far this may have affected the results is difficult to say, but the indications are that a less pure grade of metal might be more readily soluble, although possibly no more efficient so far as the formation of available hydrate is concerned. It is further to be borne in mind that the passivity of the metal is dependent upon the solvent action of the secondary compounds as well as of initial ions; and, as presented beyond, the general instability of aluminum compounds is very important in this connection.

Number of Experiments Averaged.	Electrolyte.	Rate of Decomposition per Ampere-Hour.	
		Grains	Gram.
18 (1896)	Filtered water	7.84	0.51
2	Hydrochloric acid*	11.90	0.77
2	Sulphuric acid*	9.40	0.61
2	Nitric acid*	8.80	0.57
2	Carbonic acid*	10.30	0.67
2	Carbonic acid gas	9.80	0.64
3	Hydrochloric and sulphuric acids*	8.90	0.58
3	Hydrochloric and nitric acids*	11.70	0.76
3	Hydrochloric and carbonic acids*	11.90	0.77
3	Hydrochloric, sulphuric, nitric, and carbonic acids*	8.90	0.58
3	Hydrochloric, sulphuric, nitric, carbonic acids,* and carbonic acid gas	8.80	0.57
By relative efficiency in sedimentation (section No. 6)	River water	9.42	0.61

* Dissolved in distilled water as salts of the alkaline earths in amounts corresponding to the estimated normal contents of river water. It was noted in several of these experiments that dissolved aluminum was present in the treated water, although its form was not ascertained.

Rate and Form in which Aluminum leaves the Positive Pole.

A. New Metal.

The rate at which aluminum leaves the positive pole under the action of an electric current when the electrodes were composed of bright metal plates was determined at different times and under varying conditions, as shown in the opposite table.

B. In Practice.

The results in this connection, obtained from long use of the aluminum electrodes on a large scale, are given in the next table.

On account of faulty insulation of the large electrodes no results of positive value were obtained with them previous to May 30. From this date to June 18 one or both of the large aluminum electrodes were kept in practically continuous service. They were removed, rinsed and weighed nearly every day up to June 8. The deposition of the metal and silt on the negative pole caused the weight of the electrodes to increase regularly, however, so that these first weighings were of no value. On June 8 electrodes No. 2 were dismantled and the separate plates weighed and this set rebuilt. At this time one-half of the plates was left out of the set, the space between plates doubled, and the direction of the current reversed. The second run from June 8 to 12 does not therefore represent the actual loss of metal of the positive pole, but this loss plus the loss in weight due to the removal of the deposited matter on the surface. The total ampere-hours during this run were 5850 and the loss of metal and deposit 81 pounds, or at the rate of 6.3 grams per ampere-hour.

Electrodes No. 4 were operated from June 3 to 7 and were dismantled and weighed on June 10. They were operated again from June 10 to 16, after which frequent reversals of the direction of the current prevented any study of the loss in weight of any particular portion of the set.

The results of these determinations are given in the following table:

SUMMARY OF RESULTS.

Period, 1897.	Electric Current in Ampere-Hours.	Loss in Weight of Positive Electrodes. Pounds.	Average Rate of Decomposition per Ampere-Hour.	
			Grains.	Gram.
	Electrodes No. 2.			
May 30 / June 8	45 380	16.25	2.5	0.16
	Electrodes No. 4.			
June 12 / " 15	21 470	20.75	6.8	0.44
Total...	66 850	37.00	....	....
Average	....	....	....3.89	0.25

In connection with the above data the following points are to be noted:

1. The atomic weight of aluminum is 27 and its combining weight is generally accepted as 9, or in other words its valency is 3. On this basis the amount of metal decomposed per ampere-hour, assuming that the full current is active in bringing to the anode surface decomposing ions to form normal trivalent salts, is 0.34 gram, or 5.23 grains.

2. As is generally known, certain salts of aluminum, notably those of the mineral acids, are comparatively unstable and have the power of decomposing the metal.

3. This supplementary solvent action is not limited to the formation of a basic salt, and in fact may not occur in this manner at all. The evidence indicates that under certain conditions which appear to occur in electrolytic cells, the initially formed salt becomes decomposed; the metal separates out as a more or less hydrated oxide; while the acid is free to attack new metal and form new salt, thus making the action in a measure continuous.

4. In an electrolyte composed of a combination of several acid ions it is believed that hydrochloric acid attacks the metal to the greatest extent, if not solely, and that the resultant chlorides are acted upon by the other acids, leaving the hydrochloric acid free for further solvent action.

5. According to Watts, the authority quoted in Chapter XII, the rate of decomposition of metallic aluminum is 0.51 gram, or 7.84 grains, per ampere-hour. The total average results of our experiments in August, 1896, agree with this very closely. If this rate were specifically correct, and not dependent upon circumstantial factors, it would imply that the metal left the electrodes in the form of divalent salts, as in the case of iron.

6. In view of the fact that the ultimate compound of aluminum, the hydrate, gives every indication of being in the trivalent form, it would require some atmospheric oxygen dissolved in the water in order to convert the initial compounds into the trivalent hydrate, supposing that initially they were divalent. The facts show that no appreciable diminution in the dissolved oxygen occurred; and this seems to be substantial proof against the divalent form of the initial compound, and the theoretical rate of 0.51 gram per ampere hour, as was indicated to be correct in 1896.

7. With regard to the formation of oxygen at the anode the direct observations were conflicting, but the evidence shows clearly that even with bright metal there is formed some oxygen which attacks the metal, producing a scale of alumina rust (oxide). The rust thus formed, together with a similar accumulation coming from the secondary reactions of the initial salts, produces a surface coating which not only reduces the supplementary solvent action, but also gives to the bright metal beneath the coating an acquired passivity.

8. In Chapter XII it is recorded that aluminum hydrate was obtained when metallic aluminum was used only for the negative electrodes, with the comment that it was not in harmony with the present views of electrochemistry. Except in a few instances where small amounts of aluminum were obtained in special laboratory experiments, there were no indications from the work in 1897 that the electrolytic decomposition of the negative electrodes was a factor under practical conditions. However, it is not unreasonable to suppose that under some circumstances the strong alkaline solution present at the surface of the cathode might dissolve this metal, which has the power of acting as an acid and of forming aluminates.

In conclusion it may be stated that the available evidence taken as a whole points clearly to the decomposition of aluminum under the conditions of practice only at the positive pole. Here it is initially removed from the plate as a trivalent salt of the strongest acid ions (perhaps only in the form of chloride). With bright metal the plates are not only free from marked passivity, but the initially formed salts appear to have a supplementary solvent action, with an accompanying deposition of rust upon the surface of the anode. This coating, formed in this manner and by the action of oxygen, which in small quantities is set free at the anode, gives eventually to the electrode a marked acquired passivity and reduces materially the supplementary solvent action. In consequence of this the rate at which the metal leaves the positive pole diminishes in time to almost *nil*, although at first a supplementary solvent action causes it to exceed the theoretical by a large, although variable, percentage.

Form and Rate of Deposition of Aluminum on the Negative Pole.

During the course of the experiments by the Water Company in August, 1896, it was found, as has been presented in Chapter XII, that aluminum is deposited on the negative pole simultaneously with the formation of aluminum hydrate. The reason of this seems to be the same as in the case of iron electrodes, that a portion of the metal from the positive pole, which is dissolved by the acid ions, becomes itself ionized, and acting as a negative ion or cathion transfers a charge of electricity from the positive to the negative pole, where on neutralization of the charge it is deposited on the face of the plate. It is well known that electroplating with aluminum is extremely difficult and in some cases practically impossible, owing to the rough and weakly adherent characteristics of the deposit. This is just the condition which was found to exist in the process of formation of the hydrate electrolytically, and to the character of the deposit one of the most serious factors against this process, aside from the cost of the metal, is due. It has been found in the course of many experiments that very finely divided silt or clay particles suspended in the electrolyte are deposited upon the negative pole to a greater or less extent. This deposition of silt, taking place at the same time as the deposition of the metal in its porous form, results in a combined layer or deposit of silt and metal of high electric resistance. The effect of this formation on the amount of power required is shown in one of the latter portions of this section. The amount of metallic aluminum contained in any of the deposits found in practice could not be readily determined, owing, as stated above, to the presence of silt. Some idea of the significance of this point can be obtained from the following table, in which the weights of deposits for the several runs with electrodes Nos. 2 and 4 are recorded, together with the ampere-hours of service and average rates of deposition.

TABLE OF RESULTS.

Period. 1897.	Electric Current in Ampere-Hours.	Increase in Weight of Negative Electrodes. Pounds.	Increase per Ampere-Hour.	
			Grains.	Grams.
Electrodes No. 2.				
May 30 } June 8 }	45 380	124	25.4	1.65
" 8 } " 12 }	5 830	14	24.0	1.56
Total........	51210	138	27.0	1.75
Electrodes No. 4.				
June 3 } " 6 }	15 730	10	6.4	0.42
" 12 } " 15 }	21 470	22	7.2	0.47
Total........	37 200	32	6.0	0.39
Total for both electrodes..	88 410	170	13.3	0.88

Influence on the Formation of Hydrate of the Composition of the River Water.

The formation of aluminum hydrate electrolytically is affected chiefly by three factors:

1. Initial passivity.
2. Supplementary solvent action of the salt formed when the metal leaves the plates.
3. Acquired passivity due to coatings formed on the surface of the plates.

So far as our observations went, no decisive evidence was obtained that the composition of the river water materially affected the first two of these factors, but if it did do so the result was disguised by the third factor. The formation of hydrate was influenced very materially by the surface scales or coatings (causing acquired passivity), which are next discussed with reference to the composition of the river water.

Influence on the Formation of Scale of the Composition of the River Water.

So far as the data go the indications are that the variations in the character of the river water with regard to dissolved constituents caused only a very small percentage variation in the amount of scale formation on the positive plates. The character and amount of the suspended matter, however, exerted considerable influence on the formation of the deposit on the negative plate. This is quite clearly shown by the difference in the increased weights of electrodes Nos. 2 and 4, the very finely divided suspended matter of the last days of May greatly increasing the amount of deposit on electrodes No. 2 as compared with electrodes No. 4, which were operated somewhat later. That a certain percentage of this fine material was transferred from the positive to the negative pole after reversing the direction of the current seems to be the explanation of the high rate of deposition with electrodes No. 2 from June 8 to 12. This supposition was borne out by the change in the character of the matter on the negative pole after the current was reversed, the presence of the silt being quite marked after the run from May 29 to June 8, while almost no silt was found in the scale after removal by the reversed current. Some idea of the significance of this action can be obtained from the following table, in which the initial amount of power per ampere-hour per gallon at the rate of treatment of 23.5 cubic feet per minute is given for the start of the first run of each of the two sets, after 15,000 ampere-hours, and for electrodes No. 2 at the end of the first run (see "Form and Rate of Deposition on Negative Pole," page 409).

HORSE-POWER REQUIRED PER AMPERE-HOUR PER GALLON.

Date. 1897.	Number of Electrodes.	Ampere-Hours Service Since Last Cleaned.	Electric H.P. per Ampere-Hour per Gallon.
May 30, 11.00 A.M.	2	0*	450
June 1, 5.00 P.M.	2	15 000	1 200
" 8, 6.00 A.M.	2	45 000	3 080
" 3, 6.00 P.M.	4	0	240
" 6, 8.00 A.M.	4	15 000	435

* The plates were only rinsed and not scraped at last cleaning.

After the discussion of foregoing topics it is obvious that the coatings or scales, composed of aluminum oxide (rust) and clay particles, not only increased the required amount of power very largely (shown above to be sevenfold), but also increased the acquired passivity so that with the increased power used there was actually less aluminum hydrate produced.

Influence on the Formation of Hydrate of the Presence of Scale.

The presence of coatings or scales, principally of aluminum rust, upon the surface of the plates exerts a marked influence upon the process, as follows:

1. It reduces the supplementary solvent action of the aluminum salts and thus makes the actual rate of loss of metal at the positive pole fall to the normal rate, approximately.

2. It gives to the metal an acquired passivity which makes the actual rate of hydrate formation drop far below the normal; in fact we have seen instances where the formation of hydrate was reduced to almost nothing.

3. When the scale becomes very thick and has sufficient tenacity to remain in place without breaking in pieces, we have repeatedly noted, especially for a short time after reversing the direction of the current, that practically all of the aluminum hydrate remained between the metal and the layer of alumina rust.

4. From the last table it is plain that the scale makes a large increase in the resistance to the electric current, and the reduced rate of formation is concomitant with an increased amount of electric power.

Influence on the Process of Reversing the Direction of the Electric Current.

After electrodes have been in service for some time the positive plates become covered with a scale of oxide and the negative ones with a more or less heavy coating of deposited metal and silt. Under such conditions a reversal of the electric current results in the complete removal of the deposit from the old negative poles and the cessation of removal of oxide scale from the old positive poles.

It is difficult to determine in how far the reversing of the current affects the rate of formation of hydrate. That hydrate was formed in large amounts after a reversal was evident from inspection, but, owing to the fact that the coating on the old negative plates retained a large amount of the newly formed hydrate between it and the plate, it was not possible to determine the rate of formation of the hydrate. This retention of the hydrate would be a very serious factor in practice, however, necessitating a mechanical removal of the coating when the current was reversed.

In regard to the effect of reversing the current on the resistance of the electrodes, the evidence indicates that if a suitable means could be provided to remove the coating as it cracks off the old negative plates, a considerable increase in conductivity might be gained. In practice, however, it is probable that the combination of the new deposit and old oxide scale which would form on the negative (old positive) plates after reversal would result in increasing the resistance as fast as or faster than the removal of the coating from the positive (old negative) plates would reduce the resistance. Furthermore, the almost immediate formation of a layer of hydrate which would be retained on the new positive poles would, unless removed, result in an increase of the resistance. These effects on resistance are shown by the records of potential differences on cell No. 4 on July 16, 17, and 18, in the next table.

The electrodes were rinsed at 6.08 P.M. on July 16 and the direction of the electric current reversed after 7960 ampere-hours' service since the plates were last cleaned. From 6.30 P.M. to 12.00 P.M., July 16, the resistance of the electrodes remained constant at 0.071 ohm. At 12.00 P.M. the direction of the electric current was reversed. It was again reversed at 6.00 A.M. and 12.43 P.M., July 17, and at 12.30 P.M., July 18. The records of the observed resistance are opposite.

Hour.	Resistance in Ohms.			
	July 17.		July 18.	
	A.M.	P.M.	A.M.	P.M.
12.30	0.102	0.130*	0.110	0.124*
1.00	0.120	0.104	0.104	0.088
1.30	0.116	0.157	0.103	0.124
2.00	0.111	0.168	0.104	0.150
2.30	0.094	0.164	0.108	0.160
3.00	0.089	0.157	0.108	0.162
3.30	0.089	0.144	0.110	0.162
4.00	0.086	0.131	0.112	0.185
4.30	0.089	0.131	0.113	
5.00	0.089	0.122	0.115	
5.30	0.089	0.122	0.117	
6.00	0.089*	0.124	0.117	
6.30	0.069	0.113	0.119	
7.00	0.094	0.113	0.124	
7.30	0.094	0.112	0.113	
8.00	0.102	0.108	0.117	
8.30	0.089	0.104	0.117	
9.00	0.110	0.106	0.119	
9.30	0.110	0.106	0.122	
10.00	0.110	0.106	0.119	
10.30	0.110	0.106	0.122	
11.00	0.110	0.106	0.124	
11.30	0.110	0.106	0.124	
12.00	0.139	0.104	0.124	

* Reversed direction of electric current.

Percentage of Metal Wasted in this Process.

On account of the very irregular manner in which the scale came off from the positive pole during practice, no observations were attempted to learn the relative percentages of metal removed as hydrate and as oxide. Judging from the results in July and August, 1896 (see Chapters XI and XII), and also from observations of the amounts of scale removed from the plates in cleaning during 1897, it is estimated that at least 50 per cent. of the metal removed from the positive pole was lost in the form of scale, and that from 10 to 20 per cent. more was deposited on the negative plate in a manner which made it very slightly or not at all available. During practice it would seem reasonable to figure on an average loss of about 65 per cent. of the metal removed from the plates.

Influence of Scale and Deposit on the Amount of Power Required.

This subject was referred to under the discussion of the effect of the composition of the river water. As presented there it was found in practice that the formation of scale on the positive poles and the deposit on the negative pole increased the amount of power required per ampere-hour per gallon from 240 electric H.P. with new plates (electrodes No. 4) to 3080 with old plates of 45,000 ampere-hours' service (electrodes No. 2). This increase of 740 per cent. does not probably represent the limit of the increase, as the resistances of both electrodes Nos. 2 and 4 were steadily increasing at the time they were taken out of service. Assuming an efficiency of 50 per cent. in the formation of hydrate the above figures represent an increase from 246 to 1825 electric H.P. to treat 25 million gallons per 24 hours with the equivalent of 1 grain per gallon of sulphate of alumina.

The effect of reversal on scale formation has already been presented.

So far as could be learned the only possible way to reduce the resistance of the electrodes was to remove the plates and scrape the surfaces fairly clean. This of course involves a considerable loss of metal, and its cost for labor alone would make it prohibitive. No practicable means was found of doing away with these scales and deposits with their attending effects.

Percentage of Electric Power Wasted in this Process.

In the formation of aluminum hydrate by this process power is wasted in two ways:

1. A certain percentage of the current is transferred by ions which do not attack the pole, but decompose water. This current is entirely wasted and, as power is required to produce it, such power is lost. Owing to irregularities in removal of scale it was found that determinations of the amount of hydrate formed during practice were not feasible. Basing the conclusions on the result of many laboratory tests and on the amount of scale formed during practice, it is estimated that not more than 50 per cent. of the current is available in the formation of hydrate, and there are indications that the loss might at times approach very nearly to 100 per cent.

2. The loss of power due to increased resistance of the electrodes as presented in previous sections of this chapter reached as high as 740 per cent. of the initial power required, and the indications were that the limit had not been reached. Frequent scrapings of the plates, such as would be required to prevent this increase of resistance, are impracticable.

Conclusions.

With the present knowledge of electrochemical actions, and with the present cost of aluminum in the form of plates as contrasted with equal amounts of metal in the form of commercial sulphate, the use of hydrate of aluminum prepared by the electrolytic decomposition of the metal is out of the question on account of cost. This is shown by the following summary:

1. Aluminum in sheet form costs in carload lots according to the latest quotation 27 cents per pound. In the form of sulphate of alumina one pound of metal costs 16 cents. The ratio of cost of equal amounts of coagulant prepared by the electrolytical decomposition of the metal and by the chemical decomposition of the commercial sulphate by lime is therefore 17 to 10 for aluminum alone.

2. In operating there would be a constant loss of about 50 per cent. of the metal required for the formation of the hydrate due to the passivity of the electrodes to the acid ions, the supplementary solvent action of the salts formed, and the consequent formation of oxide scale. This might at times approach 100 per cent.

3. The amount of power required would constantly increase with the age of the electrodes, necessitating at frequent intervals the removal and scraping of the plates. This last step would be very expensive. Under normal conditions probably 50 per cent. of the normal power required would be wasted in overcoming the resistance of the surface coatings. The normal amount of power would also be increased from 50 to 100 per cent. to offset the reduced rate of formation of hydrate, due to the acquired passivity of the metal.

4. In short, the process was impracticable, under the conditions of these tests, both with regard to economy and regularity of production of hydrate. While it is probable, if not certain, that prolonged investigation would improve the process by using a different grade of metal and devising mechanical appliances for the removal of scales, yet in the light of our knowledge, owing to the inherent character of the metal and the narrow range of conditions as applied to this line of work, commercial success of this process seems to be an impossibility.

Section No. 6.

Relative Efficiency of Available Coagulants, Based on Equal Weights of Metal Used and also on the Amount of Electric Current in the Case of Electrolytically formed Coagulants.

In order to arrive at the most economical coagulant to apply to the water, it is essential to know the relative efficiencies of those available for the purpose. From foregoing sections it is clear that the available coagulants are four in number, obtained by the following treatments:

1. Sulphate of alumina.
2. Persulphate of iron.
3. Electric current on aluminum electrodes.
4. Electric current on iron electrodes.

With the first two (sulphates) the comparisons are expressed in their final form with reference to the amount of metal contained in the commercial products used for the tests. This is necessary because the amount of metal which determines the quantity of hydrates varies in different lots of sulphates of the same kind. The reason that this is so important is that the coagulation is associated very closely with the volume of hydrate formed. Furthermore it may be mentioned in passing that the volume of hydrate formed depends upon the specific gravity of the metal. Thus it has been found that one part by weight of aluminum forms about three times as much hydrate as does one part by weight of iron, while the specific gravity of iron is about 2.8 as great as that of aluminum. These general comparisons will be of much assistance in understanding the different amounts of work done in this line by equal weights of the two metals. A record will be found at the foot of each table showing the amount of metal contained in the commercial sulphate used.

With regard to the electrolytic formation of hydrates of these two metals, what has been said above about volumes of hydrate and specific gravity of metals also holds good in this case.

In sections Nos. 4 and 5 it was pointed out that much of the metal left the plate in a form non-available for coagulation, and was therefore wasted. Practically it is necessary under these conditions to learn the amount of electric current necessary to decompose and convert enough available metal in form of hydrate to equal the efficiency of a known amount of metal in the form of sulphate. With this information in hand, and knowing the total amount of metal decomposed and removed from the plate, it is possible to estimate how much of the metal (and also electric power) served dircetly in producing coagulation.

The evidence obtained upon the relative efficiencies of these coagulants was obtained in two different ways, as follows:

1. As coagulants in aiding subsidence in one-gallon bottles.
2. As coagulants in connection with the Jewell filter and devices operated therewith.

In the first method the percentages of removal of suspended matter were obtained after 24 hours subsidence. The electrolytically formed hydrates were obtained regularly from bright metal electrodes, and a current was applied for such a period that the theoretical rate of decomposition would give an amount of metal equal to that in the corresponding bottle in the set with the sulphates. In all cases a series of tests was made with each of the coagulants under consideration, and for a direct comparison of efficiencies there were selected, so far as possible, those results which came midway between the results of plain subsidence and complete clarification. In this manner the fairest comparisons were made, and it is these results which are given in the tables beyond.

Concerning the second portion of the evidence in connection with the Jewell filter, it is to be stated that, of the 185 runs described and recorded in the first half of this chapter, those runs are selected which enable a direct comparison to be made of the several coagulants in the purification of similar waters under the same general conditions. It is also to be borne in mind that these conditions of the second portion of the evidence are those of practice, and as the electrodes were more or less rusty the efficiency of the electric current was less than on the first set of data, where the tests were made with bright metal.

Supplementary to these comparable data were a number of runs in which the coagulation was insufficient for satisfactory purification. Such runs cannot be included in these tables of comparable results, yet they were of much value in showing and confirming the range in relative efficiencies of the several coagulants.

TABLE SHOWING THE RELATIVE EFFICIENCY OF SULPHATE OF ALUMINA* AND PERSULPHATE OF IRON,† IN CONNECTION WITH 24 HOURS' SUBSIDENCE.

Suspended Solids in River Water. Parts per Million.	Grains of Each Chemical per Gallon.	Percentage Removal.	
		Sulphate of Alumina.	Persulphate of Iron.
360	2.25	97	94
562	2.50	93	97
1 560	4.00	96	97
216	0.75	80	80
553	1.75	89	90
416	1.75	88	90
Averages 611	2.17	90.5	91.3

* Containing 9.87 per cent. of aluminum.
† Containing 24.73 per cent. of iron.

The above data show that under these conditions sulphate of alumina and persulphate of iron, containing 9.87 and 24.73 per cent. of metal respectively, possess substantially equal efficiency, or that the advantage lies very slightly with the persulphate of iron.

TABLE SHOWING THE RELATIVE EFFICIENCY OF PERSULPHATE OF IRON* AND ELECTRIC CURRENT WITH IRON ELECTRODES, IN CONNECTION WITH 24 HOURS' SUBSIDENCE.

Suspended Solids in River Water. Parts per Million.	Persulphate of Iron.		Electric Current.	
	Grains per Gallon.	Percentage Removal.	Ampere-Hour per Gallon.	Percentage Removal.
562	2.50	93	0.054	95
1 560	2.00	91	0.050	96
243	1.25	85	0.031	87
·216	1.00	90	0.025	85
553	1.75	89	0.045	88
272	2.00	88	0.031	90
364	2.00	90	0.037	91
Aver. 554	1.79	90	0.039	90

* Containing 24.75 per cent. of iron.

These data show that 0.039 ampere-hour of electric current on bright iron electrodes per gallon was equal under these conditions to 1.79 grains per gallon of persulphate of iron, containing 24.73 per cent. of metallic iron. From this it follows that the amount of iron decomposed and converted into the form of available ferric hydrate per ampere-hour was 11.3 grains, which is 70 per cent. of the theoretical rate.

TABLE SHOWING THE RELATIVE EFFICIENCY OF SULPHATE OF ALUMINA* AND ELECTRIC CURRENT WITH ALUMINUM ELECTRODES, IN CONNECTION WITH 24 HOURS' SUBSIDENCE.

Suspended Solids in River Water. Parts per Million.	Sulphate of Alumina.		Electric Current.	
	Grains per Gallon.	Percentage Removal.	Ampere-Hour per Gallon.	Percentage Removal.
562	2.50	95	0.023	94
1 560	2.00	91	0.023	92
243	1.25	85	0.013	88
553	1.75	89	0.015	90
416	1.75	88	0.018	90
322	1.75	88	0.018	90
987	1.50	94	0.015	94
184	0.88	89	0.015	88
Aver. 603	1.67	90	0.0175	91

* Containing 9.87 per cent. of aluminum.

From the above data it is seen that 0.0175 ampere-hour of electric current on bright aluminum electrodes per gallon was equal under these conditions to 1.67 grains per gallon of sulphate of aluminum containing 9.87 per cent. of metallic aluminum. This shows that there were decomposed and converted into the form of available aluminum hydrate 9.42 grains per ampere-hour. This is 181 per cent. of the theoretical rate.

Comparing the efficiency of an electric current in the formation of coagulants by the decomposition of bright metallic iron and bright metallic aluminum, and remembering that in the last two tables 1.67 grains per gallon of sulphate of aluminum is equal to 1.65 grains of persulphate of iron, it is noted that 0.0175 ampere-hour on aluminum electrodes is equal to 0.036 ampere-hour on iron electrodes.

According to these data the electric current is twice as efficient when applied to aluminum electrodes as when applied to iron electrodes. From the theoretical rate of decomposition it would be expected that the relative efficiency of the current on aluminum and iron electrodes would be 0.9 to 1.

TABLE SHOWING THE RELATIVE EFFICIENCY OF SULPHATE OF ALUMINA * AND PERSULPHATE OF IRON,† WHEN USED IN CONNECTION WITH THE JEWELL FILTER AND ASSOCIATED DEVICES.

Number of Run.	Grains per Gallon.	Suspended Solids in River Water. Parts per Million.	Filtered Water. Cubic Feet.	Bacterial Efficiency.
		Sulphate of Alumina.		
1	1.32	336	5 004	95.9
8	1.33	586	8 540	99.2
19	3.98	452	11 986	95.3
26	3.10	347	6 041	97.6
28	3.01	347	4 356	99.1
36	1.05	231	11 296	99.2
50	1.17	136	16 282	99.4
153	3.33	352	7 679	98.7
Averages	2.29	348	8 898	98.0
		Persulphate of Iron.		
4	1.23	351	5 859	97.9
10	3.99	586	12 446	99.3
18	3.99	518	16 177	99.2
25	2.83	322	11 304	99.6
31	3.37	407	8 013	99.6
35	1.81	193	14 556	99.1
51	1.23	131	13 507	99.8
155	2.66	379	2 617	99.1
Averages	2.31	361	10 560	99.2

* Containing 8.46 per cent. of aluminum.
† Containing 24.43 per cent. of iron.

The above comparisons show that persulphate of iron containing 24.43 per cent. of iron is slightly but distinctly superior under these conditions of sulphate of alumina containing 8.46 per cent. of aluminum. This lot of sulphate of alumina was not so rich in aluminum as that used in the subsidence experiments, and it is fair to assume that the relative efficiencies stated under those conditions would hold true in connection with filtration.

TABLE SHOWING THE RELATIVE EFFICIENCY OF SULPHATE OF ALUMINA * AND ELECTRIC CURRENT WITH IRON ELECTRODES, WHEN USED IN CONNECTION WITH THE JEWELL FILTER AND ASSOCIATED DEVICES.

Sulphate of Alumina.

Number of Run.	Grains per Gallon.	Suspended Solids in River Water. Parts per Million.	Filtered Water. Cubic Feet.	Bacterial Efficiency.
98	1.56	296	5 942	98.0
117	2.14	622	....	99.2
125	3.82	454	10 381	99.6
131	2.70	288	8 034	98.9
149	2.55	464	7 618	98.0
153	3.30	352	7 679	98.7
180	0.96	140	10 322	97.9
183	0.94	173	5 457	96.6
*Averages	2.25	349	7 920	98.4

Electric Current with Iron Electrodes.

Number of Run.	Ampere-Hour per Gallon.	Suspended Solids in River Water. Parts per Million.	Filtered Water. Cubic Feet.	Bacterial Efficiency.
89	0.040	330	15 551	98.4
120	0.078	711	....	98.8
122	0.097	535	7 494	98.4
132	0.078	218	10 598	97.5
147	0.089	488	4 392	98.3
148	0.099	419	5 082	97.8
178	0.040	128	7 274	98.4
181	0.040	160	7 426	97.5
Averages	0.070	374	8 260	98.2

* Containing 8.46 per cent. of aluminum.

For the sake of a more extended comparison, sulphate of alumina is presented here instead of persulphate of iron. From the foregoing table the corresponding amount of the latter chemical may be substituted if desired.

These data indicate that the relation in question was somewhat variable but on an average 0.070 ampere-hour of electric current per gallon upon rusty iron electrodes as found in practice (with a potential difference between plates of 3 to 5 volts) was equal to 2.25 grains per gallon of sulphate of alumina containing 8.46 per cent. of aluminum. This corresponds to an electrolytic conversion of iron into the form of hydrate of 9.33 grains per ampere-hour, or 58 per cent. of the theoretical rate. The difference between this and the 70 per cent. found with bright iron electrodes was due of course to the increased passivity caused by rusting.

At this point it may be noted that in the later comparisons the relation was found to be in the ratio of about 0.10 ampere-hour, equivalent to 2.5 grains of sulphate of alumina, containing 9.87 per cent. of aluminum or to the same amount of persulphate of iron containing 24.73 per cent. of iron. From careful inspection at the time of the tests this relation was considered to be best and was so reported to you. In view of the fact that the lowest rate is the safest one upon which to base computations, we conclude that the last comparison is the safest ratio under practical conditions. On this basis the amount of iron decomposed and converted into available hydrate would be 6.17 grains per ampere-hour, or 38 per cent. of the theoretical rate of decomposition.

TABLE SHOWING THE RELATIVE EFFICIENCY OF SULPHATE OF ALUMINA * AND ELECTRIC CURRENT WITH ALUMINUM ELECTRODES, WHEN USED IN CONNECTION WITH THE JEWELL FILTER AND ASSOCIATED DEVICES.

Sulphate of Alumina.

Number of Run.	Grains per Gallon.	Suspended Solids in River Water. Parts per Million.	Filtered Water. Cubic Feet.	Bacterial Efficiency.
19	3.98	452	11 986	95.5
36	1.05	231	11 296	99.2
50	1.17	136	16 282	99.4
59	2.47	301	6 899	99.7
131	2.70	288	8 034	93.9
Averages	2.28	282	10 899	98.5

Electric Current with Aluminum Electrodes.

Number of Run.	Ampere-Hour per Gallon.	Suspended Solids in River Water. Parts per Million.	Filtered Water. Cubic Feet.	Bacterial Efficiency.
20	0.056	452	5 741	95.9
41	0.020	242	5 569	99.0
49	0.011	133	9 784	98.5
58	0.028	453	3 949	99.5
133	0.037	159	6 556	95.2
Averages	0.031	288	5 920	97.6

* Containing 8.46 per cent. of aluminum.

These data, which were obtained on the whole under favorable conditions, and when the plates were only slightly covered with oxide coating, comparatively speaking, indicate that 0.031 ampere-hour of electric current on aluminum electrodes per gallon was nearly as efficient as 2.28 grains of sulphate of alumina containing 8.46 per cent. of aluminum. One of the disadvantages of the electric treatment which is indicated by the above data is the diminution in the length of runs between washings and consequently in the quantity of water filtered per run. This was due largely to accumulations of gas, which retarded subsidence under the given conditions and closed some of the interstices of the sand layer.

Later experience with the electric current on aluminum electrodes demonstrated conclusively that the above comparison was not representative of what would occur in practice. After the plates of the composition used here (a very pure commercial grade) were continued in service, coatings of oxide made the formation of hydrate very irregular and much less than the rate indicated above.

Furthermore, as was repeatedly seen in special tests, continuous service caused a considerable portion of the aluminum hydrate to be non-available, because it became lodged between the bright metal and the surface coating.

Comparing these results with those obtained with bright aluminum electrodes it is seen that the efficiency dropped to about 75 per cent. of that recorded in the subsidence experiments. In view of the fact that under the conditions of practice the percentage efficiency steadily decreased, the regular tests with aluminum electrodes were discontinued during the latter portion of the investigations; and the conclusion was drawn that unless some practicable method of removing surface coatings could be found, the electrolytic method of forming aluminum hydrate was unsafe and impracticable, independent of its cost, on account of the very low and irregular formation of the hydrate. No practicable means of removing the surface coatings on a large plant could be devised.

Conclusions.

These comparative tests show that one grain per gallon of sulphate of alumina, containing 9.87 per cent. of aluminum, is equaled in efficiency as a subsiding and filtration coagulant by one grain per gallon of persulphate of iron, containing 24.73 per cent. of iron, and by 0.040 ampere-hour per gallon of electric current on iron electrodes. With regard to the action of an electric current on aluminum electrodes, the process as tested under the most favorable conditions which could be made applicable to a large plant, was found to be unsafe and impracticable.

SECTION No. 7.

ECONOMICAL APPLICATION OF COAGULANTS, IN TERMS OF SULPHATE OF ALUMINA, TO AID IN THE REMOVAL OF SUSPENDED MATTER BY SEDIMENTATION.

At the outset of the consideration of this portion of a system of purification applicable to the Ohio River water the following facts are to be recalled:

In the application of coagulants to this

water, as it is taken from the river, there is a great waste of chemicals, with an undesirable consequential effect upon the quality of the water from an industrial standpoint; a large percentage of the normal filter plant would have to be duplicated and held in reserve for use at times of muddy water; the suspended matter in the river water varies so rapidly in amount and character that in the absence of adequate subsidence it would be difficult to manage a plant economically and at the same time efficiently; and, to correct these difficulties, experience shows that it is essential for economical and other reasons to remove as much suspended matter as practicable from the river water by plain sedimentation before the application of coagulants.

From what has been said concerning plain sedimentation in section No. 1 of this discussion, it will be understood that during the greater portion of the year there would be required a fairly low and approximately uniform application of coagulants to the water after the removal of the bulk of the suspended matter by plain subsidence and before filtration. Yet at times during the spring and summer the amount of clay is so great and the size of the particles so small, that the application of coagulants can be divided to advantage from an economical point of view, and a portion of the coagulants employed solely as an aid to subsidence.

Many data obtained in the course of these investigations point in this direction, but the fact is brought out most clearly by a comparison of the results of runs Nos. 167 and 168, which may be briefly summarized as follows:

Number of Run.	Grains per Gallon of Sulphate of Alumina.			Suspended Solids in River Water. Parts per Million.	Filtered Water. Cubic Feet.	Bacterial Efficiency.
	Basin No. 1.	Jewell Settling Chamber.	Total.			
167	0	2.82	2.82	129	6 556	99.3
168	1.49	0.83	2.32	141	15 296	99.5

In comparing these two runs it will be noted that the quality of the river water was approximately the same, although the amount of suspended matter was slightly higher in the case of No. 168. With the latter run the total amount of the divided application of coagulants was 0.5 grain per gallon less than in the single application in No. 167. The increased provision for subsidence aided by coagulation, about 3 hours as compared with 0.5 hour, caused a further removal of suspended matter as the water reached the sand layer, as shown by the fact that the suspended matter in the water at the top of the filter in runs Nos. 167 and 168 was found to be 79 and 15 parts per million, respectively.

In consequence of this clearer but well coagulated water at the sand layer on run No. 168, the quantity of water filtered between washings was considerably more than double what it was on run No. 167, and the percentage of wash-water on Nos. 167 and 168 was 8.1 and 3.5, respectively. In brief, with the divided application of chemicals to give greater facilities for subsidence, the amount of coagulants was reduced 0.05 grain per gallon; the quality of the effluent was fully maintained; and the capacity of the filter was materially increased.

With 1.06 grains per gallon of sulphate of alumina applied at basin No. 1 and 1.10 to 1.13 grains at the Jewell settling chamber, there was a slight loss in economy with the divided application, in purifying a water containing rather more suspended matter than in the case of runs Nos. 167 and 168, as shown by runs Nos. 163 and 164.

The use of 0.65 grain per gallon of sulphate of alumina at basin No. 1, in addition to 1.20 grains at the Jewell settling chamber, was found to be inadequate for the purification of this water, as shown by runs 157 and 158.

The practical conclusions to be drawn from this experience are that with preliminary coagulation, followed by subsidence for a period of about 3 hours, the application of coagulants may be divided to advantage, and a considerable portion of the suspended matter kept off the filter, when the total amount of required coagulant ranges from 2 to 2.5 grains or more of ordinary sulphate of alumina per gallon. In the case of a water requiring more than this amount of coagulating treatment, a proper division of the application would increase the saving of coagulants and would diminish the frequency of washing the filter.

To place an estimate upon the minimum limit of suspended matter in the water where a division in the application could be profitably made is difficult, owing to the wide range in the character of the suspended matter; and, further, the period of subsidence following the preliminary application of coagulants is an important factor and was too short in these devices. Under the existing conditions it was found necessary to apply about 1.5 grains per gallon of sulphate of alumina in order to make preliminary coagulation and subsidence effective. With a longer period of subsidence this quantity could possibly be lessened somewhat. But before considering further the practical significance of these facts we will show why it is necessary to apply a certain considerable amount of coagulating chemicals in order that coagulation and subsidence may be efficient.

Relative Efficiencies in Sedimentation of Different Amounts of Coagulants.

In studying the behavior of coagulants in connection with the sedimentation and filtration of the Ohio River water, the most noticeable feature is that in the case of sulphate of alumina very little appears to be accomplished until the quantity of applied chemical reaches a certain amount, ranging with different waters from 0.75 to 1.50 grains per gallon.

The indications are that, before any practical coagulation is effected, a certain amount of coagulant must be applied in order that the absorptive and perhaps other similar capacities of the suspended matter in the water be completely satisfied. In connection with the explanation of this, reference is made to the close of section No. 2 of this discussion.

Persulphate of iron and electrolytically formed hydrates of iron and aluminum behave in a similar manner to sulphate of alumina, as shown by the results of experiments recorded in the next set of tables.

These results are representative of many data obtained in the laboratory, where subsidence for 24 hours after the application of the coagulant took place in one-gallon bottles.

Attention is especially called to the last column, where the increase in the removal of suspended matter for successive portions of the coagulant is shown.

Sulphate of Alumina.

(River water contained 424 parts per million of suspended matter.)

Applied Chemical. Grains per Gallon.	After Settling 24 Hours.		Percentage Additional Removal for Successive Portions of 0.25 Grain.
	Suspended Solids. Parts per Million.	Percentage Removal.	
None	55	70	....
0.25	47	74	4
0.50	44	76	2
0.75	35	81	5
1.00	3	97	16
1.25	1	99	2
1.50	0	100	1

Persulphate of Iron.

(River water contained 364 parts per million of suspended matter.)

Applied Chemical. Grains per Gallon.	After Settling 24 Hours.		Additional Percentage Removal for Successive Portions of 0.40 Grain.
	Suspended Solids. Parts per Million.	Percentage Removal.	
None	129	65	....
0.40	122	66	1
0.80	123	66	0
1.20	120	67	1
1.60	67	82	15
2.00	38	90	8
2.40	28	92	2
2.80	7	98	6
3.20	2	99	1

Electric Current with Iron Electrodes.

(River water contained 424 parts per million of suspended solids.)

Electrolytic Treatment. Ampere-Hour per Gallon.	After Settling 24 Hours.		Additional Percentage Removal for Successive Portions of 0.012 Ampere-Hour.
	Suspended Solids. Parts per Million.	Percentage Removal.	
None	185	56	....
0.012	180	58	2
0.018	167	61	5
0.025	161	62	1
0.031	156	63	1
0.038	144	66	3
0.044	123	71	5
0.062	26	94	23
0.096	5	98	4
0.124	0	100	2

Electric Current with Aluminum Electrodes.

(River water contained 364 parts per million of suspended solids.)

Electrolytic Treatment Ampere-Hour per Gallon.	After Settling 24 Hours.		Additional Percentage Removal for Successive Portions of 0.002 and 0.003 Ampere-Hour.
	Suspended Solids. Parts per Million.	Percentage Removal.	
None	120	67	....
0.002	96	74	7
0.005	87	76	2
0.008	82	77	1
0.010	80	78	1
0.013	44	88	10
0.015	34	91	3
0.018	20	94	3
0.020	10	97	3
0.023	3	99	2

The above results show that with these waters it was necessary to apply from 1.0 to 1.6 grains of sulphate of alumina per gallon before subsidence caused a material removal of suspended matter, in addition to that removed by plain subsidence. It is true that these waters contained more silt than ought ordinarily to be the case in practice after plain subsidence had taken place. With suspended matter of a clayey nature this minimum amount of coagulant for efficient coagulation would probably be reduced.

Just how far the conditions of practice would cause the minimum efficient amount of coagulant to depart from that indicated above was impracticable to ascertain accurately under the conditions of these investigations.

There are indications that the minimum limit, where the division in the application of coagulant would be economical, would fall below 2 grains of ordinary sulphate of alumina and perhaps as low as 1.5 grains per gallon. As it requires about 0.75 grain as a minimum application to secure coagulation prior to filtration, this would leave an equal quantity of coagulant to facilitate subsidence.

SECTION No. 8.

EFFECT OF THE PERIOD OF COAGULATION OF THE OHIO RIVER WATER BEFORE FILTRATION.

Recently there have developed in some localities differences in opinion as to the most advantageous period of time to intervene between the application of the coagulant and the entrance of the water into the sand layer. The data bearing on this point are presented in the next two tables, and the conditions under which they were obtained are outlined as follows:

Table No. 1.

In this table a comparison is made of the principal data in 13 pairs of runs showing the efficiency of the Jewell filter when the coagulant (sulphate of alumina) was applied at the inlet and outlet of the settling chamber, respectively. It will be recalled that the outlet of the settling chamber was at the top of the filter. When the coagulant was applied at the inlet to the settling chamber the period of coagulation averaged about 30 minutes, and when applied to the mouth of the pipe leading from the settling chamber to the upper compartment (containing about 1.6 feet of water) above the sand layer, the period was about 8 minutes. The character of the Ohio River water was such during these runs that the average quantity of coagulant was approximately equal to the estimated annual average amount required for the water under favorable conditions for purification.

Table No. 2.

A comparison of the principal data of runs Nos. 173, 174, and 175 with the Jewell filter is made in this table.

At this time the river water contained much less suspended matter than on the runs recorded in Table No. 1. The coagulant on these three runs was applied at the inlet to basin No. 1, the inlet to the Jewell settling chamber, and to the outlet of the latter chamber, respectively. This made the average periods for coagulation about 199, 30, and 8 minutes, respectively.

Comparing the average results of Table No. 1, it is seen that with the same character of river water the change in the point of application of the coagulant from the inlet to the outlet of the settling chamber (reducing the period of coagulation from 30 to 8 minutes) caused the quantity of water filtered

TABLE NO. 1.

COMPARISON OF THE EFFICIENCY OF THE JEWELL FILTER WHEN THE COAGULANT WAS APPLIED AT THE INLET TO THE SETTLING CHAMBER, AND WHEN IT WAS APPLIED TO THE WATER AT THE TOP OF THE FILTER.

Number of Run.	Suspended Solids in River Water. Parts per Million.	Applied Sulphate of Alumina. Grains per Gallon.	Filtered Water. Cubic Feet.	Bacterial Efficiency.
Coagulant Applied at the Inlet to the Settling Chamber.				
94	149	2.11	17 898	97.9
97	300	1.33	2 105	95.6
98	296	1.46	5 942	98.0
102	368	1.69	4 609	96.7
104	438	1.88	8 367	98.8
140	124	1.67	26 640	98.2
143	548	1.52	6 137	97.9
145	438	1.92	11 584	99.2
164	189	1.81	4 200	98.9
166	189	2.14	4 218	99.0
176	130	1.02	18 435	98.0
180	140	0.78	10 322	97.9
183	173	0.77	5 457	96.6
Averages	268	1.55	9 686	97.8
Coagulant Applied at the Top of the Filter.				
92	210	2.47	4 463	98.1
93	140	1.92	5 567	97.9
95	184	2.74	1 013	98.7
96	300	1.31	1 048	96.7
99	295	1.42	5 518	95.7
101	350	1.87	999	97.5
103	368	1.92	2 856	98.1
141	552	1.59	1 300	97.7
142	548	2.02	4 210	98.9
165	189	2.10	1 187	97.8
175	130	1.60	10 565	99.2
179	127	1.04	1 007	97.0
184	174	1.10	1 071	97.0
Averages	274	1.78	3 139	97.7

TABLE NO. 2.

COMPARISON OF THE EFFICIENCY OF THE JEWELL FILTER WHEN THE COAGULANT WAS APPLIED AT THE INLET TO BASIN NO. 1, THE INLET TO THE JEWELL SETTLING CHAMBER AND THE OUTLET OF THE LATTER (TOP OF FILTER), RESPECTIVELY.

Number of Run.	Application of Sulphate of Alumina. Place.	Application of Sulphate of Alumina. Grains per Gallon.	Suspended Solids in River Water. Parts per Million.	Filtered Water. Cubic Feet.	Bacterial Efficiency.
173	Inlet, Basin No. 1..	1.51	74	32 227	99.0
174	Inlet Jewell Settling Chamber....	1.60	73	20 438	99.0
175	Top of Filter.......	1.60	130	10 565	99.2

between washings to be diminished to about one-third; and this reduction was accomplished when the quantity of coagulant was increased 15 per cent.

The character of the filtered water was unchanged, except perhaps it should be noted in this connection that it was a failure in the quality of the effluent which caused the filter to be washed in all runs recorded in Table No. 1, excepting No. 140, on which run the rate failed with a satisfactory effluent.

This means that with the shorter period of coagulation the quality of the effluent failed more quickly than in the case of the regular period. In this connection it is to be pointed out that, while the amount of the suspended matter in the river water was the same in each case, the suspended matter in the water as collected from above the sand layer averaged 90 and 160 parts per million with the long and short periods, respectively.

With regard to the data in Table No. 2 the river water contained less suspended matter than in the case of the water dealt with in the first table, and the amount of coagulant was relatively greater, with a consequently higher bacterial efficiency.

Under these conditions the ratio of the quantities of filtered water per run, when the coagulant was applied at the inlet and the outlet of the settling chamber was 2 to 1 instead of 3 to 1, as in the case cited above. In a general way this diminution in the effect of the period of coagulation was repeatedly observed as the water became clearer.

On runs Nos. 173, 174, and 175 the suspended matter in the water on the top of the filter was found to be 21, 45, and 86 parts per million, respectively. As would naturally be expected, the longest and most satisfactory run was the one on which the amount of suspended matter going on the filter was the least. All things considered, this run, No. 173, on which the period of coagulation was about 3.3 hours, was the most satisfactory one obtained during the entire series of experiments. It brought out very clearly the fact that the period of coagulation could with marked advantage be made much longer than custom formerly supposed.

It is not to be inferred that in all cases a

period of 3.3 hours for coagulation is desirable or even admissible from a practical standpoint.

The facts as illustrated by runs Nos. 182 and 183 show that this is not true. With about 0.75 grain per gallon of sulphate of alumina applied to river water containing 172 parts per million of suspended matter, at the inlet to basin No. 1 and the Jewell settling chamber, respectively, the application at the first point resulted in the run being a failure, while in the second case fair results were obtained.

As stated in section No. 1, the decomposition of commercial sulphates in moderate amounts by the alkaline constituents of the Ohio River water is practically instantaneous. But the amount and character of the suspended matter in the water exert considerable influence upon the optimum period of coagulation for a given water. This is shown by inspection of the data, when it will be noted that different amounts of coagulants were required to yield satisfactory results from waters apparently similar, so far as could be told from amounts of suspended matter. In general terms these last observations hold true, practically speaking, for electrolytically formed coagulants.

Conclusions.

1. The Ohio River water as it comes from the river, and also after the coarse matters are removed from it by plain subsidence, requires, for its most economical and efficient treatment, different periods of coagulation at different times, according to the character and amount of suspended matter.

2. When the water is very clear the indications are that but little difference would be noted in periods of from 1 to 30 minutes; and, further, with clear water it is probable that if the period were extended beyond this range to a certain but not well-defined point, a loss in efficiency would result.

3. But when the water contains its usual amount and character of suspended matter the period of coagulation to give the best results is a variable one, and reaches several hours in length before a division in the application of coagulants (as discussed in section No. 7) becomes advisable.

4. To fix upon any given period to give uniformly, under the conditions of successful practice, the optimum degree of coagulation, or very nearly so, does not seem practicable in the light of our present knowledge; and it is recommended that for a large plant the devices for the application of coagulants be made adjustable, so as to vary the period of coagulation as the character of the water demands. Whether or not it would ever be advisable to fix the point of application, so as to give a constant period of coagulation, can only be told by practical experience.

5. With regard to the best period of coagulation for subsidence, when a division is made in the application of coagulants, it must be borne in mind that under these conditions two objects are sought, the coagulation of the suspended articles and their removal by sedimentation. While it is probable that sedimentation might take place more rapidly if the coagulation was completed before the suspended matters began to subside, than when these two actions took place simultaneously, experience indicates quite clearly that a saving is made by allowing sedimentation to take place during coagulation. The period of coagulation, being plainly the shorter, becomes therefore unimportant, as the optimum period of subsidence with coagulation would be the controlling factor.

The conditions of these investigations were not such as to allow the study of the optimum period of subsidence with coagulation, of a water which had already been partially purified by plain subsidence. It may be stated, however, that as the water after proper preliminary treatment by plain subsidence would contain only relatively fine suspended particles, the optimum period would probably be considerably longer than would be indicated by the results of subsidence with coagulation of a water which had not been properly settled. Experiments on the direct treatment of river water such as were recorded in Chapter IV, and in previous sections of this chapter, do not therefore apply to the subject in hand except in a very general way.

Section No. 9.

Degree of Coagulation of the Water before Filtration, and the Minimum Amount of Coagulant Required for that Purpose.

In all cases experience showed that for successful filtration the coagulation of the water as it enters the sand layer must be practically complete. To a trained operator of a filter this condition of the water can be noted quite accurately by inspection. It can be described by the statement that the suspended matters in the water must have a "curdled" or "flakey" appearance, which is such that ultimately the suspended matters would subside and leave the water in a practically clear condition. The rate at which such subsidence would take place depends largely upon the size and specific gravity of the matters in suspension.

It was found that the proper degree of coagulation of this water as it entered the sand layer was the *sine qua non* of economical and efficient purification by the American type of filters. From what is said in the paragraph above it is not to be inferred that subsidence alone is adequate under practicable conditions for satisfactory purification. It is essential to have filtration in order to make the purification complete. The amount of suspended matter in the water affects the degree of coagulation only in that the amount of coagulant must be sufficient to yield enough gelatinous hydrate to envelop practically all of the suspended particles, including the bacteria.

Coagulation of the water entering the sand need not if necessity be absolutely complete so far as maximum formation of size of flakes is concerned, because the friction in the sand layer will supplement this action if the volume of hydrate is sufficient. This is especially true of the middle and latter portions of runs, when considerable hydrate is accumulated in and upon the sand layer. Concerning a volume of hydrate in excess of that capable of giving the above conditions, it is to be avoided not only because it is a waste of chemicals (and unnecessarily increases the corroding and incrusting constituents of the effluent in the case of sulphates), but because it increases the frequency of washing the sand layer and consequently reduces the capacity of the filter.

In view of the fact that during the greater portion of the year the Ohio River water contains clay particles which are smaller than bacteria, the bacterial efficiency is generally satisfactory if the filtered water is clear and free from turbidity. As a matter of fact, in many cases during the tests recorded in this chapter very fair bacterial efficiency was obtained when the effluent was so turbid that the run was stopped, the filter washed, and the amount of coagulant increased for the next run. However, there are also times during the winter when the suspended matter is so coarse that comparatively little difficulty is experienced in getting a bright or even brilliant effluent, while a satisfactory removal of bacteria was a less easy matter

This consideration of the relative difficulty in removing bacteria and finely divided clay brings us to the question of the minimum amount of coagulant which can properly be applied to this water. Experience indicates that under ordinary circumstances this river water would rarely if ever reach a condition where less than 0.75 grain per gallon of sulphate of alumina, containing about 9.87 per cent. of aluminum, could be used with safety in this method of purification.

Section No. 10.

On the Conditions of Successful Filtration.

In addition to a confirmation of the evidence in Chapter IX, our knowledge upon the conditions of successful filtration was advanced in several particulars. But as it was considered feasible to operate only one filter during the tests described in this chapter, comparative data are scanty or lacking along several lines, notably those related to the character of the sand layer, such as thickness and size of grain. The principal information of practical value obtained in this connection during 1897 is as follows:

Amount of Suspended Matter in the Water Reaching the Sand Layer, and the Coagulation of the Same.

Experience during the last portion of the tests (April to July, 1897) demonstrated conclusively that for the uniform, efficient, and economical filtration of the Ohio River water it is imperative to remove the suspended matter so far as practicable from the water before it reaches the sand layer. The data confirm in a decisive manner the conclusion drawn in 1896, that filtration alone is inadequate for the successful purification of the silt and clay-bearing Ohio River water. Filtration is the last step, and a very important and essential one, in a method in which sedimentation, plain and with coagulation, precedes filtration.

By plain subsidence, supplemented at times by subsidence with coagulation, there are gained a number of distinct advantages, as were pointed out before, as follows:

1. A considerable wastage of coagulants would be prevented—an amount much exceeding the cost of subsidence.

2. The cost of construction and maintenance of a large reserve portion of a plant, to aid in handling muddy water, would be obviated.

3. The efficiency of the plant would be more uniform and satisfactory with regard to the quality of the effluent.

4. The difficulties and cost of operating a plant to purify with uniform satisfaction the very variable Ohio River water would be reduced largely. In this connection reference is especially made to the adjustment of the optimum amount of coagulant and to the cleansing of the sand layer.

At this point the very important question arises, What amount of suspended matter can be properly handled by filters of the American type?

Much thought has been directed to an expression of this amount by weight in parts per million. We have not succeeded, however, in fixing the limit in this manner, owing to the wide discrepancies obtained in handling equal weights of suspended matter of different character. Thus at times 100 parts per million of fine clay were more difficult to remove than 500 parts of silt.

The best way in which we can express this amount is by the statement that by plain subsidence, aided by coagulation when necessary, the suspended matter in this river water should be reduced to a point where, by filtration and the coagulation just preceding it, the remaining suspended matter can be removed by the final application of coagulants not exceeding 1.5 to 2 grains per gallon of ordinary sulphate of alumina, or its equivalent.

In section No. 9 it was stated that for successful filtration the final application of coagulants must be such that the coagulation of the suspended particles is practically complete. When the coagulation is complete, it follows, as shown by experience, that the period of coagulation may be extended so as to cause a still further removal of suspended matter by subsidence, and consequently an additional relief to the sand layer. This is possible with an application of chemical or electrolytic treatment sufficient to produce complete coagulation, because there will then remain, as the water reaches the sand layer, sufficient hydrate to accomplish filtration satisfactorily.

Failure to provide proper coagulation is inadmissible, as this is the *sine qua non* of successful filtration by this method.

Rate of Filtration.

The Jewell filter was operated normally in 1897, as was the case in 1895–96, at about 100 million gallons per acre daily, equivalent to 1.58 gallons per square foot per minute.

In the last operations (1897) the only point tested in this connection was the possibility of lowering the rate of filtration to advantage, with regard to a reduction in the amount of coagulant and greater uniformity in efficiency, especially just after washing the sand layer. A comparison of the efficiency of the filter at normal and half-normal rates, respectively, is shown by the following representative averages of leading data on (I) runs Nos. 67, 72, 81, and 82, and (II) Nos. 68, 70, 75, and 83:

	I	II
Rate of filtration in million gallons per acre daily	90–95	45–50
Parts per million of suspended solids in river water	181	187
Applied sulphate of alumina in grains per gallon	1.25	1.21
Cubic feet of filtered water	12 302	14 749
Bacterial efficiency	97.2	96.6

Comparative Summary.

These data, with many others which are not directly comparable, show clearly that, when the amount of coagulant is such as to give at the normal rate only a moderately satisfactory bacterial efficiency, a reduction of the rate to one-half of the normal does not increase the bacterial efficiency, although it increases slightly the quantity of water between washings. It may be safely concluded that a material reduction in a rate of filtration of 100 million gallons per acre daily would not diminish the required amount of coagulant, and there would be no substantial advantages to offset the lessened capacity of the filter.

From what has been said concerning the proper degree of coagulation of the water this fact seems to be almost obvious.

In passing it may be stated that, when by any chance the coagulation was inadequate, it was repeatedly noticed that with low rates the bacterial efficiency and appearance of the effluent departed less from the normal than in the case of the regular rate of filtration.

The evidence presented in Chapter IX indicated that under suitable conditions the rate of satisfactory filtration could be materially increased above 100 million gallons per acre daily. Our investigations in 1897 strengthened that view, although with only one filter, and electrical appliances of too small capacity, it was not considered advisable to make a study of high rates, especially with the unsubsided river water.

In the judgment of the writer it would be advisable to construct a plant on the basis of 100 million gallons per acre daily, equivalent to 435.6 square feet per million gallons per 24 hours, with the knowledge that in all probability the rate would be safely increased to a considerable degree in meeting the demand for a greater consumption of filtered water.

Available Head or Pressure for Filtration.

The total available head on the Jewell filter, as normally operated by the Water Company, was 10 feet, of which 5.5 feet was a positive head as measured from the surface of the water to the bottom of the sand layer. The remaining 4.5 feet was a negative head or suction, and was obtained by means of a siphon. So far as our observation went, no necessity for modifying this head was noted.

Negative Head or Pressure.

The claim has been advanced that a negative head possesses a specific advantage for economical and efficient filtration. All the conditions being equal, we have seen nothing to lead us to suppose that there would be any difference in practice due to the head being either positive or negative, beyond the fact that with a negative head there is ordinarily a smaller amount of coagulated water drained into the sewer and wasted just before washing the sand layer, or similar operations.

Cleaning the Sand Layer to Relieve Clogging.

There are three methods which can be employed to advantage in the removal of accumulated matters from the sand in order to relieve clogging and to keep the sand in a clean and efficient condition, as follows:

1. By washing the sand with a reverse stream of filtered water under pressure.
2. By agitation of the surface accumulations and their removal into the sewer by flushing with water standing upon the sand.
3. By the application of caustic soda, either with or without steam.

The following information was obtained upon the subject in 1897:

Washing.—Experience confirmed the early conclusion that whenever washing of the sand layer is required it should be accomplished thoroughly, so that the water passing from the top of the sand to the sewer should be comparatively clear. In the Jewell filter this was ordinarily accomplished with the aid of mechanical agitation, by about 600 cubic feet of wash-water supplied at the bottom of the sand layer at a pressure of about 7.5 pounds. The rate of delivery of wash-water ranged from 22 to 134, and averaged 71.0, cubic feet per minute.

Assuming that the voids in the normal sand layer were 35 per cent., and that the thickness of the layer when floated was increased from 30 to 33 inches, this would mean an average vertical velocity between the sand grains of 1.37 linear feet per minute.

There seems to be no room for doubt but that the use of mechanical agitation in the process of washing was a distinct advantage. In this case the teeth of the agitator extended to within three inches of the bottom of the sand layer. The indications are that it would be better to have them reach as nearly to the strainer system as safety would allow.

With regard to the effect of washing the sand layer, upon the quality of the effluent, it will be recalled that in 1896 it was concluded, from the results obtained from the Warren and Jewell filters, that with complete coagulation of the applied water and thorough washing of the sand layer there was practically no diminution in bacterial efficiency following a washing. In a strict sense this conclusion is correct, but the evidence of 1897 causes a certain modification of these views. That is to say, when the coagulation was sufficient to give a satisfactory bacterial efficiency during the latter and major portion of a run, it was repeatedly found that the coagulation might not be complete enough to yield a normal effluent, bacterially, for some little time after the sand layer was washed. This is shown by the following average numbers of bacteria obtained during the first portion of runs Nos. 84, 89, 91, 93, 102, 106, 122, 126, 130, 131, 133, 142, 147, 148, and 168.

The bacterial efficiency at the times of collection of the samples and the average number of bacteria in the river water and in the effluent, together with the average bacterial efficiency, are given. In preparing this table all normal runs on which the four or more samples were collected were averaged.

Quantity of Water Filtered between the Last Wash and the Collection of the Sample. Cubic Feet.	Average Number of Bacteria per Cubic Centimeter.	Bacterial Efficiency.
150	273	97.3
250	225	97.7
500	206	97.9
1000	178	98.2
Average, river water, entire run	9 970	....
" effluent, entire run....	186	98.1

At the regular rate of filtration the above quantities of water correspond to 6.4, 10.6, 21.3, and 42.5 minutes of service after filtration was resumed following a wash.

The difference between these figures and corresponding ones obtained in 1896 is explained by the fact that in 1897 the coagulation was relatively less, as every effort was made to keep the amount of coagulant as low as was consistent with good purification.

The entire evidence taken as a whole shows that when coagulation is absolutely complete there is no appreciable diminution in the quality of the effluent just after a thorough washing of the sand layer.

Nevertheless, when coagulation is very slightly incomplete, but sufficient to give satisfactory average purification, the data show that just after washing there is a slight diminution in efficiency. This slight diminution in efficiency, at this time, could be corrected by an extra application of coagulant for a short period; by reducing the rate of filtration, or by discharging the effluent at a normal rate (or higher) into the sewer so long as it appeared unsatisfactory. This question is one which will have to be settled by experience obtained in practice.

Surface Agitation.—Surface agitation in a manner similar to that employed in 1896 was used in 39 per cent. of all runs on which the wash and waste water was less than 10 per cent. of the filtered water, and on 49 per cent. of the runs on which the wash and waste water did not exceed 10 per cent. of the filtered water, and on which the average bacterial efficiency was 97 per cent. or over. When the Jewell filter was operated by the McDougall Company it was their custom to employ surface agitation, and after stirring up the surface accumulations to flush them off into the sewer so far as practical.

This modification is one of merit, although this filter was not constructed in a manner to allow of its performance in an entirely satisfactory way. The reason was that the top of the inner tank was about 10.5 inches above the top of the sand, and accordingly this depth of very muddy water remained on the sand after the operation was completed.

The indications are that this is the cheapest manner of removing the bulk of solid matters from the surface of the sand layer, and it seems advisable to modify the construction of filters so that this procedure can be employed to the greatest advantage.

This would call for means of removing all

of the muddy water from the sand during or after the completion of the agitation, and probably some other changes, especially in the character of the sand layer.

It must be understood that surface agitation could not completely do away with washing, and while the indications of its dispensing in part with washing are promising, how far it could be carried into successful practice cannot be foretold.

Application of Caustic Soda.—The application of caustic soda to this filter on July 3 demonstrated conclusively that it had a marked effect in cleansing the sand grains of organic matter and other materials attached to them.

As filters continue in service the use from time to time of caustic soda would doubtless be an advantage in keeping the sand layer in a satisfactory condition.

Character of the Sand Layer.

The sand layer of the Jewell filter was 30 inches in thickness and the sand grains had an effective size of 0.43 millimeter. It is the judgment of the writer that the frictional resistance of the sand could be increased to advantage; especially in an effort to reduce the cost of cleansing, by allowing the use of the partial but more frequent cleansings by surface agitation in place of thorough washing of the whole sand layer. This could be accomplished by increasing the thickness of the layer or by using a sand with a finer grain, or both. The indications are that this could be done best by maintaining the thickness of the sand layer at 30 inches, and using a finer sand.

It is recommended that a sand be employed having an effective size of about 0.35 millimeter. As the resistance of the sand to the flow of water varies inversely as the square of the effective size, this would increase the friction in the ratio of 2 to 3.

SECTION No. II.

QUALITY OF THE EFFLUENT AFTER PROPER SEDIMENTATION, COAGULATION, AND FILTRATION — INDEPENDENT OF THE NATURE OF THE COAGULANT.

Under suitable conditions for economical and efficient treatment, as noted above, the quality of the Ohio River water after purification is presented in the following paragraphs. It will be noted that the statements in this section are independent of the nature of the coagulants. Following this the effect of the several available coagulants is discussed.

Appearance.

The appearance of the Ohio River water after purification under the above conditions was very satisfactory, as it was practically free from turbidity and color.

Taste and Odor.

As a rule the taste of the effluent was somewhat different from that of the river water, in that the earthy taste due to suspended earthy matters in the unpurified water was removed. The odor of the effluent was the same as before purification, and was never found to be sufficient to be in any way objectionable.

Organic Matter.

The amount of organic matter remaining in the effluent was found to range, when expressed as nitrogen in the form of albuminoid ammonia, from .030 to .110 part per million, and averaged about .070 part, expressed as oxygen consumed the range was from 0.5 to 1.6 parts, and the average was 1.0 part.

In such small amounts the organic matter in the effluent was entirely unobjectionable.

Mineral Matter.

Upon purification the changes in the mineral contents of the Ohio River water is characterized chiefly by the complete removal of suspended mud, silt, and clay. This is unquestionably an advantage, although from a sanitary standpoint the evidence indicates that such an action does not specifically improve the healthfulness of the water, except perhaps in the case of some abnormal individuals.

From an industrial point of view the removal of suspended mineral matter is discussed below.

With regard to the dissolved mineral constituents of the effluent, they do not differ materially from those of the river, except as influenced by the nature of the coagulants as shown in the next section.

Gases.

The principal gases in the river water, carbon dioxide (uniting with water to form free carbonic acid) and atmospheric oxygen, were practically unaffected by purification except through the nature of the coagulant.

Algæ and other Grosser Micro-oganisms.

It was found that the effluent was practically free from all diatoms, algæ, and other micro-organisms which may be called large when compared with bacteria.

Bacteria.

Under favorable conditions of coagulation and filtration the bacteria in the effluent were reduced to a point which was satisfactory in the light of modern sanitary science.

Undecomposed Coagulants.

This topic is entered into in subsequent sections, and the conditions of proper coagulation as stated above in the title lead to the inference that the presence of undecomposed coagulants in the effluent is not a factor for consideration. For the sake of explicitness, however, it may be mentioned here that, with suitable conditions for the employment of subsidence to its economical limit, with commercial sulphates there would be no occasion for the chemicals to be applied in amounts exceeding that capable of complete decomposition by the river water. Concerning the use of electrolytically formed iron hydrate, it is not probable that dissolved iron would ever appear in the effluent; although it is possible that large amounts of clay in the river water in midsummer, when the amount of dissolved atmospheric oxygen in the water is least, might press closely and perhaps overreach the safe limit in the amount of iron which could be completely oxidized and rendered insoluble. If such an occasion should arise it would be of very short duration and could be obviated by the use of small amounts of commercial sulphates to supplement the electrolytic process.

In 1897 there was no instance where any difficulty was experienced in keeping the effluent free from undecomposed coagulants.

Storage of the Effluent.

The conditions of successful practice demand that between the purification plant and the distributing pipes there should be provided a reservoir in which sufficient filtered water may be stored to compensate for all inequalities in the rate of consumption at different hours of the day, and also to allow the plant to be stopped when repairs, etc., require it. The question of storage of the effluent is one of much practical importance.

While it is true that the effluent as it leaves the filter is free from algæ, diatoms, etc., it is a fact that the spores of these micro-organisms are present in the atmosphere; and the filtered water contains a considerable amount of food (principally in the form of nitrates) for the growth of these organisms, many of which give rise to objectionable tastes and odors. The growth of these organisms requires the presence of sunlight; and the effect of purification is marked in this respect, because in open reservoirs the removal of all suspended matters from the water permits the sun's rays to penetrate the filtered water, while with the river water this is impossible. This was demonstrated conclusively by microscopical examinations of the river water with different amounts of suspended matter in it during warm weather (the period of maximum growth of these organisms), as shown in Chapter I.

To estimate the period of storage during which the filtered water might be stored in open reservoirs, before the growth of algæ would begin in warm weather, is a difficult matter. It would vary widely with the temperature and the frequency of sunshiny days, the amount and specific character of the particles of floating matter coming from the atmosphere, and the amount of dissolved matter in the filtered water, adaptable as food for these organisms. Inspection of isolated portions of the Ohio River where the current was almost *nil*, lead to the belief that such a growth might occur in much less than one week. General information concerning the life history of these organisms indicates that at times the period would be as short as 4 days, but it is possible that under some circumstances it might be no longer than 2 days. It is certain, however, that it would not be safe to expose the filtered water to the rays of the sun for an average period of about 6 days, as would be the case if the uncovered reservoir at Crescent Hill were used under present conditions.

Difficulties with algæ growths may be obviated by making the period of exposure to the sun's rays very short, or by using a covered reservoir, or both. The covered reservoir would be safest, especially as it would preclude trouble from growths of organisms which might become seeded upon the walls of the reservoir.

Corrosion by the Effluent of Metal Receptacles.

This subject was discussed in Chapter IX, but in 1897 additional information of value was obtained.

In all probability there would be no difficulty whatever in the action of the effluent upon lead pipes, or iron pipes which were properly coated with a protective paint. With uncoated iron pipes or receptacles, especially those of wrought iron, the effluent would have an increased corroding action. As already explained, water normally produces corrosion by the joint action of the carbonic acid and the atmospheric oxygen dissolved in the water. This action produces iron (ferric) hydrate, just as in the Anderson process of securing coagulation. When first formed, iron hydrate is flocculent and fairly porous, and it will be understood from what has been said concerning the nature of this compound as a coagulant, that it has the power of incorporating within itself suspended matters and some dissolved matters. The resulting mass is much less porous than when no suspended matters are embodied in the hydrate. Facts show that this is of practical importance in the consideration of corrosion by the Ohio River water before and after purification.

Partial Protective Influence of Suspended Matter against Corrosion.—Comparison of the relative corroding action of the Ohio River water before and after the removal of silt and clay, by filtration through filter-paper, a Pasteur filter or other device in which the chemical character of the dissolved compound would not be materially changed in quality or amount, showed repeatedly and without exception that the suspended matter acted as a partial protection to the iron. This is illustrated by the following representative experiment, in which 8 pieces of 0.5-inch wrought-iron rods weighing 150 grams were placed in 2200 cubic centimeters of river water (chemical sample No. 985) and the effluent after passing this water through a Pasteur filter. The experiment was continued for ten days, and in order that the effluent might not be dissimilar to practical conditions by an exhaustion of carbonic acid and oxygen, air (containing these gases) was constantly passed through each water. At the end of this experiment it was found that in the case of the river water 1.1 grams of iron had been lost from the rods by corrosion, while in the effluent the corresponding amount was 2.1 grams. To prove that this was not due essentially to an action of dissolved chemical compounds (exclusive of course of carbonic acid and oxygen), this experiment was repeated for 14 days, using distilled water with 10 parts of common salt in each bottle, and in one of them some fine clay (kaolin) was suspended. The results show that in the case with suspended clay there was a loss of iron by corrosion of 0.90 milligram, while in the clear water the iron lost 1.81 milligrams.

Bearing in mind the decisive proof that on a laboratory scale the suspended matter gave a marked although incomplete protection to iron from corrosion by the water, an examination was made of the experience of this Company in the corrosion of uncoated pipes. The most notable instance of the slowness with which the Ohio River water corrodes uncoated iron is in the case of the intake at the old pumping station. This wrought-iron pipe, 0.37 inch thick and 50 inches in diameter, was put in service in 1860, and remained in continuous service without any artificial protective coating until 1894. After 34 years of exposure to the river water it was corroded to a considerable degree, but not enough to warrant its removal, and it was coated with a layer of cement and continued in service.

In concluding it may be stated that the reason that the effluent has a greater corroding action upon iron than has the river water, is because the suspended matters mixing with the hydrate diminish materially the contact of the water with the surface of the bright metal at the point of corrosion. In a measure this effect is similar to that in the case of lead pipes. The Ohio River water dissolves new bright lead rapidly, but with great promptness it forms a very thin layer of basic carbonate of lead which, practically speaking, is absolutely impervious to water and consequently arrests all further action.

Adaptability of Effluent for Boiler Use.

Compared with the average boiler waters in this section of the country, and farther West, the Ohio River water in an unpurified condition is a fairly satisfactory water for use in steam-boilers. In comparison with the clear and soft waters in the East, however, it has two marked disadvantages.

In the first place, during the greater part of the year the amount of suspended matter is so great that it forms large quantities of sludge, which at times cannot be removed by "blowing off," so that it is necessary to enter the boiler and remove it by manual labor. At such times the incrusting constituents are very low in amount and are deposited upon the separate particles of the sludge for the most part, and seem to leave the metal almost free from sulphate of lime, etc. The removal of these large amounts of suspended matters would be an advantage, unquestionably, and the effluent would therefore be superior to the river water.

The second disadvantage of the river water for use in boilers is seen at times of very low water in the river, such as is found during the fall months. At these times the water contains not only sulphate of lime and other incrusting constituents in considerable quantities (and far in excess of the average amounts), but also some very fine clay. In boilers this clay and the incrusting constituents unite and form a coating resembling cement, which is very difficult to remove from the surface of the boiler. The removal of the suspended clay from the water before its entrance into boilers would therefore improve the water for boiler use.

With regard to the dissolved chemical compounds such as incrusting constituents, there is no difference between the river water and the effluent, independent of the nature of the coagulant. Disregarding the influence of the coagulant, which is discussed beyond, the effluent is more suitable for boiler use than is the river water.

Uniformity in Quality of Effluent.

With proper conditions for sedimentation, coagulation, and filtration, and independent of the nature of the coagulant, there ought not, and need not, be any objectionable variations in the quality of the effluent in consequence of the purification. It was found that the quality of the effluent does vary owing to the inherent variations in the river water. From a practical point of view these variations would occur in the dissolved mineral compounds, especially the carbonic acid and the incrusting constituents. The evidence obtained in 1897 showed that with regard to these constituents the composition of the river water is more variable than was considered to be the case in 1896. The normal and extreme amounts of carbonic acid and incrusting constituents in parts per million in the river water are as follows:

	Maximum.	Minimum.	Normal.
Carbonic acid	133	29	70
Incrusting constituents	51	8	18

SECTION No. 12.

MANNER IN WHICH THE NATURE OF THE COAGULANT AFFECTED THE QUALITY OF THE EFFLUENT.

There are three different coagulants, each of a somewhat different nature, which have been considered as factors in this problem, namely: sulphate of alumina, persulphate of iron, and electrolytically formed iron hydrate. As stated in Chapter III, the passage of undecomposed sulphates into the effluent would not only be inadmissible, but inexcusable. Our experience in 1897 allows of no modification of this view. It may be mentioned in passing, however, that the presence of undecomposed sulphates in the effluent would be exceedingly objectionable in connection with corrosion. With regard to the electrolytic iron method there would be no danger of any iron getting into the effluent during cold weather, but in midsummer if a heavy rise in the river should occur there might not be sufficient oxygen in the water to convert all the iron into insoluble ferric hydrate. Under these circumstances it would be necessary to supplement the safe limit in this treatment with some other coagulant, or to aerate the water.

In view of the fact that it is practicable to coagulate this water properly without the passage of undecomposed sulphates or of dissolved hydrates into the effluent, and that the necessity for doing so is imperative, we will consider the nature of the effect of the several coagulants upon the quality of the effluent only when applied in permissible (but adequate) amounts.

In general terms the quality of the effluent is affected in two ways by the nature of the coagulant: first, with regard to the amount of oxygen and carbonic acid; and, second, with reference to the increase in amount of incrusting constituents in consequence of the lime and magnesia passing from the (alkaline) carbonates and bicarbonates into the neutral sulphates.

From a sanitary point of view there is no reason to believe that these factors under suitable conditions of practice would be of any practical importance. They would influence, however, the corroding and incrusting power of the effluent.

The manner in which the several available coagulants affect the quality of the effluent, expressed quantitatively in equivalent amounts of 1 grain per gallon of sulphate of alumina containing 9.87 per cent. of aluminum, is shown in the table opposite.

In order to consider the practical effect of the nature of the coagulant upon the corroding and incrusting power of the water, it is

COMPARATIVE EFFECT UPON THE QUALITY OF THE EFFLUENT OF ONE GRAIN PER GALLON OF SULPHATE OF ALUMINA,* AND ITS EQUIVALENT OF OTHER COAGULANTS.

(Changes in Constituents of Effluent expressed in Parts per Million.)

Coagulant.	Atmospheric Oxygen.	Alkalinity.	Incrusting Constituents.	Carbon Dioxide.
Sulphate of alumina	None	9.04 (decrease)	9.04 (increase)	3.97 (increase)
Persulphate of iron	None	11.78 (decrease)	11.78 (increase)	5.16 (increase)
Electrolytic iron	0.76 (decrease)	None	None	None

* Containing 9.87 per cent. of aluminum, equivalent to 18.62 per cent. of alumina (Al_2O_3).

necessary to know the amount of the above changes. This depends upon the amounts of coagulants used, and the estimated quantities of coagulants which would be required are presented in the next section. In section No. 14 the degree to which the several coagulants would affect the effluent is shown and its practical significance discussed.

SECTION No. 13.

AMOUNTS OF THE DIFFERENT AVAILABLE COAGULANTS WHICH WOULD BE REQUIRED, WITH OPTIMUM CONDITIONS OF SUBSIDENCE AND FILTRATION, TO PURIFY SATISFACTORILY THE OHIO RIVER WATER.

Taking into consideration the employment to their economical limits of plain subsidence and an extended but varying period of subsidence with coagulation, and in some cases a division in the application of coagulants, it is estimated that the annual average amounts of required coagulants for the satisfactory purification of the Ohio River water would be as follows:

ESTIMATED REQUIRED AMOUNT OF COAGULANT PER GALLON OF RIVER WATER.

Coagulant.	Max.	Min.	Aver.
Grains of sulphate of alumina*........	4.00	0.75	1.75
Grains of sulphate of iron †....	4.00	0.75	1.75
Ampere-hour of electric current on iron electrodes......................	0.16	0.03	0.07

* Containing about 9.87 per cent. of aluminum.
† Containing about 24.73 per cent. of iron.

The average amount of coagulant in the respective equivalent forms would probably range according to the rainfall and other conditions in amounts from 1.50 to 2.00 grains in the case of the sulphates, and from 0.06 to 0.08 ampere-hour of electric current on iron electrodes. The mean average is given above.

In regard to the maximum amount of electrolytic iron treatment it is to be borne in mind that the amount above given could only be safely applied at times when the amount of oxygen dissolved in the river water was relatively large. As a rule, the maximum amount of electrolytic treatment which could be safely applied would be about 0.12 ampere-hour per gallon.

SECTION NO. 14.

DEGREE TO WHICH THE SEVERAL COAGULANTS IN THEIR RESPECTIVE AMOUNTS WOULD AFFECT THE QUALITY OF THE EFFLUENT, WITH ITS PRACTICAL SIGNIFICANCE AND A CONSIDERATION OF THE ADVISABILITY AND COST OF THE REMOVAL OF THE ADDED CONSTITUENTS.

Taking the annual average amounts of the required coagulants as estimated in the last section, the amount of changes in the several constituents of the effluent which would actually occur may be taken as follows:

CHANGES IN CONSTITUENTS OF RIVER WATER.
(Parts per Million.)

Coagulant.	Decrease in Oxygen.			Decrease in Alkalinity.		
	Max.	Min.	Av.	Max.	Min.	Av.
Sulphate of alumina....	None	None	None	27.0	6.0	12.5
Persulphate of iron........	None	None	None	35.0	7.8	16.2
Electrolytic iron........	8.9	1.7	3.9	None	None	None

Coagulant.	Increase in Incrusting Constituents.			Increase in Carbon Dioxide.		
	Max.	Min.	Av.	Max.	Min.	Av.
Sulphate of alumina....	27.0	6.0	12.5	11.9	2.6	5.5
Persulphate of iron........	35.0	7.8	16.2	15.5	3.4	7.3
Electrolytic iron........	None	None	None	None	None	None

The first step in the consideration of the practical significance of these data is to note the range of these constituents as they naturally occur in the Ohio River water.

ANNUAL RANGES OF AFFECTED CONSTITUENTS AS THEY NATURALLY OCCUR IN THE OHIO RIVER WATER.
(Parts per Million.)

Atmospheric Oxygen.			Alkalinity.		
Maximum.	Minimum.	Average.	Maximum.	Minimum.	Average.
13.0	4.6	8.6	108.0	21.0	65.0

Incrusting Constituents.			Carbon Dioxide.*		
Maximum.	Minimum.	Average.	Maximum.	Minimum.	Average.
51.0	8.0	18.0	133.0	29.0	70.0

* Carbon dioxide exists in the water as carbonic acid.

Atmospheric Oxygen—Electrolytic Iron Process.

The atmospheric oxygen dissolved in the water is affected only in the electrolytic iron process. It will be seen that while the average decrease in oxygen is equal to less than half the average amount in the river water, yet the maximum (calculated) decrease is nearly double the minimum amount in the water. Owing to the influence of temperature the amount of oxygen in the water is least during the summer months. During cold weather the indications are that there would be enough oxygen for the satisfactory use of this process. An exhaustion of the oxygen and the passage of soluble iron into the filtered water is inadmissible. Such a state of affairs would probably never occur except at times when the river water might be heavily charged with clay in midsummer. To guard against this effectively it would be necessary to provide facilities for the use of sulphates to supplement, at times in hot weather, the electrolytic iron process.

With regard to alkalinity, incrusting constituents, and carbonic acid, they remain unaffected by the electrolytic iron process.

Changes in Alkalinity, Incrusting Constituents, and Carbonic Acid—Process with Commercial Sulphates.

The above data show that in this process the atmospheric oxygen is unaffected, while the alkalinity is reduced and the incrusting constituents and carbonic acid increased. In the case of persulphate of iron the changes are 30 per cent. greater than with sulphate of alumina, other conditions being equal. In view of the fact that the two sulphates are of about equal cost, the sulphate of alumina is therefore the better chemical to employ as a coagulant. As stated and explained in Chapter III, the use of this product in such amounts that it would pass through the filter in an undecomposed form would not only be inadmissible but inexcusable.

We shall therefore consider sulphate of alumina more especially in the balance of this section, but will take up the effect of each sulphate in the following connection:

1. Sanitary character of effluent in this regard.
2. Use of soap.
3. Incrustations and adaptability for use in steam-boilers.
4. Corrosion of iron receptacles.
5. Corrosion of lead receptacles.

Effect upon the Sanitary Character of Effluents due to Changes Caused by the Use of Sulphates.

So far as we have been able to learn the sanitary character of the effluent would not be appreciably affected by the reductions in the alkalinity and the corresponding increases in incrusting constituents and carbonic acid, within the ranges noted above. There is no reason to believe that the carbonic acid has any significance in this respect, and we have only to consider the effect of changing the lime (and some magnesia) from the carbonate to the sulphate. In this connection it is to be noted that during the greater part of the year the amount of sulphate of lime in the chemically treated effluent would be far less than is naturally present in the river water during the fall months. And at that season of the year the percentage increase of sulphate of lime due to applied chemicals would be very small.

Effect upon the Amount of Soap Required by the Filtered Water due to Changes Caused by the Use of Sulphates.

The amount of soap required by a water for washing purposes depends upon the total amount of lime and magnesia present in the water. This is indicated by the total hardness of the water, which is measured by the sum of the alkalinity and incrusting constituents, approximately equal to the temporary and permanent hardness, respectively. As the decrease in alkalinity and increase in incrusting constituents are proportional, the soap consuming power would be constant under ordinary conditions.

After prolonged boiling of the filtered water it would require slightly more soap, because upon the expulsion of carbonic acid gas there would be less lime in the form of carbonate to settle out than in the case of the river water.

Changes in Adaptability of the Effluent for Use in Steam-boilers due to the Employment of Sulphates as Coagulants.

The adaptability of a water for boiler use, independent of matters in suspension, is governed by the amounts of incrusting constituents, and in this respect the two sulphates in question produced relative changes substantially as follows:

PERCENTAGE INCREASE OF INCRUSTING CONSTITUENTS OF THE EFFLUENT ABOVE THOSE IN THE RIVER WATER.

	Maximum.	Minimum.	Average.
With sulphate of alumina....	300	12	70
With persulphate of iron....	400	16	90

Owing to the fact that the increase in the incrusting constituents is low when the amounts naturally present in the river water are high (fall months) the maximum amount in the filtered water as shown by these data would not be far in excess of that in the river water.

COMPARISON OF THE MAXIMUM AND AVERAGE AMOUNTS OF INCRUSTING CONSTITUENTS OF THE EFFLUENT AND OF THE RIVER WATER.

(Parts per Million.)

	Maximum.	Average.
Ohio rievr water....................	51	18
Effluent with sulphate of alumina.....	57	30
Effluent with persulphate of iron......	59	35

From the above figures it is seen that the average annual amount of incrusting constituents in the effluents when sulphate of alumina and persulphate of iron are used are only 60 and 70 per cent., respectively, of the maximum amount naturally present in the Ohio River water, and at times when the river water is least suitable for use in boilers the increase in incrusting constituents is only 12 and 16 per cent., respectively.

These additions in incrusting constituents cannot be regarded as other than undesirable, but it is quite possible, if not probable, that the practical effect of the additions when proper subsidence is availed of, would be offset by the freedom of the effluent from suspended matters. Experience alone can demonstrate this conclusively.

There is another way of looking at the applicability of the effluents obtained with commercial sulphates in connection with use in boilers. That is to compare these data with the available results showing the incrusting constituents (permanent hardness) of the water supplies of other cities. So far as they were available these data are as follows:

COMPARISON OF INCRUSTING CONSTITUENTS (PERMANENT HARDNESS) OF THE WATER SUPPLIES OF VARIOUS CITIES.

(Parts per Million.)

Supply.	Incrusting Constituents.
Unfiltered Ohio River water (average), Louisville, Ky.	18
Filtered Ohio River water with sulphate of alumina, Louisville, Ky.	30
Filtered Ohio River water with persulphate of iron, Louisville, Ky.	35
Lynn, Mass.	4
Holyoke, Mass.	18
New York, N. Y.	15
Scranton, Pa.	64
Cincinnati, O.	20
St. Louis, Mo.	48
London, England	50
Liverpool, England	57
Manchester, England	19
Bradford, England	21
Birmingham, England	64
Glasgow, Scotland	9
Paris, France	30
Geneva, Switzerland	53
Vienna, Austria	20
St. Petersburg, Russia	40

With regard to the amounts of incrusting constituents in the water supplies of other cities it is not known how widely they may vary. The data are averages of all available results from reliable sources, but as a rule only one figure was given in a single work. In the case of most of the European results the figures appear to be given as representative ones, and it is believed that they suffice for the present purpose.

While the above evidence shows that the Ohio River water, after purification in which plain subsidence preceded coagulation with sulphate of alumina or persulphate of iron, would not be an especially soft water as viewed by Eastern standards, yet as compared with the waters of the Western part of this country it would not be an objectionable one, nor would this factor be of sufficient weight to offset the advantages of filtration.

Furthermore, it is possible to remove these incrusting constituents from the water by the application of caustic soda followed by subsidence or filtration. On the basis of $1.85 per 100 pounds for caustic soda, containing 60 per cent. available sodium oxide, the cost of chemical per million gallons of water to remove 1 part per million of incrusting constituents would be 12 cents.

In the judgment of the writer this step would not be justifiable so far as the entire supply is concerned, and it is hardly probable that it would be worth while for large manufacturing establishments to adopt it.

Corrosion of Iron Receptacles due to Changes in the Effluent Caused by the Use of Sulphates as Coagulants.

It has already been explained in detail that corrosion of uncoated iron is due chiefly to carbonic acid and dissolved oxygen in a water; and in 1897 it was learned that the degree of corrosion by the water would be greater after purification due simply to the removal of the suspended matter which served in a measure as a protective coating. With adequate facilities for the proper employment of subsidence, the amount of applied sulphate could be reduced much below that employed at times in 1895-96, and the increase in carbonic acid may be considered as follows:

PERCENTAGE INCREASE OF CARBONIC ACID (CARBON DIOXIDE) IN THE EFFLUENT ABOVE THAT IN THE RIVER WATER.

	Maximum.	Minimum.	Average.
With sulphate of alumina	41	2	9
With persulphate of iron	55	3	10

Expressing these changes in actual quantities, the following comparisons are obtained:

COMPARISON OF THE MAXIMUM AND AVERAGE AMOUNTS OF CARBON DIOXIDE IN THE EFFLUENT AND IN THE RIVER WATER.

(Parts per Million.)

	Maximum.	Average.
Ohio River water	133	70
Effluent with sulphate of alumina	145	76
Effluent with persulphate of iron	149	77

At this point it is to be stated that the evidence obtained in 1897 upon the corroding action of the effluent upon iron was very different (independent of the influence of suspended matter), and much more favorable than was the case with the limited data in 1896. The reasons for this are twofold.

1. In 1896 there were times when the applied sulphate of alumina for considerable periods averaged as high as from 6 to 8 grains per gallon: while in 1897 it was learned that with a proper use of subsidence the maximum limit could be held at about one-half of that stated above.

2. The limited data in 1896 indicated that the amount of free carbonic acid in the Ohio River water ranged from 20 to 30 parts per million, while the more extended series of operations in 1897 showed that the amount reached as high as 150 and averaged about 70 parts. Further, the later results showed that it was very seldom that the amount was less than 50 parts, clearly proving that the amounts found when in 1896 were abnormally low to an extreme degree. The explanation of this is not entirely known, but it was partly due to the inaccuracies of Pattenkofer's method of determining carbonic acid.

From these and other facts it was computed that the average percentage increase in carbonic acid was about 40 per cent. under the conditions and data of 1896, and only about 9 per cent. for 1897. Another very significant condition which obtained from time to time during the latter part of the tests of 1896, and which was absent in 1897, was the presence of undecomposed chemicals in the effluent. This was of great importance in this connection, because when corrosion is once started by an effluent containing sulphuric acid, the conditions are much more favorable for a continuance of the action by carbonic acid.

As has been stated repeatedly, the presence of undecomposed chemicals in the effluents is inadmissible for many reasons, and with proper subsidence facilities its occurrence would be inexcusable.

The carbonic acid liberated by the decomposition of carbonate of lime is the same, so far as its corroding nature is concerned, as an equal amount of carbonic acid naturally present in the water. As the results of a large number of experiments, under the conditions indicated to be most suitable for practical purification, it was found that the small increase in carbonic acid produced only very slightly greater corroding action than possessed by the river water after removing the suspended matter with a Pasteur filter. In fact in a large portion of the tests made in bottles with rods of bright wrought iron the increased corrosion was not appreciable.

To remove the small amounts of carbonic acid added to the water by the application of sulphate of alumina or persulphate of iron, and leave the large amounts naturally and normally present in the river water would be impracticable. The cost of chemical per million gallons for removing 1 part per million of carbonic acid, with lime at $3.75 per ton, would be 2.2 cents. As lime is only sparingly soluble in water it would be necessary to pump daily for a 25-million-gallon plant about 1750 gallons of water in order to prepare sufficient lime-water to remove 1 part per million of carbonic acid.

In view of the fact that corrosion would affect only such iron pipes or receptacles as were not properly coated with a protective paint, it would not be justifiable to remove carbonic acid to a point where it would not possess a corroding action. A better way would be to protect the piping system as it is extended as far as possible by protective paints, and to keep the quantities of applied chemicals as low as possible by taking full advantage of subsidence. With regard to the piping system already in service, it is probable that such portions as are not already protected by a coat of paint are protected in a considerable measure by the deposit of suspended matter of the water which has passed through them.

Action of the Effluent on Lead Pipe.

As in the case of unpurified Ohio River water, the effluent would contain enough carbonic acid and carbonate of lime to form very quickly basic carbonate of lead which is insoluble and makes an impervious protective coating.

SECTION No. 15.

COMPARATIVE COSTS OF EQUIVALENT AMOUNTS OF THE SEVERAL AVAILABLE COAGULANTS, TOGETHER WITH AN ESTIMATE OF THE YEARLY COST OF TREATMENT OF THE OHIO RIVER WATER BY EACH OF THEM.

As has been shown in the preceding sections of this chapter, the coagulants available for use in the purification of the Ohio River water are hydrate of alumina prepared by the decomposition of sulphate of alumina by the lime in the river water, hydrate of iron prepared by the similar decomposition of persulphate of iron, and hydrate of iron prepared by the electrolytical decomposition of metal plates. The relative advantages and disadvantages of each have been presented at considerable length both in absolute and comparative terms, and it remains to show the exact relative and annual costs of these three coagulants. In regard to the sulphates, this evidence has already been presented in a general way, but, for completeness, they will be taken up again here.

Comparative Cost of Equivalent Amounts of the Available Coagulants.

In section No. 6 of this chapter it was shown that the amounts of treatment with persulphate of iron and with electric current on iron electrodes, equivalent to 1 grain per gallon of sulphate of alumina (containing 9.87 per cent. of aluminum) were as follows: Persulphate of iron (containing 24.43 per cent. of iron), 1 grain per gallon; electric current on iron electrodes, 0.04 ampere-hour per gallon.

In regard to the two sulphates the comparison of cost is a simple one, but in regard to the electrolytically prepared coagulant there are several separate items which must be taken into consideration.

In the following comparisons no account is taken of cost of attendance, which would be slightly greater in the case of the electrolytic treatment than in the case of the sulphates. The cost of construction of devices for the application of the sulphates is also not considered as it would be comparatively small for a gravity flow, and, owing to the limitation in the amount of safe electrolytic treatment, these devices would be required in the use of any of the coagulants.

Cost of Electrolytic Treatment with Iron Electrodes.

In the cost of preparation of hydrate of iron by the action of an electric current on iron electrodes the following items must be considered:

1. Cost of construction of electrolytic cells.
2. Cost of construction of electrodes.
3. Cost of construction of electric generating appliances, together with the necessary building to cover them.
4. Cost of operation of electric appliances.
5. Cost of metal used in the formation of the hydrate and wasted in the process.

In this connection it is considered that the Water Company owns the necessary available land on which to construct the buildings and cells.

For the several items the following estimates of cost are used:

1. Cost of Construction of Electrolytic Cells.

As will be seen the practical size of the necessary cells would be so great that open channels of masonry would be, apparently, most suitable. For ease of handling it is assumed that plates 4 feet wide, 3 feet deep, and 0.5 inch thick would be employed for the electrodes. It is further assumed that a 0.5-inch length of electrolyte (water space between the plates) would be most advantageous.

With walls and bottom 1 foot thick the masonry required on this basis would be 0.090 cubic foot, or 0.00334 cubic yard per square foot of cross-section of electrolyte. At $30.00 per cubic yard the cost for masonry would therefore be $0.100 per square foot of cross-section of electrolyte. At 5 per cent. interest per annum this would represent an expenditure of $0.0000137 per day (or per twenty-five million gallons) for each square foot of electrolyte, or $0.0137 per 1000 square feet of electrolyte.

In the following computations the letters C. S. E. will be used to represent the cross-section of electrolyte in thousands of square feet.

2. Cost of Construction of Electrodes.

The area of one side of all plates would correspond practically to the area of cross-section of electrolyte. The weight of metal required would therefore be (on the above assumption of size of plates) approximately 20.0 pounds per square foot of cross-section of electrolyte, and would cost at 2 cents per pound (in place) 40 cents. The daily interest on this amount would be $0.0554 × C.S.E.

3. Cost of Construction of Electric Generating Appliances, together with the Necessary Building to Cover Them.

From preliminary estimates on the required size of these appliances it is assumed that they could be constructed at a cost of $170.00 per indicated H.P., or allowing one-third for a reserve plant, $220.00 per actual average I.H.P. The interest on this would be $0.030 per day, per I.H.P.

4. Cost of Operation of Electric Generating Appliances.

It is assumed that a combined efficiency of 80 per cent. could be expected, and that the consumption of coal would be 1.33 pounds per I.H.P. per hour.

The required amount of current to treat 25 million gallons per 24 hours with 0.04 ampere-hour per gallon would be 41,600 amperes.

Using the average resistance of the electrolyte as presented in section No. 3 of this chapter, 7000 ohms per centimeter cube or 9.65 ohms per square foot of cross-section of electrolyte with a 0.5-inch length of electrolyte (water space between plates), the required amount of power would be $\frac{17\,900}{\text{C.S.E.}}$.

The daily cost would be $\frac{\$571.00}{\text{C.S.E.}}$.

5. Cost of Metal Used in the Formation of the Hydrate and Wasted in the Process.

As was shown in section No. 4 of this chapter, the total amount of metal used in this process is 1.05 grams per ampere-hour. To treat 25 million gallons with 0.04 ampere-hour per gallon there would be required therefore 2305 pounds of metal, which at 2 cents per pound would cost $46.10.

Summary of Cost.

The several items may now be summed up as follows:

1. Daily interest on cost of construction on electrolytic cells, $0.0137 × C.S.E.

2. Daily interest on cost of construction of electrodes, $0.0554 × C.S.E.

3. Daily interest on cost of construction of electric generating appliances, $0.030 per I.H.P., or $\frac{\$537.00}{\text{C.S.E.}}$.

4. Daily cost of generating electric power, $0.0319 per I.H.P. per 24 hours, or $\frac{\$570.00}{\text{C.S.E.}}$.

5. Daily cost of metal used, $46.10.

Total ($0.0137 + $0.0554) × C.S.E.

$$+\frac{\$537+\$570}{\text{C.S.E.}}+\$46.10.$$

This is evidently a minimum when the values of the two variables are equal, or when the cross-section of the electrolyte is 126,500 square feet.

With this cross-section the potential difference between the plates would be $\frac{8.65\times41\,600}{126\,500}$, or 3.18 volts.

The cost would be as follows:

1. Electrolytic cells, 422 cubic yards masonry, daily interest........	$1.73
2. Electrodes, 1265 tons of iron, daily interest......................	7.00
3. Construction of generating appliances, 142 average actual indicated H.P., 42 I.H.P. reserve, daily interest.................	3.90

4. Operation of generating appliances, 142 average I.H.P., daily cost	4.51
5. Metal used per day	46.10
Total cost	$63.24

Cost of Treatment with Persulphate of Iron.

In regard to the sulphates it has already been show that their value is dependent upon the amount of available metal which they contain. In the purchase of these chemicals it is necessary, therefore, to consider their composition. The persulphate of iron which was used in these tests contained 24.43 per cent. of iron and was of approximately equal efficiency to sulphate of alumina containing 9.87 per cent. of aluminum. It is stated that this chemical could be purchased in carload lots F.O.B. cars, Louisville, for $1.25 per hundred pounds. To treat 25 million gallons with 1 grain per gallon would cost, therefore, $44.62.

Cost of Treatment with Sulphate of Alumina.

During the investigations of 1897 three different lots of sulphate of alumina were employed. These lots contained different amounts of alumina and were purchased at different prices as follows:

Lot.	Per Cent. Aluminum.	Cost per Pound in Car-load Lots F.O.B. Louisville.
A	9.87	1.50 cents
B	8.46	1.40 "
C	10.41	1.65 "

As the value of a coagulating chemical depends on the amount of hydrate forming metal which it contains, the costs of these three lots of chemicals must be reduced to the cost per pound of aluminum in order to compare them. These figures are as follows:

Lot.	Pounds Aluminum per Pound Sulphate.	Cost per Pound Aluminum.
A	0.0987	15.2 cents
B	0.0846	16.5 "
C	0.1041	15.9 "

The above comparisons illustrate the necessity of purchasing these chemicals by the amount of metal which they contain. In the purchase of large lots it would undoubtedly be best to receive bids based on the amount of available aluminum in the sulphate offered. In all of these estimates lot A is used as a basis.

The cost of treating 25 million gallons of water with 1 grain per gallon of lot A would be $53.55.

Summary.

The costs of treatment of 25 million gallons of Ohio River water with the equivalent of 1 grain per gallon of sulphate of alumina containing 9.87 per cent. of aluminum, by the three available coagulants, would be as follows:

Electrolytic iron treatment	$63.24
Persulphate of iron "	44.62
Sulphate of alumina "	53.55

Annual Cost of Treatment of Twenty-five Million Gallons Daily of Ohio River Water.

The average amounts of the different methods of treatment which would be required to purify the Ohio River water at Louisville have been presented in section No. 13 of this chapter. Combining the averages given there with the relative cost of the different treatments as given above, the average annual cost of treatment by the three methods of treatment is obtained as follows:

Estimated Average Annual Cost of Treatment.

Electrolytic iron	$40 400
Persulphate of iron	28 500
Sulphate of alumina	34 300

CHAPTER XVI.

FINAL SUMMARY AND CONCLUSIONS.

FOR the sake of convenience and explicitness, the leading points of practical significance are brought together in brief terms in this chapter. The circumstances under which the investigations and tests were conducted caused the evidence upon many of the points to appear in several chapters; but with the aid of the accompanying index detailed information upon the important features of the work may be obtained readily.

Character of the Unpurified Ohio River Water.

The suspended mud, silt, and clay in the Ohio River water make it in many respects an undesirable water for a municipal supply, and the large amounts and wide variations in the size and character of the suspended matter make it a difficult and expensive water to purify. With regard to the sanitary character of the river water, the large amounts, during the greater portion of the year, of suspended organic and mineral matter cannot be considered other than as objectionable, although there is no evidence to lead to the belief that these matters exert a specifically injurious effect upon persons in normal health. In fact it is in the low stages of the river when the water is comparatively clear that its hygienic character is least satisfactory. During the fall months there were repeatedly noted unmistakable signs of contamination of this water supply by the sewage of the cities located above it; and from time to time throughout the year, the conditions manifested themselves in the presence in the water of *bacillus coli communis*, which is the most prevalent germ in the feces of man and certain domestic animals. The result of all tests for specific germs of disease, however, were negative.

Practically speaking, the significance of this is that when the river is high and the water muddy the water is not dangerous, although it is not free of suspicion for drinking purposes. When the river is low and the water clear, however, the healthfulness of the water is always questionable, and the degree of danger which its use involves depends upon the prevalence of disease in the cities higher up in the valley. If an epidemic of cholera or typhoid fever should break out in any of the upper cities, there are at present no reliable means of preventing the specific germs of disease from passing in more or less diminished numbers from the outfall sewers of the upper city by the river, to and through the reservoir and distributing mains, to the service pipes of the water consumers at Louisville. It is true that several natural agencies such as dilution and sedimentation in the river and reservoir tend to remove these germs in a large measure, but such means cannot be depended upon now. As the population on the watershed increases, with no corresponding and compensating changes in the natural conditions causing the removal from the water of sewage germs, the healthfulness of the river water will continue to decrease steadily and surely. Under these conditions it is imperative that whatever method of purification be adopted, it shall be capable of protecting the water consumers from water-borne diseases, because if this were not done the expenditure of the large sums of money necessarily involved in purification would not be justifiable.

With regard to the storage and distribution of the unpurified Ohio River water, the amount of suspended matter in the water prevents the penetration of the rays of the sun, when stored in an open reservoir, to such a degree that under ordinary circumstances no growths occur of algæ, etc., which give rise to the objectionable tastes and odors. The water contains an ample supply, however, of soluble mineral matter suitable as a food for the micro-organisms. Carbonic and oxygen gases are dissolved in the water in such amounts that the water has considerable corroding action upon iron pipes which are not coated with a protective paint. This corroding action is much retarded by the suspended matters of the water, as they serve in a measure in forming protective coatings. The Ohio River water under the conditions met with in practice has no objectionable action on lead pipes, because the water quickly forms insoluble basic carbonate of lead which gives to the pipe an impervious protective coating.

For use in steam-boilers the Ohio River water is not very desirable when compared with the soft and clear waters of the East. Nevertheless, comparing it with the still harder waters met with farther West, it is fairly satisfactory for boiler use. When the river water is muddy it forms in boilers large amounts of sludge which are removed with much difficulty on some occasions, as this sludge cannot be "blown off." At such times the amounts of sulphate of lime and of other incrusting constituents are small and they are deposited upon the sludge for the most part and not upon the metal of the boilers. During the fall months, however, when the river water is fairly clear the amounts of incrusting constituents are much larger than usual, and the fine clay in the water at such times unites with the sulphate of lime, etc., to form a scale resembling cement and which is very difficult to remove.

Applicability to the Purification of the Ohio River Water of the Three Methods Investigated during these Tests.

Three methods of purification were tested with general results as follows:

1. The general method embodying subsidence (sedimentation), coagulation, and filtration, such as was practiced in part in the Warren, Jewell, and two Western systems, is correct in principle for the practicable purification of this water. It had several weaknesses, as practiced in these tests, the most important one being the totally inadequate facilities in all cases for the employment of subsidence to its proper economical limits. This is shown more clearly beyond.

2. The Harris Magneto-Electric System was a complete failure.

3. The MacDougall Polarite System as it was tested by this Company was not applicable to the purification of the Ohio River water.

Imperativeness of the Use of Coagulants.

Owing to the fact that at times this river water contains large amounts of very minute clay particles (many of which are as small as 0.00001 inch in diameter), it may be stated in unqualified terms that at least for several successive weeks in the spring and early summer, successful and economical purification of this water makes the use of coagulation imperative in connection with subsidence.

Whether or not it is absolutely essential or desirable to employ coagulation in connection with filtration of a properly subsided water is a problem which would depend upon the rate of filtration, but upon which no specific data were obtained in these tests.

Relative Applicability of American and English Types of Filters.

With regard to the filtration of the Ohio River water after partial purification by plain subsidence and subsidence aided at times by coagulation, by the American and English types of filters, no comparisons were made during these investigations. Taking into consideration, however, the general information obtained in these tests as to the character of the water, combined with the results of the tests made with English filters in 1884, the indications point to the superiority of the American filters for this water, owing to their improved facilities for cleansing the sand layer. Here it may be noted that the tests in 1884–85 were made for about eight months in tanks 12 feet in diameter. The water passing on to the filter was subsided for about six days in the Crescent Hill reservoir without coagulants. During this period the excessive amounts of fine clay, as found frequently in the spring, were largely absent. The filters were constructed after the English plan, as recommended and described by Kirkwood, and the sand had an effective size of 0.36 millimeter. This agrees very closely with the size of sand employed in the best filters in Europe.

As a result of the tests of 1884-85 it was learned that the clay could be removed and an effluent free of turbidity secured by English filters at a net rate of about 1.5 million gallons per acre daily. But the principal point of practical significance was the marked indication of the clay passing into the sand layer, and the necessity of cleaning and reconstructing the sand layer at periods of comparatively short duration.

Removal of Coarse Matters by Plain Subsidence.

The entire absence of this very important and essential feature of successful purification of water of this character comprised the greatest weakness of all the systems tested. This subject was given considerable attention on a laboratory scale, and it was found that with ordinary muddy water about 24 hours of quiescent subsidence in one-gallon bottles caused a removal of about 75 per cent. of the suspended matters by weight. As it is well known that on a large scale the quiescent state of the water cannot be obtained in so short a time, the above period is only of passing significance in connection with laboratory experiments, and for the most practicable conditions on a large scale it is necessary to rely upon information from other sources. This subject is dealt with in section No. 1 of Chapter XV, and it may be added that in practice the period should, in all probability, be much longer than 24 hours.

Most Suitable Coagulant for the Ohio River Water.

All things taken into consideration, the most suitable coagulant at present for the treatment of the Ohio River water is sulphate of alumina. Persulphate of iron in equivalent amounts is now slightly cheaper, but the difference is not sufficient to offset certain advantages of sulphate of alumina.

The electrolytic production of aluminum hydrate from metallic aluminum electrodes is impracticable, both on the grounds of excessive cost and of irregularities in efficiency. With regard to the electrolytic production of iron hydrate from iron electrodes this process yields a satisfactory coagulant up to the equivalent of 3 grains per gallon of sulphate of alumina. Beyond this point it could not be safely employed in midsummer, when the amount of dissolved oxygen in the water is inadequate to oxidize larger quantities. Combining the cost, the limitations in the amount which can be safely applied without the presence of iron in the effluent and certain irregularities upon reversing the direction of the electric current, this process is not considered advisable.

Concerning the Anderson process for the preparation of iron hydrate directly from metallic iron, the results of laboratory tests indicate that it is not applicable for the economic and efficient purification of the Ohio River water.

Of the various chemicals mentioned in section No. 2 of Chapter XV, no others were found practicable.

Preparation and Application of Solutions of Alumina.

The method of dissolving known amounts of the chemical in known volumes of water is the best.

The passage of a stream of water through a cylinder containing the chemical is not practicable.

Concerning the application of the solutions of the chemical the Warren device was fairly automatic, but possessed several faults, the chief one of which was the failure in the operation of the device when the flow of water fell below a certain quantity. The pumps used in the Jewell and modified Western systems were satisfactory, but required great care and close attention.

Taking everything into consideration it is believed that in practice the discharge of a solution by gravity would be the most advisable.

Coagulation and Subsidence.

In addition to plain subsidence and to coagulation given to water just prior to filtration, there are times when coagulation in conjunction with subsidence can be employed to advantage in keeping clay and other suspended matters from passing on to the sand layer. Such times would occur in practice when the water after plain subsidence would require more than from 1.5 to 2.0 grains per gallon of sulphate of alumina for thorough coagulation. In this respect all of the systems were lacking, although the practical significance of this point was realized by the operators of the Warren System, as shown by their division of the application of coagulants in July, 1896.

With regard to the optimum period of time to provide for the accomplishment of coagulation and subsidence, it would vary according to the amount and character of the suspended matters present in the water after plain subsidence had taken place. The indications are that it might reach or exceed 6 hours in many instances, but the economic period would be limited by the cost of subsiding facilities.

Coagulation and Filtration.

After the river water has been properly treated by subsidence for the removal of suspended matters, it is imperative that the water as it reaches the sand layer be thoroughly coagulated from a practical point of view. In the absence of complete coagulation, or very nearly complete, the efficiency of filtration cannot be uniformly depended upon.

Concerning the optimum period of coagulation of the water prior to filtration, it would vary widely from time to time in the purification of this water. When the water contains very little suspended matter the period should probably be not more than half an hour. But as the quantity of suspended matter increases, the period of coagulation (and supplementary subsidence) should increase. In some cases the optimum period would be at least 3 hours, and probably longer. The longest period of course would be found when the amount of coagulant fell just below the point where economy demands a division in the application (1.50 to 2.00 grains per gallon).

Point of Application of Coagulant with Reference to the Period of Time Elapsing between Application and the Entrance of the Water into the Sand Layer.

The results of these investigations prove conclusively that at the present time no fixed point of application of coagulant would fulfill the demands of economy. In the light of our present knowledge, the devices for the application of coagulant should be made adjustable with reference to the point of application. Whether or not it would ever be practicable in the treatment of this water to confine the application of coagulants to a range of three or four points can be told only by experience under the conditions of successful practice.

Total Annual Average Amounts of Sulphate of Alumina Required for Coagulation.

Taking into consideration the fact that two periods of extended droughts occurred during the tests of 1895–96, the data show that with the systems tested at that time the annual average amounts of sulphate of alumina would range from 2.5 to 3.5, and average about 3.0 grains per gallon of filtered water.

By taking advantage of subsidence to its economical limit, the investigations of 1897 indicate clearly that this could be held at from 1.5 to 2.0 grains, with an annual average of about 1.75 grains.

In these comparisons it is assumed that in each case a good grade of sulphate of alumina would be used.

Filtration.

In respect to filtration proper, independent of subsidence and coagulation, the Jewell filter on the whole was found to be more satisfactory than the others examined in these tests.

The capacity of filters of this type is considered to be 100 million gallons of filtered water per acre daily. This means that to obtain one million gallons of filtered water in 24 hours it would be necessary to provide 435.6 square feet of filtering surface. To rate these filters at a lower capacity is out of question, and the indications are that when the bulk of the suspended matters is removed by subsidence, and the operation of a system placed on a practical basis, this capacity could be safely increased to meet the increased consumption of water. It is probable that this capacity under the stated conditions could be raised 50 per cent. with satisfactory results.

The Jewell filter did not contain all of the best features of filters of this type, especially when compared with the Warren filter, and it could be improved in a number of ways, both with regard to construction and operation. An outline of the more important features which successful filters in practice should comprise is as follows:

Essential Features of American Filters for the Successful Filtration of Twenty-five Million Gallons of Ohio River Water Daily.

Experience obtained during these investigations shows the practical importance of the following points:

Condition of the Water Entering the Sand Layer.—The evidence is very decisive that so far as practicable the suspended matters should be removed before reaching the sand layer, and that, at that point, the water should be thoroughly coagulated. Further, it is clear that subsidence should be employed with waters of this character to a degree where the amount of coagulant to be applied at or just before the entrance to the filter should not frequently exceed 2 grains per gallon.

Failure to make suitable provisions in this respect caused the Western gravity filter to be voluntarily withdrawn from the tests because it was unable to purify enough water, when the river water was very muddy, to wash its own sand layer; and in the two best filters, the Warren and Jewell, it may be conservatively stated that to maintain the full supply at times of heavy freshets it would be necessary to provide reserve filters equal to 75 per cent. of the normal capacity of the plant. Furthermore, the failure in these systems to remove the coarser particles by subsidence would in practice cause a large waste of coagulants, as stated above.

Structure of Filters. — For a permanent plant the use of metal, as in the case of the Western pressure filter, would be preferable to wood. The foul odors in the bottom of the Warren filter when it was removed at the close of the tests, shows an objection to the use of wood for closed compartments.

Size of Filters.—The several filters represent the prevailing size in practice, but for economy in operation the individual filters should be made much larger, the limit to be determined by the successful operation of mechanical appliances to stir the sand layer effectively while it is being washed by a reverse flow of water.

Location of Sand Layers.—The location of the sand layer near the top of the filter tank, as in the case of the Jewell filter, is an advantage, because it guards against the waste of coagulated water above the sand layer just prior to washing and it would also reduce the cost of construction.

Character of Sand Layers.—Experience indicates that in all cases the frictional resistance to the flow of water was too small. This could be remedied by using a sand of finer grain or a layer of greater thickness, or both. In the judgment of the writer it would be advisable to maintain a thickness of 30 inches and employ a sand having an effective size of 0.35 millimeter. This would increase the frictional resistance of the sand layer in the Jewell filter about 50 per cent., other conditions being equal.

Filtered Water Exits.—The Western filter did not satisfactorily meet this difficult problem, as the sand passed into the slotted brass tubes. In the Warren filter there was little chance for lateral and irregular flow of water at the bottom of the sand layer, except as caused by the supports beneath the perforated plate. All things considered, it is believed that the Jewell filter was superior in this respect, although it would probably be advisable to double the number of strainer cups.

Amount and Nature of Pressure (Head).—The indications are that 10 feet for a maximum acting head would be advisable under the conditions of practice. So far as could be learned the negative head (suction) in the Jewell filter gave directly no advantages over a positive head with regard to the efficiency of the filter. In consequence of a negative head, however, there are several advantages as noted above in connection with the waste of coagulated water and the cost of construction.

There were no indications that the use of a pressure filter, as represented in the Western pressure filter, would be advisable in purifying this water supply.

Rate of Filtration.—The evidence and conclusions upon this point are presented above in reference to the capacity of filters.

Washing the Sand Layer. — Experience showed that when the sand layer requires washing it should be done thoroughly with filtered water, and that accompanying agitation of the sand layer is an advantage. The agitator of the Jewell filter was of a type superior to that in the Warren filter, but the teeth of the rake arms should penetrate as nearly to the bottom of the sand layer as safety would allow.

Surface Agitation.—This process could be profitably employed to a greater degree in practice than was the case in the Jewell filter, the only one of these filters in which advantage of this was taken at all. In practice the filter tank should be designed so as to allow the water above the sand, together with the surface accumulations, to be flushed off into the sewer during agitation. The use of a finer sand would also be an advantage in this connection.

Application of Caustic Soda.—From time to time the use of caustic soda, to keep the sand free of matters which are absorbed and attached to it, is advisable.

Attention.—This is a very important factor in the efficiency of filters of this type in the purification of the Ohio River water, and economy as well as efficiency demands that they shall receive skilled attention, especially to prevent a waste of coagulants. With suitable provisions for subsidence, the necessary amount of care and skill would be much less than indicated by these tests, after the plant had been placed upon a practical and systematic basis of operation.

Accessibility of Parts.—Improvements in all of these filters should be made with regard to accessibility of parts, in order to facilitate examination and repairs whenever necessary.

Quality of the Ohio River Water after Purification by Coagulation and Filtration, preceded by Subsidence so far as Practicable.

With proper attention to the operation of a system as outlined above, and an adequate degree of coagulation (by sulphate of alumina) of the water as it enters the sand layer, this method could produce a quality of filtered water which would be thoroughly satisfactory under all ordinary conditions with regard to appearance and sanitary character.

Owing to the inherent character of the Ohio River water and the local conditions, the filtered water could not be stored in open reservoirs, except for very short periods, with any reasonable assurance that algæ, etc., coming from the air would not grow in the presence of sunlight and give to the water objectionable odors and tastes. To guard against this effectively the reservoir in which the filtered water is stored should be covered.

The filtered water would not give any trouble in the case of lead pipes, or in iron pipes which are properly coated with protective paints. In uncoated iron vessels the corrosive action would be somewhat greater than in the case of river water, owing principally to the removal of suspended matters, which in a measure act as a protective coating. With regard to use in steam-boilers there would be more incrusting constituents than in the river water, although the annual average amount in the filtered water would be only about 60 per cent. of the quantity normally present in the river water during the fall months. The effect of this addition would be largely if not wholly offset by the removal of the suspended matters; and, compared with the waters of other cities, it would be classed as a satisfactory boiler water.

Final Conclusion.

The general method of subsidence, coagulation, and filtration is applicable to the satisfactory purification of the Ohio River water at Louisville; but, as practiced by the Warren, Jewell, and Western systems during these tests, its practicability is very questionable if not inadmissible. By removing the bulk of the suspended matters from the water, large reductions could be made in the size of filter plant, amount of coagulant, and cost of operation. On the basis of twenty-five million gallons daily, these reductions when capitalized at 5 per cent. would represent about $700,000. There is no room for doubt but that for a less sum than this satisfactory provisions for subsidence as outlined herein could be provided, which would not only aid in furnishing a filtered water of better quality, but would also give the water consumers a better service in other regards.

Very respectfully submitted,

GEORGE W. FULLER,

Chief Chemist and Bacteriologist.

LOUISVILLE, KY., Oct. 7, 1897.

APPENDIX.

THE appendix consists of a brief technical résumé of the methods of analysis which were employed during these tests and investigations, together with some notes on the collection of samples.

COLLECTION OF SAMPLES.

The only departure from the standard methods and technique of collection of samples was in the use of a device termed the "automatic sampler."

Automatic Sampler.—For the purpose of collecting samples which should be representative of the effluent for long periods of time, the device described below was arranged and used during March, April, and early part of May. 1896, for the collection of samples from all the systems, and from May 11 to July 23, 1896, for the collection of samples for chemical analysis from the Western Pressure System. The device consisted of a brass cylinder (A) closed at one end, of about 5 cubic centimeters capacity, and with a single orifice on one side. This cylinder was ground into a covering cylinder (B) in which it was revolved by a feathering paddle-wheel in the main effluent pipe. The wheel was operated by the current and was designed to turn at a rate proportional to the flow of water through the pipe. A small pipe led from the opposite side of B to the collecting bottle. The openings for these pipes and for the orifice in A were in the same plane. An air pipe with protected end was provided from cylinder A, as was also an escape from the collecting bottle. The operation was as follows: As cylinder A revolved its orifice connected with the inlet orifice through cylinder B and water from the effluent pipe entered and filled cylinder A and the air tube. As cylinder A turned, it cut off the connection with the inlet pipe, and when one-half around, connected with the outlet orifice through cylinder B and the contents of the cylinder and air tube were discharged through the outlet tube into the collecting bottle. In this manner a small sample was taken at each revolution, the gearing being so proportioned that at the normal rate of 23.5 cubic feet per minute, about six samples were taken each minute. A gallon bottle was used as a collecting bottle. The whole device was inclosed in a wooden box.

REGULAR CHEMICAL ANALYSES.

Form of Expression.

The results of the determinations of the several chemical constituents are expressed in this report in parts by weight per million parts of water by volume. This form was adopted mainly for the reason that the results of a previous series of analyses for this Company had been expressed in this manner.

Turbidity.

During the early part of these tests, use was made of the adjectives commonly employed in describing the results of inspection of the samples as they appeared after settling over night in one-gallon bottles. During 1896 a "diaphanometer" was used for a time. This instrument consisted of a brass tube in which the sample of water was placed and through which light was reflected from a Welsbach gas lamp. The turbidity of the water was estimated as the reciprocal of the length of a column of water which would cause the image of a cross of black lines at the bottom of the tube to disappear. Fairly satisfactory results were obtained with waters of a slight but noticeable turbidity; but it appeared to be inadequate for regular use in this connection with satisfactory results upon the fairly clear effluents or very muddy river water.

Sediment.

The relative amounts of sediment in the river water were estimated in the early part of the work by inspection of the samples after settling over night in one-gallon bottles. These observations seemed to be of but little value, and later were abandoned, comparison of sediment then being made upon the parts by weight of suspended matter.

Odor.

The odor of the water at room temperature and after heating in a beaker to 100° C. was observed and recorded, respectively, as the "cold" and "hot odor," in substantially the same manner as described by Drown in the Report upon the Examination of Water Supplies by the Mass. State Board of Health, 1890, Part I.

Color.

The dissolved color of the water was measured by the platinum-cobalt standards of Hazen, as described in the American Chemical Journal, Vol. XIV, page 300.

Oxygen Consumed.

The Kübel method was used in substantially the same form as described by Drown in the Report of the Mass. State Board of Health for 1892, page 328.

In this determination the period of boiling with potassium permanganate exerts great influence on the results obtained; and, furthermore, this period differs considerably in different laboratories. It was the custom here to boil exactly five minutes after adding the potassium permanganate, the water and sulphuric acid having been previously raised to the boiling temperature. In order that the results obtained in this laboratory may be compared with previous work at other places, the following average results of a number of experiments are presented.

EXPERIMENTS TO SHOW THE EFFECT OF DIFFERENT PERIODS OF BOILING ON THE AMOUNT OF OXYGEN CONSUMED.

Sample.	Time of Boiling. Minutes.	Oxygen Consumed. Parts per Million.
Ohio River water........................	2	5.4
" " "	5	6.8
" " "	10	8.5
" " " filtered without coagulant	2	1.9
" " " " " "	5	2.3
" " " " " "	10	2.8
" " " " with coagulant...	2	0.7
" " " " " " ...	5	1.4
" " " " " " ...	10	1.4

Nitrogen as Albuminoid Ammonia.

The method of Wanklyn as modified by Drown, Hazen, and Clark was used substantially as described in the Report of the Mass. State Board of Health for 1890, Part II, page 710, and also in the American Chemical Journal, Vol. XII, page 425.

Determinations of the "total" nitrogen as albuminoid ammonia were made on the unfiltered water; of the "dissolved" after the passage of the water through filter-paper or a Pasteur filter. And the "suspended" nitrogen as albuminoid ammonia was obtained by difference.

Nitrogen as Free Ammonia.

The method of Wanklyn was used as described by Drown, Hazen, and Clark in connection with the nitrogen as albuminoid ammonia, referred to above.

Nitrogen as Nitrites.

In the determination of nitrogen as nitrites the Griess-Warrington method was used, as described by Drown and Hazen in the Report of the Mass. State Board of Health for 1890, Part II, page 715.

Nitrogen as Nitrates.

The "aluminum method" was used as modified by Hazen and Clark and described in the Report of the Mass. State Board of Health for 1890, Part II, page 711.

The following method was employed in the preparation of nitrate-free water used in blanks. Eight liters of ordinary distilled water were treated with 100 cubic centimeters of a 50 per cent. sodium hydrate solution, and 5 grams of pure aluminum foil. After some hours the water was placed in a still with 3 grams of potassium permanganate and distilled. The middle portion of the distillate was free from nitrates.

In preparing the sodium hydrate solution one liter of this water and 250 grams of the purest sodium hydrate obtainable were brought together in a porcelain dish with about 2 grams of pure aluminum foil. When the foil was all dissolved, the solution was boiled down to a volume of 500 cubic centimeters, and, after being allowed to settle, filtered through asbestos.

Two cubic centimeters of this solution with 50 cubic centimeters of water and 0.35 gram of aluminum foil, should indicate the presence of only a very slight amount of ammonia when treated in the same manner as samples for analysis.

Chlorine.

Chlorine was determined according to the method of Mohr, as modified by Hazen and described in the American Chemical Journal, Vol. XI, page 409.

Residue on Evaporation.

For this determination 100 cubic centimeters of the water were evaporated to dryness on a water bath, in a platinum dish of known weight. After drying in a steam oven (temperature 96° to 98° C.) for two hours, the dish with its contents was cooled in a desiccator over sulphuric acid and weighed. This gave the "total" residue on evaporation. A similar determination on the filtered sample gave the "dissolved" and the difference between these two gave the "suspended" residue on evaporation.

Fixed Residue after Ignition.

The fixed residue after ignition was determined by igniting the residue on evaporation at a low heat in a radiator, and weighing as usual after cooling in a desiccator.

Alkalinity.

The method of Hehner for determining the alkalinity was used as described in Leffmann's Examination of Water, edition of 1895, page 82. Owing to the fact that the color of the Ohio River water on many occasions obscures the end point when methyl orange is used as an indicator, lacmoid was employed in the hot sample. Methyl orange as procured at this laboratory was also lacking in sensitiveness. Furthermore, this indicator is incapable of showing the presence of undecomposed sulphate of alumina, a property which is possessed by lacmoid.

The determinations of alkalinity with lacmoid as an indicator, in preference to temporary hardness by the soap method, were necessary in this work for two reasons:

1. Normal carbonates, which are determined as permanent hardness or incrusting constituents by the soap method, have the power of decomposing sulphate of alumina in the same manner as the temporary-hardness constituents.

2. The presence of undecomposed chemicals (sulphates) in the effluent is not shown by the ordinary temporary-hardness determination, but is readily detected by the alkalinity determination when lacmoid is employed as an indicator, as the sulphate of alumina reacts acid to this indicator.

The alkalinity determination, therefore, is a measure of the capacity of the water for decomposing sulphate of alumina, and an acid reaction to lacmoid indicates the presence of this chemical in an undecomposed form.

Incrusting Constituents—Permanent Hardness.

The salts determined by the Hehner permanent-hardness method have been classed as incrusting constituents, and the normal carbonates have been determined as alkalinity. The reasons for this are presented above. This method is described by Leffmann in Examination of Water, edition of 1895, page 82.

Total Hardness.

In regard to the total hardness of the water as indicated by its soap-destroying power, the sum of the determinations of the alkalinity and incrusting constituents is comparable to such results, although not necessarily identical.

Dissolved Alumina.

For the determination of dissolved alumina the method of Richards was used as described in Leffmann's Examination of Water, edition of 1895, page 58.

Iron.

For the determination of iron the general method of Thompson was used, as described in Leffmann's Examination of Water, edition of 1895, page 57.

Dissolved Oxygen.

The method for the determination of dissolved oxygen devised by Winkler and modified by Drown and Hazen was used as described in the Report of the Mass. State Board of Health for 1890, Part II, page 722.

Carbonic Acid (Carbon Dioxide).

The determination of carbonic acid (carbon dioxide) in the water was made according to Trillich's modification of Pettenkofer's method, substantially as described in Ohlmüller's Untersuchung des Wassers, edition of 1896.

MINERAL ANALYSES.

Silica, Barium, Strontium, Iron, Aluminum, Nickel, and Manganese.

The methods employed in the determinations of silica, barium, strontium, iron, aluminum, nickel, and manganese, were as follows:

Silica.—One or two liters of the water (depending upon its character) were acidulated by the addition of 20 cubic centimeters of hydrochloric acid, and evaporated to dryness. The dish containing the residue was transferred to an air bath, and heated to 130° C., until the hydrochloric acid was driven off. There were then added 10 cubic centimeters of hydrochloric acid and 150 cubic centimeters of distilled water, and the whole was gently warmed. The silica was filtered off, washed, dried, ignited, and weighed. The residue was then treated with hydrofluoric and sulphuric acids, and the process repeated. The difference in weight of the residue before and after this latter treatment was taken as the amount of silica present.

Barium and Strontium.—Any residue remaining after the treatment with hydrofluoric and sulphuric acids was fused with sodium carbonate, and the barium and strontium precipitated and weighed together as sulphates.

Iron and Aluminum.—The filtrate after the removal of silica, barium and strontium was treated for iron, manganese, etc., as follows: The iron and aluminum were separated by the basic acetate method, the combined oxides weighed, and the aluminum determined by difference, the iron being first determined by the Thompson colorometric method already referred to.

Nickel and Manganese.—The filtrate from the iron and aluminum determination was rendered slightly acid by the addition of acetic acid, and nickel, if present, was precipitated with hydrogen sulphide, and the manganese separated in the filtrate after neutralization by the addition of ammonium sulphide.

Calcium and Magnesium.

The filtrate from the manganese determination was boiled and filtered if necessary, and the calcium and magnesium determined by precipitation as calcium oxalate and magnesium pyrophosphate, respectively.

Sulphuric Acid.

One liter of the water was evaporated to dryness in a porcelain dish with 10 cubic centimeters of hydrochloric acid. The silica was removed (see silica determination) and the sulphur determined by precipitation as barium sulphate.

Phosphoric Acid.

The phosphoric acid was precipitated from the filtrate obtained in the determination of the sulphuric acid by ammonium molybdate. The "yellow precipitate" was dissolved in ammonia and the phosphorus determined as magnesium pyrophosphate.

Sodium and Potassium.

Two liters of the water were evaporated to dryness in a platinum dish with 20 cubic centimeters of hydrochloric acid. The residue was taken up with water, a few crystals of barium hydrate added and the solution boiled. The solution was cooled and the precipitate allowed to settle. The volume was then made up to 250 cubic centimeters and 200 cubic centimeters were filtered off. Ammonium carbonate and ammonium oxalate in the solid form were added to the filtrate and the mixture brought to a boil. After cooling the volume was again made up to 250 cubic centimeters and 200 cubic centimeters filtered off. Manganese or nickel, if present in sufficient amount to interfere, were precipitated as sulphides.

The filtrate was evaporated to dryness in a platinum dish, sufficient sulphuric or hydrochloric acid being added to unite with the sodium and potassium. After ignition to expel ammonium salts, redissolving in hot water, filtering and evaporating to dryness, the potassium and sodium were ignited and weighed as sulphates or chlorides according to the acid added.

The percentages of potassium and sodium in the mixture were calculated after determining the common constituent (*i.e.*, the Cl or SO_3) from the formula given by E. K. Landis, Jour. Amer. Chem. Soc., Feb., 1896.

QUANTITATIVE BACTERIAL ANALYSES.

The general technique of the quantitative bacterial methods used in these investigations was substantially the same as in the case of those described by Fuller and Copeland in the Report of the Mass. State Board of Health for 1895, page 585. A brief summary of some of the principal features is as follows:

Culture Media Regularly Employed for Quantitative Work.

At the outset of these investigations glycerine agar was used as the culture medium, owing to its adaptability under the existing local conditions. The laboratory itself had a widely variable temperature, owing to climatic conditions and to the presence in the building of a number of steam-pipes used for heating and general laboratory purposes. The fact that, at a number of points on the steam-pipes between the laboratory and the boilers, steam was used from time to time in varying amounts by the experimental devices, caused the steam pressure to vary; and in consequence it was difficult to regulate the laboratory temperature. The maintenance of a uniform temperature in the thermostat was difficult, also, on account of the necessity of using gasoline gas which varied widely not only in quality but in pressure.

Under these circumstances glycerine agar was at first selected as the culture medium with the view to getting satisfactory data upon the efficiency of the filters and at the same time preventing heavy losses of data which seemed imminent with the use of gelatine. The precaution was taken, however, of making comparative studies of the numbers of bacteria obtained by glycerine agar and gelatine, respectively. As a result of these studies it was found that while satisfactory data could be obtained for comparing the efficiency of the several filters, yet the actual numbers of bacteria were normally, but not always, materially lower when glycerine agar was used than in the case of gelatine.

Accordingly, when the scope of the investigations was enlarged on Feb. 1, 1896, it was decided to adopt nutrient gelatine as the regular culture medium, and to guard against loss of results through liquefaction of the medium by employing a sufficiently low temperature for incubation.

Reaction of Culture Media.

After considerable study it was found that the reaction of media used in the regular quantitative work which gave the most satisfactory results under the local conditions was

1.5 per cent. (equal to 15 cubic centimeters of normal hydrochloric acid added to every liter of neutral medium), especially in the case of the effluent, and this reaction was, therefore, maintained throughout the tests. The relative effects of reactions ranging from 0.5 to 2.0 per cent. are shown in the following table of average results:

BACTERIA PER CUBIC CENTIMETER ON GELATINE OF DIFFERENT REACTIONS.

Sample.		Bacteria per Cubic Centimeter.			
		Reaction (per cents.).			
Source.	Number of Determinations.	0.5	1.0	1.5	2.0
River water	41	22 700	22 700	22 900	17 700
Effluent	33	118	248	298	243

Sterilization and Dilution.

Sterilization.—All glassware, such as Petri dishes, pipettes, sample bottles, etc., were sterilized for one and one-half hours in a hot-air sterilizer at a temperature of 150 degrees C., or a little higher. All media and water for dilution purposes were autoclaved for 10 minutes under a steam pressure of 20 pounds.

Dilution.—In the case of the river water when it contained high numbers of bacteria, one cubic centimeter of the sample was diluted in 100 cubic centimeters of sterile distilled water, and in the case of very turbid effluents a dilution of 1 to 10 was used.

Period and Temperature of Cultivation.

The normal period of cultivation employed was 4 days in an ice-chest 10 feet long in which the bacterial compartment and ice compartment were in the opposite ends. In some cases, however, when the temperature of the bacterial compartment fell below 16 to 18 degrees C., a longer period was allowed in order that the maximum growth might be more nearly obtained. It was deemed advisable at times, owing to the local conditions facilitating melting and liquefaction of the gelatine, to maintain a low temperature in this compartment, and thus guard more effectively against the possibility of loss of plates through liquefaction. Owing to this precautionary procedure the loss of plates due to this cause was trifling, and it is believed that it was more advantageous to prevent the possibility of loss of data upon samples which were collected under conditions which might not occur again, than to strive at all times towards the maximum possible growth. It is to be noted, further, that the conditions were the same for all samples at the same time, and thus strictly comparable results were obtained in the case of the respective filters.

The relation between the fourth and successive day growths and the influence exerted by temperatures ranging from 10 to 18 degrees C., are indicated by the results and percentages presented in the next table. In 1897 temperatures of less than 14 degrees C. were avoided so far as possible by partially opening the door of the ice-chest as occasion demanded. So far as our knowledge goes the bacterial results obtained during the investigations are very appreciably higher than would be obtained by two days' cultivation at 20 degrees C., which is the conventional procedure in Europe.

SUMMARY SHOWING THE RELATION BETWEEN FOURTH-, FIFTH-, AND SIXTH-DAY GROWTHS OF BACTERIA ON GELATINE AT DIFFERENT TEMPERATURES.

Number of Samples Averaged.	Range of Temperature. Degrees C.	Source of Sample.	Bacteria per Cubic Centimeter.			Percentage Increase.	
			Fourth Day.	Fifth Day.	Sixth Day.	Fourth to Fifth Day.	Fourth to Sixth Day.
27	10–12	River water......	20 500	29 600	31 700	44.4	54.6
39	10–12	Effluent..........	159	211	395	32.7	142.1
42	12–14	River water......	23 900	32 700	47 000	36.8	96.7
37	12–14	Effluent..........	173	397	341	129.5	97.1
10	14–16	River water......	14 500	....	19 900	....	37.2
34	14–16	Effluent..........	257	....	338	....	31.5
7	16–18	River water......	12 200	14 100	12 100	15.6	0.0
68	16–18	Effluent..........	155	167	170	7.7	9.7

In the next table are presented the monthly averages of temperatures of the quantitative bacterial compartment.

MONTHLY AVERAGES OF THE TEMPERATURE OF THE QUANTITATIVE BACTERIAL COMPARTMENT.

	1895.		1896.								1897.						Total Averages.
	Nov.	Dec.	Jan.	Feb.	Mar.	Apr.	May.	June.	July.	Aug.	Feb.	Mar.	Apr.	May.	June.	July.	
Maximum....	22.0	20.7	20.1	12.8	14.6	14.2	16.9	16.8	19.4	15.0	16.1	15.2	16.1	17.7	19.5	19.0	17.3
Minimum....	19.6	20.2	19.2	10.7	10.3	11.7	15.0	15.8	16.7	14.0	15.1	14.0	15.5	15.5	18.0	16.7	15.4
Mean........	20.8	20.4	19.6	11.8	12.5	13.0	16.0	16.3	18.0	14.5	15.6	14.6	15.8	16.6	18.7	17.9	16.4

Qualitative Bacterial Analyses.

The qualitative bacterial work was divided into examinations for sewage bacteria, notably *B. coli communis*, and a comparison of the species of bacteria in the water before and after purification, with an incidental classification of the more common forms of bacteria.

Comparison of Species.

For this purpose the methods and tests were employed as found in the best manuals, and they were usually in harmony with modifications suggested at the Convention of Bacteriologists held at New York in June, 1895.

Examinations for B. coli communis.

The method of procedure in the search for this organism was substantially the same as that recommended by Smith in the American Journal of the Medical Sciences for Sept., 1895. Dextrose and lactose broths were both used for this work and the reactions of all solutions used in the fermentation test were adjusted to an alkalinity of 1.5 per cent. A temperature of 37 degrees C. was employed in all the tests covering the examination for this species, and all cultures (with the exception of the fermentation cultures, which were allowed to develop for four days) were allowed to develop for 48 hours before observations were made. The cultures were started in flasks containing 100 cubic centimeters of sterile nutrient dextrose broth, 50 cubic centimeters of water being used each time for inoculation. Lactose litmus agar plates were made from these cultures, and from these plates colonies which presented in two days an appearance resembling that of *B. coli communis* were transferred to gelatine tube, agar tube, peptone solution, litmus milk, and fermentation tube. Observations were made after the customary period of two days on the gelatine and agar tube cultures, microscopically for size and biologically for a characteristic growth; on the peptone solution for indol production; and on the litmus milk for coagulation both before and after boiling. The fermentation culture was inspected day by day, the quantity of gas recorded; and on the fourth day the total gas, the percentage of carbon dioxide, and the end reaction were determined.

CONVERSION TABLES.

There are given in the next tables the relations which exist between different methods of expression of several quantities which are used in connection with this report. Conversion can be made from one form of expression to another by the use of the corresponding multiplication factors as given in these tables.

Table No. II is copied from Kirkwood's Filtration of River Water.

Table No. I.

CONVERSION OF STATEMENTS OF CHEMICAL COMPOSITION.

	Grains per U. S. Gallon. (231 cubic inches.)	Grains per British Gallon. (277 cubic inches.)	Parts per 100,000.	Parts per 1,000,000.
1 grain per U. S. gallon	1.	1.20	1.71	17.1
1 grain per British gallon	0.830	1.	1.43	14.3
1 part per 100,000	0.580	0.70	1.	10.0
1 part per 1,000,000	0.056	0.07	0.10	1.

Table No. II.

EQUIVALENTS OF VARIOUS MEASURES.

	U.S. Gallons.	Imperial Gallons.	Liters.	Cubic Feet.	Cubic Meters.	Cubic Inches.	Pounds Avoirdupois. (Water at 0° C.)
1 U. S. gallon	1.	0.8311	3.78520	0.13368	0.003785	231.	8.3388822
1 imperial gallon	1.20032	1.	4.54346	0.16046	0.004543	277.274	10.
1 liter	0.26419	0.22010	1.	0.03532	0.001	61.0271	2.204737
1 cubic foot	7.48015	6.23210	28.31529	1.	0.028315	1 728.	62.37916
1 cubic meter	264.18657	220.09671	1000.	35.31661	1.	61 027.0963	2204.737
1 cubic inch	....	....	....	....	....	1.	0.036099

Table No. III.

APPROXIMATE EQUIVALENTS OF VARIOUS MEASURES OF RATE OF FILTRATION.

	Million U. S. Gallons per Acre per 24 Hours.	Million British Gallons per Acre per 24 Hours.	U. S. Gallons per Square Foot per Hour.	British Gallons per Square Foot per Hour.	Cubic Feet per Square Yard per Hour.	Vertical Velocity in Inches per Hour.	Vertical Velocity in Millimeters per Hour.	Vertical Velocity in Meters per 24 Hours. Cubic Meters per Square Meter per 24 Hours.
1 million U. S. gallons per acre per 24 hours	1.	0.833	0.96	0.80	1.15	1.53	39.0	0.935
1 million British gallons per acre 24 hours	1.200	1.	1.15	0.96	1.38	1.84	46.8	1.122
1 U. S. gallon per square foot per hour	1.045	0.870	1.	0.83	1.20	1.60	40.7	0.978
1 British gallon per square foot per hour	1.255	1.045	1.20	1.	1.44	1.92	48.9	1.174
1 cubic foot per square yard per hour	0.869	0.724	0.83	0.69	1.	1.33	33.9	0.813
1 lineal inch, vertical velocity, per hour	0.652	0.543	0.62	0.52	0.75	1.	25.4	0.610
1 hundred lineal millimeters, vertical velocity per hour	2.566	2.139	2.46	2.05	2.95	3.94	100.	2.400
1 lineal meter, vertical velocity per 24 hours = 1 cubic meter per square meter per 24 hours	1.069	0.891	1.02	0.85	1.23	1.64	41.7	1.

INDEX.

A

T

W

PLATE 1.

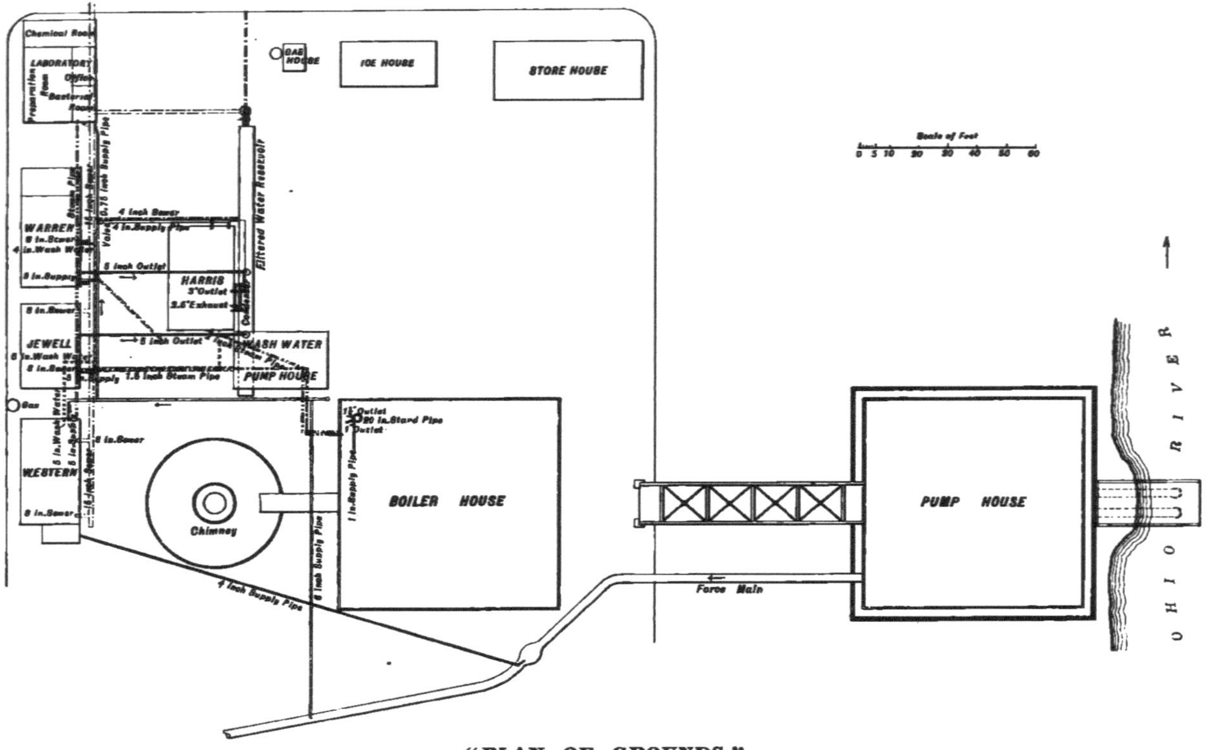

"PLAN OF GROUNDS."

PLATE II.

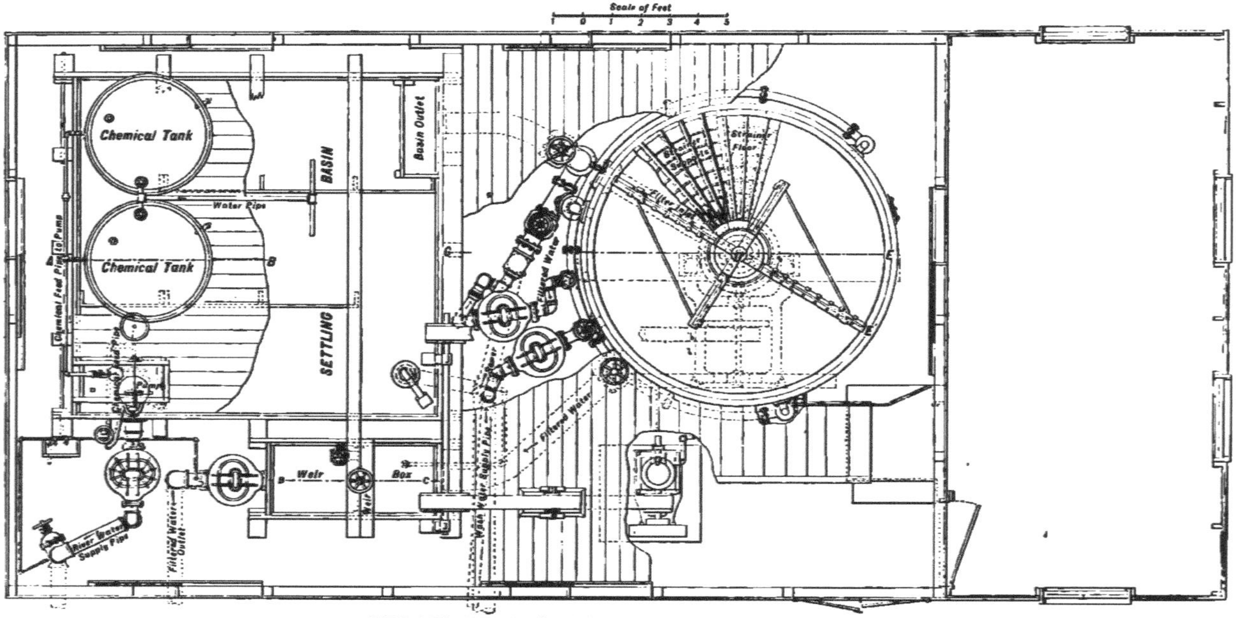

"PLAN OF WARREN GRAVITY SYSTEM."

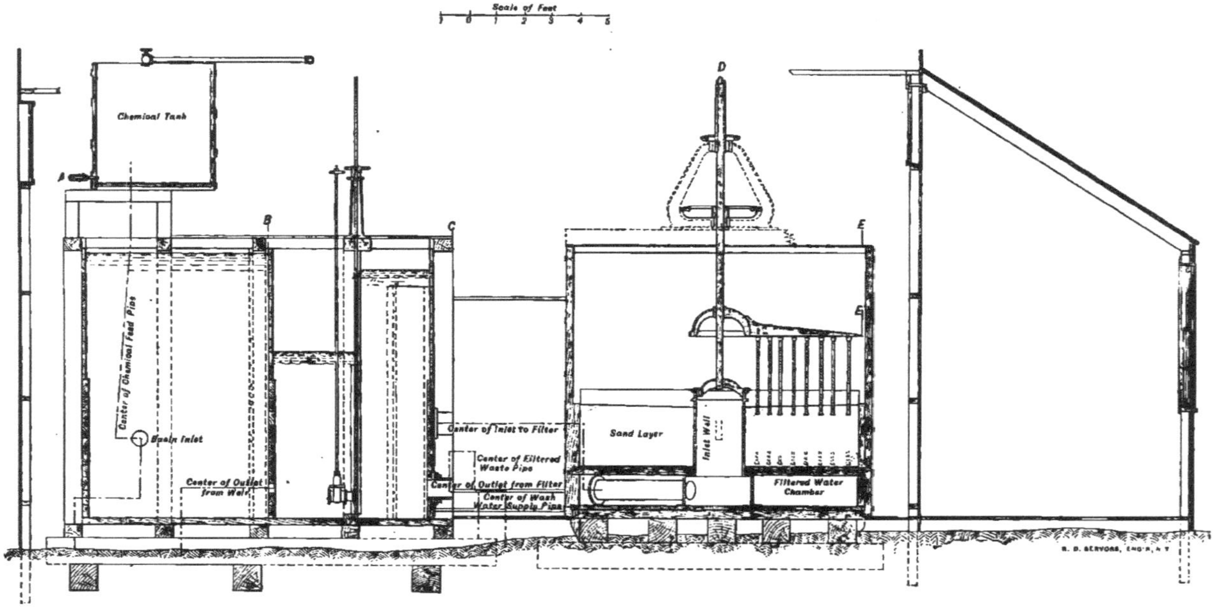

"SECTION OF WARREN GRAVITY SYSTEM."

PLATE IV.

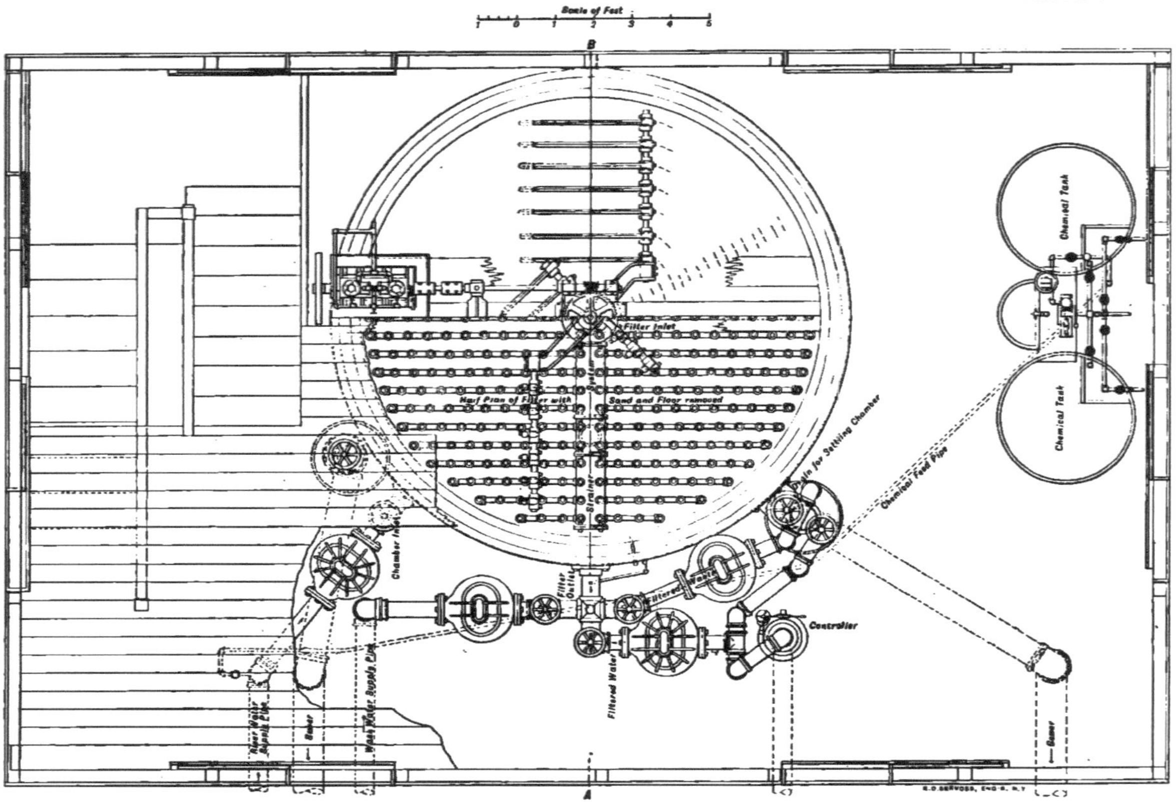

"PLAN OF JEWELL GRAVITY SYSTEM."

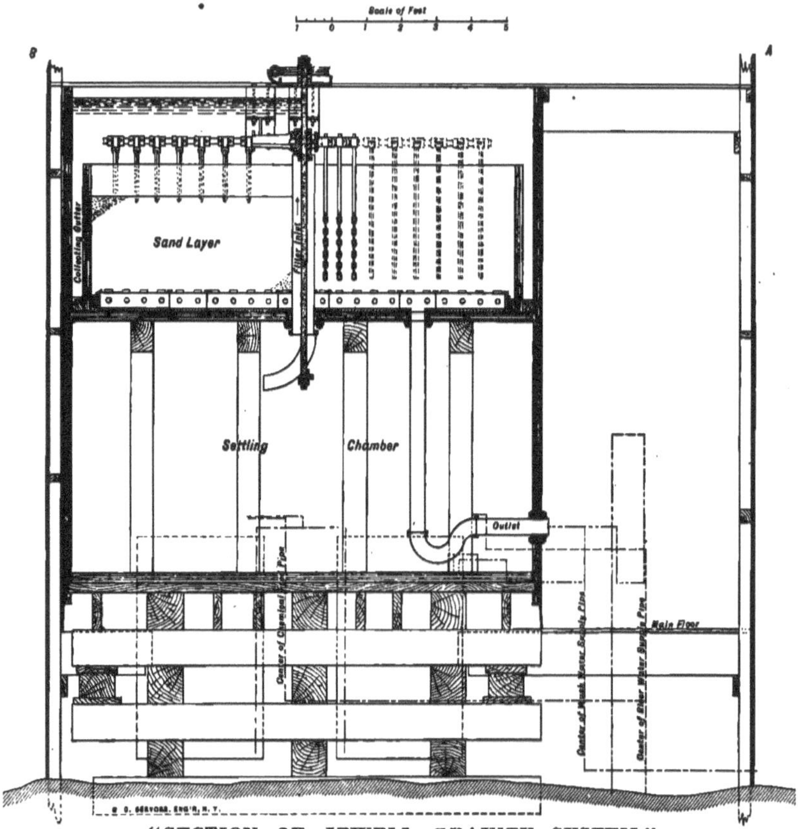

"SECTION OF JEWELL GRAVITY SYSTEM."

PLATE VI.

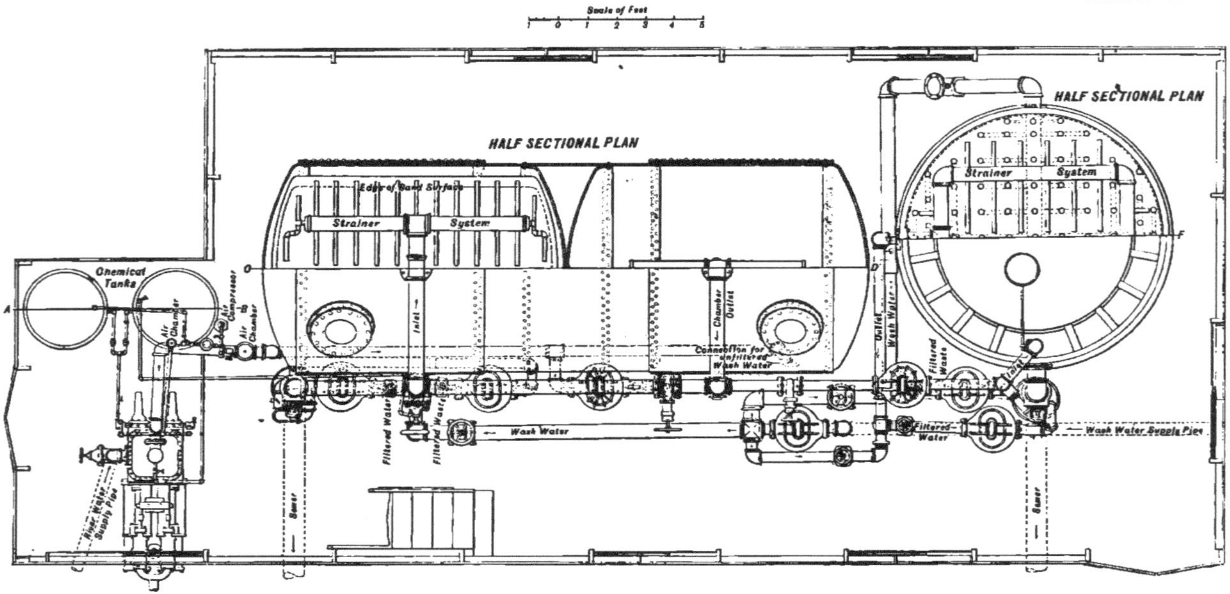

"PLAN OF WESTERN PRESSURE AND GRAVITY SYSTEMS."

PLATE VII

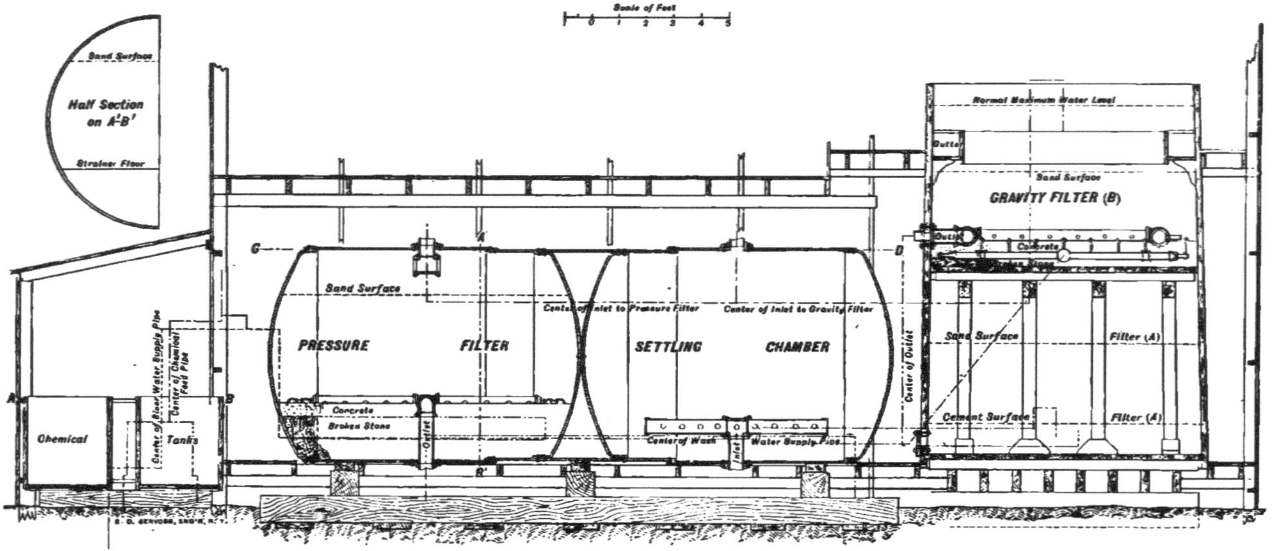

"SECTION OF WESTERN PRESSURE AND GRAVITY SYSTEMS."

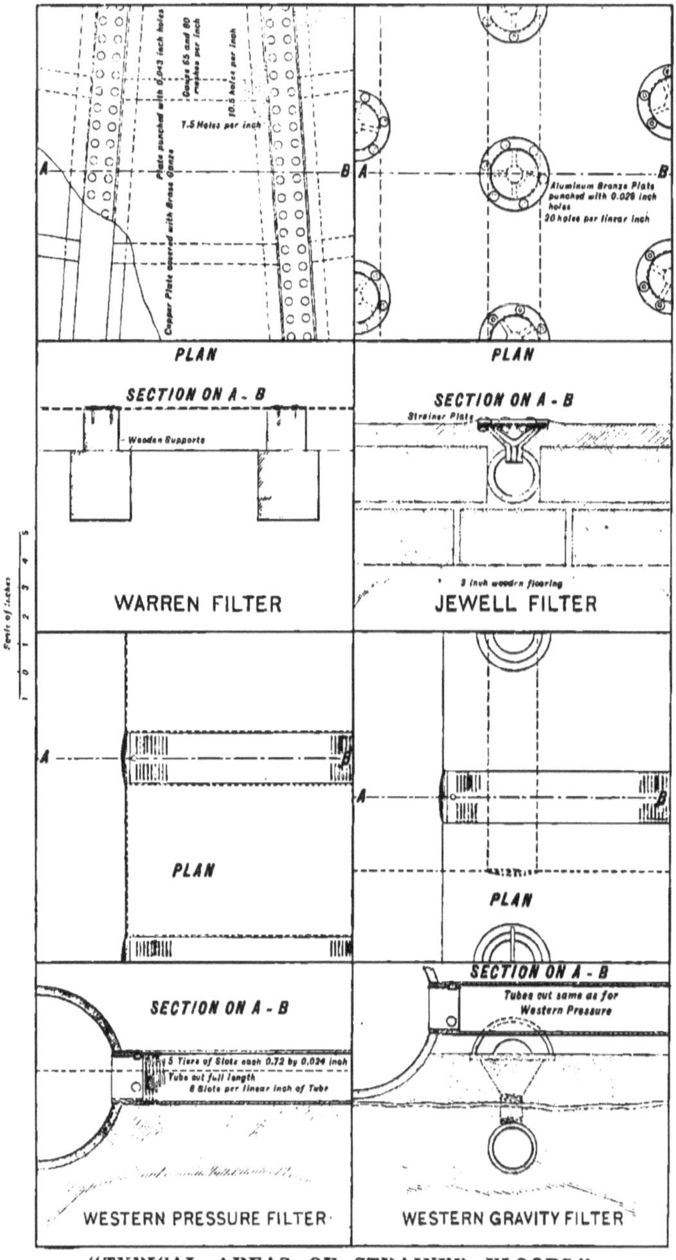

"TYPICAL AREAS OF STRAINER FLOORS."

www.ingramcontent.com/pod-product-compliance
Lightning Source LLC
Chambersburg PA
CBHW021428300426
44114CB00010B/693
* 9 7 8 3 3 3 7 1 3 9 9 4 0 *